The Cambridge Handbook of Second Language Acquisition

What is language, and how can we investigate its acquisition by children or adults? What perspectives exist from which to view acquisition? What internal constraints and external factors shape acquisition? What are the properties of interlanguage systems? This comprehensive 31-chapter handbook is an authoritative survey of second language acquisition (SLA). Its multi-perspective synopsis of recent developments in SLA research provides significant contributions by established experts and widely recognized younger talent. It covers cutting-edge and emerging areas of inquiry not treated elsewhere in a single handbook, including third language acquisition, electronic communication, incomplete first language acquisition, alphabetic literacy and SLA, affect and the brain, discourse and identity. Written to be accessible to newcomers as well as experienced scholars of SLA, the *Handbook* is organized into six thematic parts, each with an editor-written introduction.

JULIA HERSCHENSOHN is Professor and Chair in the Department of Linguistics at the University of Washington.

MARTHA YOUNG-SCHOLTEN is Professor in the School of English Literature, Language and Linguistics at Newcastle University.

CAMBRIDGE HANDBOOKS IN LANGUAGE AND LINGUISTICS

Genuinely broad in scope, each handbook in this series provides a complete state-of-the-field overview of a major sub-discipline within language study and research. Grouped into broad thematic areas, the chapters in each volume encompass the most important issues and topics within each subject, offering a coherent picture of the latest theories and findings. Together, the volumes will build into an integrated overview of the discipline in its entirety.

Published titles

The Cambridge Handbook of Phonology, edited by Paul de Lacy
The Cambridge Handbook of Linguistic Code-switching, edited by
    Barbara E. Bullock and Almeida Jacqueline Toribio
The Cambridge Handbook of Child Language, edited by Edith L. Bavin
The Cambridge Handbook of Endangered Languages, edited by Peter K. Austin
    and Julia Sallabank
The Cambridge Handbook of Sociolinguistics, edited by Rajend Mesthrie
The Cambridge Handbook of Pragmatics, edited by Keith Allan
    and Kasia M. Jaszczolt
The Cambridge Handbook of Language Policy, edited by Bernard Spolsky
The Cambridge Handbook of Second Language Acquisition, edited by
    Julia Herschensohn and Martha Young-Scholten

Further titles planned for the series

The Cambridge Handbook of Biolinguistics, edited by Cedric Boeckx and
    Kleanthes K. Grohmann
The Cambridge Handbook of Generative Syntax, edited by Marcel den Dikken
The Cambridge Handbook of Communication Disorders, edited by Louise Cummings

The Cambridge Handbook of Second Language Acquisition

Edited by
Julia Herschensohn
Martha Young-Scholten

CAMBRIDGE UNIVERSITY PRESS

CAMBRIDGE UNIVERSITY PRESS
Cambridge, New York, Melbourne, Madrid, Cape Town,
Singapore, São Paulo, Delhi, Mexico City

Cambridge University Press
The Edinburgh Building, Cambridge CB2 8RU, UK

Published in the United States of America by Cambridge University Press, New York

www.cambridge.org
Information on this title: www.cambridge.org/9781107007710

© Cambridge University Press 2013

This publication is in copyright. Subject to statutory exception
and to the provisions of relevant collective licensing agreements,
no reproduction of any part may take place without the written
permission of Cambridge University Press.

First published 2013

Printed and Bound in the United Kingdom by the MPG Books Group

A catalogue record for this publication is available from the British Library

Library of Congress Cataloguing in Publication data
The Cambridge handbook of second language acquisition / edited by
Julia Herschensohn, Martha Young-Scholten.
   pages   cm. – (Cambridge handbooks in language and linguistics)
Includes bibliographical references and index.
ISBN 978-1-107-00771-0 (hardback)
1. Second language acquisition.   I. Herschensohn, Julia Rogers, 1945–
II. Young-Scholten, Martha.   III. Series: Cambridge handbooks in language
and linguistics.
P118.2.C356   2013
418 – dc23   2012021826

ISBN 978-1-107-00771-0 Hardback

Cambridge University Press has no responsibility for the persistence or
accuracy of URLs for external or third-party internet websites referred to
in this publication, and does not guarantee that any content on such
websites is, or will remain, accurate or appropriate.

To the memory of Teresa Pica,
outstanding scholar and mentor,
whose seminal work will always be an inspiration to so many.

Contents

List of figures	page ix
List of tables	x
List of contributors	xii
Acknowledgments	xv

	Introduction *Julia Herschensohn and Martha Young-Scholten*	1
Part I	Theory and practice	5
1	Theories of language from a critical perspective *Jan Koster*	9
2	History of the study of second language acquisition *Margaret Thomas*	26
3	Theoretical approaches *Florence Myles*	46
4	Scope and research methodologies *Melinda Whong and Clare Wright*	71
Part II	Internal ingredients	93
5	The role of the native language *Claire Foley and Suzanne Flynn*	97
6	Learning mechanisms and automatization *Richard Towell*	114
7	Generative approaches and the poverty of the stimulus *Bonnie D. Schwartz and Rex A. Sprouse*	137
8	Learner-internal psychological factors *Jean-Marc Dewaele*	159
9	Alphabetic literacy and adult SLA *Elaine Tarone, Kit Hansen and Martha Bigelow*	180
Part III	External ingredients	205
10	Negotiated input and output / interaction *María del Pilar García Mayo and Eva Alcón Soler*	209
11	Second language identity construction *Elizabeth R. Miller and Ryuko Kubota*	230
12	Socialization *Georges Daniel Véronique*	251

13	Variation *Vera Regan*	272
14	Electronic interaction and resources *Astrid Ensslin and Cedric Krummes*	292

Part IV   Biological factors 313
15	Age-related effects *Julia Herschensohn*	317
16	Childhood second language acquisition *Belma Haznedar and Elena Gavruseva*	338
17	Incomplete L1 acquisition *Silvina Montrul*	353
18	Third language acquisition *Jason Rothman, Jennifer Cabrelli Amaro and Kees de Bot*	372
19	Language processing *Alice Foucart and Cheryl Frenck-Mestre*	394
20	Affect and the brain *Andrea W. Mates and Anna Dina L. Joaquin*	417

Part V   Properties of interlanguage systems 437
21	The lexicon *James Milton and Giovanna Donzelli*	441
22	Semantics *Laurent Dekydtspotter*	461
23	Discourse and pragmatics *Roumyana Slabakova*	482
24	Morphosyntax *Tania Ionin*	505
25	Phonology and speech *Ellen Broselow and Yoonjung Kang*	529

Part VI   Models of development 555
26	Explaining change in transition grammars *Michael Sharwood Smith, John Truscott and Roger Hawkins*	560
27	Stagelike development and Organic Grammar *Anne Vainikka and Martha Young-Scholten*	581
28	Emergentism, connectionism and complexity *Randal Holme*	605
29	Input, input processing and focus on form *Joe Barcroft and Wynne Wong*	627
30	Sociocultural theory and the zone of proximal development *Amy Snyder Ohta*	648
31	Nativelike and non-nativelike attainment *Donna Lardiere*	670

Appendix	692
Notes	697
Glossary	702
Selected references	737
Index	814

Figures

6.1	Schematic representation of the processing components involved in spoken language use (Levelt 1993: 2)	*page* 118
21.1	Lexical growth in learners of EFL in Greece (Milton 2009: 79)	449
21.2	Lexical growth in learners of French as a foreign language in Britain (Milton 2006)	450
21.3	Vocabulary profile of a typical learner (Meara 1992: 4)	452
21.4	Coverage of the most frequent English words presented in graph form (Carroll, Davies and Richman 1971, cited in Milton 2009: 47)	453
21.5	Coverage from written and spoken corpora in the BNC (Milton 2009: 58)	456
24.1	Structure of English negative clauses (simplified)	512
24.2	Structure of French negative clauses (simplified)	513
24.3	Structure of German negative clauses (simplified)	514
26.1	OGE: the COMBINE operation (adapted from O'Grady 2005: 8–9)	566
26.2	Modularized memory stores in MOGUL (selected examples)	572
28.1	An emergentist model of language development	610
28.2	Early stage construction learning (based on Chan 2008)	622

Tables

6.1	Operationalizing the constructs of L2 implicit and explicit knowledge (adaped from R. Ellis 2005a)	*page* 134
9.1	Stages of question formation in English based on Pienemann, Johnston and Brindley (1988)	190
9.2	Participant profile, Studies 1 and 3	191
12.1	Some approaches to sociocultural SLA research	258
17.1	Linguistic characteristics of heritage speakers	357
21.1	Base forms, lemmas and word families (Milton 2009: 11)	444
21.2	What is involved in knowing a word (from Nation 2001: 27)	445
21.3	EFL vocabulary size estimates, exam and levels of competence	448
21.4	The most frequent words, and words from the 5,000-word band, and their occurrences in the BNC (Kilgariff 2006)	452
21.5	Components and degrees of value in task induced involvement (adapted from Tsubaki 2006)	458
24.1	Suppliance of verbal morphology in L2 English: percent suppliance in obligatory contexts	517
24.2	Placement of verbs with respect to negation and adverbs in L2 English	518
24.3	Use of infinitival verb forms in finite contexts in L2 French and L2 German (Prévost and White 2000)	519
24.4	Correct vs. incorrect use of finiteness morphology in L2 French and L2 German (Prévost and White 2000)	519
24.5	Use of finite and non-finite verbs before vs. after negation in L2 French and L2 German (Prévost and White 2000)	520
27.1	Summary of Brown's (1973) stages of grammatical development in English	586
27.2	L1 and L2 morpheme orders in cross-sectional studies (de Villiers and de Villiers 1973; Dulay and Burt 1973, 1974; Bailey, Madden and Krashen 1974)	588
27.3	Question formation in L1 and L2 English	590

27.4	Stages of negation in L1 and L2 English	591
27.5	ZISA-study-based stages of development in adult L2 German (based on Pienemann 1989)	592
27.6	Hierarchy of processing resources (Pienemann 1998, 2005)	595
27.7	Stages of question formation (Pienemann and Johnston 1987)	596

Contributors

Eva Alcón Soler, Departamento de Estudios Ingleses, Universitat Jaume I
Joe Barcroft, Department of Romance Languages and Literatures, Washington University in St. Louis
Martha Bigelow, Department of Curriculum and Instruction, University of Minnesota
Ellen Broselow, Department of Linguistics, Stony Brook University (State University of New York at Stony Brook)
Jennifer Cabrelli Amaro, Department of Spanish and Portuguese Studies, University of Florida
Kees de Bot, Department of Applied Linguistics, University of Groningen, and University of the Free State
Laurent Dekydtspotter, Departments of French and Italian / Second Language Studies, Indiana University
Jean-Marc Dewaele, Department of Applied Linguistics and Communication, Birkbeck College, University of London
Giovanna Donzellii, Department of English Language and Literature, Swansea University
Astrid Ensslin, School of Creative Studies and Media, Bangor University
Suzanne Flynn, Department of Linguistics and Philosophy, Massachusetts Institute of Technology
Claire Foley, Department of Slavic and Eastern Languages and Literatures, Boston College
Alice Foucart, Department of Psychology, University of Edinburgh
Cheryl Frenck-Mestre, Centre National de Recherche Scientifique / Laboratoire Parole et Langage, Aix-Marseille Université
María del Pilar García Mayo, Departamento de Filología Inglesa, Universidad del País Vasco (UPV/EHU)
Elena Gavruseva, Linguistics Department, University of Iowa
Kit Hansen, Department of Writing Studies, University of Minnesota

List of contributors

Roger Hawkins, Department of Language and Linguistics, University of Essex

Belma Haznedar, Department of Foreign Language Education, Bogazici University

Julia Herschensohn, Department of Linguistics, University of Washington

Randal Holme, Department of English, Hong Kong Institute of Education

Tania Ionin, Department of Linguistics, University of Illinois at Urbana-Champaign

Anna Dina L. Joaquin, Department of Linguistics/TESL, California State University Northridge

Yoonjung Kang, Centre for French and Linguistics, University of Toronto Scarborough

Jan Koster, Linguistics Department, University of Groningen

Cedric Krummes, School of Creative Studies and Media, Bangor University

Ryuko Kubota, Department of Language and Literacy Education, University of British Columbia

Donna Lardiere, Department of Linguistics, Georgetown University

Andrea W. Mates, Neurobiology of Language Research Group, University of California at Los Angeles

Elizabeth R. Miller, Department of English, University of North Carolina at Charlotte

James Milton, Department of English, Chinese University of Hong Kong

Silvina Montrul, Departments of Linguistics / Spanish, Italian and Portuguese, University of Illinois at Urbana-Champaign

Florence Myles, Department of Language and Linguistics, University of Essex

Amy Snyder Ohta, Department of Asian Languages and Literature, University of Washington

Vera Regan, School of Languages and Literatures, University College Dublin

Jason Rothman, Departments of Spanish and Portuguese Studies / Linguistics, University of Florida, and Department of Modern Languages, University of Ottawa

Bonnie D. Schwartz, Department of Second Language Studies, University of Hawai'i / Department of English, Radboud University Nijmegen

Michael Sharwood Smith, School of Management and Languages, Heriot-Watt University, University of Edinburgh and English Department, University of Social Sciences, Warsaw

Roumyana Slabakova, Department of Linguistics, University of Iowa

Rex A. Sprouse, Departments of Germanic Studies / Second Language Studies, Indiana University

Elaine Tarone, Center for Advanced Research on Language Acquisition (CARLA) / Department of Second Language Studies, University of Minnesota

Margaret Thomas, Program in Linguistics / Department of Slavic and Eastern Languages and Literatures, Boston College

Richard Towell, Centre for Linguistics and Applied Linguistics, University of Salford

John Truscott, Center for Teacher Education, National Tsing Hua University

Anne Vainikka, Cognitive Science Department, Johns Hopkins University

Daniel Véronique, Department of French as a Second Language, Aix-Marseille Université

Melinda Whong, Department of Linguistics and Phonetics, University of Leeds

Wynne Wong, Department of French and Italian, Ohio State University

Clare Wright, School of Education, Communication and Language Sciences, Newcastle University

Martha Young-Scholten, School of English Literature, Language and Linguistics, Newcastle University

Acknowledgments

This volume owes a debt to its benefactors: the authors who have carefully written and revised their papers; the reviewers who graciously refereed the submitted chapters; John Riebold, the graduate research Assistant who carefully reviewed formatting of the chapters on the first draft, and graduate research assistant Allison Germain who compiled the index, the long and short bibliographies, making sure that the format was correct. We and the authors are grateful to the following scholars who helped us in reviewing the contributions: Dwight Atkinson, David Birdsong, Robert Blake, Vivian Cook, Annabelle David, Robert DeKeyser, Kevin Gregg, Holger Hopp, Georgette Ioup, Peter Jordens, Yasuko Kanno, Gabriele Kasper, Paul Kerswill, Usha Lakshmanan, Diane Larsen-Freeman, Juana Liceras, Patsy Lightbown, Alison Mackey, Theo Marinis, Thorsten Piske, Philippe Prévost, Friedemann Pulvermüller, Lisa Reed, Vivienne Rogers, Stephen Ryan, Sandra Silberstein, Neal Snape, Ianthi Maria Tsimpli, Ineke van de Craats, Marjolijn Verspoor and Steven Weinberger. We especially thank our editor Dr. Andrew Winnard and his advisers, and the Cambridge University Press team, notably Sarah Green and Sarah Roberts. Dr. Winnard provided help at every stage of the process and was always ready to send an email response to any query. Ms. Green and Ms. Roberts promptly answered our more numerous technical questions in the final stages of putting everything together and helped with production issues. And finally, we thank our partners, Michael Herschensohn and Bruce Scholten, for their patient support. We are grateful to all who have helped to bring forth this new volume in the Cambridge Handbook series.

Introduction

Julia Herschensohn and Martha Young-Scholten

Scope and overview

The volume you now hold in your hands (or see on your electronic device) aims to represent the state of what we know about how humans acquire a language in addition to their native language. This is no easy aim to achieve because what we can now call a field rather than an area of inquiry has expanded tremendously in the last half century. Some attribute this to the need for more of us to acquire a second language (L2). In reading Margaret Thomas' chapter on the history of second language acquisition (SLA), it will be apparent that this need is nothing new, and in the western world was already documented during the early days of the Roman Empire when education involved learning Greek to read the classics written in that language. There are doubtless many more individuals in absolute terms who need to acquire the twenty-first-century lingua franca, English. But for native speakers of English, there are no signs of an increased widespread need to acquire an additional language. These observations dovetail with another one: that most of the work in second language acquisition is still on English. This state of affairs is slowly changing, in no small part due to those who supervise non-native English-speaking PhD students encouraging them to work on the second language acquisition of their native language. Moreover, much of the work in second language acquisition is still on adults and still on classroom learners. This, too, is slowly changing as several chapters (one of which is dedicated to child second language acquisition) in this handbook reveal.

As Thomas' and several other chapters show, second language acquisition as a field of inquiry did not exist until researchers began to investigate the topic systematically; Lado's (1957) application of Contrastive Analysis to second language acquisition paved the way for such inquiry. Research that began as a search for better methods of teaching had by the 1980s completely divorced itself from the need to make reference to any pedagogical applications of findings presented. In keeping with trends that have only strengthened in the last two decades, few of the chapters of this handbook mention teaching. The handbook – in addition to covering the traditional issues in second language acquisition such as transfer, age of exposure, universals and other internal factors – covers as well various external factors and components of language such as syntax, phonology and vocabulary. This volume identifies new trends in issues considered relevant to the study of SLA from electronic interaction to literacy and presents a set of theories about second language development. Internal factors at the forefront of SLA research now include psycholinguistic processing and neurolinguistic functioning; perspectives range across connectionist, interactional practices, attrition, social context and related issues. Studies along these lines, as the chapters show, have contributed substantial new findings to deepen our understanding of the acquisition of a second language and its relationship to other developmental profiles.

The *Cambridge Handbook* brings together the latest work in traditional and newer areas of inquiry to provide a comprehensive and current overview of the state of the field. It deals with questions such as the following concerning non-native language acquisition: What is language? How can we investigate its acquisition? What perspectives exist from which to view this acquisition? What is the scope of research and which methodologies best address research questions? How does the learner's grammar develop? What are the internal constraints on acquisition? What external factors are held to be relevant? What is linguistic competence and how can we investigate it? In answering these questions, the handbook chapters necessarily take various perspectives from generative to cognitive to interactionist to environmental; the handbook also includes extensive information on recent relevant linguistic, psycholinguistic and neurolinguistic research, new interpretations of input, interaction and intake, and new sources of input, namely via electronic communication. Its chapters on psycholinguistic research, electronic interaction/input, conversation analysis, child L2A, third language acquisition, attrition and poststructuralist approaches to identity construction are particularly cutting-edge and point to directions in which much research is heading.

The handbook is divided into six parts whose chapters are described in detail in the transitional introductions to each area. Part I, "Theory and practice," provides the theoretical foundation of scholarship on second language acquisition. The first two chapters situate this scholarship philosophically and historically, while Chapters 3 and 4 give overviews of current approaches and methodologies. The second and third parts elaborate respectively on factors related to L2 acquisition. Part II, "Internal ingredients," includes what the individual learner brings to the task of acquisition such as cognition or native tongue. Part III, "External ingredients," covers crucial social and interactive factors involved in input and intake. The chapters in Part IV, "Biological factors," refer to physiological constraints of maturation and real-time processing, L2 acquisition within the assumed critical period, influence of the L2 on the native language, third language acquisition and the brain's processing of language. Part V, "Properties of interlanguage systems," covers the acquisition of linguistic competence in the lexicon, semantics, discourse and pragmatics, morphosyntax and phonology. The handbook closes with Part VI, "Models of development," with chapters that delineate stages and mechanisms of change in the L2A process ranging over theoretical perspectives such as autonomous induction, processability, MOGUL, Organic Grammar, input processing, emergentism and sociocultural theory. It closes with a comprehensive chapter, reviewing many themes of the collection.

We wish to make a few helpful points for users of this handbook. The following terms are used interchangeably: development, learning and acquisition; L2A, SLA and non-native language acquisition. Often native language, first language and L1 are used interchangeably and the term L2 usually stands for any language acquired subsequent to the first. The handbook includes helpful ancillary resources: a shorter end-of-volume list of selected references and an exhaustive online version, a glossary, an appendix and index. The reader will also find helpful the cross-referencing of chapters within chapters.

Please visit www.cambridge.org/herschensohn-youngscholten to access the exhaustive list of references that accompanies this volume.

Part I
Theory and practice

INTRODUCTION TO PART I

Part I, "Theory and practice," provides the themes of the handbook, namely: theories of language, central topics in SLA in the past and present, SLA theory families and research methodologies. It thus provides the theoretical underpinning for the chapters to follow and gives an overview of the range of topics covered in the handbook.

The first chapter in the handbook covers the main ways – since Plato through to Descartes, but primarily focusing on the present, the "Chomskyan revolution" and its aftermath – that knowledge of language has been viewed. It traces rationalist and empiricist theories that have influenced issues taken up in language acquisition and ultimately second language acquisition. This thought-provoking lead chapter situates contemporary theories of language with respect to their antecedents of earlier centuries. Focusing on the late twentieth and early twenty-first centuries, and invoking the traditional nature/nurture contrast, it analyzes the Chomskyan notion of biolinguistics. Koster argues that language is most appropriately described as an agentive functionality by which humans evolutionarily adapted an innate brain structure to a new cultural application.

The basic aim of the second chapter is tracing the study of L2A from its early history through the 1950s Contrastive Analysis (CA) to twenty-first-century connectionism. The chapter goes beyond mere chronology to elaborate those themes that are not new, but continue to be re-explored from fresh perspectives: the role of the L1 (cf. 1950s CA), interlanguage competence (cf. 1960s error analysis), order of acquisition (cf. 1970s morpheme order studies), access to Universal Grammar, cognitivist/emergentist proposals, and social context approaches (cf. studies starting in the 1980s). This chapter complements Chapter 1 in filling in the theoretical precedents of language and its acquisition from ancient scholars through Renaissance, Enlightenment and modern writers. Thomas traces empiricist/rationalist debates through three themes, native language influence, the role of cognition and the importance of social interaction in L2A, thus foreshadowing the main themes of the next parts.

The third chapter presents the main theory families that currently exist in L2A research. These broadly include interlanguage architecture approaches that see a role for Universal Grammar; cognitive approaches that focus on the roles of input, output, processing and memory; and sociocultural approaches that take into consideration individual and social factors such as those relating to identity and interaction. The chapter gives an overview of three major theoretical families, formal linguistic, cognitive and social. After establishing the necessity of a theoretical basis to L2 research (that links directly to the preceding chapters), Myles lays out criteria for comparing the approaches in terms of areas of inquiry, theoretical presuppositions and research findings.

The fourth chapter summarizes the range of empirical data examined and the methodologies employed for their collection in L2 research. The various methodologies to be discussed include oral production databases from longitudinal and cross-sectional studies, instructional experiments, metalinguistic and interpretive tasks, statistical analyses, ethnographic documentation, learner corpora, and conversation analysis. The chapter focuses on the methodologies – both quantitative and qualitative – that are exploited by two theoretical families, the psycholinguistic (Myles' linguistic and cognitive, the handbook's "internal ingredients") and the sociolinguistic (Myles' sociocultural or the handbook's "external ingredients"). Whong and Wright outline the paradigms of linguistic, processing and corpora-based research as well as more qualitative techniques in both naturalistic and instructed settings.

1

Theories of language from a critical perspective

Jan Koster

1.1 Introduction

Since antiquity, a central concern of theories of language has been whether language is predominantly a matter of *nature* or of *nurture*. One version of this dilemma is whether language is primarily a biological phenomenon or a sociocultural reality. British empiricism and German Romantic ideas, interacting in complicated ways, set the stage for much of nineteenth-century linguistic thinking, which culminated in the various so-called *structuralist* schools of the first half of the twentieth century. Often, this tradition emphasized culture, nurture and diversity. In the second half of the twentieth century, nativism, influenced by Chomsky and the idea of Universal Grammar, made a powerful comeback. This culminated in the "biolinguistic" idea that language has a core that can be compared to an organ, or rather, to a computational system of the kind found in mammalian vision. Instead of embarking upon the impossible task of giving an overview of all current theories of language, I will give a historical sketch of how the Chomskyan-style linguistics fared with respect to the perennial tension between culture and biology in the study of language and how this tension can be resolved with current neurobiology. It is my hope that this story suggests some lessons about other theories of language as well.

1.2 The Chomskyan revolution

During the second half of the twentieth century, linguistic theorizing was dominated by the so-called Chomskyan revolution. This type of linguistics rose to ascendancy with Chomsky's 1957 book, *Syntactic Structures*, and had its greatest popularity during the 1960s, culminated in the 1970s, but steadily lost ground after the 1980s. At the time, the Chomskyan perspective was generally seen as revolutionary, although there were always critics. It is questionable whether the new theories were as revolutionary as believed at first. In retrospect, a good case can be made that early generative grammar, rather than superseding older theories, was largely ignorant of them. Let me explain.

Pre-Chomskyan linguistics, at least in Europe, was dominated by the Saussurian idea that language is primarily a system of signs, of which words are the most important (Saussure 1916). Signs were thought to have a public face (*signifiant*) and a conceptual side (*signifié*). In the most common case the public face of a linguistic sign is formed from the sounds of speech. But the conceptual side of language was also believed to have a public aspect, as it was assumed that the concepts of a language represented particular choices from a universal but more or less amorphous conceptual space. Conceived this way, language was seen first and foremost as a sociocultural reality. Of course this did not exclude such sociocultural realities being possible only on the basis of psychological or biological capacities.

Next, signs (words) were believed to enter into paradigmatic and syntagmatic relations. If we limit ourselves to syntax, we can say that paradigmatic relations define a class of elements that can take the same position in a sentence, such as *John* and *The father of John* in (1):

(1) a. *John* left
    b. *The father of John* left

In American structuralism such a paradigm is also called a substitution class or a distribution class.

Syntagmatic relations are the horizontal relations in a phrase or clause, like the relation between *John* or *The father of John* with the following verb *left* in (1). It was generally recognized that the syntagmatic relations of language are not between single words but between *groups of words* (also known as phrases or constituents). As a result, sentences were analyzed as having a hierarchical structure. It was also recognized that parts of phrases could be "self-similar," meaning that noun phrases could contain noun phrases or clauses could contain clauses, a self-similarity referred to as *recursion*. Both phrase structure and recursion, were, terminology aside, within the scope of pre-Chomskyan structuralism.

There were claims in early Chomskyan linguistics that pre-Chomskyan theories of phrase structure were construction-bound, but this was not actually the case: the notion of a word group or phrase under structuralism is more abstract than the notion of a construction (active, passive, question, etc.). Both active and passive constructions, for instance, were analyzed in terms of word groups built up from the same ingredients (such as heads, complements and adjuncts). More generally, word groups (phrases, constituents) were seen to express the combinatorial potential of a word (the head or the core of the group). This potential was often referred to as the valency of the word (Tesnière 1959), which was ultimately believed to be a reflection of the semantic properties of the word. In somewhat anachronistic terminology, it could be said that sentence structure was seen as hierarchical and recursive, consisting of word groups projected from the lexicon. The items of the lexicon (Saussurian *signs*) were held to be sociocultural objects and part of the inventory referred to as *langue*. As syntactic structures were conceived of as the realizations of the valency of words, syntax was sociocultural in orientation as well. Matters of individual psychology were only secondary and reduction to biology was practically unheard of.

Phrase structure theory was only one element of structural linguistics. Another aspect was analysis in terms of information structure as developed by the Prague school in the 1920s and 1930s. According to this type of theory, the content of a sentence can be divided into old and new information (theme–rheme, topic–comment, focus–presupposition). Analysis in terms of information structure is also implicit in the old *Satzklammer* (or sentence bracket theory), which divides the sentence into a middle field and a left and right periphery (see Kathol 2000). Both word order variation on the middle field and specific use of the peripheries was seen in terms of what we now call information structure. Consider, for instance, the fact that a sentence consists of a DP (*Determiner Phrase*, extension of Noun Phrase) and VP (Verb Phrase). In most languages of the world, the DP precedes the VP, reflecting the fact that it is a natural organization of information that the topic of a sentence (the DP) be mentioned before something is said about it (in the VP). Especially with respect to linear order, information structure was seen as a leading principle.

What is known as the Chomskyan revolution introduced some technical innovations and sought to give the field a new metatheoretical orientation. In *Syntactic Structures* a language "L" is a set of sentences generated by the grammar. The technical notion *grammar* was algorithmic and inspired by the study of "formal language." The strings of "deep structure" (Chomsky 1965) were generated by phrase structure rules. Other sentence types, like passive sentences and questions, were derived by optional transformations. Sentence recursion was accounted for by so-called "generalized transformations," which combined phrase markers (the structures resulting from phrase structure rules and "singular" transformations) into complex structures.

According to this new metatheoretical orientation, what was formalized was not a sociocultural reality but a matter of individual psychology (ultimately biology), referred to as *competence*. All of this had great appeal at the time, as it suggested explicitness and mathematical sophistication the study of language had not seen before.

Unfortunately, it all rested on shaky ground, as became clear in the next fifteen years. The failure was not recognized as such but perceived by many generative grammarians as continuous innovation. Although transformational grammar died in the 1970s, the idea that there was a major revolution in linguistics between 1955 and 1970 has been kept alive until the present day. In fact, what came after 1980 is even believed by some to be a second revolution, while it was, in spite of some minimal innovations, in reality the beginning of a period of theoretical stagnation that, I argue, has been with us ever since.

What was problematic about transformational–generative grammar from the beginning was insufficient understanding of the fact that the formal languages used were an extremely poor tool to model natural language. First of all, to the extent that formal languages define a set of well-formed formulas, there is no close natural language (NL) equivalent. Strings of NL words are more or less "interpretable," no matter what their grammatical status is. Well-formedness in NL is a relative matter and not something absolute as generative syntacticians would have it. Compare the following two strings:

(2) a. John read the book
    b. John book read

For a native speaker of English, (2a) is fully well-formed, while (2b) is not. Nevertheless, (2b) is clearly interpretable and might even receive the same interpretation as (2a). When English is defined as a set of sentences, as a language "L," there is no non-arbitrary reason to include (2a) in that set and to exclude (2b). Of course, (2a) is optimal in a sense that (2b) is not, but the point is that there is no similar notion of optimality in artificial formal language. In the latter, a string is either well-formed or it is not.

Although this point was appreciated early in the history of generative grammar, the obvious conclusion was hardly drawn: a natural language cannot be satisfactorily characterized by an algorithm. As (2b) and numerous other examples show, semantic interpretation tries to make the best sense of any string of words, regardless of its degree of optimality from a syntactic point of view. There is another difference between formal languages and NL that played a much bigger role in the subsequent development of generative grammar. Unlike the symbols manipulated by the rules of formal languages, NL words have rich inherent properties independent of the syntactic rules in which they appear. First of all, the words of NL have a public side (*signifiant*) and a conceptual side (*signifié*) and are, in that sense, complete interface elements, even *before* entering into derivations that will be sent at the end of some *phase* to the interfaces involving sound and meaning. Furthermore, all words have a valency, predicting in which syntactic environments they may occur. Thus, the English word *book* may be preceded by an indefinite article (*a book*) rather than be followed by it (*book a*). On its right, the noun may be followed by a PP (Prepositional Phrase: *a book about linguistics*) and so on. So, each word comes with a set of potential environments that can be seen as a property of that word. Syntactic environments are partially predictable on the basis of the conceptual structure associated with a word. No such properties are associated with the symbols of formal languages, which have no properties beyond the fact that they can enter into certain rules.

Not only was the valency of words practically ignored in *Syntactic Structures*, but so was the information structure discussed by the Prague school. Thus, as briefly indicated above, a rule like S → NP VP is arbitrary in that it could just as well be S → VP NP, ignoring the fact that in the majority of natural languages, the subject (NP) precedes the predicate (VP). With some exceptions, word orders like NP–VP are universal, to be accounted for by a general theory rather than by stipulation via individual rules.

The new generative metatheory was developed partially in response to behaviorism; see for example Chomsky's (1959) review of Skinner's *Verbal Behavior*. The theory reinterpreted the sociocultural *langue* as competence, a matter of individual psychology, to be ultimately explained in terms of biology. This move had a certain plausibility thanks to the shift from word-oriented linguistics to syntax-oriented linguistics. Starting from signs (morphemes, words), claimed to be the right approach in this chapter, it is immediately clear that the reconstruction of syntax solely in terms of individual psychology is incoherent. Words, obviously, are collective property, not belonging to an individual but to a speech community.

1.3 Rediscovering the lexicon

Transformational–generative grammar received its classical form in *Aspects of the Theory of Syntax* (Chomsky 1965). According to the *Aspects* model (also known at the time as the "standard theory" or ST), a grammar consists of a phrase structure grammar and a lexicon (the "base component") responsible for the *deep structure*, which is the input for semantic interpretation. Deep structures could be modified by a series of cyclically organized transformations leading to *surface structures*. The generalized transformations of Chomsky's initial, 1957, work disappeared in this model, with recursion now being a property of the base component. This development followed the lead of Katz and Postal (1964), who had hypothesized that all semantic interpretation depends on deep structure. This trend was continued by what became known as Generative Semantics, which held that (i) syntax is partially pre-lexical, manipulating concepts rather than morphemes or words, and (ii) that the inventory of categories at the deepest level could be limited to S (proposition), V (predicate) and NP (argument). For many this suggested a simplified universal syntax inspired by formal languages once more, in this case the very poor syntax (compared to NL syntax) of predicate logic. Many linguists did not find this empirically plausible in the long run and Generative Semantics all but died out in the early 1970s.

Chomsky gave up the idea that semantic interpretation solely depends on deep structure and argued that it was transformations, particularly those modifying linear order, that also affected semantic interpretation

(Chomsky 1971). This led to the extended standard theory (EST), which dominated the field until the end of the 1970s, when the emphasis shifted to "Principles and Parameters" (Chomsky 1981, also referred to as Government-Binding theory or GB). The most important principles are locality principles, i.e. those that determine the maximal structural domain within which syntactic categories can be related. Most anaphors, for instance, do not have an antecedent outside their clause. Parameters account for crosslinguistic differences in domain-size, word order and other language-specific details. Some languages, for example, do allow an antecedent outside their clause.

The EST effects of linear order on semantic interpretation recalled the Prague-style concern about information structure, and it was the first time transformational-generative grammar interfaced with this important structuralist tradition. Much more important is the obvious fact that transformational-generative grammar actually did not survive the introduction of a lexicon in *Aspects* in 1965. Within five years, it became clear that the ensuing lexicalism was not a continuation of a revolution but a return to the basic tenets of pre-Chomskyan structuralism (particularly in some of its European forms). First of all, it became clear that context-free phrase structure rules become superfluous as soon as a lexicon with subcategorization frames is introduced. In *Aspects*, syntactic base structures are generated largely independently of the lexicon, whereas lexical items are inserted later in the derivation on the basis of, for example, a match between the subcategorization frame and a structure generated by the phrase structure rules. In the following (simplified) example, a VP is expanded as in (3a) while the verb *see* can be inserted on the basis of the verb's subcategorization frame given by the lexicon (3b), indicating that it is transitive:

(3) a. VP → V NP
    b. *see*: [+V, −NP]

If things are set up this way, the same information is given twice: (3a) gives the structure of a common VP-type and this structure is stated once more in the subcategorization frame (3b).

1.4 Not quite a revolution

Unfortunately, the implications of giving up phrase structure rules (like 3a) in favor of projection from lexical frames (like 3b) were underappreciated at the time. What was new about generative grammar in the 1950s was not something like (3b) but description in terms of rules like (3a), which were adapted from the study of formal languages and mathematical linguistics. Very few pre-Chomskyan structuralists would have objected to the idea that syntax spells out the valency of lexical items. It is therefore reasonable to say that giving up (3a) in favor of projection from the lexicon was not the next step in an ongoing revolution, but reinventing the wheel of structuralist grammar. Early generative grammar was not a revolution but a development based on the serious error that NL syntax can be largely developed independently of the lexicon.

What has been appreciated even less until the present day is that the shift from a sociocultural view of language to individual psychology was based on the same error. Obviously, lexical items are not primarily a matter of individual psychology but artefacts belonging to a shared culture. So, also in this respect, the adoption of lexicalism was an implicit return to a major tenet of Saussurian structuralism.

What about the rest of the revolution? Phrase structure grammar, although replaced again by pre-revolutionary projection of lexical valency, was never the most controversial and hence revolutionary part of transformational-generative grammar. More controversial was the introduction of transformations, together with the claim of their psychological reality. The same can be said about the closely related distinction between deep structure and surface structure. The metatheory not only made claims about the individual/psychological nature of grammars, but it was also hypothesized that in language acquisition, grammars are selected from a small class of feasible (or possible) grammars. This innate hypothesis space has been referred to as the LAD (language acquisition device) or Universal Grammar. In its most extreme form, UG is seen as a single grammar with parameters, to be set on the basis of the data the child is exposed to during the acquisition of his or her native grammar.

I will come back to how the lexicalism of around 1970 should have affected said theory of language acquisition. At this point, I will limit myself to the question of how the other two revolutionary tenets fared in the 1970s: the idea of transformational analysis and the idea of grammar with multiple levels (such as deep and surface structure). To make a long story short, both ideas appeared to be mistaken. One transformation after another disappeared; in many cases a classical transformational analysis was shown to be impossible (see, for instance, Higgins 1973; Jackendoff 1969; and Wasow 1972). In most cases, transformations were replaced by construal rules, which are rules of completion based on feature sharing (see Koster 1987: 8). For example, consider a typical reflexive, like *himself* in (4):

(4) John saw *himself*

In earlier transformational analyses, a transformation derived (4) from *John saw John*, replacing the second *John* by *himself*. *John saw John* was supposed to be closer to the deep structure and seen as a *full reconstruction* of the input level for semantic interpretation. However, full reconstruction did not work, for instance, for sentences with quantifiers: *everyone saw everyone* does not mean the same as *everyone saw himself*. So, it was concluded that a sentence like (4) only involved *partial reconstruction*: the anaphor *himself* was directly introduced at the deepest level and the only completion provided by further rules was the referential identity shared with *John* (commonly expressed by a referential index).

In most cases, partial reconstruction (by what is known as *construal*) was accepted, but for reasons that remain obscure, an exception was made for displacements, i.e. the structures derived by movement transformations. The most typical of those are NP-movement (as in the passive construction in 5a) and *wh*-movement (as in 5b):

(5) a. *John* was seen [–]
    b. *What* did John see [–]

The empty positions [–] were referred to as *traces* at the time, but that was a notion that already presupposed displacement by movement rules. The real point is that elements like [–] express the fact that the valency of a verb like *see* remains intact under displacement. This opened the door for non-transformational analysis of displacement, i.e. in terms of partial reconstruction instead of full reconstruction. In structures like (5), the reconstruction is partial because, by property sharing between antecedent and dependent element (as in (4)), the object positions only derive their lexical content from the antecedent. Their categorical status is given by the subcategorization frame of *see* in (5) (also involving theta roles and Case), hence making the reconstruction partial instead of total.

The partial-reconstruction view of displacement makes it more similar to other forms of construal, like those for anaphoric relations and agreement phenomena. This made it possible to get rid of transformations altogether, as movement was the last stronghold of transformational analysis. Important empirical confirmation of this view was provided by research in the wake of Emonds' (1970) structure-preserving hypothesis, which showed that the major movement transformations did not create any structure beyond what was given by the base structures (NP, VP, etc., generalized as "X-bar theory"). The implications were dramatic but often ignored at the time. With X-bar theory as the main device of sentence generation and transformational analysis gone, the characteristic multiple-level approach (with deep and surface structure) was gone as well, leaving generative grammar as a non-revolutionary elaboration of the more traditional ideas of structuralist syntax.

Movement lived on as *move alpha* and continued to be seen as the basis of a multiple-level theory in Chomsky (1981). Overt displacement has a clear function, namely highlighting certain categories to the listener or reader. Highlighting, often in the spirit of Prague-style information structure, crucially depends on the *visible* effects of displacements. Invisible movement does not make sense from this point of view. In early post 1980s Chomskyan syntax, this fact was masked by giving movement an entirely new rationale, namely in terms of *feature checking*. Feature checking was further divided between the checking of strong features for overt movement and weak features for covert (LF-)movement. All of this was ad hoc, unlike the earlier rationale for displacement in terms of information structure.

Altogether, this shift to arbitrary feature checking was another symptom of the decline of mainstream generative grammar.

1.5 A partial consensus

In current syntax (known as minimalism), the idea of multiple levels of representation (apart from the interfaces) is mostly given up, making monostratal syntax the consensus view, more than thirty years after the demise of transformational analysis. The operation Merge combines two linguistic categories X and Y to the set {X, Y}, and is seen as the core of syntax. An example would be the combination of a verb (V) and its object (NP) to {V, NP}. Internal Merge occurs when no external element is added but a category is merged again, so that two copies of the category are present in the structure. This is supposed to be the case for structures underlying questions like [*what* did John see *what*]. The phonological component only spells out the first copy of *what*, deriving the question *what did John see*.

Although we have latter-day minimalism (since Chomsky 1995) and other anti-lexicalist frameworks, many linguists subscribe implicitly or explicitly to the lexicalist frameworks of the 1970s. The idea that syntactic structures, with minor additions, spell out the valency of lexical items completely undermined the claim that linguistics underwent a major revolution in the second half of the twentieth century, as X-bar theory is conceptually no more than a variant of the phrase structure theories existing before Chomsky. None of this is intended to deny that linguistics has seen spectacular growth in the last several decades, both in depth of analysis and empirical scope. There also is much more (worldwide) uniformity in terminology and means of representation than what was usual in the very disconnected forms of structural linguistics seen before the 1950s. Another change of lasting importance was a methodological lesson learned from the natural sciences: *apparent* diversity of language data does not immediately falsify universal claims. What is considered the facts involves theoretical interpretation that can be just as wrong as the theory explaining the facts. (This lesson is lost on a growing number of linguists who think that theories of Universal Grammar can be falsified by just listing problematic data from a variety of languages; see, for instance, Evans and Levinson 2009 and the anti-universalist rhetoric of Tomasello 2008.) A common misunderstanding found in some of such critiques is that universals (in Chomky's sense) necessarily occur in all languages. In reality, Universal Grammar is a toolbox (like distinctive features in phonology) from which actual languages make a selection.

As a theoretical paradigm shift, however, early transformational grammar was overhyped and practically everything that was radically new about it in the 1950s and 1960s appeared to be mistaken and was gradually given up after 1970. Within the (in retrospect) rather traditional lexicalist framework of X-bar theory, some earlier ideas were successfully further developed, like the greater use of empty categories (as [–] in (5) or the "silent" categories of Kayne 2005) and the addition of functional elements (like agreement in *Syntactic Structures* and INFL/inflection for tense, agreement, aspect, etc. in later theories). This led to substantially deeper analyses than had been common, especially since the 1980s, when functional categories were hypothesized to project similarly to lexical categories (DP, CP, IP, TP, AgrP, vP, etc.). Furthermore, the idea of binary branching was more commonly adopted than in earlier forms of structuralist syntax (Kayne 1984). It is important to emphasize that all these extensions can be adhered to without assuming a conceptual break or paradigm shift in the 1950s and 1960s.

The same is true for the one area in which generative grammar really shone. What I have in mind are the constraints on what may be called secondary computation. The most important of these are known as *locality principles*. The three main types of locality principles are: (i) minimal distance principles, (ii) minimal domain principles, and (iii) command principles (Klima 1964; Reinhart 1976). Minimal distance principles go back to Rosenbaum (1967) and were further developed by Culicover and Wilkins (1984), Koster (1978) and Rizzi (1990). Minimal domain principles go back to Chomsky (1964) and Ross (1967). Locality principles are the core achievement of generative grammar, the main principles in what became known as the Principles and Parameters framework. In their standard formulation, these principles are not entirely construction-independent, as Subjacency (for movement constructions; see Chapter 31, this volume) has a form rather different from Principle A of the Binding theory (of Chomsky 1981), but, at least in principle, a construction-independent account seems possible (cf. Koster 1987). Since X-bar theory is construction-independent as well, there clearly is justification for a construction-independent perspective next to approaches that emphasize the Gestalt of constructions (Croft 2001; Goldberg 1995).

All in all, then, before the 1990s and minimalism, there was a growing generative consensus that (hierarchical and recursive) syntactic structures were projected from the lexicon to avoid the redundancy problem of the misguided forms of generative grammar of before 1970. Lexicon-driven sentence generation, it was concluded above, is not a revolutionary innovation of mid-twentieth-century generative linguistics but an elaboration of the structuralist idea that syntax reflects the valency of lexical items. Many variants of generative linguistics (Lexical Functional Grammar, Head-driven Phrase Structure Grammar, etc.) interpreted this kind of grammar as monostratal, i.e. without multiple levels of representation such as deep structure and surface structure. Since minimalism and Construction Grammar adopted the idea of monostratal representation as well, there is nowadays near-consensus on this point (see also Culicover and Jackendoff 2005 for many similar observations). Minimalism, in practice, was a partial return to the idea of lexicon-independent sentence generation. In the next section, we will see if this move was justified.

1.6 Minimalism and the biolinguistic program

Since Chomsky (1995), the Minimalist Program has been one of the mainstream frameworks in current generative grammar. So far, it has led to much empirical research but to little theoretical progress. The concerns here are not about minimalism as a program. On the contrary, the overall goal of constructing a theory that makes grammar look as "perfect" as possible and relegates as much as it can to third factor principles is an appropriate one. The problem is with how this program is carried out in practice. It can be said that little *theoretical* progress has been made since the 1980s. Part of the theoretical stagnation is due to the fact that some key problems of earlier versions of generative grammar are either unresolved or ignored. But there are deeper problems that involve the very foundations of the field.

More generally, current generative grammar is often referred to as a computational theory, but the current style of the field is so informal that it is practically impossible to find explicit accounts of what exactly is computed and how. With the low level of explicitness considered normal these days, references to recursive Merge say little beyond the traditional wisdom that syntax involves hierarchical structures with phrases within phrases of the same kind. There is nothing wrong with that insight but it is exaggerated to say that it is revolutionary.

In order to see what is problematic about standard generative grammar (including minimalism), we must have a closer look at its foundations. During most of the life cycle of standard generative grammar, it was realistically interpreted in terms of individual psychology, and from the beginning, a connection was made with biology, as in Lenneberg (1967). However, it is only recently that biological terminology has become more dominant than references to psychological reality, particularly since Jenkins (2000) and Hauser, Chomsky and Fitch (2002).

Note that neither rationalism nor the biological foundations of language in general are at issue here. We can assume that all learning is constrained by biological principles, some of them very specific. The days of behaviorism are far behind us. The view of biologically constrained learning is trivially true, and from this general perspective language is as biologically based as our ability to play chess or to drive a car. None of that can be done by other organisms, after all, and at best there is a question as to how specialized or inflexible parts of our brain are with respect to certain tasks. So, the claim that language makes use of biological, innate components is self-evident and therefore trivial. This, of course, does not mean that it is a trivial task to determine the exact nature of the biological components involved.

The non-trivial claim of current biolinguistics is more specific, namely that grammar is like a specialized organ, or rather like internal computational systems such as the ones found in the mammalian visual system. The trivial claim is true on general grounds and the non-trivial claim is false, or so, at least, it can be argued. This has to do with the meaningful distinction that can be made between biologically based functionality and culturally based functionality. Consider as an example the role of the lungs in respiration and the role of the lungs in playing a wind instrument such as the trumpet. The former is based on our genetic program and develops automatically, without human interference. Playing a trumpet, however, is based on the same innate structures – the lungs – but this time the function of the lungs is not formed by our genetic program but by coupling them with an instrument invented by humans in order to achieve human goals. The study of respiration in mammals is generally seen as biology, while playing the trumpet is generally seen as culture. This example illustrates once more that innateness is not the issue. The difference is based on the question whether the use of the same innate structures is mediated by human agency and artifacts (trumpet) or not (respiration).

So, the criterion distinguishing the trivial claim from the non-trivial claim is the involvement of artifacts. Language is only possible thanks to artifacts, namely our invented words. This simple observation suffices to refute the non-trivial claim. Whoever rejects this conclusion can choose between two ways out: either it must be shown that organs or internal computational systems (like in mammalian vision) also involve artifacts or it must be shown that the words of our language are not really artifacts. Clearly, the first option is absurd: neither organs like the heart or the kidneys nor mammalian visual computation is based on human inventions. But the second option is untenable, too; however, in practice it comes closest to a thesis defended in a certain variety of biolinguistics. But let us first see how the internalist perspective was developed in generative grammar.

Although the internalist perspective has been part of generative grammar since the 1950s, it has been characterized by its current terminology since the early 1980s. Particularly in Chomsky (1986), the notions E-language (external) and I-language (internal/individual/intensional) were discussed, with the further argument that the proper subject matter of linguistic theory (in some reasonably narrow sense) is I-language. Chomsky characterized enumerated sets of sentences as E-languages, while the actual mechanisms were characterized as I-languages, objects (grammars) selected from a narrow range by children learning their language.

X-bar theory has been promising execution of this program. This does not mean, of course, that the specific form of the X-bar theory in Chomsky (1970, 1981) was correct. As with any other empirical theory, one might hope for steady improvements over the years. In the case of X-bar theory, several modifications were proposed, for instance concerning the superfluousness of intermediate bar levels (Muysken 1982), the number of Specifiers or the nature of functional projections. Whatever the right X-bar theory, the key principle is that redundancy can only be avoided by projecting syntactic structure straight from the lexicon. This is an insight based on the firm conclusion of the first twenty-five years of generative grammar, even if it means a substantial return to the pre-generative tradition, when syntax was still word-oriented and not seen through the lens of formal languages with their lexicon-independent syntax.

A pivotal operation in minimalism is Merge, a rule that combines (merges) two syntactic objects. The optimal interpretation of Merge is not as part of a sentence-generating mechanism but as a metatheoretical characterization of the properties of subcategorization frames: all involve binary hierarchical structure with the possibility of recursion. Sentence generation can remain as the spelling out of subcategorization frames, as in X-bar theory. In a word-oriented syntax of this kind, whatever Merge stands for is *applied* in the creation of lexical items with complex combinatorial properties. In other words, there is a crucial and theoretically important difference between sentence generation *by* Merge and sentence generation as the spelling out of lexical properties *in accordance with* Merge. The former reintroduces the redundancy problem, the latter solves it.

In its application to lexical structures, then, Merge is not something biological but applied biology at best. Of course it is possible to consider Merge in abstraction from its lexical application and to reflect on its biological sources, but at that level of abstraction there is no obvious reason to say that Merge has anything to do with natural language at all. The fact that it is so successfully used in language is not a strong argument for the idea that the biological purpose of Merge is linguistic, a Panglossian view (see Gould and Lewontin 1979 who note the fallacy of reading cultural functions into biological structures).

The crux of the matter is that Merge, in abstraction from its lexical application, is not linguistically functional. It is for a reason that before the shift to syntactocentrism, the morpheme was generally seen as the smallest linguistically functional unit. This is the wisdom behind Saussure's idea that the sign with its dual nature (sound–meaning) is the core element of language. Our combinatorial capacities (as expressed by Merge) are extremely important for language as we know it. No matter how powerful it makes language as a tool, it is only an auxiliary facility. There is just as little reason to call the capacity for Merge the "faculty of language in the narrow sense" (FLN in Hauser *et al.* 2002) as there is reason to call a gasoline engine "a car in the narrow sense."

1.7 Reconciling biology with culture

The current biolinguistic interpretation of theories of grammar is only possible due to an error that also led pre-1970 generative grammar astray: the shift from a traditional, sign-based theory of grammar to a syntax-based theory (where the notion "syntax" was borrowed from the lexicon-independent algorithms designed for formal languages). The public cultural objects stored in the lexicon are the *sine qua non* of language, no matter how narrowly conceived. Without the function assigned to them by words, the hierarchical, recursive structures of syntax have no linguistic significance. This makes the project of a grammatical metatheory in terms of individual psychology or biology (in the non-trivial sense) futile.

Chomsky's distinction between empiricist and rationalist theories of language acquisition and his rejection of extreme versions of the former (e.g. Skinner's behaviorism) make good sense. Like Chomsky's own theories, such theories are selection theories, but with a hypothesis space so unconstrained that language acquisition, both in its speed and in its convergence on universal properties across languages, would become impossible. Poverty-of-the-stimulus arguments strongly suggest that language exploits innate structure (see Chapters 7 and 22, this volume).

However, nothing justifies a Panglossian interpretation of the innate structures involved. In a strictly biological context, structures have become functional in the course of evolution either by adaptation (the gradual adjustment of structures to particular functions by natural selection) or by exaptation (first selected by one function and subsequently applied and adjusted to another function, also by natural selection). *Exaptation* is a term coined by Gould and Vrba (1982), referred to as pre-adaptation in earlier theories. In fact, it is a phenomenon that was discussed by Darwin himself and discussed in the German-speaking world of the nineteenth century as *Funktionsverschiebung* (see Russell 1916). An example given by Gould and Vrba is the birds' wings that originally evolved as thermo-regulators. The notion of exaptation is extremely important because it illustrates the fact that there is no intrinsic relation between form and function. It is not predictable from physical principles which function a given structure will take in the future. Kauffman (2007) rightly takes that as an argument against reductionism, in this case the idea that biology can be reduced to physics.

How does language fit into this picture? Hauser *et al.* (2002) suggest that the faculty of language in the narrow sense (FLN) only includes recursion and that it may have evolved originally for reasons other than language. Possibilities they mention are number, navigation, and social relations. Basically, then, they claim that linguistic functionality could be a matter of exaptation.

However, neither adaptation nor exaptation will do for linguistic functionality, for the simple reason that language is based on an invention and therefore on human agency, a phenomenon found nowhere else in the biosphere. What comes to mind here is a distinction made by Searle (1995: 20), namely between agentive and non-agentive functionality. Examples he gives are the heart and a paperweight. The functionality of the heart developed by natural selection and comes about during ontogeny on the basis of our genetic program, without human interference. When we use a stone as a paperweight, however, its function is not a matter of natural selection but of human decision. We can even use an object designed for some other purpose as a paperweight, as long as it has the right size and weight. This shows an agentive version of exaptation. Agentive functionality is the right notion for language, even in the narrowest sense. This situates language outside the scope of standard biology, which has no equivalent of agentive functionality (apart perhaps from some very rudimentary use of tools among animals).

Words are tools and tools are the prototypical examples of physical structures showing agentive functionality. Moreover, words are not just tools but *cognitive* tools, something unknown even among our closest relatives, the great apes. Just as standard tools are an extension of our body, cognitive tools are an extension of our minds. Humans are not just standard biological entities but beings that live in symbiosis with objects that extend the sphere of their intentionality. Also within the human body, we can make a distinction between structures that fall within our sphere of intentionality and structures that do not. The hands, for instance, can be used as tools, while the kidneys cannot. The lungs, as discussed earlier in connection with trumpet playing, are an interesting case in that they have a non-agentive function in respiration but an agentive function in the playing of wind music. The reason is clear: unlike the heart and the kidneys, the functioning of the hands and the lungs is accessible to our control and therefore falls within the sphere of human intentionality.

These considerations also apply to the brain. Much of what goes on in the brain is not accessible to us and therefore falls outside the sphere of human intentionality. Words and their use, however, are accessible to consciousness and willful arrangement and therefore do fall within the sphere of human intentionality. This does, of course, not mean that we have conscious access to *how* the brain manages the use of words, but that is true for all tool use, including the use of a hammer or a computer. We have no idea what happens in our brain when we use a hammer. In order to be used as a tool, it suffices that a structure is under our control in one way or another.

The most important preliminary conclusion at this point is that human agency and intentionality cannot be characterized by the standard forms of functionality known from biology (viz. adaptation and exaptation). The missing concept is Searle's agentive functionality. Recent developments in neurobiology give further substance to this key notion for the understanding of the biological foundations of culture. In a very important book, Dehaene (2009) gives a neurobiological account of another form of cognitive technology, our use of writing systems. Writing and reading are interesting because it is uncontroversial that writing is a relatively recent invention, say, of 5,000 years ago. That is far too short a period for a capacity to have developed by natural selection. Nevertheless, as Dehaene shows, our use of the graphic systems (of all cultures) is governed by very specific areas of the brain, reminiscent of the classical areas of Broca and Wernicke. Dehaene and others have identified a region in the occipito-temporal sulcus of the left hemisphere that Dehaene has dubbed "the letterbox."

This is a very important discovery because it shows that even uncontroversially cultural phenomena such as reading and writing are not controlled by some mechanism of general intelligence, but by very specific areas evolved for very specific purposes. In this case, the area in question is specialized for the recognition of shapes and for object invariance (i.e. the capacity to recognize something as the same object when seen from different angles and perspectives). This is largely an evolved, innate capacity, with obvious survival value for apes and monkeys as well (hence the finding of homologous structures in their brains). However, we humans have been able to give these innate structures a new function, namely the function created by the invention of writing systems. This is the agentive form of function assignment discussed earlier and Dehaene calls it our capacity for "recycling": our capacity to give very specific, innate brain structures a new function by using them in a new, culturally invented context.

Recycling, in Dehaene's sense, is precisely the notion we are looking for, and it sets a standard for all cognitive phenomena with a cultural, agentive component, including natural language. Both spoken language and writing systems are cognitive technology, primarily memory technology. Derived from these, we have a set of linguistic tools for the support of thinking and for communication. If both are cognitive technologies, an interesting question arises as to the differences. Spoken language differs from writing, after all, in that it is universal and acquired much earlier in life and without explicit instruction. But none of this makes a difference to the logic of the problem. Nothing in the recycling hypothesis says anything about the fact that some forms of recycling are easier to obtain than others. Singing songs, for instance, is universal and acquired early in life, while playing the piano is far from universal, learned later in life, and with much more effort and explicit instruction. Nevertheless, both are uncontroversially cultural activities making use of innate capacities. It is just that some activities lean more heavily on easily accessible innate capacities than others, as can be demonstrated with numerous examples.

Another possibility is hypothesizing that language involved a certain measure of *coevolution* (Deacon 1997). That, too, is entirely compatible with the recycling hypothesis and here it is likely that the speed of access and use of language was favored by natural selection. However, that would be a matter of facilitating evolution, not function-creating evolution. Recall that the function of organs such as the heart is created by evolution, while linguistic functionality is created by human invention. Nothing of principle excludes the possibility that the use of inventions is rewarded by natural selection.

1.8 Concluding remarks

Altogether Dehaene's notion of recycling is the right concept for human capacities that integrate biological and cultural phenomena. It is confirmed in case after case and is the cutting-edge idea about the relation between the brain and its cultural applications (see also Marcus 2004: 140). It avoids

Panglossianism and the idea that we can meaningfully speak of a Universal Grammar or the LAD even before the child is exposed to the words that are a necessary condition for calling something linguistic in the first place. In general, there is no evidence for innate biological structures in the brain with intrinsic cultural dedication. Our internal organs are functionally dedicated thanks to evolution, but the brain structures involved in language are functionally dedicated by human agency, which demonstrates its power in the invention of words shared by a community.

The notion of recycling also avoids the preformationist idea that, for example, elephants were at earlier stages of their individual development or ontogeny just smaller elephants, up to the very small ones present in their father's sperm.[1] Preformationism has since long been replaced by a more epigenetic approach to embryology: what precedes elephants in their ontogeny is not elephant-like all the way back, even if there is substantial predetermination in that the process is largely controlled by elephant DNA. This lesson from biology seems to apply to language acquisition as well: there are no good reasons to assume full-fledged concepts or a language of thought before birth. Probably, then, it is not the Panglossian and preformationist rationalism of Fodor (1983) and Chomsky that is the ultimate answer to Skinner and his successors, but rather the epigenetic rationalism of Piaget and others.[2] According to Piaget, mental growth proceeds in stages that are qualitatively different from one another. This approach better suits the fact that we are born with a rich, genetically determined mental endowment but that nothing forces us to assume a *linguistic* mental state before actual exposure to the words of our community.

2

History of the study of second language acquisition

Margaret Thomas

2.1 Introduction: when does the history of second language begin?

How people learn a second language is a topic of long-standing human curiosity as well as of prime educational and social importance. Speculation about the nature of second language acquisition can be read between the lines in texts created by teachers and scholars in (what we now call) Europe, going back at least to late antiquity. This chapter addresses the backdrop to the study of second language acquisition as carried out in cultures based historically in Europe. Certainly other cultures have, for diverse reasons, valued knowledge of a second language and speculated about its nature (e.g. ancient India; the Arabic-speaking world). But the focus here is on western tradition, because (i) at present, historiography of the study of language acquisition in China, India, Africa, the Middle East, etc. is sparse; (ii) the historical sources of European-based inquiry into language acquisition are accessible to readers of this handbook; and (iii) the influence of European-based inquiry into language acquisition is now felt worldwide.

In western Europe by the sixth or seventh century CE, the Romance vernaculars had diverged from Latin to the point where Latin was no longer spoken natively. Schoolchildren therefore required foreign language instruction in order to read the classic literature of the poets and orators that Roman society prized so highly. This created a major problem, because the existing materials and practices of literary instruction had been designed for native speakers of Latin, to teach them a metalanguage for analyzing and labeling the parts of their own language. Grammarians and teachers gradually adapted the received pedagogical tradition for students who needed to learn both an analytic metalanguage and Latin itself, which by the sixth century was no longer anyone's native language (Law 1986) but had become the language of education and Christianity. In the process of adapting grammars and classroom practices, Roman scholars had to conceptualize the nature of second language learning. Implicit in the innovations they introduced are attempts to answer such questions as "What kind of exposure do learners need in order to acquire a second language?"; "What faculties do learners bring to the task of learning a second language?"; and even "What role does the social context of learning play in acquisition?"

The Romans did not, of course, come up with permanently or universally satisfactory answers to these questions. Subsequent teachers, scholars and learners up to the present day have continued to ask and answer questions about the nature of second language (L2) acquisition, framed in the different idioms of their varied social, intellectual and linguistic contexts, and their different senses of what counts as an adequate answer. Gradually, reflection on L2 acquisition has accumulated. These reflections do not form a coherent tradition in the sense that successive contributors built on each other's work, much less that they did so self-consciously to create "theories" of L2 acquisition. That came only much later. But the accumulated, heterogeneous, reflections of people who have observed L2 learning or speculated about its nature – century by century, in however fragmentary or limited a manner – constitute the history of the discipline.

Some modern scholars (Block 2003; Gass 2009; Gass, Fleck, Leder and Svetics 1998; but cf. Joseph 2010: 5–6) prefer to view the study of L2 acquisition as originating when it was identified as a scientific discipline, conventionally dated around the middle of the twentieth century. Scientific methods have certainly allowed contemporary scholars to build powerful models of L2 acquisition, which have opened up new insights into it (Jordan 2004). But to dismiss insight into L2 acquisition that existed before the emergence of twentieth-century notions of science, or to claim that scientific methods and assumptions obviate whatever predated them, is unduly restricting (Thomas 1998a, 2004). To do so closes down opportunities to understand the range of ways in which people have tried to make sense of second language learning; it perpetuates disciplinary isolation; and it impoverishes our capacity to evaluate current research.

This chapter focuses primarily on the very recent history of second language acquisition, from the 1950s to around 2000 (after which point subsequent chapters in the handbook recount the immediate-past context of their topics, as necessary). But although the mid twentieth century is the conventionally acknowledged starting point for the modern discipline, the last fifty or sixty years do not encompass all relevant reflection on the topic. They only encompass what is most accessible and expedient to readers of the handbook. The distinction is important. Part of what defines what is accessible and expedient is relevance, and historical context furnishes our sense of what counts as relevant. Historical context also helps us identify what is genuinely innovative. Therefore in narrating the late twentieth-century history of L2 acquisition, I will freely refer to pre-twentieth-century ideas and texts by way of contextualizing contemporary and near-contemporary treatment of the topic.

The chapter is organized as follows. I focus on the historical backdrop to three themes common in present-day discussion of L2 acquisition: (i) the role of a learner's first language; (ii) capacities imputed to be inherent to learners and which bear on the task of L2 acquisition; and (iii) the function of the social context in which learning takes place. In Chapter 3 of this volume, Myles provides a useful taxonomy of three "families of theories" of L2 acquisition. The three themes I will review historically each represent one of Myles' three families, namely formal, cognitive and sociocultural theories of language acquisition. Other themes subsumed under Myles' families of theories might be targets of similar historical research, but are not touched on here: linguistic subsystems that underlie learners' performance; conceptualization of L2 processing; the relationship between input and L2 acquisition. Mine are not the only themes, or even necessarily the most important ones, in modern L2 research. Rather, they are themes that are salient in the recent history of the field and that have appeared in different guises over its full-length history. Therefore (i), (ii) and (iii) provide a basis for appreciating continuities and discontinuities across the full history of second language acquisition, a history that vastly predates the twentieth-century focus in this chapter.

2.2 History of the role of a learner's native language in second language acquisition

The fact that a second language learner already knows another, native, language is so basic to modern conceptualization of L2 learning that it provides the name for the phenomenon, "*second language* acquisition." Acknowledging that in common usage what goes by this term may actually constitute acquisition of a third or fourth (etc.) language, that label prioritizes the fact that a learner has previous exposure to (at least) one other language. (There are imaginable alternatives. "Second language acquisition" might instead be labeled in a manner that focuses on the learner's age, as in "language acquisition in adulthood" or "in late childhood.") Modern observers notice that certain properties of the first language (L1) predictably surface in L2 learners' performance so that, for example, Russian-speaking learners of English typically exhibit a profile of targetlike and non-targetlike production in English that differs from the profile of Chinese-speaking learners of English. Although not entirely uncontroversial, most contemporary scholars take for granted that a learner's L1 plays some role in the acquisition of L2; what is debated is the nature of that role (see Chapter 5, this volume). However, what counts as an obvious fact today is not given by nature. The attribution of a role for a learner's L1 in L2 acquisition is a concept that was built up gradually over time.

2.2.1 Prehistory of the role of L1

In recounting the background to modern debate about the influence of a learner's native language, it is instructive to intentionally start too early, that is, to review scholarly reflection on L2 acquisition before the L1 was attributed a distinctive role. For example, the Roman rhetorician and educator Quintilian (Marcus Fabius Quintilianus, 35/40–97 CE) designed an idealized curriculum for bilingual literacy training in Greek and Latin, starting with the beginning of a child's education at age 7 (see Marrou 1956: 262–65; Hovdhaugen (1982: 83–86) provides excerpts from Quintilian's writings; Kaimio (1979) discusses Roman bilingualism). Quintilian treated the two on a par with each other, since in his day many children of the Roman elite learned Greek from servants and household slaves and thus entered school with competence in Greek as well as Latin. He stated that his aim was "to give equal attention to both languages, [so that] neither will prove a hindrance to the other" (*Institutio oratoria*, trans. Butler 1920, vol. I: 27). Implicitly, then, neither had priority over the other in Quintilian's reckoning of the nature of language learning: Latin could be a "hindrance" to Greek as much as vice versa. These assumptions mirrored the tradition of Greek/Latin bilingualism that prevailed in the relevant social class in Quintilian's day. But there is little evidence that the ancient Romans attended to other languages they encountered – Germanic, Celtic, Etruscan, Umbrian, Oscan – or that they believed that to acquire those languages was to gain access to cognitive or cultural capital of the same order as was derived from the acquisition of Greek or Latin. Therefore it is not surprising that Quintilian did not conceptualize the influence of an L1 on an L2 in general terms.

Moving ahead 1300 years, across evidence of diverse treatments of (what we now call) first versus second languages, the Florentine poet Dante Alighieri (1265–1321) made an important contribution. Dante opened his essay *De vulgari eloquentia* ("On vulgar eloquence"; trans. Botterill 1996: 3) by distinguishing natural vernacular languages, learned "by imitating our nurses," from what he referred to as artificial languages, "developed through dedication to a lengthy course of study." Dante's purpose was to praise the power and nobility of the vernacular languages at the expense of the "artificial language" Latin, inverting the usual assignment of prestige. Along the way he sharply defined two classes of languages, which differ on the basis of how they are learned and also in their inherent features: according to Dante, the one is employed by the "whole world... though with different pronunciations and using different words"; the other "a secondary kind of language" that Romans, Greeks and "some – but not all – other peoples also have" (ibid.).

In this we can see an emerging conceptualization of first versus second languages, although for Dante they seem to be so different in kind as to make an influence of one on the other remote. In 1570 a text by the humanist Benedetto Varchi (1503–65) took a different stance. Like Dante, Varchi distinguished native from non-native languages and attributed "naturalness" to the former. But Varchi viewed them as essentially commensurate outside the context of acquisition: non-native languages are "those which one does not speak naturally, but which one learns with time, effort, or from those who teach the languages, or who speak them, or from books" (Varchi 1804 [1570]: 211). In other words, for Varchi (unlike for Dante) non-natively acquired languages are not different in kind from natively acquired ones, only different with respect to a given learner's experience. What is a native language to one speaker could be a non-native language to another speaker and vice versa. This was a significant intellectual achievement in the history of conceptualization of L2 acquisition.

2.2.2 Role of L1 in twentieth-century structuralism

The gap between Quintilian's assumptions about Greek/Latin bilingualism and the essentially equal footing on which Varchi placed native versus non-native languages stretches across fifteen centuries of changing social, intellectual and linguistic circumstances. Scholars continued to explore differing epistemological bases for natively versus non-natively acquired languages. Moving forward abruptly to the middle of the twentieth century, study of language in the United States had by then claimed membership in the company of the sciences, in large part due to the initiative of American structuralist Leonard Bloomfield (1887–1949). Bloomfield worked in an era when Saussurean synchronic study of language was taking a seat next to diachronic study of language, that is, next to the historical-comparative linguistics that dominated nineteenth-century European language scholarship. For Bloomfield, identification of linguistics as a science, rather than a facet of cultural history, was a central career goal (e.g. Bloomfield 1926).[1] Not surprisingly, a shift toward treating the study of language as a science affected all facets of linguistic research, including conceptualization of the relationship of learners' first to second languages.

Two key figures were the University of Michigan's Charles C. Fries (1887–1967) and his student Robert Lado (1915–95). Fries and Lado are jointly associated with Contrastive Analysis, a pedagogical technique that focused attention on structural differences between a learner's L1 and L2. Contrastive Analysis assigns a strong role to the first language in second language acquisition, namely it assumed that learners presuppose that the properties of L1 also hold for the L2. Lado (1957) assumed a broad notion of learners' extension of the "properties of L1" to L2. Not only do learners expect the structural properties of L1 to hold in L2, but also the properties of the sound system and lexicon, and even orthographic and cultural conventions. Where L1 resembles L2, acquisition should be unimpeded. Conversely, where properties of L1 differ from those of L2, learners have to be taught to abandon the presupposition of L1/L2 identity. Therefore, second language acquisition can be facilitated by calling attention to points of contrast between L1 and L2. Fries (1945) argued that, by these lights, conducting contrastive analyses of L1 versus L2 phonology, morphology, syntax, lexis, etc. prepares teachers to teach effectively. Lado popularized the technique and demonstrated how to carry out L1/L2 contrastive analyses. For example, relying heavily on Fries' work, Lado (1957: 90–91) listed four steps for comparing L1 versus L2 vocabulary items: first, compare the forms of pairs of words; then, compare their meanings, their distributions, and their connotations. In comparing the sound systems of two languages, Lado advocated that the analyst ask three questions: do the L1 and L2 have phonetically similar phonemes? Are their allophones similar in both languages? Are those allophones similarly distributed? (1957: 13).

Fries was a structuralist (or "descriptivist") linguist in the sense that the term distinguished structuralism from historical linguistics, or synchronic from diachronic study of language. The terms in which Fries framed Contrastive Analysis were those of American structuralism, which conceived of a language as built up in levels, from the smallest units, phonemes. Phonemes combined to form units at the next level, morphemes, and then on to larger and larger units. Contrastive Analysis thus conventionally began by collecting and comparing what were considered the atomic units of the sound system of L1 versus those of L2. This was characteristic of structuralists' self-consciously "scientific" working style: they focused on the distribution of observable facts of language and analyzed them according to what they judged to be simple, ordered, explicitly defined "discovery procedures." Structuralism was also recognizably a product of an intellectual culture that placed a high value on empirical evidence which was gathered and interpreted according to "scientific" methods. Contrastive Analysis was recognizably structuralist in another sense too, namely in that it took for granted the systematicity of all languages at any point in their historical development and the analyzability of all languages using structuralist concepts and terms. Compared to Quintilian or Varchi, Fries and Lado obviously worked under vastly different assumptions about languages and attributed a different role to L1 in L2 acquisition.

By the late 1960s, however, confidence in Contrastive Analysis began to erode. It was shown to both under- and over-predict difficulty in acquisition, threatening Fries' and Lado's assumption that second language learners presuppose the resemblance of L1 and L2. Dušková (1969), for example, showed that for Czech learners of English, L1/L2 difference did not always disrupt acquisition and conversely, that L1/L2 similarity did not ensure error-free acquisition. In addition to these empirical threats, Contrastive Analysis was affected by a widespread reassessment of American structuralism that took place around that time. Generative grammar emerged to challenge structuralism's reluctance to generalize beyond the observable facts of language. Generativists viewed structuralists' empiricist orientation as a liability, in that it failed to take into account the creativity exhibited in everyday use of language, which (in generative terms) must be based in an innate language faculty, not a repertoire of memorized patterns, as assumed by structuralists. Nevertheless, generative grammar shared with structuralism certain fundamental commitments: that linguistics is a science; that linguistic phenomena can be analyzed as systematic and "rule-governed" at any point in time; and perhaps even structuralists' habit of resolving linguistic phenomena into ordered levels (see Chapter 1, this volume). These characteristics of American structuralism were inherited by a generation of linguists who dissociated themselves from some of the achievements of structuralists, including from Fries' and Lado's Contrastive Analysis and its assumptions about the role of L1 in L2 acquisition.

As an aside, it has often been claimed (e.g. by Dulay, Burt and Krashen 1982: 98, 140; R. Ellis 1985: 23; Larsen-Freeman and Long 1991: 55; and many others) that Chomsky's (1959) famous repudiation of B. F. Skinner's (1904–90) behaviorist psychology of language undermined Contrastive Analysis. Actually, Contrastive Analysis was not founded on behaviorism. Aside from Bloomfield, behaviorism was not popular among American structuralists. Fries, for example, was a thoroughgoing humanist who rejected the reduction of human behavior to stimulus-response contingencies (P. Fries 1987; Pocklington 1990: 43). Lado was also little disposed to behaviorism (1964: 35–37). It is more historically accurate to view the abandonment of Contrastive Analysis as occurring independently of the fate of behaviorism (see Thomas [in preparation]). In any case, the substantial empirical challenges that Contrastive Analysis faced were sufficient to discredit it.

2.2.3 Reconceptualizing the role of L1 in the 1970s–1980s

Loss of confidence in Contrastive Analysis led researchers to rethink the assumption that L1 had a strong formative influence on L2 acquisition. Studies by Dulay and Burt (1974b) on child learners whose L1 was either Spanish or Chinese and by Bailey, Madden and Krashen (1974) on adults of various L1s found *no* influence of the native language in the sequence of acquisition of L2 English morphosyntax. These findings in reaction to Contrastive Analysis, however, soon met with heterogeneous counter-reaction. Research from the 1970s and early 1980s documented support for the common intuition that a learner's L1 does indeed play some role in L2 acquisition: perhaps a role in the accuracy, path, or rate of acquisition, or in the incidence of avoidance strategies or in the sequence of provisional hypotheses a learner generates as he or she approximates the target-language grammar. Or, perhaps the effect of the L1 surfaces differently in different linguistic domains and different contexts of acquisition (see Gass and Selinker 2008: 136–51 for review). Flynn's (1987) study of L2 word order and anaphora started from a conviction that neither contrastive analysis nor Dulay and Burt's "creative construction" could adequately account for the course and outcome of L2 acquisition.[2]

Conceptualization of the role of L1 in L2 acquisition thus entered a state of flux in the 1970s and 1980s. During the same interval, research methodology evolved rapidly, unsettling the interpretation of many earlier empirical studies. Moreover, generative theory gained adherents – and critics – as a tool for understanding how people acquire a second language. The first pioneering attempts to apply generative theory in L2 research were merely exploratory, but gradually researchers began to take it more seriously (see White 1989, 2003a). From that developed new conceptions of the role of L1 in L2 acquisition.

A representative study from the 1980s that probed the role of L1 in L2 is White (1985). She tested whether Spanish- versus French-speaking learners differ in their grammars of an aspect of English about which generative theory made some intriguing crosslinguistic claims. Adopting a then-contemporary version of generative theory (Chomsky 1981), White accepted that a human language faculty imposes universal formal principles on the structure of natural language grammars. By these lights, differences across languages derive from a limited number of "parameter settings" built into principles of Universal Grammar, in the way a restaurant may offer diners two options for appetizer, entrée and dessert within an otherwise fixed menu. A single parameter setting was held to give rise to a cluster of related surface-level facts, making it possible (in theory) for a small collection of principles in which a finite number of parameter settings are embedded to account for a great deal of the complexity of crosslinguistic differences.

White's research (among many other studies from the same period) investigated whether, in cases where L1 and L2 select different parameter settings, the L1 setting is retained in L2. Her topic was the "*pro*-drop parameter," proposed to constrain whether a grammar allows null pronouns as subjects in finite clauses (the [+*pro*-drop] setting, as in Spanish *Tengo hambre*, literally, "Have hunger," where the first-person subject can be dropped, while the verb is marked – with *o-* for first person), or whether a grammar disallows null subjects ([–*pro*-drop], as in English, which exclusively allows "*I am hungry*," with an explicit subject). Although the *pro*-drop parameter is named for this specific property, its feature setting ([+/–]) also purportedly governs other grammatical properties. Among them is whether a grammar allows inversion of subjects and verbs in declarative sentences: [+*pro*-drop] languages like Spanish allow inversion of full (non-pronominal) subjects as in *Vino Juan* (literally "came Juan"); [–*pro*-drop] English allows only "Juan came" (White 1985: 48).

White's research assumed that Spanish is [+*pro*-drop] and English and French [–*pro*-drop]. She asked whether Spanish-speaking learners transfer their [+*pro*-drop] setting in L2 English, while French-speaking learners correctly reject null subjects and subject–verb inversion in L2 English since neither is attested in their L1. White's results were mixed. She found clear evidence that Spanish speakers do, in fact, accept many more null subjects in English than French speakers do. But the two groups performed similarly with respect to inversion.

Looking beyond these equivocal results, note that White (1985) sought evidence that learners' acceptance of null subjects co-occurred with their acceptance of subject–verb inversion, or that conversely, learners rejected both constructions together. That is, her work probed learners' abstract grammatical knowledge of the L2 as predicted by a proposed parameter setting, not the presence or absence of specific L1/L2 grammatical patterns.

Whether or not learners produced null subjects or subject-verb inversion is less telling than whether or not those two grammatical features were correlated in their grammars. In this sense generative-inspired research diverged in its conceptualization of language and of the role of L1 in L2 acquisition, compared to that of Fries and Lado. And it did so in a way that highlights its differences from mid-century American structuralism. Structuralism was attentive to the forms and distributions of linguistic units and notoriously intolerant of abstraction, whereas late twentieth-century generativism trafficked freely in abstractions and took for granted that its object of investigation was linguistic competence – that is, learners' unconscious knowledge of language, which is only partially reflected in their performance, that is, their use of language.

White (1985) and many other studies from the 1980s adopted a generativist orientation in assuming that if there is an effect of L1 in L2, it is not an effect of sounds, words or sentences of L1 serving as models for sounds, words or sentences in L2. Rather, the locus of influence (or failure of influence) of L1 on L2 would be at the level of learners' knowledge of language underlying L1 linguistic units and their patterned distribution. In that sense, universal principles and language-specific parameter settings mediate apparent L1 transfer effects. Among other important studies from the same period that shared – or challenged – these assumptions, one might mention Adjémian (1976), Clahsen and Muysken (1986), Liceras (1986) and Schachter (1989a). White (1989) surveys this work.

2.2.4 Late twentieth-century research on the role of L1

The role of L1 in L2 continues to be investigated in generative studies of L2 acquisition. Subsequent research has framed the issue somewhat differently, but shares the notion that the role of L1 in L2 is instantiated not through the surface units of the language but through learners' abstract grammatical knowledge. For example, one prominent stream of work in the 1990s sought to define the "initial state" of L2 learners, that is, to define the starting point from which learners proceed at the outset of L2 acquisition, including the role of the L1. A proposal by Schwartz and Sprouse, labeled "Full Transfer / Full Access" (1996; see Chapter 5, this volume), argued that learners' initial approach to an L2 presupposes that all the abstract properties of L1 (universal principles plus L1-specific parameter settings, or what replaced them in successive versions of generative grammar) hold in L2. Schwartz and Sprouse further argued that learners eventually reset parameter settings as needed to match their perceptions of L2 where L1 and L2 differ, since learners do not lose recourse to the full set of options. Therefore, as in the case of White (1985), Schwartz and Sprouse (1996) conceived of the role of L1 in L2 as instantiated through the underlying L1 grammar, taken as the starting point for construction of the L2 grammar.

Counterproposals to Full Transfer / Full Access emerged rapidly in the 1990s, variously exploring which abstract properties of the L1 grammar play what roles in L2 and proposing limits on the capacity of learners to abandon a property of L1 where L1 and L2 diverge. Vainikka and Young-Scholten's (1996a) "Minimal Trees Hypothesis," for example, argued on the basis of data from uninstructed learners of German that learners' initial state imposes on L2 the lexical categories of the L1 and presupposes certain principles that govern lexical categories, but that the L2 grammar is devoid of all functional categories. As learners' exposure to the target language continues, they gradually acquire an appropriate inventory of functional categories. Eubank (1996) made a different proposal about learners' initial state. His research explored the plausibility that a grammar comprising both lexical and functional categories is available to learners from the start, but that what learners must acquire is the values attributed to features associated with L2 functional (grammatical) categories. For example, language may have either "weak" or "strong" verb features. Learners of L2 English have to acquire the fact that English has "weak" verb features and as a result, the grammar of English does not generate word order patterns with the main verb "raised" over the adverb like *John plays often tennis. Learners of L2 French have to acquire its "strong" verb features, which generate precisely that word order.

It is important to note that this historical sketch of proposals about the role of L1 in L2 acquisition privileges research based on generative theory. This has the advantage of offering a gratifyingly stark contrast between 1950s Contrastive Analysis and what followed it; and since generative grammar has been widely influential, that contrast is salient to a *Handbook of Second Language Acquisition*. However, this sketch necessarily fails to represent the full range of other proposals and assumptions about the role of L1 in L2 acquisition. To take examples from anglophone literature in the 1900s, that would include the writings of Henry Sweet (1845–1912) and the "Reform Movement" (Howatt 1984); Otto Jespersen (1860–1943); Harold E. Palmer (1877–1949); J. R. Firth (1890–1960); M. A. K. Halliday (b. 1925). All of these figures wrote about second language learning and teaching, from varied points of view. Sweet ([1899] 1964: 53–5), for example, conceived of what he called cross-association between a learner's native and target languages as holding differential relevance across stages of acquisition: L1/L2 similarity facilitates early learning, but eventually impedes progress at a more advanced level. The contributions of scholars like Sweet to our understanding of the roles of L1 in L2 acquisition in a wider history of L2 studies await investigation.

2.3 History of research on the inherent capacities of second language learners

2.3.1 "Cartesian linguistics"
As in the case of the influence of L1 on L2, the question of what is given or immutable with respect to the learner has been raised in diverse terms

over the history of western linguistics. Chomsky (2009 [1966]: 98–106) cites seventeenth-century scholars, including Herbert of Cherbury (1583–1648) and Géraud de Cordemoy (1626–84), as holding a rationalist position that speakers know more about language than they could possibly have learned from the environment. Chomsky identified this stance as characteristic of what he calls "Cartesian linguistics," in reference to the French philosopher René Descartes (1596–1650), a founding figure in modern western epistemology. According to Chomsky, Wilhelm von Humboldt (1767–1835) developed a Cartesian perspective on language learning in a text published in 1836, in which Humboldt wrote that language "cannot properly be taught but only awakened in the mind; it can only be given the threads by which it develops on its own account"; and moreover that, "The language-learning of children is not an assignment of words, to be deposited in memory and rebabbled by rote through the lips, but a growth in linguistic capacity with age and practice" (trans. P. Heath, 1988: 44, 58; cited in Chomsky 2009 [1966]: 101). In these terms, Chomsky considers Herbert, Cordemoy, Humboldt and others as precursors to twentieth-century notions that humans possess an innate language faculty as part of their genetic endowment.

Chomsky's reading of seventeenth-century philosophy as comprising an outcropping of "Cartesian linguistics," a tradition within which he identifies his own work, has been highly controversial among historians of linguistics (see Thomas 2004: 109–19 for review of diverse points of view). But both preceding and following the seventeenth century there was abundant speculation about what capacities learners bring to the task of learning a language. The notion that language learning is at least in part dependent on learners' rationality – that is, dependent on their inherent powers of reasoning, induction and generalization, as opposed to dependent on the memorization of words or rules – is frequently attested in teaching materials and methods. As an extreme example, the German-born seventeenth-century grammarian and language teacher Gaspar Scioppius (1576–1649), discussed by Breva-Claramonte (1984), argued that rules of grammar are founded in logic and are therefore necessarily without exception. Scioppius attributed apparent exceptions to processes of ellipsis, or to failure of insight on the part of the grammarian. Learners therefore require only a brief summary of the properties of the L2, provided that it is prepared with adequate insight and a few examples. By exercising their natural powers of rationality, they can then induce the full range of features of the L2. On this basis, Scioppius reduced the grammar of Latin to so few rules that they "[could] be easily memorized by the average pupil in one day" (Breva-Claramonte 1984: 277).

There is, obviously, a significant gap between the powers of rationality that Scioppius ascribed to language learners (which, arguably, are a matter of self-conscious application and may be trained or sharpened with practice) and the character of an innate language faculty that some modern linguists ascribe to learners. The latter operates involuntarily, beneath the level of consciousness; its domain is, by hypothesis, specific to language; and research into its content is carried out with the tools of modern empirical research. Critics of "Cartesian linguistics" point out similar gaps between the ideas of Herbert of Cherbury, Cordemoy or Humboldt and generative grammar's conceptualization of language learning. Chomsky, however, has consistently maintained that generative grammar's conceptualization of language learning is part of an intellectual tradition that flourished in the seventeenth century, was submerged during the nineteenth century and then re-emerged in the late 1950s in the idiom of modern cognitive science.

2.3.2 Emergence of the notion of interlanguage

Without presuming to adjudicate this significant historiographical controversy, a lot has been written since the 1950s about the inherent capacities of second language learners. S. Pit Corder's (1926–90) 1967 article, "The significance of learner's [sic] errors" and Larry Selinker's 1972 article "Interlanguage" form a symbolic point of origin for contemporary L2 acquisition studies (Thomas 1998b). Corder's contribution was to argue for a notion that has become a bedrock assumption in contemporary L2 acquisition theory: that L2 learners' grammars exhibit internal consistency independent of the extent to which they approximate the characteristics of native-speaker grammars of that same language. Selinker accepted Corder's premises; coined the term "interlanguage" to label a learner's output as he or she attempted to reproduce the L2; and attributed the systematicity of interlanguages to the operation of learners' "latent psychological structures" which exist as "an already formulated arrangement in the brain" (1972: 211–15).

Corder and Selinker built their arguments by selective and rather desultory reference to existing research on L2 acquisition. The notion of interlanguage, however, gave rise to new empirical studies that probed the existence and content of learners' inherent capabilities. When Dulay and Burt (1974b) and Bailey et al. (1974), adverted to above, discredited the role of L1 in their research on the order of acquisition of English morphosyntax (see Chapter 27, this volume), they interpreted their finding of an apparently fixed sequence of acquisition as due to some (unspecified) "built-in syllabus" (a term they borrowed from Corder 1967: 166) governing L2 acquisition, emphasizing that processes learners engage in to establish an internal grammar of the L2 are ruled less by the influence of L1 than by inherent dispositions in the language faculty.

Dulay and Burt (1974b) and Bailey et al. (1974) are representative of research in this vein in that their work started by collecting a corpus of learner data. They then explicated the systematicity they discovered in the corpus and (in the absence of an obvious external source of that systematicity) attributed it to the existence of specific cognitive capacities in learners. By the 1980s the basis for L2 research shifted from a model centering on the interpretation of discovered systematicity, to the hypothesis-testing model favored in the modern social sciences. In the latter approach, the L2 researcher begins with a theoretically motivated constraint, deduces what would count as evidence for its presence or absence in learners' interlanguage and then tests those predictions against elicited or observed data (see, for example, Chapter 7, this volume). As a result, conceptualization of the inherent capacities of L2 learners is driven forward by linguistic theory. As linguistic theory has evolved, new research has followed, in the effort to discern whether L2 grammars evince a particular theoretically grounded constraint.

This stream of research – whether or not it can be conceived of as continuous with Chomsky's Cartesian linguistics – has spread since the 1980s into many domains in the study of second language acquisition, giving rise to strong claims and counterclaims about what L2 learners bring to the acquisition of phonology, morphology, lexis, semantics, syntax, etc. It takes for granted the existence of a highly articulated language faculty and its operation (whether full or partial is debated) in L2 acquisition (see Chapter 7, this volume). A representative study is Dekydtspotter, Sprouse and Anderson (1997; see Chapter 22, this volume). Dekydtspotter *et al.* interpret sentence-comprehension data from L2 learners of French to show that they acknowledge a distinction between the grammars of result versus process nominals, a distinction the learners cannot have derived from their L1 grammars, nor from their exposure to French, nor from direct instruction.

2.3.3 Reappraising the basis of L2 learners' capacities

There are also competing conceptions of L2 learners' capacities, which counterpropose that L2 acquisition can be explained without assuming the existence of a specific language faculty. Some counterproposals claim, in diverse terms, that learners' complex knowledge of L2 emerges out of multidimensional interaction among non-linguistic factors. Bley-Vroman (1990), for example, argued provocatively that L2 learning should be accounted for without positing that learners have access to a mental faculty dedicated specifically to language learning. He conceded that for child L1 learners, the speed and uniformity of acquisition of their first language and the independence of L1 from the environment of learning, implies that child learners have access to specifically linguistic faculties. But Bley-Vroman posited that a Fundamental Difference Hypothesis distinguishes L2 from L1 learners on the grounds that L2 learning is slow, unpredictable and highly individually variable. To Bley-Vroman, such characteristics are sufficient to establish that L2 learning is different in kind from L1 learning.

Bley-Vroman's Fundamental Difference Hypothesis has met with critique, for example, from Schwartz (1990, 1998a). Others have continued to explore ways to account for L2 acquisition that obviate the necessity of a language-specific mental faculty. What have come to be called "emergentist" approaches are various (see Chapter 28, this volume). Some scholars (e.g. N. C. Ellis 2002a) argue that learners attend to the relative frequency of particular form/meaning relationships in the input. On that basis, they extrapolate the grammatical structure of L2 – and they do so without access to cognitive capacities specifically dedicated to language. O'Grady (2003) has promoted a different kind of emergentism, arguing that L2 grammars can be accounted for as the products of the interaction of (for example) principles of processing efficiency with the limited capacity of working memory.

Modern psycholinguistic constructs such as language processing or working memory do not have historical precedents of much depth. But insofar as emergentist approaches in general exclude inherent, specifically linguistic, mental capacities, emergentism belongs to the empiricist tradition in philosophy. Empiricism emphasizes the origin of human knowledge in experience. In some versions, that means that everything a person knows, including about language, must derive strictly and solely from sense experience. In other versions, such as in British philosopher John Locke's (1632–1704) *Essay concerning Human Understanding* (1975 [1690]), a touchstone in the early history of empiricism, the mind has recourse from birth to the capacity for reflection, in addition to experience derived from the senses. Still other versions of empiricism admit inherent content to the mind in the form of more articulated but all-purpose capacities such as logic, the operation of memory, or the ability to make associations.

Empiricism has a long and many-branching family tree in western philosophy. It is not obvious how to best classify varieties of modern emergentism, especially since emergentism as it has developed in research on L2 acquisition is at present a work in progress. Tracing the historical background to emergentism, however, would be a rewarding historiographical task granted that the application of empiricism in the study of language has had its share of thoughtful proponents as well as incisive critics since at least the late eighteenth century, continuing up to today.[3] Notwithstanding the novelties of how empiricism is instantiated in emergentist theories of L2 acquisition, the existing reservoir of reflection on empiricism going back several hundred years supplies concepts and terms that can help us assess its applicability to questions about how people acquire a second language.

There are, of course, other facets in discussion of the inherent capacities of L2 learners. Some focus on the individual differences among learners that bear on the act of acquiring an L2 (see Chapters 8 and 15, this volume). Since the late twentieth century this includes research investigating correlations between success or failure of L2 acquisition in various domains with personal traits of diverse sorts, some fixed with respect to individual learners, some variable. Examples include age; aptitude; intelligence; motivation; psychological traits such as empathy, anxiety, or extroversion; and attitudes toward L2 native speakers and culture. Before the late 1900s, the only individual differences (aside from L1) that attracted sustained attention in discussion of L2 acquisition were age and aptitude. However, neither age nor aptitude has been well investigated historically as a factor bearing on L2 acquisition. Therefore it is premature to try to determine how either contributes to the long-range history of concepts of L2 acquisition.

In summary, there is an elaborate historical precedent to the study of inherent capacities available to all L2 learners, insofar as this is taken as a part of the debate between rationalists and empiricists. There is even a meta-debate about whether Chomsky has adequately conceived of the positions of rationalists versus empiricists with respect to language. Other kinds of inherent capacities of learners, such as the role of personal attributes in L2 acquisition, await historical analysis.

2.4 History of the role of social context in L2 acquisition

A third theme in the history of reflection on L2 acquisition is the question of whether, and if so to what extent and how, the social context of language learning is a relevant factor. Is what is most salient about L2 acquisition internal to learners – residing in their cognition – or is L2 acquisition in essence a social activity, something accomplished by interaction between people? Or (a third possibility) is the social context of language learning one among many layers of variables that bear on L2 acquisition, some so internal as to be subconscious to learners; some constituting explicit knowledge that a learner can articulate; some based in conventions of interpersonal communication external to the learner; and some extending even further, to the institutional and political environments in which learning takes place?

The question is an important one in defining the nature of L2 acquisition and has obvious ramifications for pedagogical practice. Since the early 1990s, modern versions of this question have been explored in research that (for example) analyzes conversations among L2 learners, or between L2 learners and native speakers, to show how the parties negotiate across language barriers to construct their social roles and self-representations with respect to each other. Other research has explored differences in the path and outcome of L2 acquisition depending on the social status of the L2 vis-à-vis the L1 (for example, where one is a minority-group language and the other a national language, or a language of high international prestige).[4]

2.4.1 Social interaction in L2 acquisition: fourth versus twentieth century

Inquiry into these dimensions of L2 acquisition has sometimes been carried out using quantitative social-scientific methods, but more commonly in the form of qualitative research that examines small case studies in depth. Either methodology is distinctively modern – as is the overall notion of "doing research" – but there are certainly historical precedents, where earlier scholars reflected on the role that social context plays in L2 acquisition. A famous passage in the *Confessions* of Augustine of Hippo (Aurelius Augustinus, 354–430 CE) comes to mind, in which Augustine contrasted his experiences of acquiring L1 Latin versus L2 Greek. Augustine framed that contrast not by calling attention to the different cognitive status of Latin as his first language acquired in infancy, versus that of Greek as a second language acquired as a schoolboy. Rather, he highlighted the different environments in which he learned Latin versus Greek. He wrote that he learned Latin:

> by keeping my eyes and ears open, amidst the flatterings of nurses and the jesting and pleased laughter of elders leading me on. I learned it without the painful pressure of compulsion, by the sole pressure of my own desire to express what was in my mind, which would have been impossible unless I had learnt words: and I learnt them not through people teaching me but simply through people speaking: to whom I was striving to utter my own feelings. (*Confessions* I, 14, trans. Sheed 1942: 14)

On the other hand, Augustine reported that when he studied Greek in school, he "was driven with threats and punishments to learn" and found it "hard and hateful": "the drudgery of learning a foreign language sprinkled bitterness over all the sweetness of the Greek tales" (I, 13–14, trans. Sheed 1942: 13–14). In these terms, Augustine attributed his successful acquisition of Latin at home to the context of "jesting and pleased laughter of elders" in which he strove "to utter [his] own feelings," compared to the school environment of "threats and punishments" where he failed to learn Greek. He concluded that "All this goes to prove that free curiosity is of more value in learning than harsh discipline" (ibid.).

In this passage from the *Confessions* Augustine represents, in fourth-century terms, starkly contrasting social-environmental factors in his differing experiences of language acquisition. From the late twentieth century, the discussion has been framed in terms that derive from psychology, sociology, anthropology and sociolinguistics. In particular, the work of Russian psychologist Lev Vygotsky (1896–1934) introduced in Europe and America in the late 1970s, has been influential. For Vygotsky, give-and-take between child language learners and their interlocutors within a specific sociocultural environment forms the basis for the development of cognition, including memory, logic, will and concept formation. Most importantly, according to Vygotsky (1986 [1934]), interpersonal exchange is the basis of L1 acquisition, because learners incorporate external, interpersonal, language first as private speech and eventually as silent thought. At each step of the transition from external speech, to private speech, to thought, Vygotsky asserted that the character of speech changes. But he insisted that the origin of language is in the sociocultural realm, not in cognition (see Chapter 30, this volume).

Vygotsky's claim is not merely that the social context of learning has a role in acquisition, even an important role. His claim is stronger: that learners initially appropriate language through person-to-person exchange, then internalize it as a tool for self-regulation. Vygotsky's ideas have recently been extended to L2 acquisition. A case study by Amy Snyder Ohta (2000a) of two adult learners of Japanese illustrates modern Vygotskian research. Ohta recorded and analyzed the speech and gestures used between two students as they collaborated on a peer-to-peer translation task directed at acquisition of the distribution of Japanese particles. Ohta's analysis showed that each student adopted subtle communicative signals that his or her partner accurately recognized as requests for assistance. The more advanced student waited for his partner's cues before offering assistance. As the partner's internalization of the distribution of particles advanced, she asked for (and needed) less assistance from her partner; the partner spontaneously decreased the rate in which he offered help and decreased the explicitness in which he encoded offers of help. Ohta concluded that her study confirmed Vygotsky's assertion that learning takes place through negotiated social interaction, which learners gradually incorporate as implicit self-regulated knowledge. As in Augustine's experience of "keeping my eyes and ears open, amidst the flatterings of nurses and the jesting and pleased laughter of elders leading me on," Ohta identified social interaction as the foundation of language acquisition, within which context the pair of students she analyzed evinced unstudied and sensitively regulated control over collaborative strategies. Those strategies maximized their capacity to acquire the L2.

2.4.2 Conceptualization of cognitive versus social factors in L2 learning

The precedence Vygotsky assigned to social context in the development of language and thought contrasts with the assumptions of mainstream research on L2 acquisition since the 1950s, especially in the United States. The conceptualization of L2 acquisition behind Fries' and Lado's structuralist, post-Bloomfieldian, Contrastive Analysis assumed that learning a second language is essentially a cognitive phenomenon. Later conceptualizations that supplanted Contrastive Analysis (Dulay and Burt's creative construction; White's generative grammar-based research; its successors, such as Full Transfer / Full Access) all share the assumption that learning a second language is at base a cognitive phenomenon, even as scholars have variously defined the specific cognitive resources available to L2 learners. Swimming against that mainstream, a classic 1997 article by Alan Firth and Johannes Wagner objected to what the authors perceived as a narrowly cognitive perspective on L2 acquisition, on the grounds that (for example) instead of abandoning variation in learner performance as irrelevant in a search to define what is universal in L2 acquisition, variation in performance should be and can be accounted for with respect to the diverse and mutable social-interactional situations in which language is used.

Firth and Wagner concluded that in order to reach a more comprehensive understanding of L2 learning, more research needs to be carried out about individual learners' communicative purposes and practices (see Chapter 30, this volume). Their 1997 article is sometimes identified as initiating a trend toward study of L2 acquisition in realistically idiosyncratic, non-idealized, social contexts.[5] It is a subject of debate whether sociocultural theories of L2 acquisition like that extrapolated from Vygotsky's work or that developed by Firth and Wagner are incompatible with research on L2 acquisition as a function of linguistic knowledge (or, to emergentists, as a function of language processing and working memory). For some scholars, a sociocultural approach necessarily excludes the validity of a cognitive approach (Long 1997; Johnson 2004); for other scholars, social and cognitive factors coexist within separate domains of L2 acquisition (Block 2003).

Therefore, debate about whether language is essentially a cognitive or social phenomenon is ongoing. It is useful to recognize that, in fact, the debate has been ongoing for a long time. In the eighteenth century, many scholars considered the origins of phenomena to be the best means of discerning their essential nature. Therefore the question of how the first human language developed was critical to understanding the nature of the human mind (in addition to the question's relevance to other eighteenth-century preoccupations: religion versus science; human nature versus social convention; humans versus animals). The French philosopher known as Condillac (1714–80), an admirer of John Locke, wrote one of the first treatises on the topic, *Essay on the origin of human knowledge*, in 1746. Condillac's *Essay* imagines how two pre-linguistic children who had gotten lost in a desert might invent language. By associating their natural gestures or cries (of pain, hunger, etc.) with specific objects of desire, the children would spontaneously invent relationships between linguistic signs and their referents. Condillac specified that two children would be required for this result: a single child alone would not develop language, because each needs to observe the other's gestures and cries in order to come to associate sounds with objects. By inventing language within this social context, children would create a powerful tool for analyzing their experience, on which basis they could then begin to build their cognitive faculties.

Condillac's topic proved irresistible for many scholars who followed, including Jean-Jacques Rousseau (1712–78), Wilhelm von Humboldt, Friedrich von Schlegel (1772–1829), Jacob Grimm (1785–1863), extending up to Max Müller (1823–1900). In 1769, the Berlin Academy of Science offered an award for the best essay on the origin of language. The prize went to Johann Gottfried Herder's (1744–1803) *Treatise on the Origin of Language*. Herder rejected Condillac's solution on the grounds that it offered no reason why animals might not likewise have developed language; and in any case, in the absence of language how could the children associate their cries with their objects of desire? Instead, Herder claimed that language has no discrete origin, but rather is as a product of reflection: human beings' "*first moment of taking-awareness* ... was also *the moment for the inward emergence of language*" (2002 [1772]: 128; emphasis in the original). For Herder language developed internally, then came to be employed in the world of social interaction. For Condillac language could only emerge out of interpersonal exchange, which then was a spur to cognitive development.

The issues that Condillac and Herder wrestled with are still with us today in debate about the role of language in cognitive development and the role of social context in the development of language. Those are issues that animated Vygotsky and others who have tried to sort out the relationships of language, cognition and the social world. Along with that core similarity, there are obvious differences between eighteenth-century and modern debates about cognition and social context. In the eighteenth century, scholars framed their questions by speculating about phylogeny; late twentieth-century scholars tried to answer their questions ontogentically, by looking at the development of individual L1 or L2 learners. Methods and styles of argumentation also vary since, of course, Condillac and Herder did not employ contemporary social science methods to support their claims – but neither did Vygotsky. Vygotsky characteristically presented only sketchy empirical data to support his claims, preferring to build arguments in ways not unlike those of Condillac or Herder, namely out of anecdotal evidence and by deducing the consequences of a principle presented as a matter of common sense. An eighteenth-century text on the origin of language may strike twenty-first-century readers as alien in its approach, assumptions and argumentation. The same kinds of global gaps separate some, but not all, twenty-first-century readers from Vygotskian sociocultural theory, or from Firth and Wagner's insistence that social context is formative to language acquisition. But discontinuities as well as continuities together make up the history of second language acquisition.

2.5 Conclusion

Of the three themes surveyed historically in this chapter, each animates present-day research on L2 acquisition. None is without precedent. Together, they do not exhaust the grounds on the basis of which one might look beyond the twentieth century for the backdrop to modern study of L2 acquisition. But even this small sample of issues in L2 studies, viewed historically, reveals the heterogeneity of that backdrop. The first theme, specification of a role for the L1 in L2 learning, was only articulated after western scholarship gradually came to conceptualize natively versus non-natively acquired languages. Then in the twentieth century, the issue became (and continues to be) a central, self-conscious, point of disagreement through several generations of models of L2 acquisition. The second theme, inquiry into the inherent capacities that learners bring to the task of acquiring an L2, may be understood as continuing into the twenty-first century a debate between empiricists and rationalists that some scholars (notably Chomsky) consider a long-standing and comprehensive key to the history of western linguistics. Reflection on the third theme, the question of how to evaluate the role of the social context of language, goes as far back as the fourth century. Whether language is at base a social or a cognitive phenomenon became an object of explicit speculation in the 1700s, albeit through different means and in different terms, compared to those used today.

These three historical sketches therefore illustrate some of the heterogeneous ways in which the study of L2 acquisition is connected to large-scale intellectual trends. Even a glimpse of those connections offers, I believe, a number of benefits to scholars of second language acquisition. It provides an opportunity to look beyond the boundaries that the proclivities of the modern discipline impose on the subject matter. It enhances one's capacity to imagine what it would mean to hold a very different set of assumptions about the common, basic, human experience of learning a second language. And it opens up a richer appreciation for the cultural and scientific value of the scholarship displayed in this handbook.

3

Theoretical approaches

Florence Myles

3.1 Introduction

Becoming acquainted with second language acquisition theorizing can be rather confusing for the novice, given the plethora of different and seemingly conflicting claims. This state of affairs is due to a number of reasons. First, because second language acquisition is a complex and multifaceted phenomenon, the investigation of a given aspect requires specific theoretical and methodological tools; for example, the study of the linguistic system underlying a learner's production will require the support of a linguistic theory, whereas the investigation of the neurological basis underpinning the second language will rely on neurolinguistic theorizing, and there might not be much overlap between the sets of questions investigated and the claims made. Second, different theoretical approaches adopt widely differing views of the nature of language, of the language learning process and of the language learner and his/her role in the acquisition process. Is language primarily social? Individual? Cognitive? Linguistic? Is the learning process primarily social? Individual? Cognitive? Linguistic? What is the role of the learner in this process? For example, does s/he need to amass metalinguistic knowledge or is it unnecessary? Do all learners need the same type of input and interaction or do needs vary from learner to learner according to their individual learning styles and personal characteristics?

This chapter aims to present the main theoretical families that currently exist in SLA research, thus setting the scene for the chapters that follow. By *families* is meant groups of theories which focus on the investigation of broad subdomains of SLA research. For example, one theoretical family explores the development of the linguistic system in second language learners, resorting to a range of different theories in so doing. Another family focuses on the role of social factors in SLA, again drawing on different theories to aid this exploration. And yet another group of theories concentrates on the psycholinguistic dimensions of SLA, such as the development of processing skills or the role of individual differences.

It might seem artificial to separate formal (linguistic), cognitive and social aspects of language, as of course the learning and use of language routinely involve all three at the same time. Some current theoretical approaches do argue in principle against separating language and its learning into these different aspects, on the grounds that language is primarily social and cannot therefore be removed for analysis from the context in which is situated. However, no one approach to date has succeeded in capturing all these facets and giving answers to this wide range of questions, hence the current multiplicity of approaches addressing particular dimensions of language acquisition. These approaches not only focus on different subdomains, but also differ in their methodological tools (see Chapter 4, this volume). The first section of the chapter will outline what a theory should do and be clear about, e.g. in terms of its domain of application, its research agenda and its methodology, as well as the views of language, learning and the learner which underpin it. It will then outline the main research agendas which have motivated much of SLA research over the last forty years or so. It will also summarize what SLA theorizing needs to explain, that is, the findings which empirical research has brought to light. The second section will introduce the main theoretical approaches currently active, and outline their contribution to the overall SLA research agenda.

3.2 Why theories?

3.2.1 Purpose of SLA theories

The *Oxford Dictionary* defines a theory as "a supposition or a system of ideas intended to explain something, especially one based on general principles independent of the thing to be explained." For the purposes of SLA research, we might paraphrase this definition as "a more or less abstract set of claims about the units which are significant within the phenomenon under study, the relationships which exist between them, and the processes which bring about change" (Mitchell and Myles 2004: 7). In the context of a multifaceted phenomenon such as SLA, a theory might be restricted in scope and focus on a single aspect of the acquisition process, or it might be more elaborate and comprehensive. For example, a property theory will be primarily concerned with modeling the nature of the language system underlying learner productions, while a transition theory will aim to model the changes this system is undergoing during developmental processes (Gregg 2003b; Schwartz 1998b). A theory aims at explaining the phenomenon under investigation, not merely describing it, and will therefore evolve through a cyclic process of systematic inquiry, in which the claims of the theory are assessed against empirical evidence. This may take place through a process of hypothesis testing through formal experiment, or through more ecological procedures, where naturally occurring data are analyzed and interpreted. Theory building is a reflexive process: on the basis of empirical findings, the theory is modified in order to better account for the facts that have been uncovered; new theoretical insights in turn give rise to the need for more empirical investigations to test them further.

In the context of second language acquisition research, different theoretical approaches will not only need to be explicit about which views of the nature of language, of the learner and of learning underpin them, but also about which aspect of SLA they are attempting to model or explain. As we have already suggested, a theory particularly suited to investigate the role that social relationships and networks play in the learning process might have very little to say about the role that, say, individual learner variables, or formal properties of human languages, play in this process. But whatever the particular focus of a given theory, we would expect it to be explicit about the following (Mitchell and Myles 2004: 9):

1. Clear and explicit statements of the theory's precise object of inquiry, as well as of the assumptions and claims which it is making about its view of the nature of language, of the learner, of the learning process and of how these interact with one another;
2. Systematic procedures for confirming/disconfirming the theory, through data gathering and interpretation: a good theory must be testable/falsifiable in some way;
3. Both descriptions of L2 phenomena, and attempts to explain why they are so (property theories), and proposals for mechanisms of development (transition theories);
4. Last but not least, engagement with other theories in the field, and serious attempts to account for at least some of the phenomena which are understood as common ground in ongoing public discussion.

Before outlining the main theoretical families currently in use in SLA research, and their position on each of the four points above, the principal research agendas which have motivated SLA research in the past forty years or so will be reviewed briefly.

3.2.2 SLA research agendas

The following core questions have motivated much of the SLA research carried out in recent decades (Myles 2010: 227):

Formal:

1. What is the linguistic system underlying learners' performance, and how do they construct this system, at various stages of development and in each of the following: phonology; morphology; lexis; syntax; semantics; discourse; pragmatics?
2. What is the role of (i) the native language or other previously acquired languages, (ii) the target language and (iii) universal formal properties of human languages?

Cognitive:

3. How do learners develop their ability to access and use their L2 system in real time, i.e. their processing capability?
4. What are the roles of individual differences and learning styles in shaping and/or facilitating L2 development?
5. What is the influence of the age of the learner, in shaping and/or facilitating L2 development?

Social and interactional context:

6. How does input/interaction/output facilitate, shape and/or accelerate the development of either 1 or 3 above (formal system and/or processing)?
7. How do the environment/social context facilitate, shape and/or accelerate the development of either 1 or 3 above (formal system and/or processing)?

Looking at those questions in more detail, we can say that the prime objective of the first two questions is to *document and understand formal linguistic development*. This has undoubtedly been the focus of a large part of SLA research to date, especially in the 1980s and 1990s, when much work aimed to establish developmental sequences in the domain of morphosyntax in particular (see Chapter 27, this volume). The investigation of these questions has relied on formal theories of language, not only to describe and analyze learner language (Hawkins 2001a; White 2003a), but also to explore the cohabitation and interaction of several language systems in the same mind (Cook 2003a; Cook and Bassetti 2011; Cook, Bassetti, Kasai, Sasaki and Takahashi 2006). The questions asked when attempting to explain developmental patterns in the different subsystems of language have become increasingly sophisticated, trying to account for the interplay between morphosyntactic, discursive, pragmatic and processing factors in shaping these patterns. In addressing these questions, the formal properties of both the L1 and the L2 (and increasingly any L3), as well as universal properties of language, have received much attention as possible explanatory factors, and the interplay between these different systems has been the object of much inquiry, as many of the formal properties in evidence in learner languages are not directly traceable to either the L1 nor the L2. A range of theoretical frameworks have been used to investigate these L2 formal patterns, and we will review some of these in the next section.

The third question, *how do learners develop their ability to access and use this system in real time (i.e. their processing capability)*, implies that the development of the formal linguistic system on the one hand, and the development of the ability to access and use this system in real time on the other, are two different kinds of development, relying on different types of internal mechanisms. And indeed, researchers interested in investigating the development of processing skills and of fluency have focused primarily on processing mechanisms such as automatization, and have given relatively less attention to the formal properties of the developing system (see Chapter 19, this volume). This dissociation between formal linguistic knowledge and processing skills is not, however, accepted by all researchers, and we will review theoretical approaches which consider the two types of process as interdependent and impossible to separate (e.g. associationist/emergentist frameworks; sociocultural frameworks such as N. C. Ellis 2008a; O'Grady, Lee and Kwak 2009; Vygotsky 1978, 1986 [1934]). In the main, however, SLA researchers have treated linguistic knowledge and processing as separate and drawing on different learning mechanisms, though developing in parallel (Pienemann 2005a; Towell 2003, 2007; Towell and Dewaele 2005; Towell and Hawkins 1994).

The fourth question, on the *role of individual differences and learning styles in shaping and/or facilitating L2 development*, has been motivated by the well-documented observation that learners are highly variable in the speed at which they learn foreign languages, as well as in their ultimate success, and this is in marked contrast to first language learners, who are more homogeneous in rate and success of acquisition. Even with the same input and the same opportunities for interaction in, for example, a single classroom of beginners, some learners will progress much faster than others. Researchers investigating the reasons behind this observation have focused, on the one hand, on the role of intrinsic learner variables such as aptitude and learning style and, on the other hand, on potentially more extrinsic variables such as motivation and learning context (see e.g. Chapter 8, this volume; Dörnyei 2009a; Dörnyei and Skehan 2003 for reviews).

The fifth question deals with *the age of the learner*, and how far this can be expected to influence the learning process and eventual attainment; this complex issue has attracted the attention of the general public to the field, perhaps more than any other (Birdsong 2005a; Cable *et al.* 2010; Herschensohn 2007; Hyltenstam and Abrahamsson 2001; Johnstone 2002; Muñoz and Singleton 2011; Muñoz 2006a, 2008a, b).

The sixth question focuses on the *role of the input and of interaction* in L2 development. Here, researchers have investigated what type of input and interaction might facilitate, shape and/or speed up development (see Chapter 10, this volume; Gass 1997, 2003; Gor and Long 2009; Lyster 2004c; Mackey 2007; Mackey, Oliver and Leeman 2003). They have explored whether facilitative effects related to the type of input and/or interaction found in studies relate to all sub-domains of language, or whether it is primarily evident in the development of lexis, as in negotiation of meaning studies (Gass and Varonis 1994; and see Chapter 10, this volume), or also in the acquisition of syntax, as in the study of interrogative development by Mackey (1999). The role of input/interaction/output in the development of processing skills has also been investigated, and ways of manipulating input and interaction in order to promote learning has also been an important focus in this area (see e.g. VanPatten 1996, 2002; Chapter 29, this volume).

The final question is about the *role of the social and interactional context*. More recently researchers have become interested in exploring the role of the social context, not only in terms of the social status of the speakers or languages involved, but also in terms of the specific communicative needs entailed in different social contexts (Firth and Wagner 2007; Jenkins 2007), and in terms of the co-construction of identities in multilingual communities of practice (Chapters 11, 12, 13 and 30, this volume; Norton 2000; Pavlenko and Blackledge 2004).

This list of questions is not meant to be exhaustive, but rather aims to capture the main research agendas which have prevailed in the field over the last forty years or so, and are still to a large extent shaping it today, that is:

- Question 1 (formal properties of learner language) and question 2 (role of the L1, of the L2/L3 and of universals of languages in L2 development) are concerned with the formal properties of human languages; they focus on language, with different views of language underpinning them; they have a limited amount to say about the process of learning.
- Question 3 (processing capability) question 4 (individual differences) and question 5 (age of acquisition) have mainly been understood to relate to internal cognitive characteristics and mechanisms; their main focus is on learning.
- Question 6 (the role of input and interaction) and question 7 (the role of the social environment) concern sociocognitive and social factors; the focus is on the wider social context, on interactional patterns and/or on language use, with both language and learning often receiving limited or partial attention (Myles 2010).

Before introducing the main theoretical families, it is useful to briefly outline some of the main empirical findings of SLA research in recent decades which are relevant to these questions. These findings provide a foundation for reviewing the different theoretical approaches in terms of their contribution to explaining and interpreting them.

3.2.3 Research findings

Researchers have established a number of well-documented findings characteristic of the second language acquisition process. The following provides a brief summary of these (see Myles 2010). A comprehensive review is also found in e.g. R. Ellis (2008):

- L2 learners follow developmental stages in their acquisition of a specific second (or third) language. These are largely independent of the learner's first language, and of the mode of exposure (naturalistic vs. instructed); moreover, they are often similar to the stages followed by children acquiring this same language as an L1 (e.g. the acquisition of interrogation and negation in English L2, of German word order etc.). Although the existence of developmental stages is well established (see Chapter 27, this volume), our knowledge of these stages remains rather patchy, especially in languages other than English and in areas other than morphosyntax.

- The linguistic system underlying learner production is rule-governed, but these rules do not always resemble the rules underlying the L1 or the L2 (e.g. L2 learners go through an early stage where verbs are typically uninflected, and this is found even for learners whose L1 and L2 both obligatorily inflect verbs (Housen 2002; Lakshmanan and Selinker 2001; Myles 2005)). Additionally, learners acquire subtle grammatical properties of the L2 which do not seem learnable from the input alone, and which they have not been taught explicitly (Dekydtspotter 2001; Dekydtspotter and Sprouse 2001; Hawkins 2004).
- Some properties from the L1 are likely to transfer, others not; moreover, within pairs of languages, properties often transfer one way but not the other. For example, object pronouns are placed after the verb in English (*Peter paints it*) but before the verb in French (*Peter la peint*). French learners of English do not transfer French placement and never produce *Peter it paints*, whereas English learners of French go through a stage of wrongly producing postposed object pronouns in French L2 (*Peter peint la*) (for a review, see Mitchell and Myles 2004). Thus, although transfer undoubtedly plays a part in L2 development, its role is complex and remains relatively poorly understood (see Chapter 5, this volume).
- The rate and outcome of the learning process is highly variable, with some learners arguably becoming indistinguishable from native speakers and others fossilizing at a much earlier developmental stage, sometimes in spite of plentiful input. There is some variability in the route of development, both across learners and within learners, but in comparison, it is relatively limited.

The following section presents the main theoretical families which have addressed the varied research agendas that we have briefly reviewed, specifying their domain of application, their view of language, of learning and of the learner, and evaluating their contribution to our understanding of some of the empirical findings just presented.

3.3 The main theoretical families

In keeping with our discussion so far, the main theoretical families introduced in this section are classified in terms of their focus on the formal properties of learner language (linguistic theories), on cognitive considerations such as processing or psychological makeup of individuals (cognitive theories), or on the social and interactional context of second language acquisition (interactionist, sociolinguistic and sociocultural theories). These divisions are of course somewhat artificial, and sometimes difficult to maintain in the context of approaches to language and to learning which increasingly aspire to integrate formal, cognitive and social variables. Much of the research in each of these families has continued to pursue its own specific agendas, with its own methodological apparatus.

3.3.1 Linguistic approaches

For the purpose of this chapter, "linguistic approaches" refers to theoretical approaches that focus on the formal properties of language and how these shape the development of an L2, in the context both of universal properties of human language and of specific L1–L2 pairings. For illustrative purposes, we focus primarily although not exclusively on the Universal Grammar approach, as it has been highly influential and productive within this theoretical family (see Chapter 7, this volume). Other linguistic approaches, e.g. functionalist, structuralist or Hallidayan, have contributed to SLA research, e.g. especially in the context of the European tradition, but the scope of this chapter does not allow a contrastive analysis of these different linguistic theories' contribution to the SLA research enterprise.

Domain of inquiry

The focus of linguistic approaches is the description and explanation of the formal system underlying learner production and comprehension: what is this system like at various stages of development, and why is it that way? When evaluating the contribution of linguistic theories, it is important to remember that they are theories of human language, and have therefore much broader scope than the description and explanation of (second) language production. Their domain of inquiry is vast, as outlined for example in Chomsky (1986) who sees the goals of linguistic research as providing answers to three distinct questions: (1) what constitutes knowledge of language? (knowledge in the Chomskyan sense meaning abstract underlying representations rather than conscious metalinguistic knowledge); (2) how is knowledge of language acquired? and (3) how is knowledge of language put to use?[1]

Within a very broad agenda which seeks to understand the nature of human language, first language acquisition has always been an important driving force; and Chomskyan theory building has always seen accounting for the ease with which children acquire their native language in spite of the complexity and abstractness of human language as an important goal and motivator. This ease of acquisition has been argued to be due to an innate language faculty which guides and constrains children in the hypotheses they make about the language they are acquiring. The focus of linguistic inquiry within this framework has never been on the acquisition of second languages. But as a general theory of language, this line of inquiry has been of direct relevance to the study of second languages, which are assumed to be natural languages and therefore to be governed by the constraints which operate on all human languages. Additionally, given the many similarities between first and second language acquisition, if Universal Grammar can explain the former, it will also play a part in the latter. Furthermore, UG might explain some of the differences between L1 and L2 acquisition by providing a theoretical frame for investigating constructs such as the Critical Period (whereby innate language faculties constraining first language acquisition might not be available to older L2 learners) and transfer when comparing pairs of languages in a principled way.

In spite of its potentially vast remit, most of the SLA research attention within this framework to date has been on morphosyntax, with some longstanding interest in L2 phonology (Archibald 1993; Broselow 1984; Ioup 1984; Ioup and Weinberger 1987; and see Chapter 25, this volume), and a few studies on L2 semantics (Dekydtspotter, Sprouse and Thyre 1999, 2000; Juffs 2000; and see Chapter 22, this volume). More recently there has been much interest among researchers in developing a better understanding of the interfaces between the different subsystems of language, for example between morphosyntax and semantics or pragmatics (Arche and Domínguez 2011; Domínguez 2007; Sorace and Serratrice 2009; Sorace, Serratrice, Filiaci and Baldo 2009) or phonology (Goad and White 2008). Formal linguistic approaches to SLA, whether structuralist, functionalist or UG, do not typically include any developed theory of processing, or of learning. Moreover, researchers in this tradition have very little to say about what triggers development in either L1 or L2 acquisition, apart from rather general claims such as the need to communicate/make meaning. In the context of first language acquisition, linguists claim that all that children need is language around them for it to develop, and the cognitive mechanisms driving this development are beyond their formal remit. Their domain of inquiry is seen as a property theory and not a transition theory, and it is within these parameters they must be understood and evaluated (Mitchell and Myles 2004).

Views on the nature of language

The view of language characterizing the UG approach is usually modular, with the formal properties of language being part of a distinct structure in the mind, and different aspects of language in turn being modular (syntax, phonology, etc.) (Coltheart 1999; Fodor 1983; Jackendoff 2002). Until recently, morphology and syntax have been the privileged object of study, with the focus firmly on the sentence and its internal structure, rather than any larger unit of language. Work at the level of smaller units (words, morphemes, phonemes) has also been primarily concerned with structure and how different elements relate to one another. This is one of the major criticisms by outsiders of work in this tradition; it is seen as studying language somewhat clinically, in a vacuum, as a mental object rather than a social or psychological one (Lantolf 1996; Zuengler and Miller 2006) and as rigidly separating language knowledge from language use. It is primarily interested in the former, leaving the latter to other theorists. This dichotomy between competence (the mental representations underlying language in the mind) and performance (the realization of language in real time) is central to this approach, as performance is seen as a defective window onto this mental grammar, full of imperfections due to the real-time demands of online processing.

Not all formal linguistic theories adopt the modular approach characteristic of UG. For example, the Hallidayan systemic functional school (Halliday and Matthiessen 2000) views language as essentially a set of form–function mappings in which meaning is the driving force. The main difference between this approach and Chomskyan linguistics is that syntax is not clearly separate from semantics and pragmatics (Hendriks 2005; Klein and Perdue 1992; Perdue 2000). In the context of SLA, although these approaches have contrasting views of language itself, they both focus on understanding and explaining learner language in a formal sense, as the result of the individual mind shaping learner production.

The dichotomy between competence and performance in Chomskyan approaches which we mentioned earlier has been the object of much criticism, both theoretical and methodological. The theory is preoccupied with the modeling of linguistic competence, and the study of naturalistic performance is not seen as a suitable window into mental representations of language, as it is affected by various non-linguistic performance factors (Towell and Hawkins 2004). In the context of SLA, this is seen as even more problematic, as L2 representations are less stable than those of native speakers, and therefore even more difficult to tap. Grammaticality judgment (GJ) tests (in which subjects – learners or native speakers – have to decide on the grammaticality of sentences presented to them) were long thought to be the most appropriate methodology to access native speakers' intuitions about their native language, as they usually demonstrate agreement about what is grammatical or ungrammatical in their language. L2 learners' intuitions, however, are much more likely to be unstable, and therefore less reliable, and often, data on L2 competence deriving from GJ tests are disputed and reinterpreted. (For a discussion of this problem, see Chaudron 2003; Sorace 1996.) The reason why GJ tests rather than, for example, spontaneous production have frequently been used is because it can be very difficult to get evidence about subtle grammatical properties which might not be present in learners' spontaneous output. More recently, SLA researchers within this paradigm have taken criticisms about the unnaturalness of GJs seriously, and they are using a greater variety of elicitation techniques (see Chapter 4, this volume). Thus even if use of grammaticality judgment tests is still frequent, they are usually complemented by production and interpretation data, online experiments or neurolinguistic experiments using e.g. event-related potentials (e.g. Domínguez, Tracy-Ventura, Arche, Mitchell and Myles in press; Hopp 2009; Sabourin 2009). While using a range of elicitation techniques strengthens any consistent findings, the problem of drawing inferences about L2 learners' mental representations from such data nonetheless remains.

View of the learning process

In terms of their view of the learning process, formal approaches to SLA have been criticized for leaving untouched a number of areas central to our understanding of the second language learning process. First, linguistically, the UG approach has in the past been almost exclusively concerned with syntax, though recent interest in phonology, morphology and the lexicon has started to redress the balance somewhat. Semantics, pragmatics and discourse have not been central to its endeavors, even if recent work has increasingly addressed interfaces between the different linguistic modules. To give an example, word order in Spanish appears syntactically very flexible, when in fact it is governed by subtle pragmatic rules, and researchers have been interested in finding out how syntax and pragmatics interact in SLA (Alexiadou, Anagnostopoulou and Everaert 2004; Arche and Domínguez 2011; Archibald 2004; Domínguez 2007; Hopp 2009; Rothman and Slabakova 2011; Sorace and Serratrice 2009; van Hout, Hulk, Kuiken and Towell 2003). Second, the UG approach has been exclusively concerned with documenting and explaining the nature of the L2 linguistic system, quite properly, given that it is a formal linguistic theory. And while functionalists have focused more clearly on semantics, discourse and pragmatics, their interest has also been primarily on the language system and its relationship to meaning (for example, how L2 learners present new vs. old information in discourse), rather than on the learning process (Andersen and Shirai 1994; Bardovi-Harlig 2000; Klein and Perdue 1992; Salaberry 1999; Salaberry and Shirai 2002). The social and psychological variables which affect the rate of the learning process or its ultimate outcome are beyond their remit and therefore largely ignored. This has often left educationalists frustrated, as language teaching practice is very much embedded in and shaped by social and psychological constraints.

Bearing in mind the domain of inquiry of formal linguistic approaches, however, it is unsurprising that linguists have had little to say about the learning process itself. These approaches view the learning process as the interaction between linguistic input and universal linguistic mechanisms operating within the mind of individuals. Linguistic input is thought to trigger these universal mechanisms, but little work has been carried out on this triggering process until recently (Hara 2007; Isabelli 2003; Schwartz and Gubala-Rysak 1992; White 1992). This is changing, however, with researchers such as Carroll (2001, 2009) or Truscott and Sharwood Smith (2004a) exploring the relationship between the processing of the input and formal linguistics (see Chapters 26 and 27, this volume).

View of the language learner

As we have already seen, formal linguistic approaches are only interested in the learner as the possessor of a mind which contains language; the assumption is that all humans are endowed with such a mind, and variations between individuals are of little concern. Again, the emphasis is very much on language as the object of study, rather than on the speaker or learner as a social being, and the focus is on what is universal within this mind. Native speakers of a given language community are seen as sharing the same mental grammar (notwithstanding minor local variations), which is viewed as relatively static (only the lexicon is seen as growing throughout a lifetime). By contrast, second language learners are seen as "non-native," with their learning endeavors having as objective the native-speaker norm.

This idealized, static and normative view of language and of the language learner has been criticized for being based on a monolingual speaker in a predominantly multilingual world, and for assuming second language learners have as their target the native-speaker norm, which is very often not the case (Firth and Wagner 2007; Jenkins 2007; but see earlier recognition of this, in Bley-Vroman 1983).

Linguistic approaches and SLA research agendas/findings

We summarized earlier the main research agendas within SLA as having focused on three broad areas: the analysis of the linguistic system underlying learners' L2 development, including the role of the L1 in this development; the nature of processing in the L2 and the role of psychological variables in speeding up or hindering L2 processing; and the role of the social and interactional context in L2 learning.

Formal linguistic approaches, given their domain of inquiry, have focused on the first part of this agenda. Chomskyan approaches have tended to focus primarily on morphosyntax (and on phonology to a lesser extent), until recently when interfaces between subsystems have increasingly come to the fore, whereas functionalist approaches have concentrated on semantic/discourse/pragmatic concerns when investigating learner language and developmental stages. As regards the research findings summarized above, linguistic approaches have attempted to explain aspects of many of them (indeed they have been at the origin of some of these findings), as follows:

(a) Developmental stages

The UG approach argues that, like children acquiring their L1, second language learners' hypotheses about the L2 are constrained by the restricted possibilities afforded them by UG. For example, the lack of inflected verbs in early stages would arguably be due to learners not yet having acquired the functional projection hosting tense features (the Inflection Phrase) (Hawkins 2001a; Vainikka and Young-Scholten 1994, 1996a, to appear). Functionalist approaches have modeled early L2 development in terms of three distinct universal stages (see Chapter 27, this volume, for discussion).

As mentioned before, however, what triggers development from one stage to the next has been underresearched.

(b) Interlanguage rules are unlike both the L1 and the target language

The example mentioned above is a case in point; the uninflected verb stage witnessed in many L2 learners' production does not reflect either the native grammar or the target grammar when both languages inflect verbs. The reason put forward to explain this differs, however, depending on which formal linguistic framework is adopted.

(c) Selective transfer of L1 properties

The UG approach, by comparing the formal properties of languages crosslinguistically, enables predictions to be made about transfer. In the example outlined previously whereby French learners of English do not transfer pronoun placement whereas English learners of French do, this would be due to the fact that this property in French is linked to the strength of the inflection phrase which forces verbs (and their clitic pronouns) to raise to a higher position in the syntactic tree, whereas it remains in situ in English as the inflection phrase is weak and does not trigger movement (Herschensohn 2004; White 1996a). Therefore, before L2 learners of French acquire the inflection phrase and its feature strength, the clitic pronoun would not raise and would remain after the verb.

(d) Variable rate and outcome of SLA process

This approach neither enlightens us as regards variability in the rate of learning, nor in variable outcomes with learners with the same L1/L2 combination. It has, however, provided us with some testable hypotheses about why some grammatical properties might never become nativelike for L2 learners. For example, it has been suggested that grammatical gender is not available past the Critical Period as a formal feature to L2 learners whose L1 does not have this feature (Franceschina 2001; Hawkins and Franceschina 2004).

Conclusion: contribution of formal linguistic approaches to theory building

The domain of inquiry of formal linguistic approaches is the description and explanation of the formal nature of human languages, including second languages. There is no doubt that within this agenda, the UG descriptive framework has been hugely influential. It has helped researchers formulate sophisticated and well-defined hypotheses about the exact nature of the language system (learner systems as well as the L1 and L2 systems), the interplay between the first and second language in L2 learners and the linguistic knowledge learners bring to the task of L2 acquisition. These hypotheses have been tested in a wealth of empirical studies which have enhanced our understanding of L2 morphosyntactic development in particular, but also of how different linguistic subsystems might interact.

Other formal linguistic approaches have met with some success and enlightened us on specific aspects of the SLA process. By focusing on how learners convey meaning, for example, functional-pragmatic approaches have drawn our attention to discourse organization in learner language. The domain of inquiry of linguistic approaches does not enable them to account for processing mechanisms nor social factors which are outside their remit. Understanding of these is the domain of other theoretical approaches, with which formal linguists have become increasingly engaged, and to which we now turn.

3.3.2 Cognitive approaches

Cognitive approaches see the acquisition of a second language as the acquisition of a complex skill, and here researchers believe that we can better understand the second language acquisition process by investigating how the human brain processes and learns new information, as well as how a learner's individual makeup impacts on this process. The focus is very much on the learning dimension of second language acquisition, rather than on the formal properties of learners' second languages. These approaches are generally classified as *transition* theories, that is, theories which aim to understand how learners develop over time in the L2 (Gregg 2003b; Schwartz 1998b) rather than as *property* theories, which describe and explain learners' linguistic systems. As we will see below, however, the boundary is not always clear, and some cognitive approaches consider the language system and its acquisition as one and the same thing.

Domain of inquiry

The domain of inquiry of cognitive approaches is varied, but as is the case with formal linguistic approaches, they also focus on the individual and on what happens in the human mind. However, rather than drawing hypotheses from the study of linguistic systems, cognitivists' hypotheses originate from cognitive psychology and neurology, and from what we know about the acquisition of complex skills generally. They view second language acquisition as one instantiation of learning, relying on the same mechanisms as other types of learning, rather than as language specific, as the UG approach does. Consequently, processing approaches have been interested not so much in the formal properties of language, but on how learners gradually expand their linguistic knowledge and learn to access it increasingly efficiently in online production (Ellis 2002; Harrington 2001; Juffs 2004; McLaughlin and Heredia 1996; Myles 1995; Pienemann 2003, 2007). The primary focus on the individual mind of the learner, regardless of context, also applies to a large extent to work on individual differences between learners, for example their level of intelligence or working memory capacity; the way in which constructs such as anxiety or motivation might be socially and culturally shaped has also played some part in this subfield (Dörnyei 2009a;

Dörnyei and Skehan 2002, 2003; Dörnyei and Ushioda 2009, 2011; Robinson 2002a; Sawyer and Ranta 2001; Skehan 1989).

Given this focus, cognitive SLA theorists' main focus of investigation has been the development of processing skills in L2 learners and the way in which these contribute to learning, and the role of individual differences, both in terms of cognitive factors such as intelligence, working memory or aptitude, and in terms of (socio-)affective factors such as motivation, anxiety, extroversion, learner beliefs, learning styles or learner strategies.

Views on the nature of language

The view of language within cognitive approaches is relatively underdeveloped, as the focus is on the learning process. In fact, many SLA researchers working on these approaches do not see language as a separate module in the human mind, but as just another form of information which is processed through general cognitive mechanisms. This dichotomy, between language being seen as a separate module or as an integral part of cognition, is of course somewhat charicatural; there are researchers who believe that there is a language-specific module for first language acquisition, but that the learning of second languages is different and relies on general cognitive mechanisms (see for example Bley-Vroman 1989). Even within the context of L1 acquisition, some researchers believe that some aspects of language acquisition are innate and other aspects not, and others leave the question open (Butterworth and Harris 1994; Harley 1995). The question of the specificity and innateness of the language faculty is far from resolved, in both the L1 and L2 acquisition fields, and the opposition between cognitivists and innatists should be seen more in terms of two ends of a continuum rather than a dichotomy. Even within frameworks concentrating firmly on the processing component of language learning such as Processability theory (Pienemann 1998, 2003, 2005a, 2010), the possibility of an innate linguistic module is not rejected outright; Pienemann does not take a stand on this, but deals exclusively with the growth of the computational mechanisms required for the processing of second languages. Thus formal versus cognitive approaches are increasingly seen as complementary rather than conflictual.

Cognitive theorists of SLA fall into two main groups:

(a) Processing approaches: researchers such as Pienemann (2005a, 2010), Towell (2000, 2004) and Towell and Hawkins (1994, 2004), or VanPatten (2002, 2007) who believe that language knowledge might be special in some way, but who are concerned to develop transition/processing theories to complement property theories such as UG or, in the case of Pienemann, another linguistic theory (Lexical Functional Grammar).

(b) Emergentist/constructionist approaches: theorists such as N. C. Ellis, MacWhinney, Tomasello and others (N. C. Ellis 2003, 2007, 2008b; N. C. Ellis and Larsen-Freeman 2006; N. C. Ellis and Schmidt 1998;

Goldschneider and DeKeyser 2001; MacWhinney 1999, 2001; O'Grady, Lee and Kwak 2009; Tomasello 2003), who do not think that the separation between property and transition theories is legitimate, as they believe that one can explain both the nature of language knowledge and how it is processed through general cognitive principles. In fact, they do not make the distinction between competence and performance, as they see these as being one and the same thing. In this view, the learner is seen as operating a complex processing system which deals with linguistic information in similar ways to other kinds of information.

Cognitive approaches to the role played by individual differences in facilitating or speeding up learning focus exclusively on psychological variables, and the nature of language falls outside their domain of inquiry.

View of the learning process

The learning process is the main focus of cognitive approaches, and in particular its computational dimension. *Information processing* approaches investigate how different memory stores (Short-Term Memory (STM); Long-Term Memory (LTM) – declarative and procedural) deal with new L2 information, and how this information is automatized and restructured through repeated activation. Processability theory looks more specifically at the processing demands made by various formal aspects of the L2, and the implications for learnability and teachability of L2 structure (Pienemann 2003, 2005a, 2010).

Constructivist/emergentist views of language learning share a usage-based view of language development, which is driven by communicative needs, and they reject the need to posit an innate, language-specific, acquisition device. These include approaches known as emergentism, connectionism or associationism, constructivism, cognitivism and the Competition Model (an explanation of the differences between these terms is beyond the scope of this introductory chapter; for overviews, see Chapter 28, this volume, as well as e.g. N. C. Ellis 2003; MacWhinney 1999; Plunkett 1998; Tomasello 2003; Tomasello and Brooks 1999). These approaches "emphasize the linguistic sign as a set of mappings between phonological forms and conceptual meanings or communicative intentions" (N. C. Ellis 2003: 63). Learning in this view occurs on the basis of associative processes, rather than the construction of abstract rules. Learning is seen as the analysis of patterns in the language input, and language development is seen as resulting from the billions of associations which are created during language use, and which lead to regular patterns in learner performance which might look rule-like, but in fact are merely frequency-based asssociationist preferences. These links become stronger as these associations keep recurring, and they also become part of larger networks as connections between elements become more numerous. Language in this view is seen as a set of probabilistic patterns which become strengthened in the brain of the learner through repeated activation.

For theorists interested in individual differences, the learning process is not itself the object of study, but rather how learner characteristics impact on this process (see Chapter 8, this volume).

View of the language learner

Cognitive approaches, like linguistic approaches, are concerned primarily with the individual, and do not focus on the learner as a social being. But they are interested in the learner's mind as a processor of information, rather than in the specificity of the linguistic information it contains.

Cognitive approaches view the learner as responding to the multitude of information surrounding us, processing it, organizing it and storing it. They view the human mind as having evolved a sophisticated cognitive makeup enabling it to deal with a wealth of information. A working memory of limited capacity filters new information and selects which elements are processed at any given time. Information is then stored and organized in short- and long-term memory stores, both declarative and procedural, in order to be retrieved increasingly efficiently through repeated activation, as learning occurs. As with formal linguistic approaches, the focus is not only on the individual, but also on what is universal in the makeup of the human mind, in this case in terms of the human mind's characteristics as a processor, organizer and storer of information.

The *individual differences* approach, on the other hand, focuses on individuals' specific characteristics rather than on what is universal, and on how these individual characteristics interact with the learning process. These approaches therefore view the learner as a unique sum of a range of psychological variables which will all impact on the rate and outcome of the learning process.

Cognitive approaches and SLA research agendas/findings

Cognitive approaches have primarily investigated research questions 3 and 4:

Question 3. How do learners develop their ability to access and use their L2 system in real time, i.e. their processing capability?
Question 4. What are the roles of individual differences and learning styles in shaping and/or facilitating L2 development?

In addressing these questions, cognitive approaches have put forward explanations for some of the findings we have outlined above, as illustrated (selectively) below:

(a) Developmental stages

Processability theory (Pienemann 1998, 2005a, 2008, 2010) has argued that the acquisition of processing in the second language is incremental and hierarchical, thus explaining developmental stages in a principled way, with word-level processing preceding phrase-level processing which in turn precedes sentence-level processing. In the example mentioned previously about the acquisition of object pronoun placement in French L2, the raising of the pronoun from its in situ position after the verb involves interphrasal processes which will be more costly than in the context of L2 English where the pronoun remains in situ. Connectionism also views learning as incremental as neural networks become strengthened, with developmental patterns being linked with frequency, saliency and regularity of patterns in the input.

(b) Interlanguage rules are often unlike both the L1 and the target language

As just mentioned, the processing limitations at each stage of development in Pienemann's model will give rise to learner productions which are unlike both native and target languages. In the case of the uninflected verb stage, this will be because learners have not yet gone beyond the phrase-level processing stage. Under an emergentist view, the overgeneralization of frequent patterns might lead to learner-specific productions unlike either L1 or L2 (O'Grady 2008b; O'Grady et al. 2009).

(c) Selective transfer of L1 properties

Similarly, transfer might occur one way (from a given L1 to a given L2) but not the other when the processing demands for a particular structure are greater in one language than another, and therefore beyond the current processing capabilities of the learner in the L2 in one direction but not the other (Pienemann 2003). Transfer might also be a strategy used when communicative needs go beyond the current grammar of the learner, who might then borrow an L1 structure in the absence of a suitable interlanguage form (Benson 2002).

(d) Variable rate and outcome of SLA process

This is the area in which research on individual differences has had most impact. Work on e.g. aptitude, intelligence, anxiety, motivation, etc. has found correlations between certain individual characteristics and both rate of learning and eventual success in a second language (see Chapter 8, this volume; Dörnyei and Skehan 2002, 2003; Dornyei and Ushioda 2009; Robinson 2002a).

Conclusion: contribution of cognitive approaches to SLA theory building

A wealth of studies has been carried out from the perspective of cognitive psychology, and there is no doubt that they have greatly enriched our understanding of SLA processes. As we have seen, although there are some similarities between cognitive approaches and formal linguistic approaches, in that both focus on language and/or learning within the mind of the individual learner, there are also major differences between these theoretical families, both conceptually and methodologically. Formal linguistic approaches focus on the linguistic system and its domain-specific nature, whereas the territory of cognitive approaches is the learning mechanisms involved in the SLA process and what impacts upon them. Their underlying assumption is usually that learning a language relies on similar mechanisms to those used in other types of learning, i.e. it is not domain specific. Consequently, their methodologies are very different, with cognitive psychologists making use of laboratory techniques to measure accurately performance indicators during L2 processing such as length of pauses, priming effects and reaction times. Formal linguists, on the whole, tend to apply linguistic analysis techniques to the study of L2 learners' productions or intuitions, though they tend to consider language outside the mechanisms underlying its use. Both methodologies have their advantages and disadvantages; laboratory studies have the benefit of being able to control in a precise way the variables under study. But this very fact can also be seen as a disadvantage, as it assumes one can study discrete aspects of language in isolation, without taking account of the interaction between the different language modules, or of the social context in which language use is embedded. A distinctive feature of connectionist approaches resides in the links they attempt to build with neurology and even neurobiology, and the methods used to explore this. Connectionists believe that we have to study learning within the actual architecture of the brain, and make use of neurological information: "two distinctive aspects of the connectionist approach are its strong emphasis on general learning principles and its attempt to make contact with neurobiological as well as cognitive phenomena" (N. C. Ellis and Schmidt 1997: 154).

Cognitive theories, like formal linguistic theories, have met with some success in explaining some of the results in SLA research, each bringing particular insights into specific aspects of the process. Their focus on different parts of the human mind, language or learning mechanisms respectively, has meant that their respective research agendas and research questions have often been complementary rather than contradictory. Neither of these approaches, however, have embedded the study of SLA within its social and interactional context, nor taken full account of the social dimension of language and the impact it can have on the SLA process. We now turn to the next theoretical family, which focuses on this.

3.3.3 Interactionist, sociolinguistic and sociocultural approaches

Sociolinguists, social theorists, conversation analysts and interactionists, in contrast with the two previous families, focus on the social context in which language learning takes place, and the role that this context plays in the co-construction of both linguistic knowledge and identity (see Chapters 13 and 30, this volume). This work ranges from macro-analyses of the role of social factors and contexts in the (co-) construction of identity (Firth and Wagner 2007; Jenkins 2007; Morgan 2007; Norton 2000, 2010; Toohey 2000), to micro-analyses of interactions aiming to investigate the role of scaffolding and microgenesis in L2 learning, for example (Gánem Gutiérrez 2008; Lantolf 2008; Lantolf and Poehner 2008; Lantolf and Thorne 2006; Mitchell 2004; Ohta 2010), or the way in which conversations are negotiated and co-constructed (Long 1996; Mackey 2007; Mackey, Oliver and Leeman 2003; Mackey and Polio 2009; Pekarek Doehler 2006; Pekarek Doehler and Ziegler 2007; Philp and Tognini 2009; Seedhouse 2004). Much of this work, especially in the sociocultural tradition, sees language as a cultural product, jointly constructed during social interaction, and thus often disagrees fundamentally with a cognitive view of language or of learning. Consequently, the focus has not been on understanding which formal properties are acquired and how, but rather on providing a glimpse of the actual process of acquisition taking place in real time, and of the forces at play. Much sociocultural research, however, has concentrated on *microgenesis*, i.e. illuminating small local changes in learners' L2 knowledge which arise through different types of L2 interaction and engagement, and has less to say about changes in the L2 system in the longer term. Interactionists and sociolinguists also focus on language in context, and on local variation and change in the L2 system, although the former researchers commonly situate themselves within a broadly cognitive paradigm, with the object of study the sociocognitive processes taking place in interaction. Some sociolinguistic research, however, is developmental and focuses on the acquisition of sociopragmatic norms and registers in second language learners (see Chapters 13 and 23, this volume; Bayley and Regan 2004; Dewaele 2004a; Dewaele and Mougeon 2004; DuFon and Churchill 2006; Kasper and Rose 2002; Rose 2005; Tarone 2007). So, the common thread here is the importance of the social and interactional context, with major differences in how the learning process is viewed, either as primarily social, or as cognitive/individual.

Domain of inquiry

The different approaches within this broad theoretical family have somewhat different domains of inquiry. What they have in common, however, is that they focus more on the situated context in which second language learning takes place than on the mind of the learner or on the language system. The sociocultural framework has been particularly influential in social and educational research and its domain of inquiry is the learning process as a social and inter-mental activity, in which language is seen as a mediation tool. Interactionists focus on the role played by the different types of interactions the learner may engage in. They examine not only the role that the input learners are exposed to might play, but also the role of any output produced by the learner, as well as the interactional patterns between learners and other conversational partners; their aim is to identify what kind of interactions might be maximally facilitative of L2 learning. Both sociocultural theorists and interactionists may engage in detailed analyses of interactional patterns, but using different conceptual frameworks. Researchers interested in the development of sociolinguistic and sociopragmatic competence focus on language, albeit on its social and pragmatic functions rather than its formal nature as in the case of linguistic or cognitive approaches.

Views on the nature of language

As will be obvious from the above, the views of the nature of language vary widely within this broad theoretical family. Some sociocultural theorists increasingly ally themselves with views of language associated with cognitive linguistics (Langacker 1987, 2008b; Lantolf 2011; Lantolf and Thorne 2006) or adopt a view of language as a complex system (see discussion in Chapter 30, this volume). Some sociolinguists adopt a broadly functionalist approach. The prime focus all have in common is that they see language as embedded within its social and interactional context, and they are interested in the role this context plays, in order to answer widely different research questions depending on the framework adopted. Sociolinguists are interested in studying how the complex social and pragmatic rules and conventions typical of any mature language are acquired by second language learners. These rules are often acquired late and can be very difficult for L2 learners to grasp (e.g. the distinction between formal *vous* and informal *tu* when addressing someone in French, or the wide range of honorific forms of address in Japanese (Dewaele 2004a; Iwasaki 2008)); many sociolinguists argue that it is the concern to establish a desired L2 identity (or a hybrid identity) which drives the learning of such forms, and/or the rejection of them by some learners.

Sociolinguists thus adopt a broad view of language, including its relationship with paralinguistic aspects of communication appropriate to various contexts and communities of practice, which may be seen as drivers of acquisition. Interactionists view language primarily as a source of input which can be modified in various ways in order to facilitate the learning process; by and large, they do not challenge the view of language as a separate module in the learner's mind, with a vocabulary and a set of grammar rules which have to be acquired. Sociocultural theorists, on the other hand, have a very different view of language. They view language as a tool for thought, and are highly critical of theories which view communication as primarily about the transmission of predetermined meanings and messages. Instead, they view dialogic communication as central to the joint construction of knowledge (including knowledge of language forms), which is first developed intermentally, and then appropriated and internalized by the individual. They reject the Saussurean idea of language as an autonomous abstract system, and hence Chomsky's distinction between competence and performance, preferring to adopt e.g. emergentist accounts.

View of the learning process

Unlike innatists but similarly to cognitivists, sociocultural theorists believe that the same general learning mechanisms are involved in language learning as in any other kind of learning. However, unlike cognitivists, they see learning as primarily social, rather than individual, with learners actively shaping their learning environment and co-constructing knowledge with their interactional partners. Learning in this view is not separate from language use, learning *is* language use. In fact, much of sociocultural theorists' work involves the very detailed analysis of micro-language events such as scaffolding in conversations (where learners help one another in the joint elaboration of a solution to a problem), or the use of private speech to internalize new knowledge (e.g. learners repeating silently an explanation by the teacher) (Gánem Gutiérrez 2008; Kenning 2010; Lantolf 2000; Lantolf and Thorne 2006; Ohta 2001c; Zuengler and Miller 2006).

Interactionists also focus on micro-episodes of language interactions, in order to find out what role the input learners receive plays in the learning process, and how modifications to this input might facilitate language learning. The various strategies used by learners to negotiate this input in order to make it meaningful are also a focus of attention (e.g. when a learner asks or guesses the meaning of a word; the role of recasts – when the teacher repeats what a learner has just said but without a mistake), as is the role played by *output*, that is the language produced by learners. Learning in this view is a process of enabling cognitive mechanisms to work on the language to be learnt, by actively engaging with it through meaningful interaction (Braidi 1995; Gass 2003; Mackey 2007; Mackey and Polio 2009).

Sociolinguists' focus is diverse, representing a multitude of theoretical perspectives ranging from sociolinguistic variation to identity construction, second language socialization to communities of practice, or the role of affect and emotion in second language learning. The focus is primarily on language use and the social and affective context in which learning is taking place, and how both this context and the personal aspirations of the learner for a particular type of identity can shape the kinds of encounters and any subsequent learning which may take place. In terms of their view of the learning process itself, apart from researchers who conduct quantitative studies of how L2 learners acquire the sociopragmatic rules underlying language use, sociolinguists concentrate on the social forces at play, through qualitative and interpretative analyses (Bayley and Regan 2004; Dewaele 2004a; Kasper and Rose 2002; Norton 2010; Tarone 2007; Toohey 2000).

Overall, theoretical approaches within this paradigm have tended to focus on the study of language use, which they view as the driver of language development, and their contribution to our understanding of learning has focused primarily on the detailed description of language episodes which might contribute to learning or inhibit it.

Views of the language learner

For sociocultural theorists, the view of the language learner is closely related to that of language and of learning. As described above, language is seen primarily as a tool for thought or as a means of mediation in mental activity, both within the learner, e.g. through private or inner speech, and in collaboration with others, e.g. through scaffolding and microgenesis. Learning in this view is therefore primarily a mediated process. It is mediated both through learners' developing use and control of mental tools (with language playing a central role), and it is socially mediated through interaction and shared processes such as problem solving and discussion.

Some sociolinguists view the language learner in a similar way to cognitivists, as an individual mind whose task is to acquire the rules of the L2, albeit its sociopragmatic rules in this case, rather than its grammar or vocabulary (see Chapter 23, this volume). In order to study the acquisition of these rules, they make use of (socio)linguistic or psycholinguistic methodologies. Ethnographers, on the other hand, focus on the learner as a social being situated within a specific context, affording different opportunities for learning linked to specific communities of practice, involving unequal power relationships which shape the interactional practices taking place. Learners in this view are very much seen as active social partners within complex social settings and the focus of this approach is on how they negotiate their learning in situated contexts, as well as on how their identity is shaped by these encounters (for more details, see Chapter 12, this volume).

Interactionists, as outlined above, pay attention to the interactional patterns learners engage in, and how they affect language learning. Their view of the learner is primarily as an individual engaging with conversational partners in order to develop an interlanguage system, and making use of internal cognitive and linguistic mechanisms for so doing (see Chapter 10, this volume). Within this broad theoretical family, the view of the language learner varies substantially according to the approach adopted, from an individual making use of psycholinguistic tools to assist learning, to the learner as a primarily social being negotiating new identities and power relationships.

Interactional/sociolinguistic/sociocultural approaches and research agendas/findings

Given that the main findings reported above were primarily the result of the formal and cognitive agendas which dominated the field until relatively recently, it might seem unfair to evaluate this theoretical family in terms of its contribution to research agendas it does not share. In fact, one of the main contributions of sociolinguistic and sociocultural approaches has been to question the validity of these agendas. If second language acquisition is primarily a social process, the focus on purely linguistic and cognitive mechanisms might be misplaced.

Bearing this in mind, this theoretical family has tended to concentrate on giving answers to research questions 6 and 7:

Question 6. How does input/interaction/output facilitate, shape and/or accelerate the development of either question 1 or question 3 above (formal system and/or processing)?

Question 7. How does the environment/social context facilitate, shape and/or accelerate the development of either question 1 or question 3 above (formal system and/or processing)?

In addressing (aspects of) these questions, researchers within this broad theoretical family have contributed to a better understanding of some of the findings outlined previously. For example, sociolinguists interested in the L2 acquisition of sociolinguistic and pragmatic rules have contributed to our understanding of developmental sequences by documenting the development of sociopragmatic rules in L2 learners over time (Dewaele 2004a; Regan, Howard and Lemée 2009). And although sociocultural theorists, conversation analysts or interactionists, because of their focus on investigating language use in action, have had little to say about developmental routes over extended periods of time, or about the formal rules underlying L2 productions, they have provided detailed descriptions of situated learning taking place, thus giving us insights into the kinds of learner activities, contexts and interactions which might facilitate and speed up the learning process (Aljaafreh and Lantolf 1994; Mackey and Polio 2009; Ohta 2001c; Pekarek Doehler and Ziegler 2007). The general sociocultural focus on language as a cultural tool means that some researchers in this tradition are very interested in the role of the L1 as a potential support for L2 interaction (e.g. in classroom code switching). Some sociolinguistic researchers have also concerned themselves with the total linguistic repertoire of the learner, e.g. exploring the role of codeswitching in interactional patterns and in identity construction (see e.g. Moore 2002). This is a very different perspective on the L1 from the concerns of other traditions with the extent of L1 influence on L2 linguistic form.

By investigating in great detail the kind of language use learners engage in, however, these approaches have broadened the traditional SLA research agendas, bringing L2 use into the spotlight, and enabling us to understand better how the social context shapes the kinds of interactions learners engage in. This of course can shed some light on the types of interactions and social contexts which are most facilitative or inhibitive of L2 learning, thereby contributing to our understanding of why the rate and outcome of the SLA process are so variable, but this is not the primary goal of many of these approaches. In fact, researchers within this paradigm often claim that the field has been asking the wrong kind of questions, and that the focus should shift to understanding the social factors at play in the co-construction of language and identity rather than concentrating on the learning of the formal properties of languages over time, as has been the tendency to date (Block 2003; Firth and Wagner 2007; Lantolf 2011; Lantolf and Thorne 2006).

Conclusion: contribution of interactionist/sociolinguistic/sociocultural approaches to SLA theory building

This theoretical family has given rise to a wealth of very detailed investigations of learner interaction, paying attention to factors going beyond the characteristics of the conversation itself such as the wider social processes at play and learners' own social contribution to the learning context. These detailed descriptions of interactions have given insightful glimpses of learning in action, and these approaches have been of particular interest to educationalists, who have welcomed Vygotskyan concepts such as the "zone of proximal development," scaffolding or activity theory, which lend themselves well to detailed analyses of classroom practices.

In terms of theory building, the sociocultural shift of emphasis from seeing L2 learning primarily in terms of the individual having to master a discrete linguistic system to a much more holistic view of complex social processes which cannot easily be analyzed in terms of dissociated discrete elements has contributed to a considerable broadening of the SLA research agenda, including a rethinking of its core traditional values.

3.4 Conclusion

This chapter has provided a simple map of the main theoretical families currently dominant in second language theorizing, and of their contribution to an overall multifaceted SLA research agenda. The purpose has not been to draw a comprehensive picture of the multitude of theoretical approaches used in the field, but rather to outline why a single SLA theory is currently beyond our reach, and to illustrate where all the different and sometimes conflicting approaches originate from. In doing so, attention has also been paid to drawing out the different conceptual and methodological tools behind the main theoretical families in order to evaluate them. This agenda has meant oversimplification in places, and many omissions, some undoubtedly unfortunate. Specific theories have been used to illustrate the different approaches and how these have tackled the SLA research agenda, rather than to suggest that their contribution is somewhat superior to others. The various theoretical families have all enriched our understanding of specific aspects of this complex phenomenon, and they complement each other by focusing on different theoretical and empirical agendas. Following this overview, later chapters in this book provide in-depth treatment and rich exemplification showing the ongoing diversity of the field and active development within all of the theoretical families sketched here.

4

Scope and research methodologies

Melinda Whong and Clare Wright

4.1 Introduction

There is a wide range of theoretical approaches not only to second language acquisition, but also to the fundamental question of what language is (see opening chapters of this volume). As we will see in this chapter, questions of research method are also theory-driven. Certain assumptions must be made as even the questions that form the starting point of research are going to reflect the paradigm in which the research is situated. Thus, the diversity of research methods is as broad as that of theoretical approaches to SLA. In order to consider the range of research methods, we will follow Whong (2011) who makes a broad distinction between internal, psycholinguistic approaches on the one hand, and external, sociolinguistic approaches on the other. As a generalization, this distinction corresponds to fundamental differences in one's approach to research in SLA. The psycholinguistic side of the field is primarily interested in investigating the internal, mental mechanisms of language development and takes an individual learner approach to research. This development is seen as both biological, in the sense that language is a natural feature of being human, and cognitive, as language development occurs in the brain. The sociolinguistic view recognizes the importance of external social factors in the development of the second language as every language is intricately tied to the people and the culture of the community in which that language is situated. Moreover, the second language context is often one of classroom learning; thus pedagogical factors are another external factor important to SLA as well. We will briefly consider this internal/external distinction before looking more closely at specific research associated with differing approaches to investigating SLA.

Psycholinguistic approaches have developed sophisticated methods of measuring mental processes to very precise levels (see Chapters 6, 19 and 20, this volume). In some cases, it is the difference of milliseconds determined by a computer that can give insight into mental development. This kind of research requires very specific hypotheses and tightly controlled experiments with attention to each specific variable which could affect the outcome of the data collected. While psycholinguistic research aims to show causation between variables, because of the very complex nature of language development and the fact that there are a multitude of variables involved, it is often the case that psycholinguistic research in fact shows correlations between variables, instead of true causation. Because explanations then depend upon the theoretical framework assumed, this can allow for a range of explanations for the same set of data.

Sociolinguistic research, by contrast, looks to external factors to explain second language development. These factors are often explored by observation, with researchers asking what speakers of a second language actually do in natural settings. Additionally, observation can reveal external influences on what speakers do. If the aim is to get a true picture of what actually occurs, the less interference and manipulation by the researcher the better, a phenomenon known as the Observer's Paradox (Labov 1972). Other questions exploring external factors can be answered by questioning speakers of a language. Thus, whether observation or questionnaire/interview is used, for sociolinguists, the method is not laboratory-type experimentation, but instead ethnographic observation or exploration through exchanges with participants. After all, if language is a part of society and culture, then probing people's actions and understandings will give insights which allow for explanation of trends in second language development (see Chapters 8, 11, 12 and 30, this volume).

Because the two approaches ask very different questions about second language development, it is perhaps natural that they look to different methods. Psycholinguistic approaches are usually quantitative, with results that can be captured numerically in percentages and means, and subjected to statistical testing to rule out the possibility that the results are a product of circumstance and chance. Ethnographic and questionnaire/interview data coming out of sociolinguistic research, by contrast, tends to be qualitative in nature as capturing the complexity of social factors can be undermined by pressure to represent findings numerically. While the observation and narrative involved in such research are not readily measured, research on external factors at times employs quantitative methods for capturing specific aspects of research which then support the larger qualitatively based narrative. In short, for this type of research, trends, patterns and tendencies emerge to form a narrative which is supported by documented (and sometimes quantified) behavior, argumentation and logical reasoning.

These positions are polarized and contended (see Firth and Wagner 1997), but we can nonetheless try to view them neutrally, as equally valid approaches asking interesting, albeit different questions in order to better understand the nature of second language development and use. Yet no research is neutral because of the need for a theoretical framework in which to understand the research, whether experimental and quantitative or observational and qualitative. When we step back from SLA, we see that this difference is one of fundamental opposition in social science more broadly. The quantitative approach, which developed out of the scientific method, is considered a positivist approach because researchers begin the research by anticipating the result, putting a hypothesis to the test. As such, this approach can be criticized as being a process of confirming a preconceived outcome. This contrasts with a constructionist approach which is seen as more exploratory in nature, beginning with an open question and relying on observation to suggest answers. Moreover, there is a tension between these two approaches where both are committed to certain philosophical ideals. While a more conciliatory view sees the two as compatible and leading to a more complete picture, in the heat of debate they are pitted against each other with the suggestion that one is somehow more valid than the other.

In the rest of this chapter, we consider a range of methodologies under each approach. What unifies researchers is that all are seeking to understand second language development. Like the larger volume, this chapter is organized in terms of the theoretical questions being asked in the field of SLA. We will start by considering biological factors implicated in SLA including age, native language transfer and universal constraints on language development. We will then consider both online and neurological research on the internal working of the mind/brain. This is followed by discussion of external factors, starting with questions of classroom instruction. We end with a look at affective and sociocultural factors important to second language development.

4.2 Biological factors

The guiding assumption for proponents of a biological approach to SLA is that language is a natural and inherent artifact of being human which is best understood by researching mental properties of individuals. In this psycholinguistic approach, a learner needs to acquire the constraints of a language system before s/he can freely generate language. The generative (i.e. Chomskyan) view assumes innate mechanisms in order to explain native first language acquisition. Aside from some tentative early remarks (Chomsky 1970), Chomsky himself has refrained from extending the generative view to the second language context. Many others in the generative tradition have done so, focusing mainly on questions of age, native language transfer, and universal properties of L2 development by testing specific aspects of core grammar, or competence, whether morphosyntax or phonology or the lexicon (see Chapters 21, 22, 23, 24 and 25, this volume). In this section we consider these points, highlighting issues of research methods relevant to this psycholinguistic approach.

From the beginning, generative SLA research modeled itself on first language acquisition research, including the methodology used to collect data. Researchers were also influenced by work from the 1970s which focused on child L2 learners, relying on oral production data from children in immersion-type settings. The now well-known morpheme order studies of this era asked whether young L2 children would parallel the developmental paths of the native children in Brown's (1973) study (see Chapter 27, this volume). Studying spontaneous speech from three L1 English children, Adam, Eve and Sarah, Brown found that all three acquired fourteen pre-determined morphemes in the same order, supporting a biological view of native language development. Dulay and Burt (1974b) wondered what L2 children would do. Their methodology was a semi-controlled standardized test known as the Bilingual Syntax Measure (BSM). Developed for use with children, the BSM includes a set of pictures with questions designed to orally elicit specific linguistic forms. Dulay and Burt (1974b) tested fifty-five Chinese and sixty Spanish children between the ages of 6 and 8, and found that in general, these second language learners followed the same order as native English children despite the difference in the L2 learners' native languages. They therefore claimed that natural, biological forces are also at work in second language development. This research, however, is also well known for its methodological limitations. Among various criticisms was Porter (1977), who cast doubt on the results by showing that the decision to use the BSM may have introduced a bias which led to such similar patterns in morpheme production. That is, the results were an artefact of the data collection process. While other studies using different methodologies turned out to confirm the basic findings of Dulay and Burt (1974b), we can see the important role that the choice of methodology plays in yielding valid results.

A second important point from the 1970s research is the relationship between results and conclusions. While early proponents of a biological approach found support for inbuilt language-specific internal mechanisms for language based on this research, others have used the very same results to argue for a very different theoretical claim. Cognitive linguists Goldschneider and DeKeyser (2001), for example, analyzed the morpheme results in terms of their salience, complexity, regularity and frequency in the input learners receive to argue that it is the nature of the input that leads to similar patterns of development rather than internal factors. Because the same results can give rise to competing interpretations, it is important when reporting results to clearly separate out the presentation of results from the discussion of results where conclusions are drawn and theoretical claims are made. This is crucial because a transparent and honest presentation of results outlined in a theory-neutral way can then allow for open analysis and healthy debate by researchers from a range of theoretical stances.

Other earlier age-related seminal research is that of Johnson and Newport (1989) on the question of a critical period for second language acquisition

(Lenneberg 1967). This study was carefully designed to measure specifically identified areas of inflectional morphology and syntax against two variables: age of arrival in an English-speaking environment and length of exposure to English. Their results show a correlation between increased language ability and early age of arrival for speakers who arrived before the age of 15, so they argue for a critical period with an upper limit of 15 years. However, an alternative reanalysis of the results by Bialystok and Hakuta (1994) showed age-related effects for only some of the linguistic forms and a correlation with language ability for age 20, not age 15. In other words, while those who arrived before age 15 may have had an advantage, in terms of correlation between youth and language ability, the Johnson and Newport data do not show a disadvantage for those who arrived between ages 15 and 20. This means that there is no basis in this data for positing 15 as an upper limit for the critical period. While there has been much research on the question of age since Lenneberg (1967; see Chapter 15, this volume), we again see different claims based on a single set of results. Despite much care and attention in research design, decisions made when analyzing results can lead to very different conclusions.

Another concern for generative SLA research is the question of native language influence (see Chapter 5, this volume). Early Contrastive Analysis Hypothesis (Lado 1957) research proposed that second language learning would be facilitated in constructions where the native and second language structures or forms were the same, whereas differences between the two languages would cause difficulties of acquisition. The problems with this research paradigm, especially for areas of inflectional morphology and syntax, are well known as empirical studies have found numerous counterexamples. (For discussion see Chapters 2 and 27, this volume.) Yet the assumption that there is a role for L1 transfer is largely accepted. Researchers have tended to look for L1 effects which are any features of the interlanguage that mirror the native language and are not a part of the target language. More recent research takes a much more articulated view of language to tease apart which aspects of the native language might exhibit transfer effects, from syntax to functional morphology to prosody (see Chapter 5, this volume). However, there is still no comprehensive theory of L1 transfer which predicts exactly what those effects will be, nor how they interact with other developmental effects.

One complicating factor in researching native language transfer is the methodological difficulty in separating out the native language as a variable among other variables. If there is a result in the interlanguage data which looks like an L1 effect, there is no way of knowing whether the L1 is truly the source, or whether it is a product of natural development since under the generative approach, the learner's L1 knowledge is made up of options from the set of universal constraints. Perhaps the most interesting finding in the generative SLA research is evidence for linguistic phenomena that are not part of the target language nor the native language (also see Chapter 7, this volume). Clahsen and Hong (1995) investigated whether adult Korean learners of L2 German know that German requires subjects. While thirteen of the thirty-three learners tested seemed to know that German requires subjects, two seemed to be abiding by Korean grammar, which allows null subjects. Based on the remaining eighteen learners, Clahsen and Hong (1995) argue that there are no natural UG-based constraints on L2 development because the majority of subjects do not show properties of the native language nor of the target language. White (2003a), however, reanalyzed Clahsen and Hong's results to argue that five of the eighteen learners show grammatical constraints that are neither Korean nor German, but instead reflect a different type of null subject language such as Spanish. She interprets this as evidence that there are universal guiding principles for L2 development. This would explain results that can be explained neither by the influence of the native language nor directly from the input from the target language. Echoing our theme of methodology, we have yet another case of results being interpreted differently in order to support a particular theoretical stance.

This research on null subjects also illustrates the most complicating variable in generative SLA research: L2 development. A researcher can carefully control for age and native language through deliberate selection of learners. L2 development, by contrast, is much more slippery. Models of L2 development from the mid 1990s were framed in terms of initial state – the learner's knowledge at the start of L2 acquisition – and ultimate steady-state attainment (also referred to as fossilization/a fossilized grammar). Yet even these rather stable beginning/end points are difficult to pin down. Is a learner still at the initial state after the first ten minutes of L2 exposure? Or a week? Or more? Does ultimate attainment mean no more language knowledge ever – not even new words or idioms? Even more difficult are questions of intermediate-stage learners – investigation of whom characterizes the vast majority of SLA research. Most researchers assign their learners to proficiency categories based on their academic level (e.g. second year studying English at university level) or standardized tests which the learner will have taken some time in the recent past (e.g. IELTS or TOEFL). Very few researchers actually test their learners for proficiency because doing so credibly would require as much time and energy as the test for the targeted data. When proficiency is tested, one fairly quick way of doing so is to use a cloze test in which every seventh (or so) word from a short reading passage is deleted. (See, for example, Slabakova 2001.) This has been used as a relative measure of language ability for a given sample of learners. To our knowledge, however, the validity of such tests has not been established.

Broadly speaking, there are two ways to explore development in SLA research. A longitudinal study follows the same set of learners over a certain length of time (usually at least six months) in order to document the development of individual interlanguage grammars. Hakuta (1974) and, more recently, Haznedar (2001) are examples of longitudinal studies of a single child L2 learner. Because of the demands on both the researcher and the learners studies like these are often limited to single case studies. This is problematic – particularly outside generative SLA circles – as it can be risky to generalize results from one learner to L2 development more generally. One exceptional example is the European Science Foundation (ESF) project of Klein and Purdue (1992), a longitudinal study of forty adults. Longitudinal studies are very hard to carry out for the practical reason of time – both in terms of commitment by the researcher and the continued participation by the learners. A more common way to account for L2 development is to do a cross-sectional study. If the researcher is trying to chart development, sets of learners can be tested, where learners are placed in low, intermediate and advanced proficiency groups. If learners are equivalent in other ways (native language, age of exposure, age at time of testing, type of language input, etc.) then we can assume that the groups represent points along a developmental path. Most impressive are studies that include both longitudinal and cross-sectional data. The *Zweitspracherwerb italienischer, spanischer und portugiesischer Arbeiter* (ZISA) project (Clahsen, Meisel and Pienemann 1983) collected both types of data and studied forty-five adults, with longitudinal data collection spanning two years.

Since the 1970s, the most heated debate for generative SLA researchers has been whether L2 development is constrained by UG in the same way as native language development, and since the 1980s, the traditional method for testing linguistic competence has been the grammaticality judgment task (GJT) where the speaker indicates whether a sentence presented to him/her is grammatical or ungrammatical. One advantage of the GJT is that it gives insight into the learner's grammar while removing the burden of production. It is readily accepted that what a speaker knows about the language may not be reflected by what s/he actually produces, especially if s/he feels anxious, tired or self-conscious. Most crucially, a GJT shows what a learner's interlanguage does not allow – a point which simply is not possible from either oral or written production data. From a practical point of view, GJTs are relatively easy to administer, either in pencil-and-paper form, or via computerized presentation using E-prime or other software (see below). In (1) and (2) are examples of GJTs which have been used to test L2 learners. Example (1) is from a study by Juffs (1998: 411) on the acquisition of L2 English causatives by Chinese, Korean and Romance language speakers. The second example from Hawkins and Chan (1997: 224–26) was used to test L1 Cantonese and French learners' knowledge of the properties of relative clauses in English. (Sentences which are asterisked are ungrammatical in the target language.)

(1) a. First of all, the cook melted the chocolate on the cake.
 b. *First of all, the chocolate melted itself on the cake.

(2) a. The lady that I met yesterday was my former teacher.
b. The girl that John likes is studying at the university.
c. *This is the building which they heard the news that the government will buy.
d. *The classmate whom Sally is cleverer than him reads very slowly.

The GJT has been criticized for its reliance on learners who are not trained linguists to make what are sometimes very subtle judgments (see, e.g., Bialystok 1994; Birdsong 1989; Chaudron 2003; Schütze 2005). Moreover, for any sentence a learner judges ungrammatical, it is difficult to know which part of the sentence was the cause of the rejection. Both criticisms are relevant to the above examples. An attempt to address the second criticism can, however, be seen in Juffs' construction of the ungrammatical variant in (1) which uses the same lexical items, and differs from its grammatical counterpart as a minimal pair. Another solution is for the learner to be asked to indicate which part of the sentence is problematic, or to correct the sentences s/he finds ungrammatical.

A further difficulty with the GJT is identifying whether learners vary in terms of degree of ungrammaticality; learners' intuitions appear not to be captured by "grammatical/good" vs. "ungrammatical/bad." One solution is to use a gradient scale, such as Likert scales of -2 to $+2$, where -2 equates to "I'm sure this is ungrammatical" and -1 equates to "I think this is ungrammatical" and so on. This kind of measure provides a more nuanced way of checking the degree to which learners are aware of the target constraint, how strongly they respond to that constraint, and why they may respond so variably at different times. Even if careful measures such as these are adopted, however, there remains a further problem: some aspects of grammar are not appropriate for judgments of grammaticality, but instead tap interpretation of a sentence or sentences.

In order to test interpretation, researchers, again following the lead of first language acquisition (see, e.g., Crain and Thornton 1998), have developed the truth value judgment (TVJ) task which asks learners to judge the validity of statements based on some kind of context, whether pictures or short stories. The TVJ allows for research that investigates aspects of interpretation so subtle that they go beyond what native speakers, even language teachers, consciously and explicitly know about their language. As an example, H. Marsden (2009) researched the knowledge that L1 English and L1 Korean learners of L2 Japanese have of equivalents of quantifiers like *every* and *any*. She provided her learners with pictures and asked them to decide whether each picture matched each sentence given. For the example given in (3), she included one of two pictures: (i) one girl stroking three cats, or (ii) three girls, each stroking a different cat. Unlike in English, in Japanese, this sentence only matches picture (i), with one girl stroking three cats.

(3) Dareka-ga   dono neko-mo nadeta.
    someone-NOM every cat   stroked
    "Someone stroked every cat." (H. Marsden 2009: 144)

While this may seem like an esoteric exercise, it has important theoretical implications. When the results suggest that L2 speakers have nativelike interpretations of these so-called poverty-of-the-stimulus effects, researchers can then argue for UG-constrained development among adult L2 learners – the crux of the generative SLA research agenda. (For other examples, see Chapters 7 and 8, this volume.)

Findings from GJTs and TVJs have become the canon of generative SLA research. However, researchers are well aware that these have been limited to a so-called property theory approach whereby characteristics of specific stages in L2 development are being examined, and not a transition theory approach which asks how learners move from stage to stage. Researchers in the 1980s and early 1990s were optimistic that parameter setting in Principles and Parameters theory (Chomsky 1981) could help to explain transitions in L2 development by researching parameter resetting. Because a parameter is assumed to include a cluster of properties, if a parameter is triggered and it is set (or reset), a whole range of linguistic properties would be put into place. This could explain transitions from one stage to another. The resulting studies on parameter setting and resetting exemplify sound experimentation in terms of method and logic (e.g. White 1992). However, as pointed out by a number of researchers (e.g. Carroll 2001), identifying parameters to account for syntactic variation across languages has proved problematic, thus undermining the research agenda. Again we see difficulty in the interplay between theory and method. One very recent approach to transition theory is that of Slabakova (2008), who employs a meta-analytic approach surveying a large body of generative SLA literature. By putting together many pieces of the developmental puzzle, Slabakova is able to make claims about L2 development and to provide a contribution to transition theory. Given the large amount of research that now exists within the generative SLA paradigm, more meta-analyses are needed in order to draw conclusions and address the question of transition from one stage to the next.

4.3 Cognitive factors

We turn now to look in more detail at learner-internal research that focuses more specifically on the working of the mind/brain in L2 language use. This research has commonly aimed to ask how the L2 is used *online* (i.e. in real time) and how cognitive constraints such as processing speed may affect the nature of L2 storage and use. In terms of acquisition or development, research often seeks to measure how far L2 users show increasing reliance on automatized or implicit subconscious processes, similar to mature adult L1 processing. Methodologies used in this research paradigm commonly seek to elicit data on L2 behavior in timed comprehension activities or oral production, which are seen as tapping such implicit processes.

In its focus on language development and use, cognitive-based research has often been seen as a reaction to traditional generative approaches to SLA, discussed above. Initial distinctions between linguistic competence and performance meant that in the generative paradigm, linguistic competence was distinct from general cognitive factors connected to real-time performance (Chomsky 1965; Fodor 1983). Many cognitive-based studies have indeed explored L2 development from the perspective that language involves only general learning and processing strategies. However, there is a growing awareness across the SLA spectrum that processing research can bring new insights into the nature of L2 use and development, regardless of the theoretical stance of the L2 researcher (e.g. Marinis 2003; Juffs 2004). The wealth of empirical research referred to in subsequent chapters in this handbook provides much of the detail of how these kinds of methods have driven changes in our understanding of the role of learner-internal cognitive factors in SLA.[1] We focus in this section on several key developments in technology which have fostered novel ways to understand the complex nature of L2 processing in both comprehension and production.

One valuable methodological tool is learner corpora of oral production data, which provide a vast amount of information about what kind of processes are involved in L2 development. Corpora include a wide range of L2s, ranging from data from instructed learners of French and Spanish (www.flloc.soton.ac.uk and www.splloc.soton.ac.uk) to naturalistic data from the ESF study (see above), now found in CHILDES' TalkBank (http://childes.psy.cmu.edu/data), and for recent phonological corpora, in CHILDES PhonBank (http://childes.psy.cmu.edu/phon/). Corpora focusing on analyses of speech such as MICASE (http://micase.elicorpora.info) can also allow detailed analysis of learners' patterns of language use in different situations, such as classroom discourse compared to informal speech.

Such corpora have been used to provide a wider perspective on traditional SLA research questions by allowing the researcher to tap into an extensive database, and corpora have also facilitated increasingly sophisticated research questions. For example, CLAN software on the FLLOC database allows a specific query (tapping, say, word frequency or morphosyntactic marking) to be run on multiple files at once. Analysis can thus quickly identify important factors in learner behavior, split by age group or by target phenomenon (e.g. negation, verb raising); or comparisons can be drawn for the same speaker across different tasks (e.g. to see if grammatical accuracy is task-dependent). In corpus linguistics, tools such as WordSmith (www.lexically.net/wordsmith) allow extensive analyses to track, say, learners' use of different types of explicit or implicit language knowledge and respond to different discourse situations (e.g. identifying explicitly taught chunks, the use of automatized formulaic sequences, success or difficulty with specific collocations or use of discourse-specific lexis).

SLA research is also turning to more sophisticated methods of measuring parsing to tap into participants' automatic, unconscious linguistic processing. For example, computer-generated GJTs can reveal millisecond differences in learners' speed of processing different stimuli, independently of the accuracy of their overall grammaticality judgments. Such information provides important insights into causes of learner variability, and subtle differences in processing stimuli that offline (untimed) accuracy judgments would not capture. Several of the chapters later in this handbook specifically cover research done using these techniques, so we do not go into detail here, but highlight some of the most common software packages used, and the contributions and limitations of using such techniques.

Frequently used software for psycholinguistic measures of processing and reaction times currently include E-Prime (www.pstnet.com/eprime.cfm) and NESU (www.mpi.nl/world/tg/experiments/nesu.html), although these are not easily manipulable by non-experts. Others include the freely downloadable and easy to learn DMDX (www.web.arizona.edu/~cnl/dmdx.htm), or PsyScope for Macs (www.psy.ck.sissa.it). One of the benefits of this software for researchers is the capacity to use stimuli of any kind, whether words, pictures or sound, allowing a range of hypotheses about how linguistic knowledge is stored and retrieved and the effects of different modes of presenting input.

A commonly used technique to measure ease or difficulty in processing is self-paced reading/listening, or the *moving window* technique. This procedure measures reaction times on computer-presented stimuli, such as grammaticality judgments. Participants are instructed to read through the sentence as quickly as possible, pressing a button to reveal the next words or sentence on the screen. There is usually a comprehension question afterwards to test overall understanding, to ensure participants focus on processing the sentence rather than mechanically pressing the button. The millisecond differences of speed in calling up the next word or phrase reveal differences in processing different sections of the sentence, e.g. where ambiguities need to be resolved, or traces of underlying movement have to be interpreted (such as in resolving subject or object theta roles in relative clauses, or grammatical vs. ungrammatical wh-movement).

White and Genesee (1996) and White and Juffs (1998) are examples of studies using this technique to analyze differences between L1 and L2 judgments on subjacency violations. These studies found that L2 learners responded as accurately as native speakers, but responded more slowly, and also showed greater ease with object extraction than subject extraction. In other words, using reaction time data highlighted asymmetries in how linguistic knowledge was retrieved and processed which the accuracy measurements alone did not reveal.

Priming research is another way of using computer-based tests of unconscious knowledge, where different items (such as words or structures) are presented in a sequence, usually too fast for conscious awareness or learning (e.g. less than 100 milliseconds). Priming effects are found when an item processed earlier in the sequence facilitates the subsequent processing of similar test items.

Priming has been widely used in bilingual research for studying the effects of language transfer, or for overlapping processes in lexical retrieval where, for example, judgments of *coin* as French (corner) or English (money) will be affected by the sound or form of previously presented primes (see, among many, de Groot and Kroll 1997; Green 1998). Priming can also provide information on how processing involves different modes, e.g. where cross-modal priming tests how far auditory primes may affect visually processed test stimuli (see e.g. reviews in Marinis 2003). Priming techniques in SLA can therefore provide a way of understanding more precisely the interconnections between subconscious linguistic processing of form, meaning and sound, and aid our understanding of how L2 develops.

McDonough and Trofimovich (2008) and E. Marsden (2009) provide wide-ranging overviews of priming studies in SLA, many of which have focused on different types of priming effects on parsing or lexical retrieval. Other studies have also begun to look at priming effects on L2 oral production. McDonough (2006), for example, found that grammatical structures (such as subject or object questions) showed a clear priming effect: participants produced the primed structure more frequently in a subsequent interactive oral production task.

Another technologically based technique that is becoming increasingly used in SLA research to tap unconscious or implicit processing is eye-tracking (see Chapter 19, this volume, and also Dussias 2010). Here highly precise measures of length and place of eye movements over a stimulus (e.g. text or pictures) can provide detailed information on what L2 learners are subconsciously attending to in their online decision-making processes. Longer gaze fixation shows which parts of the stimulus require greater processing, e.g. in responding to syntactic ungrammaticality or semantic anomaly. Eye-tracking thus potentially adds another dimension to the reaction-time experiments referred to above, by providing more information on the structural nature of processing L2 semantic, syntactic and other linguistic information (Dussias 2010: 156).

As our understanding of processing in SLA increases, we can become more sophisticated in asking questions about the nature and location of the language processes involved. An extension of this interest is reflected in the increasing use of neurolinguistic research in SLA. Developments since the 1990s in brain-imaging techniques, including event-related potentials (ERPs) and functional Magnetic Resonance Imaging (fMRI) have the potential to allow a greater understanding of the actual brain processes involved, giving more physiological detail to the reaction-time and eye-tracking behavioral data discussed above (see also Chapters 6 and 19, this volume, on the implications of this area of research).

In principle, these methodologies can be theory-neutral, but, in practice, one of the key research questions within this paradigm has been to identify how far L1 and L2 language processing are similar or different, which overlaps in many ways with the cognitive research outlined hitherto. For example, one of the major research questions is whether the kind of automatic processing seen in native speakers' sentence processing is absent or reduced in L2 learners and instead involves different processing, with greater reliance on conscious or explicit knowledge (see Hahne 2001; Friederici 2002 for reviews). There also seems to be ample evidence (Phillips 2006), at least for adult learners, that L2 processing is more cognitively demanding, resulting in slower ERP responses (or latencies) in an individual's L2 compared to his/her L1. Such evidence has been argued to provide a strong empirical foundation to claims that adult L2 acquisition is fundamentally different from L1 acquisition (Clahsen and Felser 2006a; Ullman 2001b).

However, concerns have been raised whether these neurolinguistic techniques reveal as much as they claim, particularly since different studies produce conflicting interpretations of L2 data (e.g. Green 2003; Paradis 2004; Perani *et al.* 1998). For example, Green (2003) suggests that there is still little or no information about how different neural regions may work together during second language production. De Bot's (2008a) review of research on neurolinguistics warns against drawing generalizations about the underlying processes of language when too much as yet remains unclear about the theoretical and empirical relation of brain activity to language function. He also highlights methodological weaknesses in operationalizing learner variables. Different studies often use different assumptions in defining levels of proficiency, age differences in acquisition, or interpretations of other individual differences. Given these differences, it is perhaps unsurprising that cognitive and neurological research remains highly specialized both in techniques and research questions, and can lead to contradictory conclusions.

4.4 Pedagogical factors

Until now, we have discussed second language research that tries to tap learners' internal mental processes using either traditional behavioral or more recent online and neurological methodologies. We now turn to external factors, starting our discussion with classroom-related research, which is at the intersection of research in education and second language learning. The main method employed in classroom research in the 1960s and 1970s was observation. Brown and Rodgers (2002) identified more than two hundred observation instruments developed for use in classrooms of which twenty-six were identified by Chaudron (1988) as specifically for second language classrooms. Observation usually relies on audio- or visual-recording of classroom activity followed by careful (usually orthographic) transcription. This yields a vast amount of data which are then subjected to analysis. One approach to analyzing these data is conversation analysis (see Markee 2000) in which *talk*, as the object of study, is seen to rely on social constraints. As with qualitative methodology in general, this kind of data requires analysis to identify trends and patterns which can then provide an understanding of features of the second language classroom, from teacher beliefs to the nature of instruction to learner participation and so on. Indeed, the sheer number of potential variables in classroom research is one main reason for taking what is generally a qualitative approach. Once trends have been identified, findings can also be captured more quantitatively through coding, a step which requires determining the unit for analysis and counting of the number of occurrences using coding techniques such as those laid out in the Communicative Orientation of Language Teaching or COLT (Spada and Fröhlich 1995).

While observation is *constructionist*, meaning that it is more open-ended than controlled experiments, the decisions made about how to make sense of what is observed can lead to bias reflecting the theoretical perspective of the researcher just as the more positivist approaches can. In other words, as we have seen with psycholinguistic research, all research is influenced by the theoretical viewpoint of the researcher to some extent. One difference, however, is the extent to which constructionist researchers have openly acknowledged this problem, especially since the shift in the 1990s to ethnographic research, which still involves observation, but adds notions from anthropology and emphasizes self-awareness on the part of the researcher. A significant limitation of observation and ethnography that remains, however, is the difficulty in researching a specific aspect of the learning/teaching process which might not naturally occur during observation, or perhaps not with sufficient frequency. This has led to methodologies in which the researcher exerts some control over the learners in order to specifically test an area of instruction and/or learning.

One influential research agenda initiated in the 1980s was Long's Interaction Hypothesis (1981) which claims that learning occurs not just in the learner's individual, subconscious response to input, but from learners themselves as they work out and work on language in interaction with others (see also Chapter 30, this volume). This has led to methodologies quite different from those which fall under the observational approach. Instead of observing what might naturally occur in the classroom, this research puts a theory about second language learning to the test by manipulation of the learning event. In the early days of this theory-driven research, the focus was on conversations between a native speaker and a non-native speaker as this theory focused on what happens when non-native speakers have to modify their output in order to be understood in interaction with native speakers. This research is experimental; the interlocutors are given specific tasks to perform, designed to include specific types of interaction (e.g. Doughty and

Pica 1986). By recording, transcribing and analyzing the data, the researcher can make claims about what types of negotiation during conversation lead to second language learning, as shown for example by the non-native speaker's ability to repair breakdown in communication and any subsequent use of linguistic features new for that speaker. Yet it has also been noted that negotiation may be more relevant to interaction between non-native and other non-native speakers, since for many learners this is more likely than interaction with native speakers. In a meta-analysis by Keck, Iberri-Shea, Tracy-Ventura and Wa-Mbaleka (2006), however, 85 percent of studies still involved native–non-native speaker interaction. Another limitation from the point of view of generalizability is that the majority of this research tends to be conducted in university settings as this is where researchers have most immediate access to learners.

This shows us that one downside of using a controlled method is the question of how appropriate the findings can be for classroom settings that differ from those in an experiment. Yet this must be balanced with the need to control the research design in order to test specific points of theory and yield results which can be analyzed. From a pedagogical point of view, research on interaction based on dyads is problematic in the context of classrooms that are not limited to pair work. Moreover, since the teaching method associated with interaction is Task-Based teaching (Long and Robinson 1998), the research question which then arises is whether Task-Based teaching is an effective method for teaching language. This research requires a different sort of method in which a class of learners is tested to see if teaching through tasks – which, by definition, are interaction-based – leads to learning in a way that more traditional modes of language teaching do not. This type of research normally requires pre-testing to measure both a control/comparison and an experimental group of learners' proficiency prior to treatment in the form of a task only for the experimental group, and post-testing both groups to measure the effectiveness of the treatment.

A wealth of studies on classroom instruction has been conducted, giving rise to what can be seen as conflicting results. However, the meta-analysis by Keck *et al.* (2006) concludes that in total, experimental groups do seem to outperform comparison groups. One problem with generalizing from a body of studies like this is that the wealth of studies also uses a wealth of experimental designs from more controlled to relatively free tasks on pairs or groups of learners performing on a range of task types. There are, in fact, many variables to control for; in addition to the usual SLA variables of native language, target language, age, proficiency, etc., there are other pedagogical variables including educational setting, type of task, type of interaction, type of participants (native–non-native, teacher/peer), target linguistic features, measurement of development and credible comparison group, to name a few. Another challenge is that any comparison group will often also show improvement – after all, they were also being taught, just not in the way that the researcher is interested in. While this is clearly good from a pedagogical point of view, it can be frustrating for the researcher. And, problematically, this raises ethical issues as it might be considered unethical to teach learners using a methodology assumed to be ineffective just so the researcher can show another method to be effective.

Another area of classroom research which has received much attention is the question of explicit versus implicit learning. This research is generally referred to as research on instructed learning, with a strict communicative approach (where no grammar teaching occurs) seen as implicit learning, known as Focus on Meaning. Within explicit teaching there is the traditional grammar teaching approach known as Focus on Forms and the more current teaching of forms within a meaningful context, known as Focus on Form (see Chapter 29, this volume). We have just mentioned a meta-analysis for research on interaction. In language teaching research, Norris and Ortega (2000) are pioneers in this approach of combining the results of a large number of studies in order to reach some general conclusions. In their meta-analysis of research on instructed language learning, they evaluated forty-nine studies published in journals between 1980 and 1998 to conclude that explicit instruction in the classroom is beneficial in comparison with implicit learning. As with the meta-analysis of Keck *et al.* (2006), Norris and Ortega (2000) had difficulty finding coherence across published studies. In deciding which studies to include, Norris and Ortega found that many studies had to be left out because of deficiencies in their methodology. In fact, one main conclusion of the meta-analysis was severe methodological weaknesses in the field. These ranged from small size of sample to lack of control group. There is also a wide range of practice in terms of reporting results as some presentations of results include comprehensive individual results while others collapse results into averages or means. Norris and Ortega also note omissions in fully reporting results, where many researchers claim statistical significance, but do not always report the basic descriptive statistics such as medians and means which would enable the reader to validate the strength of their claims.

In another more recent meta-analysis on instructed language learning by Spada and Tomita (2010) thirty of 103 studies published in journals after 1990 were analyzed, including ten which were also included by Norris and Ortega (2000). The reason for the limited number of studies was that Spada and Tomita were interested in research which focused specifically on some point of grammatical instruction. The overall finding by Spada and Tomita is, again, that explicit instruction does seem to lead to learning of grammatical forms such as past tense or passives in a way that implicit methods do not. However, as they point out, this cannot rule out the effectiveness of implicit instruction per se as it may be that implicit instruction requires more time. Moreover, as none of the studies include any more than ten hours of instruction, it is difficult judge the effects of instruction, especially in the long term.

Another area of research which is constrained by the time devoted to the treatment is research on corrective feedback. Coming out of research on interaction, research on corrective feedback in the early 1990s found that there is a large a range of types of feedback being used by teachers, from traditional explicit correction to implicit modeling, e.g. recasting correctly what the learner has said (see Russell and Spada 2006, and citations within). This research, however, has also found that a fair amount of any sort of corrective feedback seemed to be ignored by students – at least in the moment. Whether there is any long-term improvement as a result of feedback to a large extent remains an open question. The problem of length of study is a fundamental methodological problem that plagues all areas of SLA and classroom research. It is difficult to carry out research over a long period of time especially beyond any single academic year because of constraints on both the learners and researchers. A second fundamental difficulty is the aforementioned problem of the multiplicity of variables. Taken together, these two constraints make it especially difficult to be able to claim causation in classroom research. Thus, many researchers limit themselves to safer claims such as *indirect causal relationship*, meaning that there does seem to be some relationship, but the research cannot conclusively show a direct cause effect. As generally accepted, it is very difficult to demonstrate true links between interaction and L2 acquisition (Keck *et al.* 2006: 93). It is more possible to show correlations, and perhaps researchers should be satisfied with this.

In sum, instructed language research makes use of a range of methods, from observation and ethnography to investigate the language produced spontaneously by speakers, to pre- and post-testing to show the effects of a given treatment, and to quasi-experimental methods which allow for more control by the researcher. These methods vary in terms of the degree to which they focus on what occurs versus focusing on the effect of theory-based intervention or treatment. And as with all research, none of this research is neutral or unbiased, as the theoretical framework of the researcher will come into play, whether in the design of the study or in the analysis of the results. This is not inherently bad, of course, but it is a reality which must be acknowledged by the researcher.

4.5 Social factors

We now move to research methodologies focusing on learner context. We have seen that explanations of what constrains L2 development, especially intra-individual variation, have remained unclear if the research question focuses only on the nature of the grammatical competence (the *What*) or on biological or cognitive factors driving transition (the *How*). Investigations of social and affective factors have provided useful insight into the impact of the L2 context (the *Why*).

The work of Gardner (1985), amongst others, has highlighted the importance of affective factors of motivation and personality within SLA.

Investigating the role of personality, identity, attitude, motivation and learner strategy are now seen as central research questions underpinning a broad understanding of the SLA process (as reflected in the representation of such questions in this handbook, e.g. Chapters 8, 10, 11, 12 and 30). However, questions of why L2 learners behave as they do means that comparisons of L2 acquisition to L1 acquisition, common in property and processing theories of SLA, usually do not arise.

Methodologically, research here commonly tends to follow one of two paths. Firstly, the ethnographic qualitative tradition draws on theory based on data collected from individuals or small groups, where the observer avoids any presupposed empirical hypotheses. Observations, interviews, conversations, or self-reports are typical methods of gathering data, as mentioned above. The data may be used to assess types of interaction, in a classroom, for example, comparing patterns of teacher/learner discourse (Seedhouse 2005b), or the specific functions for using L1 in an L2 classroom (Macaro 1997). Another method is gathering qualitative data using self-reports or think-aloud protocols (e.g. Bowles 2010), where participants are asked to explain why they responded as they did. This is used either as a single method or to provide extra context in a quantitatively measured grammaticality judgment task.

By contrast, the psychological quantitative tradition may focus on hypothesis testing on often large data sets, usually using large-scale questionnaires, where individual accounts are not investigated but the breadth of data collected provides robust and reliable evidence of specific responses or particular trends. An interesting recent development has been how learners' use of technology has boosted both angles of these research techniques. Such data collection may include both computer-mediated communication for qualitative conversation analysis (gathered using, say, micro-blogs and social networking sites) and also web-based questionnaires for immense collections of quantitative data from learners (see Walsh 2007, and also Chapter 14, this volume).

One of the issues in social research is how to operationalize the factors being researched, as we can see from a brief overview of motivation research. Gardner's (1985) classic study of motivation identified an instrumental-integrative dichotomy in which L2 learners' motivation can either be to learn the L2 because it provides them with a necessary tool to achieve a goal such as a new job or because they want to integrate into the target language community, perhaps because of a personal relationship or desire to be accepted by that community. Another way of labelling a similar division regarding motivation is the intrinsic–extrinsic distinction (Deci and Ryan 1985; Noels 2001), where intrinsic factors include learner-internal ones such as self-development, and extrinsic factors include external material ones such as the search for a job.

Measures of motivation have been used to test how far a specific factor or cluster of factors are associated with a specific linguistic feature under investigation. For example, Gardner and MacIntyre (1991) used the Attitude/Motivation Test Battery with vocabulary test data to test hypotheses as to which type of motivation was associated with higher vocabulary scores. Developments in motivation research since the 1990s (e.g. Dörnyei and Schmidt 2001; Dörnyei and Ushioda 2009) have elaborated Gardner's standard dichotomy in more nuanced detail, building greater consensus over reliable and effective methods across the quantitative and qualitative paradigms. Dörnyei and Ushioda (2009) further identify the importance of understanding that a learner's motivation to improve linguistic performance incorporates non-linguistic factors such as the learner's engagement with task context and need for meaning, as much as motivation to acquire linguistic proficiency in itself.

However, there remain some concerns with motivation research. McGroarty (2001) points out the problem of using too constrained a model of motivation, in which L2 learners are assumed to be able to articulate their motivation in ways that fit a specific model such as intrinsic vs. extrinsic factors, whereas in reality most people would find it hard to pick such factors apart. It has been argued that standard motivation measures thus potentially skew the findings by imposing externally defined measures, so alternative methods such as self-report and narratives have also begun to be more widely used (Gimenez 2010; Woodrow 2010). Self-report has long been employed to gauge a range of measures in quantified form (via self-rating), including linguistic proficiency itself, as well as degrees of motivation (Gardner 1985). However, it is infamously susceptible to corruption or instability (Bialystok and Hakuta 1999), in that a confident participant would be happy to respond with a high self-report, compared to a more proficient but less confident participant. A more qualitative approach uses verbal reports and think-aloud protocols (see above), to try and tap participants' thought processes with more authenticity. However, data interpretation can be difficult, due to the highly subjective nature of such findings, and depends on the linguistic or metacognitive abilities of the participants to express those thought processes in ways that can be insightful for the researcher.

The increasing use of such research tools reflects a growing trend within SLA, and especially applied linguistics, for a socially realistic study of language, based on ethnographic and sociocultural theories of communication and identity dating back to Hymes (1971) and continuing through Block (2003). The prime methodological tool emphasizes naturalistic data collection, gathered through observations of real-time communicative situations such as multilingual business meetings or classroom interactions. Much of this research follows Geertz's (1975) paradigm of Thick Description, or grounded theory (Glaser and Strauss 1967), i.e. unstructured observation providing descriptive data of sufficient depth to build up post-hoc theories that are then confirmed or revised, in an iterative process of further data collection and theory testing.

Some of this research has specifically challenged the concept of language as an empirical objective reality, and thus of using cognitive scientific methods which are commonly located in classroom or laboratory settings, instead of methods which involve exploring naturalistic language as a social accomplishment (Firth and Wagner 1997, 2007). In such approaches, the traditional empirical concept of research validity or objective truth can be redefined as authenticity or trustworthiness, and is rooted in combining analyses of participant data with transparent indications of the researcher's subjective analysis (Starfield 2010: 56).

While the wider implications of the issues raised by Firth and Wagner remain open to debate (see e.g. Block 2003; Harklau 2005), nevertheless, certain methodologies allied to this research strand are increasingly common in SLA, notably conversation analysis, which we briefly discuss here. Conversation analysis (and critical discourse analysis) seeks to identify what micro-analysis of interactions, either in the classroom or in naturalistic settings, tells us about L2 identity, motivation and attitude as well as seeking to find out how language proficiency develops in a communicative setting (e.g. Sacks, Schegloff and Jefferson 1974; Markee 2000).

Methodologically, the central tool for conversation analysis (CA) research is collection of spontaneously occurring classroom or non-classroom data, usually as video files to be transcribed and coded for quantitative or qualitative analysis of interaction patterns. There are now standardized conventions of how to present the data in linguistically analyzable form, available on the CHILDES database, for example. However, the significance of CA within SLA can be seen as more than a linguistic analysis of form and function of turn-taking. Rather, CA aims to add essential information about the role of social action, identity and context in SLA. In addition, CA research, like all sociocultural SLA research, seeks to present a dynamic view of the nature of L2 competence. Rather than comparing L2 to L1 acquisition and finding a deficit of nativelikeness, CA presents competence as variable and co-constructed by participants through interaction (Seedhouse 2005b).

This discussion of social factors in SLA research shows how insights into the context of language acquisition and issues of motivation and identity play an important role in understanding the complexity of L2 acquisition. We also note that many of the qualitative methodologies are very recent in SLA, and therefore it is inevitable that controversy exists and unresolved questions remain, and insights from all aspects of SLA research are required. We reiterate R. Ellis' (1994a) support for the value of multifaceted research methodologies incorporating different approaches in increasing our understanding of SLA in all its complexity.

We finish this chapter with a recent example of a successful multifaceted SLA research design: that of Moyer (2004, 2009), whose mixture of quantitative and qualitative research methods has yielded fresh insights into L2 acquisition. Moyer's work on acquisition of L2 accent overtly promoted the dual assumption that both L2 experience and intention are key to understanding the SLA process, particularly in long-term attainment and the question of nativelikeness. She stresses how far traditional quantitative measures of factors affecting SLA, such as age of onset and length of residence, must be re-envisaged to understand the many facets of L2 experience and motivation. Her integrated view of critical influences of SLA utilized mixed methods, i.e. both quantitative techniques (such as correlational analysis of linguistic accuracy) and qualitative techniques (such as interviews to elicit open answers about identity and motivation), to identify clusters of factors focused on cognitive and social variables, which all interact in understanding ultimate attainment in SLA.

4.6 Conclusion

Perhaps Moyer's mixed methods approach offers one way to find coherence across shared research questions and methods in SLA. However, given the enormous complexity of second language acquisition, it is unlikely that even such an approach can or should capture all of the variables implicated. We have sought to show how both positivist and constructionist approaches, and qualitative and quantitative methods, have driven insightful research into SLA both despite and because of their differences. Researchers will benefit from continued technological advances in assessing internal and external factors affecting L2 learners with increasing sophistication. Methodological rigor will improve consensus in defining what constitutes L2 acquisition and use across all theoretical and empirical perspectives. As long as there are different theoretical starting points to language and second language development, there will be conflicting claims – an outcome that should not make us throw up our hands in frustration, but instead continue to refine our methodologies so that in time SLA research can yield more and more valid results.

Part II
Internal ingredients

INTRODUCTION TO PART II

Part II covers the internal ingredients held to be essential for second language acquisition. The components each chapter discusses are not necessarily neutral, given that different theorists consider the same set of ingredients from their own perspectives. Learners bring to the task of L2A their native language, their cognitive predisposition, individual characteristics, their innate capacity for language and their developed knowledge (e.g. literacy or bilingual capacities).

Focusing on the question of transfer in L2 acquisition, the fifth chapter goes beyond earlier work on native language influence, in covering more recent initial state research and discussion of long-term L1 effects. It looks at researchers' continuously evolving treatment of the role of the L1 in the developing grammar, at superficial (e.g. morphological) versus deep (e.g. syntactic) levels. This chapter traces the study of native language influence from mid-twentieth-century Contrastive Analysis, through Creative Construction and UG approaches to current work on phonology as well as morphosyntax. Flynn and Foley highlight the distinction of surface versus deep transfer and the complexities of other factors that intersect with L1 transfer.

Chapter 6 looks at L2A from a psychology-based cognitive perspective, where researchers have examined the operation of working memory, declarative/procedural memory and explicit/implicit knowledge. The roles of chunking and automatization are pivotal. This chapter explores the contribution of cognitive mechanisms such as working memory and general learning procedures to the development of L2 knowledge, both declarative and procedural. Adopting Carroll's and Levelt's models for comprehension and production, Towell then examines Anderson's, Paradis' and Ullman's proposals for proceduralization. The last section discusses the implications of these models for implicit versus explicit learning.

Establishing the logical problem of language acquisition (poverty of the stimulus, POS), Chapter 7 presents Universal Grammar (UG) as a solution. Schwartz and Sprouse present the role of Universal Grammar, UG (the language faculty) in language acquisition (L1 and L2) through a detailed discussion of poverty of the stimulus, the primary and distinctive motivation for UG accounts. The first section outlines five arguments for POS in L1A, clearly explaining and illustrating the *logical problem of language acquisition* with strong examples. The second section clarifies misunderstandings of the notion of POS, while the third provides examples of POS in non-native language acquisition.

The eighth chapter provides a comprehensive overview of the extensive research which has been carried out over the last half-century on learner-internal factors such as motivation, aptitude, interest, personality and emotion. Based on investigations of instructed L2A, it also discusses characteristics related to learning styles and strategies. The chapter investigates a range of individual cognitive and personality traits that influence a learner's progrss in L2 development. After initial overviews of attitude, motivation, aptitude and memory, Dewaele devotes the remainder of the chapter to personality traits such as extraversion, conscientiousness, risk-taking and foreign language anxiety.

Introducing the population of older learners whose development of alphabetic literacy and acquisition of L2 oral ability occur simultaneously, Chapter 9 presents research on a relatively new area of investigation, the role of reading ability as an influence on acquisition. Issues covered include emerging research on differences observed in the processing of input in the acquisition of morphosyntax and the implications of these observations for both cognitive and generative theories of L2A. The chapter first reviews background studies of the impact of literacy on native language processing and linguistic task solving. Tarone, Hansen and Bigelow then turn to studies of low and non-literate adults learning oral and reading skills in L2.

5

The role of the native language

Claire Foley and Suzanne Flynn

5.1 Introduction

The role that a native or first language may play in second language acquisition has inspired research for many decades. Changes in prevailing views on L1 influence have in fact partly defined historical development of the field (see Chapter 2, this volume). Because of its historical importance, we have organized our review of research on the role of the L1 chronologically. We begin with a brief sketch of the evolution of views on the role of the L1 from the Contrastive Analysis approach of the 1940s and 1950s through the Creative Construction approach of the early 1970s (Section 5.2). We turn next to developments of the later 1970s and 1980s, many of which shed light on the influence of the L1 on particular features of development over time, such as rate, developmental sequence, or production/avoidance of particular structures (Section 5.3). By the 1990s, views on the role of the L1 were helping to define researchers' perspectives on the initial state of L2 acquisition (Section 5.4). This historical development has led to an ever-richer range of research in the 2000s, including innovative approaches to teasing out the particular role that an L1 plays across domains of language (Section 5.5).

Across the decades, researchers have taken varying perspectives on defining *similarity* and *difference* between L1 and L2, a distinction whose importance has roots in Contrastive Analysis, where similarities between L1 and L2 were argued to facilitate acquisition, and differences to hinder it. An important distinction that has emerged across domains of linguistic knowledge is that between *surface forms* (e.g. particular words) and *abstract structures and processes* (e.g. proposed underlying representations). Researchers vary in their assumptions and hypotheses about what kinds of L1 knowledge – surface-related or abstract – might affect L2 development. In the concluding section, we return to the surface/abstract distinction, and to the fact that research on both sheds light on the nature of modularity in grammar.

In this chapter, we have attempted to include examples of research that spans the linguistic subfields of phonology, morphology, syntax and the lexicon. Space limits the comprehensiveness of our coverage, and we have also not attempted to summarize interesting research in such areas as the role of the L1 in L2 pragmatics, literacy, or discourse (but see Chapters 9 and 23, this volume). In places, we describe the design and results of a few studies in somewhat more depth to better inform some of the conclusions made in Section 5.6. While most of the research reviewed here draws on data from adult learners, transfer has been studied for child learners as well (e.g. Paradis and Genesee 1996); for research on child L2 acquisition and bilingualism, see Chapter 16, this volume. When needed, we use the convention "years; months" to express research participants' ages. Except as noted, studies reviewed here are cross-sectional. Other sources providing a comprehensive look at the role of the L1 in L2 development include Gass (1996), Odlin (2003), Major (2008: 63–7) and Gass and Selinker (2008: 89–158).

5.2 From Contrastive Analysis to Creative Construction

In the 1940s and 1950s, scholars of language and pedagogy examined similarities and differences between the L1 and the L2 (e.g. Fries 1945). Adapting a general view of transfer as the use of knowledge or skills from one context in a different linguistic context, Weinreich (1953) introduced the concept of *transfer* in L2 acquisition: use of the L1 that leads to "correct" usage in the L2. *Interference*, in contrast, involves use of the L1 that leads to "incorrect" language use.

As described in detail in Chapter 2, this volume, during the 1950s, many scholars attempted to apply analyses of combinations of L1 and L2 for pedagogical reasons. In a work on applied linguistics for language teachers, Lado (1957) developed the *Contrastive Analysis* (CA) approach to L2 acquisition. Under the Constrastive Analysis Hypothesis, learning a new language involves identifying and learning differences between the L1 and the L2. Similarities between L1 and L2 are predicted to facilitate acquisition; L2s with more differences from the L1 are predicted to take longer to learn. The CA approach encouraged careful scrutiny of similarities and differences between an L1 and an L2, and led researchers to test the prediction that more differences would mean more difficulty for learners. Through the 1950s and 1960s, studies examined the specific errors made by speakers of an L2.

Corder (1967) drew new attention to the possibility that specific learner "errors" may actually reflect knowledge of a developing system. At the same time, language acquisition researchers were influenced by the developing perspective of Chomsky (1959, 1965) that language is best viewed as a system of the mind, characterized by innate capacities. Though research explicitly testing predictions of a theory of Universal Grammar for second language acquisition emerged much later (e.g. Flynn 1983; White 1985), developments in linguistic theory proceeded alongside a focus on errors in L2 acquisition as a possible window into knowledge. In the late 1960s and early 1970s, L2 research turned attention to the systematicity in the developing L2 that errors sometimes reveal, and to the learner's developing grammar as an object of study. A signal of the importance of this focus was Selinker's (1972) coinage of the term *interlanguage*, which has endured in use to the present.

In their research on child L2 development, Dulay and Burt (1974a) explicitly tested the competing predictions of the view that L2 errors reflect L1/L2 differences and the view that errors reflect the development of a system, just as they do in L1 development. Their research used the Bilingual Syntax Measure, an experimental instrument with pictures and accompanying questions designed to elicit responses that would include English functional morphemes, such as those studied by Brown (1973) in L1 research (see the detailed review of these studies in Chapter 27, this volume). From a corpus of responses by 179 5–8-year-old speakers of L1 Spanish / L2 English, they counted errors that they attributed to *interference* (e.g. for target "They are hungry," production of "They have hunger," parallel to Spanish *[Ellos] tienen hambre*) and errors that they argued were developmental, similar to children's L1 English errors (e.g. for the same target, "They hungry"). They reported that only 4.7 percent of all errors were interference-type errors, and argued that "innate universal mechanisms" (1974a: 129) guide the Creative Construction (CC) of the new L2 system.

In another study, Dulay and Burt (1974b) compared the functional morphemes produced, and their accuracy order, by child speakers of L2 English (L1 Spanish for one group and L1 Chinese for another). They reported overall basic similarities in order of emergence for speakers across L1s (e.g. plural -s produced with overall higher rates of accuracy than third-person verbal marker -s for both L1 groups). Similarly, in a study that used the Bilingual Syntax Measure with adult speakers, Bailey, Madden and Krashen (1974) reported consistency in relative difficulty of use of functional morphemes in the L2 English production of speakers of different L1s. (Not all research in the 1970s supported an invariant order of acquisition of functional morphemes even across speakers of the same L1. See, for example, Cancino, Rosansky and Schumann (1975), who conducted a longitudinal study of six speakers of L1 Spanish / L2 English (two children, two adolescents, two adults) and reported that some individual speakers appeared to acquire morphemes in varying orders.)

Thus, by the early 1970s, the evidence from several studies using the Bilingual Syntax Measure suggested that the L1 does not play a defining role in determining the course of L2 development in the area of inflectional morphology. Research on order of acquisition of functional morphemes by speakers of various L1s continued through the later 1970s and 1980s; see Kwon's (2005: 14) citations of studies drawing on the L2 English knowledge of speakers of L1 Arabic, Chinese, Japanese, Korean, Spanish and Vietnamese. Some of this research called into question the consistent order of acquisition seen in the early 1970s studies; see the discussion of Hakuta (1976) below. For a more recent review and meta-analysis of order of acquisition studies that in fact calls for further investigation of the role of the L1 as a determinant of order, see Goldschneider and DeKeyser (2001).

5.3 Types of developmental influence

Gass and Selinker (2008) describe the later half of the 1970s as a time when research began to shift from determining whether or not the L1 had an effect on L2 development to seeking an understanding, qualitatively, of "*how* and *when* learners use their native language and on explanations for the phenomenon" (2008: 137). During the later 1970s and the 1980s, these studies included efforts to understand what might influence relative frequency of production of L2 structures for speakers of different L1s, paths and rates of development and the conditions under which the L1 might or might not influence the developing L2.

5.3.1 Relative frequency of use

One possible way a first language might influence L2 progress is in affecting frequency of use of particular forms in the L2 in the production of language under research observation. Forms might be avoided (not produced or produced relatively infrequently) or overproduced (produced more frequently than expected, or more often than other groups of speakers produce them).

An early study uncovering avoidance was Schachter's (1974) analysis of English relative clause production by L1 speakers of Persian (forty-three participants), Arabic (thirty-one), Chinese (nine) and Japanese (five). Her basic finding of more relative clause errors in the writing of Persian and Arabic speakers than that of Chinese and Japanese speakers suggested at the outset a higher level of competence in the latter group, but Schachter also analyzed the number of relative clauses attempted (either correct or incorrect). She discovered that Chinese and Japanese speakers attempted only about half as many relative clauses as Persian and Arabic speakers did and thus had fewer occasions on which to commit errors. She argued that learners' differences in production of relative clauses were rooted in a basic similarity – directionality – between English and both Persian and Arabic in relative clause syntax (the clause appears to the right of the relative clause head). In contrast, in Chinese and Japanese, the relative clause appears to the left of the head. Schachter argued that avoidance can result from an L1/L2 difference.

In a study of Arabic speakers and of Spanish and Portuguese speakers acquiring English, Kleinmann (1977) compared production of several different structures that resembled those of the L1 to differing degrees. Kleinmann controlled for comprehension of the structures through a multiple-choice test, which did not reveal significant differences between the twenty-four speakers of Arabic on the one hand and the nineteen speakers of Spanish and Portuguese on the other. A production task using pictures and conversational situations sought to elicit structures of four types: passives and present progressives (both predicted to be more difficult for Arabic speakers) and infinitive complements and direct object pronouns (both predicted to be more difficult for Spanish and Portuguese speakers). The structures predicted to be more difficult for speakers of a given L1 were in fact avoided significantly more often by those speakers for three of the four types (for present progressives, there was no significant difference among L1s).

Subsequent studies of avoidance have hypothesized that it is instead the complexity of the L2 itself, rather than factors related to the L1, that may be leading to avoidance – a hypothesis not, however, supported by the results of Laufer and Eliasson (1993). They tested avoidance of English phrasal verbs by speakers of L1 Swedish, which has phrasal verbs, and of L1 Hebrew, which does not. Results from a multiple-choice test (fifty advanced speakers of L2 English) and a translation test (thirty-seven advanced speakers) showed that speakers of L1 Swedish used significantly more L2 English phrasal verbs than Hebrew speakers. The authors argued that absence of phrasal verbs in the L1 is a better predictor of avoidance than such factors as complexity of the target (e.g. semantic complexity of different phrasal verbs). The interplay between transfer and syntactic complexity has remained important to research through the present where recent work on child bilingual acquisition, for example, has probed the role of complexity. Strik and Pérez Leroux (2011) hypothesized that less complex structures are more likely to transfer, and Prévost, Tuller, Scheidnes, Ferre and Haiden (2010) argued that computational complexity of the target affects acquisition of English *wh*-questions by child speakers of French, even to the extent of overriding L1 transfer effects.

Research has also probed relative frequency of use in the domain of the lexicon. Kellerman (1979) developed the idea that the frequency with which a learner uses a particular structure represents a decision that L2 learners may make, informed by knowledge about which L1 forms may appropriately transfer to the L2. He tested L1 Dutch learners of L2 English on various English forms involving the verb *break* (e.g. *break his leg* and *break his heart*). One factor of interest to Kellerman in this study was how core the meaning of *break* was within a structure. He defined "core" meanings as those that are closest to the usual meaning of the word – the meaning most speakers would think of first (1979: 47). Core meanings are more concrete and more frequently used. Literal meanings may also be perceived by speakers as more core than those with figurative meanings, which may be viewed as highly language-specific. The results in Kellerman (1979) suggested that a lexical item is a better candidate for transfer in structures where it is assigned its core meaning. An additional factor of interest for Kellerman was how "close" the L1 is to the L2, where closeness conditions the L2 learner's likelihood of viewing a particular L1 structure as appropriate to transfer to the L2.

5.3.2 Paths and rate

The Dulay and Burt (1974a, b) and Bailey, Madden and Krashen (1974) studies suggested a generally consistent order of development for English functional morphology. Zobl (1982) provided evidence that the general trend was more complex than it first appeared: he showed that the L1 may influence paths of the development of determiners. First, Zobl cited a longitudinal study by Huang (1971) showing that in the development of L2 English by a 5-year-old child whose L1 was Chinese, the determiner *this* appeared to precede productive use of the definite article *the*. For example, at a particular stage of development, the child produced utterances like *Yes, this is dirty* and *I want this bike*, but did not productively use *the* until a later point in development (Zobl 1982: 175–6). In contrast, Zobl cited work by Hernández-Chávez (1977) showing that a child whose L1 was Spanish productively used *this* and *the* at the same point in development, producing at the same point in time utterances like *This one . . . that truck* and *Get the car* (Zobl 1982: 177).

Other evidence from the 1970s also suggested that learners with different L1s might not traverse the same paths in acquisition of functional morphology. Hakuta (1974) reported on a longitudinal study of a native Japanese-speaking child's acquisition of English. The study was based on observations of two hours or more, every two weeks, of the young girl between the ages of 5;4 and 6;5. Hakuta analyzed her spontaneous speech during this time, arguing that results showed a different order of acquisition than the pattern seen in Dulay and Burt's (1974b) study.[1]

Finally, Zobl (1982) reviewed a range of studies bearing on the effect of the L1 on rate of development. The review included studies arguing that when the L1 marks definiteness with articles, acquisition of an L2 with definite and indefinite articles will be faster; other studies included investigation of an L2 with copulas by speakers of L1s without this category of verb (see the review and citations in Zobl 1982: 172).

5.3.3 Conditions under which the L1 might influence the L2

As is true at every time period reviewed here, researchers in the 1970s and 1980s worked to understand under what conditions L1 knowledge transfers to the L2. Viewing transfer as a process that operates in conjunction with general principles of language development (e.g. Slobin's 1973 proposed operating principles for L1 acquisition), Andersen (1983a) proposed the "transfer to somewhere" principle: "A grammatical form or structure will occur consistently and to a significant extent in interlanguage as a result of transfer *if and only if* there already exists within the L2 input the potential for (mis-)generalization from the input to produce the same form or structure" (Andersen 1983a: 178). A revision of the principle added that "in such transfer, preference is given in the resulting interlanguage to *free, invariant*, functionally *simple* morphemes which are congruent with the L1 and the L2 . . . and the morphemes occur *frequently* in the L1 and/or the L2" (Andersen

1983a: 182). Andersen's proposal thus identified several conditions under which the L1 would be more likely to influence the L2 – conditions relating both to L2 input (and indirectly, the L2 itself) and to the form that is the target of transfer.

An example of the evidence Andersen presented as compatible with "transfer to somewhere" is a study conducted by Gilbert and Orlović (see Gilbert 1983). Data were drawn from twenty-minute interviews with twenty-nine participants learning German (from four to six speakers of each language), most of whom had lived in Germany for about a tenth to about a third of their lives. An analysis of these learners of German, which has overt definite articles, showed an initial period of definite article omission by speakers of different L1s, followed by higher rates of definite article production by speakers of L1s that also have definite articles (e.g. Italian, Greek, Spanish) than by speakers of L1s that lack a free morpheme corresponding to the definite article (Serbo-Croatian, Turkish).[2]

Dulay and Burt (1974a) drew a parallel between errors in L1 development and those in child L2 development, noting that errors seem to be a necessary part of development, and that "no one has found a way to accelerate" passage through error stages in L1 development (1974a: 135). It is interesting to note that a proposal by Zobl (1980a) in fact suggested that the L1 may sometimes *decelerate* progress through a developmental point. The proposal was that some L2 errors are the result of development, but in cases when the error happens to match an L1 pattern, the L1 may reinforce the non-target form or pattern, extending a developmental stage beyond its typical length for speakers of an L1 where there is no such match. For example, under Zobl's proposal, L2 English negative constructions like *no like* and *no good* (replacing sentences) are consistent with a universal early stage in negative sentence formation: ANAPHORIC NEG (negation) + PREDICATE. When the L1 is Spanish, utterances of this form happen to align with negative constructions in the L1, where the negation system and optional omission of subject pronouns yield constructions parallel to these. Zobl suggested that in such cases, the L1 reinforces an L2 error.

5.3.4 Concluding notes on types of developmental influence

Most of the studies of the late 1970s and 1980s reviewed above paid attention to surface forms (e.g. Gilbert 1983 and Zobl 1982 research on determiners). At the same time, many began to probe the knowledge underlying the use of surface forms (e.g. the concept of core-ness underlying different meanings of a lexical item in Kellerman 1979).

5.4 Views on the initial state

The late 1980s and 1990s brought increasingly vigorous debate over the possible role of Universal Grammar (UG) in second language acquisition. The development of earlier work in that theoretical linguistic framework (e.g.

Chomsky 1965; Ross 1967) led in the early and mid 1980s to the theory of Government and Binding (Chomsky 1981) and to the Principles-and-Parameters formulation of the same approach (Chomsky 1986). The theory of UG as then formulated held that universal abstract *principles* constrain human language (e.g. all languages depend on hierarchical, and not merely linear, structure) and that crosslinguistic differences are accounted for by *parameters*, set on the basis of experience (e.g. whether a language permits null subjects or not). During the rapid evolution of the theory, through Minimalism (Chomsky 1995) and more recent work (see Chapter 1, this volume), many researchers in second language acquisition took seriously the possibility that UG might constrain the course of second language acquisition in some form. For these researchers, considering the role of UG on the one hand and of the L1 on the other hand served to more sharply define views on the "initial state" of L2 acquisition. The debate centered on such questions as (1) in what form, if any, is UG accessible to the developing L2 system? (2) in what form, if any, is the L1 accessible? and (3) how does each influence the course of development? The debate reflected attention to highly abstract properties of language (see Chapter 3, this volume).

Foundations for the debate had been laid in the 1980s, both by research in first language acquisition in this framework (e.g. Hornstein and Lightfoot 1981; Lust 1986; Roeper and Williams 1987) and by L2 research. Interestingly, work on L2 acquisition in the UG framework showed from the outset that while the theory of UG could sharpen and make possible new hypotheses about L2 acquisition, at the same time, L2 acquisition offered a critical testing ground for the theory itself. For example, Flynn (1983, 1987; also see Flynn 1996) pointed out the importance of teasing apart the influence of L1-specific features (parameter settings) and universal principles on L2 development, both for understanding SLA and for understanding the content of a proposed theory of UG. This research compared the L2 knowledge of a right-branching language (English) for speakers of a left-branching L1 (Japanese) and a right-branching L1 (Spanish). Flynn hypothesized that if the L2 English speakers had access only to the parameter setting of the L1, for L1 Japanese speakers, left-branching structures in English (such as preposed adverbial clauses, e.g. *When the actor finished the booklet, the woman called the professor*) would be more accessible (easier) than corresponding right-branching (e.g. postposed) structures (e.g. *The boss informed the owner when the worker delivered the message*). Flynn tested this prediction with fifty-one Spanish and fifty-three Japanese speakers at three levels of English proficiency. The prediction was not borne out: Japanese L1 speakers of L2 English did not more easily produce or comprehend preposed structures; advanced speakers actually preferred postposed structures. She concluded that the evidence was more consistent with awareness that Japanese and English differed in directionality, and reflected the need for L2 speakers of English to work out the consequences of the new parameter setting.

Another example of a study from the 1980s that moved the field toward more precise consideration of the role of UG in SLA is White's (1985) investigation of the possible role of the pro-drop parameter in L2 acquisition. She sought to discover whether L1 speakers of Spanish, a [+pro-drop] language, would transfer that parameter setting to a non-pro-drop L2, English; and whether, in contrast, L1 speakers of French, a [−pro-drop] language, would transfer that setting correctly to L2 English. (See Chapter 2, this volume, for the details of this study.)

Research on SLA in the 1980s that tested claims of the UG framework often did uncover or argue for a role of the L1. One characteristic these studies shared was that they approached the influence of the L1 at an abstract level, rather than at the level of surface forms and constructions. What many of them also shared was an initial acknowledgement of the possibility that *both* universal principles and knowledge of the L1 (in some form) exerted an influence on SLA.

In the 1990s, research investigating the influence of UG Principles and Parameters on L2 development flourished. The developing theory of UG influenced this work not only through its explicitness about what characterizes the initial state of the mind in L1 acquisition, and what develops, but also through the kinds of hypotheses it made possible through the explicitness of proposed theoretical apparatus, especially in morphosyntax. For example, the theory specified syntactic categories, their architecture and types of operations (such as movement). Categories of research during the 1990s can be classified according to their perspective on the initial state of SLA. These categories are pertinent to our chapter because they are partly defined by the extent to which the role of the L1 was emphasized, and they have been debated extensively since the 1990s.

5.4.1 Full access

One approach, the Full Access Model (FAM), views UG as the initial state of SLA. On the basis of evidence that there are strong similarities between the course of L1 and L2 acquisition, Epstein, Flynn and Martohardjono (1996) argued that UG is the starting point of SLA. The emphasis of this approach in the 1990s was to uncover evidence that principles of UG as formulated in the late 1980s, such as subjacency and control theory, were at work throughout all stages of SLA, and thus that UG is plausibly the initial state. While Epstein *et al.*'s article "fully allow[ed] for a role for the L1," the article "[did] not itself make any predictions about the initial state of the L2 vis-à-vis the L1" (1996: 750). Thus, though the study also implicitly acknowledged the role of the L1 (e.g. when it invokes the need to assign a new parameter setting (1996: 706)), the emphasis of this approach was on UG as the initial state for SLA.

5.4.2 Full transfer / full access

Another approach, the Full Transfer / Full Access Model, assumes that the L1 grammar is fully available as the starting point (e.g. Schwartz and Sprouse 1994; Schwartz 1998c). Under this approach, the developing L2 takes the L1 as a point of departure: "the initial state of L2 acquisition is the final state of L1 acquisition" (Schwartz and Sprouse 1996: 40–1). The grammatical system is restructured when it fails to yield L2 forms that the learner encounters, and UG is consulted in the restructuring process.

5.4.3 Minimal Trees hypothesis

Others posited a more limited role of the L1. For example, Vainikka and Young-Scholten (1994, 1996a), noting that languages vary widely in the functional categories they project, argue for an economical learning process that initially does not project functional categories. In their Minimal Trees Hypothesis, only lexical categories are available from the L1. Vainikka and Young-Scholten argue that a process of Structure Building applies in L2: functional categories are not available either through the L1 or from UG at the beginning of SLA. Later, on the basis of evidence from the L2, functional categories are projected. The full array of functional categories made possible by UG was argued not to be available at the outset, though any functional categories can be built on the basis of L2 evidence. In a subsequent development of their approach, Organic Grammar, Vainikka and Young-Scholten (2006, 2011) listed ten assumptions related to the knowledge held to underlie Minimal Trees and noted that L1-based Minimal Trees are part of the initial state for L2 learners. For a related discussion of stages in development, see Chapter 27, this volume.

5.4.4 No direct access to UG

Yet other approaches have argued that in adult L2 acquisition, there is no direct access to UG (e.g. Bley Vroman 1989, 2009; Clahsen and Muysken 1986, 1989). These approaches assign a key role to the L1; under some of them, UG is argued to be accessible through the L1.

5.4.5 Concluding notes on views on the initial state

Not all research of the 1990s focused on the nature of the initial state. For some other strands of research, the nature of the interlanguage was the primary object of study. An example is Klein and Perdue's (1997) *Basic Variety* – an initial interlanguage system that was argued to hold across different combinations of L1 and L2. The Basic Variety was argued to reflect organizational constraints common to many languages, and the role of the L1 under this approach was less important than in most other approaches.

5.5 Approaches of the past decade

From about the year 2000 to the present, research in L2 acquisition has built on the foundation described above. One strand of research has attempted to deepen the debate over the nature of transfer itself, considering the possibility that the role of the L1 may differ within different modules of language knowledge. The arguments reviewed below are from the area of morphosyntax, and other research has probed the role of the L1 within the domains of phonology and the lexicon (see relevant chapters in this volume). Finally, several other current areas of investigation include important debates on the role of the L1.

5.5.1 Morphosyntax

Several studies of argument structure (presence and position of elements required by a given verb) have suggested that the role of the L1 may not be the same at a given point in development across all modules of grammar. Montrul (2000) investigated change-of-state verbs, where the modules of argument structure and overt verbal morphology both play important roles, in L2 English, Spanish and Turkish. In all three languages, some change-of-state verbs participate in the causative/inchoative alternation, illustrated in (1) for English.

(1) a. The child broke the glass. (causative)
    b. The glass broke. (inchoative)

In Spanish, the inchoative form includes a reflexive marker on the verb (*se*), as in (2). In Turkish, for most verbs with this alternation, the causative is marked with causative morphology on the verb, and the inchoative form lacks additional overt morphology, as in (3).

(2) a. El enemigo hundió el barco.
      "The enemy sank the ship." (causative)

    b. El barco se hundió.
      "The ship sank." (inchoative)

(Montrul 2000: 234)

(3) a. Düşman gemi-yi bat-ır-mış
      enemy ship-ACC sink-CAUS-PAST
      "The enemy sank the ship." (causative)

    b. Düşman gemi-yi bat-mış
      enemy ship-ACC sink-PAST
      "The enemy sank the ship."

    c. Gemi bat-mış
      ship sink-PAST
      "The ship sank." (inchoative)

(Montrul 2000: 235)

For some Turkish verbs, the causative structure includes no additional morphology, and the inchoative verb instead includes an anticausative morpheme. Montrul carried out parallel studies for each of the three languages.

In each case, both native speakers and L1 speakers from the other two languages looked at pictures and rated the acceptability of accompanying sentences – some grammatical in the target language and some not – from the categories above. (A total of forty-seven learners of English, fifty learners of Spanish and forty-two learners of Turkish were tested; a cloze test placed all at an intermediate level, with some high-intermediate and some low-intermediate.) Some results supported universal patterns of development, while others reflected the L1. An example of the latter: for Spanish structures like (2b) above, L1 English speakers incorrectly accepted inchoative forms lacking the morphological marking *se*, while L1 Turkish speakers (even at overall lower levels of general proficiency) correctly rejected them. Since the corresponding structures in English lack overt morphology but Turkish allows overt anticausative marking, the finding appears to reflect transfer from the L1. On this basis, Montrul suggested it might be possible that the L1 is playing a stronger role in one module of grammar (overt verbal morphology) than another (argument structure).

El-Nabih (2010) also investigated the acquisition of the English causative/inchoative alternation by native speakers of Arabic. Arabic, like Turkish, requires overt morphemes on the verb in the inchoative form for some alternating verbs and overt morphemes on the verb in the causative form in other instances. Consistent with Montrul's (2000) findings for Turkish, El-Nabih reported that L1 Arabic / L2 English speakers' judgments of acceptability of English causative and inchoative structures reflected transfer from Arabic. At the same time, El-Nabih reported sensitivity by these speakers to the distinction between verbs with different argument structures, arguing that this sensitivity reflects access to UG.

Whong-Barr (2006) called for more explicit hypotheses about what transfers from the L1 in the course of L2 development, and how the transferred knowledge interacts with other processes of development. While Montrul's (2000) work began to unpack the concept of transfer by pointing out the possibility that modules of language may transfer differently, Whong-Barr suggested that in addition to modules, derivational processes may transfer. For example, in the area of functional morphology transfer, she suggested that the L2 learner might insert a verb in a derivation along with the properties the verb has in the L1, including possible requirements for functional morphemes, such as reflexive clitics. Her exploration raised questions of significance to our understanding of the nature of language itself: is knowledge of language modular? If so, what are the modules? If language is derivational, what is the nature of the derivational system?

In an article offering a processing framework to identify mechanisms for second language acquisition, Sharwood Smith and Truscott (2006) raised general questions about the nature of "full" transfer (see Chapter 26, this volume). They asked what triggers the full transfer of the L1 in L2 acquisition, and questioned what the nature of transfer is, pointing out that it must in fact be a type of "copying" rather than movement of something from the L1 elsewhere (since presumably what is transferred also remains in the L1).

Finally, recent research in L2 acquisition has approached morphosyntax through the study of formal features and the role of particular features present or absent in the L1. Lardiere (2009a) probed the way features may be viewed and categorized, and the ways L1 features may be reassembled in L2 acquisition. See the papers in Liceras, Zobl and Goodluck (2008), which explored the role of formal features in many different aspects of L2 acquisition.

5.5.2 Phonology

In the area of phonology, the distinction between more surface-related and more abstract types of knowledge has manifested itself in the treatment of phonetic segments (e.g. allophones sensitive to position) vs. abstract features, constraints (e.g. in an Optimality theory framework) and phonological processes. Here, we review several studies that acknowledge distinctions between (and even within) the surface-related and abstract types of knowledge. See Major (2008) and Chapter 25, this volume, for reviews of recent work on the role of the L1 in L2 phonology.

Over many years of research, Flege and colleagues have investigated the puzzle of L2 accent. In the 1990s, much of their research led to the increasingly explicit formulation of the *Speech Learning Model* (SLM), an attempt to account for L2 accent in its stabilized form (for an L2 speaker who has spoken the language for many years) and its relation to the age at which a learner began acquiring the L2 (see Chapter 15, this volume). Flege (1995) presented central postulates and hypotheses of the SLM, including the examples in (4)–(5) (Flege 1995: 239).

(4) Example postulate of the SLM: "The mechanisms and processes used in learning the L1 sound system, including category formation, remain intact over the life span, and can be applied to L2 learning."

(5) Example hypothesis of the SLM: "Sounds in the L1 and L2 are related perceptually to one another at a position-sensitive allophonic level, rather than at a more abstract phonemic level."

The SLM explores the possibility that L2 learners' perception of L2 segments as similar to L1 segments might hinder acquisition, since learners would tend to assume the two sounds belonged to the same category (e.g. see Flege 1995: 238). However, Young-Scholten's (2004) longitudinal study of the acquisition of word-final devoicing of obstruents in German by three L1-speakers of English provides counter evidence. She argued that the L1 played a role not through similarity of L1/L2 segments, but because resyllabification related to an L1 process (flapping) influenced the developing L2 by creating difficulties in determining where the underlyingly voiced obstruents occur to which final devoicing applies.

Brown (2000) hypothesized that a learner's L1 influences L2 acquisition of phonology, not through inventory of phonemic segments in the L1, but at a more abstract level, through the inventory of phonemic features that distinguish segments in the L1. Under this hypothesis, distinctive features in the L1 (e.g. [+/-*voice*]), not the phonological representations themselves (e.g. /p/), constrain perception and influence L2 acquisition. If learners have experience distinguishing two segments that vary along a particular acoustic dimension that corresponds to a feature, they will be able to perceive contrasts in the L2 that vary according to that feature – even contrasts that involve other segments that do not appear in the L1. Critical to testing this hypothesis is the comparison between (i) contrasting English phonemes /l/ and /r/, which are not distinctive in Japanese but are distinguished in English by [coronal], a feature not contrastive in Japanese, and (ii) contrasting English phonemes which, though they are not contrastive in Japanese, are distinguished by features which serve other contrasts in Japanese. These included [continuant], as in English /b/ vs. /v/, and [voice], as in English /f/ vs. /v/. In these pairs, either one exists in Japanese (/b/) but the other does not (/v/) or neither exists (/f/ and /v/). (See Chapter 26, this volume, for a detailed reanalysis of this study in terms of the model discussed therein.)

Brown asked fifteen native Japanese speakers (mean of eight years studying English; mean 3.5 years in North America) to complete an AX discrimination task and a picture choice task. In both, Japanese L2 learners' percentage of correct responses was significantly lower than English speakers' for the /l–r/ pair, but was not significantly different from English speakers' on the other contrasts listed above. In both tasks, Japanese L2 learners' percentage of correct responses for /l–r/ was also significantly lower than their own for the other three contrasts. On this basis, Brown concluded that the presence of particular distinctive features in the L1 can influence success in perceiving other contrasts involving the same feature in the L2. These results argue for the influence of highly abstract knowledge of the L1 – knowledge that extends far beyond surface forms – on development of the L2.

Though less frequently studied than other areas in L2 phonology, the role of L1 prosody has also been investigated in recent work. For example, Goad and White (2006) presented evidence from ten Mandarin speakers of English (described as "intermediate-level") supporting the Prosodic Transfer Hypothesis: that L1 prosody constrains L2 production. They argued that L1 effects can be overcome – for example, that new prosodic structures needed in the L2 can ultimately be built.

5.5.3 Lexicon

Because it unites several categories of knowledge in a single representation, the lexicon has been a particularly rich area for the study of L2 acquisition.

(For a detailed overview of a wide range of studies bearing on L1 influence on the L2 lexicon, also see Gass and Selinker (2008: 447–75), Juffs (2009) and Chapter 21, this volume.)

Levelt's (1989) model for lexical entries included information on meaning and syntax on one hand (the *lemma* component) and morphology and phonology on the other (see Levelt 1989, 182–8; Chapter 6, this volume). Grounded in earlier work, research of the past ten to fifteen years has clarified the role of the L1 in mapping form to meaning in L2 acquisition.

Kroll and Sunderman (2003) trace the history of a key debate: does mapping from form to meaning in L2 involve direct access to concepts, or is it mediated by the L1? Building on studies conducted in the 1980s and early 1990s, Kroll and Stewart (1994) proposed a model in which L2 learners in early stages of acquisition link L2 words with concepts via the L1 (i.e. they access the concept by virtue of the fact that it underlies meaning in the corresponding L1 word; see also Chapter 19, this volume). In later stages of acquisition, the link between the L2 word and concept strengthens. Kroll and Stewart confirmed several predictions that follow from the model. For example, if the form–concept link is stronger for the L1, then manipulating semantic variables should affect translation from L1 to L2 more than it should affect translation from L2 to L1. In a study of twenty-four fluent Dutch-English bilinguals (Dutch speakers who began to learn English at a mean age of 12), Kroll and Stewart showed that providing semantic information by grouping words to be translated into a category (e.g. vegetables, furniture, animals) affected translation from the L1 to the L2 but not from the L2 to L1.

If mapping from form to meaning is mediated by the L1, then the L1 provides preliminary access to concepts. Jiang (2002) hypothesized that the semantic information associated with the L1 form continues to be accessed even later in development – in other words, that Levelt's lemma component continues to inform the L2 lexical entry even when the meaning- and syntax-related component does not. Jiang studied L1 Chinese / L2 English (N = 25; mean 10.4 years of instruction in English; mean 1.8 years residence in the US; all with TOEFL scores of 550 or higher upon admittance to a US graduate program) and native English speakers' (N = 27) judgments of semantic relatedness for pairs of words like those in (6) and (7). All pairs were semantically related to some degree in English. Some pairs, however, had a common translation in Chinese, while others had different translations.

(6) Problem/question *Same translation: wenti*

(7) Interrupt/interfere *Different translations: daduan/ganrao* (Jiang 2002, 621)

Under Jiang's "Lemma Mediation Hypothesis," while native speakers should not differ in their semantic relatedness judgments across these types of pairs, L1 Chinese / L2 English speakers should, judging pairs like (6) more similar than pairs like (7). The prediction was borne out. Jiang (2004) replicated the finding with Korean L1 / English L2 speakers (N = 15; mean 3.8 years formal instruction in English; mean 1.9 years residence in the US).

5.5.4 Concluding notes on approaches of the past decade

Another area of current importance is research on the role of age in second language acquisition, where some scholars have argued that the L1 matters. For example, Johnson and Newport (1989) reported that for L2 English speakers whose L1 was Korean or Chinese, performance on a grammaticality judgment task measuring syntactic knowledge correlated negatively with age of arrival for participants up to the age of 15. (Performance was low for those over 15, but there was no correlation with specific age of arrival.) However, Birdsong and Molis' (2001) replication of the study with L1 Spanish speakers showed a different pattern: higher scores overall, and the decline correlated with age of arrival did not appear until after age seventeen. A second example of evidence that the L1 matters in studies of the role of age on second language acquisition is that studies reporting nativelike performance by adult L2 learners often involve speakers of L1s and L2s that are similar (e.g. Dutch and English in Bongaerts 1999). See Chapter 15, this volume, for a review of these and other studies.

An area of growing importance is the study of third language (L3) acquisition. This line of inquiry provides a critical testing ground for hypotheses about the L1's relation to the L2/L3/Ln initial state, the nature of transfer and the nature of an "endstate" to L2/L3/Ln acquisition. See, for example, Rothman and Cabrelli Amaro (2010), Rothman (2010) and Chapter 18, this volume. Finally, recent research on processing has shed light on the role of the L1. See, for example, Sabourin and Stowe (2008) and Hopp (2010).

5.6 Conclusions

The studies reviewed above show that over time, researchers have continued to differ in whether they view surface or abstract characteristics of the L1 as playing a role in L2 acquisition. For example, as shown in the review of phonology findings above, Flege's (1995) SLM tended to emphasize surface elements (e.g. see the example hypothesis in (5)), while research such as Brown's (2000) argued that the L1 influences L2 development not only at the abstract level of the phonemic segment, but at the level of distinctive features. Montrul's (2000) study of the causative/inchoative alternation pointed to the importance of L1 surface morphological marking, but for Kroll and Stewart's (1994) model of the bilingual lexicon, and also for Jiang (2002, 2004), the L1 provides a route to the abstract conceptual representations needed for L2 lexical items. The work described above on the nature of the L2 initial state supports the influence of many abstract L1 features. Whong-Barr (2006) addressed a line of inquiry about the particular abstract elements that may be transferred (e.g. constellations of requirements of particular functional elements). Research on both surface forms and abstract knowledge in L2 can inform theories of modularity in grammar: if there is evidence that one domain of knowledge develops independently of another, grammatical theory must accommodate the dissociation of those particular aspects of knowledge.

Some of the research reviewed here shows that L1/L2 similarities correspond to an advantage in production in the L2 (Schachter 1974; Kleinmann 1977; Laufer and Eliasson 1983; Zobl 1982). However, the full set of research points to a more nuanced picture, examples of which include the notion that development is affected not only by L1/L2 similarities and differences, but by characteristics inherent to the dimension of language being acquired (e.g. coreness, as in Kellerman 1979) and inherent to the L2 (e.g. Andersen 1983a).

Much of the work reviewed here also provides evidence that the role of the L1 is not the same at every point in development. Zobl (1980a) argued that similarity between L1 structures and L2 errors appearing at particular stages could influence rate of development. Research reviewed by Kroll and Sunderman (2003) suggested that the role of the L1 in providing access to conceptual representations changes over the course of development.

This body of research reflects a contrast between transfer as something automatic (e.g. at the initial state) and transfer as something that is selective, to varying degrees and in varying ways. Interestingly, the possible selectivity of transfer is a decades-old idea that has been readdressed in new ways. Kellerman (1979: 54) hypothesized that "non-transfer of potentially useable [native language] material is the biggest single argument for the existence of a strategy of transfer." Zobl (1982) sought to establish parameters for transfer, arguing that it is selective both in formal terms and developmentally. In more recent research, transfer has been viewed as selective at the highly abstract level of formal features (e.g. see Liceras, Zobl and Goodluck 2008). More broadly, the research reviewed here suggests that the L1 in some cases plays a role that is uniform across languages and/or linguistic domains (e.g. possibly in the lexicon) and in some cases the L1 plays a role that involves more selection.

6
Learning mechanisms and automatization

Richard Towell

6.1 Introduction

Second languages exist within the mind/brain of the individuals who have acquired them. But before this, these languages have to be created over a period of time. To do so requires the development of a set of learning mechanisms, the processing and storage of knowledge through the use of memory, and a way of making the knowledge acquired available for use in real time without the speaker having to think about it. How does this happen? How is the language to which an individual is exposed perceived by that individual using auditory and subsequently visual cognitive abilities? The input has to be decoded and the patterns discovered have to be stored for future use in decoding and in language production. Once the individual's initial decoding has given rise to some kind of knowledge, conscious and/or unconscious, of the patterns of the language, these must be stored in long-term memory. How might this happen? How does that knowledge develop beyond the initial storage? The decoding process and language production both call on working memory: what role does this play? Much of language learning relies on explicit instruction, how does this relate to these different factors and, specifically, can explicit instruction lead to the acquisition of implicit knowledge? In this chapter we will see what researchers have had to offer as answers to these questions.

In Section 6.2 we will consider the issue of how second language input may be perceived and decoded. To do this, we will look at the Autonomous Induction theory of Carroll (2001). In Section 6.2.2, we will examine how language is produced in real time, drawing on work by Levelt (1989, 1999) and Kormos (2006). We will then, in Section 6.3, examine how language may be stored in memory systems and especially how these systems may deal with how the knowledge develops over time. To do this we will draw on the work of the psychologist J. R. Anderson and his colleagues (1983, 1995, 1998, 2004) and see how his model has been made use of by second language acquisition researchers. There is a degree of commonality in the different research mentioned so far, as each makes use of psychological models which are similar in so far as they assume the use of production systems. There are, however, other neuropsychological models which use different methodologies and take a different standpoint. In Section 6.3.2, we will look at arguments put forward by researchers who take as their starting point neurophysiological evidence which suggests that production systems of the type proposed may not be suitable for language acquisition. Instead of a single developmental continuum, the researchers involved think in terms of parallel memory systems which must complement one another as development takes place. SLA researchers have at different times attributed the relative lack of success in second language acquisition to potential differences in working memory and we will therefore devote Section 6.3.3 to the examination of these views, drawing to some extent on the theories in Section 6.3.2, which take different standpoints in relation to working memory. In Section 6.4, we will look at how SLA researchers have conceived explicit and implicit learning. A major question has been whether explicit instruction can result directly or indirectly in implicit learning. We will look at how this debate has been and might be framed and discuss current views before concluding in Section 6.5.

6.2 Basic processes

6.2.1 Comprehension

A central question for second language acquisition is: how do learners construct knowledge of a second language on the basis of what they hear? One view of how this may happen is presented by Carroll as the Autonomous Induction theory (2001). She brings together the linguistic theories of Jackendoff (2002: Representational Modularity) and the psychological theories of Holland, Holyoak, Nisbett and Thagard (1986: Induction theory). The basic line of argument is as follows: Jackendoff's theory of Representational Modularity presents language as having a generative capacity at the phonological, the morphosyntactic and the semantic levels. At the semantic end this links to conceptual structures related to the real world and at the phonological end it links to phonetics, articulatory and acoustic. Each level has its own internal tiers and each level is linked to the other levels by interface rules. Each of the levels and each of the tiers processes information of a very specific kind by means of formation rules which are unique to them. They cannot handle information which is not expressed in the format which they use. The tiers are designed to input and output information in formats suitable for linking within the levels and the levels are linked to each other by interface rules. This sets up a very powerful linguistic system for handling and exchanging information between physical form at one end – i.e. the speech signal received by the learner in auditory or signed form – and conceptual structures at the other, whilst allowing autonomy and specificity to each of the levels of linguistic structure.

In this approach, semantic, morphosyntactic and phonological information is all presented in parallel to the generative formation rules at each level. Adult second language learners in the early stages of learning are therefore faced simultaneously with sounds, some of which may be familiar and some not, with at best partially recognizable meanings and partial assumptions about, for example, what constraints any identifiable nouns, verbs, prepositions or adjectives might have. Learners have to do their best to make what sense they can of this mass of information with processing limited capacity (see Section 6.6 below on working memory). It is in this sense that the problem clearly is one of induction. Each of the generative systems is capable of handling specific kinds of information: they are assumed to be modular processing systems. As noted above, access is at either end of the chain: via phonetic systems or via conceptual systems. Induction therefore has to be guided by whatever autonomous knowledge is in the generative mechanisms the learner possesses. Carroll assumes that some of this is derived from Universal Grammar (see Chapter 7, this volume) and that it will be influenced by the first language at some point (see Chapter 5, this volume). The *Autonomous Induction theory* (AIT) then makes use of the psychological theories to establish the learning mechanisms which will enable the learner to undertake the task of decoding the information in such a way that it feeds learning. Given the range of theories implicated in these mechanisms, it is to be expected that they will be complex and for that reason we will not attempt to detail them here. However, the contribution of the AIT is further discussed in Chapter 26, this volume.

The importance of this theory for this chapter is that it makes use of methodological assumptions that are similar to those used in the areas of second language production and second language development which will be dealt with in the next two sections. "The basic format of the Induction theory is the condition–action rule" (Carroll 2001: 141). Condition-action rules are usually formulated as IF (a certain condition is present) THEN (take a certain action) or IF Condition A holds THEN implement Action B. Such condition–action pairs operate all of the (many) mechanisms posited in the theory. Most critical is Carroll's suggestion that learning takes place during the learner's parse of incoming data. For that to happen, the learner must process an utterance in context and an effort must be made to analyse linguistic form. This is the "certain condition" or the context which provokes the action:

> the constituent to be parsed will therefore appear in the left hand side of a condition-action rule of the i-(induction) learning system. Learning will take place when a novel action is implemented, e.g. [the learner's] attaching the expression in a parse at the given level of representation, assigning it a morphosyntactic feature, or putting it in correspondence with a unit of another level of representation. (Carroll 2001: 142)

In other words, the implementation of the action in relation to the condition is what will bring about language learning. Of particular interest is what happens when a parse is not easily constructed and learners must examine all of their existing knowledge in order to find a way of parsing new structures. This will provoke new learning. (Note that all of this is assumed to operate at a largely subconscious level for the second language learner.)

The central argument presented by Carroll is that once you fully specify all the linguistic and psychological knowledge and capabilities which are available to an adult second language learner, there is no reason to believe that the learner cannot use those capabilities to construct and store knowledge of the second language. Note, however, that one of those factors is innate UG type information in the autonomous representational (symbolic) systems. Carroll's is therefore a position which argues that the general cognitive skills which an adult learner possesses are sufficient for second language acquisition given the kind of innate linguistic and psychological capabilities which are assumed. So far, producing empirical evidence to support this argument seems to have proved problematic, and the next challenge for Carroll and her colleagues will be to produce the evidence of how this works in practice. As we shall see when discussing a similar issue in relation to second language production, this is a difficult issue to confront.

6.2.2 Production

Another central question for second language acquisition is: how do learners produce a second language? Levelt (1989, 1999) presents a model of language production which also unites different kinds of linguistically and psychologically defined knowledge in constructing an integrated model of language production. It should be noted both that the Levelt model represents the knowledge and systems of a mature adult and that it concerns only the native language. The model therefore contains no concept of how the knowledge present might have been acquired or developed or a notion of how it would differ when two languages are present. Kormos (2006) has reflected in detail on how the model would need to be developed in order to be suitable for individuals with two languages and this will be considered below. The issue of development within memory systems of the kind which are implicated in the Levelt model will be presented in the next section. These involve declarative and procedural knowledge and memory systems. *Declarative knowledge* is the kind which can be made more or less explicit, such as knowledge of vocabulary (lexis) and knowledge about a language, such as pedagogic rules of grammar. To a greater or lesser degree, declarative knowledge is thought to be under conscious control. *Procedural knowledge* is the kind of knowledge which cannot be made explicit, which underlies skill development and which arises through practice, such as using a computer keyboard or driving a car. Procedural knowledge is largely not under conscious control. Each kind of knowledge has a specific memory system.

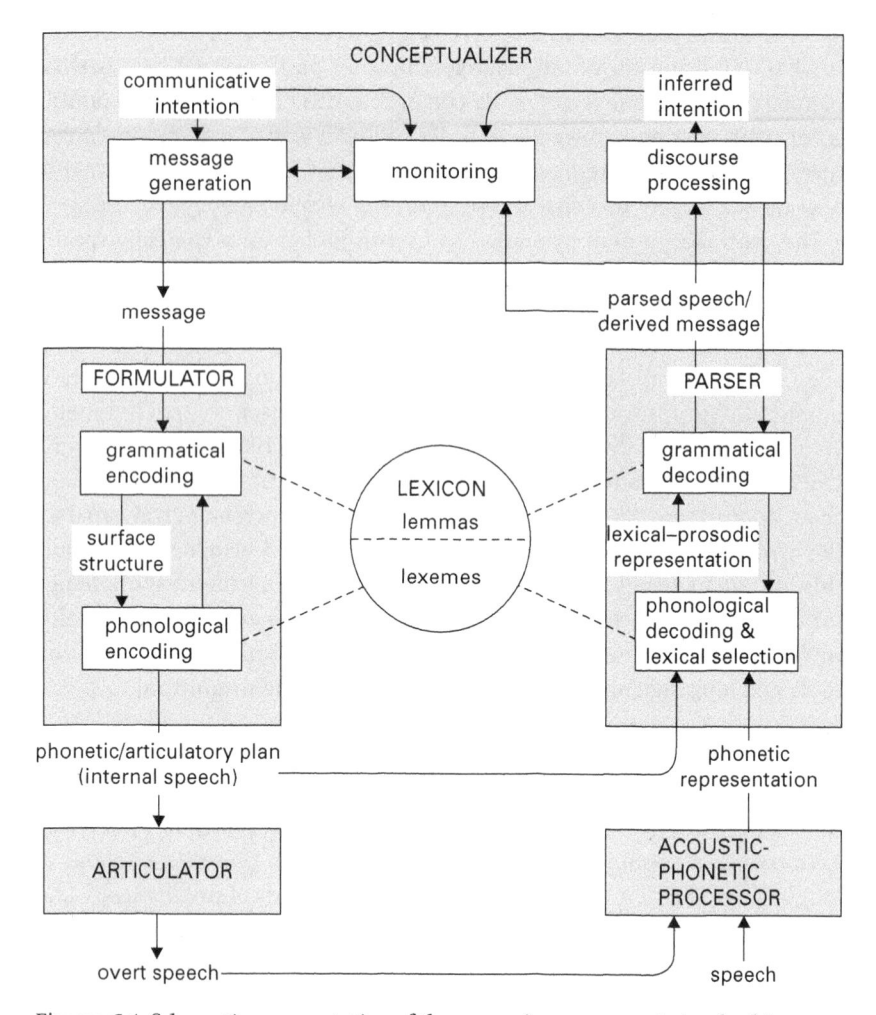

Figure 6.1 *Schematic representation of the processing components involved in spoken language use (Levelt 1993: 2)*

In Levelt's schema, the knowledge shown within square boxes is procedural knowledge and the knowledge in circles or ellipses is declarative knowledge. Language production takes place in three stages, with declarative stores of knowledge being available to feed into the language processors at each stage. Language production begins by generating the message on the basis of concepts in a production unit which Levelt calls a *conceptualizer*; this produces a preverbal message which can then be encoded in the appropriate syntax and phonology in a unit called a *formulator*; the resulting phonetic plan is passed to a third unit, the *articulator* which gives rise to overt speech. Inside each of the units are language processors. The processors are made up of procedural knowledge. These take the form of the IF...THEN condition–action pairs described above. Levelt (1989: 236–40) specifies seven main kinds of procedures necessary for the generation of surface structure:

"Each individual procedure can be written as a production – a condition/action pair of the kind IF X THEN Y, where X is the condition and Y is the action" (Levelt 1989: 240). Utterances can then be produced by a series of processing activities which work incrementally and in parallel on the different parts of the construction. First, the ideas which are to be expressed arise in the conceptualizer and draw on declarative knowledge, in this case of the world. There is a monitoring process within the conceptualizer to check the intended ideas are being brought forward. The formulator then draws on declarative knowledge from the *lexicon* in two stages, one associated with semantic and syntactic structure (*lemmas* – "bundles of *declarative* knowledge about a word's meaning and grammar," Levelt 1989: 236 italics in original) and one with phonological form. In each case, the formulator is working with procedures which have been created by a process of proceduralization and with declaratively stored lexical knowledge.

Following Kormos (2006: 56ff), for second language learners, it is assumed that choices are made at an early stage in the process of which language will be used depending on the context of use (the "language cue"). In addition, the items in the lexicon will be tagged for language. All semantically relevant lexical items will presumably be activated in response to the information from the conceptualizer but only the appropriately tagged and most highly activated item will be selected. In this way the second language learner produces interlanguage utterances as best s/he can from the resources currently available. The declarative knowledge of the growing L2 lexicon is stored in the declarative memory which already includes the L1 lexicon, and the developing procedural knowledge is stored in the processing components.

If we assume that second language learners comprehend language through the kind of autonomous induction system that Carroll describes and that they produce language through the kind of production systems which Levelt and Kormos describe, then these questions arise: how does the second language learner acquire the declarative and procedural knowledge needed for comprehension/induction? How is it stored in the learner's mind/brain? And, once the perceptual and initial storage stages have been completed, how does knowledge develop to become the basis for fluent comprehension/induction and production by the learner?

6.3 Memory and its development

6.3.1 Anderson's ACT

The attempt to answer these questions will begin with a model of learning which involves declarative and procedural knowledge and which tries to explain how, over time, knowledge develops through a process known as *proceduralization*. This is J. R. Anderson's ACT (Adaptive Character of Thought) model, the latest version of which is known as ACT-R(ational) 5.0.(2004). It has been developed over at least thirty years and has been shown to model learning effectively in a number of different areas, the most well-known of which is mathematics.

The model assumes that there are differentiated memory stores. There is declarative memory, which may have specific modules, there is a central production system containing procedural knowledge, and there are *buffers* which contain limited amounts of information and which pass this information between the declarative module and the production system. The buffers may be seen as equivalent to parts of working memory in other models (see discussion below and Chapter 8, this volume). These memories work in quite different ways, and the same knowledge may be stored in each in specifically defined manners (see below). Within the ACT model, all knowledge begins as declarative and some of it becomes proceduralized. This involves declarative knowledge both being incorporated with procedural knowledge and being recreated as procedural knowledge. Proceduralization of knowledge is essential for the performance of any cognitive skill. This is largely because working memory capacity or – in this model – the capacity of the buffers is insufficient to allow access to declarative knowledge with sufficient speed for skilled performance. Therefore, over time and through defined stages, the knowledge necessary for the performance of a cognitive skill, such as (but in no way limited to) language, must be proceduralized.

Central to the concept of procedualization are IF...THEN condition-action pairs of greater or lesser complexity. As we saw above in the Carroll and the Levelt models, the IF part of the pair specifies a context in which a given action might be appropriate, the THEN part indicates the action which should be carried out. It may then be argued that in the early stages of learning a second language, given a goal such as communicating a particular meaning, the learner builds a very long chain of IF...THEN condition-action pairs. When, by using that chain, s/he succeeds in communicating that meaning, it will be used again. As this happens repeatedly, economies are created: steps are conflated and the number needed is reduced. In spoken language, the same morphosyntactic steps are repeated over and over again (articles, adjectives and nouns are combined in noun phrases; verbs and adverbs are combined in verb phrases; noun phrases and verb phrases are combined in utterances) and so the IF...THEN chains should shorten (in terms of the time it takes to produce them) relatively quickly (see the examples from Johnson below). Each successful activation will then reduce the activation threshold needed to make the combination fire again. Any non-successful activation will raise the threshold. In this way, the *power law of practice* will eventually enable second language learners to provide a consistency of expression in their production. Over time, detailed processes of compilation, composition and tuning all lead to a point where the learner's L2 knowledge is stored in the procedural memory in the form of productions in the target language Note that in the example above, the units to be combined by the learner were grammatical categories and not individual words. The ACT system, particularly the procedural elements, works with symbols or categories of this kind, not individual words or phrases. Later on, once the combinations are established it may well be that certain repeated goals and situations require the same formulaic utterances and the system would be expected to store these in declarative memory as chunks for direct recall. The ACT model allows for patterns to be created and stored at various levels as a means of achieving defined goals.

However, storing patterns or fixed combinations could lead to complications if this happened too easily for the learner, i.e. wrong patterns could be stored and once they are combined in this way, they could not be altered by the learner, and once implemented they would run to completion. This makes these patterns powerful instruments for the performance of routine tasks but inflexible operators should circumstances change. If flexibility is needed, however, it can easily be obtained by the learner relying on his/her declarative knowledge, which has not disappeared simply because some of it has been proceduralized. But declarative knowledge can only be used in circumstances where enough time and memory is present: it is slow to access and "expensive" in working memory capacity (see Section 6.4).

Especially in the 1990s SLA researchers made use of the ACT model. There were three main ways in which it was applied and/or tested. The first involved setting out those procedures which learners might be using to produce the language and showing how these might combine and how they might reflect various strategies and competences.

Production procedures

Johnson (1996) offers the most detailed interpretation of the Anderson model for the context of second language learning and teaching. His approach requires some extension of the model to allow instant proceduralization of knowledge and it avoids the declarative stage, but otherwise his approach accepts the progression from declarative encoding to procedural encoding to tuning. He recognizes the dangers of permitting proceduralization to happen too quickly in the model, but argues that examples of fossilization and transfer show that this is a phenomenon which occurs in second language learning.

Johnson illustrates the notion of a progressive reduction in steps in a chain in the following way. P(roduction)1 and P(roduction)2 illustrate declarative encoding for the production of part of the English present perfect, with a condition–action pair:

P1 IF the goal is to form the present perfect of a verb and the person is 3rd singular
    THEN form the 3rd singular of *have*
P2 IF the goal is to form the present perfect of a verb and the appropriate form of *have* has just been formed
    THEN form the past participle of the verb.

The next stage, as these forms are practiced, enables these two to be combined into one production, what he calls a "procedural encoding":

P3 IF the goal is to form the present perfect of a verb and the person is 3rd singular
    THEN form the 3rd singular of *have* and then form the past participle of the verb

Tuning then involves determining the scope of the production, which requires both generalizing and discriminating. Generalizing is exemplified as follows, using a category symbol "X," i.e. an appropriate noun. P4 and P5 show how two productions are used to produce two utterances each with a different noun. They can then become the P6 – a production to be used with any appropriate noun:

P4 IF the goal is to indicate that a coat belongs to me
    THEN say *My coat*
P5 IF the goal is to indicate that a ball belongs to me
    THEN say *My ball*
P6 IF the goal is to indicate that object X belongs to me
    THEN say *My X*.

Discriminating then involves knowing the limitations of, for example, what X might be (a noun not a verb) and the contexts in which "My" is inappropriate and "Mine" is required instead.

O'Malley and Chamot (1990) used the same approach in the area of language strategies. Taking the various kinds of strategies and the various competences which had been proposed, they suggested that learners would use their competences in relation to specific goals and subgoals, and that the sequence of procedures would allow them to correct where necessary. To illustrate, O'Malley and Chamot (1990: 74) outline a production system for communicating in a second language as follows:

P1 IF the goal is to engage in conversation with Sally and Sally is monolingual in English
    THEN the subgoal is to use my second language.
    . . . . .
P3 IF the goal is to initiate a conversation
    THEN the subgoal is to say a memorized greeting formula (discourse competence)
    . . . . .
P13 IF the goal is to answer with the information requested, and I want to form a grammatically correct sentence,
    THEN the goal is to pay attention to word order and noun and verb endings as I respond (grammatical competence for syntax and strategic competence)

P14 IF the goal is to pay attention to word order and noun and verb endings and I notice (or Sally's reaction suggests) that I have made a mistake that impedes comprehension
THEN the subgoal is to correct my mistake
(sociolinguistic and grammatical competence)

P15 IF the goal is to correct my mistake
THEN "pop the goal" e.g. go back to P13

This sequence makes it possible to identify precisely where something has gone wrong and which competence might need enhancing. Such a specification might also assist in defining the stages through which a learner advances.

Measuring production

The second use of the ACT model has involved attempting to spot where procedural learning might be happening by examining learner production at different stages and examining how it had changed. The preferred method was the use of temporal variables to measure such elements as mean length of run, phonation/time ratio, articulation rate and speech rate. These measures could then be used as an indication of the extent to which a given learner had proceduralized certain knowledge. By asking learners to undertake the same oral language task on two occasions between which either teaching or a significant event such as residence abroad had taken place, it was thought that the temporal variables plus a detailed examination of the language used might provide an indication of whether the language had become more proceduralized. The initial research was led by the KAPPA group in Germany (Dechert, Mohle and Raupach 1984). Towell and Hawkins (1994) then reworked it as part of an overall approach to SLA. The results of the empirical studies based on this approach do, in general, demonstrate that individual learners increase on the various measures mentioned above, i.e. the length of their runs between pauses does increase, they pause less and their speech rate increases as a result of more exposure to the foreign language (Towell, Hawkins and Bazergui 1996; Towell 2002; Towell and Dewaele 2005). This can be argued to be attributable to proceduralization and automatization of knowledge.

Automatization

The third use of the ACT model was developed through a more experimental approach by DeKeyser (1997). He was interested in two main aspects of the learning theory: to what extent would it be possible for learners to acquire automatic knowledge of a language having started from a declarative or explicit explanation of the rules? And to what extent would the knowledge acquired be skill-specific? Both questions follow from the Anderson model: if language knowledge does go through the stages described, it should become automatic in the longer term. If productions are goal driven and are specific to the contexts in which they are learnt, it should be the case that they will only be performed or performed best in that context.

To answer these questions, DeKeyser devised an artificial language which allowed him to present a variety of natural language rules. Sixty-one paid volunteers (mainly undergraduates) were then explicitly taught the vocabulary and rules of this language. Once tests had shown that they had grasped the vocabulary and rules, they were given fifteen further practice sessions with tests at regular intervals. Different groups were assigned differently weighted rules and skills, ensuring that some groups practiced some rules in comprehension only and some rules in production. After twenty-one sessions in all, the twenty-second session tested the learners on all the rules in both comprehension and production.

The results largely confirmed DeKeyser's expectations. The mean performance of all participants in comprehension and production followed a "power law of practice" in progressively reducing reaction times in comprehension and error rates in production. The practice effect was shown to be skill-specific: the knowledge, although explicitly taught, was seemingly not as available for the non-practiced skill as for the practiced skill.

DeKeyser concludes that "the learning of second language grammar rules can proceed very much in the same way that learning in other domains...has been shown to take place" (DeKeyser 1997: 214). He believes that "This evidence supports the model of skill acquisition that posits that during initial practice declarative knowledge is turned into qualitatively different procedural knowledge and that subsequently a much slower process of gradual automatization takes place, which requires little or no change in task components, only a quantitative change within the same components" (DeKeyser 1997: 214). He thus adopts the notion of the two memory systems and of a qualitative transformation as knowledge is exchanged between the two, plus a notion of further development which is quantitative. He and others explore these notions further in DeKeyser (2007, 2009).

The difficulty with the Johnson and the O'Malley and Chamot applications of the Anderson model is that it is impossible to conclusively show that the productions suggested are indeed the mental representations which the learners possess. It is also difficult to show absolutely that increases in the temporal variable scores can be specifically attributed to the kind of development which the ACT model proposes (Pienemann 1998: 40). More recent work has tended not to attempt to specify the productions involved (or indeed to refer back to the Anderson model) but to accept the more general notions of proceduralization and automatization as means of explaining developmental changes without the precision attempted by Johnson. (It should be noted that applications of the Anderson model to learning in other areas, such as mathematics, are expressed in mathematical formulas and tested with great precision via computer modelling and experimental data.)

These concepts and also the temporal variable methodology are now being used in studies which attempt to combine studies of the development of complexity, accuracy and fluency (Housen and Kuiken 2009; Pérez-Vidal in press). Relatively new software PRAAT (Boersma 2009) allows the processing of real-time data much more swiftly, and Segalowitz (2010) offers a stimulating examination of the many factors which contribute to second language fluency. As we shall see later, a key element in debates in this area is whether the second language learner has simply speeded up declarative knowledge, whether there is some fundamental change in the mental representation of the language or whether there can in fact be no progression but instead two kinds of knowledge developing in parallel.

The unifying element between the approaches discussed so far is that they make use of some form of production system as a means of describing how development in comprehension and production takes place. There is in this view an assumption that learners will follow a progressive path of skill acquisition on a continuum, and that knowledge develops when practiced.

6.3.2 Declarative and procedural knowledge revisited

Not all researchers agree with this notion, and one reason seems to be that they come at the issue from a different evidential base. For those who have a neurological background, it seems very clear that declarative and procedural knowledge are separate, complementary and parallel dimensions of learning. They each have an essential developmental and performance role to play in second language acquisition but they are not on a continuum and the one does not become the other.

M. Paradis

M. Paradis (2004, 2009) comes to this issue with a wealth of knowledge from a neurophysiological background and firmly adopts the above view. He rejects the suitability of the Anderson model for language acquisition: "Anderson's model of skill learning is not readily applicable to language acquisition because...unlike most motor skills, acquisition is not the automatization of the same entities that were previously practiced" (M. Paradis 2009: 86). As far as Paradis is concerned, the entities to which the adult second language learner is exposed will mainly be lexical forms, explicit rules of the grammar and exemplar sentences, all of which are declarative. In his view there is nothing that could be done with such information through practice which could change its character as declarative and therefore its representation in declarative memory. Paradis is opposed to any notion of an interface between explicit and implicit knowledge. "There is...no direct link between the rules (as explicitly learned), the explicit processing of sentences, or the utterances themselves (as perceived) and the implicit tallying that establishes linguistic competence" (M. Paradis 2009: 99). This is not to say that explicit knowledge cannot contribute to the creation of implicit knowledge by, for example, storing examples in declarative memory which may be used as a comparator for the utterances created by implicit knowledge. But the one cannot become the other. This principled view leads him to repeat a distinction introduced into second language research between learning and acquisition (Krashen 1981; see also Schwartz 1993) where learning is a conscious and explicit process and acquisition is unconscious and implicit: "The ACT model may apply to learning, but not to acquisition. The term *proceduralization* cannot refer to the automatization of metalinguistic knowledge that would result in implicit linguistic competence procedures. Proceduralization only takes place by *acquiring* implicit procedures" (M. Paradis 2009: 87 – italics in original). Paradis argues that the evidence for this view comes from a wide spectrum: "Implicit linguistic competence and metalinguistic knowledge are distinct as suggested by neurofunctional, neurophysiological and neuroanatomical evidence, and recently confirmed by a number of neuroimaging studies on bilinguals... They have different memory sources (declarative vs. procedural)... Implicit competence and explicit knowledge coexist. Neither one becomes the other" (M. Paradis 2004: 61). Notable support for this position comes from evidence from aphasic and amnesic patients (see M. Paradis 2004: chapters 3 and 4).

Under this view, development in second language acquisition and learning takes place on parallel and complementary lines. Declarative knowledge linked to learning grows on the basis of explicit and conscious information; procedural knowledge linked to acquisition grows in response to unconscious and implicit information. The two interact in language comprehension and production but grow independently.

Ullman

Ullman has built a similar view of L1 and L2 language acquisition based on his understanding of the differing roles of declarative and procedural memory. He takes the view that declarative and procedural memories are involved in language acquisition across the lexicon and the grammar but they have separate roles. Declarative memory will be more associated with idiosyncractic information (e.g. lexical items and irregular grammatical forms) and procedural memory will be more associated with regularities (e.g. morphological and syntactic regularities). He states: "Essentially, the systems together form a dynamically interacting network that yields both cooperative and competitive learning and processing, such that memory functions may be optimized" (Ullman 2005: 147). For late learned L2, he assumes that, as adults have a more fully developed declarative memory, they will probably initially learn many forms as declarative items before they have enough information for the procedural memory to begin learning the regularities. The dynamic interaction between the two memories allows both to learn much of the same information but to store it in different ways. Declarative knowledge can be learnt quickly and recalled swiftly in the form in which it was learnt but no linkage is created between similarly structured bits of information. Procedural knowledge, on the other hand, creates links at a more abstract level and stores information in ways which look much more like systematized rules, thus for example categorising verbs into regular declensions so that their swift recall is then by means of an application of those regularities, not the recall of the form itself in isolation. Storage of this kind takes much longer to accomplish and is not under conscious control. The patterns are established by the memory system, not by the conscious application of declarative knowledge. Ullman argues for neuroanatomically defined separate memory systems with different roles and allows knowledge to be present in both in different ways and at different times.

The evidence for Ullman's position is derived from experimental studies involving neurophysiological experiments. One such study is reported in Morgan-Short, Stanz, Steinhauer and Ullman (2010). The focus of the study was the second language acquisition of gender agreement as manifested through article–noun agreement and adjective–noun agreement. It required a number of subjects (thirty healthy adult English speakers with no fluency in other languages) to study an artificial language and then be tested on the resulting knowledge whilst their brain functions were monitored by measurements of event-related potentials (ERPs), i.e. real-time electrophysiological brain activity (see Chapter 19, this volume). The participants were split into two groups for the language training. One was taught by a method of *explicit instruction* (rules + examples) whilst the other was taught by a method of *implicit instruction* (examples in context). The artificial language allowed the description of objects and actions associated with a board game and included within it variations in the form of articles and in the form of adjectives corresponding to morphological gender marking in natural languages. Previous research has established that L1 speakers react to lexical semantic violations by what is called an N400, i.e. an electrophysiological negative reaction which occurs about 400ms after stimulus onset. A rule-governed syntactic, morphosyntactic or morphophonological violation by contrast gives rise to a LAN, a left anterior negativity. Also observed in L1 speakers is a P600, i.e. an electrophysiological positive reaction which occurs about 600ms after stimulus onset in response to syntactic and morphosyntactic processing difficulties. Simplifying somewhat, it is argued that the reason for these differentiated responses is that, as suggested by the declarative/procedural distinction, the lexical/semantic information is processed in one manner by the brain (=N400) and the syntactic or morphosyntactic information in another (=LAN or P600). In order, therefore, to test Ullman's hypothesis that L2 learners, at least in the early stages, rely on declarative lexical-type knowledge and not on proceduralized syntactic-type knowledge, ERP evidence can be used. Previous experiments (see Steinhauer, White and Drury 2009) had suggested that non-native speakers, at least at a low level, did indeed process syntactic information in the L2 rather as if it were lexical information. In this experiment, the investigators not only wanted to check on whether the measurements would confirm that this was the case, they also wanted to know whether different methods of instruction would affect the outcomes.

The results showed that "at low proficiency, both adjectival and gender agreement violations yielded N400s (350–600-ms time-window) but only for the implicitly trained group" (Morgan-Short *et al.* 2010: 178) and "at high proficiency, noun-adjective agreement violations elicited N400s for both the explicit and implicit groups, whereas noun-article agreement violations elicited P600s for both group" (Morgan-Short *et al.* 2010: 178). No LANs were elicited. The P600s do suggest that these learners may be using their brains in similar ways to the way brains work in relation to the L1, but the N400s and the absence of LANs do not. The N400s suggest that both groups of learners at the end of their learning were still making use of those parts of the brain devoted to declarative memory to process noun–adjective agreements where L1 users make use of procedural memory. This was also the case at the lower level of proficiency but only for the group which had implicit training. The results therefore support the general position of the declarative/procedural model but point to complex relationships between the level of proficiency, the actual forms which are being learnt and the method by which they have been learnt. More research on this kind of experiment is reported on in Chapter 19 of this handbook.

At this stage in this chapter we have two different views on how learning mechanisms and long-term memory systems work in the development of second language knowledge. The first sees the learning mechanisms progressively building knowledge from a declarative base, proceduralizing and automatizing it over time by means of production systems. The second sees each of the two memory systems developing knowledge in the way which is appropriate to it and collaborating in comprehension and production. Under this view the implicit system has no interface with the explicit system and it cannot develop from it: it can only use explicit knowledge to monitor and correct. Both develop in parallel and work together.

As we shall see in Section 6.4, these two competing views, not always expressed in these terms, have presented significant challenges to SLA researchers. Before we look in more detail at those challenges, however, we need to consider the role of the third form of memory: working memory.

6.3.3 Working memory

Alongside the long-term declarative and procedural memories, we have *working memory* (WM). Working memory is defined by Miyake and Shah (1999: 450): as "those mechanisms or processes that are involved in the control, regulation, and active maintenance of task-relevant information in the service of complex cognition." This definition appears to encompass the two main competing conceptions of what working memory might look like at a lower level of detail.

The older of the two conceptions has been present in the literature from 1974 onwards (see Baddeley 1986, 1990, 2000, 2007) and is sometimes known as the Multiple Component Model, because it is composed of several more or less independent units. Under this conception, working memory is a separable part of the memory system in the mind: it should not, for example, be considered just the activated part of a long-term memory. Working memory has four components: a controlling *central executive*; a *phonological loop*, which contains a mechanism for limited storage which rapidly decays, and a mechanism for articulatory rehearsal; a *visuo-spatial sketchpad*, which performs a similar role for visual stimuli; and an *episodic buffer*, which is a limited-capacity temporary storage system that is capable of integrating information from a variety of sources. This latter element functions to permit information to be held for longer than the phonological loop or the visuo-spatial sketchpad can manage, largely on the basis that the information held is integrated in some way, such as being continuous prose with linked ideas. The central executive selectively determines where attention will be focused, the two slave systems execute the processes, and the episodic buffer keeps information active when it is integrated. By virtue of its integrating powers, it may also create new cognitive representations.

The limited capacity on the audio side of the WM is determined by the amount that *phonological working memory* (PWM) or loop can keep active. It is important to distinguish this effect when dealing with simple memory sets (e.g. when remembering nonsense syllables) from the effect when using natural language. It is argued that the PWM is limited to about two seconds' worth of unstructured sound-based information. This limitation is not to be expected to hold for the highly structured forms associated with natural language within which hierarchical structure chunks information in different ways (see the discussion in Gathercole and Baddeley 1993: chapter 4, and for example Engle, Kane and Tuholski 1999, Ericsson and Delaney 1999).

An alternative account of WM, to be found in many of the North American psychological theories, which relies on spreading activation, does not require that WM be a specific, separable unit. Anderson, in the 1993 account of ACT-R theory, makes it clear that the term WM is an "expository convenience" (1993: 20) which refers to that part of the long-term memories which is currently activated. In ACT 5.0 of 2004, WM is a buffer which exists between the declarative module and the production system, transferring information between the two (Anderson *et al.* 2004: 1037). These are seen as similar to the slave systems in the Baddeley model. The key factor in the development of skilled behavior is the creation of productions which contain within them all the elements which allow a complex piece of behavior to be carried out without need for any conscious control. Thus, within this approach, the way in which the limitations imposed by WM are overcome is by the creation of sophisticated productions which can control behavior without the need for declarative knowledge which consumes much more of the available space within WM.

Where we get potentially important differences of view is to do with the role WM might play (see also discussion in Dewaele 2002b). For Baddeley and those who work within his theory, WM capacity is likely to be fairly fixed as it is determined by physiological characteristics: the size of the PWM may determine how much knowledge may be put on hold whilst other parts of the system are incrementally processed. If that amount is small, we might well expect that individuals will have difficulty in establishing relationships across distant boundaries. Also, under this view we would expect WM capacity to remain stable across performances by individuals at different times and in the L1 and the L2. If an individual's WM capacity is largely a given, it would also follow that, when we observe differences in behavior, these are likely to be attributable to changes in the storage or computation of the language and not to changes in the state of the WM (although it may be the case that the central executive becomes more used to handling certain kinds of information and therefore learns to handle them faster).

For theorists who see WM as the activated part of long-term memory or a buffer, there is no physiological limit on the WM: it will be variable according to other aspects of behavior. As we have noted above, ACT-R is very much goal-oriented. It therefore follows that the degree of activation of the WM is likely to be relative to the degree of focus on the goal. Engle *et al.* (1999: 104) express this idea as follows: "Thus we assume that 'working memory capacity' is not really about storage or memory per se, but about *the capacity for controlled, sustained attention in the face of interference or distraction*" (italics in original). This opens up the possibility that behavior which is thought to call on WM to a greater or lesser degree might be variable in so far as the learner is able to pay controlled sustained attention to something in the environment. Sawyer and Ranta (2001: 342) have linked the ideas together very succinctly: "Assuming that noticing is crucial to learning, and attention is required for noticing, and attention at any moment is limited by WM capacity, then there must logically be a close relationship between amount of learning and size of WM." Under this view, there seems to be no real reason to expect WM capacity to be fixed within an individual. Rather it will vary according to the task being undertaken and specifically to the amount of attention paid to the task.

We therefore have two views on the role that WM can play. There is agreement that WM is potentially critical because it has a limited capacity. If, however, one takes the view that the limited capacity is a more or less permanent characteristic of an individual, then one would not expect to see variability in linguistic behavior which would be characteristic of an individual over time and over tasks. If, on the other hand, one takes the view that the limited capacity is not linked to any physiological characteristic but instead linked to the ability to provide sustained attention at a given point in time, then we would not expect great constancy in behavior on

WM-related tasks but instead variability across performances by the same individual depending more on how much attention that individual had paid to the task in question. The two views are not, however, necessarily mutually exclusive: it could be that we should expect to see task-based variations, but within an overall, individually defined WM capacity. In addition, M. Paradis (2009: 49) argues that WM is only relevant to those aspects of memory which can be made conscious. Given the distinction discussed above which he makes between learning (conscious, declarative, explicit) and acquisition (unconscious, procedural, implicit), it follows that from his point of view it is only learning which might be influenced by any aspect of WM, and that WM could not be a place where explicit and implicit information could interact.

A recent investigation by Mackey, Adams, Stafford and Winke (2010) shows the potential importance of WM. The researchers were interested in the ability of second language learners to modify their output as a result of interaction and feedback. Previous research established that there was considerable variability in the use which individual learners made of feedback (Mackey, Philp, Egi, Fujii and Tatsumi 2002). The question arose of whether WM might be a factor given that either model of WM would suggest that individuals with differing WM would have differences in their ability to "regulate attention during the performance of complex cognitive tasks" (Mackey et al. 2010: 504). The researchers hypothesized that learners with higher WM capacity would be more likely to produce modified output than those with lower WM (Mackey et al. 2010: 509). WM capacity was assessed in forty-two native English speaking undergraduates enrolled in Spanish classes at a major US university by means of an L1 listening test adapted from Daneman and Carpenter's (1980) listening span test. Learners had to judge sentences for plausibility (to ensure that they were processing the meaning) and grammaticality, and then at points in the tests were asked to recall the final word of the sentence (to judge their ability to store the information). They then interacted with four bilingual Spanish speakers on specified communicative tasks. The interlocutors were trained to provide feedback, mainly in the form of prompts. Broadly speaking the hypothesis was confirmed: learners with higher WM capacity measured in this way did produce more modified output. The researchers recognize that WM capacity is not the only determining variable and propose on the basis of a measure of effect size that 17 percent of the variation in the production of modified output can be explained by variation in WM.

Thus, working memory may be an important determinant of learning outcomes, at least for those aspects of learning and acquisition which are capable of conscious modification. It may be more linked to an individual's physiologically determined capability and/or it may be linked to the degree to which an individual is concentrating on the specific goals to be attained.

6.4 Explicit and implicit learning

Given that much language teaching consists of imparting to learners in a classroom an amount of knowledge about the language and the presentation of numerous examples in an explicit way followed by a greater or lesser degree of practice and exposure to the use of the language in context, it has been important for second language researchers to attempt to answer the question: does explicit instruction lead to the acquisition of implicit knowledge? From the earlier sections of this chapter, it should be clear that the answer to this question is not simple (see also for example the special issue of *Studies in Second Language Acquisition* 27 no. 2 June 2005).

6.4.1 Acquisition versus learning

We have already noted above that Krashen (1981) argued for two separate types of learning which he labelled *acquisition* and *learning*. *Acquisition* takes place implicitly and unconsciously in response to the learning environment. *Learning* takes place explicitly and consciously and can not lead to *acquisition*. This is known as the non-interface position. The primary form of learning was taken by Krashen to be *acquisition* and he (1981, 1985) claimed that consciously learnt knowledge could only be made use of in a limited number of circumstances, e.g. to monitor what the unconscious system produced and potentially to modify it. However, this could only take place if sufficient time was available and sufficient attention could be devoted to the form of the language. This and Krashen's other hypotheses were hotly contested (Gregg 1984) and the empirical basis proved unable to withstand the criticism. Nonetheless, most subsequent SLA work argues that implicit unconscious learning is the primary form of learning. Generativists argue in favor of knowledge being triggered by means of specific cues in the primary linguistic data (see White 2003a) and deny that explicit or direct negative evidence has a role to play in the acquisition of linguistic competence. Moreover, constructivists (Tomasello 2003), connectionists (N. C. Ellis 1998; see Chapter 28, this volume) and those who adopt the Competition Model (MacWhinney 1987b) argue that second languages are or at least can be learnt on the basis of exposure without any need for explicit rules, as is self-evidently the case for children learning their first language. This holds even in the classroom; for example N. C. Ellis (2002: 173) writes that "because the conscious experiences of language learning do not revolve around counting, to the extent that language processing is based on frequency and probabilistic knowledge, language learning is implicit learning."

This stands in sharp contrast to the arguments put forward in Section 6.3 of this chapter which suggest that language development involves the progressive development of language as a skill, moving from declarative to procedural or from explicit to implicit knowledge. It also stands in contrast to the results of a number of studies of second language acquisition, as listed by Norris and Ortega (2000) in their meta-analysis of a number of empirical investigations. These showed that second language learners who were exposed to explicit knowledge had in general better outcomes. DeKeyser (2003: 321-6) also cites numerous studies where the results all show this to be the case. While this might be labelled as support for the interface position, in the thirty years that this debate has been present in SLA research, the question of whether explicitly learned information (declarative knowledge) can become implicit/procedural knowledge has still not been satisfactorily resolved.

It may be that the use of binary pairs traps researchers in a black and white view of the issues. On closer inspection, there are some significant caveats amongst proponents of the non-interface position. N. C. Ellis (2005) argues that there must be some degree of attending to form in second language acquisition in order for the probabilistic learning to take place and that explicit knowledge can influence learning outcomes. Explicit language processing would assist learning in at least three ways. First, attention of some kind is necessary as the first stage in language acquisition (N. C. Ellis 2005: 317): the surface form of the language must sufficiently be attended to for the form of the language to be registered in the consciousness of the learner (cf. Carroll above). Second, "explicit memories of utterances can be used as scaffolding in the building of novel linguistic utterances that use processes of analogical reasoning and conceptual blending" (N. C. Ellis 2005: 329). Third, the use of recasts at points where learners have produced erroneous utterances may permit the reanalysis of their interim linguistic knowledge (N. C. Ellis 2005: 331; cf. Mackey *et al.* 2010 cited above). M. Paradis (2009: 61), however, in radical disagreement with N. C. Ellis, suggests that the debate has disintegrated. And the generativists' notion of triggering relates only to syntax and to some extent phonology; there is recognition that other aspects of language are learnt using general cognitive abilities.

6.4.2 Finer constructs

Two scholars have helpfully attempted to broaden the debate. At an abstract level, De Keyser (2003) has suggested that four combinations are possible, derived from the explicit/implicit and deductive/inductive binary pairs. *Explicit deductive learning* is what we recognize in traditional classrooms where presentation of rules is followed by examples and practice; *explicit inductive learning* is where examples are provided first and rules are subsequently provided to show the relationships between them; *implicit inductive learning* is where children learning their first language derive implicit rules purely from the data (under connectionist or constructivist views); *implicit deductive learning* is where children have innate knowledge of linguistic parameters which provide unconscious "rules" which are then implicitly acquired by some form of triggering (under generativist views, including

Table 6.1. *Operationalizing the constructs of L2 implicit and explicit knowledge (adapted from R. Ellis 2005a)*

Criterion	Implicit knowledge	Explicit knowledge
Degree of awareness	Response according to feel	Response using rules
Time available	Time pressure	No time pressure
Focus of attention	Primary focus on meaning	Primary focus on form
Systematicity	Consistent responses	Variable responses
Certainty	High degree of certainty in responses	Low degree of certainty in responses
Metalinguistic knowledge	Metalinguistic knowledge not required	*Metalinguistic knowledge encouraged*
Learnability	Early learning favored	Late, form-focused, instruction favored

those of second language acquisition researchers; see Chapters 7 and 22, this volume).

R. Ellis (2005a: 152) attempted in a more practical way to give an operational definition of the various constructs of the explicit/implicit distinction (see Table 6.1).

This suggests that implicit knowledge will be relied upon when the learner is focused on meaning, is under time pressure and does not have the relevant metalinguistic knowledge. It is expected that responses provided on the basis of implicit knowledge will be consistent and that if questioned, learners would express certainty that the response is correct (even when they are wrong!). This is because learners are drawing on their existing, implicit knowledge using their feel for what is right. Explicit knowledge on the other hand will be relied upon when learners are focused on form, are not under time pressure and do have the relevant metalinguistic knowledge. Reponses provided will be more variable and learners will not be very sure whether they are right. This is because learners are drawing on explicit knowledge learnt, for example, from a textbook in the same way as other explicit information, such as historical dates, which might be only partially learnt or memorized. There is no dispute that learners can acquire these two kinds of knowledge, and the article from which the table is taken contributes significantly to a confirmation that the two types of knowledge are present in learners' mind/brains and can be distinguished by carefully designed tests.

However, the wider debate is largely about whether explicit knowledge in the way that R. Ellis has outlined its characteristics here contributes to second language acquisition, and if so, how? R. Ellis attempted to answer this question in a 2002 article. His conclusion was: "Taking performance in free-production tasks (especially oral) as the measure of whether implicit knowledge has been acquired, the analysis demonstrated that FFI (form focused instruction) results in acquisition, at least sometimes, and that when it does the effects are durable" (R. Ellis 2002: 233). He is concerned, however, that these results may not be based on use of language which would have made it impossible to perform on the basis of speeded-up explicit knowledge. This highlights a major and ongoing difficulty in this area: how is it possible to know, when a learner produces a fluent oral performance, whether one is witnessing performance based on explicit/declarative knowledge which has been speeded up by virtue of intensive practice or whether one is witnessing performance based on implicit/procedural knowledge? Further studies, which are examined in detail in Chapter 19, have made use of additional methodologies using physiological measurements: it remains to be seen whether these will provide the means of separating out the various dimensions discussed above.

6.5 Conclusion

We began this chapter with some wide-ranging questions: how are second languages created within the mind/brain? What learning mechanisms are there? How is a second language comprehended, produced, processed and stored? What is the role of working memory? If an answer of some kind can be provided for these questions, how does that answer relate to language instruction and specifically to whether explicit instruction can lead to the acquisition of implicit knowledge? We now have two possible sets of answers.

The first possible set of answers would be that second languages are created within the mind/brain, going from declarative knowledge to procedural knowledge along an explicit deductive continuum. Evidence for this is hard to come by because we cannot tap the internal workings of the brain directly. But we do have evidence from some experiments, notably DeKeyser (1997), and the evidence from temporal variables and interpretation by some scholars of how production systems might function as learning mechanisms. Production systems have been shown to be powerful instruments in other types of learning undertaken by humans. They may well operate in all areas of comprehension, processing and storage as well as production. Working memory would have a bearing on how well these mechanisms worked, either because individuals have physiological differences in their WM capacity or in their ability and willingness to direct their attention to a goal. If this view is correct, we could be optimistic that learners exposed to classroom instruction would be able over time and with considerable practice and exposure to acquire second languages. Whether the resulting knowledge should be regarded as implicit is open to question but as yet we find it difficult to distinguish in many cases speeded-up explicit knowledge from implicit knowledge.

The second possible set of answers might be that second languages are created within the mind/brain within two parallel memory systems, the declarative and the procedural, which contain explicitly and implicitly created complementary kinds of knowledge. The declarative memory is conscious and contains specific information but does not become aware of patterns and regularities (or frequency and probabilistic knowledge discussed above). The procedural memory is unconscious and able to create knowledge on the basis of the patterns and regularities it recognizes. The two kinds of knowledge combine in language production and comprehension but develop along separate lines. The learning mechanisms which underlie the declarative memory involve chunking of information but it is not yet clear how the procedural or implicit memory works beyond the fact that it implicitly tallies all the information it processes and raises or lowers thresholds according to quantitative information. This suggests an implicit inductive view of second language learning if it is assumed that the data provide all the evidence needed or an implicit deductive view if it is assumed that surface data are assisted by innate knowledge (see Chapter 7, this volume). Some of the evidence for this view comes from interpretations of results from amnesic and aphasic patients and is added to by neurophysiological evidence suggesting that the brain processes the two kinds of information differently. These studies also suggest that L1 and L2 learners may not use the same parts of the brain, especially at different levels of proficiency. The role of working memory is likely to be less important where WM is seen as processing only conscious declarative information. Under this view, it is unlikely that the knowledge acquired by second language learners in the classroom should be considered implicit: it is more likely to be speeded-up explicit knowledge but in the case of learners with great exposure and practice this might be considered implicit.

Only further detailed and careful research will tell us if one or other of the set of proposed answers is correct or whether, as is so often the case, there is another set which lies either in a combination of the two or somewhere in between.

7

Generative approaches and the poverty of the stimulus

Bonnie D. Schwartz and Rex A. Sprouse

7.1 Introduction

One of the central concepts in approaches to second language research grounded in generative grammar is the *poverty of the stimulus* (POS). The purpose of this chapter is threefold: (i) to provide an overview of the principal aspects of the POS in the acquisition of natural language grammars in general; (ii) to address briefly some of the misunderstandings surrounding the POS; and (iii) to clarify how argumentation from the POS in first language research vs. second language research logically differs.

A defining property of generative approaches to non-native language (L2) acquisition is a focus on the question of whether (adult) L2 acquisition is guided and constrained by the same principles of *Universal Grammar* (UG) that are assumed by generative grammarians to guide and constrain native language (L1) acquisition. Within this broad research paradigm, some L2 researchers have claimed that UG becomes inactive or "inaccessible" at some point in the human life cycle and thus plays no role in non-native language acquisition after that (Clahsen and Muysken 1986; Meisel 1997). Others have claimed that UG remains fully active or "accessible" in the human brain throughout life and (in principle) plays the same role in both native and (adult) non-native language acquisition (or at least, UG would play the same role, if it were not for the confounding factor of previously acquired grammars) (Dekydtspotter, Sprouse and Anderson 1997; Dekydtspotter, Sprouse and Swanson 2001; Herschensohn 2000; Schwartz 1987; Schwartz and Sprouse 1996; Slabakova 2008; Vainikka and Young-Scholten 1994; White 1989, 2003a; and many others). A third group of L2 scholars has claimed that only those properties and/or categories of UG instantiated in the L1 grammar can be accessed in adult L2 acquisition (Bley-Vroman 1990; Hawkins and Chan 1997; Schachter 1989b; Tsimpli and Dimitrakopoulou 2007; Tsimpli and Roussou 1991), while yet a fourth position is that UG is selectively impaired or "partially accessible" in the adult L2 learner (Beck 1998a).

Despite competing claims about the epistemology of adult L2 acquisition, the commonality uniting all of the perspectives referenced above is the assumption that children are born with UG, that is, a body of domain-specific cognitive principles or mechanisms constraining the acquisition of language, and that UG plays a fundamental role in accounting for the observable course of L1 development in childhood. On the interpretation presented in this chapter, the basis for positing UG is the empirical fact that human children (exposed to contextualized linguistic input, i.e. primary linguistic data), systematically and without the need for specific instruction or for direct negative evidence (direct information about what is impossible, e.g. impossible strings annotated as such), acquire systems of *subdoxastic* linguistic knowledge, which cannot plausibly be inferred from the input on the basis of domain-general learning principles alone.

The enormous gap between the input available to the child (primary linguistic data) and the system of knowledge acquired, a system that includes what is possible but, crucially, excludes what is impossible, has come to be known as the *poverty of the stimulus*. (See Thomas 2002 for a history of the development of this term and its rising importance over the course of the evolution of generative linguistic theory.) As Thomas (2002) astutely points out, the "stimulus" is in fact in no way "impoverished" from the perspective of the language-acquiring child. Quite the contrary, the stimulus (ambient linguistic input uttered in contexts of the world) is entirely sufficient to allow all children, barring pathology, to develop mental grammars that appear to match those of the speech community in which they live with respect to even extremely subtle and complex properties. The standard (perhaps, defining) explanation of generative grammar for this phenomenon is that the brain/mind of human children is endowed with UG, a network of domain-specific cognitive predispositions that filter the input and narrowly constrain the set of grammars that can be projected from the input. Thus, the stimulus is "impoverished" only from the perspective of the expectations of a purely inductive domain-general learning hypothesis.

It would be counterintuitive, to say the least, to deny that there is a general POS associated with the acquisition of human languages, given that cognitively normal humans acquire the ambient language of their speech community, and no other species does so, nor do other species seem to have anything remotely like language in the sense of human language, with properties such as recursion and the generation of an infinite set of discrete sentences. There is something special about human brains that produces cognitive outcomes to the linguistic stimulus that are radically different from the cognitive outcomes produced by the brains of even our closest primate cousins exposed to the same stimulus.

However, the gap between what an "unbiased" analysis of the input would predict and the grammar actually triggered in the child's brain suggests that much more is at stake than merely the superior domain-general reasoning/learning abilities of *Homo sapiens sapiens*. To the extent that the contribution of this system of innate knowledge to language acquisition has no application outside the realm of human language, one is left with the conclusion that the human brain is equipped with domain-specific cognitive structures and operations for language (henceforth language-specific knowledge).

7.2 Five aspects of the POS in language acquisition

The severity of the POS is not uniform across the acquisition of all linguistic phenomena. While the POS is in general the gap between the primary linguistic data available to the child and the properties of the system ultimately attained, the specific nature of that gap varies from phenomenon to phenomenon. Here we sketch five types of such gaps pointing to a POS. In presenting the first four types, we progressively move to increasingly compelling arguments from the POS for the positing of UG. The fifth and final gap type we explore comes into focus only through an intriguing comparison of provisional systems children create that do not match the input they received but do correspond to other human language grammars.

7.2.1 Intricate domain-specific knowledge

Perhaps the softest type of POS phenomenon is that involving the conspicuous intricacy of the inflectional systems of many of the world's languages. It is striking that in many cases, despite an apparently chaotic array of surface forms, it is possible to capture the relevant facts through a somewhat simpler, elegant underlying system with a set of rules mapping abstract representations to surface forms.

An illustrative example is Anderson's (1982) analysis of the inflection of a certain class of transitive verbs in Georgian. Anderson provides the following forms for the present tense of the verb *xed-av-s* "to see."

(1) a. i. g-xedav   "I see you-SG"
        ii. v-xedav   "I see him"
        iii. g-xedav-t   "I see you-PL"
     b. i. m-xedav   "you-SG see me"
        ii. xedav   "you-SG see him"
        iii. gv-xedav   "you-SG see us"
     c. i. m-xedav-s   "he sees me"
        ii. g-xedav-s   "he sees you-SG"
        iii. xedav-s   "he sees him"
        iv. gv-xedav-s   "he sees us"
        v. g-xedav-t   "he sees you-PL"

d. i. g-xedav-t   "we see you-SG"
    ii. v-xedav-t   "we see him"
    iii. g-xedav-t "we see you-PL"
e. i. m-xedav-t   "you-PL see me"
    ii. xedav-t   "you-PL see him"
    iii. gv-xedav-t "you-PL see us"
f. i. m-xedav-en   "they see me"
    ii. g-xedav-en "they see you-SG"
    iii. xedav-en   "they see him"
    iv. gv-xedav-en "they see us"
    v. g-xedav-en   "they see you-PL"

(from Anderson 1982: 597 (18), 603 (25), 604 (27))

Of interest both to morphological theory and to an understanding of the intricacy of language acquisition is the observation that even once one has segmented these forms into (PREFIX)-*xedav*-(SUFFIX) and associated each form with its meaning (the latter itself not a transparent task, given that meaning is not written on the sleeve of forms – see below), there remains non-trivial analytic work to be done. This is because the individual prefixes and suffixes are not "morphemes" in the sense of sequences of phonemes corresponding to minimal units of meaning or grammatical function. For example, the suffix *-s* frequently occurs in forms denoting a third-person singular subject, the suffix *-t* frequently occurs in forms denoting a non-third-person plural subject or object, and the suffix *-en* frequently occurs in forms denoting a third-person plural subject. Since present tense verbs in Georgian have only one slot for an agreement suffix, the suffixes *-s*, *-t* and *-en* might be seen as competing for that single slot. The actual inflectional system of Georgian is such that *-t* wins out over *-s* in (1c(v)), while *-en* wins out over *-t* in (1f(iv)) and (1f(v)). To account for generalizations of this sort, Anderson proposes disjunctively ordered blocks of rules.

No one would wish to claim that children acquiring Georgian are somehow not exposed to the full range of these prefixes and suffixes, and in this sense, the stimulus is not "truly impoverished." What is striking is that the brains of children acquiring Georgian are not only extremely sensitive to the presence of these prefixes and suffixes, (correctly) extracting them from the input and generalizing them to attach to members of the class of items linguists label "verbs," but are also willing to entertain the notion of disjunctively ordered blocks of rules (or their functional equivalent in some alternative framework). One may speculate about whether the elegant system proposed by Anderson is "psychologically" real or just a convenient summary, but it is undeniable that children exposed to Georgian in naturalistic settings uniformly arrive at subdoxastic knowledge of these inflectional patterns and that these patterns reflect a highly domain-specific regimen grounded in notions of person, number and grammatical relations (subject and direct object), together with the proviso that word structure of a particular language might be such that only one of multiple suffixes or prefixes is actually realized in any given surface form.

There is little doubt that clever non-Georgian-speaking adults could figure out these patterns, given a sufficiently large corpus with helpful glosses, if they put their minds to the task. However, young children do this without the aid of "glossing," apart from their perception of the (overly rich and complex) scenes of the world in which they are bombarded with a haphazardly constituted and presented auditory corpus. Furthermore, linguists have received explicit analytic training informing them that systems of verbal inflection are likely to cross-index, e.g. person and number features with grammatical relations. Linguists also know that verbs are likely to carry inflection for the time of the event described (relevant to the time of speaking), but not, for example, for the speed, difficulty or loudness of the event, or its social, ethical or legal appropriateness (although such information could of course be encoded through other non-inflectional means). We grant that person and number are semantically relevant to the world apart from language, but grammatical relations do not readily map directly onto non-linguistic reality. In short, it would appear that something in the brains of children is "on the lookout for" the possibility of verbal inflection, potentially marking a subset of features drawn from a universal feature set, and potentially marking only a subset of those features in the context of the larger inflectional system. This is no mean feat, but it is the least impressive type of the POS we discuss in this chapter.

7.2.2 Needles in the linguistic haystack

A second level of POS involves phenomena for which the relevant stimulus may well be present in the ambient language, but tokens are very rare and particularly unlikely to occur in child-directed speech. In these instances, an account denying the existence of rich language-specific knowledge must assume that the child's brain/mind is indeed that of a "little linguist" proposing alternative hypotheses and remaining ever vigilant until the crucial datum presents itself in order to select just the correct ones.

Consider Chomsky's (1975: 30–35) classic demonstration of the principle that syntactic rules are structure-dependent, presented here in a somewhat simplified form. A child exposed to English will frequently encounter declarative sentences with a finite form of the verb *be* as well as the corresponding polarity (*yes/no*) interrogative, as in (2).

(2) a. The child is here today.
    b. Is the child here today?

Such a child might induce a rule of *be*-fronting, roughly as in (3).

(3) be-*Fronting* (Version A)
A declarative sentence with a finite form of the verb *be* may be transformed into a corresponding polarity interrogative by moving the finite form of *be* to the front of the sentence.

While Version A will be observationally adequate for most of the *yes/no* interrogatives of sentences with a finite form of *be* the child is likely to hear or produce, it is too vague to yield a definitive output for a declarative like (4).

(4) The child who is feeling ill is here today.

The vagueness derives from the presence of two instances of finite *be* in (4). This suggests two competing hypotheses, as in (5) and (6).

(5) be-*Fronting* (Version B)
A declarative sentence with a finite form of the verb *be* may be transformed into a corresponding polarity interrogative by moving the first finite form of *be* to the front of the sentence.

(6) be-*Fronting* (Version C)
A declarative sentence with a finite form of the verb *be* may be transformed into a corresponding polarity interrogative by moving the finite form of *be* in the main clause to the front of the sentence.

Version B (5) is a structure-independent rule, because it refers simply to the first linear occurrence of a finite form of *be*; Version C (6) is a structure-dependent rule, because it is formulated strictly in terms of the structural position of the finite *be*-form, namely the one in the main clause. For a declarative sentence like (7a) (=(4)), Version B yields the polarity interrogative in (7b), while Version C yields (7c).

(7) a. The child who is feeling ill is here today. (=(4))
    b. Is the child who ___ feeling ill is here today?
    c. Is the child who is feeling ill ___ here today?

The structure-dependent version of the rule, Version C, succeeds where the structure-independent version, Version B, fails. Chomsky's claim is not merely that all syntactic rules are structure-dependent; his claim is that the child never considers structure-independent versions. This is because UG restricts the hypothesis space available to the language-acquiring child to structure-dependent rules. Subsequent empirical research with children has confirmed Chomsky's intuition: Crain and Nakayama (1987) experimentally demonstrated that young children (aged 3 to 5) acquiring English uniformly produce interrogatives with the structure-dependent pattern illustrated in (7c), not with the structure-independent pattern in (7b). (Of course the structure-dependent hypothesis extends beyond finite *be* to all verbal elements that precede the subject in both *yes/no* questions and non-subject *wh*-questions: modals and auxiliary *have* and *do*.)

For the sake of the argument, let us assume that some young children have heard interrogatives like (7c) as well as relevant non-subject *wh*-questions by the time they produce their first polarity interrogatives with a relative clause embedded on the main-clause subject. Indeed, Pullum and Scholz (2002) suggest that examples such as (7c) are not absent from children's linguistic experience, based on an eighteenth-century poem by William Blake and on computer-based searches of *The Wall Street Journal*, Oscar Wilde's play *The Importance of Being Earnest*, and selected files from the CHILDES database (MacWhinney 1995), e.g. *Where's the other dolly that was in here?* (Pullum and Scholz 2002: 44 (34b)).[1] Even if this is true, a view of language acquisition that crucially relies on the availability of this kind of input to the child makes very strong and highly implausible assumptions both about the nature of the input that is uniformly available to all children acquiring (for example) English and about the child's attentiveness to such data for the purpose of resolving previously formulated alternative grammatical hypotheses. This is why we use the label "needles in the linguistic haystack" for examples of direct positive evidence that are not likely to be robust in the input available to any child and are likely to be extremely rare or absent from the evidence available to many children. Because such examples are instantiations of grammatically well-formed sentences, it is in principle possible that they may occur in the child's linguistic environment. However, in the absence of UG, one must still imagine that a child is a little linguist who is subconsciously seeking relevant data to distinguish between two (indeed many more) competing grammatical hypotheses and who indeed eventually encounters the required evidence. In the next subsection, we will see that acquiring the knowledge that strings like (7c) are grammatical is the relatively easy part; the much more severe POS is associated with acquiring the knowledge that strings like (7b) are ungrammatical.

7.2.3 Uniqueness and variability

The logical problem of language acquisition (so called, because logic would leave grammar acquisition unexplained without the aid of UG) is severely complicated by the fact that natural language syntax exhibits cases of uniqueness as well as cases of variability. (For further discussion of this point, see Fodor and Crowther 2002.) As Freidin (1991) points out, the simple fact that (7c) is well-formed does not entail that (7b) (among myriad other logically possible strings) is ill-formed. To illustrate this point, let us return to the child who has come to know that (7c) is a well-formed *yes/no* interrogative, instantiating Version C of the rule of *be*-Fronting (6). Can children who receive confirmation of Version C through examples like (7c) now confidently conclude that examples like (7b), generated by Version B (5), are ungrammatical? That is, is there some sort of principle of uniqueness of form–function mapping, such that data that are non-trivially consistent with one version of a hypothesis are necessarily interpreted simultaneously as counterevidence against an alternative version? The answer is clearly negative, since there are indeed instances of optionality or variability in natural language grammars. One example is the alternation known as Particle Shift in English, as in (8).

(8) a. Joe looked up the number.
    b. Joe looked the number up.

Sentence (8a), where the particle *up* precedes the direct object (DO) *the number*, contains precisely the same words as – and is truth-conditionally equivalent to – the sentence in (8b), where the particle follows the DO.[2]

This type of apparently free surface alternation undermines any strong version of a uniqueness strategy for the acquisition of syntax. Thus, even if we could imagine a child adopting rule (6) through exposure to examples like (7c), the child could not on this basis alone confidently exclude (for instance) rule (5) as another option.

All of this brings us back to how children acquiring English come to know that *yes/no* interrogatives like (7b) are ungrammatical. First, clearly, nothing in the child's environment can provide this information directly, because these are ungrammatical sentences that input-providers simply do not produce (qua ungrammatical sentences). Second, although we cannot rule out a priori the possibility that some children might not be exposed to examples like (7c) (during the relevant time period), it is still the case – even if all English-acquiring children do encounter them – that there is no learning-theoretical guarantee that the grammaticality of examples like (7c) necessarily implies the ungrammaticality of examples like (7b), since (6) and (5) could be rules that disjunctively apply. So, the possibility of a child hypothesizing a structure-independent rule like (5) needs to be excluded, but it is difficult to see how a structure-independent rule like (5) would violate a principle of general cognition. Thus, general cognition cannot be the source of this exclusion. Presumably, the only sources of linguistic knowledge are the environment and the child's mind, and the child's mind includes non-language-specific knowledge (including domain-general knowledge) and language-specific knowledge. If the environment and non-language-specific knowledge are not possible sources of this piece of new knowledge (the impossibility of strings like (7b)), then language-specific knowledge (i.e. UG) is the only source left.

Nevertheless, this particular example does not yet illustrate the most compelling class of POS problems. This is because rule (5), while quite plausible on its surface, is only one logically possible rule that a child might hypothesize to address interrogatives with a main-clause subject containing a relative clause, if s/he is somehow "motivated" to extend a rule like (3), designed to cover monoclausal examples. Natural analogical extension would not necessarily infer rule (5) from grammatical knowledge already acquired. In Section 7.2.4, we turn to cases where natural logic is in fact defied in language acquisition.

7.2.4 The bankruptcy of the stimulus

Finally, we turn to what we consider to be the most impressive class of POS phenomena. These are cases where the stimulus is not merely unstructured, rare or incomplete. Rather, these are cases where the input available to the language-acquiring child would be affirmatively misleading, if it were not for the filtering effects of UG which pre-inform the child prior to experience with the world that certain representations are not licit. Some of these cases appear extremely complex; others involve what appear to be relatively short, simple sentences. In virtually any case of the bankruptcy of the stimulus (Sprouse 2006a), however, natural analogical extension from positive exemplars would erroneously lead the child to anticipate that an ill-formed structure is grammatical. Furthermore, the logic of the unavailability of direct negative evidence means that, by definition, there will be nothing in the input that directly informs the child that the ill-formed structure is in fact ill-formed.

Consider the sentences in (9).

(9) a. Who thinks he is hungry?
    b. Who does he think is hungry?

The relevant aspects of the examples in (9) are that they contain both a *wh*-phrase in initial position and a third-person singular subject pronoun later in the sentence. Interrogatives of this type are not rare, not "exotic" and not "complex" (apart from the fact that the sentences contain an embedded clause). However, they differ significantly in the range of interpretations that can be associated with them. The English pronoun *he* can be used deictically. That is, *he* can be used to refer to a male whose identity is established linguistically or contextually outside the sentence in which it occurs. Suppose we are talking about Richard. The examples in (9) can then be rephrased as in (10):

(10) a. Give me the name of the person who thinks Richard is hungry.
     b. Give me the name of the person who Richard thinks is hungry.

Let us refer to this as the deictic interpretation of the pronoun.

Sentence (9a) can also have a very different interpretation, viz. where the pronoun *he* does not point out any particular individual, but is a placeholder for a second occurrence of the interrogative *who*. This interpretation of (9a) can be somewhat stiltedly rephrased as in (11):

(11) Give me the name of each person x who thinks x is hungry.

Let us refer to this as the bound interpretation of the pronoun.

Suppose that a child acquiring English has encountered both sentences (9a) and (9b) in contexts where it would be reasonable to assume that the deictic interpretation was intended by the speaker. Furthermore, let us assume that this same child has encountered (9a) in a context where the bound interpretation makes sense. If the child is keeping track, s/he might subdoxastically construct the equivalent of the table in (12):

(12)

	Deictic interpretation of *he*	Bound interpretation of *he*
Who thinks he is hungry?	yes	yes
Who does he think is hungry?	yes	

The set of sentences of any natural language represents a discrete infinity. Since the input to the acquisition process is finite, we must assume that (some version of) natural analogical extension is at work in language acquisition. Presented with the data in (12), the natural analogy would be to fill in the lower right-hand cell with "yes" as in (13). That is, natural analogical extension would lead to the prediction that a sentence like (9b) should allow the bound interpretation of the pronoun *he*.

(13)

	Deictic interpretation of *he*	Bound interpretation of *he*
Who thinks he is hungry?	yes	yes
Who does he think is hungry?	yes	*yes*

However, this does not match the intuitions of native English speakers when they are (typically, to their befuddlement) asked whether sentence (9b) can be rephrased as (14).

(14) Give me the name of each person *x* who thinks *x* is hungry.

That is, the summary of the intuitions of actual native speakers of English about the interpretation of the sentences in (9) is what we find in (15).

(15)

	Deictic interpretation of *he*	Bound interpretation of *he*
Who thinks he is hungry?	yes	yes
Who does he think is hungry?	yes	***no***

The unexpected "no" in the lower right-hand cell of the table in (15) (known as a *strong crossover effect*) is a paradigm case of the bankruptcy of the stimulus. The point is not merely that this knowledge cannot be triggered by anything in the input; what is crucial is that what is inferable from the input (dyads of the form in (16)) should lead the language-acquiring child to a non-targetlike grammar.

(16)   < (sentence [who ... he ...]), (interpretation of he) >

The observation that this does not occur (e.g. Crain and Thornton 1998; Thornton 1990) leaves as the possible source of this knowledge only something inherent in the child's brain/mind distinct from experience of the input. To the extent that this knowledge has no imaginable source of application to any non-linguistic aspect of cognition suggests that this is not merely innate knowledge, but domain-specific innate knowledge. Innate knowledge specific to the linguistic domain is virtually the definition of UG.

A common retort to the claim that knowledge of impossibility (of form and of form–meaning pairings) derives from innate language-specific knowledge is to say that learners need only rule out everything they do not encounter in their input. This is to say, the learner is strictly conservative. However, we know that at some level, learners must generalize; no one believes that language acquisition literally happens on a case by case basis of what constitutes learners' input. So, the question is at what levels generalization, i.e. abstraction, occurs. This is not an easy question to answer. Nevertheless, it is well documented that L1 children overgeneralize in the morphological domain (i.e. they are not strictly conservative); they create past tense forms like *buyed and *taked, even though they do not occur in their input. L1 children also overgeneralize in the lexical domain; from intransitive verbs like giggle, they create causatives, *Giggle me (meaning, "Make me giggle"). In the syntactic domain, children have been found to overgeneralize the dative alternation, creating sentences like *You finished me lots of rings (meaning "You finished lots of rings for me"). The point is that overgeneralization does occur in L1 acquisition, and therefore language acquisition cannot be strictly conservative, in the sense that children will necessarily infer impossibility from absence in the input. The flipside of this coin also needs to be considered; this is the case of extreme rarity in input nevertheless leading to robust judgments of acceptability (the exact opposite of what conservative learning would expect). Just such a case is illustrated in the first example in Section 7.4 below.

7.2.5   The narrow range of provisional non-target grammars

The acquisition of intricate domain-specific knowledge on the basis of haphazardly presented input, the discovery of needles in the linguistic haystack, and the bankruptcy of the stimulus are all cases of the general POS providing learnability-theoretic evidence (when coupled with the "no negative evidence" dictum) for UG. However, there is yet another kind of POS problem that developmental linguists have documented. Since the pioneering work of Brown (1973), it has been well understood that during early childhood, children are not taking "pot shots" at producing adultlike utterances and simply missing the mark much of the time. Rather, children pass through a series of developmental stages, before ultimately attaining a grammar essentially indistinguishable from that of the ambient speech community. Each developmental stage is a grammar, perhaps a grammar that is not identical to the grammar of the input-providers, but a grammar nevertheless.

Of interest here is the range of the provisional non-target grammars that children entertain during this developmental period. First of all, from the earliest discernible point, these provisional grammars appear to conform to the format of adult grammars (e.g. with respect to phrase structure, null elements, movement, etc.). Secondly, they exhibit the same sorts of restrictions as adult grammars.[3] Thirdly, and perhaps most intriguingly, in some cases children whose input is generated by a particular adult grammar will provisionally exhibit, in a given domain, the properties of a distinct adult grammar.

Consider the case of Lucernese Swiss German, the acquisition of which was studied by Schönenberger (1996, 2001). Like other varieties of German, Lucernese is a subject–object–verb (SOV) language with verb second (V2) in main clauses; but in embedded clauses with an overt complementizer, the finite verb appears in final position (i.e. not in V2 position), as schematized in (17).

(17) a. ... complementizer S X $V_{[+finite]}$
 b. *... complementizer $V_{[+finite]}$ S X
 c. *... complementizer S $V_{[+finite]}$ X

Thus none of the input to which Lucernese-acquiring children are exposed will display the surface patterns in (17b) or (17c).

However, in a longitudinal study of the spontaneous production of two monolingual Lucernese children, Schönenberger finds that their provisional grammar differs from that of adult Lucernese speakers in a very precise way. While their finite verb placement in main clauses is targetlike (respecting V2), their verb placement is not targetlike in embedded clauses. Specifically, in the total 801 utterances that require the finite verb in the embedded clause to be in final position (17a), the two children produce this pattern only 5.6 percent of the time (45/801). Instead their utterances correspond to the ungrammatical patterns in (17b) and (17c) and this continues well into their fifth year of life. Two example utterances are provided in (18) and (19).

(18) Chasch mer achli Gift geh, dass <u>werdet</u> mini Ohre au
 can me some poison give that <u>turn</u> my ears also
 bru. (cf. (17b))
 brown
 "You can give me some poison so that my ears turn brown too."
 (Target Lucernese: Chasch mer achli Gift geh, dass mini Ohre au bru <u>werdet</u>.) (from Schönenberger 1996: 665 (28))

(19) Wenn si macht es Gschenk de   törf i nid ine.   (cf. (17c))
     when she makes a   present then may I not inside
     "When she makes a present then I am not allowed to go into her room."
     (Target Lucernese: Wenn si es Gschenk macht de törf i nid ine.)
     (from Schönenberger 1996: 666 (30))

What the two children do is clearly in disregard of their input: they require what is impossible in the target language and they disallow what is required. Nevertheless, this aspect of the provisional grammar they have created is manifested in other languages, such as Kashmiri (i.e. an SOV language with V2 in both main and embedded clauses).

This state of affairs represents yet a distinct type of the POS phenomenon. From one perspective, at an early stage of development, the input is sufficient to trigger a natural language grammar but not necessarily the grammar underlying the ambient language. However, from a complementary perspective, there is a remarkable "incommensurability of knowledge to evidence" – to use a phrase suggested by Thomas (2002: 65) to replace the easily misunderstood notion "poverty of the stimulus."

7.3 Misunderstandings surrounding the POS

7.3.1 Universal Grammar vs. universals of language

Universal Grammar, at least in the sense of the term within generative grammar, is neither a grammar of all the world's languages nor a collection of properties found in all human languages. Rather, what the content of UG provides is the hypothesis space within which grammatical development is permitted to proceed. It is the subdoxastic knowledge that learners bring to the task of language acquisition. Logically, UG must simultaneously be sufficiently permissive to allow the acquisition of the grammatical properties attested in any natural language and sufficiently restrictive to account for the full range of POS types illustrated by the phenomena outlined in Section 7.2. A simple demonstration that a particular linguistic property found in many of the languages of the world is not found in a particular language would not undermine any already established POS phenomena. Thus, such a demonstration could not undermine the empirical and logical foundations of the argument for the existence of UG from the POS.

7.3.2 Learnability problems vs. specific solutions

The existence of POS problems is the primary motivation for the postulation of the existence of UG. We understand the central project of generative grammar to be the investigation of the content of UG. This project had its origin in the 1950s and in the early 1960s in the work of Noam Chomsky, his students and a handful of linguists influenced by this work. However, since that time, a number of different models of UG and a myriad of highly specific hypotheses have been proposed and tested; some have been continuously refined, while others have been abandoned. In many cases, the abandoned hypotheses proved too restrictive to allow for the grammatical properties of languages studied at a later time. In other cases, specific hypotheses were abandoned because their explanatory force was subsumed under a later set of hypotheses within a model with greater theoretical simplicity and/or broader empirical coverage. Neither the larger models of UG (i.e. the specific theories or frameworks of UG such as the Standard Theory, the Extended Standard Theory, the Principles and Parameters framework, the Minimalist Program) nor the specific hypotheses (e.g. Strict Cyclicity, the *Wh*-island Constraint, the Null Subject Parameter, the Minimal Link Condition) should be confused with UG. They are provisional attempts at capturing aspects of UG. Empirically falsifying a particular hypothesis about formal properties of UG in no way invalidates the existence of the POS problems that form the basis for claiming that UG exists.

7.3.3 Not all linguistic phenomena have (equally) probative value

A third area of common misunderstanding regarding the argument from the POS concerns the strength of arguments that can be made from various linguistic phenomena. Schwartz and Sprouse (2000) argue that the most compelling arguments for the role of UG in L2 acquisition are based in demonstrations of the most severe POS problems, not merely in phenomena that are compatible with current technical views of what UG allows. In the study of L1 acquisition, it is also true that not all linguistic phenomena have (equally) probative value.

Pullum and Scholz's (2002) attempted refutation of the POS in the realm of language is a relevant case in point. Essentially a target article in an issue of *The Linguistic Review*, Pullum and Scholz's paper appeared together with a set of (mostly critical) commentaries as well as Scholz and Pullum's (2002) reply. Here we wish to focus solely on the issue of the nature of the linguistic phenomena on which these two authors focus.

Pullum and Scholz provide a review of four specific linguistic phenomena in English, aspects of which the literature has presented as cases of POS problems (plurals in the first constituent of Noun–Noun compounds, sequences of auxiliary verbs, *one*-anaphora, and auxiliary fronting in interrogatives with a main-clause subject containing a relative clause (on this last phenomenon, see Sections 7.2.2 and 7.2.3 above)) and attempt to show that in each instance a purely data-driven approach to L1 acquisition is adequate and therefore that the conclusion of linguistic nativism drawn by others is falsified.[4] Claiming that the issue of the availability of negative evidence to children is of no direct relevance to the evaluation of arguments from the POS for language acquisition (see, e.g., 2002: 15–17), Pullum and Scholz consistently and explicitly refuse to address any and all bankruptcy-of-the-stimulus problems associated with the phenomena they have selected.[5] Furthermore, Pullum and Scholz present a five-step procedure for documenting and assessing "'the argument from the POS' (henceforth "APS")" (2002: 15):

(20) *Pullum and Scholz' (2002: 19 (4)) APS specification schema*
   a. ACQUIRENDUM CHARACTERIZATION: describe in detail what is alleged to be known.
   b. LACUNA SPECIFICATION: identify a set of sentences such that if the learner had access to them, the claim of data-driven learning of the acquirendum would be supported.
   c. INDISPENSABILITY ARGUMENT: give reason to think that if learning were data-driven[,] then the acquirendum could not be learned without access to sentences in the lacuna.
   d. INACCESSIBILITY EVIDENCE: support the claim that tokens of sentences in the lacuna were not available to the learner during the acquisition process.
   e. ACQUISITION EVIDENCE: give reason to believe that the acquirendum does in fact become known to learners during childhood.

We see this schema as methodologically and conceptually flawed. Methodologically, (20d) requires that one support a claim that perfectly grammatical sentences are unavailable to children, and it is clear that for Pullum and Scholz, "available to the learner during the acquisition process" means that someone somewhere has uttered such a sentence in a context in which a child might have been listening. However, it is virtually impossible to document non-occurrence, that is, that children never hear tokens of well-formed sentence patterns. The mere absence of tokens of a sentence type from any given corpus can never serve as documentation that such sentences are "unavailable to the learner." Conceptually, adhering to steps (20b)–(20d) makes sense only if the "lacuna" pertains to positive evidence alone. This can have an application for the phenomena discussed in Sections 7.2.1 and 7.2.2, but not for phenomena with the degree of stimulus impoverishment illustrated by the cases in Sections 7.2.3 and 7.2.4 (see below for additional comparable phenomena in the L2 context). In cases like those in Sections 7.2.3 and 7.2.4, the whole point is that the crucial lacuna in the evidence is the specification of the impossibility of sentence patterns or of sentence-meaning pairings, logically possible ones in the case of 7.2.3 and logically expected ones in the case of 7.2.4.

In sum, complex and rare phenomena pose comparatively soft POS problems. Demonstrations that rare phenomena are attested in corpora do not vitiate the need for the postulation of UG to account for the successful acquisition of the knowledge that certain logically possible and (of even more probative value) logically expected sentence patterns and sentence-meaning pairings are in fact ungrammatical.

7.4 A comparison of the POS in native vs. non-native language acquisition

One of the central concerns of generative approaches to second language acquisition is the extent to which interlanguage grammars are constrained by UG. This issue is inherently interwoven with the question of what role(s) the L2 learner's (L2er's) native language grammar plays in non-native language acquisition, on the assumption that the L1 grammar is constrained by UG. Thus, a number of logical possibilities arise. It could be that UG is not at all involved in (adult) L2 acquisition, and that native grammars and interlanguage grammars are thus fundamentally different, cut from ontologically distinct cognitive cloth. Another possibility is that UG fully restricts language acquisition in adults, just as it does in (at least young) children. (This possibility is in principle compatible with a range of hypotheses about the role of the L1 grammar in the initial state of interlanguage development.) Yet another possibility is that UG is selectively impaired in (adult) non-native language acquisition, such that some, but not all, of its restrictions apply. One more hypothesis in the literature is that only those principles of UG which are instantiated in the L1 grammar play a role in (adult) L2 acquisition.

Schwartz and Sprouse (2000) argue that the most secure basis for distinguishing among these hypotheses is to investigate the existence of POS problems in L2 acquisition. Many asymmetries that are attributable to UG are already present in the L2er's L1 grammar, but the target language may instantiate new ones that are not. Given the logical possibility that only those principles of UG which are instantiated in the L1 grammar play a role in L2 acquisition, only a demonstration of the acquisition of the UG-based asymmetries not present in the L1 (and for tutored learners, not the object of instruction) constitutes a clear piece of evidence for full UG involvement in (adult) non-native language acquisition.

Our first illustration of this concerns the L2 acquisition of a particularly subtle and complex restriction on word order in German. German is an (underlyingly) SOV language with V2 in main clauses. Consider the examples in (21).

(21) a. Ich glaube, dass Peter gestern den Wagen repariert hat.
      I believe that Peter yesterday the car repaired has
      "I think that Peter repaired the car yesterday."

   b. Peter hat gestern den Wagen repariert.
      Peter has yesterday the car repaired
      "Peter repaired the car yesterday."

   c. Gestern hat Peter den Wagen repariert.
      yesterday has Peter the car repaired
      "Yesterday Peter repaired the car."

d. Den Wagen hat Peter gestern repariert.
   the car has Peter yesterday repaired
   "The car, Peter repaired yesterday."

Example (21a) illustrates an embedded clause introduced by the complementizer *dass* "that," where the finite verb *hat* "has" obligatorily appears in clause-final position. The next three examples illustrate main clauses, where the finite verb appears as the second constituent, preceded by the subject (21b), an adverbial (21c), and the DO (21d). On traditional generative accounts of German word order, the fronted XPs in these examples are assumed to move to the Spec,CP position, and this movement is known as *topicalization*.

In addition to topicalization, German also allows (under appropriate semantic and discourse conditions) the leftward movement of DOs, as illustrated in (22).

(22) a. Ich glaube, dass Peter schon den Wagen repariert hat.
       I believe that Peter already the car repaired has
       "I think that Peter has already repaired the car."

   b. Ich glaube, dass Peter den Wagen schon repariert hat.
      I believe that Peter the car already repaired has

   c. Ich glaube, dass den Wagen Peter schon repariert hat.
      I believe that the car Peter already repaired has

In (22a) the DO *den Wagen* "the car" occupies its underlying position to the immediate left of the verb *reparieren* "repair." In (22b) *den Wagen* has moved to the left of the adverb *schon* "already," while in (22c) it has moved to the left of the subject *Peter*. This movement is known as *scrambling*.

Of further interest here is that both topicalization and scrambling can target infinitival complements, as illustrated in (23) and (24), respectively.

(23) a. Peter hat schon [den Wagen zu reparieren] versucht.
       Peter has already the car to repair tried
       "Peter has already tried to repair the car."

   b. [Den Wagen zu reparieren] hat Peter schon versucht.
      the car to repair has Peter already tried
      "To repair the car, Peter has already tried."

(24) a. Ich glaube, dass Peter schon [den Wagen zu reparieren]
       I believe that Peter already the car to repair

      versucht hat.
      tried has
      "I think that Peter has already tried to repair the car."

b. Ich glaube, dass Peter [den Wagen zu reparieren] schon
   I believe that Peter the car to repair already
   versucht hat.
   tried has

c. Ich glaube, dass [den Wagen zu reparieren] Peter schon
   I believe that the car to repair Peter already
   versucht hat.
   tried has

d. Peter hat schon [den Wagen zu reparieren] versucht.
   Peter has already the car to repair tried
   "Peter has already tried to repair the car."

e. Peter hat [den Wagen zu reparieren] schon versucht.
   Peter has the car to repair already tried
   "Peter has already tried to repair the car."

In (23a) the infinitival phrase *[den Wagen zu reparieren]* "to repair the car" appears to the immediate left of *versuchen* "try," while in (23b) it appears in topicalized (clause-initial) position. The examples in (24) show that in a *dass*-clause, the infinitival phrase can appear in its underlying position immediately to the left of the verb *versuchen* (24a) or in either of the two scrambled positions, immediately to the left of the adverb *schon* (24b) or to the left of the subject *Peter* (24c). Examples (24d) and (24e) illustrate infinitival phrases in underlying and scrambled positions, respectively.

The focus of our interest, however, is not simply the existence of "intact" topicalization and "intact" scrambling illustrated above, but the interaction of these movement operations. That is, in principle, it is possible to move YP, a subpart of a constituent (for example, the DO contained within an infinitive phrase), to the left and then to move XP, what remains of that constituent, by another instance of leftward movement. This multi-part operation is known as *remnant movement*, schematized in (25).

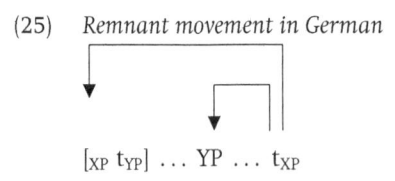

(25) *Remnant movement in German*

$[_{XP}\ t_{YP}] \ldots YP \ldots t_{XP}$

(from Hopp 2005: 38 (5))

However, such remnant movement is only possible when the two instances of movement are of distinct types (Müller 1996, 1998). For instance, remnant topicalization after scrambling is allowed, but not remnant scrambling after scrambling. This is illustrated in the paradigm in (26).

(26) a. *Intact Topicalization* (=23b)
   [Den Wagen zu reparieren]₁ hat Peter schon t₁ versucht.
   the car to repair has Peter already tried
   "To repair the car, Peter has already tried."

b. *Intact Scrambling* (=24c)
   Ich glaube, dass [den Wagen zu reparieren]₁ Peter schon
   I believe that the car to repair Peter already
   t₁ versucht hat.
   tried has
   "I think that to repair the car, Peter has already tried."

c. *Remnant Topicalization* (after scrambling)
   [t₁ Zu reparieren]₂ hat Peter [den Wagen]₁ schon t₂ versucht.
   to repair has Peter the car already tried
   ≈"Repairing Peter already tried to do to the car."

d. *Remnant Scrambling* (after scrambling)
   *Ich glaube, dass [t₁ zu reparieren]₂ Peter [den Wagen]₁
   I believe that to repair Peter the car
   schon t₂ versucht hat.
   already tried has

Examples (26a) and (26b) repeat examples of the intact topicalization and intact scrambling of the infinitival phrase *[den Wagen zu reparieren]* already discussed above as (22b) and (24c), respectively. In (26c), the DO *den Wagen* is first scrambled out of the infinitival phrase, and the resulting remnant phrase *[t₁ zu reparieren]* is then topicalized. However, after the same initial scrambling of the DO in (26d), subsequent scrambling of the remnant phrase results in ungrammaticality.

As discussed by Schreiber and Sprouse (1998) and Hopp (2002, 2005), acquiring the distinction between the grammaticality of remnant topicalization and remnant scrambling appears to represent a severe POS. Granting for the sake of argument that language acquirers have a principled distinction between topicalization and scrambling as well as a principled distinction between intact movement and remnant movement, consider the cells of a table (similar to the ones discussed in Section 7.2.4) that could be compiled on the basis of sentences in the primary linguistic data, as in (27).

(27)

	Intact movement	Remnant movement (after scrambling)
topicalization	yes	yes
scrambling	yes	

Natural analogical extension would lead to the prediction that remnant scrambling should be possible as well, as in (28).

(28)

	Intact movement	Remnant movement (after scrambling)
topicalization	yes	yes
scrambling	yes	*yes*

However, this does not reflect the intuitions of native German speakers when they are (typically to their amusement) asked whether sentences like (26d) are possible. The actual summary of their intuitions is sketched in (29).

(29)

	Intact movement	Remnant movement (after scrambling)
topicalization	yes	yes
scrambling	yes	*no*

Schreiber and Sprouse (1998) and Hopp (2002, 2005) address the question of whether adult native speakers of English, a language which lacks scrambling, (can) come to have knowledge of the distinctions between grammatical vs. ungrammatical words orders of the type in (29). If they do, they reason, this provides evidence for the continued role of UG in adult L2 acquisition. The logic here parallels that presented earlier for bankruptcy-of-the-stimulus problems but with the added twist of necessarily taking into consideration the grammatical properties of the L1.

For German natives, the grammaticality distinctions of the kind in (29) pose a POS problem. There is no doubt that tokens of intact topicalization and scrambling of non-complex XPs are aplenty in the language surrounding learners. However, as Hopp notes, citing work by Bornkessel, Schlesewsky and Friederici (2002), Hoberg (1981) and Schlesewsky, Fanselow, Kliegl and Krems (2000):

> [C]orpus studies demonstrate that the noncanonical word orders, in particular scrambling of complex XPs and remnant movement, are highly infrequent in spoken and written German... The relative statistical difference between infrequent sentences and non-occurring ungrammatical sentences is thus very small. Therefore, observing the relative discourse frequency of noncanonical orders is unlikely to lead to a reliable distinction between rare licit and non-instantiated illicit sentences. (Hopp 2005: 42)

In other words, the source of this knowledge is not external to the learner (i.e. not in the input), which leaves as the source an internal one. UG is an excellent candidate for this source, since the explanation for the phenomena seems to implicate categories (e.g. constituents), operations (e.g. distinct movement types) and a restriction (no remnant movement involving movements of the same type – or a functional equivalent to this) that pertain only to language.

The same conclusion would hold of L1-English speakers acquiring German, if they, too, come to make this distinction between possible and impossible orders, but with two important extra steps: (i) in light of the absence of scrambling in English, knowledge of such word-order impossibilities cannot stem from the L1 grammar; (ii) additionally, German language instruction does not touch upon grammaticality contrasts of the kind in (29). With these two potential sources of knowledge excluded, this brings the L1-English L2er of German back into essentially the same learning scenario (in this domain) as that of the L1-German acquirer, set out above.

And indeed, Schreiber and Sprouse (1998) found that advanced English-German L2ers displayed knowledge of the distinctions sketched in (29) on a paper-and-pencil contextualized acceptability judgment task. Hopp (2002, 2005) likewise found that intermediate to very advanced L1-English L2ers of German also make the relevant distinctions. Hopp's experiment significantly extended this inquiry to include additional paradigms of possible and impossible (remnant) movement in German. Critical items (and fillers), following discourse-favorable contexts, were presented bimodally, in writing and recordings (where intonation naturalness was highly controlled, for both grammatical and ungrammatical items), and participants judged test sentences for acceptability. Hopp's main finding is that, like native Germans, native English-speaking L2ers of German reliably make the same relative distinctions between grammatical and ungrammatical orders, at the group level and the individual level. In sum, the results offer solid evidence of targetlike adult L2 acquisition under POS, thereby implicating UG.

Non-native language acquisition also poses a qualitatively different POS problem in certain cases, one not faced by children acquiring their native language. L2ers may well be confronted with a target language that does not license something that their L1 licenses. In other words, the target language (in this domain) is more restrictive than the L1. In this configuration – on the assumption that learners approach non-native language acquisition from the perspective of their L1 (i.e. the L1 grammar is the initial state of L2 acquisition) – the learnability problem facing L2ers is coming to know that what is allowed in the L1 is not allowed in the target language without there being direct evidence for the restriction.

Precisely this kind of L2 learnability problem is tackled in the work by H. Marsden (2004, 2009) on the L2 acquisition of interpretive (im)possibilities in Japanese doubly quantified sentences. As shown in (30), both Japanese and English allow sentences with multiple quantifiers.

(30) a. Dareka-ga   dono hon-mo   yonda
       someone-NOM every book-PRT read
       "Someone read every book."
    b. Someone read every book.

The possible interpretations of such sentences differ between the two languages. Both languages allow the *subject-wide scope* interpretation sketched in (31a), whereas English, but not Japanese, also allows the *object-wide scope* interpretation sketched in (31b).

(31) a. There is some person x such that x read every book.
    b. For each book y, some person read y.

The learnability issue at stake here is whether English speakers (can) come to know that Japanese sentences of the type in (30a) are restricted to the subject-wide scope interpretation. Moreover, in order to establish that this is an L1-induced POS problem, one first needs to know whether English speakers of lower Japanese proficiency do erroneously allow sentences like (30a) to have both interpretations of (31), as English speakers do for (30b).

The results of Marsden's (2004, 2009) research attest to both these outcomes. She tested intermediate-level and advanced-level L1-English L2ers of Japanese on the interpretation of doubly quantified sentences using a picture-sentence truth-value judgment task. Participants were first shown drawings depicting either a scene where one person performed a given action on every object (cf. the meaning in (31a)) or a scene where several people each performed the same action on their own object (cf. the meaning in (31b)); a sentence was then presented both in writing and in a recording (with natural, neutral stress), and participants judged whether it accurately captured the meaning conveyed in the drawing. Marsden finds that while intermediate L2ers associate both subject-wide scope and object-wide scope interpretations to sentences of type (30a), just as the native controls do on the English version of the task with sentences of type (30b), (a subset of) advanced L2ers consistently limit their interpretation to only subject-wide scope as the Japanese natives do. Given that direct evidence for this narrowing of interpretation comes neither from input nor from language instruction, this is another instance of overcoming bankruptcy of the stimulus in adult L2 acquisition, arguing for the continued operation of UG.[6]

7.5 Summary and conclusion

The aim of this chapter has been to discuss the concept *poverty of the stimulus* as related to language acquisition, explain why its status remains key to the generative enterprise and elaborate on the probative value of different types of POS phenomena for both L1 and L2 research. We end by emphasizing that it is in fact arguments from the bankruptcy of the stimulus that are the most compelling for concluding that in the task of language learning, humans – including L2 adults – are constrained by innate language-specific knowledge. As Joseph Emonds (p.c., class lectures 1998) expressed it, one of Noam Chomsky's most enduring contributions to linguistics is the systematic inclusion of sentences with asterisks. In our view, it is those data that best exemplify the POS.

8

Learner-internal psychological factors

Jean-Marc Dewaele

8.1 Introduction

A familiar question among second language learners and second language teachers is why the learning process is a such struggle, leading to limited proficiency for some learners, while others in the same situation seem to breeze through and attain high levels of proficiency in the L2. Instinctively, learners and teachers believe that the cause must be psychological, and that some hidden internal characteristic of the L2 learner predetermines a more or a less successful outcome. Much of the early research in individual differences in SLA has tried to unearth a single source of these differences in order to establish the profile of the good language learner (Naiman, Fröhlich, Stern and Todesco 1978; Rubin 1975). This quest has turned into a search for the holy grail for "researchers, like [King] Arthur's knights, stumbling through the night, guided by a stubborn belief that something must be there, glimpsing tantalizing flashes of light from a distance, only to discover that their discoveries looked rather pale in the daylight" (Dewaele 2009a: 625).

While the search for psychological independent variables in SLA continues, more and more researchers accept that a dynamic perspective is necessary, acknowledging the complex interplay of independent variables in SLA (Dewaele and Furnham 1999; Dörnyei 2009a, b; Dörnyei and Ushioda 2009). The learner's psychological profile may play a role, but only in a particular context. Learners have unique previous histories that may, for example, determine their reaction to an L2 class and shape their future trajectories. Research on variation in L2 learners' performance at a given time and in their progress as learners and users has identified a wide range of factors linked to the individual's language learning history, his/her current linguistic practices and particular language constellation, and the educational context and the wider sociopolitical context. The driving force behind individual difference research is thus the quest to identify the interaction between learners' internal psychological characteristics and external factors. Doing so successfully might bring us closer to a Grand Unified Theory of Individual Differences (Dewaele 2009a: 625).

Personality psychology has been a source of inspiration for SLA researchers looking for variables that could be linked to various aspects of L2 learning and production. However, research on SLA and personality presents some obstacles, which might explain why – as we shall see – there are relatively few researchers working in this area. One problem facing both linguists and psychologists is finding an appropriate level of analysis for both the personality and the language variables (Furnham 1990: 92). There is an absence of:

> parsimonious, consistent, fruitful theories described specifically for, or derived from, the personality markers of speech... the theories that do exist are frequently at an inappropriate level – too molecular in that they deal specifically with the relationship between a restricted number of selected variables or too molar in the sense that by being overinclusive they are either unverifiable or unfruitful in the extent to which they generate testable hypotheses.

Linguists might feel confused by the multiplicity of theories in the field of personality research, and have difficulty accessing the personality questionnaires because they are usually not available in the general domain. The few researchers who have ventured into this area of research have combined a wide variety of independent and dependent variables, often defined differently from study to study, which has produced mixed results and makes the interpretation of the findings difficult (Dörnyei 2005).

The present chapter is organized as follows: I will start by briefly reviewing the main findings in SLA research on attitudes and motivation, which could be described as a combination of learner-internal and learner-external factors. As this area of inquiry is vast, I will restrict myself to the major developments, without going into the specifics of individual studies (see Dörnyei and Ushioda 2009 for an excellent overview). I will then look at the SLA literature on learner-internal characteristics and focus on language talent and aptitude, working memory and short-term memory, and the transfer of first language skills to the L2. In the third and final section I will look in some detail at studies that have linked language production with personality traits: four so-called super-traits (Extraversion (which has attracted most attention in SLA research), Neuroticism, Conscientiousness and Openness-to-Experience) and two so-called lower-order personality traits connected to Foreign Language Anxiety (FLA, Trait Emotional Intelligence and Perfectionism). Finally, I will propose some tentative conclusions about the role of psychological factors in SLA research.

8.2 Language attitudes and motivation

SLA researchers point to concepts such as motivation (including attitude), investment or desire as being at the heart of success in foreign language learning. Yet these are not stable personality traits, as they might appear and disappear, even over a short time span. The work of Gardner and Lambert (1972) and Gardner (1985) is generally considered to be the seminal work in SLA (MacIntyre 2007). To begin with, Gardner (1985) defines attitude as "an evaluative reaction to some referent or attitude object, inferred on the basis of the individual beliefs or opinions about the referent" (1985: 9). Attitudes form part of language learning motivation, which is defined as "the combination of effort plus desire to achieve the goal of learning the language plus favorable attitudes toward learning the language" (Gardner 1985: 10). Gardner's socio-educational model is grounded in the social environment: it articulates the impact of larger social forces such as intergroup attitudes, cultural identification and familial influence on the L2 learning process (Gardner 1985, 2010; MacIntyre, Clément, Dörnyei and Noels 1998). Learners' motivation and levels thereof do not emerge in a vacuum; they originate, are influenced and are maintained by attitudes towards the learning situation and so-called integrative orientation, i.e. that which reflects "a sincere and personal interest in the people and culture represented by the other group" (Gardner and Lambert 1972: 132), which, combined with "favorable attitudes toward the language learning situation and a heightened motivation to learn the language" (Gardner 2010: 202) is argued to lead to better results in the L2 compared to peers with lower levels of integrativeness.

Motivation can also be supported by so-called instrumentality, i.e. "conditions where the language is being studied for practical or utilitarian purposes" (Gardner 2006: 249). Learners with high levels of instrumental orientation or motivation also tend to score better than those with lower such levels on L2 proficiency measures (Gardner 2006). It is the integrative motivation concept that has been most hotly debated in discussions on motivation with some researchers defending a strong version of the concept, namely social identification and integration and others defending a weak version, namely a sense of affiliation and interest.

Ideally, motivation should explain why a given person opts for certain actions, and how long and how hard that person is willing to persist at certain activities (Dörnyei and Skehan 2003: 614). Yet after three decades of research on motivation, Dörnyei (2001: 2) noted that it is "one of the most elusive concepts in the whole of social sciences" because it is a multi-faceted, complex and composite construct: some components are more trait-like and others are more state-like and situation-specific (Dörnyei 2006: 50).[1] In the 1990s, a number of researchers had already started challenging aspects of Gardner's model, defending a more situated approach to the study of motivation (Crookes and Schmidt 1991; Dörnyei 1994; Oxford and Shearin 1994). Dörnyei argued for a stronger focus on the influence of the immediate learning context on learners' overall disposition and the effect of this motivation on concrete learning processes within a given classroom context (Dörnyei 1994). Towards the end of the 1990s, Dörnyei drew closer attention to the temporal/process aspects of motivation (Dörnyei and Otto 1998) and later presented motivation as a "dynamic system that displays continuous fluctuation, going through certain ebbs and flows" (Dörnyei 2006: 51).

Since the mid 2000s, Dörnyei has turned to new approaches to attitudes and motivation, abandoning Gardner's concept of integrativeness. This was prompted by the realization that the concept of integrative orientation is hard to apply when there is no specific group of speakers (Ushioda and Dörnyei 2009: 3), and that at least for English as a global lingua franca, it no longer belongs to the different groups of native speakers of English. An alternative interpretation would be that the recognition of English's role as a lingua franca did not fit conventional understandings of integrativeness and came as a result of continued efforts to reconsider integrativeness, rather than being the spur for those efforts. Ushioda and Dörnyei point to Yashima's (2002) revised notion of integrativeness, namely "international posture," as being better adapted to the new status of English. She defines it with reference to Japanese learners of English as "interest in foreign or international affairs, willingness to go overseas to stay or work, readiness to interact with intercultural partners, and ... openness or a non-ethnocentric attitude toward different cultures" (Yashima 2002: 57). Kormos and Csizér (2008) conclude that integrativeness is also a problematic construct in Hungary, where very few learners have direct contact with native speakers of English and instead learners' attitudes and motivation are shaped through media products and through the perceived importance of contact with foreigners (Csizér and Kormos 2008).

Dörnyei and colleagues have drawn on the psychological theory of "possible selves" to focus more on the learner's self-concept and identification aspects (Csizér and Dörnye 2005; Dörnyei 2005). A learner imagines an Ideal L2 Self, which is the representation of all the attributes that that person would like to possess, including the mastery of an L2. The learner also develops an Ought-to L2 Self, having the attributes that that person believes one should possess. L2 motivation can then be seen as the desire to reduce the perceived discrepancies between the learner's actual self and his/her ideal or ought-to L2 selves: "A basic hypothesis is that if proficiency in the target language is part and parcel of one's ideal or ought-to self, this will serve as a powerful motivator to learn the language because of our psychological desire to reduce the discrepancy between our current and possible future selves" (Ushioda and Dörnyei 2009: 4). Motivation is also linked to a third dimension,

L2 Learning Experience, which concerns situation-specific motives related to the immediate learning environment and experience (Dörnyei 2006).

While most work on attitude and motivation has been carried out with a cross-sectional design using quantitative methodology, some researchers, such as Ushioda (2001), have carried out longitudinal qualitative studies. The latter have shown that motivation for learning a foreign language is linked to various dimensions such as academic interest, language-related enjoyment, desired levels of L2 competence, personal goals, positive learning history, personal satisfaction, feelings about countries or people where the L2 is spoken as well as to external pressures. Ushioda (2001) thus sees motivation not as a cause or the product of specific learning experiences but rather an ongoing, dynamic process. Indeed, learners' preferences for specific teachers or methods can affect their motivation over a period of years and the need for more such longitudinal research into motivation has been noted by Woodrow (2012). Woodrow thus argues that "to get a deep insight into the dynamic and shifting nature of motivation longitudinal and in-depth qualitative studies are necessary." In addition, successful L2 learners typically engage more often in intrinsic motivational processes, rather than being externally regulated by the teacher. They take control of their affective learning experience, see themselves as agents of the processes that shape their motivation to sustain their involvement in language learning (Ushioda 2001, 2008). This finding echoes Rubin's (2008) observation that the good language learner is able to self-manage. Less successful learners focus more on external incentives and blame factors beyond their control for their lack of progress (Ushioda 2001, 2008). A related concept is self-efficacy, i.e. people's beliefs in their capabilities to perform in ways that give them some control over events that affect their lives (Bandura 1999). Self-efficacy has been described as an important component of motivation (Hu and Reiterer 2009; Ushioda 2012).

Several researchers working in the postmodernist tradition have criticized traditional social psychological L2 motivation research (see also Chapter 11, this volume). Norton (2000: 4) argues in favor of a comprehensive theory of identity that integrates the language learner and the language learning context. She proposes the notion of investment of learners in an L2, their effort being sustained by the understanding that the acquisition of a wider range of symbolic and material resources will enhance their cultural capital, their identity and their desires for the future. Pavlenko (2002) has criticized the monolingual and monocultural bias of social psychological approaches to L2 motivation which imply a view of the world in terms of "homogeneous and monolingual cultures, or in-groups and out-groups, and of individuals who move from one group to another" (Pavlenko 2002: 279). Kramsch (2009a) argues that more attention needs to be devoted to the subjective aspects of SLA where for some learners the desire to learn a new language reflects "the urge to escape from a state of tedious conformity with one's present environment to a state of plenitude and enhanced power" (2009a: 14). Other learners, however, have "a deep desire not to challenge the language of their environment but to find in the foreign words a confirmation of the meaning they express in their mother tongue" (2009a: 15).

Dewaele (2010: 132) reported the importance of random events in triggering the desire or motivation to learn a new language. The fictional character, originally published in German in 2004 and in English in 2008, Raimund Gregorius (in Pascal Mercier's *Night Train to Lisbon*), a Swiss-German teacher of Latin, ancient Greek and Hebrew with little interest in modern languages, experiences such an unexpected trigger event one morning on his way to school. A mysterious woman is about to jump off a bridge in the driving rain. He manages to bring her to her senses and after a short conversation in French, he finds out that she is a native speaker of Portuguese. The way she pronounces "*Português*" enchants him: "The *o* she pronounced surprisingly as a *u*; the rising, strangely constrained lightness of the *é* and the soft *sh* at the end came together in a melody that sounded much longer than it really was, and that he could have listened to all day long" (2008: 7). His infatuation with Portuguese starts right there. He hones his nascent skills at home with a record of a Portuguese language course, repeating "the same sentences again and again to narrow the distance between his stolid enunciation and the twinkling voice on the record" (2008: 22). His rapid progress triggers a second epiphany: "Português. How different the word sounded now! Before it had possessed the magic of a jewel from a distant inaccessible land and now it was like one of a thousand gems in a palace whose door he had just pushed open" (2008: 23). Gregorius takes the night train to Lisbon, where he is forced to rely entirely on his beginner's Portuguese in order to trace the author of a book he bought earlier in his hometown. He controls his communicative anxiety in Portuguese and becomes both braver and wiser in the process. His sudden passion for Portuguese could be described as a desire, an investment, a high motivation, combined with a social and geographical displacement. The enthusiasm at his new-found skills liberates him from self-imposed limitation and alters his sense of self.

Postmodernists (and others) point out that moving to the target language country is not sufficient in itself to boost learners' language skills. For example, the uniqueness of the study abroad experience is linked to very different linguistic outcomes. Kinginger (2008, 2009) found that the huge interindividual differences in grammatical and sociolinguistic competence of her American students' after their stay in France were linked to material conditions (lodged in dormitories with other foreign students or housed with guest families) but also to their life histories, aspirations, commitment and psychological factors such as gregariousness and self-image.

In sum, postmodernist researchers reject what they perceive to be the simplistic explanations of complex phenomena in SLA by social psychologists, and they defend a more socially situated, emic perspective, where learners are crucial witnesses of their own learning process over a period of time. It is this perspective that helps researchers understand individual differences in language learning achievement.

One question that arises from the observation of large amounts of variation in levels of L2 motivation/investment is whether this is linked to nature or nurture. Krashen (1981) argued in favor of nature, postulating that personality variables are linked to motivational variables under his Affective Filter. Learners with an analytic orientation are expected to have a more favorable attitude toward the general learning context and Krashen also predicted that learners with an outgoing personality, high self-esteem and low anxiety would be more successful in SLA (lowering the Filter). The latter was confirmed by Ożańska-Ponikwia and Dewaele (2012). No link seems to exist between L2 motivation and personality (Dewaele 2005b: 127), but it is possible that some aspects of personality might make learners more or less prone to experience a trigger event that might ignite a sudden passion for a new language. Such an event could be the fortuitous encounter with a speaker of a foreign language (such as Gregorius' encounter with Portuguese described above), or any cultural object that suddenly sparks an interest in that language and culture.

8.3 Language talent and language aptitude

8.3.1 The talented L2 learner

Jilka (2009) notes that the idea that a certain talent is innate and therefore reflected in a person's biological makeup is relatively straightforward when it refers to purely physical talent (see Chapter 20, this volume). However, the idea that non-physical abilities such as L2 learning could be linked to the brain is not as widely accepted, despite being a logical extension of this line of reasoning (Jilka 2009: 2). Do some people have a gift for languages? Dörnyei and Skehan (2003: 590) define language learning aptitude as a "specific talent for learning... languages which exhibits considerable variation between learners." The problem is that compared, for example, to musical, logical or spatial talent, foreign language talent consists of different independent linguistic skills and cannot be measured by a single instrument (see Chapter 6, this volume). Having language talent might involve a number of seemingly unrelated cognitive factors that interact and determine a learner's overall capacity to master a second language (Dörnyei 2006: 46). Language aptitude in itself does not predict whether or not a person is able to learn a second language, it merely predicts "the rate of progress the individual is likely to make in learning" (Dörnyei 2006: 43) under optimal conditions. When the conditions are good, learners with higher levels of talent or ability will be more successful language learners (Gardner 2006: 241). Robinson (2002c) has focused specifically on the interaction between an individual's aptitude (defined as the sum of lower-level abilities, so-called aptitude complexes, which can be grouped into higher-order cognitive abilities) and the learning situation/conditions:

> Profiling individual differences in cognitive abilities, and matching these profiles to effective instructional options, such as types of pedagogic tasks, interventionist focus on form techniques, and more broadly defined learning conditions, is a major aim of pedagogically oriented language aptitude research. (Robinson 2002c: 113)

Robinson thus views L2 learning aptitude as a highly complex and dynamic construct where clusters of learner variables interact with a range of L2 learning tasks and teaching techniques.

A number of neurobiologists in the late 1980s started looking for physical and chemical evidence of language talent in the brain of exceptional language learners. Geschwind and Galaburda (1985), for example, linked pathological (exceptional) language talent to the increased growth of particular brain areas (triggered by the delayed growth of others). Schneiderman and Desmarais (1988) argued that superior neurocognitive flexibility is helpful in SLA because the system established for L1 must be bypassed by the learner. To acquire L2 pronunciation, for example, learners need to bypass established motor pathways in order to control articulatory movements. Language talent has also been linked to specific brain anatomy or greater brain plasticity in talented individuals (de Bot 2006). Mechelli *et al.* (2004) and Golestani, Molko, Dehaene, LeBihan and Pallier (2006) have reported physical differences between the brains of bilingual learners and those of monolingual controls. Bilingual learners had greater grey matter density in the inferior left parietal cortex, a region of the brain which has been shown by functional imaging to become activated during verbal-fluency tasks. However, it is unclear whether this is the consequence of the learning of a new language, or a pre-existing characteristic of the brain affecting aptitude. Hu and Reiterer (2009) are confident that future brain imaging research on the relationship between personality and language aptitude will "provide the chance to directly map brain anatomy and activities onto psychological phenomena" (2009: 102).

Other cognitive abilities may play a role in SLA. Slevc and Miyake (2006) looked at the effect of musical ability on SLA. Their dependent variables represented four domains of L2 ability: receptive phonology, productive phonology, syntax and lexical knowledge. The independent variables included age of L2 immersion, patterns of language use and exposure, and phonological short-term memory. The authors used hierarchical regression analyses to determine if musical ability explained any unique variance in each domain of L2 ability after controlling for other relevant factors. They found that musical ability predicted L2 phonological ability (both receptive and productive) even when controlling for other factors, but did not explain unique variance in L2 syntax or lexical knowledge. L2 learners with musical skills may thus only have an advantage in the acquisition of L2 sound structure.

Nardo and Reiterer (2009) have also investigated the link between musicality and phonetic language aptitude. Statistical analyses revealed significant positive correlations between musicality and L2 productive phonetic talent (as measured by a pronunciation talent score) as well as the aptitude for grammatical sensitivity (as measured by the Modern Language Aptitude Test). The rhythm subscore, followed by the pitch discrimination score and the self-evaluated singing scores correlated positively with all the language measures.

8.3.2 Working memory and short-term memory

Dörnyei (2005) has described the SLA research into the relationship between working memory (WM) (which involves "the temporary storage and manipulation of information that is assumed to be necessary for a wide range of complex activities" (Baddeley 2003: 189)) and learning as "one of the most promising current directions in language aptitude studies" (Dörnyei 2005: 56; see also Chapter 6, this volume). Dörnyei (2005) singles out the verbal component of Baddeley's model of WM, namely the phonological loop, which he considers "to be an ideally suited memory construct for SLA" (Dörnyei 2005: 55). WM is typically operationalized as the ability to mentally maintain information in an active and readily accessible state while concurrently and selectively processing new information. Short-term memory (STM) is often operationalized as a sort of static memory that holds information for a short period of time (less than 20 seconds). It is the mechanisms of executive control that differentiate WM from STM (Baddeley 2003).

Both Robinson (2003) and Skehan (1998) have concluded that memory ability plays a crucial role in SLA after reviewing the literature on "good" to "exceptional" language learners: "Exceptionally successful foreign language learners consistently seem to be characterised by the possession of unusual memories, particularly for the retention of verbal material" (Skehan 1998: 233). Indeed, capacity in WM is the central component of language aptitude according to Miyake and Friedman (1998: 339). They point to the literature showing a link between L1 WM capacity and both L2 WM capacity and L2 language comprehension skills and acquisition. Their own empirical study with native speakers of Japanese who were advanced learners of English showed that a higher WM capacity was linked to the acquisition of appropriate linguistic cues and better comprehension of complex sentence structures in the L2 (1998: 361). Robinson (2002c) has also underlined the striking correlation between WM capacity and L2 proficiency.

To illustrate how this works, we can refer to Biedroń and Szczepaniak (2009), who present a cognitive profile of "Ann," a highly talented 21-year-old trilingual Polish learner of Japanese. The results show particularly high scores in the area of phonological, analytical and memory abilities. She did not prefer any particular learning strategy but had very positive attitudes towards Japanese, was highly motivated and she did not feel anxious, or inhibited when speaking a foreign language (2009: 15). Biedroń (to appear) then investigated the link between aptitude and WM–STM among Polish foreign language learners. She compared the results of twenty-three high-ability learners (who knew between three and ten languages) with the scores of thirty-six first-year English students who had been learning English for seven to ten years before university. The research revealed that STM and WM scores of the highly able learners were significantly higher than those of the first-year students. The differences were especially great for memory tests based on linguistic material, in particular for the (Polish) WM test, which could not be influenced by the knowledge of English. This suggests that L1 aptitude might be transferable to the L2. Similarly, Towell and Dewaele (2005) discovered significant positive correlations between speaking rate in English L1 and speaking rate in the French L2 production of twelve students before and after a period abroad. However, no significant relationship emerged between shadowing rates (the percentage of text produced on the recording that had been repeated by participants; linked to WM) in both languages.

8.3.3 Transfer of L1 aptitude to L2

One interesting avenue of aptitude research is the link between L1 and L2 language aptitude. It seems that 13- and 14-year-old children who score highly on verbal tests in their L1 do equally well in their L2, which could be evidence of an innate aptitude for languages (Skehan 1989). However, Skehan also emphasized that the L1 could only explain part of the variance because aptitude also reflects the ability to handle decontextualized language material. Dewaele (2007a) reported strong positive correlations between language grades obtained by Flemish high-school students for the L1 (Dutch) and their grades in the L2, L3 and L4 (French, English and Spanish). The same individuals thus tended to get the highest scores in all language classes, which could be related to cognitive or social factors, or to a combination of both.

Sparks, Patton, Ganschow and Humbach (2009) defend the view that a long-term crosslinguistic transfer from L1 to L2 exists. In this study the authors investigated the relationship of L1 skills in primary school and L2 learning in secondary school. Fifty-four students from a rural school district in the US were classified as high-, average-, and low-proficiency L2 learners (2009: 203). The three groups were compared on L1 achievement measures of reading, spelling, vocabulary, phonological awareness and listening comprehension administered at ages 6, 8 and 10 (2009: 203). The L2 aptitude measures were word-decoding and spelling measures while the outcome measures were oral and written L2 proficiency measures in Spanish, French and German administered at the end of two years of L2 study (2009: 203). Results showed significant differences between the three proficiency groups in the L1 achievement measures, with the high-proficiency L2 learners exhibiting stronger L1 skills and L2 aptitude than the average- and low-proficiency L2 learners. The authors conclude that: "students' early L1 skills are strongly related to their L2 learning several years later and... L1 skills may be an important source of individual differences among L2 learners" (2009: 226–27).

8.4 Personality traits

Personality traits "refer to consistent patterns in the way individuals behave, feel and think" (Pervin and Cervone 2010: 228). They thus "summarize a person's typical behavior" (2010: 229). There is widespread agreement in the psychological community that individual differences can be organized in a simple coherent taxonomy consisting of five broad, bipolar dimensions, the so-called Big Five (2010: 228). Participants who rate themselves in personality questionnaires get scores on the various dimensions.

The dimensions are Extraversion vs. Introversion; Neuroticism vs. Emotional Stability; Conscientiousness vs. Lack of Direction; Agreeableness vs. Antagonism; and Openness to new Experience vs. Closedness (Pervin and Cervone 2010: 262). Factors similar to the Big Five have been found in languages across the world and this has been interpreted by some psychologists as evidence that "the Big Five personality structure is a human universal" (2010: 265). Indeed McCrae *et al.* (2000) argue that the Big Five have a biological basis and are not influenced directly by the environment. However, Pervin and Cervone (2010) point to studies that have demonstrated an effect of sociocultural and historical changes on personality trait scores. It is not entirely clear either whether "each and every individual in the population possesses each of the five factors" (2010: 273).

Some personality questionnaires use "yes/no" feedback in response to a statement such as "Can you get a party going?" or "Are you a talkative person?" Every dimension typically has about ten items that probe typical behavior linked to that dimension. The two previous statements refer to extraversion. A participant may answer "no" to the first statement and "yes" to the second one. The score on a dimension represents the sum of ticks ("yes" or "no" depending on the direction of the question). Other personality questionnaires invite participants to choose a numerical value on a Likert scale, ranging from "disagree completely" to "agree completely." Traits are continuous dimensions of variability on some trait and they are normally distributed. In other words, more participants are situated in the middle of a dimension rather than at its extremes. It means, for example, that there are more ambiverts than either extraverts or introverts. The Big Five personality traits are situated at the summit of the hierarchy; there are many narrower facets, also called "lower-order" personality traits, that are often correlated with Big Five traits but also explain unique variance. While there is little doubt that the "super-traits" or the Big Five and "lower-order" traits determine behavior in general, it is less clear to what extent they affect foreign language behavior. I will also present a short overview of some of the SLA research linked to three personality traits, namely emotional intelligence, foreign language anxiety and perfectionism.

8.4.1 Extraversion vs. introversion

According to Eysenck and Eysenck (1985), variation on this dimension is linked to the amount of cortical arousal, which in turn leads to different behaviors. While extraverts are under-aroused, introverts are over-aroused. The consequence of this is that extraverts compensate for their suboptimal arousal levels by tending towards activities that involve greater sensory stimulation while introverts will instead try to avoid over-arousing situations. Eysenck also developed an objective measure of the extraversion dimension, namely the "lemon drop test": extraverts were found to produce more saliva than introverts when a fixed amount of juice was placed on their tongue (Pervin and Cervone 2010: 250).

Eysenck and Eysenck (1964: 8) described a typical extravert as someone who "is sociable, likes parties, has many friends, needs to have many people to talk to ... craves excitement, takes chances, often sticks his neck out, acts on the spur of the moment, and is generally an impulsive individual." On the other hand, a typical introvert is someone who "is a quiet, retiring sort of person, introspective, fond of books rather than people: he is reserved and distant except to intimate friends. He tends to plan ahead, 'looks before he leaps,' and distrusts the impulse of the moment. He does not 'like excitement'" (Eysenck and Eysenck 1964: 8).

Extraverts' low autonomic arousability and the insensitivity to punishment signals thus make them more stress-resistant while introverts have higher levels of the neurotransmitter dopamine (Lieberman 2000). Stress releases extra dopamine, which might push individuals over the very narrow range of optimal innervation in the dorsolateral prefrontal cortex and impair attentional and WM processes (Lieberman and Rosenthal 2001). This neurological difference between extraverts and introverts might explain why extraverts are superior to introverts in STM and WM (Lieberman 2000). The combination of extraverts' speed of retrieval of information from memory and their higher degree of physiological stress resistance would explain their better performance in high-stimulation environments such as a foreign language classroom.

Linguists have focused their attention on the possible effect of extraversion on success in L2 learning, the expectation being that the more talkative, gregarious extravert learners have a natural advantage in the acquisition of the L2 compared to their more introverted peers. However, studies where extraversion scores were correlated with language test scores revealed inconsistent results. In a review of SLA research that included extraversion as an independent variable, Dewaele and Furnham (1999) point out that the extraversion variable became "unloved" by researchers because of a single partially flawed study by Naiman, Fröhlich, Stern and Todesco (1978) on personality and language learning. The authors expected good language learners, i.e. Canadian secondary-school students learning French as an L2 who scored highest on the Listening Test of French Achievement and an Imitation Test, to have a distinctive psychological profile. The research was inspired by Rubin's insightful observation that "the good language learner is...comfortable with uncertainty...and willing to try out his guesses" (Rubin 1975: 45). This seems to fit the description of an extravert learner, hence the expectation of Naiman and his co-authors to find a positive correlation between extraversion and test scores. When the link failed to materialize, they questioned the construct validity of the Eysenck Personality Inventory/EPI, which was used to calculate extraversion scores (Naiman *et al.* 1978: 67), rather than wondering whether their choice of dependent variables might have affected the unexpected result. The resulting negative publicity for extraversion was so strong that researchers have generally turned away from it.

Dewaele and Furnham (1999) suggested that if Naiman *et al.* (1978) had used a wider variety of more sophisticated linguistic variables, covering not only written language but also natural communicative oral language, they might have found that the construct validity of the EPI was not to blame for the lack of expected relationships. Indeed, the few studies that have correlated extraversion scores with oral fluency measures did report significant effects. For example, Rossier (1976) found that extraverts were more fluent that introverts on a pictorial stimulus test, and Vogel and Vogel (1986) reported that more introverted German students had longer pauses – indicating a lower level of fluency – in their oral French interlanguage. Extraverts have been found to be more fluent in oral L2 production, speaking faster with fewer filled pauses (Dewaele 1998; Wakamoto 2000).

Dewaele and Furnham (2000) found significant correlations between extraversion scores of Flemish university students producing French interlanguage in dyadic conversations and the values of linguistic variables reflecting style choice, fluency and accuracy. Extraversion was not significantly linked to morpholexical accuracy rates. While the extraverts were found to have higher speech rates and fewer filled pauses, they also exhibited lower values of lexical richness, more implicit/deictical speech styles and shorter utterances than the introverts, especially in a stressful formal exam situation. We speculated that these differences are linked to the fact that L2 production is less automatic (i.e. less based on implicit knowledge) than L1 production and relies more on declarative knowledge which requires more STM capacity (Dewaele 2002b). This could be particularly problematic for introvert L2 users who have less STM capacity. Reduced STM capacity means that units of linguistic information would have to queue before being processed, causing a slowdown in processing and in fluency. Dewaele (2002b) compares the stacking of linguistic information to a bottleneck in an airport control tower, forcing planes to fly in circles above the runway. Extravert L2 users experience less disruption in the functioning of the STM and WM, allowing them to remain flexible and fluent. Extraverts are able to allocate extra resources to task completion and message preparation while taking contextual cues into account in order to readjust their speech pragmatically.

Smart, Elton and Burnett (1970) was one of the first studies to consider the link between extraversion and success in L2 learning (measured by grades and the Scholastic Aptitude Test/SAT). The authors report that in a group of eighty-four female American subjects, the thirteen with the best grades for intermediate French at secondary school and the highest academic aptitude scores were significantly more introverted. However, Chastain (1975) reported completely opposite results. He analyzed the relationship between the final grades of American university students learning French, Spanish and German in beginners' courses and personality variables including anxiety, outgoing personality/extraversion and creativity. While no clear link emerged between reserved and outgoing for the learners of French, a positive relationship emerged for the learners of Spanish and the learners of German. For no group did SAT verbal ability scores correlate significantly with any personality variable. Chastain admitted that course grades may have been calculated differently for the different languages and that grades are not the best measure of language achievement. Dewaele (2007a) found negative, but non-significant, correlations between extraversion and language grades in the Dutch L1, French L2, English L3 and German L4 of Flemish high-school students. This suggests that language students with higher grades tend to be more introverted. A separate study on the same sample showed that extraversion was also not linked to foreign language attitudes (Dewaele 2005b).

Vocabulary is the area where differences between extraverts and introverts are most likely. A weak negative relationship emerged between extraversion and vocabulary test performance in a group of EFL students in Indonesia (Carrell, Prince and Astika 1996). However, extraverts and introverts did not perform differently on tests measuring reading comprehension, grammar and writing. Clearer effects emerged in Kiani's (1997) study, which focused on the relationship between extraversion and scores on standard English proficiency tests (TOEFL, IELTS) among adult Iranian students learning English. Introverts scored higher on the subcomponent of reading comprehension and vocabulary. However, Morimoto's (2006) study of EFL learners in New Zealand failed to uncover statistically significant differences between extraverts and introverts in depth of knowledge of vocabulary and grammatical knowledge.

Level of stimulation may well play a role. For example, MacIntyre, Clément and Noels' (2007) study of the interaction between learning situation and extraversion on vocabulary test scores of Canadian French L2 learners found that introverts were found to perform best after having studied in a very familiar situation, while the extraverts performed best in conditions involving a moderate degree of novelty (2007: 296). The researchers also found an interaction between person and situation in the trait "willingness to communicate," which showed that not every extravert is more willing than an introvert to communicate. Finally, while Busch (1982) did not find a relationship between Japanese ELF learners' extraversion scores and results of written vocabulary and grammar tests, cloze tests, dictation and oral comprehension tests, the extraverts were found to score lower on pronunciation scores.

Oya, Manalo and Greenwood (2004) looked at the link between the personality of Japanese students and their oral performance in English L2. The extraverts were not significantly more fluent or accurate and their speech was not more complex than introverts. However, extraverts were perceived to be more confident and better able to establish rapport with their audience, which resulted in higher global impressions scores.

Van Daele, Housen, Pierrard and Debrugh (2006) reported equally ambiguous findings on the link between extraversion and the development of fluency, complexity and accuracy in Flemish secondary school students' L2 English and French. Extraverts scored higher on lexical complexity in both foreign languages, but the effect disappeared the following year. This could be the result of a methodological artefact, namely that the extraverts got bored with repeating the task a second time and made less of an effort (2006: 227).

One of the most in-depth studies on personality and success in SLA is Ehrman (2008), who used an updated good language learner design. She selected a sample of sixty-two language learners who had obtained a level 4 (i.e. "full professional proficiency, with few if any limitations on the person's ability to function in the language and culture" (2008: 64)) on an oral interview test (out of more than 3000 learners), this top 2 percent thus represents "the true elite of good language learners" (2008: 61). She used the Myers-Briggs Type Indicator (MBTI) to establish personality types (four scales: extraversion–introversion, sensing–intuition, thinking–feeling, judging–perceiving; combining into sixteen possible four-letter types). As the variables were nominal, she used frequencies and crosstabs analyses to determine which personality type was most frequent among the level 4 participants. Only one type was significantly overrepresented, namely INTJ types (introverted–intuitive–thinking–judging) (2008: 64). She concludes that "the best language learners tend to have introverted personalities, a finding which runs contrary to much of the literature, and, even, to pedagogical intuition. The best learners are intuitive and they are logical and precise thinkers who are able to exercise judgment" (2008: 70).

Research linking extraversion with functional practice strategies in real communicative L2 situations has shown some interesting results. Ehrman and Oxford (1990) found that extraverts tend to prefer social strategies, like cooperation with others or asking for clarification, and also use more functional practice strategies such as seeking opportunities to use a foreign language outside the class environment. This finding was confirmed by Wakamoto (2000), who found a positive correlation between functional practice strategies, social-affective strategies and extraversion among Japanese learners of English. A similar finding emerged in Wakamoto (2009), based on a similar population, where more extraverted students reported using more metacognitive and social-affective strategies than introverted students (2009: 78). Observation of teacher-fronted classes revealed that extraverts, not introverts, were using social-affective strategies; however, the latter did use more social-affective strategies in group activities and individual learning (2009: 121).

Extraverts' inclination to take risks includes linguistic risks. For example, Jay (2009) found that swearing in L1 production is positively correlated with extraversion, and more extravert L2 learners tend to use more colloquial and emotional words than their more introverted peers (Dewaele 2004c; Dewaele and Pavlenko 2002). Extraverts were also found to use more mildly stigmatized sociolinguistic variants in their French L2 (Dewaele 2004c). The research suggests that extraverts are less reluctant to use stigmatized language and more willing to engage in potentially more "dangerous" emotion-laden topics. The more risky linguistic behavior of extraverts could be linked to a superior pragmatic competence and awareness. Li, Chen and Xiao (2009) reported that extravert Chinese English majors scored significantly higher than their more introverted peers on pragmatic competence in English L2.

To sum up, it seems that both extraverts and introverts have specific strengths and weaknesses in SLA and oral L2 production. Overall, these strengths and weaknesses cancel each other out, so that it impossible to conclude which is the desirable end of the extraversion–introversion dimension for SLA and oral L2 production.

8.4.2 Neuroticism vs. emotional stability

People who score high on Neuroticism (N) tend to feel more "tense, nervous, unstable, discontented and emotional" (Pervin and Cervone 2010: 262). Those with low scores on N can be described as calm, contented and unemotional. Although personality traits are independent dimensions, some interaction can occur whereby neuroticism affects extraverts and introverts differently so that "neurotic introverts [are]... most likely to suffer... phobias, obsessional-compulsive rituals, anxiety states and neurotic depression. Neurotic extraverts, on the other hand, ... [are] most susceptible to hysteria... " (Eysenck and Eysenck 1985: 312). As is the case for other dimensions, most people are situated in the middle of this dimension (Bell curve).

Chamorro-Premuzic, Furnham and Petrides (2006: 148) reported that low-N individuals scored significantly higher on verbal ability than high-N individuals. The authors suggest that higher levels of neuroticism may impair cognitive performance, "thus moderating the effects of actual cognitive ability on tested intelligence – mainly because of their likelihood to elicit test anxiety and lack of confidence" (2006: 149). Two other studies on monolingual participants investigated the link between Neuroticism and language measures. Steer (1974) found no link between speech rate and neuroticism. However, Campbell and Rushton (1978) found that teacher ratings of Neuroticism correlated with pausing before responding during a conversation. No relationship was found between Neuroticism and foreign language attitudes of Flemish students (Dewaele 2007a), but high-N participants scored higher on Foreign Language Anxiety (FLA) (Dewaele 2002a). However, Neuroticism did not correlate with Flemish students' foreign language grades (Dewaele 2007a).

8.4.3 Conscientiousness

Individuals who score high on this dimension are systematic, meticulous, efficient, organized, reliable, responsible and hard-working. Conscientiousness is further associated with persistence, self-discipline and achievement striving (Busato, Prins, Elshout and Hamaker 2000). Furnham and Chamorro-Premuzic (2006) reported that individuals with higher fluid intelligence may make less of an effort, resulting in more able individuals being less conscientious (2006: 81). However, their own study showed that conscientious people had higher General Knowledge scores (2006: 84). Highly conscientious L2 learners would be expected to be harder-working language learners, and Wilson (2008) provides evidence in support of the prediction: British students studying French at the Open University who scored higher on Conscientiousness – measured through the OCEAN Personality Assessment[2] – were more likely to complete the course successfully.

Ehrman's (2008) description of participants who combine intuition and thinking fits the profile of high Conscientiousness. She describes them as being merciless with themselves, always trying to improve their competence and mastery of the target language. They are also more likely to be strategic thinkers, using metacognitive strategies (goal-setting, self-assessment, self-monitoring) (2008: 67). They have a penchant for analysis and love relatively fine distinctions (2008: 67). They also strive to be precise in their use of words, expressions and grammar (2008: 67).

8.4.4 Openness-to-Experience

Openness-to-Experience encompasses aspects of intellectual curiosity, creativity, imagination and aesthetic sensibility. Individuals with high scores on Openness-to-Experience would have "a greater predisposition to engage in intellectually stimulating activities that lead to higher knowledge acquisition" (Furnham and Chamorro-Premuzic 2006: 81). Openness-to-Experience is significantly related to intelligence (McCrae and Costa 1985). Young (2007) found that open mindedness was a good predictor of foreign language learning achievement. Verhoeven and Vermeer (2002) reported that Openness-to-Experience and, to a lesser extent, Conscientiousness and Extraversion were linked to the buildup of basic organizational skills involving lexical, syntactic, discourse and functional abilities, the acquisition of pragmatic skills (involving sociocultural routines), and the development of monitoring strategies in second language learning children in the Netherlands. The authors found even stronger relationships between the Big Five personality variables and linguistic measures in the children's L1. Ehrman (2008) reported that openness is correlated with intuition in the MBTI. Learners who score high on this dimension "concentrate on meaning, possibilities, and usually accept constant change" (2008: 66). They are typically seeking hidden patterns, are high-ability readers, and can pick up nativelike ways of self-expression (2008: 66). Foreign language learners who score high on Openness-to-Experience should thrive in educational settings that promote and reward critical and original thought (Farsides and Woodfield 2003).

8.4.5 Risk-taking

Risk-taking is one facet of extraversion that could have a specific impact on SLA. Extraverts tend to take more risks in the L2 class (Ely 1986: 3). This behavior could also be linked to extraverts' optimism and self-confidence, making them less likely to fear stepping out in the linguistic unknown in the L2 class, with the potential risk of making errors and social embarrassment. Risk-takers have also been found to participate more in the L2 class and to score higher on proficiency measures (Ely 1986; Samimy and Tabuse 1992). This does not mean that risk-taking "always create[s] consistent results for all language learners" (Oxford 1992: 30). Risk-taking interacts with psychological factors such as Foreign Language Anxiety, self-esteem, motivation and learning styles (1992: 30). Moreover, only careful, calculated risk-taking is likely to stimulate foreign language learning (Oxford 1992).

8.4.6 Foreign language anxiety and trait emotional intelligence

One psychological variable that has received abundant attention in the SLA literature is communicative anxiety (CA), which includes Foreign Language Anxiety and the more specific Foreign Language Classroom Anxiety (FLCA). MacIntyre (2007) has argued that early research in this area confused levels of abstraction, more specifically the distinction between trait anxiety, situation-specific anxiety and state anxiety, "each of which provides a valuable, but somewhat different perspective on the processes under study" (2007: 565). An individual with a high level of trait anxiety is likely to feel anxious in a variety of situations. This causes a diversion of attentional resources of the central executive to the source of anxiety and the decision on how to react. The anxious person might thus be distracted from his/her goals by internal (troubling thoughts) or external (threatening task-irrelevant distractors) stimuli (Eysenck, Derakshan, Santos and Calvo 2007).

At the situation-specific level of conceptualization, "the concern is for concepts that are defined over time within a situation" (MacIntyre 2007: 565). The FLCA Scale developed by Horwitz, Horwitz and Cope (1986) measures this situation-specific anxiety. For Horwitz and colleagues FLCA is "a distinct complex of self-perceptions, beliefs, feelings and behaviors related to classroom learning arising from the uniqueness of the language learning process" (1986: 128). FLCA is linked to any activity in the foreign language, but it is typically highest for speaking, and it affects foreign language learners at all levels and even non-native foreign language teachers (Horwitz 1986).

Finally, anxiety can exist at the state level, "the concern is for experiences rooted in a specific moment in time without much concern for how frequently those experiences occurred in the past or whether they might occur again in the future" (MacIntyre 2007: 565). Second language performance seems negatively correlated with higher levels of state anxiety (Gregersen 2003; MacIntyre and Gardner 1994). MacIntyre (2007) speculates that there are fewer studies on state anxiety in SLA because of the complicating factor that learners attempt "to cope with and compensate for the effects of anxiety" (2007: 565).

FLCA has been reported to interfere negatively with learning and performance (Horwitz 2001; Woodrow 2006) and high levels of FLCA in the classroom have been linked to students discontinuing their study of foreign languages (Dewaele and Thirtle 2009). FLA has been linked to introversion (MacIntyre and Charos 1996) and trait emotional intelligence (EI) – also called trait emotional self-efficacy. The construct of EI posits that "individuals differ in the extent to which they attend to, process and utilize affect-laden information of an intrapersonal (e.g. managing one's own emotions) or interpersonal (e.g. managing others' emotions) nature" (Petrides and Furnham 2003: 39). Trait EI is located at the lower levels of personality hierarchies and has been found to correlate negatively with Neuroticism, positively with Extraversion, Openness and Conscientiousness (Petrides and Furnham 2003: 48).

Dewaele, Petrides and Furnham (2008) investigated the link between levels of trait EI and levels of communicative anxiety (CA) in the L1, L2, L3 and L4 of adult multilinguals. A significant negative relationship was found between Foreign Language Anxiety in the different languages of the participants and their scores on trait Emotional Intelligence. The authors speculated that emotionally intelligent individuals are better able to gauge the emotional state of their interlocutor and feel more confident about their ability to communicate effectively. A recent study has shown that L2 users who scored highly on trait EI engaged more frequently in conversations in their L2 (Ożańska-Ponikwia 2010). In other words, a higher level of emotional intelligence might encourage L2 users to practice their L2 more regularly, which in turn increases self-confidence and boosts proficiency. Dewaele *et al.* (2008) identified another independent variable linked to FLA, age of onset of learning, which was positively linked (see Chapter 15, this volume). Participants who had learnt a language solely through classroom instruction suffered from higher levels of FLA compared to those who had also used their language outside the classroom. The knowledge of more languages was linked to lower levels of FLA, which confirmed an earlier study on multilinguals (Dewaele 2007b). A cluster of variables linked to current use of the target language (TL) was also linked to FLA: participants with a higher frequency of use of the TL who had a stronger socialization in the TL, who used the TL with a larger network of interlocutors and who felt more proficient in the TL reported lower levels of FLA (Dewaele 2010; Dewaele *et al.* 2008).

8.4.7 Perfectionism and foreign language anxiety

Perfectionism has been defined as a less exaggerated form of obsessive-compulsive disorder (Pittman 1987). Perfectionist L2 learners tend to make slower progress because the fear of making mistakes hinders their learning. They are inhibited about classroom participation, unwilling to volunteer a response to a question unless they are absolutely sure of the correct answer and they react badly to minor failures (Gregersen and Horwitz 2002). Moreover, they are counterproductively compulsive in their work habits and their productivity tends to be low because of procrastination (Brophy 1996).

Gregersen and Horwitz (2002) were struck by the similarities in the manifestations of foreign language anxiety and perfectionism and argued that the techniques developed to help overcome learners' perfectionism might also be useful in helping them overcome their FLA. The authors found that the main difference between four anxious and four non-anxious learners was their reaction to their performance. The anxious learners were found to be more perfectionist: they set themselves higher personal performance standards, procrastinated more, were more fearful of evaluation, and were more concerned about errors. The authors draw some pedagogical implications from their findings, namely that perfectionist learners should be told that their self-beliefs are hypotheses rather than facts (2002: 569), that they should try to remain calm and focus on continuing a conversation as a goal in itself, and not get side-tracked by errors (2002: 570).

8.5 Conclusion

Is there such thing as "a good language learner"? The answer seems to be positive, but no single independent variable, set of learner-internal variables or combination of learner-internal and learner-external variables can currently be put forward as the only cause behind successful SLA. One difficulty is the definition of success. Indeed, as Cook (2002b) points out, L2 users can be perfectly successful communicators, while clearly not having nativelike performance in the L2. Physiological factors such as superior memory abilities, stress-resistance, musical ability and verbal ability in the L1 combined with various personality factors of the learner can result in more rapid processing and storage of input, higher levels of intrinsic motivation, self-efficacy and self-management, relatively low levels of FLA/FLCA and a willingness to use the L2. However, the effects of many of the previous variables are determined by a complex and dynamic interaction within a potentially infinitely varying or at least unpredictable learning context. L2 learners with similar personality profiles may differ enormously in their progress and ultimate attainment because of some random trigger event, such as unhappiness with a particular teacher, an encounter with a striking text or film in the L2, or even a sudden infatuation with a native speaker of the L2, that suddenly makes the learning of the L2 – and learning it well – an absolute priority for that individual. Other equally good learners may not have experienced such an event and therefore proceed gently without pushing themselves to the limit.

In sum, while it is reasonable to assume that some psychological traits or internal characteristics of learners will make them potentially good language learners, they will have to choose whether or not to fulfill that potential. Learners' choice will be influenced by the teaching environment, by the larger sociopolitical environment and by random life events. Once the choice has been made, learners will progress in the acquisition of the L2 while reminding themselves that they can be legitimate good L2 users and do not necessarily have to sound like native speakers in their L2.

9

Alphabetic literacy and adult SLA

Elaine Tarone, Kit Hansen and Martha Bigelow

9.1 Introduction

Large numbers of adult immigrants who are not literate in any language currently settle in contexts where they must become literate and learn a second language at the same time. While we recognize and appreciate broad definitions of literacy to include, for example, visual and technological literacies, the work reviewed in this chapter focuses mainly on one aspect of literacy – the ability to decode and encode alphabetic script, mainly at the word, phrase and sentence level. The population we focus on has typically not learned in traditional classroom settings and has not had the opportunity to learn to read or write yet in their home language or the second language(s) they might speak. In many of the places they settle, in North America, Europe, Australia or New Zealand, these immigrants must become literate in an *alphabetic* script – a writing system that uses visual symbols (graphemes) to represent phonemes in the language. Such adults, who must simultaneously acquire alphabetic literacy and oral second language skills, face a considerable challenge – one that has been insufficiently studied by second language acquisition researchers. We are just beginning to understand the impact that alphabetic literacy has on adults' oral processing of a second language – specifically, it appears that adults with limited or no alphabetic literacy are relatively unable to segment, compare and manipulate linguistic units empty of semantic content, while they retain the ability to process language units semantically.

This chapter reviews what is and is not known in this important area of human experience, and discusses the implications of this work for both cognitive and generative second language acquisition theory. Our own research has focused only on the impact of literacy in an alphabetic script on L2 acquisition; this is the extent of our expertise. Others who have expertise with character- or syllable-based scripts will be able to study the impact of mastery of such non-alphabetic scripts on non-literates' oral language processing in SLA.

We first review a body of research in cognitive psychology – experimental studies comparing the phonological awareness and brain activation of matched groups of literate and non-literate adults in their native language. Next, we review four areas of research on second language acquisition by non-literate and unschooled adults: (i) longitudinal studies of unschooled migrant workers in Europe; (ii) cross-sectional studies comparing the phonological awareness of non-literate and literate adults learning a second language; (iii) an experimental study on awareness of oral corrective feedback in English L2 related to alphabetic literacy level; and (iv) cross-sectional studies on the impact of alphabetic literacy on adult second language learners' metalinguistic awareness and working memory for language. We end the chapter with an exploration of the dramatic implications of the findings in these lines of research for current theories of SLA.

9.2 Impact of alphabetic literacy on adult oral native language processing

There is considerable evidence that alphabetic literacy significantly affects one's awareness of linguistic units, particularly phonemes, in oral language, as well as one's ability to cognitively manipulate these in various ways. Indeed, cognitive psychologists now believe that alphabetic literacy leads to the awareness of phonemes and other linguistic units, and even alters the way the brain processes oral language (Castro-Caldas 2004; Goswami 2008).

This body of research began with a series of interesting experimental studies by cognitive psychologists who compared the way alphabetically literate and non-literate adults processed their native language. A good deal of the data were collected in a fishing village in southern Portugal, with findings corroborated by studies in Spain, Mexico, China and other countries. The Portuguese village's sociodemographic characteristics were such that researchers could confidently study matched groups in which the sole difference between groups was exposure to schooling and literacy (Reis, Guerreiro and Petersson 2003):

> For social reasons, illiteracy occurs naturally in Portugal. Forty to fifty years ago, it was common for older daughters of a family to be engaged at home in the daily household workings. Therefore, they did not enter school... The fishing village Olhão of Algarve in southern Portugal, where most of our studies have been conducted, is socioculturally homogeneous, and the majority of the population has lived most of their lives in the community... Literate and illiterate people live intermixed and participate actively on similar terms in this community. Illiteracy is not perceived as a functional handicap, and the same sociocultural environment influences both literate and illiterate people on similar terms. (Reis *et al.* 2003: 192)

In initiating the line of research comparing literate and non-literate adults in this village, Morais, Cary, Alegría and Bertelson (1979) argued that it was important to study adults rather than children in order to determine whether phonological awareness emerged as a consequence of age or of external factors. While previous studies had shown that schoolchildren developed the ability to manipulate phones orally between the ages of 5 and 6, it was not clear what caused this ability; it could have resulted either from the children's increased (biologically conditioned) cognitive maturity, or from learning to read. In a ground-breaking empirical study, Morais et al. (1979) studied sixty Portuguese adults, some of whom had never attended school and had not learned to read, and others who had attended school and were literate. Matched in terms of cognitive development and lifestyle, literate and non-literate participants were asked to add or delete phonemes (P, SH or M) from the beginnings of oral sequences supplied by a researcher. Results showed that when the stimulus and answer prompts were pseudo-words (not meaningful Portuguese words), the non-literate adults were correct only 17 percent of the time, while the literate group was correct 72 percent of the time; indeed, half of the non-literate adults could not do the task correctly for any words. The researchers concluded that the ability to manipulate phonemes orally is not a result of independent cognitive development, but rather a result of learning to read, in an alphabetic script. In a related study with children, Kolinsky, Cary and Morais (1987) found that children are not aware of words as phonological entities until they become literate.

Subsequent research solidified and refined that basic finding over the next two decades. One of the earliest of these studies made it clear that the ability to manipulate phonemes orally resulted from alphabetic literacy, and not other kinds of literacy. To identify the differential impacts of alphabetic versus character-based scripts, Read, Zhang, Nie and Ding (1986) replicated the Morais et al. study with thirty Chinese adults with similar ages and levels of schooling who were workers at Beijing Normal University. Eighteen of these participants could only read Chinese characters (the non-alphabetic group), and twelve (the alphabetic group) could read both characters and an alphabetic script called Hanyu Pinyin. All participants were asked to add or delete a single consonant (d, s, n) at the beginning of a spoken Chinese syllable. All syllables and targets were permissible phonological sequences in Chinese; some were words and some were non-words. The results showed that the non-alphabetic Chinese group performed much like Morais et al.'s (1979) non-literate participants: they could not add or delete individual consonants in spoken Chinese, particularly in non-words, which had to be processed entirely in terms of phonological form and not meaning. The alphabetic group could easily and accurately perform this task. The authors conclude, "it is not literacy in general which leads to [oral] segmentation skill, but alphabetic literacy in particular" (1979: 41).

To determine which oral segmentation skills are affected by alphabetic literacy, Morais, Bertelson, Cary and Alegría (1986) administered several oral tests to forty-one adult Portuguese workers, twenty-one of whom were completely non-literate and twenty who had attended reading classes for non-literate adults (twelve "better readers" and eight "poorer readers"). Several speech segmentation tasks were used, including deleting either an initial C [p] or V [ʌ] from a pseudoword supplied by the researcher, progressive free segmentation (participants progressively produce a given utterance), and detection of rhyme. Results confirmed that in deleting initial C [p], the non-literate adults were only 19 percent accurate, as compared with a 73 percent accuracy rate for the literate adults; the non-literate adults were also largely unable to produce subsyllabic units in the progressive segmentation task. Though the non-literate adults did better on vowel deletion and rhyme detection than they did on consonant deletion, they were still not as good at these as the literate group overall. The researchers concluded that alphabetic literacy specifically determines the ability to analyze oral speech into phonemes, while syllable segmentation and the ability to detect rhyme develop independently of alphabetic literacy.

Similar findings were obtained in a larger study in Spain. Adrian, Alegría and Morais (1995) compared the oral speech segmentation skills of fifteen non-literate adults with those of a group of thirty-two poorer readers and better readers. All participants were given a large battery of oral tests, including phonemic discrimination (*ta/sa*, are they the same or different?), rhyme detection (*mepu/pepu*, do they rhyme or not?), syllable detection (e.g. is [pa] contained in [pati]?), syllable deletion (take [de] from [kade], what do we have?), phoneme detection (do these words contain the same phoneme? *kar/kus*), phoneme deletion (if we subtract [t] from the syllable [tal], we have...?), word reversal (*león fiero/fiero león*), syllable reversal (*saca/casa*), phoneme reversal (*fo/of, los/sol*). Results showed that literacy did not affect phonemic discrimination (same/different) at all, but it did significantly affect scores on all tests that required conscious awareness and manipulation of phonemes (matching, monitoring, deletion or reversal). There was almost no overlap between the scores of non-literate adults and those of poorer readers on such tests. While the syllable and rhyme awareness tasks were easier than the phonemic tasks, the non-literate group was still significantly worse at these than the readers. Thus, alphabetic literacy seems to affect conscious segmentation of oral speech at virtually all levels of ability.

Reis and Castro-Caldas (1997) extended the work of Morais and colleagues, making much stronger claims about the way alphabetic literacy impacts our cognitive processing of language:

Learning to match graphemes and phonemes is learning an operation in which units of auditory verbal information heard in temporal sequence are matched to units of visual verbal information, which is spatially arranged. This type of treatment of auditory verbal information modulates a strategy in which a visual-graphic meaning is given to units that are smaller than words, and thus independent of their semantic representation... If we, as normal adult readers, are asked to spell a word, we evoke a visual image of its written form. The awareness of phonology also allows us to play with written symbols (which can be transcoded to sounds) to form pseudo-plausible words, independently of semantics. Therefore, learning to read and write [an alphabetic script] introduces into the system qualitatively new strategies for dealing with oral language; that is, conscious phonological processing, visual formal lexical representation, and all the associations that these strategies allow. (Reis and Castro-Caldas 1997: 445)

The authors supported this claim with a study of Portuguese sisters aged 50–70. These women, ten literate and twenty non-literate, who were otherwise homogeneous in terms of intelligence and cultural background, were studied in the village where they had led their entire lives (and where reading and writing skills were not needed). The three experiments below, described with the results, were designed to support claims about the way alphabetic literacy affects the ability to process language in terms of its form instead of just its meaning:

1. Word repetition. Literacy improved the participants' ability to repeat pseudo-words, which have no meaning and can only be processed in terms of their linguistic form. When asked to repeat a randomized word list containing twenty-four highly frequent meaningful words and twenty-four pseudo-words, the non-literate group made significantly more errors on the pseudo-words than the literate group, with no difference between the groups in ability to repeat the meaningful words.

2. Word pairs. Literacy significantly improved participants' ability to associate words on the basis of linguistic form. Two sets of word pairs were developed. One set of pairs was words semantically related (e.g. *fork–spoon, rose–carnation*) and the other set of pairs was words phonologically related (e.g. *mala–pala, lua–rua*). The non-literate group scored significantly worse on the phonological word pair test than they did on the semantic word pairs, and overall worse than the literate group, who scored equally well whether words were semantically or phonologically related.

3. Verbal fluency. Literacy significantly improved participants' ability to fluently access words based on their linguistic form alone. Two tasks of verbal fluency were given. In a semantic fluency task, participants were given one minute each to produce names of animals (subtask 1) or furniture (subtask 2). In a phonological fluency task, they were asked to produce words beginning with the phoneme /p/ (subtask 1) or /b/

(subtask 2). The non-literate adults performed significantly worse on the phonological fluency tasks than on the semantic ones, while the literate adults did equally well on both.

Reis and Castro-Caldas explain these results by pointing out that alphabetic literacy makes auditory units smaller than the word (whether a phoneme, or a larger cluster of phonemes) visually representable. Visual representation improves one's ability to store language sequences in a short-term phonological buffer in working memory for purposes of repetition or other explicit analysis. The model of working memory Baddeley (2007: 8) proposes (see Chapter 6, this volume) includes a "visuospatial sketchpad," the function of which is the short-term storage of visuospatial information (as used in playing chess, architecture and engineering), not, as often misconstrued, as a mediator between alphabetic script and oral language processing (see Baddeley 2007: chapter 4). That is, its function is storage of visual language sequences.

Such processing of language in terms of its form is explicit. On the other hand, semantic processing of language – for meaning – involves implicit processing of form. It is interesting that in Experiments 2 and 3, the non-literate adults did worse than literate ones on all tasks. The authors claim that this is because literate participants were able to use both semantic and phonological processing strategies, which can interact with and support each other, improving overall performance. Reis and Castro-Caldas claim: "all our results support the hypothesis that the missing of a single skill (grapheme-phoneme association) interferes significantly in the higher development of the language system" (1997: 449).

Having established that alphabetic literacy influences aspects of the auditory–verbal language system, Reis, Faísca, Mendonça, Ingvar and Petersson (2007) showed that it also influenced individuals' notion of words as phonological units, independent of lexical semantics. They found that alphabetic literacy significantly affected participants' performance on phonological word-length comparisons, confirming and extending the earlier finding that non-literate adults are biased toward semantic–conceptual–pragmatic types of cognitive processing rather than processing based only on language form.

The findings from non-literate adults in Portugal and Spain were replicated and elaborated upon in a large-scale study in Brazil (Dellatolas et al. 2003; also reported in Loureiro et al. 2004). A comprehensive battery of tests assessed the phonological skills, verbal and visual memory of ninety-seven adults and forty-one children with differing levels of literacy. The results of this study confirmed those cited above: for both adults and children, the ability to perform oral tasks involving awareness and manipulation of phonemes is dependent on alphabetic literacy – specifically, the ability to represent phonemes with graphemes. Castro-Caldas (2004) makes an important distinction between this skill, which relates specifically and only to the mastery of reading and writing in an alphabetic script, and other more diffuse effects of the "rich environment" of schooling, which produce more abstract thinking and the development of parallel processing of information.

An impressive series of research studies beginning in 1998 documented differential brain activation in literate and non-literate adults as they carried out different oral segmentation and manipulation tasks (see also Chapter 19, this volume). Castro-Caldas *et al.* (1998) studied brain activation in alphabetically non-literate and literate Portuguese adults; he used PET and statistical parametric mapping. Both groups of participants performed similarly and activated similar areas of the brain when they were repeating real words. But when asked to repeat pseudo-words, the participants who were not literate had significant difficulty, and did not activate the same neural structures as literate participants. The authors concluded that learning to read and write in an alphabetic script influences the functional organization of the human brain differently than acquiring oral language. This conclusion was supported and elaborated in Petersson, Reis, Askelöf, Castro-Caldas and Ingvar (2000), who reanalyzed these data in order to more precisely identify specific areas of the brain that might be impacted by alphabetic literacy: the interaction between Broca's area and the inferior parietal cortex as well as the posterior mid-insula bridge between Wernicke's and Broca's area. Ostrosky-Solís, García and Pérez (2004) used cortical evoked potentials to a probe click stimulus to assess cerebral activation during verbal memory tasks in literate and non-literate adults in Mexico. Their findings suggested that alphabetic literacy led to intrahemispheric specialization activating parietotemporal areas of the brain. Petersson, Silva, Castro-Caldas, Ingvar and Reis (2007) used positron emission tomography (PET) scans and MRIs to study brain activation patterns in twenty-eight Portuguese adults (fourteen non-literate) as they repeated or did cued recalls of words and pseudo-words. Their results suggested that the literate group was relatively left-lateralized in the inferior parietal cortex compared to the non-literate group, and that large-scale brain connectivity was more affected by literacy than grey matter per se. Petersson, Ingvar and Reis (2009) relate these and related brain activation findings as supporting the conclusion that alphabetic literacy alters not just the processing of phonological structure and verbal working memory, but also the corresponding structural and functional properties of the human brain in ways that are still being studied.

In summary, a considerable amount of persuasive evidence has been assembled to show that alphabetic literacy modifies the way the human brain processes oral input in one's native language. The theoretical implications of this have been explored by Ong (2002) and Olson (2002). If alphabetic literacy changes the way the human brain processes oral input in one's native language, it would be very odd if it did not also affect the way the brain processes oral input in a second language (L2). Alphabetic literacy must be a crucial intervening variable in oral second language acquisition (SLA). So what do SLA researchers know about the way the non-literate adult processes oral second language input? What research has been done on what happens when adults must develop literacy and oral L2 at the same time?

9.3 Research with non-alphabetically literate adults acquiring second languages

9.3.1 SLA research with unschooled workers in Europe

There has been only a small amount of SLA research focused on exploring the relationship between adults' literacy levels and the processes and outcomes of oral SLA. Research on adult and adolescent SLA has almost exclusively been carried out with literate participants, as noted by Bigelow and Tarone (2004). Indeed, even when SLA research has been carried out in populations known to have low levels of formal schooling, as in the *Zweitspracherwerb italienisher, portugiesischer und spanischer Arbeiter* (ZISA) study (e.g. Clahsen, Meisel and Pienemann 1983) and the *European Science Foundation* (ESF) study (e.g. Perdue 1993), the literacy levels of L2 learners have typically not been directly measured. Literacy has never been one of those individual differences identified as influential in affecting outcomes in SLA.

And perhaps this would not matter if all those acquiring L2s were literate; in that case there would be no reason to include literacy level as a variable in SLA research. However, it is easy to show that vast numbers of second language learners worldwide (mostly women) are in fact not literate (Bigelow and Tarone 2004). The literacy statistics show that, although their lot is better in some countries than others, on average, women worldwide do not have as much access to education as men. UNESCO estimates that two-thirds of the 796 million people worldwide who report not being able to read and write are women (UNESCO Institute for Statistics 2010). And many non-literate and low-literate adults have now immigrated to or live in communities where they must use more than one language. There is now a small but growing body of research exploring the degree to which alphabetic literacy affects second language learners' oral L2 processing.

The first major studies focusing on low-educated adult immigrants who were learning second languages were carried out in Europe. Both the ZISA project (Clahsen *et al.* 1983) and the ESF project (Perdue 1993) undertook longitudinal studies to examine the SLA of working-class adult immigrants in Germany (ZISA), and in Germany, France, the Netherlands, Sweden and the UK (ESF) who had "limited education" (Perdue 1993). Unfortunately, it appears that although they tracked number of years of reported schooling, neither project explicitly measured the literacy levels of these immigrants;

as a consequence they could not systematically assess the impact of literacy level per se on oral SLA outcomes. The ZISA project was important in identifying invariant orders of acquisition based on word order that held for all the L2 learners in the study; this finding became the empirical base upon which Processability theory (Pienemann 2005a) was based. It is interesting, in view of our exploration of the cognitive consequences of illiteracy, that the ZISA project found that even though word-order stages were constant for all their learners, there were two groups of learners who could be differentiated based on the degree to which they supplied morphological features in their interlanguages. One group had a "standard" orientation, and accurately supplied a set of grammatical morphemes, while the other group had a "simplifying" orientation, favoring what the authors termed communicative effectiveness at the expense of deletion of those morphemes (Clahsen *et al.* 1983). Based on the research summarized in Section 9.1, one must wonder whether literacy level might have been a key factor differentiating these two learner groups. Do non-alphabetically literate adult L2 learners, who we now know rely on semantic processing rather than phonological processing strategies, have more difficulty processing and acquiring semantically redundant grammatical morphemes in the L2? Are they the ones who primarily constitute the "simplifying" group? Do non-literate adults learning an L2 tend to delete semantically redundant morphemes more than literate adults?

9.3.2 Research with adult L2 learners on alphabetic literacy and oral language processing

The two first studies of which we are aware that explicitly examined alphabetic literacy in relation to the oral language processing of adult L2 learners were carried out in the early 1990s, not by members of researchers from the mainstream SLA research community, but rather as a kind of by-product of the body of research cited in Section 9.1. Following up on the Read *et al.* (1986) study, De Gelder, Vroomen and Bertelson (1993) explored the impact of alphabetical vs. character-based literacy on the metaphonological abilities of Chinese adults who were learning Dutch L2. Two tests (administered in Dutch with help as needed from a Chinese interpreter) compared the metaphonological abilities (i.e. ability to manipulate L2 consonants) of character-based (non-alphabetic) vs. alphabetic script readers. The non-alphabetic group had learned to read Chinese characters only and were unable to read Dutch L2 pseudo-words, while the alphabetic group that had also learned to read Pinyin scored 50 percent or better in reading Dutch L2 pseudo-words. The two tests were administered in succession, the first without corrective feedback, and the second with such feedback. The corrective feedback in test 2 occurred after each response: the participants were told whether their response was correct and if not what they should have said. Results of both tests for these L2 learners were consistent with those of Read *et al.* (1986). The alphabetic group significantly out-performed the non-alphabetic (character) group in all oral L2 consonant manipulation tasks. The tests also confirmed that as in previous L1 studies, sensitivity to rhyme was not particularly affected by alphabetic literacy. Interestingly, the corrective feedback that was supplied had basically no impact on the performance of either group of learners.

The second study, Gombert (1994), investigated the impact of training on the ability of non-literate, semi-literate and literate adults to orally manipulate linguistic units in their L2. Operating on the assumption that metalinguistic segmentation abilities are by-products of learning to read an alphabetic script, Gombert studied 21 North African immigrants who had lived in France at least three years and all "spoke and understood French [L2] quite well" (1994: 254). Their teachers at a work center identified three literacy groups: seven totally non-literate, seven partially literate (meaning they had started learning to read French L2 only within the last year) and seven literate in French L2. In a pre-test, training, post-test design, the pre-test consisted of three oral tasks: judgment of phonological length, initial consonant deletion and lexical segmentation of sentences into words. Those who did not get a perfect score on all these tasks were provided with training consisting of practice with corrective feedback and explanation until they achieved six correct answers or underwent eighteen trials, whichever came first. The post-test was the same as the pre-test. The results with these L2 learners replicated those of Morais *et al.* (1979) and others for native speakers: on the pre-test, on all three tasks, literate participants performed best, and non-literate participants worst, with partially literate participants midway between. Although De Gelder *et al.* (1993) found corrective feedback had no impact on performance, the corrective feedback and explanation used by Gombert significantly improved the post-test performance of the partially literate and non-literate participants. Finally, Gombert observed that the lexical segmentation task, which was the hardest for all three literacy groups, may have been so because French was the participants' second language, and because liaison (resyllabification between a word-final consonant and following word-initial vowel) may have made identification of word boundaries especially difficult for them as L2 learners.

9.3.3 The Minneapolis Somali literacy study

Bigelow and Tarone (2004) argued that mainstream SLA research should document the impact of literacy on oral second language production and acquisition by adults. When large numbers of non-literate and low literate Somalis began immigrating to Minnesota at the turn of the millennium, Bigelow and Tarone initiated a small-scale research study on Somali adolescents' and adults' acquisition of English L2, and the impact of literacy level on oral L2 use and development. They began by replicating some standard second language acquisition research studies in this population. The results of this study are widely reported and presented in depth in Tarone,

Table 9.1. *Stages of question formation in English based on Pienemann, Johnston and Brindley (1988)*

Stage
1: Single words or phrases *(Why? This?) (A boy? To who?)*
2: SVO word order *(This is picture?)*
3: Fronting *wh-, do*, or other word followed by SVO *(What he is doing?)* *(*Does he going home?)* *(*Is he is mad?)*
4: Inversion: *yes/no* questions with auxiliary, copula, or modal *wh*-questions with copula (but not aux) *(Is she mad about that?)* *(Can you repeat that?)* *(What is this lady? *Where are this place?)*
5: Inversion: Aux (e.g. *is*), do operator, modal in 2nd position *(Who's buying it? What's he doing?)* *(What does she hold in her hand?)* *(Where will she take this?)*
6: Negative question with do operator, grammatical tag question *(Doesn't she want to come in?)* *(He's a doctor, isn't he?)*

Bigelow and Hansen (2009; see also Hansen 2005; Bigelow, delMas, Hansen and Tarone 2006; Tarone, Swierzbin and Bigelow 2006; Tarone and Bigelow 2007; Tarone, Bigelow and Hansen 2007; Bigelow 2010).

Three areas of oral SLA research were identified for replication:

1. Interactionist research on *corrective feedback* focuses on L2 learners' responses when their spoken grammar errors are corrected; a learner's ability to accurately repeat an oral correction of grammatical errors requires metalinguistic processing and the manipulation of sequences of words and sublexical linguistic forms (see Chapter 10, this volume).
2. Research on *elicited imitation* assesses the impact of the learner's morphosyntactic knowledge on accuracy of recall for sentences or strings that exceed working memory limits.
3. Research on *oral narrative* focuses on the linguistic forms used by learners when they are focused on meaning, and so can be assumed to be acquired by the learner.

These three SLA study types were selected for replication in part because they could be administered using data elicitation procedures that were entirely oral.

The studies on corrective feedback and elicited imitation focused on the linguistic forms used by the learners in asking English questions, which are commonly believed to be acquired in a fixed ("universal") developmental order consisting of formal stages, e.g. six for Pienemann Johnston and Brindley (1988), summarized in Table 9.1.

The participants in all three studies were various subsets of a group of thirty-five adolescent and adult Somali immigrants living in Minneapolis.

Table 9.2. *Participant profile, Studies 1 and 3*

				Literacy level			Years in schooling		
ID*	Age	Gender	Mean	L1	L2	TSE prof.	L1	L2	Years in US
Abukar	15	M	5	4	6	50	0	4.5	4.5
Najma	27	F	5.5	5	6	40	7	1.5	3
Ubax	17	F	3.5	0	7	40	0	3	3
Fawzia	20	F	6	6	6	30	0	3	3
Khalid	16	M	8.5	8.5	8.5	50	0	7	7
Faadumo	18	F	9	9	9	40	0	3	3
Moxammed	17	M	9	9	9	40	0	7	7
Sufia	15	F	8	9	7	30	0	3	3

Literacy levels in both Somali and English were explicitly measured by rating participant performance as they were completing the *Native Language Literacy Screening Device* (1999). For studies 1 and 2, a subset of eight participants was selected: four with the highest mean literacy levels in the group (ranging from 8 to 9), and four with lowest mean literacy levels (ranging from 3.5 to 6). Their proficiency scores on the Test of Spoken English (TSE), a measure that includes accuracy and fluency, were balanced across the two groups.

L1 and L2 literacy scores were averaged to capture whether the participants had acquired the core notion of grapheme–phoneme correspondence. The researchers argued that it is immaterial whether that notion is acquired in L1 or L2; once it is acquired in either language, it is used in the processing of both languages. Considerable evidence supports Cummins' Interdependence Hypothesis that literacy skills (especially in grapheme–phoneme correspondence) transfer easily between L1 and L2 (Baker and Hornberger 2001; Bialystok, Luk and Kwan 2005). Bialystok *et al.* (2005) assessed the interdependence of literacy skills of Canadian 6-year-old children who were bilingual in languages that had different similarity relationships: English–Spanish (both Indo-European languages sharing alphabetical script), English–Hebrew (Indo-European vs. Semitic, both with an alphabetical script) and English–Chinese (different language families with alphabetical vs. logographic script). Children bilingual in languages that shared an alphabetic script (English–Spanish and English–Hebrew) transferred significantly more literacy skills across languages than bilinguals whose languages used different types of script (English–Chinese).

Mean literacy scores were used in Bigelow *et al.* (2006) to capture whether the participants had acquired the notion of grapheme–phoneme correspondence in either L1 or L2. The question was, did having this notion affect participants' ability to notice corrective feedback on question formation in English L2?

The data in Table 9.2 show why it is essential to use an independent measure of literacy level; self-reported years of schooling do not appear to be related to literacy level. Note that even among our eight participants, literacy levels are not at all related to years of schooling: two of the participants in both the low- and higher-literacy group claimed three years of schooling. Bigelow *et al.* (2006) discuss the reasons for this discontinuity in more detail than is possible here, but basically, a "year of schooling" in a remote resettlement camp may differ from a "year of schooling" in a metropolitan area in terms of many variables, including content of lessons, hours per week, teacher qualifications, available materials, environmental noise and basic security concerns.

The data were collected in non-school settings in one or two individual sessions carried out individually with the same researcher, with tasks given in this order: (1) introductory conversation; (2) two spot-the-difference tasks; (3) three story completion tasks; (4) three story retellings in narration; (5) two elicited imitation tasks; (6) literacy measure (L1, then L2).

Study 1: Literacy and recall of recasts

In a partial replication of Philp (2003), Bigelow *et al.* (2006) documented the relationship among literacy level, sentence length and complexity and the ability of L2 learners to recall recasts of errors they made in forming questions, for example:

Learner: Why he is mad? (Ungrammatical trigger)
Researcher: Why is he mad? (Recast)
Learner: Why is he mad? (Accurate recall/uptake)

When learners had to ask questions about a series of pictures, the errors they made in forming questions typically involved failure to change word order or omission of an auxiliary or of *do*-support. Note that such errors are formal in nature, and do not change the core meaning of the questions. When such errors occurred, the researcher provided corrective feedback in the form of a recast (a correct version of the erroneous question) accompanied by a non-verbal signal to repeat the recast. Results showed that literacy level was significantly related to the learners' ability to accurately recall these recasts, with the higher-literacy-level group performing better than the low-literacy group ($p = .043$). The superiority of the higher-literacy group was even greater in recalling complex recasts, which included two or more corrections ($p = .014$). Interestingly, length of recast was not related to recall for either Somali literacy group (it had been significantly related for Philp's (2003) college-educated subjects). In summary, the more literate the participants were, the better able they were to produce correct or modified recall of recasts of their questions. These findings suggest that literacy made corrective oral feedback on errors in the linguistic form of questions easier for L2 learners to notice. This conclusion is consistent with the findings summarized in the first part of this chapter, that alphabetic literacy improves conscious processing in terms of linguistic form (as opposed to semantic processing).

Study 2: Elicited imitation

Hansen (2005) documented the impact of literacy level on accuracy of recall of question forms in two tasks: elicited imitation (EI) and recast. Elicited imitation requires that learners repeat, one by one, a list of semantically unrelated, decontextualized, eight-syllable-long L2 questions read to them by the researcher. But before presenting the hypothesis and findings, the issue of the role of working memory in accuracy of EI recall bears examination because it makes predictions that are not completely borne out.

Decades of memory research, particularly with respect to recall of lists of items, has established that a person can hold seven units plus or minus two, in working memory's temporary store (Miller 1956). Recall accuracy is further affected by the type of units to be recalled, with words being more readily recalled than non-words, and recall accuracy for initial units and last units being greater than for those in the middle (Baddeley 2007). Viewing the L2 EI task from the working memory perspective, then, the learner's capacity can be impacted not only by the number of sentence syllables to be recalled, but also by the meaningfulness of the recall target. This is what in part led Hansen to postulate that the elicited imitation task, because it provides no meaningful context, would require more reliance on phonological processing in working memory than the recast task, which focuses on meaningful language produced in context by the learner, and so lower alphabetic literacy levels would make EI more difficult. The results of her study confirmed her predictions. Higher alphabetic literacy levels improved recall of target questions on both the elicited imitation and the recast tasks: the moderate-literacy-level group had more correct recalls, fewer incorrect recalls and fewer "no recalls" than the low-literacy-level group. The probability that these differences were due to chance was $p = .057$ on the elicited imitation task, and .014 on the recast task. In addition, both the low-literacy group and the moderate-literacy group found the elicited imitation task significantly more difficult than the recast task ($p = .008$).

But there is a wrinkle with respect to the role of working memory. If working memory capacity were a critical factor, then EI recall accuracy should be higher early in the sentence. In fact, though, learner errors, particularly those in the low-literacy group, often occurred immediately in the first or second word of the sentences, thus undermining a strict serial-processing model. Interestingly, the recall attempts had semantic content that overlapped with that of the target sentence. For example, three different learner responses to the prompt "Why does she work late on Sundays?" were as follows: "Why didn't she working last night?" "Why you work later on Sunday?" and "Why you /dada/ why you like the Sunday, Sunday?" Phonological overload in working memory may be a partial explanation, with the low-literacy group particularly affected due to their lack of literacy-based metalinguistic skills, but clearly factors such as the learner's interlanguage and the learner's need to create meaningful utterances are at work as well.

The conclusion to the EI study was that relatively higher alphabetic literacy levels significantly affected second language learners' ability to recall and repeat the linguistic units used to produce English questions. It bears repeating that the accurate use of many of the linguistic units used in questions does not affect base meaning, so that participants relying more on semantic processing and less on phonological processing can be expected to be at a disadvantage.

Study 3: Grammar forms used in oral narrative

This study (fully reported in Tarone *et al.* 2006) attempted to explore the impact of literacy level on acquisition of the linguistic forms used by the low- and moderate-literacy groups in producing oral narratives describing the same sequence of events. Of particular interest in this comparison were (a) the suppliance or absence of semantically redundant grammatical morphemes (characteristic of the "standard" vs. "simplifying" orientation of Clahsen *et al.* 1983), and (b) utterance complexity, since alphabetic literacy may affect the processing of complex linguistic forms in short-term memory. To sample use of semantically redundant grammatical morphemes, the study focused on the production of "bare verbs" (verbs with no morphological marking) as compared to verbs with morphology (accurate or not), and also on the use of "bare nouns" (plural nouns with no plural morpheme) as compared to plural nouns marked with plural morphemes. To compare complexity in utterances produced by the two groups, a count was made of the number of relative clauses, and clauses expressing causality using the connectors *because, so* or *since*.

The results confirmed a tendency for the low-literacy group to produce more bare verbs (64 percent) than the higher-literacy group (50 percent), although there was considerable variation in the data from both groups. Representative utterances for past-tense marking were:

(1) Khalid (moderate literacy):   So, she called him.

(2) Fawzia (low literacy):   Somebody call him.

(Interestingly, the low-literate group produced fewer verbs overall (321) than the moderate-literate group (458).) The more literate group produced more noun plural morphology than the low-literate group: 77 percent of plural nouns marked for plural, compared with the low-literate group's 48 percent. The low-literate group often seemed to prefer using quantifiers to indicate plurality:

(3) Ubax (low literacy):   *A lot of monkey* ... they take his <u>hat</u>

(4) Khalid (moderate literacy):   The <u>*monkeys*</u> took all his <u>*hats*</u>.

Although there was, again, considerable variation in noun plural marking across literacy groups, overall the data are consistent with the idea that literacy level may be related to the standard vs. simplifying orientation noted by Clahsen *et al.* in 1983. Finally, there appeared to be a strong tendency for the more literate group to produce more complex utterances in their oral narratives than the low-literate group. For example, the moderately literate group used more relative clauses (28 compared to 8), and more dependent and *so*-clauses (131, compared to 72) than the low-literate group in producing the same oral narratives. Thus, the results of Study 3 are consistent with the view that alphabetic print literacy level may be related to the linguistic forms (redundant grammatical morphemes and complex sentence structures) that L2 learners acquire and use in their oral learner language. The authors call for more large-scale studies to examine the overall impact of alphabetic literacy level not just on oral second language processing but on such aspects as the overall standard vs. simplifying orientation of the L2 learner and long-term acquisition outcomes. One pedagogical implication of this work is that, to facilitate processes of SLA by low-literate adult learners, teachers may need to use a balanced approach to literacy that combines a more explicit focus on formal segmental units of L2 with a focus on context that allows these learners to exercise their strengths in semantic processing (e.g. Vinogradov 2010; Bigelow 2010; Bigelow and Vinogradov 2011).

In presenting their research, the authors point out that low alphabetic literacy levels and low scores on phonological awareness tasks do not prevent their participants from acquiring considerable oral proficiency in using English. Nor does it prevent them from memorizing and reciting extremely long oral narratives in Somali. Clearly, these individuals are successfully processing a considerable amount of oral input, but SLA researchers have not studied how they do this. As non-alphabetically literate adults they appear to be structuring working memory in some way other than through segmental linguistic units. We know their awareness of rhyme, stress and rhythm is less affected by alphabetic literacy; we believe these elements may function in important but so far unknown ways to organize their working memory for oral language. Amanda Lanier (personal communication) suggests that intonation may play an important role in structuring the working memory of non-alphabetically literate adults; this idea is attractive because the intonation envelope includes the key elements of stress and rhythm. The relation between rhyme and pitch patterning should also be explored. Research is urgently needed in this area.

The Minneapolis Somali project subsequently inspired another set of studies reported in Bigelow (2010), that has focused on (a) broader processes of literacy, including contexts of language/literacy use among Somali adolescent girls; (b) the co-construction of racialized identity among Somali youth; and (c) how refugee adolescents have been constructed as uneducable, partially through use of published academic work from education and applied linguistics.

9.4 LESLLA research on literacy and SLA

Some of the most recent international research on adult second language learners with limited or no formal schooling and low print literacy has emerged in a series of international conferences specifically addressing this population. Symposia on Low-Educated Second Language and Literacy Acquisition by Adults (LESLLA) have been held in the Netherlands, the United States, the United Kingdom, Belgium, Canada, Germany and Finland, beginning with an inaugural meeting in Tilburg in 2005. Thus far, the conferences have produced several peer-reviewed collections of articles (van de Craats, Kurvers and Young-Scholten 2006a; Faux 2007; Young-Scholten 2008; van de Craats and Kurvers 2009; Wall and Leong 2010). The research reported in these volumes has mainly used experimental or quasi-experimental methods to explore questions in second language acquisition that contribute to existing lines of research, by including participants with limited formal schooling.

To explore the impact of literacy on phonemic awareness in processing second language data, Young-Scholten and Strom (2006) administered a range of oral awareness and reading tests to seventeen adult low-literate Somali and Vietnamese learners of English L2 whose study of ESL and years in the US varied widely. As in previous studies with young children and with late literate native-language-speaking adults studied by Morais and colleagues, Young-Scholten and Strom found that phonemic awareness developed only after the adult L2 participants were able to read, while notions of word, syllable, rhyme and onset awareness developed independently of reading skills. There was variation in these latter notions: Somali adults were more aware of onsets and rhymes than of syllables, while Vietnamese adults had more syllable awareness than the Somalis. Consistent with Study 3 of Tarone et al. (2009), interlanguage syntax levels of the participants appeared to be correlated with their literacy levels as well, though the direction of causality was not established. Importantly, the researchers found that, for all the participants, knowing the names of letters of the alphabet was unrelated to phonemic awareness or decoding ability. All seventeen low-literate adults knew the names of alphabetic letters in different fonts and orders, but those who could not read did not have good phonemic awareness or grapheme/phoneme correspondence. This finding suggests that learning the names of the letters of the alphabet does not lead to phonemic awareness. Rather, phonemic awareness must be explicitly taught and not be assumed to develop as a result of memorizing and reciting the names of letters of the alphabet.

Vainikka and Young-Scholten (2007b) used their Organic Grammar theory (see Chapter 27, this volume) to problematize the strong position of Bigelow et al. (2006) that alphabetic literacy *causes* an increase in L2 learners' ability to notice linguistic forms in the oral input. Rather, they proposed a weaker *indirect influence hypothesis*, that alphabetic literacy affects phonology, which in turn has an indirect effect on acquisition of L2 morphology and syntax (2006: 144). Their data showed that although lack of native language literacy appeared to correlate overall with Somali learners' production of Stage 1 or basic syntax in L2 (2006: 131), it did not account for one of their Somali speakers (S3), who had begun learning ESL with no L1 literacy, but ended up at Organic Grammar's Stage 4 in L2 morphosyntax. But, as shown in the Bigelow *et al.* study, alphabetic literacy skills can develop in either L1 or L2 – at the time S3 attained higher levels of L2 syntax, he had also attained higher levels of L2 literacy. For this reason, his achievements can still be argued to depend on his acquiring (in either L1 or L2) the tool of grapheme–phoneme correspondence and with it the ability to visualize linguistic segments. It is immaterial whether the tool of grapheme–phoneme correspondence is initially attained through learning to read L1 or L2 – once that ability to represent phonemes with graphemes is attained, it can be applied as a tool to the processing of either language.

Kurvers, van Hout and Vallen (2006) point out that there are different types of metalinguistic language skills that may or may not be conferred by the ability to read. *Phonological awareness* is the ability to break words into segments like syllables or phonemes and manipulate these. *Lexical awareness* is the ability to segment sentences into units at word boundaries, and to separate the forms of words from their meanings. There are three possible reasons for children's sudden spurt in phonemic and lexical awareness between the ages of 5 and 8: language development, cognitive development or literacy development. The authors point out that a comparison of the metalinguistic abilities of non-literate and literate adults ought to be able to test these conflicting hypotheses. Non-literate and low-educated but literate adults' cognitive and linguistic abilities have matured, and literacy is the only difference between them. "Literacy hypotheses predict major differences [in metalinguistic skills] between readers and non-readers (irrespective of their age)" (2006: 71). Their research study compared the metalinguistic awarenesses of three groups: twenty-four preschool Dutch L1 children, twenty-five non-literate Dutch L2 adults and twenty-three low-educated literate Dutch L2 adults. All Dutch L2 learners were dominant in their native languages (Tarifit, Moroccan Arabic, Somali, or Turkish). Primary oral metalinguistic skills tested were word segmentation and rhyme, sentence segmentation, word length and word/referent differentiation. Phonological tasks included rhyme production and judgment and word segmentation. Lexical/semantic tasks included word referent, word length, word judgment in L1 and sentence segmentation. A textual task examined syllogisms. Results showed that the three groups significantly differed in their performance on all but one of the language awareness tasks (the rhyme awareness task, on which all three groups did equally well). The non-literate adults scored significantly lower on the phonological awareness tasks in this study than either the literate adults or the children, but lexical awareness was even more aligned in this study with literacy than phonological awareness. The non-literate adults and pre-literate children scored significantly lower than the literate adults on word length, word judgment and segmenting sentences into words. Following the same line of reasoning as Reis and Castro-Caldas (1997), the researchers conclude:

> For most illiterate adults, language is a referential system and a medium of communication, but not an object accessible to reflection, or a string of elements that can be parsed into structural units... Illiterate adults are able to reflect on many language-related aspects: on the content, on the utterance as a whole, or on the way something is said. However, they are not able to reflect on more formal aspects of language, an ability they did probably not acquire because they did not receive literacy training. (Kurvers *et al.* 2006: 84–85)

Following on this study, other LESLLA researchers have focused on impact of alphabetic literacy on adult L2 learners' metalinguistic notion of *word*. Kurvers, van Hout and Vallen (2007) compared the performance of literate and non-literate adult learners of Dutch L2 in their ability to segment oral input in their most dominant language into words – that is, to identify word boundaries in the speech stream. (In their study, "illiteracy" meant the inability to read simple words in either L1 or L2.) The results showed a strong significant effect of literacy on the adult L2 learners' ability to segment oral language input into words. The non-literate participants tended to focus on meaning, or content only, and many found it hard to even understand task instructions asking them to divide the speech stream up. Those non-literate adults who did divide the speech stream did not tend to do so using word units; they used units such as syllables. Adult L2 learners who were alphabetically literate had significantly less difficulty dividing up the speech stream into words at accurate word boundaries. The researchers conclude that the metalinguistic awareness of the word develops as a result of learning to read, and quote Bamberg (2002: 451):

> [literacy is a force] for transforming an early form of "language knowledge" (one that is more implicit, holistic and content-directed) into a more "explicit and analytic awareness" that enables the speaker/writer to detach from content and situational context...

Other researchers who have studied word segmentation are Onderdelinden, van de Craats and Kurvers (2009); they examined the word concepts of 15 non-literate and 15 low-literate adult immigrants in the Netherlands. Their study, replicating that of Karmiloff-Smith, Grant, Sims, Jones and Cuckle (1996), found that metalinguistic awareness of words develops together with the development of literacy: on all measures of word concept, regardless of word type and number of syllables, the low-literate adults did better than non-literate adults. Those who had even a little alphabetic literacy were significantly better at identifying word boundaries in the stream of speech than their counterparts who had no alphabetic literacy.

Paralleling Reis and Castro-Caldas' (1997) study of adults' oral native language processing, LESLLA researchers have also examined the impact of alphabetic literacy on second language learners' working memory for oral L2. Kurvers and van de Craats (2007) studied fifty-seven adult learners of Dutch L2 who had had no previous schooling. They found significant correlations between all measures of working memory (a digit span task and a non-word repetition task scored two ways: number of phonemes and number of words) and literacy proficiency levels that had been established according to the Common European Framework and the framework for literacy levels and labeled: A1/A2, B1/B2, C1/C2. The researchers conclude: "all working memory scores nicely seem to grow with the literacy level the students have reached." A comparison of matched pairs of learners, differentiated only by literacy level, reinforced the significance of the non-word repetition task correlations with literacy level. As in previous studies, with these adults, vocabulary size did not correlate with working memory measures.

Kurvers, van Hout and Vallen (2009) asked whether non-literate adult immigrant second language learners might be able to learn alphabetic literacy skills incidentally by encountering print "sight vocabulary" in the communities in which they live, or whether they need formal instruction to develop alphabetic literacy skills. Results of this study showed that while non-literate adults living in the Netherlands developed a good sense of print awareness and the functions of writing by sheer exposure, they did not develop the ability to read environmental print out of context or explain what was represented in writing. They did not acquire grapheme–phoneme correspondence by exposure to print in the environment. The authors conclude that formal instruction is required in order for non-literate adults to learn that signs represent phonemes, and to incorporate that knowledge into their cognitive processing of a second language.

Finally, Young-Scholten and Naeb (2010) carried out a longitudinal study over a nine-month period of eleven adult learners, all of whom began the study of English L2 with no NL literacy skills. Results showed that the learners did make slow progress toward literacy over the time period, engaging processes similar to those of children in learning to read in their native language. It remained unknown by the end of the study whether those small steps would eventually result in full literacy.

To sum up, then, the research that has now been done to document the relationship between adults' alphabetic print literacy and ability to orally segment second languages has been entirely supportive of findings on its impact on native language metalinguistic processing. Unsurprisingly, perhaps, the same impacts have been found for both native language and second language processing. The implications of these findings for cognitive and generative theories of second language acquisition will be explored in the next section.

9.5 Conclusion and implications for theories of SLA

A growing line of research has established that the construct *phoneme* is acquired when grapheme–phoneme correspondence is acquired; this acquisition significantly alters the way auditory input is processed in working memory and even changes the organization of brain function in processing language. This line of research on native language processing provides a compelling explanation for the results of a second line of research, focused on second language acquisition, that shows that adult second language learners with little or no alphabetic literacy have significantly more difficulty than their literate counterparts both in orally segmenting L2 and in processing oral recasts of some formal linguistic elements in their ungrammatical learner language. These twin lines of research have important implications for the assumptions and scope of current theories of SLA (see R. Ellis 2008 for overview). These theories appear to be based on erroneous assumptions about the innateness of certain human language processing skills, which the research shows appear to not be innate at all but learned as a by-product of alphabetic literacy. Current SLA theories, based on a restricted dataset of alphabetically literate learners, may be limited in scope, accounting only for the way literate learners process target languages, but not for the SLA processes of the very large numbers of adults worldwide who are not alphabetically print literate.

Do current theories of SLA only provide models of brains that have been modified by alphabetic literacy? Do we really understand the human capacity for second language acquisition, or just the alphabetically literate human's capacity for SLA? Current SLA theories do not build on or even take notice of the most robust, twofold finding that is common to the studies cited in this chapter: (1) while alphabetic literacy is not related to adults' and adolescents' ability to process oral second languages semantically, (2) alphabetic literacy is significantly related to their ability to notice and process oral L2 in terms of formal, semantically redundant linguistic units and patterns.

Most current SLA theories assume that all adult second language learners are aware of formal linguistic units like phonemes and words, and can mentally compare, contrast and manipulate their order in sentences. Most of those theories do not distinguish between linguistic units that have semantic content and those that do not. For example, Schmidt's Noticing Hypothesis (recently summarized by Robinson 2006), upon which much current research on corrective feedback is based, claims that noticing is a necessary and sufficient condition for a learner to convert input to intake, and that *conscious noticing* is necessary for learning to take place. The Noticing Hypothesis does not assert this only for linguistic units and sequences that have semantic content; it applies to all linguistic units. Can semantically redundant linguistic segments be acquired at all by learners who apparently do not notice them in the input? If so, does this provide counterevidence to the Noticing Hypothesis?

The Input and Interaction Theory (Gass 2002; Chapter 10, this volume) incorporates the Noticing Hypothesis, as well as its assumptions. Alphabetic literacy level is relevant to SLA research documenting the influence of enhanced input or corrective feedback on the acquisition of core L2 syntactic structures (e.g. Mackey 2007; Mackey and Polio 2009). Such research has typically targeted syntactic structures such as simple verb tenses, question formation and negation. The assumption of work in this area is that all L2 learners have the metalinguistic awareness to notice enhanced input or corrective feedback that is focused on L2 forms – regardless of whether these forms carry meaning or not. But if L2 learners do not have the awareness or ability to consciously manipulate phonemes, morphemes and words in the L2, then we must ask whether they notice enhanced input or corrective feedback targeting those phonemes, morphemes and words. For example, if corrective feedback adds a semantically redundant morpheme like a plural marker or third person singular morpheme to a word they have just produced (e.g. /laik/ /laiks/; /trai/ /traiz/), non-alphabetically literate adults may not notice the difference between their own word and the corrected word.

Sociocultural theory (Lantolf 2006; Lantolf and Thorne 2006; Swain, Kinnear and Steinman 2010; Chapter 30, this volume) also posits that acquisition results from L2 learners' conscious manipulation of linguistic units in the zone of proximal development (ZPD), where their learning is supported by interaction with and scaffolding from more proficient interlocutors. This work in the ZPD requires metalinguistic awareness (typically) of segmental linguistic units. Again, if non-literate adult second language learners are significantly less likely to notice linguistic units that carry minimal semantic information, and less able to compare, contrast and manipulate their order in sentences, then they will have little to gain from interaction in a ZPD that requires such conscious awareness of language form.

Generative SLA theory (see Chapter 7, this volume) also relies on data the bulk of which has been gathered from L2 learners who are focused on form, not meaning; these theories aim to account for L2 learners' conscious awareness of segmental linguistic units and rules for their combination – their metalinguistic knowledge. But there is a methodological issue: how can we study the L2 competence of adult learners who are *not* literate, when such learners appear to be unable to judge the grammaticality of permissible movements of semantically redundant linguistic segments? There is also a question of scope: if non-alphabetically print literate adults have limited ability to provide the kind of data upon which generative theory relies – the conscious comparison, contrast and mental manipulation of the order of formal linguistic units in sentences – then we have to assume that generative theories of SLA have little to tell us about the cognitive processes they employ in processing and acquiring second languages.

Variationist theories of SLA (e.g. Fasold and Preston 2007; Tarone 2010; Bayley and Tarone 2011; Chapter 13, this volume) are better positioned than most to account for the learning of non-literate second language learners. First, they focus on the impact of diverse social contexts on SLA and naturally lead researchers to include unschooled learners in the database; second, they can quantitatively model the acquisition and use of linguistic units either explicitly or implicitly, either from above (from the institutionally powerful) or from below (as in popular, vernacular street talk). Variationist models

> can predict and explain *both* explicit *and* implicit second-language acquisition, using a detailed computer model (Fasold and Preston 2007) containing sociolinguistic constructs based on decades of empirical evidence from studies of language use in a wide range of social contexts, including SLA contexts. (Tarone 2010: 70)

The research reviewed in this chapter on the relative (in)ability of adults with limited or no alphabetic literacy to segment, compare and manipulate linguistic units empty of semantic content, while retaining very good ability to process language units semantically, raises questions about the scope of current SLA theories. It appears to be quite likely, based on the research cited earlier in this chapter, that non-alphabetically literate adults primarily notice those linguistic segments in the L2 input that have semantic content. If this is so, then there are some urgent questions that need answers. Do non-alphabetically literate learners fail to acquire the linguistic forms they don't notice in the input? Do such learners only acquire L2 units and sequences that have semantic meaning? If future SLA research shows that adult L2 learners who are not alphabetically literate in fact acquire discrete linguistic forms and sequences without noticing them in the input – this would be disconfirming evidence for SLA theories founded on the Noticing Hypothesis. They might suggest that unconscious processes of SLA can occur (Krashen 2003; Chapters 7 and 22, this volume). Research focused on non-alphabetically literate adult L2 learners might be uniquely positioned to test conflicting claims of opposing SLA theories like the Noticing Hypothesis and Monitor theory.

Because the centerpiece of current theories of SLA is whether, and how, *all* L2 learners process *all* L2 forms regardless of whether they carry semantic content, a truly adequate theory of SLA, one that includes *all* adult and adolescent learners, not just the alphabetically print literate ones, is an SLA theory that can predict and explain the way alphabetic literacy affects the way the human mind processes both meaningful and semantically redundant target language linguistic units in the process of second language acquisition.

Such a theory also has the potential to more adequately account for differences between the SLA processes of adults who read different types of script – for example, those who read only character-based script (e.g. some Chinese learners of English L2) – compared to those who read only alphabetic script (e.g. English-speaking learners of Chinese characters). We have seen that non-alphabetically literate adults appear to be structuring working memory in some way other than through phonemes or words. Is their working memory for oral language structured in ways similar to those used by adults who read only character-based scripts? Research on the SLA of non-alphabetically literate adults and research on the SLA of learners of English L2 who are literate only in character-based scripts may be related; what we learn about the oral SLA of one population is likely to help us learn about the oral SLA of the other. All such research will have significant implications for current theories of second language acquisition.

Part III

External ingredients

INTRODUCTION TO PART III

In contrast to Part II's focus on the individual learner's linguistic and cognitive abilities, Part III covers the external ingredients essential for L2A. In the spirit of Firth and Wagner's (1997) reconceptualization of L2A as a social process, the chapters in this part examine the importance of social interactions to L2 development. Learners require social exchange to gain input, negotiate meaning, build sociocultural identity and gain socially appropriate linguistic behavior in the target culture. The chapters cover spoken, written and electronic mediums of communication. Complexity theory (Larsen-Freeman) and Dynamic Systems theory (de Bot) have emerged from these approaches, seeing language acquisition as being in a perpetual state of adaptation (see Chapter 28, this volume).

Chapter 10 presents an overview of studies that determine how second language acquisition is driven by interactional modifications native and non-native interlocutors make in the process of understanding utterances and making themselves understood. It reaches from the early idea of comprehensible input, input modification and output, to meaning negotiation through recent ethnomethodological approaches. Tracing the Interaction Model (IM) to its origins, García Mayo and Alcón Soler define interactional modifications and then outline subsequent research on input, output and feedback. Their discussion of conversational tasks and individual differences ties this chapter to related external ingredients of L2 learning.

Starting with the idea that social and cultural knowledge is required to understand and use linguistic forms in their context, Chapter 11 examines how texts, both spoken and written, cohere to convey particular meaning. Its coverage includes power relations contributing directly to construction of identity through discourse. Elucidating post-structuralist/postcolonial perspectives, this chapter looks at the contextual use of language to explore the negotiation of hybrid identities through linguistic practices. Miller and

Kubota give an overview of a broad range of postmodern studies of the social construction of identity in L2 contexts. Viewing language use as an "act of identity" and discourse as a "system of power," the authors provide a clear theoretical foundation for L2 identity scholarship. They then exemplify identity studies through five areas: heritage learners, multilinguals, gender, race and non-native teachers.

Chapter 12 is devoted to how the acquisition of a second language is shaped by social conditions of naturalistic target environments. It furnishes a comprehensive survey of L2 socialization research, broadly inclusive of language ecology, sociocultural theory, critical theory and conversation analysis approaches. Situating current work in its historical context, Véronique describes theoretical frameworks, methodologies and areas of inquiry that have grown out of Firth and Wagner's proposal. After a presentation of conceptual frameworks, he provides French and German examples of immigrant conversations that highlight linguistic as well as social development. The chapter gives a welcome overview that links to other chapters by Regan, Ohta, Tarone *et al.*, Miller and Kubota, and Montrul.

Chapter 13 considers the growing body of research that reveals socially driven adoption of dialect and other variation features and also looks at the emergence of hybrid forms. It includes mention of related features of contact linguistics such as code switching and register shift. The chapter situates variationist sociolinguistic theory with respect to L2A, pointing out the applications of the former to the latter. After providing the historical background of earlier native and L2 studies of variation, Regan takes a postmodern perspective on the "third wave" studies of recent years. She discusses a range of scholarship using discourse-conversation analysis or performativity that explores L2 identity construction and agency by, for example, adolescents or migrants.

Chapter 14 includes coverage of the relatively new (and in some cases very new) opportunities second language learners have for increasing the input they receive and the interaction in which they engage in electronic form, both in instructional settings (computer-assisted learning) and in extra-classroom contexts (emailing, chat rooms, user lists, blogs and twitter), thereby also raising the issue of World Englishes. It considers interaction-driven approaches that adopt conversation analysis and also covers corpus-based approaches to L2A. This chapter provides a cutting-edge overview of the range of computer-mediated communication for language learning (CMCL) on L2 development, including human–machine (e.g. CALL) and the rapidly expanding human–machine–human (e.g. email or virtual gaming). After a brief overview of the background and theory underpinning CMCL, Ensslin and Krummes show pedagogical, acculturational, cognitive and identity-wise ramifications of virtual communication in the L2.

10
Negotiated input and output / interaction

María del Pilar García Mayo and Eva Alcón Soler

10.1 Introduction

Among the different explanations of the process of second language acquisition (SLA) that have been put forward in the past decades, the Interaction Hypothesis (Long 1996) is one that claims that there is a strong connection between learners' engagement in conversational interaction and second language (L2) acquisition. The process of acquisition is held to be facilitated by learners' participation in meaningful conversational interaction with other learners or with native speakers (NSs). *Negotiation* is a special type of conversational interaction that takes place between learners and their interlocutors when one of them indicates that the other's message has not been successfully conveyed, as illustrated by the well-known example from Pica (1994: 514) in (1):

(1)   Learner: the windows are crozed
           NS: the windows have what?
       Learner: closed
           NS: crossed? I'm not sure what you are saying there
       Learner: windows are closed
           NS: oh the windows are closed oh. Ok, sorry

In this conversation between an English L2 learner and an English NS while they are engaged in a task in which they have to describe a picture to their interlocutor, there is clearly a lack of understanding on the part of the NS. This is verbalized in the form of a question in the second line. The learner then produces the word "closed," which still seems problematic. The NS produces the word "crossed" to compare with "closed"; the learner finally pronounces the word properly and the NS acknowledges that the utterance has been understood. During negotiation both interlocutors attempt to *repair* communication as they work toward mutual comprehension.

The study of conversational interaction among L2 learners and their interlocutors has been central to the study of SLA since the beginning of the 1980s, and numerous empirical studies have claimed to have shown strong links between interaction and learning (e.g. Adams 2007; Mackey 1999; Mackey and Philp 1998; McDonough 2005; see especially Keck, Iberri-Shea, Tracy-Ventura and Wa-Mbaleka 2006 and Mackey and Goo's 2007 meta-analyses of interaction research). The Interaction Hypothesis could be considered a theory, as it tries to explain why interaction and learning might be linked using concepts from other areas of knowledge such as psychology. On the other hand, as Gass and Mackey (2007: 176) observe, researchers are starting to consider the Interaction Hypothesis in terms of a model of SLA, as it describes some of the processes involved when learners are exposed to input, produce output and receive feedback on that output. (See Chapter 30, this volume, for more on this.) We will thus refer to this SLA framework as the *Interaction Model* (IM).

This chapter is organized as follows: Section 10.2 presents a historical overview of the origins of research on the role of learner interaction in language learning, where we will refer to the seminal work by Hatch (1978b) and Long (1980, 1981) and the latter's important revision of the Interaction Hypothesis (Long 1996). Section 10.3 describes the major theoretical constructs of input, output and feedback and illustrates how interaction is argued to facilitate learning by providing contexts in which learners are exposed to L2 input and are "pushed" (Swain 2005) to make their output more accurate. Interaction also provides learners with an opportunity to negotiate meaning and form with their conversational partners and to receive feedback in response to difficulties that might arise during conversational exchanges. Both negotiation and feedback have been shown to play an important facilitative role in language learning (Mackey 2006; see also Chapters 29 and 30, this volume). Section 10.4 considers several factors that influence conversational interaction and Section 10.5 concludes the chapter, highlighting lines for further research within the IM.

10.2 A brief historical overview

Pica (1996: 246) points out that early researchers on conversational interaction traced their roots to ethnomethodology and conversational analysis and in particular to work by Garfinkel (1967), where the term *negotiation* was used to refer to the process by which participants in a conversation structure their social relationships, taking turns at talking and communicating meaning to each other. Negotiation as a term appeared in the SLA literature as early as 1980 (J. Schwartz 1980).

In the same way that the so-called baby-talk register was studied in research on child language development (Gallaway and Richards 1994), during the 1960s and 1970s some sociolinguists started to pay attention to the special register of NS-learner interaction. They observed that NSs tended to address foreigners with a simplified variety of the language, which was referred to as *foreigner talk*. Hatch (1978a, 1978b) argued that analyzing the properties of this register could provide information not only about social aspects of the type of language addressed to this group (Gumperz 1964, 1970) but also – and crucially – about the linguistic features of the L2 learning process. Hatch's contribution was a turning point in the study of learner language because she argued that researchers should change their assumptions about the nature of the language learning process: it was not that the learning of the L2 structures would lead to the learners' communicative use of the L2. On the contrary, the learning of the L2 is claimed to evolve out of communicative use itself (Pica 1996: 247). In her own words "One learns how to do conversation, one learns how to interact verbally, and out of this interaction syntactic structures are developed" (Hatch 1978b: 404). Thus, Wagner-Gough and Hatch (1975) showed how learners' participation in conversational interaction provided them with opportunities to process and produce the L2 and was "beyond its role as simply a forum for practice" (Gass, Mackey and Pica 1998: 300).

Hatch's view was very different from what Krashen (1982, 1985) proposed in his Input Hypothesis, which holds that the process of L2 learning by adults is incidental and implicit and that exposure to comprehensible input is both a necessary and sufficient condition for L2 learning to take place. (Editors' note: see Chapter 6 and chapters in Part V.) Linked to the hypothesis are two other ideas: (i) speaking is the result of acquisition and not its cause, and (ii) if input is understood, and there is enough of it, the necessary grammar is automatically provided. Those claims are hard to sustain in light of the empirical studies carried out in French immersion programs in Canada (see Section 10.3.2). (Editors' note: but see Chapter 7 on poverty of the stimulus.)

Long's (1980, 1981, 1983b, 1985) pioneering studies analyzed the talk directed to L2 learners by NSs and the interactions in which they engaged. He showed that although there were few linguistic differences between the talk produced in NS-NS and NS-learner conversations – as attested by several measures of grammatical complexity – there were interesting changes in the structure of conversational interaction – conversational management in learner-learner interactions regarding the use of conversational and linguistic adjustments. These adjustments were not unique to learner discourse but were significantly more numerous in instructional environments. Long suggested that those adjustments might play a role in interlocutors' provision of comprehensible input and proposed a systematic approach to linking those features to the learners' L2 development. The steps proposed by Long (1985: 378) for a systematic study of learners' participation in conversational interaction were the following:

Step 1: Show that (a) linguistic/conversational adjustments promote (b) comprehension of input.

Step 2: Show that (b) comprehensible input promotes (c) acquisition.
Step 3: Deduce that (a) linguistic/conversational adjustments promote (c) acquisition.

Long argued that the first step – that linguistic and conversational adjustments promote comprehension of input – was indirectly supported because there is no evidence of successful language learning in the absence of comprehensible input (but see White's (1987) claim that it is precisely incomprehensible input that drives the acquisition process as understood within generative theories). The second step – by making input more comprehensible, acquisition is promoted – found support in the research carried out during the 1980s and 1990s by Long himself and in the studies by Pica and colleagues (Pica 1993; Pica, Doughty and Young 1986; Pica, Young and Doughty 1987; Pica, Holliday, Lewis, Berducci and Newman 1991) and by Gass and Varonis (1985a, 1985b) among others. As Pica (2009: 475) points out, during this early stage of the research, there was a need for descriptive data on L2 classrooms. Research focused on the outcomes of NS–learner or learner–learner interactions while they performed different communicative tasks. For example, comparisons were made between the percentages of learners' utterances that lexically and/or structurally modified their prior utterances during learner–learner negotiation with the percentage of NSs' utterances that did likewise during NS–learner interaction. By documenting in detail the participants' interactional moves and the modifications produced during negotiation the studies aimed to show that interaction provided the necessary conditions to facilitate language acquisition.

In his early research Long (1980, 1981, 1983b) referred to the efforts by NS and learners to avoid a breakdown in communication as *interactional modifications*. But, how do NS and learners resolve non-understanding sequences? How do they negotiate meaning in their conversations and make input more comprehensible? Long (1983b) operationalized negotiation as confirmation checks, clarification requests and comprehension checks. *Confirmation checks* (Long 1983b: 137) are "any expressions... immediately following an utterance by the interlocutor which are designed to elicit confirmation that the utterance has been correctly heard or understood by the speaker," as illustrated in (2):

(2)   NS: I am over the deadline for this project.
       Learner: You mean you should have done the job by now?
                                              ← confirmation check
       NS: Exactly.
                                                    (García Mayo 1997)

In example (2) the learner wants to make sure that she has understood the NS's utterance properly so she paraphrases what the NS has said. The NS confirms that his message has been properly understood.

A *clarification request* is "any expression... designed to elicit clarification of the interlocutor's preceding utterance(s)" (Long 1983b: 137). Thus, by means of clarification requests the learner or the NS elicits information regarding a preceding utterance that is causing problems for the proper understanding of the conversation, as illustrated in (3), where the NS does not understand the meaning of the word *headmaster*:

(3) Teacher: So all of us want a new way of testing, so let´s create it. We are going to find the characteristics to find a good way of testing. So you start saying things and Marta will write them on the blackboard. Finally we will present an alternative to the headmaster.
Student: Headmaster? ← **clarification request**
Teacher: The person in charge of the school is the headmaster.
(Alcón Soler 1994: 87)

Comprehension checks are attempts "to anticipate and prevent a breakdown in communication" (Long 1983b: 136), as illustrated in example (4), where the teacher uses a comprehension check in anticipating that his/her interlocutor might have problems understanding a lexical item:

(4) Teacher: Today we are going to examine different brochures. Do you know what a brochure is? ← **comprehension check**
Student: *Folleto*?
Teacher: Yes, that is a brochure
(Alcón Soler 2007: 46)

In his update of the Interaction Hypothesis, Long (1996: 418) defines negotiation as follows:

> the process in which, in an effort to communicate, learners and competent speakers provide and interpret signals of their own and their interlocutor's perceived comprehension, thus provoking adjustments to linguistic form, conversational structure, message content, or all three, until an acceptable level of understanding is achieved.

and notes that

> negotiation for meaning, and especially negotiation work that triggers interactional adjustments by the NS or more competent interlocutor, facilitates acquisition because it connects input, internal learner capacities, particularly selective attention, and output in productive ways. (Long 1996: 451–52)

Pica (1994) describes with numerous examples how negotiation contributes to the language learning process because it facilitates comprehension of L2 input and draws learners' attention to L2 form–meaning relationships (through the process of repetition, segmentation and rewording). Long (1996, 2007) also highlights the role of negotiation of meaning and conversational adjustments as facilitators in the process of L2 acquisition and, most importantly, emphasizes the critical role not only of input and output as building blocks in the process but also of learners' internal cognitive capacities.

In sum, research over the last decades has shown that when interaction is modified through negotiation, learners receive comprehensible input that supplies phonological, lexical and morphosyntactic data for their learning, opportunities to receive feedback and to produce modified output (Adams 2007; García Mayo 2005; García Mayo and Pica 2000; Gass and Varonis 1989; Mackey, Oliver and Leeman 2003; Pica, Lincoln-Porter, Paninos and Linnell 1996).

As noted by Mackey (2007:10), researchers in the 1990s provided a more detailed analysis of the components of interaction and operationalized them to study their impact on the learning process. Research on interaction and negotiation is currently not so focused on establishing a connection between conversational interaction and L2 learning but, rather, on the relation between interaction, learner-internal cognitive processes and L2 learning. The following section presents the L2 learning outcomes of input, output and feedback, three major constructs of the IM, as identified by Gass and Mackey (2007), and reviews research that has shown how they facilitate L2 learning in conversational interaction.

10.3 Input, output and feedback during conversational interaction

10.3.1 Input

Input refers to the linguistic forms learners are exposed to, both oral and written, and the visual signal in the case of sign language. Different SLA theories differ as to how much input is needed to facilitate the learning process and how it needs to be organized (Gass and Mackey 2006). As mentioned above, Krashen's (1982) Input Hypothesis was a first attempt to connect input and acquisition (but see Carroll (2001) on the generative view of input, and see Chapter 26, this volume). However, his proposal met with severe criticism as, among other issues, it was not easily testable and some of its constructs were not clearly defined and/or operationalized (Gregg 1984; McLaughlin 1987).

Input presented to the second language learner can be of different types. We can talk about *authentic* or unmodified input vs. *modified input*. The latter can be modified in several ways (see Chapter 29, this volume, for specific discussions of structured input and the appendix for examples). For example, an oral or written text can be *simplified* by using shorter sentences and simpler lexical items within the range of the learner's needs. Input can also be *elaborated* in different ways. Research has tested whether one type of elaborated input, referred to as *enhanced input* (Sharwood Smith 1991) facilitates the L2 acquisition process. Input enhancement has been used in a number of studies (Alanen 1995; Alcón Soler 2005; Izumi 2002; Jourdenais, Ota, Stauffer, Boyson and Doughty 1995; J. White 1998) to attempt to increase the salience of certain target structures (English articles, possessive pronouns, speech acts, etc.) in order to augment noticing (focal awareness, Schmidt 1990) and, consequently, the amount of *intake*, that is, the subset of input that becomes available to the learner. Only Jourdenais *et al.* (1995) found significant effects of input enhancement on noticing and subsequent production. In the other studies the effects were weaker or non-existent. Obviously, this might have been due to the fact that the salience of certain features of the input depends not only on the external characteristics of the input but also on learner-internal factors (Robinson 1995).

Interactionally modified input has been claimed to be more effective than other types of modification, both in NS–learner and learner–learner conversations (Gass and Varonis 1994; Loschky 1994; Pica 1993). Consider example (5), an exchange between two learners:

(5) S1: And they have the spaceship
     S2: The what?
     S1: The spaceship
     S2: What does it mean?
     S1: Like a car to travel to the space
     S2: Ah
     S1: The astronauts use it to go to the moon
     S2: Oh *nave espacial*

(Alcón Soler 2002: 360)

In example (5), Learner 2 interrupts Learner 1's utterance to ask about the meaning of *spaceship*. Learner 1 responds by using a paraphrase. Again negotiation offers L2 input that highlights the meaning of the unknown lexical item and its use in context.

There have been several studies that have specifically tested whether interactionally modified input would make L2 input more comprehensible and, thus, facilitate the learning process. One of the earlier empirical studies was Pica *et al.* (1987). The researchers compared the comprehension of sixteen learners of English on directions to a task presented by an NS. The learners were split into two experimental conditions: the premodified input condition, where input was modified in terms of decreased complexity and increased quantity and redundancy, and the interactionally modified input condition, where the participants had opportunities to interact with the NS. The study showed that interactional modifications aided input comprehension, whereas the grammatical complexity of the input seemed to make little difference. Interaction appeared to have the greatest effect when it was accomplished through confirmation and comprehension checks and clarification requests. Gass and Varonis (1994) analyzed data from sixteen learner–NS interaction in a direction-giving task. The learners were divided into a modified input group and an unmodified input group. The groups were differentiated by the kind of input the NS gave to the learner (interactive or non-interactive). The first trial of the task measured learner comprehension and considered their performance when the NS gave directions to place objects on a board, and the second trial considered learner production, as measured by the NS's success in following the learner's directions. The hypothesis the researchers entertained was that those learners who had the opportunity to interact with the NS when they were receiving directions would be better able to give directions on the second trial, which was precisely the case.

Loschky (1994) tested whether interactionally modified input would have an impact on the comprehension of specific vocabulary items and locative constructions in Japanese. There were three groups in the experimental study performed by forty-one L2 Japanese learners: (i) the unmodified input group, where the learners received basic descriptions of objects, (ii) the premodified input group, where descriptions were simplified and (iii) the interactionally modified input group, where learners were allowed to interact with a NS. Loschky concluded that interaction facilitated the comprehension of vocabulary items but the same could not be claimed about the retention or acquisition of those same items or of the locative structure. Different results were reported by R. Ellis, Tanaka and Yamazaki (1994) in their study of two groups of Japanese ESL learners. The researchers found empirical evidence for a link between interactionally modified input and vocabulary acquisition: the learners featured a better comprehension and produced more words when the input was interactionally modified than with premodified input.

Mackey (1999) was a seminal experimental study with a pre-test–post-test design where the researcher showed that interactionally modified input actually facilitated the development of question formation in English. The experimental design was complex: the thirty-four adult ESL participants were divided into five groups: (i) interactors, those who received interactionally modified input while engaged in three tasks; (ii) interactor "unreadies," who received the same input as the interactors but were at an earlier developmental level as regards question formation in English according to Pienemann and Johnson's (1987) stages; (iii) observers, who were asked to observe the interaction but did not participate in it; and (iv) scripted, who received premodified input. There was also a control group. For statistical purposes, the groups were divided into those who took part in interaction and those that did not. Mackey showed that "the group that took part in interaction was significantly more likely to demonstrate sustained stage increase than the group that did not participate in interaction" (1999: 571).

Studies such as Pica et al. (1996) with Japanese ESL learners of a low-intermediate level of proficiency – one of the first direct empirical tests of the Interaction Hypothesis claims, together with Loschky (1994) – and García Mayo and Pica (2000), with Spanish EFL advanced learners, focused, among other issues, on the role of the learner as an input provider in conversational interactions with other learners and with NSs. Whereas the low-intermediate Japanese ESL learners were a limited source of modified input, the advanced Spanish EFL learners used a range of conversational modifications which conformed to target L2 morphosyntax yet were simpler and, thus, were a source of modified input.

Although much more research needs to be done on the role of interactionally modified input, studies carried out so far point to its importance as a facilitator of L2 comprehension and of development as it focuses learners' attention on potential gaps in their interlanguage.

10.3.2 Output

Output is the term used to refer to the language that learners produce in speaking and writing. Output has generally been seen not as a way of creating knowledge but as a way of practicing what has previously been learned or as a way of providing more input. For Krashen (1982), for example, output does not play any important role: in his model learners' production is only considered as provision of positive evidence for interlocutors in the language learning process. Krashen (1998: 177) claims that one can develop "extremely high levels of language and literacy without any language production at all."

A different perspective is provided on the basis of research carried out within Canadian immersion programs, which indicated that, after some years of schooling, immersion students communicated fluently but not accurately in French (Harley 1992). One possible explanation could be that these learners have limited access to nativelike models of the target language. Another important factor to bear in mind, however, is that they also had very little opportunity to produce language. Thus, Allen, Swain, Harley and Cummins (1990) observed that the overwhelming majority (over 80 percent) of their 8- and 11-year-old learners' utterances were simple one-clause sentences. Swain (1985), who argued that an input-rich and communicatively oriented classroom could not provide all that is needed for targetlike proficiency, proposed the *Output Hypothesis* (Swain 1985, 1995, 1998, 2005), claiming that output can not be seen merely as an end product of learning but, rather, as an important factor to promote the L2 learning process. In her own words (1995: 128):

> Output may stimulate learners to move from the semantic, open-ended, non-deterministic, strategic processing prevalent in comprehension to the complete grammatical processing needed for accurate production. Output, thus, would seem to have a potentially significant role in the development of syntax and morphology.

That is, learners should have opportunities to use the language in production rather than merely for comprehension. Consider the following examples occurring during the completion of different tasks:

(6) Learner 1: yes, and here is .. ah! But this is different! There are two people .. or maybe has a .. a ...
Learner 2: a what?
Learner 1: the hair, maybe the hair of the one is not the same
(García Mayo 2001: 141)

(7) Learner: I go home about eight and after I go swimming
NS: Huh?
Learner: I went to swimming with my friends
(McDonough 2007: 332)

In example (6) Learner 1 responds to Learner 2's clarification request *a what?* by being more detailed about the description of the character in the vignette they are working on. In Swain's terms, Learner 2 "pushes" Learner 1 to make his utterance more comprehensible to his interlocutor. In example (7) the learner reformulates his original utterance again as a response to the NS's signal of lack of understanding. The reformulation involves the change from *go* to *went* and the adding of more detailed information (*swimming with my friends*), although the utterance is still not targetlike because of the wrong use of the proposition *to*.

Swain (1995, 1998) proposed three functions that output plays in the L2 learning process. The first is the *noticing function* which posits that it is "while attempting to produce the target language (vocally or subvocally) that learners may notice that they do not know how to say (or write) precisely the meaning they want to convey" (Swain 1998: 67). There are several levels of noticing: learners may "notice the gap" (Schmidt and Frota 1986), that is, they may realize the form they produce is different from the target language form, and they may also "notice the hole" (Swain 1995), when they notice that they can't say what they want to say accurately in the target language. Williams (2005: 683) points out that noticing the gap involves cognitive comparison, which has been argued to be a crucial process in language acquisition (R. Ellis 1997a). The important role of noticing should be considered from the perspective of the claim that noticing a form in the input must occur in order for that form to be acquired. In other words, target language input becomes intake only when it is noticed. (Editors' note: but see Chapters 6 and 9, this volume.) Schmidt (1990, 2001) proposed the Noticing Hypothesis in which he emphasized the importance of attention and awareness, the latter being a requirement for learning. Several studies (Leow 2000; Robinson 1997) have provided support for the Noticing Hypothesis.

Alcón Soler (2007) and Alcón Soler and García Mayo (2008) report on data collected in foreign language classrooms exploring the relationship between focus on form, noticing, uptake and subsequent lexical gains. The database consisted of seventeen 45-minute audio-recorded teacher-led conversations, 204 learners' diaries, post-tests and delayed post-test translations from twelve EFL learners. While Alcón Soler (2007) shows a positive relationship between the teacher's pre-emptive focus on vocabulary items, noticing and subsequent post-testing of noticed items, Alcón Soler and García Mayo (2008) consider the relationship between learners' pre-emptive and reactive focus on form, uptake, noticing and subsequent lexical production of lexical words noticed. Their findings indicate that both reactive and pre-emptive focus on form episodes occur in meaning-focused activities but that successful uptake is more likely to occur when learners themselves perceive problems in their output than when the teacher anticipates those problems.

The second function of output is *hypothesis formulation and testing*. Swain (1998: 68) claims that learners may use their output "as a way to try out new language forms and structures as they stretch their interlanguage to meet communicative needs; they may use output to see what works and what does not." Consider the following example:

(8) Hiroko: a man is uh drinking c-coffee or tea uh with uh the saucer of the uh uh coffee set is uh in his uh knee
Izumi: in him knee
Hiroko: uh on his knee
Izumi: yeah
Hiroko: on his knee
Izumi: so sorry, on his knee

(Gass and Varonis 1989: 80–81)

In the conversation between the two Japanese learners, Hiroko produces the correct possessive pronoun *his* but Izumi considers that the correct form is *him*. Hiroko insists and also changes the preposition in a second turn. Finally Izumi agrees to the use of *his*. Oral interaction between learners does not always end up with their using the appropriate targetlike form. In (9), for example, Learner 1 questions up to four times the wrong use of the past form of the verb *arrive* that his partner seems to prefer, although he finally decides to go with the wrong form *arrove*:

(9) Learner 1: John arrive, arrove, arrive or arrove?
Learner 2: arrove is in past
Learner 1: arrove airport. Or arrived.
Learner 2: arrove, is in past
Learner 1: I mean arrove or arrived
Learner 2: arroved the airplane
Learner 1: arrived or arroved?
Learner 2: arrove
Learner 1: arrove the airport at 8:30 am

(Adams 2007: 48–49)

A third function of output is a *metalinguistic function*. According to Swain (1998: 68), "the learners' own language indicates an awareness of something about their own or their interlocutor's use of language. That is, learners use language to reflect on language use." For Swain, this metatalk is language used for cognitive purposes and it may help learners to understand the relationship between meaning, forms and function. In (10), for example, the two advanced learners are trying to reconstruct a text in which they were required to make all the necessary changes to produce a meaningful and grammatical paragraph. The material in italics in the interaction is part of the text. The learners disagree about whether the adjective *inclined* should be followed by *to* or by *-ing* and there is metalanguage throughout their interaction:

(10) Learner 1: *men are less incline*... it has to be an adjective... inclined to confess, you are inclined to do something...
Learner 2: to confession...
Learner 1: to confess...
Learner 2: but after a preposition ...
Learner 1: to confess... what?
Learner 2: to is a preposition ...
Learner 1: yeah ...
Learner 2: so it should be followed by ing
Learner 1: inclined to confessing...
Learner 2: yeah
Learner 1: no, because to is part of the second verb... inclined to confess... yeah
Learner 2: ok, I trust you

(García Mayo 2002: 329)

Besides the three functions Swain claims output serves in the L2 learning process, other researchers have studied the psycholinguistic mechanisms underlying the production of language. Thus, it has been argued that modified output may promote cognitive processing of syntactic and semantic aspects of language, the change from declarative to procedural knowledge and automaticity (Anderson 1983; de Bot 1996; DeKeyser 2001; see Izumi 2003 and Muranoi 2007 for a detailed review of the psycholinguistic mechanisms underlying the Output Hypothesis; see also Chapter 6, this volume).

A number of empirical studies have been carried out to identify how modified output can impact L2 learning during conversational interaction. Based on these studies' findings it is currently claimed that negotiated interaction provides opportunities to produce and modify output, claimed to be a crucial aspect of L2 learning. Following Long's logic, early work by Pica, Holliday, Lewis and Morgenthaler (1989) considered how Japanese learners of English responded linguistically when NSs signalled difficulty in understanding the learners while performing three different tasks (information gap, jigsaw and discussion). The findings of the study confirmed that comprehensible output was an outcome of linguistic demands placed on the leaner by the NS in the course of their negotiated interaction with the NNs.

Muranoi (2000) examined the impact of *interaction enhancement* (IE) – a treatment in which both input and output are enhanced – on the learning of English articles by ninety-one Japanese university learners. IE is argued to guide learners to focus on form by providing interactional modifications and to lead them to produce modified output; it turned out to be beneficial for learners regarding the specific grammar point focused on (English articles). McDonough (2005) carried out a study in which she examined the impact of negative feedback and learners' responses on ESL question development. Over an eight-week period, sixty Thai EFL learners participated in three treatment sessions, consisting of information-exchange and information-gap activities, and completed four oral production tests. The findings of the study indicated that the only significant predictor of ESL question development was the production of modified output involving developmentally advanced question forms in response to negative feedback. Like the study just described, Sato and Lyster (2007) compared the interactional patterns of learner–learner and learner–NS dyads in a foreign language setting focusing on learners' production of modified output during task completion (two-way information gap tasks) and investigated whether this interaction differs depending on the interlocutor. The researchers coded the interaction data of eight Japanese learners and four English NSs and identified language-related episodes (LREs) – "[episodes] that entail discussion of meaning or form, but may emphasize one of these more than the other" (Swain and Lapkin 2001: 104). Their findings indicate that learners modified output significantly more in learner–learner dyads than in learner–NS dyads, a result that is explained on the basis of the learners' comments in a follow-up retrospective session, where they expressed being under pressure and more passive when the interlocutor was an NS.

A fruitful line of research dealing with one of the specific functions of output, noticing, started with Swain and Lapkin's (1995) study in which they reported that their learners consciously recognized linguistic problems and modified their output while writing. Qi and Lapkin (2001) conducted a case study of two adult Mandarin ESL learners engaged in a three-stage writing task. Their findings indicated that noticing in the composing stage influenced noticing in the feedback stage. Adams (2003) and Swain and Lapkin (2002) support the important role of output on noticing (but see Truscott 1998 where he found no effect of such form-focused feedback on writing).

Work on output–input cycles (Basterrechea and García Mayo 2010; Izumi 2002; Izumi and Bigelow 2000; Izumi and Izumi 2004; Izumi, Bigelow, Fujiwara and Fearnow 1999; Leeser 2008; Song and Suh 2008) considers the role of pushed output in noticing specific target features in the input and the effect of receiving subsequent input (after production has taken place). Learners are engaged in output–input cycles and compare their production with input received subsequently in the different experimental designs. In order to determine the effect of pushed output on noticing, results of the experimental groups, who are given output opportunities in the form of text-reconstruction tasks, are compared to control groups whose learners are exposed to the same input but do not engage in output activities. Overall, the findings in these studies point to the benefits of the output groups: learners engaged in output treatments outperform those in the control groups in the comprehension of the input (Izumi 2002; Izumi and Bigelow 2000; Izumi et al. 1999; Leeser 2008) and in the noticing of the target form (Basterrechea and García Mayo 2010). A recent line of research focuses on the benefits of another form of output, referred to as syntactic priming, a speaker's tendency to produce a previously spoken or heard sentence. In McDonough and Mackey (2008) research assistants participating in a variety of tasks with ESL learners were trained to use question forms that were one developmental stage higher than the learners' current knowledge of question formation. The findings showed that the learners had a tendency to produce questions that were structurally the same as the one immediately produced before by the research assistant, a question form at a stage higher than the learners' knowledge of question formation, rather than lower-level question forms.

Although, as with any other aspect of the learning of an L2, output may be influenced by different variables such as the learners' proficiency level, age, gender and interlocutor (another learner or an NS), there seems to be increasing evidence that learners' engagement in conversational interaction may facilitate their development in the target language.

10.3.3 Feedback

Leeman (2007: 112) defines feedback as

> a mechanism which provides the learner with information regarding the success or failure of a given process. By definition, feedback is responsive and thus can occur only *after* a given process.

Feedback can be positive or negative but most L2 acquisition research has focused on negative feedback, which has been observed to serve as the starting point for negotiated interaction (Mackey and Philp 1998). Some researchers (Gass 1997; Long 1996; Pica 1994) have claimed that this feedback facilitates L2 acquisition on the basis of studies both in classroom (Doughty and Varela 1998; Mackey 2006; McDonough 2005) and laboratory contexts with instructed learners (Ayoun 2001; Leeman 2003; Mackey and Philp 1998; Mackey and Silver 2005). On the basis of the feedback received from their interlocutors during conversational interaction, learners may (i) notice mismatches between their production and the targetlike forms and (ii) modify their output.

Feedback can vary greatly in the form it takes when provided to learners and is often viewed as a continuum from explicit to implicit. *Explicit feedback* refers to situations in which the interlocutor (an NS, a teacher or another learner) provides linguistic information about the non-targetlike nature of the utterance that has been produced. *Implicit feedback* is an indirect and less obtrusive way to show that learners' utterances are problematic and is of more interest within the interactional model. The interactional modifications identified in Long's early work are examples of implicit feedback.

Research within the IM has paid a great deal of attention lately to another type of implicit feedback: *recasts*. Previously referred to as "expansions" (Chaudron 1977) or "completion or elaboration" (Pica et al. 1989), recasts are defined as "utterances that repeat a learner's incorrect utterance, making only the changes necessary to produce a correct utterance, without changing its meaning" (Nicholas Lightbown and Spada 2001: 273). Example (11) illustrates a recast:

(11) Learner: Your picture how many cat your picture?
NS: How many cats are there in my picture?   ← Recast
Learner. Yeah how many cats?
(Mackey 1999: 561)

Recasts frequently occur as responses to grammatical and phonological errors but their effectiveness as feedback is inconclusive. Studies on recasts have focused on describing their frequency and effectiveness. Their frequency, however, does not guarantee their saliency (Sheen 2006). For example, Lyster and colleagues (Lyster 1998, 2001; Lyster and Ranta 1997) studied French immersion classrooms and indicated that young L2 learners may not notice target–non-target mismatches by means of recasts. (See also Chapter 9, this volume, regarding non-/low-literate adult L2 learners' responses to recasts.) They suggest that other types of feedback, which include teacher's elicitation, metalinguistic clues, clarification requests and repetitions (which are collectively referred to as prompts (Lyster 2004a)) might be more effective in drawing learners' attention. However, Ohta (2000b) found Japanese FL learners reacted to teacher recasts provided in class. Similarly in a laboratory study, Mackey and Philp (1998) showed that intensive recast treatment had a positive effect on learners' use of target question forms but was not significantly related to L2 development. Oliver and Mackey (2003) argue that the extent to which learners modify their output after a recast is contingent on the interactional context (explicit vs. communicative language contexts) in which the recast appears. In their study, if the context made the recasts explicit, they became more salient. In any case, as Nabei and Swain (2002) mention, recasts are complex behavior and they depend on many variables such as the length of the recast and its linguistic focus, among others (see Sheen 2006, and Loewen and Philp 2006 for a review).

Modified output as a response to interactional feedback has been linked to L2 development in several studies (Loewen 2005; McDonough 2005; McDonough and Mackey 2006) and to noticing of L2 forms (Mackey 2006). Studies have also yielded evidence that learners are able to provide and respond to feedback in conversational interaction with other learners (Adams 2007; García Mayo and Pica 2000; Sato and Lyster 2007; Toth 2008), although the quality of those learner–learner interactions may differ from those between learners and NSs. The studies in Nassaji and Simard (2010) show that interactional feedback and focus on form can make a positive impact on L2 learning. An interesting line of research within the IM is that focusing on learners' cognitive processes when they receive feedback in conversational interaction. Mackey, Gass and McDonough (2000) investigated whether EFL and Italian as a foreign language learners perceived implicit negative feedback as such in task-based interaction with NSs and whether they were able to identify the element that triggered feedback. After task completion, the learners watched videotapes about their performance and, when asked to introspect about their thoughts while completing the tasks, they were found to be quite accurate in their perceptions of lexical, semantic and phonological feedback. However, morphosyntactic feedback was generally not perceived as such. A recent replication of Mackey *et al.* (2000) was carried out by Gass and Lewis (2007) with heritage vs. non-heritage learners of Italian. The findings of their study generally supported those in the original. Mackey (2002) also explored learners' roles in relation to different interactional processes, feedback being one of them (Mackey 2002: 387–89) and she concluded that there is substantial overlap between researchers' claims and learners' comments about their interactional opportunities.

Thus, research in the last several decades has shown that feedback received during interaction facilitates the L2 learning process and is linked to L2 development. However, this relationship is mediated by several factors such as the degree of feedback explicitness, the type of interlocutor and the target grammatical structure (R. Ellis 2007), among others. Much more qualitative and quantitative research is needed to support this claim. Russell and Spada (2006), in their meta-analysis of corrective feedback, did not find differences in the effectiveness of different types of responses given to learners' errors. More recently Li (2010) carried out a meta-analysis on the effectiveness of corrective feedback whose findings point to an overall effect maintained over time specifically for implicit corrective feedback.

10.4 Factors influencing conversational interaction

As we have seen above, conversational interaction is believed to facilitate the necessary connections between input, output, feedback and some learner cognitive capacities (noticing and attention). But there are several factors that can influence the development of conversational interaction, and SLA research has paid attention to these too. On the one hand, there has been increasing research on tasks, where task-based language teaching (TBLT) has been primarily informed by Long's (1996) Interaction Hypothesis (R. Ellis 2003: 100). On the other hand, there are several individual differences that may have an impact on the way conversational interaction develops. In this section we will briefly consider task-related and interlocutor characteristics and how they can affect interaction.

10.4.1 Tasks and conversational interaction

Task is a central concept in current instructed SLA research, both as a research instrument and as a construct in need of investigation (R. Ellis 2003; García Mayo 2007; Seedhouse 2005a). Researchers manipulate tasks to test their theoretical claims and various task features which are of interest to researchers in their effort to understand the intricacies of how task-based interaction in the classroom might facilitate the process of L2 acquisition.

Task type was initially studied by Doughty and Pica (1986). They claim that unless the required information exchange task is chosen, that is, one in which participants have to share information in order to complete it, learners will interact less and will modify their interaction less as well (Doughty and Pica 1986: 321). Pica *et al.* (1989, 1991) have shown that information gap tasks provide a great number of opportunities for learners to receive NS modifications. More recently Pica, Kanga and Sanro (2006) used three well-known information gap tasks (spot the difference, jigsaw and grammar communication) to generate learners' modified interaction, noticing and awareness of English articles and verb morphology in a written passage. The three tasks were effective in drawing learners' attention to the target forms and, most importantly, in the retention of those forms during text reconstruction.

Within Vygotsky's sociocultural theory (Vygotsky 1978; Lantolf 2006), which claims that human cognitive development is a socially situated activity mediated by language (see Ohta, this volume), some researchers have also considered the nature of interaction using *collaborative tasks*. Ohta (2000b) shows that learners of Japanese as a foreign language working collaboratively give each other mutual support and co-construct meaning and knowledge. In a similar vein, Alcón Soler (2002) examines the nature of collaborative dialogue in teacher–student and peer–peer interaction and supports the claim that pragmatic knowledge may emerge from assisted performance. Ohta (2001c) also argues for the importance of private speech (speech directed to oneself) in L2 acquisition. Alegría de la Colina and García Mayo (2009) looked at learners' private speech in the interaction of twelve low-proficiency Spanish EFL learners in a study focusing of the role of the first language as a cognitive tool. They conclude that the use of private speech (captured by highly sensitive microphones) was essential to complete the different tasks because it was mainly used for reflection when learners were developing understanding of the information provided. Swain and Lapkin (2002) use a case study of two 12-year-old French immersion students working collaboratively to construct a story, orally and in writing, from a series of pictures in a jigsaw task. The authors, having examined the collaborative dialogues operationalized as LREs occurring while the students wrote, noticed and reflected on their noticing, conclude that "reformulation of learners' writing . . . is an effective technique for stimulating noticing and reflection on language" (see also Swain, Brooks and Tocalli-Beller 2002, for a review of reformulation). Alegría de la Colina and García Mayo (2007) explore the effects of three collaborative tasks (dictogloss, jigsaw and task reconstruction) designed to promote focus on form and metatalk among low-proficiency adult Spanish EFL learners. They conclude that the experience was beneficial, as it was through collaborative dialogue that learners were able to construct meaning while completing the tasks. More recently, Gánem Gutiérrez (2008) studied how adult Spanish foreign language learners collaborated while they undertook three different collaborative writing tasks. She carried out a qualitative analysis of the learners' oral transcripts and suggested that collaboration plays a role in the language improvement observed during the dialogic process.

Task complexity is another key feature that has received a great deal of attention lately. The Cognition Hypothesis (Robinson 2001b, 2001c, 2003, 2005b, 2007a, 2007b; Robinson and Gilabert 2007) posits that tasks that are more complex because of higher reasoning demands are more likely to promote interactional modification. In a study with Japanese EFL learners, Robinson (2001c) showed that they produced more confirmation checks when completing a complex task, where task complexity was operationalized as [− prior knowledge] and [+ few elements], although Nuevo (2006) does not support those results. More recently, Nuevo, Adams and Ross-Feldman (2011) empirically examined the effects of task complexity (operationalized as [+ reasoning demands]) on modified output and showed that there was very little effect of complexity on the type of modified output their participants (seventy-nine intermediate ESL learners) produced. The study had a pre-test/post-test design with learners engaged in three task-based treatment sessions with past tense and locative as the target structures.

Several studies have found that learners' *task repetition* has an impact on conversational interaction (Bygate 2001; Gass and Varonis 1985a; Plough and Gass 1993). However, others (Gass, Mackey, Alvarez-Torres and Fernández-García 1999) have found little support for the prediction that doing a task again would lead to improvement in overall proficiency over time.

As tasks are the tools classroom researchers use to test their claims about the importance of input, feedback and output in conversational interaction, research on task-related features is on the increase and will hopefully shed new light on the L2 process.

10.4.2 Individual differences and conversational interaction

One important line of research within the IM focuses on learners' individual differences and the extent to which these might affect their performance in particular tasks and their linguistic development (see Chapter 8, this volume). One of the individual differences that has been studied is *motivation*. For example, Dörnyei and Kormos (2000) have suggested that learners are more willing to communicate if they have a positive attitude toward the task they are engaged in and the same researchers have also claimed (Kormos and Dörnyei 2004) that the motivation of the interlocutor also plays a role in learning. In more recent work Dörnyei and Tseng (2009) claim that self-appraisal (the learner's continuous comparison between his/her performance and the predicted one) and specific mechanisms making up the learner's motivational system when processing a task are related to general factors such as attention and noticing, two of the learner's internal capacities which have been claimed to partially account for different learning outcomes (Robinson 1995).

Attention (mentioned above) and working memory have also been claimed to play a significant role in conversational interaction. Long (1996) already argued for the role of selective attention during interaction and Swain's (2005) Output Hypothesis claims that producing language forces the learners to pay attention to L2 form. Mackey, Philp, Egi, Fujii and Tatsumi (2002) examined the contribution of working and phonological memory in the noticing of recasts and reported that learners with larger working and phonological memory spans tended to be more likely to notice errors targeted by the recasts than those with smaller spans. (See Chapter 9, this volume.) More recently, Trofimovich, Ammar and Gatbonton (2007) examined the noticing and effectiveness of recasts as a function of learners' individual cognitive factors (phonological memory, working memory, analytical ability and attention control). Probably due to methodological differences with regard to the study by Mackey *et al.* (2002), none of the cognitive factors examined predicted the rate at which the learners noticed recasts but the effect of individual differences on the learners' use of the information available in the recasts was clear. Goo, Hama and Sachs (2009) studied how working memory capacity mediates the efficacy of corrective feedback and L2 development during task-based interaction. They concluded that working memory capacity significantly predicted the efficacy of recasts but not the efficacy of metalinguistic feedback (see also Mackey, Adams, Stafford and Winke 2010).

The study of the impact of *gender* in conversational interaction dates back to work by Gass and Varonis (1986), in which they observed that male language learners tend to dominate conversations and produce more language output while females tend to initiate more conversations and receive more input. (See Chapter 8, this volume, on additional individual factors such as personality.) There is comparatively little research on this issue in SLA. As pointed out by Ross-Feldman (2007: 56), in studies by Gass and Varonis (1986), Pica *et al.* (1989, 1991) and Oliver (2002) different learners interacted under either mixed- or matched-gender dyads. In her recent study, Ross-Feldman (2007) analyzes the interactions by males and females in both types of dyad to determine whether learner gender influences the incidence of LREs. Each participant interacted in both mixed- and matched-gender dyads and the overall finding was that the gender of the learners did influence the interactional patterns. Both males and females seemed to be advantaged by working with female language learners because they were more likely to articulate what they noticed. There was no significant difference between the LREs generated by the different dyads, though. More recently, Azkaray and García Mayo (2011) analyzed the interaction of Basque-Spanish male and female EFL learners while the participants carried out four tasks, two information-gap tasks (picture description and picture placement) and two collaborative tasks (dictogloss and picture story). Their findings showed that there was no significant difference between the LREs generated by matched- and mixed-gender dyads (in line with Ross-Feldman's results) but there was a significant task effect: LREs were more common in those tasks where a writing component was included.

Some individual differences have been shown to have an impact on conversational moves during interaction but there is clearly room for much more detailed research in this area.

10.5 Conclusions and lines for further research

Research on conversational interaction during the past three decades has shown that the processes that occur while both learners and NSs engage in communication have the potential to facilitate L2 learning. Conversational interaction may bring about segmentations and modifications in learners' production, negotiation of meaning, attention to problematic formal or meaning aspects on the basis of feedback provided and, most importantly, the engagement of the learners' cognitive mechanisms in processing form–meaning relationships. Through interaction with others, language learners obtain additional linguistic information that has an impact on their performance.

The importance of various empirical studies establishing that there is a clear link between conversational interaction and L2 learning cannot be denied. However, we should also be cautious and consider whether interaction is not the cause of learning but, rather, a facilitator of the process. Interaction is claimed to be necessary for the L2 learning process, but it is clearly not sufficient.

There is no doubt that we find ourselves in a very exciting time for the IM where research has opened up new areas that could not be foreseen when the foundational bricks were laid several decades ago. There is much work to be done in different areas. For example, most research on the IM has been carried out in ESL settings but foreign languages, not just English, are taught in classrooms throughout the world. Although some work on interaction in foreign language contexts has been carried out (see Alcón Soler and García Mayo 2009; García Mayo and Pica 2000; Havranek 2002; McDonough 2004; Sheen 2004; Shi 2004; Tognini 2008; and Philp and Tognini 2009 for a review), many questions remain to be addressed. An interesting area of research has been opened at least within the European and North American contexts with the increase of Content and Language Integrated Language (CLIL) approaches, which are being implemented at different educational levels (primary, secondary and university) in different countries. A reasonable question to ask would be whether access to the more finely tuned and frequent input that CLIL programs claim to offer has an impact on the conversational interaction that takes place among learners or between learners and teachers.

This chapter has reviewed the apparent benefits of interactional practices but, as Spada and Lightbown (2009) state, there is a clear need for more longitudinal and replication studies. The former would be necessary to establish the potential connection between interaction and language development (Philp 2009), the latter to determine interactional patterns that occur in different contexts, with different populations (children, adolescents and adults) and language combinations. On the individual learner front, more research needs to be carried out on cognitive processes and how they impact on interactional behavior and also on the learners' perception of the benefits of interactional practice on their learning outcomes. In order to carry out comparable research, there is a need to establish a clear operationalization of constructs and methodologies. The suggestion to create a common database on tasks used in interaction research, with guidelines as to which interactional mechanism each one is expected to trigger, would be an interesting step in that direction.

Other lines of research that will no doubt offer ways forward in interaction research are, on the one hand, the study of *computer-mediated communication* (CMC; see Chapter 14, this volume) and the question of whether and if so how online interaction generates opportunities for L2 learning (Kenning 2010; Sachs and Suh 2007; Sagarra 2007; Smith 2009; see Ortega 2009 for a review). On the other hand, there are developing lines of research that adopt a cross-disciplinary view of interaction, including insights from "systemic-functional linguistics, Vygotskian theory, dynamic systems theory, language socialization, language identity and conversational analysis" (Philp 2009: 258).

In addition, although some studies have illustrated the value of conversation as a method for understanding classroom interaction and its potential for pragmatic learning (Ishida 2004; Kasper 2004; Young and Miller 2004), further classroom-based research framed within the IM needs to be conducted in future studies. From this perspective, Dalton-Puffer (2005), Dalton-Puffer and Nikula (2006) and Nikula (2007, 2008) explore how interpersonal aspects of communication are realized in interaction and the way contextual factors such as the object of directives (information/action) or classroom register (instructional/regulative) affect speakers' directness choices. This type of research also illustrates the potential of interaction for gaining awareness of the specific conditions of pragmatic learning during classroom interaction.

11

Second language identity construction

Elizabeth R. Miller and Ryuko Kubota

11.1 Introduction

Contemporary approaches to identity and second language learning are most frequently traced to Bonny Norton's seminal research (1995, 2000) among immigrant women in Canada in which she noted that when learners invest in learning a language, they do so because they believe that knowing the language will offer them desirable identity options in the future. Her research was not the first to consider identity in relation to L2 learning, however. Block (2007a: 47) offers a comprehensive review of how learner identity was "lurking in the wings" of SLA dating back to the 1970s (see also Ricento 2005), and he regards Gardner and Lambert's (1972) research on learners' integrative and/or instrumental motivation to learn an L2 as among the first to account for learner identity (see Chapter 8, this volume). Block also points to research on language ego (Guiora, Beit-Hallahmi, Brannon, Dull and Scovel 1972), acculturation (Schumann 1976) and learner affect (Brown 1980), among others. However, as Block acknowledges, identity as conceptualized in earlier research differs quite starkly from most contemporary approaches to identity. The most important difference is Norton's and other contemporary researchers' rejection of the notion of language learner identity (and motivation) as a relatively stable trait. Norton drew on feminist poststructural theory (Weedon 1987) in arguing that an individual's identity (or subjectivity) is dynamic and may change from moment to moment and across time; that it is influenced by unequal power relations and is always a site of struggle; that it is hybrid and multiple; and, as such, that it must always be understood as a relational rather than an individual phenomenon. If identity is a socially and historically constructed relationship within discursive practices and among individuals, social groups and institutions, then teachers, researchers, policy makers, administrators and community leaders are all implicated in the range of identities available to language learners, or as Morgan (2007:

1037) argues, this means regarding second language learning as "a shared responsibility."

More than fifteen years have passed since Norton's first article (1995) appeared in which she urged scholars to consider the central significance of identity in understanding L2 learning processes, and the response has been remarkable. It is now commonplace to comment on the abundant and varied research that can broadly be labeled as identity research. Providing an overview of this sizable and still growing body of research is necessarily selective. We have organized our chapter by first discussing two of the primary conceptual frameworks that have informed identity research, poststructural and sociocultural. We then review studies according to selected identity categories: heritage language identities, multilingual identities, gendered identities, racialized identities and non-native language teacher identities.[1] Finally, we discuss some of the future directions we believe identity research needs to take in advancing this important area of study.

11.2 Conceptual frameworks

11.2.1 Poststructuralism and other postfoundational perspectives

Norton's (1995, 2000) research on identity, though groundbreaking in the field of second language studies, has been part of an important shift across the social sciences toward foregrounding the social construction of identity. This focus is an aspect of postfoundational inquiry which rejects the modernist notion of fixed objective and universal truths, and acknowledges the fluidity and plurality of language, culture and identity, while problematizing how knowledge, including the sense of self, is constructed in power and discourse. As applied to SLA, postfoundational approaches, including postmodernism, poststructuralism and postcolonialism (see Ninnes and Mehta 2004) "explore... how identities and agencies are performed, rather than determined by closed categories of language, gender, ethnicity and sexual identities, and how a plurality of meanings can be achieved in social, educational, and political contexts" (Kubota 2008: 330–31).

Poststructuralism includes multiple, sometimes conflicting, theoretical approaches (Block 2007a; Morgan 2007; Pavlenko 2002); however, there are shared perspectives across these approaches which have informed identity research. Pavlenko (2002: 282) has described poststructuralism in relation to L2 learning as "an attempt to investigate and to theorize the role of language in the construction and reproduction of social relations." Such "language" is better described as discourses or "systems of power/knowledge (Foucault 1982) that regulate and assign value to all forms of semiotic activity" (Morgan 2007: 1036). In other words, our social, cultural, historical and political realities are constituted by discursive practices, including our multiple, changing and complex identities. As such, all instances of language use are "acts of identity" (Le Page and Tabouret-Keller 1985; see also Pennycook 2007, 2010).

While identities are constructed in discourse and within relations of power, power is not just imposed on individuals; rather it circulates, is resisted and is appropriated, thus producing contradictory and oppositional identities.

In viewing identities as constituted in discourse, one begins to see why processes of language learning are integral to identity and why identity cannot be divorced from our attempts to better understand language learning. The struggle and contestation that often emerge as language learners seek to participate in new discursive practices occur in part because learners' "taken-for-granted points of reference" are gone (Block 2007b: 864) but also because the identity options available in those practices may be undesirable, and ultimately, disempowering. For example, Bourdieu's (1977, 1991) understanding of the importance of power relations in establishing how people can be (dis)valued through the ways in which they speak further highlights the profound significance of accounting for power relations in language learning. Though one might perfectly learn a linguistic system, Bourdieu contends that such competence cannot ensure that one will be regarded as a legitimate speaker of the language. Moreover, as Bakhtin (1981: 293) has argued, language does not reside in an individual, and even the notion of an individual speaker/learner is itself a fiction; rather language "lies on the borderline between oneself and the other" and as such inevitably involves struggle (1981).

The complex identity changes entailed in second language learning are not reducible to merely gaining an additional identity or a "half-and-half proposition whereby the individual becomes half of what he or she was and half of what he or she has been exposed to" (Block 2007b: 864). Rather this involves a continuous process of creating something new, a *third space* or hybrid identity. Informed by postcolonial scholarship (Bhabha 1994) as well as poststructural theory (see Kramsch 2009), the notion of "thirdness" foregrounds the heterogeneity of discourse and culture, and the hybridity of identity. Theories of thirdness and hybridity often foreground the positive, productive effects of power (Foucault 1980, 1982). That is, the instability of discourses and identities enables changes to take place and gives space for learners to act agentively in constructing desirable identity options for themselves. Kramsch (2009: 238) adds that thirdness allows language learners the right to appropriate a language and "give it other meanings than native speakers would."

One of the tensions that emerges in poststructuralism comes from the theoretical understanding of the ever-dynamic constitution of subject positions (i.e. emergent and fluctuating identities in interaction) which often contrasts with individuals' sense of their more enduring identities and/or others' attributions of relatively fixed or essential identities (Morgan 2007). Weedon (2004: 19) acknowledges the function of ideology to "temporarily fix" and to "curtail the plural possibilities of subjectivity" (cited in Block 2009: 217). Understood as discursively constructed, identities can be reconstructed again and again and, as such, can take on durability. Such a view is advanced in Butler's (1990, 1997) performativity theory. Butler (1990: 32) has focused primarily on gendered identities and has famously proposed that gender is "a set of repeated acts within a highly rigid regulatory frame that congeal over time to produce the appearance of substance, of a 'natural' kind of being." From this perspective, our ongoing social performances become sedimented into recognizable, durable identities that persist over time; the performance constitutes "the identity it is purported to be" (Pennycook 2001: 69). Given the attention among feminist poststructural theorists to the construction of gender identities, it is not surprising that researchers who have explored gendered identities in relation to language learning (see below) have frequently aligned with Butler's theoretical approach.

Racialized identity has also attracted researchers' attention in recent years (Curtis and Romney 2006; Kubota and Lin 2006, 2009b). Critical Race theory (CRT) shares similar perspectives with postfoundational thoughts, although its origin is in critical legal studies in the Unites States. CRT recognizes that racism is still deeply ingrained in contemporary society, privileging the racially and economically dominant group while oppressing others, that the idea of race is a social construction, that processes of racialization and forms of racism are not static or monolithic, and that each racialized group is heterogeneous (Delgado and Stefancic 2001). Through counter-storytelling offered by people of color, CRT challenges the prevailing narratives that privilege Eurocentric whiteness and oppress marginalized subjectivities. As in other postfoundational approaches, CRT avoids essentializing or privileging particular experiences by recognizing the intersection of race, gender, class, language, religion, sexual identity and other social categories. While only a few publications in applied linguistics have explicitly drawn on CRT (e.g. Curtis and Romney 2006; Michael-Luna 2008, 2009), other research on race reflects the tenets of CRT, shedding light on racialized identities in second language learning.

11.2.2 Sociocultural approaches to SLA

In considering power relations, social contexts and discourse in the constitution of learner identity, identity researchers foreground L2 learning as a sociocultural process and not solely cognitive (see Chapter 30, this volume). The Communities of Practice (CofP) or situated learning conceptual framework (Lave and Wenger 1991; Wenger 1998) has been drawn on by numerous SLA researchers who have explored Lave and Wenger's (1991: 115) contention that "learning and a sense of identity are inseparable; they are aspects of the same phenomenon." Lave and Wenger (1991: 53) add that learning "involves the whole person" and that it "implies becoming a full participant, a member, a kind of person." They proposed the notion of "legitimate peripheral participation" by which newcomers to a community of practice at first can participate only in limited, or peripheral, ways. However, as they gain a space for participating in the particular practices of those communities, and if they have the resources for doing so, they have the potential to increase their involvement toward more intensive participation and to develop desirable insider identities in these communities of practice. Language learning, as with every other kind of learning, is thus viewed as a relational engagement among participants of a community, and in much of the SLA research, such "communities" consist of classrooms or other school-based collectives.

Toohey (1996, 1998, 2000) is credited with introducing the CofP theory to SLA research in her ethnographic longitudinal study of young English language learners in Canada as they progressed from kindergarten to Grade 2/age 7 (see also Day 2002; Haneda 1997, 2006, 2008; DaSilva Iddings 2005; Kanno 2003; Morita 2000, 2004; Nguyen and Kellogg 2005; Norton and Toohey 2001; Ros i Solé 2007). In adopting this conceptual framework, Toohey (2000) foregrounds the need to focus on individuals-participating-in-community rather than on isolated individuals. Importantly, Toohey also highlights the role of power relations in such communities. She notes that if learners are blocked from participation or consigned to marginal participation in a community of practice, they will not be able to learn in the same way as those individuals who enjoy full participation. In foregrounding Lave and Wenger's (1991) insistence on the inseparability of learning and social practice, i.e. learning is inevitable when one participates in a practice, no matter how fully or peripherally (see also Haneda 2006), Toohey contends that some learners' marginalized participation in school practices is not the antithesis of learning, but rather the process of learning something like "assume a minimal role in this activity" (2000: 15) or "participate in a... disempowered manner" (1999: 134). Most importantly, Toohey (2000: 75) demonstrates how "the community, in a sense, produces success and failure" for learners through the kinds of (marginalized) participation made available to them and through attributing (un)desirable identities to these individuals. Being assigned undesirable, disempowered identities can lead to learners' isolation from a community and to their ongoing limited and less powerful forms of participation or to their resistance to participation. In fact, Zuengler and Miller's (2007) ethnographic study demonstrated how an entire classroom community of practice can become marginalized based on the histories of its participants and how those histories are regarded by members of other communities of practice.

However, the notion of CofP also conceptualizes a strongly positive relationship among learners and the participation identities that develop. Viewing language learning from this perspective foregrounds the dynamic process by which language learners invest in learning a language as they aspire to participate in communities of practice which they believe will offer them desirable identity options (Norton 2001; Norton and Toohey 2001). Such aspirations allow learners to transcend their current social positions and to see language learning as useful beyond the classroom context. Of course, the kinds of identities individuals hope to achieve through learning a language may not be realized given the sociopolitical relations at work in learners' current contexts (McKay and Wong 1996; Miller 1999), but the framework allows us to understand motivation/investment as relational and socially constructed, and how communities and their individual participants contribute to a learner's changing desires and efforts to learn a language – through the kinds of identities that are made available and which learners are able to claim for themselves.

Language socialization, and to a much lesser extent, Vygotskian sociocultural theory (see Chapter 30, this volume), have also been adopted by identity scholars and these, along with CofP theory, can all be broadly labeled as sociocultural approaches to language learning, though with distinct differences among them (Duff 2007a; Lantolf and Thorne 2006; Norton 2006). Language socialization, with its roots primarily in linguistic anthropology, is succinctly defined as "socialization through the use of language and socialization to use language" (Schieffelin and Ochs 1986: 163). Researchers have investigated how participation in routine practices that define a culture or community can serve to socialize learners into the "values, practices, identities and stances of the target group" (Duff 2007a: 311; see also Zuengler and Cole 2005). Vygotskian theory has its origin in early-to-mid-twentieth-century Russian psychology and focuses on human mental functioning and development (Vygotsky 1978, 1987), and its emphasis on cultural, social and interactional mediation as the basis of cognition and learning lends itself to identity research as well. Holland, Lachiocotte, Skinner and Cain (1998), for example, note that Vygotsky's emphasis on cultural and collective resources, made salient and available to learners in social practices, provide the means by which individuals organize their thoughts, manage their feelings and control their actions. And such "social forms of organization," they contend, are basic to the formation of an identity (Holland *et al.* 1998: 282). The intersections and notable differences among all three of these sociocultural approaches to L2 learning have been ably accounted for by Duff (2007a). Though each of these gives emphasis to different aspects of the sociocultural world in mediating L2 learning, they all regard learners' identities as implicated in such learning processes.

11.3 Identity categories in SLA research

Researchers who have been highly influential in broadening second language scholarship to include social, cultural and political perspectives have also been critical of researchers' "general preoccupation with the learner, at the expense of other potentially relevant social identities" (Firth and Wagner 1997: 288). Firth and Wagner (1997: 292) argued that most researchers in the 1990s and earlier tended to treat learner identity as the only one that "*really matters*, and it matters constantly and in equal measure throughout the duration of the encounter being studied." They likewise suggested that the attributions of *native speaker* or *non-native speaker* assigned by researchers may have little "emic relevance" (1997: 292) for the individuals so named. Firth and Wagner's (1997: 296) call for researchers to be more "critically sensitive to the theoretical status" of such research categories has been addressed in numerous studies problematizing, for example, the native vs. non-native speaker binary through demonstrating its ideological basis rather than one grounded in clear linguistic distinctions among people and groups (Davies 2003; Doerr 2009; Holliday and Aboshiha 2009; Kandiah 1998; Kramsch 1997; Leung, Harris and Rampton 1997; Rampton 1990; Shuck 2004, 2006). Much of this research focuses on how simplistic identity categories such as native speaker or non-native speaker (as well as language learner) obscure the enormous complexity in identity and learning and the power relations that contribute to reifying and neutralizing such identity labels. While second language scholarship has not completely avoided essentializing individual identities, the complexity of identity acknowledged and explored in the research reviewed below has moved the field forward in positive ways. At the same time, when researchers seek to understand more about L2 learning, it seems likely that learner identities will be lurking in the wings in one way or another.

Though several of the studies reviewed below rely on surveys and questionnaires, the majority use varying kinds of ethnographic methods. A large number of these are classroom-based ethnographic studies which include the whole range of age and grade levels, from primary- and secondary- to university-level classrooms as well as adult further education classrooms. Rather than focusing on L2 instruction as a form of language input, these studies typically attend to the interactions, ideologies and cultural norms active in classrooms as sites for identity construction. These ethnographic projects frequently take the form of case studies in which few research participants are involved but which allow for rich and detailed qualitative analysis. Most of the research discussed here uses interviews as part of, or as the primary, research data. Given the central place of interviews in these studies, it is not surprising that many have adopted varying forms of discourse analysis, thematic analysis and/or narrative analysis in investigating how participants' identities are constructed in discourse.

11.3.1 Heritage learners

Blackledge and Creese (2008: 535) note that it is now "almost a truism" among heritage language researchers that learning a heritage language is a crucial part of one's identity formation. (Also see Chapter 17, this volume.) But the nature of that identity–language connection and what such an identity might entail is far from straightforward. Much of the research on heritage language learners from the past decade has given considerable attention to arriving at an adequate definition for the term while also recognizing its slipperiness and contested nature (Blackledge and Creese 2008; Jo 2001; Lee 2002, 2005; Valdés 2001; Wiley and Valdés 2000). The need for arriving at a satisfying definition of *heritage language learners* is made particularly salient as educators seek to establish appropriate curricula for language classes which frequently include both heritage and *foreign language learners* (students who have no family connections to a language and who begin with no previous linguistic knowledge of the language). Writing about the North American context, Valdés (2001: 38) has defined a heritage language learner as "a student who is raised in a home where a non-English language is spoken or merely understands the heritage language and who is to some degree bilingual in English and the heritage language." As suggested in this definition, there is a common assumption that a heritage identity correlates with some degree of linguistic awareness of the language (though research has shown that such proficiency is highly variable among students (Valdés 2001)), and with some form of family connection to a language. A number of studies have, in fact, documented that learners' affiliation to a heritage culture is one of the strongest motivators for studying a language, and as such, aspects of their identity are strongly implicated in the learning process in ways different from foreign or other second language learners (Cho, Cho and Tse 1997; Kondo-Brown 2003; Weger-Guntharp 2006; Wiley 2001).

Lee (2005: 556), too, recognized that heritage learners are often motivated to learn a language in order to "develop and define their ethnic and cultural identity," but in drawing on survey data from 530 university students in the United States she argues for the need to differentiate between heritage learners and "learners with heritage motivation." She discusses the inadequacy of the heritage vs. non-heritage binary distinction in commenting on the enormous diversity found among those identified as heritage language learners. For example, she found that some African American university students choose to learn Yoruba or Swahili to connect to their "heritage" and to "find meaning in their ethnicity" (2005: 558), even though they do not know whether their ancestors ever spoke those particular African languages, and they typically have had no previous experience in using the language. Lee (2005: 561) contends that given the broad spectrum of affiliations, the varying degrees of intensity in those affiliations and of linguistic proficiency among learners who view themselves as heritage language learners, educators and researchers must be careful "not to attach permanency to the labels of heritage and non-heritage learners."

Oriyama (2010) also found varying kinds of identity affiliations among secondary school students who attended Japanese heritage language schools in Sydney, Australia, and, somewhat unexpectedly, she discovered that their greater proficiency in a heritage language did not always correlate with stronger heritage identities. Using interviews as well as survey data to examine how the youths in her study positioned themselves as Japanese and/or Australian, Oriyama (2010: 91) found that those with the strongest Japanese language proficiency and who had attended full-time private Japanese schools for a number of years as well as weekend community-based heritage language schools tended to identify themselves "exclusively as Australian." By contrast, those who only received heritage language education at the weekend community schools and otherwise attended mainstream English-language Australian schools tended to identify more strongly as Japanese or as Japanese-Australian. These distinctions in identity affiliations were true even among siblings in the same family; for example, a brother who only attended the weekend language schools identified himself as Japanese and Australian while his sister who had attended full-time Japanese school for four years viewed herself primarily as Australian. These former full-time Japanese school students all viewed language proficiency as a necessary component of Japanese identity, and even though they were all highly proficient speakers of Japanese, they believed that their language was not strong enough for them to make a "legitimate claim to Japanese membership" (2010: 92). Oriyama found that students who only attended the weekend language classes and who had lower language proficiencies but who also had more limited contact with native Japanese speakers (other than one or both parents) tended to have far more positive views of their identities as Japanese. These youths also reported experiencing generally positive attitudes by their non-Japanese friends to their multicultural identities. As Oriyama (2010: 95) notes, rather than strong proficiency in a heritage language leading to a stronger sense of one's heritage identity, such identities seem to be dependent on one's "perceived legitimacy" in doing so, and in this case, these youths' perceptions of that legitimacy seemed to be negatively correlated with their more intensive contact with native speakers of Japanese.

Blackledge and Creese (2008) investigated a school context in which students' heritage affiliations were both contested and redefined as students laid claim to hybrid heritage identities. In their ethnographically informed case study in supplementary schools in the United Kingdom, Blackledge and Creese investigated two community-based Bengali heritage language programs for children between the ages of 4 and 16. They found that the school administrators and teachers frequently treated nationalistic ideological beliefs, important events in the national history of Bangladesh, and symbols of Bengali nationhood (such as the national anthem or the national flower) as key elements of the heritage they hoped to transmit to the students. The teachers were also enthusiastic promoters of the standard variety of Bengali. However, the students often contested these forms of heritage transmission. For example, in response to their teacher's insistence that only Bengali be used in the classroom *because they are Bengali*, one student commented that his aunt "speaks English all the time," thus offering a counter-example of someone who is Bengali but chooses to speak English (2008: 546). On another occasion, a student rejected a teacher's pronunciation of a new student's name, contending that at their British school, the same student used an anglicized pronunciation of her name. Blackledge and Creese

(2008: 547) note that this student appeared to "negotiate a subject position away from the imposed 'heritage' identity" and to oppose "ideologies which rely on the 'purity' of the Bengali language." Thus, we see that identities often become a site of struggle in the face of powerfully constraining discourses of heritage national identity. However, this study, as well as those highlighted above, also demonstrates that one cannot discount learners' agency in how or even whether they identify as heritage language learners, no matter their ancestral ties or their degrees of proficiency in the language.

11.3.2 Multilingual learners

One of the early studies that explored contemporary multilingualism is Rampton's (1995) ethnographic and sociolinguistic research among adolescent boys of Indian, Pakistani, Caribbean and Anglo descent living in the United Kingdom. As Rampton shows, these boys engaged in "language crossing" as they strategically used bits of the languages belonging to an ethnicity not their own (e.g. an ethnic Anglo boy using Punjabi expressions). Rampton argues that participants in these multilingual conversations made no claims to membership in an Other's speech community (indexing a particular ethnicity) or to desiring to improve their proficiency in a single language. Rather, their multilingual ludic interactions demonstrated a particular kind of interactional competence which allowed these boys to perform their insider identities in a new kind of multiracial community. Though the multilingual identities of these boys was very much an outcome of neighborhood friendship groups in a particular community, they point to the kinds of strategic multilingualism fostered by contemporary globalization and the mass migrations it has generated in many other contexts.

A long-held understanding of a multilingual speaker is someone who acquires and uses two or more languages (Aronin and Singleton 2008), and as such, the terms *bilingual* and *multilingual* are often used interchangeably (Pavlenko 2005). However, in considering multilingual identities resulting from processes of modern globalization, we will focus primarily on research in which identities are associated with "complex multilingual repertoires in which often several (fragments of) 'migrant' languages and lingua francas are combined" (Blommaert 2010: 7). Kramsch and Whiteside (2008: 1) have pointed to "the increasingly multilingual and multicultural nature of global exchanges" in advocating that second language researchers need to reframe the notion of who language learners are (more than likely *not* monolinguals acquiring a second language) and to think in terms of complex ecologies rather than relatively stable communities in theorizing linguistic contexts. A large number of studies addressing modern multilingual identities has been conducted in Europe (Blommaert, Collins and Slembrouck 2005; Ceginskas 2010; Cots and Nussbaum 2008; Oliveira and Ança 2009), as well as in Canada (Dagenais and Jacquet 2008; Dagenais, Day and Toohey 2006; Duff 2007b; Heller 1997), Singapore (Stroud and Wee 2007), Tibet (MacPherson 2005) and the United States (Kramsch and Whiteside 2007, 2008), among many other national contexts. The focus of this research reflects changing demographic, political and economic realities as well as the adoption of poststructural approaches to identity, and often problematizes the notion of autonomous, national languages serving as the targets of learning (Canagarajah 2007; Kramsch 2006b; Pavlenko and Blackledge 2004; Pennycook 2007, 2010).

Researchers have noted that such multilingual diversity has not negated status differentials, and that multilingual speakers of primarily minority languages are often rendered speech-less in contexts where the languages of dominant or powerful groups and individuals hold sway (Blommaert, Collins and Slembrouck 2005). Differential status can also be perpetuated as individuals reproduce language ideologies from their countries of origin. For example, Oliveira and Ança (2009), who researched adolescent immigrant students in Portugal, found that students' differential valuing of languages in their multilingual repertoires was strongly influenced by the political situations in their countries of origin; i.e. two Ukrainian students had very different personal affiliations to Russian and Ukrainian given their differing histories in the country. These varying affiliations affected how they drew on these languages in the process of learning Portuguese and English and sometimes inhibited their learning. But at the same time, research on contemporary multilingualism often takes a more celebratory stance toward what learners already know, focusing more on their strategic and symbolic competence (Kramsch 2006b) than on their linguistic deficiencies. For example, Kramsch and Whiteside (2008: 23) contend that "multilingual encounters increase the contact surfaces among symbolic systems and thus the potential for creating multiple meanings and identities."

Kramsch and Whiteside's (2008) ethnographic study of four Maya-language-speaking immigrants from Yucatan, Mexico, living in San Francisco, California, demonstrates such strategic and symbolic competence in these immigrants' everyday community encounters. They contend that these individuals' performance of their multilingual (English, Spanish and other Maya languages) repertoires "indexes the various ways in which the protagonists wish to position themselves in the ongoing discourse" (2008: 16). One of the authors observed a service encounter between a Vietnamese grocer, who had adopted the name "Juan" when interacting with his Spanish-speaking customers, and Don Francisco, one of their focal participants. Juan was observed using a mix of English and Spanish throughout the conversation while Don Francisco used only Spanish; however, as they began their leave taking, Don Francisco suddenly switched from Spanish to Maya. Kramsch and Whiteside (2008: 17) contend that this interactional move can be interpreted as another instance of Don Francisco's "resistance to a Spanish colonial discourse which holds Maya in low esteem among Mexicans." Don Francisco was often observed trying to teach the local merchants some Maya and to encourage them to use it with him. The authors note that in some neighborhoods in San Francisco the use of Maya can grant its speakers some social capital as it serves to distinguish them from other Mexican immigrants. On this occasion, Juan responds to Don Fransico's switch to Maya with some Maya-like sounds and laughter, suggesting some embarrassment at his inexpert Maya utterance but also willingness to respect his customer's language and his linguistic identity. Kramsch and Whiteside (2008: 24) conclude by noting that the symbolic competence demonstrated in such service encounters displays a "mindset that can create 'relations of possibility' or affordances" necessary for participating in "late modern" interactions. This position toward celebrating multilingualism is advocated in Stroud and Wee's (2007) classroom-based research in Singapore. They contend that in this context, allowing classroom interactions to include Mandarin, Malay and Singlish (often described as colloquial Singaporean English), in addition to English, the officially legitimated language of school, not only engaged students' multilingual identities, it also seemed to have enhanced their learning of standard English as well.

While the above studies demonstrate how multilingualism produces multiple, fluid and hybrid identities, Otsuji and Pennycook (2010) show how multilingual individuals still at times perform a fixed cultural or linguistic identity, arguing that both fixity and fluidity are co-constitutive in constructing multilingual identities and need to be incorporated into theories of language and learning.

11.3.3 Gendered learners

Research investigating the role of gendered identities in language learning processes has drawn primarily on feminist poststructural theory, and/or social constructivist approaches, which treat gender as a social process, constructed in and through relations of power (Ehrlich 1997; Norton 1995, 2000; Pavlenko, Blackledge, Piller and Teutsch-Dwyer 2001; Shi 2006). It is for this reason we refer to them as *gendered identities*, to emphasize their constructed, contested, dynamic and non-essentialist nature. As with any identity category, *gender* must be understood as a simplified label for a complex array of identity positions which intersect with race, ethnicity, age, class and sexuality (Pavlenko and Blackledge 2004). For example, in their ethnographically informed case studies in a California school, McKay and Wong (1996) found differential language learning success among four Chinese male students in their early teens, just as Miller (2003) found differential success in her school-based ethnography among Chinese and Bosnian immigrant girls at an Australian secondary school. These students' varied social contexts and family histories along with dominant discourses of race and class which intersected with their gendered identities influenced their language learning trajectories. As such, these researchers would have been hard pressed to generalize across all male or across all female learners. Some studies have found that women claim or are granted identities as superior language learners, such as in Vitanova's (2004) narrative study of Eastern European immigrant couples in the United States or in Menard-Warwick's (2008a) critical ethnography of an adult ESL class for Latina women, but these women's identities as good language learners are understood to be locally negotiated achievements rather than outcomes of a pre-given linguistically advantaged gender.

Numerous studies, many of which have focused on immigrant women, have documented the ways in which gendered identities, primarily female identities, have constrained individuals' access to target-language communities and thus their language learning opportunities. For example, Deljit, one of the focal participants in Kouritzin's (2000) life-history interview research among immigrant women in Canada, was not allowed by her husband to cede childcare to anyone else and thus was unable to attend English classes. As Kouritzin notes, the problem of access to language classes was not that such classes did not exist or that daycare was unavailable, but that women like Deljit are assigned particular gendered identities which ascribe to them full responsibility for childcare and household duties, making it difficult or impossible to attend English language classes (see also Frye 1999 and Warriner 2004 for similar observations). In doing case study research among Cambodian women living in Philadelphia, Skilton-Sylvester (2002) found that some women were asked to discontinue classes when their husbands felt threatened by their wives' expanding social networks and greater independence. One such example was Ming, who said that her husband no longer wanted her to attend language classes because he feared she would meet a boyfriend or that she would run away from home. Skilton-Sylvester (2002: 17) notes that Ming's literacy development was perceived as a threat to her husband, leading Ming to stop attending English classes because she was "unable to maintain her identity as a student alongside her identity as a wife."

Lack of access or spousal prohibitions do not, however, explain some women's ambivalence about learning the dominant language, influenced in many cases by their desire to nurture their native languages at home with their children (Kouritzin 2000; Skilton-Sylvester 2002). Using narrative analysis on her interview data, Park (2009) explores and describes the conflicted choices an economically privileged and well-educated Korean woman made in following her husband to the USA for his career enhancement though that meant abandoning her PhD studies in Turkey. Wanting her children to maintain Korean and to appreciate their Korean heritage, she invested more in her Korean identity and became a Korean teacher in the USA rather than investing in learning English more fully. The same kind of ambivalence can be found among individuals contending with dominant masculine identities. Also drawing on interviews, Teutsch-Dwyer (2001) explores the language trajectory of Karol, a Polish male immigrant to the USA, noting that over fourteen months, Karol demonstrated almost no progress in English despite substantial access to English speakers. Teutsch-Dwyer contends that it was Karol's inability to perform an acceptable male identity when interacting with American English-speaking men that led him to interact primarily with several American female co-workers. One of these English-speaking women became his girlfriend and she eventually took responsibility for all of his personal business, resulting in a kind of learned helplessness for Karol. It appears that he saw no need for developing his English skills given his domestic arrangements.

Difficulty in gaining access to English language learning opportunities is often balanced by individuals' agentive efforts to overcome many of the constraints limiting their access (Menard-Warwick 2004; Norton 2000; Warriner 2004). Further, learners exercise agency in selecting how to perform gender appropriately in given linguistic and cultural contexts. Skapoulli (2004) describes the hybrid gendered identity of Nadia, a young Egyptian girl whose Egyptian Arabic-speaking parents immigrated to Cyprus when she was 4. Drawing on her interviews with Nadia, Skapoulli observed that Nadia had become skilled in shifting from the gendered practices of her home and Coptic Christian religious cultures to those of her modern, liberal peers. Having lived in Cyprus for twelve years and been educated in Greek schools, Nadia sounded nativelike in her L2 and could move strategically between a local Greek dialect peppered with English expressions to perform her identity as a mainstream, hip teenager, to standard, formal Greek to perform her identity as a conservative, modest female, as expected by her religious community. Skapoulli comments that for Nadia "second language use is inextricably connected to gender identity and directly associated with social context" (2004: 255). One also finds evidence of western women agentively rejecting aspects of pragmatically appropriate ways of speaking Japanese, as women, because they perceive it as positioning them as "too humble" (Siegal 1996) or as "girlish" (Ohara 2001).

Researchers have also found that enhanced and empowered gender identities come to be associated with learning a language (Gordon 2004; Kobayashi 2002; Rivera 1999). McMahill (2001) used a case study approach in exploring the identity dynamics that emerged in an English language class for Japanese women, which was based on feminist pedagogy. These students recognized the "imperialist nature of English as an international language" but still saw it as a "weapon for self-empowerment" and a resource for resisting "linguistic-specific ideologies of femininity" in many contexts of Japanese culture (2001: 332, 323). Several of these students further claimed that when they spoke English they felt they could be more direct and more assertive. In Pavlenko's (2001) analysis of L2 learners' memoirs, she found that some female immigrants preferred the subject positions available to them in their new languages, finding them freeing and empowering. Pavlenko notes that these writers, of varied language backgrounds, did not blame their native languages but rather recognized oppressive ideologies and the "links between language, gender, and identity created by [them]" (2001: 142). In a comprehensive ethnographic study that included fieldwork in Laos as well as the USA, Gordon (2004) observed that many of the Lao immigrant women she came to know in Philadelphia were able to build on their developing knowledge of English to gain access to helpful resources for their families and to learn about American culture, including awareness that they could call the police in cases of spousal abuse. We see then that gendered identities intersect with L2 learning processes in highly varied ways, constructed as they are in complex relations of power, influenced by discourses of race, nationality, class and education.

Whereas the term *gender* has replaced the term sex in academic discourse (Higgins 2010, though see Rubin 2006, on the continuum of the "sex/gender system"), *sexual identity* is an emerging focus of inquiry in SLA research (Nelson 1999, 2006, 2009). Much of the work on sexual identity has focused on curriculum and materials development which incorporates varied sexual identities (De Vincenti, Giovanangeli and Ward 2007; O'Mochain 2006) or emphasizes the applicability of queer theory for language classroom inquiry (Curran 2006; Nelson 1999). Liddicoat's (2009) study is one of the few to examine how language classroom discourse may inadvertently provide (or impose) a space for self-disclosure of one's (homo)sexual identity through grammar practice activities. He examines an interaction in a Spanish language classroom in which the instructor asked a male student to describe his girlfriend while the class was practicing Spanish adjectives. The student produced a grammatically correct response using adjective endings marking masculine identity (*Mi uhm (0.2) novio es alto y:::: delgado*; "My uhm (0.2) boyfriend is tall and slim"). Over several turns, the teacher and student negotiated the correctness of the student's practice sentence, until the student finally understood that the problem was not his grammar. At that point, he reissued his original sentence, adding that his boyfriend "has a beard" to demonstrate that he was intentionally using masculine markers. Liddicoat (2009: 199, 201) comments that "the prevailing heteronormativity of the language classroom conditions a response to students' implicit coming out not as the self-disclosure of a minority sexual identity, but rather as a problem of linguistic competence" or a case of "linguistic failure." In this way, Liddicoat demonstrates the importance of developing awareness of and sensitivity to individuals' sexual identities along with their gendered identities.

11.3.4 Racialized identities

As some of the aforementioned studies indicate, race intersects with other social categories, shaping and shifting identities of second language learners, as well as teachers, in complex ways. Indeed, issues of race have attracted greater attention in SLA research in recent years. Although race is not a biologically determined notion, it nonetheless indexes the identity of Self and Other, concealing, marginalizing or affirming the sense of who we and others are (Kubota and Lin 2009b). Although scholarly publications on the racialization of identity sporadically appeared in the 1990s, it was not until recently that researchers began to pay explicit attention to race.

One earlier study on the racialization of identity was conducted by Ibrahim (1999). Using ethnography, Ibrahim exposed the ways in which immigrant students from Africa attending a Canadian high school appropriated North American black identity or *became black* through acquiring black stylized English as an L2. Drawing on the notion of performativity (Butler 1990), Ibrahim revealed how these youths, especially boys, identified with blackness represented by gangster rap language and style, whereas older girls were more eclectic in their choice of music, dress and language though they too still tended to use Black English markers. Their desire for such marginalized identities is situated in hegemonic discourses that expect them to be and perform as black. Similarly, an ethnographic study by Bashir-Ali (2006: 633) found that a high-school Mexican immigrant student desired to acquire Black English to find her identification space in the majority social group in her school and refused to speak her native language – a marker of inferiority associated with the ESL label, as well as academic mainstream English "to avoid the risk of sounding 'White.'"

While these studies reveal how high-school racial and linguistic minority students acquired non-mainstream language to identify with a counterculture and to adopt a symbol of the *cool* status in the school and in the wider racialized society, Michael-Luna (2008) conversely documented how primary-school children predominantly from Mexico identified themselves as white in her ethnographic and narrative study. Examining moment-to-moment interactions in the classroom – a modified method of Critical Race theory to accommodate the age of the research participants – Michael-Luna found that the absence of a racial/ethnic identification group for these students in the story of Martin Luther King, Jr., forced them to choose affinity with a racial category of either black or white. The stigma associated with blackness in the story as well as the marginalized status of these students in the school seemed to compel them to call out that they are all white.

As these examples indicate, even when identity options are available, the act of choosing may not be totally left to individual agency, but rather it is often constrained by power and discourse that construct symbolic meanings for various categories of identification, such as race, language, gender and so on. Although these racial minority learners might consider their ideal identity option to be an oppositional one, this option is generally not conducive to gaining cultural capital recognized as legitimate in other social contexts. This problematizes the notion of ideal identity options – i.e. *ideal* for whom?

As the studies by Michael-Luna (2008, 2009) indicate, classroom pedagogy can influence learners' investment in learning and their construction of identity (see also Harklau 2000; McKay and Wong 1996; Motha 2006). By contrasting two ethnographic studies – one involving primary-school students of Mexican origin and a white teacher and another involving African American students in preschool and kindergarten classes with white and African American teachers – Katz and DaSilva Iddings (2009) found that while the teacher in the former case did not value the students' cultural and linguistic backgrounds, including their bilingual ability, and thus negatively influenced the students' investment in their bilingual and bicultural identity, the teachers in the latter case fully affirmed and integrated students' linguistic and cultural identity.

11.3.5 Non-native teacher identities

Language teacher identities have increasingly become a focus of SLA research with the growing recognition that they are a "crucial component" of L2 learning processes in classrooms (Varghese, Morgan, Johnston and Johnson 2005). Varghese *et al.* (2005: 22) make the case that "[i]n order to understand language teaching and learning, we need to understand teachers; and in order to understand teachers, we need to have a clearer sense of who they are: the professional, cultural, political and individual identities which they claim or which are assigned to them." The identities of non-native teachers are especially relevant to SLA research in that their experiences as teachers are often situated on the same trajectory as their linguistic development.

Early studies on teacher identity focused primarily on the discriminatory attitudes and practices which many non-native teachers experience (see Moussu and Llurda 2008 for a comprehensive review of research on non-native teachers). For example, Reves and Medgyes (1994) surveyed over 200 English as foreign language teachers in ten countries and found that they felt very insecure in their linguistic competence in English and were anxious about being shown up and judged harshly by their students. The authors note that these teachers' professional insecurity often affected their classroom performance negatively, resulting in their professional self-esteem decreasing even more. Amin's (1997) interview study of "visible minority" female teachers in an ESL context in Canada similarly points to the influential role of student attitudes on teachers' self perceptions. The non-Caucasian teachers in Amin's study believed that their ESL students thought only white people could be native speakers of English and that only white people know "real" English. As such, they believed they were attributed identities of "less able teachers" in comparison to their white colleagues. Amin (1997: 581) contends that when students give such messages to their teachers, implicitly or explicitly, "minority teachers are unable to effectively negotiate a teacher identity" and "no matter how qualified they are, [they often] become less effective in facilitating their students' language learning than, perhaps, White teachers." Clearly, race becomes the identity frame through which students attribute non-nativeness to their teachers in many cases, and such deficit-oriented perceptions have real material effects on non-native language teachers. Many, for example, experience greater difficulty getting language teaching jobs than do native speakers (Clark and Paran 2007).

A number of studies have advocated changes in teacher education programs in efforts to empower non-native teachers and to enable them to construct desirable professional identities for themselves (Brutt-Griffler and Samimy 1999; Golombek and Jordon 2005; Kamhi-Stein 1999; Liu 1999; Pavlenko 2003). Pavlenko (2003), for example, investigated how classroom discourses in L2 teacher education programs can play a significant role in shaping teachers' identities positively in her narrative study of these individuals' written linguistic autobiographies. She found that exposing future teachers to research on multicompetence (Cook 2007) or the ideology of non-nativeness allows many of them to imagine themselves "as multicompetent and bilingual" rather than as deficient speakers of English (2003: 266). Ilieva (2010), however, complexifies this appropriation of identity-affirming discourses in analyzing program-final portfolios produced by non-native future English teachers. She observed that the "authoritative discourses" of teacher education programs, which include notions of legitimate peripheral participation, multicompetence, and equity often seemed "ventriloquated, or parroted" (2010: 362) in students' portfolio essays. And yet Ilieva saw evidence that these ventriloquated discourses still provided these future teachers with opportunities to construct positive new identities for themselves and cites Bakhtin (1981: 345) in noting that when "someone else's ideological discourse is internally persuasive for us... entirely different possibilities open up" (in Ilieva 2010: 362).

Though many researchers have noted that non-native language teachers are likely to be better teachers in their home contexts than native language teachers because they understand their students' culture and the locally preferred learning and teaching practices, Holliday (2009) dismisses this as a traditional view and one that is confining for these teachers. He contends that these teachers need to be understood as "out in the world expecting to do all the things that native speaker teachers do, with complex cultural identities, [who] can compete effectively in diverse professional settings" (2009: 150). Menard-Warwick (2008b) adds that the field has long overlooked one of the most highly valued capacities a non-native teacher can bring to a classroom. She advocates recognizing and promoting teachers' *interculturality* as a primary asset over mere cultural compatibility between teachers and students, what Kramsch (2005: 553) has defined as "an awareness and a respect of difference, as well as the socioaffective capacity to see oneself through the eyes of others." Menard-Warwick (2008b: 635–36) argues that teachers who develop this competence, and a meta-awareness of it, can "in sharing their personal histories of understanding and adapting to multiple cultural frameworks and thus modeling intercultural identities... open up identity options not previously imagined by their students." Merely being a non-native language teacher does not automatically result in intercultural awareness. However, non-native teachers' life experiences of learning languages and using them, and sometimes spending time in other cultures, serve as powerful resources toward developing intercultural awareness.

11.4 Future directions

We end by identifying several aspects of identity research that we feel need further consideration. We first address one of the primary research methods used in identity research, that of interview research. Interviews are particularly well suited for gaining an understanding of how learners perceive past events and experiences influencing their language learning, and how they see themselves as agents of their learning. However, we also concur with the admonitions voiced by several second language scholars not to assume that research participants' words can somehow speak for themselves, or that we can "take them at their word" rather straightforwardly (Block 2000, 2008; Miller 2011; Pavlenko 2007; Talmy 2010; Talmy and Richards 2011). Investigating learners' narratives produced in research interviews includes analysis of the content of the talk, what interviewees actually say, but as Pavlenko (2007: 167) cautions, content analysis or thematic analysis of language learners' narrated life stories is merely a "preliminary analytical step" and should not be "confused with analysis" itself. We find that theoretical and analytical coherence is sometimes lacking in research studies which adopt poststructural approaches to theorizing identity but which adopt positivist methods in analyzing the data. Using narrative accounts produced in research interviews requires careful consideration of the contexts in which they are generated, including the active participation of the researcher (Briggs 2007), as well as the linguistic forms and interactional behaviors produced by interviewees, what Holstein and Gubrium (2003) refer to as the *hows* and *whats* of interview talk. Pavlenko (2007: 180) helpfully identifies analytic approaches one can take in treating "the interdependence between context, content, and form" in language learner narratives. There is, of course, no methodological magic bullet which can accomplish this; however, we urge identity researchers to treat interview accounts as multiply complex discursive constructions rather than mere reports, and to account for how one's theories of identity help produce the conceptual categories that are explored.

Related to the above concern is the need for greater clarity in how the term identity itself is used. Some scholars fear that the term identity has become so ubiquitous across the social sciences and humanities that it is now a catch-all category which has lost its analytic purchase (Bendle 2002; Brubaker and Cooper 2000). In addressing applied linguistics research, Block (2009) discusses the inconsistency in how identity is sometimes conceptualized and in how the term is applied. While there seems to be relative consensus among researchers that identities are dynamic, hybrid and multiple, Block notes that researchers still tend to analyze identity "in terms of inscriptions" (2009: 216), such as the social, cultural or demographic categories identified in our chapter, i.e. gender, race, heritage and so on. Drawing on Weedon (1987, 2004), Block recommends that applied linguists maintain a distinction between *subjectivity* and identity, using the former to refer to the more ephemeral moment-by-moment positioning of individuals and the latter to our "more stable identities" (2009: 217). This temporary fixing of subjectivity into more stable identities (Weedon 2004) is frequently influenced by ideologies and local relations of power and is used by individuals in creating a sense of who they are, their "self-sameness over time" (Brubaker and Cooper 2000: 11). It is also deployed in assigning identities to others, making individuals "recognizable" according to socially maintained categories such as those noted above. We want to further note that distinguishing between subjectivity and identity entails more than a superficial distinction between terms; we believe that it points to the need to theorize both ephemerality and stability in the complex identity processes involved in L2 learning.

A similar call for theoretical commensurability and explicitness can be applied to examinations of *agency* in second language research. Learner agency is understood to be at work when learners choose to learn a language if they perceive that it will bring them desirable social and linguistic capital and enhance their future identities (McKay and Wong 1996; Norton 2000), or when learners decide *not* to invest in learning an L2 fully if they perceive that it will entail the loss of a former identity (Pavlenko and Lantolf 2000; Pavlenko 2001), or if they fear that their children will lose their heritage language and identities (Kouritzin 2000; Skilton-Sylvester 2002). Such agentive choices and/or actions are understood to be constrained or enhanced by the institutional processes and power relations at work in learners' environments rather than deployed solely through the power of the individual (DaSilva Iddings and Katz 2007; Kanno 2003; Miller 2010; Ros i Solé 2007; Vitanova 2005). Block (2009: 219), however, points to the rampant "fuzziness" in how agency is treated in SLA as well as in social research more generally. For example, researchers too often comment that L2 learners "have agency" or "demonstrate agency" with little theorizing of how they understand what it means to *have agency*. Our concern lies in the potential incompatibility of using poststructural theory to conceptualize identity and agency as discursively constructed while at the same time implicitly treating the human subject as autonomously agentive by definition (Davies 1991). Poststructuralism helps us understand the profoundly social and power-inflected character of the simultaneous processes of identity (re)construction and learning and such a view also frames learner agency as emergent from the overlapping social, cultural, political and linguistic processes at play in particular contexts and over time (Lantolf and Pavlenko 2001). As Ahearn (2001) notes, there are many ways to conceptualize agency (see Ahearn 2001; Butler 1997; Davies 1990, 1991; Giddens 1979; and Ortner 2006, for ongoing discussions and differing conceptions of agency among sociologists, linguistic anthropologists and feminist poststructuralists). However, we urge second language researchers to strive for theoretical commensurability in how they approach learner identity and learner agency, to explicitly discuss those theoretical approaches, and to show how one's analysis of language learning processes is informed by and compatible with those theories.

Finally, we want to note an area of identity research that is receiving increasing attention and which promises to lead to exciting new understandings regarding identity in L2 learning. Online, virtual-world communication is itself relatively new, with new forms of digitally mediated practices proliferating rapidly (see Chapter 14, this volume). These include social virtualities such as Second Life, massively multiplayer online games and synthetic submersive environments such as Quest Atlantis (Thorne, Black and Sykes 2009). The expanding communication possibilities enabled by such new technology provide "unprecedented potential for linguistic, cultural, and creative exchange across geographically dispersed sites" (Thorne et al. 2009: 804), using multiple or hybrid language forms (Lam 2000, 2004) including multiply-authored participatory composing practices (Yi 2008). Existing research suggests that these continuously developing forms of communication allow individuals to assume new and more powerful identities in the languages they are still learning, in part because they typically feel less self-conscious and receive more affiliative feedback than in classroom or other face-to-face interactions (Lam 2004) and because they are able to display themselves as experts in particular on-line communities, such as fan fiction sites (Black 2005, 2008). However, the effects of participation in many of these new digitally mediated practices on identity and language learning are still relatively unexplored and demand greater scrutiny (Thorne 2008; Thorne et al. 2009).

11.5 Conclusion

In closing, we, too, urge greater scrutiny and continued exploration of how the range of scholarly findings from identity and SLA research can be translated into accessible knowledge that can transform classroom, community and policy-making practices. The social turn in research has revolutionized the ways in which we understand the sense of self among often marginalized second language users, learners and teachers within social, cultural and ideological contexts, exposing unequal relations of power and resistance. Whether the distance between the social turn in academia and the social change in the real world can be narrowed remains an unresolved question, but it is one we feel is worthy of further exploration.

12

Socialization

Georges Daniel Véronique

12.1 Introduction

This chapter is devoted to an overview of research work on L2 acquisition as socialization, with an emphasis on adult naturalistic acquisition, and on the acquisition of L2 literacy (for chapters that deal with similar issues, see Chapters 9, 11, 13 and 30, this volume). The chapter examines the issues, both theoretical and empirical, raised by the analysis of L2 acquisition and of literacy in L2 as processes of social integration. The chapter first introduces the conceptual underpinnings of socially oriented approaches to SLA and examines how they challenge and complement mainstream cognitive SLA research. Section 12.2 sketches the development of socially oriented research in SLA and its relation to naturalistic adult SLA and to L2 literacy. The section examines the main terms of the debate between the cognitive SLA paradigm and the socially oriented SLA paradigm. Following Zuengler and Miller (2006: 35), the term *sociocultural* is also used to refer to the varied socially oriented approaches to L2 learning (see Chapter 27, this volume). Section 12.3 describes the conceptual framework of sociocultural SLA research and defines key concepts such as agency, power relations and integration. Section 12.4 sketches the historical background, presents illustrative material and analyses of naturalistic SLA, and then describes SL literacy. The last section identifies some of the problems and difficulties facing sociocultural approaches to SLA and discusses future directions for socially oriented research in SLA.

12.2 Socialization: calling for a "reconceptualization of research in SLA"

From the 1970s through the 1980s SLA research drew both on Chomsky's theory of language and on sociolinguistics and ethnography of communication. According to Juffs (2002: 88), seminal work on adult naturalistic L2 acquisition in Schumann's Harvard project (1973-75) in the USA and in Europe – namely, the *Heidelberger Forschungsprojekt "Pidgin Deutsch"* (HPD 1974-78), the *Zweitspracherwerb italienischer und spanischer Arbeiter* (ZISA 1975-79) and later the *European Science Foundation* project (1981-88) – demonstrated sociological constraints that influence language learning and use. (Note that research on linguistic socialization in the classroom emerged during approximately the same period; see e.g. Frawley and Lantolf 1985.) Sankoff (2002: 639) remarks that the development of the concept of interlanguage (Selinker 1972) in the field of SLA "parallels to some extent the notion of *vernacular* in sociolinguistics," hence the inception of "a tradition of 'variationist' or 'sociolinguistic' [research] within SLA." The impact of sociolinguistics on the study of L2 acquisition accounts for "increasingly socially situated SLA research" and for the "discernible thread of language-in-context focused research" which developed in Europe in the 1970s according to Regan (1998). Sociolinguistic perspectives are still a major component of socially oriented SLA (see Regan, Howard and Lemée 2009, and Chapter 13, this volume).

From the 1990s, the expanding field of SLA research focused mainly on the acquisition of L2 knowledge and on its cognitive and neural underpinnings (see Chapter 2, this volume). However, growing dissatisfaction by some with disembodied cognitive research and with the study of the acquisition of decontextualized L2 systems led to the vindication of socially oriented SLA research. A movement of protest against rationalist approaches to SLA gradually emerged in the same years. It is against the backdrop of this epistemological strife, vividly depicted by Jordan (2004: 1-3), that the dispute between cognitive and socially oriented SLA must be viewed. The debate between researchers who focus on the mental processes involved in SL acquisition and those who insist on the need to explore the social use of the target language by L2 learners began to reach a climax with the special issue of the *Modern Language Journal* (1997).

12.2.1 The social turn in SLA research

In 1997, Firth and Wagner called for a reconceptualization of SLA research in at least three areas. They argued in favor of an "enhanced awareness of the contextual and interactional dimensions of language use." They called for an "increased emic (i.e. participant-relevant) sensitivity" to basic categories of SLA research and advocated a broadening of the SLA database. Firth and Wagner, as well as other contributors to the 1997 special issue of the *Modern Language of Journal* (MLJ), challenged the standard identity categories in use in SLA research such as learner or non-native speaker. The terms *input, intake* and *interlanguage* were also disputed. Discussion developed about whether research should focus on the processing of input per se or study the social and linguistic affordances made available to L2 learners in view of societal integration, in a more ecological perspective (Kramsch and Vork Steffensen

2008; Van Lier 2010). Adoption of the latter perspective entails that the *agency* of the language learner in contexts and settings where linguistic affordance obtains is liable to analysis. It also implies that SLA research is in a position to answer Lantolf's (1996) query about "what people need to learn to be able to interact with other people from different cultures and speech communities." The contributors to the *MLJ* special issue and Block (2003) *inter alia* called for a study of the social cognition via language use involved in L2 acquisition instead of a focus on individual cognition. Despite early development of a sociocultural perspective in SLA research, in the 1980s and 1990s, through work on interethnic communication and on the negotiation of L2 understanding in context, progress in capturing the multidimensionality of L2 socialization needs still to be made.

Ten years later, in 2007, a special issue of the *MLJ* was published to take stock of progress in the development of sociocultural approaches to SLA. As Firth and Wagner (2007) observed, the 1997 issue kindled much interest in sociocultural SLA leading to the bloom of many projects hailing from language ecology, language emergence theory and language socialization. According to Kramsch and Whiteside (2007: 918), "opening the Pandora's box of the social dimension of language acquisition has confronted SLA research" with new questions about the universality of its concepts and the purpose of its investigations, leading possibly to "a more flexible conception of the field based on an ecological understanding of discursive, social and historical relativity."

12.2.2 Competing paradigms: L2 socialization versus cognitive approaches

Although some authors working in formal linguistic perspectives claim an essential but not exclusive role for their studies (Juff 2002), the interaction of mainstream cognitive SLA researchers with context-oriented researchers is one characterized by competition and controversy. In a survey of fundamental issues in SLA, Hulstijn (2007) comes to the conclusion that there is a small strand of SLA research which takes into account the social context of SLA and tries to include communicative interaction, learner attributes and social contexts as factors of L2 acquisition. However, he notes that "there is no detailed information concerning the *mechanism* involved or the *reason* why the factors should affect L2 learning," and adds that "finally, there does not seem to be a *direct* link between social context and the representation and processing of L2 information" (Hulstijn 2007: 199).

This critical assessment of socially oriented SLA research points to the gap between the "two parallel SLA worlds" (Zuengler and Miller 2006). Many examples of the controversy between the two paradigms are available. To quote just two of these studies, Larsen-Freeman (2007) lists twelve points where sociocultural SLA and cognitive SLA paradigms are at odds. These include (i) the role attributed in the two competing paradigms to context;

(ii) their conception of the nature of language and their objects of inquiry in language-focused research; (iii) the representation of the L2 learner and of the identity of the research participants; (iv) the philosophical orientation and degree of acceptance of the diversity of SLA theories. Zuengler and Miller (2006) analyze the controversy between the cognitive and sociocultural paradigms in SLA in terms of two major topics: L2 use *versus* L2 acquisition and the debate in theory construction between *positivism* (there exists a real world outside theory which must be accounted for) and *relativism* (theory produces the artefacts it describes).

12.2.3 Brief epistemological remarks on the debate between cognitive and sociocultural SLA research

As Zuengler and Miller (2006) observe, the contention between cognitive and sociocultural SLA is based both on different ontologies – different visions of the explanandum and of its state of being – and conflicting epistemologies, in terms of methods and procedures. The major criticisms leveled by socially oriented SLA research against cognitive approaches to SLA are:

- SLA research is in need of enlarging its research questions beyond the study of decontextualized linguistic systems and individual cognition to the analysis of socially significant L2 use.
- L2 learning must be envisioned as a social and cultural activity and L2 learners must be construed as active social agents.
- L2 acquisition and use is about becoming a member of a new social community not about the internalization of linguistic patterns.
- As a social accomplishment, L2 acquisition implies the development of social relations via social interactions, involving specific communicative tasks, the specific biographies of the second language users and the development of multiple identities on the part of language acquirers.
- The standard categories of SLA research such as non-native speaker or learner need to be replaced by more socially significant categories (Chapter 11, this volume).
- The participant's perspective (emic) on SLA should be adopted.
- The relation between the individual and the social in SLA must be thought about anew in terms of power relations and of community of practices.

Conversely, cognitive theories of SLA emphasize the fact that socially oriented approaches to SLA neglect a proper characterization of L2 knowledge and of its dynamics. They also take exception to the type of methodology, more qualitative and hermeneutic in nature (e.g. conversation analysis and learning stories, for instance) adopted by sociocultural SLA. According to Gregg (2003b), a relativist externalist theory of SLA, i.e. sociocultural SLA, is confused about the proper object of inquiry in a theory of SLA: it should not explain learner behavior but rather learner mental states. Socially oriented approaches to SLA such as those initiated by ethnography of communication or sociolinguistics, for instance, fall under the criticisms of Jordan's guidelines (Jordan 2004: 112–18) for rationalist research in SLA. Discussing a study by Willett (1995), Jordan (2004: 176) considers that the "thick description" of events provided by Willett's paper is not in the service of any explanatory theory. The style of writing is also criticized on the basis of its use of "an enormous array of pseudo-technical terms" intended to impress rather than to clarify. Discussing Schumann's Acculturation Model, Jordan (2004: 190–91) finds that it violates the guidelines set for rationalist research because it is not testable and that such constructs as "social distance" and "psychological distance," which play an important role in the model, are poorly defined.

The roots of cognitive SLA researchers' criticisms of sociocultural SLA lie both in divergent epistemologies, resulting in an inability to comprehend the objects of research and results of the other paradigm, and in the type of empirical research conducted under sociocultural approaches to SLA. Note that in the epistemological rift between cognitive and sociocultural SLA paradigms, socially oriented researchers often define their epistemological stance as constructivist rather than relativist (Firth and Wagner 2007).

Watson-Gegeo and Nielsen (2003) go further and reject the social/cognitive dichotomy as expounded in the 1997 *MLJ* issue and the ensuing debate between the two competing paradigms. Their main argument is that the debate is misconstrued because "cognition *originates* in social interaction" (Watson-Gegeo and Nielsen 2003: 156), and because there is a direct link between the construction of linguistic knowledge and social, cultural and political contexts. They propose a theoretical and methodological approach which unites cognitive research on SLA, expanded to take into account social and cultural contexts, and they suggest that sociocultural research should broaden its view of language activities and use a more complete methodological tool kit. Here the language socialization perspective on SLA will be understood as belonging to the sociocultural paradigm per se.

12.2.4 Socially oriented SLA research

Given the shared postulate that "SLA is not situated in processes but in people embedded in activity" (Lantolf 1996a), sociocultural approaches to SLA, although quite diverse, share the following assumptions:

- The focus of SLA research should be on the development of social identity (see Norton and Toohey 2002) and social meaning rather than on the dynamics of interlanguage per se (Dittmar, Spolsky and Walters 1997).
- The study of the discursive construction of identities should be a major topic of interest.
- A participant or emic perspective should be favored in the analysis of data as well as a qualitative or even hermeneutic (interpretive) perspective (Flick, Kardorff and Steinke 2009).

- Corpora for analysis should consist of contextualized, unedited and naturally occurring data. This implies paying heed to the ecology of L2 use in context and development.

Beyond these assumptions and a common conceptual framework (see Section 12.3), the sociocultural paradigm harbors a number of partly divergent approaches. This diversity may be accounted for by the historical development of the paradigm and by the type of research question that is in focus in each of these approaches.

Various classifications of sociocultural SLA approaches have been put forward. Mitchell and Myles (2004) devote two chapters of their book to approaches which view SLA as a social phenomenon, namely sociocultural and sociolinguistic perspectives, respectively. To these may be added what Mitchell and Myles call the functional/pragmatic perspective in SLA as propounded, for instance, by Klein and Perdue (1997) *inter alia*, which falls under the emergentist approach to SLA (MacWhinney 2010). Emergentism as a usage-based theory of acquisition can be seen as yet another strand within the sociocultural paradigm. In addition, conversation analysis and ethnography of communication also contribute regularly to socially oriented SLA research. As do sociolinguistic perspectives on SLA representing a systemic functional perspective (Williams 2010) and variationist sociolinguistics (see Chapter 13, this volume).

In her definition of language socialization, Riley (2010) insists on the fact that "language socialization" relates two processes: the acquisition of "sociocultural knowledge, skills and values" through verbal interactions and "engagement in social interaction" as a means to develop communicative competence. According to Duff (2010: xiii), the language socialization perspective pays "particular attention to social, cultural and interactional contexts in which language and other kinds of knowledge are learned both formally and informally" (see Ochs and Schieffiin 2010, for a historical overview of this approach). Language socialization approaches are close to ecological perspectives on SLA, although the focus of research is different. Ecological perspectives view "SLA as an emergent phenomenon, triggered by the availability of affordances in the environment, heavily dependent on an individual's perception of these affordances and his/her willingness to participate actively in their use" (Kramsch and Vork Steffensen 2008: 23). These holistic approaches share many assumptions with Lantolf and Thorne's (2006) sociocultural approach, which offer yet another perspective on SLA and socialization, hailing from Vygotsky's mediation theory (see Chapter 27, this volume) and from Marxist activity theory. Other researchers working in a sociopsychological framework study the social networks in which the agents of L2 learning interact (Gardner 2002).

It is possible to identify up to ten different strands of research within the sociocultural perspective. However, these approaches are not discrete or isolated, but interact rather smoothly with each other, very much like a bunch of flowers, to take up Lantolf's metaphor (Lantolf 1996). Although they share the same assumptions about SLA research, a pool of common concepts (see below), a partly common history and a common dissatisfaction vis-à-vis mainstream cognitive SLA, sociocultural approaches differ in the research questions they pose, in the empirical data they examine and in the methods and procedures of analysis they adopt. To illustrate this diversity, seven strands of sociocultural SLA research are listed in Table 12.1.

Table 12.1 provides an arbitrary and overly simplified picture of the diversity of the SLA sociocultural paradigm. However, it does show that some approaches such as sociolinguistics or language emergence theory are more focused on language in context, relating form, function and use, while other approaches are more critical or more pedagogical, in the sense of Lantolf and Thorne (2006).

12.3 A conceptual framework for socially oriented SLA

This section identifies some of the major concepts which form the theoretical basis of the sociocultural SLA paradigm and also presents some early developments. Various strands of research within the paradigm focus on these concepts in different ways.

12.3.1 The legacy from early influences

Although not all researchers working in the sociocultural SLA paradigm draw explicitly on Vygotsky, Bakhtin and Voloshinov, the contribution of these authors has certainly exerted a major influence. The contribution of Vygotsky (1978) is at least threefold. In the first place, he strongly emphasized the contribution of *alter* (the other) to language development and subsequently to its acquisition. Secondly, Vygotsky highlighted the role of the helper in language development and acquisition via *scaffolding* (Lantolf and Thorne 2006). In Vygotsky's model, learning through interaction results in development. In this perspective, the notion of zone of proximal development has been developed to account for teacher and peer assistance to the learner (see Chapter 27, this volume). Vygotsky's claim of a parallel between second language acquisition and the development of native language literacy has also proven to be fruitful. From the contributions of Bakhtin (1981) and Voloshinov (1973), one can single out the notion of voice, or "speaking personality, the speaking consciousness" (Wertsch 1991a: 51) and the imitation of the voices of others during learning and acquisition. Voloshinov's insistence on the importance of social interaction as the basis of verbal interaction can also be highlighted where he claims that utterances do not exist per se but are that which obtains between speakers as social acts (Voloshinov 1973: 82).

Table 12.1. Some approaches to sociocultural SLA research

	Language ecology approach to SLA	Language socialization and SLA	Vygotskian sociocultural theory	Critical theory and SLA	Conversation analysis for SLA	Sociolinguistic approaches	Language emergence theory
Primary research focus	Language and culture	Verbal interaction and social and cultural norms	Mediation and "pedagogy"	Critical discourse	Negotiation of meaning and emic categories	Variation and sociolinguistic competence	Emergent grammar and emergent lexicon
Objects of inquiry in language-focused research	Power relations and gate-keeping in L2. Identity issues	Acts of identity Development of social networks	Zone of proximal development and mediation	Learning narratives	Turn taking, Communication breakdowns in L2	Variable rules	Semantic, syntactic and pragmatic linguistic organization
Theoretical background	Critical language ecology	Linguistic anthropology	Vygotsky's theory and activity theory	Community of practice	Situated cognition	Functional sociology	Functionalism in linguistics
Type of account / explanation	Case studies and global explanation	Case studies and "thick" description	Discourse analysis	Hermeneutics (Interpretive approach)	Analysis of transcripts	Description	Description

French theory and postcolonial/postmodern thinking have greatly contributed to the development of critical discourse which, in turn, has fuelled several strands of sociocultural SLA. The critical sociology developed by Bourdieu has contributed through the key concept of symbolic capital, partly related to social and cultural origin (*habitus*) and to the strategies of the speaker as a social agent in terms of our understanding of power relations in verbal interaction (Bourdieu 1990). Bourdieu's idea of the legitimacy of specific speakers and of their right to speak has also proven fruitful. Foucault's analysis of the matrices of social thought (*epistemes*) and of the generation of texts from discourse grounded in social history have greatly contributed to the development of relativism (Foucault 1980). Derrida's deconstruction of key notions such as the linguistic sign, writing, speech acts and grammar has favored an anti-positivist stance and a renewed investigation of speech in verbal interaction.

12.3.2 Social context and setting

Defining the macro-social contexts and micro-sociolinguistic settings that are involved in the learning of a second language is an important step toward understanding SLA as a socialization process. Siegel (2003) identifies five different types of macro-contexts, ranging from *dominant L2* where the typical learners are immigrant workers immersed in the TL language environment, to *external L2* (learning the L2 in the learners' country or in *study abroad projects*), to *coexisting and institutional L2* where learners are multilingual speakers and, finally, *minority L2* where speakers of the dominant language learn the minority language. Collentine and Freed (2004) insist on the importance of identifying contexts of learning and cite study abroad programs as providing one such macro-context.

In the wake of Firthian linguistics, systemic functional linguistics has developed a theory of language "as 'a resource for meaning' in the complex socially constituted contexts within cultures" (Williams 2010: 57). Bernstein (1973) and Halliday (1978) identify four types of contexts crucial to language socialization and to social integration, via the development of adequate linguistic codes, namely instructional contexts (explaining rules), regulative contexts (strategies of control), imaginative context (narratives) and interpersonal contexts. According to Bernstein (1972: 147), "codes on this view make substantive the culture or subculture (of the learners) through their control over the linguistic realization of contexts *critical* to the process of socialization." Of the four types of critical contexts described, sociocultural SLA research has mainly studied interpersonal contexts.

Roberts and Simonot (1987: 135) describe different levels of context: "(1) The context created as the interaction unfolds. (2) The contexts of previous similar interactions. (3) The wider social contexts of living as a member of a minority ethnic group." They consider that "the white 'gatekeeper' brings to the encounter the ideology of the institution he represents. The minority ethnic client brings his or her experience of discrimination" (1987: 136). According to Roberts and Simonot, "in the ecology of second language acquisition by ethnic minority workers, the concept of interaction must go deep enough to account for the fact that native speakers, more likely than not, are not providing the support that in Long's words 'cocoons' the learner" (1987: 135).

Teasing global contexts apart from more local phenomena is a crucial step in sociocultural approaches to SLA. Candlin's (2000) proposal to distinguish between contexts and settings in terms of the macro-social factors that shape social and linguistic events and the micro-dimensions of local verbal interaction is a useful one. The different definitions of context and setting discussed above show how thinking on language socialization has moved toward a dynamic conception of context and setting, with interlocutors being the partial agents of the making of their linguistic environment. (And see Porquier and Py (2004) for a detailed and vivid list of settings where L2 learning does eventually take place.)

12.3.3 The agency of the L2 learner

According to Kern and Liddicoat (2010: 19), viewing the L2 learner as a social agent implies that the "speaker is no longer someone who speaks, but someone who acts – that is, someone who acts *through* speaking and thus becomes a social actor." For Kern and Liddicoat (2010: 19), the collocation 'speaker/actor' demands a new perspective on language use and language development. Viewing the language learner as a social agent involved in social interaction entails also a shift in focus in the way in which the learner's cognitive activities are accounted for. The cognitive architecture of the learner's mind is no longer in focus per se. It is rather the emergent nature of context-socially shared cognition – situated cognition – which is under investigation. The authors emphasize the fact that there are "speaker/actors who lack grammar skills but nevertheless function well in terms of communication and socialization, while still others may have solid grammar skills but are less adept at social interaction" (2010: 20). Block (2007b) argues that in addition to emphasis on agency, sociocultural SLA should be counterbalanced through recourse to the notion of community of practice.

12.3.4 Identity and power relations

H. C. White (2008) identifies four meanings of identity. The first sense of identity is related to the elaboration of a stable social footing. The second sense of identity is akin to *face*, i.e. a differentiated social face within some distinct social grouping. A third sense of identity arises from the fact that each social agent participates in many networks and has to adjust to social diversity. A fourth sense is the one derived *ex post*; it is an account after the fact of one's being in society. This general definition agrees with Norton's (2000: 5) definition of identity as the way "a person understands his or her relationship to the world, how that relationship is construed across time and space, and how the person understands possibilities for the future." Although Norton (2000: 116) recognizes some positive aspects to Schumann's (1978a) Acculturation Model, namely sensitivity to the sociocultural context of language learning and identification of the role of the individual learner, she calls for a different conception of the relationship of the adult immigrant learner to the target language community. (See also Chapter 11, this volume.) For Norton, power relations exist in naturalistic SLA. "Inequitable power relations may prevent members of the learner group from maximizing their contact with target language speakers" (Norton 2000: 117). When the L2 learner is estranged from the target society, s/he is liable to be the victim of gate-keeping procedures. Norton and Toohey (2002: 115) assert that "language learners are not only learning a linguistic system; they are learning a diverse set of sociocultural practices, often best understood in the context of wider relations of power." According to Norton and Toohey, social constraints are exerted on the learner in the process of L2 learning. They view learners in terms of symbolic and emotional entities.

The issue of identity is central to Regan, Howard and Lemée (2009: 2) in their definition of sociolinguistic competence. (See also Chapter 13, this volume.) According to the authors, sociolinguistic competence refers in the context of study abroad programs to the manner in which a particular L2 speaker "relates to the community or communities they are living in and may wish to be part of in some way."

12.3.5 Societal integration

Sociolinguistic and SLA research in the field of interethnic relations and target language acquisition have regularly faced the issue of societal integration. The acquisition of the TL by adults and the ability to arrange education of migrant children in both the mother tongue and language of the host country have produced a number of research projects. Societal integration is both a helping and a hindering factor of SLA in naturalistic settings. When social distance and social discrimination are strong, then the chances of becoming a legitimate speaker in one own's right are slight.

In the context of the European Science Foundation project (1981–88), attempts have been made to correlate sociobiographical data and various measures of linguistic attainment in the TL. For example, van Hout and Strömqvist (1993) show that Age and Family Status are variables that correlate negatively with lexical richness, i.e. the older, married learners acquire fewer lexical items than younger, unmarried learners. Degree of schooling in the home country correlates positively with the acquisition of L2 lexicon. Indirectly, it may be argued that younger, unmarried learners with some L1 education stand a better chance of obtaining social integration than older, married and less educated learners.

Although they may diverge on some points, sociocultural approaches to SLA share a common conceptual basis. The paradigm is sensitive to the discursive nature of central notions such as identity and power relations. Societal integration as a global concept does not necessarily imply absence of gate-keeping and of symbolic and social violence. Language life stories (see Section 12.4) show the impact of contexts and settings on L2 acquisition and L2 literacy. Agency and community of practices and sensitivity to power relations imply the capacity of understanding settings and contexts in the target community and of developing relations to the other (*alter*).

12.4 Naturalistic SLA, literacy and socialization

12.4.1 Background

The emergence of research on SLA, literacy and socialization in western societies is strongly determined by social changes related to migration, to economic expansion and to the development of an urban mode of life. This section provides a short presentation of the emergence of naturalistic SLA and L2 literacy as important components of social change. (See also Chapter 9, this volume.)

From the 1950s, in the wake of the decolonization process, western societies experienced rapid economic expansion, which spurred migration on both sides of the Atlantic. "By the late 1980s, family reunification from 1970s onwards had brought the population of immigrants to 4.4 million in West Germany, 3.7 million in France, 0.9 million in Belgium and Switzerland and 0.5 million in the Netherlands" (Alladina 1996: 331). Immigration in large cities caused various types of linguistic disruption (Dittmar, Spolsky and Walters 1997), and social and linguistic discrimination of minorities and interethnic communication emerged as important issues for integration in western societies (Ehlich 1996a: 187). Ehlich (1996b: 924–25) notes that, in the 1970s, sociological and anthropological pursuits were related to research on intercultural communication. The acculturation of migrant workers to new ways of living, including verbal communication, were analyzed in the emerging research on naturalistic L2 acquisition and, later on, on L2 Literacy.

In North America as well as in Europe, the emergentist field of SLA focused partly on immigrant workers' and on their families' attempts to acquire and use the dominant language of the host country, largely in naturalistic unguided settings (see Chapters 17 and 29, this volume). The emergence of research projects devoted to SLA by adult immigrants (see Section 12.1 above) was motivated by blatant social needs – because of miscommunication between the host society and foreign workers – and by educational reasons – a demand arose for specially designed educational programs for adult immigrant learners or their offspring (see Auer and di Luzio 1984 and Preston 1989 for early development, and Chapter 13, this volume).

Since the 1980s, there has been renewed interest in research on L2 acquisition of literacy in L2 spurred by various population movements seeking economic and political shelter in Europe as well as in North America. As Craats, Kurvers and Young-Scholten (2006b) have shown, participants in L2 literacy programs are migrant workers or political refugees, i.e. low-income and low-literate individuals, highly comparable to the participants in the major naturalistic SLA research programs, on both sides of the Atlantic.

Rockhill (1987) reports on an important early study on the acquisition of L2 literacy by Latino women in Los Angeles in the sociocultural paradigm. On the basis of a program starting in 1979, a corpus of life histories from fifty Spanish-speaking working-class adults was recorded. Rockhill showed that literacy is power and that it is gendered. *TESOL Quarterly* (1993) devoted a special issue to adult literacies in which Klassen and Burnaby (1993) surveyed the situation of literacy among adult immigrants to Canada. They advocated recourse to both quantitative and qualitative studies which have since been conducted (see above and Chapter 9, this volume).

Focus on the acquisition of L2 oral or written skills by low-educated learners, such as migrant workers or political refugees, did not necessarily imply that research would be socially oriented. In effect, a majority of research in the field of literacy has been conducted within the cognitive paradigm (see Section 12.4.3 below and Chapter 9, this volume).

12.4.2 Naturalistic data analysis

Sociocultural approaches focusing on the broader context have been successful in drawing attention to the identity of the adult naturalistic SL learner, to the social contexts and settings where s/he interacts. This perspective has involved taking a closer look at L2 biographies, and identity and gatekeeping processes to which the speaker/learner might be subjected have also been described. In her study of a group of female adult learners of English as a second language, Norton (2000) closely examines the researcher and the researched relationship before moving into a detailed study of the life stories of her five informants. She provides a larger picture of migration to Canada and draws attention to the fact that "opportunities to practice English cannot be understood apart from social relations of power in natural or informal settings" (Norton 2000: 72). Her scrutiny of the minute details that five immigrant women provided of their language acquisition through pratice as migrant workers in Canada led Norton to the conclusion that "the relationship between the individual and the social in the context of second language learning should be reconceptualised" (Norton 2000: 124). Positing that L2 acquisition is part and parcel of the practice of migrants in their new environment, she demonstrates that identity is an evolving construct in direct relation to the balance of power developed by the non-unitary migrant person in her new social and communicative world.

Language-focused sociocultural approaches have tried to explain the management of understanding and communication in L2 as the result of the basic learner varieties in the context of inequitable verbal interactions.

Managing L2 understanding

Since the 1980s, a large body of research has been devoted to interethnic communication and understanding in L2. Most analyses combine conversation analysis and ethnography of communication methodology. Studies show that interethnic communication is liable to misfire and minority speakers spend much time and energy in signaling or repairing linguistic breakdowns and managing understanding. Negotiating understanding in L2 depends on the capacity to produce meaningful, though not necessarily grammatical by TL standards, utterances and to understand power relations and be able to put one's meaning and intent across. L2 communication is in no way simply a matter of processing linguistic input. It implies the capacity to identify gate-keeping procedures, to become a legitimate speaker and to stand on one's own.

Below is an extract from an authentic conversation between a German lawyer (A) and a Turkish client, Herr Kaya, who is a foreign worker living in Germany (first presented in Becker and Perdue 1984). The verbal interaction between the Turkish client and the German lawyer takes place in the latter's office. The conversation misfires on sociocultural and strategic grounds. As will become clear through an analysis of the transcript, there is a divergence between the two partners about the interpretation of the sequence of events. In this extract, power relations, identity and conversational strategies are involved. In the conversation in the lawyer's office, Herr Kaya and the lawyer pursue different scripts: the lawyer wants his client to develop a proper appraisal of the situation. He wants him to understand the practical implications of "parental custody." Herr Kaya, however, is worried about possible new expenses to be incurred.

Extract 1

1. Lawyer A: *im moment gehts hi/ also in DIESEM verfahren gehts doch NICHT um das*
    at (this) moment the topic he/ OK in THIS case it is NOT a question of
2. *GELD sondern es geht darum wer die elterliche SORGE hat Herr Kaya*
    MONEY but it has to with who gets parental CUSTODY Herr Kaya
3. Herr Kaya: *ja elterniche sorge natürlich [...] aber ich hab vierunvirezig tausent mark war*
    Yes parental custody OK [...] but I have forty-four thousand marks (was)+

4. Lawyer A: *SCHULDEN nä? Sie hat KEINE pfennig mehr schulden Sie verdient fünfzehn hundert*
DEBTS isn't it? She has no longer any pfennig left She earns fifteen hundred
5. Herr Kaya: *Mark ich ver-*
Marks I ea
6. Lawyer A: *Nee he / herr Kaya noch mal*
No Mister/ Mister Kaya once again
7. Herr Kaya: *Ja bitte*
Yes please
8. Lawyer A: *Das gericht hat ENTSCHIEDEN dass IHRE frau die elterliche sorge bekommt*
The court has DECIDED that YOUR wife has obtained parental custody
9. Herr Kaya: *Ja + ja*
Yes +Yes.

Conflicting scripts leads the lawyer to negate Herr Kaya's statement (lines 1 and 2: "it is not a question of money") stressing both the negation marker *nicht* and the word *Geld* ('money'). In line 6, the lawyer rebuts Herr Kaya's position again and goes on to repeat the same piece of information about "parental custody" (lines 1, 2, 8). Herr Kaya is deferential and polite (line 7) but follows his own line of argumentation. His main concern is to save money in this legal procedure not to lose parental custody.

The differences in expectations and scripts between the two interlocutors are related to the social status and function of the lawyer in relation to his client and to the client's misunderstanding of the situation. Because he is set on his own purpose (no further expenditure), Herr Kaya misunderstands the technical expression *elterliche Sorge* "parental custody." He even coins a new derivational adjective *elterniche* on the basis of *eltern* "parents."

Responding to a social investigation

A functional linguistic approach to learner varieties differs from a formal approach because it is sensitive both to linguistic properties and to contextual factors. It is postulated that social factors provide the drive for learner varieties to evolve while languages in contact may shape the internal properties of these varieties. According to Dittmar *et al.* (1997: 1721), "social and linguistic integration into a target culture can be examined by looking at identity through grammaticalization, the process whereby an adult second language learner devises, selects, produces, and repeatedly develops formal means for expressing intentions in a second language." Klein and Perdue (1997) postulate that naturalistic learners build an early *basic variety* shaped by pragmatic – topic first and focus last – and semantic – controller first – principles which yield a limited, yet sufficient, knowledge for the learner to fulfil prototypical narratives and other discourse tasks. Social and communicative factors are the pushing factors that will lead the *basic variety* to evolve in the direction of more advanced L2 varieties.

The following text is an extract from an authentic encounter between an unemployed Moroccan immigrant worker, Abdelmalek (A), and an unemployment interviewer Bernard (B) at the unemployment bureau. B needs to check whether A has been looking seriously for a job. The following extract shows how A explains the steps he has taken to find a job. He must convince B that he has taken the proper steps to find a job. If B is not convinced, Abdelmalek will be sanctioned.

Extract 2

1. B: *Vous avez une idée pourquoi vous avez pas retrouvé du travail?*
"Do you have any idea why you have not (yet) found a new job?"

2. A: *Parce que Ø /le parti/ l'agence + /jãna/ pas /done/ l'agence comme le certificat nom de patron*
Because Ø left for the (unemployment) office + there's not give the office as the certificate the name of the employer
"I went to the unemployment office. They did not give me any document with the name of the boss to contact."

3. *L'adresse moi je /parte/ patron il /madi/ moi complet je /ne/ pas travail moi*
Address me I left (the) boss he said I am full I have no job me
"I went to the job's address. The boss told me he was 'full'. He had no job to offer."

4. *Il / madi/ cachet /saje/*
He said stamp ok "He said, I will stamp your form, OK"

5. B: *Oui mais ça suffit pas d'aller à l'agence*
"Yes but it is not enough to go to the unemployment office"

6. A: *non*
"no"

7. B: *Qu'est-ce que vous faites d'autre + pour trouver du travail*
"What else do you do to find a job?"

8. A: *du travail + ça /fe/ euh je /part/ toujours Ø /ʃerʃe/ / janpa/*
work + it makes euh I go always (to) look for there isn't
"Jobs, I always look for jobs, there isn't any"

9. B: *où est-ce que vous allez+ comment vous faites?*
"Where do you go? What do you do?"

10. A: */ʃet/*
do.

In Abdelmalek's learner variety, reference to the speaker on stage is marked through pronouns *moi* (me), *je* (I) or zero anaphora Ø. He uses connectors *parce que* (because), *comme* (as), adverbs such as *toujours* (always) and *madi* (told me) to introduce reported speech. Verbs are not inflected. In this passage, all utterances produced by Abdelmalek follow a pragmatic Topic–Focus organization as in 2, or 3:

2. A: *Parce que [Ø]*_{Topic} *[/le parti/ l'agence]*_{Focus}

3. *[L'adresse]*_{Topic} *[moi je /parte/]*_{Focus}

In 2, the Topic, which is implicit, is marked by zero anaphora.

Presentational /jãna/ (there is) introducing thetic constructions is used for side comments, as in 2:

2. A: /jãna/ pas /done/ l'agence comme le certificat nom de patron (there's not give the bureau as the certificate the name of the employer).

In this utterance, the agent *l'agence* (the unemployment bureau) is demoted from first position because of presentational /jãna/ and the thetic construction.

In this extract, Abdelmalek's line of argument is to show that he has been active in looking for a job. He narrates the job interview he obtained through his own initiative, not because of help from the unemployment bureau (lines 2–4). As the supervisor closes on him (line 7), Abdelmalek produces a general statement (line 8):

8. A: *du travail* + *ça /fe/ euh je /part/ toujours Ø / ʃerʃe/ / janpa/* (work + it makes euh I go always (to) look for there isn't).

A repeats the topic *du travail* (work), from the supervisor's question (line 7), and follows up with a sentence focus which is another thetic construction, + *ça /fe/ euh je /part/ toujours Ø / ʃerʃe/ / janpa/*. Abdelmalek is cornered and the interaction breaks down in line 10, where he is just able to repeat the supervisor's last word. This extract illustrates both the efficiency of Abdelmalek in the use of his basic variety and the imbalance of the interview. Recourse to thetic constructions on the part of the migrant worker Abdelmalek provides a clear illustration of the inequitable relations that hold between the supervisor and the person being interviewed.

12.4.3 Literacy practices

In his introduction to Norton (2000), Candlin (2000) contrasts research on literacy and SLA research, arguing that the former field is marked by social engagement while SLA research seems disconnected from social concern. Since Rockhill's seminal work in the field of L2 literacy (Rockhill 1987; see Section 12.4.1 above), there has been a growing interest in the development of L2 literacy for low-educated learners, which has brought together SLA and literacy research (see Chapter 9, this volume).

Contrasting approaches to SL literacy

L2 literacy studies exhibit the same divergent cognitive and sociocultural approaches as SLA research. If the question posed by Young-Scholten and Naeb (2010: 63), "Can adult immigrants without native language education or literacy learn to read in a second language?", is shared by various strands of research involved in literacy studies, the types of answers provided diverge. Some working within the field of Low-Educated Second Language and Literacy Acquisition (LESLLA), for instance, focus on the linguistic and cognitive processes underlying reading development by adults with little or no schooling. Others develop mainly quantitative measures to longitudinally assess literacy programs (see Reder and Bynner 2009). In spite of Rockhill's pioneer study on SL literacy, and Klassen and Burnaby's plea for qualitative research in SL literacy, there has been little sociocultural research in the domain of L2 literacy.

Cognitive research projects on L2 literacy

In addition to Young-Scholten and Strom's (2006) small-scale study of the acquisition of SL literacy in English by Vietnamese- and Somali-speaking adults reported on in Chapter 9, this volume, Condelli, Wrigley and Yoon (2009) report on a project called "What works" for adult literacy students of English as a second language "who lack basic literacy skills and have minimal proficiency in English." The 495 students who participated in the project were very low literate and had minimal oral language skills in English. Data were collected from thirteen ESL programs in seven US states over a two-year period. A system of "study liaisons" from the same social environment and communities as the students enabled the program to keep track of the students over an extended period. The average age of the participants to the study was 40 and the students, 72 percent female, had an average of 3.1 years of native language schooling, with the thirty-eight Hmong students having 0.3 year of school attendance on average. Students participated in the program for an average of sixteen weeks and received 128 hours of instruction. Attendance measures and test scores for English literacy and language were computed. Two student variables, age and years of formal education, were significantly related to growth in basic reading skills, confirming Young-Scholten and Strom's results. Adult ESOL literacy student who entered the class with some basic reading skills showed significant progress in reading skills but this took time to appear. The same students with higher basic reading skills when the class began ended up with higher English oral skills. Three instructional strategies proved to be related to growth in student literacy and language learning: connection to the outside world (using materials from everyday life); use of the students' native language for clarification in instruction; and varied practice and interaction.

Sociocultural approaches to L2 literacy

Bingman (2009) reports on a mixed-methods longitudinal study of adult literacy in Tennessee. Ten out of the 450 participants in the project were interviewed about their life histories. These were tales of struggle against poverty and racism. One of the conclusions of the paper is worth quoting: "The quantitative data can give power to the conclusions and qualitative data add the depth of context and the complexity of life as lived" (Bingman 2009: 310). McDonald and Scollay (2009) also chose to use both qualitative and quantitative methods in their three-year project on acquiring/improving basic literacy skills. Seventy percent of the 132 participants in the study were multilingual L2 literacy students. The qualitative approach to the literacy program enabled the researchers to understand the betterment of life obtained through literacy and the nature of the relation developed with tutors. Maclachan, Tett and Hall (2009) also studied interconnections developing literacy, self-confidence, learner identity and social capital in an evaluation of the Scottish Adult Literacy and Numeracy Strategy. It is unclear how many of the 600 participants on the project were L2 literacy acquirers. However, the methodology and the conclusions regarding the benefits accruing to the learners in enhancing their social confidence and the positive modification of learner identity also apply to this population.

12.5 Concluding remarks

12.5.1 Problems and difficulties within sociocultural approaches

Among the challenges facing socially oriented SLA research is the diversity of approaches practiced within its realm. Although there is no urge to unite the different strands of research, it would prove fruitful in the future to work toward some form of convergence. This section discusses some of the challenges facing socially oriented SLA, which could pave the way for future development. Besides diversity, three types of challenges confront sociocultural SLA research: its epistemological status and the ensuing methodology, and its relation to the cognitive and linguistic issues involved in SLA.

Methodological and epistemological challenges

Qualitative hermeneutic research produces significant results and insights in the process of L2 acquisition (see Section 12.4.3 above). However, it must avoid the pitfall of stressing the dichotomy between the language user and his/her social environment (Williams 2010: 58). It must also clarify the question of its explanatory power. By definition, sociocultural SLA research rejects idealization of data and modeling. Does this epistemological stance preclude the possibility of drawing general conclusions and explaining the mechanisms and factors at play in a given situation? Answers to these questions are related to the types of accounts that sociocultural SLA wishes to produce. A case in point is the status of freighted descriptions. Rationalist SLA research is critical of the explanatory value of this type of account (see Section 12.1.3 above). For ethnographic researchers, there is no better way to render the complexity of individual lives. Following McDonald and Scollay (2009: 314), sociocultural research seems to be pulled by opposing forces: "how to adequately represent the individuals" versus the fact that "conclusions cannot be based only on anecdotes and stories." The choice of a partly rationalist and of a partly constructivist stance to research might find a way out of this epistemological dilemma.

Relation to the issue of cognition

Although situated cognition as a shared practice offers some form of answer to the question of explicating the cognitive processes involved in SL acquisition and use, handling the cognitive side of L2 learning remains a sore point for SLA sociocultural approaches. A close analysis of verbal interaction will not always provide all the necessary insights into the acquisition process (see Porquier and Py 2004).

Relation to language focused research

Various strands of sociocultural SLA research are suspicious of linguistic descriptions, possibly following the Critical Discourse strand. Fortunately, sociolinguistics, conversation analysis and emergentist linguistics examine language and the development of linguistic knowledge as social practices and as rule-governed behavior. As shown in Section 12.4.3, the minute analysis of emergent linguistic categories does not contradict the need to place these linguistic features in the broader picture of sociolinguistic settings and social context, and of questions of power and identity.

These epistemological and methodological caveats apply both to the fields of naturalistic L2 acquisition and L2 literacy. Although it might be tempting, as in mainstream cognitive SLA, to tease apart social and psychological factors on the one hand and linguistic and cognitive features on the other, an integrated research perspective is highly desirable. Adult learners who may have suffered from social and psychological trauma due to the circumstances of their lives (economic migration, political asylum, etc.) cannot be sliced into neat components for the sake of elegant research.

12.5.2 Future directions

Studying naturalistic L2 acquisition and L2 literacy in their social context is a complex process. Socially oriented SLA has to define a research agenda which will take advantage of the varied nature of research carried out under its banner. It must obviously develop and expand its methodological tool kit. Moving out of positivistic quantitative data collection and analysis implies paying heed to the quality and the significance of the data collected as well as to the procedures of data analysis. Socially oriented SLA research must develop both descriptive and explanatory capacities in view of a more comprehensive approach of its explanandum. As shown by research in the field of L2 literacy, sociocultural SLA research can and should combine qualitative and quantitative research.

Despite a real interest in qualitative and contextualized studies of SLA and L2 literacy, sociocultural research has still to improve its procedures of analysis and its accounts. However, it is to be expected that the global SLA scene will confer legitimacy on research questions related to aspects of L2 socialization as distinct from acquisition.

The chapter has surveyed various aspects of SLA socialization and discussed how various social and sociolinguistic factors affect L2 learning and use. The attempt to establish a causal link between social context and L2 use and knowledge requires both the development of an adequate conceptual framework – the emergence of the notions of identity and power in SLA research has produced a positive effect on knowledge – and a renewal in the approach to empirical phenomena.

13

Variation

Vera Regan

13.1 Introduction

Language is inherently variable; this applies whether we are talking about a speaker's first, second or third language. Yet linguistics in the twentieth century tended to focus on the invariant and variation was considered to be a marginal issue. However, focus has increasingly been shifting to variation in linguistic studies. For instance, in a 2010 article in *New Scientist*, Kenneally says that Evans and Levinson (2009) "believe that languages do not share a common set of rules...their sheer variety is a defining feature of human communications... Language diversity is the 'crucial fact for understanding the place of language in human cognition.'" Whether or not one agrees that all languages share a set of rules (Editors' note: e.g. Universal Grammar; see Chapters 1, 2, this volume), it is increasingly accepted that variation is an important aspect of language.

All language may be variable; however, second language is particularly variable. This chapter will address why variation in L2 is considered important, and what more we have learnt about SLA by taking variation into account. One approach to the investigation of L2 variability is the variationist perspective on language. Recent interest in SLA and variation (see Bayley and Regan 2004) is demonstrated in descriptions in standard works on SLA (e.g. Bayley and Tarone, in press; Doughty and Long 2003; R. Ellis 1994a; Mitchell and Myles 2004). This chapter is an account of the contribution of research from within the variationist paradigm, particularly to SLA research, especially SLA in social context.

Variationist sociolinguistics places variation centrally in linguistic description and analysis. Generally speaking, variation refers to differences in linguistic form, or to two or more ways of saying the same thing. Researchers then find correlations between these forms and social facts. At any point where speakers can make a choice in discourse, this is a potential site for a linguistic variable, such as *-in/-ing* alternation or use of quotative *like* in English, or *ne* deletion in French. For example, we can say:

(1) *I'm go**in** to the shop* or *I'm go**ing** to the shop*

(2) *I'm **like** "not in a million years"* or *I **said** "not in a million years."*

(3) *je **ne** vois pas ça* or *je 0 vois pas ça* 'I don't see that'

Before variation studies, it was felt that these alternatives were in *free variation*, that is, choice of form was random. In fact, we now know that variation is systematic (Labov 1966; Weinreich, Labov and Herzog 1968). Numerous fine-grained, quantitative studies since the 1960s have demonstrated that the choice of variants (or forms) (*-in* vs. *-ing*) by the speaker is not arbitrary but conditioned (or affected) by the simultaneous effect of multiple factors, linguistic and social. Many of these have been studies of non-standard dialects. Social factors might include age, sex, social class, style of speech, ethnicity and so on. Linguistic factors could include factors such as the previous speech segment, or verb type. The variable *-in/-ing* is composed of two variants: *-in* and *-ing*. Variationists have also found that forms in different language varieties tend to occur "more or less often," rather than "always or never." For the variationist, it is a matter not only of determining *what* occurs, but on what occasions and how often, which factors (social and linguistic) affect what occurrences and how this knowledge forms part of the mental grammar of the speaker.

Descriptions of variation research, its methods, concepts and theoretical frameworks in relation to first (native) language will be briefly described in this chapter (more comprehensive accounts can be found in, for example, Guy 1993; Labov 2001; Poplack 2000; Tagliamonte 2006; Walker 2010). It should be noted that despite the title of the field of Second Language Acquisition research, in reality, most speakers in the world are speakers of many languages and in this chapter second language speaker also implies third, fourth and multilingual speaker. After this general discussion, there will be a discussion of the role of variation in SLA and, in turn, a discussion of some of the areas of acquisition affected by variation, the contribution of variation theory to L2 research, use of variationist methodology in the investigation of L2 acquisition and likely future contributions of the "third wave" in variation theory and practice to SLA research. While some of these topics are dealt with elsewhere in this volume (Chapters 11 and 12), this chapter will present specifically variationist perspectives on these issues.

13.2 Background

13.2.1 Variationist sociolinguistics

Psychologists have long been interested in probabilistic behavior. Adamson (2009: 79–80), for example, describes how experiments in probability matching showed that people can accurately gauge the proportion of different events. People also have a sense of probability in relation to language patterns, which may be part of language competence. This has implications for all language learning including SLA. Variationists investigate how the learner's mental grammar accommodates the variation found in every speech community, and see it as a probabilistic grammar (a "more or less") not a categorical one ("either or") (Adamson 2009).

Variationists seek to model the variable grammar of language and languages. Variation has always been linked to a theory of language change by variationists such as Labov (1994, 2001), and the theory confronts the paradox of the coexistence of fixed structure in language and also the fact that language is changing. Given variation theory's ability to model change in linguistic systems, it seems unsurprising that variationists interested in SLA saw the possibilities of using this type of modeling in the investigation of the development of variable and constantly changing L2 systems.

Variationist research methods are mainly quantitative but have important qualitative implications, having emerged from a strong anthropological tradition (e.g. Sankoff 1980). Classic variationist research involves conducting detailed analyses of naturally occurring speech data to account for variation patterns. These data are collected through what is known as the sociolinguistic interview, audio-recorded conversations using standard "modules" developed by Labov. These modules, or series of designed questions, produce shifts in topic and style in response to the interviewer's questions, covering topics such as danger of death, childhood, education and others. Relative frequencies of linguistic phenomena in the discourse are counted. Variationists are concerned, as we saw, not only with what is possible (as a categorical, either/or approach would), but with what is likely and unlikely and in what proportions (a probabilistic approach). Crucially, a variationist approach correlates linguistic forms with social factors and tries to account for both. Variationist research has revealed robust patterns of language use in numerous speech communities. For example, studies of -in/-ing alternation in English have revealed similar patterns of use in different English-speaking communities; -in usage is higher amongst working-class speakers, among men and in informal speech. In multiple large-scale analyses of urban communities groups of people tended to use the same relative proportions of variants of a variable. For instance, most people in the same speech community, in casual speech, would use more -in than -ing. Despite differences in rates of use, the relative patterns were similar in groups described as *speech communities*.

Modelling variation in speech takes as given the fact that multiple factors contribute to the variation. Therefore a heuristic tool, Varbrul (*variable rule analysis*), was designed by Labov and his colleagues (Rand and Sankoff 1990). The term variable rule is now rarely used. Originally, variable rules were adapted from generative syntax's optional rules but built probabilistic information into their formulation. While the term is no longer used, probabilistic modeling is still a goal of variation analysis. Varbrul is a set of computer programs designed to deal with naturally occurring speech data. It models patterns in discourse and determines how the choice process is affected by the factors in the environment in which the form appears. These factors are said to constrain the choice. A multiple regression analysis shows those factors which are significant in the production of the variant as well as their relative size. The results of the variable rule analysis show whether the effect is statistically significant, the size of that effect (the range between the highest and lowest factor weight) and the constraint hierarchies (involving the ordering of factor weights; see Poplack and Tagliamonte 2001: 92–93). *Constraint hierarchies* refer to the fact that the constraints affecting the choice of variant can be ordered in a hierarchy, depending on the importance of the effect they have on the choice of form. For instance, in relation to *-in/-ing* alternation within the factor group "gender of speaker," the factor "female" will emerge as more important than "male" in use of *-ing* and so will be attributed a higher ranking in the constraint order.

Variationists have noted an asymmetry of form and function in language; as we have seen, several forms may be used variably to express the same function. This asymmetry has been evident especially at the site of change in language, often characterized by instability, where two competing forms are in flux. One form may "win" and be maintained, and the other lost. Alternatively, both may maintain an existence in the language. Variationists are sensitive to the inherent instability of form and function as the implications are valuable both in predicting language change and for the social implications of synchronic variation. Given that learner language is also characterized by an asymmetry of form and function and by constant change, variation research tools are useful in researching variability in second language (Young 1996). L2 longitudinal studies, as we will see later, can particularly benefit from this aspect of variation analysis. Such studies help in understanding the progression of the L2 speaker from early stages to greater proficiency.

Variation analysis depends on having "good data" (spontaneous, unmonitored speech which constitutes, according to Labov, the most systematic language). The interviewer captures this by obviating the "observer's paradox," that is, eliciting relaxed speech despite the fact that the speaker is aware of being observed. Strategies for overcoming such obstacles include encouraging speakers to talk about topics in which they are emotionally invested (see above), thus avoiding focus on form and conscious choice between alternants. Feagin (2002), Labov (1984), Milroy (1987), Milroy and Gordon (2003) and Tagliamonte (2006) all provide excellent guides to field work. Narratives in particular tend to produce spontaneous speech, and Labov and Waletzky (1967) elaborated a system for the analysis of these. Current poststructuralist work on variation has referred to the role of narrative, as Labov described it, in the enterprise of obtaining ethnographic data on the lives of individuals in a local context; Eckert (2000) is an example of such ethnographic work.

While much variationist linguistic research focuses on social aspects of speech, psycholinguistic and psychological aspects of variation in acquisition have also been explored (for example, Dewaele 2009b; Dewaele and Furnham 2000; Pavlenko and Blackledge 2004; Sia and Dewaele 2006). Newly developing connectionist approaches have much to offer in this area also, in that both connectionist networks and variation theory deal with probabilities (Adamson 2009: 12–13); Mitchell and Myles (2004: 121) outline how connectionist linguistics and cognitive linguistics are compatible with variationist theory.

13.2.2 Variation and SLA

We can see the evolution of variationist research in SLA as dividing roughly into phases: an early phase, roughly the 1970s and 1980s where pioneering studies explored the possibilities of variationist research methods in SLA; a middle stage, roughly the 1990s, consolidating these openings in a number of detailed variation studies; and the current phase, since approximately 2000, where ethnographic approaches to SLA are taken by variation sociolinguists, some of this being poststructuralist in approach. This section will trace the development of these phases.

Variationist sociolinguistics (as developed by Labov) and SLA research (e.g. Corder 1967; Selinker 1972) developed in parallel during the 1960s and 1970s, with little reference to each other. However, in the 1970s, a number of variationist researchers began to make connections between the two fields and to see that they shared several research agendas (for instance, Adamson and Kovac 1981; Dickerson 1974, 1975; and Tarone 1979, 1982). They began to apply variationist models, constructs and research methods to studies of SLA. It became apparent that variationist sociolinguistics had benefits to offer SLA research. Its probabilistic, as opposed to deterministic, models looked promising in the investigation of the variable nature of L2 speech.

Variationist sociolinguistics and SLA research were both interested in particular speech varieties: SLA in interlanguage, and variation studies in nonstandard dialects. Both investigated speakers' underlying systems, especially to see whether the varieties were systematic or simply random. Sociolinguistic approaches to SLA were established on both sides of the Atlantic. In Europe, for example, the Heidelberger Forschungsprojekt "Pidgin-Deutsch" showed that social factors were an important contribution to acquisition (Meisel 1983). In the US, studies of SLA used variation research methods. Tarone (1988) is a description of this early socially oriented research on SLA; see also Adamson and Kovac (1981), Beebe (1980), Beebe and Zuengler (1983), Berdan (1996), Dickerson (1975), Tarone (1982) and Wolfram (1985). They all concluded that variability in L2 data was indeed systematic, as indeed variationists had demonstrated for L1 speech. (This does not ignore some random developmental variability in learner language; performance errors, processing limits and so on. [Editor's note: this remains a problem for non-variationist L2 researchers; see Chapter 31, this volume.])

A particular benefit of variationist research on L2 acquisition was the significance of change in L2 speech over time, because of its focus on the mechanism of language variation and change. In SLA research, this can be used to chart changes in rates as well as changing constraint hierarchies in relation to L2 development, especially in longitudinal studies (Hansen 2006; Liu 2000; Regan 2004a). Young (1991) demonstrates that learners restructure their grammars as they progress through various stages of variability, where they use different forms (target and non-target) towards categorical usage; that is, they use one particular target form finally.

One problem with the early studies was that they attributed variation to one factor alone, for example to attention to speech, linguistic environment, proficiency of speaker and others. However, we now know that multiple factors contribute to the variation in L2 data. The multivariate analysis used by variationists models the simultaneous effect of multiple linguistic and social factors on L2 speech.

In the 1990s, a series of Variation Varbrul studies followed which addressed the 1980s problem of multifactoriality (Adamson and Regan 1991; Bayley 1991; Regan 1996; Young 1991). Young and Bayley (1996: 253) summarize the area in two principles: "the principle of quantitative modelling and the principle of multiple causes" and applied these in studies of Chinese speakers of English L2. Young investigated plural marking and Bayley, past tense marking. Adamson and Regan investigated *-in/-ing* use by Vietnamese and Cambodian speakers of English L2, and Regan investigated *ne* deletion by Irish speakers of L2 French. These studies showed that the variation in L2 speech was constrained by a number of linguistic and social factors and they confirmed first-phase findings that variation in L2 speech was indeed systematic. The studies further demonstrated that Varbrul was a powerful heuristic and analytical tool for the analysis of these highly variable L2 speech data. But further variation studies were still needed and Bayley and Preston (1996) produced a volume answering this need, consisting of seven variationist studies.

13.2.3 Sociolinguistic competence: native speaker variation speech patterns

So far, the variationist studies of SLA discussed had mostly been studies of the acquisition of the categorical in language; that is, where the learner acquires the elements in language where no choice is involved in target-like structures, for example the structure of negation in English: *I don't see* (as opposed to learners' use of *I not see*). A new strand in variation SLA research began in the 1990s which focused on the acquisition of what is variable in language, that is, where the native speaker exercises choice: *I was running* vs. *I was runnin'*, in this case between two targetlike possibilities where one is non-standard. The categorical and the variable can be represented as two axes (Corder 1981): the vertical axis represents developmental progression, and the horizontal axis progression on the sociolinguistic dimension, the use of non-categorical native-speaker patterns of variation. On the vertical axis, the L2 speaker may say variably *I no walk* and *I don't walk*; i.e. a target and a non-target form may be used variably until the target form finally wins out. On the sociolinguistic axis, the speaker progresses along a continuum of sociolinguistic competence.

Just as native speakers choose one variant rather than another, so do L2 speakers. In the earlier phases of SLA research there was a tendency to view the learner as acquiring a monolithic target language and prestige norm varieties, frequently in a formal classroom. In reality, L2 speakers' experiences are far more complex. They may be naturalistic learners with exposure to a multiplicity of varieties, many stigmatized. In addition, L2 speakers are not necessarily literate (see Chapters 9 and 12, this volume). SLA variationist research has begun to address this complexity.

Recent studies of how L2 speakers acquire target language variation patterns assume that this type of variation is part of linguistic competence, not simply relevant to performance. In addition, as this type of variation involves choice, it forms an important part of the speaker's identity construction, self-presentation in interaction and establishment of relations with their interlocutor (see Chapter 12, this volume). This area of sociolinguistic competence is an important part of acquisition for variationists, and social approaches in SLA now take it into account (Bayley and Regan 2004). It has become part of the current "third wave" phase.

13.2.4 The acquisition of native-speaker variation patterns: naturalistic and formal settings

Studies of acquisition in different settings have shown that context is a major causal variable. Adamson and Regan (1991), Bayley (1996) and Major (2004) examined the acquisition of target language variation patterns in naturalistic situations. As Schumann's Acculturation Model (Schumann 1978b) had suggested earlier, contact with native speakers was important for language development. These studies provided evidence that naturalistic learners who have contact with native speakers (NS) tend to approximate NS rates and constraint orderings in relation to NS variation patterns. Other studies provided a comparison in terms of learning context, by examining more formal settings (e.g. the year abroad, the immersion classroom and the traditional classroom). Year abroad is an interesting context for acquisition in that it is neither only classroom setting nor only naturalistic, but a mixture of the two (Byram and Feng 2006; DuFon and Churchill 2006; Regan, Howard and Lemée 2009). Exposure to the two environments can potentially provide ideal conditions for the acquisition of a variety of registers and norms. Regan (1995) is a longitudinal study of six Irish English study-abroad learners of French and their acquisition of speech patterns in relation to *ne* deletion. The Varbrul results demonstrated that both the rates of deletion and the constraint ordering of the conditioning factors changed after the learners' year in France. These L2 speakers moved significantly closer to NS French patterns. In addition, contrary to the hypothesis that the speakers would "de-colloquialize" after a year back in a formal classroom, these changes were, in fact, maintained. Contact with native speakers was crucial in interindividual variability (which concurs with other findings already noted). Agency also seemed to be involved in the degree of interindividual variation (for instance, some of the speakers actively sought out the company of native speakers more than others). Other variationist year abroad studies also demonstrate that L2 speakers approximate native-speaker patterns (Lemée 2002; Sax 2000, 2003), but do not match them. Length of stay was also a significant affecting factor, with those who stayed longest attaining more targetlike patterns.

Research on the acquisition of variation patterns in the immersion classroom by Canadian researchers, principally Mougeon and colleagues (Mougeon 2010), provides an interesting comparison with the year abroad experience and thus further findings on context of acquisition. Mougeon's Varbrul studies of the acquisition of variation patterns investigated several variables connected with varying degrees of formality in the spoken French of Canada by anglophone learners (e.g. F. Mougeon and Rehner 2010; Rehner, Mougeon and Nadasdi 2003). Results showed that, despite a degree of acquisition of native speech variation patterns, the immersion speakers in Canada did so considerably less than the year abroad Irish students (see Lemée, Howard and Regan 2007). Dewaele and Regan (2001) also found, in relation to Dutch and Irish learners of French, that classroom learners acquired only a restricted colloquial vocabulary; see also Sankoff *et al.* (1997) and Blondeau, Nagy, Sankoff and Thibault (2002) on Canadian anglophone L2 learners in naturalistic settings acquiring the NS French norms.

Combining these results, which provide evidence across a range of situations, we can see a steady increase, in quantitative terms, from least contact with native speakers to most contact (Lemée *et al.* 2007) in the acquisition of vernacular speech patterns. We will further develop this below.

13.3 Contribution of variation theory to SLA

The analysis of L2 language variation has contributed to broader theoretical discussions of SLA by providing empirical evidence in a number of domains. These include social and psychological factors: the role of input, transfer, age and gender, context of acquisition, and as dependent variables, morphosyntactic phenomena such as tense and aspect, or various phonological phenomena. Preston (1996) has illustrated how quantitative work in SLA has clear implications for our understanding of language transfer, effects of exposure to the L2 and language universals in SLA. This section provides an overview of some areas in which variationist research has been instrumental in evaluating competing theories of SLA, where it either confirms earlier predictions or provides contradictory evidence, indicating the necessity for further investigation. In addition, new findings on L2 acquisition have emerged through variation research on SLA. A brief description follows of how these topics have been approached by variationists.

13.3.1 Tense

Adamson, Fonseca-Greber, Kataoka, Scardino and Takano (1996), Bayley (1994), Howard (2002) and Jia and Bayley (2008) have all studied tense in SLA from within a variationist framework. An example is also Berlin and Adamson (2009), who conducted a Varbrul analysis of English irregular past tense marking by Chinese children. Results suggested that children learned irregular past tense verbs individually while adults tend to learn them in classes. The children correctly marked verbs in obligatory past tense contexts in background clauses more than in foreground ones. Speakers expressed background information when they had more linguistic resources and could therefore be more accurate. The authors also found support for Andersen's prototype hypothesis and Bayley's transfer hypothesis. That is, the participants marked telic verbs as past tense more frequently and earlier in the acquisition process. They relied on telicity to indicate past in the earlier stages and, as proficiency increased, relied less on perfective verbs. The fact that Varbrul can take into account the multiple combinations of constraints on past tense marking permits researchers to discover which combination best accounts for the variation observed in the L2 speech in relation to past tense. This study also contributes to previous findings on prototypes in SLA research, findings on clause type and tense (Adamson *et al.* 1996; Hansen 2001; Wolfram 1985; Young 1991) and also to the notion of saliency (Wolfram 1985), where age makes a difference to its effects. This last finding has implications for variation analysis of the development of L2 speech over time. Through its use of Varbrul, the study thus contributed to several key themes in SLA: transfer; the path of tense acquisition, the factors which affect performance and at which stages of the process; the role of proficiency level; the role of clause types; and prototype theory. These topics feed into major overarching themes in SLA, such as the relationship of L1 to L2 and routes and rates of acquisition.

13.3.2 Input

L2 research investigates the extent and nature of input, and more recently the question of the input to which the L2 speaker has access. The role of input in SLA is discussed among others by Gass (2003), Pica and Doughty (1985) and Rast (2008). An important contribution of variation linguistics is that it makes precise input available to L2 speakers by means of fine-grained descriptions of the speech in communities where L2 speakers live. Communities' speech norms are frequently non-standard, and variationist research since the 1960s has produced a stream of detailed information about target languages across the world. We need to know what the target input is to be able to estimate the effects of crosslinguistic influence, if any. An example of variation research contribution to the issue of input is Ghafar Samar (2000), cited in Bayley and Lucas (2007: 137), who shows that L1 transfer, previously thought to play an important role in the use of resumptive relative pronouns in the English of Farsi speakers, did not, in fact, account for them. Once again quantitative analysis, taking multiple factors simultaneously into account, was useful in providing robust data on the issue under scrutiny; here, the role of L1 influence.

13.3.3 Group versus individual variation

Whereas the issue of group and individual variation had been convincingly demonstrated by variationists dealing with native speakers (Guy 1980), the relationship between group results and individual performance has been more problematic in SLA, given the multiplicity of variables involved and the well-documented L2 interspeaker variation. It is important to establish the appropriateness of proceeding with group results. Specifically, is it inappropriate to bunch together groups of individual speakers: might this mask individual effects? The issue of group results also relates to notions of speech communities. If variationist analyses, for instance, find evidence that linguistic factors have different effects, or that these factors change over time, then we might conclude that speakers have different internal grammars, or that these change over time as in the case of L2 acquisition. This is invaluable empirical information for studying the process and route of acquisition.

In relation to L2 speakers, Bayley and Langman (2004) and Regan (2004) analysed the relationship between group and individual. Regan (2004) investigated five Irish English learners of L2 French, comparing longitudinal results from three different testing phases and two different learning contexts (year abroad and classroom learning). Analyses of *ne* deletion in both group and individual speakers over three phases showed that rates remained similar for group and individual. Bayley and Langman (2004) studied the acquisition of English by speakers of three different first languages: Chinese, Hungarian and Spanish. They also found that individual variation patterns closely matched group patterns on several dimensions. The results from the two studies (one cross-sectional and one longitudinal) provide crosslinguistic evidence that it is, in fact, reasonable to group results in

L2 research. It is, however, necessary to continue to verify these conclusions given that individual L2 learner differences may lead to more diversity in the speech communities of which they are a part than traditional native speech communities.

13.3.4 Gender

Gender has recently been the focus of much SLA research (see Chapter 8, this volume; Kinginger 2004; Marriott 1995; Norton 2000; Polyani 1995) and emerges as a crucial variable here, too. For example, Adamson and Regan (1991) found interesting behavior relating to gendered use of language for *-in* and *-ing* in L2 English by Vietnamese and Cambodian speakers. Male L2 speakers in Philadelphia were found to accommodate to male speech norms, rather than adopting the overall community norms. Both male and female speakers, like native speakers, used more *-in* in casual style, for instance. But male speakers used *-in* even in careful style and went to considerable efforts to approximate male norms. The Varbrul analysis showed that gender seemed to be more important than style. Along the same lines, Major (2004) examined gender and stylistic differences in the English of native speakers of Japanese and Spanish. He studied four phonological processes widespread in all varieties of American English and found that gender stratification (that is, differences between genders) is acquired before style stratification. There is also evidence in variationist SLA research of gender differences in L2 speech in instructed contexts, immersion classroom and Year Abroad (Lemée 2003; F. Mougeon 2006; R. Mougeon, Nadasdi and Rehner 2002; R. Mougeon and Rehner 2001; Sax 2003).

13.3.5 Age

Age is an important causal variable in SLA research (e.g. Singleton and Ryan 2004; Chapter 15, this volume). For many years, the perspective taken in SLA research on age was mainly a psycholinguistic one; little research had been done from a social perspective before the development of variationist studies of SLA. However, age interacts with many social factors such as context, gender and social class, and consideration from a social standpoint as well as a language-internal one is important for a full picture of the role of age in SLA.

A central issue in the literature relating to age and acquisition is the Critical Period Hypothesis (CPH). Research in SLA has generally accepted the importance of the CPH and that age can play a major role, particularly in relation to pronunciation. That age is not the sole factor is illustrated by Flege, Munro and MacKay (1996), who investigated age and the acquisition of the English phonetic system. They analysed the production of word-initial English consonants by Italian L1 speakers who began learning English at different ages from childhood to adulthood. Using multiple regression, they found that, although an important factor, age was not an overriding issue. Certain speakers who learnt English after childhood produced English consonants like native speakers. This quantitative study concurs with research which found that Dutch learners of French and English in a classroom setting after age 12 attained pronunciation levels which native speakers rated as nativelike, and in some cases in the English study more highly than natives due to L2 speakers' more standard accents (Bongaerts, van Summeren, Planken and Schils 1997; Bongaerts, Mennen and van der Silk 2000). This is contrary to previous notions that older people are incapable of "sounding like native speakers." This particular variationist research complements and confirms psycholinguistic results.

13.3.6 Context

Context as a causal factor has figured prominently in the SLA literature; from the seminal work of European researchers such as Meisel (1983), who showed how crucially the process of grammaticalization was affected by social factors in general and context in particular, by Véronique (1990), who investigated arabophone speakers in France, to research on the other side of the Atlantic (Andersen 1984; Schmidt 1983; Schumann 1978b). Meisel showed that the speech of migrant workers in Germany with most contact with native speakers was significantly more grammaticalized than that of those with less NS contact. Unlike those with little contact, they tended to use grammatical morphemes not crucial to meaning but having the effect of making them sound more nativelike and therefore affecting how they related to German society. Social networks played a significant role. Subsequent Varbrul studies confirmed these findings. Bayley (1991) found that contact with more native speech (mixed native English-speaking and Chinese social networks, as opposed to Chinese-only networks) increased the likelihood of learners' past tense marking. Regan (1995) found that contact with native speakers was important in the acquisition of target-language patterns by Irish speakers of French. Likewise, Nagy, Blondeau and Auger (2003) found that contact with native speakers was crucial to the acquisition of target-language patterns. In this area, variationist research brought attention and fine-grained empirical evidence to an aspect of L2 acquisition previously relatively neglected.

This research left no doubt as to the importance of social context in accounts of acquisition. Since then, studies of variation and SLA, especially NS variation patterns, have produced quantitative information on context and language use as varied as the traditional classroom (Dewaele and Regan 2001, 2002), immersion classrooms (R. Mougeon, Nadasdi and Rehner 2010; Rehner *et al.* 2003) year abroad (Howard 2002; Lemée and Regan 2004; Regan 1995; Regan *et al.* 2009; Sax 2003) and naturalistic contexts (Blondeau 2010; Blondeau *et al.* 2002).

13.3.7 Summary

In this second phase of variationist research on SLA, the range of topics summarized demonstrates the integration of variationist perspectives into mainstream SLA research. It offered powerful tools for investigating aspects of interlanguage which would be difficult for other approaches to reach. Detailed multivariate analysis using statistical tools is able to reach the finest grain of L2 speech, demonstrating the numerous intersecting factors, social and linguistic, which all result in the variation in this speech. Variation research has become a part of any research program within SLA, whether that research is on age, gender, input or any of the other domains of SLA research. Variationist perspectives have perhaps been most useful in the area of language acquisition in social context, but this area has recently become one of the central issues in SLA research. Indeed, so central has social context become that variationist research has, itself, begun to focus on problems in the analysis of social context that were not previously explicitly enunciated.

13.4 Recent developments in variationist SLA research

After the growth of variationist research in SLA during the 1990s (in particular acquisition in social context), researchers began to feel the need for a more subtle account of the experience of L2 speakers. They began to refine the social categories on which analysis had been based. As seen earlier, it was not the case that early variationist work was unaware of the limitations of the essentialist and predetermined categories (age, sex, etc.) adopted from sociology, but these limitations were counterbalanced by the research results that emerged. (Some superb early studies combined subtle ethnographic and quantitative analysis.) However, as L2 variation research developed, these limitations increasingly seemed a barrier to a full exploration of the situation of the L2 speaker in society. This perception was part of a general shift in research, as issues of globalization and migration in the twenty-first century seemed to demand a multilayered, more nuanced ethnographic description of the L2 speaker's experience.

The work which followed aimed at greater sensitivity and subtlety in relation to how exactly these categories of age, sex and so on are expressed in different social groups. Eckert's (2000) L1 variationist study of the "Jocks" and the "Burnouts" has been influential not only in L1 studies, but also in L2 research. The study was based on participant observation of adolescents in a Detroit secondary school and showed that an overly simple interpretation of sex as a social category did not account for the variation in the speech of the subjects. Eckert emphasized that neither sex nor social category (whether the youngsters were Jocks or Burnouts; Jocks were those who were school- and sports-focused and Burnouts those focused on social activities outside of school) was sufficient in themselves to explain the variation, but rather the combination of the two was necessary, and this could only have been evident from ethnographic work in the particular community. Replacing the old sociological category of sex with that of gender as a social construct enabled a dynamic concept which, by taking on new shapes and complexions according to context and community, could yield richer accounts of the variation in that particular group. Other scholars produced similar studies in L1 speech (e.g. Cheshire 2002; Holmes and Meyerhoff 2003; Mendoza-Denton 2008). While categories are used in quantitative analyses to show patterns or tendencies, researchers now present these findings as pointing to (or *indexing*), rather than defining, the social meanings associated with linguistic forms. Focus is at a local rather than a structural societal level, and the concept of *community of practice*, defined as a group of people whose mutual interaction and communication is built around common activities (Lave and Wenger 1991) has proved useful in the explanation of linguistic and social behavior which does not fit neatly into the older essentialist categorizations. Following on from this shift in L1 research, variation SLA research similarly increased its emphasis on ethnographic research. Tarone and Liu (1995) is an early example of work which brings together the two approaches. A combination of qualitative ethnographic work and quantitative work on L2 data seeks to obtain as full a picture as possible of how variation in speech interacts with people's life histories (Regan 2010).

13.4.1 Identity and variationist SLA

Identity has emerged as central to the recent, more ethnographic, variation SLA research, as well as its relation to style in speech (for example, Block 2009; Pavlenko and Blackledge 2004; see also Chapter 11, this volume). Postmodern thinking on identity has been strongly influenced by Giddens (1991), which has led to a dynamic concept of identity as constructed through interaction; the individual's life narrative is acted out through time and space. It is generally accepted in this research that individuals are shaped by the structures within which they operate just as they themselves shape these structures. And during this process, identities are created by the way individuals present themselves and also by the roles ascribed to them by those who interact with them. Accommodation theory and monitoring (paying attention to speech) involve the way a speaker presents him/herself and how the speaker's audience affects what is said, and are closely linked with the process of identity construction.

Numerous frameworks explore the issues of identity; for instance, discourse analysis (Benwell and Stokoe 2007), conversation analysis (Markee 2000), narrative analysis and positioning theory (Bamberg 2004), performativity (Butler 1990) and language socialization (Bayley and Schecter 2003). Ethnomethodological research investigates identity construction and language practices (for example, Rampton 1999). People are constantly engaged in the process of identity construction, finding a place for themselves in the social world by negotiating their positions in various intersecting communities of practice in which they participate. Bakhtin (1986) portrays the individual's selfhood as emerging from struggle with their surroundings. L2 speakers are even more intensely caught in the maelstrom of different communities as they cross borders of various kinds – geographical, psychological and social. For L2 or multilingual speakers, by the nature of the multiple worlds they inhabit and the fluidity of their relationships to these worlds, the process must be managed with great subtlety. Identity construction involves more than language; there is increasing research on the role of gesture, clothes, body language and facial expression in identity construction. However, we focus here on the role language plays in identity construction as this has been to date easier to investigate. Whether we link this with style, as Coupland (2007) does, or see it as the acquisition and use of variation patterns (Bayley and Regan 2004; Regan and Ni Chasaide 2010), the L2 speaker chooses from his/her linguistic repertoire in the process of identity creation. The speaker uses variation patterns in order to construct identity, to index aspects of persona and forge new links between place and persona. The speaker also uses these variable patterns in adopting stances vis-à-vis the norms and ideologies which are encountered in day-to-day interactions. The fact that the speaker has a choice between different variants available means that this type of variation is closely bound up with identity construction. Bucholtz's "tactics of subjectivity model" (2003: 408) says "identities emerge from temporary and mutable interactional conditions, in negotiation, and often in contestation with other social factors and in relation to larger, often unyielding structures of power."

An additional element for L2 speakers is that, depending on their level of proficiency, the sort of "bricolage" (Hebdige 1984) which native speakers engage in to construct identities is infinitely more complex. The L2 speaker, even if highly proficient, has limitations on the linguistic resources available to him/her in a way a native speaker does not. And, as we saw earlier, forms can be used for functions different from those used by native speakers. As postmodern researchers remind us, language is a practice, not a static entity. L2 speakers use targetlike variation patterns in highly creative ways. Regan and Ni Chasaide (2010) investigates identity and the acquisition of these patterns. Several of the studies in the volume show how the use of variation patterns functions as an element in self-presentation and identity construction as performativity.

Among the choices available to the multilingual speaker are dialect or vernacular features, register and language choice. Choice of language, and the point at which switches are made from one language to another, can be highly significant moves in identity construction. Equally, choice of variant is significant. Where sometimes it has been supposed that a feature has not been acquired by the L2 speaker, or is not targetlike, in fact, L2 speakers may be carefully choosing to use certain non-standard features to identify with certain aspects of their interlocutors. The male speakers in Adamson and Regan (1991) overuse the non-standard variant in order to emphasize differential gender use. In terms of choice of language, Blondeau (2010) finds that anglophone Canadian speakers in Montreal are now choosing to use French in order to emphasize their identity as bilinguals, whereas previously they chose English. Adolescents in an Irish immersion school (Ni Chasaide and Regan 2010) reject the norms insisted upon by the school and choose instead to construct their own brand of spoken Irish because it better expresses their chosen identity as young, urban, East coast Ireland adolescents speaking Irish (as opposed to the identification of Irish with rural, elderly, West coast Ireland, traditional associations by school norms).

Variationist researchers are also increasingly focusing on migrant language (Kerswill 2006). To understand the kinds of choices L2 speakers make, we need to know what type of input is available to compare possibilities. For example, we can only evaluate the extent to which language change is being affected by newcomers to a country if we have exact measures of variation both in the migrants' and in traditional speakers' use. There is much comment both in the linguistics literature and in the popular press about the effects of migrants on language in various communities (e.g. McCrum, 2010; Kerswill, Torgenson and Fox 2008; Weise 2009). The language variety with which the L2 speaker has contact is not always a standard variety; speakers may be living or working in areas where non-standard varieties are commonplace. Due to lack of professional qualification equivalents or language proficiency, people from one social class in their country of origin may find themselves living and working in the context of a different social class in the host country. This can result in feelings of dislocation or even *anomie*, with implications for identity. Nestor and Regan (2010) and Regan, Nestor and Ni Chasaide (2010) found in terms of non-standard input, Polish people living in Ireland, for instance, are likely to have Irish English as input, and, depending on their social networks and workplace, probably a particular regional variety of Irish English, not standard RP British English. Walker and Hoffman (2010), dealing with ethnic orientation and linguistic variation in Toronto English, investigate popularly held beliefs about Canadian English by analysing the use of two sociolinguistic variables in the speech of Chinese- and Italian-speaking immigrants in Toronto. The variationist quantitative analysis provided evidence of agency on the part of the speakers from the two ethnic groups, showing they appear to use overall rates of certain variants to express ethnic identity.

How immigrant speakers relate to stable and incoming variables can reveal much about where they situate themselves in the society in which they are living: they may pick and choose within the available variants, old and new. Thus, Bayley and Regan (2004) suggest investigating the acquisition of incoming as well as stable variables. Age-grading and gender are indications regarding whether a variable is stable or new. If it varies by geographical region, but not age or gender, then a variable is most probably stable. If, on the other hand, it varies according to age and sex, the possibility is that it is an incoming change. We need to investigate how L2 speakers react to all aspects of the variable grammar of the community, not just what is held up to immigrants as the ideal variety.

For instance, Meyerhoff, Schleef and Clark (2009) analysed *-in/-ing*, and how it was being adopted by Polish adolescent migrants in Edinburgh and London. They examined the linguistic factors constraining *-in/-ing* but also L2 "Polish-specific" factors. They investigated attitudes toward life in the UK, friendship networks, self-assessment of proficiency in English, time spent learning English and age of arrival. They discovered that, despite having been in the UK for quite short periods of time, the Polish teenagers were replicating NS variation in relation to *-in/-ing*. Overall frequencies of the apical *-in* were higher amongst the Edinburgh teenagers (as opposed to the London dwellers), like the higher NS frequencies in Edinburgh. So the L2 speakers approximate NS patterns in relation to this stable variable.

In contrast to the stable *-in/-ing*, a new variable which has appeared in varieties of English throughout the world is the use of *like*, both quotative (as has emerged from adolescent English from (California) Valley Girl speech) and discourse. This has been extensively studied in the variation literature on native English (for example, D'Arcy 2005). An interesting question is whether L2 speakers adopt the incoming variable and then how they pattern in relation to this variable. Do they have the same constraint ordering and rates as the local community or do they, instead, pattern like a more "globalized" manifestation of the variation in *like*? Regan *et al.* (2010) contrasted the acquisition of the new variable *like* (discourse) and the stable *-in/-ing* by Polish speakers in Ireland. High degrees of interspeaker variation were found. Preliminary results suggest that this variation is primarily linked to age, but also gender and social networks. In addition, the L2 speakers favored *like* in clause-marginal positions, similar patterning to that of *like* in Irish English native speech (Schweinberger 2010).

13.4.2 Identity and agency

As mentioned earlier, identity construction, as it relates to language use, is increasingly seen to have an agentive element (Goldstein 1996; Norton 2000 are examples of identity construction and agency in L2 speakers). Wei and Wu (2009), in a study of Chinese children's acquisition of English, demonstrates that there can be a considerable degree of agency in relation to how, or even whether, L2 speakers access linguistic input. Regan and Ni Chasaide (2010) examine the acquisition of variation patterns in two languages (L2 and L3), using participant observation and sociolinguistic interviews. They studied Irish adolescents learning French and Irish in an Irish-immersion school. The youngsters used the two languages differently depending on their stance in the construction of different identities. For instance, they switched into English from Irish in a systematic way. The switches to English were domain related (technology and contemporary music). The study showed that they have their own vocabulary, patterns of code switching different from native speakers and different from those insisted on by the teachers in the school. In relation to quotative *like*, the students behaved differently from native Irish speakers. They chose to use *like* in the same way as it is used in the adolescent anglophone culture throughout the world. Given that the students know an Irish equivalent of *like* (*mar*), and could have used it, it is interesting that they borrow it from English and seem to use it as an adolescent linguistic identity marker, as other English-speaking adolescents do. Their use of quotative *like* is different from that of bilingual Montrealers who appropriate *comme* instead of *like* in their French (Sankoff et al. 1997). The students' use of *like* is not an indication of developmental deficit (they are high-proficiency Irish speakers), but seems to be rather an index of their construction of complex linguistic and cultural identities.

Identity construction becomes acute in the case of migrants and those who are, to some degree, marginalized in society. The migrant situation is fluid, identities are constructed and reconstructed, communities are formed and reformed, and language use is accordingly variable and affected by constantly changing factors. As noted earlier, the process of identity construction is defined by individual choices by the speaker: the degree of integration the person may wish for in the host community, the degree to which s/he wishes to learn the language of the host community and the degree to which s/he wishes to maintain their L1. The choice is not unconstrained, of course, by society; self-determination is circumscribed. Regan and colleagues have investigated issues of identity and language practices in relation to the Polish and Italian communities living in Ireland in an urban East coast and a rural West coast setting (Nestor and Regan 2010; Regan and Nestor 2009; Regan et al. 2010).[1] Nestor and Regan (2010) investigate the issue of agency in a case study of one Polish adolescent girl, Ola. She saw learning English as an investment in her future: "I think it's very good because I learn, like, English a lot and I think that will help me in the future." She herself was an active agent in her own learning; she sought opportunities to use English. Ola was the only Polish child in her school for several years; she enjoyed her "different" status and was a model student. However, this situation was shattered with the arrival of a large group of other Polish children during the economic boom in Ireland. In a process of "distinction" (Bucholtz and Hall 2010: 24) the other Polish students resisted the model-minority identity, and instead created a counterdiscourse to construct alternative identities such as "the Polish speaker," "the lazy student" and so on. This resistance undercut Ola's own sense of self. She felt alienated from her own ingroup and, through the new students' resistance, her identity became a site of struggle. As a result, she renegotiated her own identities in order to challenge the counterdiscourse of her peers. She remained a "model student," but rejected a national identification as Polish. She used variation patterns, in relation to quotative and discourse *like*, as they embed in "Irish English" rather than global English and made phonetic choices which were locally relevant (she spoke with a local regional accent). She thus renegotiated her national identification away from both dominant identifications in the school – Polish or Irish – to position herself in a third, undefined space in between.

Ola's experience is an example of how turbulent the experience of identity construction can be for migrant speakers, and how variable. Where Ola, due to local circumstances, rejected her Polish identity, there is evidence that many Polish speakers in France and in Ireland make strenuous efforts to maintain this Polish identity (Regan forthcoming; Regan and Nestor 2009). Ethnographic research applied in a study of Polish speakers living in Paris found that family dynamics were constructed around this maintenance, both linguistic and cultural. This includes the whole extended family, including grandparents, helping to ensure the children were taken to Polish school on Wednesday (in France a school half day) and Saturday, where they learned Polish, spoken and written, Polish culture, and where they met other Polish children. They also returned regularly for summer holidays in Poland with family, particularly grandparents. In one interview, a mother recounted a bad experience her son had at school when another student called him *Sale Polonnais* "Dirty Pole." Her son reacted passionately to this insult by saying to his mother in recounting the experience; "*Maman, pourquoi elle m'a parlé comme ça. Je suis fier d'être polonnais; toi, tu es polonnaise, mon père est polonnais!*" "Mum, why did she speak to me like that?! I'm proud to be Polish. You're Polish. My father is Polish." Alongside this fierce determination to maintain Polish identity, language and culture, there was an equal determination to "become" French.

13.5 Conclusion

Research on variation and SLA in social context has recently taken an interesting direction, with linguistic analysis of speech being combined with ethnographic research and "thick descriptions" to produce rich accounts of L2 acquisition. Earlier work in variationist SLA often focused on quantitative analysis, with analysis of the ethnographic data collected often secondary in the analysis. However, recent research has demonstrated the benefit of combining the two types of data to produce a multilayered representation of the experience of the L2 speaker. Detailed quantitative evidence produced by classic variationist analyses helps us to understand the nature and the unfolding of the acquisition process. This two-pronged approach shows which factors simultaneously constrain the variation in L2, and how the acquisition process unfolds, by charting the changes in effects of factors over time at different stages of development. Many of the central areas and themes of SLA have been further developed by good quantitative research in the past two decades. In addition to the quantitative analysis, we also have a richly layered description of the process of acquisition as it takes place in the day-to-day existence of the speakers, using ethnographic methods.

We can observe speakers in the community of practice in which they participate, enabling a more subtle understanding and hence a more nuanced description of the roles they play, the personae they create and the degree of agency involved in the process.

In the future, research which combines quantitative and ethnographic research methods (with longitudinal as well as cross-sectional studies) is set to provide some of the most complete analyses to date of variation in SLA. Neither method, quantitative nor qualitative, on its own is as powerful as the two combined, as each method has its deficiencies. Ethnographic data provide subtle interpretations and do not require essentialist variables such as social class or gender, but it depends very much on individual interpretation of behavior. However, the recording of these data, which other researchers can then analyze, requires video as well as audio-records, and this is both time and labor consuming. In contrast, recording speech for linguistic analysis has the advantages of an objective recording and subsequent notation system which others can analyze, but such social analysis tends to depend on categories such as sex or social class. It is through observing the indexical relations between language and the context in which it occurs that the fullest explanation of language use emerges.

Further studies of migrant and non-literate speakers are needed, in naturalistic settings, and studies of both children and the elderly will prove a rich source of information about diversity in society in the twenty-first century as well as indications regarding the future directions for language and society. The information gathered from this type of research will not only contribute to both sociolinguistics and SLA theory, but also be valuable in educational planning and language policy at program level.

14

Electronic interaction and resources

Astrid Ensslin and Cedric Krummes

14.1 Introduction

This chapter investigates the ways in which second language development can be and has been aided by electronic interaction in the sense of instructor- and learner-led use of the rapidly involving digital technologies, by increasing learners' input and interaction among themselves, with instructors and native speakers (rather "expert users"; see Section 14.4). "Electronic interaction" here stands for two interrelated processes (see Barnes 2002): (i) human–computer interaction in terms of individuals using computer hardware and software online and offline, including desktop and mobile devices, designated learner software, websites and corpus tools; and (ii) human–computer–human interaction, where learners communicate remotely with other people, mediated by networked media, most importantly the Web 2.0 with its focus on social, user-generated content, and its concomitant phenomena such as social networking, macro- and microblogging, the wikification of knowledge (Dvorak 2005), participatory and fan culture (Jenkins 2006), and virtual worlds (e.g. Boellstorff 2008).

As Lamy and Hampel (2007: 36) demonstrate, there are distinct affordances and constraints associated with the computer as a mediating tool. These derive from its technical functionalities as an online and offline medium and these include browsing; artefact creation and manipulation; displaying, storing and retrieving artefacts; sharing textual and audiovisual tools; graphical user interfaces; asynchronous and synchronous communication (e.g. email, wall posts and chat); voice-over internet (e.g. Skype); and the use of diverse communication platforms, e.g. video-conferencing. In the context of SLA, these material and interactional qualities lend themselves to considerations of language learning potential, of learner fit, meaning focus, authenticity, learning strategies, literacy (e.g. "new literacies"; see Lankshear and Knobel 2006) and adequacy of resources (see Chapelle 2001: 8).

To give just one example of how the material and interactional characteristics of CMC (*computer-mediated communication*) provide both opportunities and challenges for learners and teachers of a second language, let us consider email communication. Its affordances as a technology allow asynchronous communication, repeated editing and redrafting, formatting, multimodal enhancement and the identification of specific addressees. These foster for example peer collaboration, giving and receiving closed or open feedback, and extended, reflective commentary (Lamy and Hampel 2007: 39). On the other hand, because email is considered to be a more formal medium than, for instance, instant messaging or chat, certain netiquette skills are required which may be incompatible with the learners' own cultural backgrounds, or indeed their level of linguistic competence in the language used with respect to register and style. It is difficult for moderators and instructors to control and balance the quantity and volume of messages posted by L2 learners; and, as is the case with much computer-mediated learning, the amount of feedback required to negotiate errors, rules and idiomacy inside or outside the classroom may pose considerable challenges to instructors.

Electronic interaction can take place both in instructional settings (computer-assisted learning) and in extra-classroom contexts (emailing, chat rooms, user lists, social networking, blogs and wikis). With the emergence of text-based multi-user virtual worlds, called MUDs (Multi-User Dungeons), and, more recently, 3D Multi-User Virtual Environments (MUVE), the divide between virtual and real has shifted, and with it the ready-made assumption that classroom-based learning is by default situated in the physical world. After all, the experience of interacting in a virtual environment is perceived by many users as equally real as the physical world (Castronova 2001; Taylor 1999; Turkle 1997). We shall therefore use the term *actual* to refer to offline learner interaction (see Linden Lab's *Second Life*™ MUVE, 2003–10; henceforth *Second Life*), where learner interaction takes place in the physical world, and *virtual* to refer to interaction in cyberspace.

Section 14.2 provides a broad overview on the rather short history of computer-mediated SLA and its many terminological, conceptual and pedagogic ramifications. We shall then move on to discuss the two theoretical approaches to SLA that are most relevant to second language development and electronic interaction, namely generative and interaction-driven frameworks. Especially the latter, coupled with interculturalist approaches, leads on to the question of what role language varieties, including the notion of the native speaker, might play in an increasingly globalized, networked, intercultural and multilingual learning environment.

Internet-based CMC is a global phenomenon yet dominated by a small number of world languages, including English (27.3 percent of all Internet users), Chinese (22.6 percent), Spanish (7.8 percent), Japanese (5.0 percent), Portuguese, German, Arabic, French, Russian and Korean (all between 2.0 and 4.2 percent).[1] English is used (online and offline) by more people as an L2 or L*n* than as an L1 (Crystal 2003: 69), and it is increasingly difficult to draw categorical boundaries between so-called native and non-native varieties. This raises the question of target norms, considering that linguistic forms and registers used in CMC across languages are as fluid, creative and inconsistent as the contexts in which they occur (Bazzanella 2010: 21; see also Herring 1996, Crystal 2001). Section 14.4 therefore focuses on the role of non-standard varieties in CMCL (computer-mediated communication for language learning; see Lamy and Hampel 2007), the deconstruction of the native speaker and the pedagogical implications inherent in these developments. In Sections 14.5 and 14.6 we then move on to CMCL applications. Due to the growing popularity of online learning and teaching (Meskill and Anthony 2010: 2), we put particular emphasis on internet-based SLA activities. In drawing partly on Lamy and Hampel's (2007) collection of case studies, we first exemplify various types of current and emerging CMCL, such as asynchronous and synchronous platforms; video conferencing; mobile devices; Web 2.0 facilities and virtual environments. Finally, we discuss another recent form of human–computer interaction in SLA: electronic corpora as learning tools within and outside the classroom.

14.2 From CALL to CMCL

Electronic interaction as a feasible alternative to face-to-face or handwritten communication in SLA first emerged in the 1990s with the increasingly widespread use of graphical user interfaces, local area networks, user-friendly software and, not least, the arrival of the World Wide Web/WWW. The development of networked media has "created enormous opportunities for learners to enhance their communicative abilities, both by individualising practice and by tapping into a global community of other learners [and speakers of the target language]" (Hanson-Smith 2001: 107).

Overall, the historical development of CALL (computer-assisted/aided language learning) can be seen roughly as a three-stage process (Warschauer and Healey 1998). Early approaches revolved around issues relating to the benefits of the digital medium to learning, and the question of whether the machine could and would ultimately replace the instructor, as opposed to merely serving as an additional learning tool (Higgins and Johns 1984). Pedagogically, pre-WWW CALL was typically behaviouristic in nature, with the computer being used mostly as a drills provider to individual learners, and as a reading and writing tool for offline input and output (Lamy and Hampel 2007: 9).

Through the 1980s, CALL came to be considered by many to be highly compatible with communicative (Krashen 1982), content-based (Cantoni-Harvey 1987) and task-based approaches (Nunan 1989, 1995) to SLA, as well as with the then newly developed constructivist principles of learner autonomy (e.g. Little 1991; Dam 1995), learner-centeredness, and the interplay of extrinsic and intrinsic motivation (Dörnyei 1994, 2001).

The third and final move from communicative to *integrative* CALL (Warschauer and Healey 1998) happened through the 1990s and into the twenty-first century, with the increasing democratization and multimedialization of the internet and its most recent manifestations of user-generated content, share-ware, upgrade and fan culture, social networking and micro-blogging. For SLA, spoken and written language outputs became increasingly accessible from networked, multimedia-enabled computers, thus facilitating integrative interaction with authentic learning materials across a wide spectrum of virtual contexts. For language learners, the implications are that "[s]everal skills can be deployed at once, approximating communication in non-computer-mediated environments much better. It also means that learning and teaching online can be group-based, affording the possibility that CALL can accommodate socio-cognitive and collaborative pedagogies" (Lamy and Hampel 2007: 9) such as group-based situated and task-based learning, as well as peer-to-peer feedback. The move to the participatory Read/Write Web (cf. Warschauer and Grimes 2007) has gone hand-in-hand with a perceived increase in the importance of learner creativity, both in terms of learners' selecting tools according to their own needs (Mangenot and Nissen 2006) and in the sense of linguistic, stylistic creativity, as studied by Ensslin (2006) in a hypertext-based SLA creative writing environment.

As a result of the distinctly social and communicative evolution of digital, networked multimedia, research into instructed language acquisition and electronic interaction since the 1990s has particularly concentrated on questions and research methods pertaining to discourse analysis and conversation analysis (DA and CA), the study of written and, increasingly, oral learner participation and interaction, and aspects of motivation arising from collaborative and participatory activities. These have the potential to foster and develop not only communicative but indeed intercultural competence in learners (Lamy and Hampel 2007: 18; cf. Ensslin 2001). As these focal areas seem to shift increasingly toward human-computer-human interaction, the theories and analytical practices of CMC are becoming more and more salient in SLA, for which reason Lamy and Hampel (2007: 8) replace CALL and its cognate terms (e.g. CALI, CELL, CBLT, HALL, ICALL, MALL, NBLT, TELL and WELL)[2] with CMCL (computer-mediated communication for language learning).

Following Bax (2003), we use CALL as an inclusive term, comprising both CMCL and more traditional offline and data-carrier-based activities. Moving away from distinct terms for distinct types of computer-aided language learning seems plausible not least because the computer-aided L2 curriculum will increasingly be dominated by an integration of offline and online and of classroom-internal and external tools and interaction. Furthermore, with the advent of cloud computing, the storage, retrieval and processing of communicative data, conventionally done locally (at the user end), will increasingly happen online, via web servers, portable and online applications. Finally, the ubiquitous nature of smartphones, tablet devices and application software will have a considerable impact on how learners perceive spatiality, mobility and presence. As a result, offline and online, face-to-face and computer-mediated activities and materials will increasingly be merged and perform in a variety of old and new physical and virtual contexts. This requires careful reflection, planning and monitoring on the part of instructors, who typically find themselves acting as technological and linguistic facilitators, advisors and commentators in the electronic "feedback loop" (Lamy and Hampel 2007: 105). Similarly, integrating social networking roles such as "friends" (e.g. *Facebook*, *Second Life*), "followers" and "followed" (e.g. *Twitter*), CALL teachers may increasingly operate at the same social – and often affective – level as their students.

14.3 Theoretical and methodological underpinnings

This section considers the two main theoretical approaches underpinning CALL (as well as SLA research more widely): psycholinguistic SLA theories on the one hand (see Part II, "internal ingredients," this volume), and sociocultural theory on the other (see Part III, "External ingredients," this volume). The former are informed by generative approaches, which see language acquisition as a largely internal, cognitive process and look at the activities contributing toward these developmental processes. The latter, inspired by Vygotsky's (1978) social interactionist theory, is more interested in the social and situative contexts and activities that trigger learning processes, as well as aspects of learner identity. As Levy (1998: 93) observes, "both theoretical positions have the potential to inform research and practice in...CALL," and should be regarded as complementary rather than mutually exclusive.

The most potent metaphor for the cognitive SLA framework thus far is that of the human brain as a computer which processes input data by filtering out meaningful data from intake and storing aspects of these data as L2 knowledge and which produces, on the basis of such stored information, new informational output (see R. Ellis 1997b: 35; Robinson and Ellis 2008). Among the most influential ideas based on this concept is Krashen's Input Hypothesis (1981, 1985), which assumes that only *comprehensible* input (or intake), i.e. input that "is just a little beyond the learner's competence but is nevertheless understood" (Lamy and Hampel 2007: 20), can contribute to the development of new cognitive structures. As "the major function of the second language classroom is to provide intake for acquisition" (Krashen 1981: 101), a CALL-oriented methodology needs to ensure comprehensible input, i.e. the stimuli received by and pitched at learners in terms of going "just a little beyond" their current competence levels. SLA theorists have been highly critical of Krashen's views, however, not least because the stimuli received – the primary linguistic data – do not always have to be comprehended to lead to acquisition. For example, when a learner for whom all subjects are agents fails to comprehend an utterance such as

Mary's leg was stung, incomprehensible input can prompt acquisition of the passive (e.g. White 1987). Similarly, in authentic CMC, a rigid comprehensible-input view can pose major challenges as learners will have to acquire very specific types of communicative competence in order to adapt to platform- and user-group-specific registers. Therefore, a flexible approach to Krashen's ideas, coupled with learner-led trial-and-error activities (such as hypothesis-testing), may be adopted as a compromise in the highly dynamic pedagogic sphere of CALL.

Complementing Krashen's Input Hypothesis is Swain's theory of comprehensible output, which provides learners with "the opportunity for meaningful use of [their own] linguistic resources" (Swain 1985: 248; see also Chapter 10, this volume). Output is useful to the learning process as it raises the learner's consciousness of existing lexical, grammatical and pragmatic gaps; it helps learners test hypotheses; and it enables learners to reflect on and negotiate their output on a metalinguistic level (see Pica, Holliday, Lawis and Morgenthaler 1989; Shehadeh 2002; Hong 2002). In a CMCL environment, output is readily confirmed or corrected by interlocutors (see Pellettieri 2000: 83), and it has to be within the remit of a CALL instructor to monitor appropriateness levels and intervene in cases of verbal abuse (e.g. flaming).

This implies that neither input nor output alone can suffice for learners to develop their interlanguage, and cognitivists claim that "interaction between learners and other speakers, especially, but not only, between learners and more proficient speakers and [to a slightly lesser extent] between learners and certain types of written texts" (Long and Robinson 1998: 22; see also Gass, Mackey and Pica 1998 and Chapter 10, this volume) is key to acquisition. For this reason, CMCL can be considered a powerful methodological toolkit within CALL, although its design and implementation needs careful planning and piloting.

As interaction-driven approaches are conceptually linked to the cognitivist concept of the "black box" and are therefore mostly interested in what in the environment stimulates internal processes, they typically neglect influences that are external to the learner. Undeniably, however, interaction is contextually determined (Wertsch 1991b), and it has been the prime interest of sociocultural SLA theorists to look at the social aspects of interaction-driven learning (see also Chapters 12 and 27, this volume). Tarone (1983), for instance, sees interlanguage (not unlike expert user language) as a stylistic continuum, which ranges from careful to vernacular style (for a recent discussion on the controversial boundaries between World Englishes, Standard English and English as a Lingua Franca and the debates surrounding Interlanguage theory, see Kilickaya 2009). Learners are likely to adapt their stylistic choices to the communicative situation at hand. In CMCL, asynchronous communication, and its inherent quality of allowing planning and editing, enables careful style, whereas synchronous chat will, due to time constraints, invariably lead to more vernacular uses. These differences in context require learners to develop the communicative and strategic competences needed to adapt to a variety of medium-specific and socially contingent levels of formality and in-group registers.

Closely associated with the use of different interlanguage styles is the importance of social accommodation (Beebe and Giles 1984; Rogerson-Revell 2010) and acculturation (Schumann 1986; Mady 2010). SLA has been identified as a process of "long term convergence" (R. Ellis 1997b: 39) between learners and their perceived expert-user norms (native speakers). This can only succeed, however, if learners are willing to engage with and develop a positive attitude toward the target-language group and their cultural practices. Both psychological and social distance needs to be minimized to maximize learning outcomes, and common emotional factors such as language shock and motivation play an important part in the social conditioning of SLA (see Chapter 8, this volume). In this respect, CMCL's specific communicative parameters play an important part in stimulating accommodation and acculturation. As Walther (1996) observes, written CMC is typically characterized by a lack of audiovisual and paralinguistic cues such as body language, physiognomy, pitch and intonation, which are among the key affordances of face-to-face interaction. Thus, in CMCL, scaffolding, collaborative dialogue and instructional conversation (van Lier 1996) need to adapt to a communicative context in which cues are filtered out by increasing the amount of verbal explication and the negotiation of meaning for the learner.

A predominant theme within new media theory has been the concept of hyperidentities (Filiciak 2003). As simultaneous co-habitants of multiple (text-based, 2D and 3D) virtual environments, contemporary CMC users often develop multiple, malleable identities and, as a whole, contribute toward a fluid, ever-changing and socially dynamic view of selfhood (Poster 1990: 128; see also Turkle 1997). These identities are researched via textual markers such as email signatures, the choice of user names and, more generally, textual choices such as syntactic complexity (clause structure), lexis and morphology (such as clipped forms, abbreviations, acronyms and leetspeak[3]), and various non-standard uses of punctuation, fonts, formatting and emoticons for emotive language and modality (Yates 1997). The concept of hyperidentities in SLA underscores the importance of learners being subject *to* and the subject *of* social conditions, and as users of creative virtual environments (such as Second Life, Facebook, MySpace), learners can significantly shape their social learning context, thus increasing their cultural capital and ability to assert themselves as equal participants in the target language community (Peirce 1995). As Warner (2004), for instance, observes, learners in a synchronous networked CMC environment (a MOO) negotiate their identities in playful ways, by playing with form (such as the sound of new word combinations), meaning (e.g. idiomatic phrases and modifications thereof) and pragmatic frame (such as commenting on and satirizing roleplay).

Kern (2006: 27) states that CMCL "is not a genre in itself but more a collection of genres, each with its specificity, partly depending on the communication channel chosen (IRC, SMS, chatting, emailing, blogging, instant messaging, MOO) and partly due to the social and cultural context as well as the circumstances surrounding the communicative act under scrutiny." Teachers should therefore aim not only at communication per se but include meta-communication as well, by "exploring the relationship between language, culture, contexts and technological mediating tools." This underlines the importance of interculturalist models of learning to CMCL, which makes use of networked media, thus fostering connectivity and global communication. Interculturalist pedagogy in CMCL therefore needs to draw learners' attention to differences, for instance, in institutional cultures (Belz 2002) and interaction styles (Belz 2003) and to work toward resolving misunderstandings that invariably result from cultural diversity (Ware 2003), as well as drawing attention to the fluidity and complexity of learner identities (Lemke 2002; Goodfellow and Hewling 2005; Kramsch 2009a).

Methodologically, the focus on interaction and social context in CALL has given rise to discourse analysis/DA and conversation analysis/CA research frameworks. After all, "CMCL produces large quantities of interactional texts, and ... the computer-based nature of CMCL activities allows these data to be captured with ease through digital recordings of the visual, aural and written traces of human interactions" (Lamy and Hampel 2007: 51). As Santacroce (2004) points out, DA and CA share an interest in naturally occurring conversation, its sequentiality and underlying logic. Due to a difference in methodological heritage, however, DA tends to focus more strongly on structural and content-related elements (linguistic, textual and semiotic patterns in context) than does CA, which is more interested in the social implications and shared rules of interaction. CA therefore focuses on phenomena such as turn-taking, politeness and tensions between self-interest and interlocution interest in conversation (see Tudini 2010 on CA and online chat). Applications of DA and CA to CMCL largely include research into grammatical, pragmatic and discursive aspects of learner language (Pellettieri 2000; Sotillo 2000; Williams 2003); communication research into strategies and learner engagement with native speakers (J. S. Lee 2002; Schwienhorst 2004); studies of intercultural competence and politeness (Belz 2003; Davis and Thiede 2000); as well as work on the affordances of digital media (Simpson 2005) and pedagogical implications for teacher training, power and equality online (Meskill 2005; Meskill, Mossop, DiAngelo and Pascuale 2002).

14.4 Encounters of the native kind

In this section, we look at the significance of language varieties in relation to electronic interaction, thereby deconstructing the notion of the native speaker. With the term "language variety" we cover both standard languages and their dialects and various accents, whether these are standardized, prestigious or not. (Also see Chapter 13, this volume.) As mentioned above, all second language learners, whether within or outside the classroom, will come across various registers and styles in online interaction. On a microlevel, the continuum will range from a careful style to more vernacular uses; on a macro-level, learners will come across, for instance, Iberian Spanish, North-American Spanish, South-American Spanish, but other varieties too.

Starting off with a cartoon found in the *New Yorker* (Steiner 1993) depicting two computer-savvy dogs with the caption "On the Internet, nobody knows you're a dog," we observe that the nature of electronic interaction is often anonymous. This makes it difficult for language learners or anybody else to know whether or not the language used in an online venue has been spoken or written by a native speaker. In the Luxembourgish lessons on YouTube provided by one co-author of this chapter, for instance, some users are unsure (or even wrong) about the author's/language instructor's identity. One commentator speculates that the instructor learned Luxembourgish "[f]rom being a nosy brit [sic]" (Krummes and Hotham-Gough 2007–10), whereas another asks in Luxembourgish *Ass daat lo e letzebuerger oder en englenner ????* "So is that a Luxembourger or an Englishman????" (Krummes and Hotham-Gough 2008–10). CMC, especially when anonymous or falling within Lange's (2007) dichotomy of "publicly private" and "privately public," thus raises the question "whether the native speakers and second-language learners invariably recognize one another" (Davies 2003: 199).

Davies further on argues that "[r]ecent evidence suggests that there is no discrete borderline and that the NS-NNS connection is a continuum" (2003: 15) and distinguishes between five "flesh-and-blood or reality definitions" (2003: 214):

1. native speaker by birth (that is by early childhood exposure),
2. native speaker (or native speaker-like) by being an exceptional learner,
3. native speaker through education using the target-language medium (the *lingua franca* case),
4. native speaker by virtue of being a native user (the postcolonial case) and
5. native speaker through long residence in the adopted country.

Appreciating the complex identity of native speakerhood in terms of how one speaks a language, Prodromou (2003) suggests for the case of English the term "successful users of English" (SUE). In discussing Prodromou, O'Keefe, McCarthy and Carter (2007: 30) explain that "SUEs are highly successful L2 communicators, but they will achieve this goal by strategic uses of their resources in ways different from those of native speakers. It makes more sense, therefore, not to see SUEs as failed native speakers, but to look upon all successful users of a language, whether native- or non-native speaking, as 'expert users.'" Tomlinson (2005: 6) reports on Prodromou's SUEs that "they have a virtually flawless command of grammar and vocabulary and even seem to have a wider range of lexis than native speakers. However, proficient non-native users of English use less ellipsis and fewer idioms and rarely make use of 'creative idiomaticity.'"

With this in mind, we advocate the conflation of L1 native speakers and L2 (or L*n*) expert speakers and refer to Belz and Vyatkina's (2005a) term *expert user*. In the light of potential anonymity, of learning a language as a second, foreign or even auxiliary language (Luke and Richards 1982), learners of a language aim at the language spoken by expert users, whether these speakers are native speakers or not. Clearly, learners cannot assume that all their target electronic interaction partners will be native speakers. Boundaries are blurred between who is an expert speaker, and the canonical homelands of native speakers are in competition with other language communities. The important thing is that learners get the input they want and need.

14.5 Varieties of CMCL

This section provides examples of case studies carried out by CMCL researchers on asynchronous and synchronous communication platforms and interaction, video conferencing, mobile devices, some recent Web 2.0 facilities such as blogs, wikis and social networking, and virtual environments such as MUDs, audiographic environments and graphical virtual worlds such as Second Life. In so doing, we assume as given that the Web as a huge repository of authentic language material, and the concomitant challenges for learners and teachers to distil input that is both meaningful and beneficial for L2 acquisition. To emphasize the importance of freely available participatory online services, commercial products such as TELL ME MORE™ and RosettaStone™ (see Godwin-Jones 2010) are sidelined in this discussion.

14.5.1 Asynchronous and synchronous CMCL

In this section, we look at the two oldest and most established forms of CMCL: asynchronous fora and email, and synchronous chat. Due to its user-friendly, low-tech nature and its common use by the majority of the population on the empowered side of the digital divide, asynchronous CMCL has received a large amount of interest among researchers. Holliday (1999), for instance, found that "electronic [and specifically email] communication provides a range and distributive frequency of linguistic features comparable to other genres of writing and speaking" (quoted in Hanson-Smith 2001: 109). He further established that email interlocutors tend to refer to and comment on each other's messages, thereby negotiating meaning and using scaffolding mechanisms for long-distance communication (see also Peyton 2000). An extensive study of how to implement learner email projects is offered by Warschauer (1995), who provides information on where to obtain suitable online teaching and learning materials and on how to establish international exchanges (see also Rosenthal 2000: 366).

Asynchronous fora are discussion platforms centered around specific areas of interest, allowing users to negotiate controversial issues, to ask and answer questions, and to obtain alternative opinions from a wide range of people from different cultural backgrounds. These discussion platforms came to be used as language learning tools in the mid 1990s (Lamy and Hampel 2007: 107), and have been researched, for instance, in terms of how they contribute to L2 acquisition through uptake, peer-sharing of lexical units, collaborative dialogue and communicative strategies (Savignon and Roithmeier 2004). Another study, by Weasenforth, Biesenbach-Lucas and Meloni (2002), looked at how fora offer opportunities for effective L2 acquisition following a constructivist agenda, which focuses on "active, collaborative construction of knowledge instead of knowledge transfer from one person to another" (Weasenforth et al. 2002: 58). More specifically, Weasenforth et al. examined the conditions that allow instructors to implement collaborative technologies in such a way as to enable a learner-centered approach. Working with a sample of fifty-two advanced-level graduate (mostly East Asian) ESL learners (aged from mid twenties to early thirties) over a period of eighteen months, the researchers arranged a participation pattern requiring the learners to contribute new forum threads on a weekly basis, and to join a total of twelve discussions revolving around course content (Weasenforth et al. 2002: 61). The sample was divided into six classes, and the instructors were asked to observe, participate in and trigger discussions, to evaluate learner performance and give examples of appropriate discourse. For the online forum assignments, the classes were split into groups of three or four students.

Using an analytical framework that involved cognitive and metacognitive factors (e.g. strategic thinking, learning context, goals of the learning process), motivational and affective factors (emotional influences, intrinsic motivation and effects of motivation on effort), developmental and social factors (such as physical, intellectual and social constraints on learning) and individual learner differences, the research surveyed learners' assessment of the benefits of the assignment. The study established that asynchronous fora give learners time to "read ... and compos[e] postings," which "encourages reviewing and responding to classmates' arguments" (Weasenforth et al. 2002: 74), as well as reflection in introverted students. Although not all participants in their study could be encouraged to engage with the technology, overall, it was found to be conducive to a constructivist learning framework with respect to social, cognitive, affective and individual principles of learning (2002: 59). Like many other CALL researchers, however, they emphasize the importance of careful integration in curriculum design and of providing sufficient tutor support in response to learners' differing participation patterns and the discrepant need for guidance and moderation.

Synchronous CMCL occurs in either written or oral form and is either embedded in websites, wikis, social networking sites and virtual environments, or offered as stand-alone "channels." Because chat and instant messaging exchanges can be logged with relative ease, instructors and researchers can readily access transcripts of student conversations for assessment and analysis (Lamy and Hampel 2007: 115). Regarding register, written synchronous CMCL comes closer to oral than written discourse (Weininger and Shield 2003: 329) and has therefore been studied particularly for its contribution to the development of oral L2 skills in negotiating meaning (e.g. Chun 1994; Ortega 1997). Blake (2000: 132) found that carefully designed chat exercises allow linking between remote learners as well as "promot[ing] learners to notice gaps in their lexical interlanguage [i.e. their vocabulary] in a manner similar to what has been reported in the literature for oral learner/learner discussion" (see Varonis and Gass 1985). Grammatical gaps, however, were not as readily negotiated by learners in Blake's (2000) study. However, a contrastive study by Salaberry (2000: 5) on the development of past tense verbal endings in L2 Spanish in an instant messaging scenario found that "the first signs of change in developmental stages of morphosyntactic development are more clearly identified in the computer based interaction task than in the face-to-face oral task."

In a study centered around mediational factors, Thorne (2003: 38) sought to "develop a conceptual framework for understanding how intercultural communication, mediated by cultural artifacts (i.e., Internet communication tools), creates compelling, problematic, and surprising conditions for additional language learning." To do so, he looked at three case studies examining telecollaborative exchanges between university students from the US and France (aged between 18 and 24), where two of the three used instant messaging facilities. Working with interview and observational video-recorded data, Thorne established that, despite synchronous CMCL facilitating classroom-external and therefore individual learning, it may necessitate "the mediation of another person, specifically an age-peer... willing to provide immediate and explicit linguistic feedback as part of a socially meaningful relationship" (Thorne 2003: 51). Interpersonal online mediation can thus be used strategically by learners to replace and indeed outperform individual dictionary consultation. (On such scaffolding, see Chapter 27, this volume.)

14.5.2 Video conferencing

Digital or desktop video conferencing allows "the real-time sharing of video and audio information between two or more points," thereby enabling interlocutors "to communicate synchronously while being able to view the person at the other location" (Dudding 2009: 179). The most popular forms in use today operate via Internet Protocol and via dedicated web-based applications such as Skype. Offering a "manageable context for... real communication" (Butler and Fawkes 1999: 46), video conferencing has, since the

1990s, become a frequently used and documented tool in SLA (see O'Dowd 2006). That said, students' responses to seeing themselves and their interlocutors on screen tend to be mixed due to the medium allowing the inclusion of potentially alienating paralinguistic features resulting from a clash of cultural expectations. On the one hand, video enables learners to gain an insight into the body language(s) used in the target culture (O'Dowd 2000), thereby helping them develop intercultural competence. On the other, delays in transmission can impair turn-taking and the meaningful decoding of body language, thus creating a somewhat unnatural, potentially discouraging communicative situation (Goodfellow, Jefferys, Miles and Shirra 1996; Zähner, Fauverge and Wong 2000). Therefore, it is important to surround video conferencing activities with reflective and evaluative offline tasks and discussions (Kinginger, Gourves-Hayward and Simpson 1999; O'Dowd 2000; Zähner et al. 2000), and to train instructors in the most effective and logistically realistic uses of the medium.

14.5.3 Mobile devices

The current generation of mobile devices, especially smartphones, personal media players, personal digital assistants, tablet computers, e-readers and handheld gaming devices offer a growing diversity and convergence of communicative activities (texting, telephone, email, multimedia messaging, typing, stylus-handwriting and voice and video recording), downloadable software applications, web services and games, thus giving rise to a wide range of new and potential functionalities for intra- and extra-classroom learning. Today's learners "have resources to interact from a distance, through an ever more sophisticated array of communication technologies (and prominently mobile technologies)," which has sparked "[t]he development of 'connected presence,' in which social relationships are accomplished through a seamless web of frequent face-to-face encounters and variously mediated interactions at a distance" (Licoppe 2009: 1925).

The term MALL (Mobile-Assisted Language Learning; cf. "mobile device-assisted language learning," Lamy and Hampel 2007: 150–51) was first used by Chinnery (2006), and many experts agree that, due to its distinct spatial, creative and social qualitites, it should be treated as a separate area of investigation and practice within CALL/CMCL. Not only do contemporary mobile technologies offer a host of language learning facilities in the form of "apps" (specialized applications that can be downloaded onto smartphones and tablet computers), such as flashcards (e.g. AccelaStudy, Study-Cards and Flash My Brain), vocabulary and pronunciation building tools (MyWords) for numerous languages "that allow comparison of learner's pronunciation with that of a model native speaker using the iPhone's recording and playback functions" (Godwin-Jones 2008a: 4). Equally importantly, Kukulska-Hulme (2007: 123) highlights MALL's affordances for contextual learning, whereby learners can, for instance, when located in a specific building and "walk[ing] into node areas indicated on a map," use GPS-enabled mobile phones to collaboratively produce spatially sensitive walk-throughs. The context-sensitive lexical labeling of actual-world locations and objects through mobile devices in augmented reality scenarios, as well as concomitant communication and social networking facilities integrated in state-of-the art mobile devices greatly improves learners' access to authentic material, and makes it relevant to their individual spatiotemporal contexts.

To manage the rapidly diversifying uses of mobile technologies in terms of both hardware and software, practitioners intending to use MALL in their teaching may wish to (i) critically reflect on the repertoire of possibilities and the potential for learning and teaching vis-à-vis the cost involved in ensuring learners have equal access to the proposed learning materials; (ii) examine how contextual learning may be facilitated in view of learners' needs and communicative habits; (iii) consider the likely social and emotional effects of each communicative genre available to learners; (iv) think about the physical environments in which specific mobile devices are likely to be used by learners; (v) take advantage of already existing networks and online communities; (vi) explore possibilities for immersion and flow; (vii) be prepared for unexpected learning outcomes and social side-effects (see Kukulska-Hulme, Evans and Traxler 2005).

14.5.4 Web 2.0: blogs, wikis, social networking

By the end of the first decade of the twenty-first century, highly interactive Web 2.0 applications such as (macro- and micro-)blogs, wikis and social networking tools are no longer emerging technologies. They have become largely normalized as everyday communication and data-exchange platforms. However, their potential for SLA has only begun to be explored, especially with respect to the "new opportunities and incentives [they entail] for personal writing" and the "reading-to-write culture," which "challenge[s]...language teachers...to extend students' Internet world beyond their first language, to leverage participation in the read-write Web as a learning opportunity for language self-development, and to find means to link informal and recreational writing with formal and academic writing" (Godwin-Jones 2008b: 7).

Blood (2002: 12) defines blogs as "website[s] that [are] updated frequently, with new material posted at the top of the page." Whilst macro-blogs are non-restrictive in the size and layout of posts, so-called micro-blogs such as Twitter and status updates in Facebook only allow a certain number of characters per post, thus leading to specific stylistic and abbreviative adaptations. Two-way communication is enabled by comment and reply functionalities, which, however, preserve a certain communicative hierarchy and put the initiator of a communicative strand, who can delete any undesired posts or block individual users, at a social advantage. Wikis, by contrast, are websites designed in such a way as to give users quasi-equal edit and share rights, thus constituting the most democratic type of collaborative website. Social networking sites, such as Facebook, Bebo and LinkedIn, may be circumscribed as sophisticated, multimedia and multifunctional communication and file-exchange fora. They include chat, email, wall posting and status updating functions and enable intensive identity management through a combination of self- and other-representation, enriched by communal and individual applications such as online games, quote and proverb feeds and playful personality surveys.

The CMCL potential of the above technologies for instruction-based and classroom-external language learning is considerable. Ward (2004: 3) sees the "un-charted creative potential" of collaborative online platforms in their "ability to accommodate multiple authors." With respect to wikis in particular, Lund and Smørdal (2006) highlight possibilities for collective knowledge building and for including instructors in student-centered activities. As Pinkman (2005) warns, positive effects on the development of learner autonomy, independence and empowerment can be expected only if there is careful planning and integration with other activities.

14.5.5 Virtual environments

The earliest internet-based virtual environments, commonly referred to as Multi-User Dungeons (MUDs) or Multiple Object-Oriented Environments (MOOs), were text-based and therefore similar in discursive structure to chat but with some very distinctive properties. Both MUDs and MOOs operate on the basis of text (commands and conversational turns) entered by users, and whilst MUDs specialize in roleplay and socializing, MOOs integrate databases of objects that users can create, manipulate, share and use. MOOs require users to construct mental images of spatial metaphors used in the text-based descriptions (such as a virtual living room, where users can "hang out" and chat about any non-private issues), and these spatial metaphors, or allegories, can easily take on the form of typical resource and learning environments such as virtual universities, libraries and classrooms. By the same token, objects in a learning MOO might include virtual projectors, notes and recording devices (Peterson 2004: 40–44). Regarding CMCL, the idea of social and spatial immersion, as well as imagined ownership and emotional involvement, have been found to have particular learning potential: "building rooms in the MOO is not just a pretend exercise, which students hand in and then forget. Instead, their rooms become part of the environment that the students construct and use for their language learning" (von der Emde, Schneider and Kötter 2001: 215).

Viewed from an interactionist point of view, MUDs and MOOs provide opportunities for socio-affective exchanges and quasi-anonymous role-playing activities (Lamy and Hampel 2007: 125–26), which "may not only prompt learners to experiment with unfamiliar structures, but... may likewise stimulate them to explore (and exploit) the connotations of the language they are using and encountering in more depth than in a traditional classroom or non-extendable chatroom" (Kötter 2003: 150). This may happen via tandem learning, self and other repair, and the metalinguistic exploration and evaluation of learners' and expert users' responses to the creation and labeling of individual objects in the self-created metaphorical environment. Furthermore, virtual environments allow learners to interact critically with interlocutors from different cultures and to negotiate openly conflict and misunderstandings derived from cultural differences observed in virtual environments (Schneider and von der Emde 2006).

The first decade of the twenty-first century saw a productive co-development of the open-source read/write Web and radical improvements in 3D graphics programming, improving bandwidths, CPU capacity, storage space and graphics processing, which boosted the development of graphical, 3D virtual environments (GVEs). Among the most popular GVEs at the time of writing are Massively Multiplayer Online Role-Playing Games (MMORPGs) such as *World of Warcraft* and socially, creatively, commercially and educationally oriented Multi-User Virtual Environments (MUVEs) such as *Second Life* (SL). An overview of interactional and collaborative learning in *World of Warcraft* is offered by Childress and Braswell (2006), and Sykes, Oskoz and Thorne (2008) explore the potential of so-called synthetic immersive environments (visually rendered environments that combine virtual gameplay with actual-world learning objectives) for interlanguage pragmatic development.

Second Life allows its so-called residents to "create the world of [their] choice replete with gizmos and widgets that do things (like play recordings and slide shows...), [and their] avatar[s] can defy gravity and fly at will. [They] can teleport from place to place, world to world, and you [they] ride all manner of conveyances if available" (Stevens 2006). Users can customize their avatars (in-world representations) almost infinitely, thus experimenting with alternative representations of self and the resulting social interactions with other learners and expert users of the target language.

Like the GVE's *Active Worlds* and *Quest Atlantis* (Peterson 2006; Zheng, Brewer and Young 2005), *Second Life* has been used for language learning. Previous research into MUVE-based CMCL has established that it enables tandem learners to carry out and negotiate diverse tasks in the target language. This involved transactional communication and interactional strategies, and it was found that "the use of avatars facilitated learner interaction management during real time computer-mediated communication" (Stevens 2006, cf. Peterson 2006). *Second Life* currently hosts a plethora of SLA places and groups, which are either remediations of offline SLA institutions or *Second Life*-specific sites and call out for close ethnographic, conversation and (multimodal) discourse analytical examination (Ensslin 2010). For an examination of implications of *Second Life*-based SLA for resource provision in academic libraries, see Hundsberger (2009).

14.6 Corpora and SLA

In this section, we explore how interactive language learning can be augmented by electronic corpora – digitized collections of texts that have been collected and documented according to pre-established demands and specifications. These texts, whether spoken, written or signed in one or several language varieties, can be accompanied by metadata and linguistic annotation.

There are three ways in which language learners can be involved with corpora. First, corpora can provide data to the researcher for a learner corpus (see Chapter 4, this volume); second, learners can use corpora directly in and outside the classroom; and third, learners can use materials that are based on corpora.

14.6.1 Language learner corpora

Granger (2002: 7) writes that learner corpora are "electronic collections of authentic FL/SL textual data assembled according to explicit design criteria for a particular SLA/FLT purpose." Regarding "explicit design," Belz and Vyatkina (2005a: 5) add that "the majority of learner corpora consist of (argumentative) written essays, often produced under experimental conditions." In order to illustrate these, we examine ICLE, the International Corpus of Learner English; FALKO, the Error-Annotated Learner Corpus of German; and Telekorp, a bilingual computer-mediated communication corpus of learners of German and English. (Editors' note: see also the primarily oral (or signed) language corpora on CHILDES, TalkBank and PhonBank.)

The ICLE project consists of essays of over 3 million words "of EFL writing from learners representing 16 mother tongue backgrounds (Bulgarian, Chinese, Czech, Dutch, Finnish, French, German, Italian, Japanese, Norwegian, Polish, Russian, Spanish, Swedish, Turkish and Tswana)" (Faculté de philosophie, arts et lettres 2010: n.p.). All participant learners are university students and their essays are meant to be argumentative rather than "[d]escriptive, narrative or technical" (Granger 2009: n.p.).

The FALKO corpus, which is modeled on the ICLE, consists of a subcorpus of expert users of German and various subcorpora of learners of German with different language backgrounds. Whereas the experimental conditions of the design of the corpus are quite liberal in ICLE, FALKO does not permit participants to use paper-based or electronic language tools (e.g. dictionaries, grammar references and spellcheckers); it took ICLE's suggested essay questions and made four of them compulsory. Participants also provide their own metadata through a questionnaire, and their level of German is determined by doing a C-test: a cloze test where participants are rated on the CEFR (Common European Framework of Reference for Languages) scale (e.g. A1 through C2). ICLE and FALKO not only share corpus design principles, but they also share the same methods of data analysis. Following Granger's (1996) contrastive interlanguage analysis (CIA), they "compar[e] learner data with native speaker data (L2 vs. L1) or compar[e] different types of learner data (L2 vs. L2)" (Granger 2008: 267). One application of CIA in FALKO is to look at over- and underuse of lexical and grammatical items across the different learners' language backgrounds compared to the expert users of the German control group (Zeldes, Lüdeling and Hirschmann 2008).

The Telekorp corpus relies on a different data collection design. The corpus consists of computer-mediated communication genres, including both synchronic texts (chat) and asynchronic texts (messages). Student participants did not perform under experiment conditions; rather, 64 US and 87 German university students had to communicate in English and German with each other in a classroom setting. The "[t]ransatlantic telecollaborative interactions consisted of a variety of tasks centred on the mutual reading/viewing of parallel texts" (Belz and Vyatkina 2005a: 5). Telekorp is longitudinal, including language production of over eight weeks. Belz and Vyatkina (2005a, 2005b) avoided doing a "slash and burn" (Dörnyei 2003: 90) by not only collecting corpus data from their language learners, but also by providing them with feedback on their performance. This leads us to our second approach to language learners and corpora, namely learners using corpora.

14.6.2 Learners using corpora

Whereas the previous section shows that learners' output can be compiled into a learner corpus to be used by researchers, another way for learners to interact with corpora is data-driven learning (DLL), a term coined by Johns (1986, 1990). Johns (2002: 108) states that his "approach was rather to confront the learner as directly as possible with the data, and to make the learner a linguistic researcher." This usually entails using corpora and KWIC (key word in context) concordances (in handout format or electronically) in a language classroom (O'Keefe, McCarthy and Carter 2007). Johns (2002), for instance, includes a cloze test activity with nouns that learners have to correctly identify through an alphabetical list of ten items. For each noun, there are five KWIC concordances in which the item has been removed. For accessible instructions on using corpora and especially concordances with learners, Tribble and Jones (1997) provide basic information, tables and figures to illustrate their materials.

Another corpus activity requires learners to figure out the semantic meaning and function of a word. Möllering (2004) compiled KWIC concordances of German modal particles and turned them into worksheets, inviting learners to notice the various uses of the German *ja* ("yes") in their different contexts (see Möllering 2004: 238–43). However, Belz and Vyatkina (2005a: 4) criticize Möllering's (2004) approach for not giving learners "the opportunity to see how their own uses differ from those of expert users." In their own research, the authors (Belz and Vyatkina 2005a, 2005b) asked their own US student participants to go through the Telekorp corpus to which they contributed and examine the usage of modal particles as produced by the expert users of German and by themselves.

Not every language tutor needs to compile his/her own corpus for classroom teaching, and Reppen (2010) provides a few suggestions on how to use online general language corpora with learners. Activities consist of a mixture of reading key words in context (KWIC) concordances to determine the meaning and use of different words or word clusters and/or determining frequencies, especially if the search item shows a difference in usage depending on the registers or genres of corpus texts (e.g. spoken, fiction, magazine) as in the Corpus of Contemporary American English, COCA (Davis 2008-10).

14.6.3 Learners using corpus-based materials

O'Keefe *et al.* (2007: xi, emphasis ours) observe that "corpus information, in recent years, seems to be becoming *de rigeur* as the basis of the compilation of major reference grammars, and, more and more, as the major feature of coursebooks." A good case study of textbook materials is McCarthy, McCarten and Sandiford (2005), where the syllabus has been influenced by using data from the Cambridge International Corpus. The aim of such a textbook is to teach "authentic and useful" North American English (McCarthy *et al.* 2005: iv). In conversations, for instance, the textbook shows a horizontal bar chart indicating that the phrase *I'm* is more common than *I am* (McCarthy *et al.* 2005: 5). At a later stage (McCarthy *et al.* 2005: 39), the textbook explains the discourse marker *well* and states that, in conversation, it is "one of the top 50 words."

McCarthy *et al.* (2005) might be considered as a flagship textbook in terms of its corpus-based syllabus design. However, O'Keefe *et al.* (2007: 274) warn that one "must not assume that the profession at large will rush to share its enthusiasm for everything to do with corpora." Indeed, many textbooks contain sentences or multiword expressions unattested in corpora (Römer 2004), thus presenting learners with constructed texts.

Corpus linguistics is thus not only be beneficial for SLA researchers in terms of learners providing authentic data on their production. Corpora can also provide a range of authentic and systematically compiled input for learners, be it in the form of using corpora and concordances themselves, or using materials based on corpus evidence.

14.6.4 The effectiveness of corpora in SLA

Because corpus linguistics is a relatively new user-friendly methodology and/or research discipline, there is an identifiable gap in the research into the effectiveness (i.e. with control groups) of using the above-mentioned materials in classroom teaching. Boulton (2008: 13) investigated "several hundred papers linking corpora and L2 teaching/learning" and only found thirty-nine studies "which report some kind of evaluation of DDL beyond the researcher's opinion." One of those studies (Koosha and Jafarpour: 2006) shows that data-driven learning (DDL) groups performed better than control groups in the learning of collocations of prepositions in English produced by Iranian EFL adult learners. Allan's (2006) findings also confirm DDL groups outperforming control groups, but Allan also mentions that DDL learners show a greater language awareness. Boulton (2010) even suggests that DDL materials do not have to entail hands-on concordancing on a computer: they can also be useful via the printed medium, either via paper KWIC lines or corpus-informed learning and teaching materials. Of all corpus-informed materials, Boulton (2010: 18) finds the COBUILD *Concordance Samplers* series, such as Capel (1993), the closest to hands-on DDL: "more data, fewer exercises, less mediation, with more of the responsibility falling on the learner (who may as a result learn more and become more autonomous)."

However, Boulton (2010) also observes that the corpus research has not been put into DDL teaching practice to the extent predicted by Leech (1997). On the one hand, some publishers are unaware of DDL and others are unwilling to introduce DDL materials to the market. On the other hand, teachers may be "hostile to any use of [information and communication technology] or CALL" (Boulton 2010: 3). Boulton (2010: 8) observes that "[h]owever simple the corpus interface, however well DDL is integrated with other functions, however user-friendly the program – the very fact of having to use computers will deter many." Whether the reasons are market-driven or affective, the number of corpora and their application in learning and teaching are on the rise. Although more theoretical corpus research will be carried out in the future, it is hoped that further research will engage in the effectiveness of corpora in the classroom setting.

14.7 Concluding thoughts

Clearly, a summative handbook chapter on as rapidly an expanding area as CALL and CMCL cannot aim to cover all its elements exhaustively. In this chapter, we have therefore sought to present readers with a broad overview of the relatively new (and in some cases very new) opportunities second language learners have nowadays for increasing the input they receive and the interaction in which they engage in electronic form, both in instructional settings and in extra-classroom contexts, thereby also raising the issue of language varieties as attested in various language corpora, and the deconstruction of native speaker in favor of "expert speakers." In a move to integrate recent trends in learner corpus research and its implications for the SLA classroom, we have also looked at how online and offline corpora and corpus-analytical tools can sensibly be integrated into the syllabus, thereby raising learner awareness vis-à-vis the problems inherent in uninformed and uncritical uses of the Web as a resource of authentic target language material. We have connected these issues to theoretical concerns relating to the receipt of comprehensible input (and primary linguistic data) under generative approaches to L2 acquisition and to interaction-driven and sociocultural approaches that adopt discourse and conversation analytical frameworks. For issues revolving around CALL-based assessment, mediation, multimodality, learner-centered curriculum design, oral language skills development and a more extensive focus on (combined) teaching and research methodological frameworks within CMCL, we recommend Lewis (2002), Felix (2003), Lamy and Hampel (2007) and Meskill and Anthony (2010).

Despite the sheer number of existing studies on CMCL, there can be no doubt that considerably more empirical research into all the areas covered in this chapter needs to be undertaken. Not only are we dealing with a highly dynamic field of research, but the ways in which recent augmented-reality technologies and (playful) social practices have widened the scope of immersive educational tools and methods leads to the question of how the bridging of virtual and actual reality (see Ensslin and Muse 2011) might impact learner identities and their communicative needs and expectations.

Part IV
Biological factors

INTRODUCTION TO PART IV

Part IV includes chapters that consider language acquisition from a biological standpoint relating to maturation, i.e. age of acquisition, and chapters that specifically address (neuro)biological or purely cognitive (rather than mentalist) aspects of second language acquisition. It also includes studies of acquisition and loss across the lifetime for spoken and written language. Many of the chapters indicate the interplay between maturational and socioeconomic factors that emerge in bilingual populations.

After introducing Lenneberg's (1967) notion of a critical period for first language acquisition, Chapter 15 reassesses findings relating L2 grammatical deficits to age of acquisition onset (AoA). It reconsiders the Fundamental Difference Hypothesis (Bley-Vroman 1990) in the light of recent studies demonstrating evidence both pro and con, and reviews a range of data by comparing endstate achievement of adult and child learners to native speakers. After providing background on the notion of a maturationally sensitive period, Herschensohn presents studies of age effects in phonology, morphosyntax and language processing. The last section summarizes the influence of maturation, processing resources and native language, showing that no single influence determines ultimate L2 competence.

Following a brief overview of children's native language acquisition and varying definitions of bilingualism, Chapter 16 discusses child L2A, comparing and contrasting development and endstate achievement to that of L1A on the one hand, and adult L2A on the other. It reviews various recent studies that elucidate these ideas in extensive investigations of child language. The chapter notes a distinction between early (3–7 years) and late (8–13 years) L2 learners. Haznedar and Gavruseva reconsider studies on L2 initial state, functional category implementation, morphological variability and atypical development. The chapter's comparison of child L1 and L2A with adult L2A links it to age effects and incomplete L1A.

Chapter 17 discusses asymmetric bilingualism and native (often heritage) language attrition, considering transfer, language dominance, input, education and literacy. It examines bilingual populations in terms of both their mental representations of language and social context. The chapter describes the linguistic competence of bilingual speakers of majority (socially dominant) and minority languages. Montrul first defines the sociopolitical influences that shape acquisition and attrition by minority speakers, and then presents evidence of minority language abilities in phonology, the lexicon, morphology and especially syntax. She also touches on related issues such as language prestige, code switching and areas of vulnerability at the discourse-pragmatics interface with syntax.

Chapter 18 investigates third language acquisition, exploring the idea of multicompetence and the role of previously learned languages in the acquisition of later ones. Linking to the previous chapter, it deals with grammatical influence among the languages acquired as well as the role of social factors (e.g. prestige), input, literacy, education and AoA. Rothman, Cabrelli Amaro and de Bot devote sections to multilingual education (exploring the teaching of lingua francas and minority languages) and to multicompetence across the lifespan (highlighting multilingual abilities). The second half of the chapter presents findings on multilinguals' competence in the linguistic subdomains of the lexicon, syntax and phonology.

Chapter 19 builds on the basics covered in Chapter 6, assessing psycholinguistic research on language processing in early and late bilinguals (child and adult learners) as compared to baseline monolinguals. It covers lexical access, syntactic anomalies and ambiguities, production, perception and integration (syntactic, semantic). In a first section Foucart and Frenck-Mestre discuss behavioral studies (e.g. reaction time, eye movement) of lexical access and syntactic processing. They then turn to neurolinguistic methodologies (ERPs and neuroimaging) that investigate the brain's real-time interaction with language. The last section considers the implications of this research for theories of language, acquisition and processing. The chapter also outlines the Shallow Structure Hypothesis and evaluates the feasibility of inferring L2 abilities and grammatical knowledge from behavioral and EEG data.

Recent cognitive research has focused not only on the obvious cortical regions that include the well-known left hemisphere areas of Broca and Wernicke, but also subcortical areas involved in emotion and memory. Chapter 20 investigates what is known about affective factors such as motivation, anxiety level and L2 identity with respect to their cerebral correlates (e.g. the amygdala). The chapter situates individual differences among language learners in terms of neurobiological distinctions that can presumably be traced to cerebral maturation during infancy. Mates and Joaquin attribute affective responses – from motivation to anxiety concerning L2 use – to Schumann's idea of Stimulus Appraisal. They explain the role of subcortical structures such as the amygdala in L2 development.

15

Age-related effects

Julia Herschensohn

15.1 Introduction

The idea that childhood is the optimal time for language acquisition appears obvious to the casual observer today as it has in the past. For example, the French writer Montaigne (1962 [1580]: 172–73) recommends starting a supplementary language (such as Latin, which he learned from infancy) at a very early age. The evidence for a critical period for first language acquisition seems clear, given that all typically developing children learn the language(s) in which they are immersed to gain native speaker competence as adults (Guasti 2002; Meisel 2008; Prévost 2009). For extensive discussion of age-based issues related to typical and atypical (e.g. SLI, Downs Syndrome, Williams Syndrome) first language acquisition (L1A), see Herschensohn (2007). Indeed, these facts and a number of other biological phenomena are adduced by Lenneberg (1967) to argue for a critical period for learning the native tongue, starting at age 2 and closing at age 12, i.e. puberty. However, Lenneberg is more cautious in addressing acquisition of subsequent languages, yet nonetheless concludes that "automatic acquisition from mere exposure" (1967: 176) is not possible beyond childhood. In the ensuing decades, his idea of a critical period was extended from its initial application to L1 acquisition to L2 acquisition in a range of research that appeared to corroborate age effects in L2A. Age of onset of acquisition (or AoA, sometimes referrring to age of arrival for immigrants but also used to refer to initial exposure; details of use of the term are beyond the scope of this chapter) shows an inverse relationship with incidence of nativelike attainment in sampled populations, with increasing AoA roughly correlating with decreasing proficiency as measured, for example, by pronunciation accuracy (Scovel 1988) and grammatical accuracy (Johnson and Newport 1989). The clear existence of such age effects does point to an advantage in language acquisition for younger learners, but it is not sufficient to establish explicit temporal limits for a biological critical period (Birdsong 1999b;

Herschensohn 2007). This chapter summarizes earlier and more recent work exploring the character of L2 age effects, the evidence for a critical period, and the role of factors other than age in L2 ultimate attainment. The first section situates the critical period debate in terms of maturation and experience, contrasting categorical critical period approaches (e.g. Bley-Vroman 1990; DeKeyser 2000) with more relativistic ones (e.g. Singleton and Ryan 2004; Herschensohn 2009). The second section presents evidence for AoA effects in phonology, grammar and processing in child and adult learners of L2, while the third section discusses intersecting factors such as literacy, motivation, social identity and first language influence.

15.2 Critical periods, maturation and experience

Lenneberg's (1967) influential arguments for the biological foundations of human language grew out of earlier work by Penfield and Roberts (1959) on language, and by a range of biologists on critical periods (e.g. Lorenz 1978 [1937]; Gray 1978 [1958]; Hubel and Wiesel 1965). For example, Hubel and Weisel patched one eye of a young kitten during the period of hypothesized binocularity formation; the kitten – deprived of the visual stimulation in one eye – was never able to develop depth perception. A strict definition of a biological critical period involves a developing organic system that is genetically scheduled to respond to a maturational event (e.g. visual response to stimulation for vision or a shift in hormones at puberty) at the onset of a critical period, and reaches its terminus when the development is complete (cf. Bornstein 1987a, b). If the process is interrupted, it may result in incomplete or failed development of the organ in question, as in Hubel and Wiesel's eye-patched kitten which ultimately failed to develop depth perception. The evidence for a developmental schedule for L1A may appear compelling (Lenneberg 1967; Guasti 2002), but the same question for L2A is more complex and has been a subject of debate, leading most scholars to agree that the broader term sensitive period (Knudsen 2004; Bialystock and Hakuta 1999; Flege 1999) is preferable since it implies softer boundaries. For L2A, prior experience with a native language affects learning of subsequent languages (Flege and Liu 2001; Birdsong 2005a, 2006a; see also Chapter 5, this volume), and a number of non-linguistic factors outlined below can impact L2A as well. This section discusses two approaches to AoA effects in L2 learners, those advocating a categorical difference between adult and child L2A (Bley-Vroman 1990; DeKeyser 2000), and those supporting a more gradient difference (Singleton and Ryan 2004; Montrul 2008; Herschensohn 2009), thus setting the themes that will be examined in subsequent sections.

15.2.1 A categorical critical period for L2
This section looks at the evidence for a sensitive period (rather than a critical period) for language acquisition and what its dimensions might be. The

evidence for a critical period for first language acquisition (L1A) includes its predictable and relatively short schedule crosslinguistically, its inevitability even in cases of disruption such as left hemisphere brain lesions and its dissociation from other cognitive functions (Lenneberg 1967; Guasti 2002; Herschensohn 2007). In addition, there is a marked decline in grammatical processing and automaticity in cases of L1 deprivation (Curtiss 1977; Newport 1994 [1990]) relating insufficient input to insufficient brain development. In L1A, the infant's brain uses linguistic input to forge new synaptic pathways and to prune others, resulting in implicit knowledge that will permit very rapid speed of native language processing in adulthood (M. Paradis 2004, 2009). Late L1 learners (most often deaf children with delayed onset of sign language) provide evidence for age effects (e.g. morphosyntactic deficits) in L1 attainment: Newport (1994 [1990]) finds an inverse correlation between morphosyntactic accuracy and AoA in L1 learners of sign language whose onset age ranged between 4 and 12 years. Research on deaf sign language learners whose first exposure was beyond age 12 is scarce and anecdotal (Curtiss 1988; Schaller 1995), but it is clear that L1A of morphosyntax is significantly incomplete (Newport cites only 50 percent accuracy of those with AoA greater than twelve years on *grammaticality judgment* or GJ tasks). Curtiss and Schaller document two case studies of language-less deaf individuals, Chelsea and Ildefonso, who only achieve modest gains in vocabulary after beginning acquisition as adults (see Herschensohn 2007 for more detailed discussion of L1A by deaf and so-called feral children who received no language input during childhood). Using gross measures of grammatical mastery, one could designate 0–4 years as the "very sensitive" period (the cutoff for native attainment according to Meisel 2008), and 5–10 as the offset for L1A of morphosyntax. For the native language, acquisition of implicit phonological and morphosyntactic knowledge, including very rapid online processing, is best accomplished with a very early start, at birth (Herschensohn 2007).

The evidence for a sensitive period for L2A is less clear, robust and definitive. Infants exposed to sufficient input in two languages learn both with native ability in a pattern and time frame similar to that of monolinguals (Bialystok 2001; Meisel 2004, 2008; Genesee, Paradis and Graco 2004). With sufficient continuing input, social interaction and the faciliation of literacy (Montrul 2008), they can become balanced bilingual adults. However, when these ideal conditions are not met, bilinguals favor a dominant language (the mother tongue or the subsequent one) and may have incomplete command of the other language (see Chapter 17, volume).

On a categorical view, single cases of purported competence might serve to provide support against a critical period: "a single learner who began learning after the period closed and yet whose underlying linguistic knowledge (not just performance on a limited production) was shown to be indistinguishable from that of a monolingual native speaker would serve to refute the claim [of a critical period]" (Long 1990: 255). Scholars on both sides of the debate have adduced evidence to maintain the view that older (post-puberty) learners can achieve competence (as measured by linguistic metrics) within the native range (e.g. Ioup, Boustagui, El Tigi and Moselle 1994; Bongaerts 1999; Obler and Gjerlow 1999) or that they cannot (e.g. DeKeyser 2000; Hyltenstam and Abrahamsson 2000).

High achievers aside, L2 learners generally show declining ability with increasing AoA, an indisputable tendency that many scholars seize to claim a critical period as a given of post-puberty L2A (DeKeyser and Larson-Hall 2005). For example, proponents of an L2 morphosyntactic deficit (e.g. Hawkins and Franceschina 2004; Hawkins and Casillas 2007) or of the Interpretability Hypothesis (e.g. Tsimpli and Dimitrakopoulou 2007) argue that morphosyntactic features (e.g. gender, tense) non-existent in L1 are unavailable or problematic: "uninterpretable [grammatical] features are difficult to identify and analyze in the L2 input due to persistent, maturationally-based, L1 effects on adult L2 grammars" (Tsimpli and Dimitrakopoulou 2007: 217; cf. Birdsong 2009a).

Scovel (1988) argues that the sensitive perod applies to speech production (pronunciation) and perception, essentially sparing morphosyntax. Johnson and Newport (1989) and many replications of their study (Bialystok and Hakuta 1994; Birdsong and Molis 2001; Jia and Aaronson 2003) indicate morphosyntactic decline inversely correlated to AoA. Diminished processing speed, as well as accuracy, also characterize the decline of the sensitive period offset (Guillemon and Grosjean 2001; Clahsen and Felser 2006a, b).

There is, however, no empirical corroboration for a single definitive age of terminus for a critical period since research shows that different subdomains of language are affected at different ages (Seliger 1978; Moyer 2004; Abrahamsson and Hyltenstam 2008, 2009). Furthermore, true critical periods are strictly biological and linked to maturation, whereas L2A is impacted by a range of non-biological factors (Birdsong 1999a; Moyer 2004). Finally, the distinct roles of maturation and experience in L2A cannot be separated, and some scholars maintain that the latter – exposure to the TL – is more important than the former (Flege and Liu 2001).

15.2.2 Age effects from a gradient perspective

In contrast to the view that there is a categorical divide between pre- and post-critical period L2 learners, a more gradient view of age effects in L2A takes into account a number of factors (see Singleton and Ryan 2004; Herschensohn 2007, 2009; Dörnyei 2009a). Evidence cited above indicates there is a maturationally sensitive period for L2A, with offset decline beginning at age 4, and steeper decline occurring through the teen years, but with no definitive terminus (Herschensohn 2007). There is no strictly delimited biological critical period (definitive onset, offset and terminus) for acquisition of L2 grammar (phonology, morphosyntax, semantics): "no study has as yet provided convincing evidence for the claim that second language speech will automatically be accent-free if it is learned before the age of about six years and that it will definitely be foreign-accented if learned after puberty" (Piske, Mackay and Flege 2001). Adult L2 learners resemble child and teenage L2 learners in endstate competence in many respects; differences are often quantitative, not qualitative. For example, late bilinguals, even very proficient ones, show lower grammatical accuracy and slower but not a different sort of processing (longer reaction time) than native speakers and early bilinguals, given standardized proficiency measures such as those used in experimental tests (Hyltenstam and Abrahamsson 2000, 2003).

Adult and child learners – rather than showing categorical distinctions in the process of acquisition – share a number of patterns in L2A. An obvious shift in cognitive functions of the maturing individual includes a reduction of implicit learning and an increase in explicit learning with age (M. Paradis 2009), but this shift cannot singularly explain age effects. Contrasting adult and child L2A under the same circumstances reveals both similarities and differences in path and ultimate achievement (Schwartz 1992, 2003). For example, Unsworth finds that for both stylistic movement of direct objects (2005) and gender agreement with determiners (2008a) in L2 Dutch, children and adult learners perform alike, indicating, she argues, comparable acquisition patterns and competence.

The next section examines similarities and differences between native speakers and L2 learners in terms of their grammars (phonology, morphosyntax), the lexicon and processing.

15.3 Ultimate attainment in L2A

The terms endstate and ultimate attainment in L2A refer to a putative stage after which there is very little change in L2 competence; this state or stage may represent a highly incomplete grammar (due to inadequate input, instruction, motivation, etc.) or a highly proficient level of achievement (see Chapter 31, this volume). This stage has been characterized as one of fossilization or stabilization (Long 2003). Studies of age effects ideally look at individuals who have stabilized after receiving adequate input under optimal conditions; they do not look at individuals who are fossilized with a highly incomplete grammar or are at an intermediate stage of acquisition. The benchmark for most age-related studies (criticized by Bley-Vroman 1983 as the comparative fallacy) usually has been native-level achievement. Native speakers are essentially at ceiling on both speed of processing and accuracy (under normal, not stressed circumstances). As this section documents, L2 learners show decreasing proficiency with increasing AoA in all areas of linguistic competence, phonology, morphosyntax, lexicon and processing.

15.3.1 Phonology
Beginning with Asher and Garcia's (1982 [1969]) investigation of Cuban Americans with varied AoAs, a number of studies in the ensuing decades tested

native speakers' perceptions of adult immigrants' nativeness in their L2 pronunciation as perceived by native listeners (Scovel 1988; Moyer 1999; Flege et al. 1999; Piske et al. 2001) or in their perception of L2 speech (Oyama 1978, 1982; Bradlow et al. 1995; Yamada 1995; Flege and Liu 2001; Flege and MacKay 2004; Lekiu, Raphiq, Zohar and Shimon 2009). In his comprehensive work on immigrants with a range of AoAs, Scovel (1988) found that native speakers' perception of non-native speakers' phonology was far more accurate than their perception of non-native morphosyntax. In reference to the Polish writer, he terms this the Joseph Conrad effect: L2 learners with higher AoAs were perceived as possessing a less nativelike accent than those with lower AoAs. In written production, however, learners of various AoAs were perceived as nativelike in morphosyntactic accuracy, leading him to claim that phonology but not syntax was susceptible to a critical period.

More extensive and carefully controlled studies of immigrant learners (Moyer 2004, English L1, German L2; Abrahamsson and Hyltenstam 2009, Spanish L1, Swedish L2) support the role of AoA in L2 phonological mastery. Moyer's (2004) investigation of twenty-five anglophone L2 German learners (AoA mean 12 years) in terms of four production tasks (word list, paragraph, spontaneous speech, proverbs) revealed "phonetic, suprasegmental, lexical and syntactic fluency" (2004: 69). The speakers were then judged by native speakers of German whose rankings of nativeness were statistically evaluated in terms of thirty-five non-linguistic factors the speakers had reported in a questionnaire (e.g. AoA, motivation, instruction, frequency of usage). AoA and length of residency (LoR) were by far the most significant of the factors, while aspects such as motivation or professional need had little influence on the subjects' fluency as perceived by native Germans. Moyer concludes (2004: 93) "while age of onset may exert independent influence on attainment, it does not provide a satisfactory explanation for non-native outcomes in SLA." Although physiological maturation plays an important role in phonological mastery, Moyer finds that factors related to social integration, cultural identity, or education are also important to the L2A of phonology.

Abrahamsson and Hyltenstam (2008, 2009) – extending their already well-established research in age effects – investigate age effects in a group of highly proficient L2 Swedish learners (LoR ten years+) whose L1 is Spanish and who have varying AoA. The first criterion is for the subjects to be perceived as nativelike by native speakers of Swedish, a selection accomplished through the familiar use of native-speaker perceived ranking. For the study, 195 volunteer advanced Swedish learners and 20 natives were recorded in telephone interviews. The Swedish native-speaker judges listened to 20–30 second snippets of the recording and then rated these as mother tongue or not, giving a perceived nativeness (PN) score of 1–10. Native controls scored 9.9, early learners (<11 years) 7.9, and late learners (>12 years) 2.5. A more detailed age breakdown shows a clear decline of PN with increasing AoA. The authors subsequently conducted a series of tests on learners whose PN was 6+ from early and late learner groups. They administered ten cognitively challenging tasks (going beyond the type of test hitherto used for AoA such as a simple grammaticality judgment (GJ) task or native perception of accent), four of which involved phonological production and perception of voice onset time (VOT) and perception in babbling and white noise environments. In scrutinized nativeness (SN, the more stringent criteria represented by the challenging tasks), the authors found "a significant difference in mean SN scores between the early and late learners" (2009: 281). While the early learners outperformed the late ones on all tests, the difference was most dramatic (nearly double the achievement level) for the VOT tests and babble perception. These carefully conducted experiments clearly show the importance of age to the acquisition of the L2 sound system, both in perception and production.

In contrast, recent studies with instructed groups of learners (Muñoz 2006a, 2008a, b; Larson-Hall 2008) offer little support for an age advantage in learning L2 phonology. Larson-Hall (2008: 53), who tested 200 early (AoA mean 8.3 years) and late (AoA mean 12.5 years) Japanese learners of L2 English, found a "statistical difference between the groups for the phonemic discrimination task," [l] vs. [w], which she nonetheless characterizes as modest. She infers a number of non-linguistic factors such as aptitude, motivation and amount of input, rather than maturation, to be influences on this outcome. Muñoz reports on the *Barcelona Age Factor* (BAF) project (1995–2004) which collected data from four groups of Spanish-Catalan learners who began instruction in L2 English at different AoAs (8, 11, 14, 18+), and who were all tested after 200, 416 and 726 hours of instruction, respectively. The project is informative in covering a large population (hundreds of subjects) and in giving a long-term longitudinal perspective (nearly a decade). However, the project points up differences between naturalistic and instructed L2A (especially with child learners), the latter sharing more traits with instruction in other academic topics than with naturalistic learning. In the introductory chapter Muñoz furnishes a very informative discussion on the history of investigation of (non-)benefits of early instructed exposure, including work by Snow and Hoefnagel-Höhle (1978). Unlike naturalistic exposure, instructed exposure to an L2 does not show a clear advantage for earlier learners; there is often an advantage for higher AoA, for the older learners have more developed cognitive skills and academic strategies that furnish an advantage in instructed language learning (as any other academic topic). Furthermore, as Fullana (2006) points out, formal instruction provides a fraction of the input of full-time immersion (and see Moyer 2004 above). Fullana describes the BAF learners' performance on phonetic perception and production tasks, noting that the younger learners generally do not show a great advantage. At Time 1 (200 hours) on the phonetic discrimination task, the older learner groups for all AoAs showed higher scores, but by Time 3 (726 hours) the youngest learners (AoA age 8) caught up and then surpassed all other groups. For production, in contrast, AoA was not significant for perceived accent scores, although most judges tended to rate AoA age 8 learners as more foreign-accented than AoA age 11. Closer examination of production of distinct vowels (e.g. [a] vs. [i]) revealed variability in pronunciation for all age groups. Other aspects of English that were examined in this overall study show clear advantages to the older learners in an academic setting, although phonological mastery is an area where there does seem to be some advantage to early learning.

Since for the BAF phonetic perception was the only area in which lower AoA seemed significant, the view that phonology is more susceptible to age effects than other linguistic domains may be supported. There are, nevertheless, high-achieving adult L2 learners in other studies who are perceived by native judges to have native phonology (Neufeld 1980; Moyer 2004; Bongaerts 1999; Bongaerts, Planken and Schils 1995, 1997). For example, of the twenty-five near-native adult L2 German learners in Moyer's (2004: 71) investigation of factors contributing to perceived proficiency, nine fell into the native range. Likewise, Bongaerts (1999) and colleagues (Bongaerts *et al.* 1995, 1997) have demonstrated perceived nativeness in adult AoA Dutch learners of L2 French and L2 English. All of the highly successful Dutch learners of L2 English in the 1995 study were rated as native on several criteria by native anglophones. Although L2 phonology is one of the most elusive linguistic domains for adult L2 learners to master, the foreign accent criterion should not be the only one used in evaluating nativeness, a topic discussed below.

15.3.2 Morphosyntax

Morphosyntactic non-nativeness is less obvious to native perceivers than foreign accent (Scovel 1988), yet a wealth of literature has documented adult L2 morphosyntactic deficits and declining grammatical proficiency with increasing AoA. Following up on Patkowski's (1982) study of immigrants, Johnson and Newport (1989) established a battery of 276 GJ sentences that were either correct or grammatically flawed. Administered to forty-six immigrants (Chinese or Korean L1, AoA ranging 3–39 years), the results showed that the earliest AoA subjects clustered within native-speaker scores (around 270), whereas the late learners (AoA 17+) showed significantly lower scores (210 and below). The methodology and conclusions of the authors have been questioned (e.g. Bialystok and Hakuta 1994, 1999; Birdsong and Molis 2001), but the test has been replicated by numerous scholars, always supporting the inverse correlation of AoA and nativelike morphosyntactic judgment (e.g. DeKeyser 2000; Birdsong and Molis 2001; Jia and Aaronson 2003). Birdsong and Molis' results highlight the importance of L1 influence, for their subjects, who were Spanish L1 speakers, scored generally much higher than Johnson and Newport's, and had higher scores with later AoAs (see also Chapter 5, this volume). DeKeyser (2000) elucidated the advantage for L2A of high verbal aptitude, a trait of individual learners whose influence on ultimate attainment has been corroborated in L2 Swedish by Abrahamsson and Hyltenstam (2008).

The two large studies examined in the previous section on naturalistic L2 Swedish (Abrahamsson and Hyltenstam 2009) and instructed L2 English (Muñoz 2006a) provide similar results in morphosyntactic competence to those in phonology. Recall that the Swedish study administered the final battery of tests only with learners whose L2 speech was deemed nativelike by Swedish judges. The subjects were given GJ tasks in both auditory and written contexts, and their reaction times were also measured. The scores of the early AoA 1–11 and late AoA 13+ (LoR ten years+) learners differed significantly: for accuracy of auditory GJ, 58 percent early to 40 percent late, and of written GJ 65 percent early to 50 percent late (the numbers indicate percentages of subjects within the range of native Swedes). The authors chose this grouping "because these may be thought of as representing L2 learning before and after the closure of a critical period" (2009, 262). For reaction times, early learners were 94 percent within native range, whereas late learners were only 60 percent. The results corroborate earlier findings concerning the inverse relation of increasing AoA with morphosyntactic nativeness, and thus the difference between early and late learners, even very good ones. The results also underscore the apparent biological foundation of speech – the real-time implementation of perception, production, comprehension and judgment. What the authors emphasize, however, is not how well the child learners performed (which they indeed did, essentially passing for native with suedophones), but rather that they did not perform at the ceiling level of the native Swedes. They conclude "that nativelike L2 proficiency is, in principle, never attained by adult learners" (2009: 289), and "that one may consider it a myth that L2 learning that begins in childhood easily, automatically and inevitably results in nativelikeness" (2009: 290).

In stark contrast to these naturalistic learners whose abundant input and often early exposure to the L2 resulted in near-nativeness (despite not being at ceiling), the instructed learners described in the Muñoz collection (e.g. Fullana 2006; Mora 2006; Muñoz 2006b, c) did not show an advantage for younger age. "The descriptive data show that the late starters [AoA 11 years] always obtained higher scores than the early learners [AoA 8 years]" (Muñoz 2006b: 24). Furthermore, the slight advantage that the early learners eventually had for phonology in the long run was not paralleled by a long-term catch-up in morphosyntax, narration and other domains, where the higher AoA learners showed higher scores at every testing time. Mora (2006), who analyzes an oral narrative of a cartoon for fluency development, uses criteria such as speech rate in words and syllables, L1 word ratio, mean length of sentence, dysfluency and pauses. These measures, while a gauge of perceived fluency, also reveal the learners' ability to engage lexical retrieval, morphology, syntax and discourse constraints in real-time implementation of the grammar. She concludes that the L2 learners are far less fluent than the native controls and that "late learners outperform early learners on the basis of their faster speech rate, much lower restricted use of L1 words and the use of longer fluent runs" (2006: 84). The BAF studies underline the difficulties of evaluating age effects in learners who are not endstate, since when studied these instructed students were far from stabilized in their knowledge and practice of L2 English.

Torres, Navés, Celaya and Pérez-Vidal (2006) find similar results from the BAF corpus in their analysis of writing ability as shown through compositions that were judged on fluency (essentially quantity), lexical complexity (breadth of vocabulary), grammatical complexity (complex sentences) and accuracy. As with Mora's analysis of oral narration fluency, for the four writing criteria the older learners (AoA 11) outperformed the younger ones in a statistically significant manner for 15/17 of the subcriteria. Unsurprisingly, amount of instruction time correlated positively with improved scores in all areas, and generally the older learners outperformed the younger ones at the same level of instructional hours. However, the younger group, while still showing lower scores at Time 3 (726 hours of instruction), was no longer systematically inferior to the older group. Once again, it appears that a sufficient quantity of input coupled with advancing skills in explicit learning may help the younger learners.

These analyses and the others reported from the BAF project provide ample evidence for the age advantage in instructed foreign language learning; in such environments, older learners are more adept at using explicit learning strategies, while younger learners make more use of implicit learning (M. Paradis 2004, 2009; DeKeyser 2003; DeKeyser and Larson-Hall 2005). This research provides extensive evidence corroborating the age advantage for older learners in initial stages that had been observed in earlier studies (Snow and Hoefnagel-Höhle 1978, 1982 a, b), but it also clearly shows the necessity of sufficient input to the development of a broad range of L2 skills (Piske and Young-Scholten 2009). With sufficient input, as in a naturalistic setting, children are much better eventually at L2A than adults, but the disadvantage that older learners have in implicit acquisition is partially compensated for by their advantage in explicit learning. In this sense, they are able to take advantage of an instructional setting to bootstrap the L2. Another observation that emerges from the BAF studies is the independence and interdependence of various aspects of L2A. The distinct developmental patterns of phonology as opposed to morphosyntax have long been recognized (Seliger 1978), and the BAF studies show additional distinctions and differing trajectories for other areas such as narration or composition as well.

15.3.3 Processing and lexical access

In addition to ceiling performance in phonology and morphosyntax, native speakers enjoy automatized and rapid speech (see Chapter 6, this volume, for discussion); child L2 learners often share these processing advantages (Clahsen and Felser 2006a, b). In contrast, adult L2 learners are far less accurate and quick in morphosyntactic processing, although lexico-semantic knowledge is fairly comparable for native and second languages (Osterhout, McLaughlin, Kim, Greenwald and Inoue 2004; Hopp 2007; Tanner 2011). The distinction is not surprising in that lexical learning goes on throughout the lifetime in any language, and depth of lexical knowledge correlates with a number of non-grammatical factors such as frequency, neighborhood density (similarity to other words), word length and sociopragmatics for both L1 and L2 (Hirsch, Morrison, Gaset and Carnicer 2003; Kutas and Schmidt 2003; Silverberg and Samuel 2004). It is then instructive to compare L2 learners' real-time processing of speech with that of native speakers to determine that they show the same basic division and are sensitive to the same external factors, and furthermore to ascertain which areas are most influenced by AoA (Frenck-Mestre 2005a; Grosjean 2004).

This section briefly looks at evidence from two sorts of psycholinguistic studies, behavioral and electrophysiological (see Chapters 19 and 20, this volume). Behavioral studies infer mental procedures from physiological responses to baseline events compared to various sorts of experimental task responses (linguistic, in the case at hand). Common techniques include measuring reaction time (RT) to a facilitating or inhibiting trigger compared to the baseline, or examining eye movements in a reading task (Frenck-Mestre 2005b; Siyambalapitiya, Chenery and Copland 2009). Longer RT or rereading can reveal that a given task requires more cognitive effort to process, resulting in slower or more laborious behavior that is less automatized (hence less speedy). For example, for native speakers of English sentences with verb disagreement – such as *the key to the cabinets were rusty* – require longer RTs than grammatical ones (Tanner 2011). Tanner examines perceptual responses in native and L2 English to this type of ungrammatical sentence (an agreement attraction error, with the plural attractor noun *cabinets* next to the plural verb) that is frequently observed in native English production.

Electrophysiological studies track the time course of the electrical pulses that constitute activation of neural networks in the brain (Osterhout *et al.* 2004; Osterhout, McLaughlin, Pitkänen, Frenck-Mestre and Molinaro 2006). Electroencephalography (EEG) portrays a graph of negative and positive activity recorded at a given site on the scalp, where a gel-coated electrode picks up signals through the skull. Typical responses to a sentence such as *I drink beer* can be compared to experimental atypical responses, particularly with respect to lexico-semantic and morphosyntactic anomalies that have been observed through these *event-related potentials*, or ERPs. For monolinguals, the EEG for a semantically anomalous word in a sentence such as *books* in *I drink books* results in a negative wave produced 400 ms after the word (N400). In contrast, the response to a morphologically anomalous word such as *drinks* in *I drinks beer* is a positive wave about 600 ms after the word (P600). The N400 and P600 have been well documented crosslinguistically and with a range of anomalies that belong to these two classes: lexico-semantic (e.g. wrong words, non-words) or morphosyntactic (e.g. verb disagreement, gender mismatch).

Osterhout and colleagues (2004, 2006, 2008), in longitudinal ERP studies with beginning French L2 learners during their first year of instruction, found L2 responses similar to those of monolinguals. The L2 learners registered an N400 response to lexical anomalies (non-words) after only 14 hours of instruction, but their explicit conscious judgments of whether an item is a word or non-word were at chance. On selected grammatical phenomena (e.g. verb agreement), the learners developed an N400 response after five months of study, a response that indicates a lexico-semantic anomaly for monolinguals. However, by the eighth month of the year, the L2 learners responded to the grammatical anomaly with a P600 (as do native speakers), a development that the researchers attribute to the grammaticalization of verb agreement in the L2. The ERP responses have been documented for advanced L2 learners as well. For example, in a study of verb agreement/disagreement in very proficient native Spanish learners of L2 English, Tanner (2011) found that the L2 learners demonstrated ERP responses that are qualitatively similar to native responses by English speakers, not only in terms of the overall pattern (P-600 / N-400), but also with respect to non-linguistic factors such as the presence of an attractor plural noun next to the verb (*key to the cabinets was/were*). For natives and L2 learners lexico-semantic processing shows greater similarity than does morphosyntactic processing, but the two categories are not mutually exclusive (Frenck-Mestre 2005a; Grosjean 2004).

Lexical access – the ability to retrieve a word's meaning instantaneously – might appear to be a lexico-semantic phenomenon. However, the morphosyntactic correlates of a word also impinge on its retrieval. For example, languages with noun gender indicated by grammatical concord on a prenominal determiner give a prelexical cue to a noun's gender and lead to a shorter RT in lexical access to identify the word. Native speakers demonstrate congruency/incongruency effects by showing faster recognition of nouns with congruent (agreeing) than with incongruent gender marking on determiners and adjectives (for Spanish and French, see Antón-Méndez, Nicol and Garrett 2002; Grosjean, Dammergues, Cornu, Guillelmon and Besson 1994). Hence the seemingly redundant nature of gender concord actually bootstraps lexical processing. For L2 learners, Guillelmon and Grosjean's (2001) auditory word repetition task reveals that natives and early (AoA 5 years) but not late (AoA 24 years) English–French bilinguals demonstrate congruency/incongruency effects similar to monolinguals (Grosjean *et al.* 1994). These data suggest that early L2 learners behave more like natives than do their late counterparts, a finding that has been repeated in other studies (cf. Clahsen and Felser 2006a, b). However, this facilitation is mitigated by various other variables, especially proficiency level, which is overall a better diagnostic than simple AoA (Perani and Abutalebi 2005).

Although adult L2 learners show quantitative differences from early bilinguals and monolinguals in RT, and at initial stages show little sensitivity to factors natives take into account (e.g. verb disagreement), they can eventually gain qualitative patterns that resemble those of native processing. Foucart

(2008) and Sagarra and Herschensohn (2010, 2011) examine gender processing in L2 French and Spanish, respectively. Foucart uses eye movement and event-related potentials (ERPs) in comprehension and production tasks with L1 English, German and Spanish learners of L2 French to compare their processing of concord and discord with that of French natives. She finds that despite quantitative differences (L2 learners have slower RTs, and L1 influences speed of processing as well; cf. Sabourin, Stowe and de Haan 2006), the learners show qualitative similarities to monolinguals (P-600 response to gender disagreement). She concludes that gender representation is similar for both late bilinguals (i.e. older L2 learners) and natives (whether or not the L1 is gendered), but that gender computation is less automatic in the L2 than in the L1. She underscores the idea that highly proficient bilinguals may reach nativelike representation and processing of gender, regardless of AoA or L1 influence.

Sagarra and Herschensohn (2010, 2011) examined beginning (first-year university students) and intermediate (third-year students) adult anglophone learners of Spanish in online (RT) and offline (GJ) tasks on sentences with noun–adjective gender/number agreement/disagreement. Results indicate that all participants were highly accurate in the (self-paced) offline task, but that only intermediates and Spanish native controls showed sensitivity to gender and number violations in the online task for the 2010 study. Their 2011 study shows similar results, with intermediates and monolinguals demonstrating sensitivity to concord/discord and to animate versus inanimate nouns. Intermediates and Spanish monolinguals have longer reading times in sentences with gender discord than in sentences with concord, and in those with animate rather than inanimate nouns. These results suggest that intermediate learners display targetlike patterns that are more qualitatively similar to those of natives than do beginners. The overall findings suggest that adult learners can develop processing patterns qualitatively similar to those of native speakers.

Clahsen and Felser (2006a) compared the processing of adult L2 learners with that of native children and adults and explained similar strategies for children and adult natives as examples of continuity, although native children have slower RTs than native adults. In contrast, they argue that L2 processing of complex syntax (e.g. relative clauses) remains non-nativelike, a difference they attribute to the learners' preference for lexico-semantic or linear information (termed shallow structure parsing) over nativelike full parsing that makes use of non-linear structural relationships for phrase structure and filler–gap dependencies. The divide is not categorical, though, since native speakers use both shallow and full parsing, and extremely proficient late bilinguals (older L2 learners) may, in principle, use full parsing as well as shallow. In contrast, Hopp (2007) attributes differences between native and L2 processing to factors such as L1 influence or computational limitations. In German, scrambling (the movement of verbal arguments) is a stylistically complex construction that is sensitive to a number of semantic and morphological features. Hopp investigated scrambling in L2 German by late bilinguals (L1 Dutch, English, or Russian) in offline and online tasks. He argues that the results reveal L2 morphosyntactic control as well as interpretation and processing strategies that resemble those of natives. The open questions of how similar natives and non-natives are will be further explored in the next section.

15.4 Influences on L2A

The ample evidence presented in the preceding section on age effects in grammatical competence, foreign accent and speed of processing shows clearly that there is a sensitive period for learning a second language: earlier is better. The evidence also indicates that this period does not include a threshold set at a specific age after which L2A is impossible, as a true biological critical period would. The categorical view of a critical period does not hold, but the exact nature of the L2 sensitive period and its underlying causes require further investigation here. Clahsen and Felser (2006b), in discussing non-native processing, describe four factors distinguishing L2 from native processing: variable levels of grammar knowledge (proficiency), L1 influence, cognitive resource limitations and maturation, all of which contribute to L2 variability and incompleteness. The last three factors are not limited to processing, but can be seen in other areas of L2 competence and furnish the themes for this section.

15.4.1 Maturation and the brain

The importance of AoA points to maturation as an important factor for mastery of a second language. The early establishment of neural networks for L1 phonology figures importantly in later restrictions on the brain's ability to gain L2 phonology (Kuhl 1991, 2004; de Boysson-Bardies 1999). Kuhl (2004: 831) points out that "infants are 'primed' to learn the regularities of linguistic input when engaged in social exchanges," and that they are sensitive to two main phenomena during the first year of life, prosody and distributional frequencies of the sounds of the ambient language. Armed with a predisposition to learn language by segmenting the stream of speech (Guasti 2002; Jusczyk 1997), they hone perception skills whose potential phonemic categories and statistical generalizations (e.g. the ability to recognize segmental sequences, syllables and eventually words) are later used to shape their production of first words, phrases and eventually sentences. The early establishment of neural networks in the brain supporting linguistic development indicates that phonology is one of the first acquired abilities, one which is the most difficult to overcome when trying to gain a new L2 phonology in later life. Kuhl points out that experience and maturation are interdependent, and that "neural commitment to the statistical and prosodic regularities of one's native language promotes the future use of these learned patterns in higher-order native-language computations [and ...] interferes with the processing of foreign-language patterns that do not conform to those already learned" (2004: 838).

Many scholars see a categorical difference in the learning patterns, implicit versus explicit, that characterize child and adult skill development. The learning that occurs as neural networks are established by the infant is obviously unconscious and implicit. The contrast between this implicit learning of procedural routines can be contrasted with the typical explicit learning patterns of adults gaining declarative knowledge in a range of domains in addition to language. Explicit learning patterns result in declarative knowledge for those (overwhelmingly instructed) adult learners studied thus far (see Chapter 6, this volume). In L1A the maturing brain develops its dedicated linguistic areas, especially in the left frontal and temporal lobes, while also connecting to other regions in the right hemisphere and subcortex (Schumann et al. 2004). Just as Lenneberg cited automatic acquisition from mere exposure as a characteristic of L1A, other scholars cite implicit learning as the defining property of L2 learning in childhood (DeKeyser 2000, 2003; Ullman 2001b; M. Paradis 2004, 2009), contrasting it with the explicit learning of adults (for both naturalistic and instructed environments). DeKeyser (2000) further demonstrates that for individual learners, higher verbal analytical skills (better explicit learning techniques) contribute to greater ultimate achievement in adult L2A. Ullman links the two means of learning and memory to different brain areas: declarative in the medial temporal lobe and procedural in the left frontal lobe and basal ganglia. Implicitly learned procedural patterns are established early in life, whereas explicit learning becomes more important with increasing age. M. Paradis (2004) agrees that late L2 learners rely on explicit learning, resulting in "a cognitive system different from that which supports the native language" (59). M. Paradis (2009) places even more emphasis on the differences between the two learning mechanisms and memory types, essentially excluding procedural language learning by adults. He recognizes that very fluent L2 adults may appear to have cognitive systems similar to natives, but he proposes (without testing) that they may simply have speeded up processing due to extensive practice. Paradis' view is not accepted universally, since many psycholinguists argue that L2 learners have qualitatively similar grammatical representation and processing to native speakers (e.g. Osterhout and colleagues; Foucart 2008; Hopp 2007; Tanner 2011; see also Chapter 7, this volume, on what cannot be learned explicitly, yet is nonetheless acquired).

Despite the obvious advantage imparted by early establishment of linguistic neural networks through implicit learning, the categorical version of implicit learning as the sole factor in age effects requires mitigation. Some learners become proficient and implement procedural storage of L2 grammar, as indicated by psycholinguistic studies, leading Ullman (2001b: 110) to say that "practice as well as age of exposure should affect both grammatical proficiency and the degree of dependence on procedural memory for grammatical computations." The abilities of proficient late bilinguals/older

L2 learners who exhibit procedural mastery in the L2 (Hopp 2007), the qualitative similarity of L1 and L2 processing (Perani and Abutalebi 2005), the fact that even intermediate learners show evidence of implicit learning (Sagarra and Herschensohn 2010) require a more nuanced version of the implicit/explicit divide. Perani and Abutalebi (2005: 205) note that in L2 processing, "the patterns of brain activation associated with tasks that engage specific aspects of linguistic processing are remarkably consistent among different languages, which share the same brain language system." Dörnyei (2009a: 257) points out that implicit proceduralization plays an important role in adult L2A, a tendency not predicted by restricting adults to explicit learning alone. Indeed, the distinction between declarative and procedural ability can be illustrated by the contrast between instructed learners who know declarative grammar rules but don't yet have procedural abilities. Sagarra and Herschensohn's (2010, 2011) beginners – who had clearly documented declarative knowledge of adjective agreement in Spanish in the grammar test, yet lacked sensitivity to adjective discord in the online task – contrasted with the intermediates who showed both declarative and procedural abilities that were qualitatively similar to those of monolingual Spanish speakers.

The question of whether neural commitment in early learning through implicit acquisition is definitively completed in childhood (as in a critical period threshold) is weighted toward childhood, but not categorically so. Adult L2 learners also demonstrate procedural learning and implicit knowledge of which they may be consciously unaware. For example, Osterhout et al. (2004, 2006) document continuing brain plasticity in adult language learners who develop implicit sensitivity to lexical grammatical anomalies in the L2. Osterhout et al. (2008) describe an increase in gray matter density over five weeks of intensive Spanish (cf. Mechelli et al. 2004). Pallier (2007) and Pallier et al. (2003), who studied Korean adoptees who learned L2 French at various ages of childhood, found that the adoptees completely lose their L1 and replace it with L2 French as evidenced both by behavioral tests and neuroimaging. Pallier concludes that these experiments "argue against irreversible modifications occurring in the first ten years of life, either because of maturational constraints or as a byproduct of learning the L1" (2007: 164). The evidence for continuation of brain plasticity leading to implicit learning and procedural knowledge is compelling and indicates that plasticity, although greatly reduced in adults as compared to young children, is still available to mature brains. The maturation and continuing plasticity of the brain constitute one factor contributing to sensitive rather than critical period effects; the persistent influence of the native language is another factor to be examined next.

15.4.2 Influence of the native language

The influence of the mother tongue on acquistion of subsequent languages has long been recognized (Lado 1957), but recent research has revealed more subtle aspects of the role of the native language in L2A. In one vein, studies using the immigrant AoA paradigm have shown quite differential results depending on the native language. Experimental studies looking at specific grammar points (e.g. adjective gender concord) also have exposed different L2 competence related to different L1s.

Several studies replicating the Johnson and Newport (1989) GJ tests used L2 learners with different L1s (the 1989 study had Chinese and Korean as L1s). Birdsong and Molis' (2001) results with L1 Spanish speakers differ substantially in raw scores (generally higher) and onset of decline (generally later) from the earlier study with East Asian L1 speakers. The two articles by Bialystok and Miller (1999), who looked at L1 Spanish and Chinese, and McDonald (2000), who looked at L1 Spanish and Vietnamese speakers, both showed higher achievement in L2 English by the Spanish speakers. As an Indo-European language, Spanish is distantly related to English, whereas the East Asian languages have no genetic relationship to English and are structurally quite different as well.

The influence of the native language is also a function of the learner's AoA. For example, a reprise of the immigrant phonology study mentioned above is provided by Aoyama, Guion, Flege, Yamada and Adahane-Yamada (2008) who compared Japanese L1 adults (mean AoA 40) and children (mean AoA 10) longitudinally over a year (Time 1 and 2) on production and perceived accent of English L2 consonants. At Time 1 (.5 year), the adults outperformed the children, but by Time 2 (1.6 years) the children had definitively outpaced the adult learners, although they were not accent-free. The authors conclude that earlier is definitely better for L2A, but that early does not guarantee nativelike accent. The study is useful also in documenting the longitudinal progression of adults versus children that has been reported previously in more anecdotal terms. Dimroth (2008) likewise finds child/adult differences in acquisition of tense and negation in her case study of two Russian learners of L2 German (AoA 8, 14). Native language influence is partially determined by AoA.

Structural and morphological similarity also play a role in L1 influence. Sabourin and Stowe (2008) compared L1 Romance (French, Italian, Spanish) and German learners of L2 Dutch on ERP responses to verbal (inflection) and nominal (agreement of determiner and noun) anomalies, and they found a nativelike response to the former but not the latter by Romance speakers. Both conditions elicited a P600 for the German subjects, but only the verbal anomaly did so for the Romance subjects. They conclude (2008: 422) "the difference between L2 groups found in Experiment 2 suggests that in the case of gender, it is not sufficient to have gender in the L1, but that the systems must be very similar to that of the L1, down to the lexical level, in order for the processes eliciting the P600 effect to be employed in the L2." Their results are similar to those of Sabourin et al. (2006), who measure gender concord in relative pronouns in L2 Dutch. They found chance accuracy in L1 English, better performance by L1 Romance and best performance by L1 German subjects. The genetic relationship of German and Dutch and their similar morphology are cited as important factors for both studies (surface transfer), with abstract gender feature (deep transfer, as for Romance) as a secondary source of L1 facilitation. The relatively poor performance on Dutch gender as opposed to tense may in part be due to the very opaque gender concord system in Dutch that is not mastered by native Dutch children until the age of 7 (Blom, Polišenská and Unsworth 2008) and is quite related to lexical frequency (Unsworth 2008a). Hopp (2006), who looked at advanced and near-native learners, found no L1 related difference in his very proficient L2 learners of German whose L1 was either Dutch or English, but rather found that proficiency level was the most important factor in mastery of various aspects of subject–object ambiguities.

Gender agreement is also the topic of a Spanish–English study of two bilingual populations, heritage speakers (individuals whose mother tongue is a minority language that gives place to the social majority language in which they gain literacy) and adult Spanish L2 learners (Montrul, Foote and Perpiñán 2008), who differ in terms of AoA and input. Comparing the two groups (about 70 subjects each, 22 native controls) on two written comprehension tasks and one oral production task, the authors found that the adult learners outperformed the heritage learners in literacy tasks, while the heritage Spanish speakers were better on the oral task. In contrast to the error-free monolingual Spanish controls, both experimental groups made errors (10–25 percent overall), indicating incomplete grammars (cf. Montrul 2008; see also Chapter 17, this volume). The two populations – who differ in AoA, in amount of oral and written input, and in mode of acquisition – show no distinct advantage for earlier AoA and no consistent grammatical deficit for adult AoA. Contra advocates of critical period limits on grammar acquisition, the overall results point toward differences between the early and late learners that do not define a categorical critical period for language acquisition. If, however, the oral task is taken to be indicative of implicit knowledge (and the written one of metalinguistic explicit knowledge), the AoA advantage is clear. The authors conclude that "both L2 learners and heritage speakers know something about grammatical gender in Spanish, but such knowledge might be stored, represented and deployed differently" (2008: 542). The next section examines in greater detail how grammatical knowledge may be implemented.

15.4.3 Cognitive resources, experience and other variables

While brain plasticity and L1 transfer affect L2A, there are other factors – cognitive abilities, education, identity and input – that impact acquisition in additional ways. External influences such as literacy, education and amount of input are significant, as are individual characteristics such as verbal acuity and sociocultural identity. Moyer's (2004) study underlines the less significant role of these additional factors compared to AoA, yet other research has demonstrated measurable differences in acquisition ability due, for example, to cognitive aptitude and education.

Abrahamsson and Hyltenstam (2008) retested DeKeyser's (2000) premise that verbal analytical ability facilitates L2A in their extensive study of perceived nativeness in Swedish L2 speakers. DeKeyser used an adaptation of the MLAT aptitude test while Abrahamsson and Hyltenstam adapted five subtests of the Swansea LAT (phonetic memory, lexical-morphological analysis, grammatical inferencing, aural memory and sound–symbol associations). DeKeyser found the predicted AoA advantage, with child learners outperforming adults, but with a mitigating effect: his L1 Hungarian learners of L2 English with high AoAs exhibited greater L2 accuracy correlated with their verbal analytical ability. Abrahamsson and Hyltenstam (2008, 2009) explore this cognitive advantage with a larger battery of tests, and they found that the advantage extended to childhood learners as well as adult learners. Comparing their Swedish learners to native speakers, they found that not only did the late learners benefit from higher language aptitude (confirming the DeKeyser thesis), but also the early learners: "a majority of those early learners who scored within the native-speaker range on the GJT [grammaticality judgment task] also had above average aptitude, and most of those who scored below the native-speaker range exhibited below-average aptitude" (Abrahamsson and Hyltenstam 2008: 499).

The interaction of individual cognitive skills with AoA and language processing is the topic of McDonald's (2006) comparison of adult L2 English learners (L1 Spanish and Vietnamese) with native speakers. Assuming that working memory capacity and decoding ability could be important factors for language processing speed, she compared the L2 learners' performance on word detection and GJ tasks with that of native monolinguals. Under normal circumstances, learners – as is well documented – process the L2 more slowly and less accurately (as indicated by the GJ task) than natives. However, under stress conditions of various types (e.g. added noise) the monolinguals likewise showed reduced speed and accuracy. Furthermore, the cognitive factors were significant for both L2 learners and natives: higher memory and decoding ability correlated with increased accuracy in GJs in both L2 learners and stressed native speakers. It is possible "that late L2 learners actually have a large overlap in grammatical knowledge with native speakers; they are just processing the sentences under difficult conditions, analogous to natives listening through noise, or maybe with an extremely high memory load" (McDonald 2006: 397).

Another important variable affecting age and acquisition is education, the compensatory nature of which can be seen in the explicit learning that L2 learners exploit, as evidenced in the BAF studies. Tomiyama (2008), who looks at attrition of L2 English by two Japanese siblings, concludes that the older one, whose L2 English was more solidly established at his departure from North America and remained more robust than that of the younger sibling, "spent more years in the educational setting providing him with more opportunity to solidify his literacy skills" (2008: 271; see also Chapter 9, this volume). The educational advantage even carries through cross-modally (Prinz 1998), as greater cultivation of linguistic skills in American Sign Language (ASL) helps development of written L2 English. Prinz (1998) points out that continuing use of ASL in school (e.g. honing narrative skills, problem solving in ASL) is beneficial to developing literacy skills in L2 English, hence overall academic performance. Chamberlain and Mayberry (2008) examine the role of ASL proficiency in skilled and less skilled English readers and find that it is indeed a significant factor.

The role of cultural identity, prestige and social integration must also be taken into account as contributors to the motivation of L2 learners (see Chapters 8 and 12, this volume). The ability to use a language or to be perceived as a native speaker of a majority language is especially important for minority members of a heterogeneous society such as the United States (Valdés 2004, 2006). Education in the majority language, the sway of siblings and peers, media images that promote majority language and culture are all influences that contribute to L2 learning of the majority language by immigrant children (Montrul 2008).

Finally, robust quantity and quality of input is crucial to language development and maintenance (Piske and Young-Scholten 2009). It appears that even knowledge of vocabulary is dependent on quality of input, as Abrahamsson and Hyltenstam's (2009) child learners reveal in their less than nativelike mastery of formulaic language (e.g. proverbs). This shortcoming could be attributed to their reduced exposure to traditional Swedish formulaic language, given their immigrant family home environment. Trofimovich and Baker (2006, 2007) demonstrate that learners require sufficient long-term experience with suprasegmentals (e.g. prosody and fluency factors) as well as segmentals (phonemes) for L2 phonology. They compare designated inexperienced and experienced adult (LoR three months vs. ten years) and child (LoR one year vs. eleven years) L2 learners; experienced learners outperform the inexperienced in both age groups, and the long-term child learners are often perceived as native. Summarizing, AoA is an important variable, but L1 influence, cognitive acuity, experience with the L2 and other external factors all have a role in L2 acquisition.

15.5 Conclusion

There is ample evidence that the human brain is experience *expectant*, biologically programmed to seek the necessary linguistic input (Bruer 1999) to learn a first language. Children learn language in a very systematic way cross-linguistically from birth to 4 years, with linguistic deficits if the trajectory is severely thwarted in some respect. The trajectory requires sufficient input received within an appropriate time frame. For subsequent languages, the human brain is experience *dependent*, biologically capable of learning another language, but not necessarily destined to do so. The L2 will, like the L1, show concomitant deficits if sufficient input is not received within an appropriate time frame. Birth to 4 years is the very sensitive period for L1A or bilingual L1A; after 4 years L1A or additional language acquisition results in measurably deficient scrutinized proficiency (phonology, morphosyntax, lexicon or processing). Late childhood from 5 to 10 – during which time the brain continues to consolidate neural networks – is a period of offset in acquisition aptitude, resulting in deficits in L2 proficiency as perceived by native speakers. The decline in acquisition potential increases during the teen years and continues into adulthood as the brain's ability to establish new neural networks diminishes. The general decline in language learning aptitude with increasing AoA is paralleled by a decline in implicit learning and inverse increase in explicit learning (M. Paradis 2009).

Deficits in endstate L2 include phonology, morphosyntax and processing differences from native monolingual performance. Pronunciation may deviate from the native profile in vowel space, consonant features and suprasegmentals. Morphosyntax is less vulnerable than phonology, but often reveals problems with features non-existent in the L1 and morphological performance errors. Comprehension and production in real-time processing also show deficits in slowed reaction time, lower accuracy and non-native processing strategies. Finally, as Abrahamsson and Hyltenstam emphasize, proficiency is not a monolithic and homogeneous ability comparable in all learners – individuals show different areas of expertise or deficit in L2 subdomains. So is there a sensitive period for L2A and what are its dimensions? The range of evidence presented in this chapter indicates that childhood is indeed a more sensitive period for acquiring a post-maternal language, but the period is not a critical one; it does not have a categorical terminus and its dimensions vary individually due to a number of additional external and internal factors.

16

Childhood second language acquisition

Belma Haznedar and Elena Gavruseva

16.1 Introduction

This chapter focuses on recent empirical and theoretical advances in the field of child second language acquisition (cL2A) research, also referred to as *successive or consecutive bilingualism*, with specific emphasis on the studies conducted within the framework of Universal Grammar. Until recently, the child L2 label has embraced a population of learners whose exposure to a second language may begin as early as age 3 (Lakshmanan 1995, 2009; McLaughlin 1987; Meisel 2008; Schwartz 2004). More recent studies, however, subdivide L2 children into early successive bilinguals who fall into the age range of 3 to 7 and late successive bilinguals who begin L2A after the age of 7 but before puberty (Blom 2008; Blom, Polišenská and Unsworth 2008; Chondrogianni 2008; Ionin 2008). Meisel (2008) places a stricter upper limit on cL2A, arguing that adult L2A begins at age eight. (See Blom and Unsworth 2010 for discussion of challenges in defining cL2A; also see Nicholas and Lightbown 2008, who emphasize cognitive and environmental factors in shaping cL2A.) This more fine-grained distinction is suggested by the findings that point to some interesting differences between early and late child L2 acquirers in error profiles (L1 transfer errors, in particular), degree of L1 influence, ultimate attainment and likelihood of fossilization. In addition to pre-pubescent age and knowledge of L1 (the extent of which naturally varies with age), the typical child L2 learner in studies thus far acquires the target language in a naturalistic setting, with minimal or no instruction, and continues to use her/his L1 at home. However, some recent generative work has expanded cL2A investigations to instructional settings (Myles 2005; Pladevall-Ballester 2010).

Child L2A emerged as a subarea of second language research in the 1970s, with its research foci being driven by the tradition of Contrastive Analysis (CA) that dominated the field of L2A at the time (Fries 1945; Lado 1957).

Most of the earliest studies focused on English as an L2 and were concerned primarily with descriptive facts regarding developmental universals and natural sequences as revealed by the order of emergence of English morphemes, a research agenda inspired by Brown's (1973) work in L1 acquisition, L2 developmental stages (negation, *wh*-questions), individual differences, etc. (Cancino, Rosansky and Schumann 1978; Dulay and Burt 1974b; Ervin-Tripp 1974; Hakuta 1974, 1976; Milon 1974; Ravem 1978; Wagner-Gough 1978; Wode 1977; among others). For many researchers, the basic assumption of the CA hypothesis – similarities imply ease and differences imply difficulty – did not seem to receive support in empirical studies of either child or adult L2 learners. Richards (1974) and Selinker (1972) cited many examples which were not attributable to the learner's L1, but were mainly developmental. Moreover, some errors never occurred, although they were predicted by the CA framework (Dulay and Burt 1974b). For others, L1-related errors varied depending on the learner's age and proficiency (Taylor 1975). There is no doubt that there were some discrepancies in terms of the classification of errors. For Dulay and Burt, for example, most of the seemingly L1-related errors were ambiguous in that they are also found in L1 acquisition. Also, certain types of errors, known as *intralingual* errors, were produced by L2 learners regardless of their L1 background.

The fact that similar errors were found in the speech of L2 learners regardless of their L1 led some researchers to hypothesize that L1A and L2A were similar processes (e.g. Dulay and Burt 1972, 1973, 1974b). For them, such errors were simply of a developmental kind and therefore L2 acquisition was proposed to be as creative as L1 acquisition. Overall, the primary goal of early child L2 studies was to uncover developmental errors that could provide evidence against the CA position that learners' L1 overwhelmingly influences and drives L2. As the term *interlanguage* (Selinker 1972) gained prominence, the aim was also to compare learners' utterances with target language forms and to account for inconsistencies in terms of learner-driven hypotheses. While this early research placed the language learner into the focus of investigation, a substantial body of acquisition data remained descriptive in nature, mainly because of the lack of strong connections between linguistic theory and language acquisition theory.

Recognition of the need to account for the acquisition patterns in a learner's interlanguage as well as advances in linguistic theory in the 1980s and 1990s led to the adoption of a new research framework. Of particular theoretical interest were the questions of whether the principles of Universal Grammar constrain L2A (see Chapter 7, this volume) and whether language development can be explained in terms of parameter-setting processes. In child L2A, these questions were taken up in the work of Hilles (1986, 1991), Lakshmanan (1991, 1993/94, 1994) and Lakshmanan and Selinker (1994), who each investigated some core properties of syntactic structure (e.g. Case filter, the complementizer system) and the pro-drop parameter in the L1-Spanish/L2-English child population (see Lakshmanan 1995, 2009 for an overview). In the mid to late 1990s, generative child L2A turned to the following three major issues: (i) the L2 initial state, (ii) the availability of functional categories in early L2 grammars, primarily Inflectional Phrases (IPs) and Complementizer Phrases (CPs), (iii) morphological variability (e.g. Armon-Lotem 1998; Grondin and White 1996; Gavruseva and Lardiere 1996; Haznedar 1997; Haznedar and Schwartz 1997; Paradis, Le Corre and Genesee 1998; Prévost 1997; Prévost and White 1999; Rohde 1996; among others). These issues were inspired by the research trends in child L1 acquisition such as the Optional Infinitive Hypothesis (Wexler 1994) and the Truncation Hypothesis (Rizzi 1993/94), on the one hand, and by the question of access to UG that defined much of adult L2 in the 1990s, on the other (Clahsen and Muysken 1986; Clahsen 1988; Bley-Vroman 1990; Hawkins and Chan 1997; Vainikka and Young-Scholten 1994, 1996a, b; Eubank 1993/94; Epstein, Flynn and Martohardjono 1996; Schwartz and Sprouse 1994, 1996). The term *access* designates domain-specific learning principles and implies the modular nature of the language faculty.

Current child L2A studies continue to explore the syntactic component of the language faculty, as researchers expand into more specific areas of syntax and extend empirical studies of interlanguage systems to more languages (e.g. Dutch, German, French, Italian, Spanish, Greek): the acquisition of Determiner Phrases (DPs) in the framework of the Fluctuation Hypothesis (Ionin, Ko and Wexler 2004; Zdorenko and Paradis 2008) or in comparison to clitics (Chondrogianni 2008), acquisition of tense agreement (Haznedar 2001, 2003; Ionin and Wexler 2002; Kakazu and Lakshmanan 2000; Prévost and White 1999, 2000) and tense-aspect systems (Gavruseva 2002, 2004, 2008a; Gavruseva and Meisterheim 2003; see also Haberzettl 2003 and Rocca 2007 for studies in a functionalist framework), interaction of D-elements (determiners and clitics) with the acquisition of tense–agreement–aspect (Belletti and Hamann 2004; Gavruseva 2008b), acquisition of gender agreement in DPs (Blom et al. 2008; Hulk and Cornips 2006), acquisition of direct object scrambling (Unsworth 2005), acquisition of verb placement (Blom 2008).

In empirical inquiries, researchers with a generative orientation have employed a range of methodologies to investigate interlanguage patterns. Longitudinal studies that track children's L2 development over a period of one or more years remain a methodological staple of much of the research, to be reviewed below. Spontaneous production data audio- and/or video-recorded during children's play, consisting of interactions with a researcher or with same-age playmates, has allowed for a detailed study of children's L2 development over time, with specific attention to individual variation and idiosyncrasies of interim linguistic systems (see Lakshmanan and Selinker 2001 for discussion of pitfalls in the analysis of naturalistic data, in particular, the technique known as "obligatory context counts"). Elicited production methods have also been employed to supplement spontaneously produced language samples or as the primary methodological technique. The common props used in elicitation methods are books with pictures that depict a cohesive series of events (e.g. children are asked to narrate a story), picture stimuli designed to elicit specific structures in a sentence-completion format (e.g. children are prompted to use a sentence that contains a determiner–adjective–noun phrase) or a fill-in-the-blank format (e.g. children are asked to provide a single verb form). Picture stimuli are also used by investigators to ask questions that facilitate a dialogue with children (e.g. "Why is he so fat?", as in Dulay and Burt's (1974b) technique). Grammaticality judgment tasks are also increasingly employed, although at more advanced developmental stages. As more experimental methods are being introduced in child L2 studies, study designs include L2 children of various proficiency levels whose acquisition data are compared to child L1 and/or adult L2 learners tested in similar task formats. The field of SLA is rapidly embracing more innovative and comprehensive experimental designs that allow for cross-learner-group comparisons.

In the overview of studies that follows, we focus on some central findings that hold promise for opening up new avenues in future cL2A research. The chapter is organized as follows. Section 16.2 presents an overview of current theorizing on the L2 initial state and the role of L1 in children's syntactic representations. In Section 16.3, we discuss the research on functional categories that has defined much of child L2A work over the past decade. Section 16.4 addresses morphological variability in child L1/L2 acquisition. Section 16.5 highlights the differences/similarities between child L2 learners and language-impaired child populations. Section 16.6 concludes the chapter.

16.2 L1 and the initial state in child L2 acquisition

In L1 acquisition, UG is assumed to be the initial state of the child's knowledge of language (Chomsky 1981). In L2 acquisition, however, there is an ongoing debate about whether UG or L1 constitutes the initial state (e.g. Bley-Vroman 1990; Flynn and Martohardjono 1994; Schwartz and Sprouse 1996). For some, the L2 learner is assumed to start off with UG and L1 grammatical representations, either in toto (Schwartz and Sprouse 1996) or in part (Vainikka and Young-Scholten 1994, 1996a, b, 1998). According to Schwartz and Sprouse's Full Transfer/Full Access Hypothesis (FT/FA), for instance, UG and the L1 grammar in its entirety characterize the L2 initial state, apart from morphophonological representations of lexical items. For others, the interlanguage initial state is not a particular grammar but rather UG itself (e.g. Platzack 1996; Epstein, Flynn and Martohardjono 1996, 1998). It should be noted that neither the Full Access Hypothesis of Flynn and Martohardjono (1994), Flynn (1996) and Epstein *et al.* (1996, 1998), nor the Fundamental Difference Hypothesis of Bley-Vroman (1990) is proposed as an initial-state hypothesis specifically for child L2A. (Also see Chapter 5, this volume.) Several longitudinal studies attribute certain syntactic patterns in cL2A to L1 transfer of lexical projections and functional feature values, providing support for the FT/FA.

The first pattern concerns the headedness of lexical and functional projections. Haznedar (1997) reports recurring head-final VP word order in early productions of an L1-Turkish/L2-English child, Erdem (AoA 4 years), which is consistent with the VP structure of Turkish (e.g. *I something eating*). Similarly, Mobaraki, Vainikka and Young-Scholten (2008: 220) report robust evidence for transfer of VP-headedness in two Farsi-L1/English-L2 children (AoA 7 and 8) (e.g. *We tennis play, This chicken on the tractor sitting*). In a study of an L1 Korean/L2 English girl (age 3;6 at the onset of L2A), Kwon and Han (2008: 314) report sentence-final placement of the English negative marker *no*, which corresponds to a Korean negative construction (e.g. *I'm the friend your no* = "I'm not your friend"). What is common in these non-adult word order patterns is that they are reported in the earliest language samples collected from the respective children. Interestingly, adult L2 learners are argued not to transfer the headedness parameter of lexical heads into L2 (cf. Clahsen 1988 on adult L1-Turkish learners' use of SVO word order in L2 German).

The second pattern deals with the use of structural case on subjects of predicates realized as bare (uninflected) lexical verbs in main clauses. In L1A research, uninflected predicates (in Wexler's 1994 terms, *optional infinitives*) were shown to exhibit a number of unique properties such as co-occurrence with null and non-nominative subjects (e.g. *Me eat this* = "I ate this" or *Ø fighting* = "He is fighting"). In the studies of child L2 English, the use of bare lexical predicates is widely reported (Armon-Lotem 1998; Gavruseva and Lardiere 1996; Haznedar 2001; Kakazu and Lakshmanan 2000; Mobaraki *et al.* 2008), with some divergent findings about the case forms of subjects. In Gavruseva and Lardiere (1996), Haznedar (2001), Haznedar and Schwartz (1997) and Kakazu and Lakshmanan (2000), an L1-Russian 8-year-old, an L1-Turkish 4-year-old and an L1-Japanese 5-year-old consistently produced nominative subjects with uninflected predicates (e.g. *He eating* = "He is eating"). To account for this prominent child L1/child L2 difference, transfer of the tense feature from the respective L1s was proposed (in the generative framework, T^0 is assumed to check structural case).

By contrast, Mobaraki, Vainikka and Young-Scholten (2008) report null and non-nominative subjects in the early development of two L1-Farsi children, ages 7 and 8 at the onset of L2A. Null subjects are reported to occur at the rate of 38 percent and genitive subjects at 53 percent in the database of 108 predicates, compared to 6 percent of nominative subjects. (Interestingly, in copular constructions, non-nominative subjects correlate with copula *be* omission (e.g. *My not a girl* = "I'm not a girl"), which is a pattern observed in child L1 English.) It is significant that the subject case patterns are nevertheless attributed to the influence from Farsi, a language that makes use of the same pronominal forms to mark all cases, unlike Turkish and Russian, which have rich case paradigms. As the authors put it, "what we may be observing is the strengthening of an existing, L1-based tendency to initially misanalyze pronoun forms as non-case-marked" (2008: 230).

Along the same lines, Belletti and Hamann (2004) also suggest that L2 children may be influenced by the morphological properties of pronominal paradigms in their L1. In the study of an L1-German/L2-French child (age 4 at the onset of data collection), the researchers report word order errors with the pronoun *ça* ("that") (e.g. *Tu peux pas ça faire* = *Tu peux pas faire ça* "You cannot do that"), as well as placement problems with subject and object clitics (e.g. *avec le* = *avec lui* "with him"). The child also used nominative clitic pronouns in non-finite clauses (e.g. *mais JE maman* = *mais moi, je suis la maman* "but I'm the mommy"). These patterns are in stark contrast with what is reported for child L1 French, where nominative pronouns are hardly ever misused and overwhelmingly occur with inflected predicates. Belletti and Hamann (2004: 160) propose that transfer from German may be involved, where nominative and accusative determiners can be used as demonstrative/personal pronouns. Thus, it seems that L2 patterns can be influenced by morphological paradigms in children's respective L1s, at least in the pronominal domain.

The third pattern concerns the use of uninflected/bare lexical verbs as predicates, a developmental error that is reported both for main and subordinate clauses in child L2, at least, in child L2 English data (e.g. *She know when he come*). Because the properties of bare predicates in child L2 acquisition are generally distinct from what is observed in child L1A, some researchers propose to view them as morphologically deficient spell-outs of a fully specified syntactic structure. In child L2, then, we observe underlyingly finite predicates with "missing surface inflection" (Haznedar and Schwartz 1997), in other words, *pseudo*-optional infinitives.

Recent work on aspectual systems in child L2A suggests that aspectual features can also be subject to L1 transfer. Ionin (2008) discusses misinterpretation of the aspectual marker -*ing* in the cross-sectional child L2 data from L1-Russian/L2-English children (ages 5–11). One child in particular was prone to using -*ing* with perfective meaning (e.g. *I'm buying watch* = "I bought the watch" [context: shows her watch to the investigator]), in contrast to the other children who were generally on target in assigning progressive meaning to -*ing*. Ionin proposes that this child may have transferred an aspectual feature from Azerbaijani, a language that she knew in addition to Russian. It is also possible that the child's age (roughly 10) at the onset of L2A may have facilitated the L1 influence. Rocca (2007) also argues for aspect-related L1 transfer in the two groups of child L2 learners she studied longitudinally. For the Italian-L1/English-L2 children, ages 7–8, Rocca (2007: 133) reports systematic overextension of progressive -*ing* to stative predicates (e.g. *Foxie wanting to catch her* = "Foxie wanted to catch her"), which she attributes to the semantic patterns of *Imperfetto* in the children's L1 Italian (*Imperfetto* is prototypically connected to states). Alternatively, the L1-English/L2-Italian children, ages 7–8, overused the past participial construction (*Passato Prossimo*) with statives to indicate the background of situations (e.g. *Ø vivuto-past.part. dentro uno bellissima casa* = "I lived inside a very beautiful house"; Rocca 2007:

187). This is a non-targetlike pattern because adult Italian requires *Imperfetto* in such contexts. Rocca argues that the L1 English child learners associate progressive aspect in English with *Imperfetto* forms in Italian and therefore go through a stage where they underuse *Imperfetto* on states (progressive is prototypically linked to activities in English). Although Rocca's work is functionalist in spirit, one could construe an account of these patterns by proposing transfer of syntactic aspectual features.

Recent work on the acquisition of DPs demonstrates that the effects of transfer extend beyond the VP-AspP-TP domains. For instance, data from the acquisition of articles and clitic pronouns show that both elements could be subject to L1 transfer. In the adult L2A of German, Parodi, Schwartz and Clahsen (2004) argue for L1 transfer on the basis of varying determiner omission rates, with naturalistic L2 learners from [+article] languages (Romance languages) omitting determiners less frequently than L2 learners from [−article] languages (Turkish and Korean). In child L2A, Chondrogianni (2008) compares the acquisition of determiners and clitics in L1-Turkish/L2-Greek children (ages 3–11) of varying proficiency levels. She points to L1 transfer because her participants omitted both elements initially and demonstrated targetlike production rates at higher proficiency levels only for determiners (despite the morphological sameness of determiners and clitics in Greek). However, Chondrogianni points out that transfer alone cannot account for the developmental differences between the two D-elements. Similarly, Meisel (2008: 62) reports clitic errors in German-L1/French-L2 children: nominative clitics sometimes appear as subjects of non-finite predicates (e.g. *et il jou[e]* = "and he play.non-finite"). He argues that this error type separates child L2 learners from child L1 learners of French (where such errors are unattested), which points to a difference in the initial state. Thus, clitics seem to be more problematic for L2 children than determiners, a finding that needs further empirical corroboration and theoretical explanation. In addition, just like pronominal subjects, clitics in child L2 productions seem to separate this population of learners from L1-acquiring children.

Alternatively, Zdorenko and Paradis (2008) argue for a limited role of L1 transfer in the acquisition of determiner semantics. Like previous adult and child L2 studies, Zdorenko and Paradis observe that omission is a more frequent error type in child learners from article-less languages (Chinese, Korean, Japanese), but only at the earliest stages of language development. The authors propose that L1 influence is observed in attaining at-ceiling accuracy rates, with child learners from [−article] languages lagging behind their [+article] peers. Interestingly, L1 background did not seem to affect determiner misuse errors (e.g. overuse of *the* in indefinite contexts or the use of *a* in definite contexts), as there were no statistically significant differences between the two child population groups. According to Zdorenko and Paradis, the evidence from determiner errors suggests that L2 children, unlike L2 adults, have full access to UG. Here, the Fluctuation Hypothesis proposed by Ionin, Ko and Wexler (2004) provides a promising framework for future investigations.

In more recent studies, the effects of transfer in successive and simultaneous bilingualism have been addressed from the perspective of the syntax–pragmatics interface (e.g. Hulk and Müller 2000; Serratrice, Sorace and Paoli 2004; Tsimpli, Sorace, Heycock and Filiaci 2004). Since linguistic knowledge at interfaces is assumed to be more vulnerable (e.g. prone to optionality), L1 influence may affect the interfaces to various degrees, with possible consequences for fossilization (e.g. Tsimpli and Sorace 2006; Sorace and Serratrice 2009). Indeed, much current work in adult L2 explores the Interface Vulnerability Hypothesis and the differences in vulnerability between external (e.g. syntax–discourse) and internal interfaces (syntax–semantics, morphology–syntax, morphology–semantics, etc.) (Slabakova 2008; White 2009). As for cL2A, however, limited work has focused on external vs. internal interfaces. In a recent study, Pladevall-Ballester (2010) provides evidence for L1-transfer at the syntax–discourse interface by showing that L1 English/L2 Spanish 5-year-olds overuse overt subjects and SV word order in the contexts that require inverted VS (e.g. focused subjects of unergative predicates). We believe that the Interface Vulnerability Hypothesis could also provide a fruitful framework for future child L2A research.

16.3 Functional categories in child L1 and child L2 acquisition

One central area of research in L1 acquisition concerns the knowledge of functional categories, which constitute formal properties of grammar such as agreement and tense. In regard to the status of functional categories in early child grammars three hypotheses can be identified: (i) the *Maturation Hypothesis*, (ii) the *Strong Continuity Hypothesis* and (iii) the *Weak Continuity Hypothesis*. As young children's speech initially lacks functional elements (e.g. determiners, tense-agreement markers), it has been proposed that child grammars initially project only lexical categories whereas functional categories are subject to developmental maturation (e.g. Guilfoyle and Noonan 1992; Platzack 1990; Radford 1990). Consequently, syntactic properties attributed to functional categories should be absent in children's early productions (e.g. NP-movement, verb movement, *wh*-movement, etc.). This articulation of the maturational view entails that emerging grammars are fundamentally different from adult grammars.

Proponents of the Strong Continuity Hypothesis, on the other hand, argue that child grammars have the same clausal structure as adult grammars (e.g. Boser, Lust, Santelmann and Whitman 1992; Guasti 1993/94; Hyams 1992; Pierce 1992; Poeppel and Wexler 1993); this is what Universal Grammar provides. The main idea is that early child clauses are characterized by a full CP projection; that is, all functional projections are present from the beginning. Evidence in support of the Strong Continuity Hypothesis is based on data from the acquisition of languages such as French, Italian and German. In these languages, young children produce tense/agreement inflections at an early age and hardly ever make agreement errors (although non-finite predicates may be produced). Furthermore, children's early utterances provide evidence for the syntactic processes such as verb raising and verb second, which require the presence of functional categories (e.g. Clahsen 1991; Déprez and Pierce 1993; Hyams 1992; Meisel and Müller 1992; Pierce 1992; Poeppel and Wexler 1993).

An intermediate position between the Maturation and Continuity Hypotheses is argued for by Clahsen, Eisenbeiss and Vainikka (1994) and Vainikka (1993/94), according to which functional categories are initially not available, but emerge gradually via interaction between input and X-bar theory under UG. At first sight, the Weak Continuity Hypothesis appears to be similar to maturational accounts of linguistic development in that both models allow for an early stage where functional categories are not instantiated. The Weak Continuity Hypothesis, however, differs from the maturational view in that functional categories develop gradually, through lexical learning, and in predictable developmental order. The underlying prediction is that while the child's grammar initially consists only of lexical categories, functional categories follow a developmental sequence in which the VP is acquired first, followed by IP, which is in turn followed by CP. This view is also referred to as the Lexical Learning Hypothesis. (For more on developmental sequences, see Chapter 27, this volume.)

The acquisition of functional architecture has been addressed in many child L2A studies, with important implications for the maturational and continuity positions. Since child L2 learners have an L1 system with fully specified functional projections, the development of functional categories in the L2 grammar could either follow in the steps of L1 children (which could constitute evidence against developmental maturation in L1A) or take a distinct path, with some variations depending on children's first language (which could constitute evidence for the maturational position in L1A). Our aim in this section is to review work on functional categories in child L2 grammars.

In one of the pioneering studies on functional categories in child L2 English, Lakshmanan (1993/94) examines longitudinal data from a $4\frac{1}{2}$-year-old Spanish child, Marta (data from Cancino, Rosansky and Schumann 1978). On the basis of her consistent use of copula *be*, auxiliary *be* and negated utterances, as well as her analysis of *for* in utterances with no main verbs (e.g. *The girl for tamboron* = "The girl is playing the tambourine"), Lakshmanan argues for the presence of the functional category IP in Marta's L2 English. Her conclusion is that early stages of L2 acquisition provide evidence for functional projections, such as IP and the related mechanisms such as case assignment.

Another study on the acquisition of functional categories in child L2 English was conducted by Gavruseva and Lardiere (1996). The data from an 8-year-old Russian child are examined for the availability of functional projections in early L2 acquisition. Gavruseva and Lardiere's analysis specifically addresses Vainikka and Young-Scholten's (1994, 1996a, b, 1998) structure-building approach to L2 acquisition (i.e. the implicational stage-like development of VP–IP–CP). With respect to the production of IP- and CP-related elements, Gavruseva and Lardiere examine obligatory contexts for the use of agreement, auxiliaries, modals and past tense forms, case on subject pronouns, subject–auxiliary inversion and clausal VP-complements, concluding that both functional categories are present in the child's L2 English.

Haznedar (2001, 2003) also argues for the availability of functional categories in child L2 English. Based on the data from an L1-Turkish 4-year-old (previously mentioned in Section 16.2), Haznedar analyzes the acquisition patterns of copula and auxiliary *be*, case marking of overt pronouns in subject and object positions, *wh*-questions and embedded clauses over an eighteen-month period. The data reveal that copula and auxiliary *be* were used consistently from the early stages, subject pronouns were always nominative (regardless of whether lexical predicates were inflected or not) and null subjects were virtually non-existent (despite Turkish being a null subject language). Based on these findings, Haznedar argues that the child's interlanguage grammar engages functional categories in early syntactic representations.

Gavruseva (2002, 2004, 2008a, b) explores the status of aspectual projections in child L1-Russian/L2-English, arguing that the emergence of finiteness (tense/agreement) is driven by the acquisition of aspectual features. One pattern that is typical of child L2 English is the asymmetry in the uses of the morpheme *be*: children acquire *be* as a copula much faster than its function as an aspectual auxiliary in progressive contexts. Gavruseva (2008a) attributes the delay in the acquisition of auxiliary *be* to the ongoing development of aspectual features [−bounded/+progressive], arguing that copula *be* is the spell-out of tense/agreement only; therefore children reach target rates of production (90 percent) much sooner. Furthermore, Gavruseva reports that similar error profiles are found across various acquisition contexts, including first language and specific language impairment. Given this similarity, the Maturational Hypothesis can be rejected in favor of Strong Continuity.

Taken together, the studies that explore functional architecture in cL2A have contributed to isolating the characteristics unique to this population on the one hand, and have highlighted the patterns specific to child L1A contexts. The next section provides an overview of the studies that have addressed morphological variability from a similar comparative perspective.

16.4 Morphological variability in child L1 and child L2 acquisition

Crucially related to the issue of full/partial access to UG is the long-standing debate on the nature of syntactic representation in L2 acquisition. In particular, with respect to the morphology–syntax interface, there is considerable disagreement over the relationship between overt verbal/nominal morphology (e.g. inflections, determiners) and the knowledge of abstract properties of L2 syntax. Discussions on variability in the use and omission of inflectional morphology in L2 production data are closely associated with generative theories of L1 acquisition.

Wexler's (1994, 1996, 1998) Optional Infinitive (OI) Model can be viewed as one of the most influential hypotheses that accounts for the acquisition patterns of verbal morphology in L1 acquisition. According to Wexler, young children acquiring non-null-subject languages (Dutch, English, German, Norwegian) go through a period in which they alternate between finite and non-finite verbs in declarative main clauses (e.g. *Daddy go* vs. *Daddy goes*) (see Boser, Lust, Santelmann and Whitman 1992; Haegeman 1995; Hoekstra and Hyams 1996; Phillips 1995; Poeppel and Wexler 1993; Rizzi 1993/94; Sano and Hyams 1994; Schütze and Wexler 1996). It should be noted that rates of optional infinitives are noticeably low in pro-drop languages (see research on Italian (Guasti 1993/94), Spanish (Grinstead 2000), Catalan (Torrens 1995)). Given the prevalence of optional infinitives in some child grammars, Wexler proposes a maturational account, according to which the early absence of obligatory tense marking is part of a biologically determined program for language acquisition. The important point here is that despite the use of infinitive forms at this stage, children's syntactic knowledge associated with finiteness is held to be intact. More specifically, children do not use verbs randomly in different syntactic positions but know the distribution of finite and non-finite verbs. In an analysis of French L1A data, Pierce (1992), for instance, observes that the negative element *pas* is correctly placed either to the right of finite verbs or the left of non-finite verbs. This suggests that French children know the syntactic distribution of finite and non-finite verbs and hence the properties of head movement.

Concurrent with the investigations of the OI stage in children, L2 researchers have also examined the properties of root infinitives in both adult and child L2 learners, as Wexler's proposal also has implications for L2 acquisition (Haznedar and Schwartz 1997; Lardiere 1998a, b; Prévost 1997). While a group of researchers argues that the optionality of tense marking may be characteristic of early L2 acquisition (Prévost 1997; Paradis, Le Corre and Genesee 1998), for others, child L2 grammars are not compatible with the characteristics of the OI stage (e.g. Haznedar and Schwartz 1997; Ionin and Wexler 2002; Geçkin and Haznedar 2008). Of the two major camps considering this phenomenon, some argue for a dissociation between overt morphology and abstract syntax in L2 acquisition (Haznedar and Schwartz 1997; Lardiere 1998a, b; Prévost and White 2000), where absence of surface morphology does not entail absence of the associated syntactic representation. For others, the dissociation in performance on L2 syntax and morphology reflects a syntactic deficit and thus suggests the unavailability of UG (e.g. Meisel 1997; Beck 1998a).

The issue of morphological variability can also be viewed from the perspective of similarities vs. differences between child L2 and child L1/adult L2 acquisition. While a group of researchers argues that morphological variability could be attributed to the same grammatical principles in both child L1 and child L2 acquisition (e.g. Gavruseva 2002, 2004), others maintain that child L2A and adult L2A are more similar and so stand apart from child L1 acquisition. As has been discussed in the previous section, given the well-known assumptions regarding the level of attainment in cL2A, Schwartz (1992, 2003, 2004) formulates this question in more specific terms: is cL2A more like child L1 acquisition or more like adult L2 acquisition? For Schwartz (2003), cL2A resembles child L1 acquisition in regard to the domain of inflectional morphology, whereas in the domain of syntax, cL2A is more like adult L2 acquisition (Schwartz 2003: 47). Following her proposal, Unsworth (2004) shows that for a syntactic phenomenon, namely object scrambling in L2 Dutch, L1-English children and adults go through similar developmental stages based on their production. In comprehension, however, discourse-pragmatic factors also influence both L1 and L2 children. On similar grounds, Blom and Polišenská (2005) provide evidence for similarities and differences between child L2 and adult L2 learners. In a study on the acquisition of morphosyntax by Moroccan Arabic and Turkish-speaking children and adults acquiring Dutch as an L2, they argue that even though both child and adult L2 learners go through an optional infinitive stage, child L2 learners are more accurate in verb placement, producing word order patterns similar to child L1 learners. As can be seen in this chapter, the issue of whether or not child L1, child L2 and adult L2 acquisition are guided by the same processes is one of the major themes addressed in recent cL2 acquisition research and is currently far from being settled. In addition to comparisons concerning cL1, cL2 and adult L2 learners with typical language development, recent work compares L2 children to monolingual age peers with specific language impairment (e.g. J. Paradis 2008; Marinis and Chondrogianni 2010). The next section explores how cL2 acquisition research informs atypical linguistic development.

16.5 Comparing typical and atypical child L2 acquisition

Recent years have witnessed significant interest in research showing parallels between cL2 learners and their monolingual/bilingual age peers with specific language impairment (SLI). It has been shown that difficulties with finiteness and tense marking are not confined to typically developing child L2 learners (e.g. Gavruseva and Lardiere 1996; Haznedar 2001; Ionin and Wexler 2002; Lakshmanan 1994; J. Paradis 2005, 2008), but are also found in the speech of children with SLI, both in L1 and L2 acquisition (e.g. Grüter 2005; Håkansson 2001; Paradis and Crago 2000, 2004; J. Paradis 2004). (For more recent and comprehensive discussions on parallels between typically developing (TD) monolingual children, TD L2 children and SLI children, the reader is referred to Paradis' (2010) keynote article in *Applied Psycholinguistics* and all the commentaries therein.) For instance, English-speaking children with SLI were found to experience serious problems with the suppliance of tense morphemes, suggesting that morphosyntax is one of the highly unstable linguistic domains in SLI (e.g. Cleave and Rice 1997; Conti-Ramsden 2003; Rice and Wexler 1996; Rice, Wexler and Cleave 1995; Rice 2004). Rice and Wexler (1996) argue that the development of finite verb morphology in SLI children shows characteristics of an *Extended* Optional Infinitive (EOI) stage, which persists until around age 9. To this end, the acquisition of tense morphology has been regarded as a clinical marker in identifying SLI children (e.g. Conti-Ramsden 2003; Rice and Wexler 1996).

In a series of studies, Paradis and her colleagues have examined the EOI profile in cL2 learners with typical development and those with SLI. Based on the production data from TD monolingual French children, monolingual French children with SLI and TD L1 English/L2 French learners, Paradis and Crago (2000) examine the use of tense morphology, temporal adverbials, agreement morphology and distributional contingencies associated with finiteness. Their findings reveal that (i) the cL2 learners and SLI children had similar accuracy rates of tense with auxiliary verbs, and (ii) both groups had lower accuracy rates than their typically developing monolingual peers. In a follow-up study, Paradis and Crago (2004) examined the development of nominal morphology in the same group of children and found that both cL2 learners and SLI children showed high and equal accuracy with most aspects of the determiner phrase. These results suggest that SLI children have more difficulties with verbal than nominal morphology, which is in fact consistent with the predictions of the OI stage (e.g. Bedore and Leonard 1998). Paradis (2005) also examined the production of tense and non-tense morphology in children with various L1 backgrounds. Similar to previous findings, she found that cL2 learners of English were less accurate with tense- than non-tense-marking morphemes and the majority of errors were omission errors rather than commission errors. Paradis (2005) also highlighted an uneven profile in the use of tense morphology, with 3sg-*s* and past tense marking being more affected than auxiliary and copula *be*. In comparison to a much higher accuracy rate of *be* (60.2 percent), the L2 children performed poorly with 3sg-*s* (16.6 percent), regular past tense -*ed* (22.6 percent) and irregular past tense forms (12.7 percent). This is in line with previous findings reported in typically developing child L2 acquisition research (e.g. Haznedar 2001; Ionin and Wexler 2002).

On similar grounds, Paradis, Rice, Crago and Marquis (2008) worked with three groups of English-learning children: cL2 learners of English, monolingual English-speaking children with SLI and monolingual TD English-speaking children. Analyzing tense-marking morpheme data from the Test of Early Grammatical Development (TEGI, Rice and Wexler 2001), Paradis *et al.* (2008) found similar abilities among all three groups regarding the use of *be* morphemes, and between the cL2 learners and the SLI children in identifying ungrammatical uses of *be* morphemes. Thus, they argued that cL2 learners' acquisition patterns were compatible with the characteristics of an EOI profile. Paradis *et al.* (2008) also showed that the same L2 children were less accurate than L1 children with SLI matched by age and MLU and L1 younger controls matched by MLU in the production of 3Psg -*s* and past tense. Based on the data from two cL2 learners of English (one was a late talker, the other had SLI), J. Paradis (2008) also reported that both children had higher scores with non-tense than tense morphemes and very low scores with tense morphology until the end of the first two years of exposure. Paradis notes that the EOI profile in the cL2 data continues after the initial stage of acquisition, and hence presents overlaps with monolingual children with SLI, whose difficulties with verbal morphology persist for more than two years. In J. Paradis (2008), it was only after three years of exposure that TD cL2 learners demonstrated relatively high scores with tense morphology. (For further discussion on years of exposure to an L2, see Marinis and Chondrogianni (2010).) Based on the data from thirty-eight TD Turkish child L2 learners of English and thirty-three monolingual English-speaking children, Marinis and Chondrogianni argued that four or more years of exposure to English was sufficient for the L2 children to score within norms for L1 children on the TEGI that assesses tense marking. This is important because on the one hand, cL2 learners with little exposure to L2 have difficulties with inflectional morphology at an early stage of development; on the other hand, their development shows striking similarities to the development of SLI children. As Marinis and Chondrogianni (2010) correctly point out, this similarity leads to difficulties in discriminating between TD cL2 learners and SLI cL2 learners in that the TD children could be misdiagnosed with SLI. It is therefore crucial to have a better understanding of the profile of TD cL2 learners. Further research into TD cL2 acquisition has great potential to shed light on issues related to typical and atypical linguistic development in children.

16.6 Conclusion

Recent studies within a generative framework attempt to pave the way for a discussion of the implications of child L2 acquisition for other related research areas, namely L1 acquisition, adult L2 acquisition and SLI, expanding the research program since the mid 1990s. In this overview, we showed how investigations in cL2 acquisition have informed and enriched the theories of both cL1 acquisition and adult L2 acquisition, while building on the discoveries in both fields.

On similar grounds, recent studies further our understanding of the theories of child L2 by expanding methodology that consists not only of naturalistic production data and basic elicitation methods but also includes some novel experimental techniques. For instance, Unsworth (2008b) has proposed a new proficiency measure, the Age-sensitive Composite Proficiency Score (ASCOPS), which takes into account the intrinsic differences between adult and child L2 learners. She correctly points out that careful comparisons of child L2 development with adult L2 development have the potential to contribute to our understanding of adult and child L2 acquisition. She also specifically highlights methodological and conceptual problems, noting that in order to evaluate differences and similarities between L2 adults and L2 children in their acquisition of a particular target language property, it is crucial to control variables such as L1, age and proficiency. To this end, in order to ensure that appropriate children are compared with appropriate adults, L2 proficiency should be carefully controlled for. Low-proficiency children should be compared with low-proficiency adults, high-proficiency children with high-proficiency adults. Overall, these views highlight the need for more careful comparisons of child L2 development with adult L2 development, which will bring with it a number of methodological and conceptual perspectives. For a detailed discussion on comparisons of child L2A with adult L2A as well as experimental methods in language acquisition research, the reader is referred to Blom and Unsworth (2010).

A noteworthy milestone in recent cL2A advances is the inclusion of more language combinations into the research program and the comparison of cL2 learners of varying proficiency levels. The range of topics in cL2 has expanded to include some new variables in the long-standing issues of L1 transfer/influence and access to UG. For example, more insights into L1 influence are to be gained if L2 children are subdivided into groups based on the properties of their L1 (e.g. +/−article, +/−pro-drop, +/−verb movement, etc.) or based on their age of exposure to L2. In fact, age of first exposure is emerging as an important variable in recent cL2 studies that have reported the effects of transfer. Age 8 appears to be a cut-off point between the younger and the older L2 children, a divide in learners that highlights age gradations within the critical period, with important implications for developmental stages and ultimate attainment. Future studies on cL2 acquisition will serve the field by pursuing these issues further through comparisons of acquisition contexts in typical and atypical contexts.

17

Incomplete L1 acquisition

Silvina Montrul

17.1 Introduction

An important factor in the nature and outcome of bilingual acquisition in a post-immigration context is the sociopolitical status of the languages in question. For speakers of minority languages, bilingualism is not a choice, but a question of survival. Very often in such cases, acquisition of the majority language as second language has detrimental effects on the linguistic development of the first language and results in subtractive bilingualism. This chapter discusses the syntactic competence of minority language speakers, their linguistic development from childhood to adulthood and the conditions under which the minority language can turn out to be incompletely acquired or undergo loss (attrition). I present the most recent research on minority language speakers and also discuss how this particular bilingual population speaks to classic theoretical debates about the nature of language and its acquisition, representation and use.

17.2 Minority languages

17.2.1 Minority language speakers

Another important factor in the study of bilingualism in an immigrant situation is when in life the languages are acquired. (See also Chapter 15, this volume.) Terms that are applied are early bilingualism, which refers to the acquisition of two languages before puberty. Late bilingualism, or adult L2 acquisition, typically occurs after puberty. Whether the two languages develop at the same time or one after the other is also important in early (child) bilingualism: simultaneous bilingual acquisition refers to the acquisition of two languages since birth, whereas sequential bilingualism in childhood is typically considered after at least age 3 to 4, when the basic foundations of the L1 are assumed to be in place (Rothweiler 2006).

However important, age of acquisition is not a sufficient condition to predict linguistic outcomes by adulthood: what I emphasize in this chapter is that the sociopolitical status of the two languages plays a fundamental role in the degree of acquisition and in the eventual linguistic dominance as well, particularly for younger bilinguals.

Very often, the dominant language in young bilinguals growing up in an immigrant situation tends to be the majority language. Majority languages are languages spoken by members of an ethnolinguistic majority group, who may or may not be members of a state, in the political sense. That is, majority languages typically (but not always) have official status and recognition, are used in the media, and are the language of instruction in education. Meeting these criteria are English in the UK, USA Canada, Australia and New Zealand, Spanish in Spain and in Spanish-speaking Latin America, and French in France. Minority languages, on the other hand, are the languages of ethnolinguistically minority groups. The language and culture may be a demographic minority or may be numerically significant in population but be considered a minority by virtue of its low social, cultural and political status due to factors surrounding immigration, colonization or marginalization. Examples of minority languages are indigenous languages in America (Inuktitut in Canada, Quechua in Peru) and in Australia (Dyirbal and Warlpiri), French in Canada, national languages in Europe (Irish in Ireland, Welsh in Wales, Basque in Spain, Catalan in northeastern Spain – despite in these examples meeting the status criteria) and immigrant languages all over the world. Some languages can in fact have dual status as minority or majority languages depending on where the speakers are located. For example, Spanish is a majority language in Spain and Spanish-speaking Latin America, but a minority language in the US. Similarly, Hindi is an official majority language in India, but a minority language in the UK and in the US.

When majority-language-speaking children learn a second language, either in a second language context (e.g. English-speaking children who learn French in Montreal) or in a foreign language context (children who learn English all over the world), their native language is rarely compromised or negatively affected by learning the second language (see Genesee 2004 for a detailed synopsis of this research). These children add another language to their linguistic repertoire by choice, and such a type of additive bilingualism has been shown to be socially, cognitively and academically beneficial to children.

Many studies have shown that the situation is radically different for children whose native language is a minority one (see e.g. Paradis, Genesee and Crago 2010). Children who speak a minority language at home must learn the majority language to succeed socially and academically when they start school, even if they attend bilingual schools. At a very young age children realize that the majority language is spoken by the wider speech community and is highly valued. Despite parental efforts to speak the minority language at home, studies have shown that children as young as 2 years old already prefer to speak the majority language (Döpke 1992; Lanza 2001). Unfortunately, for these children and families, gaining proficiency in the second language – the majority language – typically has detrimental effects on the first language – the minority language. Several studies have shown that after a period of balanced bilingualism, as proficiency in the second language increases, proficiency in the minority language decreases for minority-language-speaking children, either due to incomplete acquisition of the minority language, attrition of what they have acquired, shift in language dominance, or all of these factors (Jia and Aaronson 1999, 2003; Kohnert, Bates and Hernández 1999). As a result, minority language speakers growing up in subtractive bilingualism environments represent cases of unbalanced bilingualism, a fact already established by the seminal work of Lambert (1977).

17.2.2 Incomplete L1 acquisition vs. attrition

Before describing the typical linguistic profile of minority language speakers and the grammatical properties of the weaker language, it is important to define "incomplete" L1 acquisition. A distinction must be made between incomplete L1 acquisition and acquisition followed by attrition. Both are processes and outcomes of language loss at the individual level rather than at the society or group level, the latter particularly being the realm of sociolinguistic studies of language contact and change (Thomason 2001; see also Chapter 13, this volume). From an acquisition perspective, incomplete acquisition implies that some grammatical aspect of the language did not reach age-appropriate levels when the bilingual child was still in the process of acquiring the family language. Incomplete acquisition of the family language typically occurs in childhood, since adults are assumed to have reached their full linguistic development. For example, Anderson (1999) in a longitudinal study followed two Puerto Rican siblings for two years soon after their immigration to the US. The study focused on control of gender agreement in noun phrases, which typically developing monolingual Spanish-speaking children master with close to 100 percent accuracy by age 3 (see details in Montrul 2004a). The younger sibling did not show mastery of gender agreement with nouns at age 4;7 and the error rates increased dramatically two years later at age 6;5 after intense contact with English through daycare. Silva-Corvalán (2003) longitudinally investigated the linguistic development of seven Spanish–English bilingual children. Two of the children did not produce present subjunctive forms at ages 5;5 and 5;6, when more fluent bilingual children already do. Because many minority language speakers may not be exposed to a sufficient amount of language exemplifying the grammatical property in question, a linguistic property that emerges and is mastered during monolingual early language development can remain only partially mastered in these bilingual children, never fully reaching a nativelike level, as was the case for gender agreement in nouns with Anderson (1999).

Attrition, on the other hand, implies that a given property of the language reaches a stable endpoint of acquisition at a given age, but is subsequently lost, again due to reduced exposure to speakers of the language or written text in the language after the onset of schooling in the majority language. Attrition is much easier to document and measure in adulthood than in childhood, although the effects of attrition in adulthood seem to be minor as compared to the effects in childhood (Köpke 2007; Montrul 2008). In some reported cases, the effects of L1 attrition have been minimal: after more than thirty years of language disuse Schmid (2002) found that German Jewish immigrants living in the US and no longer using their German exhibited some transfer from English but very few actual morphosyntactic errors that could be attributed to L1 attrition. No adult undergoing attrition in a bilingual environment has been shown to regress in their language to such an extent as to forget how to conjugate verbs, ask questions, or produce and discriminate native sounds (Keijzer 2007).

But when attrition occurs in childhood, the effects are more evident. For example, unlike the younger sibling in Anderson's case study, the older sibling was producing gender agreement in nouns with 100 percent accuracy at age 6;7 but two years later, at age 8;5, she exhibited a 5.8 percent error rate. Nico and Bren, two of the children followed longitudinally by Silva-Corvalán (2003) from age 2;10, exhibited a much more reduced tense–aspect and mood system at age 5;6 than at ages 3;0–3;3.

It is also possible for incomplete acquisition and attrition to coexist in two different grammatical domains (e.g. gender agreement vs. subjunctive), or for incompletely acquired aspects of grammar to undergo further attrition. Suppose a child shows mastery of verbal morphology with 70 percent accuracy at time A and two years later, at time B, mastery drops to 40 percent. How can we tell if such decline is due to attrition, for example? The only way to tease apart incomplete acquisition and attrition and their potential coexistence is with longitudinal studies of children focusing on both early and late acquired structures in the two languages, as Merino (1983) did. Merino investigated production and comprehension abilities of Spanish and English in immigrant children attending an English-only school in San Francisco, focusing on early acquired structures (tense, agreement, gender) and late acquired structures (relative clauses, subjunctive, conditional) in both Spanish and English (where relevant). The cross-sectional part of the study tested children from kindergarten (age 5) to fifth grade (age 10), while the longitudinal part tested the kindergarten children two years later. Results showed progressive gains in English production and comprehension by age and grade level and progressive loss in Spanish abilities. The cross-sectional results revealed that the fifth graders had less knowledge of Spanish than the children in kindergarten. The longitudinal results further showed that the later acquired structures (relative clauses, subjunctive,

Table 17.1. *Linguistic characteristics of heritage speakers*

Generation	Possible language characteristics	
Bilingual individual	*Minority language*	*Majority language*
1st generation (parents)	monolingual	incipient L2 learner
2nd generation (children)	more or less dominant	more or less dominant
3rd generation (grandchildren)	some knowledge to none	dominant to monolingual

conditionals) suffered more severe decline than the early acquired structures (tense, agreement, gender), which was taken as evidence of attrition. There are many possibilities for why late acquired structures were more affected than the early acquired structure, including input frequency, complexity of the structures and linguistic vulnerability of the structures. Clearly, more studies of this type are needed. When we are dealing with stable but incompletely acquired systems in adults, it is hard to extrapolate the processes that may have led to the speaker's present state. Nonetheless, and for lack of a better term, I use the term "incomplete L1 acquisition" to refer to the ultimate non-targetlike attainment of adult minority language speakers, who, as we will see next, display a number of linguistic characteristics that set them apart from monolingual native speakers and fully bilingual speakers.

17.3 Profile of minority language speakers

Both linguistic and cultural identity within a group is a characterizing feature of minority language speakers (see Chapter 11, this volume). At the same time, the bilingual profiles of these speakers vary greatly, depending on a number of complex and interrelated factors. Consider the case of immigrants, or heritage speakers in the context of the US. Heritage speakers are individuals who emigrated in early childhood with their parents and other family members, or children of immigrants. While the parents are either monolingual or dominant in a variety of their language (e.g. Arabic, Bengali, Chinese, Hindi, Korean, Mandarin, Russian, Spanish, Tagalog, Urdu), the children grow up in a context where English and the immigrant language of the family are spoken.

Sociolinguists often relate generation of immigration and degree of bilingualism to acculturation patterns (Silva-Corvalán 1994). Table 17.1 illustrates some characteristics of heritage speakers based on generation and degree of bilingualism.

For example, first-generation immigrants immigrate to the host country as adults (after age 18). They are typically monolingual speakers of their minority (heritage) language, and most of them learn (imperfectly) the majority language as a second language late in life. Command of the minority language is strong in this immigrant group, although there can be some attrition after more than ten years where exposure to the majority language is intense (Schmid and Köpke 2004).

The children of the first generation are the second generation immigrants. This group may include the children of first-generation immigrants born in the host country to at least one first-generation parent. Second generation also refers to immigrant children who come to the host country before the age of 5 (prior to schooling). In terms of types of bilingual profile, the second-generation group may include (i) simultaneous bilinguals, those exposed to the minority and the majority language before the age of 5; (ii) sequential bilinguals, those exposed to the minority language at home until age 4 or 5, and to the majority language once they start pre-school as well as (iii) late child bilinguals or L2 learners, children monolingual in the minority language, who received some primary schooling in their home country and immigrated after age 8.

It is in the second generation when language shift in the home typically occurs, due to the fact that children are schooled in the majority language and have a strong desire to fit in with the new society, even in cases where some heritage language schooling is available, as in community or church schools common among East Asian immigrants in North America (see Kondo-Brown 2006). With language shift, there are concomitant changes in the bilingual balance of second-generation children until adulthood. Similar shifts and language dominance changes are also attested in children who speak non-immigrant minority languages, such as Inuit children in Arctic Quebec in Canada (Allen, Crago and Presco 2006), or Irish in Ireland (Ó'Giollagáin and Ó'Curnáin 2009). As children begin to use the majority language more than the home language, the heritage language may start to lag behind in development. Many of these children are either monolingual or dominant in the heritage language in early childhood, but as bilingualism progresses and changes during primary school, they can go through a period of balance in the two languages (Kohnert and Bates 2002) and eventually become dominant in the majority language (Kohnert, Bates and Hernández 1999). Typically, when they reach adolescence, minority language speakers are already dominant in the majority language, and by the time they are adults the majority language is both stronger and dominant in overall proficiency in all domains of use. (The situation depicted in Table 17.1 for non-first-generation immigrants will depend on various factors including continued migration of speakers into a given community; see e.g. Hamid 2011 on language maintenance among Bangladeshis in the UK.)

Due to such rapid shift, which is common even in cases of continuous immigration and influx of new immigrants in already established communities as in the US, by the third generation minority language speakers are native speakers of the majority language. Some may have some command of the minority language, while most do not. By the fourth and subsequent generations, the language is no longer used in the family; this includes

Spanish in the US (Valdés, Fishman, Chávez and Pérez 2006). When exposure to and use of the majority language intensifies in immigrant families, it typically brings about reduced exposure to and use of the minority language. A similar pattern of loss occurs in cases of non-immigrant minority languages, such as Irish in Ireland where, despite government and education efforts to protect Irish, there are not enough monolingual native speakers of Irish, and the language is currently not being transmitted completely to the next generation (Ó'Giollagáin and Ó'Curnáin 2009).

One common characteristic of heritage language speakers is that they are exposed to the family language since birth, either exclusively or in conjunction with the majority language. Acquisition of the minority language occurs in a naturalistic environment, through the aural medium. Depending on the language, the culture and socioeconomic status of the family, minority language children may also be exposed to printed language and written registers. However, the vast majority of immigrant children are not, especially when the languages spoken have different scripts from the majority language (e.g. do not use the Roman alphabet) (Moag 1995; Polinsky and Kagan 2007) or are not written (e.g. the Southeast Asian language Hmong). In general, adult heritage speakers' aural comprehension skills are better than their oral production and written skills. It is typical in these families for parents to speak the family language to the children but for the children to respond in English or the majority language when speaking to their parents (Montrul 2011a), and that is why their oral production skills may not be as strong as their auditory comprehension. Thus many children are familiar with the spoken colloquial variety and have little to no experience with formal or written registers (again, depending on the language; Rothman 2007; Albirini, Benmamoun and Saddah 2011). Because communication in the minority language is typically limited to interactions with parents and some older relatives, and to a much lesser extent with siblings and friends, restricted use of the language in a variety of social and academic contexts leads to register contraction, and along with this comes lack of acquisition of vocabulary and grammatical structures used in more formal registers. As a result, the language of these speakers is very different from the language of the parents and of peers raised in their home countries, in the case of immigrants. They exhibit smaller vocabularies in the language, less syntactic variety and high error rates in use (Polinsky 2006).

17.4 The weaker language in minority language speakers

Given these profiles of minority language speakers, an important question is what the structural characteristics of their weaker language are. Recent linguistic, psycholinguistic, sociolinguistic and pedagogical research has identified a series of areas affected in minority or heritage language grammars. These include vocabulary, morphosyntax (regular and inherent case, verbal and nominal agreement, tense, aspect, mood), pronominal reference, article semantics, word order, relative clauses and conjunctions, among many others.

17.4.1 Phonetics and phonology

Although the language of heritage speakers is usually perceived as having non-native and non-standard features, pronunciation is the linguistic domain most spared from this impression. In comparison to areas of morphosyntax, heritage speakers are typically described as having good phonology, especially when they are compared to adult L2 learners of similar morphosyntactic proficiency. For example, Au, Knightly, Jun and Oh (2002) and Oh, Jun, Knightly and Au (2003) studied the phonetic perception and production abilities of Korean and Spanish heritage speakers with very low productive proficiency in the languages (referred to as *overhearers*). Tests of pronunciation and voice onset time (VOT) measurements for Spanish voiceless stops (labial /p/, dental /t/, velar /k/) and for the dental-alveolar Korean stops (aspirated /t^h/, plain /t/, tense and /t'/) revealed that the heritage speakers were significantly more nativelike than comparison groups of second language learners who had not been exposed to Korean or Spanish since childhood. Nonetheless, the heritage speakers also displayed some non-native phonological features. Yeni-Komshian, Flege and Liu (2000) report measurable non-native effects in pronunciation of Korean as a heritage language. And Godson (2004) found that the vowel quality of Western Armenian heritage speakers showed some transfer from English in two of five Western Armenian vowels, and the quality of other vowels was also different from the quality of these vowels for monolingual and fluent bilingual Western Armenian speakers. To date, the pronunciation of heritage speakers remains an understudied area. The few available studies suggest that there are measurable systematic differences between monolinguals and heritage speakers worth investigating, especially to address theoretical debates on the role of early input for phonological abilities in bilinguals.

17.4.2 Vocabulary

Heritage language speakers also have marked gaps in their vocabulary and find it difficult to retrieve words they do not use very frequently. Polinsky (2005) investigated knowledge of word classes in Russian heritage speakers of very low proficiency. She found that heritage speakers had better command of verbs (as measured in word recognition and translation accuracy) than of nouns and adjectives. These findings are not surprising, given the fact that in language attrition situations nouns are more frequently used in code-switching and borrowings than verbs and adjectives. Note, too, that anomia is more common for aphasics than problems with retrieval of verbs. Furthermore, as Polinsky explains, verbs are semantically more dense and heavier than nouns (containing both lexical and structural information), and hence more costly for the grammar to lose. Polinsky (1997, 2007) found that vocabulary proficiency correlated positively with structural accuracy in Russian heritage speakers: those speakers who knew more basic words from a list of 200 items exhibited better control of agreement, case markers and subordination in spontaneous speech. The relationship between morphosyntax and the lexicon needs to be explored more closely, especially if, as several authors suggested, it has pedagogical and assessment potential for both second language learners and heritage language learners (Fairclough 2008; Lam, Pérez-Leroux and Ramírez 2003).

17.4.3 Morphosyntax

The linguistic area most noticeably affected in heritage language grammars is inflectional morphology. Heritage speakers of languages with overt gender, number and case marking on nouns produce a significant number of errors as compared to native speakers or even their own parents. For example, Russian has a three-way gender system (masculine, feminine, neuter) and Spanish has a two-way system (masculine, feminine). Although monolingual Russian- and Spanish-speaking children control gender marking by age 4 with almost 100 percent accuracy (with the exception of irregular, less frequent forms), Polinsky (2008a) and Montrul, Foote and Perpiñán (2008) have independently shown that heritage speakers display very high error rates with gender marking (ranging from 5 percent to 25 percent). In Russian, neuter gender and feminine are most affected. Indeed, Polinsky found that while higher-proficiency Russian heritage speakers still displayed a three-way gender system, lower-proficiency speakers had a two-way distinction, consisting of only masculine and feminine, and no neuter. Similarly, Montrul et al. (2008) found that when Spanish heritage speakers made gender errors, these were most frequent with feminine nouns and with nouns with non-canonical or non-transparent word endings. If masculine gender is considered the default in Spanish and feminine is the marked form, clearly Spanish heritage language grammars also show simplification of marked forms and retention of the default. Case marking is another candidate for attrition and imperfect mastery in heritage language grammars. Monolingual adult Russian has a six-way distinction in nouns: nominative, accusative, dative, instrumental, oblique and genitive. According to Polinsky (2006, 2008b), the case system is severely reduced from six to only two cases – nominative and accusative – in heritage speakers of Russian. Case omission patterns have also been reported in Korean by Song, O'Grady, Choo and Lee (1997). Although nominative and accusative case markers are typically dropped in spoken Korean, monolingual children and adults gain full control of the case system, including the discourse-pragmatic conditions under which case markers can be dropped or retained. Song et al. found that while 5- to 8-year-old monolingual Korean children were 86 percent accurate at comprehending

OVS sentences in Korean with nominative and accusative case markers, 5- to 8-year-old Korean heritage speakers performed at less than 34 percent accuracy. They tended to interpret OVS sentences as SOV sentences, ignoring the case markers. As for case marking in Spanish, Montrul and Bowles (2009) showed that adult Spanish heritage speakers omit the dative preposition *a* "to" (known as *Differential Object Marking* or DOM) with dative experiencer subjects with *gustar*-type verbs (**Juan le gusta la música* instead of *A Juan le gusta la música* "Juan likes music"), and they omit the same preposition when it appears with animate direct objects (**Juan vio María* instead of *Juan vio a María* "Juan saw Maria"). Second language learners of Spanish in a non-immigrant context have been shown to have similar patterns of incomplete acquisition with DOM in Spanish and with dative experiencers (Bowles and Montrul 2009; Guijarro-Fuentes and Marinis 2007; Montrul 1998).

The verbal domain exhibits similar morphological problems in heritage language speakers, especially with subject–verb agreement and with tense paradigms. Heritage speakers of Russian and Spanish seem to control regular forms of the present and past tenses but confuse aspectual distinctions between perfective and imperfective forms (Polinsky 2006; Silva-Corvalán 1994, respectively). The subjunctive mood (in both present and past) is poorly controlled by Spanish heritage speakers in production and in comprehension (Montrul 2007; Silva-Corvalán 1994), and so is the conditional (Silva-Corvalán 1994). These types of errors are not common in speakers who have full control of their native language, even when matched for education and social class.

17.4.4 Syntax

The erosion of case and agreement morphology characteristic of many heritage language grammars has consequences for basic clause structure and pronominal reference. In languages with flexible word order, case markers allow the speaker and hearer to keep track of the participants (and grammatical relations). As a result, Russian and Spanish heritage speakers tend to rely on SVO word order, while Korean speakers prefer SOV order (Song *et al.* 1997). Montrul (2010) found that while Spanish heritage speakers accepted and comprehended SVO sentences at more than 90 percent accuracy, they were much less accurate with sentences with preverbal objects.

A typical consequence of the loss of agreement and more rigid word order relates to the licensing of subjects, especially in null subject languages such as Russian, Spanish and Italian. In these languages, both null and overt pronouns are possible grammatically because the person and number information is recoverable from the agreement morphology. However, the distribution of null and overt subjects is licensed by discourse-pragmatic factors, such as topic continuation, topic shift, or switch reference, as amply discussed by Sorace and collaborators for Italian in the context of L1 attrition and advanced stages of L2 acquisition.

Sorace (2000a) observed that near-native speakers of Italian produced more overt subjects in Italian than native speakers, in contexts that pragmatically require null subjects. Sorace and Filiaci (2006), and later Belletti, Bennati and Sorace (2007), confirmed similar results in an interpretation task in which near-natives showed a clear overextension of the scope of overt subject pronouns, which led to the production and acceptance of these pronouns in the presence of a topical antecedent, as in (1b) and (2b), respectively (examples from Belletti et al. 2007).

(1) a. Perchè Giovanna non è venuta?
        "Why didn't Giovanna come?"
     b. Perchè **lei** non ha trovato un taxi.
     c. Perchè ___ non ha trovato un taxi.
        "Because she couldn't find a taxi"

(2) a. La vecchietta saluta la ragazza quando *pro* $_{i/?j}$ attraversa la strada.
     b. La vecchietta$_i$ saluta la ragazza quando lei$_i$ attraversa la strada.
        "The old woman greets the girl when ø/she crosses the road."

Sorace (2000a, b) and Belletti et al. (2007) did not find overextensions of null subjects to overt subject contexts in these studies. Sorace claims that the null/overt pronoun asymmetry is not caused by influence of the dominant language (a non-pro-drop language if it is English), but rather it is related to the processing and grammatical integration of syntax and discourse in a bilingual situation. Similar asymmetries – problems with overt subjects but not with null subjects – were observed in earlier studies of the second language acquisition of Spanish by Liceras (1988). In first language attrition and child bilingualism, Silva-Corvalán (1994) was among the first to notice this phenomenon with Spanish heritage speakers and first-generation immigrants. Since then other studies have found that Spanish as well as Russian heritage speakers tend to overuse overt subjects in topic shift and switch reference contexts where a null subject would be pragmatically more appropriate (Montrul 2004b; Polinsky 2006).

Another vulnerable domain in heritage language grammars is long-distance dependencies, including pronominal reference within and beyond the sentence, as with reflexive pronouns (anaphors like English *himself*). Korean has three reflexives – *caki*, *casin* and *caki-casin* – which differ in their distribution and interpretation. *Caki* is subject oriented and prefers long-distance antecedents (beyond the clause). *Caki-casin* requires a local antecedent (within the clause). *Casin* can take local or long-distance antecedents. In English, reflexive pronouns (*himself/herself*) are typically subject oriented and take local antecedents (i.e. in *Paul said that Peter hurt himself*, *himself* refers to *Peter*, the subject of its own clause, but in a language like Korean it could refer to *Paul*, the subject of the more distant main clause). Kim, Montrul and Yoon (2009) found that long-distance preferences were affected in adult Korean heritage speakers. Heritage speakers preferred local binding for *caki* and seemed to treat *casin* and *caki-casin* indistinguishably, as if they had a two-anaphor system. These speakers' interpretations differed sharply from those of monolingual Korean speakers. Other problems with reflexive pronouns are reported by Polinsky and Kagan (2007) in Russian heritage speakers.

Furthermore, heritage speakers have been shown to have problems with more complex structures, like relative clauses. Polinsky (2008c) tested comprehension of subject and object relative clauses in Russian heritage speakers, and so did O'Grady, Lee and Choo (2001). They both found that heritage speakers had significant difficulty with object relative clauses (*The cat that the dog is chasing*) as opposed to subject relative clauses (*The dog that is chasing the cat*), which may suggest that heritage speakers do not have a syntactic representation for object relative clauses. Thus, in terms of relativization, there is an advantage for subjects as opposed to objects in heritage language grammars, as in many languages of the world (e.g. Malagasy).

To summarize, under reduced input conditions, minority language speakers develop some core aspects of their family language but their grammatical systems show a marked tendency toward simplification and overregularization of complex morphological patterns and stricter word order. Additionally, heritage language speakers also possess incomplete knowledge of forms of address and other pragmatic elements that interact with discourse and sociolinguistic conventions. The question that arises is what internal factors drive these processes, and an obvious suspect is structural transfer from the dominant language (see Chapter 5, this volume).

It is possible that the shape of the incompletely acquired adult grammars described above may be triggered by transfer from English, the dominant language in most of the empirical studies on immigrant communities conducted to date (Albirini, Benmamoun and Saddah 2011; Cuza and Frank 2011; Keating, VanPatten and Jegerski 2011; Kim *et al.* 2009; Montrul 2002; Montrul and Bowles 2009; Montrul *et al.* 2008; Montrul, Bhatt and Bhatia 2012; O'Grady, Kwak, Lee and Lee 2011; Polinsky 2006, 2008b, c; Rothman 2007; Silva-Corvalán 1994; Zapata, Sánchez and Toribio 2005). After all, English has strict SVO order and does not have overt case markers, null subjects, subjunctive morphology, gender or different types of reflexive pronouns. Ideally, studies of the same heritage language with different contact languages should be undertaken to investigate the extent to which transfer from the dominant language influences the degree of incomplete acquisition found in heritage language grammars. A study of this sort is Kim (2007), who investigated the local and long-distance properties of the three Korean reflexives *caki*, *casin* and *caki-casin* in Korean heritage speakers residing in the US (dominant language English) and Korean heritage speakers residing in China (dominant language Mandarin). Although Korean and Chinese have long-distance binding while English does not, Kim found that the Korean heritage speakers preferred more local than long-distance binding regardless of contact language. Kim's results indicate that the contact language is not always the main cause behind the preferences observed with binding.

However, a recent study by Montrul and Ionin (2012) on the semantic interpretation of definite articles with plural noun phrases supports the role of transfer in heritage language grammars. In both Spanish and English, the syntactic and semantic distribution of definite and indefinite articles is largely similar, but the two languages differ in the expression and interpretation of plural noun phrases. For example, Spanish plural noun phrases with definite articles can express generic reference (*Los elefantes tienen colmillos de marfil* "Elephants have ivory tusks") or specific reference (*Los elefantes de este zoológico son marrones* "The elephants in this zoo are brown"). English plurals with definite articles can only have specific reference (the latter sentence), while generic reference is expressed with bare plural noun phrases (the former sentence). Montrul and Ionin found that the Spanish heritage speakers incorrectly accepted bare plural subjects with generic reference in Spanish (**Cebras tienen rayas* "Zebras have stripes") and interpreted definite articles as having specific rather than generic reference, as in English.

Although Kim's (2007) study presents evidence for simplification and Montrul and Ionin's (2012) provide solid evidence for transfer, a given phenomenon can also be due to both transfer and simplification. Montrul and Bowles (2009) demonstrated Spanish heritage speakers' attrition of differential object marking (DOM) (the preposition *a*) with animate and specific direct objects. According to the diachronic evolution of Spanish, the emergence of DOM was an innovation from Latin not shared by other Romance languages (except Romanian). Even though this marker is currently extending from animate to inanimate objects in some Spanish-speaking regions, heritage speakers of Spanish omit this preposition very often in production and accept ungrammatical sentences in grammaticality judgment tasks, as in **María besó el niño* vs. *María besó a el niño* "Maria kissed the boy." Since English does not overtly mark animate direct objects, this apparent simplification in Spanish heritage grammars seems to be driven by transfer.

There is also evidence that the observed incomplete acquisition in adulthood may be due to attrition throughout childhood and not to transfer. Polinsky (2011) compared comprehension of object and subject relative clauses in child and adult Russian heritage speakers. Unlike in English, relative clauses in Russian exhibit word order differences (SV vs. VS in object relatives and OV vs. VO is subject relatives), regulated by information structure (topic vs. contrastive focus). The neutral and more frequent order is VS and VO. Polinsky predicted that heritage speakers who are dominant in English may follow the English word order for Russian relative clauses (i.e. SV and VO). However, this prediction was not borne out. While the child heritage speakers performed at ceiling with both subject and object relative clauses, the adults exhibited very poor performance on object relative clauses, regardless of word order. Not only does this study demonstrate indirectly that heritage language systems undergo attrition and restructuring throughout the lifespan, but it also suggests that dominant language transfer does not operate across the board.

Another interesting perspective on this issue is offered by Rothman (2007) and Pires and Rothman (2009), who studied adult heritage speakers of Brazilian and European Portuguese. The focus of the two studies was knowledge of inflected infinitives. They found that while European Portuguese heritage speakers raised and schooled in the US had very good command of inflected infinitives as compared with a control group of European Portuguese native speakers, the Brazilian heritage speakers had very poor knowledge of inflected infinitives. Rothman (2007) and Pires and Rothman (2009) assumed that the Brazilian and European heritage speakers were comparable in all regards and thus questioned the source of the different patterns of incomplete acquisition. Clearly, transfer from English cannot be an explanation in this case. The explanation, instead, has to do with the nature of input as it relates to dialectal variation. While inflected infinitives are frequent in both standard and colloquial European Portuguese and in standard Brazilian Portuguese (which resembles European Portuguese), they are not part of colloquial Brazilian Portuguese. Since most heritage speakers in the US rarely receive literacy instruction in Brazilian Portuguese and are exposed to the colloquial variety at home, it seems that inflected infinitives are not in the input that Brazilian Portuguese heritage speakers receive. By contrast, European Portuguese heritage speakers are exposed to inflected infinitives in their spoken variety and thus develop knowledge of these verbal forms. Brazilian native speakers learn inflected infinitives at school.

In short, although transfer from the majority language could be at play in many cases, it is not the only factor that may lead to incomplete acquisition: simplification and attrition without transfer, and incomplete acquisition due to properties of the input (e.g. restricted to oral registers and limited literacy) are also possible. Overall, the specific factors that independently or collectively contribute to the degree of simplification and structural convergence observed in heritage language grammars at different levels of structural analysis is a matter for further investigation.

17.5 Theoretical issues in the study of incomplete L1 acquisition

The linguistic ability of minority language speakers raises several questions about the nature of language, the necessary ingredients for successful L1 acquisition and the conditions under which a native language acquired in childhood can undergo attrition. Successful language learning and maintenance in monolingual children not only involve the operation of Universal Grammar but also optimal input (in quantity and quality) at a very early age, and continuous use of the language in a variety of meaningful contexts (see

Chapter 15, this volume). Minority language speakers receive early input at home in a naturalistic setting, but exposure to optimal input and uses of the language gradually decrease after a certain age in childhood. Montrul (2008) shows how the critical period hypothesis is also relevant for attrition, since the earlier in childhood there is reduction in input, the more attrited or undeveloped the language ends up. I now consider the role of literacy, age effects and child–adult comparisons.

17.5.1 Literacy and later language development

The typical age when severe reduction in input and use of the language occurs in minority-language-speaking children coincides with schooling, especially if education is delivered exclusively in the majority language, as is common in the US. (Even though some schools may offer some type of bilingual programs, these are not available for all minority language children and for all minority languages.) We know that the essence of native speaker competence is developed by the time children enter school; native command of oral language is the foundation for literacy (Nippold 2004). We also know that significant language learning occurs during the school-age period, including expansion of vocabulary, acquisition of complex syntax, semantics and pragmatics and register variation (Berman 2004, 2009; Oller and Jarmulowicz 2009). Pires and Rothman (2009) demonstrate that despite marked differences between vernacular and standard dialects of Portuguese, the fact that all educated learners of a particular language come to know properties of the standard dialect which are absent from their colloquial dialect must mean that literacy in the standard dialect contributes to grammatical knowledge.

Therefore, when one looks at the situation of immigrant minority languages in North America, it is easy to conclude that absence of schooling in the minority language contributes significantly to the demise of language skills in minority-language-speaking children. Merino (1983) conducted a cross-sectional and longitudinal study of the Spanish and English comprehension and production abilities of Mexican immigrant children attending an English-only school in the San Francisco area. As mentioned earlier, the study looked at early acquired and late acquired grammatical phenomena in the two languages. Merino observed that as English language abilities increased from kindergarten (5- to 6-year-olds) to fifth grade (9- to 10-year-olds), Spanish language ability declined: fifth graders had the Spanish language abilities of first graders, and the most affected areas were production of late acquired structures (relative clauses, subjunctive and conditional). A similar fate for the minority language after the onset of schooling in the majority language is reported by Wright, Taylor and Macarthur (2000), who followed sixty-two Inuit children from Northern Quebec from kindergarten. While half of the children continued their education in the minority language (Inuktitut), the other half went to English schools or French schools.

Results of a battery of tests in the three languages (completed at the beginning and end of each academic year) showed that the children who continued education in Inuktitut showed sustained growth and development in their native language, whereas the children receiving schooling in French or English exhibited significant native language stagnation, slow development and even decline in Inuktitut.

There is evidence that while schooling in the minority language is a necessary condition, it is not a sufficient condition for minority language growth and maintenance. Evidence for this comes from national languages in Europe, such as Irish and Welsh, which coexist with English as official languages of Ireland and Wales. Despite government efforts to provide monolingual or bilingual education in these minority languages and in English, recent research shows that not all children become highly competent in Irish or Welsh. For Welsh, Mueller-Gathercole and Thomas (2009) found that all children develop high ability in English (the majority language) regardless of language background and language of schooling, whereas linguistic ability in Welsh was correlated with the amount of input in Welsh at home and at school. They even found that maintenance of Welsh in adulthood was contingent upon continuous exposure to Welsh. The situation of the Irish language is even more dire. Harris (2008) documents significant decline from 1987 to 2002 in the Irish-speaking abilities of children receiving some instruction through the Irish medium in ordinary schools; children who receive full immersion in Irish perform much better. A reason for this decline is that there are very few speakers of Irish and even fewer monolingual speakers even in the Irish-speaking areas, and despite receiving instruction in Irish at school, children prefer to use English with each other and outside school.

17.5.2 Age effects versus experience

Understanding the linguistic abilities of minority language speakers is very relevant for second language acquisition, for both theoretical and pedagogical reasons. Today it is typical in the US to see many heritage speakers taking L2 classes, especially at universities; this holds especially for East Asian Languages, Russian, Spanish and the less commonly taught foreign languages (Arabic, Farsi, Hindi, Modern Greek and Turkish). In certain political circles, heritage language learners represent a valuable national resource, as they can potentially fulfill the need for advanced and competent speakers of critical languages (Campbell and Rosenthal 2000). But language teachers and program directors recognize that heritage language learners are a different breed of learner whose partial knowledge of the language presents a unique set of challenges to language teaching practices. We therefore need to understand how and how fast minority language speakers can learn their heritage language in a classroom setting, and whether it is realistic to expect them to come to resemble educated native speakers.

Pedagogical practices must be informed by a deep understanding of what L2 learners and heritage speakers have or do not have in common. On the one hand, heritage language learners and L2 learners differ in the age of acquisition of the target language, the type of exposure (input) and the context of acquisition (naturalistic vs. instructed). By some theoretical accounts, the learning mechanisms deployed in childhood and adulthood are very different, and therefore the outcome of L1 and L2 acquisition is also different (see the recent issue of *Studies in Second Language Acquisition* 2009 on the *Fundamental Difference Hypothesis* and also Chapters 6 and 15, this volume). In general, adult heritage speakers have good or better aural comprehension skills than oral production and written skills. By contrast, L2 learners typically have better written skills than oral skills, by virtue of having learned the language primarily in a formal setting with limited opportunity for interaction with native speakers. Their language learning experience may play a role in how they process and learn the language further in the classroom (Bowles 2011; Montrul 2011a).

But heritage speakers also share some characteristics with L2 learners, including non-native attainment and transfer errors from the dominant language (Montrul 2008). In fact, recent research has revealed that many of the problem areas typical of second language learners, such as inflectional morphology, for example, seem to be problem areas for heritage speakers as well (Au *et al.* 2002; Montrul 2011a). Given these findings, it is crucial to carry out systematic comparisons of L2 learners and heritage speakers in order to understand the linguistic ability of the two types of learners, as well as areas of differences and similarities. What has occupied the emerging field of heritage language education so far has been what to teach and how to best organize programs that address the linguistic and affective needs of the growing and changing (as new language groups immigrate) heritage language speaker population (Brinton, Kagan and Bauckus 2008). Therefore, pinpointing specific areas of linguistic knowledge in which the heritage language speakers and L2 learners may differ is an important first step in informing any type of classroom-based instructional intervention, materials development or language program. For second language acquisition, the study of heritage language learners can also inform classic theoretical debates on the nature of linguistic knowledge as a function of age and experience in L2 learners. Studies that have addressed these questions are Häkansson (1995), Montrul *et al.* (2008), Montrul (2010, 2011a, b), Montrul and Ionin (2010), Montrul and Perpiñán (2011). Some of these studies have found no differences between L2 learners and heritage speakers (Montrul and Ionin 2010), while others have reported differences related to language experience: Montrul (2010) found that Spanish heritage speakers were more nativelike than proficiency-matched L2 learners on clitic left dislocations in an untimed grammaticality judgment task and a speeded online comprehension task, probably because clitic left dislocations are more frequent in spoken than in written Spanish. Montrul (2011a) showed that L2 learners make more morphological errors with gender agreement, tense, aspect and mood morphology and with differential object marking in oral than in written tasks, whereas heritage speakers show the opposite pattern: more errors in written than in oral tasks. So far, results have not revealed significant effects of age of acquisition, or linguistic advantages for heritage speakers who were exposed to the target language much earlier over L2 learners with exposure to the language after puberty. But these are avenues of investigation worth exploring in future research.

Although comparing L2 learners and minority language speakers with different ages of onset of bilingualism can only indirectly shed light on age effects in bilingual acquisition, studies of attrition may yield better results. Montrul (2008, 2011b) and Bylund (2009) have independently concluded that there are age effects and even maturational constraints in L1 attrition in a bilingual situation, with an estimated cut-off point of susceptibility to attrition between the ages of 8 and 10 for Montrul or 10 and 12 for Bylund. That is, the earlier in life there is reduction in input to one of the languages and increased exposure to the other language, the more attrition (or incomplete acquisition) there will be. After a careful review of existing literature, Montrul (2008) concludes that minority language speakers who are simultaneous bilinguals tend to exhibit more attrition in the minority language than sequential bilingual children (who have more hours of exposure to the minority language in childhood than simultaneous bilinguals whose daily linguistic input is always divided between two languages). However, sequential bilingual children are more prone to attrition than postpuberty L2 learners and adults. Internationally adopted children adopted in infancy, who experience interrupted input in their native language altogether, are the most vulnerable to total attrition in childhood (Montrul 2011b). Although internationally adopted children become highly competent L2 users, they quickly lose their L1. Language loss occurs more rapidly, within the first year after adoption, in infants than in toddlers, and more rapidly in toddlers than in older children (Gindis 1999; Glennen 2005). Some studies have even reported almost complete language loss in adults who were adopted as children between the ages of 3 and 10 years old (Pallier *et al.* 2003; Ventureyra 2005). The hypothesis of age effects in L1 attrition remains to be tested empirically (Bylund 2009; Hyltenstam, Bylund, Abrahamsson and Park 2009; Montrul 2008), with cross-sectional studies that include adult minority-language-speaking bilinguals with different ages of onset of bilingualism ranging from childhood to adulthood and reduced exposure to the minority language.

17.5.3 Child–adult comparison: attrition vs. incomplete acquisition

An admittedly thorny problem in describing the outcome of minority language acquisition is whether the grammatical systems observed in adults are the result of incomplete acquisition or attrition in childhood. Although longitudinal studies are ideal to tease apart these two possibilities, another way to address these questions is by comparing child and adult heritage speakers. Studies of this sort are, however, very scarce, and the two available are small-scale in nature. Polinsky (2008b) offers a description of the narrative skills and grammatical accuracy of a 9-year-old Russian heritage speaker who arrived in the US at age 5 and one 25-year-old Russian heritage speaker who moved to the US in childhood as well. Polinsky found that the Russian of the adult heritage speaker was significantly more reduced in case marking, tense and aspect than the child's. A similar finding is reported in Polinsky's (2011) study of child and adult Russian native speakers and Russian heritage speakers (more than twenty subjects per group). Polinsky found that the adult heritage speakers were significantly less targetlike than the child heritage speakers and the two monolingual control groups (child and adult), in their aural interpretation of subject and object relative clauses. She concludes from these studies that incomplete acquisition in adults is not only due to incomplete acquisition of some aspects of the grammar but also to attrition.

Other comparisons that may shed more light on these and other theoretical issues worth pursuing in future research are between minority language speakers and monolingual children, as well as minority language children and simultaneous bilingual children who had more opportunity to receive exposure and use the two languages more equally throughout their lifespan.

17.6 Conclusion

This chapter has shown that compared to L1 acquisition in a monolingual environment and adult L2 acquisition, the linguistic development of minority language speakers is a very complex phenomenon, where linguistic and psycholinguistic, in addition to affective and sociolinguistic factors (which we were unable to cover more extensively in this chapter, but see Chapter 13, this volume), are intimately connected and difficult to tease apart. Many adult minority language speakers display stable grammars that differ in significant ways from the grammars of fluent speakers of the language, especially in the degree of simplification at different levels of linguistic analysis. The study of minority language speakers raises crucial questions about the nature of native speaker competence and the conditions under which it develops or not, opening several avenues of investigation for further research.

18

Third language acquisition

Jason Rothman, Jennifer Cabrelli Amaro and Kees de Bot

18.1 General introduction: L3

Like any instance of language acquisition, the acquisition of a third (L3) or more (Ln) language can be studied from various linguistic traditions or paradigms. Although each paradigm has its own set of specific questions, one thread transcending paradigmatic lines is a common empirical emphasis on determining how language acquisition affects the process of L3/Ln acquisition (i.e. transfer). The importance of determining this is relevant in different ways depending on the aims of that paradigm, ranging from the more complete understanding of mental linguistic representation, to informing cognitive models of language acquisition and linguistic processing, understanding the unique sociolinguistic variables that arise in multilingualism, determining whether L3 learning is distinct and how L3-specific pedagogical practices can be facilitated. Given the recurrent theme of transfer, we dedicate considerable portions of each subsection to this underlying topic.

In the past two decades in particular, there has been a sharp increase in rigorous L3/Ln acquisition studies. One might reasonably ask why in the first place there should be a differentiation between L2 and other subsequent language acquisition in adulthood. In truth, many researchers do not make this important distinction, including for L3/Ln learners in so-called L2 populations. Implicitly, such a practice assigns the label L2 to cover any instance of non-primary adult language acquisition (see De Angelis 2007 for discussion). Additionally, even among researchers who study multilingualism, the parameters used to determine what constitutes a third language are not universally defined. For some, L3 acquisition is simply chronological; the third language acquired in the literal sense. For others, the L3 is any language currently being learned in adulthood after at least two other languages have been acquired whereby the so-called L3 could actually be, in a chronological sense, the fourth or more language learned. For still others, the attainment of proficiency in previous languages is the ultimate criterion used to qualify a subsequent language as L3/Ln (see Hammarberg 2010 for discussion). Whatever the case, failing to properly differentiate true L2 from L3/Ln can have an inadvertently damaging impact on important questions studied under the guise of a broadly defined SLA (see De Angelis 2007). For example, if there is any credence to the so-called additive effect of bilingualism on L3 learning (Cenoz 2003), the superior metalinguistic skills/knowledge of bilinguals is a variable that must be controlled for in L3 learning research. Previous linguistic experience is also an important factor when examining linguistic processing given, among other confounds, the possibility that all linguistic systems are simultaneously activated when acquiring and processing a third, fourth and nth language. From the perspective of multicompetence (Cook 1991b, 2003a), keeping L2 distinct from L3 is paramount for empirical prudence since it is assumed that L2 learners have different grammars than monolinguals, even for their L1, as a result of the L2 acquisition process. From a formal (generative) linguistic perspective that assumes adult accessibility to the biologically endowed language faculty (i.e. UG-continuity), it follows that L3 learners have access to more grammatical properties (the underlying feature representations of two languages) when it comes to initial hypotheses that feed into L3 interlanguage development. Thus, properly differentiating between types of adult language learners is a concern of all L3/Ln researchers even if the functional reasons for doing so are distinct depending on the paradigm one adopts.

The goal of this chapter is to introduce the reader to the nascent, yet growing field of L3 acquisition. In doing so, we provide a (non-exhaustive) review of the current trends, working models and key questions of importance to the various subdisciplines of linguistic inquiry that study L3/Ln acquisition as a unique instance of adult language learning. By unavoidable circumstance, the research covered in the chapter is European and North American centered given that the overwhelming majority of available research comes from these areas. Much of the increase in the acquisition of third/nth languages in Europe and North America has been the result of educational policies that have recognized multilingualism. We therefore begin with an overview of L3/Ln acquisition in education, which is closely aligned with the social factors involved.

18.2 Educational and sociolinguistic approaches

18.2.1 Educational approaches

Although fewer than 2 percent of the nations of the world have two or more official languages, the number of multilinguals in the world far outweighs the number of monolinguals. In addition to multilingual societies that are essentially extensions of the nations that they border (e.g. Switzerland, Luxembourg), there are other factors that have contributed to an increase in official multilingualism and multilingual education in both industrialized and developing nations that had previously subscribed to monolingual or bilingual education models. Under the Council of Europe's definition, multilingualism is the co-occurrence of two or more languages in society, while plurilingualism refers to the diversification of an individual's use of languages. In this chapter, we assume the European Commission's definition of multilingualism, which is "the ability of societies, institutions, groups and individuals to engage, on a regular basis, with more than one language in their day-to-day lives" (European Commission 2007: 6). Effects of globalization in terms of multilingualism, or more specifically multilingual education, can be seen in the increase in programs such as Australia's National (East) Asian Languages and Studies in Schools, dedicated to the promotion of the acquisition of languages used by Australia's principal trading partners, and the Council of Europe, whose Common European Framework of Reference for Languages (CEFR) promotes individual multilingualism to increase educational, social, economic and political mobility. We have also witnessed increased immigration and a change in status of many minority languages throughout the world, which has resulted in the incorporation of non-majority languages in education systems and higher rates of successive (as opposed to simultaneous) multilingualism. Here we observe several types of learners in research on multilingual education, including those raised speaking three or more languages from infancy and simultaneous bilingual speakers (often migrant children) acquiring an L3 (Jessner 2008). This section begins with a discussion of a model of multilingual education that can account for all of these learners, followed by an overview of current trends in multilingual education research.

While recent definitions of multilingual education such as those of Cummins (2008) define the term as the use of two or more languages as languages of instruction, rather than as subjects, Cenoz (2009) proposes a goal-oriented definition of multilingual education that encompasses its various contexts: *Multilingual education implies teaching more than two languages provided that schools aim at multilingualism and multiliteracy* (2009: 32). Jessner (2008) divides these contexts into two categories, the first of which is elite multilingualism. This category of multilingual contexts includes double immersion, multiple languages of instruction and multiple foreign languages as subjects of instruction, and tends to maintain strict boundaries between languages. It accounts for the majority of multilingual education contexts, for example at international schools found in over 100 countries. Most such schools employ English as the sole language of instruction, with at least one additional language offered as a subject. The second category is that of minority contexts, discussed in detail below. Research such as that of García, Skutnabb-Kangas and Torres-Guzmán (2006a) and García (2009) calls for a change of context to support the implementation of "multiple multilingual education" programs that foster dynamic rather than additive multilingualism, such as those more likely to be found in India and Africa. These contexts are explored in greater detail as we discuss a recent model proposed to account for all the linguistic, sociolinguistic and educational variables that different typologies of multilingual education comprise.

Despite a large body of typologies of bilingual education, these do not always apply to multilingual education given the increased complexity of multilingualism involved. Cenoz and Genesee (1998) note that multilingual education can take different forms due to its relationship to the local sociolinguistic context, making it difficult for one model to apply universally. Those multilingual models which exist include the Factor Model (Hufeisen 1998; Hufeisen and Marx 2007), in which a series of neurophysiological, learner-external, affective, cognitive and linguistic factors influence the acquisition process at different stages (see Baetens Beardsmore 1993; Ytsma 2001 for more limited typologies). Cenoz (2009) has developed the Continua of Multilingual Education in reference to educational and sociolinguistic variables and linguistic distance. By taking this approach, she moves beyond other models that rely solely on dichotomies. She accounts for contexts in two categories: the first is that of a whole population, such as the 1960s French/English immersion programs in Canada, current education models in Spain involving Spanish and Basque or Catalan in addition to English, or double immersion programs such as Hebrew/French in Canada (e.g. Genesee 1998). The second category comprises contexts involving specific groups, such as the European Schools initiative by foreign civil servants for provision of multilingual/multicultural education for their children, and the 1981 Foyer project in Belgium designed to accommodate the multilinguistic reality of immigrant children considered the key to social integration in Dutch-speaking schools in French-dominant Brussels, with gradual introduction of Dutch and a focus on the mother tongue as the basis for learning (Baetens Beardsmore 1993). Other European nations also offer mother-tongue instruction to immigrant students in for example Finland, Sweden and Switzerland.

Cenoz's (2009) model accounts for another dichotomy in multilingual education: that of foreign languages as a subject versus foreign or multiple languages as languages of instruction. Content and Language Integrated Learning (CLIL) is a descendant of the French immersion schools in Canada and North American Content-Based Instruction (CBI) (see e.g. Brinton 2003) and is the teaching of subjects in a different language from the mainstream language of instruction (Marsh 2007: 233). While research in this area is relatively limited given its recency and concentration in Europe (see Dalton-Puffer 2011) (although growth in CLIL has occurred in Asia and North and South America) Genessee (1998) and De Graaff, Koopman, Anikina and Westhoff (2007) conclude that CLIL is the most effective way to increase proficiency. There has been a sharp increase in research in the last several years, as demonstrated by the *International CLIL Research Journal* started in 2008 and a 2011 edited volume by Ruiz de Zarobe, Sierra and Gallardo del Puerto dedicated to CLIL in Europe that covers different strands of research conducted from Spain to Estonia. Dalton-Puffer (2011) notes a sharp increase in research questions, and these focus on the debate of language vs. subject pedagogies, the generalizability of findings on CLIL via English to other CLIL languages, along with a call for theory to feed practice and vice versa. Thus far, there is evidence from research in Spain's Basque country of overall better proficiency via CLIL (ISEI-IVEI 2007), as well as increased lexical richness (Jiménez Catalán, Ruiz de Zarobe and Cenoz 2006) among students. Cenoz (2009) has shown that CLIL contributes to a multilingual perspective in language teaching and softens the boundaries between languages at multilingual schools. She claims that CLIL research is important because of the complexity of several languages of instruction in comparison to L3s taught simply as subjects. Yet research on multiple foreign languages as subjects is sparse in comparison to CLIL research, and Azpillaga, Arzamendi, Exteberria, Garagorri and Lindsay (2001) note that classroom research is necessary to fully understand this type of multilingual education. One example is Ruiz de Zarobe's (2008) longitudinal study of English comparing English as a foreign language (EFL) students with CLIL students in Basque schools in which the CLIL students outperformed the EFL students on production, receptive and lexical measures. Goikoetxea (2007) analyzed various areas of communicative competence among EFL learners, and found that students had more problems with sociocultural and discourse competence than with linguistic competence. Sociolinguistic issues such as these are discussed at length in the next section.

Despite the differences among the many contexts of multilingual education, there are several trends that reveal a common thread and which link to other paradigms on L3 acquisition, including use of prior linguistic knowledge (see Cots 2007), language awareness, cross-language approaches (see García 2009), crosslinguistic influence and teacher multilingualism.

A relatively new aspect of multilingual education is also the fostering of minority and heritage languages, that is, languages acquired in a setting where the dominant language of the society is not (exclusively) spoken (e.g. Clyne 2004; Olshtain and Nissim-Amitai 2004). Hélot and de Mejía (2008) see great opportunity in the use of minority/heritage languages in conjunction with mainstream languages in education, and studies of their successful incorporation have been carried out on six continents. While space limitations preclude us from elaborating on these and the research, the following is a short list, with examples, of such situations across the globe: Europe (Basque in the Basque Country, Catalán in Catalonia, Frisian in the Netherlands and Ladin in the Ladin Valleys in Italy), South America (indigenous languages in Peru and Bolivia; Hornberger and López 1998), Mexico (indigenous languages; Hamel 2008; Ogulnick 2006), North America (Native American / First Nation languages; McCarty 2008, 2010), South

Asia (India; Mohanty 2006), Africa (Botswana; Adeyemi 2008) and Australia (indigenous and immigrant languages). We also direct the reader to a volume edited by Heugh and Skutnabb-Kangas (2010) dedicated to multilingual education in Asia, Africa, South America and North America. Many of these cases support mother-tongue medium education, with the introduction of additional languages after several years of primary school. In 1998 Baker and Prys Jones noted progress in minority languages in education in efforts to foster acquisition and ensure continued use; such progress is seen as vital for the survival of these languages (Baker 2007: 142). There are many challenges including a lack of qualified teachers and materials and debate about which variety of a given language to teach. In addition, for each successful program incorporating minority languages, there are situations in which speakers of these languages suffer subtractive bilingualism, a phenomenon in which a second (in this case the majority) language is added with first language loss as a result (see Chapter 17, this volume, and García et al. 2006).

Jessner (2008) notes that achieving multilingualism means addressing learners, teachers, educators and policy makers, and that multilingual education can only be successful if language teaching is restructured and oriented toward multilingual norms. Cenoz (2009) echoes Jessner's sentiments, observing that "schools are not only influenced by society but can also have an important effect on society. Specific studies...need to take into account the whole phenomenon (of multilingualism)" (2009: 3). In addition, assessment in multilingual education is an important area requiring more work on, for example, the development of norms for the testing of multilingual proficiency (see e.g. Grosjean 2008; Rothman and Iverson 2010). A broadening of the scope of research in this area is crucially needed; while Asia, Africa and South America have the most linguistic diversity in the world, most research focuses on Western Europe and some parts of North America despite the fact that these continents account for just a small percentage of the world's languages and multilingual education situations.

18.2.2 Sociolinguistic approaches

Group and individual multilingualism encompass both naturalistic and educational contexts, spanning communicative competence, motivation/investment, attitudes, communicative anxiety, metapragmatic awareness, emotions and sociocultural transfer. As the number of languages in any given situation increases, the sociolinguistic variables increase, and with multilingualism becoming (or being recognized as) the norm, there is a need for the non-monoculturally biased study of the sociolinguistic factors affecting multilingual societies and their learners. Cenoz (2000) notes that one of the primary differences between L2A and L3A/multilingualism is the number of sociolinguistic factors at play; space does not allow for an exhaustive overview of this broad subfield of multilingualism. Here the factors presented are those at a macro-level such as language status and sociobiographical and psychoaffective factors. The reader will observe that these categories are not mutually exclusive.

Language status is one of the most studied factors in multilingualism. Take for example the Basque Country, where multilingualism has flourished due to the increased status of Basque through preservation efforts, institutional support and use as a language of instruction, and compare this to parts of the world where there continues to be prejudice towards multilingualism, such as African regions in which national European languages are seen as more prestigious than minority languages (e.g. Wolff 2000). "Multilingualism with English," both as a lingua franca and a common L3 was briefly discussed in Section 18.2.1 and is another widely studied phenomenon (e.g. Aronin and Singleton 2008; Gorter 2006). Cenoz and Jessner (2000) have called for further research on the sociolinguistic effects of English on minority languages given the growing number of contexts in which this multilingual situation is a reality. Among concerns about the dominance of English as a Lingua Franca/ELF are Pavlenko's (2005) that it will lead to the universalization of emotions, Heller's (2003) that it is Mcdonaldsizing the linguistic landscape and Skutnabb-Kangas' (2000) view of ELF as an agent of linguistic genocide.

In their studies of gender, researchers such as Piller and Pavlenko (e.g. Piller and Pavlenko 2004, 2007) show gender to be an important factor in multilingualism, particularly in economic production and social reproduction. To illustrate this, Piller and Pavlenko (2007) show how the new economic order has allowed minority women in the tourism industry to turn their multilingualism into a commodity, and the authors discuss how other employment opportunities have arisen that require multilingual skills. They also discuss gender and language choice for the purpose of romantic desires and regarding bilingual parenting. In addition to their work, many European studies have found gender to determine attitudes toward a speaker's languages (e.g. Huguet and Llurda 2001; Ytsma 2007; but see e.g. Safont Jordà 2007 on the non-significance of gender).

The study of socioeconomic status (SES) and multilingualism has also produced mixed results. While Sanz and Lado (2008) note that variables such as language status are an important component of L3 acquisition and Lasagabaster (1998) found SES to be a predicator of L3 English proficiency, Dewaele (2005b) found frequency of exposure to language to be more important than SES. Related to SES, language choice and code switching and/or code mixing (both situational and addressee-based) have been observed extensively in multilingual contexts (e.g. Dewaele, Petrides and Furnham 2008; Wolff 2000), and are employed most by those with higher levels of education to preserve group or cultural identity, as well as for socioeconomic advancement in society (Ennaji 2005).

Turning to individual factors, multilinguals have been found to have better communicative competence (e.g. Baker 2006; Wolff 2000), and Fouser (1997, 2001) and Safont Jordà (2003, 2005), among others, have found heightened metapragmatic awareness in multilinguals. Some research has proposed that motivation has an important role in L3 acquisition (e.g. Bernaus, Majgoret, Gardner and Reyes 2004; but see Lasagabaster 1998). The study of attitudes toward multilingualism has yielded results linked to individual factors such as age (Cenoz 2003) and dominant home language (Sagasta 2003), and to language status and sociobiographical factors as well. However, the study of individual attitudes has shown no differences between bilinguals and trilinguals (e.g. Brohy 2001). There is also evidence of more positive attitudes from native speakers of a majority language towards L3 acquisition (Lasagabaster 2001), towards the L1 of a non-native speaker of the majority language (e.g. Huguet 2007), toward an elite L3 (e.g. Mettewie and Janssens 2007), as well as toward the majority language, regardless of its status as an L1, L2 or L3 (Bernaus et al. 2004). Dewaele (2005b) linked social factors such as sociopolitical relations to attitude toward acquisition of French and English in Belgium; but see Bernaus et al. (2004) on no such link for immigrant students in Spain learning Catalan, Spanish and English. Another extensively explored area has been that of multilingualism and emotions (e.g. Dewaele 2004b, 2008; Pavlenko 2005), and it has been found that languages may create individual emotional worlds, revealing how emotion is encoded and processed in the multilingual lexicon. Finally, with respect to communicative anxiety, Dewaele (2002a, 2007b, 2008) and Dewaele et al. (2008) have shown that multilinguals suffer less anxiety than bilinguals, due to increased communication skills, socialization, language use outside a classroom environment, self-confidence and perceived competence.

We now turn to internal factors in L3/Ln acquisition.

18.3 Multicompetence and language throughout the lifespan

Multicompetence is a term coined by Cook in 1992 to refer to the knowledge of two or more languages in one mind. Its introduction meant a breakthrough in several respects. First, in contrast to earlier views (e.g. Weinreich's 1953 seminal *Languages in Contact*) languages are not seen as separate entities but as part of a larger system: "Since the first language and the other language or languages are in the same mind, they must form a language supersystem at some level other than be completely isolated systems" (Cook 2003b: 2). The notion of multicompetence was in a way a reaction to the notion of "interlanguage" as developed by Selinker (1972), which refers to a system of stages in between the first and second language. The restriction to two languages was typical of the thinking at the time, which may reflect the

Anglo-Saxon tradition in Applied Linguistics whose focus was English as a second or foreign language. Second, there has been a change in view of transfer or crosslinguistic influence/CLI. Transfer was seen as the impact of the first language on the second, but with the introduction of multicompetence, came awareness of the multidirectionality of CLI: during acquisition languages influence each other, and that influence is not restricted to the L1 ≫ L2 direction. This has led to a considerable body of research studying CLI from this perspective, with specific focus on the impact of the L2 on the L1 (e.g. the contributions in Cook 2003a; Dussias 2001; Kecskes and Papp 2000).

The third respect in which multicompetence constituted a breakthrough follows from the claim that languages in multilinguals are connected in a larger system whereby changes in one language may have an impact on the other languages. This implies that languages are constantly changing and that growth and decline are normal phenomena in development. A language that has been acquired is not viewed as a stable system in which knowledge, once stored, is invulnerable to change. There is a wealth of research on language attrition which shows that the language system and its subsystems show signs of decline when not used. This holds for first languages (Schmid 2010; Seliger and Vago 1991), but also for second and third languages (Bardovi-Harlig and Stringer in press; de Bot and Weltens 1995). The notion of multicompetence holds that no language is immune to decline, but rather the process of growth and decline is influenced by a large set of factors, partly sociolinguistic and partly psycholinguistic (Clyne 2003).

Connected to this is a final issue that, by some measures, has become apparent when thinking in multicompetence terms: there is no true endstate in language development. While the *endstate* is a common term in UG-based studies on language development (e.g. White 1989; Chapter 31, this volume), it is considered a misnomer under a view in which languages are viewed as being in constant flux, with acquisition as well as attrition as natural components of language development. Multicompetence has led to a more dynamic perspective on language development and multilingualism; see e.g. Herdina and Jessner's pioneering 2002 book including language development based on the notions of Dynamic Systems theory (see Chapter 28, this volume). In the last few years this new line of thinking has gained prominence as a promising approach to language development and multilingualism (de Bot, Lowie and Verspoor 2007, 2010; Larsen-Freeman and Cameron 2008).

The connection between multicompetence and L3/Ln acquisition is not only intuitive, but fundamental insofar as it makes inevitable predictions: with each language acquired, the possibility of changes to the supersystem and thus the subsystems of specific languages in the multilingual mind grows exponentially. Ultimately, the notion of multicompetence might prove explanatory for researchers of all paradigms, as its core tenets are compatible with virtually any existing formal theory of acquisition, inasmuch as it can account for individual variation and unexpected developmental patterns that follow from more restricted views of the static nature of mental linguistic representation.

18.4 Cognitive approaches to L3 grammar acquisition

We now examine the research within specific linguistic domains of the lexicon, syntax and phonology and present models from cognitive approaches to language acquisition relevant for L3 acquisition. Although we are sensitive to the differences between these approaches to language acquisition, given the space at our disposal in this chapter, we provide only necessary details of differences. We instead focus on what these approaches share: the belief that acquisition of language is first and foremost a cognitive phenomenon which takes place in the brain of an individual. One important issue where cognitive theories diverge is the extent to which language and its acquisition are domain-specific. UG-based approaches (e.g. Chomsky 2007a; see Chapter 7, this volume) maintain that language and its acquisition are biologically predetermined and acquired independently of other cognitive functions, while emergentist and usage-based approaches (O'Grady 2005; Tomasello 2003; Chapter 28, this volume) maintain that language does not follow from inborn mechanisms of specific linguistic design, but rather from mechanisms of general human cognition. Psycholinguistic studies, which most often follow specific instantiations of the above-mentioned general cognition-driven acquisition, often examine processing. Current models of bilingual and multilingual processing from all paradigms are essentially steady-state models that present a "frozen" picture of an individual's system. In focusing on different states of the language system at different moments in time, these models cannot inform us, at least with precision, how grammatical acquisition moves from one state to the next (but see recent work referred to above which adopts a Dynamic Systems / complexity theory perspective, de Bot *et al.* 2007, Larsen-Freeman and Cameron 2008 and also Chapter 28, this volume). Problems with cognitive models notwithstanding, the study of L3 linguistic competence permits researchers to test their models further in novel ways and challenges them to think about the overall process of language acquisition more openly.

18.4.1 The lexicon

Most of the psycholinguistic work on multilingualism has focused on the lexicon. The core questions are whether the addition of an L3 slows down processing, what mechanisms underlie code switching and whether the lexicons of different languages are separate or form one system.

Some of the earliest experimental studies on multilingual lexical processing come from Mägiste (1979, 1986), who studied groups of bilingual and trilingual adolescents in Sweden. They were tested on various speeded tasks: word naming, number naming, picture naming and decoding. All participants learned Swedish and/or German in school, and came from a variety of language backgrounds. The data show that the trilinguals were slower in decoding for word naming tasks, while both the bilinguals and trilinguals were slower in the other naming tasks. However, there was no clear definition of what constituted the first/second/third language or information on the relative use of the languages, so it can only be hypothesized to what extent the results reflect differences in use rather than more complex processes of crosslinguistic influence.

In another study, reported on in Mägiste (1986), a Stroop test was used and trilinguals were again found to be slower when the findings were corrected for age, length of residence and intelligence. Similarly, other language influence can be assessed by having subjects name the print color of words in different languages. For example, French/English bilinguals see *maison* "house" printed in black vs. *noir* "black" printed in black or red. If the languages are totally separate no crosslinguistic influence is expected, but most results show influence.

Van Gelderen *et al.* (2003) included word recognition (lexical decisions) as a part of a larger project on Dutch monolingual and bilingual adolescents learning English. The bilinguals had a Turkish, Moroccan or Surinam background. For both English and Dutch the bilinguals were slower in their second (Dutch) and third (English) language than monolinguals, but the differences were significant though rather small ($\approx$ 30ms). In the data analysis, word recognition skills were not a significant component of general reading skills. A similar study on minority language speakers in the Netherlands learning English in primary education by Sanders and Meijers (1995) found no differences for lexical skills between bilinguals and trilinguals.

There is also work on bilingual and multilingual code switching (CS) and findings have been used extensively to inform theories and models. Here we only touch on some of the issues in so far as they are relevant for our understanding of multilingual lexical processing. A relevant point is whether trilingual CS is functionally and structurally different from bilingual CS, and whether speakers thereby express their social and cultural identity in each language. Pittman (2008) reports on CS behavior in two trilinguals and found that patterns reflected differences in the structure of the languages involved and recency of use of these languages. There is also more switching between two languages than between three, in line with findings from Stavans and Swisher (2006). This most likely reflects the fact that there are more situations in which two languages are appropriate than three or more. Thus far, research does not point to the need to develop models that cater specifically to multilingual code-switching.

One of the issues debated extensively in the recent literature is the extent to which the different languages act as separate systems within the larger language system (as under multicompetence; see above). Psycholinguistic and neuropsychological research provides no clear evidence for this: separate languages do not appear to have their own distinct substrates in the brain, and psycholinguistic research also shows that languages cannot be completely switched off, which can be interpreted as evidence for an integrated system. However, at the same time, the fact that multilinguals can choose to use one and not the other language shows that the systems can be separated. A new dimension to this discussion has been added through investigation of whether switching between languages involves costs in terms of time: the typical task used is a cued naming task in which the task is to name a picture or word in one of the languages in the experiment. The cue for language choice is typically the color of the screen or the word/picture to be named (see e.g. Costa, Santesteban and Ivanova 2006; Meuter and Allport 1999; Philipp, Gade and Koch 2007). Results indeed point to a cost in terms of time, indicating therefore that there are different systems because in an integrated system no switch costs would be found. However, a serious issue here is whether such tasks have any validity for our understanding of normal, spontaneous code-switching behavior where anticipation and contextual cues play a role.

As already mentioned, the structure of the multilingual lexicon is one of the most hotly debated issues (see Costa *et al.* 2006; Kroll and de Groot 2005 and Dijkstra 2005 for overviews) but few of the large set of studies actually focus on multilinguals rather than bilinguals. In one of the rare studies of trilingual CS, Pittman (2008) concludes: "Even though the amount of trilingual code-switching was lower than the bilingual code-switching, there is sufficient evidence in this study for the existence of three separate systems" (2008: 137). It is not clear from what basis this conclusion is drawn: the data presented show patterns of the three languages in combination and much convergence in trilingual CS when compared to bilingual CS. It is obvious that the two sisters reported on in this study have developed a way of speaking between them in which they more or less freely combine elements that from a linguist's perspective originate from different languages but that in the mind of the speakers may well have merged to a large extent.

Crosslinguistic influence may also be task specific. Sercu (2007) reports on a study with tri/quadrilinguals in Brussels. She had adolescents in their final year of secondary education compose a text in their self-chosen first language on the basis of a cartoon and then translate the text into their other two or three languages. She found relatively few crosslinguistic influence phenomena in the translations, which suggests that the participants were quite good at keeping their languages apart in this specific task and setting. If there was CLI, only two of the languages were typically involved, and better-mastered languages were more likely to influence the weaker languages than the other way around. Sercu points out that differences in strategies reflect learners' histories in acquisition and use: "Depending on the learner's language history, task perceptions or perceptions of contextual features, one learner's version of a language may be very different from that of another learner as well as from the language as it is described by linguists in grammar books and dictionaries" (2007: 70). The impact of learning history is very clear in a study by Kujalowicz and Zajdler (2009), who asked Polish learners of English and Chinese to translate words. In the Polish context, Chinese is learned through English, so the learners are used to translating between Chinese and English, while Polish hardly plays a role. The participants' task was to translate concrete nouns from Chinese (L3) into English (L2) and Polish (L1). Translation into English was much faster (400 ms) than into Polish. While the authors explain this finding by referring to the bilingual learning setting, there may also be an effect of activation of the larger Polish set compared to the smaller English one. The data on switching times in experimental CS studies (such as Meuter and Allport 1999) show that it takes longer to switch back to a larger system, such as the L1 than to a smaller system, such as the L2.

A sharp contrast with the formal, school setting of a translation task is the switching between different languages in Quebec rap music, as described by Sarkar and Winer (2006). They show that rappers fluently switch between various languages, including ones they are only partly fluent in. Several factors appear to play a role in the choice of elements from different languages, such as facilitating internal rhyme and discourse marking. For many of the lyrics, there is no clear base language and there do not seem to be limits or constraints on the quality and quantity of CS, suggesting that "language" is in fact a minor cue in the selection of elements in production. (Also see Chapter 14, this volume, on multilingualism in the context of digital communication.)

One of the debates in the literature on bilingual and multilingual processing is whether lexical items are labeled for language. Wei (2006: 96) clearly favors the view that there is labeling. While this position seems to have considerable support (see Dijkstra 2005 for an overview), others have claimed that such tagging is not necessary to explain experimental findings on the mental lexicon. Laheij (2005) argues that in lemma and lexeme selection there is already sufficient information to select the intended item without the addition of language labels as cues. His view is in line with the idea that language selection is in fact the selection of linguistic elements that are associated with specific language use settings. Language is one of the cues in the selection of elements in language production, but its status may be overrated; there is also a set of elements that is, for instance, associated with a hospital context (doctor, nurse, operation, needle and so on), but no one would claim that we have a hospital lexicon as such. Similarly, the use of elements may be associated with settings in which certain types of utterances are customary, and one of the principles we might observe is that elements come from systems that at a metacognitive level would be labeled as different languages, but whether they are therefore also labeled and processed as such in the multilingual brain is another issue (de Bot in press).

18.4.2 Syntax

A good amount of work within the domain of L3/Ln syntax has focused on the status of the initial state for multilingualism as it relates to the extent to which previous language learning makes this state different from L2 acquisition, or L1 acquisition (see García Mayo and Rothman in press; Rothman, Iverson and Judy 2011). There are four logical possibilities relating to the knowledge the learner brings with him/her to the task of acquisition; the initial state in L3A could involve: (a) no transfer, (b) absolute L1 transfer, (c) absolute L2 transfer or (d) either L1 or L2 transfer (see Chapter 5, this volume). Such possibilities are amenable to empirical scrutiny and provide the backdrop from which the current initial state models derive.

Given the observed patterns of both L2 and L3/Ln initial state syntactic behavior, it is at present relatively uncontroversial to claim that there is some level of transfer (but see Epstein, Flynn and Martohardjono 1996), and there have not been any strong claims suggesting that there is no transfer at the L3/Ln initial state. Yet absolute or full transfer of an L1 at the L3/Ln initial state has never been systematically advanced, at least within cognitive paradigms (but see Na-Ranong and Leung 2009). Absolute L1 transfer is predicted from two distinct lines of reasoning: (a) the L1 acts as a filter, blocking (direct) access to acquired L2 properties or (b) L1 syntactic representations are the only possibility of transfer assuming a position akin to the Fundamental Difference Hypothesis under which it is argued that new syntactic acquisition in any additional language by post-puberty learners, at least, is impossible (see Bley-Vroman 1989, 2009).

A privileged role for the L2 has also been advanced, formalized under Bardel and Falk (2007) and Falk and Bardel (2011). Their L2 Status Factor Hypothesis maintains that the L2 takes on a considerably stronger role than the L1 in the initial state of L3 syntax. Essentially, it is proposed that the L2 acts as a filter to the L1 grammar. Evidence comes from Bardel and Falk's (2007) examination of two different groups: L1 verb second (V2) /L2 non-V2 and L1 non-V2/L2 V2, learning either Swedish or Dutch as an L3, focusing on the placement of negation. Their data showed the L2 Dutch/German group, who did not have a V2 L1, outperformed the L2 English group, whose L1 is V2, in producing postverbal negation. They maintained that only a privileged role for the L2 is corroborated by the data.

The L2 Status Factor is a particularly strong hypothesis since, like an absolute L1 transfer position, it makes straightforward predictions that are testable irrespective of language pairings. However, just as showing L1 transfer would only be consistent with absolute transfer under certain methodologies and language pairings, demonstrating L2 transfer might only be consistent with the possibility of L2 transfer as opposed to falsifying alternative explanations. Rothman and Cabrelli Amaro (2010) mention this in a study which examines properties related to the Null Subject Parameter, a formal classification that divides the languages by whether or not they allow null subjects (e.g. Spanish, Italian) or require overt ones (e.g. English, French). Their data are entirely consistent with the L2 Status Factor predictions. However, they cannot differentiate between an L2 Status Factor effect and (psycho)-typological influences since the choice of L2 and L3 in their methodology conflated both variables (i.e. English was always the L1, Spanish was always the L2 and the L3 was either French or Italian).

At present, there are two existing models of the L3 initial state that hypothesize the possibility of syntactic transfer from all previously acquired languages. The *Cumulative Enhancement Model* (CEM) proposed by Flynn, Foley and Vinnitskaya (2004) is both a model of the initial state as well as a theory of development and ultimate attainment. Although some formal linguistic work in L3 syntax existed sporadically before the mid 2000s (e.g. Klein 1995), it is fair to say that Flynn *et al.* (2004) provided the first L3/Ln initial state model. The second model proposing multiple sources of transfer in multilingual syntactic acquisition is the *Typological Proximity Model* (TPM; Rothman 2010, 2011), which can be viewed as a more restricted version of the CEM. What both models share and what differentiates them from models of absolute L1 or L2 transfer is that neither predicts categorical transfer. The CEM states that multilingualism is conditioned by a cumulative effect of previous linguistic acquisition. While the TPM shares this point, it views transfer as being conditioned by factors related to psychotypology between the languages at play. For both models, all previously acquired properties are in theory available to the L3/Ln learner. Transfer is not predicted by either the CEM or TPM to be random.

For the CEM, transfer at the initial state and even beyond is predicted to be maximally facilitative. The CEM maintains that developmental patterns are not redundant and that language acquisition has a collective bootstrapping or facilitative effect in that any prior language can either enhance subsequent language acquisition or, crucially, remain neutral. Previous linguistic knowledge is thus predicted to transfer in multilingual development only when it has a positive effect; otherwise, transfer is expected not to occur.

Differently from the CEM, however, the TPM hypothesizes that transfer is constrained by either actual typological proximity or perceived proximity between the three grammars and thus non-facilitative transfer is possible. Since the CEM and TPM make different predications regarding non-facilitative transfer, they are testable against one another under the right conditions. Rothman (2010) tested the L2 Status Factor, the CEM and the TPM by examining the L3 acquisition of Brazilian Portuguese, contrasting two sets of L3 learners: (a) L1 speakers of English who were highly successful learners of L2 Spanish and (b) L1 speakers of Spanish who were highly successful learners of L2 English. He tested word order restrictions and relative clause attachment preference. This pairing is especially relevant since despite the fact that Spanish and Brazilian Portuguese are typologically similar, Brazilian Portuguese patterns much more like English than Spanish in these related domains. The data demonstrate that Spanish was transferred irrespective of its order of acquisition and despite the fact that English would have been a more facilitative choice. Rothman concludes that these data provide evidence in favor of the TPM and against the predictions of the L2 Status Factor and the CEM. Rothman (2011) examined the domain of adjective placement and its semantic entailments under a similar mirror-image methodology and shows comparable results.

There is a comparatively shorter research tradition in L3/Ln syntax development and ultimate attainment from a formal linguistic perspective as compared to the also understudied L3 initial state. Klein (1995) was one of the first to explicitly contrast L2 and L3 acquisition in her study of lexical verbs that require prepositional complements and related syntactic properties of preposition stranding in a group of L2 learners and a group of multilingual learners of English. Interestingly, she found that the L3 learners significantly outperformed the L2 learners both in correct verbal subcategorization and in preposition stranding, despite being matched for proficiency in target non-primary English, thus showing some type of advantage for syntactic acquisition related to previous linguistic experience.

Considerable work from the Basque Country with balanced Basque–Spanish bilinguals learning English as in L3 in a school context by García Mayo and colleagues has provided interesting results in recent years (e.g. García Mayo, Lázaro Ibarrola and Liceras 2005, 2006; García Mayo and Villarreal Olaizola 2011; Gutierrez Mangado and García Mayo 2008; Perales, García Mayo and Liceras 2009). Stemming from a large corpus of longitudinal speech that employs the use of the famous "frog story" for elicitation and thus ensures comparability across many hundreds of subjects, this research has been able to examine L3 interlanguage development for a multitude of morphosyntactic properties such as weak and strong pronouns, morphological insertion of place markers, subject pronouns, long-distance *wh*-questions, suppletive and inflectional morphological suppliance, among other properties. This research informs epistemological debates in L2 acquisition (see also e.g. Cabrelli Amaro, Iverson and Judy 2009; Iverson 2009, 2010; Jaensch 2008, 2009; Leung 2001, 2005) by highlighting how L3/Ln development can inform perennial developmental debates in generative non-native syntax (see Chapter 24, this volume, and White 2003a for L2 review).

Although much of the work in L3/Ln syntax on development has focused on the acquisition of English, there are also studies examining German (Jaensch 2008, 2009), French (Foote 2009; Leung 2007), Spanish (Foote 2009; Lozano 2002) and Brazilian Portuguese (Montrul, Dias and Santos 2011). Some of this work provides evidence in favor of typologically determined transfer well into higher levels of development, adding support for the TPM (Foote 2009;

Montrul et al. 2011). Yet other studies test the extent to which L2 theoretical positions can explain similarities and asymmetries between L2/L3 production, such as Goad and White's (2006) Prosodic Transfer Hypothesis, Prévost and White's (2000) Missing Surface Inflection Hypothesis and Hawkins and Hattori's (2006) Failed Interpretable Feature account (e.g. Slabakova in press). What is still lacking in this line of research are independent L3/Ln models for development and ultimate attainment. Future research, however, promises to fill this gap and continue to demonstrate how the study of L3/Ln acquisition breaks new ground for determining with greater precision the mental architecture of linguistic design and how the process of acquisition in general unfolds.

18.4.3 Phonology

Twenty-five years ago, Ringbom (1987: 114) observed that "the effect of grammar and phonology [of a non-native language in a European context] is accorded much less space and importance. Phonology Ln-influence seems to be rare, since it is hardly mentioned in any studies." In 1997, Hammarberg also acknowledged the dearth of research in this area, expressing surprise given the interest taken in phonology in earlier contrastive linguistics and the fact that the pioneers of interlanguage research in the 1970s viewed transfer as a driving force in L2 phonology acquisition. However, Missaglia (2010) attributes this lack to the fact that adult learners have been the focus of L3 studies. Since L2 adult learners outperform young learners in the early stages of lexical and grammar acquisition but children outperform adults in phonetic and phonological acquisition, she states that it makes sense that researchers have focused on the domains that adults master earlier in both L2 and L3 research (see Chapters 15 and 17, this volume). Regardless of the reasons for which L3 phonology has not been a research focus in the past, its growth just over the last few years has been appreciable, with a primary focus on the elements of transfer.

In addition to the possibility that young bilinguals (both simultaneous and successive) might be able to acquire new phonological systems with greater ease, efficiency and to a greater level of proficiency, there are now two candidates for transfer, which can allow us to work toward answering many questions regarding the economy and architecture of non-native phonological systems. In addition, the observation of transfer is very important in its ability to tell us about the endstate of the L2, which informs what can in fact be acquired in an adult non-native system. Given these facts, recent research on L3 phonology has primarily observed progressive (as opposed to regressive) transfer and crosslinguistic influence in an attempt to determine the factors involved. As we have seen above, studies of other domains indicate that typological distance (perceived or actual), the status of the L1 and L2, language universals, recency of use, proficiency in the L2, and psychoaffective factors might all play a role in crosslinguistic influence in L3A, but we demonstrate that additional research is necessary to determine the role of each of these variables.

Much research on transfer in L3 phonetics and phonology points to a privileged status for the L1 (e.g. García Lecumberri and Gallardo del Puerto 2003), although we see below that new research moves away from this idea. Ringbom (1987) claimed that practically all adult learners, even at an advanced stage of learning, retain a foreign, L1-based accent in their speech, at least in their intonation, and that L2 transfer to L3 is relatively rare. However, he notes that recency or intensity of use can lead to occasional L2 phonological transfer. He goes on to state that the extent to which phonology is transferred from an L2 also depends on psychotypology, or the perceived typology between two languages, and these are all issues that are discussed in more detail below.

Pointing to a strong role for the L2 in terms of facilitative influence are studies such as that of Tremblay (2007), who observes the *voice onset time* (VOT) of L1 English / L2 French learners of L3 Japanese. While English has voiceless aspirated stops and French has voiceless unaspirated stops, Japanese has voiceless stops with a VOT intermediate to that of English and French. Tremblay found that learners transferred their L2 English VOT value to L3 Japanese. Here there is no possibility for psychotypological influence. Other studies have found evidence of such influence as a driving factor that can apply to individual items or the entire system. However, without certain methodological considerations, it is difficult to tease apart a straightforward L2 transfer factor from psychotypology, as can be seen in Wrembel (2010). She found L2 influence in her study of L1 Polish / L2 German learners of L3 English, but due to the language pairings, was unable to determine whether transfer was driven by an L2 status factor or psychotypology. Llama, Cardoso and Collins (2010) used experimental groups with L1/L2 mirror images (L1 French / L2 English and L1 English / L2 French) acquiring L3 Spanish to investigate transfer of VOTs, and such pairings made it possible to tease apart L2 status and psychotypology, finding in favor of a privileged L2 status.

Wrembel (2010) cites several possible explanations for an L2 status or "foreign language mode" in L3 phonological acquisition. Hammarberg and Hammarberg (2005) posit a foreign-language cognitive mode that promotes interlanguage transfer and acts as a coping strategy at the beginning of L3 acquisition when the phonetic form is too unfamiliar to master, overriding L1 transfer. Additionally, Wrembel's observation that more advanced speakers were more often identified correctly as speakers of their native language than the L2 provides evidence that the L2 is a stronger source of crosslinguistic influence at the initial stages, and that the tendency to resort to L2 articulatory settings becomes less powerful with the development of L3 proficiency. She also posits the possibility that L3 acquisition might reactivate the L2 due to similarities in mechanisms and processes involved in non-native language acquisition.

Other factors have been posited in order to explain an L2 effect, such as psychoaffective factors, as we can see by reports such as Hammarberg and Hammarberg (2005) of a subject's desire to suppress her L1 in an effort to sound non-foreign. Another possible reason for L2 transfer is that of L2 proficiency. The participant in Hammarberg and Hammarberg (2005) transfers only her near-native L2 German to L3 Swedish, and not her L1 English or less-proficient Italian and French. Psychotypology could also be a factor in this case, given the relationship between German and Swedish, but was not considered. It has also been proposed that high L2 proficiency might reduce L1 influence in favor of L2 influence, as evidenced in Gut's (2010) study that implemented a mirror-image methodology to test vowel reduction and speech rhythm in L2 English / L3 German and L2 German / L3 English by L1 speakers of Hungarian, Polish and Russian. However, Rivers (1979) showed L2 influence from a language that had nearly been forgotten (Italian) in a study of Spanish acquisition by an L1 English speaker, in which phonetic resemblance facilitated transfer.

Research has also found multiple sources of transfer for L3 phonology or instances in which prior knowledge of two typologically similar languages influence L3 acquisition, a process De Angelis (2007) refers to as combined transfer. In the only longitudinal study that has been done in L3 phonology, while L2 influence was found during the first eight months of development, Hammarberg and Hammarberg (2005) found evidence of overall L1 phonological influence as L3 proficiency increased. Barkley (2010) observed influence of both L1 and L2 grapheme–phoneme correspondence rules, as well as variation within groups, acknowledging that additional factors were likely at play. Other studies such as Gut (2010) and Pyun's (2005) investigation of L1 Korean / L2 English / L3 Swedish learners have found evidence of universals interacting with different source languages. Finally, in the only study to our knowledge to observe L3 phonology in an Optimality theory framework, Louriz (2007) observed L1 Moroccan / L2 French learners of L3 English at the initial state of acquisition and found evidence of influence from universals (in this case, a constraint that aligns primary stress with the left edge of the word) that blocked the transfer of L1/L2 stress patterns, and asserts that transfer from the L1 or L2 can occur, but only when the two languages tie in a certain constraint ranking.

Although the majority of research focuses on progressive transfer from the L1 and/or L2 to the L3, there is also the possibility for L3 regressive transfer, that is, crosslinguistic influence in which the L3 affects the L2 and/or L1. This is an important area to explore, as it can provide additional evidence for or against a critical period for phonological acquisition, as well as inform debates regarding the mental constitution of native vs. non-native language systems via observation of the (in)stability of native and non-native phonological systems when exposed to an L3. While Gut (2010) did not find any L3 to L2 influence in her study of vowel reduction and stress rhythm in L2 English/L3 German and L2 German/L3 English, preliminary findings by Cabrelli Amaro and Rothman (2010) show that an L2 steady-state phonological system is more vulnerable to L3 influence than a native (simultaneous bilingual) L1 system. They continue to investigate the effects of L3 Brazilian Portuguese phonology on native and non-native Spanish systems, observing spirantization and vowel raising to determine the degree of vulnerability to L3 influence.

18.5 Discussion and conclusions

The study of L3/Ln acquisition is in its infancy within all subdisciplines of linguistics that investigate it, despite the proliferation in recent years of high-quality research dedicated to multilingualism. As is true of any understudied area, there is much opportunity for innovative research. To close this general introduction to L3/Ln acquisition and take steps to move future empirical endeavors forward, we venture to highlight here some of the important issues that work must address at the level of multilingual epistemology and we point out some directions for research domains that would be especially productive.

Although there are many areas one could single out that would benefit from a more precise empirical examination, we highlight here four distinct areas crucial for future research: (a) the issue of which parameters should be used to define an L3/Ln speaker; (b) the issue of the comparative fallacy applied to L3A; (c) creation of independent measures of proficiency; (d) conveying how the understanding of the process of L3 acquisition sheds light on various subfields of linguistic inquiry, from theory to practice.

The issue of determining what inclusive and exclusive parameters should be applied to L3/Ln learners (a) is an important matter of empirical prudence in general and becomes extremely relevant when one considers how lack of such a standard renders cross-study comparisons impossible. Of course, to some extent, these parameters must be dictated by specific research questions and thus vary to some degree even if standards are eventually agreed upon. This raises the question of whether L3 acquisition should simply be considered chronologically. For example, should timing of acquisition matter whereby a simultaneous bilingual or a child L2 learner could be taken as an adult L2 learner in the case of learning what is chronologically an L3 if the present language being learned is the first language acquired in adulthood? What about the case of an adult who has learned two previous languages as a young adult to a level of high proficiency and attempts a chronologically fourth language? Is s/he an L3 learner or an L4 learner? Should proficiency or recency of linguistic acquisition be factored in? For some, these factors contribute considerably to the label used to describe learners whereby one can be a multiple L2 speaker learning an L3 that is in fact a fourth, fifth or more language. For Hammarberg (2010), for example, the important issue is to make true L2 acquisition distinct from L3. For him and many others this can be accomplished by labeling L3 as the current language past a true L2 that is being acquired even if it is chronologically L4, L5 and so on. While this distinction accomplishes the goal of keeping true L2 separate from Ln, it fails to take into full account the extent to which transfer at the level of underlying grammatical competence and at the level of metalinguistic knowledge and strategy can be dynamic. We would like to suggest that maintaining an empirical difference between true L3 and Ln is as prudent as it is for the L2/L3 difference on which researchers in this area seem to agree uncontroversially.

As it relates to the comparative fallacy of comparing L3 knowledge to native speaker monolinguals (b), L3 acquisition does not stand alone. If one takes seriously Cook's notion of multicompetence, then this comparison is even more problematic since the L3 learner would be starting the process of L3 acquisition with grammars and lexicons slightly different from monolinguals even in the case of his/her L1. The question then becomes what the standard of comparison should be to gauge L3 knowledge, or whether there should even be any comparison at all. In part, the answer to such a question depends on the L3 research questions examined in a study-by-study basis. Certainly, for initial-state studies looking specifically at transfer, the comparison might necessarily be different from that of an ultimate attainment study. If the focus is on the initial state, we suggest along with Rothman (2010, 2011) that a comparison to a native control group might not be necessary. Conversely, testing the individual L3 learners in the L1 and L2 and then comparing the initial state of L3 for these same properties could yield a sharper picture of the source of transfer.

Regarding independent measures of multilingual proficiency (c), we are far from honing in on standardized measures (see Cruz Ferreira 2010; Rothman and Iverson 2010). Again, if the notion of multicompetence is on the right track, then it is not clear what normative measures could or should be based on. It might seem fairer to assess the proficiency of adult learners of a language, be it an L2, L3, Ln, as measured against the norms of childhood bilingual judgments/productions, as has been suggested by some. However, while this might move us in the right direction for a more fair comparative benchmark for L2 acquisition, it fails to show the same promise for adult multilingualism since there are simply too many variables that differentiate the linguistic and sociolinguistic experiences of naturalistic bilingual acquisition in childhood from adult multilingualism. Steps forward in this area are especially welcome in light of the increased importance of multilingualism across the globe, but especially in areas like Europe, Africa and Asia where multilingualism is the norm.

Finally, we are confident that as the study of L3/Ln acquisition develops and increases in scope of domains studied, language pairings and methodologies employed, new insights into the cognitive underpinnings of language as well as into the dynamic nature of the social influences on language development will be uncovered. Future research in L3/Ln acquisition from all paradigms should keep in mind the macro-interest in multilingualism research when designing studies such that they are able to meaningfully contribute to larger questions about the nature, cognitive and sociological, of language more generally.

19

Language processing

Alice Foucart and Cheryl Frenck-Mestre

19.1 Introduction

Being bilingual implies having to deal with two languages within one brain. In this chapter, the term "bilingual" refers to all speakers who have some command of two languages, independently of their proficiency (i.e. low or high). Bilinguals can be distinguished in two groups: *early* bilinguals, who have learned their second language (L2) from birth or in the early years of life; and *late* bilinguals who have learned their second language later in life, usually at school (around age 12), also called L2 learners. (See also Chapters 16 and 17, this volume.) The case of bilingualism is a challenge for psycholinguists who aim to understand how the two (or more) languages of a bilingual are represented in the mind, whether they are organized similarly and how bilinguals manage to keep their languages apart when processing only one of them. In this chapter, we first review studies that have investigated the organization of the two languages in the brain and whether the two languages interfere with each other during access to the lexicon and syntactic representations. In the second part of the chapter, we report neurolinguistic studies that have examined cognitive processes and neural perspectives in monolinguals and bilinguals, with a special focus on factors that seem to influence bilingual language processing such as proficiency and age of acquisition (AoA). Finally, in the third part of the chapter we present current theories on L2 processing and we discuss the studies presented earlier in relation to these theories.

19.2 The bilingual mind

19.2.1 Lexical access in bilinguals

Lexical access is the mental process of retrieving information about words, such as orthographic, phonological and semantic properties. While these features can generally be retrieved from the mental lexicon effortlessly, in the case of bilinguals the question is whether the first language (L1) and L2 can be accessed independently or if they are mutually and irrepressibly activated. Many studies have suggested that information from both languages is activated when reading, listening or speaking one of the two languages. In this section we review a selection of these studies (for a review, see Costa 2008; Dijkstra 2005; Kroll and Dussias 2004).

Orthographic information

Various studies have investigated the retrieval of orthographic information in bilinguals.[1] In an early study, Van Heuven, Dijkstra and Grainger (1998) examined the possible interaction between L1 and L2 orthographic properties by means of progressive demasking in a lexical decision task involving orthographic neighbours (i.e. words appeared one letter at a time and participants had to press a button when they recognized the word). Orthographic neighbours are words that share all letters but one, and whose letters are in the same position. For example, the words *pin* and *pun* are neighbours of the word *pan* whereas *nap* is not. Studies on monolinguals have shown that the smaller the number of neighbours a given word has, the faster that word is recognized. For Dutch–English bilinguals, Van Heuven *et al.* (1998) reported slower response times to English target words in conjunction with an increase in the number of neighbours in Dutch, thus suggesting parallel activation of words in an integrated L1–L2 lexicon. Evidence of permeability of the "language barrier" is also provided by studies of interlingual homographs, words that are spelt the same way in two languages but do not share the same meaning or phonological representation (e.g. *pin* means "pin" in English, but "pine" in French). In a go/no go task, in which participants have to react only to one of the two languages, Dijkstra, Timmermans and Schriefers (2000) found that Dutch–English bilinguals were faster to respond to control words than to interlingual homographs. However, subsequent studies reported varying patterns of results, from response inhibition to null effects, depending upon task and list composition (see Midgley, Holcomb and Grainger 2009 for a discussion).Whether inhibition or facilitation is reported, both are nonetheless evidence of interlingual interaction.

Interaction between L1 and L2 has also been shown with cognates, which are recognized faster than non-cognate words, even when only one of the two languages of a bilingual is at task (Lemhöfer, Dijkstra and Michel 2004). The cognate effect has been investigated with various tasks such as lexical decision (Cristoffanini, Kirsner and Milech 1986; Van Heuven, Schriefers, Dijkstra and Hagoort 2008), naming (Gollan, Acenas and Smith 2001; Schwartz, Kroll and Diaz 2007; Van Heuven *et al.* 2008), progressive demasking (Dijkstra, Grainger and Van Heuven 1999), word translation (de Groot, Dannenburg and van Hell 1994) and picture naming (Costa, Caramazza and Sebastian-Galles 2000; Costa, Santesteban and Cano 2005). The cognate effect tends to be stronger from L1 to L2 than from L2 to L1, but this may vary depending on proficiency (Jared and Kroll 2001).

Phonological information

Orthographic and phonological information are often intertwined and only a few studies have focused particularly on the interaction between L1 and L2 phonological information (for a more detailed discussion see Duyck 2005; Haigh and Jared 2007). The overall findings have shown that bilinguals are faster to recognize a word (written output) in their L2 if it is preceded by a pseudohomophone in their L1 (oral output), and vice-versa (Brysbaert, Van Dyck and Van De Poel 1999; Duyck 2005; Duyck, Diependaele, Drieghe and Brysbaert 2004; Van Wijnendaele and Brysbaert 2002). In a word naming study, Jared and Kroll (2001) also reported that French–English bilinguals were slower to name a word in their L2 (e.g. *bait*) when part of this word is pronounced in a different way in their L1 (e.g. *fait* "done," pronounced [fɛ] in French). The reversed effect (influence of L2 on L1) was found only if the experimental block was preceded by the naming of L2 words, and this effect varied as a function of proficiency. An interaction between L1 and L2 phonological information has also been shown in auditory studies; however, the effect was found when bilinguals were processing their L2 but not when processing their L1 (Marian, Spivey and Hirsch 2003; Weber and Cutler 2004). Further evidence of activation of phonological information in both languages comes from two studies involving phoneme recognition (Colomé 2001; Hermans 2000). When presenting a picture to Spanish–Catalan bilinguals and asking them whether a Catalan phoneme was present, Colomé (2001) found longer response times when the target phoneme was also present in the Spanish translation of the picture. For example, when presented with the picture of a table (which in Catalan is *taula*) and asked whether the phoneme /m/ was present (in Spanish "table" is *mesa*), participants were slower to answer than when asked whether the phoneme /n/ was present. The author concluded that this was due to the fact that the phonological properties of the Spanish word were activated even when bilinguals were processing Catalan. Hermans (2000) obtained similar results with Dutch–English bilinguals.

Semantic information

Semantic representations (concepts), unlike lexical representations (words) largely overlap in the two languages of a bilingual. For instance, the concept CHAIR in English refers to the same concept as *chaise* in French (Francis 1999, 2005). Two studies used the picture–word interference paradigm to examine semantic representations in bilingual language production; they obtained conflicting results (Costa, Miozzo and Caramazza 1999; Hermans, Bongaerts, de Bot and Schreuder 1998). Costa et al. (1999) had Catalan–Spanish early bilinguals name pictures in Catalan while ignoring *distractor* words presented in either Catalan or Spanish. Among other results, they found shorter naming latencies, i.e. participants were faster to name the picture when the picture and the distractor were identical in the same language, as well as when the picture was presented with its translation in the other language, compared to unrelated picture–word pairs. For example, participants were faster to name a picture of a table in Catalan (i.e. *taula* "table") when presented with an identical distractor (i.e. *taula*) or its Spanish translation (i.e. *mesa*), than with unrelated distractors (e.g. *gos* and *perro* "dog" in Catalan and Spanish, respectively). The authors assumed that the effect was due to the extra activation that a target picture receives when the distractor is the translation of the picture name, since a distractor activates both its own lexical node and its translation. Thus, the production of the target picture is facilitated when picture–word pairs are related (extra activation is received, e.g. *taula–mesa*), than when they are unrelated (e.g. *taula–perro*). These results differ from those obtained by Hermans and colleagues (1998) who asked Dutch–English bilinguals to name a picture in their L2 (i.e. English) while ignoring auditory distractor words presented in their L2 or L1 (i.e. Dutch). Picture–word pairs were either semantically or phonologically related, or unrelated. For example, the name of the picture MOUNTAIN (*berg* in Dutch) was associated with either a semantically related distractor (e.g. L2, "valley"; L1, *dal*), a distractor phonologically related to the target language (e.g. L2, "mouth"; L1, *mouv*, [sleeve]) or to the translation of the non-target language (e.g. L2, "bench"; L1, *berm*, [verge]), or unrelated (e.g. L2, "present," L1, *kaars*, [candle]). Naming latencies were longer when picture–word pairs were semantically related, but shorter when they were phonologically related. This effect was found regardless of whether pictures and distractors were processed in the same language. The authors concluded that the translation of the L1 word had to be activated in order to interfere with L2 selection. The presence of a distractor which is phonologically related to the L1 translation (e.g. "bench"–*berm*) increases the activation of this lexical node, thus provoking a competition for selection with the picture name. Costa *et al.* (1999) suggested that the difference between the results of their study and Hermans *et al.*'s (1998) may have been due to the response language (L1 in Costa *et al.* vs. L2 in Hermans *et al.*) and the proficiency of the participants (the restriction of lexical selection is easier for highly proficient bilinguals, as examined in Costa *et al.*). Studies in language production have also provided evidence of interaction between the two languages of a bilingual during language processing (for a review of semantic representations in bilinguals, see Francis 1999, 2005).

Lexical access in sentence context

In everyday language, however, words are generally not presented in isolation but embedded in sentences. To date, only a few studies have investigated L1–L2 interference when words are processed in sentence context. The overall findings have suggested that despite the fact that a word is embedded in one language context, there is still an interaction effect across L1 and L2 (Chambers and Cooke 2009; Duyck, Van Assche, Drieghe and Hartsuiker 2007; Elston-Güttler, Gunter and Kotz 2005; Libben and Titone 2009; Schwartz and Kroll 2006; van Hell and de Groot 2008). In a recent eye-tracking study (which involves recording participants' eye movement when they are performing a task), Chambers and Cooke (2009) investigated the effect of sentence context on spoken language comprehension. English-French bilinguals were presented with a visual display while listening to sentences in French. In the display a picture of the target noun appeared (e.g. *poule* "hen" in French) as well as the picture of a near interlingual homophone (e.g. *pool*). A crosslanguage competition effect was revealed by the participants' temporary eye movements to the homophone. However, this effect was reduced when the homophone was semantically incompatible with the auditory sentence (e.g. *fraise* "strawberry"). The effect was not modified by the proficiency level of the participants, suggesting that even high-proficient bilinguals cannot control crosslanguage competition.

Effects of non-selective lexical access were also found in an eye-tracking study involving cognates (e.g. *divorce*) and interlingual homographs in low (e.g. "Because they owned a lot of property around the world, the expensive *divorce* was a disaster") and high ("Because of the bitter custody battle over the kids, the expensive *divorce* was a disaster") semantic constraint sentences (Libben and Titone 2009). Such sentence pairs refer to whether a word is highly expected from the context, e.g. the word *divorce* is more expected after the phrase *custody battle* than *owned a lot of property*. The eye movements of French-English bilinguals revealed cognate facilitation and interlingual homograph interference at an early stage of processing for both low- and high-semantic-constraint sentences, but only at a late stage in processing for low-constraint sentences. The authors concluded that in high-semantic constraint contexts, non-selective lexical access is rapidly resolved.

Lexical access: summary

The studies reported above clearly suggest that information from both languages of a bilingual is activated during language processing. In language comprehension, when bilinguals are presented with letter strings, word candidates from both their L1 and L2 are activated. In language production, the activation of both languages suggests that when a word is to be produced, the same amount of activation is sent to the lexical nodes of both languages, but only those of the language in use are considered for selection by the lexical mechanism (Colomé 2001; Costa and Caramazza 1999; Costa et al. 2000; Costa et al. 1999; Roelofs 1998). The relevance of these results for L2 models will be discussed in the last part of this chapter.

The observed influence of one language of a bilingual on the other also raises the question of language switching; the various available models make different assumptions concerning the processes involved in language switching (see among others, de Bot and Schreuder 1993; Green 1998; Grosjean 2001; Poulisse and Bongaerts 1994). This debate falls outside the scope of the present chapter; however, it seems that capacity for switching from one language to the other, similarly to the interaction between the two languages, depends on L2 proficiency (Costa and Santesteban 2004; Green 1998; Meuter and Allport 1999).

19.2.2 Syntactic processing

Once the meaning of a word and its properties have been retrieved, the word is usually processed within a sentence. In an utterance, words are linked to each other following syntactic rules. These rules can be similar or different across languages, and the two languages of a bilingual may not follow the same rules. To investigate crosslinguistic influence most studies have directly compared syntactic processing in monolinguals and bilinguals.

Error production

Nicol and Greth (2003) investigated the factors involved in the production of subject–verb agreement errors. It has been shown that when a verb is separated from the head noun by another noun that disagrees in number, monolinguals are more likely to produce subject–verb agreement errors. However, it seems that speakers of different languages process agreement in different ways due to crosslinguistic divergence. In English, subject–verb agreement is realized syntactically (Bock and Miller 1991) whereas in Spanish, Italian, French and Dutch subject–verb agreement involves semantic representations (Vigliocco, Butterworth and Garrett 1996; Vigliocco, Hartsuiker, Jarema and Kolk 1996). For example, when having to complete a sentence such as *The picture on the postcards...*, speakers of languages in which semantic representations are involved in agreement would be more likely to produce *are* (as opposed to *is*) because *picture* is conceptually plural (since there are several postcards, there are several pictures). Nicol and Greth (2003) examined subject–verb agreement errors in English–Spanish bilinguals. Interestingly, rather than finding language-specific mechanisms they found nearly identical error patterns in the two languages of the bilinguals. Hence, the authors concluded that speakers develop a way of processing agreement in their L1 (either syntactically or semantically) and they apply the same procedure in their L2 instead of adopting the procedure used by native speakers of the second language.

Priming

Priming studies have recently been used to investigate L2 production. Syntactic priming refers to the observable tendency of speakers to use a syntactic structure when it has recently occurred in the previous discourse (Bock 1986; Branigan, Pickering and Cleland 2000). Hartsuiker, Pickering and Veltkamp (2004) had Spanish–English bilinguals describe cards depicting an action to each other; a naive participant spoke English and a confederate spoke Spanish. Prime sentences consisted of active and passive sentences. They observed that participants were more likely to produce an English passive sentence when preceded by a Spanish passive sentence than when preceded by an active sentence. This suggests that syntactic representations are language non-specific and therefore are shared between languages. Similar results were found with German–English bilinguals for active sentences (Loebell and Bock 2003). Schoonbaert, Hartsuiker and Pickering (2007) used the same paradigm as Hartsuiker *et al.* (2004) to test syntactic priming within and across languages in Dutch–English bilinguals. In four experiments they tested whether the naive participant would repeat the same syntactic structure as previously used by the confederate. They used two constructions, a prepositional object (e.g. *The cook shows a hat to the boxer*) and double object (e.g. *The cook shows the boxer a hat*) and four directions of priming (L1 to L1, L1 to L2, L2 to L2 and L2 to L1). Their results showed a syntactic priming effect in all conditions, thus providing further support for the hypothesis of common syntactic representations across languages.

Desmet and Declercq (2006) also used priming to investigate the attachment of relative clauses to noun phrases. They used sentences such as *Someone shot the servant of the actress who was on the balcony*. In this type of sentences, the relative clause can be attached either to *the servant* (high attachment) or *the actress* (low attachment). It has been shown that monolinguals are more likely to produce high-attachment relative clauses (e.g. *the servant*) when preceded by high attachment primes than low-attachment primes (e.g. *the actress*) (Scheepers 2003). Desmet and Declercq (2006) replicated the same experiment with Dutch–English bilinguals who were asked to complete beginnings of sentences. Participants were more likely to use a high-attachment clause in English after completing a high-attachment prime in Dutch compared to after completing a low-attachment prime. These results again suggest that syntactic representations are shared between languages.

Syntactic ambiguity

Ambiguous sentences have also been used to compare L1 and L2 parsing. In a seminal study, Frenck-Mestre and Pynte (1997) recorded the eye movements of French native speakers and late English–French bilinguals during the processing of (written) syntactically ambiguous sentences. They manipulated lexical properties of the critical verb to determine whether this would affect syntactic ambiguity resolution. Both native and non-native readers showed an effect of verb subcategorization information on ambiguity resolution. In a second experiment, they again tested French–English and English–French bilinguals during the processing of syntactic ambiguities; however, this time sentences contained verbs that had different properties in the bilinguals' two languages, as opposed to having similar structure as in the first experiment. Results showed that bilinguals hesitated in their second language when reading structures containing conflicting lexical information across their two languages. However, despite this momentary localized effect of transfer, similar patterns of eye movements were obtained for both groups when the ambiguity was resolved. These experiments are in line with other bilingual studies using eye movement recordings, which suggest that native and non-native immediate syntactic parsing are similar and influenced by the same factors (Hoover and Dwivedi 1998; Juffs and Harrington 1996). For reviews on eye movements during syntactic processing in a second language, see Frenck-Mestre (2002, 2005b).

In contrast, some studies have suggested that effects of syntactic structure observed in native speakers seem to be absent in adult L2 processing (Felser, Roberts, Gross and Marinis 2003; Papadopoulou and Clahsen 2003). For example, Papadopoulou and Clahsen (2003) examined how older L2 learners parse temporarily ambiguous sentences containing relative clauses. They compared Spanish, German and Russian advanced learners of Greek to a group of native speakers. Their results showed that L2 learners used relative-clause attachment preferences that were different from those of the native speakers; however, these preferences were different than the preferences found in L1, as might have been expected if it was direct transfer from their L1. The authors concluded that, in contrast to native speakers who use both lexical cues and phrase-structure-based parsing strategies, adult L2 learners rely on lexical cues but not on syntactic information in parsing. A similar conclusion was drawn by Marinis and colleagues (Marinis, Roberts, Felser and Clahsen 2005), who examined how adult L2 learners of English from different language backgrounds (Chinese, Japanese, German and Greek) parsed long-distance *wh*-dependencies while reading sentences in English. They argue that their results showed that, unlike native speakers, these L2 learners did not use intermediate syntactic gaps during processing, supporting the claim that L2 learners cannot process their L2 in a nativelike manner because they underuse syntactic information when processing sentences in their L2.

Crosslinguistic transfer

Ambiguous sentences have also allowed researchers to investigate crosslinguistic transfer, i.e. whether the rules of one language of a bilingual influence parsing in the other language. It has been shown that the ambiguous sentences are not processed in the same way in all languages (Cuetos and Mitchell 1988; Frenck-Mestre and Pynte 2000a, 2000b). For example, when processing the sentence *Someone shot the servant of the actress who was on the balcony*, Spanish speakers favor high attachment (i.e. *the servant*) whereas English speakers favor low attachment (i.e. *the actress*). In a series of studies, Dussias (2003, 2004; Dussias and Sagarra 2007) predicted that Spanish speakers who have received enough exposure to English should, like native speakers, favor low attachment when processing ambiguous sentences. Her results showed that Spanish–English bilinguals tend to prefer low attachment compared to Spanish monolinguals and Spanish–English bilinguals who had not been exposed to English much. Similar results had been obtained in a previous study by Fernandez (1998). In addition, Frenck-Mestre (2002) reported developmental changes of ambiguity resolution in a cross-sectional eye-movement study of English native speakers acquiring French. Initially, these learners resolved syntactic ambiguities in the L2 according to the grammatical rules of the L1. With more experience (several years on), bilinguals resolved the same ambiguous structures in the L2 according to L2 frequency and grammatical rules, and much like native speakers. These studies suggest that L2 parsing is indeed influenced by the knowledge of an L1, at least in initial stages, and they provide evidence of crosslinguistic transfer.

Syntactic anomalies

Parsing in monolinguals and bilinguals has also been compared during the processing of syntactic anomalies; however, these have been used more often with event-related brain potentials (ERPs), hence, we will report more studies in the next section. To our knowledge, not many studies have investigated syntactic anomalies using eye-tracking (but see Foucart 2008; Keating 2009). Recently, though, Keating (2009) examined the performance of Spanish native speakers, comparatively to that of beginning, intermediate and advanced English-Spanish late learners. He manipulated gender agreement between the noun and adjective in either the determiner phrase or the verbal phrase, in either the main or a subordinate clause. Results for beginners and intermediate L2 learners showed no online sensitivity to gender agreement violations, independently of the grammatical role or position of the adjective in the sentence. On the other hand, advanced learners revealed a similar pattern to Spanish native speakers (i.e. longer fixation times for violations), but only when violations occurred in a local context (i.e. within the determiner phrase). In contrast, when the noun and the adjectives were not juxtaposed (i.e. for violations in the verbal phrase and across a clausal boundary), advanced L2 learners did not show online sensitivity to gender agreement.[2] These results are in line with those obtained by Sagarra and Herschensohn (2010, 2011) for beginner and intermediate English-Spanish learners on both online (self-paced reading) and offline (grammaticality judgment) measures of sensitivity to gender agreement for attributive adjectives. These studies suggest that high-proficient late L2 learners can reach native-like processing even when agreement involves features that do not exist in the learner's L1; however, it seems that processing predicative adjective agreement may be more demanding than processing attributive adjective agreement due to the distance between the agreeing elements as well as working memory costs.

Syntactic processing: summary

The studies in language production reported above suggest that syntactic representations are shared between languages at least in relation to the organization of syntactic information into structures for sentence production. They suggest crosslinguistic interaction; however, whether this interaction may vary with proficiency level still divides researchers. A similar debate is taking place in language comprehension. The findings will be further discussed in the views of L2 models in the last part of this chapter.

The studies reported in this section have provided important information about lexical access, semantic and syntactic representations in bilinguals. However, most behavioral and eye-tracking studies have investigated the question of crosslinguistic interference between the L1 and L2 without consistently integrating factors that may influence it, such as proficiency or age of acquisition. Other methodologies such as event-related potentials (ERPs) and neuroimaging techniques (fMRI, MEG) have focused on the effect of these factors on L2 processing, and have compared native speakers to early and late bilinguals. In the next section, we report the findings gathered using these methodologies.

19.3 The bilingual brain: neurolinguistic methodologies

19.3.1 ERPs in native, early and late bilinguals
ERP methodology
Event-related potentials (ERPs) are the record of brain activity in response to auditory or visual stimuli, obtained by means of electrodes placed on the scalp. They have been used to study online processing of words or sentences for two decades and, more recently, to examine the stages of lexical access in production. The ERP wave is composed of a series of positive and negative peaks which can vary, depending on the type of stimuli and task requirements, in onset, amplitude and scalp distribution. These peaks are named according to their polarity (i.e. N for negative; P for positive) and their position on the waveform (e.g. N1 is the first negative peak; P1 the first positive one) or their latency (e.g. P600 is a positive peak with a peak latency of 600ms). Latencies on the waveform can provide information in relation to the processes triggered by different types of stimuli. Compared to offline behavioral methodologies which provide information on explicit processing (e.g. grammaticality judgment tasks), ERPs can also reveal implicit processing. However, unlike other neuroimaging methodologies such as fMRI and MEG, ERPs do not indicate precisely which region of the brain is activated. Instead, they represent the activity of a large number of neurons that can be detected at some distance from their source. So, generally, the scalp distribution of an effect does not allow one to directly determine the cortical region activated by a certain process in the brain.

ERPs have relatively recently started to be used to investigate L2 processes and they have already provided crucial information that complements findings obtained with other methodologies (for reviews, see Frenck-Mestre, 2005b; Mueller 2005). The studies conducted so far have shown that lexico-semantic processing in L1 and L2 is very similar, though sometimes with delayed latency and reduced amplitude in L2 speakers; on the other hand, syntactic processing has been claimed to differ in L1 and L2 depending on AoA, proficiency and language similarities.

ERPs and AoA

One of the earliest studies to tackle the question of AoA was undertaken by Ardal, Donald, Meuter, Muldrew and Luce (1990). They visually presented semantically anomalous sentences to early and late bilinguals (L1 French, L2 English), and to English native speakers. Semantic violations provoked an N400 effect both in monolinguals and bilinguals, but the effect was slightly delayed for bilinguals. The results were obtained for bilinguals regardless of the age of acquisition.

Weber-Fox and Neville (1996) also compared native and non-native speakers to examine semantic and syntactic processing. They addressed the issue of the critical period hypothesis by testing Chinese–English bilinguals ranging from young to older (1–3, 4–6, 7–10, 11–13, >16 years) age of acquisition. Native speaker controls showed an *Early* (125ms, ELAN) and a late *Left Anterior Negativity* (300–500ms, LAN), as well as a P600 effect in response to syntactic category violations, and an N400 effect in response to semantic anomalies. The results obtained for the bilinguals revealed no early left negativity, except for one group (age of acquisition between 11 and 13 years), but because of a larger bilateral distribution rather than being left-lateralized, the authors concluded that it could not be considered a genuine ELAN. The late negativity was found for all L2 groups, but was more widely distributed for groups with age of acquisition above 11. Bilinguals who acquired their L2 up to the age of 10 showed a pattern similar to that of native speakers for the P600 effect. The 11–13 group revealed a delayed P600 effect to violations, whereas no effect was found for later learners. The authors concluded that semantic processing is similar in nature in L1 and L2 (only differing in latency and amplitude), but that syntactic processing in L2 is influenced by the age of acquisition. The similarity of pattern for early bilinguals suggests that the achievement of nativelike processing in L2 is possible when the L2 is acquired early in life. In contrast, as revealed by the delayed latency, late learners apparently always show some differences in comparison to native speakers, even with enough exposure, although this conclusion has recently been seriously challenged as outlined below.

In a series of studies, Kotz (2001) and Kotz and Elston-Güttler (2004) examined lexical and conceptual processing in bilinguals. These studies used categorical (e.g. *boy–junior*) and associative priming (e.g. *boy–girl*) on early (before the age of 4, Kotz 2001) and late (after the age of 11, Kotz and Elston-Güttler 2004) German–English bilinguals. Early bilinguals displayed an N400 effect for both types of priming, as did native speakers. In contrast, late bilinguals showed an N400 effect only for associative priming; no effect was found for conceptual priming. Moreover, the authors reported a larger N400 effect for high-proficient than for low-proficient bilinguals. The authors concluded that the conceptual link in L2 depends on the age of acquisition.

Recently, Gillon-Dowens and colleagues (Gillon-Dowens, Vergara, Barber and Carreiras 2010) compared ERP sensitivity in Spanish native speakers and English–Spanish late learners (AoA after 20 years old, with at least twelve years immersion). They manipulated gender and number agreement between the determiner and the noun and the noun and the predicate adjective. The results revealed similar patterns for native and L2 speakers in the case of syntactic violations between the determiner and the noun (i.e. early negativity and P600 effect), but not in the case of violations between the noun and the predicate adjective (i.e. early negativity and P600 effect for native speakers but only P600 effect for L2 speakers). The authors concluded that late L2 learners can reach nativelike processing; however, they suggested that agreement processing may be more demanding in complex structures due to the distance between the agreeing elements as well as due to working memory costs.

ERPs and proficiency

In two studies Hahne compared native speakers of German, Russian learners of German (age of acquisition <10, Hahne 2001), and Japanese late L2 learners of German (AoA <21, Hahne and Friederici 2001) in response to phrase structure anomalies and semantically anomalous words. Japanese speakers had overall lower proficiency than the Russian speakers, as revealed by their grammaticality judgments. Semantic violations elicited an N400 effect for the native speakers and both L2 groups; however, the effect obtained in the bilingual group had reduced amplitude and later peak latency. Native speakers displayed an early left anterior negativity (ELAN) and a P600 in response to syntactic anomalies; Russian L2 learners did not show an ELAN but a delayed P600 was present, and Japanese L2 learners did not show any online effects even though they were able to detect these anomalies offline, as revealed by the grammaticality judgment they had to make at the end of each sentence. The authors concluded that the presence of a P600 effect in case of syntactic violations depends on proficiency.

In a more recent study, Hahne, Mueller and Clahsen (2006) examined the processing of inflected words by Russian-speaking advanced learners of German. In response to incorrectly inflected past-participle forms (e.g. *gelauft* instead of *gelaufen* "run"), these L2 learners showed an anterior negativity followed by a P600. For incorrect inflection of noun plurals, L2 learners displayed a P600 when the regular pattern was generalized (i.e. -s replaced the -n; e.g. *Tuben* vs. *Tubes*), but an N400 effect when the irregular pattern was generalized. The authors concluded that high-proficiency L2 speakers were able to process inflectional morphology in a nativelike manner in cases where the rules are systematic, but are less capable of such for more complex rules such as those governing nominal pluralization in German.

The conclusion that L2 learners can reach a nativelike processing level was further supported by Rossi, Gugler, Friederici and Hahne (2006), who presented sentences containing word category violations, or morphosyntactic agreement violations or both types of violations to high- and low-proficiency German and Italian L2 learners. The results for high-proficiency learners were similar to those found for native speakers (albeit with some differences in amplitude): an ELAN and P600 effect for word category violations and a LAN and P600 effect for morphosyntactic violations. In contrast, low-proficiency learners did not show any LAN effect and displayed a delayed P600 effect. The authors concluded that late L2 learners who achieve high proficiency can process language similarly to native speakers provided there is sufficient exposure to the L2. The importance of these findings for L2 models will be discussed in the last part of this chapter.

The role of proficiency has also been tested with an artificially constructed miniature language "Brocanto." Friederici, Steinhauer and Pfeifer (2002) exposed German native speakers to Brocanto; after enough exposure, participants reached high proficiency both in comprehension and production. Participants' sensitivity to violations of phrase structure word order was then tested with ERPs; a biphasic effect consisting of an early anterior negativity and a P600 was found. Even though it is not clear whether the mechanisms underlying artificial language processing are similar to those underlying natural language processing, this study confirms the key role of proficiency in L2 syntactic processing.

ERPs and language transfer

ERPs also allow one to investigate the influence of L1 on L2 processing depending on crosslinguistic differences/similarities. Tokowicz and MacWhinney (2005) examined the phenomenon of language transfer in English–Spanish learners. They tested learners' sensitivity to (a) tense marking, which is formed similarly in English and Spanish; (b) nominal number agreement, which is formed differently in the L1 and the L2; and (c) nominal gender agreement, which is specific to the L2. The results showed a P600 effect in response to violations that occurred in structures that were similar in L1 and L2 (i.e. tense marking) and structures that were unique in L2 (i.e. gender agreement), but not in structures that were different across languages (i.e. number agreement). The authors suggested that structures that are similar in L1 and L2 and structures that exist only in the L2 should be acquired faster than those that are in conflict (or "competition") between the two languages.

Kotz, Holcomb and Osterhout (2008) obtained a comparable effect of "positive transfer" when comparing highly proficient Spanish L2 speakers of English (AoA less than five years) and native English speakers. A similar P600 effect was found for native and L2 speakers in response to phrase structure violations and temporarily syntactically ambiguous sentences. The constraints in the phrase structures were similar in English and Spanish, whereas the temporary ambiguity was only possible in English, not in Spanish. These results support the claim that early L2 speakers can process structures that are crosslinguistically similar and language-specific to L2 in like fashion to native speakers.

Recently, Foucart and Frenck-Mestre (2011) found an effect of "negative transfer" when comparing French native speakers and German-French learners' sensitivity to gender agreement violations. Both native and L2 speakers showed a P600 effect when violations occurred in structures that obey the same syntactic rules in L1 and L2 (i.e. agreement between singular determiner and noun). In contrast, German L2 speakers of French did not show this effect when L1 and L2 syntactic structures conflicted (i.e. plural adjective agreement). These results confirm that syntactic processing in L2 is affected by the similarity of syntactic rules in L1 and L2.

ERPs and L2 learning

ERPs can also reveal the different stages in L2 learning. Mueller, Hahne, Fujii and Friederici (2005) had German native speakers learn a miniature version of natural Japanese. Once learners had reached high proficiency, the authors compared Japanese native speakers and learners' sensitivity to syntactic violations. Native speakers revealed an anterior negativity and a P600 effect for word category violations, and an N400 and P600 for case violations. Learners only showed a P600 effect for both types of violations. The results suggest different neural mechanisms in L1 and L2 online syntactic processing.

Recently, Osterhout and collaborators (Osterhout, McLaughlin, Kim and Inoue 2004; Osterhout, McLaughlin, Pitkänen, Frenck-Mestre and Molinaro 2006) have investigated the neurological changes that occur in learners' brains over time with increasing proficiency and/or exposure to their L2. Although their findings are preliminary, they claim that it may be possible to establish *what* aspects of the L2 have been learned and *when* they have been learned. From several longitudinal studies, they showed that L2 learners usually display a typical N400 effect in response to semantic violations, and this effect is consistent throughout the acquisition. In contrast, it seems that at early stages of acquisition, the processing of syntactic violations is also reflected by an N400 effect and not a P600 effect as is usually expected for this type of violation. However, when proficiency increases, the N400 effect gradually switches to a more classic P600 effect. The authors claim that the gradual change of ERP responses reflects the various stages of L2 acquisition.

Last, in two recent studies, we have shown that the same input factors that affect L1 syntactic processing apparently affect L2 processing (Frenck-Mestre, Foucart, Carrasco and Herschensohn 2009; Frenck-Mestre, McLaughlin, Osterhout and Foucart 2008). In both native speakers and L2 learners, the presence of overt oral cues to morphosyntactic agreement has been shown to enhance the ERP response to agreement violations, whether of verbal or nominal agreement. Interestingly, this effect is apparently linked to L2 proficiency, as it was obtained for both intermediate and advanced L2 (French) learners, but was not observed in the ERP record for learners in the first stages of acquisition (McLaughlin et al. 2010).

Overall, ERP study findings converge regarding semantic processing but are still controversial regarding syntactic processing. While semantic processing seems to be similar in L1 and L2 (reflected by the N400, sometimes delayed and smaller in L2), ERPs have revealed that nativelike syntactic processing in L2 not only depends on AoA and a critical period, but also very much on proficiency and language transfer.

19.3.2 Neuroimaging in native, early and late bilinguals
Neuroimaging methodologies

Recently, neuroimaging methodologies have been adopted to study the neural mechanisms of first and second language processing. These methodologies provide complementary types of information. Magnetic resonance imaging (MRI) uses a magnetic field to construct an image to produce a structural image of the brain. MRI images are then used as a template for those obtained using functional magnetic resonance imaging (fMRI), which reveal the activity of the brain during processing. fMRI is sensitive to regional changes in blood flow, which thus allows one to infer the areas in the brain that are activated when performing specific tasks. This methodology is preferred over positron emission tomography (PET) for long tasks. Indeed, like fMRI, PET is sensitive to changes in blood flow; these changes are perceived by detecting positrons, positively charged particles emitted by radioactively labeled substances injected in the blood stream and which reveal brain activity, i.e. changes in blood flow, in the different regions of the brain. PET and fMRI provide high spatial resolution but low temporal resolution in contrast to magnetoencephalography (MEG), which provides both high spatial and temporal resolution of neural activity. Similarly to ERPs, MEG is revealing as regards the timing and the nature of linguistic processes. This is reflected through negative and positive peaks in the electrophysiological trace recorded with these measures, which are defined according to their amplitude, latency and distribution. Different patterns of activity are then correlated to different types of processing performed by the brain. MEG offers a more precise spatial resolution than ERPs but imposes additional constraints due to the use of magnetic fields and the physical risks this can entail.

Neuroimaging methodologies were first used in the field of language studies for clinical investigations of bilingual aphasia. Overall, the results of dozens of studies have revealed a very mixed picture, from selective damage to only one of a bilingual's two languages by a brain lesion, to complete recovery of both (for recent reviews, see Hull and Vaid 2007; M. Paradis 2004, 2008). Based on these results, claims have been put forward for both selective loss of one of a bilingual's two languages, thus implying distinct neural organization for each (M. Paradis 2004) and, on the contrary, common neural underpinnings for both languages. Indeed, more recently, neuroimaging methodologies have focused on the impact of factors such as AoA and proficiency on the activation of the language areas of the brain in native, early and late bilinguals, and have suggested that neural differences in L1 and L2 may decrease as proficiency increases (Green 2003). In the next section we review a few of these studies.

Neuroimaging, AoA and proficiency

Neuroimaging studies have generally addressed the question of AoA and proficiency together. The influence of these factors was first investigated in a PET study by Perani *et al.* (1998) in which they compared high-proficiency late Italian–English bilinguals (AoA >10) and early Spanish–Catalan bilinguals (AoA <4). The results for these two groups were contrasted to those obtained for a group of low-proficiency late Italian–English bilinguals from a previous study (Perani *et al.* 1996). When bilinguals listened to stories in L1 and L2, neural activity comparable to that found in L1 was revealed in the two high-proficiency groups independently of the AoA, but not in the low-proficiency group. The authors concluded that previous reports of differences in the neural substrate underlying the two languages of a bilingual had failed to sufficiently account for the effect of proficiency in the L2. A subsequent fMRI study testing high-proficiency late Chinese–English bilinguals in a syntactic judgement task (Luke, Lui, Wai, Wan and Tan 2002) also suggested that neural processing mechanisms involved in syntactic processing do not vary in native speakers and high-proficiency bilinguals.

In contrast to the above studies, Wartenburger and colleagues found an effect of AoA for syntactic processing (Wartenburger *et al.* 2003). In an fMRI study they compared the neural activity of three groups of Italian–German bilinguals, namely high-proficiency early bilinguals (from birth), high-proficiency and low-proficiency late bilinguals (after age 6), during grammatical and semantic processing of sentences. Their results revealed nativelike neural activity for syntactic processing only in early bilinguals, whereas late learners showed broader activity (increased activation of the inferior frontal gyrus (IFG)). These results were supported by another fMRI study conducted by Hernandez and colleagues investigating a gender decision task for regular and irregular words (Hernandez, Hofmann and Kotz 2007). They scanned early and late high-proficiency English–Spanish bilinguals and revealed overlap of L1 and L2 activation with an increased activation of the IFG for irregular words for late bilinguals compared to early bilinguals. In a series of studies, Kubota and colleagues obtained similar results while investigating syntactic processing in L1 speakers and L2 high-proficiency Japanese learners of English using MEG (Kubota, Ferrari and Roberts, 2003, 2004; Kubota, Inouchi, Ferrari and Roberts 2005). The peaks of activation found for native and non-native speakers were similar in response to certain types of syntactic violations but not to others. The authors concluded that some syntactic structures are more prone to be learned and automatically processed by bilinguals than others. On the other hand, Wartenburger and colleagues showed that high-proficiency late bilinguals activated the same areas as early bilinguals for semantic processing, unlike low-proficiency bilinguals who showed different activation in areas related to memory and executive processing. Similar patterns of increased activation in L1 and L2 speakers were found by Rueschemeyer and colleagues in a study investigating semantic processing in German native speakers and high-proficiency Russian–German bilinguals (Rueschemeyer, Fiebach, Kempe and Friederici 2005). In another fMRI study, Xue and colleagues (Xue, Dong, Jin, Zhang and Wang 2004) examined semantic processing in Chinese native speakers and low-proficiency Chinese–English bilinguals. Despite the fact that L2 speakers performed worse than L1 speakers in the semantic judgment task, a similar activation pattern was found for L1 and L2 speakers.

Overall, these findings suggest that neural processing mechanisms of semantic processing are affected by proficiency while those of syntactic processing depend on AoA as usually revealed by an increased activation of the IFG (Dodel et al. 2005; Golestani, Alario, Meriaux, Le Bihan, Dehaene and Pallier 2006; Rueschemeyer et al. 2005).

Neuroimaging and language transfer

The effect of syntactic similarity on neural activation was investigated by Jeong and colleagues in an fMRI study (Jeong et al. 2007). They tested Korean trilinguals in Japanese and English (equivalent proficiency in both languages). Participants were scanned when performing auditory sentence comprehension tasks in Japanese (similar to Korean), and English (different from Korean). The results showed similar activation patterns in the three languages, however, with additional activation of the IFG for English due to crosslinguistic differences. This study supports the claim that syntactic similarities/differences in L1 and L2 affect neural processing mechanisms.

Neuroimaging and L2 learning

The neural mechanisms underlying language acquisition were investigated in an fMRI study by Tettamanti and colleagues (Tettamanti, Alkadhi, Moro, Perani, Kollias and Weniger 2002) examining the acquisition of grammatical and ungrammatical syntactic rules by adults. The authors reported an activation of a network in the left hemisphere, including Broca's area, for grammatical rules but not for ungrammatical rules. This activation increased with proficiency. Similar activation of Broca's area was found in a study by Musso and colleagues (Musso et al. 2003) in which they examined German native speakers learning a sample of "real" grammatical rules of English and Japanese. These two languages are quite distinct, but according to the authors, they both follow principles of Universal Grammar. The same native speakers also had to learn "unreal" rules, i.e. rules that, the authors believed, violated the principles of Universal Grammar. Activation in Broca's area was found for the real rules only, suggesting that, interaction between biological constraints and language experience in this specific area is necessary to enable linguistic competence for a new language. Activation of this region has been reported in other studies using artificial grammars, indicating that it is involved in the processing of complex syntactic structures and is required during the acquisition of rules (Bahlmann, Schubotz and Friederici 2008; Friederici, Bahlmann, Heim, Schubotz and Anwander 2006; Opitz and Friederici 2004).

19.4 Drawing conclusions from behavioral and neurolinguistic data

Behavioral, eye-tracking and neurolinguistic studies have all been motivated by the same issues concerning bilingualism such as the organization of the two systems in the brain, language control, the effect of AoA and proficiency, and crosslinguistic influence. Behavioral studies usually collect data using response times or error rate, whereas eye-tracking and neurolinguistic studies allow one to detect more subtle differences occurring during L1 and L2 language processing. These different methodologies have reached similar conclusions for some aspects of bilingual processing (e.g. semantic representations; Kotz and Elston-Güttler 2007) but conflicting for others (e.g. syntactic processing; Kotz 2009; van Heuven and Dijkstra 2010). Conflicting results can be accounted for by the fact that methodologies provide different types of information, i.e. fMRI, PET and MEG provide *spatial* information (areas of the brain activated during processing), ERPs, MEG and eye-tracking provide *temporal* information (when processing occurs), and ERPs and MEG are informative on the *nature* of the processing (i.e. semantic or syntactic). Moreover, the procedure required for each methodology may also affect the results obtained (e.g. word-by-word presentation for ERPs). Hence, it is interesting to have an overall look at the complementary data collected with the different methodologies to shed light on crucial aspects of L2 processing. In this part of this chapter, we attempt to draw conclusions from these findings and we discuss them in the framework of L2 models.

19.4.1 Lexical access and semantic representations

Lexical access in bilinguals has been largely investigated with behavioral studies (for a review, see Costa 2005; Dikjstra 2005) but neurolinguistic studies have also addressed this issue and have often reached similar conclusions. For instance, neurolinguistic studies have investigated bilingual language control (see for reviews, Abutalebi 2008; Abutalebi and Green 2007; Moreno, Rodríguez-Fornells and Laine 2008; van Heuven and Dijkstra 2010) and most of the findings converge with those obtained in behavioral studies, suggesting that lexical access is non-selective, i.e. that information from both languages of a bilingual is activated during language processing (Holcomb, Grainger and O'Rourke 2002; Kerkhofs, Dijkstra, Chwilla and de Bruijn 2006; Martin, Dering, Thomas and Thierry 2009; Midgley, Holcomb, van Heuven and Grainger 2008; Thierry and Wu 2007; van Heuven et al. 2008). Similar types of materials were used across methodologies; for example, Midgley and colleagues (2008) used interlingual neighbours in an ERP study with French–English bilinguals and found that words with a large number of neighbours across languages provoked a larger N400 effect than words with fewer neighbours. Similarly, Kerkhofs and colleagues (2006) showed that the N400 effect was influenced by the frequency of inter-lingual homophones (in Dutch and English).

These findings support models of bilingual production that argue that selection is language specific (Colomé 2001; Costa and Caramazza 1999; Costa et al. 1999, 2000; Roelofs 1998). According to these models, lexical nodes are tagged depending on the language they belong to. When a word is to be produced, the conceptual level sends the same amount of activation to the lexical nodes of both languages, but only those that are tagged for the language in use can be selected. Consequently, there is no competition for selection between the lexical nodes across languages. For example, when a French–English bilingual wants to produce the word *chair* in English, the semantic concept CHAIR sends activation to both the French lexical node *chaise* and the English lexical node *chair*, but only *chair* will be considered for selection because it is tagged as being an English word.

Behavioral and neurolinguistic findings also support language comprehension models that claim that lexical access is non-selective, such as the Bilingual Interactive Activation (BIA) model (Dijkstra and van Heuven 1998) and its more recent version, the BIA+ (Dijkstra and van Heuven 2002). This model proposes four levels of linguistic representations: letter features, letters, words and language tags that are activated in turn when a bilingual is presented with a word. There is competition between the representations of both languages at each level; for example, language tags inhibit the word candidates from the other language. Following this inhibition/activation process, a lexical candidate is activated. The level of activation across the two languages depends on proficiency in L1 and L2.

Overall, the data from behavioral and neurolinguistic studies suggest that L1 and L2 share semantic representations and processing mechanisms. In addition, neurolinguistic studies have revealed that the time-course and the brain areas related to semantic processing vary according to proficiency more than as a function of AoA. ERP studies have shown that the N400 effect is elicited in the L2, but that it is often delayed in late bilinguals compared to native speakers, especially for those with low proficiency (Elston-Güttler and Friederici 2005; Kotz and Elston-Güttler 2004; Weber-Fox and Neville 1996). This suggests that even though some information takes longer to be processed in L2, the essential semantic processing mechanisms are similar in L1 and L2. In addition, fMRI studies have generally revealed that the areas recruited for L1 and L2 semantic processing are shared (Indefrey 2006a); however, additional areas might be activated in L2 and the level of activation may also vary compared to L1 (Kotz and Elston-Güttler 2007).

19.4.2 Syntactic processing

While the findings from the different methodologies seem to converge regarding lexical access and semantic representations, findings related to syntactic processing are still controversial (Frenck-Mestre 2005a; Kotz 2009; Mueller 2005). Overall, it seems that syntactic processing is more dependent on AoA, proficiency and language transfer than is semantic processing, yet this remains unclear. For example, ERP studies investigating syntactic processing, largely using syntactic anomalies, have obtained conflicting results. On the one hand, a P600 effect similar to that found in native speakers was found in L2 learners in case of syntactic anomalies (Foucart and Frenck-Mestre 2012; Frenck-Mestre et al. 2008; Frenck-Mestre 2005b; Hahne 2001; Hahne, Mueller and Clahsen 2006; Sabourin 2003; Weber-Fox and Neville 1996), suggesting that nativelike syntactic processing can be achieved in L2. On the other hand, this effect was not found for all L2 learners (Hahne 2001; Hahne and Friederici 2001; Sabourin 2003). Moreover, until recently, the absence of a left anterior negativity (LAN) in bilinguals that was present in monolinguals (Hahne 2001; Hahne and Friederici 2001, Weber-Fox and Neville 1996) was interpreted as evidence that late L2 learners could not reach a nativelike level for syntactic processing (but see Frenck-Mestre 2005b; Osterhout et al. 2004; McLaughlin et al. 2010). However, the LAN component was recently found in late L2 learners (Gillon-Dowens et al. 2010; Rossi et al. 2006), which suggests that a nativelike level can indeed be reached by high-proficiency bilinguals even when they learn their L2 late in life. These results are in line with Hopp's (2007) *Fundamental Identity Hypothesis*, which argues that grammatical representation and processing are similar in native and non-native speakers and that if differences are found, they are not due to a critical period but to factors related to L2 acquisition such as L1 transfer or performance factors (see also Herschensohn 2000, 2007 and Chapter 15, this volume; Hopp 2010).

The claim that nativelike competence can be reached in L2 contrasts with the *Shallow Structure Hypothesis* (SSH) proposed by Clahsen and Felser (2006a). The SSH argues that L1 and L2 processing differ in that the syntactic analysis engaged in by late L2 speakers during language comprehension is not as in-depth as that of native speakers. Among other differences, according to the SSH, L2 learners cannot process sentences in their L2 in a nativelike manner because, unlike native speakers, they seem to rely on lexical cues and not on syntactic information, hence they do not process long-distance dependencies (e.g. relative clause ambiguities) as native speakers do (Felser *et al.* 2003; Marinis *et al.* 2005; Papadopoulou and Clahsen 2003). Furthermore, the SSH claims that L2 learners should experience greater difficulty processing agreement between distant elements (e.g. noun–adjective agreement) due to limited processing resources when reading in the L2 and be unable to retain information required for agreement in working memory while processing other lexical items/relations intervening between the two agreeing elements. Some evidence of just such difficulties has indeed been provided by recent eye-tracking studies of L2 morphosyntactic processing (Keating 2009, but see Foucart and Frenck-Mestre 2011). It is important to note, however, that the argument that readers sometimes opt for a superficial parse of complex structures is not limited to L2 processing (Christianson, Hollingworth, Halliwell and Ferreira 2001; Ferreira and Patson 2007). Moreover, the SSH has not gone without criticism (Dekydtspotter, Schwartz and Sprouse 2006; Frenck-Mestre 2006; Hopp 2007, 2010).

Last, another more recent model of L2 processing based on neurolinguistic data is that proposed by Ullman (2005). The *Declarative/Procedural* (DP) model (Ullman 2001a) outlines two memory systems; the declarative memory system is related to lexical learning and processing and underlies knowledge of facts and events, whereas the procedural memory system is related to grammatical acquisition and processing, and underlies cognitive skills and "habits." (See also Chapter 6, this volume.) These declarative and procedural systems are found in separate neural areas, namely the medial temporal lobe regions and the frontal-basal ganglia structures, respectively. The declarative memory contains information about words such as sounds, meaning and form, and the procedural memory involves syntactic rules and the building of complex structures. In L1 acquisition, Ullman (2001a) predicts that children first learn word features in declarative memory and gradually acquire syntactic rules in procedural memory. Ullman (2005) claims that the same process cannot be applied by late L2 learners; in Ullman's terms, procedural memory progressively declines in life whereas declarative memory increases, hence L2 learners tend to rely more on declarative memory even for functions that would be related to procedural memory in L1. This use of declarative memory will be suitable for simple structures but may not be for more complex structures such as sentences involving non-local agreement. The DP model and SSH agree on this point. However, unlike the SSH, the DP model predicts that with enough L2 experience (depending on various factors like L2 exposure, learner's characteristics, etc.), L2 learners will rely on procedural memory as do L1 speakers and L2 syntactic processing will be nativelike for highly proficient bilinguals.

This prediction is supported by neurolinguistic data showing a gradual change of ERP effects and of neural activation for syntactic processing as proficiency and/or L2 exposure increase. As reported above, Osterhout and collaborators (Osterhout *et al.* 2004, 2006; McLaughlin *et al.* 2010) recently showed changes in learners' neural response to syntactic manipulations during L2 acquisition in a series of longitudinal studies. In response to syntactic violations Osterhout's group has reported an N400 effect during initial stages of learning that gradually evolves into a P600 effect. This pattern supports the proposal that in the early stages of grammatical learning, whether in children or in adult L2 acquisition, learners rely on item-based schemas or formulaic strings which allow them to communicate but which have little or no internal structure. Beyond this early "non-decompositional" stage, learners unpack these formulaic chunks and induce abstract grammatical categories and productive rules (for recent accounts, see Tomasello 2000; Wray 2002). The same line of argumentation has been forwarded for L2 acquisition of verbal inflection, whereby in an initial stage learners may first memorize the stem and affix as an undecomposed *chunk* only to gradually learn to decompose these elements later in development (Zobl 1998). In sum, these findings support the proposal that L2 learners go through various stages of syntactic learning; they first memorize chunks of words and morphemes (e.g. *talked*), and only later do they integrate syntactic rules (e.g. *talk-ed*). Neuroimaging studies also support Ullman's (2005) prediction that L2 learners only start using procedural memory later. Studies have revealed greater activation in the medial temporal regions in L2 learners (region related to declarative memory) when processing sentences, but this difference of activation between L1 and L2 speakers is reduced or absent in high-proficiency bilinguals (Perani *et al.* 1998).

In sum, recent findings support the claim that nativelike syntactic processing can be attained even by late bilinguals (Foucart and Frenck-Mestre 2011; Gillon-Dowens *et al.* 2010; Hopp 2010; Keating 2009; Luke *et al.* 2002; Rossi *et al.* 2006). These findings were obtained using different methodologies and, hence, revealed important information on when and where L2 processing occurs. This claim contrasts with the models of L2 processing that assume "representational deficits" or limitations in processing, but is in line with models which argue that with enough L2 experience, L2 syntactic processing should be as automatic as in L1 (Herschensohn 2000, 2007; Hopp 2007, 2010; Schwartz and Sprouse 1996).

19.5 Conclusion

In this chapter we gave an overview of studies investigating the bilingual brain. We focused on different aspects of L2 acquisition and processing such as lexical access, semantic representations and syntactic processing, and reported findings from studies using behavioral, eye-tracking and neurolinguistic methodologies. Overall, the findings across these methodologies converge in relation to lexical access and semantic representation, suggesting that lexical access is non-selective and that fundamental semantic processing mechanisms are similar in L1 and L2 but depend on proficiency. In contrast, findings for syntactic processing are more controversial, with some supporting the idea that L2 processing will never reach L1 automaticity and others suggesting that nativelike syntactic processing can be attained even by late bilinguals. In addition, syntactic processing seems to depend not only on proficiency but also on AoA and language transfer. The present chapter also emphasized the necessity to combine different types of methodologies to better understand the linguistic and neurophysiological processes involved in L2 language processing.

20
Affect and the brain

Andrea W. Mates and Anna Dina L. Joaquin

20.1 Introduction

When we read autobiographies by language learners, note their answers on surveys and examine their test results, it is clear that individuals have unique experiences, different rates of progress and different outcomes in acquiring a second language. These experiences are not so unique that second language acquisition researchers have not found a set of contributing or causal factors known as *individual differences* (IDs), but there is enough variation in individual experience and outcome to make the task of pinpointing these contributing factors difficult. This chapter goes beyond Chapter 8 which also covers IDs to look at these with respect to the brain, particularly the subcortical brain with its ties to emotional processing and learning, to provide a lens on processes and outcomes in SLA. We begin in Section 20.2 by discussing the factors contributing to different brains being distinct from one another as the biological underpinning of IDs. Then, in Sections 20.3 and 4, we focus on two affective characteristics that vary among individuals – motivation and anxiety in SLA. In Section 20.3, we discuss motivation as the outcome of stimulus appraisals and propose a neurobiology that supports the making of such appraisals. In Section 20.4, we use Porges' Social Engagement System as a way to understand anxiety in SLA. Section 20.5 discusses the implications of this neurobiological approach on SLA research and the language classroom.

20.2 Different brains are distinct

While IDs in aptitude, motivation, anxiety, age of arrival and other categories may correlate with second language attainment, each individual also has a unique underlying biology shaped by the ongoing interplay of genetics, developmental selection and experiential selection. This biological uniqueness and the processes that bring it about serve to remind us that language learners have brains that share similarities but are also truly different and change over time. The implications of these individual differences will be explored in a number of ways throughout this chapter, and we begin by discussing how these differences arise.

20.2.1 Synaptic connections

Schumann *et al.* (2004) emphasize that all brains are different – as different as faces – as a result of both genetic and epigenetic factors (Edelman 1987, 1989). Each cause of variation is a process that begins long before one undertakes learning an L2. Humans, as products of sexual reproduction, receive approximately half of their genes from each parent. Thus siblings do not receive identical sets of genes from their parents, resulting in the mixes that produce the visible differences we observe among siblings. Even identical twins' brains are different. Contrary to popular belief, offspring with presumably identical sets of genes may be born with genetic differences. This phenomenon arises because of structural variation in DNA known as *copy number variants* (CNV). Typically, people carry two copies of every gene, one from each parent. However, there are regions that deviate from this two-copy rule and may have anywhere from zero to over fourteen copies of a gene-producing CNV. As a result, identical twins' DNA may differ at various points of their genome resulting in differences, including the expression of diseases, temperament and personalities (Bruder *et al.* 2008; Casselman 2008).

Genetic factors account for the general formation of the brain. Just as they account for the characteristics of the eyes, nose and mouth, these account for variation in size and shape of the brain's lobes, ventricles and major tracts (Edelman 1987) whose formation varies from individual to individual. And just as a broken nose in childhood may permanently affect the appearance of one's face, developmental and environmental selection contributes to the unique connectivity between neurons and their organization into neuronal groups. *Developmental selection*, the combined effect of genes and engagement with the perinatal environment, results in brains that are anatomically similar in a macro-sense, but vary considerably in micro-structure. Thus, although identical twins may have identical genes, different early experiences mean that brains are not identical, e.g. identical twins may have differing gyral patterns (Bartley, Jones and Weinberger 1997; White, Valenzuela, Kozlowska-Macgregor and Leung 2002).

In addition to genetic factors and development-induced neuronal variation, one's individual experiences, particularly social interaction, also produce differences. We know this in part from evidence that human beings do not survive isolation well. During the 1970s and 1980s, government policies in Romania resulted in far more children in state-run orphanages than resources to care for them. Caregivers provided children's basic medical and nutritive needs but at a ratio of 1:20, workers spent little time with individual children. When the Ceauşescu regime was toppled, the world saw results of social deprivation that horrifyingly resembled those of Harlow's famous monkey experiments (Carlson and Earls 1997; Fleming, O'Day and Kraemer 1999). Fleming et al. (1999: 681) noted that "children reared in orphanages in Romania exhibit disrupted physiological, sensory-motor, emotional, and cognitive development reminiscent of that observed in socially isolated rhesus monkeys." Additional research reveals that children raised in such conditions have lower levels of the neuropeptides *oxytocin* (OT) and *vasopressin* (AVP), which are associated with social bonding, stress regulation, social communication and understanding and perceiving emotions (Wismer Fries, Ziegler, Kurian, Jacoris and Pollak 2005; Carter 2005). These deficits arguably arise because the human brain has been adapted for interaction, an interactional instinct, which motivates infants and young children to orient to, seek out and become like others in their sociocultural domain (Lee 2009).

The formation of *synaptic connections* and *neural networks* is the process associated with learning, and interaction with caregivers and with the shared environment strengthens or weakens synaptic connections in a process known as *experiential selection*. In this process, networks of neurons that fire together are more likely to fire together in the future, and the more they fire together the stronger their connection becomes. For one child, the sounds that form the phrase *dinner time* are reliably associated with smells of roasts and potatoes, and for another child, smells of stir fry and rice. For one child, the response to *dinner time* is to go wash hands and for another, to round up siblings. Experiential selection thus results in unique neural networks that process *dinner time*. If one of these children moves to a place where the call to dinner is occasioned by a phrase in a different language, his/her *dinner time* network will cease to be reinforced and over time will weaken while new networks responsive to this new environment are developed and strengthened. Thus, one experience leads to the strengthening of one neuronal group, while the lack of another experience leads to the weakening or pruning of other synaptic connections. Repeated exposure to a stimulus can lead to massive strengthening of connections in a learning process that may result in stored *declarative* information ("what") or *procedural* routines ("how"; see Chapter 6, this volume, for discussion). The impact of experience and, more specifically, of different experiences on the individuality of brains cannot be underestimated. Because individuals not only experience different things but also experience the same things differently, even for hypothetically cloned individuals, experiential selection will begin to exert its influence on the neural circuitry of each clone's brain such that in any given area their brains would not have precisely the same synaptic structures. Thus as much as genetics contributes to differences among brains, experiences add yet another layer of profound difference.

Because our interactional proclivities motivate us to interact and experience our social environment, we observe, listen-in, participate in activities, imitate other humans, receive instruction and are evaluated for our actions (Joaquin 2010; Rogoff 2003; Rogoff et al. 2007). Thus, we acquire the relevant cultural schemas used to relate to other members appropriately. This socialization is another experiential process that contributes to individualized expectations, preferences and aversions. This was alluded to in the *dinner time* illustration, and helps us see how socialization is a particular way in which experience contributes to variations in learner preferences, styles, strategies, traits and so on.

20.2.2 The outcomes of different brains being different

Setting aside for now the influence of experience on brain development, let us look briefly at structural differences across brains and their relation to specific skills. Einstein's brain provides a particularly interesting case of individual differences in brain structures. Hours after Einstein died at the age of 76 of a ruptured aneurysm, his brain was preserved. Research on his brain found that he had a wider, more spherical, and 15 percent larger parietal lobe than controls (Witelson, Kigar and Harvey 1999). In addition, Einstein also had more of the glial cells known as astrocytes and oligodendrocytes in his parietal lobe (Diamond, Scheibel, Murphy and Harvey 1985). *Glial cells* provide support and nutrients to the brain and form *myelin*, a sheath around the neuron that increases transmission of signals. The findings on the structure of Einstein's brain are particularly interesting as "[v]isuospatial cognition, mathematical thought, and imagery of movement are mediated predominantly by right and left posterior parietal regions" (Witelson et al. 1999: 2149). Earlier research had also shown that other notable physicists and mathematicians (i.e. Gauss, Osler and Siljestrom) had expanded inferior parietal lobes as well (Spitzka 1907). Such research suggests "that variation in specific cognitive functions may be associated with the structure of the brain regions mediating those functions" (Witelson et al. 1999: 2152).

While differences in brain structure and connectivity can lead to differences in function, the phenomenon of *degeneracy* reminds us that differences do not necessarily lead to observable behavioral differences or measurably different cognitive capacities. Degeneracy describes a situation where multiple causes produce the same effect such as when different sequences in DNA code for the same protein (Edelman and Galley 2001). Another example comes from findings about protein albumin in humans. It was once thought to be indispensible in transporting certain hormones, maintaining normal blood pressure and other processes. However, protein albumin was found to be completely absent in some individuals and those critical functions performed by other systems (Beuhler 1978). Likewise, degeneracy shows that it is possible for two or more structurally different neural systems to perform the same function or yield the same output.

Keeping all these factors in mind when we pursue an understanding of biological factors that contribute to variation in SLA, we begin with an understanding that each brain is uniquely shaped by that individual's genetic endowments, developmental selection and experiential selection, all of which interact. Examples such as Einstein's brain demonstrate that anatomical difference can imply functional difference, but degeneracy reminds us that differences do not ensure functional differences. The same or similar outcomes can be achieved by different means. In the next section, we examine the neurobiology of stimulus appraisal and how brain differences apply to affect in SLA.

20.3 Stimulus appraisal system: affect and the brain

Schumann (1997; Schumann et al. 2004) has proposed a *stimulus appraisal* approach to understanding affect and motivation in SLA. He begins with Scherer's (1984) conceptualization of how we assess stimuli in our environment by making appraisals across five categories – whether the situation is *novel* or *pleasant*, whether it contributes to one's *goals or needs*, whether we feel we have the *coping potential* to deal with its consequences, and how our engagement within a situation may affect our *self and social image*.

There are always at least these five categories of appraisal at play, and the primacy or salience of one category does not mean that one of the other categories is not also involved. Since SLA research frequently looks at classroom settings, we use classroom learners to provide an illustration. For example, two students attend to the same stimulus – a lecture – yet, they make different appraisals. The heritage language learner who has exposure to the language at home but little formal grammar instruction (see Chapter 17, this volume) may feel pride about material covered that has been internalized and shame over material that is new but seemingly basic. However, by the time the lecture is over and a classroom activity begins, this learner has regained confidence and believes he can participate without threatening self or social image. The novice learner finds novelty exciting and typically approaches the challenges of sitting through lectures and participating in practice activities with enthusiasm. These kinds of appraisals provide the basis for preferences and aversions and as such are antecedents for motivation; across individuals appraisals will vary because brains differ. In other words, genetic and developmental influences cause the neurobiological systems supporting stimulus appraisal to vary from individual to individual. Yet imagine that the hypothetical novelty embracing student is not feeling well and would rather be at home. Her appraisal of the unpleasantness of being sick and in class overtakes any other positive appraisals of the classroom situation that day. Thus experience also colors every encounter and appraisal.

Lee et al. (2009) take the neurobiology of stimulus appraisal that Schumann (1997) presented, expand on it, and discuss individual differences in the neurobiology of stimulus appraisal (see also Chapter 8, this volume). In this section, we use this as one avenue for understanding individual differences in SLA.

20.3.1 Stimulus appraisal and SLA

Schumann (1997) demonstrated the relevance of stimulus appraisal to L2 acquisition by examining the questions on the *Aptitude/Motivation Test Battery* (AMTB) developed by Gardner and colleagues (Gardner 1985; Gardner and MacIntyre 1993). These questions were designed to measure several attributes of L2 learning including *motivation, integrativeness, attitude* toward the learning situation and *language anxiety*. Schumann argued that the questions measured these attributes "by directly eliciting the learner's stimulus appraisals or by assessing the learner's actual, intended, or desired behavior, which is based on stimulus appraisal" (1977: 68). He classified each question item according to the stimulus appraisal(s) it elicited – novelty, pleasantness, goal/needs significance, coping potential, and/or self/social image. For example, *I am studying French because it will help me understand French people and way of life* was an item on the orientation index, involving instrumental and integrative motivation. Agreeing with this statement appears to reflect an appraisal along the goal dimensions (Schumann 1997 citing Gardner 1985: 182). Another statement, *I am afraid the other students will l laugh at me when I speak French*, elicits an appraisal of the learner's projected self and social image in the classroom, in conjunction with the subject's coping potential and the pleasantness of the classroom environment. Gardner defined attitude as "an evaluative reaction to a referent" (Schumann 1997: 81 citing personal communication with Gardner 1995). This suggests that all dimensions of attitude and motivation, as delineated in the AMTB, are based on stimulus appraisals. Schumann found further empirical support for the role of stimulus appraisal in SLA as he examined learner diaries and autobiographies in which learners described their individual assessments of particular language learning situations, environments and milestones.

20.3.2 Stimulus appraisal and other perspectives

The stimulus appraisal system is another way to approach Csizér and Dörnyei's (2005) conceptualization of the internal structure of L2 motivation. While giving prominence to Gardner's integrativeness and instrumentality, they break it down to *integrativeness, attitudes toward the second or target language (L2) speakers/community, cultural interest, instrumentality, vitality of the L2 community, milieu and linguistic self-confidence* (Csizér and Dörnyei 2005). The attributes were then measured in a questionnaire administered to teenage language learners as part of an ambitious longitudinal research study to measure attitudes and motivations toward learning an L2.

In their model, a learner's integrativeness reflects his/her motivation due to a positive perception of the L2 and its culture, resulting in the learner wanting to become similar to people of the target culture. Such a perception is related to the appraisal of pleasantness (of the L2 and culture) and of the contributions to a learner's self/social image when s/he becomes similar to members of the desired culture. Attitudes toward the L2 speakers/community and cultural interest are related to the novelty and appraised pleasantness of the language and culture, which may also direct one's goals. The instrumentality of a language refers to the benefits of L2 proficiency, including its "pragmatic incentives . . . as well as the importance of the particular L2 in the world, and the contribution its proficiency makes to becoming an educated person" (Csizér and Dörnyei 2005: 21). In other words, instrumentality may be the perceived ability of L2 learning to aid in achieving one's goals. The vitality of the L2 community concerns the perceived importance and wealth of the L2 communities and milieu the perceptions of significant others including parents, family and friends. These can be seen as appraisals of how language learning contributes to achieving one's goals and benefits to one's self/social image. Linguistic self-confidence involves a learner's beliefs about his/her abilities to reach language goals successfully, a self-assessment of the learner's coping potential. These motivational factors interact with each other. For example, instrumentality is affected by milieu; in the same way, attitudes toward the L2 speakers/community are affected by the perceptions of the vitality of the L2 community. These components of motivation, according to Dörnyei (2001), are, by definition, antecedents to learner behavior, in the same way that "appraisals guide SLA" (Schumann 1997: 2).

In reviewing the results of the studies, Dörnyei's (2005) research interestingly shows that of all the possible factors affecting motivation, it is integrativeness, instrumentality and attitudes toward the L2-speaking community that stand out consistently as the most important variables, with integrativeness playing a "principal role in determining the extent of a learner's overall motivational disposition" (Dörnyei 2010: 77). However, integrativeness also turns out to be a key motivating factor "in an environment where 'integrating' was not very meaningful (since there was nothing to integrate into). Furthermore, integrativeness was closely associated with two very different variables: faceless pragmatic incentives and attitudes toward the L2 community" (Dörnyei 2010: 78). To reconcile such findings, Dörnyei applied the psychological conceptualization of *possible selves* (Markus and Nurius 1986) – particularly the *Ideal L2 Self* and the *Ought-to L2 Self* as part of *the L2 Motivational Self-System* (Dörnyei 2009c, 2010; Ushioda and Dörnyei 2009; see discussion in Chapter 8, this volume). The Ideal L2 Self is associated with mastery of the L2, including being a successful professional. The Ought-to L2 Self is related to attributes that one ought to possess. Dörnyei also applied *self-discrepancy theory* (Higgins 1987), to suggest that motivation involves the desire for people to reduce the discrepancy between their actual and ideal/ought selves. The third component of the L2 Motivational Self System is the L2 Learning Experience, which concerns the situated motives related to the immediate learning environment and experience (e.g. the impact of the teacher, the curriculum, the peer group, the experience of success). Dörnyei's perspective clearly has helped the field understand Gardner's integrativeness better and has a provided a way to look at its relationship to instrumentality as our ideal L2 self may also be professionally successful. It is also a theoretical perspective that is aligned with the Stimulus Appraisal Model with particular parallels to the self/social image dimension. The L2 Learning Experience component, depending on the stimuli, lines up with other appraisal dimensions.

Because appraisals are gained through experiences and colored by individuals' genetically endowed nervous systems, which as we have seen differ across learners, different learners will make different appraisals about language learning in general and also specific language learning contexts. This will set each learner on a separate language learning trajectory. One learner may find learning French unappealing due to her own and her family's disdain of the French and their culture. They find all things French unpleasant and believe that becoming like the French in any way would not benefit one's self/social image. This learner certainly would not appraise learning French as something that contributes to personal goals or needs. However, the same learner may have opposite appraisals for Chinese and consider China an exotic, interesting land with fascinating people. The family believes that China will play a bigger and bigger role in the world economy. These appraisals encourage the learner to learn Chinese. While in the beginning the learner finds the novelty of learning Chinese appealing, a few weeks into the course the learner finds that she is unable to cope with the rapid pace of instruction. Despite her family's encouragement, she only finishes the first introductory course. Such anecdotes illustrate how the constructs and components of L2 motivation point toward stimulus appraisal.

20.3.3 The neurobiology of stimulus appraisal

In his 1997 work on the neurobiology of affect and L2 acquisition, Schumann focused on the mature brain and the roles of the amygdala, orbital frontal cortex and the body proper. Elements of the *limbic system* embedded in the mid-brain regulate hormones and relate to emotional behavior. The *amygdala* is located deep in the medial temporal lobes and has a primary role in processing and storing memories associated with emotional events; related to the basal ganglia, it is characterized as determining fight–flight responses. The *orbital frontal cortex* is located in the prefrontal cortex and is involved in decision making (especially as related to reward and punishment); it is linked to the limbic system. The *cortex*, the wrinkled exterior layer of the brain, takes care of higher mental functions such as reasoning, language and vision. Stimulus appraisal begins from birth as infants newly encounter the sights, sounds, tastes, smells, tactile sensations and inhabitants of the world, and the stimulus appraisal system is built on top of the neurobiological structures available to newborns. Thus we begin this neurobiology of stimulus appraisal with the infant's interactional instinct and then reflect on how the amygdala, orbital frontal cortex and body proper build on those systems and the experiences newborns have.

Opiates and dopamine along with the corticobulbar tracts

Lee *et al.* (2009) detail the new experiences of infants from the perspective of our consummatory and appetitive reward systems as described by Depue and Morrone-Strupinsky (2005). One way to think of consummatory and appetitive rewards is to think of consummatory rewards as rewards for finding and appetitive rewards as rewards for seeking. In the earliest moments after birth, infants, via their nervous systems, experience a cacophany of new stimuli. In that setting, gentle touch and nursing promote the release of opiates from the hypothalamus, which facilitate a calming of the aroused infant nervous system. This is the infant's first experience of what Depue and Morrone-Strupinsky (2005) call consummatory reward; consummatory reward being characterized by feelings of satiety and pleasure and a resting state associated with activation of the parasympathetic portion of the autonomic nervous system, the system that governs visceral states like heart rate, breathing, digestion and perspiration.

While newborns lack fine motor control over their hands and feet and certainly cannot move themselves across any significant distances, they are born with working connections between the cortex and cranial nerves called corticobulbar connections (Porges 2003, 2005, 2011). These connections allow for an impressive range of socially oriented behaviors when newborns are just minutes old. For example, neonates followed face-like stimuli for 180 degrees through a coordination of both eye and neck movement (Cohen and Cashon 2003; Johnson, Dziurawiec, Ellis and Morton 1991; Goren, Sarty and Wu 1975); imitated interlocutors in socially meaningful ways (Nagy and Molnar 2004; Kugiumutzakis 1999; Meltzoff 2002; Mazokopaki and Kugiumutzakis 2009) and displayed facial and emotional expressions (Charlesworth and Kreutzer 1973; Ekman and Rosenberg 2005).

Additionally, newborns have the ability to bind together the contextual features of an experience with conditions for reward. In other words, infants can unconsciously register what conditions produce what rewards. These associations are formed in the *nucleus accumbens shell*, a deep brain structure and part of the basal ganglia that is sensitive to sensations of reward and pleasure. The connection of being held or fed with the result of a satisfying calmness, and the ability to manipulate eye gaze, head position, vocalizations and facial expressions provide the infant with enough resources to seek previously experienced consummatory rewards; this seeking process is facilitated by the appetitive reward system.

The appetitive reward system revolves around the release of dopamine to the nucleus accumbens shell during the process of seeking out a goal. Dopamine is released in response to rewards-along-the-way in the course of "incentive motivated behaviors" (Depue and Morrone-Strupinsky 2005). While opiates are released by close interactions such as gentle touches, nursing, grooming, or for adults, mating, in the process of infant affiliation, dopamine is also released by the more distant signals that some social interaction is imminent – familiar maternal smells, friendly faces, pleasant vocalizations and other such stimuli. As adults, we can recycle this system for non-social goals. We experience appetitive rewards when we walk toward the kitchen, and open the freezer, and see the bucket of ice cream, and pick it up sensing that the bucket isn't empty. As we eat the ice cream, we begin to experience consummatory reward.

This whole system of consummatory rewards, affiliative memories and appetitive rewards remains available to adults. As adults experience needs or develop goals, these same systems mediate seeking and finding within the framework of both immediate and long-term goals. In other words, the work of opiates and dopamine in the nucleus accumbens shell acts as a neurochemical substrate for stimulus appraisal. An individual can take his/her current environment and plan next courses of action according to the perceived likelihood of achieving appetitive or consummatory rewards.

The amygdala, orbital frontal cortex and the body proper

In addition to neurochemical systems subserving stimulus appraisal, there are particular nervous system components that make special contributions to assessing the environment. The first, and perhaps focal, component in Schumann (1997) is the amygdala, the previously mentioned subcortical brain region associated with processing emotional stimuli. The amygdala receives sensory input both directly through the thalamus, a structure nestled under the cortex and at the top of the brain stem that is the first waypoint for most sensory information, and also indirectly from thalamic inputs that stop by the cortex first. The direct inputs from the thalamus arrive first and provide a basic picture of the environment in case there is some threat that requires immediate reaction, such as a snake lying by the path. Indirect inputs arrive later after the cortex has had a chance to interpret the stimuli and attach emotional valence to it – the snake is actually a non-threatening loop of rope (LeDoux 1996).

One particular cortical region that innervates the amygdala is the orbital frontal cortex (OFC). The OFC is anatomically linked to the amygdala and plays an important role in emotion and social behaviors (Blakemore and Choudhury 2006; Sowell et al. 2003; Mates, Mikesell and Smith 2010). The medial surface of the OFC, the surface between the two lobes, is the cortical region that plays an overview role in the previously described process of creating memories for affiliative reward (Depue and Morrone-Strupinsky 2005). It receives direct sensory information from the thalamus, reward information from the amygdala, as well as contextual information from the hippocampus. These connections are mostly reciprocal in that the OFC sends integrated assessments of a situation back to those same regions thereby coloring the very process of perceiving. Finally, the body proper is part of the stimulus appraisal system. Changes in heart rate, breathing and perspiration feed back up to the brain to signal affective changes (Schumann 1997). More about the body proper will be discussed when we discuss the social engagement system and anxiety.

Genetic and developmental influences on the neurobiology of stimulus appraisal

There remains much to be discovered about the genetic and developmental influences on the various neurobiological systems that have been described; however, Lee *et al.* (2009) believe that enough is known to at least begin the discussion. First, there appears to be wide, genetically based variation in dopamine and opiate receptor density. Greater receptor density suggests greater sensitivity to those neurochemicals making certain people more likely to find particular stimuli rewarding. Additionally, receptor density changes over an individual's lifetime, reaching its peak at ages 3 to 4 years before a rapid decline up until puberty where the rate of decline tapers dramatically. Opiate receptor density appears to follow a similar peaking and rapid decline phase, but this happens at an earlier age when infants are most dependent on close caregiver interaction. These developmental changes suggest that sensitivity to certain kinds of rewards not only differs from person to person, but also at different time points in the same person's life.

Section 20.3 discussed how our affective, emotional responses to the environment in general and language learning contexts in particular are built on stimulus appraisals. In turn, these stimulus appraisals are based on a neurobiological system involving neurochemical processes of reward via dopamine and opiates as well as a tripartite system consisting of the amygdala for low-level assessment of threats in the environment, the orbital frontal cortex for an integration of emotionally salient stimuli, and the body proper. The stimulus appraisal system is not only shaped by an individual's unique experiences but also by unique genetic and developmental influences. Because each language learner is equipped with their own unique stimulus appraisal system, they evaluate each second language learning opportunity differently. In this section, the illustrations tended to present learners' more global attitudes toward a particular target language or language learning. In the following section, research on anxiety in SLA and the neurobiology of social engagement is presented to consider appraisals that may be more moment-by-moment.

20.4 Anxiety in SLA: the view from the limbic system

Whatever a learner's cognitive capacities are, affective factors can facilitate or inhibit language learning that these capacities otherwise equip them for. In Gass's SLA model (1988), affective factors are a key regulator of the needed apperceived input. And in Krashen's view (1982), one's success in second language learning is determined by the relationship between comprehensible input and *affective filter* levels; a high affective filter will result in comprehensible input not reaching the part of the brain responsible for language acquisition and a lower or weaker filter will allow such input to strike deeper (1982: 31). (Note however, when introduced, these ideas had not been subject to empirical scrutiny.) As suggested previously, the motivational component of affect is part of cognition, and a learner's affective response to the learning environment is believed to impact the trajectory of SLA. In this section, we focus on anxiety as a particular affective response and then an underlying neurobiology of anxiety to suggest why anxiety impacts SLA and why it impacts different learners differently.

20.4.1 The effect of anxiety on language learning
Anxiety has been defined as the subjective feeling of tension, apprehension, nervousness and worry associated with an arousal of the autonomic nervous system (Horwitz 1986, 2001; Spielberger 1983). MacIntyre (1995: 2) discusses how anxiety can impact language learning:

> [A] demand to answer a question in a second language may cause a student to be anxious; anxiety leads to worry and rumination. Cognitive performance is diminished because of the divided attention and therefore performance suffers, leading to negative self-evaluations and more self-deprecating cognition which further impairs performance and so on... For some students this is a frequent course of events, and anxiety becomes reliably associated with any situation involving the second language. Once established, this association leads students to become anxious at the prospect of second language learning or communication.

Second language research has long been concerned that anxiety-producing environments inhibit language learning and in 1978 Scovel suggested that different levels of anxiety affect language acquisition differently, arguing that mild anxiety can be beneficial, or *facilitating*, insofar as it can motivate a learner to approach and apply him/herself to a new learning task. On the other hand, too much anxiety can be harmful, or *debilitating*, insofar as it may motivate a learner to flee or avoid the new task (1978: 132). Scovel attributes the "source of all affective arousal," and thus, facilitating and debilitating anxiety, to the limbic system (1978: 139).

Anxiety can be further specified into subcategories. For example, social anxiety is concerned with how one is perceived in relation to others. This type of anxiety can inhibit behavior and lead to avoidance of social situations. Anxiety has also been divided into three categories: trait, state and situation. *Trait anxiety* is a stable personality trait or the tendency to react in an anxious manner. *State anxiety*, on the other hand, is a temporary condition experienced at a particular and definite moment. *Situation specific anxiety*, however, is a trait that recurs at specific situations and events (Geen 1991: 392). From the L2 acquisition perspective, anxiety is typically thought of as the "apprehension experienced when a situation requires the use of a second language with which the individual is not fully proficient" which is manifested in "feelings of apprehension and physiological processes such as increased heart rate" (Gardner and MacIntyre 1993).

In bridging variables in language learning, including affective factors such as anxiety, MacIntyre and colleagues (MacIntyre, Baker, Clément and Donovan 2003; MacIntyre, Clément, Dörnyei and Noels 1998) introduced the construct of *Willingness to Communicate (WTC)* in SLA, which is "a readiness to enter into discourse at a particular time with a specific person or persons, using a L2" (MacIntyre *et al.* 1998). It is also the "consistent tendency to move toward or away from communicating, given the choice" (Dörnyei 2005). This model essentially asks: "Why do some choose to use a L2, and some do not within a given situation?" Such research has been important, as it is a widespread belief that the use of the target language is necessary for acquisition (Seliger 1977; Swain 1995).

MacIntyre's WTC model proposes a multilayer pyramid model including a range of linguistic and psychological variables that affect WTC including linguistic self-confidence, the desire to affiliate with a person, interpersonal motivation, intergroup attitudes, motivation, parameters of social situation, communicative competence and experience, and various personality traits (MacIntyre *et al.* 1998, 2001). Of these variables, the two strongest predictors of WTC is communication anxiety and perceived communication competence. Communication anxiety refers to the general level of fear associated with actual or anticipated communication, while perceived communicative competence refers to one's self-evaluation of one's ability to communicate appropriately in a given situation that ultimately determines one's decision to communicate (Baker and MacIntyre 2000; MacIntyre *et al.* 2001, 2003; McCroskey 1977, 1982).

Evidence from language learner diaries

Bailey (1995) appeared to find evidence of these different effects of anxiety in examining diary studies. Learners were reporting ways in which anxiety not only motivated competitiveness, a desire to gain the teacher's approval, and an interest in or lack of concern with tests and grades, but also could induce withdrawal from the language learning experience (1995: 195–96).

For example, in one of Bailey's own diary entries while enrolled in a French class she wrote:

> I hope Marie will eventually like me and think that I am a good language learner... The girl who has been in France seems to think that she's too good for the rest of use, but she didn't do all that well today. I want to have the exercises worked out perfectly before the next class. Today I was just scared enough to be stimulated to prepare for next time. If I were any scareder I'd be a nervous wreck. (Bailey 1980: 41)

In her entry, Bailey compared herself to others, which resulted in facilitating anxiety that "stimulated" her enough to work harder and to prepare for the next time, and not enough to withdraw from trying. However, the day after, Bailey's entry reads:

> I am absolutely worn out. I floundered through the class, making at least four stupid mistakes out loud. I felt so lost!... Today my palms were sweating and I was chewing my lip through the entire class. My emotional state wasn't helped by the blond girl who sat next to me, she had already taken French 3 and was just looking for a 3-unit course. (Bailey 1980: 42–43)

This entry reveals how she was "a learner who was very uncomfortable and extremely anxious about the class" (Bailey 1995), and again she found herself ranking herself and competing against a classmate. Then, seeing herself as weaker than the other students motivated her to study French in order to avoid public errors. However, the feeling that she could not compete in class became so intense that she soon withdrew from this painful situation (1995: 173) as she wrote:

> Over the weekend I had planned to do a total review of the French grammar book, but I didn't get to it because I had so much department business to do. Last night I began reading the assigned chapter but I got bogged down and discouraged and I quit. Coming to school today I vowed to leave my office an hour before class so I could prepare. Some things came up though and twenty minutes before the class was supposed to start, I decided to skip class and use the time to review instead. Then I discovered I had left my French books at home! I feel very anxious about this class. I know I am (or can be) a good language learner, but I hate being lost in class. I feel like I am behind others and slowing down the pace. (Bailey 1980: 43–44)

Evidence from experimental methods

In addition to diary studies, anxiety in the language learning context has been examined using other methods as well. Horwitz, Horwitz and Cope (1986) report a study by Kleinmann (1977) which elicited different sentence structures from participants (i.e. passive) under relaxed and anxiety-producing conditions. The study found that anxiety affects the quality of communication strategies; anxious participants tended to avoid more complex and difficult phrasings. Steinberg and Horwitz (1986) explored the effects of induced anxiety on oral descriptions of pictures by twenty Spanish-speaking ESL learners. There were two conditions: anxiety and non-anxiety. In the anxiety condition, a "stressful environment was fostered" – the subject was "brusquely" seated just a few feet away from the experimenter, who made sure to note the presence of the audio- and video-recorders and conspicuously played with the controls during the interview. Subjects were also told that the exercise reflected their basic English skills and that "good performance was crucial to the success of the experiment." In the non-anxiety condition, subjects were greeted in a "warm, personal manner," were seated comfortably in an armchair and were not subjected to the presence of video camera. Subjects were also told that while they hoped that the subjects would perform their best, "the experience was supposed to be interesting and enjoyable for them and they were not to worry about being evaluated" (Steinberg and Horwitz 1986: 133). The results showed that subjects in the anxiety condition described visual stimuli literally and less interpretively than their counterparts. The researchers concluded that students in classrooms may be less likely to discuss personal reactions and interpretations in a stressful environment. Studies on writing and anxiety (Daly and Miller 1975; Daly 1977) also show that students with higher anxiety levels write shorter compositions, use less intense words and qualify their writing less. These studies strongly suggest that anxiety has a measurable impact on SLA.

Stimulus appraisal and anxiety

Overall, while the discussion on anxiety in SLA may emphasize different perspectives, what is clear is that assessments of language use in context are valuable. That is, "to study language anxiety is to study the interaction of the person in the situation producing that anxiety. Some situations arouse anxiety while others do not, so both individual and the context must be taken into consideration" (Endler 1980). SLA research has typically treated anxiety as situation specific and related to a learner's current perception of their lack of language and communicative abilities, the difficulties of the task they are faced with, and their fear of being less competent than other students or being subject to evaluation. This chapter suggests that such perceptions are stimulus appraisals that may lead to physiological responses and can affect behavior and language learning. Anxiety may arise from perceived lack of pleasantness in the language learning/use process, estimated effects on self/social image via a self-evaluation of language ability possibly in comparison with others, doubt as to one's ability to cope with the difficulties of the tasks at hand, or some combination of such appraisals. For example, in Bailey's diary studies mentioned above, she describes the anxiety she felt when she made "four stupid mistakes ... out loud" which led to her palms sweating and lip chewing, and how this anxiety was increased by observing a more competent classmate next to her. Her diary entry reveals how her anxiety was the result of a confluence of appraisals of the situation: lack of pleasantness, the effects of her mistakes on her social image and her coping potential. (See, for example, the Foreign Language Classroom Anxiety Scale developed by Horwitz et al. 1986.)

20.4.2 Subcortical regions implicated in anxiety

Anxiety impacts the language learning process in very immediate ways in that it can motivate choices to engage or withdraw from language learning contexts and opportunities. As suggested previously, it results from stimulus appraisals of the ongoing environment in conjunction with memories of previous experiences. Where the previous neurobiological discussion in Section 20.3 focused on systems that may subserve stimulus appraisal, here we wish to connect those systems to action via Porges' (2003, 2005, 2011) Social Engagement System (SES). In fact, the fight-flight response does not stand alone, but is one part of a tripartite system for social engagement. Porges' SES argues that our evolved vagal system which manages instincts for fight, flight or freeze through autonomic nervous system regulation of our heart rate, respiration and digestion is foundational to our capacity for social engagement. Communicating with others comes after a determination that the situation is not dangerous or life threatening along with a corresponding inhibition of fight, flight or freeze responses from the visceromotor system (Hardacre 2009).

According to Porges (2003, 2005, 2011), encounters with the environment undergo a process called *neuroception*, nervous system perception, where the brain unconsciously assesses whether the person is in a life-threatening situation, in danger or safe. Threats in the environment result in stimulation of the amygdala, and if the threats are life-threatening, the amygdala in turn stimulates the ventrolateral periacqueductal grey (vlPAG) in the brain stem which coordinates a freeze response by activating the unmyelinated visceral vagus which governs the part of the autonomic nervous system, the parasympathetic nervous system, that brings about reduced heart rate and respiration and promotes digestion. The vlPAG also sends signals that inhibit the connection of the cortex with voluntary muscles. With voluntary muscles frozen and heart rate and breathing reduced, an immobilization or "freeze" response is produced. If the threats are dangerous but not life-threatening, then the amygdala sends signals to a different portion of the PAG, the dorsolateral and lateral regions, which inhibit the visceral vagus and activate the sympathetic portion of the autonomic nervous system. The sympathetic nervous system readies the body for arousal and response by increasing heart rate and respiration, dilating the pupils and preparing motor neurons for action through fight or flight responses.

Porges' SES asserts that a necessary, but not sufficient, precursor to social engagement is a neuroception of a safe environment. Under this condition, cortical brain regions linked to face recognition send inhibitory signals to the amygdala which leads to inhibition of fight, flight or freeze responses. With the amygdala inhibited, the myelinated vagus and somatomotor systems are available to facilitate social interaction. This enables the myelinated vagus to quickly tune heart rate, blood pressure and breathing to an appropriate level for engagement; not so high as to promote fight or flight, and not so low as to immobilize (freeze).

The unpacking of this portion of our neurobiology raises several thoughts about L2 acquisition. A point which was not elaborated on above is that the SES begins with neuroception, a determination of whether the environment is safe or not. Porges does not elaborate on the nature of neuroception, but we believe that neuroception is another form of stimulus appraisal. Seen this way, the SES shows one way that stimulus appraisals are linked to action. Stimuli that are seen as safe allow for inhibition of fight-flight-freeze responses through the inhibition of the amygdala and activation of corticobulbar tracts that control head and neck muscles that we use for social engagement. Stimuli perceived as threatening, on the other hand, inhibit the SES and cause the amygdala to activate the PAG which, depending on the circumstances, induces a flight, fight or freeze response. As individuals make different appraisals of learning environments and language use opportunities, they will differentially activate their individually tuned SESs.

It must be noted that Porges' neurobiological model is for social engagement and not all language learning activities necessarily require social engagement, nor do all learners treat all components of learning as such. This may explain Scovel's (1978) proposal that some anxiety could create a facilitating fight response. It is possible that a language learning fight response could involve fewer social activities that are part of the classroom learning environment; activities such as memorizing vocabulary or completing exercises, but probably not activities like participating in a group activity or asking a native speaker for directions on the street.

20.5 Discussion: implications for research

The closer one gets to the neurobiological substrate of human behavior the clearer it becomes that as researchers we face an epistemological challenge. We are trying to explain why language learners exhibit large variations in their rates of progress and ultimate attainment when the brains they are using are complicated, non-linear systems. Our experimental methods are more suited to isolating variables than modeling non-linear systems in which variables feedback on one another. Nevertheless, the field has sought to measure the influence of various constructed attributes; intelligence, aptitude, motivation, personality, attitudes, learner styles and learner strategies are all learner attributes that manifest with considerable variation across individuals. These attributes in turn may consist of different subtypes; subtypes which may interact with one another. And then, environment and contexts must considered.

Aptitude, for example, has been thought to comprise two broad cognitive abilities: analytical ability and memory, but it is also dependent on the specific instructional context (Robinson 2002c) and influenced by motivational and affective factors (Robinson 2005a; also see Chapter 8, this volume). Cognitive styles may also differ in terms of how information is processed. Learners may be field dependent or field independent (Chapelle and Green 1992), reflective or impulsive, holistic or analytic, and so on (Ehrman and Leaver 2003). Using motivation as an example, attitudes toward the specific learning contexts affect motivation (Dörnyei 1994), where some suggest that perceptions of whether learning the target language will contribute to one's ideal L2 self is also a factor (Csizér and Dörnyei 2005). Of course, affective factors, particularly anxiety, can affect language acquisition as well. However, studies have found skill level, age and IQ to be related to the effects of anxiety among learners (Verman and Nijhawan 1976; Gardner, Smythe, Clément and Glicksman 1976; Schumann 1975). Thus, Scovel (1978) in his review of anxiety and second language acquisition at the time, though optimistic about research, stated that the more we study language learning, the "more complex the identification of particular variables becomes" (1978: 166). When discussing human behavior it is tremendously difficult to say that X definitely results in Y where X is a particular learner attribute. Such a view of a stable and monolithic learner experience is what Dörnyei (2009a) refers to as "the individual differences myth."

Despite the nature of research methods commonly used in ID research, our reasoning must beware of linear models of causality. Complexity theory and a Dynamic Systems approach provide a different perspective on second language acquisition – one in which manifestations of differences in individual attributes are numerous and environmental factors differ resulting in variations in learner acquisition (Dörnyei 2009a; Larsen-Freeman 1997; Larsen Freeman and Cameron 2008; Verspoor, de Bot and Lowie 2011; see also Chapter 28, this volume). As Dörnyei (2009a: 194) states:

> [W]hen we look more closely, individual learner characteristics appear to be rather different from the meaning we tend to assign them in everyday parlance and traditional professional discourse: They are not stable but show salient temporal and situational variation, and they are not monolithic but are complex constellations made up of different parts that interact with each other and the environment synchronically and diachronically.

Research in neuroscience may help us to gain traction on such challenges. The brain as a complex, adaptive system requires researchers to grapple with non-linearity; this may serve as a model for how to approach non-linear systems. Ocean and atmospheric research also deal with non-linear systems, but neuroscience has the added benefit of examining what we need examined – the brain. The brain and the enculturated brain is what learners have to work with.

There are a number of ways that the brain can be made relevant to the concerns of SLA. First, for the factors that impact language learning outcomes, what is their biological instantiation? In this chapter, we have proposed that motivation is based on stimulus appraisals guided by appetitive and consummatory rewards, in conjunction with the amygdala, orbital frontal cortex and the body proper. Porges (2003, 2005, 2011), on the other hand, looked to the evolution of the vagal nerve to postulate a social engagement system. Following this method, we can ask what insights do new findings in neurobiology offer to our understanding of SLA?

20.6 Conclusion

This chapter has attempted to present two neurobiological narratives that provide insight into processes and outcomes in SLA. First, learners have brains that differ and change over a lifetime. Constructs and taxonomies of individual differences should take this reality seriously. Second, learners have specific neurobiological systems that help them make stimulus appraisals which motivate them to engage or withdraw from language learning processes. With different neurobiological endowments, different learners may make different appraisals under similar conditions. And with an ever adapting neurobiology, the same learner at different time points may make different appraisals of similar situations. The neurobiology of stimulus appraisal gives insight into the impact of affect on SLA within a single learner and across learners.

Part V

Properties of interlanguage systems

INTRODUCTION TO PART V

This penultimate part of the handbook covers what is currently known about learners' systems in the linguistic domains that have been most widely studied to date. It includes five chapters that delineate L2 competence in a range of areas.

Chapter 21 emphasizes the importance of vocabulary building for L2A in terms of both communicative range and grammatical mastery. It explains incidental and intentional learning of the lexicon, the interaction of processing load with vocabulary acquisition and use, and the parameters of lexical storage. In covering acquisition of the L2 lexicon, it notes similarities in learning, storage and accessing to that of native lexical knowledge. After defining the notion and concomitant features of a *word*, Milton and Donzelli devote the bulk of the chapter to how L2 words are learned. They clarify the incidental/intentional dichotomy, input/uptake and word storage and retrieval.

Chapter 22 examines the development of interpretive knowledge in the L2, including phrasal semantics, lexical semantics and grammatically computed pragmatic inferences. It explores how L2 learners interpret sentences of the target language at different stages of development input, with particular focus on poverty-of-the-stimulus phenomena that cannot be traced to direct input or instruction. The chapter describes the nature and development of L2 semantic knowledge, demonstrating acquisition of subtle interpretations that are neither self-evident in the input, transferred from L1 nor taught. Dekydtspotter presents examples of these phenomena from French, Spanish, Japanese, Italian and Korean. He argues that the development of semantic interpretation is directly linked to the L2 learner's mastery of morphosyntactic features.

The use of a second language in culturally appropriate ways is a necessary component of endstate knowledge and also interfaces with the syntax as, for example, with verbal aspect. Chapter 23 explores how pragmatic competence, discursive abilities and sociocultural acuity (e.g. appropriate speech act production) develop. The chapter focuses on development of discourse and pragmatic constraints on the grammar. After a section discussing speech acts and conversational implicatures, Slabakova reports on three areas of linguistic competence, anaphora, definiteness and deixis. The final section explores work on information structure (syntax/discourse interface).

L2 learners generally seem to master core syntax earlier and better than morphology, as evidenced by inflectional errors in production. Chapter 24 investigates the question of morphosyntactic competence in the light of hypotheses addressing the morphology/syntax divide. The chapter provides an overview of the extensive research on L2 morphosyntax done in the UG framework, succinctly illustrating theoretical perspectives through well-chosen examples of verbal phenomena. Using L2 English, French and German, Ionin contrasts three approaches to L2 morphological deficits – syntactic impairment, missing surface inflection and prosodic transfer – while explaining the role of Distributed Morphology. She concludes with a discussion of Lardiere's Feature Reassembly.

Chapter 25 assesses research on acquisition of the L2 sound system, touching on methodology, recent findings and currently unresolved problems. The chapter gives an overview of L2 phonology and speech, providing extensive empirical evidence while delineating the theoretical issues that have been debated. Broselow and Kang very clearly explain basic phonological terms and processes to render their discussions of L2 research accessible to non-phonologists. The substantial introduction presents three themes – each with intersecting roles – that characterize L2 phonological research: L1 transfer/linguistic universals; phonetics/phonology; perception/production. The subsequent sections review L2A of segmental phonology (phonemes), phonotactics (combinatorial constraints) and suprasegmentals (e.g. intonation, stress) in terms of these themes.

21

The lexicon

James Milton and Giovanna Donzelli

21.1 Introduction

The distinguished nineteenth-century English linguist and phonetician Henry Sweet once observed that, "the real intrinsic difficulty in learning a foreign language lies in that of having to master its vocabulary" (Sweet [1899] 1964: 64). In order to become fluent in a foreign language, a foreign language lexicon totaling thousands of words is required. The fluent foreign language user also needs considerable knowledge of each of these words: what part of speech they are, whether and how new word forms can be derived (e.g. *friendly* from friend; *punishment* from *punish*), whether they can be inflected (e.g. *-ing* or *-ed* for verbs; *-s* or *-es* for nouns), what other words they can occur with, and the social situations where these words can and cannot be used. It is an enormous task and it appears there is no short cut in this learning for either the L1 or L2 learner. Communicability and comprehension are likely to be compromised if the learner's vocabulary knowledge is deficient. Laufer and Sim (1985) report the learner observation that a lack of vocabulary knowledge is the greatest barrier to comprehension in a foreign language, greater even than lack of grammatical and syntactic knowledge or knowledge of the subject matter involved. The reason for this is not hard to imagine. As Wilkins (1972: 111) puts it, "without grammar very little can be conveyed, without vocabulary *nothing* can be conveyed."

After a period of time where, in academic circles at least, the contribution of vocabulary knowledge to foreign language learning was down-played, vocabulary has more recently been described as "the core component of all the language skills" (Long and Richards 2007: xii), and arguments are beginning to emerge at a theoretical level that vocabulary knowledge is the driver in the acquisition of a foreign language. In N. C. Ellis' Lexical Learning Hypothesis (N. C. Ellis 1997), for example, vocabulary knowledge is indispensable for the acquisition of grammar. As Milton (2009: 240) points out, this is a far cry from the structuralist approaches to language learning and teaching which were common in the latter half of the last century, where it was thought the number of vocabulary items necessary for learning could be limited only to what was strictly necessary to exemplify or use the grammar.

The task of learning a foreign language lexicon adequate for use may be a considerable one but, nonetheless, many learners do master it and become fluent. What is it they are learning, and how do they become successful and develop such extensive knowledge? The main themes dealt with in this chapter, and in this order, are:

- Words: what a word is and how words are counted
- What it means to *know* a word: incidental versus intentional learning of the lexicon
- How words are acquired: the relationship between *input* and *uptake*
- How words are stored and retrieved for use

21.2 Types of vocabulary knowledge and lexical storage

In order to understand the process of learning the words that comprise a lexicon, it is essential to understand what is being learned and how learners manipulate word knowledge. This is more difficult than might at first appear. If a learner is confronted with a word and the suffixes used to express the regular plural forms as in English, *cat* and *cats*, or in the Italian equivalents *gatto* and *gatti*, are these two words one word or two different ones? In one sense they are clearly two different words since they have different spelling and different pronunciation. There is also an important difference in meaning between the two: the presence of the suffixes -*s*/-*i* indicates plurality which the singular forms lack. But this kind of definition may not be helpful in understanding how learners handle words and how the learning process works in growing a large lexicon. If every different form of a word is counted as a separate word, and these words are learned and stored separately, then in order to master a language, several hundred thousand words might be needed. Early estimates of the vocabulary size of native speakers were made in precisely this way and suggested that a knowledge in the region of 200,000 or 250,000 words was required (reported in Milton 2009: 7) – arguably an impossible learning task for the foreign language learner.

More recent approaches to language learning have surmised that a lexicon is not acquired in this way and that learners of both first and additional languages (often subconsciously) recognize very early in the acquisition process that words often have a base form that can be regularly inflected. To use the English example in the previous paragraph, learners recognize that there is a meaning with a base form *cat* and that by applying a rule where -*s* is added to the end, as with many other words in English, one can create a plural form. Also, in the English verbal agreement paradigm, while there is no plural number affix as all plural forms look the same as the first- and second-person singular forms, learners need to notice the use of the suffix -*s*/-*es* to the stem of the word for the third-person singular of the present simple tense. In other languages like German or Italian, the situation is more complicated, and the processing load of the learner increases as s/he needs to notice that, for example, the plural of a subject is expressed by adding the suffix -*en* (in German) and -*iamo* (in Italian) to the verb, respectively, *ich arbeite / io lavoro* "I work" (singular) and *wir arbeit-en / noi lavor-iamo* "we work" (plural). Similar rules also occur in a number of languages in the use of prefixes and infixes

Such rule-based changes or inflections are a feature of language and represent a short cut to the acquisition of a lexicon. Rather than having to learn every word form as a separate item, if a learner learns one form and applies these rules for inflection, many different word forms are created. While English tends to use comparatively little inflection, we nonetheless can refer to the past by adding -*ed* to verb stems and the comparative and superlative by adding -*er* and -*est* to adjectives. It makes sense, therefore, to model the lexicon and its acquisition not in terms of separate word forms but in terms of *lemmas*: a base form and meaning which can be regularly inflected without changing the part of speech. This approach forms much of the basis of theory about how the lexicon works. In Pienemann's Processability theory (Pienemann 1984, 1985) this idea of an inflected base word, a lemma, is the principle which underlies all subsequent language learning in children. The idea of the lemma is also central to Levelt's (1989) Model of Speech Production in which the lexicon is divided into two parts – one containing *lemmas* and the other *forms*. While the latter comprises knowledge of the morphological (form) as well as of the phonological (sound) identity of words, the former contains information on meaning and syntactic categories (verbs; nouns; adjectives; etc.) into which words fall. Levelt claims that lemmas and forms are linked to each other in the same way as meaning is linked to the morphophonological form of a word (see also Nation 2001). We have evidence that L2 learners also grasp the idea of the lemma very early on in the learning process and that regular inflections are learned early (Kwon 2005).

Some scholars of second language acquisition take this process a stage further and choose to analyze words as larger word families rather than the more limited lemma. For example, Coxhead's (2002) Academic Word List uses the word family as the basis of analysis. This reflects the fact that in language word forms can change not just by inflection but also by derivation through affixation. In English, for example, derivational affixes change the part of speech of a word, as in *large* and *enlarge* where an adjective becomes a verb, and also significantly change the word's meaning, as in *associate* and *disassociate*, where the prefix *dis*- creates an opposite meaning. A word family consists of a base word and many if not all of its derived forms even when these significantly change the meaning or part of speech of the word.

Table 21.1. *Base forms, lemmas and word families (Milton 2009: 11)*

Base form	Forms which might be included in a lemma	Forms which might also be included in a word family
week	weeks	weekly, mid-week
govern	governs, governed, governing,	government, governance, governess, governor, ex-governor, governable, misgovern
wide	wider, widest	widen

An illustration of how far this process might extend, and the differences between lemmas and word families is given in Table 21.1.

Derived forms of words often tend to be less frequent in a given language and less regular, and in first language acquisition, these forms are learned comparatively late and may still be developing during adolescence when the lexicon is already well-formed and sizable. It is thought, too, that derived forms of words are stored and analyzed differently from regularly inflected word forms; they appear to be stored and processed as separate words (Aitchison 2003). Slips of the tongue which involve incorrectly used inflections are common, but slips involving incorrectly used derivation are very rare indicating different storage. There is some evidence that the same storage and analysis holds in second language lexicons since these less frequent derivational forms are learned later than inflected forms (Kwon 2005).

Treating words as lemmas or word families makes a considerable difference to the scale of learning required to achieve a lexicon sufficient for communication or nativelike fluency. Measurements of the vocabulary size of educated native speakers of English made using word families suggest figures of 17,000 to 20,000 words (Goulden, Nation and Read 1990) or as low as 9,000, among 18-year-olds entering university (Milton 2009). These figures are much more approachable in scale for non-native language learners than the earlier estimates of hundreds of thousands of words, and understanding the principle of the lemma serves to explain how learners can reach nativelike levels with regard to the lexicon.

This type of analysis appears to work at a very shallow level of word knowledge where the lexicon in the second language consists only of items where a meaning is linked to a form, and where the form might vary according to the inflectional rules of the language. However, we have understood for a century or so that there is more to knowing a word than merely linking a form to its meaning. As Nation's list in Table 21.2 of what is involved in knowing a word indicates (Nation 2001: 27), knowing a word also includes an understanding of the concepts, referents and associations which relate to the word and its meaning, particularly where these are different from the learner's native language. It will also include knowledge of the grammatical functions of a word and the kind of patterns of use this dictates. The definite article *the* in English often occurs before nouns but the patterns of use of

Table 21.2. *What is involved in knowing a word (from Nation 2001: 27)*

Form	spoken	R	What does the word sound like?
		P	How is the word pronounced?
	written	R	What does the word look like?
		P	How is the word written and spelled?
	word parts	R	What parts are recognizable in this word?
		P	What words parts are needed to express meaning?
Meaning	form and meaning	R	What meaning does this word form signal?
		P	What word form can be used to express this meaning?
	concepts and referents	R	What is included in the concept?
		P	What items can the concept refer to?
	associations	R	What others words does this word make us think of?
		P	What other words could we use instead of this one?
Use	grammatical functions	R	In what patterns does the word occur?
		P	In what patterns must we use this word?
	collocations	R	What words or types of word occur with this one?
		P	What words or types of words must we use with this one?
	constraints on use	R	Where, when and how often would we meet this word?
		P	Where, when and how often can we use this word?

(R = receptive, P = productive)

the can be very different from the equivalent article in other languages and these differences have to be learned. Knowing a word also includes an appreciation of the restrictions on use of words and their collocational patterns, that is, the other words they associate with (see Chapter 14, this volume, on corpora and collocations). Finally, there is a receptive/productive distinction to be drawn between words that are recognized in context when listening or reading, and the subset of words which are available to the learner at any one time for speech or writing.

In an effort to make better sense of this variety of lexical knowledge it is common to think of word knowledge in terms of dimensions that are often seen to contrast with each other and which operate relatively independently. Daller, Milton and Treffers-Daller (2007) contrast *lexical breadth*, *lexical depth* and *fluency* to create a three-dimensional lexical space within which a learner's lexical knowledge can be placed. Lexical breadth is seen as the number of words a learner knows irrespective of how well they are known. Lexical depth is how well they are known; how well learners know the subtleties of use and meaning of the words they have. Fluency is the ease and speed with which these words can be retrieved for use in speech and writing. Learners' lexicons might therefore be qualitatively different, and this three-way classification is a potential means of characterizing these differences. As Meara and Wolter comment (2004: 95), "we might find learners with similar vocabulary sizes, but very different degrees of organisation in their lexicons." Such a classification might identify learners with lots of words but poor knowledge of their use and lack of fluency, and could distinguish these learners from others with few words but considerable depth, for example. This might explain, to some extent, the degree of variability in lexical proficiency among native speakers as well as some of the differences among second language learners and, in particular, in the way learners with the same volumes of vocabulary knowledge can sometimes perform very differently in academic exams and informal communication.

Although it is common to test these dimensions of vocabulary knowledge separately in order to better characterize a learner's knowledge, it is by no means certain that in the learning of a second language lexicon these dimensions function entirely independently. Scores from tests of vocabulary breadth and depth often produce very high correlations (a study by Gyllstad (2007), for example, showed a positive correlation of 0.93 between breadth and depth). Vermeer (2001) suggests these are in fact one dimension, and one interpretation of this is that the quality of depth, the ability to appreciate the subtleties of word meaning and use, is a feature only of lexicons which are already large. Depth can thus be seen as the end of the breadth dimension since choices in the vocabulary to be used can only realistically be made when the learner has a large vocabulary from which to choose. This is certainly the implication of descriptive hierarchical scales of ability such as the Common European Framework of Reference (CEFR) Council of Europe (2001). The Vocabulary Range criteria in the CEFR clearly indicate that the qualities of depth, "idiomatic expressions and colloquialisms, [and] connotative levels of meaning," are only to be found in the highest level of performance (C2) where the lexicon is characterized as "very broad" (Council of Europe 2001: 112). It is less clear that receptive and productive knowledge are so closely linked but since productive vocabulary is a subset of receptive vocabulary it is not perhaps surprising if knowledge tested in these areas also commonly produces good correlations. The conclusion to be drawn from this is that in acquiring a second language lexicon which will allow a learner to function fluently and appropriately, the learner will have to acquire a very large number of words and use them with some sophistication. This leads to a number of questions: how many words need to be acquired and which words should they be, how fast can they be acquired, and what are the processes of exposure and learning which can optimize the learning process?

21.3 Norms of vocabulary growth

As Schmitt (2008) notes, we now have good research data which can tell us much about how second language vocabulary is learned, even if this information has been slow to filter into, for example, mainstream foreign language teaching pedagogy. This information allows us to model the numbers of words that learners need before they have a lexicon that will allow them to become fluent.

In order to become fluent, and therefore be able to retrieve and use the words the learner knows with some degree of readiness and automaticity (Daller *et al.* 2007), s/he will need to develop a second language lexicon containing thousands of words, even if words are calculated as lemmas or word families. Nation (2006) suggests that 8,000 or 9,000 word families are necessary to read a range of authentic texts such as novels or newspapers in English and slightly fewer, 6,000 or 7,000, for listening activities such as watching a film in English. This calculation is based on coverage in the British National Corpus (BNC) where just over 98 percent of the written texts tested comprised words in the most frequent 9,000 word families in the BNC, and where over 98 percent of the spoken text comprised words in the most frequent 7,000 word families. These estimates compare well with data drawn from receptive tests of vocabulary size such as the Eurocentres Vocabulary Size Test (EVST) (Meara and Jones 1990) which estimates a learner's knowledge of the most frequent 10,000 lemmatized words in English and where a learner would need to score 7,500 words or more to be able to pass a test at CEFR C2 level such as Cambridge Proficiency in English. The slight difference may well be due to the way EVST calculates vocabulary size, which is likely to underestimate (Al-Masrai 2010). We think that these quantities of words represent real thresholds in the growth of a lexicon to the scale where fluency is possible in English. While learners may vary in the skill with which they can use the lexical resources they have for communication and comprehension, if they lack a vocabulary size of this scale they are likely to be severely hindered in most language activities and could not be seen as really fluent. It will be noticed that these figures – a vocabulary size approaching 9,000 word families – are very similar to the figures obtained for native-speaking students entering university (Milton 2009). While figures may vary from one language to another, it seems likely that a learner of any language will need a lexicon of comparable scale.

Learners who are not yet fluent and who are in the process of developing their lexical knowledge and have smaller vocabularies have additional difficulties. Research suggests there is a strong relationship between vocabulary size and literacy in a second language. Good correlations have been found between vocabulary and reading comprehension (e.g. Stæhr 2008), writing skill (for example, Stæhr 2008) as well as in listening ability (Zimmerman 2004; Stæhr 2008; Milton, Wade and Hopkins 2010) and speaking (Milton *et al.* 2010). In English we have some idea of the vocabulary size needed to reach certain levels of performance. CEFR B2 (upper intermediate) level, for example, requires a lexicon of about 3,000 word families or 4,000 to 5,000 lemmas. This kind of figure is arrived at both by text coverage calculations (Laufer 1992) and through testing the vocabulary sizes of learners at this level using EVST. The calculation of text coverage – the proportion of a text covered

Table 21.3. *EFL vocabulary size estimates, exam and levels of competence*

EVST Score	ESU[a] level	Cambridge	TOEFL	IELTS	CEFR level
10,000	9 Expert		650	9	
8/9000	8 Very good		630	8	
7500/8000	7 Good	CPE[b]	620	7	C2
6500/7500	6 Competent	CAE[c]	600	6.5	C1
5500/6500			550	6	
4500/5500	5 Independent	FCE[d]	500	5.5	B2
3500/4500			450	5	
About 3000	4 Threshold	PET[e]	400/350	4.5	B1
About 2000	3 Waystage	KET[f]	300	4/3.5	A2

[a] ESU = English Speaking Union system; [b] CPE = Certificate of Proficiency in English; [c] CAE = Certificate of Advanced English; [d] FCE = First Certificate in English; [e] PET = Preliminary English Test; [f] KET = Key English Test.

by a vocabulary of a given size – has become in recent years a standardized procedure in order to address issues such as the goals of vocabulary learning at different levels of proficiency and the ease or difficulty of particular texts (Brown 2010). Nation (2001) also suggests there is a threshold at about 2,000 word families in English below which even grasping the gist of authentic spoken or written language is near impossible and learners cannot function independently. Milton (2009: 69) proposes a similar figure, as a threshold for basic communicability, for French as a foreign language. In Table 21.3 we summarize vocabulary size calculations for English as a second language at various stages in the process of learning from elementary/beginning to fluent and show how these link with familiar exams. The information for this is drawn from a number of studies (Al-Masrai 2010; Al-Qasmi 2010; Kindred 2010) and from placement testing in Swansea University.

It will be apparent that the acquisition of a second language lexicon, even to a point of basic communication, is a sizable task and is not one that will be accomplished quickly. Milton (2009: 76) suggests that in instructed language learning it might make sense with a large-scale undertaking such as this, to divide the task into smaller and more manageable elements and to spread these over the course of learning. Gairns and Redman (1986: 66), for example, have suggested that learning eight to twelve new productive words, probably lemmas, per hour would be a reasonable aspiration for instructed learners, but they assume that the further language learning progresses, the more efficiently learners will be able to learn. The upper figure they suggest is suitable for more advanced learners and the lower figure for elementary levels. This might occur if the more advanced learners are able to use their advancing knowledge of lexis and morphology to commit to memory new derivations or word combinations. Nation (2001), however, points to the importance of the most frequent vocabulary in a language and

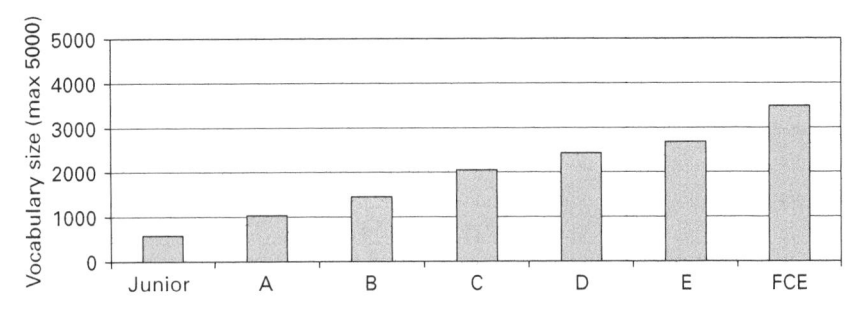

Figure 21.1 *Lexical growth in learners of EFL in Greece (Milton 2009: 79)*

suggests that every effort be made to teach this set explicitly at the outset of learning. It is also possible to hypothesize the opposite of what Gairns and Redman (1986) suggest, a spurt of vocabulary growth at the outset of language learning which subsequently slows down. Milton (2009: 76) calls this "front-loading." This seems particularly relevant to the vocabulary learning curve of young learners in formal instructional settings. Research (Vassiliu 2001; Donzelli, Milton and Daller in press) suggests that the amount of words children hear (from teachers) and read (in textbooks) in class is indeed closely related to the amount of lexis they actually acquire. Donzelli's (2010) research suggests that the vocabulary made available from the teacher to pupils in their first year of foreign language instruction seems to show a much higher frequency of repetition than the vocabulary addressed to their older peers. Teachers thus enhance the chances for incidental acquisition to occur (Tang and Nesi 2003) and for words to be *noticed* and eventually stored in the learner's mental lexicon (Aitchison 2003).

On the other hand, there is little evidence to suggest that a "front-loading" curve is the way lexicons are optimally acquired. Milton (2009) points to the development of vocabulary in what is believed to be a successful learning environment where highly regular vocabulary development is observed over the course of seven years of learning from carefully regulated vocabulary input. This is summarized in Figure 21.1.

EFL vocabulary learning in Greece is contrasted with the learning of French in UK schools (Figure 21.2), which is characterized as less successful and where the then Chief Inspector for Modern Foreign Languages stated that "pupils make less progress over the five years of compulsory secondary education than in most other subjects," as reported by Häcker (2008: 225). Observations include a conspicuous plateau in years two and three where there appears to be little or no vocabulary development and it appears that the input of new vocabulary in any quantity is missing in these years (Tschichold 2012).

Learners in Figure 21.1 (EFL in Greece) appear on average to add lemmatized words to their lexicon fairly regularly at about five words per teaching

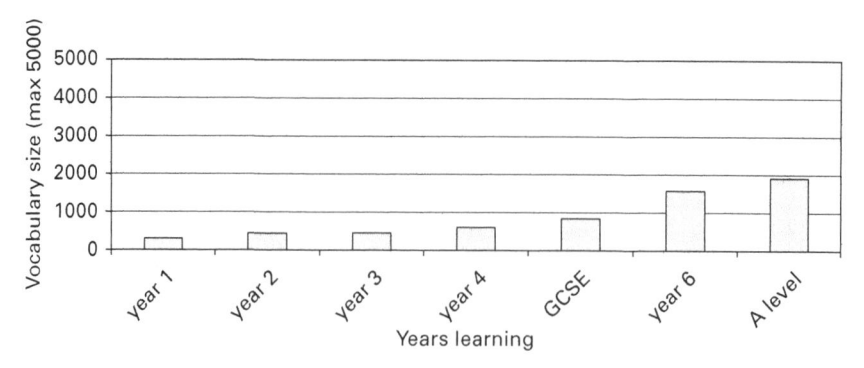

Figure 21.2 *Lexical growth in learners of French as a foreign language in Britain* (Milton 2006)

hour. There are periods in Figure 21.2 (French in Britain) where learners appear to be acquiring on average less than one word per classroom hour. These figures fit well with reviews of lexical uptake where Milton and Meara (1998) suggest that learners in Europe and the Far East consistently acquire vocabulary at three to four lemmatized words per contact hour, and where Laufer (2010) suggests that learners, presumably mostly in the Middle East, acquire between two and three lemmatized words per contact hour.

Even if it can be concluded that learners will optimally acquire vocabulary in an environment of regular and carefully graduated lexical input in class, these figures for progress appear to confirm that acquiring a lexicon is a lengthy process which must, it seems, involve thousands of hours of work. This raises the question of what the language input should be to expedite vocabulary learning in an instructed context.

21.4 How words are acquired

21.4.1 Input and uptake of vocabulary

Terminology in this area makes a clear distinction between *input* and *uptake* in learning (see Chapters 10 and 30, this volume). Uptake is the volume and proportion of the input available to learners from the environment that is successfully processed and to some extend *taken in* and acquired so it can be recognized and used in communication. Vocabulary input, is a more complex notion and is not necessarily the sum of the words that are presented in the textbook or the classroom (or outside the classroom). It should be noted at the outset that there appears to be no critical period in the learning of vocabulary although it is thought this may exist for other elements of language (see Chapter 15). Corder (1967: 165) states that "input is what goes in not what is available for going in." Input might not, therefore, include all the words of the textbook if the conditions of their presentation mean they are not available for learning for some reason. Chaudron (1982) defines *input processing* as the early stages of intake, when the learners' initial perception and segmenting of the input takes place. VanPatten's Model of Input Processing (1996, 2004, 2007) expands this idea and defines input processing as a particular stage in the input–output continuum which is only concerned with the initial data gathering from input and with how learners make form–meaning connections or project syntactic structure onto a sentence (i.e. by starting to differentiate between parts of speech like *nouns* and *verbs*).

There are very obvious differences between the vocabulary input in naturalistic second language and instructed foreign language environments. Second language acquisition has traditionally been addressed (see Mitchell and Myles 2004, for a review of studies) as the learning of any other language, other than the mother tongue, that is spoken in the wider community or region. The opportunity for vocabulary exposure and uptake arises in a wide variety of everyday contexts where learners reside in the target language country. In contrast, foreign language acquisition (FLA) generally refers to the acquisition of a language in formal instructional settings where explicit teaching of grammar and vocabulary is more likely to occur (R. Ellis 2008) and where input is restricted to the classroom (Häcker 2008). In both circumstances there are conditions applying to the exposure to words which learners have, which affect uptake, the words which are learned and used. In the following sections we do not distinguish between SLA and FLA.

21.4.2 Frequency, repetition and vocabulary learning

One of the most important factors in modeling how a foreign language lexicon is built is our understanding of the relationship between frequency of occurrence and word learning. As long ago as 1917 Harold Palmer summarized this relationship in commenting that the most frequent words in a language will be the most useful and the easiest to learn (1917: 123). The relationship is not an absolute one, and there appear to be a number of factors at play here. One thing that seems to be happening is that provided foreign language input is relatively typical (in that it comprises a spread of vocabulary which represents a balanced proportion of the lexis available in, for example, general English) then the chance of encountering a frequent word is far greater than encountering an infrequent word. Learners cannot learn words they never encounter, so learning will tend to be focused on frequent vocabulary. Frequent words will by definition also tend to be repeated, and repetition is a factor that can be linked to success in word learning although the relationship is not necessarily a simple one. For example, words should not merely be repeated in isolation, but repeated in a variety of meaningful contexts. The most frequent words in English also tend to be qualitatively different from less frequent ones, as Table 21.4, which compares the most frequent ten unlemmatized words in the BNC with words at the beginning of the 5,000-word frequency band, demonstrates.

Table 21.4. *The most frequent words, and words from the 5,000-word band, and their occurrences in the BNC (Kilgariff 2006)*

Rank	Occurrences	Word	Rank	Occurrences	Word
1	618,726,7	the	5001	1188	regulatory
2	423,963,2	be	5002	1188	cylinder
3	309,344,4	of	5003	1187	curiosity
4	268,786,3	and	5004	1185	resident
5	218,636,9	a	5005	1185	narrative
6	192,431,5	in	5006	1185	cognitive
7	162,085,0	to	5007	1184	lengthy
8	137,563,6	have	5008	1184	gothic
9	109,018,6	it	5009	1184	dip
10	103,932,3	to	5010	1184	adverse

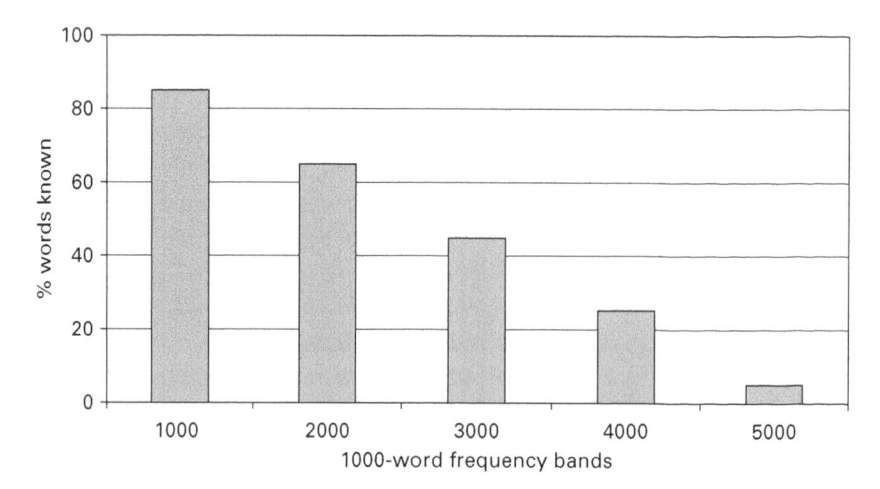

Figure 21.3 *Vocabulary profile of a typical learner (Meara 1992: 4)*

The most frequent words tend to be function words: articles such as *the*; auxiliary verbs such as *be* and *have*; prepositions such as *of* and *in*; and conjunctions such as *with*. These words may carry little semantic meaning in themselves. Infrequent words tend to be lexical or content words and carry the burden of semantic meaning in an utterance. The 5,000 word range includes *regulatory*, *cylinder* and *cognitive*.

Knowing that this relationship exists allows Meara (1992) to model how an emergent second language lexicon, in any language, appears and grows. Figure 21.3 illustrates this.

Column 1 represents knowledge of the first thousand most frequent words in a language, column 2 the next most frequent 1,000 words, and so on. A typical learner's knowledge, Meara suggests, is high in the frequent columns and lower in the less frequent columns giving a distinctive downwards slope from left to right. Learners will tend to know more of the high-frequency

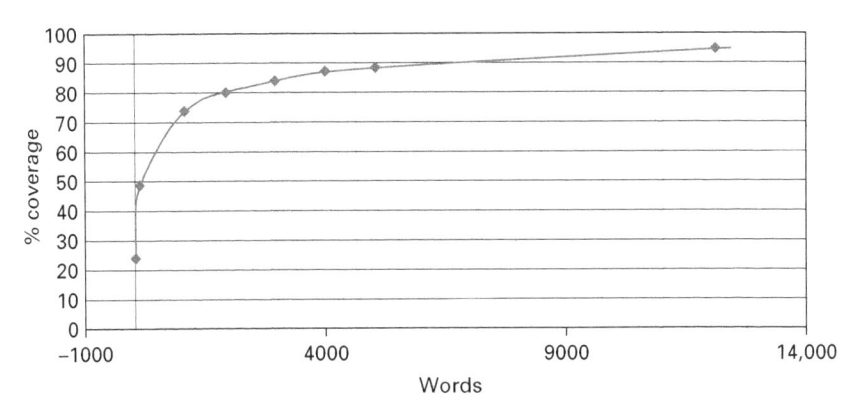

Figure 21.4 *Coverage of the most frequent English words presented in graph form (Carroll, Davies and Richman 1971, cited in Milton 2009: 47)*

words than they do of the lower-frequency words. As the learner's knowledge increases, the profile moves upwards until it hits a ceiling at 100 percent (all the words in this frequency band are known) when the profile flattens out at the most frequent levels and the downwards slope, left to right, shifts to the right into less frequent vocabulary bands. Where this relationship is tested, particularly among groups of learners, it appears to be a very strong one (e.g. Milton 2007; Richards and Malvern 2007; Aizawa 2006). A learner's lexicon, it seems, is likely to be concentrated among the most frequent lexical bands.

An important effect of learning the most frequent words early in the development of a lexicon is observed: these words make a substantial contribution to coverage and, therefore, to the ability to comprehend and communicate. The disproportionate contribution of the most frequent words to coverage is illustrated in Figure 21.4.

In Figure 21.4 the curve rises steeply on the left-hand side and in this area each additional word contributes significantly to text coverage. The most frequent ten words account for about a quarter of all the words to be encountered in normal written English, and even more in spoken English. Knowledge of about 1,000 words in English means that a learner will recognize and understand about three-quarters of the words in normal text. Knowledge of about 2,000 words in English means that about 80 percent of the words in normal text will be understood. It is thought (Milton 2009) that similar figures obtain in other languages. So, if learners learn these words then they will know a large proportion of the texts they read or hear, and, it might be argued, stand a better chance of understanding them. The logic behind Palmer's (1917) claim that the most frequent words are also the most useful is very clear. This also explains why writers such as Nation (2001) place such emphasis on the teaching of these words to second language learners so they can move to independence and communicability at the earliest opportunity. A lexicon which comprised purely infrequent and arcane words such as *reamer*, *traduce* and *mawkish* would be far less useful to learners for communication.

However, as Milton (2007) notes, a model of a lexicon characterizing knowledge in this way is likely to mislead in that it is unable to accurately reflect knowledge of infrequent vocabulary that learners should have encountered. Teaching texts cannot be organized strictly by frequency data, and if they are to have the thematic content necessary to give them meaning and interest then they must include infrequent vocabulary spread across many infrequent bands. Where a text is very highly specialized and contains subject-specific vocabulary then, as Konstantakis (2010) demonstrates, this vocabulary, rather than the more frequent and general vocabulary, is crucial to comprehension. A feature of an emerging lexicon, therefore, is that it must contain large quantities of infrequent vocabulary in addition to the crucially important highly frequent vocabulary. Milton (2009) proposes that a characteristic of good texts for learning at the outset is that they contain words in roughly equal proportions from inside and outside the most frequent 2,000 word bands. A feature of more advanced texts is that they are very heavily loaded with infrequent vocabulary.

21.4.3 Incidental and explicit learning

The previous sections have suggested how large a second language speaker's lexicon needs to be and the rate at which it is typically learned. As noted above, even learners in good learning situations appear to add words to their lexicons at a comparatively modest five words per classroom hour. Since classroom hours are so limited but the size of the lexicon is so large, this has led to an assumption by some writers that the majority of words must be acquired outside the classroom, and that the impact of classroom teaching on the lexicon is relatively small. For example, Harris and Snow state unequivocally that, "few words are retained from those which are *learned* or *taught* by direct instruction" (2004: 55), and they suggest that learners "extend their vocabulary through sub-conscious acquisition" (2004: 61). And R. Ellis suggests that "most L2 vocabulary is learned incidentally, much of it from oral input" (1994b: 24). There is a debate, therefore, as to whether vocabulary is best learned incidentally or is best taught and explicitly learned.

At the heart of this debate is a confusion of terminology, and writers can have two very different ideas in mind when they write about incidental learning. As Rieder (2003) points out, in language learning the concept of implicit learning is insufficiently distinguished from the concept of implicit learning in psychology. In psychology there is a crucial distinction made between implicit and explicit learning, where by implicit learning requires the absence of conscious operations in the learning process, and the learner by this definition is not deliberately testing a hypothesis or searching for a structure in the language s/he is exposed to. In language learning, incidental learning may refer to learning in the sense that psychologists typically use it, and Harris and Snow clearly have this view of learning in mind when they talk of the "subconscious absorption of words as they crop up incidentally" in other activities (Harris and Snow 2004: 55). This approach appears to suggest that every word present in the environment is available for uptake. But in language learning, incidental learning can also include explicit learning. For Huckin and Coady, therefore, incidental vocabulary acquisition is the learning of new words as a by-product of a meaning-focused communicative activity, such as reading or listening, and interaction. It occurs through "multiple exposures to a word in different contexts" (Huckin and Coady 1999: 185). The learner might be making a conscious note of new vocabulary, in a communicative activity, or testing out new vocabulary, which can make the focus on vocabulary fairly explicit for the learner, but any learning would still be called incidental because the focus of the activity was considered to be communication rather than vocabulary acquisition. Milton (2008) calls this kind of learning *informal*, in order to distinguish it from genuinely incidental learning where the learner is not paying specific attention to the vocabulary and acquisition is not deliberate.

Research suggests that Harris and Snow are quite wrong in assuming that large amounts of vocabulary can be soaked up without deliberate effort by learners, or without the learner even noticing that this is taking place. The research we have on genuinely incidental learning, vocabulary learning from extensive reading programs for example, suggests that uptake is negligible, one or two words only from texts which might be several thousand words in length (Horst and Meara 1999). Harris and Snow are probably quite wrong, too, in claiming that vocabulary uptake in the classroom is small. Carefully controlled studies of the language of the classroom and the words acquired from this exposure suggest that this is the principal source of vocabulary learning for most learners, particularly at the outset of learning (Donzelli 2010), and that uptake can be large. The learners in Vassiliu's study of beginners at a *frontisteria* in Greece were exposed to about 1,000 lemmatized words in their first year of study and when tested at the end of the year, recognized on average about half of these. Good learners had learned most of the vocabulary they were exposed to. As noted earlier, the rate of uptake was five lemmatized words per classroom hour on average.

There is reason, too, for not concluding that a large lexicon can be developed from purely aural input. We are thinking here of a lexicon of the kind required for fluent language use in the way we usually do, in academic circles, and which would involve the ability to read quality newspapers and journals with understanding, and to write in a variety of styles including formal academic prose. A feature of spoken language is that frequent words are even more frequent in this genre than they are in writing. This is demonstrated in Figure 21.5, which compares coverage from the written and oral subcorpora of the BNC (there are actually two spoken subcorpora: context

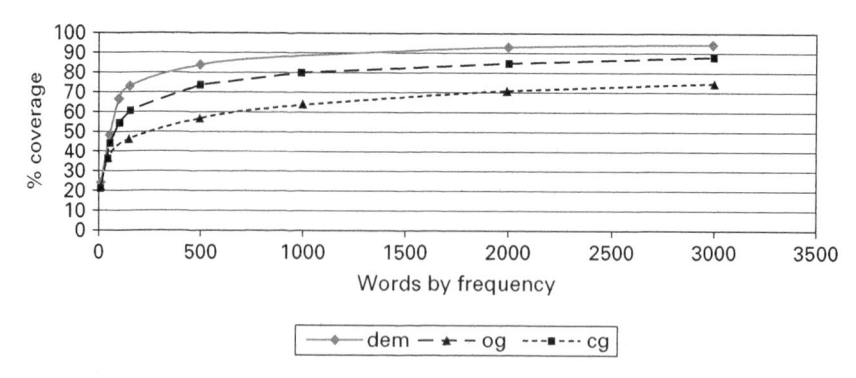

Figure 21.5 *Coverage from written and spoken corpora in the BNC (Milton 2009: 58)*

governed (cg), which includes transcripts of lectures, sermons and the like; and demographic (dem), which includes conversational material).

The predominance of the frequent vocabulary is clear from the way the most frequent words provide more coverage in the spoken subcorpora than in the written one. The most frequent 500 lemmatized words provide 84 percent coverage in the demographic subcorpus but only 57 percent coverage in writing, for example. The significance of this is that spoken language contains much less infrequent vocabulary than writing but exposure to this vocabulary is essential if a large lexicon is to be grown. If, as R. Ellis (1994b) suggests, learners grow second language lexicons predominantly from aural input, then the lexicons which develop must be small and contain overwhelmingly frequent vocabulary, which would severely compromise comprehension and communication in any but the most limited and predictable language environments.

If the words which form the lexicon do not come from oral interaction, and are not learned in any kind of quantity in the classroom, where are these words learned? The answer may lie in the kind of informal language learning activities which well-motivated learners engage in; things like listening to songs in the second language and learning the words, or watching films and TV programs with subtitles, and reading. In Swansea University we have run a number of detailed case studies to try to track the lexical gains and these studies suggest the volumes of word learning can be surprisingly large. Horst and Meara (1999), for example, examined vocabulary learning when a selected learner read and reread a *Lucky Luke* comic book. In this case the learner selected the comic he wanted to read, which contained about 6,000 words of text. He was pre-tested on the lexis of the comic then read the comic through once a week every week for eight weeks, which, he reported, took him about an hour each time. He was tested every week on the vocabulary of the comic and the results suggested that in the course of each reading he gained over thirty new lemmatized words per hour. This finding is made even more impressive when a translation revealed that over 90 percent of these words were known both productively and receptively. Milton (2008), using a similar methodology to the Horst and Meara (1999) study, investigated vocabulary uptake from listening to songs over the course of eight weeks where the learners listened to a CD of Greek ballads from films while reading the lyrics with a translation, and singing along. Once again surprisingly large volumes of lemmatized words were learned; over thirty words per hour from the activity. In this case as well the learner could translate over 90 percent of these words, but could also provide the lexical and grammatical contexts these words occurred in. Milton (2008) also reported a study of a learner who watched a film with subtitles and found about sixteen lemmatized words per hour were learned. It will be noted that these informal activities all involved reading (if not an actual book, then translation and subtitles) and all were given a very specific vocabulary learning direction through the presence of repeated vocabulary tests. Nonetheless, it is thought these studies simulate the kind of informal activities that learners genuinely engage in, and the volumes of vocabulary acquired may go a long way to explain how very large lexicons can be developed by motivated learners. Learning time is enhanced, because these activities typically take place outside the classroom, and the volumes of vocabulary gained are greater, often far greater, than can be achieved in the normal classroom where the focus of work cannot be purely dedicated to vocabulary and must encompass all the other elements of language required for exams and more general communication.

21.5 Focus on form and processing load

There is an argument that all successful vocabulary learning has to be explicit, given some of the features which are necessary for any learning to take place at all. Input is not all the vocabulary in the environment, therefore, but only what is noticed in some way. Laufer and Hulstijn (2001: 3) draw attention to Schmidt's (2001) *noticing hypothesis* since "attention... appears to play a crucial role in both implicit and explicit language learning" (2001: 9). It is not enough for a learner to be surrounded by meaningful language. As Laufer (2005: 223) argues, meaningful input might be a requirement of language learning, but is insufficient for acquiring vocabulary; *focus on form* is an additional essential component of successful learning. The learner must pay deliberate attention to a new word; note its form, its context and the possibilities of its meaning. The results from studies which investigate the guessing of unknown words suggest that where the meaning of an unknown word is obvious from the context and it does not need to be noticed in any detail, then the word is not easily recalled subsequently (Mondria and Wit-de Boer 1991). By moving so directly to meaning, the form of a new word is ignored and learning of that new word cannot take place. By contrast, Laufer and Hulstijn (2001: 11) note several further studies which suggest that where words have to be looked up, or where attention is paid to the form of the word, then recall is enhanced.

Table 21.5. *Components and degrees of value in task induced involvement (adapted from Tsubaki 2006)*

Component	Degree of involvement	Explanation
Need	0 (none)	No perceived need to learn the word
	1 (moderate)	Learner is required to learn the word
	2 (strong)	Learner decides to learn the word
Search	0 (none)	No need to learn word meaning or forms
	1 (moderate)	Word meaning is found
	2 (strong)	Word form is found
Evaluation	0 (none)	No comparison with other words
	1 (moderate)	Word is compared with other words in provided context
	2 (strong)	Word is compared with other words in self-provided contexts

The need for involvement by the learner in the process of acquisition has been developed into an *involvement load model* of vocabulary learning by Laufer and Hulstijn (2001). This has its origins in Craik and Lockhart's (1972) Depth of Processing Model, which suggests that information that is processed at a deeper level is better retained. If a learner simply notes whether a new word that occurs in the course of reading is in upper or lower case, then processing is shallow. It is unlikely to remain in memory. However, if the sound form of the word is added to the written form, then processing is deeper and it is more likely to be retained. Craik and Tulving (1975) expanded this theory with the notion of elaboration. Where new information is connected to information that is pre-existing in memory, it is enriched and is more likely to be retained. While this is a superficial explanation of the learning process, and difficult to operationalize, it still adds an explanation of why simple repetition may not aid the learning of new vocabulary as much as repetition in a variety of forms and contexts that allow a new word's meaning, associations, denotation and usage to be more fully appreciated.

Laufer and Hulstijn's (2001) and Hulstijn and Laufer's (2001) Involvement Load Hypothesis draws on these ideas of depth of process and elaboration, and adds motivational and cognitive factors to provide a fuller explanation of the process of vocabulary learning. It lists three components of task-induced involvement: need, search and evaluation. Each of these components has three degrees of value: strong, moderate and none. These are summarized in Table 21.5.

The need component is the motivation to learn the new word, and the stronger the motivation, the more likely the word is to be learned. Search involves the noticing and connecting of word form and word meaning rather than the noting of meaning in the course of reading, for example, and glossing over the form. Where meaning has to be sought and explicitly linked with form in the course of reading, then a new word is more likely to be retained. Evaluation involves the comparison of the new word with other words, and the idea here suggests that where learners are involved in making a choice of a new word from memory, as in writing an essay, then the word is more likely to be retained than in less productive tasks such as a blank-filling task where a list of words is given.

The validity of this hypothesis is checked by comparing the vocabulary uptake of learners from various different tasks which, it is argued, exemplify different degrees of task-induced involvement (Hulstijn and Laufer 2001). One group that was set the task of reading a letter with target vocabulary glossed for meaning in order to answer comprehension questions was thought to be involved in a task low in involvement. A second group was given the same letter with the target words left blank but with translations and explanations additionally provided. Subjects had to fill in the blanks in the text in addition to completing the comprehension questions. A third group was set a task involving the highest involvement load; they were given target words and explanations and were then required to write a letter using the target words. When tested on retention of the target vocabulary, this third group out-performed the other two groups. While this may be seen as giving general support to the hypothesis, there were factors, such as the length of time spent on task, which were not controlled and which may have contributed to the results which emerged. The third group, which scored highest, also spent longest on the task.

In a relatively unscientific way, therefore, it is possible to use these theories to explain why some of the techniques used by learners described in this chapter are more successful than others. Casual reading of second language teaching texts would clearly have low involvement and would require only shallow processing, and research duly reports low lexical uptake from these activities. Learners who set themselves the task of learning the words of second language songs and understanding their meanings are clearly high in motivation and task involvement, and therefore the task involves deeper processing and higher involvement. Research shows this sort of activity can lead to high vocabulary uptake. Even if involvement and processing load as contributors to success in learning foreign language lexis have not been firmly established, they nonetheless constitute the best and fullest theoretical model we have for the acquisition of a lexicon.

21.6 Conclusion

The acquisition of a second language lexicon appears to involve the learning of words where learners have a good idea that they consist of base forms that may be altered by rules. Knowledge and application of these rules, of the inflections and derivations that a word can have, is extended as learning progresses. Estimates of the growth of the lexicon suggest that a size approaching some 10,000 lemmatized words, at least in English, is required if a learner is to become highly proficient. Learning seems to be highly related to word frequency and, in addition to the sheer numbers of words required for proficiency, a learner will also need to know the majority of the several thousand most frequent words in a language, because of the coverage that these words give. Learning on this scale is not done quickly or easily. Much of this vocabulary, it appears, can be acquired in the classroom from well-constructed textbooks, but it also appears to involve considerable personal effort from the learner to achieve this. Vocabulary does not teach or learn itself and it seems that new vocabulary items must be systematically introduced, explicitly noticed by the learner, and deliberately learned and practised. To become very highly proficient, however, and in addition to classroom and textbook language, the learner will need considerable informal input, and it is beginning to appear that good learners can do this through activities like watching foreign language films and listening to songs as well as through extensive reading. The growth of the lexicon is closely associated with general language development yet it is not yet clear if vocabulary knowledge drives the development of other aspects of language, as some theories suggest. It does appear to develop in a very close relationship with the development of grammar, pragmatic knowledge and other aspects of communicative skill.

22

Semantics

Laurent Dekydtspotter

22.1 Introduction

The acquisition of meanings that mediate between linguistic representations and context/world knowledge constitutes a central challenge facing an L2 learner (see Chapter 21). Indeed, lexical meaning specifications of content vocabulary vary greatly. Thus, English *desk* denotes a piece of furniture whereas the French counterpart *bureau* also denotes a physical space. This much can be instructed to the L2 learner. On the form–meaning specifications of lexical items in interlanguage, Sprouse (2006b) argues that L2 lexical acquisition involves phonological relabeling, whereby L2 lexical entries have the semantic values of their closest L1 counterparts. This induces misalignments between the interlanguage and the target-language input, requiring a myriad of adjustments during the learning process (Stringer 2007, 2010). Although native speakers (NSs) are conscious of the information content of certain expressions, such as *the elephants* versus *elephants*, the knowledge on which this is based is not available to introspection: The semantics of *the* alternating with Ø is below the speaker's level of awareness and in L2 acquisition cannot be directly instructed in ways that would be useful to learners. Furthermore, movement rules in syntax have subtle semantic effects of which naive NSs are not conscious at all. Conditions on the acquisition and timing of the development of semantic knowledge in a range of domains can provide a window on such semantic effects and indeed into the character and process of L2 acquisition.

Semantic interpretation involves an interface between purely formal morphosyntactic knowledge and a semantic component of the mind involving the ability to conceptualize complex mental notions including individuals, events, situations, time intervals. This interface governs the derivation of complex functions that provide semantic values to natural language expressions and allow the computation of the propositional content of sentences. It determines the range of possible semantic specifications of functional categories and aspects of their hierarchy, as well as the rule-by-rule interpretation of morphosyntactic computations. The semantic development associated with the acquisition of morphosyntax reveals computations whereby subconscious mental semantic knowledge is accessed as the learner analyzes the input and it is enhanced with morphosyntactic knowledge. In this chapter, we shall look at how across a range of phenomena and L1/L2 language constellations, the continued operation of innate domain specific knowledge (i.e. Universal Grammar) for L2 learners drives crucial aspects of semantic acquisition.

22.2 Ways of developing semantic knowledge

Studying L2 semantic development first requires a solid understanding of what is at stake in acquisition. Aspects of form–meaning mappings in vocabulary learning might be the subject of instruction or be extracted from speech situations via induction and analogical extension from a known pattern. Acquiring the French word *loup* "wolf" means establishing a vocabulary entry that associates phonological and syntactic features with the concept WOLF that carves the members of the species *canis lupus* out of the domain of individuals. Such information can be imparted through translation, through demonstration, or inferred by the learner from what is being said about a state of affairs in view of world knowledge whether in a dictionary entry or not. For other aspects of L2 (or L1) semantic knowledge, however, the feasibility that meanings are learnable in view of context is remote. The meaning of new types of interrogatives casts in a particularly clear light the extent of the poverty of the stimulus (see Chapter 7, this volume). For example, where a declarative sentence denotes a proposition that characterizes the set of circumstances that make it true, an interrogative sentence does not. Hamblin (1973) argues that interrogative sentences have the set of their possible true answers as semantics. That is, an interrogative characterizes a set of propositions but requests the hearer to identify the propositions that are true of the situation under discussion. This makes the problem of identifying the semantics of new interrogative sentences particularly difficult.

Consider the *qui de célèbre* construction studied by Dekydtspotter (2001) and discussed in detail in Chapter 31, this volume. In French, certain *wh*-expressions which involve discontinuous quantification allow not only structures such as (1a) in which *qui* "who" and its adjectival restriction *de célèbre* "of famous" form a continuous constituent, but also structures such as (1b) in which *qui* "who" and its adjectival restriction *de célèbre* "of famous" form a discontinuous constituent. Sentence (1a) asks for the identity of someone famous at the time the event happened or for the identity of someone famous at the time of utterance. In contrast, (1b) asks only for the identity of someone famous at the time the event happened. The second meaning is missing.

(1) a. Qui de célèbre fumait au   bistro dans les années 60?
       who of famous smoked in-the bar in the years 60
       "Which famous person used to smoke in bars in the 60s?"

   b. Qui fumait de célèbre au   bistro dans les années 60?
       who smoked of famous in-the bar   in the years 60
       "Which person, who was famous, used to smoke in bars in the 60s?"
                             (Dekydtspotter and Sprouse 2001: 3, ex. 1, 2)

The authors tested two levels of learners and native French speakers. With no relevant direct exposure, English speakers showed evidence of constraints on the meanings available to French-like morphosyntactic forms not licensed by their grammar.

The set of meanings available for L2 structures that do not exist in English cannot be grasped from context. Developing knowledge of the semantics of discontinuous interrogative structures in English–French acquisition cannot be due to meanings grasped from context because grasping meanings requires knowing what the speaker knows. Thus, semantic knowledge is latent in grammatical architecture, based on Universal Grammar and it grows in a specific language as an outcome of the more efficient processing resulting from the development of an interlanguage grammar which licenses discontinuous quantification. In grammatical architecture, knowledge of the semantics of the discontinuous (1b) develops as a by-product of the acquisition of the (case-licensing) role of *de* in discontinuous quantification.

The semantic intuitions of English speakers in their acquisition of discontinuous quantifiers in L2 French involve a cluster of properties that support the scenario described here (Dekydtspotter 2001; Dekydtspotter, Sprouse and Swanson 2001; Dekydtspotter, Sprouse and Thyre 1999/2000; Dekydtspotter and Hathorn 2005; Dekydtspotter and Outcalt 2005). The degree to which an acquisition scenario under which speakers are not conscious of certain properties is generally applicable to other domains and is crucial to our understanding of the nature and development of semantic knowledge.

22.3 Acquiring new ways of referring

22.3.1 Reference to kinds

The acquisition of new mappings between words and their meanings requires among other things the learner's re-assignment of semantic values to morphological realizations of the category D (Determiner). Expressions can refer *extensionally* to entities in a particular situation but also *intensionally* to entities across situations. Entities referred to may be collections (or sums) of individuals in situations, e.g. *the elephants*. Crucially, the mind can also abstract *kinds*, denoting generic collections of entities across situations. The

English expression *the elephants* denotes a collection of all the elephants in the current situation. In contrast, in English *elephants* without a definite article can denote the entire species abstracting over situations. Here, there are interesting differences in the expression of reference to kinds among closely related languages.

In Italian, the expression *gli elefanti* "the elephants" may refer to the same extensional plural entity as English *the elephants* but also extends intensionally to the entire species. The (singular) common noun denotes the property of being an elephant, and pluralized *elefanti* is comprised of collections (or sums) of such animals. In its extensional use, the definite article *gli* identifies the maximal such grouping of individuals. In its intensional use, *gli* abstracts over/across situations extracting the species. Thus, *gli* maps to the extensional semantic function of English *the* and to its intensional article-less counterpart.

In English, the "kind" denotation is associated with the bare plural, *elephants*, because the intensional semantic function that allows reference to kind has no morphosyntactic specification. The semantic function applies in lexical semantics for Chierchia (1998) and in phrasal semantics for Longobardi (2001). Moreover, English bare plurals lacking a determiner (D) can also be interpreted as indefinites (e.g. *Elephants are at the water hole*), i.e. an existential interpretation which is generally available to bare plurals. This is presumed to be a default quantificational interpretation (i.e. the first one the speaker considers). Article-less plurals as well as indefinites in English allow generic readings via quantification by adverbs (e.g. *An elephant/elephants is/are always hungry*). Thus, an absent article in English may be ambiguously interpreted via kind reference or via quantification. Italian also exhibits bare, article-less plurals, but kind reference is not available to these bare plurals, because the semantic composition involved in kind reference requires an article in view of conditions on morphosyntactic spell-out of the referential D category in this language. Having a semantic function bound to this morphology blocks the whole species/kind interpretation of bare plurals: syntactically driven computations dispense with the need for context-dependent computations when grammatical architecture exists in which morphosyntactic computations mediate between lexical representations and discourse representations.

A learnability problem of the kind that is classic under Universal Grammar (see Chapter 7, this volume) arises for the L1-English L2-Italian acquirer. Thus, English (2) can mean that some white elephants will appear at the Final Judgment tomorrow at five o'clock (Meaning 1) or that all white elephants as a kind will undergo the Final Judgment tomorrow at five o'clock (Meaning 2). The Italian (3) only receives Meaning 1.

(2)   White elephants will undergo the Final Judgment tomorrow at 5.

(Slabakova 2006a: 501, ex. 3)

(3) Elefanti   di colore bianco passerano   il   Giudizio Universale
    elephants of color   white   undergo-FUT the Final   Judgment
    domani   alle 5.
    tomorrow at   5
    "White elephants will undergo the Final Judgment tomorrow at 5."
                                             (Slabakova 2006a: 501, ex. 4)

It is possible for bare plurals to describe the whole species in (3) as English (2) demonstrates. In learning Italian, English speakers would need to notice that Meaning 2 is absent, whereas it is in principle possible. However, if the speaker does not encounter Meaning 2 in context, this might be due to the vagaries of what the speaker's intentions are, not necessarily what Italian grammar is like. The inductive generalization that Italian bare plurals cannot be used to describe whole species could be disconfirmed by any observation to the contrary, even if this is reached in error. In fact, Italian input exhibits disconfirming evidence to such a generalization: determiners following verbal phrases may be null, creating the illusion of bare plurals referring to kinds (Chierchia 1998). Lastly, generic interpretations of bare plurals in subject position arise due to quantification over time slices introduced by habitual aspect and adverbs. Learning restrictions on Italian bare plurals is a daunting task for the learner, with plenty of counterexamples to be dealt with.

The learnability problem which applies to bare plurals is actually avoided by a morphosyntactically driven acquisition mechanism. Italian morphosyntax provides cues that the determiner in reference cannot be absent. Under general considerations of economy (in Minimalist syntax; see Chapter 1, this volume), a semantic value for a category assigned to a morphological exponent of this category cannot apply in the absence of its morphological exponent (Chierchia 1998). Indeed, in a grammatical architecture in which syntax mediates between the lexicon and discourse representations, syntactically driven computations eschew the need for the speaker's dependence on context. As a result, the intensional use of *gli* prevents bare nouns from referring to kinds. The morphosyntactically driven semantic acquisition of Italian is thus blind to the availability of generic interpretations of bare plurals through other means.

The unavailability of reference to kinds for bare plurals should be felt in other parts of Italian grammar. Thus (4) may mean that large cats have a high opinion of themselves only individually, although they may not think highly of the species in general (Meaning 1). Alternatively (4) may mean that large cats have a high opinion of large cats as a species, although this may not distribute to all the individual members (Meaning 2). When kind reference is not available, as in Italian, Meaning 2 drops out (5).

(4) Large cats think very highly of themselves.
                                             (Slabakova 2006a: 501, ex. 5)

(5) Gatti di grossa taglia hanno un'alta opinione di se
    cats of large dimensions have a high opinion of
    stessi.
    self
    "Large cats think very highly of themselves."

    (Slabakova 2006a: 501, ex. 6)

Examining the acquisition of Italian by English speakers, Slabakova (2006a) noted that the meanings of bare nouns are not discussed in textbooks or discussed by instructors of Italian. L1-English L2-Italian learners of intermediate and advanced proficiency and NSs of Italian were tested with a truth-value judgment task that included eight story-sentence pairs examining the interpretations available to sentences such as (2, 3) and eight story-sentence pairs examining the interpretations available to sentences such as (4, 5). Sixteen fillers were also included, balanced between True and False answers. Examples of scenarios are provided in Samples 1 and 2. A Cloze test provided an independent proficiency measure and a grammaticality judgment task which examined syntactic knowledge in the noun phrase was also administered but will not be detailed here.

Sample 1. Sample experimental item: generic story paired with bare plural (infelicitous description of what happened in Italian)

In a story that I heard somewhere, some animals ask for God's help. He is to decide who is right. A number of white elephants are arguing with some brown elephants about whose color is better. God is going to see them separately: the white ones at 5 and the brown ones at 6.

Elefanti di colore bianco passerano il Giudizio Universale
elephants of color white undergo-FUT the Judgment Final
domani alle 5.
tomorrow at 5
"White elephants will undergo the Final Judgment tomorrow at 5."

(adapted from Slabakova 2006a: 509)

Sample 2. Sample experimental item: kind reading story paired with bare plural (incorrect description of what happened in Italian)

I don't like small cats, but I adore large ones. The thing I like most about them is this: they think that every large cat in the world is smart and handsome. They just like each other very much. What a happy group of animals!

Gatti di grossa taglia hanno un'alta opinione di se stessi.
cats of large dimensions have a high opinion of self
"Large cats think very highly of themselves."

(adapted from Slabakova 2006a: 509)

Accuracy rates for items such as (3) showed no statistically significant differences between the groups in acceptance rates of licit, Italian-like interpretations: intermediate learners 64 percent, advanced learners 76 percent and Italian NSs 68 percent; and in rejection rates of illicit interpretations: intermediate learners 59 percent, advanced learners 66 percent and Italian NSs 67 percent. For items such as (5), the two learner groups' accuracy differed significantly from the NSs ($p < .001$): licit interpretations were accepted (intermediate learners 65.7 percent, advanced learners 67.4 percent and Italian NSs 88.4 percent) and illicit ones generally rejected (intermediate learners 62.7 percent, advanced learners 65 percent and Italian NSs 72.3 percent).

Despite a learnability problem, L1-English L2-Italian learners developed knowledge of constraints on the interpretation of Italian bare plurals. As Slabakova (2006a: 521) states: "No amount of pattern noticing can bring forward knowledge of a missing interpretation." Knowledge of interpretation, even in the area of reference, has to be derived from learners' morphosyntactic knowledge, via UG. In fact, development seems to be channeled in such a way that aspects of morphosyntax signal to learners that the determiner position involved in reference must be filled by a definite article. Thus innate domain-specific constraints on free application of semantic operations ultimately determine the interpretations available to bare plurals.

22.3.2 Result and process nominals

Morphosyntactic parameterization below the category D can also have a significant effect on reference. This was first illustrated in French by Dekydtspotter, Sprouse and Anderson (1997) and further discussed in Dekydtspotter, Anderson and Sprouse (2007). In French, a so-called dyadic noun such as *démonstration* "proof" in (6) allows both a complement *du théorème* "of the theorem" and an agent *le professeur* that may be introduced by the preposition *par* "by" as in (6a) or by the preposition *de* "of" as in (6b).

(6) a. La démonstration du théorème par le professeur était
     the proof   of-the theorem by the professor was
    très intéressante.
    very interesting

   b. La démonstration du théorème du professeur était très
     the proof   of-the theorem of-the professor was very
    intéressante.
    interesting
    "The professor's proof of the theorem was very interesting."
                           (Dekydtspotter *et al.* 1997: 80, ex. 3a, b)

(6a) and (6b) differ in the range of licit interpretations available to them. (6a), with the agent introduced by *par*, can refer either to a result (e.g. the professor's proof reproduced in a textbook) or to a process (e.g. the classroom event during which the professor proved the theorem). (8b), with the agent introduced by *de*, can refer only to a result, but not to a process. This is yet another instance of a missing interpretation. The learnability challenge for L1-English L2-French learners is far from inconsequential. English requires either a prenominal genitive agent (e.g. *the professor's proof*), or a postnominal *by*-marked agent (*the proof by the professor*). Hence, (6a) has an English counterpart (7a), but (6b) does not: English does not license the double-*of* pattern (7b).

(7) a. The proof of the theorem by the professor was very interesting.
    b. *The proof of the theorem of the professor was very interesting.
                                    (Dekydtspotter *et al.* 1997: 80, ex. 5c, 6c)

L2 learners might know that French allows dyadic nouns with *par*-marked agents and that this pattern is compatible with both result and process interpretations and encountering dyadic nouns with *de*-marked agents, yet nothing would uniformly force learners to assume that dyadic nouns with *de*-marked agents are restricted to result interpretations. As Schwartz and Sprouse (2000) point out, when it comes to context, there are many circumstances where the speaker might intend to convey information about the resultant object and where the process creating the object might well be equally plausible. Tracking interpretations means knowing the mind of the speaker, which is ultimately impossible. Thus, a speaker might utter (6a) or (6b) to indicate an interesting formulation on the blackboard. In this situation, it is quite likely that the event during the class session was also very interesting. The speaker who uttered (6a) can be understood in that way, but not the speaker who uttered (6b).

Anderson (2007) replicated Dekydtspotter *et al.* (1997) using items selected on the basis of judgment data from the native French speakers in the previous study. NSs, L1-English L2-French learners and English NS controls with no exposure to French were tested. The task involved twenty-eight context-stimulus sentence pairings (seven sentences with nouns under a result interpretation, and seven sentences under a process interpretation, presented once with a *de*-marked agent and once with a *par*-marked agent). French NSs accepted *de*-marked agents with results significantly more than with process, at 44.97 percent versus 7.94 percent ($p < .001$). The 44.97 percent rate for result interpretations is similar to the stylistic awkwardness of multiple *de*-marked arguments discussed in Milner (1977, 1982) and Ruwet (1972). Intermediate learners produced a crucial distinction between result and process with *de*-marked agents. This was already evident at the second-year level of instruction in French. Thus, the acceptance rate for result, at 61.08 percent, is statistically different from the acceptance rate for process, at 44.83 percent ($p < .01$). This remains the case for French learners at the third year of instruction (63.39 percent versus 41.96 percent; $p < .01$), fourth year of instruction (52.91 percent versus 26.28 percent; $p < .001$) and at more advanced levels (50.00 percent versus 14.29 percent; $p < .001$). Presented with word-for-word translations of the French test sentences, English NS controls produced asymmetries in acceptance rates of multiple *of*-marked dyadic nouns in result contexts, at 23.18 percent, and process contexts, at 14.29 percent ($p < .05$), despite their ungrammaticality in English. Once again, a form–meaning pairing latent in speakers' innate grammatical architecture becomes accessible to intuition as processing is enhanced in response to morphosyntactic properties of the L2 input.

Anderson (2007) also examined the interaction of the interpretation of pre- and post-nominal placement of variable adjectives with the semantics of the definite determiner as in *la lourde valise* "the heavy suitcase" versus *la valise lourde* "the heavy suitcase" in French. In the pre-nominal position, the DP presupposes a unique suitcase, which is in addition heavy, in the relevant context and refers to it. In the post-nominal position, the DP presupposes a unique suitcase that is simply heavy, and refers to it. The latter allows for the possibility of other suitcases. Adjective placement certainly is the object of traditional classroom instruction in French, but crucially instruction is limited to adjectives with lexical meaning changes. By the third-year level of university French, learners demonstrated semantic knowledge of adjective placement despite the fact that they would not normally expect such adjectives to occur in that position (on the basis of explicit rules and classroom input) and are not taught the relevant interpretive asymmetry. Anderson (2008) also discussed the acquisition of the semantics of adjective placement for which formal instruction is given. He noted a timetable seemingly internal to each learner that cuts across the form of evidence available to learners. Adjective placement also interacts with the definite plural determiner. Investigating adjective placement in Spanish, Rothman, Guijarro-Fuentes and Pires (2010) showed that L1-English L2-Spanish learners also acquired sensitivity to the pre-nominal (versus post-nominal) placement of adjectives in interaction with plural definite determiners.

22.4 Acquiring aspectual systems

A formidable challenge lies in the acquisition of a targetlike aspectual system in view of the many layers of computations involved. A sentence describes an eventuality – an event or state. Sentential aspect morphology imposes a perspective on this eventuality. In Spanish and French, for instance, perfective and imperfective past tenses can co-occur with all predicate types, but they induce meaning changes. The perfective past tense requires that the eventuality be seen as complete/whole bounded in time. The imperfective sentence describes an incomplete/partial eventuality: a process or a state unbounded in time. In addition to sentential aspect, verb phrases also have aspectual import: *build a house, arrive home* characterize culminating events; *run* and *dance* characterize processes; and *know the answer* and *love Amy* characterize states. The perfective viewpoint imposed on a process requires mapping the process to its event counterpart, by adding a culmination to the process. It appears that the aspectual shift operations which are possible in which context depend on the particular language (Jackendoff 1996). (This discussion ignores adverbs, although they present parallel issues.) Thus, in addition to the semantics of verbs and arguments of verbs, acquiring an aspect system requires:

(a) identifying the relevant functional morphology;
(b) selecting the viewpoints imposed on the eventualities by the functional morphology;
(c) determining the semantic characteristics of predicates on the basis of verb and object denotations (Slabakova 2001); and
(d) selecting the contextual aspect shift operations among a range of functions.

22.4.1 Acquisition of aspect in Romance languages

Certain biases have been observed in L2 development across languages (Bardovi-Harlig 1992, 2000). Thus, for L1-English L2-French learners, the rates of use of the perfective past tense (*passé composé*) were the highest with event-denoting predicates, reduced with process-denoting predicates (which require an aspectual shift by adding a culmination) and even fewer with stative predicates (which require an aspectual shift by viewing the state as bounded) (Bardovi-Harlig and Bergstrng 1996). The rate of use of the imperfective past tense was highest for state predicates, and lowest for achievement predicates that denote punctual events without a process stage. This cannot be due to the L1 English aspectual system, since the progressive is ungrammatical with stative verbs and the English past tense does not induce aspectual shifts. Similar asymmetries have been found in a wide variety of languages, as well as across tutored and untutored learners. This seems suggestive of an innate predisposition to compute aspect.

Against this backdrop, Montrul and Slabakova (2002) reported on a study of L2 Spanish which examined the acquisition of semantic intuitions crucially reliant on the acquisition of robust knowledge of imperfective and perfective past tenses as in (8a, b).

(8) a. La clase era (imperf) a las 10 (√ pero empezó a las 10:30).
      "The class was (imperfective) at 10, but started at 10:30."
    b. La clase fue (pret) a las 10 (#pero empezó a las 10:30).
      "The class was (perfective) at 10, but started at 10:30."
                            (Montrul and Slabakova 2002: 131, ex. a, b)

Imperfective (8a) characterizes a preparatory stage and is compatible with a statement that the preparatory stage did not culminate until later

(√ indicates this compatibility). Perfective (8b) characterizes a bounded event, which is incompatible with a continuation incompatible with these bounds (# indicates this infelicity).

Adult L1-English learners of Spanish, including advanced and intermediate learners, judged the felicity of combinations as in (8a) versus (8b). Participants indicated whether the two clauses made sense together on a scale ranging from −2 (contradiction) to 2 (no contradiction). A test of morphology was also administered. The advanced learners and those intermediate learners who scored above 80 percent accuracy on the morphology test reliably computed the infelicity, having therefore acquired the semantics. Those intermediate learners who did not control the morphophonology could not reliably compute the infelicity. Robust performance was approached only by advanced learners, and Montrul and Slabakova (2003) showed convergence on native speaker norms in Spanish in learners of superior and near-native proficiency. Likewise, Slabakova and Montrul (2003) showed biases for the generic interpretation of *se* "one" in imperfective sentences with intermediate learners. However, this translated into targetlike behavior across the perfective/imperfective aspectual paradigm only in advanced learners. Examining the accidental/non-accidental entailments of the perfective/imperfective values of past tenses in Portuguese, Rothman and Iverson (2008) arrived at a similar developmental profile.

22.4.2 Japanese

The acquisition of specific form–meaning mappings of sentence-level aspectual morphemes is not the only mapping to be acquired. The computation of verb phrase semantics is also highly language dependent. Thus, in English the verb phrase *write a letter* describes an event, which is specifically an accomplishment, whereas the verb phrase *write letters* describes an iterative process. The contribution of the nominal complement to the aspectual value of the verb phrase is clear. As Gabriele (2010) notes, computations contributed by the noun phrase morphology in English require contextual computations in Japanese in the absence of morphosyntactic information. In Japanese, verb phrases with bare nouns receive iterative process or event interpretations (9, 10). With a specified cardinality of a count noun as in *write two letters* (11), then an event interpretation obtains in both languages. Learners and NSs are not expected to differ. This was experimentally verified and will not be discussed further here.

(9) Sam-wa tegami-o kakimashita.
 Sam-TOP letter-ACC write-PAST.
 "Sam wrote a/the letter."
 "Sam wrote (some) letters." (Gabriele 2010: 383, ex. 16)

(10) Sam-wa jyuusu-o nomimashita.
Sam-TOP juice-ACC drink-PAST.
"Sam drank juice/the juice." (Gabriele 2010: 383, ex. 14)

(11) Sam-wa ni-tsū tegami-o kakimashita.
Sam-TOP two-CL letter-ACC write-PAST.
"Sam wrote two letters." (Aiko McPhail p.c.)

Form–meaning mappings in the nominal system in Japanese and English do not align. In English, *letter* is a count term that can be pluralized and counted, with a denotation that includes indivisible individuals, also called atoms. The mass term *juice* cannot be pluralized or directly counted: juice can only be counted after it is measured out. Likewise, the English term *furniture* cannot be pluralized, although its denotation presumably includes atomic individuals. Terms such as *furniture* seem inherently plural, lexically specified as denoting a plural domain, so that plural formation cannot apply (Chierchia 1998).

The acquisition of the Japanese referential system should have repercussions for the aspectual characteristics of (9) and (10). Such acquisition is presumably guided by constraints on morphology and semantic operations: morphologically bound operations cannot apply freely. In L1-English L2-Japanese acquisition, certain semantic operators that serve as morphologically dependent semantic values for articles (exponents of the category D) in English must be freed from article dependence in L2 Japanese. Semantic values for the category D must then be selected contextually. Bare mass nouns such as Japanese *jyuusu* "juice" allow kind reference as in English. Hence, the L1-English L2-Japanese acquisition of *jyuusu* "juice" is straightforward as the grammars match. However, the interpretation of *jyuusu* as "the juice" comes about by application of the relevant extensional maximizing determiner function in the semantics. Context determines which semantic function is appropriate as morphosyntax is silent; there are no articles in the L2.

As Gabriele (2010) points out, the acquisition of the Japanese counterparts to English's count terms requires a switch in the type of the denotations of most nouns. There is, however, morphosyntactic evidence at the determiner level and below: bare singular count nouns found in Japanese input are ungrammatical in English. This constitutes a trigger for grammatical change for the L2 learner. But the presence of singular count nouns alone does not require the adoption of a Japanese-like system. Indeed, Slavic languages are also null determiner languages that allow bare singular count nouns with otherwise familiar denotations. There is, however, positive evidence in the input that Japanese is yet different. In Japanese, counting also requires the mediation of a classifier system (11). This classifier system provides morphological evidence of different NP denotations. Thus, for English speakers, acquiring Japanese-style reference requires changing the denotations available to count nouns, thereby reclassifying all count terms as receiving inherently plural denotations similar to English *furniture*. Counting then requires individuation by a classifier. Determiner denotations must also apply freely, as lexical specifications of determiner forms and meanings must be abandoned. Thus, Japanese *kagu migaita* "furniture polished" will be equivalent to *polished furniture*, *polished some furniture* and *polished the furniture*, since determiner denotations apply freely.

Acquiring the whole Japanese reference system is undoubtedly tricky for the English speaker. Given L1 transfer, the parser can analyze (9) by freeing determiner denotations but keeping NP denotations intact. This is the minimal necessary change. A Japanese sentence with a classifier as in (11) presents evidence indicative of a different way of denoting. Two ways of denoting can coexist. Indeed, the same set of objects in a house can be referred to with a pluralized term, *les meubles* "the furniture items" or with an inherent plural term, *le mobilier* "the furniture." The acquisition of Japanese by English NSs requires eliminating a way of referring that is not fully supported by the input. Access to L1-induced denotations may become inhibited, as access to inherently plural denotations is enhanced as the full range of classifiers are acquired.

Gabriele (2010) reports on two studies, each featuring a truth-value judgment task among other tasks. These tasks examined the acquisition of the semantic interpretations available to verb phrases with bare count noun counterparts (9) versus mass noun counterparts (10). Intermediate and advanced L1-English L2-Japanese learners and Japanese NSs participated in the study. In both studies, participants were presented with scenarios in Japanese supported by three pictures. Each scenario had two possible endings: in one, the process was fully realized; in the other, the process was partially realized. After the narrative, a sentence presented orally and in writing was offered to the participant as a description of what happened in the scenario. An example of a scenario–sentence pair is provided in Sample 3 for Study 1 and in Sample 4 for Study 2.

Sample 3. Sample experimental item: scenarios paired with a bare count noun (complete and incomplete interpretations allowed in Japanese)

Today is Ken's birthday. He received four presents. He wants to write thank you cards to his friends. Ken writes three cards. Then he starts to write the last card.

Complete: he finishes the last card. Then he gives the cards to his friends.

Incomplete: but Ken has to go to school so he cannot finish the last card.

Ken-wa   tanjoobi-ni   kaado-o   kakimashita.
Ken-TOP   birthday-on   card-ACC   write-PAST
"Ken wrote card on his birthday."

(adapted from Gabriele 2010: 387, ex. 17)

> Sample 4. Sample experimental item: scenarios paired with a bare count noun (complete and incomplete interpretations allowed in Japanese)
>
> Kensuke sees hearts on the blackboard in the classroom. He hates hearts and wants to erase them. Kensuke starts to erase the hearts. Look at what Kensuke did!
>
> Complete picture: all hearts have been completely erased.
>
> Incomplete picture: all hearts have been partially erased.
>
> Kensuke-wa haato-o keshimashita.
> Kensuke-TOP heart-ACC erase-PAST
> "Kensuke erased heart."
>
> (adapted from Gabriele 2010: 394, ex. 20)

Participants judged each test sentence on a scale of 1–5, evaluating its compatibility with the story they had just listened to. There were 24 experimental items and 12 fillers in random order.

Results were similar in both studies. Japanese NSs mapped verb phrases with bare noun objects to either complete or incomplete scenarios, showing that incomplete/partial and complete events were equally accessible. L1-English L2-Japanese learners also interpreted verb phrases with bare mass nouns in object position as ambiguous between incomplete/partial and complete events. This is expected from transfer. L1-English L2-Japanese learners, however, were biased in favor of culminated events in the case of bare count nouns, although some learners did not show it. This bias was also still in evidence in advanced learners.

Gabriele (2010) argues that learners computed the predicate *kaado-o kakimashita* (card-ACC write-PAST) in Sample 3 as an accomplishment predicate and were not able to retreat from this interpretation. Indeed, retreating from an initial interpretation seems harder in L2 processing. Given the context in Sample 3, it seems that most respondents took *the thank you cards that Ken needed to write* as the topic of discourse. In view of this initial structuring of discourse, respondents assigned the object *kaado-o* (card-ACC) the meaning of *the cards* deriving an accomplishment. The incomplete interpretation requires changing one's perspective on the story to what Ken managed to accomplish: getting cards written. This is not merely a change in the semantic value assigned to the category D, but a change in contextual perspective. Studies on quantification show that changes across modules of the grammar are costly (Dekydtspotter 2001; Dekydtspotter, Sprouse and Swanson 2001). Study 2 clearly points to the role of pragmatics. The scenario in Sample 4 examines the conditions under which *the hearts on the blackboard* can be considered as erased. If they are totally erased, the issue is simple. If they are partially erased, what is required to call the hearts erased? Community use potentially plays a large role here. In Japanese, it is grammatical to say something like *I ate the cake but there's still some cake left* canceling an asserted event (Tsujimura 2003). Still, even for the Japanese NSs in Gabriele (2010), the case where the objects were completely affected was by far simpler. This derives from the Presupposition of Indivisibility (Löbner 2000: 239), according to which "whenever a predicate is applied to one of its arguments, it is true or false of the argument as a whole." Learners and NSs diverged in the limit cases in terms of the standards under which the sentence could be accepted as a true statement, although a few learners were within NS range. This study highlights the many layers of computations required for targetlike interpretation.

22.4.3 Other languages

Findings on the acquisition of aspectual systems converge. For example Slabakova (2001) finds early evidence of telicity calculations in L1-Bulgarian's L2-English, but target convergence only in the advanced learners. Slabakova's (2005) study of the acquisition of the aspectual values of verbal prefixes in L1-English L2-Russian supports similar conclusions. Gabriele (2005, 2009) documents the complexities involved in the acquisition of the aspectual value of Japanese *te-iru* and V-*ing* in L1-English L2-Japanese and in L1-Japanese L2-English. With accomplishment predicates (e.g. *paint a portrait*), Japanese and English grammar lead to similar intuitions. With achievement predicates (e.g. *arrive*), however, Japanese and English grammar lead to contradictory semantics. Thus, English V-*ing* characterizes preparatory stages of an event, and in combination with an accomplishment predicate focuses on the preparatory process inherent in the event described, as in *Mary is writing a novel*. In combination with an achievement predicate which denotes only a culmination, V-*ing* requires a contextual coercion where a preparatory process part is added, changing the very nature of the event. In contrast, Japanese *te-iru* characterizes a state that holds true as soon as a segment of an event is in evidence: with accomplishment predicates the preparatory steps satisfy this, and the *te-iru* sentence characterizes the process state inherent in the event; with achievement predicates that denote only a culmination, the segment is the culmination *itself*, so that the *te-iru* sentence characterizes the state resulting from the event. Assuming Full Transfer/Full Access (Schwartz and Sprouse 1994, 1996; see Chapter 5, this volume), learners transferred L1 syntax-to-semantics mappings to new morphemes, and retraction from these mappings proved challenging, though not impossible. The cost of aspectual shifts was also observed. The semantic evidence in the domain of aspect suggests that reliable lexical encoding of new feature values of categories and lexical items develops slowly, and research on aspect highlights the complexities of the form–meaning mappings and the layers of computations – morphological, syntactic, semantic and pragmatic – required for L2 learners to develop nativelike behavior.

22.5 Feature reassembly and semantic development

As Lardiere (2009a) points out, L2 acquisition involves the development of matrices for the L2 functional (grammatical) lexicon, and in subsequent *feature reassembly* these morphosyntactic features are redistributed in the L2 grammar. Ionin (see Chapter 24, this volume) provides a detailed discussion of Lardiere's proposal in terms of determiner semantics. Likewise, Song and Schwartz (2009) investigate *wh*-expressions in L1 English L2 Korean. The feature matrix of the Korean proform *mwues* is distinct from that of English *what*. Indeed, *mwues* translates as *what* in (13) but as *something* in (12).

(12) Amwuto   mwues-ul   sa-ci   anh-ass-ni?
      anyone   something-ACC   buy-*ci* NEG-PAST-Q
      "Didn't anyone buy something?"

      (Song and Schwartz 2009: 330, ex. 7a)

(13) Mwues-ul amwuto sa-ci   anh-ass-ni?
      what-ACC anyone buy-*ci* NEG-PAST-Q
      "What didn't anyone buy?"   (Song and Schwartz 2009: 330, ex. 7b)

Song and Schwartz (2009) examined the development of knowledge of the semantics of the interrogatives in (12) and (13). In view of the enormous challenge in acquiring the semantics of interrogatives in an L2 that go beyond the constraints found in the L1, it is clear that the development of such knowledge requires that learners be guided to perform certain syntactic computations with semantic effects given certain lexical specifications. Crucially, these computations require the acquisition of a different arrangement of features in the specification of lexical items. In initial stages of L1-English L2-Korean acquisition, learners identify *mwues* with the closest English equivalent. As the marker *ni* indicates a question, *mwues* will be interpreted as *what*, until which time the matrices are reassembled (Choi and Lardiere 2006; Lardiere 2009a). The development of semantic intuitions across proficiency levels can provide a window on the reassembly of feature matrices for functional lexical items.

Song and Schwartz's (2009) study provides a glimpse into the process of feature reassembly across child and adult L2 acquisition. Four groups of participants completed the study: child and adult L1-English L2-Korean learners and child and adult NSs of Korean. Respondents were at least 5 years of age, as part of the experimentation involved written word or phrase cards. An independent measure of proficiency was obtained with a picture-narration task (Whong-Barr and Schwartz 2002). Song and Schwartz determined relative proficiency using complexity and accuracy measures combined with equal weight to indicate L2 learners' proficiency level. Their experiment included an interpretive judgment task with a total of 32 experimental items: 16 as in (12) and 16 as in (13). Each question type was divided in four conditions crossing constituents and *yes/no* answers, so that only in one experimental item out of four was *yes* the target response. Thirty-two fillers including *wh*-questions and *yes/no* questions were, therefore, skewed to positive responses. Each item consisted of a scenario – in English for L1-English L2-Korean learners – backed by two pictures matching the description. The experimenter asked Bbung Bbung, the puppet, questions using four Korean word or phrase cards. Bbung Bbung answered either with a noun phrase, indicating a constituent question, or with a *yes/no* answer, indicating a *yes/no* question. Participants were instructed to give a *yes* response when Bbung Bbung's answer was correct and a *no* response when it was incorrect. Respondents were asked to provide an explanation when they supplied a *no* response. Only correct justifications were counted. An example item is provided in Sample 5.

Sample 5. Sample experimental item: NP answer with *yes/no* interpretation word order

Picture 1: The family was hunting for bugs. Although they felt hungry at lunch time, they did not eat any food because it was so fun.

Picture 2: The family wanted to have lunch after bug hunting. Father ate sausage, mother ate a hamburger, Tom ate bread, and Jenny ate chicken. Nobody ate a sandwich.

Experimenter: Amwuto akka   mwues-ul   mek-ci anh-ass-ni?
              Anyone before something-ACC eat-ci NEG-PAST-Q
"Didn't anyone eat something before?"

Bbung Bbung: A sandwich
Is this true? A *yes* answer is non-targetlike, a *no* answer is targetlike.
                    (adapted from Song and Schwartz 2009: 347)

Matched by proficiency, the accuracy rates of L2 children and adults were similar, and the L2 learners' results were therefore collapsed. Low to intermediate L2 learners accepted OSV structures as in (13) as constituent questions and rejected them as *yes/no* questions, with accuracy rates above 87.5 percent. However, these learners also incorrectly interpreted SOV structures as in (12) as constituent questions, systematically rejecting them as *yes/no* questions. This is expected if L1-English L2-Korean learners analyzed *mwues* as if it were *what*. High-proficiency child and adults L2 learners both knew that structures as in (13) were constituent questions and structures as in (12) were *yes/no* questions, with accuracy rates at 80 percent. In the L1, the Korean children correctly accepted OSV structures as in (13) as constituent questions and rejected *yes/no* questions, with rates at or above 91.3 percent accuracy. Korean children were adultlike in their interpretations of strings in (13). The SOV structures as in (12) did, however, show evidence of computational complexity: Korean children rejected constituent questions at

64.1 percent, accepting *yes/no* answers at 59.8 percent. This behavior of Korean children is different from Korean adults, with accuracy rates at or above 90 percent.

Song and Schwartz (2009) showed that child and adult L2 learners followed similar development, empirically validating the proposal that semantics is not affected by a putative critical period in which semantic functions or form–meaning mappings not instantiated in the native grammar are not acquirable in adulthood (Slabakova 2006b). The performance of advanced L2 learners of Korean in (13) again points to a specific grammatical architecture in which the morphosyntax of the language constrains the range of licit interpretations by blocking access to certain meanings. In the case of L2 acquisition, there was a clear effect from the start directly attributable to English-like lexical specifications, which seemed to take a significant time to eliminate.

The task of assignment of semantic values to functional lexical items is far from trivial. Marsden (2008) highlights the problem of acquiring the semantics of the reversible Japanese quantifier *daremo*, which sometimes receives a universal meaning and sometimes a negative meaning in a manner to some degree reminiscent of the English polarity item *anyone*. She does so by examining the semantics of questions such as (14) in Japanese interlanguage.

(14) Nani-o   daremo-ga   katta   no?
      What-ACC everyone-NOM bought Q
      "What did everyone buy?"   (Marsden 2008: 190, ex. 1b)

L2 learners no doubt mostly encounter *daremo* in *daremo...-masen*, "nobody" in which *masen* forces a negative interpretation. Learners also encounter universal uses as in (14). On the basis of the interpretation of interrogatives such as (14), Marsden argues that intermediate L1-English L2-Japanese learners assigned a universal quantifier denotation to *daremo*, although this denotation is illicit in native Japanese. Advanced learners appeared to have retreated from such a semantic assignment. It can be shown that L2 learners' observation of uses of structures as in (14) could not logically lead to their loss of this interpretation. This suggests that the relevant semantics they have acquired are due to specific computations, after morphological decomposition of *daremo* in which the particle *-mo* like English *any* is associated with a requirement that truth is preserved as the domain is widened (Kawashima 1994). This differs from English *everyone* and its Japanese counterpart *minna*. *Daremo* is indeed related to *daredemo* which translates as "anyone at all". Acquiring *daremo* as a reversible quantifier seems achievable only through morphological decomposition.

Thus, the question *What did everyone buy?* allows an individual answer (e.g. *apples*) as well as a pair-list answer (e.g. *Sam, apples; Jo, bananas; Sally, cherries..., etc.*). The pair-list answer is generally assumed to be due to a functional interpretation of the interrogative expression, so that for each member in the relevant domain of individuals, the function provides the objects that were bought (Chierchia 1992). The interrogative in (14) does not allow a pair-list answer. Saito (1999) argues that the functional interpretation is ruled out in computing the semantics of (14) as a result of the domain-widening property of *daremo*. A *wh*-interrogative presupposes that there is a choice among possibilities. On its functional reading, the question presupposes the existence of more than one function that maps the domain of relevant individuals to the things that they each bought, and asks for the one that continues to hold as the domain is widened. However, under the requirement that truth be preserved as the domain is widened, all functions continue to hold or none do. The question is vitiated. Thus, in response to *What can anyone buy? Apples* constitutes a fine answer; on the other hand, *Sam, apples; Jo, bananas; Sally, cherries...* constitutes a very strange answer indeed. One can picture a situation and intuit the intended question in view of the answer, but this interrogative form does not compute to the required question. This does not arise with the wording *What can everyone buy?* Marsden experimentally confirmed that English speakers accepted pair-list answers of interrogatives such as *What did everyone buy?* And Japanese NSs disliked pair-list answers in response to interrogatives such as (14), suggesting that the functional reading is computationally excluded.

Marsden also investigated L2 learners of Japanese from Chinese and Korean backgrounds. But I will only focus on the L1-English L2-Japanese learners. Marsden's (2008) English-speaking intermediate learners accepted both types of answers equally (individual answers: 86.60 percent, pair-list answers: 85.71 percent). This was true of intermediate learners in general. This is clearly a case of semantic overextension, given that this was across learners. Intermediate learners apparently treated *daremo* in this usage as a universal quantifier like *every/all/all the*. However, advanced learners tended to reject pair-list answers and to accept individual answers (acceptance of individual answers: 90.00 percent versus pair-list: 58.34 percent) much like the Japanese NSs (acceptance of individual answers: 94.44 percent, pair-list: 36.66 percent). It is important to note that the intuitions are subtle; these asymmetries are statistically and theoretically significant, and the individual results placed some of the advanced learners within NSs' Japanese range.

On the morphosyntactically driven acquisition examined here, the intermediate learners' semantic analysis of *daremo* as a universal quantifier reflects no morphological decomposition. Advanced learners identified the semantic features of *daremo* with its domain-widening property as its morphology became transparent. The alternative to rule-by-rule computations is that learners attempted to determine the range of interpretations available to interrogatives such as (14) in view of question–answer pairs in Japanese input. If they attempted to do so, it was to no avail: not encountering a pair-list answer in the input is not evidence that a functional interpretation is impossible. Not only could this state of affairs be an accident of the situations of use encountered by the learner, but the answer (*Everyone bought*) *apples* is compatible with both an individual question and a functional question interpretation of *What did everyone buy?* No situation of use will disabuse the L1-English L2-Japanese learner that the functional interpretation is illicit. L1-English L2-Japanese learners come to certain semantic computations under a morphosyntactic reflex.

22.6 Conclusion and perspectives

Non-language-specific abilities of the mind to analyze, categorize and generalize from data in the input (through, for example, low-level pattern matching and the information content in the input; see e.g. Bley-Vroman 1990; Clahsen and Muysken 1986; Felix 1985; Meisel 1997; Schachter 1988 as well as Chapter 29, this volume) are woefully inadequate in explaining the development of L2 semantic knowledge as described above. L1–L2-difference-oriented research now proposes that L2 sentence processing and L2 acquisition might involve a subset of cognitive structures of the language faculty (Bley-Vroman 2009; Clahsen and Felser 2006a; Hawkins and Hattori 2006). Indeed, aspects of L2 semantic development provide epistemological evidence that meanings are computed in a mental architecture devoted to language that remains in use across the life span, for child and also adult L2 learners (Dekydtspotter 2009). New interface research highlights the guiding role of the syntax–semantics interface, in which lexical semantics acquisition comes with knowledge of word order in the hierarchy of categories. Despite gaps in the lexicalization of prepositional modifiers across languages, L2 learners' lexical acquisition of degree (e.g. right/straight), flow (e.g. on/back) and trajectory (e.g. through/down/up/over/across) modifiers of prepositions in English (e.g. straight to / back to / through to) led to robust knowledge of the fixed word order of multiple modifiers (e.g. straight on through to) across language backgrounds, with development modulated only by processing load (Stringer, Burghardt, Seo and Wang 2011).

Knowledge of L2 semantics grows in the UG-constrained cognitive substructure devoted to language in which target language input is parsed and interpreted. This is the case even if the parses guiding the interpretation are not licensed by the current interlanguage grammar. Form–meaning relations exist in the learner's mind as latent potentials in the unlicensed parses in his/her interlanguage and then become fully realized as the processing of the L2 becomes more efficient when the relevant morphosyntax is acquired. Although L2 parses are computed in a domain-specific computational system, the task of morphological decomposition and establishment of the semantic values of morphemes cannot be underestimated. In this respect, Slabakova (2008) sees morphology as a bottleneck in L2 acquisition, in view of universal semantic operations. In an extension of Lardiere's (2009a) conceptualization of the acquisition of L2 grammars as the (re)assembly of feature matrices of functional categories and their morphological exponents, Slabakova (2009b) argues that the greatest costs in L2 acquisition come from assigning discourse-licensed, freely applying semantic operators as values to L2 morphemes. This is not an uncontroversial claim, as Lardiere (2009b) notes. However, the task of assigning semantic values to morphological exponents of categories is definitely complex. A body of work by Ionin and colleagues shows that L2 learners (from L1s without articles) experience a period of fluctuation in the values assigned to articles along the dimensions of definiteness and specificity (Ionin, Ko and Wexler 2004).

In the architecture of the language faculty, the costs inherent in identifying the semantic values assigned to functional lexical items seem offset by the benefits of morphosyntactic mediation between the lexicon and discourse-representation. Cost burdens of feature reassembly in L2 acquisition across language constellations in the face of severe poverty of the stimulus might also be understood in terms of relative computational loads across the acquisition sequence. Indeed, across a range of domains and L2s in which the acquisition task differs but the poverty of the stimulus is most severe, the development of robust semantic knowledge is shown to await efficient morphosyntactic processing by the L2 learner. This is probably not an accident given the range of computations implicated in the growth of semantics. We have seen in the research discussed above that the syntactic derivation of interpretations, the assignment of semantic values, the cross-module computations involved in the contextual selection of semantic representations and the decomposition of morphological paradigms all incur substantial costs. Non-targetlike semantic intuitions result from target-deviant semantic values as well as from a reduced ability to change interpretations especially when changes of perspectives are required. Understanding L2 learners' semantic development more fully will require understanding the processing loads associated with the detection of semantically relevant morphological paradigms, with the (re)assignment of semantic values and with the computations across modules involved in a change of contextual perspective.

23

Discourse and pragmatics

Roumyana Slabakova

23.1 Introduction

Recent research in second language acquisition acknowledges the prime importance of pragmatic and discourse knowledge for using a second language effectively. When Hymes (1966) argued against the perceived inadequacy of the terms *linguistic competence* and *performance* (Chomsky 1965) and introduced the term *communicative competence*, he was implying that the latter is a superior modeling of language knowledge and use. In the SLA literature and in the language teaching literature, linguistic competence has often been interpreted very narrowly as little more than knowledge and use of morphosyntax. However, there is a large part of linguistic competence outside morphosyntax that regulates comprehension and production of situationally and contextually appropriate sentences and discourse. Thus "linguistic competence" and "communicative competence" should not be seen as being in opposition, since effective communication cannot happen without the underlying linguistic-pragmatic competence. The existing research on interlanguage pragmatics to date has focused inordinately more on some aspects of pragmatic competence in preference to others. This chapter will survey the literature on interlanguage discourse (sensitivity to linguistic context) and pragmatics (knowledge of the world, maxims of co-operation and other universal pragmatic principles) with a view to highlighting important new developments in underresearched areas and focusing on pragmatics as another example of the acquisition of linguistic knowledge. One can argue that discourse and pragmatics are in a set–superset logical relationship. Sensitivity to linguistic discourse context is only part of pragmatic knowledge of the world, and universal pragmatic principles are used to decode and encode linguistic messages.

The *Handbook of Pragmatics* edited by Laurence Horn and Gregory Ward (2004) lists implicature, presupposition, reference, deixis, definiteness and speech acts as the domain of pragmatics. These largely overlap with what

Levinson (1983) identifies as the five main areas of pragmatics: conversational implicature, presupposition, deixis, conversational structure and speech acts. L2 pragmatics, however, has traditionally investigated areas considered to be in the purview of sociolinguistics, such as institutional talk in and outside classrooms (Bardovi-Harlig and Hartford 2005). Indeed, Rose and Kasper (2001) characterize pragmatics "as interpersonal rhetoric – the way speakers and writers accomplish goals as social actors who do not just need to get things done but must attend to their interpersonal relationships with other participants at the same time" (Rose and Kasper 2001: 2).

Thus the three areas that have largely been studied in L2 pragmatics are speech acts, conversational management and conversational implicature. Theoretical perspectives from which these topics are studied include conversation analysis and classroom discourse analysis, sociocultural theory as well as cognitive approaches to SLA (Kasper 2009). As will be shown in this chapter, speech acts have garnered the lion's share of attention within these approaches, with the latter two topics lagging far behind in research interest. While nominal reference and (in)definiteness have been extensively investigated within generative as well as non-generative L2 acquisition research, it is safe to say that deixis marking and presuppositions are severely understudied (Bardovi-Harlig 2011). On the other hand, topic and focus marking at the discourse–syntax interface is enjoying a positive surge in generative SLA studies, with Sorace's Interface Hypothesis (Sorace 2003, 2011; Sorace and Serratrice 2009) an influential idea in spurring research endeavours in the first decade of the twenty-first century.

In this review, pragmatics will be approached from a linguistic competence perspective. I use the term "linguistic competence" more broadly than is presently the case in the applied linguistic literature (e.g. Bachman's 1990 organizational competence used in opposition to pragmatic competence). The pragmatic component of linguistic competence regulates the production and comprehension of, for example, deictic expressions, implicatures and pronouns, among many other linguistic structures. Pragmatic competence involving sociodiscursive actions in human communication will not be the focus of this chapter. Rather than repeat the information already available in excellent recent overviews which survey the prevalent research perspective on pragmatics as language-mediated social action (Bardovi-Harlig 2011; Kasper 2009), I will complement these by focusing on developmental L2 research of discourse and pragmatic constraints on the grammar. The critical look taken into each area of pragmatics will be based on describing language universals as well as L1–L2 meaning mismatches within that area. I will echo and extend Bardovi-Harlig's (2005) call to recontextualize L2 pragmatics using a wider definition of communicative competence which includes knowledge of pragmatic universals and overcoming pragmatic transfer. The perspective in this chapter is thus strictly in complementation of, and not in opposition to, the perspective of interaction and sociodiscursive dimensions of pragmatics. Finally, I will identify the areas of further research interest likely to increase our knowledge of interlanguage pragmatic development.

23.2 Interpersonal rhetoric

23.2.1 Speech acts

The L2A research in this area is mainly based on *speech act theory* (Austin 1962; Searle 1969). According to these authors, a human utterance as part of communication represents the simultaneous performance of multiple acts: a locutionary act (i.e. propositional meaning of the sentence), an illocutionary act (i.e. the force associated with the use of the utterance in a specific context) and a perlocutionary act (i.e. the effects on the recipient of the performed speech act). The illocutionary act is at the heart of L2 pragmatics research because it captures the essence of the speaker's intention or goal in producing a particular conversational turn.

As mentioned above, definitions of L2 pragmatics clearly reflect the dominance of speech acts as a primary area of inquiry. For example, Blum-Kulka (1982) makes a distinction between social, linguistic and pragmatic acceptability but identifies incorrect illocutionary force as the most salient characteristic of non-native speech act realization. Thomas (1983) introduces the division between sociopragmatic and pragmalinguistic competence. In Kasper's (2001) definitions:

> Pragmalinguistic knowledge requires mappings of form, meaning, force and context... Sociopragmatics refers to the link between action-relevant context factors and communicative action (e.g., deciding whether to request an extension, complain about the neighbor's barking dog) and does not necessarily require any links to specific forms at all. (Kasper 2001: 51)

While both types of knowledge have been studied extensively (see Kasper and Rose 2002; Kasper 2009; Bardovi-Harlig, 2005, 2011 for reviews), it is sociopragmatics that has been better operationalized in the literature and has received more attention in general. The development of pragmalinguistic knowledge, the conditions, environments and the types of classroom instruction that influence it positively are still in need of more research attention (Kasper 2001). It is also interesting to observe that the L2A literature on speech act development is much richer than the L1A literature on the same topic. Therefore, it has become standard for researchers in the field to describe (but not always test) how native and non-native speakers perform a specific speech act and to compare the two (e.g. Hassall 2006; Barron 2006, among many others). Although there is a clear understanding in the literature (von Stutterheim and Klein 1987; Kasper 2009; Bardovi-Harlig 2011) that learners can and do access universal pragmatic resources such as the notions of politeness, cooperation and turn taking, positive pragmatic transfer in the conditions of L1–L2 similarity has been understudied. Perhaps understandably, researchers tend to focus on linguistic situations where speech acts in the L1 and L2 mismatch. There is significant evidence, surveyed in Kasper (2009), that forming new pragmatic knowledge presents considerable challenges to learners. However, similar L1–L2 speech acts, conversational routines and conventional expressions can give us very interesting insights into the other side of the issue: if learners can transfer the sociopragmatic knowledge from their native culture, how do they use their pragmalinguistic resources to apply the transferred competence?

Research into interlanguage pragmatics also includes an examination of the role of classroom instruction. The rationale for examining effects of instruction is based on Schmidt's Noticing Hypothesis (Schmidt 1990, 1993) observation that mere exposure to the target language is not sufficient for pragmatic competence to be picked up effortlessly, even after prolonged exposure. Furthermore, Bardovi-Harlig (1999) argues forcefully for the teaching of pragmatic skills because uninstructed learners differ from native speakers not only in production but also in perception of pragmatic norms. An implicit assumption of authors who urge the teaching of speech acts is that grammatical competence and pragmatic competence (in the sense of knowledge of politeness) do not go hand-in-hand in most learners' linguistic development.

To take an example, Koike and Pearson (2005) attempt to tease apart the effects of explicit and implicit instruction on the complex speech act of giving suggestions. Anglophone learners of Spanish at roughly intermediate proficiency level were divided into five groups: those that received explicit versus implicit pre-instruction crossed with those that received explicit versus implicit feedback; a control group that received no instruction on this speech act was also included. Results of a post-treatment test and a delayed post-test indicate that learners can indeed learn and maintain pragmatically appropriate behavior when they are instructed on the speech act and responses before further practicing with exercises. The researchers also note that explicit instruction seems to help learners understand the speech act while implicit instruction helps them to produce it more appropriately (Koike and Pearson 2005: 495). Jeon and Kaya (2006) also concluded in their recent meta-analysis based on thirteen quantitative studies that explicit instruction is generally superior to implicit instruction in the realm of speech acts.

Since polite behavior is to some extent a matter of personal choice and upbringing, not only of linguistic knowledge, studies comparing university-age L2 learners (the majority of studies) would benefit from demonstrating that the same polite behavior is indeed the norm for these individual learners in their native language. Furthermore, it should be a priori established whether or not the native language and the target language differ measurably in the respective speech act so that learners have something pragmatic to learn beyond the set linguistic expressions of the speech act under investigation in the L2. For example, Holtgraves (2007) performed a very interesting experiment to ascertain that speakers of a language activate a specific speech act construct in their mental grammar upon understanding that a speech act has been performed in the current communication. However, the non-native speakers in his experiment came from a large variety of native languages so it is not clear which of the speakers had to learn a new speech act and which had to map the L2 speech act onto their native one.

More generally speaking, the L2 speech act acquisition research is working towards a detailed and better-operationalized comparison of speech acts across languages of the world. To this end, if no independent language comparisons exist in the pragmatics literature, L2 experimental studies should include at least two native control groups (L1 and L2) as well as learner groups. Furthermore, it should be ascertained that learners notice, recognize and comprehend speech acts in listening, so that they can then appropriate them in their individual grammars (Bardovi-Harlig 2009).

23.2.2 Conversational implicature

Conversational implicature is a linguistic phenomenon related to speech acts in the sense that both capture the ability of the hearer to recognize the additional meaning and intention encoded in a speaker's utterance. While speech acts are more often culturally acceptable conventions and rules of speaking, conversational implicature refers to the universal ability to recognize the speaker's underlying intention over and above the compositional semantic meaning of the utterance. For many L2 pragmatics researchers, comprehension of implied meaning is a speech act among many others. However, literal and intended meaning interpretation is a linguistic computation much wider in its application: it is part of almost any communication not limited to conventions and rules of speaking. Consider the following example of a well-known pragmatic inference:

(1) Some professors are smart.

Most people would agree that, in hearing the utterance in (1), they understand that the speaker has conveyed the assumption in (2).

(2) Not all professors are smart.

Notice that (2) is neither encoded by the speaker's utterance in (1), nor is it part of what the speaker has *said*. Rather, (2) is an assumption inferentially derived by the hearer on the basis of what the speaker has said. Logically speaking, *some* means *some and possibly all*. But if the speaker had meant *all professors are smart*, she would have uttered (3) or (4), being maximally informative, and not (1). Since she didn't, then we can safely assume she means (2).

(3) Professors are smart.

(4) All professors are smart.

The first systematic attempt to explain how the inference in (2) is derived is due to the philosopher of language Paul Grice. In a series of lectures presented at Harvard in 1967, published later as Grice (1989), he offered a comprehensive framework of the mechanisms of inferential communication. More specifically, he suggested that communication is essentially governed by certain rational expectations about how a conversational exchange should be conducted, which he called "maxims." According to Grice's five maxims, interlocutors are normally expected to offer contributions that are truthful, informative, relevant to the goals of the conversation and appropriately phrased. These expectations about the rational conversational conduct of interlocutors constrain the range of interpretations hearers are entitled to entertain in interpreting utterances. These expectations can also be violated (or exploited) to create a variety of effects. According to Grice's maxims, in producing (1) and meaning (2), the speaker has used part of the following maxim:

(5) Quantity maxim
  i. make your contribution as informative as is required,
  ii. do not make your contribution more informative than is required.
  (Grice 1989: 26)

The speaker has chosen a relatively weak term among a range of words ordered in terms of informational strength: *some... most... all*. Assuming that the speaker is trying to be cooperative and will say as much as she truthfully can, the fact that she chose the weaker term (*some*) gives the listener reason to think that she is not prepared to make the stronger statements in (3) and (4). This leads to the inference that the stronger statement does not hold, that is, it leads to (2). The assumption in (2) is called a conversational implicature, and more specifically, a scalar implicature, since the propositions which *some... most... all* give rise to are ordered on a scale of informational strength (Horn 1972; Gazdar 1979). Implicatures are studied from the perspective of *Relevance theory* (Sperber and Wilson 1986) and from a neo-Gricean perspective (e.g. Levinson 2000).

Note that conversational implicature is universal, it is purportedly part of human language, and all languages should exhibit a similar process of implied meaning inferencing. Therefore, the issue of transfer from the native language plays out in an interesting way in this area of linguistic pragmatics. The mechanisms of scalar implicature computation, whatever they are, can readily be transferred from the native language of the learner. On the other hand, implicature in certain situations certainly depends on the lexical knowledge of set expressions, or chunks.

A pioneering series of studies on knowledge of conventional implicature was carried out by Bouton (1988, 1994). Initially based on a cross-sectional picture, Bouton followed the development of several types of conversational implicature such as relevance and implied criticism. He tested two groups of students after they had been in the US for seventeen months and after fifty-four months. The general conclusion from his findings was that the learners were capable of computing implicature in English after a period of study in the US. The only area of uncertainty and difficulty remained "specific points of American culture and not the type of implicature involved" (Bouton 1994: 163). Bouton's findings confirmed that implicature is a cognitive process distinct from cultural knowledge, and that its acquisition does benefit from instruction and longer exposure to the target language.

The effect of the learning environment, in the target language country or in the native language country, was taken up by Röver (2005). The study included ESL and EFL learners and tested, among other conditions, comprehension of two types of implicatures: formulaic implicatures, e.g. indicating agreement that should have been patently obvious to the interlocutor by saying *Is the Pope Catholic?*, and conversational implicatures that had to be computed online without the benefit of conventional expressions (Q: *Are you coming to the party?* A: *I have to work*, where the answer means *No*). Results revealed no effect of L2 exposure (target language vs. native language context) on learners' comprehension of implicatures but a significant proficiency effect. Taguchi (2008) also examined the comprehension speed and accuracy of Japanese ESL and EFL learners. She employed a pragmatic listening task with indirect refusals and indirect opinions and she administered it twice: before and after a five- to seven-week period of instruction. Results indicate that both learning groups improved in speed and accuracy, suggesting that the learning environment does not have a decisive effect on interlanguage pragmatics. In other words, even a foreign language classroom affords sufficient input for learners to make gains in pragmalinguistic competence. In this respect, these two studies contradicted earlier findings suggesting that instruction in a study-abroad situation was particularly beneficial for pragmatic development (Bardovi-Harlig and Dörnyei 1998).

There is an extensive literature on scalar implicature computation demonstrating that children cannot answer experimental questions in a pragmatic way until the ages of 5 to 7 (Guasti *et al.* 2005; Papafragou and Musolino 2003). A central question of the child acquisition literature is whether scalar implicature computation development depends on the maturation of some cognitive capacity, or on processing abilities. If scalar implicature calculation depends on the maturation of some cognitive capacity in children, we expect adult learners to be much better at it than children learning their mother tongue. Not only are adults cognitively mature, but their native language is in a position to assist them in inference calculation. If, on the other hand, scalar implicature computation depends on processing capacity because it involves choice of an optimal competitor within a narrowly constructed set of options (a sentence with *some* versus a sentence with *not all*), we could expect adult L2 learners to have more difficulty than adult and young native speakers.

These predictions were tested in Slabakova (2010) and Lieberman (2009). Slabakova investigated the L2 acquisition of scalar implicatures by L1 Korean–L2 English learners. In one experiment the participants had to judge the felicity of underinformative sentences without context as in (6) and had to say whether they agreed with the statement.

(6) Some elephants have trunks.

A positive answer represents the logical option since *some* and indeed *all* elephants have trunks. However, the sentence is pragmatically infelicitous in that it is not maximally informative; the negative is the pragmatic answer. The test sentences were translated into Korean and administered to Korean native speakers, as well as to English natives in English. Slabakova found differences in the Korean speakers' performance in their native and in their second language. They gave around 40 percent pragmatic answers in their native language (not significantly different from the English native group) and about 60 percent pragmatic answers in their second language. The results suggest that L2 learners have no problem computing scalar implicatures; indeed they do so more often than native speakers. In the second experiment with added context, the learners gave pragmatic answers over 90 percent of the time. Slabakova (2010) argued that the difference between native and second language speakers was due to processing resources. Since the logical responses are arguably due to conjuring up alternative contexts in order to agree with the logical use of *some* (only some elephants have trunks because some others may have been injured, or born without trunks; Guasti et al. 2005), speakers may have a harder time coming up with these alternative contexts in their second language.

Lieberman (2009) continued the investigation of scalar implicature computation, focusing on the issue of processing resources. He tested the acceptance of computationally demanding implicatures, as in (7), and compared them to less demanding sentences, as in (8).

(7) Max didn't read all of the books.

(8) Max read some of the books.

A sentence such as (7) involves an indirect implicature because of a scale reversal and is harder to process than the direct implicature in (8), even for native speakers (Gillingham 2007). Lieberman tested L1 Japanese–L2 English learners on the scales <*sometimes, always*>, <*partly, completely*>, as well as *every* in the scope of negation. Participants had to evaluate the felicity of sentences in short contexts. When forced to judge the acceptability of single test sentences, native speakers as well as L2 learners had difficulty computing the indirect implicatures compared to the direct ones. The non-native speakers were even less accurate than the natives, suggesting that in these cases there is indeed a processing problem and that the native/non-native differences are a matter of degree. When the processing load was reduced by presenting the participants with two alternatives, one felicitous and one infelicitous, the non-native speakers had no trouble with the task and performed similarly to the native speakers. It is interesting to note that neither in Slabakova (2010) nor in Lieberman (2009) was proficiency a factor in the learners' performance.

A very interesting dimension of child–adult comparisons and processing resources is highlighted by studying bilingual children. There is a well-established effect of bilingualism on executive functioning (involving attention, inhibition and focusing) in children and adults. Bialystok (2001), Bialystok and Senman (2004), Bialystok and Martin (2004) and others have shown that bilinguals often exhibit significantly superior executive functioning and attentional abilities that are associated with better responses on metacognitive and metalinguistic tasks. Thus it is possible that the bilingual advantage is also a factor in pragmatic development.

This research question is examined by Siegal, Iozzi and Surian (2009), which compared pragmatic competence in bilingual and monolingual children. Children participating in this study were bilingual in Italian and Slovenian, or monolingual in either language. The researchers tested 3- to 6-year-old children on a conversational violations test to find out whether they would obey Gricean maxims. Results of two experiments in Siegal, Iozzi and Surian (2009) show that there is a definite advantage of the bilingual children over the monolingual ones on four Gricean maxims: Quantity ii, Quality, Relation and Politeness. Bilingual children were more accurate in choosing non-redundant answers, true answers over false ones, answers that were relevant to the questions, and polite answers over rude ones. The only maxim on which all the children performed equally well and hovered at around 60 percent pragmatic responses was the Maxim of Quantity i. Here is a test item:

(9) Question: "What did you get for your birthday?"
    Logical but underinformative answer: "A present."
    Pragmatically appropriate answer: "A bicycle."   (Siegal *et al.* 2009: 116)

Results of 60 percent pragmatic answers for children before the age of 6 are largely in line with other studies in the literature on scalar implicature computation in children. More importantly, however, Siegal *et al.* (2009) do not establish an advantage for bilingual children comprehending underinformative sentences. Thus it is possible that comprehending underinformative sentences involves different semantic–pragmatic calculations than detecting relevance and rudeness.

In this section, studies were summarized comparing conversational implicature knowledge with the knowledge of scalar implicature in L2 speakers. Findings suggest that when universal computation mechanisms are at play, learners have no trouble comprehending them; when culturally specific knowledge or formulaic expressions are involved, learners are less accurate. In addition, the bilingual advantage may only be afforded with respect to the latter but not the former.

23.3 Reference

23.3.1 Anaphora resolution

While reference in linguistic pragmatic theory is concerned with the "aboutness" of the utterance very broadly construed, research in acquisition of reference focuses on a variety of contextual factors that lead to the introduction of a new referent in a discourse, the linguistic form that the speaker chooses on its first mention, the linguistic forms employed for repeated reference to the same entity and the interaction between linguistic (encoded) and contextual (inferred) cues that determine the hearer's identification of the intended referent. Two influential theoretical proposals on reference resolution within generative linguistics are Chomsky's (1981) Binding theory and Reinhart and Reuland's (1993) Reflexivity theory. While the former uses predominantly syntactic concepts to formulate its constraints, the latter uses semantic and argument-structure constructs in addition to syntactic ones.

A number of studies on interpretation of anaphora (Zribi-Hertz 1989; Reinhart and Reuland 1991; Pollard and Sag 1992; Pollard and Xue 2001) have pointed out serious problems for any purely syntactic account and proposed that interpretation of anaphora is determined not only by syntactic constraints, but also by pragmatic constraints. The discourse principles have been claimed to involve such notions as logophoricity, contrastiveness and discourse prominence. *Logophoricity* refers to the phenomenon in which the perspective of an internal protagonist of a sentence or discourse, as opposed to that of the current, external speaker, is being reported by some morphological and/or syntactic means (Huang 2005: 310). *Contrastiveness* refers to the usage of emphatic pronouns which highlight a contrast to current expectations or involving a "he and not anyone else" type of interpretation. *Discourse prominence* captures the fact that some discourse referents are more prominent than others in a given discourse situation. Huang (1994, 2000) proposes a neo-Gricean pragmatic theory of anaphora in which determining referents of anaphora is pragmatically constrained. He argues that in several languages, such as Chinese and Korean, pragmatics plays a central role and thus, binding of reflexives may be primarily subject to principles of language use, while in English, syntactic constraints, such as c-command and locality, are fundamental factors in reflexive binding. The interpretation of a reflexive is subject to the I-principle, a principle of "inference to the best interpretation" (Atlas and Levinson 1981): implicature may cancel some possible interpretations until it finds an antecedent for the reflexive that gives the most informative, stereotypical interpretation consistent with our knowledge of the world. To illustrate, note the Chinese example in (10).

(10) Yang Danian$_i$ danxin nüer$_j$ bu ken cihou ziji$_{i/j}$.
 Yang grandma worry daughter not willing look-after self
 "Grandma Yang$_i$ is worried that her daughter$_j$ is not willing to look after her$_i$/herself$_j$."

In English, *herself* and *Grandma Yang* cannot corefer on syntactic grounds. In Chinese, the reflexive can be referentially dependent on the local subject and on the long-distance subject. However, the local subject interpretation can be rejected when it is inconsistent with our knowledge of the world. The anaphor *ziji* in (10) is preferably interpreted as referentially dependent on the embedded subject, in this case *nüer* "daughter." But this is not the best interpretation since it contradicts our knowledge of the world: stereotypical expectations are that younger people look after older people. The main verb *danxin* "worry" suggests that the person who the daughter is not willing to look after is not the daughter herself, but the grandma. Therefore, the interpretation is canceled, and the I-principle promotes an interpretation that *ziji* is referentially dependent on the matrix subject, *Yang Danian* "grandma."

Only a few studies have addressed the role of pragmatic factors in the acquisition of L2 reflexives, so this is a significantly underresearched area. Thomas (1989a) examined the interpretation of English reflexives by native speakers of twenty different languages including two large subgroups, Chinese and Spanish. Although Thomas focused on the issue of the resetting of parameters and of L1 transfer within the generative framework, she also looked at the pragmatic influences on the interpretation of reflexives. She concluded that unlike native speakers, L2 learners frequently permit non-local binding in biclausal sentences, whether or not the NP is pragmatically favored. Therefore, according to Thomas, pragmatic bias failed to induce L2 learners to allow long-distance binding, suggesting no important role of pragmatics in L2 learners' interpretation of reflexives.

Demirci (2000, 2001), on the other hand, argues that pragmatic knowledge plays an important role in the L2 learners' interpretation of reflexives, and interferes with the learners' acquisition of locality conditions in English reflexive binding. Demirci studied the acquisition of English reflexives by Turkish learners of English at five proficiency levels. Unlike English reflexives, which only allow an antecedent in the same clause, Turkish reflexives allow both local and non-local binding. Furthermore, unlike other long-distance reflexives, such as Chinese reflexive *ziji*, Turkish reflexives can be bound by both subject and non-subject antecedents. Therefore, Turkish native speakers need to rely on inference, context and knowledge about the world in order to choose among several possible antecedents. Demirci (2000) contrasted pragmatically neutral and biased (in favor of a local NP and of a non-local NP) finite and non-finite biclausal sentences by world knowledge. She concluded that the L2 learners transferred pragmatic principles from L1 to L2; however, they were not able to overcome the transfer and to acquire fully the purely syntactic rules of English reflexive binding.

Lee (2008) also used pragmatically biased and neutral test items to check the reflexive interpretation choices of English and Korean native speakers as well as Korean-native ESL learners. The surprising finding was that less than 40 percent of the English control group chose a local antecedent in biclausal sentences (the expected English choice) when the contexts of the sentence favored a non-local antecedent. Learners were also swayed by the context to choose a long-distance antecedent. This suggests that a pragmatic factor, that is, a given context in the task, induced the native speakers as well as the L2 learners to choose a grammatically illegitimate, but contextually favored antecedent.

The study of pragmatic factors influencing anaphora resolution in second language acquisition deserves a lot more attention than it has received in the literature so far. The research findings to date suggest that even native speakers of languages that have syntactically constrained binding are influenced by context in interpreting anaphora. A linguistic theory unifying syntactic and pragmatic binding constraints should spur acquisition studies that take both factors into account. We will come back to the interpretation of pronouns in Section 23.4 on the syntax–discourse interface.

23.3.2 Definiteness/indefiniteness and specificity

Like anaphora resolution, L2 acquisition of definite descriptions and specificity marking has largely been treated from a semantic point of view (see Chapter 22, this volume). However, the calculation of definiteness and specificity happens in real discourse situations, so it is vitally dependent on how the speaker and hearer encode and decode contextual cues.

Research on article acquisition (Huebner 1983; Thomas 1989b, among many others) has established that L2-English learners, particularly those speaking a native language without articles, have persistent difficulties with articles. They often overuse *the* with indefinites and/or overuse *a* with definites. A number of proposals have been made to account for these patterns of article misuse, including purely syntactic accounts, such as (the Representational Deficit Hypothesis (Tsimpli and Roussou 1991) and the Prosodic Transfer Hypothesis (Goad and White 2004b). In this section, we focus on explanations involving the role of speaker vs. hearer discourse-dependent knowledge.

Within Bickerton's (1981) Language Bioprogram Hypothesis (which proposes that the similarity of creoles is due to their being formed from a prior pidgin by children who share UG capacity) article misuse in L2 English could be explained by the choice of learners to associate the definite article *the* with the features [specific referent] or [hearer knowledge]. The success of this explanation has been questioned on the grounds of insufficient empirical coverage (Thomas 1989b) and on imprecise semantic definitions of these features (Ionin 2003). Starting from Ionin (2003), a fruitful line of studies of the acquisition of definiteness has developed that assumes a discourse-related definition of definiteness. An informal definition of definiteness based on presupposition of uniqueness (Heim 1991) states that if a nominal phrase is definite, then the speaker and hearer presuppose the existence of a *unique* individual in the set denoted by the NP. Ionin's definition of specificity encompasses grammatical and pragmatic specificity and is based on Fodor and Sag's (1982) definition of "speaker intent to refer." A specific reading of an indefinite NP is characterized by the certainty of the speaker about the identity of the referent, the speaker having the referent in mind, the speaker being able to identify the referent, etc. A crucial difference between the two features is that definiteness encodes a shared state of knowledge between speaker and hearer while specificity is knowledge held only by the speaker (see examples in (11) below).

Based on these definitions, Ionin (2003) and Ionin, Ko and Wexler (2004) proposed the Article Choice Parameter with two settings in languages that have an indefinite and definite distinction. In one type of language, articles are distinguished on the basis of specificity; in the other type articles are distinguished on the basis of definiteness. This linguistic situation presents specific difficulties for learners whose native language does not mark these features morphologically. Assuming continued operation of UG and the universality of the Article Choice Parameter, L2 learners will go beyond their L1 setting to fluctuate between the two settings of the Article Choice Parameter until the input leads them to set this parameter to the appropriate target language value. This is known as the Fluctuation Hypothesis and it makes very concrete predictions for the pattern of errors in L2 acquisition: learners are predicted to make errors overgeneralizing *the* in specific yet indefinite situations and *a* in non-specific yet definite situations.

We illustrate how crucial pragmatic knowledge is for supplying and interpreting articles with examples from Ionin, Ko and Wexler (2004: 22–23). The target sentences are in italics and the expected article is in bold.

(11) [−definite, +specific]: target *a*, predicted learner pattern: overuse of *the* Meeting on a street
Roberta: Hi, William! It's nice to see you again. I didn't know that you were in Boston.
William: I am here for a week. *I am visiting (**a**, the, −) friend from college – his name is Sam Brown, and he lives in Cambridge now.*

(12) [+definite, −specific]: target *the*, predicted learner pattern: overuse of *a*
Bill: I'm looking for Erik. Is he home?
Rick: Yes, but he's on the phone. It's an important business matter. *He is talking to (a, **the**, −) owner of his company!* I don't know who that person is – but I know that this conversation is important to Erik.

Ionin et al. (2004) tested beginning, intermediate and advanced learners of English with Russian or Korean as their native languages. Both Russian and Korean lack articles. The researchers employed a forced-choice elicitation task and a production task, as in examples (11) and (12), as well as in [+definite, +specific] and [−definite, −specific] situations. Group results from the Russian learners largely supported the Fluctuation Hypothesis in the sense that learners overused articles in precisely the predicted learning conditions. However, the individual results presented a more complex picture where a number of individual learners did not exhibit the expected pattern. In addition, learners' production results revealed that they overused *the* with specific indefinites, but did not overuse *a* with non-specific definites.

The series of studies by Ionin and colleagues has proved highly influential and has inspired a number of following studies. For example, Zdorenko and Paradis (2008) found that in the case of child L2 learners of English, all informants fluctuated between definiteness and specificity, no matter what their L1 was, though only children from article-less L1s exhibited article omission. García Mayo (2009) used the same English forced-choice elicitation task used by Ionin et al. (2004) with two groups of native speakers of Spanish, one of low-intermediate proficiency in English and the other of advanced proficiency. Results show no evidence for fluctuation even at the low-intermediate proficiency level. However, Spanish and English articles share the encoding of definiteness, although Spanish articles additionally encode gender. Ionin, Zubizarreta and Bautista-Maldonado (2008) replicated García Mayo's study and found that L1 transfer took precedence over fluctuation in the case of Spanish learners of English. Snape (2009) confirmed the fluctuation findings with Chinese learners of English while only half of Tryzna's (2009) Polish native speakers learning English showed the expected pattern. Finally, overuse of *a* with definites was practically non-existent in the performance of Zdorenko and Paradis' children.

Ionin, Zubizarreta and Philippov (2009) modified the original Fluctuation Hypothesis proposed in Ionin et al. (2004). Linguistic research has showed that instead of distinguishing between articles based on specificity and not definiteness, Samoan distinguishes specificity, but within indefinites only (Fuli 2007; Tryzna 2009). Since the universal specificity distinction is only demonstrated within a part of the article space, children and L2 learners are expected to overuse *the* with specific indefinites, but not overuse *a* with non-specific definites. Ionin et al. (2009) argue that only specificity-related errors with indefinites, not specificity-related errors with definites, reflect L2 learners' access to the semantic universal of specificity. Their revised proposal was anticipated in some of the results from Ionin et al. (2004) and receives support from further findings with L1-Russian children acquiring English.

Trenkic (2008) takes issue with Ionin et al.'s operationalization of specificity as in items designed as [+specific] in their experiment such as those in (11) above, where there is an explicit statement of the speaker's familiarity with the referent. She argues that the semantic universal of specificity is not really at play in the learners' grammars; rather, what they are sensitive to is "explicitly stated knowledge." Based on her critique of Ionin's test items, Trenkic provides an alternative explanation: L2-English learners are mis-analyzing *the* and *a* as adjectives, and assigning the meanings of "identifiable" and "unidentifiable" to them. Ionin *et al.* (2009) argue against Trenkic's explanation of article mis-analysis and provide their own explanation in terms of adult learners' explicit strategies.

In this section, we reviewed L2 learner's choice of definite and indefinite articles based on the discourse information provided by the utterance context. The current findings suggest that some adult L2 learners fluctuate between marking definiteness and specificity, other groups of learners at similar proficiency levels do not fluctuate much, and child learners only overuse *the* with specific indefinites but not *a* with non-specific definites. We also reviewed two versions of the Fluctuation Hypothesis, an influential current explanation for the error patterns. There is still more to explain in the findings to date. The burden of proof is on the researchers providing theoretical explanations to support them with replicable empirical data.

23.3.3 Deixis

A search of the terms *deixis* and *second language acquisition* in the LLBA database yields a miserly number of published articles, five or six altogether. At the same time, deixis underlies all pragmatics and is such a fundamental property of human language that without it no human communication would exist. Thus this section will list linguistic properties that are still awaiting their second language acquisition researchers and whose acquisition patterns will give us important insights into the language acquisition capacity.

Deixis refers to the necessity of contextual information to determine the meaning of certain words and phrases in an utterance. Words that have a fixed semantic meaning but have a denotational meaning that constantly changes depending on time and/or place are deictic. Classical examples involve the meaning of personal pronouns and adverbs such as *tomorrow* and *here*. Deixis is a pervasive and complex linguistic phenomenon that covers diverse aspects related to time, space and social aspects of the communicative context.

Levinson (2004: 103) cogently points out that there is a dynamic coexistence between the indexical sign and its object of reference. Deictic linguistic expressions are not sufficient to achieve reference without contextual support, but that support is provided "by the mutual attention of the interlocutors and their ability to reconstruct the speaker's referential intentions given clues in the environment." A programmatic chapter in Klein (1986) is chapter 7, entitled "The embedding problem." "Any utterance, whether belonging to a learner variety or to the target language, is embedded in the speaker's and hearer's informational set-up, composed of current perception, recollection of preceding events and utterances, and knowledge of the world (Klein 1986: 112)." Klein discusses the necessity to always assess second language knowledge and performance embedded in context. He gives the example of the utterance in (13) produced by a migrant worker in a bakery, which can be considered ungrammatical if its context is not taken into consideration.

(13)   Me bread.

While the indexical properties of the utterance are impeccable, considering that it is produced in a place that sells bread, the sentence may not even be ungrammatical if uttered *after* the shop assistant says:

(14)   Here's your apple pie, Madam. Now, what would *you* like, Sir?

In order to understand an utterance, a learner must possess shared knowledge of the *origo* of the speaker, the lexical meaning of the deictic word and where to draw the line about the origo (*now* may mean "today" or "this year" or "in recent years" depending on the situation). The origo is the "ground zero" around which the deictic field is organized (Bühler 1935): it consists of information about the speaker, the time and place of speaking. In order to produce an appropriate utterance, the learner must take into account the origo as well as the contextual knowledge of the hearer. While certain aspects of Klein's embedding problem have found their researchers, many other aspects of the problem remain severely underresearched.

Among the different types of deixis, one that has attracted traditional attention is person deixis, having to do with the personal pronouns *I, we*, etc. Note that when Sally produces *we* in (15) and in (16), the denotation of *we* is different and it depends on an active listener to understand.

(15)   We went to the cinema last night.

(16)   We live longer than men.

Another type is space deixis, where demonstratives and adverbs like *here* and *there* are discussed. Unless otherwise specified, space or place deictic terms are generally understood to be relative to the location of the speaker, as in (17), where the speaker and the shop are positioned on opposite sides of the street.

(17)   The shop is across the street.

Languages usually show at least a two-way referential distinction in their deictic system: *proximal*, i.e. near or closer to the speaker, and *distal*, i.e. far from the speaker and/or closer to the addressee; English exemplifies this with such pairs as *this* and *that*, *here* and *there*, etc. In other languages, the distinction is three-way: proximal, i.e. near the speaker, *medial*, i.e. near the addressee, and distal, i.e. far from both. The three German demonstrative pronouns, *hier*, *da*, *dort*, corresponding to *here*, *here/there*, *there*, may be analyzed that way. Some systems combine both speaker- and addressee-anchored systems, as in the Yélî Dnye demonstrative determiners (Levinson 2000).

Niimura and Hayashi (1996) and Gajdos (2011) are among the very few studies that have examined the L2 acquisition of a deictic mismatch. Niimura and Hayashi compare English *this* and *that* with Japanese demonstratives *ko*, *so* and *a*. They argue that the choice is highly subjective and psychological, rather than physical, although proximity is a determining factor in both language systems. However, in English, focus, or the degree of attention on the referent, is the critical determinant, whereas in Japanese the overriding factor is whether or not the referent is in the domain of the speaker's direct experience. Niimura and Hayashi (1996) studied natives' and L2 learners' choices of demonstratives in cartoon strips in Japanese as well as in English. In the person focus system (English), there was more variety in demonstrative choice than in the situation focus system (Japanese). Therefore, L2 learners of Japanese had answers more widely distant from native answers compared to learners of English, but on the whole even advanced learners diverged considerably from the natives' performance. The findings of Gajdos (2011), who studied L2 acquisition of German *hier*, *dort* and *da* by native speakers of English, point to the same conclusion. On a picture and text acceptability judgment task, all of Gajdos' participants demonstrated nativelike knowledge of *hier* and *dort*, which are equivalent to English *here* and *there*. Even near-native speakers did not accept the spatial adverb *da*, which has no equivalent in English, as often as the natives did. However, the large variability in the judgments of the native speakers (48-95 percent on various test items) underscores the difficulty of the learning task.

Temporal deixis ensures that time is marked in an utterance or a sequence of utterances in relation to the speaker's deictic *origo*, the hearer's knowledge and the situational context. From this marking, the hearer should be able to infer the time of the event and its position on the time line. Klein (1986: 125) describes four kinds of factors involved in time marking: a common time conception shared by speaker and hearer; a common point of reference such as the deictic *origo* (e.g. the moment of speech); means for marking temporal spans or relations such as adverbials and verb tenses; certain discourse rules based on common knowledge, for example the Principle of Natural Order (unless marked otherwise, the sequence of events mentioned in an utterance corresponds to their sequence in real life).

The marking of temporal deixis has been studied in the so-called *Basic Variety* (Klein and Perdue 1997), the speech of naturalistic (uninstructed) learners in the European Science Foundation (ESF) corpus. The corpus incorporates longitudinal data from adult migrant workers in five European countries with target languages English, French, Dutch, German and Swedish (Dietrich, Klein and Noyau 1995; Klein and Perdue 1997; Perdue and Klein 1992; Meisel 1987; see also a review of these studies in Bardovi-Harlig 2000, ch. 2). The main finding is that the uninstructed learners "are perfectly able to express temporal reference and relations despite the complete absence of verbal morphology and even verbs in a large proportion of their utterances" (Dietrich et al. 1995: 6). An example of an utterance conforming to deictic temporality marking is given below:

(18) Türkei Urlaub zurückkomm, meine Mann krank.
Turkey vacation come-back, my husband ill
"After he came back from vacation in Turkey, my husband was ill."

The competent pragmatic marking of temporality in uninstructed learners is confirmed by non-European studies as well. For example, Sato (1990) examined the development of L2 past tense inflection (among other properties) in two Vietnamese-speaking brothers aged 10 and 12 adopted in a US family. During the ten-month period of observation, the brothers did not mark temporality with morphological means and relied on other means, such as adverbials and the interlocutor's marking of past tense. Findings of this type highlight the fact that deictic (pragmatic) marking of temporality is indeed universal and is the foundation for the development of morphological marking. It is also clear from this literature that the development of aspectual and tense morphology beyond the Basic Variety happens over a long period of time and emerges with a lot of errors and omissions.

The marking of temporality in instructed learners proceeds very differently from that of uninstructed learners. There is a vast literature on this topic, surveyed in Bardovi-Harlig (2000), among many others. Bardovi-Harlig (2000, ch. 2) shows that learners develop functional, and often rich, means of temporal expression before the acquisition of verbal morphology, and the use of lexical adverbials to mark temporality continues long after the acquisition of tense morphology. While the marking of temporality through morphological means is beyond the purview of this chapter (but see Chapter 24, this volume), it is important to note that the study of deictic temporal marking should be expanded beyond the morphological means to include the pragmatic means of that marking. For example, this deictic marking of the time line and temporal relations becomes crucially important when a learner whose native language marks temporality morphologically (say English) approaches a language that does not (say Mandarin Chinese). It is expected that such learners will have access to the universal temporal deictic schema, but this access is not empirically supported as yet.

Finally, social deixis marks the social role or status of the participants in the speech event. Special expressions exist in many languages, including the honorifics of Southeast Asian languages (Thai, Japanese, Javanese, Korean) and the so-called T/V distinction in Slavic languages, Spanish, German and French. The T/V label is based on the Latin pronouns *tu* "you-sg" and *vos* "you-pl" (Brown and Gilman 1960): when addressing a single interlocutor, *tu* and its equivalents are informal, while *vos* and its equivalents are a formal means of address implying social distance. While the linguistic structures involved are simple, the cultural context in which they are deployed is complex and involves an understanding of how interpersonal relationships are constructed and communicated in the languages which distinguish T/V pronouns. These distinctions are widely studied in the L2 pragmatics literature on conventional expressions (e.g. Dijkstra 2006; Liddicoat 2006; Dewaele 2004d, among others). Findings suggest that while perception of the pragmatic distinction is not a problem (Dijkstra 2006), the targetlike production of these lags behind perception for a long time (Lyster 2004b).

In summary, the universal concept of deixis describes the embedding of every human utterance in the surrounding context and is a much more pervasive feature of language than usually recognized. While some aspects of deictic marking have been studied widely, e.g. social deixis, others have not enjoyed much attention, e.g. person and space deixis. After twenty-five years, the bottom-line message of Klein's (1986) chapter 7 still rings true: there is a lot of work that still remains to be done on context embedding in learner varieties. The most important distinction to be made is between universal deictic properties versus language-specific ones.

23.4 Information structure (the syntax–discourse interface)

The marking and comprehension of information structure, or topic and focus, has enjoyed prime attention in the generative L2 literature in the last decade. Much attention has been paid to explaining L2 behavioral patterns through principled solutions based on independently motivated distinctions. Generative linguists assume a language architecture that is modular: the linguistic system consists of language modules (e.g. phonetics/phonology, syntax, semantics) within which specialized internal linguistic processes go on, for example feature checking and displacement of constituents within the syntax module. Between each two modules, however, another type of linguistic process occurs, the so-called interface processes. The latter take units of one module and map them onto units in another module (Jackendoff 2002; Chomsky 1995). Thus interface processes are by definition more complex and involve keeping more information in short-term memory compared to intra-modular processes.

The syntax–discourse interface has a privileged position in this language architecture. For some scholars (e.g. Jackendoff 2002), topic–focus calculation is part of the conceptual (largely semantic) module. For others (e.g. Reinhart 2006), it is outside the semantic module and is an interface between language and extralinguistic reality. Whether one or the other approach is correct is actually an empirical question. However, under both approaches the syntax–discourse interface is the meeting place between language and other cognitive systems.

Looking into the endstate competence of near-native learners, the Interface Hypothesis (Sorace 2003; Sorace and Filiaci 2006) proposed that if these learners' grammars diverge from native speakers', the divergence is more likely to be within the syntax–discourse interface than at other interfaces. A more recent version of the hypothesis (Sorace and Serratrice 2009; Sorace 2011) argues that linguistic structures at this interface are prone to lasting optionality of judgment (in the sense that learners treat the acceptable and the unacceptable versions of the construction equally) and hence even near-native learners exhibit non-native grammatical competence. For an excellent review of recent research at the linguistic interfaces and the Interface Hypothesis, see White (2011). In agreement with White, in this section I will review some seminal research findings and suggest that the sweeping proposal that all properties at the syntax–discourse interface are problematic is perhaps too strong.

The interrelated notions of *topic* (or theme, what a given sentence is about, thus *discourse-old* information) and *focus* (or rheme, what is predicated of this topic, hence *discourse-new* information) have been studied ever since the Prague school of linguistics in the 1930s. In second language acquisition, researchers have been preoccupied with whether learners encode and comprehend these notions through the use of null and overt subjects (in languages that allow null subjects in the first place), word order (postverbal versus preverbal subjects) and clitic-doubling of displaced topics. Research findings have been decidedly mixed. First of all, at lower proficiency levels, learners do not demonstrate sensitivity to discourse-new and old information (Lozano 2006; Hertel 2003; Ivanov 2009; Rothman 2009). At near-native levels, some studies find complete convergence, while others find subtle but persistent divergence. We will look at some concrete studies below.

Findings in Belletti, Bennati and Sorace (2007) present a prime example of difficulties and optionality at near-native levels. The study investigated knowledge of null subject grammars by near-native learners of Italian whose native language was English. One of the tasks of the study was a picture verification task where participants were given a test sentence and three pictures identifying the pronoun antecedent as either the matrix subject, the matrix complement, or an external referent. The null subject is appropriate when the subject of the embedded clause is the same as the matrix subject (the old lady) as in (19) below. However, if the speaker wants to shift the topic from the matrix subject to the matrix object (the girl), she will use an overt pronoun to mark topic shift as in (20). Thus the non-optional appearance of overt or null embedded subject pronoun signals topic shift or topic maintenance.

(19) La vecchietta$_i$ saluta la ragazza$_j$ quando pro$_{i/?j}$ attraversa la
 the oldlady greets the girl when crosses the
 strada.
 street

(20) La vecchietta_i saluta la ragazza_j quando *lei*_{*i/j} attraversa la
 the oldlady greets the girl when she crosses the
 strada.
 street
 "The old lady greets the girl when Ø/she crosses the street."

In processing sentences such as (20), Italian near-native speakers were found to interpret the overt pronominal subject of the embedded clause as coreferential with the lexical subject of the main clause 30 percent of the time, while the natives only interpreted it in this way 5 percent of the time, a significant difference. At the same time, 65 percent of near-native answers and 85 percent of native answers converged on the native-preferred interpretation (embedded subject refers to matrix complement). Thus the Italian near-natives in this study were less sensitive than the native speakers to topic shift discourse situations.

Rothman (2009) investigated a very similar acquisition situation: contrastive focus in English–Spanish interlanguage. One of the tasks of his study was a pragmatic-felicity judgment task, in which he gave a context story and a test sentence to judge for acceptability. Unlike Belletti *et al.*'s near-natives, Rothman's advanced speakers performed similarly to the native speakers in all conditions of this particular task.

Another property demonstrating discourse sensitivity whose acquisition has received much attention is clitic doubling as a marker of topic (Valenzuela 2005, 2006; Ivanov 2009, Parodi 2009). Topicalization in Spanish and Bulgarian may involve a dislocation of an object that has a discourse antecedent and the clitic-doubling of that object. Note that Spanish and Bulgarian clitic-double the dislocated object while English does not, because clitics are not part of its grammatical system.

(21) Context: Where did you buy these shoes?
 a. These shoes, I bought in Madrid. (English)
 b. Estos zapatos, **los** compré en Madrid. (Spanish)
  these shoes, Cl I-bought in Madrid
  "These shoes, I bought in Madrid."
 c. Tezi obuvki **gi** kupix v Madrid. (Bulgarian)
  these shoes, Cl I-bought in Madrid
  "These shoes, I bought in Madrid."

There is a crucial requirement that when the object is specific, clitic doubling is obligatory. However, when the object is non-specific or generic, native speakers allow less categorical judgments, demonstrating subjective interpretations of the situation (see Slabakova and Ivanov 2011, for more discussion). Near-native speakers of Spanish in Valenzuela (2005) were 100 percent accurate on observing the specificity requirement in a sentence-felicity judgment task. Very advanced learners of Bulgarian in Ivanov (2009) were indistinguishable from native speakers in a very similar task. On the other hand, Valenzuela's near-natives demonstrated variability in judging generic dislocated objects, perhaps supported by the larger variability in the input, as ascertained by the native results. In contrast, Ivanov's advanced learners again patterned with the natives on judging the inappropriateness of clitic-doubling in focus contexts. Finally, Parodi (2009) used a grammaticality judgement task and contrasted definite and indefinite objects. She found that advanced learners of Spanish patterned like the native speakers while advanced learners of Greek do not.

We shall compare two online processing studies next, which, although they do not investigate the same property, come to a similar conclusion. Roberts, Gulberg and Indefrey (2008) studied the online and offline performance of Turkish (a null subject language) and German (non-null subject) learners of Dutch (another non-null subject language) with respect to ambiguous pronoun resolution. The Turkish speakers chose a clause-external antecedent for an ambiguous pronoun more often than the German learners. Recall that there is a discourse preference for an overt pronoun in null subject languages to signal a topic shift (see Italian example in (20) above). Thus Turkish learners were essentially showing L1 transfer in the offline task of this study. However, in the online task both advanced learner groups diverged from native speaker behavior, suggesting that processing of ambiguous pronouns where the choice of antecedent depends on the context is difficult, even if the native language of the learners gives them an acquisitional advantage.

Hopp (2009) also investigated ultimate attainment at the syntax–discourse interface, specifically, discourse-related word order optionality in German. English, Dutch and Russian speakers who were advanced-to-near-native speakers of German were tested on an offline acceptability judgment task and an online self-paced reading task. Hopp's results indicate that convergence at the syntax–discourse interface is in principle possible in adult L2 acquisition, both in offline knowledge and online processing, even for L1 English speakers, whose L1 does not correspond to L2 German in discourse-to-syntax mappings. At the same time, just like Roberts *et al.*'s conclusions, Hopp points to the fact that L2 speakers have computational difficulties in the matching between discourse and syntactic information even when their native language has very similar properties to the ones they are acquiring. The challenge for future research at the syntax – discourse interface, then, will be to reconcile the findings of the online studies (Roberts *et al.* 2008; Hopp 2009) with the discrepant findings of the offline studies (Belletti *et al.* 2007 versus Rothman 2009; Valenzuela 2005 versus Ivanov 2009). More online studies of various properties at this interface involving more languages as L1s and L2s will shed light on the issue of computational resources as the bottleneck of this type of discourse-related word orders and meaning construals.

23.5 Conclusion

This chapter has taken the point of view of pragmatics as a field of linguistic inquiry rather than a non-linguistic component of communicative competence. In this respect, it adheres to the Anglo-American conception of pragmatics of Grice, Carnap and Peirce as opposed to the more sociological conception of other, especially European-based, traditions such as Mey, Crystal and Verschueren. Pragmatics was defined as pertaining to all context-dependent aspects of meaning encoding and decoding. As in all modules of the linguistic system, in pragmatics there exist universal properties as well as language-specific properties, where mismatches between L1 and L2 can occur. It was pointed out that not all areas of L2 pragmatics have enjoyed equal attention and inquiry. For example, research on presuppositions is practically non-existent while research on speech acts is abundant. Rectifying these imbalances in the coming decades will elucidate the big question of how second language speakers bring context to bear on syntactic and semantic computations and process both *what is said* and *what is meant* by the linguistic message.

24

Morphosyntax

Tania Ionin

24.1 Introduction

Over the last three decades, many generative SLA studies have examined the acquisition of morphosyntactic phenomena, including, but not limited to, tense/agreement marking on verbs, verb placement, number marking on nouns, gender marking on determiners and adjectives, *wh*-movement and clitics. The central question in generative approaches to the L2 acquisition of morphosyntax is whether L2 learners (in particular adult L2 learners) are capable of constructing a targetlike syntactic representation, especially in those domains where the learners' native language and their target language differ. This chapter provides an overview of morphosyntax studies in SLA, addressing the theoretical debates in the field and illustrating the theoretical claims with studies on verbal morphosyntax, which is one of the most explored topics in generative SLA. Before proceeding to a discussion of specific studies and proposals, this chapter outlines the theoretical framework that generative studies of morphosyntax commonly adopt.

24.1.1 Parameters vs. features

The debate about adult L2 learners' ability to acquire a targetlike representation was originally framed in terms of *parameters*. In the Principles and Parameters framework (Chomsky 1981), parameters were conceived of as sources of constrained variation among languages: while principles hold invariably in all languages, parameters have a finite set of values (or "settings"). Parameters were originally viewed as governing whole clusters of properties. For example, the Pro-drop or Null Subject parameter (Rizzi 1982; Hyams 1986) was viewed as governing such seemingly unrelated properties as the possibility of subject drop, the existence of postverbal subjects, and the relative richness of verbal agreement morphology (which indeed applied to Romance pro-drop languages). The notion of parameter has been very useful in SLA research, allowing researchers to examine whether L2 learners transfer linguistic knowledge in the form of parameter settings from their native language to the target language, whether they are able to reset the parameter to the target language value, whether the different properties associated with a given parameter are acquired at the same time, and/or whether the acquisition of just one of the properties associated with a parameter serves as a trigger for the resetting of the parameter (for an overview of parameter-based SLA studies, see White 2003a; see also Chapter 5, this volume, on the role of the native language in SLA). The Full Transfer / Full Access Model of SLA (Schwartz and Sprouse 1994, 1996), which is framed in terms of parameters, predicts that the initial state of learners' grammar is constrained by the parameter settings of the native language, but that parameter resetting to the target language value is possible, via access to Universal Grammar (UG). For more discussion of the role of UG in SLA, see Chapter 7, this volume.

Over the past two decades, the focus of generative SLA studies has shifted away from parameters and towards *features*, following a similar shift in generative syntax. In the Minimalist framework (Chomsky 1993, 1995, 1998, 2001), parametric differences among languages are restricted to differences in formal features on functional items. In this framework, functional elements (e.g. the past-tense *-ed* marker, the plural *-s* marker, the determiner *the*, the question word *what*) are prespecified in the lexicon with formal features such as [+/−past], [+/−plural], [+/−definite] and [+/−wh]. These inflectional elements head inflectional categories, such as D (determiner), T (tense) and C (complementizer). Learning new parameter settings is now viewed as a matter of lexical learning of the corresponding functional items.

A further important distinction in minimalism is between *interpretable* and *uninterpretable* features. Interpretable features are syntactic features which also have semantic content, whereas uninterpretable features do not; they are not usable by the semantic component and are essentially grammatical (Pesetsky and Torrego 2001). While interpretable features express information inherent to a category (e.g. gender and number on a noun), uninterpretable features express information that signals a dependency between a functional category and a dependent element (e.g. gender on a determiner in Spanish, or person/number on a present-tense verb in English). In Minimalist syntax, uninterpretable features must be checked and deleted in the course of the derivation, through a connection between the functional head and the lexical item. For example, the uninterpretable [gender] feature on Determiner must be deleted against the interpretable [gender] feature on the noun in Spanish. In the simplest case, the connection is accomplished through an *Agree* operation (Chomsky 1998) between the functional head and the lexical item: the features of the functional head and those of the lexical item enter into the Agree relation, but no overt movement of the lexical item takes place. In some instances, however, a feature may have an Extended Projection Principle (EPP) property, which requires that, following the Agree operation, the entire lexical item undergo overt movement to the environment of the functional head. The EPP is responsible for overt movement of lexical items, such as movement of *wh*-words to first position in English or verb raising in Romance (to a position preceding negation, which is discussed in more detail in Section 24.2.2).

In an influential paper, Lardiere (2009a) has argued that the notion of parameter is no longer useful for SLA research. Lardiere argues that macro-parameters which govern clusters of properties are not successful at capturing crosslinguistic facts, and that the lexical micro-parameters associated with formal features are of little use either in helping the L2 learner or in explaining the nature of SLA. Lardiere proposes replacing parameters with the notions of feature selection and feature assembly, as discussed in more detail in Section 24.6.

24.1.2 Approaches to features in SLA

SLA studies of morphosyntax since the 1990s have focused on learners' ability to acquire new feature values not present in their native language. These include studies of L2 learners' acquisition of the uninterpretable [gender] feature on determiners and adjectives in a language like Spanish, when the native language, English, does not morphologically mark gender; or studies of acquisition of the [past] feature in a language like English, when the native language, Chinese, does not morphologically mark past tense.

No one disputes that learners make many errors with the morphology of the target language, omitting and/or misusing tense/agreement marking, determiners, gender marking and clitics. What is much debated, however, is the source of such errors. A variety of representational impairment accounts, discussed in more detail in Section 24.3 below, have argued that learners are incapable of acquiring new features in the L2 that are not present in their L1. Many of these accounts propose that learners have specific difficulty with *uninterpretable* features: for example, L1-English L2-Spanish learners never become targetlike with gender agreement between nouns and determiners/adjectives, since this requires acquiring uninterpretable [gender] features on determiners and adjectives. For impairment accounts, learners' age is an important consideration: adult L2 learners past the critical period for language acquisition are incapable of selecting and/or valuing new uninterpretable features (see Chapter 15, this volume, on age effects in SLA).

An alternative approach to representational impairment argues that problems with the morphology do not necessarily reflect problems with the syntactic representation; rather, missing or incorrect morphology is reflective of problems with the retrieval of lexical items (see Section 24.4), and/or difficulty with the L2 prosody (see Section 24.5). For these theories, unlike impairment theories, learners' age is not a very important factor: child as well as adult learners have been argued to have difficulty retrieving the target morpheme (at the same time, the patterns of errors made by child vs.

adult L2 learners exhibit some differences, as discussed in more detail in Section 24.4).

Both types of accounts – representational impairment vs. problems at a more surface level – have often been framed in the Distributed Morphology (DM) framework (Halle and Marantz 1993). In the DM framework, lexical items compete for insertion into syntactic nodes; in order for lexical insertion to take place, the features on the lexical item must form a subset (but not necessarily a proper subset) of the features on the syntactic node. If multiple items are in principle compatible with the syntactic node, the most highly specified item wins. For example, a lexical item specified as [+past] would be inserted into a syntactic node specified as [+past]; if no [+past] lexical item exists in the language, then an item underspecified for the [+/−past] feature is inserted. As discussed in Section 24.4, the notion of underspecification has proven quite useful in explaining why learners overuse some types of forms (e.g. verbal infinitives, or masculine determiners) more than others.

24.1.3 Organization of this chapter

Questions of representational impairment vs. surface morphological difficulty have been explored in many different morphosyntactic domains in SLA research, most notably the verbal domain (verb placement and verbal inflection), the nominal domain (determiners, gender and plural marking) and *wh*-movement. The research on these different areas is too extensive to be covered in a single chapter, and the present chapter therefore focuses on verbal morphosyntax as fairly representative and illustrative of SLA research in other areas of morphosyntax. References to related work in other domains (such as gender and *wh*-movement) are provided in the corresponding sections. See also the papers in Liceras, Zobl and Goodluck (2008) for studies of the L2 acquisition of formal features in a variety of linguistic domains, and the papers in García Mayo and Hawkins (2009) for recent work on the L2 acquisition of articles.

The rest this chapter is organized as follows. Section 24.2 provides the necessary background on the linguistic properties of verb morphosyntax. Sections 24.3, 24.4 and 24.5 review three different approaches to errors with inflectional (and specifically, verbal) morphology: representational impairment, missing surface inflection and prosodic transfer. Section 24.6 considers an alternative way of looking at L2 morphosyntax in light of Lardiere's (2009a) recent proposal. Section 24.7 concludes the chapter.

24.2 Verbal morphosyntax

There has been much research on the L2A of verbal inflection (specifically, tense/agreement marking) and its relationship to verb syntax. As first shown in the morpheme order studies (Bailey, Madden and Krashen 1974; Dulay and Burt 1974b; Larsen-Freeman 1975), omission of tense/agreement morphology is characteristic of the speech of L2-English learners, children as well as adults (see Zobl and Liceras 1994 for an overview). Many L2 studies since then have found high omission rates of bound morphemes that mark tense (as in (1)) and agreement (as in (2)), and to a lesser extent, of free tense/agreement morphemes, including the *be* auxiliary (as in (3a)) and the *be* copula (as in (3b)). The errors in (1) through (3) are all errors of omission: e.g. the past-tense *-ed* suffix is missing in (1), the third-person singular *-s* marker is missing in (2) and a form of *be* is missing in (3). Such omission errors have been found in the naturalistic speech of L2-English learners from a variety of native languages, including L1s that lack tense and agreement marking, such as Chinese (Lardiere 1998a, b, 1999, 2003, 2007), but also L1s which have rich tense/agreement paradigms, such as Turkish (Haznedar 2001) and Russian (Ionin and Wexler 2002). Omission of inflectional morphology is also found in the L2 acquisition of languages with richer verb morphological paradigms than English, such as French and German (e.g. Prévost and White 2000). Omission of inflectional morphology is known to be highly variable, with the same learners sometimes marking tense/agreement, and sometimes failing to mark it, as illustrated in (1a) and (3a).

(1) a. ...went to school and learn English
      (Lardiere 2003: 178)
    b. one time I watch this movie
      (Ionin and Wexler 2002: 106)

(2) a. he have the uh, inspiration to say what he want to say
      (Lardiere 1998a: 19)
    b. he go to school at eight
      (Haznedar 2001: 27)

(3) a. he is crying and we crying
      (Haznedar 2001: 9)
    b. Mary so funny
      (Ionin and Wexler 2002: 106)

Before proceeding to different theoretical views of the nature of morphological problems in SLA, it is important to consider the underlying properties of both verbal inflection and verb syntax. This chapter considers these properties in English, French and German, the three languages which have been most explored in the SLA of verbal morphosyntax.

24.2.1 Verbal inflection

A distinction central to the study of verb morphosyntax is that between *finite* and *non-finite* verbs. Verbs specified as [+finite] are tensed verbs, further specified as [+past] or [-past]: for example, the verb *watch* is [−past] in (4a–b) and [+past] in (4c). In English, the past tense is morphologically marked with the *-ed* suffix, as in (4c), for regular verbs, or else with an irregular past-tense form.

In contrast, [−finite] verbs, such as infinitives and participles, are not tensed (and hence do not bear a [+/−past] feature): the verb *watch* when used as an infinitive has the same form regardless of whether the entire sentence is in the present tense (4d) or the past tense (4e); the tense is reflected on the finite verb, in this case *want*. Similarly, the participial form *watching* is the same in both a present-tense sentence (4f–g) and a past-tense sentence (4h–i), with tense expressed on the auxiliary *be*, which is finite.

(4) a. The child watches movies.
    b. The children watch movies.
    c. The child/children watched movies.
    d. The child wants to watch a movie.
    e. The child wanted to watch a movie.
    f. The child is watching a movie.
    g. The children are watching a movie.
    h. The child was watching a movie.
    i. The children were watching a movie.

Finite verbs can furthermore show agreement with the subject in person and/or number. The English agreement paradigm is fairly impoverished, with person/number overtly marked only in the third-person present tense singular (4a). Finite forms used in other person/number combinations in the present tense (e.g. (4b)) are morphologically indistinguishable from the infinitival form (4d–e), and agreement is not marked in the past tense in English (4c). The only exception is the verb *be*, which shows agreement marking in the past tense (4h–i) as well as in the present tense (4f–g); all finite forms of *be* are, furthermore, morphologically distinct from the infinitival *be* form. Given the nature of the English verbal inflectional paradigm, studies of finiteness marking in the acquisition of English typically look at three types of obligatory contexts for inflectional morphemes: third-person present-tense singular contexts, past-tense contexts and contexts which require a *be* copula or auxiliary.

In contrast to English, French and German have quite rich tense/agreement paradigms, with different forms for different person/number/tense combinations (see Prévost and White 2000 for illustrations of the French and German agreement paradigms in the present tense). Studies of the acquisition of finiteness marking in French and German therefore look at all person/number/tense combinations, excluding (in studies of oral production) those cases where a finite form is homophonous with a non-finite form (e.g. in French, *chanter*, the infinitival form of the verb "sing," is homophonous with *chantez*, its finite second-person present-tense plural form).

24.2.2 Verb syntax

In English, finite *thematic* or *lexical* verbs (i.e. all verbs other than *be*, auxiliary *have* and modals) must follow rather than precede sentence-internal adverbs

(5a) as well as follow sentential negation (5b). The opposite is true for forms of *be*, both as an auxiliary (6) and as a copula (7), and is also true of the *have* auxiliary and modal auxiliaries.

(5) a. Jen often reads books. / *Jen reads often books.
　　b. Michael does not read books. / *Michael reads not books.

(6) a. Jen is often reading a book. / *Jen often is reading a book.
　　b. Rob is not reading. / *Rob not is reading / *Rob does not be reading.

(7) a. Jen is often in Paris. / *Jen often is in Paris.
　　b. Rob is not a doctor. / *Rob not is a doctor / *Rob does not be a doctor.

As shown by the above examples, finite thematic verbs in English (such as *reads*, (5)) behave exactly like non-finite participial verbs (such as *reading*, (6)), in that both forms are placed after adverbs and after negation. In contrast, in French, finite thematic verbs precede adverbs (8a–b) and the negative element *pas* (8c–d), just like auxiliary and copular verbs (the negative element *ne* is analyzed as a preverbal clitic, and is optional in spoken French; Pollock 1989). On the other hand, non-finite verbs in French must follow *pas* (9b) and may optionally follow or precede adverbs (9a) (examples from Pollock 1989).

(8) a. Jean mange souvent de la soupe.
　　　John eat-3SG often　　some soup
　　　"John often eats soup."

　　b. *Jean souvent mange de la soupe.
　　　John often　　eat-3SG some soup

　　c. Marie (n')aime　　pas Jean.
　　　Mary (neg)like-3SG not John
　　　"Mary does not like John."

　　d. *Marie ne pas aime　　Jean.
　　　Mary neg not likes-3SG John

(9) a. *Presque oublier* /*oublier　presque* son nom, ça
　　　almost forget-INF /forget-INF almost his name this
　　　n'arrive　pas fréquemment.
　　　NEG comes not frequently
　　　"To almost forget one's name doesn't happen frequently."

　　b. Ne *pas sembler* /**sembler　pas* heureux est une condition
　　　NEG not seem-INF /*seem-INF not happy　is a　　condition
　　　pour écrire　des romans.
　　　for　write-INF novels
　　　"To not seem happy is a condition for writing novels."

Pollock (1989) attributes the differences in verb–adverb and verb–negation orders between English and French to the differing verb raising possibilities

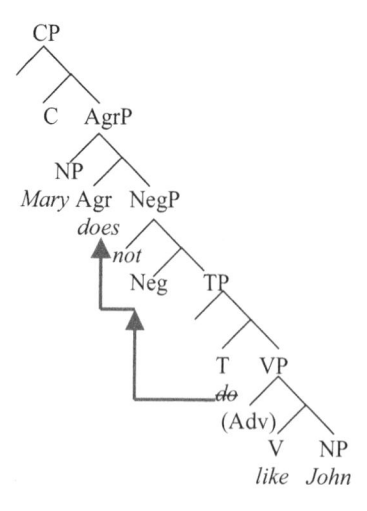

Figure 24.1 *Structure of English negative clauses (simplified)*

of these two languages. He argues that French verbs raise to Infl, the functional head underlying verbal inflection. Since Infl is higher in the structure than either negation or adverbs, the verb necessarily precedes both *pas* and adverbs in French. In English, on the other hand, thematic verbs may not raise to Infl and must remain in situ, thus following negation as well as adverbs such as *often*, which are adjoined to the left of the VP. (There are many accounts of why auxiliaries and the copula *be* raise in English, unlike thematic verbs; see, e.g., Chomsky 1993; Pollock 1989; Roberts 1998.)

Pollock additionally argues for a split Infl: there are actually two functional heads underlying verbal inflection, Tense (T) and Agreement (Agr). He uses placement of French infinitives (see (9a)) as support for this argument. Pollock argues that the Negation Phrase (NegP) is placed lower than T but higher than Agr. While finite verbs in French must raise all the way up to T, thus preceding negation, infinitives may raise only as far as Agr, which places them below negation. However, they may precede adverbs such as *almost*, which are in the specifier of the VP, thus lower than all functional heads. Simplified structures of English and French declarative negative clauses, with a split-Infl, are given in Figures 24.1 and 24.2, respectively. While the finite French verb in Figure 24.2 moves all the way from V, through T and Neg (where *ne* cliticizes onto it) to Agr, the English finite verb stays in V; a form of *do* is inserted into T and then raises to Agr (in an affirmative sentence, with no *do*-support, the tense/agreement affix is lowered onto the verb).

In the Minimalist framework, the verb has uninterpretable T and Agr features which it must check against the corresponding functional heads; the T and Agr heads have uninterpretable V features, which must check off against the verb. In English, the feature-checking takes place via the Agree relation, whereas in French, the verb must undergo overt movement. The parametric difference between English and French originally posited by Pollock (1989) therefore resides on the functional heads.

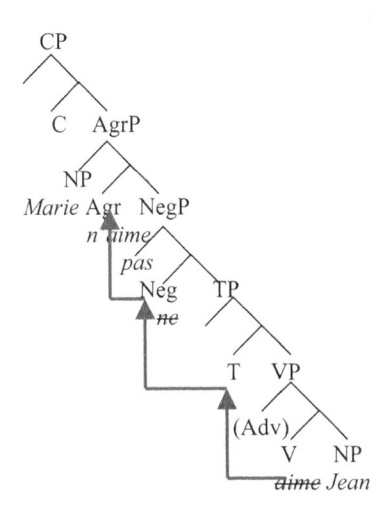

Figure 24.2 *Structure of French negative clauses (simplified)*

German presents a third option to English and French for the placement of the verb within the sentence. In a sentence containing an auxiliary as well as a non-finite verb, the non-finite verb has to follow the object, as shown in (10). Finite verbs obligatorily appear in the second position of the sentence; this holds both for auxiliaries (10) and for finite thematic verbs (11). Another phrase, e.g. the subject (11a), the object (11b) or an adverb, has to fill the position in front of the verb. Since the finite verb is obligatorily in the second position in the sentence, this is called the Verb-Second (V2) effect. Negation has to follow finite verbs – both thematic verbs (12a) and auxiliaries (12b–c), and precede non-finite verbs – both participles (12b) and infinitives (12c).

(10) a. Hans darf Maria treffen.
Hans may Maria meet-INF
"Hans may meet Maria."

b. *Hans darf treffen Maria.
Hans may meet-INF Maria

(11) a. die Kinder sahen den Film
the-NOM children saw the-ACC film
"The children saw the film."

b. den Film sahen die Kinder
the-ACC film saw the-NOM children
"The children saw the film."

(12) a. Hans raucht nicht.
Hans smoke-3SG not
"Hans does not smoke."

b. Hans hat nicht geraucht.
Hans have-3SG not smoke-PART
"Hans has not smoked."

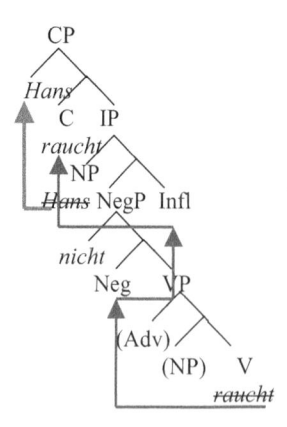

Figure 24.3 *Structure of German negative clauses (simplified)*

c. Hans will nicht rauchen.
   Hans want-3SG not smoke-INF
   "Hans does not want to smoke."

German is generally analyzed as having a head-final VP (hence the SOV order observed in (10)), and on some analyses, it also has a head-final IP (den Besten 1983); on some analyses (Grewendorf 1990), the negative element *nicht* is analyzed as being in the specifier of NegP. The German structure is shown in Figure 24.3. In German (unlike French and English), the finite verb raises from V, through Neg if it is in the structure, through Infl, and to C (whether Infl is split in German is not relevant for the present discussion). The V2 effect is captured because the verb, in C, is in second position in the sentence, with another element obligatorily moving to the specifier of the CP.

The following sections consider the L2 acquisition of verbal inflection and verb morphosyntax in English, French and German, and the different theories that have been proposed to account for the facts.

24.3 Impairment at the level of syntactic representation

A number of related but distinct proposals have been put forth in which adult L2 learners have impaired syntactic representation. Names for specific variants of the *impairment* approach have included the Weak Transfer / Valueless Features Hypothesis (Eubank 1993/94, 1996), the Local Impairment Hypothesis of (Beck 1998a), the Failed Functional Features Hypothesis (Hawkins and Chan 1997), the Representational Deficit Hypothesis (Hawkins 2003) and the Interpretability Hypothesis (Hawkins and Hattori 2006; Tsimpli 2003; Tsimpli and Dimitrakopoulou 2007; Tsimpli and Mastropavlou 2008). While there are important differences among these proposals, they all take the position that the syntactic representation in L2 learners' interlanguage (IL) grammar is in some way impaired, and that errors with morphology are indicative of deeper problems with syntax.

These proposals have largely focused on which formal features can vs. cannot be acquired in adult L2 acquisition: specifically, they have focused on whether adult L2 learners are capable of acquiring formal features that are not part of their L1 grammar. On the influential Failed Functional Features Hypothesis (FFFH) of Hawkins and Chan (1997), L2 learners are argued to have only those features in their syntactic representation that are available in their L1, and they cannot acquire new features. For example, under this proposal, L1-Chinese L2-English learners cannot acquire the [wh] feature on C, which is responsible for overt *wh*-operator movement (present in English, but absent in Chinese). Later formulations of the FFFH (e.g. Hawkins and Hattori 2006; Tsimpli and Dimitrakopoulou 2007; Tsimpli and Mastropavlou 2008) have argued that adult L2 learners are specifically unable to acquire uninterpretable formal features. Tsimpli and Dimitrakopoulou (2007), examining resumptive pronouns in Greek, argue that L1-English L2-Greek learners can make use of interpretable features such as animacy, but cannot acquire uninterpretable Case and Agreement features. Hawkins and Hattori (2006) argue that the uninterpretable *wh*-feature on C is unavailable to L1-Japanese L2-English learners. Franceschina (2001, 2005) and Hawkins and Franceschina (2004), examining the acquisition of gender in L2 Spanish, propose that the uninterpretable gender features on determiners and adjectives cannot be acquired by L2 learners whose L1, such as English, does not instantiate the gender feature. (See also Sabourin, Stowe and de Haan 2006 for more discussion of the nature of L1 transfer in the L2 acquisition of gender.)

In the domain of verbal morphosyntax, Hawkins and Liszka (2003) found much lower suppliance of past-tense -*ed* marking in obligatory contexts among L1-Chinese L2-English learners (63 percent suppliance) than among L1-Japanese L2-English learners (92 percent suppliance). Since Japanese has past-tense marking and Chinese does not, Hawkins and Liszka argue that the Chinese learners' errors are due to syntactic transfer: under their analysis, adult L1-Chinese L2-English learners are incapable of acquiring the uninterpretable features required to realize past-tense marking, because these features are not part of their L1 grammar (according to Hawkins 2009, who modifies the original proposal of Hawkins and Liszka, the relevant uninterpretable features are the V and Agr features on T). This impairment proposal is in direct opposition to the accounts of missing tense marking discussed in the following sections.

24.4 Missing Surface Inflection

According to the Missing Surface Inflection Hypothesis (MSIH) (Haznedar and Schwartz 1997; Lardiere 2000; Prévost and White 2000), problems with

L2 morphology are not due to any underlying syntactic deficits, but rather to a mapping problem between syntax and morphology. The MSIH is thus fully compatible with Full Access to UG models of L2 acquisition (e.g. Schwartz and Sprouse 1994, 1996), under which adult L2 learners are capable of acquiring a targetlike syntactic representation. Most of the work on the MSIH has been done on verbal inflection and verb placement, as discussed below, but see also Bruhn de Garavito and White (2003), White, Valenzuela, Kozlowska-MacGregor and Leung (2004) and Montrul, Foote and Perpiñán (2008) on evidence for the MSIH in the acquisition of gender marking; see Grüter (2006) for an MSIH approach to clitics.

MSIH studies on the acquisition of verbal inflection have largely focused on several interrelated questions: (i) whether learners' errors with tense/agreement morphology take the form of omission or of misuse; (ii) whether learners are accurate in verb placement with respect to adverbs and negation; and (iii) whether learners are successful on other phenomena which, according to syntactic theory, are related to the acquisition of the Tense (or Infl) category. In syntactic theory, Tense licenses overt subjects and assigns Nominative Case (Chomsky 1993, 1995), so the use of overt, Nominative case subjects is often taken to be an indication that the Tense category has been acquired. Other contexts that are taken to be indicative of finiteness are use of full CPs (e.g. *wh*-questions, embedded clauses and relative clauses), on the assumption that projection of a CP entails projection of phrases lower in the structure (cf. Rizzi 1993/94); and, in Romance languages, use of subject clitics, since these can occur only with finite verbs.

24.4.1 MSI in L2 English

In the case of English, several different studies (Haznedar 2001; Haznedar and Schwartz 1997; Ionin and Wexler 2002; Lardiere 1998a, b, 2003, 2007; White 2003b) have converged on highly similar findings, discussed below, despite large differences in the age, level of attainment and native language of their study participants. Lardiere (1998a, b, 1999, 2003, 2007) reports on a longitudinal study of Patty, an adult L1-Chinese L2-English learner who was recorded after ten years of US residence and again nine years later; there was little change between the two recording times, indicating that Patty was an endstate learner. White (2003b) reports on a similar longitudinal study of SD, an L1-Turkish L2-English endstate learner, who was recorded after ten years of English exposure, and again 1.5 years later, with little change between the two recording times. Haznedar and Schwartz (1997) and Haznedar (2001) examine the longitudinal data of a 4-year-old L1-Turkish L2-English child, Erdem; the results reported here are pooled from the first eighteen months of recordings, during which Erdem's grammar underwent rapid changes. Ionin and Wexler (2002) report on a cross-sectional study with twenty L1-Russian L2-English children, ages 3 to 13, who had between several months and two years of exposure to English.

Table 24.1. *Suppliance of verbal morphology in L2 English: percent suppliance in obligatory contexts*

Study	Third person singular -s (%)	Past tense (%)	Forms of *be* (%)
Haznedar 2001	47	26	89
Ionin and Wexler 2002	22	42	75
Lardiere 1998a, b	4	35	90
White 2003b	79	81	98

First, all of the above studies found high omission rates of tense/agreement morphology, as shown in Table 24.1 (based on pooled results from White 2003b). While the actual rates of omission differ, with SD being the most accurate and Patty the least accurate, the overall pattern of higher omission rates for affixal inflection (third-person -s and past-tense -ed) than omission of *be* copula and auxiliary forms holds across all of the studies. The fairly high suppliance of *be* forms has been used to argue that the learners have the category of Tense in their grammar, and that their problems are specific to suppliance of affixal morphology.

Second, misuse of verbal morphology was essentially non-existent: for example, compared with the high omission rates of third-person -s reported in Table 24.1, misuse of third-person -s with non-third-person singular subjects was only 5 percent in Ionin and Wexler (2002), and 3 percent in Haznedar (2001) as well as White (2003b). This indicates that when an inflectional morpheme is produced, it is produced appropriately, reflecting the corresponding tense and agreement features. Proponents of the MSIH (e.g. Lardiere 2000; Prévost and White 2000) have argued, following Borer and Rohrbacher (1997), that missing functional categories or impaired functional features should result in essentially random use of inflectional morphology, for example, use of third-person -s with non-third-person subjects. However, this is not what happens, with the prevalent error being omission rather than misuse.

Third, even though tense/agreement morphology is often missing in the learners' production, properties associated with the presence of Tense/Agreement categories, notably overt subjects and Nominative case marking on subjects, are attested. The production of overt, Nominative Case subjects is reported at 98 percent and above in Ionin and Wexler (2002), Lardiere (1998a) and White (2003b). While Erdem, the child in Haznedar's (2001) study, initially dropped subjects at a high rate – possibly due to transfer from Turkish, a null subject language – overt subjects were used consistently after Sample 7 (two months of recording), well before affixal morphology was productive; furthermore, the overt subjects produced by Erdem were nearly always Nominative, in sharp contrast to younger child L1-English

Table 24.2. *Placement of verbs with respect to negation and adverbs in L2 English*

Study	Placement of *be*	Placement of thematic verbs with negation	Placement of thematic verbs with adverbs
Haznedar 2001	nearly at-ceiling with correct *be*–Neg placement	not discussed	not discussed
Ionin and Wexler 2002	100% correct *be*–Neg placement (33 tokens) 100% correct *be*–Adv placement (8 tokens)	100% correct Neg–V placement (53 tokens)	94% correct Adv–V placement (15 out of 16 tokens)
Lardiere 1998b	not discussed[a]	100% correct Neg–V placement (112 tokens)	99% correct Adv–V placement (121 out of 122 tokens)
White 2003b	not discussed	100% correct Neg–V placement	both Adv–V and V–Adv orders attested

[a] While placement of *be* is not discussed by Lardiere (1998b), Lardiere (2006) notes that Patty correctly places finite *be* forms before negation and adverbs nearly all of the time.

learners, who are known to produce Accusative Case subjects early in their development, before Tense and Agreement are fully acquired (see Schütze and Wexler 1996); see Chapter 16, this volume, for more details.

Fourth, as shown in Table 24.2, all of the above studies found correct verb placement with negation and adverbs, with the single exception of White (2003b), who found some errors of verb placement before adverbs in SD's data. Following up these findings with a preference judgment task, White (2003b) found that SD was willing to accept both V–Adv and Adv–V orders, while being 100 percent accurate at rejecting incorrect V–Neg orders with negation. On the other hand, both Patty (Lardiere 1998b) and the L1-Russian children (Ionin and Wexler 2002) were highly accurate at placing thematic verbs after adverbs.

To sum up, the findings from L2-English acquisition of verbal morphology suggest that learners' problems are primarily of failing to supply the target morpheme. When morphemes are supplied, they are placed correctly; the syntactic properties of English verbs, such as correct verb placement and production of overt, Nominative Case subjects, are attested across studies. However, English does not allow for an examination of the relationship between verb placement and verb finiteness, since, as discussed in Section 24.2.2, all thematic verbs – finite and non-finite – do not raise but instead stay inside the VP in English. In order to address the question of finiteness and verbal morphology, it is necessary to look to other languages, such as French and German.

Table 24.3. *Use of infinitival verb forms in finite contexts in L2 French and L2 German (Prévost and White 2000: 118, based on table 6)*

L2 French		L2 German	
Abdelmalek	Zahra	Ana	Zita
(25.9%) 237/914	(25.9%) 217/837	(10.5%) 36/343	(21.7%) 72/332

Table 24.4. *Correct vs. incorrect use of finiteness morphology in L2 French and L2 German (Prévost and White 2000: 120,122, based on tables 8 and 9)*

	Regular verbs	Irregular verbs
Abdelmalek (L2-French)		
correct inflection	447 (95%)	264 (98%)
incorrect inflection	25 (5%)	6 (2%)
Zahra (L2-French)		
correct inflection	552 (94%)	156 (99%)
incorrect inflection	39 (6%)	2 (1%)
Ana (L2-German)		
correct inflection	218 (80%)	298 (94%)
incorrect inflection	55 (20%)	19 (6%)
Zita (L2-German)		
correct inflection	193 (81%)	127 (98%)
incorrect inflection	46 (19%)	3 (2%)

24.4.2 MSI in French and German

Prévost and White (2000) examine the L2 acquisition of tense/agreement morphology and related syntactic properties, including verb placement, in L2 French and L2 German. They examine longitudinal data from four learners from the European Science Foundation (ESF) Project on L2 acquisition by Adult Immigrants (Perdue 1984, 1993). Two of their subjects are Abdelmalek and Zahra, L1-Moroccan Arabic L2-French learners, interviewed for their first three years of exposure; the other two subjects are Ana and Zita, L2-German learners whose L1s are Spanish and Portuguese, respectively, interviewed for their first two years of exposure.

Consistent with the results of the L2-English studies discussed above, Prévost and White found high rates of omission of finite inflectional morphology in both L2 French and L2 German: the learners frequently used infinitival forms in place of finite forms in clearly finite contexts (with clitic subjects, with overt DP subjects and in full CPs, such as questions and relative clauses). The numbers and percentages are reported in Table 24.3.

Table 24.4 next reports on the learners' misuse of *finiteness* morphology – i.e. use of agreement morphemes with an incorrect person/number

Table 24.5. *Use of finite and non-finite verbs before vs. after negation in L2 French and L2 German (Prévost and White 2000: 117, based on table 5)*

	V–Neg order (correct for finite verbs)	Neg–V order (correct for infinitives)
Abdelmalek (L2 French)		
use of finite verbs	90 (97%)	3 (3%)
use of non-finite verbs	6 (12%)	44 (88%)
Zahra (L2 French)		
use of finite verbs	135 (100%)	0 (0%)
use of non-finite verbs	7 (58%)	5 (42%)
Ana (L2 German)		
use of finite verbs	82 (98%)	2 (2%)
use of non-finite verbs	9 (43%)	12 (57%)
Zita (L2 German)		
use of finite verbs	74 (95%)	4 (5%)
use of non-finite verbs	13 (31%)	29 (69%)

combination. As Table 24.4 shows, all learners were highly accurate in their use of finiteness morphology with irregular verbs, and the L2-French learners were also quite accurate with regular verbs (compared to their high use of infinitives in place of finite forms, see Table 24.3). While the L2-German learners often misused finiteness morphology with regular verbs, these errors largely involved misuse of the suffix *-e*, and Prévost and White discuss the possibility that this suffix may be misanalyzed by the learners as the German infinitival suffix *-en*.

Prévost and White also consider the placement of finite vs. infinitival verbs with respect to negation. As discussed in Section 24.2.2, in French and German, finite verbs raise out of the VP, and precede negation, while infinitives have to follow negation. Meisel (1997) argues for global representational impairment in adult SLA on the basis of the fact that infinitival and bare stem forms are commonly used in finite contexts (e.g. before negation) in L2 German. For Meisel, this indicates a breakdown in the link between verbal morphology and verb syntax. In contrast, Prévost and White point out that if verbal morphology and verb placement are truly unrelated, then we should expect to see not only non-finite verbs in finite positions, but also the reverse, namely finite verbs in non-finite position. However, this is not what Prévost and White observe. As shown in Table 24.5, the L2-French and L2-German learners in their study quite often placed non-finite verbs before negation, but practically never placed finite, inflected verbs after negation. The same pattern held (even more strongly) when Prévost and White considered all unambiguously finite contexts (before negation; with clitic or DP subjects; and in full CPs) and all unambiguously non-finite contexts (after auxiliaries; after prepositions; and after other verbs): non-finite verbs were very frequently used in finite contexts, but finite verbs were hardly ever used in non-finite contexts.

Herschensohn (2001) found a similar pattern of performance with two L1-English L2-French adolescents. These two learners achieved a high accuracy of tense/agreement marking, but also used infinitival forms in finite contexts, like the adults in Prévost and White's study. While the two adolescents in Herschensohn's study never used non-finite forms with negation (nearly all of their negated utterances were with finite verbs, and the correct V-Neg order), they used infinitives in other finite contexts, for example, with full DP subjects and with clitics. Like Prévost and White, Herschensohn argues in favor of the MSIH.

Rule and Marsden (2006) used an elicited production task to examine verbal morphology and verb placement in the L2 French of sixty English-speaking adolescent classroom learners. Consistent with the MSIH, Rule and Marsden found non-finite verbs often used in place of finite forms, and did not find misuse of finiteness morphology. Comparing learners across three different years/levels of instruction, Rule and Marsden found an increase in verb production, correct V-Neg order and use of finite verb forms with increased instruction. Rule and Marsden argue that learners at the initial state lack the functional category of Tense (or Infl), as evidenced by a preponderance of verbless utterances, low suppliance of finiteness morphology, and lack of verb raising in the earliest stages of development. They further argue that once Tense emerges, it is fully specified, and that the performance of higher-level learners is consistent with the MSIH.

24.4.3 The MSIH and Distributed Morphology

The above findings led Prévost and White (2000) to argue that L2 learners have a fully specified syntactic representation, with Tense and Agreement categories and features fully in place, and that their problems are of a more surface nature. Prévost and White suggest that learners have particular difficulties retrieving inflectional morphemes, especially in spoken production, and as a result use infinitives (and, in German, also the target finite form ending in -*e*) as default forms. Prévost and White advance a proposal within the Distributed Morphology framework, proposing that for L2 learners, infinitival forms are default forms which are underspecified for finiteness, and which are therefore compatible with a [+finite] syntactic node. If the learner has acquired an inflected finite form, it should in principle win over an underspecified default form in lexical insertion: for example, if an L2-French learner needs to insert a form into a node marked [+finite, −past, +second person, +plural], then the finite form which bears these features should win over the underspecified infinitival form. However, if the learner is unable to retrieve the finite form, possibly because of processing difficulties and communication pressures, then the underspecified infinitival form is used instead. This proposal can account for the variable suppliance of finite forms observed by Lardiere (1998a, b): even when a finite form has been acquired, it is not always successfully retrieved.

Interestingly, the use of infinitival forms in French and German as default finite forms appears to be a property of adult but not child L2 acquisition. Prévost (2004), studying L2 production of two 5-year-old L1-English L2-French children and two 8-year-old L1-Italian L2-German children, found a different pattern than that exhibited by the adult L2-learners in Prévost and White (2000). While the children sometimes produced infinitival forms in place of finite forms, they placed the infinitival forms after negation and did not use them in truly finite contexts such as full CPs (consistent with what has been found for child L1 acquisition, e.g. Pierce 1992; Poeppel and Wexler 1993). The child L2 learners appeared to treat non-finite forms as true infinitives (root infinitives; see Rizzi 1993/94; Wexler 1994), rather than as default finite forms. Prévost (2003), studying longitudinal production of a 3-year-old L1-English L2-German child, argues that this child used bare (uninflected) German forms in finite position, as a default, but used true infinitival forms in non-finite position. A similar pattern was found by Blom (2008) in an elicited production with L1-Turkish and L1-Moroccan Arabic L2-Dutch acquirers: while adult L2-Dutch learners often used infinitival verbs in finite position, child L2 learners placed infinitives in non-finite position (after negation), and used bare verb forms in finite position. Taken together, these crosslinguistic findings suggest that the infinitival form is a default in adult L2 acquisition, while the bare, uninflected form is a default in child L2 acquisition (in the acquisition of English, the two possibilities cannot be teased apart, since the infinitival form is identical to the bare form).

24.4.4 Morphological Underspecification Hypothesis

McCarthy (2007, 2008) puts forth a proposal that is an alternative both to syntactic impairment approaches and to the MSIH. McCarthy agrees with MSIH proponents that learners' errors are a reflection of morphological rather than syntactic difficulties. However, McCarthy also provides evidence against the MSIH, through task comparison. The MSIH predicts that learners will make errors primarily in production (especially oral production), due to difficulties with lexical retrieval of the fully specified finite form. In comprehension or judgments, where learners are not under the same pressure to retrieve lexical items, learners are predicted to be more targetlike. However, McCarthy found, in examining gender marking with L2-Spanish learners, that learners were non-targetlike in both elicited production and comprehension tasks.

These findings led McCarthy to argue for the Morphological Underspecification Hypothesis, under which learners' errors are at the level of morphological competence (cf. Lardiere 2008, 2009a), rather than performance. At lower proficiency levels, learners have not yet acquired all the feature specifications (such as the [feminine] specification of the [gender] feature), and therefore exhibit symmetrical error patterns (both feminine marking in place of masculine marking, and vice versa). More advanced learners have acquired the [feminine] specification, and as a result, do not misuse feminine forms in masculine contexts, but do misuse the underspecified masculine forms in feminine contexts. What is not entirely clear is what, under this proposal, distinguishes the grammars of advanced learners from those of native speakers: since underspecified forms are (in the Distributed Morphology framework that McCarthy adopts) a property of native grammars, it is not clear what leads learners to overuse underspecified masculine forms in contexts where native speakers use the more highly specified feminine forms.

24.5 The Prosodic Transfer Hypothesis

Until recently, the main approaches to L2 morphosyntax have argued for difficulties either at the level of representation (syntactic or morphological), or at the level of mapping from abstract syntactic forms to morphological items. Recently, a third alternative has emerged which places the problems in the phonology. This proposal is in principle compatible with the MSIH, since its aim is to pinpoint exactly why learners have difficulty using specific morphemes. It also has the potential to explain the differential rates of omission exhibited by L2 learners from different L1s. For example, Patty, a Mandarin speaker (Lardiere 1998a, b, 2003, 2007) was found to exhibit much higher rates of omission than SD, a Turkish speaker (White 2003b) (see Table 24.1) – a fact potentially traceable to the different prosodic structures of Mandarin and Turkish, as discussed below.

Lardiere (2003, 2007), continuing to analyze the L2 English data of Patty, argues that Patty's omission of verbal morphology is a result of phonological difficulties. Given that all varieties of Chinese (including Mandarin and Hokkien, the two varieties that Patty speaks) disallow final consonant clusters, Lardiere suggests that Patty's frequent omission of the past-tense -*t*/*d* marker is a result of phonological transfer. Support for this proposal comes from three findings: (i) Patty was much more accurate at supplying the past-tense marker in written email production (78 percent suppliance) compared to oral production (35 percent suppliance); (ii) Patty also deleted final -*t*/*d* in monomorphemic words ending in consonant clusters, such as *pact*; and (iii) Patty was much more accurate at supplying past-tense marking for irregular verbs (46 percent suppliance) than for regular verbs (6 percent suppliance), which is not surprising given that many irregular past-tense forms in English do not have final consonant clusters.

Lardiere's phonological account of past-tense omission was challenged by the study of Hawkins and Liszka (2003) discussed in Section 24.3; the two L1-Chinese L2-English learners in their study exhibited higher rates of final -*t*/-*d* omission in past-tense contexts (37 percent omission) than in monomorphemic words (18 percent omission). Hawkins and Liszka point out that

Bayley (1996), looking at data from twenty Chinese learners of English, similarly found more -t/-d omission in past-tense contexts (63 percent) than in monomorphemic words (37 percent). Furthermore, as noted above, the L1-Japanese L2-English learners in the Hawkins and Liszka study exhibited much lower rates of omission than the L1-Chinese learners, despite the fact that Japanese, like Chinese, lacks consonant clusters. Hawkins and Liszka therefore argue for a syntactic rather than a phonological explanation of past-tense omission by Chinese speakers. However, as pointed out by Goad and White (2006), the representational impairment account of Hawkins and Liszka cannot explain why the L1-Chinese L2-English learners in their study performed better with irregular past-tense forms than with regular past-tense forms (84 percent vs. 63 percent suppliance); the regular–irregular discrepancy (also found by Bayley 1996 and Lardiere 2003) is not expected under representational impairment accounts, since the syntactic features of regular and irregular forms are assumed to be the same. Here Hawkins and Liszka suggest that irregular past-tense forms may be acquired as independent lexical items, without a syntactic [+past] feature.

Goad, White and Steele (2003) and Goad and White (2006) propose a phonological explanation for the omission of past-tense marking on the part of L1-Chinese L2-English learners. This proposal, the Prosodic Transfer Hypothesis (PTH), adopts a hierarchical view of prosodic constituents (e.g. Selkirk 1986), under which syllables are organized into a foot, feet are organized into a prosodic word (PWd), and prosodic words are organized into a phonological phrase. Goad *et al.* (2003) show that the prosodic structure of words ending in consonant clusters is different for regular past-tense verbs than for monomorphemic words (including irregular past-tense verbs). As shown in (13), the final -t/-d consonant adjoins to the PWd when it is a separate inflectional morpheme, but is part of the PWd when it is part of the root morpheme. Goad *et al.* further argue that in Mandarin, adjunction to the PWd is impossible, and provide evidence that aspectual morphemes in Mandarin attach inside the PWd, as shown in (14), which contrasts Mandarin with English. After motivating the prosodic structures of English and Mandarin, Goad *et al.* propose that L1-Mandarin L2-English learners have particular difficulty with adjunction to the PWd in English, since this adjunction does not exist in Mandarin. As a result, learners have more difficulty with final consonant clusters in regular past-tense verbs than in monomorphemic words, including irregular past-tense verbs.

(13)   a.   Regular inflection: [hijp-t] "heaped"
               [PWd [PWd [Ft [σ hij]] [σ p]] [σ t]]

         b.   Irregular inflection: [wɛpt] "wept"
               [PWd [Ft [σ wɛp]] [σ t]]

         c.   Uninflected: [ədɛpt] "adept"
               (ə) [PWd [Ft [σ dɛp]] [σ t]]

(14) a. English tense and agreement: "yelled/yells"
[PWd [PWd [Ft [σ jɛl]]] [σ d/z]]

b. Mandarin aspect: "bought already"
[PWd [Ft [σ mai3] [σ lə5]]]
buy PERF

Goad et al. (2003) empirically tested the PTH using a picture description task with twelve L1-Mandarin L2-English learners. The learners performed at ceiling in a grammaticality judgment task of tense and agreement, and exhibited omission rates in production comparable to those in previous studies (see Table 24.1); they also supplied past-tense morphology more with irregular verbs than with regular verbs (78 percent vs. 57 percent suppliance), as predicted. Goad et al. furthermore found that while some learners deleted inflectional morphology across the board, others did so only variably. Learners in this "variable deletion" group produced agreement marking more in those contexts where the agreement marker could be accommodated without PWd adjunction (e.g. where the agreement marker could be reanalyzed as a coda, or as the onset of the first syllable in the following word). This provides evidence that omission of inflectional morphology is traceable to transfer of the L1 prosodic representation.

While Goad et al. (2003) argue that recovery from prosodic transfer is impossible, this position is modified in Goad and White (2004b, 2006). Goad and White (2006), using a sentence-completion task with ten L1-Mandarin L2-English learners, found high levels of accuracy in their production of past-tense marking; through a careful phonological analysis of the data, they show that the learners have acquired the prosodic structure of English past-tense verbs, with PWd adjunction.

The PTH is quite compatible with the MSIH, since both hypotheses assume an unimpaired syntactic representation. The PTH furthermore offers a nuanced explanation of why particular morphemes in an L2 are difficult for speakers of particular languages to produce. In addition to omission of tense marking by L1-Chinese L2-English learners, the PTH has been used to explain the pattern of article omission and article stress with L1-Turkish as well as L1-Chinese L2-English learners (Goad and White 2004b, 2008, 2009a, b; Snape and Kupisch 2010; see Trenkic 2007 for an alternative explanation in terms of processing limitations).

24.6 New directions: the Feature Reassembly Hypothesis

As discussed above, most of the work done on SLA of morphosyntax has argued in favor of one of three positions: that L2 learners have a temporarily or permanently impaired syntactic representation; that L2 learners have a fully specified syntactic representation, but difficulty retrieving inflectional morphemes; and that L2 learners' production of inflectional morphology is constrained by the prosodic properties of their L1s. Another direction in the investigation of L2 morphosyntax has been proposed under Lardiere's (2008, 2009a) Feature Reassembly Hypothesis. On this approach, framed within the Minimalist Program (Chomsky 1995, 2001), the learner's task is to select the relevant features for lexical items in the target language: for example, the [+past] feature for the -ed suffix, the [+plural] feature for the -s suffix, etc. The inventory of possible features is assumed to be universal, part of the human linguistic computational mechanism. However, not all languages make use of all the possible features, and languages differ from one another in exactly how these features are bundled together into individual lexical items and functional categories.

A child L1 learner's job is to select the appropriate features for each item in the target language. An L2 learner, unlike an L1 learner, comes to the learning task already in possession of the L1 system in which features have been selected and assembled in a particular way. The L2 learner therefore has both to select new features for the L2 (in the case of features that are not selected in the L1) and to reassemble the existing features (in the case where features are assembled differently in the L1 and the L2). Lardiere gives an example from plural marking. An English speaker acquiring Chinese or Korean has already selected the feature [+plural] for the plural -s suffix in English. While Chinese also has a plural suffix, -men, this suffix bears the features of [+human] and [+definite] in addition to [+plural], and is furthermore absent after numerals and quantifiers where the English plural marker is obligatory (e.g. *three books*). The Korean marker -tul has an even more complex distribution, conditioned by a variety of syntactic and semantic factors (see Lardiere 2009a for the details). Assuming syntactic L1 transfer, an L1-English L2-learner of Chinese or Korean will transfer the [+plural] feature, but this will not be enough: the learner will also need to select other features related to definiteness/specificity/animacy, and to pay attention to different conditioning environments. Some of the features may already be part of the learner's L1 grammar (e.g. while the [+definite] feature is not marked on the plural suffix in English, it is marked on the article *the*), so the features have to be reassembled in new ways.

The Feature Reassembly Hypothesis is different in an important way from most formulations of representational impairment. While representational impairment accounts place emphasis on *parameterized* features – for example, the existence of a [+/−plural feature] in a language – Lardiere argues that the picture is much more complex: as discussed above, English, Chinese and Korean all have a [+plural] feature, but differ in which other features are bundled up with this feature, and in the conditioning environments in which the plural marker can be used. Similarly, in the domain of tense/agreement marking, Lardiere (2003) argues that the task of an L1-Chinese L2-English learner is not just to acquire the [+/−past] feature; the English past tense also marks perfective aspect, and is also used to express counterfactuality (Ludlow 1999). Framed in terms of Lardiere's (2009a) approach, we might say (as one possible hypothesis) that an L1-Chinese L2-English learner has to reassemble the [+perfective] feature (which is selected by an aspectual marker in Chinese) and bundle it together with the [+past] feature for English past-tense verbs.

The Feature Reassembly Hypothesis goes beyond the question of whether specific syntactic features are acquirable, and looks at whether the fine-grained semantic properties of a given feature can be acquired: for example, successful acquisition of English past-tense marking means not only using *-ed* in past-tense contexts, but also using it appropriately with perfective aspect, for habitual as well as one-time events, and in counterfactuals. Montrul and Slabakova (2003) address precisely this type of question, examining whether L1-English L2-Spanish learners can interpret perfective and imperfective forms in Spanish appropriately, given cross linguistic differences in form–meaning mappings. For example, while English uses the perfective past for both one-time events (*John robbed somebody yesterday*) and for habitual events (*John robbed people on a regular basis*), Spanish uses the perfective past in the first case, and the imperfective past in the second case. In terms of feature reassembly (see also the discussion in Slabakova 2009a), L1-English L2-Spanish learners have to reassemble the [habitual] feature from the perfective form in English onto the imperfective form in Spanish. A large proportion of the advanced and near-native learners tested by Montrul and Slabakova (2003) performed in a targetlike manner on this and other aspectual contrasts, providing evidence against those formulations of representational impairment which hold that adult L2 learners are incapable of acquiring uninterpretable features or reassembling interpretable features. For other work on the L2 acquisition of the semantics of tense and aspect, see Slabakova (2002, 2003) and Gabriele (2005, 2009), among many others. See Slabakova (2008) and Chapter 22, this volume, for more discussion of the L2 acquisition of semantics.

Lardiere's (2009a) proposal does away with parameters altogether, and places the focus on the selection and assembly of features. Montrul and Yoon (2009) argue, contra Lardiere, that micro-parameters based on formal features do not present a learnability problem, since these micro-parameters are lexicalized (to individual functional elements) and lexical learning may in fact be easier than learning a cluster of properties associated with the macro-parameters of Principles and Parameters theory. Montrul and Yoon pose a number of questions that need to be addressed by Minimalist approaches to SLA, such as the inventory of formal features in UG, the constraints on feature assembly, and the question of whether the different feature-based parameters are independent of one another (if they are not, then setting the value of one parameter may lead to the setting of a value of another parameter). Other commentaries on Lardiere's (2009a) paper (Liceras 2009 and Slabakova 2009b) also argue, on independent grounds, against dispensing with the notion of parameter. Montrul and Yoon (2009), as well as Birdsong (2009a), also bring up the question of whether feature selection and feature assembly work any differently for interpretable vs. uninterpretable features (Lardiere argues against any such difference).

24.7 Conclusion

As discussed in this chapter, the deceptively simple question of why L2 learners omit inflectional morphology has received many answers: omission of morphology may be due to syntactic impairment, problems with morpheme retrieval, prosodic transfer, or unsuccessful feature reassembly. (See Chapter 28, this volume, for yet another view.) In principle, more than one of these explanations may be correct, for the same learner or for different learners. Logically, it is possible to have an impaired syntactic representation coupled with prosodic transfer, or to have difficulty reassembling formal features as well as problems retrieving the target morphemes. In order to tease apart the various explanations of L2 acquisition of morphosyntax, experimental studies continue to examine different aspects of morphosyntax, with different L1/L2 combinations, using a variety of methodologies, and paying attention to fine-grained syntactic, semantic and prosodic distinctions. On the theoretical level, as the discussion in generative SLA shifts from macro-parameters to features, researchers are considering the issues brought up by Lardiere (2009a) and commentaries about the nature of formal features and the constraints on the acquisition of formal features by L2 learners.

25

Phonology and speech

Ellen Broselow and Yoonjung Kang

25.1 Introduction

The acquisition of a second language (L2) sound system poses significant challenges for learners, who must acquire a new system of sound contrasts, new restrictions on where sounds may occur, and a new prosodic system. The challenges facing researchers are to understand the characteristics of L2 speech and to explain how and why those characteristics arise. In this chapter, we focus on three major issues that guide research on the acquisition of L2 sound systems: (i) the influence of L1 and of linguistic universals in L2 speech sound patterns; (ii) the level of representation (phonological vs. phonetic) at which L2 acquisition occurs; and (iii) the relationship between the perception and the production of the second language.

25.1.1 Transfer and universals

Almost all studies on the acquisition of L2 sound systems address the question of how and to what extent L1 influence (*transfer*) contributes to shaping L2 learners' sound patterns (see e.g. Major 2008). Lado's (1957) *Contrastive Analysis Hypothesis* (CAH) predicted that those aspects of L2 that are similar to the L1 will be easily acquired, while those aspects that are different from the L1 will be difficult. While L1 transfer is undeniably a major factor in L2 acquisition, two recurring phenomena pose problems for the claim that L2 errors are based *solely* on the difference between the L1 and the L2. First, certain L2 structures not present in L1 appear to be more easily acquired than others, regardless of the particulars of the L1 and the L2 involved. Second, the speech of L2 learners in many cases exhibits patterns that are coherent and systematic, but are nonetheless distinct from those of both the target L2 and the native language. Phenomena of both types have frequently been attributed to *universal principles* such as *markedness*, where unmarked structures are generally considered to be those that are more basic, typologically common, and phonetically easier to perceive and produce than more marked structures (see Kager 1999; Rice 2007). Eckman (1977) proposed that the *Contrastive Analysis Hypothesis* must be supplemented by the *Markedness Differential Hypothesis*, which states that marked L2 structures are more difficult to acquire than equally novel but less marked structures (see also Eckman 2008). Similarly, interlanguage patterns that appear to be rooted in neither the L1 nor the L2 can be analyzed as resulting from universal preferences for unmarked structures or patterns.

Markedness has been encoded in theories of grammar in various ways. In a theory that views a grammar as a set of parameters (see Chapter 24, this volume, on parameters) with different possible settings (for example, a parameter allowing consonant clusters in syllable onsets, which may be set either on or off), the preference for less marked structures can be viewed as encoded in default parameter settings (e.g. Hayes 1995). More recently, within the framework of *Optimality theory* (OT; Prince and Smolensky 2004), markedness is encoded in the form of universal constraints that favor less marked structures. These constraints are assumed to be present in the grammars of all languages, but may be rendered inactive by more highly ranked constraints; for example, a constraint banning consonant clusters in onsets may be outranked by a constraint demanding that lexical forms be realized "faithfully." Exposure to L2 data may trigger resetting of parameters (e.g. Archibald 1993, 1994, 1995b) or rerankings of constraints that may allow formerly dormant markedness constraints to become active (e.g. Broselow 2004; Eckman 2004; Hancin-Bhatt 2000, 2008).

As the cases discussed in this chapter illustrate, teasing apart L1 transfer effects from the effects of universal tendencies is not a trivial undertaking. Complicating this issue is the fact that a number of researchers have argued that similarity to pre-existing L1 structure may actually have a negative effect on the accurate perception and ultimate attainment of some aspects of L2 structure, particularly the acquisition of new phonemic contrasts. A number of models recognize a tendency for L2 sounds to be interpreted in terms of L1 sounds, giving rise to problems when, for example, two contrasting sounds in the L2 map onto a single L1 category. The tendency to map L2 sounds to similar but not necessarily identical L1 phoneme categories is recognized in the *Speech Learning Model* (SLM; Flege 1995), where it is termed "equivalence classification"; in the *Perceptual Assimilation Model* (PAM; Best 1995); and in the *Native Language Magnet theory* (Kuhl and Iverson 1995), each of which outlines the ways in which this process may interfere with the accurate acquisition of L2 sounds, though the degree of L1 interference may be modulated by factors such as degree of experience with the L2, age of L2 exposure, and speech rate, attention and language mode in experimental conditions (Antoniou, Best, Taylor and Kroos 2010; Flege 1991; Ioup 2008; Piske, Mackey and Flege 2001; among others). Finally, Major and Kim (1996) propose that while L2 sounds that are dissimilar to L1 sounds are initially difficult, performance on these improves quickly, while performance on L2 sounds that are similar to L1 sounds stays the same or progressively worsens (the *Similarity Differential Rate Hypothesis*).

25.1.2 Phonology vs. phonetics

A second major issue in the acquisition of L2 sound systems concerns whether the characteristics of L2 sound patterns are best explained from the perspective of *phonology* (an internalized system of abstract rules or constraints defining the possible sound patterns of a language) or of *phonetics* (the physical implementation of speech sounds in production and the interpretation of fine-grained acoustic cues in perception). Various accounts have assumed that the reason learners fail to produce L2 structures correctly is because their phonological grammar does not sanction them, causing L2 forms to be modified by the L1 grammar. In this approach, L2 acquisition involves moving from the starting point (the L1 grammar) toward an L2-like grammar in response to L2 input, which may trigger (depending on one's model of grammar) resetting of parameters, changes in phonological rules (Eckman, Iverson, Fox, Jacewicz and Lee 2003; Young-Scholten 2004); or, in Optimality theory, changes in the ranking of constraints (e.g. Broselow 2004; Escudero and Boersma 2004; Hancin-Bhatt 2008). However, evidence has emerged supporting the position that some if not all the modification of L2 forms may take place not in phonology but rather at the level of phonetics, where speakers may simply fall short in mastering the correct articulation (Colantoni and Steele 2007; Davidson 2010). (The question of whether modification may also reflect misperception is addressed in the next section.)

A related issue concerns the units of representation involved in L2 acquisition (Kang 2008) – that is, whether the L2 is perceived and produced in terms of abstract phonological concepts such as phonemes or phonological distinctive features (e.g. Brown 2000; Hancin-Bhatt 1994; Larson-Hall 2004; Weinberger 1997; among others); in terms of surface phonetic features (Brannen 2002; de Jong, Hao and Park 2009; de Jong, Silbert and Park 2009); or in terms of more phonetically based notions such as articulatory gestures (Best and Halle 2010).

Researchers beginning from the perspective of phonology have proposed that the attainability of L2 structures is a function of the availability of corresponding phonological structures in the L1 (Archibald 2005; Brown 2000; Goad and White 2006). Distinctive features (which serve both to distinguish contrasting sounds of the language and to organize sounds into natural classes sharing a particular feature) have been appealed to for explanations of crosslinguistic differences in L2 perception as well as in phoneme substitution. For example, to explain the finding that speakers of Mandarin Chinese were better at discriminating English /l/ and /ɹ/ than speakers of Japanese, though both L1s lack the phonemic contrast of /l/ and /ɹ/, Brown (2000) argued that the difficulty of acquiring a new L2 phoneme contrast depends on whether the L1 employs a phonological feature to encode that contrast. She explained the Chinese speakers' relatively good perception by proposing that the Chinese contrast between alveolar and retroflex fricatives (e.g. /s/ vs. /ʂ/) requires a feature to encode subcoronal place contrasts, which can then be extended to the English contrast. The fact that no subcoronal contrast (and consequently no appropriate feature) exists in Japanese makes this contrast difficult for Japanese speakers. Similarly, Hancin-Bhatt (1994) argued that phonological features can explain the choice of L1 phoneme to replace an illegal L2 sound (for example, why English /θ/ is typically replaced with /t/ by speakers of Turkish but with /s/ by speakers of Japanese, even though /t/ and /s/ are present in both L1 phoneme inventories). Investigating the differential substitution patterns for English interdental fricatives by speakers of German, Hindi, Japanese and Turkish, Hancin-Bhatt proposed that the likeliest L1 substitute is one that preserves those features of the L2 sound which carry the highest functional load in the L1 (that is, the features that encode the largest number of contrasts in the L1 phoneme inventory).

However, other studies have suggested that at least some L2 patterns must be described in terms of surface phonetic features rather than contrastive phonological features. According to Brannen (2002), the English interdental fricative /θ/ is replaced by /s/ in European French and by /t/ in Quebec French, although the two dialects have identical phoneme systems and consequently identical phonological feature inventories. The crucial difference between the two dialects therefore rests not in their phonological feature inventories but rather in their articulatory patterns: in European French, the coronal fricative /s/ has a dental place of articulation, while in Quebec French, /s/ is alveolar, a phonetic detail that is not considered to be contrastive in either dialect. Based on these findings, Brannen (2002) argues that L2 substitution may be sensitive to phonetically salient features, regardless of the contrastive status of the features.

Evidence suggesting that both phonological features and the mastery of articulatory routines play a role in L2 acquisition comes from comparing the rate at which contrasts defined by the same phonological feature are acquired. De Jong, Silbert and Park (2009) and de Jong, Hao and Park (2009) found that Korean learners' ability to perceive the English stop–fricative contrast both for labial /b-v/ and for coronal /d-ð/ proceeded similarly, suggesting that the learning of one contrast defined by the feature [continuant] generalized to continuant contrasts across all places of articulation. However, this effect in L2 perception was not accompanied by the same effect in the Korean speakers' production of English, where the accuracy of the continuancy contrasts in labial and coronal place did not correlate, presumably because implementation of /b-v/ involves articulatory gestures that differ from those involved in /d-ð/. There was, however, a correlation between the production accuracy of learners' stop–fricative contrasts in voiced labials /b-v/ and voiceless labials /p-f/, since in this case the gestures for producing the manner contrast are similar across the voiced and voiceless pairs.

Just as abstract features are realized differently in different phonemes, individual phonemes are realized differently in different contexts. Flege (1995) proposed that segmental acquisition takes place on the basis of contextual allophones, at a level more abstract than surface phones but less abstract than phonemes. This view is supported by numerous studies showing that a given L2 segment is not perceived or produced with uniform accuracy across different segmental contexts; rather, the same novel segment is acquired earlier in certain positions (e.g. onset, word-initial, etc.) than in others (e.g. coda, word-final, etc.). Some attribute such positional variation to phonological markedness, while others seek explanations based on perceptual similarity, articulatory ease and input frequency. For example, Trofimovich, Gatbonton and Segalowitz (2007) showed that the production of English /ð/ by French speakers was more accurate in some positions (e.g. sentence-initial) than in others, and concluded that the target sound is more easily learned in positions where it was perceived as phonetically distinct from L1 sounds, as well as in positions where it more frequently occurred. Clearly, the problem of separating phonological from phonetic explanations is not trivial (see e.g. Archibald 2009), and a full account of L2 speech will require detailed analysis of both the phonology and the phonetics of the L1 and L2 systems.

25.1.3 Perception and production

A third area of longstanding interest in L2 phonological acquisition research is the extent to which misproduction reflects misperception and the question of whether L2 *perception* and *production* develop in tandem. While it is generally assumed that in children's native language acquisition, accurate perception precedes accurate production (Smolensky 1996), many L2 researchers, most notably Flege (1995), have suggested that many of the difficulties in L2 production stem from inaccurate perception of L2 targets. As in so many other areas, the literature provides conflicting evidence. For example, Hayes-Harb and Masuda (2008) found that some English speakers learning Japanese were successful at perceptually discriminating the singleton–geminate consonant contrast in Japanese, but were unable to implement this contrast in production. They suggest that this may not reflect a problem in production per se; rather, the English learners were able to notice the presence of novel contrasts as familiar vs. unfamiliar, but had not established an accurate lexical representation of the short–long contrast, which in turn led to failure to produce the contrast. Conversely, Weber and Cutler (2004) and Cutler, Weber and Otake (2006) suggest that lexical encoding of a contrast does not necessarily lead to auditory discrimination. Using eye-tracking technology to examine the auditory processing of L2 speech, Cutler et al. (2006) found that when Japanese learners of L2 English presented with four different pictures heard English *rock*, they looked at both the picture of a rock and the picture of its minimal pair competitor, a lock.

However, the confusion was asymmetrical; when the participants heard *lock*, they converged on the lock picture. This asymmetry suggests that the learners had encoded the /l/ vs. /ɹ/ contrast lexically but could not perceive the contrast in the online auditory word-identification task.

In addition to cases showing production lagging perception, the L2 literature reveals cases showing the reverse; for example, both Goto (1971) and Sheldon and Strange (1982) found that some Japanese learners of English were more successful in producing the English /l/ vs. /ɹ/ contrast than in discriminating these sounds. Similarly, Kijak (2009) found, in a study discussed below, that learners of various L1 backgrounds generally performed better on production than on perception of Polish stress.

In the remainder of this chapter, we will survey results of L2 acquisition research in the context of the questions outlined above. Section 25.2 will discuss L2 segmental acquisition – the perception and production of consonants and vowels; Section 25.3 will discuss phonotactics – the restriction on possible combinations of segments; and Section 25.4 will discuss the acquisition of prosody – stress, tone, pitch accent and intonation.

25.2 Segmental acquisition

The vastness of the literature on L2 segmental acquisition makes it impossible to provide a comprehensive review, so we will limit our discussion to the major research results on the production and perception of three groups of sounds – stops, vowels and liquids.

25.2.1 Voicing contrasts in stop consonants

Languages differ in their realization of the stop voicing contrast along the dimension of *Voice Onset Time*, or VOT (the time between the release of stop constriction and the onset of voicing on the following vowel). Even languages that share a two-way voicing or laryngeal contrast may implement this contrast differently. For example, English speakers produce /p t k/ with a *long lag* in VOT, resulting in aspiration, and /b d g/ with a *short lag*, so that voicing begins simultaneously with release of the stop into the following vowel. In Spanish, French, Dutch, Greek and Portuguese, however, /p t k/ have a short lag (are unaspirated), while for /b d g/ voicing begins during the stop closure (i.e. a negative VOT). Many studies have found that when the L1 and L2 differ in phonetic realizations of voicing contrasts, L2 stops tend to show compromise VOT values intermediate between the L1 and the L2 stops (Antoniou, Best, Taylor and Kroos 2010; Flege 1991; Fowler, Sramko, Ostry, Rowland and Hallé 2008; Hazan and Boulakia 1993; Kang and Guion 2006; Sancier and Fowler 1997; among others; see Zampini 2008 for a recent review). For example, Flege (1987b) found that the mean VOT duration of French /t/ for less experienced English-speaking learners of French was similar to the mean value for English /t/ produced by monolingual English speakers. For more experienced learners, however, the VOT was intermediate between the French norm and the English norm. These and similar findings are consistent with the claims discussed above that learners tend to map L2 sounds onto similar L1 phoneme categories, even when the L1 and L2 categories may differ in phonetic detail (Flege 1995; Best 1995; Kuhl and Iverson 1995).

Another common finding is that L1 phonetic implementation patterns are not necessarily uniformly transferred. Learners whose L1 contrasts long-lag unaspirated stops with prevoiced stops, such as Spanish, French and Dutch, tend to produce English voiceless aspirated stops as targetlike, i.e. with a long lag, but they produce English voiced stops as prevoiced, showing transfer from the L1 (Hazan and Boulakia 1993; Simon 2009; Williams 1977, among others). It is puzzling that the short lag stop category is not correctly produced in the L2 even though it is already available in the L1, particularly given the fact that short lag stops are usually the first to be acquired in L1 acquisition (see Kager, van der Feest, Fikkert, Kerkhoff and Zamnner 2007 cited in Simon 2009). Simon (2009) proposes possible explanations for this asymmetrical transfer of L1 structure based in both phonetics and in abstract phonological representations. First, the long VOT of aspirated stops is perceptually salient and therefore more easily heard by learners Second, if the Dutch contrast between voiceless unaspirated and prevoiced stops is represented by a single phonological feature [voice] (which is specified for /b d g/ but absent in /p t k/), the stops specified for [voice] enjoy a privileged status and are therefore more likely to be transferred.

L1 transfer plays a role in the perception of L2 voicing contrasts as well as in their production. Curtin, Goad and Pater (1998) examined English speakers' perception of the Thai three-way contrast of voiced–voiceless–aspirated stops. English speakers who heard an auditory stimulus and were then asked to choose a matching picture over a minimal pair competitor were better at perceiving the Thai voicing contrast (b vs. p) than the aspiration contrast (p vs. p^h), presumably due to transfer of the L1 voicing contrast. However, in an auditory discrimination task requiring participants to decide which of three stimuli were the same, the aspiration contrast was more accurately perceived than the voicing contrast. Curtin *et al.* (1998) suggest that the picture task, which associates sound differences with meaning differences, taps into a more abstract level of processing, while the discrimination task taps simple auditory processing, where discrimination is facilitated by the perceptual salience of aspiration (see Strange and Shafer 2008 for a review of task effects in L2 perception). A later study (Pater 2003) found significantly better performance on the more salient aspiration contrast than on the voicing contrast, regardless of task type, suggesting a stronger role for acoustic salience. On the other hand, the association of sound differences with lexical contrasts was found to facilitate acquisition of a new contrast by Hayes-Harb (2007), who found that in an artificial language learning experiment, English speakers performed better in distinguishing pseudo-words that contained voiced [g] and voiceless unaspirated [k] (which do not normally serve a contrastive function in English) when stimuli were presented with contrastive meanings ([ga] "pot" vs. [ka] "mouse") than when they were presented with non-contrastive meanings ([ga], [ka] "pot") or when no meaning was attached.

25.2.2 Vowel contrasts

In an early influential study on cross-language vowel perception, Stevens, Libermann, Studdert-Kennedy and Öhman (1969: 1) suggested that unlike consonant perception, vowel perception "is relatively independent of... linguistic experience." Subsequent research, however, has revealed that both the perception and the production of L2 vowels is strongly influenced by listeners' L1, with abundant evidence that non-native speakers have difficulty perceiving certain L2 vowel contrasts not found in their L1. For example, English speakers identified a (synthesized) French [y] vowel as English [u] while Portuguese speakers identified it as Portuguese [i] (Rochet 1995), equating the L2 vowel with an L1 category in perception (Best 1995; Flege 1995; Kuhl and Iverson 1995). This perceptual distortion was also reflected in these speakers' imitative production of French [y]: English speakers' production of [y] was often judged to be [u] by French native speakers while Portuguese speakers' was judged to be [i], consistent with the claims of Flege, Takagi and Mann (1997) that learners' perceptual difficulties with novel L2 vowel contrasts are reflected in production difficulties.

In perceiving L2 vowel contrasts, speakers may rely on acoustic cues that are different from those utilized by native speakers of the L2; furthermore, when several cues to a contrast are present, L1 and L2 speakers may weight them differently. For example, many L2 learners of English who have difficulty perceiving the English [i]–[ɪ] contrast may rely on a durational difference rather than vowel-quality differences, which are the primary cues for native speakers of most dialects of English to distinguish the vowels. Such a pattern is found not only for speakers whose L1 has durational contrasts in vowels – German (Bohn 1995) and Finnish (Ylinen *et al.* 2009) – but also for speakers whose L1 has no durational contrasts – Spanish, Mandarin, Korean, Russian and Catalan (Bohn 1995; Cebrian 2006; Escudero and Boersma 2004; Flege *et al.* 1997; Morrison 2009). Escudero, Benders and Lipski (2009) found that the "over"-reliance on duration for L2 vowel distinction is not specific to L2 English but is also found in the perception of the Dutch /aː/–/ɑ/ contrast by Spanish speakers of L2 Dutch.

The reliance of L2 speakers on durational cues has been explained in terms of both language transfer and universal tendencies. Bohn (1995) proposes that when the vowel space containing two L2 vowels corresponds to a single vowel in L1, listeners will be "desensitized" to spectral distinctions in the region. He proposes furthermore that durational cues are universally salient, leading these to be the first cues used by inexperienced L2 learners.

However, Kondaurova and Francis (2008) suggest that the use of duration for L2 vowel contrasts by Spanish and Russian speakers can be analyzed as transfer, since durational cues may be used in the L1 as a secondary cue for distinctions in stress and consonant voicing. Escudero and Boersma (2004) also challenge the claim that reliance on duration reflects a universal tendency, arguing that the sensitivity to duration evidenced in their studies followed from listeners' sensitivity to the statistical patterns of the input data, where duration did play a contrastive role, albeit a secondary one. Because duration was not used in the L1, the correlation of durational differences with different vowel categories in L2 was readily acquired, while the acquisition of spectral differences was hindered by influence of the L1. Further evidence against the view that duration is a universally accessible cue for L2 contrasts comes from McAllister, Flege and Piske (2002) and Ylinen *et al.* (2005), who found that quantity distinctions in L2 vowels (Swedish and Finnish) are better perceived by speakers whose L1 uses duration to signal vowel contrasts (Estonian) than by speakers whose L1 (Spanish, Russian) does not contrast long and short vowels.

The acquisition of L2 vowel contrasts is complicated by the fact that individual vowel sounds are typically realized somewhat differently in different contexts. Levy and Strange (2008) found that the perception of the /u-y/ contrast in Parisian French was generally difficult for American English speakers, but that inexperienced L2 learners showed more errors in the context of alveolar consonants, where English /u/ is allophonically fronted and therefore more similar to /y/, than in bilabial contexts, where it is not. Although the /u-y/ contrast continued to be difficult for experienced speakers, the consonantal context effect disappeared, indicating that L2 learning includes all language-specific variations within phonetic categories. Similarly, in production, Oh (2008) examined the degree of coarticulation in alveolar stop + /u/ sequences in French and English speakers' L1 and L2, and found that English had more extensive C-to-V coarticulation while French had more extensive V-to-C coarticulation. Although many learners acquired both target values and coarticulation patterns, some acquired only target values, suggesting that coarticulation patterns are language-specific and must be learned independently of the target vowel values.

25.2.3 Liquid contrasts

The majority of research on L2 *liquids* (/r/ and /l/) has focused on Japanese learners' acquisition of the English /l/ vs. /ɹ/ contrast, which is notoriously difficult for Japanese speakers (e.g. Aoyama, Flege, Guion, Akahane-Yamada and Yamada 2004; Bradlow, Akahane-Yamada, Pisoni and Tohkura 1999; Bradlow, Pisoni, Yamada and Tohkura 1997; Goto 1971; Logan, Lively and Pisoni 1991; Takagi 2002, among others; see Bradlow 2008 for a recent review). Where English uses the /l/ vs. /ɹ/ contrast to distinguish words, Japanese has a single liquid whose distribution in the acoustic space straddles the two English categories. It has been shown that while native English speakers rely on the third formant (F3, a measure of acoustic resonance) for discrimination of English /ɹ/-/l/, Japanese speakers rely on the second formant (F2) (Iverson et al. 2003). Aoyama et al. (2004) examine how the degree of perceived phonetic dissimilarity influences L2 learners' success in acquiring L2 phonetic segments. The Japanese liquid /ɾ/ is considered more similar to English /l/ than /ɹ/, so in earlier stages of acquisition, /l/ is more accurately pronounced, showing the advantage of similarity to an L1 category. Later, however, /ɹ/ shows more improvement, presumably because its greater distance from L1 liquid prevents its assimilation to an L1 category (cf. the *Similarity Differential Rate Hypothesis*; Major and Kim 1996).

Research on acquisition of this contrast supports the view that the mapping of L2 sounds to L1 phoneme categories takes place not as a mapping from phoneme category to phoneme category; instead, learners map positional allophones (the variant pronunciations of a phoneme in different contexts) to L1 phoneme categories (Flege 1995). Ingram and Park (1998), examining the perception of the English /l/-/ɹ/ contrast by Korean and Japanese speakers in various phonetic contexts, found contextual variation in the acquisition of this contrast. Korean speakers were better at perceiving the /l/-/ɹ/ contrast in intervocalic or cluster position, where the English /ɹ/-/l/ contrast can be equated with the native Korean contrast between singleton [r] vs. geminate liquid [ll], than they were in initial position, where no singleton vs. geminate contrast is available in Korean. Japanese speakers, on the other hand, who have no comparable singleton vs. geminate liquid contrast in L1, showed generally poorer perception of the English /l/-/ɹ/ contrast than Korean speakers, but the Japanese speakers' perception was better in intervocalic and initial positions, where acoustic cues are generally more perceptible, than in clusters. This is a problem for the claim of Brown (2000) that Japanese speakers' difficulty in perceiving the English liquid contrast stems from their lack of an L1 phonological feature to encode the contrast, since the feature specification of the English liquids would be the same in all positions. Ingram and Park (1998) conclude that L1 background and general acoustic discriminability, but not universal markedness, affected the perception pattern.

Colantoni and Steele (2007), examining the production of French rhotic /ʁ/ by intermediate- and advanced-proficiency English-speaking learners, found additional evidence for the role of phonetic salience and articulatory ease in acquisition. The voiced uvular fricative realization of the French rhotic presents difficulties for English speakers not only because English lacks a dorsal fricative but also because the antagonistic articulatory requirements of voicing and frication make voiced fricatives inherently difficult to produce, particularly in dorsal place. The results show that the English learners produced frication at a level comparable to native speakers but failed to produce voicing correctly. Colantoni and Steele (2007) argue that because frication is a more salient acoustic property of the French rhotic than voicing, the L2 learners preserve the more easily perceived property of the novel sound at the expense of the less salient property.

25.3 Acquisition of restrictions on syllable structure and of phonotactics

In addition to differences in segment inventory, languages may differ in the number and types of segments that may be grouped into syllables and in restrictions on the types of segments that may occur in specific positions within a syllable. In general, while L2 segmental acquisition tends to show more obvious effects of L1 transfer than of universal tendencies, research on the acquisition of *phonotactics* and related phonological processes in the L2 sound system has been the source of a number of arguments for the role of universal markedness effects in L2 acquisition.

25.3.1 Consonant clusters within and across syllables

The perception and production of non-native consonant clusters has been extensively studied, in large part because this area provides evidence for emergent hierarchies independent of the L1 or L2, as certain non-native cluster types seem to be acquired earlier than other equally novel clusters across various L1s and L2s (Berent, Lennertz, Jun, Moreno and Smolensky 2008; Berent, Lennertz, Smolensky and Vaknin-Nusbaum 2009; Broselow, Chen and Wang 1998; Broselow and Finer 1991; Davidson 2010; Eckman and Iverson 1993; Hansen 2004; Hancin-Bhatt 2000, among others). Many of these studies address the question of whether ease of acquisition is related to sonority, assuming a *universal sonority scale* consisting of stops < fricatives < nasals < liquids < glides < vowels, organized from least to most sonorous. Two proposed universal principles govern the organization of segments within syllables: consonant clusters should increase in sonority approaching the vocalic nucleus, favoring rising sonority onset /pr/ over falling sonority onset /rp/; and consonants within a cluster should be distant in sonority, favoring onset /pr/ over onset /pn/, whose members are closer on the sonority scale.

Broselow and Finer (1991) examined the production of English pseudo-words containing /Cj/ and /Cr/ onset clusters by speakers of Japanese and Korean, where the only onset clusters allowed are obstruent-j. Lower error rates were found for clusters with larger sonority distance such as /pr/ (stop-liquid) than for clusters with smaller sonority distance such as /fr/ (fricative-liquid). Similarly, studies of speakers' perception of unfamiliar cluster types have shown an effect of sonority: Berent *et al.* (2008) and Berent *et al.* (2009) argue that English and Korean speakers perceived non-native onset clusters of rising sonority in pseudo-words more accurately than clusters of falling sonority. Berent *et al.* (2009) further argue that the sonority effect found in

English speakers' perception of non-native clusters cannot be derived from the statistical generalizations of the English lexicon. However, Davidson (2010), in a study of English and Catalan native speakers' productions of pseudo-words containing non-native word-initial clusters, argued that neither phonological markedness (as defined by sonority distance) nor analogy to L1 clusters was a good predictor of production accuracy, which was better predicted by general phonetic factors such as articulatory ease (voiceless obstruent clusters are easier to produce than voiced obstruent clusters) and perceptual salience (fricative-initial clusters contain more salient cues to the identity of the first consonant than stop-initial clusters).

While factors independent of L1 seem clearly to be a factor in the acquisition of L2 syllable structure and phonotactics, native language restrictions clearly affect not only the production but also the perception of L2. For example, Japanese speakers typically alter English words to fit the more restrictive syllable structure conditions of their native language; English "pub" is borrowed as *pabu* with a vowel inserted after [b] because [b] cannot occur in Japanese syllable codas (except in geminates). Dupoux, Pallier, Kakehi and Mehler (1999) investigated the perception of illegal structures such as the pseudo-word *ebzo*, which constitutes a legal structure in French but not in Japanese. Presented with a series of stimuli ranging from, for example, *ebzo* to *ebuzo*, with a vocalic portion of varying length (from null to a full vowel), the majority of the Japanese speakers perceived an "illusory vowel" in the illegal consonant sequence – that is, they perceived *ebzo* as a possible native language structure *ebuzo* even when there was no vocalic signal in the stimulus. In contrast, the majority of French speakers, for whom *ebzo* is a possible structure, perceived a vowel between [b] and [z] only when the vocalic portion was at least 50ms long. In a follow-up study using ERP (Event-Related Potential) methodology, Dehaene-Lambertz, Dupoux and Gout (2000) found that the illusory vowel effect held at early stages of speech processing. However, discrimination of CC–CvC can improve when the difference is associated with lexical contrasts; Davidson, Shaw and Adams (2007) found that American English speakers asked to distinguish pseudo-words containing a non-native CC sequence vs. a CvC sequence in picture-naming tasks performed better when the stimuli were presented with contrastive meanings.

Matthews and Brown (2004) and Idsardi and Kabak (2006) present additional evidence that illusory vowels arise in response to syllable structures that are illegal in the L1. Matthews and Brown's (2004) study investigating the ability of native speakers of Japanese and Thai to discriminate heterosyllabic [k.t] vs. [kVt] revealed that the Thai speakers were better able to discriminate [k.t] vs. [kVt] than Japanese speakers, even though the sequence [kt] is not possible in either language. This difference in performance arises, they argued, from the fact that [k] is a possible syllable coda in Thai (so long as it is not followed by [t]) but not in Japanese. Matthews and Brown (2004) conclude therefore that perception of an illusory vowel is triggered by native language constraints defining possible syllables, rather than simply by constraints on sequences of segments across syllable boundaries (see Kabak and Idsardi 2007 for similar arguments based on perception data from speakers of Korean). Further evidence for ascribing the illusory vowel effect (failure to distinguish CC vs. CvC) to the native language phonological system came from the fact that the failure to discriminate was found only when the interval between stimuli was long enough (1500ms) to force the listeners to access phonological representations stored in memory rather than rely on purely acoustic discriminatory skills.

While vowel insertion in both production and perception is most frequently motivated by differences in L1 and L2 syllable structure, Korean speakers' production of English word-final stops presents a case of vowel insertion that is unmotivated by phonotactic restrictions of L1. Korean speakers frequently insert a vowel after a word-final stop of English (e.g. *tape* is pronounced as [tʰeipʰɨ] ~ [tʰeip]) both in L2 speech and in loanword adaptation even though voiceless stops are allowed in coda position in Korean. Kang (2003) proposes that this seemingly gratuitous vowel insertion is due to the differences in the phonetics of final stops in English, where final stops are optionally released, and Korean, where no audible release is possible.

25.3.2 Restrictions on segments in the syllable coda

Many languages place restrictions on the types of consonant contrasts that can be realized in syllable-final position, in *codas*. One common pattern is a prohibition on voiced obstruents in the syllable coda (as in Dutch, German and Russian), resulting in a lack of obstruent voicing contrasts in coda position. Acquisition of an L2 that allows both voiceless and voiced obstruents in coda is expected to cause problems for learners of languages that disallow such contrasts, particularly since voiced obstruents in coda position are considered to be marked. In an investigation of German speakers' L2 production of the English voicing contrast in word-final stops, Smith, Hayes-Harb, Bruss and Harker (2009) found that the German speakers produced more voicing contrasts for English word-final stops than for German words but that their English production still fell short of L1 English speakers' performance, showing a transfer of L1 final devoicing to L2. The fact that German speakers managed to partially acquire the voicing contrast in coda position may be attributed simply to the influence of English input or, alternatively, to the fact that many German speakers actually exhibited *incomplete neutralization* of the German voicing contrast – i.e. German speakers actually do make a subtle voicing distinction in their production of these coda consonants, although the difference is barely perceptible.

Final devoicing has attracted much attention in L2 phonology mainly because one often observes an emergent pattern that is not straightforwardly accounted for by either L1 transfer or L2 input – namely, patterns in which learners devoice final obstruents in their L2 production even though neither the L1 nor the target L2 manifests any evidence for such devoicing (Broselow *et al.* 1998; Flege and Davidian 1984; Flege, McCutcheon and Smith 1987; Wissing and Zonneveld 1996; Yavaş 1994b, among others). Broselow (2004) proposed an OT analysis of such emergent patterns whereby a universal markedness constraint against voiced obstruents in coda position which remains dormant in the L1 becomes visible as constraint rankings fluctuate in the process of L2 acquisition. Broselow acknowledges, however, that because voicing of obstruents in coda position is articulatorily difficult and perceptually not very salient, it is likely that L2 speakers may fail to produce final voiced obstruents not because their phonological grammar forbids them but because at least some of the final devoicing takes place during perception and/or production. Similarly, Simon (2010) examined final obstruent devoicing and voicing assimilation across word boundaries in a corpus of L2 English conversations between native speakers of Dutch. The results show that while both L1 processes are frequently transferred into L2 English, a hierarchy emerges that is not motivated by the L1: final voiced fricatives are more frequently devoiced than final voiced stops. They attribute this asymmetry to the aerodynamic difficulty in producing voicing in final fricatives; while voicing requires adduction of the glottis, frication requires a sufficient airflow through the glottis.

Another hierarchy emerges in Cardoso's (2007) examination of Brazilian Portuguese speakers' production of English word-final stops. Although Brazilian Portuguese allows only /N l r s/ and no stops at all in coda, coronal stops are more frequently attested than stops at other places of articulation, in line with the observation that crosslinguistically, coronal place of articulation is the least marked of the three major places of articulation, namely dorsal, coronal and labial (Paradis and Prunet 1991).

The hierarchies of difficulty discussed above are horizontal, revealing different rates of acquisition for different members of a class. In addition, James (1987a, b) suggests a vertical hierarchy whereby the lexical level of L2 phonological representation (e.g. phonemes and word-level accents) is acquired before higher levels of representation (i.e. phrasal and rhythmic properties). We turn now to the acquisition of prosodic systems as they are realized at the word, phrase and sentence levels.

25.4 Prosodic systems: stress, pitch accent, tone and intonation

Like the acquisition of L2 segments and phonotactics, the acquisition of prosody shows evidence for the role of the L1 as well as for universal principles not obviously grounded in either the L1 or the L2 input. We begin with some discussion of the typology of prosody. Languages are most often classified into three categories: *tone* languages, *pitch accent* languages and *stress* languages. In a tone language such as Mandarin Chinese, morphemes can be distinguished in meaning solely by their pitch (e.g. *ma* with high level tone is "mother" while *ma* with falling tone is "horse"). Pitch accent languages such as Tokyo Japanese also use pitch to signal lexical contrasts, but the inventory of pitch patterns on words is generally restricted, with specific syllables within a word (accented syllables) associated with invariant tonal contours (Hayes 1995: 49–50). Hyman (2006) argues that pitch accent should not be thought of as a discrete category of languages; rather, pitch accent languages may combine features of stress-based and tone-based systems. The defining characteristic of stress, according to Hyman (2006: 231), is that each lexical word contains exactly one syllable "marked for the highest degree of metrical prominence (primary stress)." Prominence is typically signaled by a combination of acoustic cues, including duration, intensity and pitch changes, and is connected with the rhythmic organization of words and phrases. The function of pitch in a stress language like English is generally to signal sentence-level intonation. Intonational melodies convey "meanings that apply to phrases or sentences as a whole, such as sentence type or speech act, or focus and information structure" (Ladd 2008: 6), and stressed syllables may vary in pitch according to the intonational melody of the utterance in which they appear.

Languages characterized as stress-based may differ along a number of dimensions. A language may allow one or multiple stresses per word, and the position of stress may be lexically specified or phonologically predictable (or some combination of the two). In languages with predictable stress, the position of stress may depend on various factors. In a *fixed stress* language, stress is determined purely by word position, as in Polish, where stress falls on the penultimate syllable of each word, or Hungarian, where the initial syllable is stressed. In *quantity-sensitive stress* languages, the position of stress may vary depending on syllable weight, as in Cairene Arabic, where stress falls on a penultimate syllable only if that syllable is heavy (containing a long vowel or a final consonant). Languages may also employ different *foot types*, with German for example favoring trochaic (strong–weak) feet and Choctaw (southeastern United States) favoring iambic (weak–strong) feet. Languages may also impose a minimal size on feet (typically two syllables or moras, where the mora equals a weight unit within the syllable). Furthermore, languages may require all syllables to be contained within feet (giving rise to patterns of alternating stress), or they may allow or even require syllables to be unfooted; for example, the English tendency to avoid stress on the final syllable of nouns (as in verb–noun pairs such as *reCORD/REcord*) is often analyzed as a requirement that the final syllable of a noun be extrametrical, i.e. outside a foot. Thus, even learners whose L1 is stress-based may encounter substantial differences between the L1 and L2 stress systems, which are generally characterized as differences in settings of parameters or different rankings of constraints.

Another dimension distinguishing languages is rhythm, with languages classified as *stress-timed* (English) vs. *syllable-timed* (Spanish) or *mora-timed*

(Japanese). Impressionistically, English syllables tend to be of unequal duration and the intervals between syllable peaks tend to vary, while in Spanish or Japanese, syllables or moras (vocalic nuclei and coda consonants) tend to share similar durations and to be spaced at regular intervals. While cautioning that stress timing vs. syllable timing represent ends of a continuum rather than discrete categories, Dauer (1983) identifies two characteristics of stress-timed languages: (i) a tendency to reduce vowels in unstressed syllables and (ii) a larger inventory of syllable types than in syllable-timed languages. Both infants and adults have demonstrated sensitivity to rhythmic differences in both native and second languages, and such differences have been argued to play a role in L1 learners' ability to segment the speech stream (see Ramus, Nestor and Mehler 1999 for a review).

25.4.1 Acquisition of stress and rhythm

Since many studies have focused on L2 stress production or perception but not both, we will consider these areas separately.

Production of L2 stress

Comparison of learners from various L1 backgrounds supports the claim that typological similarity confers an advantage in acquiring an L2 stress system. Learners whose L1 is a stress language, even when the placement of stress differs in the L1 and L2, appear to do better in producing L2 stress; for example, Altmann (2006) argued that native speakers of Arabic (a language with predictable stress, though with different parameter settings than English) were more successful in producing English-like stress than were native speakers of Mandarin, a tone language. Learning also appears to be facilitated by overlap between L1 and L2 stress systems: in Kijak's (2009) study of the acquisition of L2 Polish, a language with fixed penultimate stress, learners whose L1 included penultimate stress as a possible option (English, German, Italian, Russian and Spanish) showed an initial advantage over those whose L1 allowed only final stress (French) or initial stress (Czech), or was a tone language (Mandarin).

The types of errors found in L2 stress production also support transfer from the L1 grammar. The most common error in Archibald's (1993, 1994, 1995b) studies of speakers of L1 fixed stress languages – Polish (penultimate) and Hungarian (initial) – involved placement of stress in the L1 position. Speakers of a quantity-sensitive L1 also showed a preference for maintaining L1 stress patterns; Youssef and Mazurkewich (1998) found that Cairene Arabic speakers produced near-perfect stress placement for English words whose stress was consistent with the Arabic pattern of stress on a superheavy (CVCC or CVVC) final syllable (*volunTEER*) or on a heavy (CVC or CVV) penultimate (*moMENtum*), while words whose stress deviated from the L1 pattern were produced correctly less than half the time, with the vast majority of errors involving putting stress in the appropriate L1 position (*bariTONE*, with final CVVC, and *cyLINder*, with penultimate CVC). In Kijak's study of L2 Polish by speakers of both fixed stress and variable stress L1s, "the positions of the majority of non-L2 stresses produced were the possible positions for stress in the L1" (Kijak 2009: 322). Speakers of the tone language Mandarin, who presumably did not need to overcome a native language stress system, "were quite successful and consistent in their discovery of the correct word edge at which main stress in Polish is located" (Kijak 2009: 312–13), and they most frequently placed stress on the penultimate or (less frequently) the final syllable. In this case, as with segmental acquisition, the distance between the L1 and L2 actually seemed to facilitate learning by preventing equivalence classification based on similarities.

Another area of transfer involves the choice of acoustic cues used to convey stress. Aoyama and Guion (2007) found that Japanese speakers used a wider pitch range on stressed syllables than did English speakers, suggesting that the Japanese speakers tended to rely on their native cue for pitch accent rather than the combination of acoustic cues for stress used by English native speakers.

L1 influence also appears in rhythm, associated in stress-timed languages such as English and German with the reduction of unstressed syllables. English vowel reduction has been shown to be problematic for speakers of Spanish (Flege and Bohn 1989), Japanese (Aoyama and Guion 2007) and Mandarin (Zhang, Nissen and Francis 2008). A study of the L2 German of Korean and Spanish speakers (Young-Scholten 1993) showed that Spanish and Korean speakers learning German had difficulty in producing L2 inflectional affixes containing reduced vowels.

While transfer is clearly a factor in L2 production, some patterns have emerged that appear independent of both the L1 and L2, but which nonetheless conform to patterns found in human language. Studies of the acquisition of English stress by speakers of Hungarian, Polish and Spanish (Archibald 1993, 1994, 1995b, 1997, 1998) and by speakers of Canadian French (Pater 1997) have been argued to present cases of this type, though Pater (1997) and van der Pas and Zonneveld (2004) suggest that some of the patterns Archibald describes can in fact be analyzed as a reflection of L1 transfer. One universal factor that receives support from several studies, both in production and perception, is a preference for assigning stress to heavy (CVV or CVC) as opposed to light (CV) syllables and in particular to syllables containing long vowels. Kijak (2009) found that learners of L2 Polish, in which stress falls on the penultimate syllable regardless of syllable quantity, tended to prefer stress on closed syllables in Polish, even when their L1 was also quantity-insensitive, suggesting that "there may be a universal bias to perceive closed syllables as prominent" (Kijak 2009: 314). Guion, Harada and Clark (2004) and Guion (2005) found a similar preference for placing stress on long vowels in studies of English L2 produced by speakers of Spanish and of Seoul Korean. In the pronunciation of English-type pseudo-words, learners were more likely to place initial stress on CVVCVCC than on CVCVCC pseudo-words, and final stress on CVCVVC than on CVCVC. This pattern is not motivated in any direct way by either Korean or Spanish, but whether it can be said to be motivated by the English input depends on the degree of influence one is willing to grant to statistical tendencies rather than absolute requirements. While the grammar of English does not require stress to fall on long vowels, a corpus study of English examining the relationship between vowel length and stress reveals that long vowels are roughly twice as likely to be stressed as are short vowels (Guion, Clark, Harada and Wayland 2003).

A related finding from crosslinguistic studies of native language systems is a tendency for vowels of higher sonority (i.e. vowels that are lower in height) to attract stress (De Lacy 2006), presumably since higher sonority correlates with greater inherent duration. The existence of a natural bias toward this stress–sonority link was supported by an experiment in which both English and French speakers had more difficulty learning an artificial language in which lower-sonority vowels attracted stress than one in which stress fell preferably on vowels of greater sonority (Carpenter 2010), even though neither English nor French appears to provide direct support for such a pattern (though a corpus study of frequency might conceivably reveal some tendency in this direction). The stress–sonority correlation is also attested in different varieties of English; Peng and Ann (2001) report a correlation between inherent vowel length and stress in Singapore English and Nigerian English, as well as the English of native Spanish speakers, with pronunciations like CHInese, where [aj] of the first syllable attracts stress in preference to the inherently shorter [i] of the second syllable. Loanword phonology also provides a number of cases in which prosodic prominence (i.e. a pitch accent or a contour tone) is placed on a heavy syllable in borrowed words, rather than on the originally stressed syllable of the input language (Kang 2010). The preferences for stressing heavier syllables and more sonorous vowels are therefore strong candidates for universal biases that may play a role in both language acquisition and language contact.

To summarize, the body of research on the acquisition of L2 stress and rhythm suggests a correlation between the similarity of the L1 and L2 prosodic systems and success in the acquisition of L2 prosody, as well as a tendency for L2 stress errors to reflect the native language stress system. Furthermore, studies support a role for universal biases favoring the placement of stress on heavier over lighter syllables and on longer over shorter vowels, which appear to emerge even in the absence of direct evidence from the L1 or L2. What is striking, however, is the relative paucity of studies taking languages other than English as the target language, even though the fact that English stress is not fully predictable makes it less than ideal for the investigation of a consistent L2 stress pattern.

Perception of L2 stress

Some of the studies discussed above argue for transfer in the perception of L2 stress as well as in production. In fact, Kijak (2009) suggests that "the properties of an L1 stress system stand much more in the way of successful L2 perception than in the case of production" (Kijak 2009: 326). Two major sources of difficulty in perception have been identified: learners fail to attend to stress in the L2 input because L1 stress is fully predictable (*stress deafness*), and learners tend to misinterpret L2 acoustic cues in terms of the different functions that these cues serve in the L1.

Arguments for stress deafness come from a set of native language studies in which native speakers of languages with fixed, predictable stress (Finnish, French and Hungarian) exhibited higher error rates and slower reaction times on tasks involving discrimination of stress differences than on tasks involving discrimination of phoneme differences. In this, the Finnish, French and Hungarian speakers differed from speakers of Spanish, in whose native language stress is to some extent lexically determined (Dupoux, Pallier, Sebastián-Gallés and Mehler 1997; Dupoux, Peperkamp and Sebastián-Gallés 2001; Peperkamp 2004; Peperkamp and Dupoux 2002; Peperkamp, Dupoux and Sebastián-Gallés 1999). The authors of these studies hypothesized that speakers of a language with fully predictable stress do not store stress in their phonological representations; thus, stress deafness should appear not at the level of acoustic processing, but rather in processing tasks that increase the load on working memory, requiring reference to a stored abstract representation of stress. Tasks that involved increased memory load (such as increasing the number of stimuli to be identified) did, as predicted, impair accuracy and reaction time for the speakers of predictable stress languages, though not for the Spanish speakers. However, although speakers of the predictably stressed languages, namely Finnish, French and Hungarian, differed significantly from Spanish speakers, the Hungarians also differed from both the French and Spanish groups. Even more surprisingly, Polish speakers, whose native language has predictable stress, did not differ significantly from the Spanish speakers in their ability to hear stress differences. In a follow-up study, Peperkamp, Vendelin and Dupoux (2010) confirmed that Polish speakers fell into an intermediate category between speakers of languages with non-predictable stress and speakers of predictably stressed L1s Finnish, French and Hungarian. They attributed this to the fact that Polish does have some lexical exceptions to the general pattern of penultimate stress, therefore defining stress deafness as gradient, correlating with the degree of predictability of stress in the speaker's language.

If stress deafness persists in an L2, we would expect speakers of languages with fully predictable stress to have difficulty accurately perceiving L2 stress. However, this is not necessarily the case. In Kijak's (2009) study, speakers of Czech, which has regular word-initial stress, performed very well in the perception of Polish stress, which is similarly predictable but falls in a different position. Kijak explains this result by pointing out that stress may serve functions other than signaling lexical contrasts: "stress fulfills an important 'demarcative' function which has been shown to be crucial in speech segmentation" (Kijak 2009: 320). Thus, Czech speakers would have good reason to attend to stress in their L1, as it can help them in segmenting the continuous acoustic stream into words (see Jusczyk 1997 on stress in child language acquisition). One might then ask why French speakers should not also attend to stress, where word-final stress could be expected to aid in segmentation. However, the analysis of final prominence in French as reflecting stress has been challenged by a number of researchers who argue that final prominence reflects an intonational accent assigned not to individual words but to the final syllable of a phrase (e.g. Jun and Fougeron 2002), making the prosodic systems of French and Czech crucially different.

Additional support for the claim that listeners do attend to stress which serves a demarcative function comes from loanword adaptation, where languages with fixed word-edge stress often truncate stress-peripheral material. For example, the initially stressed Spanish word *ígado* "liver" is adapted into Huave (spoken in Mexico), a language with word-final stress, as *ik*. Broselow (2009) argues that the Huave speakers, for whom stress always signals the final syllable of a word, have assumed that material following the stress belongs to a different word (though see Kang 2010). Additional evidence that learners' segmentation of L2 strings into words is affected by L1 patterns is provided by Altenberg (2005), who showed that Spanish-speaking learners of English were significantly worse than native English speakers at identifying the position of word break in phrases such as *keep sparking* and *keeps parking*, finding it difficult to use cues to word position (such as aspiration) that are not relevant in their L1 (see also Broselow 1984/87).

If a pattern of fully predictable word stress in L1 might interfere with learners' ability to attend to L2 stress, what about the absence of stress in the native language? Here, as with production, evidence suggests that the distance between the L1 and L2 plays a role. For example, Guion (2005) found that Korean–English bilinguals were less like English L1 speakers in their perception of English stress than were Spanish–English bilinguals, presumably because Korean is not a stress-based language. Similarly, in Kijak's (2009) study of the perception of Polish L2, Mandarin speakers showed very poor perception, a result she attributes to the lack of overlap between cues for Polish stress and the acoustic cues that are important in the prosodic system of Mandarin. This hypothesis is bolstered by other studies suggesting that speakers are biased by their L1 to ignore acoustic cues that are crucial in the L2 but serve a different function (or no function) in their L1. In an investigation of Mandarin and English speakers' judgments of stress position in English words like DEsert/deSERT, Zhang and Francis (2010) found that the two groups differed in their weighting of four main cues to stress (vowel quality, pitch, duration and intensity), with Mandarin speakers ignoring intensity cues when vowel-quality cues were available.

Stress in English may function not only as a feature of words but as an indication of the relationships among words (*BLACKberry* vs. *black BERRY*). As with word stress, speakers of other languages may have difficulty interpreting the acoustic cues signaling these relationships. Nguyen, Ingram and Pensalfini (2008) investigated the ability of speakers of Vietnamese (a tone language) to discriminate English compounds, which typically assign greater prominence to the initial constituent (*BLACKberry*), vs. phrases, which normally assign prominence to the phrase-final head (*black BERRY*). Pitch and duration were manipulated to determine which cues listeners used in their discrimination. Nguyen *et al.* found that beginning learners were not able to discriminate compounds from phrases using duration alone, because duration is not distinctive in Vietnamese. However, the Vietnamese speakers were more successful in discriminating phrases differing in the position of the focus, which is signaled in English by an intonational pitch accent on the focused element. For phrases with broad focus (*What is this? It's a black BERRY*) vs. phrases with narrow focus on the adjective (*It's not green, it's a BLACK berry*), the Vietnamese speakers "had no problem in manipulating the f_0 and intensity contrastive levels on the accent-bearing syllables as a result of positive transfer from lexical tonal pitch."

Loanword adaptation offers additional examples in which the acoustic cues of a foreign language are interpreted through the filter of the L1. Words borrowed from stress languages into tone languages are most commonly assigned high tone to the source word stressed syllables (e.g. Yoruba $to^M MA^H to^L$, $gua^M ran^M TEE^H$ (Kang 2010), where the stressed *MA* and *TEE* in *tomato* and *guarantee* are each assigned a high tone). This suggests that cues associated with stress in the lending language are interpreted as an indication of high tone in the borrowing language. A similar phenomenon was demonstrated by Chen (2007) for Mandarin-speaking learners of Spanish, who tended to interpret Spanish words with stress on the penultimate syllable as having a lexical rising tone on the stressed syllable and a falling tone on the following syllable.

In addition to differences solely related to the L1 (Korean, Spanish and Thai), a series of studies (Guion 2005; Guion *et al.* 2004; Wayland, Guion, Landfair and Li 2006) found systematic differences between early and late learners of English. Early learners were similar to native speakers in recognizing the influence of syllable structure and noun–verb differences on stress, while "late learners of English may rely more heavily on word-by-word learning of stress patterns and are less likely to abstract generalities about stress placement by syllable structure and lexical class" (Wayland 2006 *et al.*: 298). However, Davis and Kelly (1997) found that older speakers from fourteen different L1 backgrounds did show awareness of the preferred noun–verb stress patterns in L2 English (as in noun *REcord* vs. verb *reCORD*). Participants who were asked to create an English sentence using a pseudoword tended to use bisyllabic words with initial stress as nouns and with final stress as verbs, and were faster and more accurate in classifying actual words as nouns or verbs when the stress pattern conformed to the preferred structure for that category. They conclude that "despite large individual differences in native language, age of arrival in the United States, and years of exposure to English, non-native speakers have learned the English noun–verb stress difference" (Davis and Kelly 1997: 457).

The question of the level of attainment that learners can be expected to reach is still very much an open one. In a survey of L2 stress research, van der Pas and Zonneveld (2004: 125) claim that "despite more optimistic claims, the bulk of this literature fails to demonstrate that [parameter] resetting may occur." While numerous studies demonstrate some degree of success in mastering L2 stress, it is difficult to determine whether these successes represent acquisition of the L2 grammar, particularly when the L2 is English, in which stress is partially lexically determined. Even in studies using pseudo words (Guion 2005; Guion et al. 2004; Wayland et al. 2006), which would seem to avoid the possibility that learners are simply relying on their knowledge of individual words (as in studies of L2 English), a major determinant of L2 stress position was the phonological similarity of the pseudo-word to existing English words. In parameter-setting models of L2 stress acquisition, no consensus has emerged on whether particular parameters are more or less amenable to resetting, though Pater (1997) suggests that L2 restrictions on foot size and foot headedness may be learned before other parameter settings. Although the Optimality theory literature offers explicit models of the interplay between linguistic data and constraint ranking (or reranking in the L2 from the L1 grammar), we are not aware of attempts to test these models against a body of L2 stress data.

25.4.2 Acquisition of tone, pitch accent and intonation

Studies on the acquisition of L2 tone, pitch accent and intonation are relatively rare. Wang, Jongman and Sereno (2006) review several studies on the production of Mandarin tones by English-speaking learners, showing high rates of error in tone production by English speakers. Ioup and Tansomboom (1987) studied the production of both tone and segmental aspects of Thai by four adult second language learners and four children, two of whom were learning Thai as a second language. They found that tone was one of the last aspects of Thai to be mastered by the adult learners but one of the earliest for the children learning Thai, either as L1 or L2.

Studies of crosslanguage tone perception involving participants who do not know the second language can be taken to offer some insight into the initial state for language learning. Such studies suggest that an L1 system in which pitch is used to realize lexical contrasts confers some advantage in tone perception; for example, Lee, Vakoch and Wurm (1996) found that native speakers of Cantonese performed better than English speakers in identifying pairs of Mandarin syllables as same or different in tone, even though the Cantonese tone inventory is different from that of Mandarin. Similarly, So and Best (2010) found that native speakers of Hong Kong Cantonese (a tone language) and Japanese (a pitch accent language) outperformed English speakers in identifying the tones of Mandarin syllables. However, the Cantonese speakers were actually disadvantaged in some respects by their L1 knowledge; the Mandarin tones that they found most difficult to discriminate were those that fell within the range of a single tone category in Cantonese, a pattern reminiscent of equivalence classification in the perception of phonemes. The error patterns of the Cantonese speakers were quite distinct from those of the Japanese and English speakers, whose error rate correlated more closely with the inherent acoustic similarity of the tonal pairs. Apparently, "the effect of linguistic experience is more related to the constraints of the phonological systems of listeners' native languages than the degree of tonality use" (So and Best 2010: 290).

One type of equivalence classification involves interpreting pitch cues used for lexical contrasts in the L1 in terms of the intonational patterns of the L2. So and Best (2010) found evidence that English speakers were significantly less accurate in identifying Mandarin Tone 4 than were speakers of Cantonese and Japanese, and that Tone 4 was identified less accurately than the other tones. Since Mandarin Tone 4 is a falling contour similar to the intonation contour typically found at the end of English statements, it seems likely that English speakers assimilated this lexical tone to an L1 intonational contour. Consistent with this, Broselow, Hurtig and Ringen (1987) found that for English speakers who received training in identifying the four Mandarin tones (but were not learning Mandarin), identification of Tone 4 was significantly less accurate when Tone 4 occurred in final than in non-final positions, where it is less likely to be confused with a sentence-final declarative fall. Furthermore, the most frequent error involved (mis)identification of Tone 4 in final position as the high level Tone 1, presumably because English listeners take the falling pitch of Tone 4 to be associated with the sentence-final intonation and interpret only the high starting point of the syllable as signaling the lexical tone.

Even where the L1 and L2 have similar uses of pitch, L1 influence may emerge when the meanings of intonation contours differ in the two languages. In tasks designed to determine how English-speaking learners of Portuguese and Portuguese-speaking learners of English interpreted L2 intonational contours, Cruz-Ferreira (1987) found that where the same meaning was conveyed by similar intonational contours in L1 and L2 the learners in both groups performed similarly to native speakers. Learners had difficulty, however, in cases where the match between meaning and intonation differed in L1 and L2.

A second source of L1 influence may come from differences in the phonetic realization of pitch contours. Mennen (2004) studied two languages with relatively similar intonational systems, Dutch and Modern Greek. In both, declarative intonation includes a (non-final) rise (LH*), but the languages differ in the alignment of the highest point of the rise: in Dutch, the peak occurs on the accented syllable, while in Greek, the peak occurs following the accented syllable. Comparison of Dutch and Greek sentences produced by L1 Dutch and L1 Greek speakers revealed that four out of five speakers produced patterns of peak alignment that differed from both L1 Greek and L1 Dutch, suggesting that learners had developed an interlanguage system intermediate between the L1 and the L2.

25.5 Conclusion

Much research in L2 sound patterns has focused on whether L2 acquisition patterns should be understood as effects of L1 transfer or of universal preferences for particular linguistic structures; whether acquisition patterns should be explained at the level of abstract phonology or at a phonetic level; and whether patterns in L2 production correlate with patterns in L2 perception. Our goal in this chapter was to demonstrate that although these questions have provided a productive program for L2 research, the dichotomies they presuppose are overly simplistic. The literature has provided both plausible examples of transfer from the native language and emergent patterns that appear not to be motivated by input from either L1 or L2. Similarly, some L2 patterns seem to be well explained with reference to abstract phonological structures while others can only be explained as effects of phonetic salience and/or articulatory ease; furthermore, since much recent work in phonology assumes that the constraints of the phonological grammar are grounded in phonetics (e.g. Hayes, Steride and Kirchner 2004), the boundary between the two components is increasingly blurred. Nor has a simple explanation of the relationship between production, perception and lexical representations emerged, with accurate perception appearing to lag behind production in some areas and to precede it in others. Clearly, L2 speech represents a complex interplay of numerous factors, and despite many advances, no model has yet emerged to provide a fully comprehensive and predictive account of the patterns found in segmental and prosodic L2 speech. Furthermore, much work remains to be done. There is a regrettable dearth of studies charting longitudinal development, particularly the development of L2 prosody. Sorely needed are more studies of L2 stress that take languages other than English as their L2, studies that investigate production and perception simultaneously, and studies that tap into both auditory and lexical levels.

However, there are grounds for considerable optimism, as methodological advances in the field of language study transform the way research into L2 sound acquisition is conducted (Schmid and Dusseldorp 2010). Behavioral probes such as eye-tracking methods and neurolinguistic tools, in particular ERP studies (see Chapter 19, this volume), provide fine-grained temporal information concerning the time course of L2 speech processing (Escudero, Hayes-Harb and Mitterer 2008; Strange and Shafer 2008), and the availability of ultrasound imaging and electropalatography allow direct observation of articulatory patterns (Gick, Bernhardt, Bacsfalvi and Wilson 2008;

Mennen, Scobbie, de Leeuw, Schaeffler and Schaeffler 2010). And while the role of input in L2 acquisition has always been recognized (e.g. Young-Scholten 1994), increasingly large databases and increasingly sophisticated search tools may make possible the discovery of statistical tendencies in L2 input that might not otherwise be apparent (e.g. Guion *et al.* 2003), and developments in modeling statistically driven acquisition (Boersma and Hayes 2001; Hayes and Wilson 2008; Albright 2009) may shed light on the extent to which L2 patterns which are seemingly unmotivated by L1 transfer or L2 input may be accounted for by the L2 learners' probabilistic knowledge of the learning data (Wilson and Davidson, to appear). Furthermore, artificial grammar learning experiments (e.g. Carpenter 2010), by allowing experimenters to strictly control access to learning input, provide a tool to determine whether typological tendencies reflect genuine learning biases or simply a function of linguistic change (e.g. Blevins 2004). Finally, within Optimality theory, explicit models have been offered to describe the mapping from the acoustic signal to phonological representations (e.g. Escudero and Boersma 2004; Escudero 2009), an area long neglected in formal theories of phonology. Inevitably, new paradigms will emerge in this swiftly evolving field to offer fresh perspectives on the perennially intriguing problems posed by second language speech patterns.

Part VI
Models of development

INTRODUCTION TO PART VI

The distribution of chapters in this handbook demonstrates the relative dearth of research on what is responsible for development in a second language. The majority of studies in SLA concern themselves with the properties of learners' systems at a given point in their development or with the conditions and factors which might influence second language use, rate of development or ultimate attainment. Far fewer studies rise to the challenge of explaining how the learner moves from one point in development to the next. The chapters included in Part VI are attempts to do just that. This final part includes five theoretical models of development or transition that hark back to the themes introduced in Part I, which have been elaborated throughout subsequent chapters.

The aim of a theory of SLA is not only to account for how the ingredients (as presented in Parts II and III) involved in acquisition actually bring about both socially appropriate communication and grammatical knowledge (Part V) but also to account for how the learner acquires language in real time. Part VI includes chapters that each present currently prominent theories of learner progress.

The lead chapter furnishes a comprehensive introduction to the section on theories of development, not only elaborating three models, but also giving a welcome overview of the rationale and design criteria for such frameworks. Sharwood Smith, Truscott and Hawkins start by introducing the problem at hand: how does the L2 learner makes sense of the raw data? Three transition theories, O'Grady's Emergentist Model, Carroll's Autonomous Induction theory (AIT) and Sharwood Smith and Truscott's MOGUL framework are then described. This last theory proposes a middle-ground approach, that accounts for transition by the parsers' building representation based on a best-fit interpretation of the input. The authors then outline the need for a transition theory and then the tasks involved to effect L2A. They consider how the learner takes acoustic (or visual) signals and converts these into a systematic grammar, and how the L2 learner makes use of both domain-specific and general cognition. Using the illustration of the /r–l/ phonemic contrast in L2 English as learned by L1 Japanese speakers, they specify details of the transitional models, contrasting them on both theoretical and empirical grounds.

Vainikka and Young-Scholten in Chapter 27 cover the main proposals on paths of second language development since the 1970s. After an initial discussion of L1A, the authors discuss the pivotal morpheme order studies of the 1970s before investigating recent frameworks that examine stages of development. They focus in much more detail on approaches from the 1990s and beyond which continue to attract attention, i.e. the Basic Variety, Processability theory and Structure Building / Organic Grammar. These theories have all emerged from similar sets of data, namely from studies of migrant workers, primarily in Europe. This chapter thus provides the morphosyntactic part of the body of research on uninstructed adult immigrant learners referred to in Véronique's chapter. Since the mid 1990s, these sorts of studies have been extended to contexts outside Europe and to the study of instructed learners and child L2 learners, leading to new versions of these theories

In Chapter 28, Holme covers proposals that dispense with language-specific mechanisms involved under a nativist approach to L1A and L2A. These proposals assume that the learner's ability to detect and categorize patterns in the ambient input is sufficient for accomplishing the task of second language acquisition. Holme presents models of L2A that characterize this process as skill learning (as is L1A) based on external factors such as frequency and saliency, and on internal factors such as L1 influence and U-shaped learning. In addition to defining crucial concepts such as chunking, emergence and parallel processing, the author gives a clear description of learning models represented by constructionism, Processability, Competition, Connectionist and Dynamic Systems.

Chapter 29 gives an overview of characteristics, from linguistic to extralinguistic, of learner input and discusses what is known about its impact on L2 development. This chapter complements García Mayo and Alcón Soler's chapter in Part III in concretizing one model of the input/interaction approaches. In so doing, Barcroft and Wong uniquely in this handbook focus exclusively on what happens in the classroom to effect changes in learners' interlanguage grammars. There is therefore considerable coverage of the role of certain aspects of classroom input, attention to form(s) rather than meaning, to noticing and input processing. The chapter explores models of L2A that are premised on the importance of input, most particularly VanPatten's highly influential model of Input Processing (IP). After an overview of L2 approaches based on input, the authors present the model, explaining its principles (e.g. Primacy of Meaning) and illustrating them with empirical evidence. The final section discusses pedagogical applications of the model.

Like Chapter 29, Chapter 30 deals with classroom-based research. It covers the ideas underpinning the idea of a social turn, emphasizing interaction in L2 social networks. Ohta argues for a paradigm shift in recent work. Here approaches to L2 acquisiton are sociocultural in their view of language as a cultural product and contributor to socialization through communities of practice. Under this view, early stages of learners' development rely on supportive interaction with others (e.g. scaffolding) through the co-construction of knowledge (Vygotskian approaches). The chapter exhaustively discusses the adaptation of Vygotsky's concept of the zone of proximal development (ZPD) to L2A. After a critical reassessment of the historical foundations of sociocultural theory in Vygotskian developmental psychology, Ohta explores four areas of contemporary applications of the ZPD in L2A: L2 skills development, mentor feedback, peer collaboration and future directions.

The chapter that ends the handbook fittingly covers endstate competence in L2 acquisition. Lardiere notes learners' near-complete mastery of core syntax as opposed to greater optionality in their grammars in areas of interface vulnerability (e.g. syntax/pragmatics interface). The chapter also looks at endstate disparities between different grammatical areas (e.g. nominal vs. verbal domains). This final chapter appropriately recapitulates the themes treated throughout the volume and the philosophical questions posed at its outset. After a substantive introductory section covering those topics, Lardiere discusses methodological concerns for researching nativelike competence and fossilization. She then turns to specific areas of linguistic competence (e.g. semantic interpretation, morphological production) that constitute strengths and weaknesses in ultimate-state learners. Adult L2 learners have been the focus of most of the chapters of this volume, and Lardiere appropriately closes the handbook with a discussion of future directions in research on the question that remains one of the central issues in SLA: why do older second language learners fail to attain nativelike competence? Answers to this question will come not from one line of inquiry but from the many lines of research presented in the chapters of this handbook.

26

Explaining change in transition grammars

Michael Sharwood Smith, John Truscott and Roger Hawkins

26.1 Introduction

Language acquisition is about change. It is self-evident that the systematic, visible or audible performance of L2 learners tends to change, albeit at differing rates in individual learners, as the number of encounters they have with the target language increases, until they appear to reach a plateau (see Chapter 31, this volume). An early learner of English producing utterances like *every people happy* may well produce the more targetlike *everyone is happy* with longer exposure to the language. What precisely is the process whereby exposure to instances of the copula *be* triggers change in learners' mental grammars leading ultimately to the appearance of the construction in their own performance? A fundamental challenge for research into second language acquisition is explaining how such changes come about.

Despite a large number of accumulated findings about L2 speaker performance, and much discussion over the past forty years of the implications of these findings for our understanding of how L2 grammars change, it turns out that most studies have not really addressed the detail of just how change in a speaker's underlying L2 system occurs. In other words, the focus has been on studying linguistic properties that are manifested in learner performance and coming up with explanations of L2 data in terms of one or other version of linguistic theory. This is a problem if acquisition theory is required not only to deal with the *linguistic* structure of L2 systems in various stages of development, including comparison across stages, but also to account for the *psycholinguistic* mechanisms that engineer the transition from one L2 system to the next identifiably different system.

There are currently a small number of interesting responses to this *transition* challenge. Three such responses will be briefly introduced in this chapter: the first one treats the growth of language as not essentially different from other kinds of cognitive development (see Chapter 28, this volume), whereas the second two both assume humans have innate linguistic knowledge that is one of the *modules* of mind among other cognitive capacities (see Chapter 27, this volume). The final part of this chapter will be devoted to illustrating one of these modular approaches in greater detail without insisting that it represents the only feasible solution to explaining transition. The chapter begins by describing two concrete examples (phonological and morphosyntactic) of changes that occur in the L2 English of learners at different proficiency levels. These two examples will be used to demonstrate the nature of the transition problem and one of the examples will be given a particular psycholinguistic interpretation in the account selected for further elaboration. The need to draw a distinction between a theory of *what* L2 learners know and a theory of *how* they come by this knowledge is discussed in the following section. Section 26.2.3 explains why processing is a key element in how L2 knowledge changes. Section 26.3 describes a non-modular explanation of change in second language grammars (O'Grady's 2005 Emergentist Model; see also Chapter 28). Section 26.4 describes the first of the modular approaches (Carroll's 2001, 2007 Autonomous Induction theory). In Section 26.5 the second modular approach – Truscott and Sharwood Smith's (2004a) Modular Online Growth and Use of Language (MOGUL) framework – is outlined and then applied to the explanation of one of the typical examples of second language performance described earlier.

26.2 A transition theory for L2A

26.2.1 Two typical examples of second language performance

The first example to be considered involves the perception by L2 speakers of phonological contrasts (see Chapter 25, this volume), and the second involves the production of sentential negation (see Chapter 24, this volume). Brown (2000) tested the ability of L1 speakers of Japanese learning L2 English in a predominantly tutored setting in Japan to discriminate one phonological contrast that is made in both Japanese and English (/p/∼/b/) and two that are only made in English (/b/∼/v/ and /r/∼/l/). Japanese has no /v/ phoneme and, according to Brown, [r] and [l] are allophonic variants of a single /r/ phoneme. Thirty-five L2 learners divided into low- and high-proficiency groups, together with a control group of native speakers, were asked (a) to listen to minimal pairs like *boat–vote* or *boat–boat* and to decide whether the pairs they heard were different or the same; (b) to select one picture from a pair on the basis of a heard word. The pairs of pictures depicted referents whose lexical forms involved a minimal phonemic contrast, like *rake–lake*. Results show that, as expected, the native controls were highly accurate in deciding whether words differed, and in selecting the appropriate picture. The Japanese participants were not significantly different from the native controls on the /p/~/b/ contrast that also exists in Japanese. The low-proficiency speakers were significantly different from the controls both on the /b/~/v/ contrast and the /r/~/l/ contrast, although they were better on the former than the latter. The high-proficiency group had acquired the /b/~/v/ contrast and were indistinguishable from the control group. However, they continued not to discriminate the /r/~/l/ contrast. Their performance was at the same level as the low-proficiency group, and statistically different from the native controls. Taking the responses of the low- and high-proficiency learners as representative of the kind of development to be found in knowledge of English phonology by Japanese-speaking learners, the questions they raise are why Japanese speakers can, with a certain level of proficiency, acquire a /b/~/v/ but not a /r/~/l/ phonemic contrast, and how change in their grammars is implemented such that it produces this asymmetric outcome.

The second case can be illustrated from a study by Stauble (1984) of the use of sentential negation in English by six L2 speakers, three with L1 Japanese and three with L1 Spanish. These informants were immersion learners in the USA who had had at least ten years of residence. Spontaneous production data were collected from a two-hour individual interview with each informant. On the basis of the data, informants were grouped by Stauble into three proficiency levels approximately characterizable as low intermediate, intermediate and advanced. In each two-person group, one participant was an L1 Japanese speaker and the other an L1 Spanish speaker. Stauble examined intended examples of sentential negation produced by the informants in copula contexts like *She isn't tall* and main verb contexts like *He doesn't like watching TV*. Results show that the predominant form of sentential negation used by both low-intermediate-proficiency speakers (in over 75 percent of contexts) was *She no tall, He no watch TV*. By the intermediate proficiency level, the form of the negator had switched from *no* to *n't/not* in over 85 percent of contexts, with the copula *be* used optionally (*She isn't tall, She not tall*), and the form *don't* predominating with main verbs (in over 60 percent of contexts: *He don't watch TV*). The advanced-proficiency speakers were producing targetlike *She isn't tall* in over 90 percent of contexts, and were differentiating *don't* from *doesn't* and *didn't* with main verbs. Thus speakers of typologically very different L1s appear to go through similar stages over time in their productive use of English sentential negation. Again, taking the patterns of response found in these low-intermediate-, intermediate- and advanced-proficiency speakers to be representative of the pattern of development that would be found in individual L2 learners of English with Japanese and Spanish as their L1s, similar questions arise to those asked about the development of /b/~/v/ and /r/~/l/ in Japanese learners of English: why do learners develop knowledge of English sentential negation in the particular way illustrated (and not in other imaginable ways), and how is change from an initial stage of using *no* + *adjective/verb* to targetlike use at the advanced proficiency level implemented?

26.2.2 The need for a property and a transition theory in explaining L2 development

Gregg (1996), drawing on the ideas of Cummins (1983) about the explanation of psychological phenomena in general, has suggested that, to answer questions like those raised in Section 26.1, two types of theory are needed: a *property theory* that specifies the features, categories and computations necessary to describe what an L2 speaker knows at any stage of development, and a *transition theory* that specifies how the interaction between input (samples of the target language) and the human mind gives rise to the development of knowledge in just the ways observed in examples like those described above.

Much of the L2 research that has been inspired by the work of theoretical linguists on the formal properties of languages has focused on the application of property-theoretic reasoning to understanding the nature of L2 knowledge at different stages of development. For example, Brown argues that the reason why her Japanese informants were able to acquire the /b/~/v/ contrast was because the relevant feature for establishing that contrast ([continuant], distinguishing fricatives from stops) is already present in the phonemic inventory of Japanese for the representation of other contrasts (/p/~/s/, /b/~/z/). Because this feature is present in the L1, L2 learners can use it (unconsciously) in analyzing L2 input. The feature that is crucial for distinguishing /r/~/l/ in English, according to Brown, is [coronal] (referring to sounds produced by releasing air over the top of the tongue rather than down the sides of the tongue, which are [lateral]), and this feature is not used by Japanese for making phonemic contrasts. It is the absence of this feature in the L1 that causes Japanese speakers persistent difficulty in identifying the difference between words like *rake* and *lake* in English.

In the case of the production of English sentential negation, a property theory might point to the crucial role played by a functional category for Tense/Agreement that hosts light verbs like *be*, *have*, *do* and the contrast between anaphoric *no* (negation used to answer *yes/no* questions) and quantificational *n't/not* (which can negate constituents of various kinds, including whole clauses). In early proficiency, L2 learners appear to already allow *no* to have quantificational properties, but either have not established a Tense/Agreement category in their grammars, or have established it but do not require it to be phonologically overt. In later development, *n't/not* takes over the role of quantificational negator and overt forms of Tense/Agreement appear, albeit only optionally for a while.

Both of these explanations tell us what kinds of knowledge speakers have (and do not have) at certain stages of development – they are hypotheses about the types of properties involved. They do not tell us, however, how changes in the way properties are represented in L2 grammars come about. For this, a theory of transition is needed. This is the topic of the following sections.

26.2.3 Online processing as a key element in development

When a mature native speaker of English hears a continuous complex acoustic sound-wave (a linguistic message produced by another speaker) of the kind represented in (1) by a very approximate orthographic gloss, a number of different analyses must be performed before the meaning of the message "Tim meets Kim at the bus-stop every morning" can be arrived at.

(1) Timmeetskimatthebusstopeverymorning

First, sensory receptors must convert the raw acoustic signals into neural signals that are sent to the brain (Gallistel and King 2009: 1). Then, a phonetic analysis must be performed on the neural signals (Jusczyk 1997: 215). This analysis will identify, among many other things, the fact that in (1) the [tʰ] of *Tim* is aspirated, the [tˢ] of *meets* is affricated (produced a bit like a fricative under the influence of the following [s]) and the [t]s of *at* and *stop* are unaspirated. As it happens, none of these differences is relevant for distinguishing the meaning of English words. *Tim* will still mean *Tim* whether it is pronounced [tʰɪm], [tɪm] or [tˢɪm] (although such features are relevant for distinguishing meaning in other languages: in, for example, Thai words can differ minimally on the basis of an aspirated or non-aspirated stop). To determine which sounds are relevant for distinguishing meaning, a further phonemic analysis must be undertaken. Jusczyk (1997: 215) conceives this as a process of "weighting" phonetic features: "The weighting scheme basically amounts to routines that focus attention on the features that are most critical for processing contrasts between words." The phonemic information that is produced, together with a speaker's knowledge of the phonotactic constraints (what clusters of sounds are possible and what are not) and stress assignment in the language, will lead to the identification of word-sized units like *Tim, meets, bus-stop*, etc. that are then matched to morphemes that a speaker already knows and that are stored in the mental lexicon (*Tim, -s* [3p present sing], *bus, stop,* etc). Once morphemes are identified, and their linguistic category information is retrieved, phrase structure information can be assigned, followed by the extraction of propositional meaning based on the lexical meaning of the morphemes and their function in the phrase structure of clauses.

A language learner, whether first or second, has to break in to this system and identify the phonemic contrasts, the morphemes, their category membership (whether they are nouns, verbs, members of a Tense category, etc.) and the phrase structure properties and syntactic operations (how questions are formed, how negation is used, whether there is subject–verb agreement, etc.) of the target language. All approaches to transition assume that this is achieved through the learner's repeated exposure to samples of language and the application to these samples of a set of (unconscious) processing procedures. Accounts differ in what they assume the properties of the processing procedures to be. Three such accounts, and what they claim about development in language learners, will be discussed in the rest of this chapter: O'Grady's (2005) Emergentist Model of L2 development, Carroll's (2001, 2007) Autonomous Induction theory and Truscott and Sharwood Smith's (2004a, b) modular online growth and use of language framework. Due to space limitations, neither Processability theory (Pienemann 2007) nor the Input Processing Hypothesis (VanPatten 2007), both of which represent potential contributions to fully fledged explanations of transition, will be considered here, but the reader is directed to Chapters 27 and 29, this volume, for coverage of these frameworks.

26.3 O'Grady's (2005) Emergentist Model (OGE)

O'Grady (2008a: 448) offers the following definition of an emergentist approach to linguistic knowledge and language acquisition: "The phenomena of language are best explained by reference to more basic non-linguistic (i.e. 'non-grammatical') factors and their interaction – physiology, perception, processing, working memory, pragmatics, social interaction, properties of the input, the learning mechanisms and so on." Unlike a number of other implementations of this idea, O'Grady's own approach does not involve the rejection of symbolic representations, but it does see acquired linguistic properties as the outcome of an interaction between samples of language encountered and an efficiency-driven linear processor working on that raw linguistic material segment by segment, morpheme by morpheme. This takes place without the aid of any innate grammatical principles constraining development (commonly referred to as Universal Grammar – UG) nor indeed with the assistance of some special language acquisition device (LAD). Linguistic development proceeds in the same manner as any other kind of cognitive development as the outcome of repeated exposure to, and processing of, linguistic utterances. In the case of language acquisition, this means the gradual emergence of operations and sequences of operations that are required to form and/or interpret sentences (O'Grady 2005: 93).

Following O'Grady's 2005 account, during the parsing of incoming input, the (not specifically linguistic) *Combine Operation* is governed by a single imperative: "MINIMIZE BURDEN ON WORKING MEMORY" plus the following simple *Efficiency Requirement*: "RESOLVE DEPENDENCIES AT THE FIRST OPPORTUNITY." Figure 26.1 provides a simple example (*Mary speaks French*) of how combining works. This assumes that the "functor" (here, verb) *speak* in the lexicon carries the information: two arguments, one left, one right (the reader is referred to O'Grady 2005 for more detailed explanation). At an early stage in processing, since some form–meaning relations can be inferred without syntactic knowledge (O'Grady's "bootstrapping assumption"), a word is assigned an interpretation, and a conceptual structure for the incoming sentence begins to be projected (O'Grady 2010a, b). Words are processed one by one. With verbs, arguments belonging to the verb in

Time line

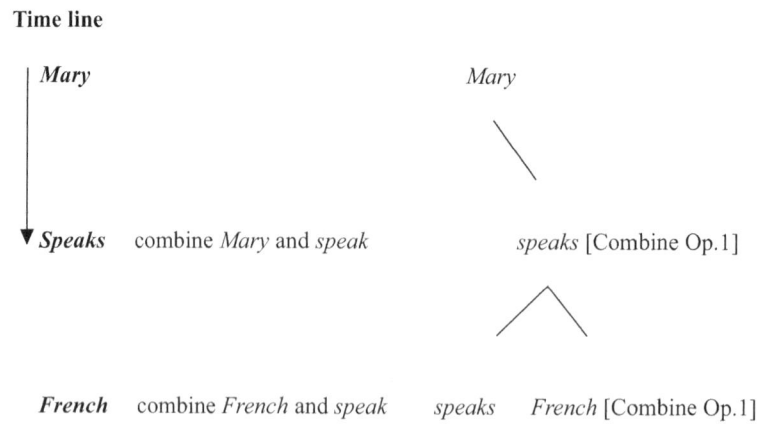

| *Mary* | | *Mary* |

▼ ***Speaks***   combine *Mary* and *speak*   *speaks* [Combine Op.1]

French   combine *French* and *speak*   *speaks*   *French* [Combine Op.1]

Figure 26.1 *OGE: the COMBINE operation (adapted from O'Grady 2005: 8–9)*

the lexicon are sought: the nominals to the left and/or right are given an appropriate interpretation (say, agent or theme).

Once the *Combine Operation* has been carried out, a *Resolve* operation will, at the first opportunity presented, match the nominal with the argument requirement in the functor (verb) so, in this example, *Mary* can be, and is, immediately matched, with the appropriate argument provided by *speak*. This is called *index copying*. O'Grady acknowledges that the lexical properties of words may not always facilitate processing, but the efficiency-driven processor does, in his terms, the best it can "given the hand it is dealt with" (2005: 12).

As more and more input is processed, the learner develops computational routines to handle (initially) the L1 or, more aptly put, computational routines "emerge." As far as the self-correction of errors is concerned, it is important to understand that there is no language acquisition device monitoring progress and stepping in to repair and adjust the current L2 grammar. A verb-final L1 will result in the emergence of efficient processing routines for handling the L1 that may turn out to be inefficient in processing verb-initial English. O'Grady states that the computational system will err from time to time. In the case of L2, initially dominant L1 routines will be easier to implement but some of these will prove to be inefficient. New computational routines will evolve not because any error is detected and repaired by a language acquisition device but simply in accordance with the efficiency requirement. Provided the errors have detectable consequences, for example a nominal is superfluous, a dependency is not resolved or an interpretation is implausible, faulty computational routines will be eliminated in favor of routines that avoid such problems. The latter will be strengthened, again, without any appeal to grammatical principles. So, in O'Grady's emergentism (OGE), learning consists "largely of the emergence of efficient computational routines" (2005: 193). The addition of "largely" reflects the fact that the development of routines is usage-based so that a transitive verb, say, could initially look for both of its arguments to the right but on encountering English, the learner will develop the appropriate left and right look routine (2005: 195).

OGE, in common with all processing-based accounts of development, places great emphasis on the idea of competition. Processing-based accounts are all competition models in this general sense. The difference is in their characterization of what precisely is doing the competing and the manner in which competition is resolved. In the case of OGE, it is computational routines that compete following general cognitive principles of construction. In the case of the next two accounts to be discussed, such operations are constrained by innate principles unique to language.

26.4 Carroll's (2001, 2007) Autonomous Induction theory (AIT)

26.4.1 Jackendoff's account of the language faculty

Whereas O'Grady's Emergentist Model assumes no UG, both AIT and Truscott and Sharwood Smith's Modular Online Growth and Use of Language framework (MOGUL) do. Since there are different theoretical approaches to UG (for example, the Minimalist Program (Chomsky 2002) or Lexical Functional Grammar (Bresnan 2001)), it might seem surprising that both models adopt the same – Jackendoff's (2002) – architecture of the language faculty. The attraction of Jackendoff's framework for those committed to the idea of a domain-specific language faculty lies in the degree to which it goes beyond syntax and phonology to elaborate, more than any other model, on the connections or *interfaces* between these two core aspects of language and of cognition in general. In addition, ever since his 1987 book, Jackendoff has incorporated in his model an account of language processing. And thirdly, the modular architecture that he proposes allows for some flexibility as to which linguistic theory can be deployed to explain syntactic and phonological properties, although his own preferences have naturally come to the fore, particularly in more recent publications (Culicover and Jackendoff 2005; Jackendoff 2002).

Before embarking on a description of AIT and MOGUL, it is worth introducing some basic features of Jackendoff's approach expressed in online processing terms, this being the aspect that is most relevant to the models to be discussed. This means, in particular, including an account of how memory operates, a feature left out of a purely property-based description.

Very briefly, the language faculty, in its narrowest sense (that is, the domain-specific faculty that is part of our biological endowment), consists of two separate largely autonomous modules, one dealing with phonology and the other with (morpho)syntax. There is an *internal interface* that puts phonological properties "in registration with" syntax properties, and *external interfaces* that put syntactic properties "in registration with" items in the conceptual system and phonological properties "in registration with" those sensori-motor systems which handle perception and production. This means that a lot of language-related processing occurs outside the core system, including semantic and pragmatic computations, and this is language in the broader sense (see discussion in Hauser, Chomsky and Fitch 2002; Pinker and Jackendoff 2005).

To be a little more specific, what are referred to as "properties" above include those linguistic primitives that have been identified as being part of UG (depending on which theoretical account has been adopted). A property may be either a single primitive or it might be a combination of primitives that have been created as a result of the attempt to parse utterances in a particular language. New representations are not created from scratch but always built with existing primitives. Note that such terminology should be treated with due caution when talking about processing in real time. "Properties," "structures" or "representations" are certainly all terms familiar from property accounts and may have various connotations. To minimize confusion, the generic term "item" will be used in later sections to refer to any object of processing.

Again, the Jackendoff notion of "putting into registration with one another" should not be understood as "translating" one thing into another: so, as it is built up in response to ongoing auditory input, a complex phonological structure like /skuls/ (*schools*), say, will get coindexed with a complex syntactic structure like Noun $_{plural}$, for example. The phonological module is the only place where phonological structures can be formed and processed, and the same holds for syntactic structures and the syntax module. As a consequence of this, lexical items or entries do not exist as such: they are better described either as "rules" coindexing structures across completely separate systems or, alternatively, as processing "chains" consisting of a phonological structure (PS) in registration (coindexed) with a syntactic structure (SS). This selfsame SS is accordingly coindexed by the SS/CS interface, linking syntax and elements of meaning, with a given conceptual structure (CS) thus: PS ⇔ SS ⇔ CS, with the bidirectional arrows indicating the interfaces. In other words, the processing of incoming speech involves the following:

Auditory–acoustic processing ⇔ phonological processing ⇔ syntactic processing ⇔ conceptual processing

The arrows are bidirectional because processing is incremental and can work in both directions. Several competing chains are temporarily maintained in working memory so a best-fit can be achieved. This means there are some repeated passes through the separate modules before a chain of representations is selected. Also the same system is implemented in reverse in order to move from meaning (conceptual structure) through to speech.

Memory, in this framework, is modularized: not only is there a separate conceptual memory, but also a syntactic memory and a phonological memory, each with their own unique types of structure. Processing within a module involves a dedicated processor assembling items (properties, structures, representations) within its own memory store. Only a subset of items in memory can be processed at any given moment: processors handle only those items from that store that appear in working memory. Taking the perception of the word *school* as an example, the incoming acoustic signal is processed, triggering operations by the interface between the auditory–acoustic system and phonology. This leads to the assembling of phonological structure using activated items which appear in phonological working memory. At the same time, across the PS–SS interface, candidate syntactic structures will be appearing in syntactic working memory for coindexing with items currently in phonological working memory (/skul/). And items will appear in conceptual working memory to complete the process of building an appropriate PS–SS–CS chain, the Jackendoff equivalent of a lexical item. In sum, both parsing and memory conform to Jackendoff's fine-grained version of modularity. Strictly speaking, one should talk of parse*rs* and memor*ies* in the plural and so, in both cases, the singular form should be treated here as shorthand for what is actually a set of separate systems.

Finally, one should note an area where AIT and MOGUL are also in agreement, and that relates to metalinguistic processing. Jackendoff seems not to pursue the question of how knowledge about language, that is knowledge that is accessible to conscious awareness, can be characterized. Both AIT and MOGUL agree that this type of linguistic knowledge is encoded in conceptual structure so that, to use Carroll's own example, the metalinguistic concept FEMININE is crucially different from the morphosyntactic gender feature required for languages like French but not English. In other words explicitly learning about French gender and related concepts is quite different from creating appropriate representations in the phonological and morphosyntactic systems described above (Carroll 2001: 152ff; Truscott and Sharwood Smith 2011). The particular ways in which operations within this architecture are interpreted in AIT and MOGUL in order to account for transition will now be introduced.

26.4.2 Autonomous Induction theory (AIT)

Carroll's account of change in L2 grammars is based on the notion of *failure-driven* learning (see also Wexler and Culicover 1980; Schwartz 1999). Each of the levels of linguistic representation, and the interface rules that map one level of representation to another, have a given set of properties at a given point in the development of language. When the input to a level of representation is entirely consistent with the current state of the system, there is no reason for change, except in the (important) sense of strengthening the current state. However, when target language input is encountered by the learner that cannot be assigned a full representation by the current configuration of properties (by the learner's interlanguage) there is *parsing failure*. At this point learning mechanisms come into play. Development means changing the properties of the formation rules at the relevant level of linguistic representation or the interface rules that map input to that level in order to accommodate novel stimuli.

The learning mechanism or the language acquisition device (LAD) is driven by induction. However, this is not induction as a general problem-solving strategy: Carroll (2001) adapts Holland, Holyoak, Nisbett and Thagard's (1986) induction theory to conform with the principles of Jackendoff's architecture. This means that, instead of working in an unconstrained fashion for all types of cognition, induction is constrained. Accordingly it works not just at a conceptual level but, in the case of language acquisition, "autonomously" on linguistic (i.e. phonological and morphosyntactic) representations. In this way, induction-based explanations are rendered compatible with a UG perspective on L1 and L2 acquisition. To distinguish it from general induction, Carroll calls this domain-specific version *i-learning*.

Carroll (2001: 131) describes i-learning as "the novel encoding of information in a representation" and the encoding strictly follows the unique set of principles that constrain possible initial, intermediate and end states appropriate to, respectively, phonology and syntax. This novel encoding is triggered when parsing cannot analyze current input with the existing parsing procedures (2001: 135). For example, when encountering what is actually an adjective following a determiner, like *French* in *the French teacher*, the current state might instead favor triggering N(oun) after Det *the*. Since there are other possibilities in English, an end-state (nativelike) parser would of course allow Det N, Det Adj and Det Adv. It is assumed there will be feedback, that is, cues in the input from other levels (phonological, conceptual) that will ultimately lead to the construction of parsing procedures selecting one of these three possibilities as appropriate. At intermediate stages, however, these possible analyses for the novel form should compete until such time as N is not automatically favoured to follow Det (2001: 136). Carroll's LAD checks for consistency between the input into, respectively, phonology, syntax and conceptual structure with the current state: any differences that are identified trigger one or more operations which are aimed at reducing the inconsistency. These operations create new representations that are close to the current ones because change in LAD is very conservative. Initially, L2 input will be mapped on L1-based representations wherever possible. The (minimally different) new representations will compete with the old ones until their strength is established via further exposure to the language. If the new intermediate state is found to be still inconsistent – say when, to use the above example again, the possibilities of Det+N as well as Det +Adj are accounted for but not yet Det+Adv – further subgoals are defined and the operators are reapplied.

26.5 Modular Online Growth and Use of Language (MOGUL) framework

26.5.1 Sharwood Smith and Truscott: acquisition by processing

The question now arises whether, on grounds of parsimony, transition can be accounted for without the need for an acquisition device, in line with OGE but at the same time retaining constraints imposed by UG like AIT. The component of the *Modular Online Growth and Use of Language* (MOGUL) framework that supplies a positive answer to this question is *Acquisition by Processing theory* (APT) where acquisition is characterized as "the lingering effect of processing" (Truscott and Sharwood Smith 2004a). APT, like OGE, rejects the need for any separate developmental mechanism (such as i-learning). Hence it is not in any obvious sense "failure-driven" (parsing failure triggering "repair"). Transition is accounted for by the operations of the parsers to build strings of representations on the basis of the best overall fit for the current input. To do this, available primitives at each level of representation are accessed, some of which will be more easily accessible as a result of repeated prior exposure. These will compete with items that provide a better fit until those items, after repeated use, will gain a level of accessibility that yields consistent use of the new "rule." The competition takes place in the system described by Jackendoff as a normal consequence of the parsers attempting a best-fit interpretation of incoming L2 utterances. There is no (re)construction of parsing procedures within a separate LAD as described in Carroll's account of i-learning. Rather, growth is the outcome of the parsers' continuing attempts to find the best overall fit for input: items that are ultimately selected in response to given input will, as a result, gain in strength and acquire an improved chance of being selected in future.

Working memory (WM) in MOGUL is defined as the set of currently activated items in *long-term memory* (LTM), following Cowan (2001). This means that a WM is not seen as a separate unit into which LTM items are retrieved. Rather, processors within modules, for example the processor responsible for processing syntactic items, and interfaces matching items across modules, for example the syntax/phonology interface, all operate on items that have been highly activated within their respective memory stores. Thus syntactic LTM refers to all items in the syntax memory store. Syntactic WM is then a subset of those items which are undergoing activation. WM can be conceptualized as the store's upper surface up to which certain items have "risen" (see Figure 26.2). This differs from Jackendoff's characterization of WM where items from LTM are written on to a separate "blackboard." This architecture is generic to all memory systems including those not specific to language, for example conceptual and auditory memory. Only those interfaces that link items across WMs that are relevant to this discussion have been included.

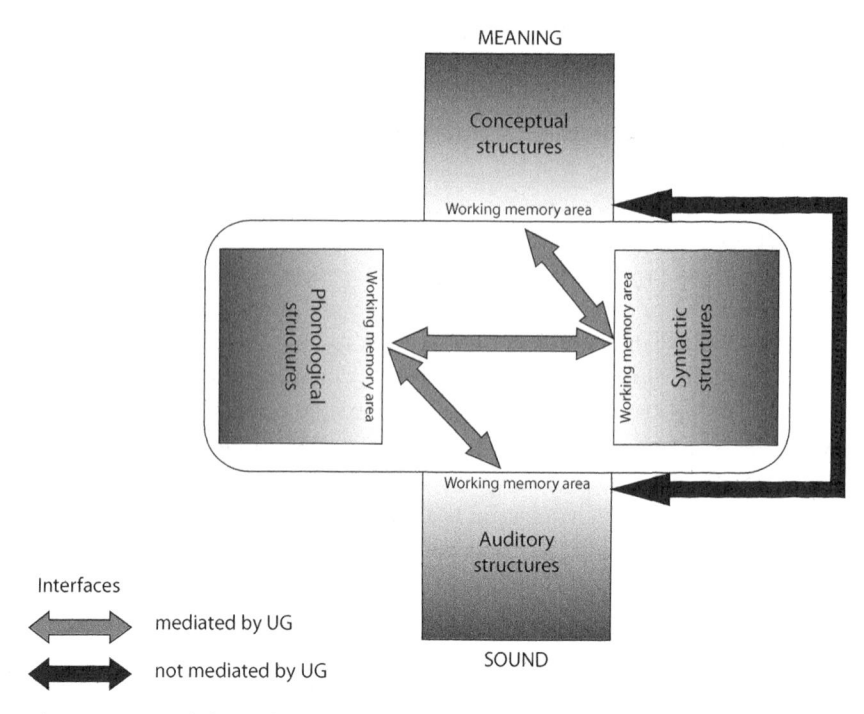

Figure 26.2 *Modularized memory stores in MOGUL (selected examples)*

It can be seen from Figure 26.2 that MOGUL incorporates some aspects of OGE but is otherwise much more akin to AIT. As stated earlier, MOGUL will be further elaborated, in Section 26.5.2, to illustrate how transition works in practice.

26.5.2 MOGUL and the transition problem

In the light of the architecture of how the language faculty mediates between acoustic signals and messages, presented in Figure 26.2, any account of transition must explain how events taking place in working memory affect memory in the longer term. Differences between performance at one point in development and performance at some later point indicate that changes in long-term memory have occurred. *Acquisition by Processing theory* (APT), within the MOGUL framework, seeks to explain these changes, again, in terms of the principle "acquisition is the lingering effects of processing." In Section 26.2 we described two cases that are relevant to a transition theory, one phonological and the other syntactic/semantic. In this section we first give a somewhat more detailed account of this approach to transition and then reconsider the case of phonological development, an important topic that has received little attention within MOGUL. The goal is to illustrate the way that transition accounts can be formulated within the framework.

Acquisition by Processing theory (APT)

The APT claim is actually less radical and more natural than it may at first appear. Uncontroversially, processing means manipulating items in working memory while acquisition means altering items in long-term memory. In MOGUL, LTM is simply the contents of the various stores – auditory, phonological, etc. – while working memory is by definition the subset of items in LTM that are currently active, so representations in working memory are also present in long-term memory. Thus, as described above, any new representation constructed during comprehension by the syntactic processor, for instance, is present in syntactic structures, i.e. syntactic LTM.

Whenever construction of an adequate representation for current input requires a processor to establish a new item, it does so purely for the purpose of processing its current input. This construction does not represent an intelligent generalization or a best guess (hypothesis) regarding the proper form of the grammar. It is simply an effort to deal with the current input. As a result, it is likely to be flawed, maybe fundamentally and maybe in a number of ways. Only a fraction of the representations constructed in this way will lead toward a nativelike grammar. Successful acquisition depends on *some* of them having this value. Whatever its value ultimately turns out to be, a new representation will remain in its store for some time after the initial processing is complete. This is one of the lingering effects of processing, which APT equates with development.

The other lingering effect involves activation levels. If an item has its current level raised during processing, when it falls back afterwards its new resting point will be slightly higher than its previous level, in much the way that the strength of a muscle is slightly greater after exercise. While this change could be seen as a form of learning – a learning mechanism selectively rewards muscles that participated in the exercise – a more appealing perspective is that it is simply in the nature of muscles, an entirely unintelligent process. This is essentially the perspective underlying work on lexical access (see Murray and Forster 2004): the speed with which a given lexical item can be accessed (i.e. its resting activation level) is a function of how frequently it has been encountered. A related view can be found in the implicit learning literature, in which a number of authors have tied implicit learning and implicit memory to priming effects (e.g. Chang, Bock and Goldberg 2003; Cleland and Pickering 2006), and even equated the two (Roediger 2003): repeated use of an item in processing allows that item to indefinitely influence future processing, which is to say that its resting activation level rises with use. Returning to APT, the small but lasting increase in resting level that comes with each use of a representation makes it more readily available for future processing. An overall representation of a typical sentence will not receive further use in comprehension or production and so should fade quickly (with exceptions, including perhaps "I don't know" at early levels of learning). New items created as pieces of the sentence's representation might well suffer the same fate but are in general more likely to prove useful and so to undergo increases in activation level.

In MOGUL, the issues for successful transition are thus (1) whether the desired representation will be constructed in the course of processing, as a way to deal with some particular input, and (2) if so, whether it will receive enough use in subsequent processing for its resting activation level to rise to a point at which it can dominate processing. If these conditions are met, then learning – *growth* is a more suitable word – will have occurred. If one of them is not met, the grammar will remain flawed and performance will be non-nativelike in the relevant aspect. There is in this process no sequence of hypotheses gradually leading up to the correct target form (there are no hypotheses at all) and no "Eureka" moment in which the system finally discovers that form. Instead, normal processing leads to the creation of a great many representations, whose fate depends on how useful they prove in subsequent processing over the long term.

In the following sections we will apply these ideas to the problem, described earlier, of how Japanese-speaking learners do and do not acquire certain phonological distinctions of English. These learners show good progress in acquiring /v/, despite its absence in Japanese. The /r∼l/ distinction, in contrast, continues to be very troublesome even for high-proficiency learners. A transition account should explain how the change occurs in the first case and why such serious problems occur in the second.

Transition in MOGUL: the case of English /b∼v/

As discussed above, Brown's (2000) explanation for the relative success learners have in acquiring /v/ is that the [continuant] feature, distinguishing it from /b/, is used in Japanese for other phonemic contrasts and so is available for establishment of the new /v/ in L2 English. It is successfully acquired because the English input is not consistent with sole use of the existing /b/, a situation that leads to restructuring of the system. In MOGUL terms, [continuant] is a representation in *phonological structures* (PS), a component of the /b/ and /v/ representations, with a high activation level by virtue of very extensive use. The /v/ item may or may not have been created at some point in the processing of Japanese input; if it has, it will not have received extensive use. So at the beginning of English learning /v/ either is present on PS with only a very low resting activation level or is not represented at all, except latently as a potential combination of more low-level representations already there, i.e. the set of distinctive features that are the innate contents of PS.

Successful development of /v/ begins with processing at the level of *auditory structures* (AS), because representations there are the input to PS. When the /v/ sound is processed by the auditory module in response to English input, the word *victory* for example, its low-level features are activated in AS and so become available for processing, meaning that they can be combined by the auditory processor, in accordance with its in-built principles, to form the [v] representation (if it does not already exist). In MOGUL, AS representations are written in italics within brackets while PS representations use the traditional phonemic form, e.g. /v/. This new combination then competes with [b], which is activated by AS input because it shares much of the component structure of [v]. This competition is based, as always, on current activation level. [b] has the advantage of a much higher resting level, while [v] owes its current level to its close fit with the current input from earlier levels of the auditory module, which should allow it to win at least some of the time.

In PS, the activation of the two AS representations will result in activation of both /b/ and the component features of /v/ (or /v/ itself if it already exists): an interface does not wait for the conclusion to the competition in one module before activating coindexed items in the adjacent module. The outcome of this competition will, however, determine which PS representation continues to receive stimulation from the interface and which is left to fall back toward its resting state (subject to influences from other sources); in other words, it determines whether a particular representation will undergo only a small and fleeting rise in its current activation level, with negligible long-term effects on its resting level. In the resulting competition between active items at PS for inclusion in the overall representation of *victory*, /b/ has the advantage of a much higher resting level, paralleling the situation at AS, while /v/ depends on greater stimulation from its AS counterpart, resulting from its closer match with input from the auditory module. In this situation, /b/ might well triumph in most cases. The essential point is that /v/ should win *some* of the time. Every time it does win, in comprehension or in production, its resting activation level rises slightly, making it more competitive.

This gradual rise in activation level should not be a linear function of the number of times the item is used; the relation should be logarithmic, as has been found in the analogous case of lexical access (e.g. Murray and Forster 2004). In other words, resting level does not go up by a fixed amount with each additional use. Instead, the rise is relatively quick early in the process and then tapers off, eventually reaching the point at which further use, no matter how extensive, has no discernible effect (see Truscott 2006). The muscle analogy is also appropriate here. The strength of a muscle can be increased relatively quickly with consistent exercise but the rate of increase will gradually decline, ending in a more or less stable state. The implication for the development of English /v/, and for second language acquisition in general, is that extensive experience can gradually reduce the gap in resting level between the second language item, /v/ in this case, and the native item that it must compete with (/b/), because the latter will have reached a plateau long before. As the gap becomes narrower, the greater activation that /v/ receives by virtue of better matching the second language input (as processed by the auditory module) can put its current level above that of its competitor, allowing it to triumph in the competition.

The result should be a gradual increase in the percentage of correct uses. This is an essential point of the MOGUL/APT account of transition, that learning will be gradual and that the possibility of the wrong item being used in any given case will remain, the transition being characterized by a gradual decline in the likelihood of this occurring (see Sharwood Smith and Truscott 2005; Truscott 2006).

Metalinguistic knowledge, centered in *conceptual structures* (CS), might also play a role in the creation and subsequent strengthening of the /v/ representation. Knowledge that /v/ exists distinct from /b/ and that it appears in particular English words would naturally come from explicit instruction and from the learner's own observations, especially of the written language. If the CS representations of this knowledge are active while some English input is being processed, they will further activate the [v] representation in AS. This support will in turn make the establishment and strengthening of a corresponding PS more likely. It should at least be expected to hasten the process. Given the a priori uncertainty regarding the outcome of the /b/-/v/ competition in processing, as described above, we cannot rule out the possibility that this metalinguistic support is a necessary part of any success.

When problems occur in transition: the case of English /r/~/l/

Brown's (2000) explanation for the continuing difficulty of the /r/~/l/ distinction, despite learners' extensive experience with English, is that the [coronal] feature, distinguishing /r/ and /l/, is not present in Japanese and so the distinction cannot be acquired by adults. From a MOGUL perspective, the essential point is that both sounds, when processed in the auditory module, will result in the activation of a single PS representation, regardless of whether the input is more /r/-like or more /l/-like. We will refer to this representation, rather crudely, as /r-l/, not suggesting that it is literally a combination of the two items but rather that it is sufficiently similar to each to be strongly activated by either. This seems to be the gist of most theorizing on this subject, that /r/ and /l/ are so perceptually similar to /r-l/ that it absorbs any input that should be processed as one of these two English sounds (e.g. Best, McRoberts and Sithole 1988; Flege 1987a; Flege, Schirru and MacKay 2003). There is then little English input that will result in the system using an alternative to this entrenched /r-l/ representation. We will explore these points in more detail in the following.

Consider first the initial state of English second language acquisition. As with the case of /v/, the /r/ and /l/ representations might or might not have been created in the course of Japanese processing. If they have been, they will have received only limited use, ensuring that their resting activation level is quite low, especially relative to that of /r-l/, and so the latter will dominate processing. On AS, [r-l] is also strongly present, again due to processing experience with Japanese. The [r] and [l] representations are either present or can be readily constructed and used, as shown by the finding of Miyawaki *et al.* (1975) that Japanese speakers, prior to any experience with English, are able to make the distinction between /l/ and /r/ specifically when they occur in a non-speech context. This is to say that when the language module (PS in particular) is not very active the /r-l/ representation will not exert a strong enough influence on AS processing to block the use of [r] and [l] there. When it is highly active (i.e. when speech is being processed), /r-l/ will strongly activate its AS counterpart, giving it a large advantage in its competition with these representations and so making their use unlikely. Thus, while distinct [r] and [l] representations are present in AS and available for use, in linguistic processing their presence is hidden by the far more active [r-l] representation.

This is the background for later development of an English second language grammar. When the auditory module receives the English word *lake*, say, its processing results in activation of AS [l] and [r-l], which in turn leads to activation of PS /l/ and /r-l/. The latter dominates the processing at PS and so is incorporated in the overall representation of *lake* being constructed there. The PS /l/ will also receive some activation, because it is coindexed with an active AS representation, but the level will not be nearly high enough for it to compete with /r-l/, because the latter has an enormous advantage in resting level and is close enough to the input sound to be strongly activated by it, largely canceling the advantage that /l/ would enjoy if it were competing with a less similar sound. This triumph of /r-l/ should be the outcome every time English /r/ or /l/ is encountered in the input. Any activation of /r/ or /l/ will therefore be weak and fleeting.

The implication is that successful transition simply through ordinary experience with the second language is unlikely; learners should be stuck indefinitely with the inability to distinguish /r/ and /l/ in their English comprehension and production. A possible way to get around the problem would be through the use of metalinguistic (CS) knowledge, as in the case of /v/. If a person gains explicit knowledge, through instruction or simply experience in reading, that there are two distinct forms and is repeatedly told which is which in the spoken input, this assistance might be expected to help. Within the MOGUL framework this means raising the activation levels in AS in the hope that this will encourage the use of the corresponding representations in PS, as in the case of the /b/~/v/ distinction. The problem is that each AS representation, again, will activate the combined /r-l/ PS in addition to /r/ or /l/. This activation, in conjunction with its high resting level, should ensure that /r-l/ will still consistently win the competition, leaving /r/ and /l/ with only a brief period of activation. Thus, serious problems should still be expected for development of the /r/~/l/ distinction. On the other hand, the stronger activation of [r] and [l] in AS means that this brief activation of their PS counterparts should be considerably stronger than it otherwise would be, creating the theoretical possibility of a meaningful, if very small, rise in resting level. While this is far from the ideal scenario for development, it does raise the possibility of genuine improvement occurring.

This theoretical possibility appears to match the empirical findings. Extensive research has found that while progress is quite difficult and the end state is likely to fall short of native ability (see especially Takagi 2002), improvements do result from training and practice in making /r/∼/l/ distinctions (see Hazan, Sennema, Iba and Faulkner 2005; Lively, Pisoni, Yamada, Tohkura and Yamada 1994; Takagi 2002). McCandliss, Fiez, Protopapas, Conway and McClelland (2002) showed that quick and substantial improvements could be obtained through the use of exaggerated instances of /l/ and /r/, though their testing was quite limited, leaving open issues regarding the durability and generalizability of these findings. There is also evidence that substantial gains can occur under more ordinary learning circumstances (Flege, Takagi and Mann 1995; MacKain, Best and Strange 1981).

The gains made in at least most of these cases are best explained by the involvement of metalinguistic knowledge as described above. What role such knowledge played in the case of McCandliss *et al.* (2002) is less clear. Input that differed significantly from that which normally activates the /r∼l/ representation apparently had the effect of significantly strengthening the /l/ and /r/ representations (and may have even been responsible for the initial creation of those representations). It is quite possible that this occurred simply because the input was more perceptually different than normal input from /r-l/ and so did not activate it as strongly as normal input does, giving /r/ and /l/ a better chance to compete. It is difficult to know, however, how much of a role was played by learners' awareness that two distinct sounds were involved. In any case, learners who have extensive experience can show considerable, if typically limited, improvement in their ability to distinguish /r/ and /l/, and metalinguistic knowledge may play a crucial role.

Brown's (2000) account of the /r/∼/l/ case crucially involves a critical period: very young children have the ability to make all possible phonetic distinctions but lose this ability as they get older, when they have great difficulty using sounds other than those of their native language. This phenomenon is well established (see, for example, Strange and Shafer 2008) but is open to alternative interpretations. In the MOGUL/APT account it is a natural consequence of processing experience. When certain representations are used very extensively, they acquire high resting activation levels and become so dominant in processing that it is very difficult for new sounds to compete with them. This account has clear parallels with ideas of Best (see Best *et al.* 1988) and Flege (1987a). All three share the prediction that second language sounds that are closest to established first language phonemes will be the most troublesome, a prediction that is supported by research findings (e.g. Best *et al.* 1988; Flege *et al.* 2003). The /r/∼/l/ case provides an example. English /r/, which is somewhat more distant from Japanese /r/ than is English /l/, is also less troublesome for learners (Aoyama, Flege, Guion, Akahane-Yamada and Yamada 2004). In MOGUL/APT such findings are expected because sounds that are more distant from an existing first language phoneme will not activate that representation as much as those that are nearer, giving the appropriate second language representation a better chance to compete.

Finally, we should note evidence that a thorough understanding of the phenomena considered in this section may require an extension of the account to include lower levels of auditory processing. Iverson *et al.* (2003; see also Iverson, Hazan and Bannister 2005) suggested that the /r/~/l/ problem is due to inappropriate weighting of acoustic cues in low-level processing, resulting from experience with the first language. Specifically, Japanese speakers attend to cues that are appropriate for their native language but are not helpful when it comes to distinguishing English /l/ and /r/. As the lower levels of auditory processing have yet to receive any development within the MOGUL framework, we will not pursue this possibility here.

26.5.3 MOGUL: nature, goals and limitations

MOGUL is a framework rather than a theory, and this is both its strength and its limitation. The goal of the project is to provide a framework within which specific theories can be constructed for particular transition cases. This framework is intended to provide a number of fundamental features that should be present in any transition account, including the gradual, quantitative character of transition and the simultaneous presence of two mutually exclusive forms in a learner grammar. It also aims to incorporate plausible accounts of the general roles played by Universal Grammar, the first language, metalinguistic knowledge and consciousness. With such a framework established, specific linguistic and psycholinguistic theories can then be provisionally incorporated to specify the details of the processing principles built into each processor and the representations in the various stores, including the primitives and the more complex items constructed from them.

MOGUL thus leaves open a vast array of specific questions, for which the answers must come from specific theories of processing and from property theories of whatever domain is being investigated. Regarding the example considered above, MOGUL assumes that, within PS, there is an innate universal inventory of primitives, but takes no firm position on what exactly these primitives are, nor does it adopt a position on the details of phonological processing. These are issues to be explored within the framework rather than issues of the framework itself.

The scale of the project (it has been called a theory of everything, with some justification) inevitably means that a great many aspects have not been developed in any detail, or not at all. Given this scale, it is perhaps not surprising that the proposal is at a higher level of abstraction than the field is accustomed to, creating obvious limits for testability of the framework as a whole (as opposed to specific theories constructed within it). The eclectic, mix and match character of MOGUL has also drawn expressions of concern from some (Carroll 2004; Dijkstra and Haverkort 2004; Pienemann 2004), though these concerns remain hypothetical (see Truscott and Sharwood Smith 2004b).

26.6 Conclusion

This chapter has addressed the topic of how change in the performance of L2 speakers over time might be explained. While many researchers agree that such an explanation requires both a property theory and a transition theory (Gregg 1996), few studies have proposed a detailed account of what a transition theory might look like. Three approaches were described. The first one, O'Grady's (2005) Emergentist Model, assumes that general processing mechanisms derive linguistic knowledge in the same way that other kinds of knowledge are derived. The second two assume innate linguistic knowledge and build on the "representational-levels-with-interface-rules" model of the language faculty, where each level has its own code (Jackendoff 1987, 1997, 2002). The Autonomous Induction theory of Carroll (2001, 2007) proposes that change occurs when there is parsing failure and then appeals to an independent set of learning mechanisms to effect changes in the representational levels and interface rules. In the MOGUL framework of Truscott and Sharwood Smith (2004a, 2011), the proposal is that "development is the lingering effect of processing" and includes neither the concept of parsing failure nor an independent set of learning mechanisms to effect change in the system. The components and operating principles of this latter approach were described and then applied to one specific example of documented L2 development: the use, by L1 Japanese speakers, of two English phonological contrasts (b~v and r~l) that do not exist in Japanese.

27

Stagelike development and Organic Grammar

Anne Vainikka and Martha Young-Scholten

27.1 Introduction

This chapter examines the idea of stages in grammatical development, in particular as attested in naturalistic (uninstructed) L2 language acquisition by adults; background from children's L1 acquisition will also be provided. While the chapter focuses on morphosyntax, where a fair amount is known about paths of development, this is not meant to imply that no ordered development occurs, for example, in the acquisition of the lexicon or phonology. Here we refer the reader to Chapters 21 and 25. We focus exclusively on acquisition, but see Chapters 17 and 28 for discussion of attrition, where regression seems to mirror progression (de Bot, Weltens and van Els 1985).

An incontrovertible fact about L2A is that – by definition – the learner already knows another language, i.e. a first or native language. It is therefore unsurprising that L1 influence or transfer is at the top of the list of issues in the field of second language acquisition; see Chapter 5. Indeed, L1 influence has certainly been observed since humans speaking different languages came into contact with each other, and discussion of this issue has been systematically documented at least since Fries (1945) and Lado (1957); see Chapter 2 for even earlier documentation. How the L1 as a whole or its components influence L2A could certainly be random and development asystematic. Yet SLA researchers realized early that not only is development systematic, but that the L1 is only one of several influences on interlanguage (Selinker 1972); half a century of research has shown that acquisition proceeds along a path or route of ordered stages. In his discussion of how one goes about not simply describing but explaining language acquisition, Gregg (1996: 51) delineates two lines of inquiry. The *logical problem* addresses what equips humans to acquire language and involves property theories (e.g. Universal Grammar; see Chapters 7 and 22). The *developmental problem* addresses the role of observed processes in acquisition and involves transition theories. For Gregg the latter is defined in Cummins' (1983) terms where the behavior, phenomenon or event under scrutiny involves some other event which precedes it and can be seen as its cause. In the investigation of stagelike development, progress can be made towards the elusive goal of identifying the mechanisms that enable the learner to move from one interlanguage grammar to the next.

There is a tight connection between theories of children's acquisition of their first language and adults' acquisition of a second language; in principle the two processes either work the same way, or they differ in definable ways. We therefore begin this chapter with discussion of L1A. Since we know that normal children attain the adult grammar, that is, they learn to speak their mother tongue, any theory of how this happens is illuminating for SLA research, even when the target grammar may not be attained to a native-like level. In this chapter we will upon occasion refer to the endstate in L1 acquisition (the adult grammar) and in L2 acquisition (the target language grammar); however, the object of investigation is the child's or L2 learner's grammar at various points in time. This does not entail a focus on errors; Bley-Vroman (1983: 4) refers to this as a *comparative fallacy* when the researcher focuses on non-acquisition of the categories of the target language rather than on the learner's grammar as a system unto itself. Consequently, from the earliest generative literature on acquisition in the 1970s to the present, research on L2 learners has been inspired by research on L1 learners (which is first subject to the influence of linguistic theories, as noted back in 1987 by Lightbown and White). We first present relevant background on L1A and on syntax, and then the remainder of the chapter concentrates on L2A.

We begin the L2A discussion with the morpheme order studies, followed by early research on stages in the acquisition of negation and questions. We then turn to more recent research, in particular on the L2A of German and then outline four recent approaches involving stages of grammatical development, namely the Basic Variety, Finiteness Linking, Processability and Organic Grammar. We conclude by briefly considering English and the theoretical and practical ramifications of the idea of stages.

27.2 Defining the notion of stage

The question of how children, who invariably (even in most cases of cognitive impairment) become adult members of their language community, hear or see (in the case of signed languages) finite input in their environment and develop a specific language has long occupied researchers. That young children follow an ordered route of development with regard to a range of behaviors has long been observed, and before considering some early research, we need to clarify just what is meant by *stage*.

Ingram (1989) devotes an entire early chapter in his book to a discussion of stages, starting with their definition. Although Ingram is referring to L1A, what follows here also applies to L2A. While noting a multiplicity of uses of "stage," Ingram arrives at common requirements for calling a developing behavior a stage. Expanding somewhat on his discussion, the possible criteria for stages that we will consider here are (i) plateau, (ii) transition to a further stage; (iii) acceleration; (iv) implicationality; (v) internal consistency; and (vi) underlying principle.

When a particular behavior unfolds over time and we can isolate points along a developmental continuum, these are candidates for stages. The case for these points being stages is strengthened when the behavior temporarily *plateaus*. However, development cannot permanently halt if that behavior is to be characterized as a stage; rather, there must be a *transition* from that plateau to a subsequent stage. If we consider children's development of walking, there is a clearly identified stage known as crawling, and various subsequent stages such as standing-with-support and toddling. Ingram adds another criterion, that of *acceleration*. Studies of children's development have shown that prior to temporary stabilization at a plateau, a behavior will often rapidly increase in frequency. An additional requirement is that of *implicationality*: stage 1 logically precedes stage 2, and stage 2 logically precedes stage 3 and so forth. While there is debate about the extent to which Universal Grammar guides L2A (see Chapter 7), the notion of a stage has proven to be fruitful. Among the first authors to describe grammatical stages in L2A were Meisel, Clahsen and Pienemann (1981) for German; they further argued that passage through each stage was obligatory and stages could not be skipped.

A stage may either refer to a single behavior or a cluster of behaviors that are held to be related. An early example of the latter are Piaget's stages of the development of intelligence under which the sensorimotor and the cognitive are held to be closely linked by internal structures (e.g. Piaget and Inhelder 1969). A further criterion is thus *internal consistency*, that is, the behavior – or cluster of behaviors – exhibited at a particular stage follows a uniform pattern, or set of patterns. For example, during the L1 or L2 acquisition of German, various word order patterns are attested; at a particular stage, one of these orders might be dominant, occurring with a less dominant alternative word order possibility. Once the pattern is established as consistent, there is potential for an explanation. In noting the distinction between a stage that simply describes a behavior / set of behaviors and one that explains them, Ingram argues that the term stage should only be used for the latter, where an *underlying principle* accounts for the occurrence or co-occurrence of behavior(s). In the case of German word order (discussed below), an explanation for why certain word orders emerge in a particular fashion predicting specific stages (in terms of both word order and inflectional morphology) is preferable to mere description of the data.

One of the criteria for stages discussed above is that there be a transition from one stage to the next. This raises the question of how the learner ends up progressing to the next stage. We referred above to Gregg's (1996) transition theory discussion whereby a behavior observed to occur prior to another could be considered its cause. This idea relates to the notion of *triggers*, namely elements in the input that, in effect, propel the learner forward – perhaps because the triggering words or grammatical forms in the input cannot be incorporated in the learner's present grammar (for seminal work, see Fodor 1998 and Gibson and Wexler 1994). Unlike what is assumed under some theories of L2 acquisition (see Chapter 10) this does not involve conscious awareness or noticing of the mismatch between one's interlocutor's forms and one's own non-target forms. The notion of trigger has been predominant in the generative literature where for crosslinguistic syntactic variation expressed as parameters such as the obligatory vs. null subjects, specific triggers have been posited for the setting of parameters (for recent relevant work, see Biberauer, Holmberg, Roberts and Sheehan 2010). A further idea concerning triggers is Vainikka and Young-Scholten (1998) on L2 German (see Hawkins 2001a on L2 English). The idea is that free morphemes act as triggers for syntactic structure in L2A; however, in children's L1A, bound morphemes act as triggers. Access to triggers is thus a possible source of the differences we observe between L1A and L2A.

From our discussion thus far one might conclude that each stage represents an encapsulated system. Even early on it was pointed out (see Piaget and Inhelder 1969) that a stage of cognitive development should not be seen as static or neatly separated from what precedes or follows it. Decades later, evidence of learners sliding back to a previous stage is also noted by SLA researchers such as Dimroth (2002) and Vainikka and Young-Scholten (2011). The *stage seepage* that points to lack of neat encapsulation is less problematic if we take as key the idea of sequential development.

27.3 Syntactic background – functional projections

The idea of a syntactic structure that resembles a tree has been the backbone of the generative study of syntax, of sentence structure, ever since the founding works of Chomsky (1957, 1965; see Chapter 1, this volume). In these early versions of the theory, little structure was posited for each sentence. However, since the advent of Government-and-Binding (GB) theory (Chomsky 1981), two things have become clear. First, grammatical or closed-class morphemes such as tense, case, subject–verb agreement, determiners (articles) and complementizers (subordinating conjuncts) form interesting patterns with each other. Second, other syntactic phenomena such as word order are related to these functional morphemes. To account for these patterns in the languages of the world, the notion of *lexical* and *functional projections* was born. Lexical projections or phrases involve open-class words or classes such as noun (Noun Phrase, NP), verb (Verb Phrase, VP), and adjective (Adjective Phrase, AP); we do not include prepositions or a PP in this list due to the unclear membership of prepositions in the lexical vs. functional category. In the earliest generative work, functional projections consisted of just S[entence] or IP (Inflectional Phrase, or a simple sentence) and S' or CP (Complementizer Phrase, or a more complex sentence); in the GB framework, DP (Determiner Phrase, or a nominal phrase) was added. Since Pollock's (1989) groundbreaking proposal for the split IP (both tense and person agreement) and then Rizzi's (1997) expansion of the left periphery for the CP, each of these projections is seen as consisting of further subprojections. Syntacticians disagree about the exact number of functional projections and even whether subprojections exist. There is presently no consensus for any language on a set of subprojections. For further theoretical discussion, see Belletti (2004), Cinque (2002) and Rizzi (2004). While in the most recent version of generative syntax, minimalism (Chomsky 1995, 2001, 2008), the idea of subprojections is to some degree replaced by a new idea of phases, in our own work, we maintain Pollock-type subprojections. (For more details on minimalist accounts of data similar to what is covered in this chapter, see Chapter 24.)

In work on the L2A of German by uninstructed adults in immersion settings (naturalistic learners), we have found these IP subprojections extremely useful: TP (Tense Phrase for tense marking), AgrP (Agreement Phrase for subject–verb agreement) and NegP (Negation Phrase for sentential negation), and we argue that Organic Grammar (Vainikka and Young-Scholten 1994, 1996b, 2011) provides a case for the existence of these functional projections. For CP and DP, subprojections are not required to account for patterns in our L2A data, but this is likely to be due to the relative lack of relevant acquisition data from naturalistic adults. The approach under Organic Grammar to functional projections is a hybrid between Minimalism and GB theory (Chomsky 1981), which according to Hornstein (2010) is still implicitly assumed in the Minimalist Program (Chomsky 1995, 2001, 2008). Organic Grammar is described in detail further below.

27.4 Grammatical stages of development in L1 and L2 acquisition

The layperson's portrayal of L1A is of the young child passing from a one-word to two-word to telegraphic stages prior to arriving at the adult grammar (Brown 1973; Leopold 1949; Miller and Ervin 1964). Broadly speaking, studies on children's development of English and other Indo-European languages

Table 27.1. *Summary of Brown's (1973) stages of grammatical development*

Stage	MLU range	New development exhibited by the child
1	1.00–1.99	Basic word order; intra-sentential relations are semantic
2	2.00–2.49	Initial appearance of grammatical morphemes
3	2.50–2.99	Auxiliaries in various functions (see Klima and Bellugi 1966)
4	3.00–3.99	Appearance of embedded clauses
5	4.00 +	Conjoined clauses

follow these stages (see description of children's acquisition of various languages in Slobin 1985 and 1992). It is Brown's (1973) US longitudinal study of Adam, Eve and Sarah (pseudonyms) that is a classic on stages of development. The three children were studied from the ages of 1;6 (Eve) and 2;3 (Adam and Sarah) until 2;3 (Eve) and 3;6 and 4;0 (Adam and Sarah, respectively). The study began when they started to string words together (the two-word stage), and from the varying starting and ending ages for each child, one notes that rate of development was not at issue. Table 27.1 shows these stages; they are preceded by a period during which the child's utterances consisted only of single words, or multiword unanalyzed chunks. Brown pointed out that "the whole development of any one of the major constructional processes is not contained within a given stage" (1973: 59).

To analyze the data, Brown pioneered the notion of *suppliance* of a particular grammatical morpheme or functor *in an obligatory context*. This involved considering utterances produced by the children where it was possible to tell which morphemes the adult grammar required. Percentage of occurrence was arrived at by totaling obligatory contexts for a given morpheme in the child's utterances during a particular data collection session and then dividing by the suppliance of that morpheme. Following Nice (1925), Brown used as the points on the children's developmental continuum a span of *Mean Length of Utterance* (MLU). This entailed counting the morphemes in an utterance and dividing the number of morphemes per utterance by total utterances in a sample. MLU is a controversial notion for two reasons. First, it is unclear what is responsible for the length constraint on children's early utterances. Second, methodological difficulties arise when calculating MLU for agglutinative languages such as Turkish where multiple morphemes comprise a word.

Given the developments in the theory of functional projections outlined above, we take a brief detour and attempt to combine Brown's L1 English morpheme order with specific functional projections. This is possible under the Weak Continuity / Structure Building approach to acquisition (described in more detail below) whereby syntactic structure develops from the bottom up, one projection at a time; that is, each stage corresponds to acquiring a new syntactic projection. Note that this is a somewhat radical view;

Strong Continuity, under which the entirety of syntactic structure is available to the child via UG from the start of acquisition, is assumed by the majority of acquisitionists. Under Weak Continuity, Brown's earliest stage corresponds to a bare VP projection, before acquisition of functional projections, while Stages 2–3 involve the development of IP-level functional projections such as TP and AgrP. Stages 4–5 involve the acquisition of the CP or its subprojections. Throughout this chapter, we will point out possible connections between acquisition stages and the development of functional projections.

Brown's (1973) study is better known for the common order of acquisition for fourteen grammatical morphemes claimed for three unrelated and unacquainted children whose contexts of development could have easily produced considerable differences. Brown's order of morpheme development for Adam, Eve and Sarah was subjected to scrutiny with a cross-sectional study whose results were also published in 1973. The study was carried out by de Villiers and de Villiers on twenty-one children between 16 and 40 months old, and children's percentages of suppliance in obligatory contexts were averaged and morphemes ranked. A comparison of rankings from Brown's longitudinal study and de Villiers and de Villiers' cross-sectional study revealed correlations so impressive that Brown enthused they had discovered "a developmental phenomenon of substantial generality" (1973: 277). The resulting order of acquisition of verb-related morphemes from these studies is provided in (1), abstracting away from contractible vs. uncontractible forms of *be* (only regular past was included in Brown 1973):

(1) progressive *-ing* > irregular past > copula *be* > regular past > 3sg *-s* > aux *be*

Studies showing that route of development is not determined by the environment (the input) or "goal-directed practice" (Lenneberg 1966: 220) began to provide evidence in the 1970s for Chomsky's new nativist theory of language under which linguistic mechanisms determine both the nature of human language and its acquisition by children (cf. Chomsky 1959).

Under a structure-building approach, English-speaking children's morpheme order represented in (1) corresponds to this order of acquisition of IP-level functional projections:

(2) Aspect Phrase [-ing] > TP [regular past] > AgrP [3rd sg -s]

There is little research to date on the order of acquisition of specific functional (sub-)projections in L1A, but the results nonetheless obtained so far confirm the predictions for L1A, in particular as shown for English in Ingham (1998) for TP and AgrP. Legendre, Hagstrom, Vainikka and Todorova (2002) provide data from children's acquisition of French showing that TP is

Table 27.2. *L1 and L2 morpheme orders in cross-sectional studies (de Villiers and de Villiers; Dulay and Burt; Bailey, Madden and Krashen)*

deV & de V: L1A	D & B: L2 children	B, M & K: L2 adults
Plural -s	Plural -s	Progressive -ing
Progressive -ing	Progressive -ing	Contractible copula -'s
Irregular past	Contractible copula -'s	Plural -s
Articles	Contractible auxiliary -'s	Articles
Contractible copula	Articles	Contractible auxiliary -'s
Possessive -'s	Past irregular	Past irregular
3rd person sg -s	3rd person sg -s	3rd person sg -s
Contractible auxiliary	Possessive -'s	Possessive -'s

acquired before AgrP. In Vainikka and Young-Scholten (2011), an overview and analysis of the data on the L1A of German, points to children first positing a NegP, then a TP, then an AgrP, and finally a CP, corresponding to the order in which the projections occur in the adult grammar. We discuss stages in the acquisition of negation (related to NegP) and questions (related to CP) below, after a review of morpheme order studies in L2A.

When Brown was publishing results from Adam, Eve and Sarah's acquisition of English, researchers interested in whether L2A involved more than transfer began to investigate possible L1A and L2A similarities. Among the first forays into L1–L2 comparisons were Dulay and Burt (1973, 1974b) and Bailey, Madden and Krashen (1974). With the validity of cross-sectional methodology having been established by de Villiers and de Villiers (1973), Dulay and Burt collected data in such a manner from 151 Spanish-speaking (1973) and sixty Spanish- and fifty-five Chinese-speaking (1974b) 6- to 8-year-olds learning English. Bailey *et al.* (1974) collected data from seventy-three adult English learners from twelve language backgrounds. Table 27.2 indicates that despite different language backgrounds and pre- vs. post-puberty exposure to English, child L2 and adult L2 learners exhibited similar accuracy orders; these orders were, however, dissimilar to L1 children's.

In what sense does an order of accuracy or difficulty entail stages? As discussed above, there should be an overarching linguistic or cognitive principle or principles to account for this order. In the 1970s and 1980s a range of papers criticized the morpheme accuracy studies on grounds of arbitrary selection of morphemes, methods of data elicitation, methods of analysis and generalizability of findings due to near-exclusive focus on English. Only a few studies treated languages other than English, e.g. van Naerssen (1980) on L2 Spanish and Bye (1980) on L1 Quiche Mayan. Surprisingly few researchers, as Gregg (1996: 68) notes, attempted possible explanations based on environmental factors or general cognitive or linguistic factors; see Flavell (1972).

However, Goldschneider and DeKeyser (2001) have done just this in their re-examination of twelve existing studies. A multiple regression analysis indicates that a combination of perceptual salience, semantic complexity, morphophonological regularity, syntactic category and input frequency can predictably account for the order. Such factors notwithstanding, Vainikka and Young-Scholten (1994, 1996b, 2011) argue that a single linguistic principle accounts for morpheme order, and accordingly for stages of development. Under Organic Grammar, the observed morpheme order is the product of syntactic structure itself, as discussed below. Dulay and Burt's (1975) idea of grouping these morphemes into the hierarchies shown in (3) was a step in the right direction, yet linguistic theory was too underdeveloped in the 1970s to make sense of how functional morphemes might be syntactically related.

(3)	Group I	Group II	Group III	Group IV
-ing	auxiliary *be*	past irregular	past regular
copula *be*			3rd person singular *-s*
plural *-s*	articles	possessive *-s*	

In Hawkins (2001a), the verbal morphemes in the top two rows were finally grouped into morphosyntactic stages for L2 English. In the discussion above on similar data in child L1A, we suggested that children's acquisition order might correspond to their acquisition of specific functional projections. If the same can be applied to L2A (as first suggested in Vainikka and Young-Scholten 1994), we then have an overarching linguistic principle for the order of acquisition: the development of new syntactic projections, during both L1A and L2A. Following the Structure Building approach applied by Vainikka and Young-Scholten (1994, 1996b) to L2 German data, Hawkins (2001a) identifies the following stages for L2 English:

(4)   VP > AspP > TP > AgrP > CP

Below we discuss similar stages in the L2A of German, but before doing so, we continue to examine earlier relevant work.

Starting in the 1960s (e.g. Klima and Bellugi 1966), L1A researchers began to write grammars for children's syntactic development, and this entailed looking for stages in the development of certain constructions in English, most commonly question formation and negation. L2 researchers quickly took up the challenge of investigating whether L2 learners followed suit, and like L1 researchers, they collected production data – usually, but not always, oral data. On this basis, the stages proposed for children's question formation shown in Table 27.3 were claimed to be followed by L2 learners. However, L2 learners tend not to produce utterances consisting of only one and then two words at the start.

Much of the data came from longitudinal studies of the acquisition of English by younger L2 learners, for example from Ravem's (1968) study of

Table 27.3. *Question formation in L1 and L2 English*

Stage 1	Stage 2	Stage 3	Stage 4	Stage 5	Stage 6
Use of memorized chunks and prefabricated routines.	Declarative word order with use of rising intonation	Subject-auxiliary inversion in yes/no questions	Redundant auxiliary inversion and incorrect verb forms ("did you saw").	Inversion in most yes/no and WH questions	Inversion erroneously generalized to all contexts

his Norwegian son, Milon's (1974) study of a Japanese 7-year-old, Wode's (1981) study of his four German children and Cancino, Rosansky and Schnmann's (1978) study of six Spanish speakers (two children, two teenagers, two adults). While the majority of the work on acquisition of negation and question formation in the 1970s and early 1980s was on English, researchers began to look at the acquisition of other languages (e.g. Hyltenstam 1977, on Swedish).

Comparing the question formation stages shown in Table 27.3 to the Hawkins-type development of sentence structure discussed above, Stage 1 (and perhaps also Stage 2) involves an early stage without functional projections. (See below for details.) Stage 3 involves the development of IP-level projections such as TP and AgrP, while the CP projection is acquired by Stage 4. Stages 4–6 in the table involve the acquisition of Rizzi's (1997) subprojections of the CP.

In considering oral production data on questions in both L1A and L2A, we confront the problem of learners using unanalyzed, formulaic chunks. These, like words, are stored in the learner's lexicon. We have already noted above how young children at the one-word stage produce unanalyzed holophrases that in the adult grammar consist of more than one word. If formulae such as *What's that?* and *What's your name?* are produced before there are any other indications in that learner's data of inversion in *wh*-questions, the researcher will prudently assume inversion has not been acquired (see earlier work by Wagner-Gough 1978 and more recent work by Myles 2004). In L2A there is the further possibility that if data are from classroom learners, instruction may prompt learners to produce memorized utterances more advanced than their current stage, giving the appearance that they have skipped stages (recall Meisel et al.'s 1981 claim that L2 learners do not do so). Bolstering the likelihood that early targetlike questions produced in the classroom are formulae is R. Ellis' (1989, 1990) and Cook's (1991a) conclusion that while classroom instruction might influence other aspects of learners' emerging proficiency, route of development appears not to be one of these.

Stages proposed for the acquisition of negation differ slightly for L1 and L2 learners, with L2 learners attaching the negator to modal and auxiliary

Table 27.4. *Stages of negation in L1 and L2 English*

Stage 1 L1 and L2A	Stage 2 L1 and L2A	Stage 3 L1A	Stage 3 L2A	Stage 4 L2A
External negation where negator (*no; not*) precedes or follows an utterance.	Internal negation where negators (*no, not, don't can't*) appear between subject and main verb.	Negator attaches to modals and auxiliaries.	Negator attaches to modals.	Negator attaches to auxiliaries (in particular to *do*).

verbs over the course of two stages, as shown in Table 27.4 (for L1A see Klima and Bellugi 1966; for L2A see Cancino *et al.* 1978; Milon 1974).

In terms of the structure of the sentence, Stage 1 corresponds to an early stage without functional projections, while stages 2–4 involve the development of the IP-level functional projections TP and AgrP. Further details are provided below.

The careful reader will note that while the morpheme order/accuracy studies typically analyze the data in terms of suppliance of morphemes in obligatory contexts, studies of question formation and negation do not do so. One cannot simply tally up contexts for questions and for negation; rather, one must look at negated utterances and attempts at asking questions and note word order and use of relevant morphemes. The comparative fallacy (Bley-Vroman 1983) notwithstanding, most researchers still seek to determine when a learner has acquired something vis-à-vis the target language. The issue of how to determine acquisition continues to occupy researchers, who provide their own rationales for using the non-production or low rates of production of a certain construction to rule out acquisition and adopt a particular percentage of target-likeness to conclude acquisition. This inevitably leads to debate at conferences and in the pages of academic journals.

27.5 Grammatical stages in research in the 1980s and onwards

Converging developments in syntactic theory in the early 1980s shifted attention away from morpheme orders and route of development of various constructions to the Principles and Parameters of Universal Grammar (Chomsky 1981). With these explicit proposals on the contents of UG, L1 and L2 researchers started to search for evidence of the operation of principles and the setting or resetting of parameters. Generative SLA research since the 1980s has been characterized by close examination at a given point in time of the properties of L2 learners' interlanguage grammars (Gregg 1996; see

Table 27.5. *ZISA-study-based stages of development in adult L2 German (based on Pienemann 1989)*

Stage 1	Stage 2	Stage 3	Stage 4	Stage 5
Canonical SVO order	Adverb preposing	Verb separation	Inversion	Verb end
Die Kinder spielen mim ball. "The children play with the ball."	**Da Kinder spielen* "There children play." (*Da spielen Kinder.*)	*Alle Kinder muss die Pause machen.* "All children must take a break." (*müssen*)	**Dann hat sie wieder die Knocht gebringt.* "Then she brought the bone again." (*Knocke...gebrungen.*)	*Er sagte, dass er nach hause kommt.* "He said that he'll come home."

above). In L1A, this means that at all points during development, the child's grammar is UG-constrained, representing a possible natural language. For example, children's subject omission patterns in English are consistent with what is found in languages of the world that allow null subjects (see Biberauer et al. 2010). In L2A, the question is framed in terms of whether there is post-puberty access to UG: is the adult learner's interlanguage grammar at a given point in time constrained by UG? The search for typically very subtle evidence is the cornerstone of such research; see Chapters 7 and 22, this volume. When it comes to subject omission in interlanguage grammars, if the patterns observed for learners are found neither in the learner's L1 nor the L2, if patterns conform to a possible language, this then is evidence for the continued operation of UG.

27.5.1 Studies of L2 German word order

At the same time, European research dating back to the 1970s was beginning to bear fruit that catapulted German and stages of development in that language onto the center stage in L1 and L2 acquisition research. It was initially unclear whether L1 children and L2 adults followed similar developmental pathways. In work on the L1A of German, Clahsen (1976, 1980, 1991) established stages of development that he and colleagues (Clahsen, Meisel and Pienemann 1983; Meisel et al. 1981) then compared to the acquisition of German by migrant workers who were not receiving instruction due to the expectation that they would return home after their contracts ended. Studies of these naturalistic adult learners have made an invaluable contribution to what we know about how L2 learners systematically and without the overlay of learned knowledge (in the sense of Krashen 1985 and Schwartz 1993) organize their internal grammars. Table 27.5 summarizes the stages proposed for fifty-seven Italian, Portuguese and Spanish adult migrant workers learning German (taken from twelve whose data were collected longitudinally), in the (Zweitspracherwerb italienischer, portuguesischer und spanischer Arbeiter) ZISA study. In the table, based on Pienemann (1989), the phenomena that define each stage are underlined, non-target utterances are marked with an asterisk and correct forms are given in parentheses.

Learners' syntactic advances are not always targetlike: adverb preposing at Stage 2 involves the verb in a position incorrect for German. Pienemann (1989) is unique in applying these stages to teaching; he proposes that it is beneficial to provide instruction targeting structures at the next higher stage only; instruction is incapable of assisting learners in skipping a stage. This follows Krashen's (1985) input hypothesis of i+1 notion (current interlanguage stage + input at the next stage up).

In their comparison of L2 adults' development with what they had established for L1 children, Clahsen and Muysken (1986, 1989) argued that unlike for children, adults' interlanguage development was not driven by UG. Their evidence was twofold: learners' non-UG-sanctioned movement of the non-finite verb to final position at Stage 3 / verb separation and lack of the same correlation between acquisition of agreement and verb raising found for L1 children. Clahsen and Muysken explained the highly systematic and non-L1-influenced development they found for L2 adults in terms of their use of general cognitive principles, where learners were responding to linear surface patterns displayed by the input rather than drawing on the deeper knowledge of hierarchical syntactic structure UG provides. Stages and their linguo-cognitive basis are subject to reanalysis, and Clahsen and Muysken's publications elicited responses from researchers who argued for UG-constrained development (e.g. duPlessis, Solin, Travis and White 1987) and proposed that Stage 3 / verb separation revealed UG-driven development of syntactic structure when the Romance learners with SVO word order switched to SOV (Schwartz and Tomaselli 1990).

Research on uninstructed immigrant adults continued, under a European Science Foundation (ESF) project which, like the ZISA project, involved the longitudinal collection of oral production data and extended research to L2 learners of Dutch, English, German, French and Swedish. Described in Klein and Perdue (1992), the focus of ESF research has been largely on utterance structure / information structure rather than on morphosyntax, with exceptions that we discuss presently.

27.5.2 The Basic Variety

A range of studies has followed in Clahsen and colleagues' steps in proposing developmental stages based both on cross-sectional and longitudinal designs. Myles (2005) is one example of a longitudinal study, albeit of instructed 12- and 13-year-old English speakers learning French. Dimroth's (2002) cross-sectional study of forty Croatian, Russian and Turkish uninstructed adult immigrants in Germany is another, with work that fits under the ESF information structure umbrella. While her main aim in this paper was to examine learners' use of topic-related additive words such as *auch* "also/and," Dimroth also placed her learners at three levels. The first of these levels compares to the *Basic Variety* (BV) proposed by Klein and Perdue (1992, 1997). The BV covers the early period of acquisition in all learner languages, including children's, and with respect to the latter, loosely resembles Slobin's (1985) Basic Child Grammar, Givón's (1979) specific pragmatic mode and Bickerton's (1984) Protolanguage. For L2A, Klein and Perdue propose a set of constraints on the form and order of constituents, on the case role properties of arguments and on discourse pragmatics, in combination with minimalist syntax (Chomsky 1995). BV properties include (a) SVO word order; (b) no functional morphology; (c) optional determiners; (d) some aspectual distinctions; (e) no subordination or overt complementizers; and (f) no movement. Because the uninstructed adult immigrants learning English, Dutch, German, French and Swedish in the ESF study upon whose data the Basic Variety approach is based typically remain or fossilize at one of these stages, Klein and Perdue use the term variety rather than stage.

The Basic Variety, as presented in a keynote article by Klein and Perdue, was critically examined in a 1997 special issue of *Second Language Research*. Commentators criticized the BV on empirical grounds, arguing that it neither represented only the earliest, most basic, stage of acquisition, nor took into consideration obvious L1 influence. The BV was re-examined in Vainikka and Young-Scholten (2006), where they suggest that the properties listed in (a)–(f) above entail three well-defined stages: Stage 1, no verbs; Stage 2, L1 word order in the VP but no functional morphology or complex syntax; Stage 3, SVO word order.

27.5.3 Finiteness linking

More recent work emerging from those analyzing the ESF data and new data includes Jordens (2008, 2009). His theory of *Finiteness Linking* identifies three stages: Stage 1: Holistic Stage; Stage 2: Conceptual Ordering; Stage 3: Finiteness Linking. At all three stages the learner expresses explicitly or implicitly a topic and a state of affairs in relation to that topic; this is referred to as validation. At Stage 1, validation is pragmatic and early verbs may be predicates rather than real verbs. At this stage, the grammar involves only lexical projections; there is no finiteness, no head movement, no specifier position, no topicalization, no *wh*-questions and no inversion. Learners instead make use of purely lexical means of expression. At Stage 2, validation is lexical rather than pragmatic, and word order is based on principles of information structuring. Topics are initial, as anchors, and the predicate is final (representing state of affairs); the predictate can now

Table 27.6. *Hierarchy of processing resources (Pienemann 1998; 2005)*

Level 1	Level 2	Level 3	Level 4	Level 5	Level 6
Lemma access: no sequence of constituents (words acquired)	Category procedure: canonical word order	Phrasal procedure: phrasal morphemes (acquisition of processes associated with word categories)	Simplified S-procedure: sentence-internal exchange of information (phrases built based on these categories)	S-procedure: Further internal exchange of information (acquisition of sentences)	Subordinate clause procedure (relationships between main and subordinate clauses)

include the main verb. A linking element occurs between the topic and predicate which can be a scope particle such as *auch* "also" or a modal verb. An intermediate stage involves the projection of the functional category AUX (auxiliary). At Stage 3 validation becomes morphosyntactic, the learner's syntax is constrained by X-bar theory (see Chapter 1) and the category FIN (finiteness) is projected.

27.5.4 Processability theory

The stages or hierarchy presented in Table 27.6 comprise Processability theory (PT) and originate in the same naturalistic German ZISA data Clahsen and Muysken (1986, 1989) drew on, and indeed for PT the idea comes from how inter-learner variation was accounted for under Meisel *et al.*'s (1981) Multidimensional Model. Similar to Clahsen and Muysken, Pienemann (1998, 2003, 2005a) excludes from PT the operation of UG and instead argues that the source of the "highly regular way in which phrase-structure rules are gradually expanded in an on-going way" is general cognitive processing (Pienemann 1998: 50). Based on Levelt's (1989) ideas on processing and on Lexical Functional Grammar (Bresnan 1982; Kaplan and Bresnan 1982), stages result from learners' steps up an implicational hierarchy of processing resources. The earliest stages of development are not syntactic because of the learner's inability to identify grammatical categories and thus locate syntactic and morphological elements; evidence for this is the miscategorization of nouns as verbs (1998: 58). Under PT a Formulator incrementally translates conceptual structures into lexical structures, where the procedural grammar lexically activates language generation. The learner's online processing of the input in terms of salience, linearity and distance between features (short distances being easier) further unifies these steps or stages of development. While PT allows some L1 influence in the form of native language processing procedures when the Formulator requires reconstruction to deal with the target language, the proposed stages are common for learners from all L1

Table 27.7. *Stages of question formation (Pienemann and Johnston 1987)*

Stage 1	Stage 2	Stage 3	Stage 4	Stage 5	Stage 6
One-word and two–three-word questions with declarative word order and rising intonation.	Declarative word order in questions. Fronting of *wh*-words	Inversion in *yes/no* questions. Declarative order in *wh*- questions.	Inversion in all questions (but not fully established).	Inversion in all questions but not always in negative questions.	Inversion generalized to embedded questions.

backgrounds. Canonical word order (Stage 2) in PT was originally SVO, as in Clahsen and Muysken (1986, 1989), but revisions of PT have allowed for learners' early-stage reliance on their L1 word order, e.g. SOV by Turkish learners of English or German (Pienemann 2003).

Evidence supporting PT comes from the aforementioned German data (also see Clahsen *et al.* 1983) as well as from those working on PT since (e.g. Håkansson, Pienemann and Sayehli 2002). Table 27.7 shows how PT-driven acquisition unfolds for English question formation.

27.6 Organic Grammar

Earlier in this chapter we discussed functional projections, where the coupling of properties (verb morphology with word order) corresponds to specific functional/grammatical projections in the syntax. Here we elaborate on Vainikka and Young-Scholten's theory of Organic Grammar. To begin with, a finite clause in any language typically contains at its core a VP projection with the verb and its arguments, and layered on top, functional projections such as a TP (tense phrase), an AgrP (agreement phrase) and a CP (complementizer phrase).

In generative grammar since the 1980s, the role of development – or stages – has been marginalized in learners' acquisition of functional projections since it is typically assumed that UG provides the full syntactic tree in L1A, and that UG and the learner's native language provide the tree in L2A. This approach bears one of two names: the Strong Continuity Hypothesis or the Full Competence Hypothesis (Boser, Lust, Santelmann and Whitman 1992; Poeppel and Wexler 1993) in the study of child language. In L2A the approach is known as Full Access / Full Transfer (Schwartz and Sprouse 1996; see also Epstein, Flynn and Martohardjono *et al.* 1996, Lardiere 1998b and White 2003a, and Chapter 24, this volume). An alternative to an approach under which acquisition begins with the full L1 syntactic tree is the idea that functional projections develop during acquisition. This so-called Weak Continuity approach has slowly gained momentum over the last twenty years, beginning with Radford's (1988, 1990) idea that children start acquisition by projecting only a bare VP, and functional projections then develop. This entails Structure Building, an idea which has become more relevant in recent syntactic theory under minimalism (Chomsky 1995, 2001, 2008) whereby syntactic trees are derived, from the bottom up (as opposed to earlier versions of syntactic theory where no derivation occurs). Radford assumed that children's functional projections matured all at once, but it is now clear – especially when considering L2A data – that neither maturation nor a sudden combined appearance are attested. Since Radford, there have been various related proposals in L1A, all of which fall under the category of Structure Building approaches (Clahsen 1991; Guilfoyle and Noonan 1992; Lebeaux 1988; Platzack 1990; Vainikka 1993/94; Rizzi 1998, 2000 can also be included here). In L2A, the Minimal Trees approach points to Structure Building based on data from naturalistic English, Italian, Korean, Spanish and Turkish speaking adults learning German (Vainikka and Young-Scholten 1994, 1996b, 1998, 2002, 2003, 2006, 2007a, 2009 and 2010). Note that along with Hawkins' (2001a) Modulated Structure Building variant, there are also researchers who accept Weak Continuity / Structure Building in L1A but reject this approach in L2A (e.g. White 2003a).

Work on Structure Building in L2A has culminated in Vainikka and Young-Scholten (2011), where the most fully articulated – both in terms of theoretical and empirical coverage – approach in L1 and L2 acquisition to date is presented as the theory of Organic Grammar. OG crucially involves stages of syntactic acquisition; each functional projection, such as NegP, TP and AgrP, corresponds to a stage in development. Throughout this chapter in discussing traditional stages, we have already exposed the reader to applying OG analysis to morpheme orders and paths of the development of questions and negation. Under OG, these stages are predicted to occur in the same order in which they occur in the adult syntactic tree (building from the bottom up). In addition to the acquisition of the functional morphology associated with each projection and its word order, it is predicted that additional phenomena associated with a particular projection (such as perhaps null subjects with AgrP) will be acquired together with the emerging projection. Organic Grammar also imposes economy constraints on possible adult trees in that only projections for which there is overt evidence can be posited by the learner. This results in a fairly standard structure for English, but a slightly modified one for German.

Organic Grammar is applicable to both first and second language acquisition. Vainikka and Young-Scholten (2011) discuss how children's L1 development across languages of the world (such as those featured in the Slobin 1985, 1992 volumes) reveals the general pattern that syntactic elements associated with IP-level projections (such as aspect, tense and agreement) develop earlier, around age 2, while syntactic elements associated with the CP (such as relative pronouns or complementizers) develop later (typically around age 3). More specifically, Ingham (1998) argues that in child L1 English, the TP is acquired before the AgrP; similarly, Legendre *et al.* (2002) show that in child L1 French, the TP is acquired before the AgrP. Focusing on German, Vainikka and Young-Scholten (2011) argue that existing data from studies of the L1A of German either support or are consistent with the syntactic stages predicted by Organic Grammar. The most extensive evidence for the Organic Grammar approach comes from the naturalistic L2 acquisition data from three American secondary school students, Joan, Paul and George, who spent an exchange year in Germany (without knowing any German when they arrived). As described in detail in Vainikka and Young-Scholten (2011), they lived with host families and attended German secondary schools where they followed much the same courses they would have followed back in the USA. Production and elicitation data were collected from them monthly for eleven months, and in Vainikka and Young-Scholten (2011) it is argued that these teenagers began with the bare VP projection in their German, then posited the NegP, then the TP, then the AgrP, and finally the CP projection. It turns out that these young uninstructed but fully immersed learners took only about two months to develop a new projection, although it took them longer to sort out the correct headedness of the AgrP and CP projections. Crucially, it is argued that the order of acquisition directly results in the order found in the target grammar, whereby each stage corresponds to a new layer in the target structure.

Vainikka and Young-Scholten (1994, 1996b, 2011) have argued that only the beginning of the structure building process, i.e. the VP projection (containing the verb and its arguments), is transferred from the L2 learner's first language. Functional projections are not transferable due to the tight connection under this approach between the projections and the corresponding functional morphology. That is, in order to transfer, say, a TP projection from L1 English to L2 German, the associated tense morpheme (*-ed*) would also have to be transferred from English to German (note that such transfer can occur between very closely related languages such as Dutch and German). However, English-speaking learners of German appear only to transfer the VP projection (with its associated word order). Functional projections are then acquired similarly to what happens with children, one projection at the time, from the bottom up. This results in the gradual building of the target structure and the researcher can then observe stages of acquisition associated with the functional projections mentioned above.

Inflectional morphology is involved at each stage in terms of how the syntax projected allows realization of particular functional morphology. These stages might be thought of as combining the insights of the 1970s/1980s morpheme order studies and the studies of negation and question formation; the stages are also akin to those proposed for the ZISA learners. However, unlike Clahsen and Muyksen (1986, 1989), Vainikka and Young-Scholten assume UG access.

Preliminary work on L2 English using Organic Grammar stages has been conducted by Young-Scholten and Strom (2006) and Young-Scholten and

Ijuin (2006); several examples from a cross-sectional study of Somali- and Vietnamese-speaking immigrants are provided in (5):

(5) a. [VP stage]
   You my car hit here teacher.
   This is car

b. [TP or AgrP stage]
   The woman is cry.
   Because too bad.

c. [CP stage]
   Someone's die because he have accident.
   Car hit the kid that's lie down on the street.
   When you reverse, you have to see anybody behind.

Example (5a) corresponds to a bare VP stage; although learners use copula *is*, there is no evidence of functional projections (and word order is transferred from the L1). Example (5b) corresponds to the acquisition of an IP-level projection (TP or AgrP) and also suggests that CP has not yet been acquired (although *because* is an early complementizer, it does not occur in embedded contexts with a full sentence yet). (5c) shows clear evidence of progression to the CP stage.

We now provide a sample of the stages found in the our data from the three American teenagers discussed above (Vainikka and Young-Scholten 2011). The target German structure has the stage order VP NegP TP AgrP CP, moving from the bottom of the tree upwards, and each of these predicted stages is confirmed in the data from the three learners and illustrated below with examples from Paul. In addition, there are two substages for the VP stage, namely before and after switching of headedness (VO to OV); note that while in general the stages occur in chronological order, the switching of the learner's L1 headedness of the VP to the target language order (Stage VP-ii) appears in these data to overlap with the development of the early functional projections. (Target German given in parentheses when relevant.) We have boldfaced the verbs and other important morphemes.

(6) a. VP(i) stage:
   Peter **lernen** die Buch. (Paul, file 1)
   Peter learn-INF the book
   (Peter liest das Buch.)
   "Peter reads the book."

b. VP(ii) stage:
   Der klein Jungen – Wasser **trinken**. (Paul, file 3)
   the little boy water drink-INF
   (Der kleine Junge trinkt das Wasser.)
   "The little boy drinks water."

(7) NegP stage [all four uttered in succession]:
   a. Der Mann **fahren**   die Auto **nicht**, nichts – no – (Paul, file 2)
      the man   drive-INF the car   not
      (Der Mann fährt das Auto nicht.)
      "The man doesn't drive the car."

   b. Die Mann **nicht fahren**   die – no – (Paul, file 2)
      the man not   drive-INF the
      (Der Mann fährt nicht das...)
      "The man doesn't drive the..."

   c. Die Mann [laughs] **nicht** Auto **fahren**.   (Paul, file 2)
      the man   not   car drive-INF
      (Der Mann fährt das Auto nicht.)
      "The man doesn't drive the car."

   d. Die Mann **nicht**, uh, die Auto **fahren**   or der Auto
      the man not   the car drive-INF or the car
      fahren. (Paul, file 2)
      drive-INF
      (Der Mann fährt nicht das Auto.)
      "The man doesn't drive the car."

(8) TP stage:
   a. Die Frau [euh] nichts   Kaffee **getrunken**... (Paul, file 4)
      the woman   nothing coffee drunk-PST
      (Die Frau hat Kaffee nicht getrunken.)
      "The women didn't drink coffee."

   b. Sie hast   uh **hast** Brot **gekauft**.   (Paul, file 4)
      she has-*2SG   bread bought-PST
      (Sie hat Brot gekauft.)
      "She bought bread."

(9) AgrP stage:
   Sie **sprechen** so schnell und es ist   wie ein lang deutsch
   they speak-3PL so fast   and it is-3SG like a   long German
   Wort. (Paul, file 5)
   word
   (Sie sprechen so schnell und es ist wie ein langes deutsches Wort.)
   "They speak so fast and it's like a long German word."

(10) CP stage:
   Was **hat**   der Mann **getrunken**, getrinken? (Paul, file 7)
   what has-3SG the man   drunk-PST   drunk-PST
   (Was hat her Mann getrunken.)
   'What did the man drink?'

Paul first transferred the English VO word order at the VP stage, as exemplified in (6a), and switched the headedness to the target OV order fairly soon (6b). There is at this point little evidence for functional projections, although negation is acquired early (overlapping with the second VP stage), reflecting a NegP stage in (7). Note that all the early examples involve the non-agreeing (and non-target) infinitive form, comparable to what occurs in German L1 acquisition. Example (8) is from a later stage at which past-tense marking has developed (and thus the TP projection); subject – verb agreement has not yet been acquired, and even auxiliaries have not fully developed (required in the target language for past-tense marking). Example (9) shows the yet later acquisition of subject – verb agreement and thus the AgrP projection; by file 5, Paul's subject – verb agreement is nearly correct. Finally, the development of the CP is exemplified in (10).

Despite the interesting patterns uncovered under Organic-Grammar-based analysis, there is an advantage in assuming that complete syntactic structure is provided to the L2 learner at the beginning of acquisition, as in the Full Transfer / Full Access hypothesis of Schwartz and Sprouse (1996), and to the L1 learner in the Strong Continuity / Full Competence approach as in Boser *et al.* (1992) and Poeppel and Wexler (1993). No theory of how acquisition of syntactic structure develops is needed: UG provides all the required syntactic projections for the child for free, and either UG – or the L2 learner's L1 (or both) – provide the full structure for the learner from the so-called initial state onwards. But Full Transfer offers no stages involving the development of syntactic structure that might also explain the morpheme order study and other relevant study data. (See Vainikka and Young-Scholten 2011 for further problems.) Under Strong Continuity / Full Competence in child language or Full Transfer / Full Access in SLA, acquisition of syntax involves filling in / refilling existing positions, and there is no expectation that one position will be filled before another, nor is there a reason why in L2 acquisition, the learners' L1 syntactic tree begins to approximate the target grammar in any particular order. We might, for example, expect acquisition orders where material involving a morphological paradigm is more difficult to acquire than single words. The prediction would be that sentential complementizers (*because, if*) are acquired earlier than subject–verb agreement in morphologically rich languages. But this order is unattested in L1A and L2A (for L1A see Slobin's 1985, 1992 crosslinguistic volumes, and for L2A see Vainikka and Young-Scholten 2011). The observed order is instead consistent with the learner positing AgrP (subject–verb agreement) before CP (complementizers), as these projections are located in all the target grammars studied so far in generative acquisition research.

Organic Grammar implies a tight coupling during acquisition of grammatical morphemes and the corresponding syntactic structure. Those who argue against Organic Grammar (or the 1990s Minimal Trees / Structure Building) consider this coupling unjustified because L2 learners, most notoriously adult L2 learners, fail to consistently produce target inflectional morphology even when there is good evidence for their having projected the associated syntax (see extensive discussion in White 2003a). The tools of Organic Grammar developed in Vainikka and Young-Scholten (2011) make it plausible to maintain even in adult L2A a tight connection between the development of syntactic structure and the development of the corresponding grammatical morphology.

27.7 Conclusion: theoretical and practical considerations

We can propose stages of L2 acquisition along with the underlying principles responsible, but until we explain how the learner moves from one stage to the next, we will not have arrived at a full account of the development of morphosyntax in a second language. This, however, requires agreement on what underlies patterns observed in the input. As we saw with Clahsen and Muysken's (1986, 1989) use of stages in their arguments against UG-constrained development in L2A, and Organic Grammar's controversial coupling of syntax and morphology, patterns in data are open to reinterpretation. We might observe a learner moving through what appears to be an ordered process of development, and what we identify as stages might represent a systematic interlanguage. If we argue that linguistic and/or cognitive constraints shape an interlanguage at any given point in time, we also need to know what mechanisms actually drive development over time. Assuming Structure Building, Vainikka and Young-Scholten's (1998) and Hawkins' (2001a) proposals for triggers in the input that prompt learners to project functional syntax is one avenue of investigation. Another avenue of investigation is the work by Pienemann and colleagues on Processability theory discussed above, which aims to bring together mental representations and processing considerations. (For a full discussion of transition theory work, see Chapter 26, this volume.)

In addition to providing evidence for a particular account of language and its acquisition, and in addition to the use of stages in language teaching under Pienemann's (1989) idea of focusing instruction on the next stage, ordered patterns of development have long been used to assess learners. Certainly the most common use within L1A is diagnosis of children whose linguistic development is suspected to be atypical. Among other things, this involves application of hierarchical scales that grade morphosyntactic features in terms of their expected order of appearance during development by typically developing children (Crystal and Varley 1993: 176 and Stromswold 2000; see also Clahsen 1976 on profile analysis for child German). In L2A, those researchers who have proposed stages of development have also applied this to the assessment of learners. The ZISA study stages shown above have been applied by Clahsen (1985) and by Pienemann, Johnston and Brindley (1988) for assessment of L2 German and other languages.

Vainikka and Young-Scholten have taken their ideas about how L2 learners build syntactic structure and, based on an expanded and elaborated theory of Organic Grammar (Vainikka and Young-Scholten 2011), adapted for English and applied these to assessment of US adult ESL students (Young-Scholten and Ijuin 2006); see examples above in (5). Young-Scholten and Ijuin's data differ from Vainikka and Young-Scholten's L2 German data on two counts. First, although like the German L2 learners studied, the English L2 learners were in an immersion context (in the USA), they were receiving instruction. Second, the data were not oral but from a written production task presented as a memory task where learners had to view a set of PowerPoint slides and write what they recalled. It is noteworthy that patterns of development observed in the written production data were much the same as those found in the German L2 data and also resembled the data from Young-Scholten and Strom's (2006) study of low-literate L2 English learners exemplified above. This further strengthens R. Ellis' (1989) claim that instruction does not influence route of development. The Young-Scholten and Strom study also serves to reveal how uneducated adult learners' problems with morphosyntax might in part underlie their difficulties in learning to read (see also Chapter 9, this volume).

Levels and benchmarks are also entailed in the measurement of oral and written proficiency. One such set of levels is the increasingly popular Common European Framework of Reference shown in (11); see also proficiency measures such as the twelve-point Canadian Benchmarks ESL scale (Pawlikowska-Smith 2000). The CEFR is intended to capture in a language-neutral manner the L2 learner's growing communicative competence (Hymes 1972) and through readily observed behavior is held to even permit self-assessment. The CEFR covers the entire breadth of second language behavior from (i) linguistic competence (syntax, morphology, phonetics/phonology, the lexicon/semantics and orthography), (ii) sociolinguistic competence (social relationships, politeness conventions, register and accent/dialect) to (iii) pragmatic competence (conveyance of information in terms of topic, focus, sequencing, cohesion along with imparting and seeking information and expressing attitudes and socializing).

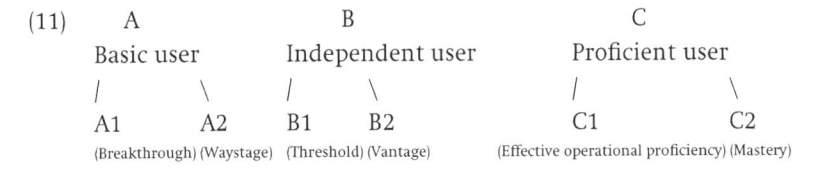

(11) A   B   C
      Basic user   Independent user   Proficient user
       /   \   /   \   /   \
      A1   A2   B1   B2   C1   C2
    (Breakthrough) (Waystage) (Threshold) (Vantage)   (Effective operational proficiency) (Mastery)

Like the stages we have been discussing, the descriptors for each of the six levels (see www.coe.int/t/dg4/linguistic/cadre_en.asp) express what the learner can do rather than what s/he cannot do. This is a much-needed advance in the assessment of proficiency. Yet these and other current levels and benchmarks are not stages; in their coverage of the entire spectrum of communicative competence, the behaviors included are too wide-ranging to be derived from even a handful of underlying principles. Linguistic competence has been largely absent in this and other such schemes, and where language is referred to, the terms used are often relative ones such as simple vs. complex to describe the grammars of, for example, CEFR A1 vs. C2 speakers (see Young-Scholten and Ijuin 2006). To give development stages their rightful place in assessment, research needs to take more seriously the challenge of correlating communicative descriptors with the sort of linguistic descriptors discussed in this chapter. This is not a new idea (see e.g. Bachman 1990), but the additional challenge here is to provide linguistic descriptors that can apply across target languages.

28

Emergentism, connectionism and complexity

Randal Holme

28.1 Introduction

In this chapter we examine a view of second language acquisition that treats the structures of language as motivated by their expression of meaning. This is the "what-you-see-is-what-you-get" approach to language (Goldberg 2006), which treats it straightforwardly as the utterances that language users produce. Language acquisition, then, is not the abstraction of hidden structures from input but the learning of the forms that the learner actually encounters. Like other forms of learning, language acquisition can be modeled materially, as the physical activity that occurs in the brain itself.

Treating language acquisition as complex skill learning suggests that we learn our first and second languages in much the same way. Our focus in this chapter will therefore be largely on these generalized learning processes and the models of language and of the cognition that they assume. MacWhinney (2008) calls this a unified theory that treats first and second language acquisition as fundamentally similar. Nonetheless, any model of SLA must acknowledge that second language learners have more knowledge about language and meaning than first language learners. The issue of what this knowledge is and how it transfers will be discussed in so far as it bears on the cognitivist perspective adopted, but I leave to other chapters in this volume the difficult topic of how far learners are aware of this knowledge, and the extent to which it makes them conscious of their learning.

In this chapter, I first set out a broad view of cognition, examine how it affects our view of language and then consider how that linguistic model impacts our theories of language learning. I complete the circle by returning to cognition and to thinking about theories of brain processes necessary to support this learning model. Finally, I explore how far this model may need to recast future research by treating L2 acquisition as what is called a *dynamic system*.

To achieve the above, the chapter first looks at the idea of an *enactive* cognition and at how it is expressed by its use of *categories, construal operations* and *image schemas* to organize reality. Then follows an outline a functional model of language, discussing an idealized model of how form is *emergent* from *usage* and an exploration of the concept of language learning as *construction* learning. The chapter then moves on to consider the relationship between this language model and what we need to do to acquire it. I therefore discuss these facets of cognition as a sensitivity to *pattern, intention* (Tomasello 2003), *saliency* (Slobin 1973, 2006), *frequency* (e.g. N. C. Ellis 2002a) and as a kind of neural *competition* among forms and their meanings (Bates and MacWhinney 1987). I further outline how our methods of learning may in part emerge as facets of the stages of learning that we attain (Holich, Hirsh-Pasek and Golinkoff 2000; Pienemann 1998). In the course of this discussion, I consider how models of language and learning can account for such well-known features of acquisition as *natural orders, U-shaped learning, knowledge transfer* and *interference*. After, I map this model of language and learning onto *parallel processing* models of cognition. The discussion of parallel processing models, frequencies and flow affects leads to a consideration of research implications and a discussion of how *complexity* or *Dynamic Systems theory* (DST) may shape studies in SLA. The chapter concludes with a summary of the necessary elements of a *cognitivist* model of language learning and some thoughts about future research.

28.2 An embodied and enactive cognition

The cognitivist models put forward here reject how Cartesian philosophy treats the mind and body as separate entities where the former tries to exert rational control over the unruly nature of the latter. In this chapter, cognition and the body are treated as mutually dependent and fashioned from each other. For example, *proprioception* expresses how we know where our limbs are in relation to ourselves and can therefore constantly track their movements in space (e.g. Gallagher 2005). To achieve this, the brain requires a body map and the nervous system must be understood as distributing cognition through the body. Language and physical movement are also bound up with each other. This is self-evident in speech in terms of how the articulation of meaning as sound is achieved by muscular movement. It can also be understood by looking at language and seeing how meaning develops out of the interaction of the body and the world. Infants move to learn, and their early experience consists of grasping, weighing, or wrapping themselves around the forms of their immediate environment (e.g. Gallagher 2005). Theories of embodied cognition also argue that because meaning originates in the body's shaping of our world, language begins in bodily action, or gesture (McNeil 1992). Infants gesture before they talk and adults point to objects to give the infant a shared focus of attention and hence a source of meaning, something higher animals such as primates do not do (Tomasello 2006). Gesture, then, is less a prop to meaning and more a resource from which meaning is fashioned. Gesture is therefore an enduring expression of our conceptual processes, or of how we shape meaning from bodily movements and their relationship to the world.

The networks of imagery represented in language which are derived from these early physical experiences are called image schemas. For example, when we bleed we experience our body as a container of liquid, building a *container* image schema (Johnson 1987). Our need to resist and exert force creates an image schema of *force dynamics* (Talmy 2000) and the experience of standing upright establishes one of *balance* (Johnson 1987).

From image schemas and from our life experience of things and actions we *conceptualize* categories. Categories gather our experiences of related phenomena. Almost all meanings result from the conceptualization of a *category*. If they did not, we would need to name every tree in a forest or every person in a crowd. A category implies a cognitive process of differentiation as between the experience of a "flower" and a "shrub" or one of organization and inclusion as when we give the name of "tree" to our experience of specimens as diverse as "oaks," "palms" and "eucalypti." Infants often overextend the few categories they know to give a conceptual home to the new phenomena they experience. For example, on first seeing a "donkey" they may call the animal a "doggie" until they learn how to categorize animals according to the conventions of their language and culture. We categorize things, processes and the relations between them often using image schemas to help us do so. When representing a process, we might, for example, use the image schema of force dynamics to associate "smash" with throwing and "break" with a more direct exertion of force, as with the hands.

We further use what are called *construal operations* to conceptualize abstract meanings from physical experience (e.g. Croft and Cruse 2004). One such operation is *metaphor*. Thus our concept of time is derived from image schemas of space through metaphor. Metaphors that use this schema are time as distance (*a long time*), time as an object moving in space (*Christmas is coming*) or as a resource heaped in space (*I'm running out of time*) (Lakoff and Johnson 1980, 1999). In English, our use of the preposition *in* often marks our common exploitation of the container schema, for example, with time, *in a minute, in a while* or situations that, like containers, are difficult to get out of, *in difficulties, in a mess*. The metaphors combine with others to provide many of the idioms used in language, for example construing us as contained by liquid or water: *in deep, in over our heads*.

Construal operations typify how cognition is enactive and embodied. They show that we do not just experience "time" and make a meaning, we conceptualize it in different ways and form a category. In other words, we are constantly structuring and restructuring experience (e.g. Gallagher 2005;

Gibbs 2005; Johnson 1987, 2007; Lakoff 1987). Language learning is part of that process of restructuration. The categories a language represents to its learners will partly restructure those that their experiences provide. L1 categories may be used in the L2 but will sometimes need restructuring to cope with different methods of construal.

28.3 Construction-based models of language: an emergent grammar

Although the above summary of embodiment indicates how meaning is derived from experience it does not give us much understanding of how we derive the grammars that can fit meanings together and show the relations between them. I will now sketch out how this might happen.

Languages evolve to express meaning and the assumption of functional grammars is that grammatical form is motivated by how it was evolved to express meaning, in much the same way as lexis. Arguably, we can take this a step further and ask whether it is not in fact possible to see grammatical form and meaning as emergent from lexis. To understand this better, let's look at an idealized model of how learners may actually create their grammar as they learn it.

28.3.1 Construction grammars

To see how a grammar emerges, contrast the meaning of a typical noun, *tree*, with that of a typical verb, *break*. *Break* represents a process and *tree* a fixed thing. Treating form as motivated by meaning presupposes that noun and verb are themselves categories that represent a basic experiential distinction between stable "things" and unstable "processes" (e.g. Langacker 1987, 1990, 2008a). Processes are only perceptible through things. Thus *break* is a meaning derived from what is being broken and who or what is doing the breaking. In short, the word achieves meaning by expressing a relationship between two others and this creates the rudiments of a grammar.

To understand this, let us imagine that a hypothetical language learner hears the sentence *Sammy broke the cup* after witnessing this event. This combination of words can be called a *construction*. Words, phrases and clauses are all *constructed* from other forms and are, therefore, in a sense, constructions. The grammatical construction is straightforwardly words that together obtain a meaning they did not individually have or stem words and inflections that do the same (e.g. *call+ed*) (Goldberg 1995, 2006; Croft 2001; Croft and Cruse 2004). Thus the meaning of *Sammy* does not necessarily predict that he will break things or that of *cup* that it will be broken.

Let us further imagine that at a subsequent moment our hypothetical learner hears: *Jane broke the jug*. A different type of meaning is now starting to establish itself. The *breaker* that *break* needs to complete its meaning is no longer just Sammy but also "Jane" whilst "the jug" is another breakable thing. What is now happening is that the verb *break* is now starting to establish a more general meaning for our *break* construction. This happens in the same way that our different experiences of things that are trees allows us to establish them as a single category. Here, our experiences of different "breakers" (Sammy and Jane) and different "things that break" (the cup and the jug) allows us to establish the categories, "breaker" and "breakable things." We can now specify the construction as: "Breaker+*break*+breakable thing."

The *break* construction's meaning allows some meanings but excludes others. For example, we can say *I broke my pen* and, through metaphor, *I broke her heart*, but not *I broke his paper*. This last meaning is therefore ungrammatical. Ungrammaticality, then, is a disjuncture between lexical and constructional meaning. It is not a transgression of a rule, but a matter of slippage from a meaningful construction to a less meaningful one (Langacker 2008a). We can now see that the rules of this construction *emerge* from the semantic relationship of the two forms. Thus common features in the meanings of *Sammy broke a cup* and *Jane broke a jug* start to create a rule that tells us what can come before the verb (a plausible breaker) and after the verb (a breakable thing). Further, the construction is *productive* because there is a vast array of things that can cause a breakage and a substantial number of objects that can break.

Now we of course need other verbs for different types of relationship between meanings. For example, *I bought a chicken / Jack cooked the bird / Sara ate the fish*. A hypothetical learner can see some similarities between the meanings profiled by each of these different verbs. Thus, in the above examples, *I*, *Jack* and *Sara* all mean something that instigates an action, or are *agents*, whilst *chicken*, *bird* and *fish* all mean something affected by processes, or are *patients*. The construction is becoming still more *productive* by developing a meaning I expressed as "agent+process+patient." The agent is now anything that instigates a process and the patient anything affected by one. As the construction becomes more productive something is happening to the meanings that are profiled.

To be productive the construction establishes what is called a *schematic meaning*. "Schema" derives from the Greek word meaning a shadow and hence outline. Imagine beginning a drawing with an oval. This oval has a highly schematic meaning in the sense that it could become a face, a table top or the body of a mouse. However, there are some meanings it could not represent, for example a book or a horse, so there is a sense that the oval is a semantic constraint. In other words, it is a meaning that requires *instantiation* or specification by other shapes if it is to be truly complete. In Cognitive Linguistics, grammatical meanings are schematic meanings that require instantiation by more precise lexical ones very much as ovals need instantiation by other shapes to become a face or something else (Holme

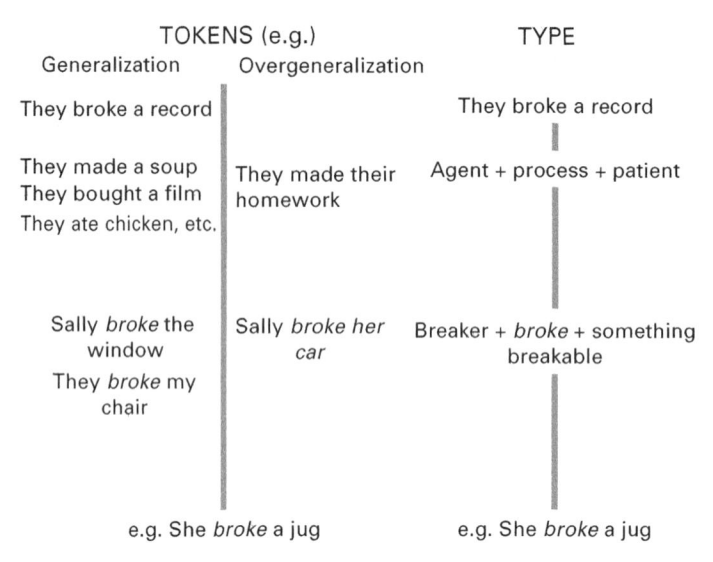

```
        TOKENS (e.g.)                              TYPE
   Generalization    Overgeneralization

They broke a record                          They broke a record
                                                      |
They made a soup     They made their         Agent + process + patient
They bought a film   homework
They ate chicken, etc.
                                                      |

Sally broke the      Sally broke her         Breaker + broke + something
   window               car                         breakable
They broke my
   chair
                                                      |


e.g. She broke a jug                         e.g. She broke a jug
```

Figure 28.1 *An emergentist model of language development*

2010). "Agent+process +patient" in fact describes an extremely productive series of constructions called *transitives*. Like the items of lexis of which they are comprised, such constructions are symbolic.

Words also have schematic meanings. What are traditionally called functional or closed class terms, or such items as determiners, prepositions and auxiliary verbs, are highly schematic because they exist to specify relations and always require completion by more precise terms (Talmy 2000). Thus the determiner, *the*, or preposition *in* needs to be followed by nouns, and means little when alone. Effectively such words open the semantic space into which a more precise nominal meaning must be inserted. Inevitably, schematic meanings are difficult to pin down or define. This is one reason why learners find it difficult to acquire grammatical meanings that do not exist in their own L1.

28.3.2 An emergentist model of construction learning

We can now see how a schematic and productive construction meaning, in this case, "agent+verb+patient" could emerge from a series of lexicalized examples of that meaning. Each of these examples will be a less schematic instance of that meaning. This process is illustrated in Figure 28.1.

The left line represents *tokens*, or words and constructions that are heard and reproduced. The right shows the *types* that are stored by the user. In the first instance type and token are the same in so far as the learner can reproduce what s/he hears. Next, a more schematic form emerges. Type and token match each other less closely. The acquired example can now be *generalized* as forms that the learner may never have heard. As with *Sammy broke a cup, Jane broke the jug* and *I broke the car* but not *I broke the house*, the learner will be testing the semantic constraints of the form. Generalization can therefore lead to *overgeneralization*. Finally, we can also note how the learner may also start to acquire other fixed exemplars of the construction such as *break a record*. Two questions now arise. The first asks whether this pattern of emergence fits with what learners do. The second concerns the processes that such learning requires.

28.3.3 Verb islands, chunking and construction generalization
A long-standing observation of first and second language acquisition is that learners move from single words to *chunks* or fixed phrases then to a more productive use of form (e.g. Wong-Fillmore 1976; Myles, Mitchell and Hooper 1999). Accordingly, much grammatical knowledge of early first language learners revolves around specific verbs or what have been called verb islands (Tomasello 1992). Thus *Doggie kiss me* will develop no further than a form that is still item based, for example Kisser+*kiss*+ kissee, affording the child the ability to say *Doggie kiss* but not *Mummy hug me* which must be learnt as a separate, hugger–huggee construction. In other words the schematic "agent+process+patient" takes a while to establish itself (Tomasello and Brandt 2009).

Goldberg and Casenhiser (2008) have studied how child language learners show an unprompted aptitude for construction generalization. The crucial prerequisite for construction generalization is acquiring a strong lexicalized example. In conjunction with other examples it makes the construction's meaning and pattern transparent, thus transforming it into the basis for generalization. N. C. Ellis (2002a) argues that sensitivity to type in second language acquisition encourages the abstraction of lexicalized forms into grammatical schemas. Thus more schematic types will begin to be extrapolated as more tokens are used. N. C. Ellis' argument is supported by Gries and Wulf (2005) in a study of the grammars of proficient L2 users of English with a German L1. Gries and Wulf found that their speakers operated at the interface of lexis and grammar with a proficiency that was equivalent to that of native speakers and processed constructions in much the same way.

Although the emergence of grammar allows a more productive use of form, creative construction use is not the sole hallmark of proficient learner discourse. A growing consensus from corpus studies shows much discourse consists of constructions with fixed lexis or limited lexical choice (e.g. Sinclair 1991) and much speech production consists of the same (Kormos 2006). Basically, words that mean more together stay together. When a construction sums up a central area of human experience, it may become widely used by a speech community, giving rise to an idiom or fixed phrase. A major part of the language learning burden therefore rests in these lexically instantiated constructions. In contrast, an impoverished repertoire of these fixed forms has come to be seen as a feature of non-native language (e.g. Boers and Lindstromberg 2008).

In the earlier stages of learning, therefore, learners may not have the lexis to understand or use the number of tokens needed to build a more schematic type. In the later stages, it can still be difficult to acquire the prefabricated constructions that make up so much of the native speaker's repertoire. Learners may also be unaware of the forms of conceptualization on which idioms depend for their meaning and so be unable to network them with similarly conceived forms, a point we will shortly explore in greater depth.

28.3.4 Syntactic bootstrapping

This model suggests a strong relationship between grammatical and lexical meaning and means that we learn much syntax from how lexis is combined with lexis. Less evident, but also possible, is that we may learn lexis with the help of syntax. This may explain data showing how our rate of lexical learning suddenly accelerates before dropping off again (Meara 2006; see also Chapter 21, this volume).

Bootstrapping refers to broadly using one knowledge form to help acquire another. Syntactic bootstrapping (Bloom 2002) is using syntax to learn vocabulary. In a construction-based model, this works as follows. Let us suppose that the learner acquires multiple tokens of a construction, *there is a _____ in my house*. The clause in fact establishes a type of category which we can call "things in a house." We can imagine a more productive locative category of things placed somewhere as "house" becomes "fridge" or "park." The use of the token itself establishes schematic meanings from the relationship between the located things. Effectively, by using the construction we are giving a new conceptual home to the lexical items we acquire and we can network them as part of a pattern of meanings. Lexis and grammar therefore help build each other. Knowing more lexically instantiated forms of a construction, and therefore more lexis, helps us establish the construction's schematic meaning. Knowing more schematic meanings allows us to network words together and store them more easily.

We now turn to closer a consideration of what cognition has to do for learning to occur.

28.4 Cognition and learning

28.4.1 Learning processes: intention sharing and pattern finding

Tomasello explores how two fundamental cognitive processes enable first language acquisition, *intention sharing* and *pattern finding* (2003). Intention sharing explains how, when an interlocutor points to an object and names it, the learner can enter their zone of attention and know what is being talked about. This is a human predisposition. Pattern finding explains how we can identify construction tokens (e.g. *Sammy broke a cup / Jane broke a jug*) as belonging to same schematic type and generalize its pattern to other forms.

Pattern seeking relates closely to categorization and is fundamental to animal cognition – all living things must sort phenomena on the basis of some perceived pattern. We know that frogs learn to categorize other animals as predators or prey and that amoeba make different chemical responses to different environmental stimuli. Categorization is fundamental to human visual processing since the data received by 100 million retinal detectors in the human eye must be transmitted along only one million neural fibres (Feldman 2006). Pattern sensitivity is also evident in phonological discrimination. For example, infants are sensitive to sound patterns in non-words, rejecting those that do not conform to the patterning in the languages they hear around them (Treiman and Danis 1988).

28.4.2 Learning processes: frequency

Pattern extrapolation cannot be disassociated from the frequency of an item in the input, however. Understanding a construction as a semantic relationship such as "agent+verb+patient" requires exposure to the tokens that illustrate that relationship and hence some *frequency* of occurrence. Forms which are found more frequently tend to be acquired more easily, though of course the learner must be able to register their occurrence. A strong common feature of first and second language findings is that learners seem to acquire grammatical morphemes in similar orders whatever their circumstances and whatever their first language (see discussion in Chapter 27, this volume). In SLA it was argued as long ago as 1975 that the order in which the morphemes are acquired corresponds to the frequency with which they occur in the input (Larsen-Freeman 1975).

When we look later at models of the brain and of the physical form taken by language knowledge we will note that this knowledge arises from stronger connectivity, as between a word and the phonemes from which it is assembled, and that word and a meaning. Stronger connections can result from more frequent exposure in sensory data and the perception of patterned relations of forms as somehow part of the same network, though not wholly so. Other features come into play, as we shall see.

28.4.3 Learning processes: perceptual saliency

Perceptual saliency refers to a general cognitive attribute whereby in a given scene we perceive one feature as more outstanding than others. This can affect our perception of meanings and the acoustic signals on which language depends (e.g. Slobin 1997; Goldschneider and DeKeyser 2001). A given entity will be made salient by its reoccurrence and thus attract greater cognitive attention, positing a strong link between saliency and frequency. For example, earlier research into Universal Grammar noted how Japanese learners of English found it straightforward to acquire what were called head-first constructions in English despite speaking what is categorized as a head-last language (Flynn 1987). Therefore, reproducing an English phrase *break the table* rapidly becomes straightforward for learners with a Japanese L1 despite the fact that the Japanese "head-last" equivalent might be *the table break*. This could be attributed to two levels of saliency. The first lies in the obviousness of the contrast between the word orders used to express the same meaning and the second to the frequency with which pattern reoccurs. Some more recent research has also shown how saliency is important in the acquisition of idioms (Lauren, Denhières, Passerieux, Lakimova and Hardy-Bayle 2006). The measurement of ERPs (event-related brain potentials) is an increasingly popular way to study brain activity because of how the procedure offers a non-invasive method of recording brain activity (see Chapter 19, this volume). Using such techniques to study our processing of idioms, Lauren et al. (2006) have shown how the salient elements in an expression are processed with relative ease and that this is unaffected by whether their meaning is figurative or not.

Another factor is Slobin's (1997) insight into how forms where learners identify a one-to-one relationship with a meaning are more easily acquired than those that presented them with multiple meanings. Using the assumption of this *one-to-one hypothesis*, Goldschneider and DeKeyser (2001) rated the simplicity or complexity of the item's form–function mapping. They further calculated an item's frequency from a corpus and using the assumption that sound patterns make an item salient, graded its saliency from its phonological characteristics. The finding was that variations in morpheme acquisition can be explained by a combination of the item's frequency, its perceptual salience and the straightforwardness of its meaning.

28.4.4 Frequency, saliency and first language effects

It has also been noted how the nature of the L1 imposes more variability in L2 acquisition than first thought (Kwon and Han 2008). Learners with some L1s skip stages in the natural order of morpheme acquisition, or never pass through others despite an otherwise high level of second language knowledge (see Chapter 5, this volume). Perception in a second language may also be affected by saliencies in the first (Holme 2009; see also Chapter 25, this volume). Our processing of any sensory data, whether it is visual or linguistic, involves its conceptualization. Thus Cantonese requires its speakers to look for key semantic information in vowels and their tones. When they encounter a language such as English, they will therefore treat the final consonants in English words in the input as lacking in salience, missing the key grammatical information encoded there.

28.4.5 Learning processes as emergent

Syntactic bootstrapping suggests how acquiring a construction's schematic meaning establishes an organizational principle that can further develop acquisition of lexis. Essentially, it expresses a principle where we learn to learn. Holich *et al.* (2000) set out a larger model for word learning by first language acquirers that accounts for the same exponential increase in the rate of vocabulary acquisition by showing how children attend to different cues at different moments in their development. Some of these cues relate closely to the strategies outlined. Thus an early cue may be intentional, as when an caregiver points out an object, connecting it to an utterance, whilst later a focus on salient items might itself be forced by the way in which learners are confronted with too many cues. Last, as language develops then language itself becomes a prop to further learning through context or even schoolroom definition.

28.5 Processability and competition

28.5.1 How language provides the means for its own learning

The principle of syntactic bootstrapping shows how language itself provides us with ways to learn more language. Pienemann's *Processability theory* can be read as illustrating this type of *emergentist* process in grammar learning (e.g. Pienemann 1998, 2005a). Pienemann sees the acquisition of one form before another as part of a larger need to assemble the more complex from the more straightforward, or to operate incrementally. The operation is achieved by what he calls a *language processor* that is acquired with the language itself. Thus, for example, we are initially unable to produce the verb+s morpheme in *the child speaks slowly* because our incremental learning pattern means that we are confined in the boundaries of each constituent, or phrase, in the clause (e.g. Pienemann 2007). This can be reinterpreted in terms of the construction-based model just outlined.

At an early stage the learner manages a grammatical utterance, *the child*, and perhaps another, *speak slowly*, but is confined by the boundaries of each, saying *the child speak slowly*. This is because the learner has not yet acquired the larger Agent+process construction needed to weld two semantic units into one. The learner is adding phrase to phrase whilst lacking the larger form and its sense of a schematic pattern to hold the phrases together.

28.5.2 Conceptualization and meaning

Image schemas are also important to our acquisition of lexical and constructional meanings. The example of a "*break* construction" revealed constraints on the meaning of the verb and hence upon its complementation that may not be evident to the learner at first. For example, English construes breakage from fracturing something with the hands, making *break a car* implausible unless *a car* refers to a toy or "the breaker" to a huge machine. Grammatical constructions also possess category meanings (e.g. Lakoff 1987; Langacker 2008a). Thus the image schema of force dynamics allows language learners to conceptualize the category meaning of what is called a caused motion construction (e.g. Goldberg 2006) and establish a common schematic meaning for such lexically different forms as *I pushed him out of the room, I knocked the castle down* or *I brushed the topic aside*.

Goldberg (1995) argues that infants learning basic constructions match their forms and associated experiences to pin down an already rich array of image schemas derived from their physical experience. Goldberg, Casenhiser and Sethuraman (2003) propose that when we acquire certain verbs, they act as "pathbreakers" to help us acquire clausal constructions, showing a more straightforward match between a construction's meaning and these image schemas. Thus *push* is a verb that identifies the caused motion construction's meaning and imagistic basis more clearly in *I pushed him out of the room* than the metaphorical *brush* in *I brushed the topic aside*. The message for language teachers is clear (Holme 2012). We can also note how the metaphorical and idiomatic *I brushed the topic aside* may be acquired more easily when the learner has a secure "caused motion" schema to give it a conceptual home.

28.5.3 Thinking for speaking: the problem of conceptual transfer

Our common anatomy and its experience of such universal environmental features as gravity, space and temperature ensure a common image schematic resource. This guarantees that many meanings are shared across languages, and that translation is a plausible activity. Second language learners do always need to work out the category boundaries implicit in newly encountered form–meaning pairings. They can instead reapply those they have already established for the first language. All languages, however, do not conceptualize phenomena in the same way, so that many idiomatic phrases are not always directly translatable. This may account for why obtaining a native speaker's idiomatic control of a language may be difficult.

Abstract meanings such as those associated with time are products of greater conceptual effort than ones which are derived from our experience of concrete phenomena, and are therefore more prone to vary (Lakoff 1987). As a consequence, operating and using a new language grammar to represent relationships such as those of time also requires an adjustment in the way these meanings are conceptualized. Image schemas evolve from human beings' common experience of phenomena such as light, heat, gravity, containment and solidity, but the representation of such concepts in different languages may also vary, creating, for example, different metaphorical representations (e.g. Gibbs 1994; Kövesces 2005). An extreme example comes from one or two languages that, like Aymara in Chile, conceive of time as space but treat the future as behind because it is hidden and the past as in front because it is known (Lakoff and Johnson 1999). The example is rare and extreme but it reveals how speaking a different language may oblige us to conceptualize reality differently.

Slobin (1996, 2007) proposed that we "think" to "speak," and that the idiosyncratic modes of conceptualization proposed by a language may cause its speakers to give a different emphasis to what they attend to in the world. Learning an L2 can then be made difficult by the use of modes of thinking for speaking, or conceptualizations that were established by the L1. Movement, color and spatial relations have been a particular focus of interest (Cadierno 2010). When looking at motion, Talmy (2000) proposed that languages divide between those that are satellite-framed (*S-languages*) and those that are verb-framed (*V-languages*). S-framing places the path of motion outside the verb and is the preferred type of construction in Germanic languages. Thus *go back* is a more common English expression than *return*, which derives from the V-framed French (*rentrer*). Because S-framed languages place the path outside the verb they can use the verb meaning to construe manner. English is particularly rich in verbs that construe manner but not path of motion (*stumble*, *stagger*, *trudge*, *trot*, etc.). Studies have claimed that learners show effects from how their L1 construes motion when learning an L2. Thus speakers of S- and V-framed L1s talk about motion differently when using an L2 (e.g. Slobin 2006). For example, Danish is S-framed, so speakers whose L1 is V-framed have more difficulties with its expressions of motion than those whose language is also S-framed (Cadierno 2010). In relation, Odlin (2008), when looking at learner narratives, has shown how learners derive movement, spatial and temporal relations from the L1's conceptual perspective.

A difficult issue concerns how far we can actually change patterns of conceptualization acquired with a first language when we learn a second, or whether we think to speak with the wrong modes of conceptualization and are continually weak when making a finer use of language. Studies in this area have focused on how gesture is itself a conceptual resource which expresses how we think. Kellerman and Van Hoof (2003) showed how we may start to change the way we gesture as we become fluent in an L2. Negueruela, Lantolf, Jordan and Gelabert (2004) studied Hispanic American bilinguals and showed that they tended to use English motion verbs with gestures that were a better match for their V-framed L1 Spanish. More recent studies support Kellerman's conclusions, however, arguing that new image schemas can be acquired with new languages (Choi and Lantolf 2008; Stam 2010).

Though methods of conceptualization may change over time, there seems to be little doubt that the use of schematic patterns derived from the L1 may cause problems in the second language. Further, if a language lacks a given conceptual distinction it will make the acquisition of related grammatical forms difficult, as when Chinese learners of English find it difficult to develop a full understanding of the meanings of English determiners (see also Chapter 24, this volume).

28.5.4 U-shaped learning and the Competition Model

Another important feature of both L1 and L2 learner language concerns *U-shaped learning*. Thus both L1 and L2 learners sometimes seem to unlearn irregular chunks such as *went* when they assemble erroneous forms such as *go-ed*. Finally, they sort out forms into regular and irregular (Cazden 1968). Thus learner development often follows a U-shaped path, beginning with a correct form–meaning pairing then oscillating back and forth between a successful and unsuccessful use of a form before it is finally sorted out. The overgeneralization of a form that seems to create the U path can be attributed to our eagerness for pattern seeking or our readiness to find a pattern. The sorting out of regular and irregular forms can be explained through another model, namely MacWhinney's *Competition Model* (Bates and MacWhinney 1987; MacWhinney 2005, 2008). The Competition Model proposes how we sort competing linguistic cues, describing language representation, processing and learning. U paths offer evidence of competition in learning and regular and irregular representations of a past tense might be seen as competing. The learner thus oscillates back and forth between competing forms until the frequency of one in the input ensures that the correct irregular establishes itself by strengthening the mental network of which it is a part and inhibiting that network's overlap with a "verb-*ed*" schema. Likewise a regular form establishes itself as the representation for those verbs whose past tense has never been encountered and where the input provides no competing irregular. This does not imply, however, that a verb-*ed* schema is a default form and that language adheres to a regularity principle. The brain is tabulating frequencies. Regular verbs that are used frequently may also be stored ready for use, for example *called* or *looked*. MacWhinney is proposing what is almost a Darwinian model of language acquisition. Larger formal networks dominate and extinguish smaller ones in the absence of competing data whilst being part of a larger verb+*ed* schema.

The Competition Model shows clearly how learning can map onto our increasing understanding of the human brain and the neural models through which it is explored. We therefore now turn to these. This means that we should first give some thought to the nature of the learning brain and then to the computer models used to represent its functions in ways that accord with what we know about language learning. The assumption will be that thought, and hence language, takes material form in the brain and so requires representation as such. Models of mind are therefore irrelevant.

28.6 Connectionism and complexity

28.6.1 Parallel processing models: the brain that learns

Parallel processing models assume that the larger part of cognitive processing is not specific to the sensory mechanisms from which knowledge of the world and of language is acquired. Called *connectionist*, such models replicate how the brain performs mental operations by making connections across *synapses* with *neurons* with degrees of strength established by usage.

The brain is essentially a network of different *connections* that are made, inhibited or let fall into disuse in response to how they are electrically excited by data that is fed into them through the senses. *Neurons* are nerve cells that respond to the stimulus of electric current and will bind to *synapses*, thus creating connections (see Chapters 19 and 20, this volume). The neuron's molecular structure changes its shape to become a channel through which the charge can flow. The biological basis of thought therefore involves tissue whose plastic nature allows it to process different types of data, particularly in infants and children (Deacon 1993). The changes in shape enable the neuron to send a signal through the synapse. The multiple shape changes caused by data passing through a network captures thought as a wave effect or flow, with each neuron responding to the current passed through it (Feldman 2006). This also means that connectivity is described in terms of weights, with the assumption of adjusted degrees of strength in the connections made.

At the level of language, differently weighted network connections could represent, for example, whether an entity is captured as the binding relationship between a word or construction and a network of category meanings, or as the fleeting recognition of such a relationship in a new language that is subsequently forgotten. It is also important to understand how knowledge exists in network relationships. Thus, when we return to our notion of pattern seeking and construction building, the networking of *Sammy broke a cup* and *Jane broke a jug*, or of the elements of which they are composed, will itself establish their schematic relationship. Essentially, the schematic meaning of the constructions can be conceived *as* their relationship. In other words, to network *a cup* and *a jug* one has to inhibit their specific meaning thus forcing the emergence of their common "breakable things" meaning.

A neuron can be recruited for different functions in the way that a node or point in a network may be connected to many others. Each neuron can receive signals from as many as 10,000 others and can combine these signals into a different transmission. In this sense, neurons are multifunctional. Learning is thought dependent on chemical change to the receiving and transmitting sides of the synapse. Learning is the excitation or inhibition of networks of units by usage. Elements of a task such as form–meaning recognition will be processed as minute and simultaneous processes.

Knowledge is basically a network of synaptic connections. Thus if one considers categories one can treat each as a network of subsidiary meanings and other knowledge. Thus our concept of an apple could be a network that involves possible colours, forms, taste, edibility and typical examples, all of which will be assembled from sensory data. Such networks model both the distinctive and interrelated nature of human knowledge, and language knowledge in particular. Since the number of neurons in a human brain is 10–100 billion with each having downstream connectivity to as many as 10,000, processing constraints do not appear to be an issue. In fact learning is better seen as specialization in how some of this capacity is used.

28.6.2 Parallel processing models: computer simulations

These neural networks are computer-based simulations of the type of learning just explained. Such parallel processing models tally the frequency of a given form by allocating it stronger or weaker network connections. They can further assemble data into more complex forms and therefore reflect the construction-based nature of language or thought. A basic network has two types of connections: input through which data is received and output through which information is sent to other networks. The input nodes connect to output nodes and information flows from input to output. The network simulates the different degrees or weights of connectivity found in the synapses of the brain. It can also inhibit the same.

The model imitates what is known as *recruitment learning*, where a network is formed on the basis of need. Thus the need to learn recruits the network through which the learning will be achieved. This also accounts for why some data are acquired rapidly, with a network rapidly being recruited and others lost or needing more effortful engagement (Feldman 2006). Rapid recruitment may be on the basis of an engagement of a network with other powerful schema, a factor that could show the influence of affect. Thus when a form is associated with a meaning which we find important, it will recruit a network more straightforwardly.

Image schemas can also be simulated with the associated network being defined. For example, the container schema is represented by the parameters, "inside, outside and boundary"; these are endowed with representation as a type of entity, thus "inside/outside" are regions and "boundary" is a "curve." Equally, to simulate how we elucidate the meaning of a category we can connect the image schema to a meaning such as "house," with the latter being partly associated with its containment of its inhabitants (Feldman 2006).

The grammars that these networks can account for remain at a rudimentary stage but they do, in principle, offer one of the few coherent explanations of how a language and its imagery could map onto the structures of the brain. Further, connectionist models are learning networks that modify themselves in response to new data. Their problem is that they cannot yet begin to recreate the massive parallelism afforded us by the brain's neuronal structure.

28.6.3 Neural nets and language learning

The computer programmes that simulate the brain's connectivity and learning from frequency effects was demonstrated by a pioneering experiment showing the U-shaped learning of the English past tense (Rumelhart and McClelland 1986). First Rumelhart and McClelland trained the network to reproduce ten common irregular verbs. The network "knew" only these verbs and produced their past tenses appropriately. Next they fed in 400 more verbs along with the ten irregular forms already used. The network now started to overgeneralize the irregular forms in the way just mentioned. As input built up, the computer started to get it right very much as the human infant does, and much as a Competition Model would predict, sorting regular from irregular forms (Rumelhart and McClelland 1986). Rumelhart and McClelland's model was subject to considerable criticism, however. Starting a debate that has continued ever since, Pinker and Prince (1988) claimed that the data in the input did not match that of the human infant because there was a sense in which the model knew what it was learning. The model also produced some strange forms never produced by any child because it could not always straightforwardly reproduce the stem of a regular verb, saying, for example, *membled* instead of *mailed*.

In opposition to the construction-based model of grammar advanced above, Pinker and Prince (1988) assumed that the mind was endowed with two systems, one of which used a rule-based algorithm to produce regular forms, adding *-ed* to an English verb stem, for example, and another which stored an irregular verb and called it up through the same mechanisms that connect word forms to their meaning (see Chapter 21, this volume). This principle has sought support from data showing how, when new verbs are derived, they take a regular form rather than following the principle of pattern-based similarities that the Construction Model assumes. Thus a Connectionist Model suggests we should say *wung* not *winged* because *fling–flung* / *sting–stung* set up a pattern for these verbs. Connectionists could claim, however, that this was predictable from their model because *-ed* is the most frequent form and therefore the one most likely to be generalized. More difficult for the connectionist argument was a claim that learners of German, who confront five types of plural morpheme (0, *-s*, *-e*, *-en* and *-er*), will use *-s* as a default plural when it has been calculated as applying to only 4 percent of forms in the input (e.g. Clahsen 1999). However, the data for German plural morpheme studies have been questioned. Most significantly the basis of comparison was *-s* and *-er*, with the latter being the least prevalent in the input (Dąbrowska 2004).

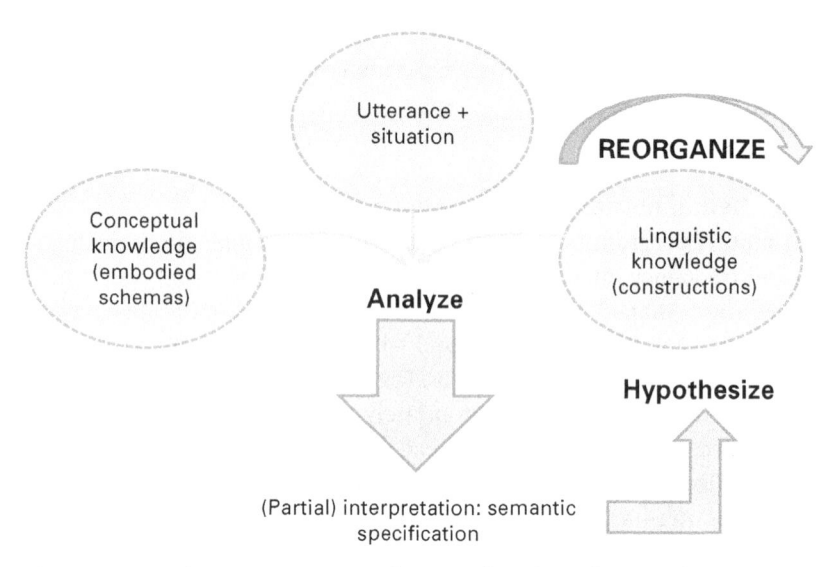

Figure 28.2 *Early stage construction learning (based on Chan 2008)*

Less contestable were studies done on the Polish genitive, or an inflection showing the possessive relation, as in the English *the cat's milk*. Despite the Polish genitive having no easily identifiable default form, and hence no probable rule-based algorithm, children seemed to learn its different forms quite easily, with frequency and patterning the most plausible explanation for why (Dąbrowska 2004). Connectionist models have also been modified by adding other levels of representation (Plunkett and Marchman 1991, 1993) and have demonstrated similar effects in the acquisition of the morphology of other languages such as the plural system of Arabic (Plunkett and Nakisa 1997).

Nelson (2007) criticizes connectionist models as potentially inapplicable to SLA because they do not separate out knowledge as memory and so cannot mimic the influence of one language on another. However, newer adaptive models are overcoming such defects (Larsen-Freeman and Cameron 2008). Nelson's criticisms also ignore how the model is basically one gigantic knowledge system where memorization is dependent on the strength of connectivity in a given network. Different networks have the hypothetical ability to engage in "cross talk" or interference and transfer of the kind that I have just characterized as part of language learning.

Chan (2008) has put forward a connectionist simulation of an early stage model of early first language, multiword construction learning. I illustrate this in Figure 28.2.

In this model the utterance and its situation are analyzed and the meaning of a construction computed by referring both to the infant's already acquired conceptual knowledge and to the constructions that the infant has previously stored. On the basis of this, a hypothetical form–meaning pairing may be added to those already stored. This results in the constant restructuring of the construction knowledge, a process that is ongoing as the form's hypothetical meanings are confirmed or rejected by their further occurrence. A second language model would differ because of first language influence. Though conceptually simple, L1 influence would be difficult to model. As discussed, it will occur at the semantic, formal and conceptual levels. Thus it will affect conceptual knowledge, semantic knowledge and construction knowledge, whilst constantly influencing how these restructure themselves.

28.6.4 Chaos and complexity

The Connectionist Model is based on a network where the reweighting of one connection can have a flow effect that will adjust to others. It is therefore dynamic, as Chan's (2008) model illustrates.

The interconnected nature of the neural model and the billions of neurons on which it depends cannot be grasped as a static or straightforwardly predictable learning system. We are studying not "individual variables," but "changes to systems" (Larsen-Freeman and Cameron 2008: 122). One consequence for research has been to try to capture language learning as a "flow model" or a dynamic system where different variables can be represented as constantly creating different consequences. Some proponents of emergentist views of acquisition, therefore, now look to complexity and chaos theory models from the physical and mathematical sciences to explain SLA (de Bot, Lowie and Verspoor 2007; N. C. Ellis 2005; N. C. Ellis and Larsen-Freeman 2006; Larsen-Freeman and Cameron 2008).

In the natural sciences and mathematics, researchers use flow models to capture complex phenomena that are constantly recreating the conditions of their own development. The need to understand such models has established what has become known as *complex* or *dynamic systems theory* and *chaos theory*. The meteorologist Edward Lorenz famously referred to how a variable as slight as "the flap of a butterfly's wings in Brazil" could trigger a "tornado in Texas." Chaos theory is something of a misnomer, however, since it does not suppose a subject that cannot be modeled. It rather stresses the non-linear nature of the processes at play, emphasizing how a given effect may not be fully predictable. The mathematical models such systems require, therefore, whether they are neurological, biological or climatic, look at flow effects, probabilities and what might emerge from them.

Dynamic systems tend to show non-linearity in development and can therefore represent the emergentist principle of an output that might be more than the sum of the input or at least point to a general "discrepancy between input and effects" (de Bot 2008b). In SLA, for example, Larsen-Freeman and Cameron (2008) view Meara's model of vocabulary acquisition as showing dynamic effects in how gradual learning leads to sharp exponential increases in knowledge then a dropping away of progress (Meara 2006;

see also Chapter 21, this volume). Evidence for the value of this approach is also drawn from Pienemann's (1998) Processability theory, where the acquisition of one grammatical item constructs the conditions for the attainment of another, thus creating what is interpreted as a flow model of acquisition.

Verspoor, Lowie and Van Dijk (2008) present a variety of evidence that shows the non-linear nature of progression in language acquisition, showing, for example, what Bates and MacWinney (1987) would call competition effects as a struggle of competing systems and subsystems. For example, they apply a cognitive concept of *carrying capacity* to SLA where growth is limited by the cognitive resources that the learner can make available. In the Connectionist Model of recruitment learning just shown, this is not a fixed limitation like a flow bottleneck but evolves from how cognition must recruit networks to make them available for new knowledge, perhaps in competition with old. In this respect, a study by Robinson and Mervis (1998) tracks how the rate of the acquisition of lexis will decelerate as that of multiword constructions picks up. One thus has a convergence of multiple developmental paths with each affecting the other in the manner that characterizes a dynamic system.

Dynamic Systems theory (DST) proposes that acquisition must be studied as an accumulative process that creates its own conditions and constantly adjusts to them. This claims some broader research implications. *Cross-sectional* sampling is thought to be questionable because it reduces a flow to static snapshots taken at intervals (Larsen-Freeman and Cameron 2008). *Longitudinal approaches*, on the other hand, can track language as flow-effects over time and within the larger environment which it affects and by which it is affected. *Micro-development* (Thelen and Corbetta 2002), or observing short instances in great detail, can also reveal the dynamic interaction of the many variables of learning.

Micro-development studies also promise an exploration of the relationship between how we develop DST in relation to *sociocultural theory* (SCT; see Chapter 3, this volume). SCT saw individual and societal development as dynamic processes where individual learning was achieved through an individual's larger modification of his/her own sociocultural and physical environment (Vygotsky 1978 [1933–35]). More concretely, a learner in conversation with a native speaker hears a construction s/he does not understand. The learner asks for an explanation. The explanation is provided but the learner is unsure. The learner repeats back what has been heard. The repetition reshapes what the interlocutor said as what the learner now feels s/he wanted to say. Cognition and the socioculture are therefore mutually developmental. Cognition is further distributed across society through such collective developments as literacy, and so achieves a magnified effect upon the individual's ability to learn. In a metaphorical sense, one thus perceives flow effects between the learning individual, the situation in which the individual learns and the cognitive networks this recruits.

In what is effectively a representative episode of this micro-genesis, Atkinson (2010) explores an embodied cognition as a *distributed* one. Thus Atkinson (2010) studies how apparently simple learning episodes come to possess an interaction of variables that could not be captured by a straightforward linear model. So when a Japanese girl learns English with a worksheet and a helping relative, the physical and spatial nature of the episode requires comprehension as language is externalized into a sociocognitive problem space between the girl and her helper by the worksheet. The worksheet is not seen as a passive source of language input or practice, nor even as the straightforward product of a distributed cognition. Essentially the worksheet is being recreated by the way the different participants pass it, point to it or whatever. This means the worksheet is not a mere object of use but becomes a significant factor in the shaping of the learning episode and the grouping of the participants in the learning space.

It remains debatable, however, first, whether these examples really model a dynamic system in the way their advocates assume, and second, whether if they do they can result in an understanding that goes beyond the co-construction of an elaborate metaphor of human learning. For example, the analysis of Meara's (2006) model of vocabulary acquisition may typify the misapplication of the flow metaphor. Though exponential, the rate of increase in vocabulary acquisition is linear and therefore does not model the probable paths from a convergence of multiple forces that a dynamic system assumes (Gregg 2010). Even Robinson and Mervis (1998) are extrapolating correlations from distinct learning paths and not tracking the mathematically more difficult processes of modeling their mutual flow effects. A risk is that if such variables could be modeled as dynamic effects they might be less well delineated than in linear studies. In other words, by showing how every variable impacts every other, each finally becomes unavailable for study as it vanishes into a gigantic flow effect. In the physical sciences, chaos and dynamic systems effects are the subject of involved mathematical modeling. A complex system such as climate can therefore be given some probable outcomes. SLA researchers have not yet shown whether they can model learning with such instruments. While the flow metaphor may help students of SLA to rethink what they do, it has yet to show if it will uncover more than the time-honoured problem of researching a process where the variables are hard to control and where each may have an impact on another.

28.7 Conclusion

In this chapter we have looked at how language can be acquired through usage as an emergent system. We have also looked at how the complexity of language is like that of an organism, emergent, or a product of aggregation and adaptation. Usage not only makes acquisition possible, it also creates the apparent complexity of the entity that is acquired. We have looked at a model of cognition that would make this picture of acquisition possible, where we can view the brain as a massive parallel network that, among other things, acquires language. In outline, therefore, we have a theory where knowledge of language can be given a perhaps hypothetical physical form. A challenge for the future will be to fit such models to the increasingly accurate picture we now have of the brain and its functions. Additional challenges will be to resolve how far language is stored and operated as lexical strings and how far these are abstracted into more productive schemas that afford language the productivity and creativity it can possess. Other future issues concern modeling within this framework how different languages affect each other, and understanding how learners can rework conceptual systems to cope with new linguistic meanings. Finally, we need a better understanding of how models should incorporate the learner's ability to represent language with language and so benefit from instruction.

29

Input, input processing and focus on form

Joe Barcroft and Wynne Wong

29.1 Introduction

Input is what drives language acquisition. Whereas production may also play an important role, without input, language acquisition cannot happen because it contains the linguistic information, or data, needed for a learner's second language system to develop over time (see also Chapter 10, this volume). Both generative (various chapters in this volume) and emergentist (Chapter 28, this volume) theories of the acquisition of syntax include roles for input. In generative theory, input interacts with Universal Grammar (UG) to trigger a series of expected stages of acquisition of syntax (see Chapter 27, this volume). In emergentist theory, evidence provided by the input shapes the development of syntax by interacting with lower-level learning mechanisms in the absence of UG (there is general rather than domain-specific knowedge, according to emergentist theory) or any other type of pre-existing constraints that are specific to language.

In this chapter we provide an overview of research and theoretical developments related to input and input processing as well as some intructional approaches that are aimed at providing learners with L2 input, in particular input enhancement. *Input* refers to meaningful samples of a target language to which a language learner is exposed in a meaningful context. This type of meaning-bearing input is also known as *primary linguistic data*. Primary linguistic data may be written or oral and contain instances or exemplars of various grammatical forms and other linguistic information that the learner attends to for meaning. Examples of input can range from spoken and written varieties of a story, a small piece of text or a series of individual sentences (e.g. *Please get into groups of three. Open your books to page ten*) in the second language classroom, to phrases (e.g. *Paper or plastic?*) or a single word (e.g. *Stop!*). An important feature of input is that there is a message for learners to attend and respond to.

Whereas input and input processing can be analyzed across multiple levels of linguistic analysis (phonology, morphology, syntax, discourse) and with regard to the acquisition of different linguistic subsystems, such as with regard to lexical and discourse-level competence, the primary focus of this chapter is input and input processing related to the acquisition of L2 grammatical features, such as morphosyntax and long-distance dependencies. Some key issues related to input processing and L2 lexical acquisition are also included.

The rest of the chapter is divided into the following sections: a definition of input; a historical overview of theoretical advances on input and input processing; an analysis of the concept of input in terms of levels of input; modalities of input; characteristics of input; consideration of input and the development of form–meaning connections; discussion of VanPatten's Model of Input Processing (including the relationship between attention to form and meaning); and input and L2 instruction (including techniques such as textual enhancement and processing instruction). The chapter closes with limitations and directions for future research.

29.2 Brief historical overview of theoretical advances on input and input processing

In 1967, Corder published his seminal essay on learners' errors, which many associate with the birth of contemporary SLA. Corder was the first to make a distinction between *input* and *intake* and helped to move the field forward by emphasizing the importance of focusing on processes of SLA rather than on product alone. *Intake* refers to the subset of input that becomes available as data or linguistic evidence available to the learner's developing linguistic system. The process by which input becomes intake is known in VanPatten's framework as *input processing* (1996: 10).

Over the past half century, research and theoretical developments in the field of SLA have advanced our understanding of the role of input, taking us from a general understanding of the importance and necessity of input for SLA to more precise and multifaceted accounts of how input is processed, why certain components of input become intake, how input processing leads not only to the acquisition of syntax and morphosyntax but also to the acquisition of other linguistic subsystems, such as lexis.

29.2.1 Krashen's Input Hypothesis

In the late 1970s and early 1980s, Krashen (1977, 1981, 1982, 1985) is noted for having proposed several important hypotheses about SLA in his Monitor Model. Krashen is credited with making a distinction between *acquisition* and *learning*. According to Krashen, acquisition is a subconscious process that is involved in constructing a new linguistic system and is outside of learners' awareness. For example, learners may intuitively know that one can say *redo* or *retake* but that *resleep* is not possible without being able to articulate why. Learning, on the other hand, is a conscious process. When learners rely on rules or explicit information about a grammatical form to complete a task or activity, they are relying on their "learned" (explicitly learned) system and are generally aware of this process. For Krashen, what learners *learn* is not necessarily what they have *acquired*. Therefore, teaching and error correction do not affect acquisition; they only affect learning. In what was known as the *Input Hypothesis*, Krashen claimed that comprehensible input is a necessary and sufficient ingredient for SLA. According to Krashen, formal instruction is not necessary. Acquisition occurs when learners have access to comprehensible input. If learners have access to an optimal amount of appropriate comprehensible input and their affective filter is low (i.e. anxiety is low), then acquisition is "unavoidable" (Krashen 1985: 4). Krashen describes optimal input as $i + 1$ input, or input with structures slightly beyond one's current level of competence.

Krashen's views have been criticized for being untestable and vague. For example, how can we measure the i in $i + 1$, and how much input is considered optimal? Despite such criticisms and whether or not one subscribes to Krashen's hypotheses, Krashen has made an impact in the field for underscoring the importance of the role of input in SLA.

29.2.2 Input and interaction

Long (1981) expanded on Krashen's proposals by focusing on the critical role of *interaction*, in tandem with input, for SLA (see Chapter 10, this volume). According to Long, interaction provides L2 learners with opportunities to negotiate meaning, and this process has, as one of its many benefits, the effect of rendering input more comprehensible (e.g. requests for clarification such as *What?* or *Excuse me?* during interaction can prompt an interlocutor to rephrase and circumlocute until the intended message is understood) (see also Long 1996, on the role of the linguistic environment in L2 acquisition). Therefore, one of the important functions of interaction is to generate more comprehensible input.

29.2.3 Input and input processing

In the 1990s, the work of VanPatten (1996) and Gass (1997) further advanced our understanding of the relationship between input and SLA with more fine-grained consideration of the relationship between input and other processes in SLA from the perspective of information processing. In VanPatten's model of SLA, at least three processes can be identified.

Input → Intake → Developing linguistic system → output
I. Input Processing   II. Restructuring   III. Access

The first process, input processing, deals with the creation of intake from input. Input that learners attend to and process is converted to intake, the subset of input that is actually usable for acquisition. If intake becomes internalized, it is incorporated into the learner's developing linguistic system and restructures the linguistic system. Intake that has been internalized may in turn be accessed for output.

Gass's (1997) model is similar to VanPatten's in that it also posits that only input that has been processed is usable for acquisition.

Input → Apperceived input → Comprehended input → Intake → Integration → Output

In Gass's model, input must first be apperceived (the learner knows there is something out there to pay attention to), and then comprehended before it becomes intake. Intake that has been integrated into the learner's developing L2 system may eventually be retrieved as output.

What both VanPatten's and Gass's models underscored in the 1990s was that acquisition is dependent on input and not output, and that only input that has been attended to and comprehended in some way is usable for acquisition. Note that steady-state language speakers who have acquired a language also process input, but the linguistic systems of these individuals will not continue to be *restructured* per se. However, input continues to provide opportunities for language development, such as opportunities for vocabulary learning, throughout one's lifespan.

Two other perspectives on input processing are those of Carroll (2001), who focuses on the role of parsing, and O'Grady (2003), who focuses on the role of computational complexity (see also Chapter 26, this volume). According to Carroll, acquisition takes place by means of a series of parsing failures. When the in-born parser in the learner's mind/brain parses input in a way that does not correspond to the real-world information conveyed by the input, opportunities arise for the parser to make adjustments. Consider, for example, that a learner processes the sentence *A María la mira Elena* as "María is watching Elena" instead of correctly as "Elena is watching María" because the learner's parser assigns the role of subject to the first noun (María) without making use of the direct object marker *a*. If the learner hears this sentence but observes that in the real world Elena is watching María (and not vice versa), the learner's parser has an opportunity to *notice* the failure and make appropriate adjustments. If the parser manages to make the adjustment, acquisition proceeds into a new stage of development. As Carroll has indicated, however, opportunities such as the one described may not be readily available; the real-world information provided by input may continue to be missed, denying the parser needed opportunities to respond to processing failures and to make appropriate adjustments.

O'Grady's (2003) perspective on processing focuses on computational complexity, or the structural distance between items that are coreferential (see

Chapter 19, this volume). Distance here does not refer to length, such as in sentence length, but to the number of syntactic nodes that intervene in cases of coreference. Consider, for example, the following two sentences:

(1) The horse raced past the barn and fell.

(2) The horse raced past the barn fell.

Sentence 2 is a fairly commonly known *garden path sentence* in which the phrase *raced passed the barn* is an adjective phrase that modifies *horse* (in other words, someone raced the horse past the barn before the horse fell). Sentence 2 is more computationally complex than sentence 1 (but shorter) because *raced* initiates an intervening adjective phrase and is not just part of the verb phrase. The increased computational complexity of sentence 2 is apparent even to native speakers of English, so imagine the difficulty it might pose for L2 learners of English. According to O'Grady, sentences with more computationally complex coreference are more difficult for L2 learners to process. O'Grady, Lee and Choo (2003) have provided convincing evidence for this assertion in a study on speakers of English processing Korean sentences. The Korean sentences contained subject relative clauses or direct object relative clauses, the latter being more computationally complex. As would be predicted, the learners interpreted sentences with subject relative clauses correctly more often (73.2%) than they did sentences with direct object relative clauses (22.7%), and reversal errors were strikingly more common with direct object relative clauses (43.4%) as compared to subject relative clauses (9.8%).

29.3 Breaking down the concept of input

29.3.1 Levels of input

Input and input processing can be analyzed at multiple levels with regard to the acquisition of different linguistic subsystems. Suppose that an L2 learner of Spanish hears the following sentence: *Quiero que anotes dos goles en el partido de fútbol mañana* "I want you to score two goals in the soccer game tomorrow." Consider how much information is being presented in this one sentence about Spanish as a linguistic system. Regarding morphosyntax, the sentence contains information about the meaning of Spanish verb morphology (*-o* marking first-person singular and *-s* marking second-person singular) and mood (*anotes* as the subjunctive form of the verb *anotar* "to score"). In terms of vocabulary, the learner is exposed to a number of lexical items and a context from which to try to infer the meanings of new words. If the learner had never heard of the verb *anotar* "to score" previously, the learner may be able to infer the meaning of this word from context. Given that all L2 learners have limited processing capacity (i.e. learners can only process a limited amount of information at any given time), the learner may not be able to attend to all of this information, but the information is there.

29.3.2 Modalities of input

The physical sources used to produce and perceive input vary depending upon whether one is learning a spoken language, a signed language, a tactile signed language, or another tactile form of communication such as Braille. For spoken languages, input is spoken but also may appear in written form. When spoken, it is the result of modified sounds produced by the vocal tract and, of course, is often accompanied by other modalities of input, such as the visual during the use of gestures or tactile when a caregiver hands a child an item and says the name of item, demonstrating that spoken languages are not constrained to the spoken modality only (see Chapter 9, this volume). When written, language may be handwritten or typed in one of the many scripts of different languages spoken throughout the world. Unlike what is typical for children learning their L1, adolescent and adult L2 learners are often exposed to written input in the target L2 while they are learning the spoken form of the language (children learning L1 typically acquire the spoken variety before learning the written). For signed languages, input is visual in nature, involving different contrastive features than those used for spoken languages. Whereas spoken languages make use of acoustically based contrastive features such as place and manner of articulation and the presence or absence of voicing in the vocal tract, signed languages make use of visually based contrastive features such as hand shape, movement, location. Finally, individuals who are both blind and deaf can communicate using a tactile rather than visual variety of a signed language. In this case, learners perceive input tactically with their hands by feeling the signs of another individual. Another type of input available for individuals who are blind and deaf or who are blind only is Braille, a system of communication based on raised dots that can be perceived by running one's fingers over them.

29.3.3 Amount of input and length of utterances

In addition to the different basic types of input, the characteristics of input can vary greatly, depending upon the nature of individual(s) who are providing the input and the manner in which they create and provide the input. To begin, the length or overall amount of input provided on any given occasion can vary greatly. Depending upon the nature of the linguistic environment, language learners (both L1 and L2) may be provided with input that varies in length of utterance from continuous extended discourse for hours (e.g. reading a book to a child or discussing literary aspects of a novel) to single words produced in isolation. Interestingly, Brent and Siskind (2001) found that isolated words constituted 9 percent of the spoken input provided to children while they are aquiring their L1, demonstrating that input of this nature is substantial and not an anomaly when it comes to naturally occurring input produced by caregivers.

Modified and unmodified input

Input also can be either modified or unmodified. *Unmodified input* is unaltered in the sense that the speaker (or writer or signer) providing the input does not change the form or content of the original message conveyed. *Modified input*, on the other hand, is input that is altered in some way by a speaker (or writer or signer) for a particular purpose. Input can be modified so that it is (or sounds) more complex, such as if one were to say *Observe how quickly Jane is darting across the roadway* as a modified version of *See Jane run*. When it comes to being understood by language learners, however, modification in the opposite direction, toward more *simplified input* (e.g. *See Jane run* instead of the other sentence) is often necessary.

Hatch (1983) listed a series of general and specific characteristics of simplified input that is provided for L2 learners. These include *slower rate* (e.g. fewer reduced vowels and contractions, longer pauses, more stress on nouns); *simplified vocabulary* (e.g. more higher frequency vocabulary, providing definitions, more use of gestures, pictures, or both); *simplified syntax* (e.g. shorter sentences, more repetition and rephrasing, more postverbal modification than preverbal modification); *simplified discourse* (e.g. speaker includes comprehension checks such as via response choices and tag questions); and a *more familiar speech setting* (meeting and communication in the same place each day).

Some might argue that certain languages do not lend themselves to such simplification of input, making it difficult to provide input solely in the target language from the very first day of instruction in a second language, but this is simply not the case. As with children who learn their L1s while being exposed to input in their L1 only, *any* L2 can be taught entirely in the target language from the very first day. If learners do not understand an instructor speaking in the target language, it is likely that the instructor needs to simplify the input s/he is providing to a greater degree, by, for example, taking into consideration the above list. On the first day of class, for example, the instructor might focus on using the phrase *This is... / These are...* and name a series of items in the classroom (*This is the chalkboard. These are the windows. This is my cell phone...*). Even this very basic phrase, along with the various items it helps the instructor to name, is an example of meaning-bearing input. Naming items in the real world is meaningful, and by repeating a single phrase of this nature while adding new lexical items one at a time (and then repeating those as well as appropriate), an L2 instructor is able to provide input that is meaningful and comprehensible, at the level of $i + 1$ in Krashenian terms on the very first day of class (while still acknowledging that the construct of $i + 1$ may be difficult to define precisely when it comes to language instruction across different levels, or to operationalizing experimentally).

Interactional and non-interactional input

Input can be either interactional or non-interactional. As noted previously with regard to the work of Long (1981), *interactional input* tends to be more comprehensible because it allows for negotiation of meaning. *Non-interactional input* is more challenging (e.g. listening to the radio) because there is no negotiation of meaning. Consider, for example, the following segment of an interaction between a native speaker (NS) and a non-native speaker (NNS) of English (from Long 1983a: 180):

(3) NS: Do you like California?
 NNS: Huh?
 NS: Do you like Los Angeles?
 NNS: Uhm...
 NS: Do you like California?
 NNS: Yeah, I like it.

In this conversation, which could occur either in a classroom or in a more naturalistic setting (immigrants learning an L2 in the absence of formal instruction), meaning is negotiated until the learner is able to understand the intended question of the native speaker. The provision of an alternative proper name (Los Angeles as a proxy for California) provides the non-native speaker with an additional opportunity for understanding the intended question. Then, when asked the original question a second time, the non-native speaker is able to respond. Note also that NNSs also may provide input to one another, and then the input will reflect characteristics of their interlanguage.

Acoustically varied and acoustically consistent input

Input can be acoustically varied versus acoustically consistent in varying degrees. One of the defining features of human speech is that acoustic realizations of individual linguistic forms vary. Acoustic properties of individual words and sentences vary when produced by different talkers or by a single talker on different occasions. Interestingly, studies (Barcroft and Sommers 2005; Sommers and Barcroft 2007) have demonstrated that increasing the variability of certain acoustic features of input positively affects L2 vocabulary learning. (See also Chapter 21, this volume.) Holding the total time of exposure and number of exposures to target L2 words constant, increased acoustic variability based on the use of multiple talkers, multiple speaking styles (produced by a single talker) and multiple speaking rates (based on a single talker) yield positive and additive effects on L2 vocabulary learning. Whereas the use of one talker resulted in productive vocabulary accuracy mean score of 38 percent, for example, the use of three talkers resulted in a mean score of 45 percent, and the use of six talkers resulted in a mean score of 64 percent. These substantial gains speak to the potential of using acoustically varied input in the L2 classroom and as part of L2 instruction in general.

Naturalistic, enhanced structured input

Finally, L2 input can either be completely naturalistic, enhanced or structured in some manner in an attempt to draw learners' attention to a target form, to require learners to process a target form in a more effective manner, or both. If input is modified for the purpose of making it more comprehensible, that is, for the purpose of being understood by a listener, such input can still be considered *naturalistic*. In fact, modifications of this nature are oftentimes unconscious on the part of the speaker. If input is enhanced or structured for pedagogical purposes, on the other hand, input of this nature falls out of the category of being naturalistic, even though it may still be meaning-bearing. Options for using input enhancement and structured input in L2 pedagogy are discussed in greater detail below; the appendix furnishes examples of structured input.

Is explicit information input?

If delivered in the L2, explicit information may be another type of input that one finds in some L2 classrooms. When instructors are explaining a particular grammar point to learners in the L2, they are communicating a message to students, and in that sense, we can say that meaning-bearing input is also involved. However, it must be noted that the "input" in explicit information about a particular target item does not necessarily provide input containing that target item; it only talks *about* the target item as a topic and may or may not include the target item itself. For example, we can say to students, "To make a noun plural in English, you add an *s* to the noun. If the noun already ends in *s*, you add *es*." While this explicit information contains a message for learners to attend to, it does not contain any plural forms of nouns. The explicit information only speaks about plural forms as a topic.

29.4 Input and the development of form–meaning connections

When we speak of input as being the driving force for SLA, we are speaking of input that is meaning-bearing and comprehensible, at least to a substantial degree. Why is it that input needs to be meaning-bearing and largely comprehensible for successful SLA? The answer to this question concerns a critical cognitive construct and mechanism underlying SLA and language acquisition in general: *form–meaning connections (or mapping)*. In order to aquire a language successfully, learners must connect (or map) a wide range of linguistic forms onto their meanings. If the input is not meaning-bearing or sufficiently comprehensible, learners have nothing onto which they can map the form. They might hear a new form in the input, but if they cannot ascertain its meaning from the larger linguistic context, they cannot make an appropriate form–meaning mapping.

With L2 vocabulary learning, for instance, we find a very basic yet telling situation regarding the relationship between form and meaning. L2 learners need to attend to three critical components of a new word: its form, its meaning and the mapping between form and meaning. Take the word "rose" as an example. An L2 learner of English must (i) learn the phonological form and written form of this word; (ii) learn its meaning, including basic referential and conceptual properties (has petals, is often red, often appears among the thorns) and a host of semantic properties and associations, many of which can be quite personal and ideolectic in nature (e.g. "I like roses but prefer Gerbera daisies"; "Roses are so much less expensive in Ecuador than in other places"); and (iii) make connections between the form and meaning of the word (the form *rose* and the meaning of "rose"). Input and input processing allow the learner to advance in all three of these subprocesses over time.

When it comes to syntax and morphosyntax, the nature of the form–meaning mapping, or the *form–function relationship*, may be less direct and can be redundant with lexical items, context, or both in terms of the meaning it conveys. Syntactic and morphosyntactic forms have meaning, such as past-ness, future-ness, direct-object marking to indicate who did what to whom, but these can be challenging to acquire because their meanings are sometimes hidden due to the history and evolution of language. Grammatical gender in Spanish is one example. We say *la casa blanca* "the white house" to comply with rules of grammatical gender (in this case, feminine) in Spanish, but little referential meaning is lost if one violates this rule and says *la casa blanco (even though other costs many ensue, such as slower reaction times from native speakers; see Chapter 19, this volume). Another example is third-person *-s* in English. Because of required overt subjects in English, this *-s* is redundant with the information conveyed by the subject of the sentence. For this reason, instructional interventions such as structured input (see explanation and examples below and in the appendix) can be designed so as to create contexts that highlight or revive what remains of the *meaning* (or the *inherent semantic value* as per VanPatten 1996) of the (morpho)syntactic feature in question or to make the learner's parser fail and adjust, as under Carroll's (2001) perspective.

Of course output and output processing also help to promote acquisition via the development of form–meaning connnections. Here one must distinguish between *output with access to meaning* versus *output without access to meaning* (see Lee and VanPatten 2003). The former is truly communicative in nature whereas the latter is a parroted type of output, such as what one might produce during an audiolingual repetition or substition drill (see, e.g., Fries 1945). Output without access to meaning (the parrot variety of output) can affect L2 acquisition negatively. In the area of L2 vocabulary acquisition, for example, Barcroft (2006) demonstrated a decrease in intentional L2 vocabulary learning when learners were required to copy target L2 words while viewing word-picture pairs (a form of output without access to meaning) as compared to when they were not required to copy them (but simply to view them and try to learn them).

29.5 VanPatten's Model of Input Processing

Learners are *limited capacity processors* in that they cannot attend to and process everything to which they are exposed in the input all at once. In consideration of previous research on challenges involved in attending to more than one task at a time (e.g. Wickens 1984) and related research in the area of SLA (e.g. VanPatten and Cadierno 1993), VanPatten (1996) proposed a *Model of Input Processing* and a series of input processing (IP) principles and subprinciples that were designed to begin to account for how L2 learners allocate their limited processing resources when presented with sentence-level input.

29.5.1 Principle 1: The Primacy of Meaning Principle

The first principle and subprinciples of the IP Model (VanPatten 2004) postulate that learners process input for meaning before they process it for form. Therefore, it is expected that learners will attend to more meaningful grammatical forms before less meaningful ones.

> Principle 1 (P1). The Primacy of Meaning Principle. Learners process input for meaning before they process it for form.
> P1a. The Primacy of Content Words Principle. Learners process content words in the input before anything else.
> P1b. The Lexical Preference Principle. Learners will tend to rely on lexical items as opposed to grammatical form to get meaning when both encode the same semantic information.
> P1c. The Preference for Non-redundancy Principle. Learners are more likely to process non-redundant meaningful grammatical form before they process redundant meaningful forms.
> P1d. The Meaning before Non-meaning Principle. Learners are more likely to process meaningful grammatical forms before non-meaningful forms irrespective of redundancy.
> P1e. The Availability of Resources Principle. For learners to process either redundant meaningful grammatical forms or non-meaningful forms, the processing of overall sentential meaning must not drain available processing resources.

P1f. The Sentence Location Principle. Learners tend to process items in sentence-initial position before those in final position and those in medial position.

Following VanPatten, a concept that is useful when considering whether a learner will process a given form is *communicative value* of the form. The more communicative value a form has, the more likely it will be attended to when it appears in the input. Communicative value is determined by two components: (i) the *inherent semantic value* of the form and (ii) *redundancy*, or the extent to which the meaning conveyed by a form is redundant in a given context. The more inherent semantic value a form has, the higher its communicative value. The more redundant a form is, however, the lower its communicative value. Consider the following sentence:

(4)   Last night Martha watched television.

Past tense is encoded in two ways in (4): *last night* and the morphological form *-ed* on the end of the verb *watch*. The morphological form *-ed* is considered redundent because the meaning it encodes, i.e. past, is already expressed by the phrase *last night*. Therefore, we say that this form has low communicative value. The Model of Input Processing would predict that this form will be less likely to be attended to by learners to get the meaning of past because learners are more likely to attend to forms with higher communicative value (e.g. *last night*) than forms of lower communicative value. Furthermore, the sentence location subprinciple (P1f) would also predict that because the form *-ed* is in a medial position, the least salient position, this would make it even more difficult for learners to process this form.

However, efforts can be made to reduce the extent to which a target form appears in a redundant context in order to force learners to attend to whatever inherent semantic value the form may have, such as in the following sentence:

(5)   Martha watched television.

The *-ed* in (5) has a higher communicative value than it did in (4) because learners cannot rely on anything else but the *-ed* in (5) to understand that the tense in this sentence is past tense. Therefore, input may be *structured* so that forms of lower communicative value can take on a higher communicative value to increase the likelihood that learners may process it.

As another example, many L2 English learners continue to have difficulty with third-person singular *-s* despite its high frequency in the language. Drawing on P1 of the Model of Input Processing, this difficulty may stem from the fact that this form has no communicative value. Third-person singular *-s* is always a redundant form because English is not a pro-drop language. As illustrated in (6), third-person singular *-s* is always present along with its subject pronoun.

(6)   **He** read**s** the newspaper everyday.

Therefore, communicative value as opposed to frequency only may be needed to explain this phenomenon.

29.5.2 Principle 2: The First Noun Principle

The First Noun Principle (P2) deals with how word order affects processing strategies. This principle postulates that learners have a tendency to assign the role of agent to the first noun in a sentence or utterance even when the first noun is not the subject.

> Principle 2 (P2). The First Noun Principle. Learners tend to process the first noun or pronoun they encounter in a sentence as the subject or agent.
>
> P2a. The Lexical Semantics Principle. Learners may rely on lexical semantics, where possible, instead of word order to interpret sentences.
>
> P2b. The Event Probabilities Principle. Learners may rely on event probabilities, where possible, instead of word order to interpret sentences.
>
> P2c. The Contextual Constraint Principle. Learners may rely less on the First Noun Principle if preceding context constrains the possible interpretation of a clause or a sentence.

For example, in the following sentence, P2 would postulate that learners will think Tom kissed Jane because Tom is the first noun they encounter in the sentence.

(7) Tom was kissed by Jane.

However, the subprinciples of P2 also predict that lexical semantics, event probablities and contextual constraints, can override the first noun strategy such as in (8).

(8) The canary was eaten by the cat.

In (8), learners would correctly identify the cat as the animal who ate the canary because they know that canaries do not eat cats.

29.5.3 Empirical support for VanPatten's Model of Input Processing

In a study by Musumeci (1989), learners of French and learners of Italian were required to assign tense to input sentences in one of four conditions: (i) verbal inflections accompanied by adverbials of time; (ii) verbal inflections accompanied by a teacher's gestures (e.g. thumb over one shoulder to denote past) but no adverbial marker of tense; (iii) verbal inflections accompanied by an adverbial and a physical gesture; and (iv) verbal inflections only as the only source of information about the tense of a sentence. Musumeci found that participants who received both verbal inflections and adverbials, and participants who received verbal inflections plus adverbial plus gesture outperformed the two conditions that did not receive adverbials. This finding suggests that the presence or absence of a temporal adverb played a significant role in tense assignment and supports the primacy of meaning principle that learners will process lexical items over grammatical markers when both encode the same information. In a similar study by Cadierno, Glass, VanPatten and Lee (1991), the researchers found that learners of Spanish also performed better on tense assignment of sentences when they had access to temporal adverbs as opposed to being provided with verbal inflections alone.

In another study using online and offline procedures, VanPatten and Keating (2007) investigated whether L2 temporal reference processing is influenced by L1 processing procedures, and whether L2 learners can achieve nativelike processing abilities. Native and non-native speakers of Spanish were asked to read Spanish sentences that contained an adverb that either matched or did not match the inflection of the verb. Using eye-tracking and comprehension questions, results showed that beginning and intermediate learners of Spanish relied on adverbs to resolve temporal conflicts while advanced learners and native speakers relied on verb inflections. In the second part of the experiment, the researchers found that L1 English speakers relied much more on adverbs to resolve temporal conflicts in their L1. This finding suggests that the beginning and intermediate learners in the first part of the experiment were using an L1 strategy to interpret the Spanish sentences. In the third part of the experiment, data from Spanish L1 speakers learning ESL showed that these beginning English learners also relied on adverbs and not verb inflections, suggesting that there was no transfer from Spanish. VanPatten and Keating thus concluded that (i) the reliance on adverbs is a universal strategy (at least as a starting point) for processing temporal reference (supporting the Lexical Preference Principle), and (ii) nativelike processing is attainable in adult SLA (at least for the type of processing they investigated).

The trade-off that can arise between processing for form and meaning with sentence-level input also can be seen at the level of lexis. Studies on *lexical input processing* have demonstrated that increased semantic processing (increased focus on the meaning-related properties of words) can decrease L2 word form learning, such as when learners make pleasantness ratings, address specific questions about word meaning, or write target words in sentences (Barcroft 2002, 2003, 2004). Although increased semantic processing can facilitate recall of previously acquired (known) words, as predicted by the *levels-of-processing* (LOP) framework (Craik and Lockhart 1972), the negative impact of increased semantic processing on *novel* L2 word form learning is not unintuitive if one considers the difference between these two tasks (memory for known words in a list versus *new* word forms). The predictions of Barcroft's (e.g. 2002) *type of processing – resource allocation* (TOPRA) model are consistent with the positive (LOP) effects of increased semantic processing on recall of known words and the negative (inverse-LOP) effects of increased semantic processing on learning new L2 word forms. According to the TOPRA model, form processing, semantic processing and processing for mapping are dissociable. As one of these three types of processing increases, the other two types of processing must decrease in order to accommodate, and the learning counterparts for each type of processing reflect trade-offs of this nature. For example, attending to questions about the meaning of target words can decrease one's ability to learn the written forms of target words (Barcroft 2003).

Support for the first noun principle (P2) may be found in the pre-test data of VanPatten and Wong (2004), who investigated the French causative structure. The causative structure in French is formed with the verb *faire* "to make, do."

(9) Jean fait promener le chien à Marie.
John makes to walk the dog to Marie
"John makes Mary walk the dog."
(VanPatten and Wong 2004: 99)

When learners were asked "Who walks the dog?", they answered "Jean" because Jean is the first noun in the sentence. In VanPatten and Wong (2004), participants were given a set of similar sentences to process. When asked to indicate who was doing the action, all participants consistently selected the first noun of each sentence as the agent of dog-walking. Other studies with data to support the observation that learners tend to rely on the first noun as the agent of sentences include Lee (1987), LoCoco (1987), Gass (1989) and McDonald and Heilenman (1992).

To summarize, the principles in VanPatten's Model of Input Processing describe how L2 learners process input to create intake. Given that input is something that second language teachers can maniupulate, we now turn to the pedagogical implications of this model.

29.6 Input and L2 instruction

The recognition that input is a fundamental ingredient of successful L2 acquisition has led to the development of many pedagogical interventions that attempt to provide L2 learners with the right type of input for acquisition in addition to helping them focus on the formal features of input. Many of these techniques are known as input enhancement techniques.

29.6.1 Input enhancement

A term coined by Sharwood Smith (1981, 1991), *input enhancement* refers to pedagogical interventions that attempt to make specific features of L2 input more salient so that learners will be more likely to pay attention to these features (1991: 118). Rutherford and Sharwood Smith (1985) offer the following as examples of input enhancement:

> A simple example would be the use of typographical conventions such as underlining or capitalizing a particular grammatical surface feature, where you merely ask the learners to pay attention to anything that is underlined or capitalized. Another example would be the deliberate exposure of the learner to an artificially large number of instances of some target structure in the language on the assumption that the very high frequency of the structure in question will attract the learner's attention to the relevant formal regularities. (1985: 271)

Input flood

The technique of exposing L2 learners to an artificially large number of exemplars of a target form in input is known in the research literature today as *input flood*. Input flood may be used with either written or oral input. In the written mode, input is modified so that many instances of the target form may be embedded. In the oral mode, the target form may be embedded in speech or it could be embedded in written input and then read aloud to learners. The rationale behind input flood is that if a particular form appears over and over again in input, learners may be more likely to notice it. Gass (1997), for example, has proposed that the frequency of a target structure can have an impact on the liklihood that learners will notice it.

Empirical studies that have investigated the impact of input flood suggest that while this technique may be beneficial for showing learners what is permissible in an L2, it may be less effective when the goal is to help them see what is not possible in the L2. Trahey and White (1993), for example, examined whether input flood could be used to teach adverb placement in English to 10- to 12-year-old French-speaking EFL learners. The rules for adverb placement in French are different from English. While both English and French allow an adverb to appear after the object ("John watches TV often" / *Jean regarde la télé souvent*), French does not allow the adverb to precede the verb like English does ("John often watches TV" / **Jean souvent regarde la télé*). Additionally, French prefers that an adverb comes between the verb and object (*Jean regarde souvent la télé*) but this construction is not allowed in English (***"John watches often TV"). Trahey and White (1993) found that while input flood was effective in helping learners learn which adverb placement positions were possible in English, it was not effective in helping them learn which positions were not permissible. The subjects came to know that it was possible to place an adverb before the verb ("Bill carefully drives his Porsche") but they also thought that sentences such as "***Bill drives carefully his Porsche" (permissible in French but not in English) were possible. Thus, it appears that input flood as an input enhancement technique may help learners know what is correct or what might be lacking in their linguistic system but it may not be as effective as showing them what is not correct.

Typographical input enhancement

The technique that involves using typographical conventions such as underlining grammatical forms in input that Rutherford and Sharwood Smith described is known today as *typographical input enhancement* or *textual enhancement*. Textual enhancement is typically carried out in the written mode and minimally involves the following: (a) learners are engaged in reading written input for referential meaning and (b) particular features of the written input are enhanced via the use of typographical cues. The typographical manipulation in textual enhancement may involve changing the font style, enlarging the character size, underlining, **bolding**, using *italics*, highlighting with color or any combination of these. Textual enhancement is typically carried out by embedding the desired target structure in authentic texts and then making those structures salient through the manipulation of typographical cues. In many cases, input in the text may need to be modified to allow for the embedding of multiple exemplars. The goal of textual enhancement is to render more salient targeted features of written input that may not be perceptually salient in hopes that learners will be more likely to pay attention to these elements.

How textual enhancement might impact L2 development has been investigated by a number of studies since the late 1990s and has been the focus of some review articles (Simard 2002; Han, Park and Combs 2008) as well as a meta-analysis of the research (Lee and Huang 2008). As these review articles have pointed out, any role that textual enhancement might play in SLA is inconclusive at this time. When enhanced conditions were compared to unenhanced conditions, some studies demonstrated significant benefits for textual enhancement (Jourdenais, Ota, Stauffer, Boyson and Doughty 1995; Shook 1994; Lee 2007), some reported no effect for textual enhancement (Leow 1997, 2001; Leow, Egi, Nuevo and Tsai 2003; Jourdenais 1998; Overstreet 1998; Wong 2003) and others showed only partial effects for textual enhancement (Alanen 1995; Izumi 2002). Because the target features, experimental conditions, exposure time, level of learners and assessment tasks (among other things) have been very diverse in these studies, it is a challenge to attempt to synthesize and interpret this body of research. Furthermore, while some studies set out to compare enhanced to unenhanced conditions only, many studies investigated textual enhancement along with other variables to examine whether textual enhancement and other types of enhancement, together or separately, might positively impact learning. Some factors that appear to have an impact on whether textual enhancement is effective are the choice of the target form, and whether learners have had some previous exposure to the target forms.

Processing instruction and structured input

Processing instruction is an input-based pedagogical technique that is based on VanPatten's Model of Input Processing discussed in the previous section.

Based on the model's predictions of what L2 learners do and do not do during input processing, activities are designed to help learners use more efficient strategies to process input better. The activities in processing instruction are called structured input activities because the input has been manipulated to help learners create better intake for acquisition. In its original conception (VanPatten and Cadierno 1993), processing instruction included three components: (i) explicit information about the target form, (ii) information about processing strategies and (iii) structured input activities. However, studies that have isolated the components of processing instruction (VanPatten and Oikkenon 1996; Benati 2004; Wong 2004) have shown that it is the structured input activities and not the explicit information that is responsible for the positive effects that have been found for processing instruction. The appendix provides concrete examples of these sorts of pedagogical activities.

As discussed earlier, one of the principles of VanPatten's Model of Input Processing is the First Noun Principle: *learners tend to interpret the first (pro)noun they encounter in an utterance as the subject/agent*. According to this principle, learners assume (regardless of their L1) that the first noun is the subject of a sentence even in object-first sentences such as English passive constructions, object pronouns in Spanish and the causative structure in French. To help learners abandon this incorrect assumption, structured input activities may be designed to push them to process sentence structure correctly in order to interpret the meaning of sentences. In a typical processing instruction treatment, structured input activities may require learners to listen to and read different sentences with varying word orders and then indicate who did what to whom via tasks such as picture selection, answering follow-up questions, translation or other means (VanPatten 2012). VanPatten calls these activities referential activities because they have right or wrong answers to allow instructors to assess whether learners are making correct form–meaning connections. While engaging in these activities, learners are pushed to abandon the first-noun strategy and to rely on other cues that lead them to interpret the sentences correctly. After working with these referential structured input activities, learners engage in a series of affective activities in which they must provide information about themselves or rely on their world knowledge to provide a response. There is not necessarily a right or wrong answer in affective activities. The purpose of affective structured input activities is to provide learners with additional meaning-bearing input that contains exemplars of the target form in a communicative context to reinforce the input processing that the referential activities started.

Processing instruction is qualitatively different from other input enhancement techniques such as input flood and textual enhancement because it goes beyond embedding target structures in input. What makes processing instruction unique in relation to other techniques is that the activities are based on a theory of input processing and the input in activities has been manipulated so that learners are pushed to process it correctly. In other words, the structured input activities in processing instruction are designed to encourage learners to make form-meaning connections.

Dozens of studies and many books have examined the effectiveness of processing instruction. Some of the main findings include the following:

- Processing instruction is always as effective or better when compared to other instructional treatments on a variety of target forms and L2s (e.g. VanPatten and Cadierno 1993; Benati 2001; VanPatten 2004; VanPatten and Wong 2004; VanPatten, Inclezan, Salazar and Farley 2009).
- Positive gains for processing instruction have been observed on a variety of different measures including comprehension and production tasks, sentence-level and discourse-level input, and in both oral/aural and writing (e.g. Sanz and Morgan-Short 2004; Uludag and VanPatten in press; VanPatten 2004).
- The positive effects of processing instruction are due to the structured input activities and not to the explicit information that is used (e.g. VanPatten and Oikkenon 1996; Benati 2004; Wong 2004). However, for some structures, explicit information may help speed up how quickly learners make form-meaning connections with structured input (e.g. Farley 2004; Fernández 2008).
- Processing instruction can have an impact on structures that were not the focus of treatment. Learners who received processing instruction treatment for a particular form have been found to make gains not only on measures that assessed that target form, but also on novel forms that were not part of the treatment they received (Benati and Lee 2008).
- The effects of processing instruction are durable. VanPatten and Fernández (2004) have data to show that the effects of processing instruction are observed for up to eight months.

29.7 Conclusion: limitations and directions for future research

To date, research and theoretical advances have led us to an improved understanding of the centrality of input and input processing in SLA. Input provides learners with the necessary formal elements of any language regardless of its modality, along with opportunities to map these formal elements onto meaning, and of course, without input, nothing happens. Different theoretical perspectives related to input processing have emphasized the following points (among others): the need for input to be largely comprehensible; the utility of interaction in making input more comprehensible and useful; the applicability of the information processing perspective (input > system > output) to L2 input processing, including the idea that only a subset of input becomes intake; the roles of limited processing capacity and processing resource allocation during input processing; the idea that attention to form and attention to meaning are (at least largely) dissociable and that processing for one may decrease a learner's ability to process for the other; the proposal that learners' parsers need to experience failure in order to adjust and move acquisition forward; the proposition that computational complexity determines how challenging processing different types of structures are for L2 learners; a series of proposed principles about how learners should attend to different parts of sentence-level input and which aspects of sentence-level input are privileged during processing; and the proposal that input enhanced via typographical or other types of enhancement may be attended to and utilized more readily.

Clearly, our understanding of the role of input and input processing in L2 acquisition has come a long way in the last half century, but as a whole this line of inquiry could benefit from new and innovative research in order to address a variety of current limitations. First, advances in EEG and different neuroimaging techniques can be utilized to assess questions that previously could not be assessed, such as whether constructs that have been proposed to be dissociable (implicit versus explicit learning, monitoring versus no monitoring, form versus semantically oriented processing) are indeed dissociable in terms of the amounts of neural activity they invoke and the localization of the neural substrates that subserve them in the brain. Comparisons with groups of native speakers would be useful in this more neurologically oriented research. Involvement of other more online measures, such as eye-tracking, should help to move beyond the limitations of pre-test/post-test observations as well. Second, input processing research needs to continue to address the critical issue of the extent to which improved performance on post-test measures may be a function of monitoring instead of fluent language use. Although the interpretation and production tasks in PI studies situate participants in contexts that may encourage unmonitored language use, participants in fact may be monitoring in varying degrees. Additional provisions, such as post-experiment questionnaires asking participants if they monitored or not during their responses, may be useful in this regard, in addition to the more neurologically oriented and online measures mentioned above. Third, more studies are needed on the long-term effects of instructional interventions such as structured input, as are more longitudinal studies that provide learners with the instructional interventions of interest for more than just one day in the L2 classroom and that assess the effects of different frequency patterns of instruction (such as different massed versus spaced interventions) over longer periods of time.

In addition to these issues, research on input processing should benefit from continuing to open up and to move beyond research on sentence-level input processing only. This process has already begun within the larger field, as evidenced by, for example, work on input and the acquisition of L2 phonology in recent years, such as the studies reported in Piske and Young-Scholten (2009); input processing and vocabulary learning, such as some studies mentioned in this chapter; and input processing for discourse-level input, such as in the volume by Lee and Benati (2010). Along with these positive developments, new research that focuses on multiple levels of input processing in tandem should lead to important new insights as well. To provide just one example, one could ask: do the positive additive effects of talker, speaking-style and speaking-rate variability on L2 vocabulary learning appear in any way when learners are processing spoken input at the sentence and discourse levels? If not, why not? And if so, what is the nature of the effects?

Another issue that may be addressed in future research concerns the search for new instructional techniques that address learners' processing challenges. A number of studies have demonstrated the effectiveness of PI – in particular the structured input component of PI. The effectiveness of this approach has been attributed largely to how it addresses learners' processing challenges, leading them toward making appropriate form–meaning (or form – function) connections. Other alternative instructional techniques that also address learners' processing challenges may remain to be developed, however, and if these arise, they too can be tested for their effectiveness and compared to what currently exists.

Finally, affirming the centrality of input and input processing in no way should deny the importance of output and output processing in SLA and in language development in general. In this light, more research on the combined effects of input processing and output processing is in order and should be enlightening. This proposal makes particular sense if one considers current theoretical movements in reseach on human memory. It is currently *retrieval* and not study that is being tied to improved memory performance. Roediger's (2009) keynote address at the annual meeting of the Pyschonomics Society provides highly convincing evidence of this turn, if not paradigm shift, in memory research. As always, it is important to note that what counts as target items in the context of language acquisition may differ substantially from target items in memory experiments. Specificity with regard to type of processing and expected learning outcomes is always critical, but given the convincing case for the role of retrieval in memory, it makes sense to continue to explore what additional insights may be gained from new research on output processing and how different combinations of both input and output processing affect the acquisition of L2 forms.

30
Sociocultural theory and the zone of proximal development

Amy Snyder Ohta

30.1 Introduction

There has been increasing interest in perspectives on second language acquisition that are grounded in discourse, culture and ecologies, interpenetrating mind and learning with social interaction, culture and society, and considering L2 developmental processes as they occur in multiple settings of language use; such approaches have grown so much in recent years that Swain and Deters (2007) recognize a "'new' mainstream" emerging in SLA theory (2007: 820).

Sociocultural theory, a neo-Vygotskian theory of human cognitive, psychological, social and historical development, born of Russian cultural historical psychology, is one approach impacting research and thinking in the field of L2 development. The *zone of proximal development* (ZPD) is arguably the most widely applied construct from sociocultural theory, not only in educational research, but also in inquiry related to second and foreign language acquisition. Vygotsky (1978 [1933–35]) defined the ZPD as

> the distance between the actual developmental level as determined by independent problem solving and the level of potential development as determined through problem solving under adult guidance or in collaboration with more capable peers. (Vygotsky 1978: 86)

The purpose of this chapter is, after theoretically situating the ZPD in sociocultural theory and considering how the ZPD is introduced in Vygotsky's writings in contrast to how it is used today (Kinginger 2002; Chaiklin 2003), to examine selected socioculturally oriented SLA research relevant to the ZPD. Along with considering how the ZPD is useful in understanding SLA processes, the chapter also considers expanded notions of the ZPD that contribute to understanding L2 development.

30.2 Background

30.2.1 Sociocultural theory

Sociocultural theory (SCT) is an integrative approach to human development and cognition built upon the work of Vygotsky, his students and colleagues, and contemporary scholars (see also Chapter 11, this volume). Lantolf and Thorne (2007) provide an overview of SCT, tailored to those interested in SLA; sources that are helpful in understanding Vygotskian thought include, of course, works such as Vygotsky (1978 [1933–35], 1987 [1934]) and Van der Veer and Valsiner (1994), as well as secondary sources, such as Wertsch (1985), Moll (1990), Newman and Holzman (1993) and Van der Veer and Valsiner (1991). Application of SCT to L2 learning focuses on Vygotsky's genetic, or developmental, method, and the mediated origin of the individual's higher mental processes in social processes. These are two of the three major themes of Vygotsky's work according to Wertsch (1985). The third, which focuses on understanding the tools/signs that mediate human mental processes, has received less attention. In this section, I will focus on the first two of these three major themes in Vygotsky's work, considering Vygotsky's genetic method and the role of mediation in human higher mental processes, followed by a brief explanation of activity theory. Following this background, I will then move to the main topic of this chapter, the ZPD.

Vygotsky's genetic method

In SCT, the word *genetic* means *developmental*. Vygotsky's genetic method, an approach which considers development-in-process, differentiates sociocultural theory from traditional western approaches to science. SCT integrates theory and method into a "tool-and-result" (Newman and Holzman 1993) approach: namely, factors that have traditionally been considered to cause development are dynamically integrated such that human cognition is interactively formed through social interactional and cultural historical processes that cannot be separated from either the cognitive processing or cognitive mechanisms being formed. The genetic method is concerned with analysis of wholes and avoidance of reductionisms, because when processes are decomposed, they may not be properly understood. Vygotsky recommended using "units" of analysis, with a unit being a part of the whole, comprising all of the key characteristics of the whole (Vygotsky 1987: 46). Vygotsky died before fully fleshing out this approach, but scholars working in sociocultural theory work to preserve the integrity of the processes they are studying.

Mediation

Mediation is the most important notion in sociocultural theory, referring to the process through which human activity, including mental activity, incorporates a range of tools, and how these tools function to transform activity and mind. Mediation means that thinking incorporates "culturally constructed artifacts, concepts and activities," including language (Lantolf and Thorne 2006: 79). The origin of human mental processes is the mediation of mind via historically and culturally embedded social interactive processes. Human psychological and cognitive processes are mediated throughout the lifespan and continually formed through these processes. The idea of mediation encompasses physical tools, which not only work to change the physical environment but also become integrated in human culture and cognition, as well as psychological, semiotic tools, the most prominent of which is language. The incorporation of semiotic tools into human mental functioning occurs from the earliest human development, when language is used by caregivers to interact with and regulate the child's functioning via social mediation. The idea of *regulation* also relates to mediation, whether the individual is *object regulated, other-regulated, or self-related*, three types of regulation that are understood to be on a continuum, moving toward higher mental functions.

What Vygotsky termed the *general genetic law of cultural development* relates to the role of socially mediated activity in human development, with cognitive development proceeding through a process of other-regulation:

> Every function in the child's cultural development appears twice: first, on the social level, and later, on the individual level; first, between people (interpsychological), and then inside the child (intrapsychological). This applies equally to voluntary attention, to logical memory, and to the formation of concepts. All the higher functions originate as actual relations between human individuals. (Vygotsky 1978: 57)

Human development's socially mediated nature is also seen in the role of language activity in human development. Language is actively internalized through interactive processes such that it becomes a meditational means through which people regulate mental functions, including consciousness and thinking. Sociocultural scholars are interested in *private speech*, that is, speech for the self, and how it develops through internalization processes into *inner speech* and thought. L2 development is conceptualized as a process of re-mediating human mental processing with a new set of semiotic tools – the language being learned. Private speech provides a window on these developmental processes (Ohta 2001c; Guerrero 2005; Woodall 2002; Negueruela, Lantolf, Jordan and Gelabert 2004; J. S. Lee 2006).

Activity theory

Activity theory (Engeström 1987, 2001) is a sociocultural-theoretic approach that focuses on the role of human activity in cognitive development to a greater degree than did Vygotsky, who was more interested in semiotic mediation of human higher mental processes (Lantolf and Thorne 2006). Some L2 researchers identify most strongly with activity theory and use this term, rather than SCT, to describe their theoretical framework. However, it is important to keep in mind that activity theory and SCT cannot be distinctly separated. Activity theory is part of a sociocultural approach to development whose influence is most strongly seen in understandings of how social practice underlies and permeates human psychological and cognitive development.

30.2.2 The zone of proximal development

The ZPD brings together the concepts of mediation, its role in the regulation and development of higher mental functioning, and the transformative role of imitating in internalization and development. The ZPD can be best understood as a kind of activity, as mediational processes whereby a person is enabled to do more than s/he could have accomplished individually through some sort of assistance. Incorporating assistance means that the individual's activity and thinking are facilitated, shaped, or guided by another's, words, tone of voice, gesture, eye gaze, facial expressions and deployment of other artifacts (visual aids, writing, etc.). The ZPD strongly relates to the general genetic law of cultural development, showing the earlier developmental processes where new knowledge and skills are realized collaboratively between people.

Vygotsky's ZPD

In Vygotsky's time, the ZPD was originally applied (and intended to be applied) to understanding mental age levels of children for the purposes of better projecting a child's educative potential (Van der Veer and Valsiner 1991). Vygotsky's definition, cited in the introduction (Vygotsky 1978), talks about an actual and a potential developmental level of a child, and how that potential level can be determined by seeing how a child is able to solve problems in collaboration with an adult. Van der Veer and Valsiner (1991) discuss Vygotsky's concern that IQ testing was being used to establish a child's mental age by investigating what a child could do without assistance. Children of widely varying abilities received the same IQ score, resulting in inaccurate educational placements. Vygotsky suggested that if, instead, the mental age/IQ were to be compared with what a child could do with some assistance, one could more effectively determine a child's educability, and make better educational placements.

The ZPD today

Most researchers today use the ZPD differently than Vygotsky intended (Chaiklin 2003; Kinginger 2002). It is most often applied to better understand learning processes, classroom interaction and human development, including SLA, while still also being applied as a tool integrating assessment and instruction, as in Dynamic Assessment (DA) (Poehner 2007). The ZPD today is still applied to child development and now it is also common to apply the

ZPD to adult learning in formal and informal settings (McCafferty in press). The original formulation's mention of a teacher or more expert peer has been replaced today with an understanding that ZPDs also form in interactions between true peers who may or may not have greater expertise (Ohta 2001c), and between individuals as well as in groups (Guk and Kellogg 2007). In addition, mediation in the ZPD is understood to reveal potential development at the time of these collaborative experiences while also impacting the whole development of the person and mind. In this sense, today's ZPD is understood both as an assessment and as a developmentally significant activity related to the forming of mind. The dialogicality and social character of cognition developed via the ZPD is retained through adulthood in the development of help-seeking and help-incorporating processes that include a variety of media (books, electronic resources, social media) in addition to face-to-face interaction (Ohta 2006, 2010). It is also the case that researchers today may talk about processes that could be called the ZPD or which are related to the ZPD, but do not name them as such, and thus may not refer to the ZPD when it would be relevant to do so. For example, Knouzi, Swain, Lapkin and Brooks (2010) describe development in terms of the internalization of social speech leading to self-regulation for particular language-related tasks, processes that are often understood as part of the ZPD.

There are some concerns regarding certain modern applications of the ZPD. Chaiklin (2003) and Kinginger (2002) point out that contrary to Vygotsky's own emphasis on wholistic thinking and integration of tool-and-result, it has become rather common in educational circles to apply the ZPD in a cause-and-effect manner as a pedagogical technique. This tends to occur when the ZPD is taken out of context and not integrated into the broader theory which gives the ZPD its meaning. Chaiklin's (2003) particular concern is that Vygotsky developed the ZPD as an assessment tool, not as a metaphor to guide our understanding of collaboration in human development. In terms of collaboration, Chaiklin insightfully notes that the effectiveness of collaboration was accepted by Vygotsky, who said that it is a "well known fact that with collaboration, direction, or some kind of help the child is always able to do more and solve more difficult tasks tha[n] he can independently" (Vygotsky 1987: 209). Vygotsky's innovation was suggesting that this "well known fact" be applied in determining a child's mental age or educability: "The child's potential for moving from what he can do to what he can do only in collaboration is the most sensitive index of the dynamics of development and the degree of success that will come to characterize the child's mental activity" (Vygotsky 1987: 210).

Chaiklin's (2003) careful readings of original source materials and explication of the original meanings of the ZPD in Vygotsky's work and application are helpful for understanding the context and original meanings of the term. However, through the applications of the ZPD to diverse teaching and learning contexts, instructional content and learning across the lifespan, including to adult SLA, the ZPD has come to mean something somewhat different than it did in Vygotsky's time. While we need not accept all applications of the ZPD as legitimate, L2 researchers Lantolf and Thorne (2006) also caution against taking a doctrinal approach to the ZPD; SCT and the ZPD are living concepts. It is legitimate for L2 researchers to apply the ZPD differently than Vygotsky did. Contextualizing the ZPD in Vygotsky's work and SCT goes far in avoiding mechanistic applications. A broadening of the ZPD's applicability has been useful and meaningful in L2 research.

30.2.3 L2 research and the ZPD

SLA, including L2 teaching and learning, presents a wide range of problems for L2 researchers to consider. Sociocultural theory, in its integration of research and practice, embodies Vygotsky's concern about solving the problems of his day and is readily applied to modern contexts. Lantolf (2008), for example, echoes Vygotsky's commitment to *praxis*, a commitment to interconnections between practice, research and theory.

Socioculturally oriented L2 researchers are most interested in development in the context of SLA – that is, as *L2 development*, not general cognitive development. The words *development, learning and acquisition* are often used interchangably, as in this chapter. Depending on the study, L2 development may mean that learners showed progress in listening comprehension through teacher-mediated dynamic assessment (Ableeva 2002), more expertly used L2 syntax via peer collaboration (as in Ohta 2000a), or developed a higher level of linguistic and metalinguistic awareness via collaboration with peers or tutors (as in Swain and Lapkin 1998, 2002; Lapkin, Swain and Smith 2002; Guerrero and Villamil 2000; Aljaafreh and Lantolf 1994). All of these are examples of L2 developmental processes. Because language activity is what is being examined, and language use varies according to different settings, the question of whether particular forms are learned or acquired may or may not be considered. Some researchers conduct follow-up work, such as post-tests to investigate what learners have retained from classroom interventions (such as Lapkin and Swain 2000), and/or conduct longitudinal studies which show evidence of development over time (Ohta 2001c).

Sociocultural L2 research is deeply process-oriented, valuing the understanding of how development unfolds in situ. Moment-by-moment analyses of discourse are often used to reveal developmental processes, called *microgenesis* (Wertsch 1985). In terms of the ZPD, while microgenetic linguistic development may or may not mean that the learner will be able to perform similarly later, or in a different context later – the ZPD shows *potential* development (Negueruela 2008). And, in embracing a view of the whole learner, in and out of the classroom, SCT-oriented L2 researchers also investigate SLA in a wide variety of contexts: classroom instruction including pedagogies from communicative-approach college foreign language classrooms that incorporate a variety of collaborative tasks (Anton 1999; Ohta 2000a), to elementary school classrooms (Poehner 2009), to teacher-fronted EFL classrooms abroad (Sullivan 2000); language learning in and out of classrooms abroad (Kinginger 2008); and advanced Asian language learning in classroom, self-study and study/soujourn abroad (Ohta 2006, 2010).

In the next section, several L2 studies related to the ZPD will be presented using a taxonomy developed by expanding that of Lantolf and Thorne (2006). L2 studies that are relevant to understanding and using the ZPD will be discussed in the following categories: (i) L2 skills development; (ii) dynamic Assessment and tutor/teacher feedback; (iii) peer collaboration; and (iv) expanding the ZPD. Any taxonomy is difficult to apply because these are overlapping, not discrete categories. Considering the contributions of particular studies in certain areas outlined here does not, of course, limit the broader range of contributions made by each study.

30.3 L2 studies and the ZPD

30.3.1 The ZPD and L2 skills development

L2 skill building has been considered to be linguistic or metalinguistic (Kinginger 2002), though the two can be difficult to tease apart. Linguistic skill building may be conscious or unconscious, and has a reflective/metalinguistic component, though these components may or may not be visible in the words transcribed for the discourse data analyzed in various studies. For example, beginning learners, guided in teacher-fronted or peer learning settings to manipulate the nuts and bolts of a new grammatical system, are building a foundational level of familiarity and expertise with new forms and how to make and use them. A basic understanding and ability to produce and recall forms is needed for the language to be manipulable in the learner's speech and verbal thought, which form the basic tools of oral and mental manipulation and rehearsal, including metalinguistic reflection. Two studies which have implications for skill building in the ZPD will be considered here: Swain and Lapkin (1998) and Ohta (2001c).

Swain and Lapkin (1998) investigated the interactions of French immersion middle-schoolers. Their detailed analysis of two middle-schoolers working on a jigsaw speaking and writing task allows insight into how learners assist each other with form–meaning connections in both French and their L1, English. This study provides examples of linguistic and metalinguistic skill building in the ZPD. Swain and Lapkin address a particular problem in French immersion programs: grammar instruction that focuses on "isolated rules, paradigms and the manipulation of form, rather than on relating form to function" (1998: 325).

Swain and Lapkin's analysis focuses on language-related episodes (LREs), which they define as "any part of a dialogue where the students talk about the language they are producing, question their language use, or correct themselves or others" (1998: 326). This includes supportive interactions in the ZPD. Their data show how the pair gave and received assistance, mostly settling on correct forms, but not always. The forms that the learners collaboratively agreed upon, whether correct or incorrect, were selected by students as correct answers in individually tailored post-tests. This evidences the power of the ZPD in L2 skill building (students learned in the ZPD, at least in the short term), but also leads to the question of whether collaboration might cause students to build up misunderstandings or learn incorrect forms. However, it is important to note that this was a research study and not an ordinary classroom setting; teachers were not permitted to intervene. When students disagreed on a form, teachers were not available to answer questions or help to resolve differences in opinion. Had the task been implemented in a regular classroom context, the results might have been quite different because a teacher would have been available to help resolve learner questions. For example, Ohta (2001c) found that in ordinary college foreign language classrooms, students in pairs/groups who disagreed on forms asked the circulating teacher for assistance, or realized their mistakes during follow-up whole-class review led by the teacher. Swain and Lapkin (1998: 333), following their analysis, recommend that classroom tasks involving collaboration "must be followed by opportunities for teacher feedback" to minimize the potential for learning incorrect forms.

Ohta (2001c) followed college-level learners of Japanese over an academic year of instruction. In terms of linguistic skill building, the study documents growth in learner use of listener responses over the period of the study, skills which were modeled by teachers, with assistance provided in teacher-fronted contexts tapping into a whole-class ZPD. Data from early in the academic year show that learners did not utter listener responses, but produced consecutive initiation/response (question/answer) pairs, or, sometimes, laughing (Ohta 2008) or pausing between initiation/response sequences. The following example from Ohta's corpus shows this lack of follow-up turns. Ungrammatical Japanese production is reflected in ungrammatical English translations. However, the nature of the grammatical errors is different. The purpose of these translations is to give the flavor of the Japanese, not to precisely pinpoint the nature of the errors.

(1) 1 S: Uh (.) biiru o nomimasu?
        Uh (.) you drink beer?
     2 C: Iie (.) uh (.) nomimasen
        No (.) uh (.) I don't.
     3 S: Nihongo no benkyoo o shimasu ka?
        Do you do Japanese's study?
     4 C: Hai (.) hai uh (.) benkyoo shimasu.
        Yes (.) yes uh (.) I do.
     5 S: Eiga (.) ni (.) ikimasu ka?
        Do (.) you (.) go to movies?

6 C: Iie (.) ikimasu (.) ikimasen. Eiga:: eiga ni (.) ikimasu ka.
    No (.) I go (.) I don't go. Do you (.) go to movies?
7 S: Hai ikimasu
    Yes, I do.(11/27)

Learners at this early stage did not evidence errors in the follow-up turn; rather, they simply failed to produce any language in the follow-up turn. These turns, however, are very important in Japanese, where verbal listener responses, called *aizuchi*, are much more common than in English (Maynard 1989; Ohta 1995, 1997, 1999). These turns provide an opportunity for aligning responses which create a related, friendly tone in conversation. The classroom data show how teachers provided instruction on how to do these responses. This, however, was not sufficient to result in learner production of these turns, as students still did't produce them. In addition to instruction, teachers also, then, provided support during learner production tasks, in both teacher-fronted and pair-work settings, allowing students an opportunity to immediately produce such turns. In the following excerpt, a teacher, observing various pairs during a pair interview task, created a whole-class ZPD by calling out a reminder to the entire class, asking them to include the listener response *Aa soo desu ka* "Oh really?":

(2) 1 R: Ah shimbun:: (.) o yomimasu?
        Do you read the newspaper?
    2 D: Sorry? (.) Hai (.) o shimasu
        Sorry? (.) Yeah (.) do.
    3 R: Dono: (.) yomimasu ka?
        Which (.) you read
    4 D: (3) Um (3) USA Today hehe (.) o yomimasu. USA Today o: (.) o yomimasu
        (3) Um (3) I read hehe (.) USA Today. I read (.) USA Today.
→   5 T: ((from a distance)) Minasan itte kudasai yo:: aa soo desu ka::.
        Everyone please say "Oh really?"
→   6 R: Ah soo desu ka::.
        Oh really?
    7 D: Koohii de- koohii o nomimasu?
        Coffee with- do you drink coffee? (11/27)

(adapted from Ohta 2001c: 197)

Note in the above example that Rob and his partner did not produce listener responses after their first two initiation/response (question/answer) sequences, but Rob uttered a listener response in line 6 after the teacher's line 5 exhortation.

By the end of the academic year, all of the students showed greater skill in producing appropriate follow-up turns, including the affective marking with *ne* that is critical for assessments (content-related emotional or evaluative comments) to be appropriate in Japanese. The following example from Ohta's corpus illustrates a student's appropriate use of such a response, which was common by the year's end:

(3) 1 C: Ka- kase o hiku: (.) um (.) kaze o hiku (.) toki doo shimasu ka?
When you ha- have a culd (.) um have a cold (.) what do you do?
2 S: Uh soo desu ne::. Ha- hot mizu o uh hot mizu o nondari nemasu. Uh netari shimasu.
Hmmm. I drink ha- hot water uh, I drink hot water sleep. Uh and sleep.
3 C: Unn ii desu ne.
Oh that's good. (5/22)

Skill development relates to both linguistic and paralinguistic skills. Haught and McCafferty's (2008) study of two Russian ESL learners relates the ZPD and skills development to development of language, prosodic features and gestures in weekly drama workshops. This study addresses the problem of language learning as development of the whole person, and how language development is a more holistic process than has been considered in much SLA research. Haught and McCafferty are particularly interested in the relationship between thinking and gesture in language development (for a review, see Stam in press and Gullburg in press). They consider the mediational role of gesture, prosody and body movements in ZPDs formed in the interactions between the students and their drama instructor.

In these drama workshops, activities revolved around "theater games, improvisations, tongue twisters and the rehearsal of written dramatic scripts" (Haught and McCafferty 2008: 151). The students were uncomfortable with improvisation, but enjoyed working with written scripts – they reported learning words and expressions through these opportunities. Activities included acting out scenes and discussing characters, situations and points of view. Discussion revolved around how to deliver these lines effectively, including talk about the meaning of the lines and their cultural context. Haught and McCafferty found that the students learned more than their lines – they also mirrored the actor-instructor's prosody and gestures, incorporating these into their growing L2 repertoire, and increasing both linguistic and paralinguistic awareness. Repeatedly practicing delivery while imitating the instructor's prosody and gesture of emotionally laden lines in context provided learners with the opportunity to use language with high emotional and cultural content and to connect form, meaning, prosody, posture, facial expression and gesture in unique ways as the actor-instructor coached their performances. Haught and McCafferty found that the drama workshops comprised a context for learners to be supported in developing a range of L2 skills in the ZPD. It is also a good example of *learner agency* in the ZPD: learners followed their own interests in a drama workshop where they focused on their own areas of focus in working to develop their L2 proficiency.

30.3.2 Dynamic Assessment and tutor/teacher feedback in the ZPD

Research on *teacher feedback*, or corrective feedback, in SLA has tended to focus on what type of feedback, for example, explicit or implicit, might be most effective for SLA (R. Ellis, Loewen and Erlam 2006). From a sociocultural approach, it is understood that feedback must be individually tailored and provided with sensitivity to the learner's developmental level; in this view, the best type of corrective feedback for a particular situation will vary depending on learner needs. SCT researchers are most interested in how various types of feedback, flexibly, responsively and collaboratively provided, are involved in moment-by-moment developmental processes. SCT-oriented studies of teacher feedback focus on interaction between teacher and student(s), and how feedback relates to learners' unfolding needs as revealed, moment-by-moment in the discourse. There are a number of interesting sociocultural studies considering the role of tutor or teacher feedback on language development in the ZPD, in both individual tutoring sessions (Aljaafreh and Lantolf 1994; Nassaji and Swain 2000) and teacher-fronted classroom instruction (Anton 1999; Ohta 1995, 1999, 2000a, 2000b, 2001a, 2001b, 2001c; Yoshida 2009, 2010; Poehner 2009; Lantolf and Poehner 2011). In this section, three classroom studies will be considered: Ohta's longitudinal classroom study (Ohta 2000b, 2001c), Poehner's case study of an elementary classroom language learning game, from a DA perspective (Poehner 2009; Lantolf and Poehner 2011), and Yoshida's classroom study that incorporated stimulated recall to better understand the characteristics of corrective feedback noticed by learners (Yoshida 2009, 2010).

Ohta (2000b, 2001c) expanded the notion of classroom corrective feedback by teachers to include considering how a teacher's feedback to an individual learner impacts others in the class. This was accomplished via individual recording of learners' private speech, utterances for the self. Private speech data reveals how learners who were not directly addressed, uttered replies sotto voce, which Ohta termed *vicarious response*, and benefited from what Ohta termed *incidental recasts*; the latter emerge when a vicarious response containing an error contrasts with the teacher's utterance. Data captured private speech episodes where, as learners struggled to produce a vicarious response in private speech, a ZPD emerged as a contrasting, correct form was provided by the teacher and incorporated into the learner's utterance. In this way, Ohta's study shows how ZPDs form in teacher-fronted, whole-class contexts as students benefit from feedback the classroom teacher provides to nominated individuals.

Yoshida's (2009, 2010) socioculturally oriented study of classroom interaction builds upon Ohta's work by incorporating stimulated recall data. Yoshida analyzed teacher feedback in her ten-week study of six Australian learners enrolled in the second year of university Japanese classes. She also found teacher feedback to impact learners beyond the particular student being addressed. Analyses of stimulated recall data show that the usefulness of teacher feedback to non-addressed students depends on the students' level of verbal engagement. The learners who were engaged in vicarious responses while the teacher called on and interacted with others were most likely to report noticing and attending to feedback addressed to their classmates. The results suggest that the level of learner engagement may relate to the extent to which a learner partakes in a whole-class ZPD.

Poehner and Lantolf (Poehner 2009; Lantolf and Poehner 2011) further investigate the idea of the role of teacher feedback in a whole-class ZPD in their study of an elementary school Spanish teacher's implementation of a language learning game in a Spanish lesson. They present the teacher's methodology as an application of Dynamic Assessment (DA) (Poehner and Lantolf 2005; Poehner 2007, 2008, 2009; Lantolf and Poehner 2011), an interactive, instructional approach to assessment and instruction in the ZPD. Previous L2 literature in this area to date has applied DA to individual teacher/learner interaction during tutoring sessions. In their study, the teacher created her own rubric to guide her provision of feedback to students who made language errors, as follows:

1. Pause
2. Repeat the erroneous phrase with question intonation
3. Repeat just the error
4. Ask the student what is wrong with the utterance
5. Point out the incorrect word
6. Ask an either/or question
7. Provide the correct language
8. Provide an explanation

(adapted from Poehner 2009: 481)

In applying this rubric to implementation of a game involving the description of animals (the grammatical structure being taught was adjective–noun agreement), the teacher moved through these prompts in sequential order, from less to more explicit feedback, depending upon whether or not a child was able to produce the correct form. Her implementation of this rubric resulted in strongly form-focused interaction during the classroom game.

Analysis shows how three children varied in the number of prompts the teacher implemented before they produced the correct form. In some ways, feedback caused misunderstanding: for example, prompt 2, repeating the error with question intonation, means that the teacher uttered incorrect language. In the data, a student misinterpreted such a prompt, an NTRI (next-turn-repair initiation), as a content-related correction (See Foster and Ohta 2005 for a discussion of the ambiguity of NTRIs); the student did not understand the teacher was speaking incorrect Spanish, something that might not be expected teacher behavior. This misunderstanding, however, also revealed the student's lack of awareness of the error and lack of facility with Spanish grammar. The teacher then provided more focused feedback, using five more prompts until finally, using prompt 6 (ask an either/or question) resulted in the child's provision of the correct form. All in all, the class seemed to benefit from these corrective procedures as measured by how two subsequent learners played the game, requiring less mediation. Lantolf and Poehner (2011) argue that, while they cannot be sure why subsequent learners required successively less intervention by the teacher, the learners most likely benefitted from participation in a "collective ZPD" (2011: 24); in other words, the teacher's feedback, though tailored to an individual student, tapped into the ZPD of the entire class, allowing others to benefit from the dynamic assessment process.

The studies of teacher feedback reviewed above show developmental processes as learners interact with the teacher's corrective feedback. Poehner and Lantolf show how teacher feedback, moving from implicit to more explicit feedback, functioned in an L2 classroom game, as children performed more accurately as the game proceeded. Via analysis of vicarious responses, Ohta's and Yoshida's research shows learners making use of corrective feedback addressed to classmates. Yoshida takes this a step further in her finding that learners who witness teacher feedback to classmates are much more likely to notice that feedback when they, themselves, are verbally engaging in the classroom activity. Through these processes, teacher feedback allows whole-class ZPDs to emerge as learners are assisted to better understand and produce utterances beyond their current developmental level, showing their developmental potential. Yoshida's findings also underscore the importance of learner characteristics – in this case, level of engagement, understood here as verbal participation in classroom activities – as it relates to the impact of assistance in the ZPD.

30.3.3 Peer collaboration and the ZPD

Vygotsky's definition of the ZPD requires an adult or more capable peer. Modern researchers applying Vygotsky's ideas have considered how ZPDs emerge in interactions between true peers. Analyses of *pair and group work* of L2 learners have produced repeated findings that ZPDs form, even among true peers, thus expanding our understanding of the ZPD in L2 learning settings. Donato (1994) is one such early study showing formation of ZPDs in small group learning settings, as learner collaboration allowed individuals to function at a higher level. Many researchers cited already in this chapter have built on this early work. More recently, Guk and Kellogg (2007) studied how ZPDs form among elementary school students doing group work in their foreign language classes. Along with collaboration allowing students to share their strengths, which Donato termed *collective scaffolding*, Ohta (2001c) suggests other mechanisms at work that promote the formation of ZPDs, even when greater expertise may be lacking. Pair and small group collaboration allows learners to take on different roles, as speaker, addressee, or auditor (conversational participant who is not currently addressed).

These terms are borrowed from Bell (1984), a sociolinguist interested dialectical variation and how speakers adapt their language to their interlocutors, depending upon whether the interlocutor is an addressee, auditor, overhearer (present in the area and known to participants, but not part of the conversational group) or eavesdropper (present in the area but unknown to participants). Ohta (2001c) applies Bell's terms in understanding the impact of various participant roles on cognitive processes in language learning. While the speaker is encumbered by the speaking role and has little working memory available to solve language problems emerging during online production, addressees and auditors are actively involved in the pragmatic notion of *projection* (Levinson 1983), mentally moving beyond the speaker's words to what might be coming next. Projection involves anticipatory thought, as the listener tracks the speaker's utterances, including potentially formulating what might come next in inner speech. For learners engaged in pair or group work, projection allows the listener to chime in to help the speaker with problems that emerge, even in cases where the listener could not have produced the entire utterance him/herself.

Simply being placed into groups and assigned language tasks, however, is not sufficient for ZPDs to form. Peers vary in how collaborative and mutually supportive their interactions are (Storch 2002). In addition, the classroom context is critical in supporting peer interaction. DiNitto (2000) shows the importance of context for the emergence of ZPDs in classroom group work. She studied group work in an intact Japanese language class that was ordinarily conducted using a teacher-fronted instructional approach where learners performed and adapted memorized dialogues in class while the teacher promptly corrected all errors (Noda 1998). DiNitto, who taught the class, was trained in this teaching methodology. However, one quarter she added occasional group work tasks into her curriculum without modifying her pedagogy in other ways. These tasks were different from the dialogue recitations that dominated her pedagogy; they involved situations that were different from those presented in memorized material, such as using new vocabulary to create maps, giving and receiving directions, role-playing restaurant ordering scenes and talking about the content of short reading passages. During one of these tasks, DiNitto video- and audio-recorded group work conducted by the students in two groups of four. While one of the groups collaborated and showed interactions of the type DiNitto expected, another reflected the norms of the teacher-fronted classroom – one student, Walt, took on the role of teacher and conducted the group work in a teacher-fronted fashion. DiNitto notes that the language used in Walt's group reproduced the norms of her methodology, including: "the explicit recitation of grammar rules, the IRF [initiation/response/follow-up sequence]-style response, the roles of expert and novice, and the privileging of form over meaning and accuracy over communication" (2000: 201).

In terms of the ZPD, clearly the broader context in which group work is embedded appears to be critical for its success – while DiNitto was at first surprised by the non-collaborative group's performance, she cites Coughlan and Duff's (1994: 190) assertion that "second language data cannot be neatly removed from the sociocultural context in which [they were] created or collected." She states:

> Students were experiencing group work as a new activity, one for which they were ill-prepared and which was by nature at odds with the classroom setting they had acclimated themselves to over the previous twenty weeks of instruction. This last point is key, for as Barnes and Todd (1995: 16) argue, "for success [in small group work] it is essential for the teacher to help students grasp what kind of learning is required." This did not happen in the classroom under review. However, I believe that "help[ing] students grasp what kind of learning is required" implies much more than teaching the students how to collaborate in the L2. It requires an underlying philosophy of language learning that was not present in this classroom. (DiNitto 2000: 201)

She concludes by questioning:

> We could ask why Walt's group did not succeed, but a more revealing question is, Why should they have succeeded? Why should they have opted for a model of learning other than the dominant learning style of the classroom? (DiNitto 2000: 201)

DiNitto (2000) does point out that the classroom environment is not the only factor determining whether or not learner collaboration can be productive – one of the two groups in her class did construct interactions where learners supported each other's language use in the ZPD. Her main goal in presenting analysis of the classroom and two group task performances is to highlight the power of the dominant classroom methodology and underlying ideology and its influence on learners and learning.

Ohta (2000b, 2001a, 2001b, 2001c) investigated the interactions of learners in their first or second year of college Japanese language classes. Ohta's longitudinal study provides insight into the process of learning a new language that is typologically distant from the learners' L1s. She collected audio and video data in intact classes as implemented by the lecturers and teaching assistants in charge of instruction, without any intervention by the researcher. Close miking of students enabled collection of student talk during group work and private speech, whispered talk to the self, that occurred during whole-class, teacher-fronted instruction.

In terms of the peer collaboration in the ZPD, Ohta's analyses of interaction in learner–learner pairs show numerous examples of peers providing one another with finely tuned, developmentally appropriate support. Aljaafreh and Lantolf (1994) point out how assistance in the ZPD, in order to be effective, must give the speaker increasing responsibility for his/her own performance, and that assistance must be negotiated, with the goal of providing "just enough assistance" (1994: 469). Ohta's (2001c) Japanese language learners naturally seemed to follow a principle of providing just enough assistance, moving from more implicit to more explicit forms of assistance as needed. For example, a common form of peer assistance was to *wait*, allowing the partner time to finish an utterance or to self-correct. In the following excerpt Kuo-ming's pauses evidence his peer interlocutor's strategy of *waiting*. Pause length is shown in seconds (i.e. "(1)" meaning 1 second) or, where less than one second, the notation "(.)" is used.

(4) 1 Km: um (1) um (1) suteki no:: (.) um ske-suteki na sofa desu ka?
        (2) Desu ne or desu k- (.) haha desu ne:, (.)
        um (1) um (1) is it the (.) nice ((wrong particle)) um ni-nice ((correct particle)) sofa ((wrong final particle))? (.) ((re-states copula with corrected final particle and wrong final particle)) (.) ((chooses correct final particle)) (Ohta 2001c: 90)

Another common form of assistance was the *prompt*, where a peer assisted by providing a partial repetition, stopping before the trouble-source to allow the partner to do his/her own reformulation.

(5) 1 Pf: Anoo sumimasen.
        Um excuse me.
     2 Sr: Hai
        Yes
     3 Pf: Ima nanji desu ka?
        What time is it?
     4 Sr: Um (2) kuji?
        Um (.) Nine o'clock?
     5 Pf: Kuji
        Nine o'clock
→   6 Sr: I guess that's ten after (.)
→   7 Pf: Kuji:::
        Nine 'oclock:::
     8 Sr: juppun desu.
        Ten minutes (("kuji juppun," literally "nine o'clock ten minutes," is the correct way to tell the time)). (Ohta 2001c: 91)

Besides prompting, peers also assisted via co-construction, chiming in what the partner needed to produce an utterance. In these and other ways, peers tailored their support, allowing their interlocutor to do more than s/he could have done individually.

Ohta (2001c) also found that negotiating assistance was about more than just providing nudges of support to classmates – in fact, students were sensitive to their own needs and limitations. Students who expressed doubts about a form received help from peers, and when a peer wasn't sure, inquiring of the circulating teacher, or if the teacher wasn't accessible, making a note to check the form later. These findings underscore the importance of the agency of the learner in working together with the teacher and classmates to create contexts effective for language learning not only by providing developmentally appropriate assistance to one another but also by judging for themselves when they needed such assistance, and by making notes of what required further inquiry. Ohta (2001c) found that learners were able to make use of a variety of learning activities, from the traditional to the innovative, mechanical to creative, in their language learning. Interestingly, findings suggest that while some task types may be more effective than others in terms of providing a context for linguistic skill building in the L2, this also depends on the learners' own orientations toward tasks, again highlighting the role of learner agency in SLA. As mentioned in the previous section, another important finding related to the ZPD is that learners also received assistance during whole-class, teacher-fronted interactions that they vicariously participated in.

Kitade (2008) investigated peer collaboration in advanced content-based Japanese language classes in the context of asynchronous computer-mediated communication (ACMC) with Japanese key-pals (see Chapter 14, this volume). ACMC refers to email exchanges in this case. Kitade investigated both how Japanese key-pals, native-speaking email partners assigned to pairs of American learners of Japanese, adjusted their messages in order to better suit the learners' developmental levels, as well as analyzing the collaboration between the paired American learners that occurred offline, during the process of reading email messages by their Japanese key-pals and co-authoring responses. Kitade's goal was to more fully understand the impact of ACMC in providing language learning opportunities. Like earlier studies of collaborative dialogue (i.e. Swain and Lapkin 1998), Kitade also included individually tailored post-tests to investigate whether learners retained the knowledge co-constructed in collaboration with their peers. Kitade found that collaboratively working in class on reading and replying to Japanese key-pal emails was quite productive for the students, as students were able to provide and receive assistance in the ZPD from each other and from instructors, incorporating this assistance into their email replies.

Kitade explains how the in-class collaboration provided important developmental opportunities: had they done these assignments at home, working independently, they would have missed the language learning that occurred via metalinguistic talk during peer collaboration (2008: 77). Consistent with results of previous research on collaborative writing (see, for example, Storch and Wigglesworth 2007; Wigglesworth and Storch 2009), Kitade found that peers working together produced higher-quality texts than did students who worked alone. And, dyad-specific post-tests demonstrated the effectiveness of peer collaboration: 73 percent of post-test items were correct, consistent with previous research findings (Swain and Lapkin 1998). Collaborating during production (writing messages) appeared to have a different effect than collaboration during receptive tasks (reading messages). Collaborative writing resulted in greater retention of new vocabulary than did collaborative reading and discussion of messages received. All in all, collaboration during email writing tasks enhanced learning by providing a context for mutual assistance in the ZPD:

> Although ACMC [asynchronous computer mediated communication] activities are frequently conducted as outside-the-classroom assignments, the findings in this study indicate the significance of the in-class ACMC activity, since this entails the beneficial aspects of offline talk. Although reference to online dictionaries is useful, the learners' retrospective interviews suggest that there are limitations in the scope of these dictionaries. Unlike the receptive mode (reading), which requires only comprehension, the productive mode requires the selection of the correct linguistic knowledge and awareness of how to apply that knowledge in a particular context. [The] collaborative peer context is able to meet such complicated demands that cannot be solved using dictionaries. (Kitade 2008: 78)

Kitade found variability among dyads in how helpful collaboration was, and in how successful they were in managing the interaction in productive ways. For example, some pairs made good use of the instructor's availability to solve intractable problems, while others did not. Overall, however, she found that the opportunity for collaboration was beneficial to students who chose to collaborate.

30.3.4 Expanding the ZPD

For adult learners, benefitting from giving and providing assistance in the ZPD is not only dependent on having opportunities to collaborate, as Kitade (2008) pointed out, but also on individual differences in how learners manage challenges that arise during language learning. The ZPD is the locus of semiotic mediation in learning and development; in the ZPD, learners interactively incorporate assistance in their activity in a way that shows learning as a "process of the present (actuality) on the basis of anticipation of immediate future possibilities and through construction of reality out of these anticipated possibilities" (Valsiner 2001: 86). And, studies such as those reviewed above have shown how opportunities for interaction and collaborative assistance not only show learners' developmental potential, but also promote development of linguistic skills that serve as resources to learners beyond the present task.

Recently, some studies have begun to shed light on how, for adults, the ZPD is not only a place of mediation by other persons, but that ZPDs also form when adults actively engage with a variety of resources in language learning. Bickhard (2005) calls this sort of process *self-scaffolding*: the individual (for our purposes, an adult language learner), supports his/her own development by using "external notes, supports, reminders, intellectual and physical prostheses, and so on" (2005: 171), that include collaborative interaction with other persons, but also other artifacts available to the learner. This includes the adult's structuring of the problem, breaking it down into manageable parts, considering possible solutions, and interacting with appropriate help sources, including people and other resources – notes, dictionaries, databases, etc. – dialogically incorporating these into his/her functioning. Self-scaffolding is a process of ZPD management.

Self-scaffolding results in the formation of a ZPD to the extent that the assistance is developmentally appropriate, allowing the individual to outperform his/her current abilities; as in social interactive ZPDs, collaborative (person + assistance) performance indicates potential for future development. Knouzi et al. (2010) relate self-scaffolding to SLA in a way that is pointedly relevant to the ZPD. Knouzi et al.'s study is about *languaging* – that is, learners' metalinguistic talk about the L2, including their engagement in using the L2. Their study subjects were instructed to speak aloud as they worked through a set of self-study cards designed to teach verbal aspect in French. While there was no interlocutor present, the task was an interactive one, involving the learner and a set of supportive instructions, with which they interacted both verbally (languaging) and non-verbally (visually accessing the materials), as the cards provided a textual source of instructional support. The most successful learners, in terms of gaining command of French aspect, were those who most intensively interacted with the material by talking to themselves and deeply considering the material being taught:

> the more the students languaged, the more insight they gained into the meaning of the explanatory card they had just read. This shows that the students do not reach a full understanding of the meaning of a card right after finishing the first reading (Lantolf and Appel 1994). It is through the act of languaging that the students made sense of each card and its relation to other conceptual units read previously. In other words, understanding stems from a combination of reading and languaging. (Knouzi et al.: 35)

Languaging involved learner interaction with a textual source of support: the informational grammar cards, which they accessed while languaging.

In the study, the authors operationalized *reading* as the activity of reading aloud, but did not consider reading that was not verbalized, such as learners' visual engagement (as eye gaze, pointing to the text, etc.) when not reading aloud or while languaging. Languaging gave the researchers access to the learners' metalinguistic processes, but we must take care not to infer a cause-and-effect ("languaging causes learning" or "languaging causes SLA") interpretation of these findings. Rather, the intensity of a learner's interaction with the assistance provided is key in development. This study is a good example of adult L2 development through a process of ZPD management; students who did more languaging were more intensely involved in interacting with the material. They sought assistance by going back to the information on the cards to receive further support. They actively managed their own ZPDs, working to gain information needed to understand the linguistic problem at hand.

Ohta (2010) considers the ZPD to be an individual's process of incorporating assistance into cognitive functioning whether the process occurs between people, or between person-and-text or other help source; Ohta posits that the adult's ability to manage and form ZPDs to promote their own learning is a skill that is gradually developed and internalized as the child matures. In this way, along with participating in ZPDs formed by the assistance of others, the child, then adolescent, then adult, progressively gains facility in creating, monitoring and managing their own ZPDs, by actively engaging with a variety of help sources to promote their own development. In essence, ZPD management means that the learner, seeking to move forward in his/her own development, actively engages with a variety of sources of assistance and support in order to learn and use the L2, creating ZPDs through this process and adapting their own help-seeking behavior, including selection of interlocutors or other sources of assistance, in order to receive developmentally appropriate support.

Ohta studied a group of advanced Asian language learners, interviewing them about their learning experiences and how they managed the L2 problems they encountered (Ohta 2010). She also queried them regarding what happened with new vocabulary they encountered during social interactions. Ohta found that learners related retention of new language with their level of engagement with language-to-be-learned. The learners who reported developing stronger L2 skills abroad also reported how they followed up on incidents of social interactive ZPDs where they received lexical assistance, by subsequently seeking further information about the new vocabulary from textual and other interactive sources, creating more ZPDs between themselves and these materials or persons in the process. All of the learners interviewed reported receiving interactive assistance, but those who reported learning new vocabulary through such interactions discussed their further engagement with the new language, such as writing down the new words and following up with further dictionary work, interaction and/or note-taking. Successful learners reported that they quickly forgot new vocabulary unless they engaged in these subsequent activities. It was not enough simply to receive interactional support.

Ohta's findings suggest ZPDs are not equal in terms of their developmental potential; whether or not that potential is realized in future language development may depend on the learners' own *voices* in the ZPD, that is, their goals and interests and level of engagement in the language learning process. Learners who were concerned about their difficulty retaining new language from the collaborative constructions that occurred in social interactions with locals *acted differently* from learners who were satisfied to simply have been able to communicate. The latter did nothing – they did not follow up. They did not take notes or work to further engage with the new language. They were simply pleased to have successfully participated in a particular conversation. The former, however, pounced upon these new items, whether immediately, or subsequently, or both. These learners were expert at managing their own ZPDs by creating contexts where ZPDs would emerge to support their development. They reported engaging repeatedly in these kinds of activities, engaging in an iterative process of ZPD management and self-scaffolding. Ohta's findings suggest that the extent to which participating in ZPDs relates to language learning is deeply connected to the individual learner's engagement in creating and managing a series of ZPDs, moving toward increased independence and self-regulation of L2 skills.

30.4 Conclusion

The ZPD is not a pedagogical technique or recipe for learning, nor a prescription about how instruction should proceed. Chaiklin (2003) and Kinginger (2002) share concerns that this is how the ZPD has been misunderstood by some western researchers using the construct in their work. While Chaiklin (2003) recommends limiting the term to meaning what it did in Vygotsky's time, and Kinginger (2002) is concerned about applications of the term that may serve to validate the L2 instructional status quo, modern L2 researchers have broadened the meaning and use of the ZPD to a wider variety of settings. Rather than being problematic, these uses of the ZPD have served to forward our thinking about L2 development. These various uses of the ZPD in L2 research have allowed a better understanding of the mediated nature of mind in L2 development, and the developmental potential that emerges when learners and teachers, learners and learners, or more broadly, learners and various sources of assistance, engage in interaction, allowing the learner to accomplish more than would have been possible without that support.

The ZPD is a critical construct for understanding mediation in L2 development. Learners connect with language through interactive inter-mental (between people) means, whether reading or listening, writing or speaking, and whether alone accessing texts or online help, or in collaboration with another person. Increasing L2 proficiency, however, requires more than simply understanding language and more than simply being assisted. For retention and learning to occur requires an active process of engaging with help sources that allows the learner to understand and produce language that s/he could not have understood or produced without assistance. It seems that contexts involving production, such as those presented in the studies discussed here, are quite powerful for L2 learning, as the level of attention and processing necessary to produce language engages a broader range of activities than does comprehension. Active engagement and interaction with sources of assistance allow the learner to move beyond his/her established proficiencies. Then, it is up to the learner whether to continue engaging with the language-being-learned such that these new linguistic words, structures, or concepts become resources for the future as well. The ZPD shows what is developmentally possible, but actual development depends on the learner's own activity and agency to move from the present into the future.

31

Nativelike and non-nativelike attainment

Donna Lardiere

31.1 Introduction: overview of ultimate attainment in SLA

This chapter examines the *endstate* grammatical knowledge, or *ultimate attainment*, of adult second language learners. Other terms for the developmental period under consideration in this chapter are found throughout the linguistic and psycholinguistic literature, e.g. *steady state* (Chomsky 1986), *asymptote* (Birdsong 2009b) and *stable state* (Eubank and Gregg 1999). There are, of course, many kinds of non-native language learners, including child L2, learners of L3 . . . L*n*, and heritage language speakers and discussion of the endstate is also relevant to their acquisition. Carroll (2006: 53–54) remarks on the difficulties of establishing criteria for identifying and labeling bilinguals, as opposed to (endstate or non-endstate) learners. Sorace (2011) suggests that advanced L2 learners, native bilinguals and L2 speakers undergoing L1 attrition should be unified under the more general label of "bilingual." For discussion in this volume, see Chapters 16 and 17. Due to space limitations, this chapter focuses on adult learners of a second language who may be considered bilingual.

In the field of SLA, the term *ultimate attainment* refers to the outcome of grammatical development; that is, the state of knowledge actually attained at a stabilized endpoint of development in a particular domain. The domain may be specified broadly (such as knowledge of the L2 phonology, morphology, syntax, etc.) or more narrowly (such as knowledge of final obstruent devoicing or past-tense marking or restrictions on *wh*-movement), but it should always be specified. There are certain domains for which it would be strange or inappropriate to speak of ultimate attainment, such as the learning of new lexical items and idioms, which is ongoing throughout one's lifetime in both native and non-native languages. Additionally, as pointed out by Birdsong (2009b: 401), linguistic systems are dynamic in the sense that both the L1 and L2 may continue to mutually influence or assimilate to each other (see also Sorace 2003); thus, endstate competence is an idealization of finality used by researchers to describe a stabilized representation of the abstract features of the underlying grammatical system of a particular language for a particular speaker.

Ultimate attainment in any given domain in a second language may be nativelike or not. Unlike L1 ultimate attainment, which is widely presumed under normal circumstances to be eventually inevitably successful, there is no presumption of success or failure inherent in the term when used for L2 acquisition.[1] Although it has long been observed that ultimate attainment is non-nativelike for most post-adolescent L2 learners for some domains (to be discussed below), that might not necessarily be the case for any given individual learner. Birdsong (1999b: 14–15), for example, argues for a 10–15 percent success rate of nativelike L2 attainment among the relevant population, that is, among learners who have been immersed for a substantial length of time in an environment that favors language acquisition.

31.1.1 Why is the study of L2 ultimate attainment interesting?

For L1 acquisition, as mentioned above, it is widely accepted that all normal children are eventually ultimately successful at converging on the target grammar of their native language. It is the task of L1 acquisition research to explain how such convergence is possible.[2] This description is compatible with use of the term here. Linguistically informed approaches to acquisition rely on models of linguistic theory that are typically based on the intuitions and/or attested language data of mature native speakers; researchers then work backwards to try to figure out how and at what developmental point such knowledge could have been acquired. Generative research in particular, following Chomsky (1981, 1986), has attempted to determine what innate properties must be attributable to the human language faculty that could account for the nature of the complex system of knowledge ultimately attained by native speakers of a language, especially for those aspects of grammatical knowledge for which there is a hypothesized *poverty of the stimulus* (see Chapters 7 and 22, this volume).

It is also widely accepted that mature second language learners, on the other hand, typically do not achieve nativelike convergence in all respects for the target language grammar they are acquiring. But *can* they? It is a tantalizing question – one that has long intrigued second language researchers, and that has led to further questions: if it is possible to achieve nativelike knowledge, is the source of such knowledge the same as that of native speakers? Does the developmental path differ substantially, and if so, how? If achieving nativelike knowledge in all respects is not possible, are certain linguistic domains more vulnerable than others? Is the nature of the divergence a truly qualitative one, or more a matter of quantitative degree? What is the nature of the attained system? In the remainder of this chapter, we will touch on these issues.

31.1.2 Focusing on what can be attained

Similar to L1 acquisition research (particularly research from a formal linguistic perspective), one way to better understand the L2 endstate is by examining what has actually been acquired and then working backwards to try to account for how such knowledge could have been acquired in principle. In other words, L2 researchers interested in more formal aspects of grammatical development assume that a model of exactly *what* is acquired – a linguistic description – must underlie our understanding of how it could come to be acquired. Highly articulated models of generative grammar have provided the basis for substantial linguistic investigations into L2 grammatical knowledge to date; therefore in this chapter I primarily focus on research results obtained within this framework.

To the extent that L2ers also succeed within a poverty-of-the-stimulus learning situation (see Schwartz and Sprouse 2000, and Chapter 7, this volume; White 1989, 2003a) – that is, in cases where a learner acquires knowledge of the L2 that could not have been induced from the linguistic environment nor transferred from the grammar of a previously acquired language – then in *some* respect, the acquisition of a second language is fundamentally similar to that of children's native language acquisition. That result would be interesting if it contributed to isolating those aspects of the human language faculty that appear to be innately determined and identifying which (if any) remain intact among adult language learners. As mentioned above, the domain must be specified as precisely as possible and often depends on the particular theoretical framework adopted by researchers. The many studies that have looked at L2 knowledge of restrictions on *wh*-extraction (subjacency constraints), for example, have been primarily concerned with investigating whether nativelike intuitions about ungrammaticality are acquirable within a particular poverty-of-the-stimulus learning condition, informed by various but quite specific formulations of generative syntactic theory.[3] I return to a brief overview of the findings of such studies in Section 31.3 and consider the issue of using nativelikeness as a criterion for successful attainment in Section 31.2.1.

As White (2003a: 22) has pointed out, if the goal of a particular study is to investigate whether specific Universal Grammar (UG) principles are still available to adult L2 learners, then it is not necessary for learners to acquire knowledge that is nativelike in all respects; rather, it is sufficient to show that they have attained properties of language that could not have been induced from experience. Indeed, investigating aspects of UG-governed knowledge has been the goal of most generative-oriented SLA research, as well as the basis for claims regarding maturational critical periods for language acquisition (see Chapter 15, this volume). Note, however, that as the theoretical landscape of generative research has continued to shift within the Minimalist Program framework (Chomsky 1995, 2001, 2005, 2007b), so have the goalposts. More specifically, various grammatical properties that had previously been considered part of core syntax – and thus subject to testable hypotheses about the acquirability of particular UG constraints – have since been reassigned to the computational system's interfaces with the sensorimotor (phonology/phonetics) and conceptual–intentional (semantics/ pragmatics) systems (R. Hawkins 2008). Although the problem of defining precisely what lies within the scope of genetically programmed core knowledge has been with us at least since the inception of the Principles and Parameters Program in the 1980s, the radically diminished role of the narrow syntactic component within the Minimalist Program has forced researchers "to renew their interface credentials" (Marantz 1995: 381) in order to account for attained (or unattained) knowledge. We return to the issue of interfaces in Section 31.4.

31.1.3 Focusing on what is not attained

As mentioned above, most mature second language learners typically do not uniformly converge in all respects on the target language grammar they are acquiring. Moreover, their performance may be persistently variable in areas that generally do not fluctuate so widely for native speakers, such as in producing regular inflectional morphology. This variability can occur even if their L2 grammars appear to reflect knowledge of hypothesized UG features and/or constraints (see Lardiere 2007 for a detailed adult L2 case study demonstrating just this point). Therefore, in addition to examining whether particular UG features, principles and/or parametric options are acquirable, research in L2 ultimate attainment also conversely seeks to understand why some elements of the L2 grammar, such as certain phonological contrasts or morphological inflections, might *never* be reliably acquired even when the evidence for them is abundantly present in the linguistic environment – that is, even when the stimulus is not poor. In other words, L2 endstate *nonconvergence* (or *fossilization*) is also theoretically interesting for SLA researchers because it is the more usual outcome even though it is not yet exactly clear why that should be the case, given the availability of evidence in the input.

R. Hawkins (2001b: 352–53) points out that, even though investigating the attainment of poverty-of-the-stimulus phenomena "provides a strategy for countering claims that SLA is 'fundamentally different' from FLA," from children's acquisition, it is still necessary and in fact more informative for both a theory of UG and a theory of SLA to isolate the source(s) of the obvious differences in outcomes between L1 and L2 acquisition. He therefore advocates "difference-oriented" approaches that seek to explain why the performance of L2 acquirers often lags behind that of native speakers and/or exhibits persistent variability. These approaches are also necessarily informed by one's view of linguistic (and psycholinguistic) theory. As Hawkins points out, for example, if one adopts a "full access to UG" position, then any observed differences in ultimate attainment between first and second language acquisition must be attributed to the interaction of UG with other factors, such as persistent L1 influence, language processing or other extragrammatical factors, for which a theory needs to be developed in order to explain the observed interactions.

In focusing on L2 non-convergence, it is worth keeping in mind a couple of additional points. First, there is a theoretical distinction between "difficult to acquire but nonetheless acquirable" and "impossible to acquire." So-called *Representational Deficit Hypotheses*, for example, and *Critical Period Hypotheses* more generally, hold that nativelike attainment is in principle not possible, and that even apparently nativelike knowledge is only just that – apparent – most likely arrived at by fundamentally different means from those used by native speakers (e.g. Bley-Vroman 1990, 2009; Felix 1985; Hawkins and Hattori 2006; Newmeyer 1998; on critical periods see Chapter 15, this volume).

Second, just as the particular formal linguistic domain must be specified, as mentioned earlier, so too must be the type of cognitive ability we are investigating; in other words, it is necessary to distinguish between language use (performance) and the attained language knowledge (competence) that underlies and informs such use. Linguistic performance typically includes the real-time retrieval and integration of information across all relevant interfaces in the parsing and production of language, i.e. language processing.

On the one hand, some studies have suggested that it is possible for the underlying L2 representations of certain features or categories to be similar or identical to those of a native speaker even though the overt morphological exponents of those features are only variably produced, for reasons that might involve performance factors such as lexical retrieval or perceptual or articulatory difficulties, or difficulty mapping the relevant features to the correct morphophonological form (e.g. Herschensohn 2001; Lardiere 1998a, 2000, 2007; Prévost and White 2000). On the other hand, other studies have argued that, despite native or near-nativelike performance (typically in production), underlying competence is nonetheless non-nativelike and/or arrived at via very different means (e.g. Abrahamsson and Hyltenstam 2008, 2009; Bley-Vroman 1989; 2009; Coppieters 1987; DeKeyser 2000; Hawkins and Hattori 2006). For researchers who subscribe to the distinction between competence and performance, the theoretical possibility of a double dissociation – nativelike competence but non-nativelike performance and vice versa – requires attempting to understand the nature of L2 grammatical representations and to locate where in the course of a derivation or parse non-targetlike breakdowns occur.

31.1.4 Organization of the chapter

The remainder of this chapter is organized as follows: Section 31.2 introduces some methodological considerations in the use of *nativelikeness* as a criterion for L2 attainment, and in establishing whether a grammatical endstate has been achieved. Section 31.3 focuses on the issue of acquirability – that is, whether there are any grammatical features of a target language that are simply not ultimately acquirable for any (late) learner. This section presents a few representative examples of research studies that have investigated this question, especially from within a generative grammar framework under conditions in which the L1 and L2 differ in some relevant respect. Section 31.4 considers the issue of lack of nativelike attainment, or *fossilization*, and, more specifically, which areas seem to be more typically vulnerable. Finally, Section 31.5 offers a summary and some concluding thoughts.

31.2 Some methodological issues

31.2.1 The use of NS data in SLA ultimate attainment studies

In this section, we briefly consider the issue of setting adult native speaker performance as the benchmark criterion against which L2 endstate data are assessed. As mentioned above, success in acquisition research is typically defined in relation to degree of nativelikeness. Indeed, the use of nativelikeness as the standard for ultimate attainment in SLA is so ingrained and pervasive in the field that Birdsong (2005b: 319) has written: "Without learner departures from nativelikeness, the field would never have come up with the construct of fossilization or the Critical Period Hypothesis as it applies to L2A." Most SLA researchers make use of some type of NS data, either explicitly – by the use of actual NS controls in their studies, or implicitly – by relying on their own NS intuitions. White (1996b: 91) points out that the use of current proposals of linguistic theory to inform acquisition research is another kind of implicit use of NS data, presumably since such proposals often rely on their authors' own intuitions. Many researchers have rightly insisted that learner interlanguages (ILs) are interesting objects of inquiry in their own right, and have cautioned against analyzing IL data solely in relation to NS grammars, as this may obscure a fuller understanding of learners' actual knowledge and result in incomplete or misleading assessments of that knowledge, a problem Bley-Vroman (1983) referred to as the *comparative fallacy*.

In avoiding comparative fallacy problems, however, we do not want to throw the baby out with the bathwater. Language acquisition does not take place in a vacuum, but rather in a particular environment – a community of language users. If a learner's primary source of target language input is a community of native speakers' output, then we should be quite surprised if that learner's IL grammar bore little resemblance to any aspects of NS grammars. Birdsong (2006c: 179–80) discusses various good reasons for assessing learner performance in relation to that of NS controls: NS performance establishes a central tendency and a range of performance against which meaningful comparisons can be made for individual learners; observing NS behavior allows us to empirically confirm or establish rather than simply presume native norms (say, on the basis of theoretical linguistic predictions).

For purposes of comparing L1 vs. L2 success in acquisition research, Birdsong (2005b: 321) moreover advises that the precise aspects or domains of native-likeness be defined from the outset, and that such aspects be reasonable. For example, we would not want to consider the non-nativelike production of an unknown L2 low-frequency vocabulary item (e.g. *diamétricalement* instead of *diamétralement* in L2 French by a native English speaker) as indicative of defective L2 learning mechanisms. Lardiere (2007: 5) observes that the terms *(non-)targetlike* and *(non-)nativelike* in SLA are researcher constructs, implying something along the lines of "From the researcher's perspective this is what appears to be the case in comparison to what we have observed or hypothesized about native speaker grammars."

Finally, Bley-Vroman (2009, following Pullum and Scholz 2002) replaces the terms *success* and *failure* with *reliable* and *non-reliable* when comparing L2 outcomes to the target grammar, suggesting that the former are "too loaded, too evaluative, too likely to be thought of as applying to struggling human learners rather than to acquisition models" (2009: 193). He points out that many L2 learners with (non-reliable) grammars that diverge in some respects from those of NSs are nonetheless able to operate successfully in the L2 environment.

31.2.2 Determining if a grammatical steady state has been achieved

How should the researcher construct of ultimate attainment be operationalized; that is, how can we decide whether or when a grammatical steady state has (most likely) been achieved by the learner? As mentioned above, the linguistic domain(s) of inquiry must first be specified. Then, like many other decisions in language acquisition research, such as how we set a criterion for deciding when a particular linguistic contrast has been acquired or where to set p values for assuming statistical significance, we apply the criteria we think make the most sense for the type of study being carried out. Long (2003) discusses this issue at some length in regard to fossilization (which of course is one possible outcome of L2 ultimate attainment). He points out the need to consider "a constellation of methodological factors" such as longitudinal duration of the study, number and comparability of data samples including "all the usual sociolinguistic parameters of speech or writing," the learner's minimum years in the target language environment and extent of motivation and opportunity to learn the L2 and, all other things being equal, a preference for studying advanced-proficiency learners whose IL errors are more likely to be "potentially permanent" than those of less proficient learners (2003: 498).

Lardiere (2007) discusses a similar range of factors underlying the rationale for her choice of informant in a longitudinal case study on L2 ultimate attainment. That informant, Patty, was a native Chinese (Mandarin and Hokkien) speaker who immigrated to the USA at the age of 22, and had lived, studied and worked in the target-language (English) environment for about ten years prior to the start of data collection. At the start of and throughout the period of data collection, Patty was married to a native speaker of American English and spoke only English at home with her husband (and later, also her daughter). She had completed undergraduate and masters degrees in American universities, was working in an exclusively English-speaking office environment in a managerial capacity, and participated in various organized cultural, professional and personal development activities nearly exclusively in English. Thus, the quantity and quality of both spoken and written environmental input was not in question (cf. Sorace 2003, who writes that persistent L2 optionality is a consequence of insufficient exposure to L2 data); nor was her integrative motivation in question (see Schumann 1997). Naturalistic spoken and written data samples, in addition to elicited and acceptability judgment task data, were collected over a period of about fifteen years, enabling the researcher to establish that various aspects of Patty's L2 English grammar had indeed stabilized. (We return to some specific findings from this and other L2 endstate studies in Sections 31.3 and 31.4.)

Finally, a caveat about using L2 *proficiency* to make claims about ultimate attainment: in principle these are distinct notions and should not be confounded. It is not uncommon to find in the SLA literature statements apparently conflating L2 ultimate attainment with nativelike levels of proficiency (however the latter is assessed). For example, Hopp (2007: 19) defines ultimate attainment and the L2 endstate as "denoting an interlanguage system after prolonged and sustained exposure *and high levels of proficiency* that is structurally stable in the sense that further acquisition other than vocabulary is not likely" (my emphasis). In a recent article on the status of the Interface Hypothesis (IH) in SLA, Sorace (2011: 9 and 26) writes "Recall that the IH was proposed for *the highest possible level of ultimate attainment* in L2" and "it predicts that the speakers *at the highest level of L2 ultimate attainment* will exhibit residual optionality only with respect to overt pronouns" (my emphasis). While it is possible, or perhaps even likely, that highest-proficiency learners have indeed attained a stable endstate grammar in regard to whatever domain is being tested, this is not necessarily the case, and the converse almost certainly does not hold; in other words, learners at less-advanced proficiency levels may nonetheless have developmentally stabilized endstate grammars. As mentioned earlier, ultimate attainment in SLA refers to the state of L2 knowledge actually attained at a stabilized endpoint of development, rather than to native- or near-nativelike proficiency in a specified domain (although such proficiency is one possible outcome of development).

Practically speaking, in examining whether particular aspects of an L2 grammar *can* be attained to nativelike levels, it certainly makes sense to select as participants those learners who are most likely to have done so, that is, those at the most-advanced proficiency levels one can find, especially for those linguistic areas which are known (or hypothesized) to pose the greatest difficulties for learners. However, the researcher should keep in mind that this selection process carries with it additional complications in turn, such as how such proficiency will be assessed and questions regarding the extent to which formal language instruction or study is required to attain nativelike levels of proficiency (an issue discussed by Abrahamsson and Hyltenstam 2008; DeKeyser 2000; Lardiere 2007; Schmidt 1983; among others) and whether the kind of proficiency achieved via such study is relevant or even useful to the kind of language knowledge being investigated (see, for example, Schwartz 1993; Belikova 2008).

31.3 What is most likely to be fully acquired?

It is an open question whether the possibility of late learners' achieving nativelike proficiency across the board in all discernible aspects of a second language is theoretically interesting; it is not at all clear that it is. (Of course, it may be of immense practical importance to individual learners for sociocultural reasons and/or certain communities such as intelligence agencies.) It would certainly be theoretically interesting if depressed performance across a range of linguistic domains – phonological, morphological, syntactic and semantic – could be linked to a single cognitive source, such as difficulty in lexical access (caused in turn by the failure to establish facile processing of phonological structure during childhood) as argued by Mayberry and Eichen (1991) in their study of late L1 acquisition of ASL.[4] However, a claim regarding a single source has not generally been advanced or entertained in SLA research, where a wide variety of factors (e.g. lack of integrative motivation, low language aptitude, L1 influence, unspecified maturational constraints) have been argued to contribute to global non-nativelikeness (see also Chapter 8, this volume). It seems unlikely that, say, the source of loss of discriminatory ability in detecting phonemic contrasts tied to voice onset time is likely to share the same ontological status as failure to fill in all the right words on a cloze task testing knowledge of L2 proverbs (as in the battery of tasks used by Abrahamsson and Hyltenstam 2009 to bolster their support for the Critical Period Hypothesis). Therefore, as Birdsong (2005b: 322) points out, we need to draw a line somewhere in determining which departures from non-nativelikeness are truly indicative of a faulty language-learning mechanism.

Studies that have examined late second language learners' abilities across a variety of language areas have typically found that a subset – usually a smallish subset – of participants perform within the same range as that of native-speaker controls for at least some of the areas tested (e.g. Abrahamsson and Hyltenstam 2008; Birdsong 2006c; Marinova-Todd 2003). On the basis of results such as these, in which there is no particular domain of performance in which *all* near-native learners fall outside the range of nativelikeness,

Birdsong (2006c: 182) advances the theoretically interesting hypothesis that no particular feature of an L2 is ultimately unlearnable. In the following subsections, we take up this issue of acquirability. We turn to studies that have directly tested this hypothesis in the domains of (morpho)syntax and semantics within a generative grammar framework, in which the theoretical construct of *feature* has a more formal status.

31.3.1 UG-constrained syntactic feature selection

Within the Minimalist Program framework (see Chapter 1, this volume), acquiring a language involves the selection of a language-particular subset of features from a hypothesized universal feature inventory, and packaging or assembling these features into language-specific morphemes (a lexicon). These morpholexical items then enter into syntactic computations that derive expressions pairing (phonological) form and meaning (Chomsky 2001). In this framework, crosslinguistic variation arises because languages may select different features and/or assemble them differently within their particular lexicons. (See also Chapter 24, this volume.)

For second language acquisition, learners have already completed this selection and assembly process for their native language(s) and bring this knowledge to the task of acquiring another language. Can they successfully (re)select and (re)assemble the features of the morphemes of the target language? Various studies have addressed this issue of acquirability within the context of the study of advanced stages of development and ultimate attainment. In particular, several studies have asked, in cases for which the L1 has not selected certain features that are required by the L2: are those features still accessible?

One approach that attempts to predict the precise conditions under which nativelike acquisition is ultimately doomed to fail is a grammatical impairment model. This is referred to variously as the *Failed Functional Features Hypothesis* (Hawkins and Chan 1997), the *Representational Deficit Hypothesis* (Hawkins 2003; Hawkins and Liszka 2003), or the *Interpretability Hypothesis* (Franceschina 2005; Hawkins and Hattori 2006; Tsimpli and Dimitrakopoulou 2007; Tsimpli and Mastropavlou 2008). I adopt the cover term *representational deficit approaches* here to represent this perspective. The specific prediction is that in cases where a particular morphosyntactic feature is present in the L2 but was not previously activated in the learner's L1, that feature will simply no longer be acquirable, due to some sort of maturational or critical period effects (see the Chapter 15, this volume). In the more recent studies cited above, an additional requirement is that the feature in question be an *uninterpretable* feature – that is, a purely formal feature with no semantic content of its own, such as those that trigger movement and/or enter into agreement relations.

On the other hand, several studies have suggested that the ultimate attainment of new features, including uninterpretable ones, is indeed possible. To give readers a flavor of the types of arguments employed within these competing views, let us turn to the acquisition of a specific feature that has been extensively investigated within the generative L2 literature – namely, [+wh], an uninterpretable formal feature hypothesized within syntactic theory to drive *wh*-movement (to clause-initial position); see Adger 2003 for a detailed account. Many studies have addressed whether L1 speakers of languages lacking overt *wh*-movement, such as Chinese, Japanese and Korean, are able to acquire this feature in an L2 that requires it, such as English. On the one hand, the fronting of *wh*-words and phrases is evident in the linguistic environment; learners can observe it and in fact they do reliably learn that *wh*-words and phrases in English must occur clause-initially. However, there is some debate over whether clause-initial positioning of *wh*-words reflects actual knowledge of feature-driven *wh*-movement, which includes knowledge of constraints on such movement, such as so-called subjacency-type violations, exemplified in (1b). More specifically, learners who observe in the input a *wh*-phrase such as *which professor* in clause-initial position in a sentence like (1a) must nonetheless come to know that the same phrase in the same position is illicit in sentences like (1b):

(1) a. Which professor did Stanley claim had written a book about syntactic features?
    b. *Which professor did Stanley read a book about syntactic features had written?

Evidence of knowledge of these constraints on movement has served as a diagnostic for acquisition of *wh*-movement (and by implication a [+wh] feature value) in many studies that have explicitly discussed this issue (e.g. Hawkins and Chan 1997; Hawkins and Hattori 2006; Lardiere 2007; Li 1998; Martohardjono 1993; Miyamoto and Iijima 2003; White and Genesee 1996; White and Juffs 1998; Yusa 1999; among others).

The findings in such studies have been mixed, with some learners demonstrating impressive nativelike knowledge of feature-driven movement in quite complex sentences. One of the best known of these studies, for example, is that of White and Genesee (1996), which focused specifically on near-native speakers of L2 English who were presumed to have attained a stable grammatical endstate. White and Genesee reported that their study participants were highly accurate on a grammaticality judgment task that included both grammatical and ungrammatical instances of *wh*-extraction; there was no significant difference between the performance of the near-native L2 speakers and the NS controls. Yusa (1999) found that not only did all participants in his study produce targetlike *wh*-fronting and subject–auxiliary inversion, but several of them were sensitive to constraints on *wh*-movement and able to correctly form clauses that did not violate such constraints (e.g. so-called "superiority constraints" involving multiple *wh*-words such as *I wonder who first bought what*), suggesting that they had acquired feature-driven *wh*-movement. Lardiere's (2007) L2 ultimate attainment case study of Patty found that she not only consistently rejected subjacency violations of the type tested by Hawkins and Chan (1997), but also robustly produced preposition stranding in oblique object relative clauses for which her L1 Chinese would require an overt resumptive pronoun (e.g. *I have a girlfriend that I can introduce you to; you don't know who you should associate with*), also suggesting *wh*-movement rather than simple base-generation of a clause-initial *wh*-phrase. Miyamoto and Iijima (2003) found that higher-proficiency L1 Japanese learners of L2 English correctly rejected sentences which violated so-called Specificity Condition constraints on extraction from specific nominals such as **How many does Mary know girls?* (the equivalent of which can presumably be derived via scrambling in Japanese).

Despite these findings of apparently successful *wh*-feature acquisition, representational deficit proponents argue that such nativelike convergence is really only apparent. The study by Hawkins and Hattori (2006) exemplifies this view. Using a truth-value judgment task, they probed native Japanese speakers (and English NS controls) on their interpretation of multiple *wh*-questions in English such as *Who did Sophie's brother warn Sophie would phone when?* in which three different responses to a preceding scenario were all pragmatically plausible (i.e. "true" on the task) but required interpreting the test question according to varying degrees of (theoretically hypothesized) ungrammaticality. Participants were asked to choose "all appropriate answers to the question" (2006: 290; test item from pp. 286–87; answers 1–3 presented in order of increasing hypothesized ungrammaticality in relation to interpreting the test question):

(2)   Sophie was angry. Her holiday had been ruined because the hotel she had booked through a travel agency was full, and she had to sleep in a tent. Sophie's brother was a friend of Norman who owned the travel agency. He spoke to Norman on Thursday and told him that Sophie would be phoning his manager, Mrs. Smith, the following day to ask for her money back.

Question: Who did Sophie's brother warn Sophie would phone when?

Answer 1. He warned Norman that Sophie would phone on Friday.

Answer 2. He warned that Sophie would phone Mrs. Smith on Friday.

Answer 3. He warned Norman on Thursday that Sophie would phone.

Hawkins and Hattori found that, although there was no significant difference between the learners and the NS controls in accepting responses that did not violate any movement constraints (in relation to the test questions), the Japanese speakers were significantly more likely than the English NS controls to fail to reject sentences that did incur such violations (e.g. response types 2 and 3 above).[5] The authors concluded from their study that the learner group was drawing on the grammatical possibility of scrambling in Japanese, which is arguably not subject to *wh*-movement constraints, and that they had therefore not selected the required [+wh] feature in their L2 English. A review of the individual data produced only one Japanese speaker (out of nineteen) whose performance fell within the range of the English NS control group, but the authors discerned a possible response bias for this particular participant. They thus interpreted their findings as providing empirical support for claims of a representational deficit. In particular, they caution against interpreting nativelike performance as evidence that L2 speakers have the same underlying grammatical representations as native speakers.

Note that Hawkins and Hattori are not arguing against the acquisition of UG-constrained L2 knowledge per se, but rather only a specific piece of it – the selection of new uninterpretable features. Their claim that the L1 Japanese speakers failed to reject violations in this study is not the same as arguing that their L2 grammars are not UG-constrained, but rather that they rely on (UG-constrained) L1 features and operations to get to a similar-looking L2 result. However, it is not clear whether any of these learners' L2 grammars were at a developmental endstate (the participants were chosen on the basis of results on a syntax test, and their length of residence in an English-speaking country ranged from only nine months to eighteen years) and that therefore they ultimately *couldn't* acquire the relevant L2 features, which is what the representational deficit viewpoint requires. To the extent that a grammatical endstate can be established (as discussed in Section 31.2), not having established one for any of the experimental participants poses something of a methodological problem for the representational deficit approach in principle, because in the case of apparent non-acquisition, one might always speculate that further development could still take place.[6]

Finally, it is clear that positive evidence for constraints on *wh*-movement is underdetermined in the target language environment and acquiring these constraints thus constitutes a genuine learnability problem that must be explained. However, assuming the operation of the same few invariant computational principles in the grammars of all languages (as minimalist theory now requires), it may not be possible to pinpoint the exact source of attained L2 knowledge of movement constraints, whether nativelike or not. (See Belikova and White 2009 and Hale 1996 for additional discussion of this point.) To summarize, an overall review of the L2 literature on the acquirability of feature-driven *wh*-movement suggests that some learners in some studies (and not necessarily only those at an L2 endstate) do demonstrate nativelike attainment of constraints on *wh*-movement in the face of a poverty of the stimulus, to the extent this can be revealed via hypothesized theoretically derived effects using the tools currently available to us to test for these effects. In other words, the preponderance of available evidence suggests that, at least for some learners, the acquisition of an uninterpretable [+wh] feature is ultimately possible. By extension, there is no reason to suppose that any other syntactic feature (along with its consequent derived word order) is ultimately unacquirable as well. This conclusion is further supported by much research, including studies showing ultimate acquisition of scrambling in L2 German (Hopp 2006, 2007) and L2 Dutch (Unsworth 2005), knowledge of verb (non-)raising in L2 Mandarin (Yuan 2001) and L2 English (Lardiere 2006), and noun–adjective word order in L2 French (Gess and Herschensohn 2001).

31.3.2 Attainment of semantic knowledge in SLA

Among the most comprehensive surveys of research on ultimate attainment in L2 semantics (see also Chapter 22, this volume) are those by Slabakova (2006b, 2008), who found that knowledge of properties related to truth-conditional meanings of contrasting morphological forms (such as tense/aspect distinctions) "emerged gradually but surely" over the range of proficiency levels tested, from beginner to near-native (Slabakova 2008: 200). In several studies of L2 semantic knowledge acquirability under poverty-of-the-stimulus conditions, (at least) the most advanced learners have demonstrated that, like native speakers, they are able to distinguish between grammatical and ungrammatical interpretations.

One example of such a study is that of Dekydtspotter and Sprouse (2001), who investigated native English speakers' L2 French acquisition of constraints on interpreting continuous vs. discontinuous modified interrogative expressions discussed in Chapter 22, this volume.

In a study different to Dekydtspotter and Sprouse in which there is no poverty of the stimulus, but rather a crosslinguistic difference in the way the features of *wh*-expressions are distributed, Choi and Lardiere (2006) and Choi (2009) investigated the interpretation of variable expressions in L2 Korean by native English speakers. Unlike English *wh*-items such as *what* or *who*, *wh*-expressions in Korean are variables that do not include an inherent *wh*-operator or +Q[uestion] feature; for example, the Korean variable expression *mues* "non-human thing" can mean either "what" or "something" depending in certain cases on morphological particles inflected on the verb, as shown in (3a) and (3b), respectively:

(3) a. John-un   Mary-ka   *mues*-ul   sass-*nunci*   an-ta.
       John-TOP Mary-NOM   "thing"-ACC   bought-Q   know-DECL
       "John knows *what* Mary bought."

   b. John-un   Mary-ka   *mues*-ul   sass-*ta*-ko   an-ta.
       John-TOP Mary-NOM   "thing"-ACC   bought-DECL-C   know-DECL
       "John knows that Mary bought *something*."

Native Korean-speaking controls performed perfectly on distinguishing the two interpretations, but even advanced L1 English speakers acquiring Korean overlooked the interpretive contingency between *mues* and the particular morphological inflection on the verb, tending to overgeneralize its interpretation as the [+Q] *wh*-expression "what" even when the verbal morphology licensed only the [−Q] indefinite interpretation "something." Only four out of twenty-four of the most advanced learner group correctly interpreted the variable expressions associated with declarative and question inflection in both production and judgment tasks; none of the intermediate learners were able to do so.

Although most learners tested did not attain anything like nativelike performance in these studies, the fact that four learners did manage it comports with Birdsong's suggestion that no feature is ultimately unacquirable for at least some learners. The difficulty here seems to be primarily morphological (or morpholexical, in the sense that the relevant grammatical features such as [±Q] are distributed differently in Korean vs. English lexical items). English speakers acquiring Korean are failing to observe the contingency between the verbal inflection and the interpretation it licenses on a different word – the variable expression. This finding supports Slabakova's (2006b) contention that morphology is the primary stumbling block or bottleneck in the acquisition of universal semantic features and principles (see Chapter 24, this volume). Once the morphology is mastered, target interpretations are attainable.

Interestingly, a more recent study by Yuan (2010) investigated native English or Japanese speakers' knowledge of similar interpretive constraints of variable expressions in Mandarin Chinese. For example, the variable word *shenme* can mean "what," "something," "all" or "anything" depending on different contextual licensing expressions, as shown in (4a–c), from Yuan (2010: 220, his (1a–c), italics added):

(4) a. Ni xiang mai *shenme* (ne)?
     you want   buy *what*   (wh-Q)
     "*What* do you want to buy?"

   b. Wo *shenme* dou   xiang mai.
      I   what   each want   buy
      "I want to buy *everything*."

   c. Wo bu   xiang mai *shenme*.
      I   not want   buy what
      "I don't want to buy *anything*."

Yuan tested L2 Mandarin learners' knowledge of a range of potential licensers for the existential polarity interpretation of variables (e.g. "something"/"anything"). He found that his most advanced learners, whom he deemed to be at a developmental endstate, were able to correctly construe Chinese variable expressions for some kinds of co-occurring licensing expressions, but not others. If the licenser was a lexical word such as a non-factive verb (e.g. *renwei* "think"), negator (e.g. *meiyou* "did not"), adverb of uncertainty (e.g. *keneng* "possibly") or conditional (e.g. *ruguo* "if"), then both groups of learners successfully interpreted the licensing relation. However, for morphological licensers such as the sentence-final question particle *-ma* and inferential marker *-le*, learners' judgments remained indeterminate.

Yuan concludes that bound-morpheme licensers are more difficult to acquire than free-morpheme ones, and indeed, may never be acquired. However, it is the case that such particles were only "moderate," as opposed to "strong," licensers even for the native Chinese controls in his study, thus complicating the coding. (The lexical-word licensers were "strong" for the NSs and for both advanced-proficiency learner groups.) Moreover, as Yuan points out, it is clear that learners can establish a syntactic and semantic representation for the existential polarity interpretation of variable expressions, particularly when these co-occur with certain (lexical-word) licensers. This view is further supported by Lardiere's (2007) observations in her case study of Patty, whose productive use of existential polarity in L2 English (which lexicalizes it in expressions such as *something* and *anything*) was perfect. In line with Slabakova's (2006b) morphological bottleneck metaphor, Yuan's study appears to confirm that functional morphology presents the greatest obstacle to establishing the required licensing relation and is highly vulnerable to fossilization.

31.4 Fossilization in the L2 endstate

It is a perpetually interesting and baffling observation about adult second language acquisition that the same learner who exhibits sophisticated L2 knowledge of subjacency restrictions or interpretive constraints in the absence of direct positive or negative evidence may nonetheless fail to consistently produce or parse a simple agreement inflection on verbs or supply correct gender marking on nouns even though there is abundant evidence for the distribution of these in the environment. Such inconsistencies may persist into the L2 endstate and form part of the landscape of ultimate attainment. Fossilization is not a global phenomenon, but rather describes an L2 endstate that is non-convergent with that of native speakers in one or more particular domains. As mentioned in the introduction, the domain may be specified broadly or narrowly, but it must be specified. In the following sections, we survey areas where many learners exhibit persistent difficulty: in the acquisition of functional morphology and in interface phenomena, including L2 processing.

31.4.1 Variability in morphological inflection

Numerous L2 studies have by now documented persistent difficulties with inflectional morphology (for a good general overview and list of references, see DeKeyser 2005). As mentioned above, Slabakova (2006b: 324) refers to it as the bottleneck and tight spot of L2 grammatical acquisition, which, once acquired, allows for the unproblematic availability and application of universal semantic principles in the interpretation of a second language.

Lardiere (1998a, 2007), in her detailed longitudinal case study of Patty, found that production of inflectional morphology – particularly affixal morphology – had fossilized in Patty's endstate L2 English grammar at somewhat-to-very low levels of suppliance in obligatory contexts, depending on the inflection and to some extent the context (spoken vs. written production). However, Patty's knowledge of English in many syntactic areas associated with that morphology was targetlike. Although inflectional finiteness marking (tense and agreement) was typically not supplied, Patty's pronominal case marking on subjects as a function of clausal finiteness was perfect, as was her knowledge of verb raising and adverb placement, and null vs. overt subject marking. She often omitted inflectional affixes on regular past participles but her NP-raising in passive constructions was also fine. As mentioned above, she had excellent control of question formation (including correct use of *do*-support and subject auxiliary inversion when auxiliaries were supplied), relative clause formation and *wh*-movement in general, including knowledge of constraints on movement. Although she occasionally omitted articles (84 and 76 percent correct suppliance for definite and indefinite articles, respectively), she showed good knowledge of the more abstract properties of definiteness including a complete absence of definiteness-effect violations among her many existential *there* constructions. In short, there was a notable dissociation between Patty's successful attainment of L2 syntactic knowledge and her much less successful acquisition of inflectional, particularly affixal, morphology.

In another case study, White (2003a) investigated the role of L1 influence in fossilization for SD, a native Turkish speaker acquiring L2 English who had lived in Canada for about ten years at the time she was first recorded. White looked at SD's acquisition of definite and indefinite articles as well as verbal and plural inflectional marking. She hypothesized that if L1 influence played a role in the acquisition (and ultimate attainment) of morphology, SD's production of articles should be significantly lower than her production of verbal and plural affixes, because Turkish has rich verbal inflection and plural marking but no articles. She also hypothesized that SD's production of verbal inflection (and plural) should be significantly higher than that of Patty, since Turkish has such inflection whereas Chinese does not. Both of these hypotheses were supported, suggesting a persistent effect for L1 influence in the acquisition of morphology. (See Orr 1987 for a similar finding in relation to the L2 acquisition of the complex Chichewa (Bantu) noun class system by L1 speakers of Gujarati – a language with (only) three genders – and L1 speakers of Chingoni – another Bantu language with a highly complex noun class system quite similar to that of Chichewa.) White suggests that the presence of overt morphology in the L1 "appears to sensitize the L2 speaker to the requirement for overt morphology in the [L2]... and to facilitate its use" (2003a: 23).

An experimental study that supports this conclusion is that of Hopp (2007, 2010), who tested L1 speakers of Dutch, English or Russian grouped into advanced and near-native levels of proficiency in L2 German on their knowledge and processing of scrambling, case and subject–verb agreement inflection in German. He found that all three L1 near-native groups showed nativelike convergence on an offline grammaticality judgment task and self-paced reading task, suggesting that they had acquired nativelike representations of inflectional marking as a means to correctly assign syntactic functions to scrambled sentences in German. On a speeded grammaticality judgment task, however, only the L1 Russian near-native group demonstrated nativelike performance on reliably detecting case-marking violations; the L1 English and Dutch near-native groups did not. Hopp attributed this result to persistent L1 influence affecting L2 processing efficiency; that is, the processes used to access and compute grammatical features are less automatized than those of native speakers. (Neither English nor Dutch has case marking on full DPs, whereas Russian does.) For the less-proficient "advanced" group, several of whose L2 German grammars had most likely fossilized, only the L1 Russian group showed convergent judgments on even the self-paced tasks; neither the L1 English nor the L1 Dutch group were able to reliably use case marking for determining syntactic order (Hopp 2007: 339).

The findings of these studies suggest that inflectional morphology is difficult, and ultimately subject to fossilization for many learners. Its acquisition appears more likely to be affected not only by whether particular features (and combinations of features) are similarly overtly expressed morphologically in the L1, but possibly also by prosodic features of the L1 (Goad and White 2004a, 2006), to be further touched on below.

Additionally, the formal complexity of the paradigmatic contrasts of inflectional morphemes and the conditions under which they must, can or cannot be expressed must be considered. DeKeyser (2005), in his discussion of what makes inflectional morphology so difficult to acquire, invokes paradigm complexity in addition to low transparency of form-meaning mappings. He writes that "difficulty of form could be described as the number of choices involved in picking all the right morphemes and allomorphs to express these meanings and putting them in the right place... Morphology in L2 is hard" (2005: 5–6). For example, whereas English has suppletive, attenuated case distinctions on pronouns only (which might explain why case is not so difficult for L2 English learners to master), German case marking is more complex, with more distinctions; it is marked on determiners, so these must also be acquired; German has lexical as well as structural case; and case interacts with scrambling (Hopp 2007). In a study of the acquisition of pronominal clitics in L2 Greek, Tsimpli and Mastropavlou (2008) ascribe difficulties in acquiring the case and agreement distinctions of third-person accusative clitics as opposed to first- and second-person clitics and genitive clitics to a hypothesized theoretical distinction in interpretability between the various agreement and case features of the clitics in question. However, a much simpler explanation is available: third-person accusative clitics in Greek exhibit a six-way formal distinction in their morphological paradigm (i.e. distinct forms for each of three genders and two numbers), whereas first- and second-person clitics and genitive clitics have only a three-way distinction. There are literally only half as many forms to learn.

The variable omission of functional morphology may also be due to phonological factors, particularly crosslinguistic differences in the way functional structure is prosodified. In a series of papers espousing this view, Goad, White and Steele (2003) and Goad and White (e.g. 2004a, 2006, 2007, 2008, 2009a) have proposed the Prosodic Transfer Hypothesis, arguing that native-like attainment of morphology will be difficult (under the weaker version) or even impossible (under the stronger version) when a learner must construct a prosodic representation in the L2 that does not exist or is illicit in the learner's L1. In this case, the discrepancy between the native and target language representations will result in the learner either variably omitting or persistently mispronouncing the relevant morphemes in the target language.

As mentioned above, White (2003a), in her case study of SD, a native Turkish speaker acquiring English, reported that SD's English production of articles was considerably lower than that of verbal and plural affixes. Goad and White (2004a), in a reanalysis of the data, suggested that, while it was possible for SD to adapt prosodic structures from Turkish to accommodate appropriate representations for English tense, agreement and plural morphology, this was not possible for articles. Consequently, SD variably omitted English articles, particularly in article+adjective+noun sequences, or mispronounced them by inappropriately stressing them. The latter finding was confirmed by an acoustic analysis of SD's data carried out by Snape and Kupisch (2010), who concluded that the results supported the stronger version of the Prosodic Transfer Hypothesis. Because phonology is an area in which later L2 learners typically exhibit lingering, prominent L1 effects (see Chapters 15 and 25, this volume), its impingement on other grammatical areas such as the production of functional morphology is not surprising.

31.4.2 Fossilization at the interfaces

In contrast to representational deficit approaches, Sorace (2003, 2011) and Sorace and Filiaci (2006) have proposed that "narrow" syntactic properties (including the uninterpretable formal features that drive syntactic movement) are ultimately completely acquirable in second language acquisition, whereas interface properties involving syntax and "another cognitive domain" such as discourse conditions and/or pragmatic information structure may not be fully acquirable. This proposal, which seeks to account for observed persistent optionality in the L2 endstate, is known as the *Interface Hypothesis*. According to this hypothesis, one possible source of such optionality may be the inability to acquire interpretable features that are present in the L2 but lacking in the L1, and that relate syntactic structure to discourse/pragmatic interpretation.

For example, the use of null vs. overt subjects in null-subject languages is pragmatically determined; one explanation is that the interpretable feature [+Topic Shift] maps to overt subject pronouns in Italian, whereas [−Topic Shift] maps to null subject pronouns (Sorace 2003, 2011; Tsimpli, Sorace, Heycock and Filiaci 2004). Studies have shown that near-native L2 acquirers of Italian (a null-subject language) who are native speakers of English (a non-null-subject language) are significantly more likely to overgeneralize overt pronominal subjects in contexts where native speakers would use null subjects (e.g. Belletti, Bennati and Sorace 2007; Sorace 2003, 2011; Sorace and Filiaci 2006). In this case, the learners' L1 English has a less restrictive option (no need to distinguish between [±Topic Shift] on subject pronouns because they are always overt), or, as Belletti *et al.* (2007: 672) write: "the L2 near-natives have a wider range of options available to them for the realization of pronominal subjects than native speakers typically have."

More generally, L2 learners' persistent difficulties with integrating pragmatic, contextual factors at the syntax–discourse interface have been amply documented (e.g. see White 2009 for a brief overview and Sorace 2011 for a more extensive one). Slabakova and Montrul (2008: 457) point out that such difficulties mirror the developmental path of child L1 acquisition, in which the pragmatic knowledge needed to appropriately interpret pronominal anaphora and certain temporal and aspectual distinctions develops much later than the relevant syntactic knowledge. In order to go beyond literal interpretation to another level of contextually relevant interpretation, they observe, grammatical and lexical information must necessarily interact with discourse-pragmatic interpretation. Fernández (2006: 63) similarly points out that it is likely that the L2 application of both prosodic and discourse/pragmatic principles "are not fully learned until very late in the acquisition process, and are subject to high between-speaker variability."

Another explanation for persistent L2 optionality is that it stems from computational complexity and/or insufficient processing resources to access and integrate multiple types of information, both linguistic and non-linguistic, in real time, leading to performance problems such as the insertion of morphologically underspecified or default forms (including a zero-form, or omission). Earlier work on L2 processing, such as that of Juffs and Harrington (1995, 1996), had already established that L2 learners' parsing of complex sentences containing long-distance *wh*-extractions or garden path constructions was slower and less automatic than that of NSs, although syntactic knowledge appeared to be completely acquirable. Since then, numerous studies have attempted to investigate whether (adult) L2 processing is fundamentally, qualitatively different from that of (monolingual) native speakers, thereby precluding truly nativelike ultimate attainment. In more recent work such as Sorace (2011), the (mis)allocation of processing resources has increasingly taken center stage as the locus for persistent L2 indeterminacy (or optionality) within research involving the Interface Hypothesis.

In their review of the L2 processing literature, Clahsen and Felser (2006a: 28) cite several studies "that have examined [L2] learners at or near the top end of the L2 proficiency scale" and that have found discrepancies between learners' grammatical competence and their processing performance. Clahsen and Felser propose the Shallow Structure Hypothesis, which argues that, although L2 learners' use of lexical, semantic and pragmatic information can reach nativelikeness, their syntactic representations remain "shallower and less detailed" than those of native speakers. However, because shallow processing seems to be a useful and computationally less costly option even for native speakers, several researchers (e.g. Avrutin 2006; Dekydtspotter, Schwartz and Sprouse 2006; Frenck-Mestre 2006; Gillon-Dowens and Carreiras 2006; Hopp 2007; Indefrey 2006b; Sabourin 2006; Sekerina and Brooks 2006) have questioned whether there is truly a discontinuous qualitative difference between L1 and L2 processing, at least for some L2 learners and some native speakers. Gillon-Dowens and Carreiras (2006: 51) point out that the studies examined by Clahsen and Felser may not have involved endstate learners:

> It is interesting that [C and F] appear to be taking it for granted that their highly proficient L2 adult participants have reached a fixed, immutable stage of L2 competence beyond which they cannot progress and that whatever processing strategies the participants were using in these studies will remain unchanged; presumably because, as seen from the low number of errors, these strategies are effective for successful L2 comprehension. However, this need not necessarily be the case. Even when L2 late learners demonstrate high levels of L2 knowledge and competence in some measures (particularly off-line measures) there could still be room for "improvement" or change in terms of greater processing automaticity, or perhaps even change in the parsing options, as a result of longer exposure to the L2, or more intensive experience of the particular language structures in question.

Other researchers (e.g. Birdsong 2006b; Carroll 2006; Sorace 2011) caution against assuming that bilingual speakers' language processing, even that of native or early bilinguals, will be the same as that of monolinguals. Carroll (2006: 53), for example, points out that "having two languages in one's head will mean, at least in certain circumstances, that both languages are activated and accessed during processing."

Finally, although Clahsen and Felser minimized the role of L1 transfer in L2 processing, the study by Hopp cited above (2007, 2010) explicitly addressed this issue by comparing L1 Dutch, English or Russian near-native speakers of L2 German. As mentioned above, all three near-native learner groups attained nativelike sensitivity to case marking and subject–verb agreement in an offline acceptability judgment task and self-paced reading task, indicating knowledge of the relevant grammatical contrasts. In a speeded grammaticality judgment task, however, only the L1 Russian near-native group demonstrated nativelike performance in reliably detecting case-marking violations; the L1 English and Dutch near-native groups did not. Hopp hypothesizes that these L1 differences relate to asymmetries in the automaticity of L2 processing; that is, native Russian speakers bring L1 routines of accessing functional features and matching them to morphophonological forms to these tasks in L2 German (2007: 359). A similar type of processing explanation, he argues, could also account for the L1 effects observed in Franceschina's (2005) study of the acquisition of gender concord in L2 Spanish by native speakers of other Romance languages and English.

31.5 Conclusion

Is there any particular aspect of a second language grammar that is impossible to acquire? An overview of the research on ultimate attainment suggests that, for some learners, at least, the answer is "no." However, it is certainly not the case that most endstate L2 learners achieve nativelikeness in all respects – in fact, most do not. We have largely sidestepped the area of phonology in this chapter (see Chapter 25, this volume), but research on the interaction between prosody and the production of functional morphology, as exemplified by the studies on the Prosodic Transfer Hypothesis, cited earlier, suggest that this particular interface is especially vulnerable to fossilization. So, apparently, is the acquisition of interpretive constraints that rely on the interaction between syntax and discourse/pragmatic knowledge.

On the other hand, many studies by now have converged on the ultimate acquirability of core areas of syntax, such as constraints on extraction, scrambling, verb-raising, adverb placement, adjective placement within noun phrases and so on. Despite variability in morphological production, many learners do manage to acquire the interpretive contrasts associated with morphosyntactic features such as case, genericity/specificity, polarity and tense/aspect distinctions. As discussed by Slabakova (2006b, 2008) and Dekydtspotter (Chapter 22, this volume), nativelike semantic knowledge is acquired by many learners, especially knowledge that is "latent in grammatical architecture" (p. 463 above), such as scope ambiguities.

In the area of L2 processing, the consensus appears to be that the processing routines of late L2 learners are slower and usually less efficient than those of native speakers, although this may be a characteristic shared by all bilingual speakers. The study by Hopp (2007) suggests that nativelike L2 processing is ultimately attainable among speakers of congruent L1–L2 pairs, that is, for those languages that share similar relevant morphological characteristics. One of the greatest and most interesting challenges ahead is the ongoing attempt to disentangle the myriad factors (e.g. proficiency level, working memory span, L1 effects, grammatical complexity, task demands) that could further inform and clarify our knowledge of the relationship between grammatical competence and performance.

Appendix

Examples of structured input activities

This appendix provides four examples of structured input activities. The first two are a referential activity and an affective activity that focus on the third-person singular -s in English. The other two are a referential activity and an affective activity that focus on the use of the subjunctive mood in adjective clauses in Spanish. English translations are provided for the sample activities in Spanish.

Third-person singular -s in L2 English

A. *Referential activity on political views*
Jason is a college freshman in Dayton, Ohio, USA. In his political science class, Jason expresses views that are typically very different from the views of his classmates. Read the sentences below and indicate with an "X" whether each view expressed belongs to Jason or to Jason's classmates and then indicate whether Jason is politically more to the right or the left of his classmates, based on all of the sentences.

Jason... His classmates...
_____ _____ ...despises taxes that fund welfare programs.
_____ _____ ...want to legalize marijuana nationwide.
_____ _____ ...thinks abortion should be illegal.
_____ _____ ...support women's right to equal pay in the workplace.

_____	_____	...believe that same-sex couples should be able to marry.
_____	_____	...feel that high schools should provide birth control.
_____	_____	...feels that women should stay at home with their children.

Choose one:

_____ Jason is more liberal than his classmates.

_____ Jason is more conservative than his classmates.

B. *Affective Activity on the Typical Student*

Read the following sentences. Are they true for a typical student at your school?

The typical student...

1. gets up at 7:00 a.m.
2. skips breakfast.
3. makes their bed everyday.
4. skips at least one class a week.
5. studies in the library, not at home.
6. works part time.
7. cooks dinner every evening.
8. watches TV at night.
9. goes to bed after midnight.

Your instructor will now read each statement and then ask you to raise your hand if you marked it as true. Someone should keep track of the responses on the board.

Explanation. The processing problem with this target structure concerns its low communicative value given that English always requires overt subjects. Many learners of English have a tendency to drop the -s when the verb is in the third-person singular form because the -s is redundant with the meaning expressed by the overt subject (a proper noun, a personal pronoun such as *he, she* or *it*, etc.).

The above activities therefore were designed to force learners to pay attention to verb forms (i.e. -s or the absence of -s) in order to get meaning.

Subjunctive in adjectival clauses in L2 Spanish

A. *Actividad Referencial sobre lo que tenemos y lo que queremos...*

Paulina acaba de cumplir los 25 años, y se ha puesto a pensar en las cosas que tiene en su vida y en las cosas que no tiene pero que le gustaría obtener.

Después de pensarlo, Paulina decide escribir una lista de las cosas que tiene y las cosas no tiene pero que quiere conseguir en su vida. Indica con "X" las cosas que Paulina tiene y las cosas que quiere obtener. Luego indica si la afirmación se te aplica a ti también basado en lo que tienes y quieres en tu propia vida.

Paulina...		¿Se te aplica?	
tiene	quiere	Sí	No

...una computadora que funcione muy rápido.
...un coche que no es muy fiable.
...un coche que sea lujoso y que nunca se descomponga.
...un perro que la quiere y que la protege.
...otro perro que se lleve bien con el perro que tiene.
...un teléfono celular que saque fotos digitales.
...un trabajo que le ayuda con las cuentas que debe pagar.
...un trabajo diferente que le fascine y que le inspire.
...un televisor que tenga una pantalla muy grande.
...un libro que explique bien la astronomía.

¿Coinciden tú y Paulina con respecto a lo que tienen y lo que quieren obtener?
_____ Sí _____ No

English translation:

A. *Referential activity on what we have and what we want*

Paulina just turned 25, and she is reflecting on the things that she has in her life and the things that she would like to have. After thinking about it, Paulina decides to write a list of things that she has and things that she does not have but would like to have in her life. Indicate with an "X" the things that Paulina has and the things that she would like to have. Then indicate whether the statement applies to you as well based on what you have and what you want in your own life.

Paulina...		Does it apply to you?	
has	wants	Yes	No

...a computer that functions very quickly.
...a car that is not reliable.
...a car that is luxurious and never breaks down.

......a dog that loves her and protects her.
......another dog that gets along well with the dog she has.
......a cell phone that takes digital photos.
......a job that helps her with the bills she must pay.
......a different job that fascinates and inspires her.
......a television set that has a very big screen.
......a book that explains astronomy.

Are you and Paulina similar in terms of what you have and what you want to get?
_____ Yes _____ No

B. Actividad afectiva sobre la pareja ideal

Indica con "X" las oraciones aplicables con respecto a tu pareja ideal.

Quiero una pareja...

_____ que me ayude a aprender cosas nuevas todos los días.
_____ que cocine muy bien.
_____ que se quede conmigo cuando me siento triste.
_____ que me deje solo cuando me siento triste.
_____ que se lleve bien con toda mi familia y todos mis amigos.
_____ que se levante muy temprano todos los días.
_____ que sea extraordinariamente atractivo/a.
_____ que sea muy atlético/a/.

Translation:

B. Affective Activity about the perfect partner

Indicate with an "X" the sentences that are applicable with regard to your ideal partner.

I want a partner...

_____ who helps me learn new things everyday.
_____ who cooks really well.
_____ who stays with me when I feel sad.
_____ who leaves me alone when I feel sad.
_____ who gets along with all of my family and all of my friends.
_____ who gets up early everyday.
_____ who is extraordinarily attractive.
_____ who is very athletic.

Explanation. The processing problem with this target structure also concerns its low communicative value given that the meaning of the subjunctive mood is redundant with the meaning of the verbs that trigger the subjunctive (e.g. *want* already conveys desire). Therefore, learners of Spanish may attend to the lexical information contained in the verb and not pay sufficient attention to the form in the subjunctive in order to get meaning.

For these reasons the activities above were designed so that learners are forced to pay attention to verb forms (in subjunctive versus indicative, e.g. *sea* versus *es*) in order to get meaning.

Notes

Chapter 1

1. For a historical perspective, see Westfall (1977: 100) and Hankins (1985: 141).
2. See Piattelli-Palmarini (1980) and also Koster (2009). For Skinner's views on language, see Skinner (1957).

Chapter 2

1. Identification of linguistics as a science had also emerged in Europe in the work of the Anglo-German Friedrich Max Müller (1823–1900) and the Danish scholar Louis Hjelmslev (1899–1965) – granted that varied notions existed of what constitutes "science" and what the consequences are of subsuming linguistics under science.
2. Recently, Lardiere (2009: 176) has proposed a "rehabilitation" of contrastive analysis that returns to foundational questions not posed by Fries and Lado, namely, questions about how to define what counts as similarity or dissimilarity across L1 and L2.
3. For discussion of empiricism in language studies from diverse modern perspectives, see Aarsleff (1982), N. C. Ellis (1998), Gregg (2003a) and Jordan (2004).
4. See Siegel (2003) for an overview of relevant research, and citation of numerous studies in this vein.
5. See, for example, the commentary that accompanied publication of Firth and Wagner (1997) in volume 81, continuing into volume 82 (1998), and, ten years later, the 2007 issue of the same journal (volume 91), which commemorated Firth and Wagner (1997) and assessed its importance.

Chapter 3

1. Chomskyan linguists have focused primarily on answering question 1, while recognizing the importance of the other two questions.

Chapter 4

1. We are unable to cover all aspects of research into internal factors, such as discussions of aptitude, or research into memory, especially short-term memory, due to limitations of space, but refer readers to later chapters of the handbook.

Chapter 5

1. An anonymous reviewer notes that Hakuta's methods and criteria differed from those of Brown (1973) and colleagues, which makes comparisons complicated.
2. An anonymous reviewer points out that Hawkins' (2001a) Modulated Structure Building approach can be viewed as an update to Andersen's "transfer to somewhere" approach. See, for example, Hawkins (2001a: 73–4).

Chapter 7

For helpful critical discussion, we wish to thank Julia Herschensohn, Holger Hopp, Martha Young-Scholten and two anonymous reviewers.

1. It is worth noting, however, that the underlying order of this question, the most common type of question Pullum and Scholz cite from CHILDES, is in fact ambiguous:

   (i) a. The other dolly that was in here is there.
       b. There's the other dolly that was in here.

   Only if the question is derived from (ia) is their *where*-question relevant to the claim that input to children includes exemplars of *yes/no* or non-subject *wh*-questions with a main-clause subject containing a relative clause. Given the ambiguity in (1), then, even such questions (*Where's the other dolly that was in here?*) are not truly of the right kind.

2. The sentences in (8a) and (8b) seem to be equivalent in terms of information structure as well; that is, there seems to be no discourse context in which one variant would be felicitous and the other not. Curiously, though, fully free alternation of the two surface patterns breaks down syntactically when the DO is an unstressed pronoun, in which case only the second word order is permitted:

   (i) a. *Joe looked up it.
       b. Joe looked it up.

3. One source of debate here has been whether there are particular principles common to adult grammars that mature in children's brains at a point when children have already passed through the earliest stages of language acquisition. If this is the case, maturation of particular aspects of UG itself accounts for the forms/interpretations and timing of particular aspects

of child language (see, e.g., Borer and Wexler 1987 and Hirsch, Orfitelli and Wexler 2007). We will not pursue that possibility here since, first, it has no bearing on the existence of POS problems in L1 acquisition and, second, such maturation, if correct, happens only once and so would be irrelevant to any language acquisition that takes place after the ostensible maturation point, e.g. in adult L2 acquisition.
4. This demonstration is generally done by listing attestations of grammatical sentences in corpora ranging from *The Wall Street Journal* to the CHILDES database (MacWhinney 1995).
5. In their response, Fodor and Crowther (2002: 122) cogently observe: "It is like an economist saying that a study of poverty should include only people with insufficient money, not those with none at all."
6. See H. Marsden (2009: 154–58) for a technical discussion of what precisely L1-English L2ers learn about the features of [*dono...-mo*] such that UG restricts scope interpretation in Japanese.

Chapter 8

1. See the Section 8.4 for the distinction between traits and states.
2. OCEAN is a short version (fifty items) of a Big Five personality test which is available free of charge online from the International Personality Item Pool (2001), a public domain personality resource. It measures Openness, Conscientiousness, Extraversion, Agreeableness and Neuroticism.

Chapter 11

1. We recognize that these foci do not exhaustively cover identity research in SLA and encourage readers to refer to Block (2007a) for reviews of research on identity in foreign language and study abroad contexts as well as Ricento (2005) for more comprehensive coverage of non-native speaker identity, explored more narrowly here as non-native language teacher identity.

Chapter 13

1. This research is part of a three-year project on "Second language acquisition and native language maintenance in the Polish diaspora in Ireland and France," funded by the Irish Research Council for the Humanities and Social Sciences.

Chapter 14

1. These figures are available from internetworldstats.com, accessed on 24 March 2011.

2. The abbreviated forms in parentheses stand for "Computer-Assisted Language Instruction" (CALI), "Computer-Enhanced Language Learning" (CELL), "Computer-Based Language Teaching" (CBLT), "Hypermedia-Assisted Language Learning" (HALL), "Intelligent CALL" (ICALL), "Mobile technology-Assisted Language Learning" (MALL), "Network-Based Language Teaching" (NBLT), "Technology-Enhanced Language Learning" (TELL) and "Web-Enhanced Language Learning" (WELL).
3. Leetspeak refers to a specific CMC register, which replaces letters with other ASCII characters, such as numbers. "Leet," for instance, is often spelt "1337."

Chapter 19

1. By convention, the first hyphenated language is always the native language, for example, Dutch–English bilinguals are native speakers of Dutch speakers of English as an L2.
2. A learner's offline grammatical competence refers to the knowledge of grammatical rules, whereas his/her online capacities refers to the ability to apply these rules when processing language.

Chapter 31

1. Duffield (2009: 276) suggests that even monolingual teenagers may not yet have acquired adult nativelike knowledge of grammatical feature values and that "the road to ultimate attainment may be a long one, even for native speakers."
2. The term *convergence* has recently been given the following characterization in regard to L1 acquisition by Bley-Vroman (2009: 177), following Pullum and Scholz (2002): "end[ing] up with systems that are so similar to those of others in the same speech community."
3. The reader is referred to J. Hawkins (2004: 273) for an alternative non-generative approach to knowledge of subjacency effects. While still acknowledging the learnability problem for L1A ("one does have to explain how the child learns the limits on the set of possible sentences that go beyond the positive data to which he or she has been exposed"), Hawkins proposes that innate hierarchies of processing ease vs. complexity may structure initial hypotheses about the target grammar. This type of proposal appears compatible with recent suggestions by Chomsky (2005, 2007b) that the burden of accounting for (much of) language acquisition be shifted from the genetic endowment to "language-independent principles" of data processing, structural architecture and computational efficiency (2005: 9); also see Chapter 1, this volume.
4. It is important to emphasize that Mayberry and Eichen's (1991) study focused on ultimate attainment in late-onset L1, not L2, acquisition of ASL, thus supporting the more widely accepted claim of a critical period for L1

acquisition. In fact, Mayberry (1993) and Mayberry, Lock and Kazmi (2002) showed that late-onset L2 acquirers of ASL ultimately outperformed late-onset L1 acquirers of ASL when age of acquisition was matched across both groups.

5. However, consider the response in relation to interpretation of the test question; it is possible (and disconcertingly easy) to bypass the test question itself and to simply check each response against the story in determining whether a particular answer is "appropriate" or not, as is typical on standardized tests of reading comprehension; that is, "he did warn Norman," "Sophie would phone Mrs. Smith on Friday," "Sophie would phone on Friday," and the warning to Norman did take place "on Thursday," etc., thus rendering all the responses true and "appropriate." A native speaker might get sidetracked wondering why Mrs. Smith would be "his manager" if he (Norman) were in fact the owner of the agency as indicated. The example illustrates how difficult devising such tasks can be and why "performance or pragmatic factors" (Hawkins and Hattori 2006: 292) may have led the NS controls into also accepting answers that violated *wh*-movement constraints to the extent that they did (21–33% vs. 58–75% for the L1 Japanese learner group).

6. It is worth pointing out that over 40 percent of the English NS controls in the Hawkins and Hattori study were disqualified for failing the syntax screening test and/or choosing all three answers in more than 5 of the 29 test items, and the judgments obtained from the remaining English NS controls appear quite fragile.

Glossary

access to UG: Full Access: in generative approaches to second language acquisition, the view that all the innate properties of Universal Grammar are accessible to the L2 learner at the onset of L2 acquisition. This approach does not take a stand on the role of the L1.

access to UG: Full Transfer / Full Access: in generative approaches to second language acquisition, the view that all the innate properties of Universal Grammar are accessible to the L2 learner at the onset of L2 acquisition, and that the L1 is the starting point of L2 acquisition.

access to UG: Partial Access: in generative approaches to second language acquisition, the view that some, but not all, the innate properties of Universal Grammar are accessible to the L2 learner at the onset of L2 acquisition.

accommodation: the process whereby speakers adjust their speech in relation to the person to whom they are speaking. Speakers can modify their speech to resemble that of their interlocutor (convergence) in order to suggest solidarity with them, or in order to put a distance between themselves and the person they are addressing (divergence).

acculturation: the process of adapting to a new culture. Schumann developed the Acculturation Model in relation to second language acquisition. Acculturation implies social integration and so involves contact with the second language group. The model relates rate of acquisition with the degree of acculturation.

activation: with respect to memory (in the form of groups of features, interlinked nodes, phrase fragments or larger units of stored information), the strength of the memory for a stored item is determined by how "active" it is in recent and current language processing events. If, for example, the topic of conversation is "apples" and the word *apple* has been used on several occasions, it will have a high level of activation. The *stimulus* (the word *apple*) has activated the path to the representation of the word *apple*. All items stored in memory have a *resting level* of activation, which is the strength of the memory when it has not been used recently.

affixation: the process of adding a grammatical element (e.g. letter or word part, called a morpheme) to add extra information to a word. In European languages these are usually added before or at the end of a word but in other languages they can be placed within the word. An affix that goes on the end of a word (e.g. *-ing*) is called a suffix. One that goes at the beginning (e.g. *pre-*, *re-*) is a prefix, while one that is placed in the middle of a word is an infix (e.g. *-ell-* in the Italian word *incasellare*, from the word *casa*, meaning "home").

affordances: a term used in design and media theory to describe the communicative, creative and collaborative possibilities of a medium, material or *artefact* from the point of view of its users. Some theories include limitations or constraints as well as possible uses.

age of acquisition onset/arrival (AoA): the age at which acquisition is believed to begin; often also the age of arrival in the target environment.

agency: following Giddens *inter alia*, sociocultural approaches to language learning and language interaction use this notion to highlight the role of the speaker/learner in the shaping of his/her social environment. The speaker/learner is viewed as a social agent who reacts to the opportunities offered for social and verbal interaction, to the affordances in his/her environment through multiple activities. This social engagement implies reciprocity of perception and action. It also implies power relations and relation to social structure and control.

agreement: in languages with overt morphology, the matching of features of one syntactic constituent to those of another to which it is syntactically linked. For example, in English the verb must agree with its subject in (e.g. singular) number (*he*-sing *walk-s*-sing), and in French the article must agree in gender with the (e.g. feminine) noun it modifies (*la*-fem *pomme*-fem "the apple"). Nominal agreement with determiners and adjectives is also referred to as concord.

allophone: a predictable variant of the same phoneme; one of (what is often) several variant realizations of the same minimal sound unit, depending on the phonetic context in which that sound unit appears.

alphabetic script: a writing system that uses visual symbols (graphemes) to represent phonemes (minimal units of speech) in the language.

anaphor (anaphoric expression): an expression/element that derives its interpretation from some other expression in the discourse (called the antecedent). Usually, an anaphoric expression is represented by a pronoun (personal, reflexive, reciprocal).

anaphora resolution: the process of resolving what a pronoun, or a noun phrase, refers to in the preceding discourse. See also **Binding**.

anomia: a type of aphasia characterized by problems recalling words or names.

aphasia: a language disorder reflected by the difficulty to speak, write and sometimes read. It is caused by damage to the parts of the brain responsible for understanding and using language. Aphasia can be triggered by strokes, severe brain injuries, brain tumors or progressive neurological conditions (e.g. Alzheimer's disease). The most common types of aphasia are Broca's aphasia, Wernicke's aphasia and global aphasia.

aptitude: a specialized form of intelligence; in language probably linked to working memory, that, in interaction with context or treatment, can be predictive of success in SLA.

argument structure: elements required by a given verb that specify the participants in the state or activity expressed by the verb. Example: the verb *meet* requires two arguments, represented by the subject and object in *Chris met the president*.

artefact: human-made entity, such as a text or work of art, which is concrete, or tangible, as opposed to mentefacts, which are the underlying mental concepts of artefacts.

articles: functional elements located in the Determiner position in the syntactic tree (e.g. *the* and *a* in English), which express semantic properties such as definiteness/indefiniteness and specificity.

articulatory settings: movement patterns of muscles and the jaw used for the articulation of speech.

aspect (grammatical): also known as viewpoint aspect, a grammatical category that characterizes the temporal flow of the situation as viewed by the speaker. Viewpoint aspect can be marked by inflectional or derivational morphology, or by auxiliaries. Types of grammatical aspect include perfective, imperfective, progressive and perfect.

asynchronous interaction: computer-mediated communication which does not require sender and recipient to be online at the same time (e.g. email). See also synchronous interaction.

attrition: the loss of language skills due to disuse and forgetting in a bilingual environment.

automatization: sometimes this term is used by researchers to mean the same as proceduralization. For those who view the establishment of skills as a process going from potentially conscious to unconscious knowledge, proceduralization may be an early stage and automatization a later stage.

auxiliary fronting: the positioning of finite perfective *have*, finite periphrastic *do*, modals (e.g. *can, will*) and all types of finite *be* immediately before the subject in the same clause. The basic generative analysis of auxiliary fronting, known commonly as "Subject–Auxiliary Inversion," moves the element from I to C, as in polarity questions (i) and *wh*-questions (ii):

(i) [$_{CP}$ [$_{C'}$ Is$_i$ [$_{IP}$ John [$_{I'}$ t$_i$ [$_{VP}$ sleeping]]]]]?
(ii) [$_{CP}$ What$_j$ [$_{C'}$ will$_i$ [$_{IP}$ John [$_{I'}$ t$_i$ [$_{VP}$ do t$_j$ next]]]]]?

AX discrimination task: an experimental method used in studies of phonetics in which a respondent hears two stimili and must note whether they are the same or different.

Basic Variety (the): for Klein and Perdue (1992, 1997), the earliest stages or fossilized system (particularly for low-educated adult immigrants) in language acquisition where the relevant constraints are both syntactic and pragmatic.

behavioral study: in psycholinguistics, behavioral studies involve the investigation of participants' behavior during language-based experiments. The experiments are controlled and allow for precise observations and subsequent conclusions about language production and comprehension. For example, participants' reaction times to stimuli presented in different conditions can be recorded and analyzed to provide relevant information for models of language comprehension.

behaviorism: a school of psychology that flourished in the United States in the early twentieth century. Behaviorists (e.g. Skinner) stressed the study of observable behavior to the exclusion of concepts of mind, emotion or consciousness. Extended to the study of language, behaviorists aimed to account for the acquisition of language as the outcome of conditioning shaped by external stimuli.

bilingual Stroop test: the bilingual version of a test that measures the ability to ignore irrelevant information. In the test, participants are presented with a word in different color text and have to name the color of the font. When the word refers to a color name other than the one the word is printed in, this leads to a slower reaction time. In the bilingual version, the color word is sometimes in another language than the test language, and this leads also to slowing down of reaction times, suggesting a merged rather than separated bilingual lexicon.

Bilingual Syntax Measure: developed in the 1970s, this way of measuring the proficiency of children in their second language focused on development of inflectional morphology.

Binding: The association/relationship between a pronoun and its antecedent. The theory/module of grammar that explains how the interpretations of anaphoric expressions are assigned.

bottom-up processing: processing in which the interpretation of incoming language data is based solely on the data, without access to higher level knowledge; also known as data driven processing.

c-command: a relationship between nodes in a linguistic tree (phrase marker). Originally defined by Tanya Reinhart (1976), c-command is a shortened form of "constituent command." It corresponds to the idea of "siblings and all their descendants" in family trees. A node A c-commands node B if and only if:

(a) A does not dominate B
(b) B does not dominate A
(c) The first branching node that dominates A, also dominates B.

Cambridge Proficiency in English Test: an advanced test of English language proficiency created and administered by the University of

Cambridge Local Examination Syndicate. It comprises subtests of reading, writing, listening, speaking and use of language.

categories: in cognitive linguistic theory, meanings are not derived directly from the world in a fixed one-to-one relationship with lexical and grammatical forms. Meanings are instead complex overlapping networks that are developed by acts of conceptualization and may include encyclopedic knowledge about an item's context of use and an understanding of its associated imagery.

causative/inchoative alternation: the two different syntactic structures projected by particular verbs. The causative form includes an argument representing the causer; the inchoative does not. Example: in English, *The child broke the glass* (causative) vs. *The glass broke* (inchoative).

ceiling/floor achievement: in tests measuring accuracy, individuals may score consistently near 100 percent, a ceiling effect, or near zero, a floor effect. For example, native speakers show ceiling effects in their performance on use of their native language.

character-based script: a writing system that uses visual symbols (graphemes) to represent morphemes (minimal units of meaning) in the language.

CHILDES: the *Child Language Data Exchange System* (http://childes.psy.cmu.edu) is a database of corpora, primarily of first language acquisition data, but with some SLA corpora as well. It also contains sophisticated freeware for the transcription and analysis of learner data.

Chomskyan: relating to the American linguist Noam Chomsky who established the branch of generative theory beginning with the publication of his *Syntactic Structures* (1957). In this view, children acquire language thanks to an innate capacity, Universal Grammar, that also characterizes universal properties of human language.

clitics: neither independent words nor affixes: they "attach" themselves or *cliticize* to other words. French subject or object pronouns are examples of clitics.

cloze test: a written test of language knowledge, where words are extracted from a passage in a set pattern (e.g. every tenth word); learners' capacity to provide the required lexical or function word serves to indicate their level of proficiency.

coarticulation: in phonetics, the way articulation of segments is systematically colored by the articulation of adjacent segments.

code mixing / code switching: the use of more than one code (language/dialect/style/register) in written or spoken language production. Code switching in particular has grammatical constraints that determine fairly consistently acceptability and predict points within a sentence where a switch will take place.

Cognition Hypothesis: this hypothesis (Robinson 2001) states that tasks that are more complex because of higher reasoning demands would be more likely to promote interactional modifications in learners' conversation.

cognitivist: in SLA, theories that do not see the mind/brain as having a specialized apparatus for language learning. Instead, language is a more general property of our ability to learn and symbolize concepts.

collaborative tasks: tasks in which learners work in collaboration, provide one another with mutual support and co-construct meaning and knowledge.

Common European Framework of Reference: the six levels of the CEFR's "can do" descriptors reflect the communicative approach to language teaching and describe targets of second language proficiency in a language-neutral manner.

communicative competence: term used in applied linguistics to describe the comprehensive pragmalinguistic capabilities of a nativelike language user, which go beyond Chomsky's idea of grammatical competence and include language and culture-specific linguistic, pragmatic, social and interactional knowledge and skills. The term was coined by Dell Hymes in his ethnography of communication (1971) and later revisited and expanded by Canale and Swain (1980), who suggest three subcategories: grammatical, sociolinguistic and strategic competence.

community of practice: a social collective whose members have some sense of a common purpose and identity and pursue joint endeavors. Membership entails participation in the particular activities or practices which constitute a given community. In contrast to the view that learning entails the acquisition of decontextualized knowledge, Jean Lave and Etienne Wenger understood learning to occur as peripheral members develop the capacity to participate more intensively and more expertly in the practices of a community.

comparative fallacy: a term introduced by Bley-Vroman (1983: 6) to describe the mistake of studying the systematic character of one language (i.e. the L2 interlanguage) by comparing it to another (i.e. the target language) rather than studying it in its own right.

competence: term used by generative linguists to refer to the unconscious innate knowledge of a language underlying *performance*.

competing chain: During the attempted processing of an utterance, in the MOGUL approach, individual representations that have been activated in various working memories (auditory, phonological, syntactic, conceptual, etc.) are matched up to form a chain of representations. Within any memory store, there will always be a competition between representations for selection so, at any given moment, alternative competing chains may be created and temporarily maintained across the various working memories. Ultimately, the chain with the best overall fit for the target utterance will be selected as the one to represent the utterance in question. This applies to both comprehension and production.

Competition Model: a model of second language acquisition and processing where learning is held to be incremental so that what is learned in the first stages may be used in later ones. Learning develops as a competition between forms for a given role, as when a learner might produce *goed* or *went*. Such competitions are resolved by cue support, completeness, or whether the item has a complete or partial match with another known one, and the activation of previous knowledge.

comprehensible input: a term coined by Stephen Krashen (1982) in his Comprehensible Input Hypothesis. According to him, learners acquire grammar and vocabulary by receiving and understanding language that is slightly beyond their current level of competence. By understanding comprehensible input, learners will develop fluency in the target language they are exposed to.

comprehension: in language processing, the stages and procedure through which an external message is converted into meaning.

conceptualization: a process by which meaning is brought into being. It assumes that meaning is not derived directly from the world but is a product of how cognition structures reality.

concordance: in corpus linguistics a concordance is a set of search results in which the search item is displayed in the middle of the screen with and a left and right context (a variable number of words). A concordance can be sorted alphabetically according to search results or context (e.g. second word to the right of the search item).

constituents: words or group of words which function as single syntactic units within the hierarchical structure of human language, and which form the basis for language computation.

construct validity: this refers to the certainty researchers have of actually measuring what they think they are measuring.

construction grammar: construction grammars see grammatical form as consisting of combinations of words and morphemes where the items that are brought together acquire somewhat different meanings in combination to those which they held when separate. Grammar is thus derived from lexis and from the relations between lexical items.

constructivism: this school of thought confers a major role on the social actor in the construal of reality and of world knowledge. Knowledge of self and society, categorization of the world are deemed to be the outcome of the cognitive and social activities of the social agent. Various brands of constructivism, such as Piaget's genetic epistemology or Vygotsky's socioconstructivism, emphasize diversely the contribution of the social agent, of his/her social networks and of situated cognition in the inception of reality and of world knowledge.

Contrastive Analysis Hypothesis: the view that second language acquisition begins with a learner's assumption that properties of the L1 hold for the L2. Where the L1 and the target language are similar, acquisition is predicted to be facilitated, and where they are different, acquisition is predicted to be more difficult.

conversation analysis: first developed by Harvey Sacks, this examines the fine details of how people in conversation manage who speaks when (turn sequencing) and seek to understand how human social order is constructed in these local moments of talk.

conversational implicature: H. P. Grice (1913–88) coined the term "implicature" for communicated non-truth-conditional meaning. A conversational implicature is an inference that can be drawn from an utterance, as from one that is seemingly illogical or irrelevant, by examining the degree to which it conforms to the canons of normal conversation and the way it functions pragmatically within the situation, as when *The phone is ringing*, said in a situation where both speaker and listener can clearly hear the phone, can be taken as a suggestion to answer the phone.

critical discourse: this broad label refers to various schools of thought that deconstruct received philosophical and social categories (*language, sign, bilingualism*, etc.), that emphasize predetermined discourse formats (Foucault), that analyze social events, facts and deeds in the light of postcolonial and postmodern thought. Critical discourse examines the social and ideological circumstances and the underpinnings of theoretical constructs that are produced in the postmodern postcapitalist era.

Critical Period (also Sensitive Period): in biological terms, a fixed span of time during the maturation of an organism when a predictable development occurs, prompted by an internal (e.g. hormonal change) or external (e.g. change in daylight hours) trigger. For example, kittens develop depth perception at a specific point of maturation only if both their eyes are exposed to visual stimuli. The Critical Period is marked by an onset, a developmental peak, an offset and a terminus, after which the organism may no longer undergo the developmental milestone.

crossover effects: the violation that arises when a coindexed pronoun intervenes between a trace and its A-bar binder. *Strong Crossover* arises when the intervening pronoun c-commands the pronoun trace as in (i):

(i) *Who$_i$ does he$_i$ think Mary likes t$_i$?

Strong Crossover is accounted for as a violation of Condition C of the classic Binding theory in Chomsky's (1981) *Lectures on Government and Binding*, because an A-bar-bound trace is locally bound by an element in an A-position.

Weak Crossover arises when the intervening pronoun does not c-command the trace as in (ii):

(ii) ?*Who$_i$ does [his$_i$ mother] think Mary likes t$_i$?

Several competing accounts of the Weak Crossover effect have been offered. See also **wh-movement**.

cross-sectional studies: within language acquisition, research that includes data collected from sets of participants who are at different levels of proficiency while all other variables are deemed comparable; results are then analyzed in order to show paths of developments across the data sets.

crosstabs (cross tabulation): the creation of a contingency table from the multivariate frequency distribution of continuous and/or nominal scaled variables, for example, gender and number of languages known in a sample of participants.

data-driven learning: in the realm of language, the proposal that the input to which children are exposed is the primary, if not sole, explanation for acquisition.

declarative knowledge: this information includes encyclopedic, situational, discursive knowledge, concepts which speakers use to categorize the world, and knowledge of the meaning and forms of the specific language or languages which the speakers know. All of this knowledge can be made conscious.

declarative memory: that part of the mind/brain where knowledge of "facts" is stored. It is assumed that these facts can be accessed in a conscious way.

definiteness/indefiniteness: a semantic concept expressed by articles, such as *the* and *a*, the definite and indefinite articles in English. Depending on the semantic theory, definiteness involves uniqueness and/or familiarity, while indefiniteness is the absence of uniqueness/familiarity (e.g. *Mary saw the dog* is felicitous if there is a unique dog in the discourse, familiar to both speaker and hearer; whereas *Mary saw a dog* carries no such requirements). Definiteness is also expressed by lexical items other than articles, such as demonstratives (*this/that*) and pronouns.

deixis: the phenomenon wherein understanding the meaning of certain words and phrases in an utterance requires contextual information. Words are deictic if their semantic meaning is fixed but their denotational meaning (who and what they point to) varies depending on time and/or place. Words or phrases that require contextual information to convey any meaning – for example, English pronouns or the adverb *today* – are deictic.

dialogicality: a characteristic of human mind/cognition as socially formed such that formation of the person is shaped by their own creativity and unique characteristics combined with the always-changing history of their interactions with others, experiences and environment. Human mind and language are ever-dialogical and never fixed, with moment-by-moment changes resulting from the dynamic interaction between various factors.

differential object marking (DOM): the overt morphological marking of direct objects that are semantically or pragmatically more salient/ prominent than their unmarked counterparts.

discourse analysis: as a hybrid field of inquiry, discourse analysis differs among scholars from disciplines such as linguistics, applied linguistics, sociolinguistics, sociology, culture studies, discursive psychology, linguistic anthropology, among others. Discourse analysts investigate how social meanings, identities and power relations are constructed in social practices, spoken interactions, written texts and/or multimodal media.

discourse: can be used in different ways depending on the field from within which it is defined. Discourse is generally a section of language longer than a sentence. It can be text or conversation. Discourse is described sometimes as the language used in a specific context, for instance, journalistic discourse. In a broader sense, discourse is used to mean the sort of language which suggests worldview, belief systems or ideology.

Distributed Morphology (DM): a theoretical framework concerned with how vocabulary items are inserted into syntactic terminal nodes. One of the main tenets of DM is that in order for a vocabulary item to be inserted into a terminal node, the item must match all or a subset of the features on that node. A vocabulary item cannot be inserted into a terminal node if it bears any features not present on the node. If multiple vocabulary items are compatible with the terminal node, the most highly specified item wins. The least specified element in a paradigm is a default or "elsewhere" form that is inserted into a terminal node when no other form has features compatible with that node. The DM framework is adopted by the Missing Surface Inflection Hypothesis in order to explain why second language learners overuse default or underspecified forms.

distributional contingency: a pattern of developmental errors that can be traced to the same linguistic property. For example, during the optional infinitive stage, non-finite verb predicates co-occur with null or non-nominative subjects, which can be traced to the omission of tense. Alternatively, subject clitics and nominative subjects co-occur with finite verb predicates, which is attributed to the presence of tense in the syntactic structure.

domain-specific/domain-general: domain-specific aspects of cognition and language are thought to be specialized biologically for specific function, while domain-general mechanisms lack situational content.

dominant language: in bilingualism, the dominant language is the language that is used more often and widely. It can also be stronger in terms of grammatical proficiency.

dopamine: a chemical messenger called a neurotransmitter produced in midbrain structures, primarily the substantia nigra, but also in the ventral tegmental area. It is involved in processes that regulate movement and emotion including reward and pleasure.

E-language/I-language: a distinction made by Chomsky (1986) between E(xternalized)-language, or performance, and I(nternalized)-language, or grammatical competence.

ecology: in sociocultural theory, ecologies are social and cultural environments. Ecologies vary across settings and situations, and the individual's integration into different ecologies has an impact on cognition and social interaction.

elicited imitation fluency task: a task in which participants hear once and are asked to repeat a prompt whose content and structure are controlled to highlight what the researcher is examining.

emergentism: a theory of language evolution and learning where grammar emerges from how language is used and learned. Thus grammatical rules emerge from how we match forms to meaning, and different learners may model language knowledge differently, with one, for example, creating a form, *eyes*, by adding *eye* to *-s* when they utter it and another uttering a preassembled unit. Essentially, the knowledge that emerges amounts to more than the sum of the parts received in the input.

emic/etic: etic analyses are based on carefully defined concepts from the analytic language of social sciences, while emic analyses use the language of the participants to present their perspectives and interpretations.

empiricism: a philosophical stance that accepts that valid knowledge is necessarily solely derived via sensory experience, and does not have a source in reasoning or logic. Empiricists generally deny the existence of innate knowledge or capacities, basing all derived knowledge on externally based experience. Empiricism has traditionally been compared to rationalism, often characterized as favoring nurture (the external input) over nature (innate capacities).

epistemology: a branch of philosophy that deals with the nature of knowledge (episteme) and how it is acquired.

equivalence classification: a cognitive mechanism by which humans perceive variable signals as instances of a single category. In second language speech, this concept is employed to describe how a second language sound that is similar, but not identical, to a native language sound category may be equated with the native category by the second language learner, most notably in the work by James E. Flege.

errors: L2 forms that do not match corresponding target language forms. Example: omission of required agreement or tense morphology on a verb.

ESF study: longitudinal study of naturalistic adult learners of English, Dutch, German, French and Swedish; funded by European Science Foundation.

essentialist: from the notion that objects have properties that are essential to them. Current sociolinguistic research questions the "essentialist" character of the traditional sociological categories used by sociolinguists such as age, gender, social class, ethnicity, and holds that these are more complex than previously supposed. For instance, in relation to gender, what it really means to be male or female in a particular society can only be determined by understanding that society.

ethnography/ethnographic: a research methodology which involves intensive and long-term engagement in a social setting, typically referred to as participant observation. Such immersion in a social context enables researchers to learn about the practices and values of the people involved. Written field notes produced by participant observers are frequently supplemented by videotaped interactions, recorded interviews, written questionnaires, as well as collected artefacts and documents. By comparing, or triangulating, these varied types of data, ethnographers hope to gain an insider's perspective of the researched social setting. Researchers who do not undertake a full ethnography, but who adopt some of the data collection practices associated with ethnography often describe their methodology as "ethnographic."

Eurocentres Vocabulary Size Test: a placement test designed to estimate a learner's knowledge of the most frequent 10,000 words.

event-related brain potentials (ERPs): a technique used to record brain activity by means of electrodes placed on the scalp while participants process stimuli. ERPs correspond to the voltage difference between a reference electrode and all the other electrodes placed on the scalp, and represent the sum of post-synaptic activity of a large number of cortical *pyramidal neurons* that can be detected at some distance from their source. While the temporal resolution of ERPs is millisecond precise, spatial resolution is comparatively poor. The ERP wave can be decomposed into a series of components, characterized by their scalp distribution, polarity and latency. Different components emerge depending on the type of stimuli and task requirements, and variations in amplitude and latency are the most often employed measures. The components are informative about the nature and the timing of processing.

executive control: refers to the executive functions, situated in the frontal lobes of the brain, which are responsible for working memory, inhibitory control and planning (see the work by Bialystok on the superior executive control of bilingual children compared to monolingual peers).

Extended Projection Principle (EPP): in generative syntactic theory, the EPP refers to the requirement that a syntactic clause must have a subject. Under minimalism, the EPP feature is a feature on a functional head (such as Tense) that requires overt movement of a phrase to the specifier of the head.

extensive reading: an approach to language learning, including foreign and second language learning, which seeks to aid the process by means of large amounts of reading. Extensive reading exposes the learner to large amounts of vocabulary and from context the meaning of new words can be inferred; the effectiveness of the approach is disputed.

eye-tracking: a technique used to determine eye-movement and eye-fixation patterns; it provides an online record of the processes involved in "natural" reading. Several time measurements can be distinguished, mainly "first pass" (i.e. from the first time the eye enters a region to when it exits, to the left or right), "second pass" (i.e. subsequent re-fixations in a region) and "total reading time" (i.e. the sum of all fixations). For example, sentences can be divided into regions of interest and analyses are usually run on "first fixations" (first time the eye enters a region) and "gaze duration" (sum of all fixations from when the eye initially enters a region until it moves on to another region, to the left or right). Other measurements such as length of saccades, the percentage of skipping a region of interest or regressions (rereading of a region of interest) can reveal differences in processing difficulty.

F-values: in speech, the formants (named F1, F2, F3, etc.) refer to the resonant frequencies of the vocal tract. Vowels and sonorant consonants of different quality are acoustically distinguished by their formant frequencies.

feature checking/deletion: under minimalism, this refers to a relationship between two elements which check their features against each other: for example, the [wh] feature on a *wh*-phrase must be checked against the [wh] feature on Comp. Uninterpretable features (such as the [wh] feature on Comp) are deleted when they are checked against the corresponding interpretable features. All features must be checked, and all uninterpretable features deleted, in the course of a derivation. Feature-checking drives overt movement: if a [wh] feature carries an uninterpretable EPP feature, the *wh*-phrase must move to the specifier of CP, resulting in *wh*-fronting, as in English (e.g. *What did you see?* not *Did you see what?*).

feature reassembly: the reconfiguring of sets of grammatical features that occur in morpholexical items and functional categories in the native language (L1) into sets of features that are appropriate to the L2.

feature: in linguistic theory, a formal property of language that distinguishes some formal contrast, such as Number (e.g. contrasting singular vs. plural) or Tense (e.g. contrasting non-past vs. past), etc. In generative linguistic theory, features may have semantic content (interpretable features), or may be purely formal with no inherent semantic content of their own (uninterpretable features), as is often found in agreement systems; features may also trigger the movement of some element from one position in a sentence to another.

feedback: the information provided to the learner in response to his/her oral or written production. It is often viewed as a continuum from *explicit*, where linguistic information about non-targetlike utterances is provided, to *implicit*, a more indirect and less obtrusive way to indicate that some utterance is problematic.

filler–gap dependencies: in psycholinguistic terms, syntactic constructions that have a displaced constituent (the filler) that does not occur in the canonical position (the gap). For example, in *wh*-questions such as *What did you see ___?*, the *wh*-word is displaced sentence initially, leaving a gap in the postverbal position.

finiteness: verbs which are finite are tensed, as past, present or future; verbs which are non-finite (such as infinitives and participles) do not carry information about tense. Depending on the language, finiteness may have morphological consequences (e.g. in English, the *-ed* suffix marks past tense) and/or syntactic consequences (e.g. in French and German, finite verbs precede negation while non-finite verbs follow negation). It is possible to have a syntactically finite verb which does not carry any overt tense morphology (e.g. the present tense in English is not morphologically marked in any person/number combinations except the third-person singular; the form *walk* is a finite present-tense verb in *I walk every day* but a non-finite verb in *I like to walk*).

Firthian: refers to the school of thought developed by British linguist John Rupert Firth (1890–1960) who contributed to a definition of language in situation and context. According to the Firthian view, speech is produced in the context of culture, i.e. the larger social and cultural patterns that define society, and in the context-of-situation, defined in turn by the context of culture. In this theoretical perspective which closely knits culture and society, the function of a linguistic item is defined by its embedding in a range of contexts starting with the word and the prosodic unit, the ultimate encompassing context being the context of culture.

foreigner talk: adjustments native speakers make when conversing with non-native speakers who are considered to have limited command of the language. These adjustments are done at various linguistic levels (prosodic, phonological, lexical, morphological and syntactic).

formants: concentration of energy in particular frequency range in sounds.

fossilization: a term introduced by Selinker (1972: 216) used to characterize ultimate attainment that is non-nativelike in some clearly specified domain. Also termed **stabilization**.

functional Magnetic Resonance Imaging (fMRI): a magnetic resonance imaging technique that measures the changes in blood flow and oxygen consumption related to neural activity in the brain. This type of scan allows one to infer the areas in the brain that are activated when performing specific tasks. fMRI provides high spatial resolution but comparatively poor temporal resolution.

functional morphemes: morphemes that primarily carry syntactic, rather than lexical, meaning, and that perform grammatical functions in a phrase or sentence. Examples: plural morpheme -*s* in English marks grammatical number on some nouns; -*ed* marks past tense on some verbs.

functionalism: in linguistics, refers to theoretical approaches which relate language utterances to their context and to discourse. Functionalist approaches deny the autonomy of syntax and analyze the syntax and the semantics of utterances together in the broader pragmatic context of discourse.

gate-keeping: since K. Lewin (1890–1947) coined the notion within mass communication studies to describe the role of key social actors in the dissemination of goods and information in society, it has been widely used in various areas of research to refer to situated social practices and talk. In various social encounters (i.e. job interviews, counseling, etc.), micro-analyses have demonstrated the use of social, cultural and linguistic resources to enforce social discrimination and the means mustered to overcome domination and misjudgments. Such social situations that exhibit power relations have been called gate-keeping situations.

generative grammar: a school of linguistics associated with American linguist Noam Chomsky. Generative grammarians aim to create a theoretical model of the human language faculty that accounts for the apparently effortless, rapid and convergent acquisition of any language by child learners, under conditions where they confront "the poverty of the stimulus," that is, where the model of language that children are exposed to is inherently limited.

Government and Binding theory: also known as Principles and Parameters, this theoretical framework evolved during the 1980s as a branch of generative syntax growing out of Chomsky's (1981) *Lectures on Government and Binding*. In addition to proposals concerning domains of government and binding (see also **anaphor, binding**) a pivotal idea was that of principles – universal constraints that characterize all languages (such as structure dependency) – and parameters – syntactic properties that vary between languages. For example, the Null Subject Parameter characterizes languages as either allowing null subjects (as Spanish *[el] habla* "he speaks") or disallowing them (as English **speaks*).

grammar: the implicit knowledge of phonology (sound system), morphology (word composition) and syntax (word combination) that makes it possible to hear and understand a language.

grammaticality judgment task: a methodology used primarily by linguists from the Chomskyan generative framework, this experimental tool is valued because of its ability to show what a speaker of a language does not allow as grammatical. Subjects are asked to judge the grammaticality of sentences.

grapheme–phoneme correspondence: in an alphabetic script, the use of units of the writing system to represent the minimal units of speech of the language.

gray/white matter (brain): gray matter contains neuronal cell bodies, while white matter consists mainly of myelinated axon tracts.

Hallidayan: refers to a view of language developed by M. A. K. Halliday in the late 1950s, also called *systemic linguistics*, which argues that language is an interrelated system of choices available to speakers for expressing meaning.

heritage language: a term coined in the United States, a heritage language is an immigrant language spoken by immigrants and their children.

hermeneutic: explanatory, interpretative; relates to the interpretive process and encompasses all forms of communication and expression.

homo sapiens sapiens: the subspecies of humans to which modern humans belong. In contrast to other subspecies of *Homo sapiens*, such as *Homo sapiens neanderthalensis* or *Homo sapiens idaltu*, *Homo sapiens sapiens* exhibit fully articulate human language.

hybridity: a notion denoting linguistic, cultural and identity mixing brought about by contacts across geographical borders in the postcolonial and globalized world. It challenges the colonialist and modernist understanding of language, culture and identity as homogeneous, essentialist and fixed, and instead highlights their heterogeneity and fluidity. Homi Bhabha is an oft-cited scholar.

image schemas: schemas derived from experience that are used to build lexical and grammatical meaning. For example, we experience forces in infancy when we are pushed or push another. Arguably such a schema gives meaning to a basic transitive sentence *I hit the ball* as a similar interplay of forces.

imperfective aspect: a type of grammatical aspect. Imperfective aspect takes an internal view of the situation, focusing on the internal structure of the event rather than on the endpoints. The progressive aspect in English (marked by the *be* auxiliary plus *-ing*) is a subtype of the imperfective: e.g. *Mary was eating an apple* reports on the ongoing event of apple-eating, which may or may not be complete.

incidental/intentional lexical storage: incidental lexical storage is unintentional or unplanned learning of new words that results from other activities. It contrasts with intentional learning where the learning of new words is the focus of a lesson or activity.

induction: a way of discovering the properties of some phenomenon without using one's prior knowledge to "deduce" those properties. Learning that goes "from the particular to the general, from examples to rules" (DeKeyser 2003).

infix: morphemes placed within the word itself, e.g. in Italian the noun *profeta* "prophet" becomes *profet-izz-are* "to prophesy" when changed into a verb, with the suffix *-are* and with the addition of the infix *-izz-*.

information structure (IS): the division of an utterance into parts denoting old (given) and new information, see also **Topic and Focus**. IS is construed broadly as comprising structural and semantic properties of utterances relating to the discourse status of their content and the participant's prior and changing attitudes (knowledge, beliefs, intentions, expectations, etc.).

initial state: linguistic knowledge characterized by universal principles and binary parameters that L2 learners bring to the acquisition process prior to L2 input exposure. Under some proposals, L2 learners start out with grammatical representations derived from the native language, in whole or in part. Under other proposals, the initial state is proposed to be Universal Grammar itself, similar to L1 acquisition.

inner speech: speech that is not uttered or articulated, but exists as an elaborated form of thought. When articulation is involved, inner speech becomes private speech.

input: samples of the target language to which learners are exposed in their linguistic environment, including multiple varieties of spoken, written, visual (e.g. signs, gestures) and tactile (e.g. Braille, tactile signing) language.

intake: the subset of input that has been attended to and processed such that it becomes available to the learner's developing linguistic system for further processing, which may lead to restructuring of the system.

integration: in general the extent of participation in various domains (social cultural, linguistic, political, economic in a host country). In relation to second language acquisition, integration is usually described in relation to motivation. According to Lambert (1977), who studied anglophone speakers of French in Canada, an integrative orientation involves a sincere interest in the people and culture represented by the other group. He opposes this stance to an instrumental orientation, which involves the practical benefits of learning the L2. Gardner (1985, 2010) found a positive relation between integrative motivation and proficiency.

intensional/extensional: in semantics, the distinction between sense, the abstract meaning of a word, and reference, the external manifestation of that word in the real world. Expressions can refer *extensionally* to entities in a particular situation (e.g. this *chair* I see) but also *intensionally* to entities across situations (e.g. the abstract idea of *chairs*).

interface vulnerability: a proposal that singles out linguistic interfaces (e.g. syntax/semantics, syntax/pragmatics) as a domain of developmental difficulties. For example, if a grammatical marker is used under a specific set of discourse conditions, learners are predicted to display lower rates of accuracy on various types of tasks, even at advanced stages of acquisition. (Compare a plural marker in Chinese, which is used in pragmatically determined definite contexts and is affixed to +human nouns, to the plural marker *-s* in English, which attaches to all +count nouns, both + and − human, regardless of definiteness.)

interlanguage: a term coined in the 1970s to label an L2 learner's internal grammar, applicable to any stage from initial exposure to near-native capacity. The term implies that learners' grammars of L2 are natural languages, that is, that they essentially comprise systematic and rule-governed linguistic knowledge.

interpretation task: in second language acquisition or experimental linguistics, this is a task that tests knowledge of grammatical structures via comprehension.

intonation: linguistic use of pitch, typically over a sentence, to convey emotion or differences such as statement vs. question.

Joseph Conrad effect: presumably reflecting novelist Joseph Conrad's abilities in his second language English, this eponymous characterization implies very good command of written syntax but lack of mastery of the spoken language, particularly pronunciation.

language acquisition device (LAD): in early generative grammar (e.g. Chomsky 1965) it was proposed that human infants have a special mental function – the LAD – whose job it is firstly to analyze the samples of language a learner encounters and assign those samples grammatical descriptions. Secondly, it must evaluate the set of possible grammars that results from this process to find the one that best fits all the primary linguistic data. The LAD is sometimes interpreted, misleadingly, as a device which not only imposes limits on grammatical development but guides the actual order in which structures are acquired. Generative linguists now prefer to use the concept of Universal Grammar.

languaging: in sociocultural theory, learners' metalinguistic talk about the language being learned. More broadly, languaging may refer to an individual's use of spoken language to learn or to solve problems, when alone or with others.

latency: the latency of an ERP component indicates the time in milliseconds when a component occurs on the waveform. For example, the latency of the P600 component is generally considered to be 600ms, occurring between 500 and 800ms post-stimulus onset, with a peak response at 600ms post-stimulus onset.

learner corpora: digitized collections of learner production (speech or writing) which can now be analyzed using computerized search techniques to identify specific patterns of language use, interlanguage forms or other elements of learner language.

left dislocation: in syntax, a left dislocation is the movement of an argument or an adjunct to the left of the main clause boundary.

lemma: the part of the lexical item in psycholinguistic models of production and perception that links the conceptual meaning of a word with its syntactic characteristics and form.

length of residence (LoR): for immigrant L2 learners, the time elapsed since the beginning of their immersion in the target language environment.

LESLLA (Low-Educated Second Language and Literacy Acquisition – for Adults): an organization for those interested in adults and adolescents with limited or interrupted formal schooling. LESLLA has an annual meeting and publishes proceedings on their website: www.leslla.org.

lexeme: the part of the lexical item in psycholinguistic models of production and perception that connects the word form to the articulatory pattern.

licensing: a syntactic configuration or a feature that determines the presence of another constituent or category. For example, a *pro* subject (a null pronominal subject) is allowed to occur in syntactic structure provided that there is a syntactic head that can check (or license) the appropriate phi-features (e.g. person, number, gender) on *pro*.

light verb: a light verb typically cannot be used as a main verb, but must co-occur with another verb or adjective. *Do* is a light verb in *She doesn't read magazines, Does she read novels?* It cannot appear on its own here: *She *doesn't magazines*, **Does she novels?* Some light verbs are also used as full main verbs: *make* is a full main verb in *He made a snowman*, but is a light verb with a causative meaning in *He made the snowman disappear*.

linguistic relativity: theories of linguistic relativity see language as shaping how we think to some degree. Different cultures with different languages develop different ways of looking at the world and acquiring these can be an additional aspect of language learning.

literacy: the ability to read, write and engage with print; the term is inclusive of a range of skills with digital, oral and visual texts across cultures and contexts.

literate: a description of a person who is able to decode/encode the script of a language; the term also used to describe individuals able to navigate a wide range of digital, visual and oral texts across cultures and contexts.

locality: in linguistics, locality refers to the proximity of elements in a linguistic structure. Theories of generative syntax attempt to explain restrictions on phrase movement using syntactic locality constraints. Constraints on movement invoke locality to explain why moving a certain expression to one place gives rise to a legitimate structure, while moving it to another place yields an ungrammatical utterance. In general, the shortest move is best.

logical problem of language acquisition: also known as Plato's Problem, the input available to the language learner is too impoverished to result in the highly complex linguistic system acquired.

long-distance dependency: this term refers to the relationship between a *wh*-word or a pronoun and the antecedents to which it refers.

longitudinal studies: within language acquisition, research that includes data collected from the same set of participants over time in order to measure development.

magneto-encephalography (MEG): a technique recording the magnetic fields produced by the brain. The recordings reflect the brain activity through negative and positive peaks in the electrophysiological trace. The peaks are defined according to their amplitude, latency and distribution and reveal different types of processing performed by the brain. MEG provides high spatial and temporal resolution of neural activity.

majority language: the language of a politically dominant group, which usually has high status, is the official language of a nation, is used in the government and is imparted through education.

markedness: asymmetrical relationship between linguistic structures in contrast, whereby the *unmarked* member of the contrast is deemed more basic, less complex, acquired earlier, typologically more common, of higher frequency and phonetically easier to perceive and produce than the *marked* counterpart.

mean length of run: the average amount of time (usually measured in seconds) taken by a given speaker between pauses. However, different researchers use different periods of silence, e.g. .25 sec or .4 sec, to define pauses, so care must be taken when comparing results.

mean length of utterance (MLU): a gross indication of a child's level of development of language, MLU is calculated by counting the morphemes in each utterance in a sample and the number of utterances in that sample and then dividing the total number of morphemes by total number of utterances.

mediation: a concept in sociocultural theory / cultural-historical psychology that refers to a person's use of cultural or social tools in cognitive, social or behavioral functioning. For example, labor is mediated by tools; language mediates thought. The assistance of one person may mediate the learning, thinking, and/or cognitive development of another.

memory: those parts of the mind/brain where knowledge is stored.

Merge: the combination of two syntactic objects to form a new one, for example, the merging of a determiner and a noun to form a Determiner Phrase. See also **minimalism**.

meta-analysis: a critical overview of research studies on a particular theme or using a comparable methodology; especially used to evaluate empirical results in terms of consistency in definitions of key concepts and/or methodological practices.

metalinguistic knowledge: conscious knowledge about the grammatical structures of a language, *explicit knowledge*, as opposed to *implicit knowledge* that is not available to conscious reflection. It is possible to have learned/explicit knowledge without being able to verbalize this. For most researchers, this would not be metalinguistic knowledge, which requires that one both knows the rule consciously, and can state what the rule is.

minimalism: a theoretical framework of generative syntax deriving from Chomsky's (1995) Minimalist Program, which advocates a minimum of levels and operations in the syntax. The central process is Merge, the combination of two syntactic objects to form a new one, for example, the merging of a determiner and a noun to form a Determiner Phrase.

minority language: a language that does not have high political status or prestige and is typically not an official language.

module/modularity: the idea that mental functioning in complex organisms is subserved by discrete, specialized areas of brain and/or cognitive activity. For example, in humans it has been claimed that the language faculty is a module that processes linguistic experience, vision is a module that processes visual experience, hearing processes auditory experience and so on. While all three might be called on and integrated in the comprehension or production of utterances, their internal representations and processes are quite distinct. Some have claimed that linguistic knowledge itself is modular, resulting from the interaction of submodules of syntactic processing, semantic processing and phonological/phonetic processing.

Monitor Model: a term that has been used to describe the five hypotheses proposed by Krashen (e.g. 1981, 1982, 1985): the Acquisition/Learning Hypothesis; the Natural Order Hypothesis; the Monitor Hypothesis; the Input (and $i + 1$) Hypothesis; and the Affective Filter Hypothesis. (1) The Acquisition/Learning Hypothesis proposes that the conscious process of learning rules about a language ("learning") is not the same as the subconscious process of constructing a mental representation of linguistic knowledge ("acquisition"). (2) The Natural Order Hypothesis proposes that every learner has an internal syllabus for acquiring different aspects of a target language over time. (3) The Monitor Hypothesis proposes that rules learned about language can only be used to "edit" (consciously) one's performance when one has sufficient time to do so. (4) The Input Hypothesis proposes that acquisition occurs when learners are provided with meaning-bearing comprehensible input, in particular, input at the level of $i + 1$, which refers to input at a level slightly beyond the learner's current level of competence. (5) The Affective Filter Hypothesis proposes that acquisition occurs optimally in an environment where a learner's affective filter is low, that is, when the learner's anxiety level is low and the learner is engaged; in this way, input can be processed more efficiently.

morpheme: the smallest unit of meaning in a language, either a word or a part of a word. The word *tree-s* consists of two morphemes, *tree* and *-s*, the plural marker (which can only appear bound to a noun).

morphosyntax: the branch of linguistics that deals with grammatical processes or items that bear on both the morphological and syntactic components of a grammar.

motivation: biological motivation encompasses both the impetus toward goal-directed action as well as those actions that lead up to goal attainment.

movement rules (move α): a linguistic computation whereby a constituent is moved from one position to another. For example, in the sentence *Which book did the professor buy?*, *which book* is the object of the verb *buy* and is said to have moved from the postverbal position typical of objects, to the beginning of the sentence, in order to indicate a question is being asked.

multilingualism: the use of multiple languages by an individual or a community of speakers.

Native Language Literacy Screening Device: an assessment which gauges an individual's literacy level in the primary language(s); intended for use placing students in second language or literacy classes; used for research purposes to determine literacy level.

nativelike: conforming to or within the range of the performance or intuitions of native speakers, defined for a particular domain of investigation; one standard by which the attainment of a second language is often assessed.

nativism: the hypothesis that an organism is born with certain predispositions that guide its interaction with its environment. O'Grady (2001) has proposed that humans are born with general information-processing mechanisms that allow the acquisition of various kinds of knowledge including linguistic knowledge ("general nativism"). Chomsky has proposed that humans are born with language-specific knowledge (often called Universal Grammar). O'Grady refers to this as "special nativism."

natural analogical extension: the generalization of an already existing pattern to a novel item. For example, if you already know (through experience) that white cats like to hunt, that black cats like to hunt and that white dogs like to hunt, natural analogical extension leads you to suppose (even in the absence of experience) that black dogs like to hunt.

natural language / natural language grammars: any attested human language, which is (or was at one time) used in a human speech community; contrasts with "artificial language," an artificially created language such as a computer language.

naturalistic/instructed learners: a distinction drawn mainly by generative SLA researchers between types of language learners (beyond childhood) based on amount of formal instruction; highlighted in early SLA research (by Krashen and others) to justify a fundamental difference between acquisition and learned knowledge, but now often assumed not to be a critical distinction, at least in route of L2 development.

negation: in syntax, the grammatical means of indicating reversal of an affirmative; a sentence may be negated as *He did not leave*, or a noun may be negated as in *non-departure*. Sentential negation is often viewed as a developmental benchmark that may be achieved by learners in a stepwise fashion.

negative evidence: in the realm of language evidence that a given string or the pairing of a given string with a given interpretation is ungrammatical. By definition, direct negative evidence is not present in a language acquirer's primary linguistic data.

negotiation: a type of conversational interaction in which one of the interlocutors signals a breakdown in communication and his/her conversational partner makes efforts to solve it.

netiquette: set of online behavioral rules ("network etiquette" or "internet etiquette") that allow smooth and considerate communication between sender and recipient(s) (e.g. don't type in all caps or it looks as though YOU ARE SHOUTING).

Noticing Hypothesis: this hypothesis (Schmidt 1990) states that what learners notice in the input is what becomes intake for learning and that noticing is a necessary condition for L2 acquisition. Swain (1985) claims that one of the functions output plays in the L2 learning process is precisely the noticing function.

noticing: a concept referring to learners paying conscious attention to the input they receive when learning a language. According to Schmidt's

Noticing Hypothesis, what learners notice in the input is what becomes intake for learning. In Swain's Output Hypothesis, noticing is one of the functions that is fostered when learners produce the target language.

null subject (pro-drop) language: a language in which a sentence with a finite verb may lack an overt subject. The identity of the subject can be retrievable from discourse, or – in some pro-drop languages – can be identified on the basis of verbal morphology. Various proposals attribute null subject, or pro-drop, languages to the effects of a specific parameter setting of Universal Grammar, a setting that arguably has other grammatical consequences for such languages.

object-regulation: regulation of the person (or animal) by an object. For example, a person who checks his email every time he passes by a computer is object-regulated. A dog who chases a ball each time it is thrown is object-regulated.

ontology: a branch of philosophy which deals with the nature of being (*ontos*). It accounts for the mode of existence of given entities for their definition and reference and for the way they relate to the real world.

opiates: opiates produced by the body in the hypothalamus and pituitary are neuropeptides which act as neurotransmitters. They produce a feeling of well-being and are involved in pain relief. Opiates also include drugs derived from the opium plant such as morphine and codeine which bind to opiate receptors found primarily in the brain and spinal cord.

optional/root infinitives: an early stage in the acquisition of non-pro-drop languages during which children alternate between producing finite and non-finite verb predicates in main clauses.

order of acquisition: the sequence in which pieces of language knowledge are argued to emerge in language acquisition. Example: sequential order in which children acquiring English produce different functional morphemes (e.g. plural marker, regular past-tense markers).

other-regulation: regulation of the person (or animal) by another. The child who brushes his/her teeth when asked to do so is other-regulated. A dog who would normally chase a thrown ball, but does not do so if given the command "stay," is other-regulated.

output: the term used to refer to the language learners produce in speaking and writing.

parameters: syntactic properties that vary between languages. For example, the Null Subject Parameter characterizes languages as either allowing null subjects (as Spanish *[el] habla* "he speaks") or disallowing them (as English **speaks*).

parse: in language processing, that part of the comprehension process which interprets the syntactic information.

perceptual assimilation: a process by which a speech signal, in SLA usually a foreign speech sound, is perceived as an instance of a native sound category.

perfective aspect: a type of grammatical aspect. Perfective aspect takes an external view of the situation, viewing the event as a whole (including initial and/or terminal points), and entails completion. In English, the simple past tense (marked by *-ed*) is perfective: e.g. *Mary ate an apple* reports on the complete apple-eating event.

performance: the actual production of utterances in real time, potentially affected by non-linguistic factors. This term is used by generative linguists to contrast with *competence*.

performativity: a poststructuralist notion developed by Judith Butler positing, for example, that gender identity is not biologically predetermined but is performed through a set of repeated acts that are socially and discursively constrained. Viewing gender as doing rather than being highlights the fluidity and multiplicity of identities and the possibilities for performing subversive acts. The notion is applied to other identities.

phonation/time ratio: the amount of time spent actually producing speech sounds as a percentage of the total time taken to produce a spoken text.

phoneme: a unit of speech (segment) that is used contrastively in a language, generally shown in slanted brackets //.

phonological/phonemic awareness: awareness of those sound units of the language that are represented in the alphabetic writing system.

phonology: the branch of linguistics that studies the underlying system of sound rules governing languages, and which seeks to explain how sounds encode linguistic form and meaning at word level and sentence level.

phonotactics: restrictions on possible sequences of segments in a given language.

pitch accent: the use of pitch to give prominence to a particular syllable or syllables within a word. In pitch accent languages such as Japanese, each word has one of a restricted set of possible pitch patterns.

polarity item: a polarity item, such as *any* in English, is an expression which must occur in certain contexts (*he did **not** receive **any** gifts*). Negative polarity contexts preserve information to subsets. Positive polarity contexts preserve information to supersets.

positive evidence: positive evidence in the realm of languages is evidence that a given string or the pairing of a given string with a given interpretation is grammatical. A language acquirer receives positive evidence through experience of primary linguistic data.

positivism: an intellectual position in which knowledge is assumed to exist in a form which can be measured and quantified.

positron emission tomography (PET): a technique that is used to detect neural activity in the different regions of the brain. It reveals changes in blood flow; these changes are perceived by detecting positrons, positively charged particles emitted by radioactively labeled substances injected into the blood stream. PET provides high spatial resolution but comparatively poor temporal resolution.

postfoundationalism: an umbrella term embracing poststructuralism, postmodernism and postcolonialism.

postmodernism: an intellectual movement that raises skepticism about modernist perspectives on knowledge, variously referred to as positivism, enlightenment and/or Eurocentrism, which seek to discover universal truths through scientific approaches to inquiry. Postmodernism critiques such decontextualized and essentialist understandings of social phenomena and instead emphasizes the situatedness in time and space, fluidity, and instability of knowledge and/or truths.

poststructuralism: a philosophical theory represented by scholars such as Michel Foucault, Jacques Derrida and Judith Butler. It scrutinizes the notion of objective and neutral truths in understanding human experiences and social structure, while providing an alternative understanding that politicizes and historicizes them in relation to notions such as discourse, the discursive construction of knowledge, power, regimes of truth, governmentality and performativity.

poverty of the stimulus: the apparently effortless, rapid and convergent acquisition of any language by child learners, under conditions where the model of language that children are exposed to is inherently limited.

power: one of the central notions of poststructuralism. Whereas Marxism tends to understand power as possessed by some or imposed upon others, Michel Foucault conceptualized it as circulating to produce force relations of domination, subordination and resistance. Power, from a poststructural perspective, is thus viewed as unstable, fluid and multifaceted. Power is also understood to circulate through discourse, producing knowledge as a regime of truths.

praxis: the dialectical relationship between theory, research and practice.

prefix: morphemes placed before the stem of a word: *pre-*heat; *re-*write, etc.

presupposition: a proposition assumed to be true in the evaluation of an expression. *Why did John go to the store?* presupposes that John really did go to the store.

priming effects: an implicit memory effect found when the processing of a target stimulus is affected by a preceding stimulus. For example, in a picture-naming experiment, participants are expected to be faster at naming the picture "dog" if it is preceded by the picture "cat," which share the same semantic category of animals, than if it is preceded by the picture "fork." This is called semantic priming, but priming can also be found with syntax and phonetics, for example.

primitive: the smallest unit of analysis in a hypothesis or theory. Primitives are the basic units from which terms, rules and principles are constructed. For example, [voice] and [stop] might be claimed to be primitives of a phonetic/phonological theory if they are assumed not to be further subdividable into smaller components within that theory. Larger units can be built from them, for example the consonant [b] with the features [voice, stop, bilabial].

private speech: utterances spoken not for social communication, but for individual cognitive or regulatory purposes. Private speech may be spoken, whispered or soundlessly articulated.

problematizing: refers to an analytic perspective which questions taken-for-granted knowledge. It invites exploration of how such knowledge has come to be regarded as true and what effects it may have. For example, in problematizing or questioning a seemingly objective notion such as "non-native speaker," numerous second language scholars have pointed to the ideological processes that are complicit in creating such a widely accepted category of knowledge.

procedural knowledge: this set of abilities constitutes knowledge of how to put the concepts together to generate a message, how to encode that message in the syntax and phonology of a given language and how to articulate that message in the speech sounds of that language. This knowledge cannot, in general, be made conscious.

procedural memory: that part of the mind/brain where knowledge of "skills" is stored. Whilst parts of skills may be accessible to the conscious mind, skills are largely performed without conscious awareness.

proceduralization: the process by which the ability to perform skills in an unconscious way is established in the mind/brain. Different researchers have different views on how this is done, notably on whether declarative knowledge can be the basis for procedural knowledge.

Processability theory (PT): a theory and a model of second language acquisition developed by Manfred Pienemann in the 1990s. It explains learning in terms of the systematic development of language structures which become progressively more nativelike. PT enables the learner to predict the course of development of linguistic forms in language comprehension and production.

processing online (real-time): the use a speaker makes of his/her linguistic knowledge to comprehend speech/writing while listening/reading is in progress, or to produce spontaneous speech/writing him/herself.

production: in language processing, the stages and procedures through which a meaning is converted into an external message.

prompt: a form of assistance where a peer or teacher provides part of a word or phrase needed by the learner, or provides partial assistance, stopping to allow the learner to complete an utterance.

property theory: theories of second language acquisition which aim to characterize and explain the nature of the linguistic system underlying learner grammars. This term is usually used to contrast with *transition theories*.

prosody: study of the rhythmic and melodic properties of speech.

prototype: related to categories human beings assign things to. In terms of language, for instance, some verbal or nominal forms are more prototypically "verb-like" or "noun-like" than others.

pseudo-word: a task prompt which has word-like properties in that it adheres to the allowable phonological sequences of the target language, but is meaningless.

quantification: refers to the means with which quantities are expressed.

quantifier: a linguistic expression, such as *much, few, some, all, no,* etc., that together with a noun phrase and a predicate make statements about quantities.

quantitative/qualitative studies: usually seen as a contrasting pair of approaches to research. However, in reality in linguistics, the approaches are not dichotomous but rather part of a continuum. Qualitative research emerges from sociology and anthropology and is used in social science research. Various approaches have been developed including case studies, ethnography, narrative inquiry. Data collection methods include participant observation, sociolinguistic interviews, diaries, verbal reports, discourse analysis and conversation analysis. Qualitative studies tend to focus on data which is difficult to quantify. Quantitative studies express their findings in numbers. Statistics are normally crucial to quantitative research. Recently a third category is being added to quantitative and qualitative, that of "mixed methods," which is a combination of the two that proposes to offer the best of both.

rationalism: a philosophical stance that accepts that valid knowledge is not necessarily solely derived via sensory experience, but rather may have a source in reasoning or logic. Rationalists may accept the existence of innate knowledge or capacities. The real world exists independently of any philosophical claims that may be formulated as to its mode of existence. A rationalist aims at providing refutable accounts of the real world in scientific quests.

reaction time: in psychological experiments, the amount of time required for a participant to respond to a given stimulus. For example, the number of milliseconds between the onset of a prompt and the button-pushing reaction of the participant.

recasts: a term used both in first and second language studies to refer to the formal correction by the interlocutor of the child's or the learner's non-target utterances. The meaning of the utterance is maintained but its non-target form is modified. Within an interactionist model of L2 learning (Long 1996) recasts are considered a type of implicit feedback.

reductionism: simplification of a problem or phenomenon by eliminating complexity. Avoiding reductionism means embracing complexity and considering all aspects of a problem or phenomenon, including interrelated problems and phenomena.

reference: expressions can refer *extensionally* to entities in a particular situation but also *intensionally* to entities across situations. Entities referred to may be collections (or sums) of individuals in situations, e.g. *the elephants.*

Crucially, the mind can also abstract *kinds*, denoting generic collections of entities across situations.

register: the variety of language used in particular settings and for specific purposes. Registers range from more to less formal and vary depending on the interlocutor, the situation and the mode (visual or oral). The term is especially relevant for Systemic Functional (SF) theory, which views language as a resource people use to accomplish their purposes by expressing meanings in context.

regulation: in sociocultural theory, the process of controlling one's own behavior, whether mental, physical or social. In human mental and skill development, there is a continuum from object-regulation, to other-regulation, to self-regulation, though all three levels of regulation are utilized by mature adults, depending upon the demands placed on the individual.

relativism: an epistemological position that postulates that the existence of reality and of the real world cannot be construed outside a specific theory of knowledge. In other words, the existence of the world and of its artefacts is dependent on the words that depict them.

remnant movement: movement of a constituent from which a proper sub-constituent has been extracted.

resting level: frequency is a major factor associated with resting level of activation. This is not so much frequency of exposure to given linguistic structures in the external environment as the frequency with which items are processed internally. In other words, items that are frequently processed have higher levels of resting activation than those less frequently processed.

Saussurean: relating to the Swiss linguist Ferdinand de Saussure (1857–1913), considered the founder of modern synchronic linguistics and the precursor to structuralism, especially known through his *Cours de linguistique générale* (*Course in General Linguistics*).

scaffolding: a form of mediation, where support provided from one person to another, or by cultural tools or artifacts, assists a person in performing beyond his/her individual capacity. In self-scaffolding, the individual supports his/her own performance through strategic use of external helps such as notes, dictionaries or other people.

schemas: the mental patterning of information. In cognitive linguistics a schematic meaning is seen as one that needs instantiation by another. Thus the preposition *on* only becomes fully meaningful when we say what is *on* what. Schemas are therefore productive or patterned in the way that many different things can be *on* each other.

scope (wide and narrow): scope refers to the domain of application of an operator over a linguistic expression. Scopal interaction can arise when a given linguistic expression contains two (or more) operators. For example, an expression like (i) can be associated with the distinct interpretations in (ii) and (iii).

(i) Fred did not pet three cats.
(ii) It is not the case that there exist three cats that Fred petted.
(iii) There exist three cats for which it is not the case that Fred petted them.

Sentence (i) contains both negation (¬) and existential quantification (∃). On the interpretation sketched in (ii), ¬ has wide scope and ∃ has narrow scope, while in (iii) ∃ has wide scope and ¬ has narrow scope.

scrambling: the relatively free varying of word order within a language, often based on pragmatic considerations.

self-regulation: regulation of the individual's behavior by him/herself, through his/her own volition and control. The child who brushes his/her teeth without being asked or reminded is self-regulated for this behavior. A person who can resist object-regulation by applying self-discipline, will power, or mental control, is self-regulated.

semantic entailment: the relationship between a sentence / set of sentences (the entailing ideas), and restrictions on the meanings available that fall out from the underlying syntactic structure.

semantics: the branch of linguistics that studies the meaning of words and sentences. It refers to the mechanisms whereby linguistic expressions receive denotations and to the module of language devoted to meaning.

semiotic: this term refers to the creation of meaning in sociocultural contexts. Language is regarded as one aspect of this meaning-making activity but is not treated as separable from other social resources.

shadowing: an experimental technique used by psycholinguists where participants repeat speech immediately after hearing it.

sonority: inherent loudness of a sound. The ranking of sounds from lowest sonority (stops) to highest sonority (vowels) is called the sonority scale or sonority hierarchy.

specific language impairment (SLI): a condition that conventionally describes a markedly delayed language development in the absence of any other apparent cognitive impairment.

specificity: a semantic concept that is closely related to definiteness. In many semantic theories, specificity involves referentiality, speaker knowledge and/or speaker intent to refer (other approaches to specificity analyze it in terms of partitivity, or membership in a previously mentioned set). Crosslinguistically, specificity can be expressed by articles, by adjectives (e.g. *certain* or *particular* in English) and by case marking. Specificity is often conflated with definiteness (e.g. in *Mary saw the dog*, the speaker refers to a specific dog, which is known to both speaker and hearer), but indefinites can also be specific (e.g. in *Mary saw a certain dog*, the speaker but not necessarily the hearer knows what dog it is). According to some SLA proposals, learners of English misanalyze *the* as a marker of specificity rather than definiteness.

speech act: an utterance that serves a specific function in communication. A given speech act may be done with a variety of communicative aims in mind, such as making a request, asking a question, giving an order, making a promise, giving thanks, offering an apology and so on. In linguistics, an utterance defined in terms of a speaker's intention and the effect it has on a listener.

speech rate or speaking rate: this is usually expressed as syllables per minute and indicates the average number of syllables produced per minute. It is arrived at by counting the number of syllables produced, dividing those by the total amount of time taken (which includes pause time) expressed in seconds and multiplying by sixty.

stabilization see **fossilization**

strategic competence: a term introduced by Canale and Swain (1980: 30) as an expansion of Hymes' concept of *communicative competence*. Strategic competence refers to the "verbal and non-verbal communication strategies that may be called into action to compensate for breakdowns in communication due to performance variables or to insufficient [grammatical or sociolinguistic] competence."

stress: relative prominence of a syllable or syllables within a word, phrase or sentence.

Stroop test: a test where participants are presented with words in different print colors. Some of the words are actually names of colors and the general finding is that it is more difficult to name the print color of words that are the name of a different color (e.g. *house* printed in black vs. *red* printed in black).

structural/inherent case: in generative theory, structural case is assigned or checked by a functional head in a specific structural configuration (for example, nominative case is checked against Tense in the TP projection). Inherent case, on the other hand, can be assigned by a lexical category which also assigns a theta role to the noun. For example, in <NP_1 NP_2> sequences in Russian, the second NP receives a possessor theta role and inherent genitive case from the first noun.

structuralism: a linguistic theory of the twentieth century that aims to describe the systematicity of language and its structure that flourished in both Europe (e.g. Martinet 1960) and in the United States (e.g. Bloomfield 1926). It is based on strict classifications of observed data and hence is considered empirically based.

structure dependence: refers to the fact that language structure is hiererarchical rather than linear, with words regrouping together to form phrases which form the basis of linguistic structure and are the units used for linguistic operations such as *movement rules*.

subdoxastic knowledge: mentally represented information that underlies intuitions and behavior, but to which individuals do not have direct access through introspection. Subdoxastic knowledge is knowledge below the level of conscious belief. Linguistic competence, in the sense of Chomsky (1965), is a type of subdoxastic knowledge.

suffix: a letter or word part, with no semantic attributes of its own, added to the stem of another word to add extra information. The *-s* on the end of *girls* indicates that it is plural, and the *-ed* on the end of *closed* marks the regular past simple tense, for example.

suppliance in obligatory contexts (SOC): refers to Roger Brown's use of identifiable contexts in which grammatical morphemes such as third-person singular *-s* are obligatory in the adult grammar and whether these morphemes are supplied by the language learner. Also used in L2 studies.

switch reference: a term used in linguistics to refer to a morpheme (or pronoun) that signals whether arguments in adjacent clauses corefer, or whether reference has shifted since the previous clause.

syllable: a unit of organization containing one or more speech sounds. A syllable contains a nucleus consisting of a vowel or syllabic consonant which may be preceded and/or followed by additional segments, most often consonants.

synchronous interaction: computer-mediated communication which requires both sender and recipient to be online at the same time (e.g. videoconferencing). See also **asynchronous interaction**.

syntactic impairment / representational deficit: here, an impairment in the syntactic representation of a second language learner's interlanguage. In some SLA theories, learners have an impaired syntactic representation, with missing and/or underspecified syntactic categories or features. In the verbal domain, the deficit has to do with finiteness/tense (e.g. an error of *She walk* in place of *She walks* may reflect an underspecified or impaired tense node in the syntactic representation). Some theories argue for global impairment, in which the impairment affects the grammar globally; others argue for more local impairment, in which the impairment is constrained to particular types of categories or features.

syntax: the branch of linguistics that studies the principles and rules for the construction of grammatical sentences and phrases.

temporal variable methodology: an analysis of continuous speech which measures time-based elements such as phonation time ratio, mean length of run, speech rate.

temporality: refers to existing in time or having some relationship with the concept of time. In linguistics, temporality signifies the meaning of time (past, present, future) expressed through linguistic means, e.g. a tense inflectional ending.

tense: a grammatical category that characterizes the time of the event in relation to the speech time; tense can be past, present or future and is closely related to finiteness. In generative syntactic theory, Tense is the head of the Tense Phrase (TP), located above the VP and below the CP in the syntactic tree. Verb raising / Verb movement of finite verbs involves movement of the verb from its base position to (or though) Tense, for the purposes of feature checking/deletion.

text coverage: the percentage of words in a text known to a reader or which appear in a word list. For example, if the Academic Word List (AWL) provides 10 percent coverage of a text then this means that 1 in 10 of the words in the text can be found in the AWL.

thematic/lexical verbs: verbs which assign theta roles (such as agent, patient, instrument, etc.) and have lexical content; auxiliaries (such as *be* and *have* in English) are non-thematic/non-lexical verbs. In some languages (including English), the distinction between thematic and non-thematic verbs is relevant for verb raising / verb movement.

thetic construction: in linguistics, a construction which states the existence of an entity or an event. Thetic constructions include presentational clauses, existentials and identificational sentences. In terms of information organization, thetic constructions are often described as sentence-focus or argument-focus structures. They may include information about the time of reference of the state of affairs depicted in an utterance, about the permanent entities mentioned or about the location of an event. In narratives, thetic constructions often provide background information.

third space: often attributed to cultural studies scholar Homi Bhabha, the concept of third space points to the experience of cultural heterogeneity and dynamism in the "same" space in a postmodern, postcolonial world. Such experience with difference, with alterity, enables new cultural forms, ideologies and meanings to emerge. Second language scholars such as Claire Kramsch use this metaphor to critique dichotomies such as L1 vs. L2, native culture vs. target culture or self vs. other, in order to show how these dichotomies are constructed (i.e. we create a sense of Self in relation to our understandings of an Other) and to encourage the development of "critical" L2 pedagogies and non-essentialist understandings of culture.

tone: the use of pitch differences to signal lexical or grammatical contrasts.

top-down processing: processing in which the interpretation of incoming language data is influenced by prior knowledge and expectations.

Topic and Focus: parts of an utterance from the point of view of the communicative needs of the interlocutors. Topic (given) stands for the old information while Focus (comment) stands for the new information within the same utterance. Human languages tend to structure utterances on the basis of the "given before new" principle – that is, in any particular sentence, information that is assumed to be familiar, or given, tends to be placed before that which is assumed to be new.

topicalization: in linguistics the topic is what is being talked about. Topicalization is the linguistic operation by which a topic is marked by intonation or word order permutations.

transfer (role of native language/L1): the use of knowledge from the L1 that leads to targetlike use of the L2. Positive transfer contrasts with *interference*, the use of knowledge from the L1 that leads to errors in the L2.

transition theory: theories of second language acquisition which seek to explain learner's development from one stage to the next, and what might trigger this development. This term is usually used to contrast with *property theories*.

trigger: an element in the learner's input that serves to prompt the language learner to set a parameter at a particular value (under Government and Binding syntax) or to otherwise restructure their current linguistic competence.

truncation: a syntactic account according to which the child's structure can be truncated at any maximal projection below CP. Under this account, root IP-only, Neg-P only, VP-only sentence structures are possible in child grammars, although in the adult language roots are assumed to be CPs.

truth-value judgment: a methodology in which speakers are asked to judge whether the meaning of particular sentences is true or not, usually based on a given scenario. This method can thereby provide data as to semantic interpretation within a person's grammar.

typically developing (TD): children with no unexpected and unexplained variation during the language acquisition process.

typological (typology): the study and classification of languages according to their structural features.

ultimate attainment: the state of knowledge, which may or may not be nativelike, attained at the endpoint or steady state of grammatical development, after which further grammatical development appears to have ceased.

unanalyzed chunks: multimorphemic/multiword sequences that the first or second language learner uses as if they were monomorphemic; also referrred to as formulae and holophrases.

Universal Grammar / UG (language faculty): as used by American linguist Noam Chomsky from the middle of the twentieth century, Universal Grammar is a theory of the necessary formal constraints on all human grammars, imposed in advance of experience by the structure of an innate human language faculty. Universal Grammar provides learners of every language with an abstract basis for the construction of a natural language grammar. The observable language-particular properties shape the expression of UG within any specific language.

usage: a view of first and second language acquisition as largely a process where forms are acquired by using them, both through our encounter with them in the input and through our use of them in output.

Varbrul: a set of computer programs developed by Rand and Sankoff (1990) designed to analyze variation in natural speech, where data are not evenly distributed. It discovers the differential effects of constraints on the choice of variant of a variable. The significance, contribution and hierarchy of effect of these constraints are determined by multiple regression.

variable, independent/dependent: in experimental design, the independent variable is the one being manipulated and the dependent variable is the observed result, or the consequence of the manipulation. For example, the effect of age of onset of acquisition of the L2 (independent variable) on pronunciation in the L2 (dependent variable).

variationist: an approach from within empirical linguistics established by William Labov which investigates language structure and use. It holds that much linguistic variation has social significance. Variationist research methods are usually quantitative. A variationist approach to language analysis has demonstrated the mechanism of language change by studying language variation.

verb final / verb second (V2): in languages with verb-second (V2) word order, a finite verb must appear in second position from the left edge of a sentence. In languages with verb-final (V-final) word order, a finite verb must appear in final position, on the right edge of a sentence.

verb raising / verb movement: in generative syntactic theory, syntactic movement of the verb from its base-generated position inside the VP to a higher syntactic position, such as Tense or Comp. Verb movement can be overt (with consequences for the word order) or covert (taking place at Logical Form). Verb movement is related to finiteness/tense, with finite verbs moving higher than non-finite verbs (e.g. in English, finite forms of the *be* auxiliary precede negation, as in *She is not sleeping*, but non-finite *be* forms follow negation, as in *She has not been sleeping* or *She will not be sleeping*). In English, thematic/lexical verbs do not undergo overt verb raising, and therefore must follow negation (as in *She does not sleep*, rather than *She sleeps not*).

VOT (voice onset time): the amount of time between the release of a stop consonant and the onset of voicing, or vocal fold vibration, this is a phonetic feature of stop consonants used to distinguish among voiced, voiceless and voiceless aspirated stops.

***wh*-movement (subjacency, islands)**: in generative linguistics, the theoretical displacement of an argument or adjunct in a sentence from the position where it was generated to a more external position. Example: in *What$_i$ did Miguel see t$_i$?* the form *what* is argued to have moved from the position marked by its trace (t$_i$) to the sentence-initial position. See also **crossover effects**.

working memory: that part of the mind/brain where knowledge is stored for a short time before being stored in another part of the mind/brain. It is normally thought to have limited capacity.

X-bar: in generative syntax, an abstract schema that describes the structural patterns of projections of syntactic categories. Noun Phrase (NP), Verb

Phrase (VP), etc. are characterized as XP, with subordinate expansions as complements (e.g. N-bar, an intermediate level above N, the head noun) or superordinate specifiers (as a determiner above a noun).

ZISA study (*Zweitspracherwerb italienischer-, portuguesischer- und spanischer Arbeiter*): cross-sectional and longitudinal study of adult migrant workers in Germany.

Selected references

Please visit www.cambridge.org/herschensohn-youngscholten to access the exhaustive list of references that accompanies this volume.

Aarsleff, H. 1982. *From Locke to Saussure*. Minneapolis, MN: University of Minnesota Press.
Abraham, W. (ed.). 1983. *On the formal syntax of the Westgermania*. Amsterdam: John Benjamins.
Abrahamsson, N. and Hyltenstam, K. 2008. The robustness of aptitude effects in near-native second language acquisition. *Studies in Second Language Acquisition* 30: 481–509.
  2009. Age of onset and nativelikeness in a second language: listener perception versus linguistic scrutiny. *Language Learning* 59: 249–306.
Abutalebi, J. and Green, D. 2007. Bilingual language production: the neurocognition of language representation and control. *Journal of Neurolinguistics* 20: 242–75.
Adamson, H. D. 2009. *Interlanguage variation in theoretical and pedagogical perspective*. New York and London: Routledge.
Adamson, H. D. and Regan, V. 1991. The acquisition of community norms by Asian immigrants learning English as a second language: a preliminary study. *Studies in Second Language Acquisition* 13: 1–22.
Adger, D. 2003. *Core syntax: a minimalist approach*. Oxford University Press.
Adjémian, C. 1976. On the nature of interlanguage systems. *Language Learning* 26: 297–320.
Adrian, J. A., Alegría, J. and Morais, J. 1995. Metaphonological abilities of Spanish illiterate adults. *International Journal of Psychology* 30: 329–53.
Aitchison, J. 2003. *Words in the mind*, 3rd edn. Oxford: Blackwell.
Aizawa, K. 2006. Rethinking frequency markers for English–Japanese dictionaries. In M. Murata, K. Minamide, Y. Tono and S. Ishikawa (eds.), *English lexicography in Japan*, 108–19. Tokyo: Taishukan-shoten.

Alanen, R. 1995. Input enhancement and rule representation in second language acquisition. In R. Schmidt (ed.), *Attention and awareness in foreign language learning. Technical report #9*, 259-302. Honolulu: University of Hawai'i.

Albirini, A., Benmamoun, E. and Saddah, E. 2011. Grammatical features of Egyptian and Palestinian Arabic heritage speakers' oral production. *Studies in Second Language Acquisition* **33**: 273-303.

Albright, A. 2009. Feature-based generalisation as a source of gradient acceptability. *Phonology* **26**: 9-41.

Alcón Soler, E. 1994. Negotiation, foreign language awareness and acquisition in the Spanish secondary education context. *International Journal of Psycholinguistics* **10**: 1-14.

 2002. The relationship between teacher-led versus learners' interaction and the development of pragmatics in the EFL classroom. *International Journal of Educational Research* **37**: 359-78.

 2005. Does instruction work for pragmatic learning in an EFL context? *System* **33**: 417-35.

 2007. Incidental focus on form, noticing and vocabulary learning in the EFL classroom. *International Journal of English Studies* **7**: 41-60.

Alcón Soler, E. and García Mayo, M. P. 2008. Focus on form and learning outcomes in the foreign language classroom. In J. Philp, R. Oliver and A. Mackey (eds.), *Second language acquisition and the younger learner: child's play?*, 173-92. Amsterdam: John Benjamins.

 2009. Interaction and language learning in foreign language contexts. *International Review of Applied Linguistics in Language Teaching* (special issue) **47**: 3-4.

Alegría de la Colina, A. and García Mayo, M. P. 2007. Attention to form across collaborative tasks by low-proficiency learners in an EFL setting. In M. P. García Mayo (ed.), *Investigating tasks in formal language learning*, 91-116. Clevedon: Multilingual Matters.

 2009. Oral interaction in task-based EFL learning: the use of the L1 as a cognitive tool. *International Review of Applied Linguistics in Language Teaching* **47**: 325-46.

Aljaafreh, A. and Lantolf, J. P. 1994. Negative feedback as regulation and second language learning in the zone of proximal development. *Modern Language Journal* **78**: 465-83.

Amin, N. 1997. Race and the identity of the nonnative ESL teacher. *TESOL Quarterly* **31**: 580-83.

Amsel, E. and Byrnes, J. P. (eds.). 2002. *Language, literacy, and cognitive development: the development and consequences of symbolic communication*. Mahwah, NJ: Lawrence Erlbaum.

Andersen, R. 1978. An implicational model for second language research. *Language Learning* **28**: 221-82.

 1983a. Transfer to somewhere. In S. Gass and L. Selinker (eds.), *Language transfer in language learning*, 177-201. Rowley, MA: Newbury House.

Andersen, R. and Shirai, Y. 1994. Discourse motivations for some cognitive acquisition principles. *Studies in Second Language Acquisition* 16: 133–56.

Anderson, B. 2007. Learnability and parametric change in the nominal system of L2 French. *Language Acquisition* 14: 165–214.

2008. Forms of evidence and grammatical development in the acquisition of adjective position in L2 French. *Studies in Second Language Acquisition* 30: 1–29.

Anderson, J. R. 1983. *The architecture of cognition*. Cambridge, MA: Harvard University Press.

2000. *Cognitive psychology and its implications*, 5th edn. New York: Worth.

Anderson, J. R., Bothell, D., Byrne, M. D., Douglass, S., Lebiere, C. and Qin, Y. 2004. An integrated theory of the mind. *Psychological Review* 111.4: 1036–60.

Anderson, S. R. 1982. Where's morphology? *Linguistic Inquiry* 13: 571–612.

Antoniou, M., Best, C. T., Tyler, M. D. and Kroos, C. 2010. Language context elicits native-like stop voicing in early bilinguals' productions in both NL and L2. *Journal of Phonetics* 38: 640–53.

Aoyama, K. and Guion, S. 2007. Prosody in second language acquisition: an acoustic analysis on duration and F0 range. In O.-S. Bohn and M. J. Munro (eds.), *The role of language experience in second-language speech learning: in honor of James Emil Flege*, 281–97. Amsterdam: John Benjamins.

Aoyama, K., Flege, J. E., Guion, S. G., Akahane-Yamada, R. and Yamada, T. 2004. Perceived phonetic dissimiliarity and L2 speech learning: the case of Japanese /r/ and English /l/ and /r/. *Journal of Phonetics* 32: 233–50.

Archibald, J. 1993. *Language learnability and L2 phonology*. Dordrecht: Kluwer.

1998. *Second language phonology*. Amsterdam: John Benjamins.

(ed.). 2000. *Second language acquisition and linguistic theory*. Malden, MA: Blackwell.

2009. Phonological feature re-assembly and the importance of phonetic cues. *Second Language Research* 25: 231–33.

Ardal, S., Donald, M. W., Meuter, R., Muldrew, S. and Luce, M. 1990. Brain responses to semantic incongruity in bilinguals. *Brain and Language* 39: 187–205.

Aronin, L. and Singleton, D. 2008. Multilingualism as a new linguistic dispensation. *International Journal of Multilingualism* 5: 1–16.

Au, T., Knightly, L., Jun, S. and Oh, J. 2002. Overhearing a language during childhood. *Psychological Science* 13: 238–43.

Auer, P. and di Luzio, A. (eds.). 1984. *Interpretive sociolinguistics. Migrants – Children – Migrant children*. Tübingen: Gunter Narr.

Augustinus, A. 1942 [c. 397]. *The confessions of St. Augustine*, books I–X, trans. F. J. Sheed. Kansas City, MO: Sheed and Ward.

Austin, J. L. 1962. *How to do things with words*. Oxford University Press.

Avrutin, S. 2006. The usability of syntax. *Applied Psycholinguistics* 27: 43–46.

Baddeley, A. D. 2007. *Working memory, thought and action*. Oxford University Press.

Baddeley, A. D. and Logie, R. H. 1999. Working memory: the multiple component model. In A. Miyake and P. Shah (eds.), *Models of working memory: mechanisms of active maintenance and executive control*, 28–61. Cambridge University Press.

Bailey, K. 1980. An introspective analysis of an individual's language learning experience. In R. Scarcella and S. Krashen (eds.), *Research in second language acquisition: selected papers of the Los Angeles second language research forum*, 58–65. Rowley, MA: Newbury House.

1995. Competitiveness and anxiety in adult second language learning, In H. D. Brown and S. Gonzo (eds.), *Readings on second language acquisition*, 163–205. Upper Saddle River, NJ: Prentice Hall Regents.

Bailey, N., Madden, C. and Krashen, S. D. 1974. Is there a "natural sequence" in adult second language learning? *Language Learning* **24**: 235–43.

Bakhtin, M. M. 1981. *The dialogic imagination: four essays by M. M. Bakhtin*, ed. M. E. Holquist and C. Emerson, trans. M. E. Holquist. Austin: University of Texas Press.

Bamberg, M. 2002. Literacy and development as discourse, cognition or both? *Journal of Child Language* **29**: 449–53.

Barcroft, J. 2002. Semantic and structural elaboration in L2 lexical acquisition. *Language Learning* **52**: 323–63.

2003. Effects of questions about word meaning during L2 lexical learning. *Modern Language Journal* **87**: 546–61.

2004. Effects of sentence writing in L2 lexical acquisition. *Second Language Research* **20**: 303–34.

2006. Can writing a new word detract from learning it? More negative effects of forced output during vocabulary learning. *Second Language Research* **22**: 487–97.

Barcroft, J. and Sommers, M. S. 2005. Effects of acoustic variability on second language vocabulary learning. *Studies in Second Language Acquisition* **27**: 387–414.

Bardel, C. and Falk, Y. 2007. The role of the second language in third language acquisition: the case of Germanic syntax. *Second Language Research* **23**: 459–84.

Bardovi-Harlig, K. 1992. The relationship of form and meaning: a cross-sectional study of tense and aspect in the interlanguage of learners of English as a second language. *Applied Psycholinguistics* **13**: 253–78.

1999. The interlanguage of interlanguage pragmatics: a research agenda for acquisitional pragmatics. *Language Learning* **49**: 677–713.

2000. *Tense and aspect in second language acquisition: form, meaning and use*. Oxford: Blackwell.

2009. Conventional expressions as a pragmalinguistic resource: recognition and production of conventional expressions in L2 pragmatics. *Language Learning* **59**: 755–95.

Bardovi-Harlig, K. and Bergström, A. 1996. Acquisition of tense and aspect in second language and foreign language learning: learner narratives in ESL and FFL. *Canadian Modern Language Review* **52**: 308–30.

Barron, T. 2006. Learning to say "you" in German: the acquisition of sociolinguistic competence in a study-abroad context. In M. DuFon and E. Churchill (eds.), *Language learners in study abroad contexts*, 59–88. Clevedon: Multilingual Matters.

Bartley, A., Jones, D. W. and Weinberger, D. R. 1997. Genetic variability of human brain size cortical gyral patterns. *Brain* **120**: 257–69.

Bates, E. and MacWhinney, B. 1987. Competition, variation and language learning. In B. MacWhinney (ed.), *Mechanisms of language acquisition*, 157–93. Mahwah, NJ: Lawrence Erlbaum.

Battro, A. M., Fischer, K. W. and Lena, P. J. (eds.). 2008. *The educated brain: essays in neuroeducation*. Cambridge University Press.

Bayley, R. 1996. Competing constraints on variation in the speech of adult Chinese learners of English. In R. Bayley and D. R. Preston (eds.), *Second language acquisition and linguistic variation*, 97–120. Amsterdam: John Benjamins.

Bayley, R. and Preston, D. R. (eds.). 1996. *Second language acquisition and linguistic variation*. Amsterdam: John Benjamins.

Bayley, R. and Regan, V. 2004. The acquisition of sociolinguistic competence. *Journal of Sociolinguistics* **8**: 323–38.

Bayley, R. and Schecter, S. R. (eds.). 2003. *Language socialization in bilingual and multilingual societies*. Clevedon: Multilingual Matters.

Bayley, R. and Tarone, E. 2011. Variationist perspectives. In S. Gass and A. Mackey (eds.), *The Routledge handbook of second language acquisition*, 41–56. New York: Routledge.

Beachley, B., Brown, A. and Colin, C. (eds.). 2003. *Proceedings of the 27th Annual Boston University Conference on Language Development (BUCLD)*. Somerville, MA: Cascadilla Press.

Beck, M.-L. (ed.). 1998b. *Morphology and its interface in L2 knowledge*. Amsterdam: John Benjamins.

Becker, A. and Perdue, C. 1984. Just one misunderstanding: a story of miscommunication. In G. Extra and M. Mittner (eds.), *Studies in second language acquisition by adult immigrants*, 57–82. Tilburg University.

Belikova, A. and White, L. 2009. Evidence for the fundamental difference hypothesis or not? Island constraints revisited. *Studies in Second Language Acquisition* **31**: 199–223.

Belletti, A. (ed.). 2004. *Structures and beyond: the cartography of syntactic structures*, vol. III. Oxford University Press.

Belletti, A. and Hamann, C. 2004. On the L2/bilingual acquisition of French by two young children with different source languages. In P. Prévost and J. Paradis (eds.), *The acquisition of French in different contexts: focus on functional categories*, 147–74. Amsterdam: John Benjamins.

Belletti, A., Bennati, E. and Sorace, A. 2007. Theoretical and developmental issues in the syntax of subjects: evidence from near-native Italian. *Natural Language and Linguistic Theory* **25**: 657–89.

Belz, J. A. 2003. Linguistic perspectives on the development of intercultural competence in telecollaboration. *Language Learning and Technology* **7**: 68–99.

Belz, J. A. and Vyatkina, N. 2005a. Computer-mediated learner corpus research and the data-driven teaching of L2 pragmatic competence: the case of German modal particles. *CALPER Working Papers* **4**: 1–28.

2005b. Learner corpus analysis and the development of L2 pragmatic competence in networked intercultural language study: the case of German modal particles. *Canadian Modern Language Review / La Revue canadienne des langues vivantes* **62**: 17–48.

Benati, A. 2001. A comparative study of the effects of processing instruction and output-based instruction on the acquisition of the Italian future tense. *Language Teaching Research* **5**: 95–127.

2004. The effects of structured input activities and explicit information on the acquisition of the Italian future tense. In B. VanPatten (ed.), *Processing instruction: theory, research, and commentary*, 207–25. Mahwah, NJ: Lawrence Erlbaum.

Benati, A. and Lee, J. F. 2008. *Grammar acquisition and processing instruction: secondary and cumulative effects*. Clevedon: Multilingual Matters.

Best, C. 1995. A direct realist view of cross-language speech perception. In W. Strange (ed.), *Speech perception and linguistic experience: issues in cross-language research*, 171–204. Baltimore: York Press.

Best, C. T. and Hall, P. A. 2010. Perception of initial obstruent voicing is influenced by gestural organization. *Journal of Phonetics* **38**: 109–26.

Best, C. T., McRoberts, G. W. and Sithole, N. M. 1988. Examination of perceptual reorganization for nonnative speech contrasts: Zulu click discrimination by English-speaking adults and infants. *Journal of Experimental Psychology: Human Perception and Performance* **14**: 345–60.

Bhatia, T. K. and Ritchie, W. C. (eds.). 2004. *The handbook of bilingualism*. Malden, MA, and Oxford: Blackwell.

Bialystok, E. 1994. Analysis and control in the development of second language proficiency. *Studies in Second Language Acquisition* **16**: 157–68.

2001. *Bilingualism in development: language, literacy and cognition*. Cambridge University Press.

2007. Cognitive effects of bilingualism: how linguistic experience leads to cognitive change. *International Journal of Bilingual Education and Bilingualism* **10**: 210–23.

Bialystok, E., Luk, G. and Kwan, E. 2005. Bilingualism, biliteracy, and learning to read: Interactions among languages and writing systems. *Scientific Studies of Reading* **9**: 43–61.

Biberauer, T., Holmberg, A., Roberts, I. and Sheehan, M. (eds.). 2010. *Parametric variation: null subjects in minimalist theory*. Cambridge University Press.

Bickhard, M. H. 2005. Functional scaffolding and self-scaffolding. *New Ideas in Psychology* **23**: 166-73.

Biedroń, A. and Szczepniak, A. 2009. The cognitive profile of a talented foreign language learner: a case study. *Psychology of Language and Communication* **13**: 53-71.

Bigelow, M. 2010. *Mogadishu on the Mississippi: language, racialized identity and education in a new land*. New York: Wiley-Blackwell.

Bigelow, M. and Tarone, E. 2004. The role of literacy level in SLA: doesn't *who* we study determine *what* we know? *TESOL Quarterly* **38**: 689-700.

Bigelow, M., delMas, B., Hansen, K. and Tarone, E. 2006. Literacy and the processing of oral recasts in SLA. *TESOL Quarterly* **40**: 1-25.

Bingman, M. B. 2009. The Tenessee Longitudinal Study of Adult Literacy Program participants. In S. Reder and J. Bynner (eds.), *Tracking adult literacy and numeracy skills: findings from longitudinal research*, 296-311. New York and London: Routledge.

Birdsong, D. (ed.). 1999a. *Second language acquisition and the Critical Period hypothesis*. Mahwah, NJ: Lawrence Erlbaum.

2005b. Nativelikeness and non-nativelikeness in L2A research. *International Review of Applied Linguistics in Language Teaching* **43**: 319-28.

2006a. Age and second language acquisition and processing: a selective overview. *Language Learning* **56**: 9-49.

2006b. Dominance, proficiency, and second language grammatical processing. *Applied Psycholinguistics* **27**: 46-49.

2006c. Why not fossilization. In Z.-H. Han and T. Odlin (eds.), *Studies of fossilization in second language acquisition*, 173-88. Clevedon: Multilingual Matters.

2009a. Uninterpretable features: psychology and plasticity in second language learnability. *Second Language Research* **25**: 235-43.

Birdsong, D. and Molis, M. 2001. On the evidence for maturational constraints in second-language acquisition. *Journal of Memory and Language* **44**: 235-49.

Blackledge, A. and Creese, A. 2008. Contesting "language" as "heritage": negotiation of identities in late modernity. *Applied Linguistics* **29**: 533-54.

Blakemore, S. and Choudhury, S. 2006. Development of the adolescent brain: implications for executive function and social cognition. *Journal of Child Psychology and Psychiatry* **47**: 296-312.

Bley-Vroman, R. 1983. The comparative fallacy in interlanguage studies: the case of systematicity. *Language Learning* **33**: 1-17.

1990. The logical problem of foreign language learning. *Linguistic Analysis* **20**: 3-49.

2009. The evolving context of the fundamental difference hypothesis. *Studies in Second Language Acquisition* **31**: 175-98.

Block, D. 2003. *The social turn in second language acquisition*. Edinburgh University Press.

2007a. *Second language identities*. London: Continuum.

2007b. The rise of identity in SLA research, post Firth and Wagner (1997). *Modern Language Journal* **91**: 863–76.

2009. Identity in applied linguistics: the need for conceptual exploration. In V. Cook and L. Wei (eds.), *Contemporary applied linguistics: language teaching and learning*, 215–32. London and New York: Continuum.

Blom, E. 2008. Testing the Domain-by-Age Model: inflection and placement of Dutch verbs. In B. Haznedar and E. Gavruseva (eds.), *Current trends in child second language acquisition: a generative perspective*, 271–300. Amsterdam: John Benjamins.

Blom, E. and Unsworth, S. 2010. *Experimental methods in language acquisition research*. Amsterdam: John Benjamins.

Blondeau, H., Nagy, N., Sankoff, G. and Thibault, P. 2002. La couleur locale du français L2 des Anglo-Montréalais. *AILE: Acquisition et Interaction en Langue Etrangère* **17**: 73–100.

Bloomfield, L. 1926. A set of postulates for the science of language. *Language* **2**: 153–64.

Boersma, P. 2009. www.fon.hum.uva.nl/praat

Bohn, O.-S. and Munro, M. J. (eds.). 2007. *The role of language experience in second-language speech learning: in honor of James Emil Flege*. Amsterdam: John Benjamins.

Bongaerts, T. 1999. Ultimate attainment in L2 pronunciation: the case of very advanced late L2 learners. In D. Birdsong (ed.), *Second language acquisition and the Critical Period hypothesis*, 133–59. Mahwah, NJ: Lawrence Erlbaum.

Borer, H. and Wexler, K. 1987. The maturation of syntax. In T. Roeper and E. Williams (eds.), *Parameter setting*, 123–72. Dordrecht: Reidel.

Bornkessel, I., Schlesewsky, M. and Friederici, A. 2002. Grammar overrides frequency: evidence from the on-line processing of flexible word order. *Cognition* **8**: B21–30.

Boulton, A. 2010. Data-driven learning: on paper, in practice. In T. Harris and M. Moreno Jaén (eds.), *Corpus linguistics in language teaching*, 17–52. Bern: Peter Lang.

Bourdieu, P. 1990. *The logic of Practice*. Palo Alto, CA: Stanford University Press.
1991. *Language and symbolic power*. Cambridge: Polity.

Bouton, L. 1994. Can NNS skill in interpreting implicature in American English be improved through explicit instruction? A pilot study. In L. Bouton (ed.), *Pragmatics and language learning* (Monograph Series 5), 88–109. Urbana-Champaign: DEIL, University of Illinois.

Bowles, M. and Montrul, S. 2009. Instructed L2 acquisition of differential object marking in Spanish. In R. Leow, H. Campos and D. Lardiere (eds.), *Little words: their history, phonology, syntax, semantics, pragmatics and acquisition*, 99–110. Georgetown University Round Table. Washington, DC: Georgetown University Press.

Bowles, M., Ionin, T., Montrul, S. and Tremblay, A. (eds.). 2009. *Proceedings of the 10th Generative Approaches to Second Language Acquisition Conference (GASLA 2009)*. Somerville, MA: Cascadilla Proceedings Project.

Bradlow, A. R. 2008. Training non-native language sound patterns: Lessons from training Japanese adults on the English /ɹ/–/l/ contrast. In J. G. H. Edwards and M. L. Zampini (eds.), *Phonology and second language acquisition*, 287–308. Amsterdam: John Benjamins.

Brame, M. 1978. *Base generated syntax*. Seattle: Noit Amrofer.

Brent, M. R. and Siskind, J. M. 2001. The role of exposure to isolated words in early vocabulary development. *Cognition* **81/82**: 33–44.

Bresnan, J. 2001. *Lexical functional syntax*. Oxford: Blackwell.

Brinton, D., Kagan, O. and Bauckus, S. 2008. *Heritage language education: a new field emerging*. New York: Routledge.

Broselow, E. 2004. Unmarked structures and emergent rankings in second language phonology. *International Journal of Bilingualism* **8**: 51–65.

Brown, C. 2000. The interrelation between speech perception and phonological acquisition from infant to adult. In J. Archibald (ed.), *Second language acquistion and linguistic theory*, 4–63. Malden, MA: Blackwell.

Brown, D. 2010. An improper assumption? The treatment of proper nouns in text coverage counts. *Reading in a Foreign Language* **22**: 355–61.

Brown, H. D. and Gonzo, S. (eds.). 1995. *Readings on second language acquisition*. Upper Saddle River, NJ: Prentice Hall Regents.

Brown, J. and Rodgers, T. 2002. *Doing second language research*. Oxford University Press.

Brown, R. 1973. *A first language: the early stages*. Cambridge, MA: Harvard University Press.

Brown, R. and Gilman, A. 1960. The pronouns of power and solidarity. *American Anthropologist* **4**: 24–39.

Bruhn de Garavito, J. and White, L. 2003. The L2 acquisition of Spanish DPs: the status of grammatical features. In A.-T. Pérez-Leroux and J. Liceras (eds.), *The acquisition of Spanish morphosyntax: the L1/L2 connection*, 151–76. Dordrecht: Kluwer.

Brysbaert, M., Van Dyck, G. and Van de Poel, M. 1999. Visual word recognition in bilinguals: evidence from masked phonological priming. *Journal of Experimental Psychology: Human Perception and Performance* **25**: 137–48.

Bucholtz, M. and Hall, K. 2010. Locating identity in language. In C. Llamas and D. Watt (eds.), *Language and identities*, 18–28. Edinburgh University Press.

Bulowa, M. (ed.). 1979. *Before speech: the beginning of interpersonal communication*. Cambridge University Press.

Busch, D. 1982. Introversion-extraversion and the EFL proficiency of Japanese students. *Language Learning* **32**: 109–32.

Bye, C. 1980. The acquisition of grammatical morphemes in Quiche Mayan. Unpublished PhD dissertation, University of Pittsburgh.

Bylund, E. 2009. Maturational constraints and first language attrition. *Language Learning* **59**: 687–715.

Cabrelli, J., Iverson, M., Judy, T. and Rothman, J. 2008. What the start of L3 tells us about the end of L2: N-drop in L2 and L3 Portuguese. In H. Chan, E. Kapia and H. Jacob (eds.), *A supplement to the proceedings of the 32nd Boston University Conference on Language Development (BUCLD)*. http://128.197.86.186/posters/32 (29 June 2010).

Cabrelli Amaro, J. and Rothman, J. 2010. On L3 acquisition and phonological permeability: a new test case for debates on the mental representation of non-native phonological systems. *International Review of Applied Linguistics in Language Teaching* **48**: 275–96.

Cabrelli Amaro, J., Iverson, M. and Judy, T. 2009. N-Drop at the L3 initial state and its relationship to the L2 steady state. In A. Pires and J. Rothman (eds.), *Minimalist inquiries into child and adult language acquisition: case studies across Portuguese*, 177–98. Berlin and New York: Mouton de Gruyter.

Cabrelli Amaro, J., Flynn, S. and Rothman, J. (eds.). In press. *Third language (L3) acquisition in adulthood*. Amsterdam: John Benjamins.

Campbell, A. and Rushton, J. 1978. Bodily communication and personality. *British Journal of Social and Clinical Psychology* **17**: 31–36.

Campbell, R. and Rosenthal, J. 2000. Heritage languages. In J. W. Rosenthal (ed.), *Handbook of undergraduate second language education*, 165–84. Mahwah, NJ: Lawrence Erlbaum.

Cancino, H., Rosansky, E. and Schumann, J. 1975. The acquisition of the English auxiliary by native Spanish speakers. *TESOL Quarterly* **9**: 421–30.

Cardoso, W. 2007. The variable development of English word-final stops by Brazilian Portuguese speakers: a stochastic Optimality Theoretic account. *Language Variation and Change* **19**: 219–48.

Carpenter, A. 2010. A naturalness bias in learning stress. *Phonology* **27**: 345–92.

Carrell, P., Prince, M. and Astika, G. 1996. Personality type and language learning in an EFL context. *Language Learning* **46**: 75–99.

Carroll, S. 2001. *Input and evidence: the raw material of second language acquisition*. Amsterdam: John Benjamins.

  2004. Acquisition by Processing Theory: a theory of everything? *Bilingualism: Language and Cognition* **7**: 23–25.

  2006. Shallow processing: a consequence of bilingualism or second language learning? *Applied Psycholinguistics* **27**: 53–56.

  2007. Autonomous induction theory. In B. VanPatten and J. Williams (eds.), *Theories in second language acquisition: an introduction*, 155–74. Mahwah, NJ: Lawrence Erlbaum.

  2009. Re-assembling formal features in second language acquisition: beyond minimalism. *Second Language Research* **25**: 245–53.

Casselman, A. 2008. Identical twins' genes are not identical. *Scientific American*. 3 April 2008.

Castro-Caldas, A. 2004. Targeting regions of interest for the study of the illiterate brain. *International Journal of Psychology* **39**: 5–17.

Castro-Caldas, A., Petersson, K. M., Reis, A., Stone-Elander, S. and Ingvar, M. 1998. The illiterate brain: learning to read and write during childhood influences the functional organization of the adult brain. *Brain* **121**: 1053–63.

Cebrian, J. 2006. Experience and the use of non-native duration in L2 vowel categorization. *Journal of Phonetics* **34**: 372–87.

Cenoz, J. 2003. The additive effect of bilingualism on third language acquisition: a review. *International Journal of Bilingualism* **7**: 71–87.

  2009. *Towards multilingual education: Basque educational research in international perspective.* Clevedon: Multilingual Matters.

Cenoz, J., Hufeisen, B. and Jessner, U. (eds.). 2001. *Cross-linguistic influence in third language acquisition: psycholinguistic perspectives.* Clevedon: Multilingual Matters.

Chaiklin, S. 2003. The zone of proximal development in Vygotsky's analysis of learning and instruction. In A. Kozulin, B. Gindis, V. Ageyev and S. M. Miller (eds.), *Vygotsky's educational theory in cultural context*, 39–64. Cambridge University Press.

Chambers, J. K., Trudgill, P. and Schilling-Estes, N. (eds.). 2002. *The handbook of language variation and change.* Oxford: Blackwell.

Chang, F., Bock, K. and Goldberg, A. E. 2003. Can thematic roles leave traces of their places? *Cognition* **90**: 29–49.

Chaudron, C. 1982. Vocabulary elaboration in teachers' speech in L2 learners. *Studies in Second Language Acquisition* **4**: 170–80.

Chen, Y. 2007. From tone to accent: the tonal transfer strategy for Chinese L2 learners of Spanish. *Proceedings of ICPhS XVI*: 1645–48.

Choi, M.-H. and Lardiere, D. 2006. The interpretation of *wh*-in-situ in Korean second language acquisition. In A. Belletti, E. Bennati, C. Chesi, E. DiDomenico and I. Ferrari (eds.), *Language acquisition and development: proceedings of GALA 2005*, 125–35. Newcastle upon Tyne: Cambridge Scholars Press.

Chomsky, N. 1957. *Syntactic structures.* The Hague: Mouton.

  1959. Review of B. F. Skinner, *Verbal behavior*. *Language* **35**: 26–58.

  1965. *Aspects of the theory of syntax.* Cambridge, MA: MIT Press.

  1970a. Remarks on nominalization. In R. Jacobs and P. Rosenbaum (eds.), *Readings in English transformational grammar*, 184–221. Waltham, MA: Ginn.

  1975. *Reflections on language.* New York: Pantheon.

  1981. *Lectures on government and binding.* Dordrecht: Foris.

  1986. *Knowledge of language.* New York: Praeger.

  1993. A minimalist program for linguistic theory. In K. Hale and S. J. Keyser (eds.), *The view from Building 20: essays in linguistics in honor of Sylvain Bromberger*, 1–52. Cambridge, MA: MIT Press.

  1995. *The minimalist program.* Cambridge, MA: MIT Press.

  2000. Minimalist inquiries. In R. Martin, D. Michaels and J. Uriagereka (eds.), *Step by step: essays on minimalist syntax in honor of Howard Lasnik.* Cambridge, MA: MIT Press.

2001. Derivation by phase. In M. Kenstowicz (ed.), *Ken Hale: a life in language*, 1–52. Cambridge, MA: MIT Press.

2002. *On nature and language*. Cambridge University Press.

2005. Three factors in language design. *Linguistic Inquiry* **36**: 1–22.

2007b. Approaching UG from below. In U. Sauerland and H.-M. Gärtner (eds.), *Interfaces + recursion = language?*, 1–29. Berlin: Mouton de Gruyter.

2008. On phases. In R. Freidin, C. Otero and M. L. Zubizarreta (eds.), *Foundational issues in linguistic theory*, 133–63. Cambridge, MA: MIT Press.

2009 [1966]. *Cartesian linguistics*, 3rd edn. Cambridge University Press.

Chondrogianni, V. 2008. Comparing child and adult L2 acquisition of the Greek DP: effects of age and construction. In B. Haznedar and E. Gavruseva (eds.), *Current trends in child second language acquisition: a generative perspective*, 97–144. Amsterdam: John Benjamins.

Cinque, G. (ed.). 2002. *Functional structure in DP and IP: the cartography of syntactic structure*, vol. I: 91–120. Oxford University Press.

Clahsen, H. 1980. Variation in early child language development. *Michigan Germanic Studies* **6**: 219–46.

1985. *Profiling second language development: a procedure for assessing L2 proficiency*. Clevedon: Multilingual Matters.

1986. *Die Profilanalyse: ein linguistisches Verfahren für die Sprachdiagnose im Vorschulalter*. Berlin: Marhold.

1990. The comparative study of first and second language development. *Studies in Second Language Acquisition* **12**: 135–53.

1991. Constraints on parameter setting: a grammatical analysis of some acquisition stages in German child language. *Language Acquisition* **1**: 361–91.

Clahsen, H. and Felser, C. 2006a. Grammatical processing in language learners. *Applied Psycholinguistics* **27**: 3–42.

2006b. How nativelike is non-native language processing? *Trends in Cognitive Science* **10**: 564–70.

Clahsen, H. and Muysken, P. 1986. The availability of Universal Grammar to adult and child learners – a study of the acquisition of German word order. *Second Language Research* **2**: 93–119.

1989. The UG paradox in L2 acquisition. *Second Language Research* **5**: 1–29.

Clahsen, H., Meisel, J. and Pienemann, M. 1983. *Deutsch als Zweitsprache: Der Spracherwerb ausländischer Arbeiter*. Tübingen: Narr.

Cleland, A. A. and Pickering, M. J. 2006. Do writing and speaking employ the same syntactic representations? *Journal of Memory and Language* **54**: 185–98.

Common European Framework of Reference www.coe.int/T/DG4/Portfolio/?L=E&M=/documents_intro/Data_bank_descriptors.html

Condelli, L., Spruck Wrigley, H. and Kwang Suk Yoon. 2009. "What works" for adult literacy students of english as a second language. In S. Reder and J. Bynner (eds.), *Tracking adult literacy and numeracy skills: findings from longitudinal research*, 132–59. New York and London: Routledge.

Condillac (Étienne Bonnot, Abbé of Condillac). 2001 [1746]. *Essay on the origin of human knowledge*, ed. and trans. H. Aarsleff. Cambridge University Press.

Cook, V. 1991a. *Second language learning and language teaching*. London: Edward Arnold.

  1992. Evidence for multicompetence. *Language Learning* **42**: 557–91.

  (ed.). 2002a. *Portraits of the L2 user*. Clevedon: Multilingual Matters.

Cook, V. and Bassetti, B. (eds.). 2011. *Language and bilingual cognition*. New York: Psychology Press.

Cook, V. and Wei, L. (eds.). 2009. *Contemporary applied linguistics: language teaching and learning*. London and New York: Continuum.

Coppieters, R. 1987. Competence differences between native and fluent non-native speakers. *Language* **63**: 544–73.

Corder, S. P. 1967. The significance of learner's [sic] errors. *International Review of Applied Linguistics in Language Teaching* **5**: 161–70.

Costa, A. 2004. Bilingual speech production. In T. K. Bathia and W. C. Ritchie (eds.), *The handbook of bilingualism*, 215–23. Malden, MA, and Oxford: Blackwell.

Coughlan, P. and Duff, P. A. 1994. Same task, different activities: analysis of SLA task from an activity theory perspective. In L. P. Lantolf and G. Appel (eds.), *Vygotskian approaches to second language research*, 173–93. Norwood, NJ: Ablex.

Council of Europe. 2001. *Common framework of reference for languages*. Cambridge University Press.

Coupland, N. 2007. *Style: language variation and identity*. Cambridge University Press.

Cowan, N. 2001. The magical number 4 in short-term memory: a reconsideration of mental storage capacity. *Behavioral and Brain Sciences* **24**: 87–185.

Coxhead, A. 2002. The Academic Word List: a corpus-based word list for academic purposes. In B. Ketterman and G. Marks (eds.), *Teaching and Language Corpora (TALC) 2000 conference proceedings*, 73–89. Atlanta, GA: Rodopi.

Craats, I. van de and Kurvers, J. (eds.). 2009. *Low-educated Second Language and Literacy Acquisition: proceedings of the 4th Annual Forum*. Utrecht: Landelijke Onderzoekschool Taalwetenschap.

Craats, I. van de, Kurvers, J. and Young-Scholten, M. (eds.). 2006a. *Low-educated Second Language and Literacy Acquisition: proceedings of the 1st Annual Forum* (LOT Occasional Series 15). http://lotos.library.uu.nl/index.html. Utrecht: Landelijke Onderzoekschool Taalwetenschap.

  2006b. Research on low-educated second language and literacy acquisition, In I. van de Craats, J. Kurvers and M. Young-Scholten (eds.), *Low-educated Second Language and Literacy Acquisition: proceedings of the 1st Annual Forum* (LOT Occasional Series 15), 7–23. http://lotos.library.uu.nl/index.html. Utrecht: Landelijke Onderzoekschool Taalwetenschap.

Craik, F. and Lockhart, R. 1972. Depth of processing: a framework for memory research. *Journal of Verbal Learning and Verbal Behavior* **11**: 671–84.

Craik, F. and Tulving, E. 1975. Depth of processing and the retention of words in episodic memory. *Journal of Experimental Psychology: General* **104**: 268–94.

Crain, S. and Nakayama, M. 1987. Structure dependence in grammar formation. *Language* **63**: 522–42.

Crain, S. and Thornton, R. 1998. *Investigations in Universal Grammar: a guide to experiments on the acquisition of syntax and semantics*. Cambridge, MA: MIT Press.

Croft, W. 2001. *Radical construction theory: syntactic theory in typological perspective*. Oxford University Press.

Cruz-Ferreira, M. 1987. Non-native interpretive strategies for intonational meaning: an experimental study. In A. James and J. Leather (eds.), *Sound patterns in second language acquisition*, 102–20. Dordrecht: Foris.

Crystal, D. and Varley, R. 1993. *Introduction to language pathology*. London: Whurr.

Csizér, K. and Dörnyei, Z. 2005. The internal structure of language learning motivation and its relationship with language choice and learning effort. *Modern Language Journal* **89**: 19–36.

Culicover, P. and Jackendoff, R. 2005. *Simpler syntax*. Oxford University Press.

Culicover, P. and Wilkins, W. 1984. *Locality in linguistics theory*. Orlando: Academic Press.

Cummins, R. 1983. *The nature of psychological explanation*. Cambridge, MA: MIT Press.

Curtin, S., Goad, H., and Pater, J. 1998. Phonological transfer and levels of representation: the perceptual acquisition of Thai voice and aspiration by English and French speakers. *Second Language Research* **14**: 389–405.

Cutler, A., Weber, A. and Otake, T. 2006. Asymmetric mapping from phonetic to lexical representations in second-language listening. *Journal of Phonetics* **34**: 269–84.

Cuza, A. and Frank, J. 2011. Transfer effects at the syntax–semantics interface: the case of double que questions in heritage Spanish. *The Heritage Language Journal* **8**: 66–89.

D' Arcy, A. F. 2005. *Like: syntax and development*. University of Toronto.

Daller, H., Milton, J. and Treffers-Daller, J. (eds.). 2007. *Modelling and assessing vocabulary knowledge*. Cambridge University Press.

Daly, J. and Miller, M. D. 1975. Apprehension of writing as a predictor of message intensity. *Journal of Psychology* **89**: 175–77.

Daneman, M. and Carpenter, P. A. 1980. Individual differences in working memory and reading. *Journal of Verbal Learning and Verbal Behavior* **19**: 450–66.

Dante Alighieri. 1996 [c. 1305]. *De vulgari eloquentia*, ed. and trans. S. Botterill. Cambridge University Press.

DaSilva Iddings, A. C. and Katz, L. 2007. Integrating home and school identities of recent-immigrant Hispanic English language learners through classroom practices. *Journal of Language, Identity, and Education* **6**: 299–314.

Davidson, L., Shaw, J. and Adams, T. 2007. The effect of word learning on the perception of non-native consonant sequences. *Journal of the Acoustical Society of America* **122**: 3697–709.

Davies, A. 2003. *The native speaker: myth and reality*. Clevedon: Multilingual Matters.

De Angelis, G. 2007. *Third or additional language acquisition*. Clevedon: Multilingual Matters.

de Bot, K. 2008a. The imaging of what in the multilingual mind? *Second Language Research* **24**: 111–33.

In press. Multilingual processing: from a static to a dynamic perspective. In J. Cabrelli Amaro, S. Flynn and J. Rothman (eds.), *Third language (L3) acquisition in adulthood*. Amsterdam: John Benjamins.

de Bot, K., Weltens, B. and van Els, T. (eds.). 1985. *Language attrition in progress*. Dordrecht: Foris.

de Groot, A. and Kroll, J. 1997. *Tutorials in bilingualism: psycholinguistic perspectives*. Mahwah, NJ: Lawrence Erlbaum.

de Jong, K. J., Hao, Y.-C. and Park, H. 2009. Evidence for featural units in the acquisition of speech production skills: linguistic structure in foreign accent. *Journal of Phonetics* **37**: 357–73.

de Villiers, P. and de Villiers, J. 1973. A crossectional study of the acquisition of grammatical morphemes in child speech. *Journal of Psycholinguistic Research* **2**: 267–78.

Deacon, T. 1997. *The symbolic species: the co-evolution of language and the brain*. New York: W.W. Norton.

Dechert, H.W., Mohle, D. and Raupach, M. 1984. *Second language productions*. Tübingen: Gunter Narr.

Dehaene-Lambertz, G., Dupoux, E. and Gout, A. 2000. Electrophysiological correlates of phonological processing: a cross-linguistic study. *Journal of Cognitive Neuroscience* **12**: 635–47.

DeKeyser, R. 1997. Beyond explicit rule learning. *Studies in Second Language Learning* **19**: 195–221.

2000. The robustness of critical period effects in second language acquisition. *Studies in Second Language Acquisition* **22**: 499–533.

2001. Automaticity and automatization. In P. Robinson (ed.), *Cognition and second language instruction*, 125–52. Cambridge University Press.

2003. Implicit and explicit learning. In C. Doughty and M. H. Long (eds.), *The handbook of second language acquisition*, 313–49. Oxford: Blackwell.

2005. What makes learning second-language grammar difficult? A review of issues. *Language Learning* **55**: 1–25.

2007. *Practice in a second language*. Cambridge University Press.

2009. Cognitive-psychological processes in second language learning. In M. H. Long and C. Doughty (eds.), *The handbook of language teaching*, 119–38. Malden, MA: Wiley Blackwell.

DeKeyser, R. and Larson-Hall, J. 2005. What does the Critical Period really mean? In J. F. Kroll and A. de Groot (eds.), *Handbook of bilingualism*, 88–108. Oxford University Press.

Dekydtspotter, L. 2001. The universal parser and interlanguage: domain-specific mental organization in the comprehension of combien interrogatives in English–French interlanguage. *Second Language Research* 17: 91–143.

2009. Second language epistemology: take two. *Studies in Second Language Acquisition* 31: 291–321.

Dekydtspotter, L. and Hathorn, J. C. 2005. *Quelque chose... de remarquable* in English–French acquisition: mandatory, informationally encapsulated computations in second language interpretation. *Second Language Research* 21: 291–323.

Dekydtspotter, L. and Outcalt, S. D. 2005. A syntactic bias in scope ambiguity resolution in the processing of English–French cardinality interrogatives: evidence for informational encapsulation. *Language Learning* 1: 1–37.

Dekydtspotter, L. and Sprouse, R. A. 2001. Mental design and (second) language epistemology: adjectival restrictions of *wh*-quantifiers and tense in English-French interlanguage. *Second Language Research* 17: 1–35.

Dekydtspotter, L., Anderson, B. and Sprouse, R. A. 2007. Syntax–semantics in English–French interlanguage: advancing understanding of second language epistemology. In D. Ayoun (ed.), *French applied linguistics*, 75–103. Amsterdam: John Benjamins.

Dekydtspotter, L., Sprouse, R. A. and Anderson, B. 1997. The interpretive interface in L2 acquisition: the process–result distinction in English–French interlanguage grammars. *Language Acquisition* 6: 297–332.

Dekydtspotter, L., Sprouse, R. A. and Swanson, K. 2001. Reflexes of mental architecture in second-language acquisition: the interpretation of *combien* extractions in English–French interlanguage. *Language Acquisition* 9: 175–227.

Dekydtspotter, L., Sprouse, R. A. and Thyre, R. 1999/2000. The interpretation of quantification at a distance in English–French interlanguage: domain specificity and second-language acquisition. *Language Acquisition* 8: 1–36.

Dellatolas, G., Braga, L. W., Souza, L. N., Filho, G. N., Queiroz, E. and Deloche, G. 2003. Cognitive consequences of early phase of literacy. *Journal of the International Neuropsychological Society* 9: 771–82.

Demirci, M. 2000. The role of pragmatics in reflexive interpretation by Turkish learners of English. *Second Language Research* 14: 325–53.

Depue, R. and Morrone-Strupinsky, J. V. 2005. A neurobehavioral model of affiliative bonding: implications for conceptualizing a human trait of affiliation. *Brain and Behavioral Sciences* 28: 313–50.

Dewaele, J.-M. 2002a. Psychological and sociodemographic correlates of communicative anxiety in L2 and L3 production. *International Journal of Bilingualism* 6: 23–39.

2002b. Individual differences in L2 fluency: the effect of neurobiological correlates. In V. Cook (ed.), *Portraits of the L2 user*, 221–49. Clevedon: Multilingual Matters.

2005a. *Focus on French as a foreign language*. Clevedon: Multilingual Matters.

2005b. Sociodemographic, psychological and politico-cultural correlates in Flemish students' attitudes toward French and English. *Journal of Multilingual and Multicultural Development* 26: 118–37.

2007a. Predicting language learners' grades in the L1, L2, L3 and L4: the effect of some psychological and sociocognitive variables. *International Journal of Multilingualism* 4: 169–97.

2007b. The effect of multilingualism, sociobiographical, and situational factors on communicative anxiety and foreign language anxiety of mature language learners. *International Journal of Bilingualism* 11: 391–409.

2010. *Emotions in multiple languages*. Basingstoke: Palgrave Macmillan.

Dewaele, J.-M. and Furnham, A. 1999. Extraversion: the unloved variable in applied linguistic research. *Language Learning* 49: 509–44.

2000. Personality and speech production: a pilot study of second language learners. *Personality and Individual Differences* 28: 355–65.

Dewaele, J.-M. and Pavlenko, A. 2002. Emotion vocabulary in interlanguage. *Language Learning* 52: 265–324.

Dewaele, J.-M. and Regan, V. 2001. The use of colloquial words in advanced French interlanguage. In S. Foster-Cohen and A. Nizegorodcew (eds.), *EUROSLA Yearbook* 1: 51–67. Amsterdam: John Benjamins.

2002. Maitriser la norme sociolinguistique en interlangue francaise: le cas de l'omission variable de "ne." *Journal of French Language Studies* 12: 123–48.

Dewaele, J.-M. and Thirtle, H. 2009. Why do some young learners drop foreign languages? A focus on learner-internal variables. *International Journal of Bilingual Education and Bilingualism* 12: 635–49.

Dewaele, J.-M., Petrides, K. V. and Furnham, A. 2008. The effects of trait emotional intelligence and sociobiographical variables on communicative anxiety and foreign language anxiety among adult multilinguals: a review and empirical investigation. *Language Learning* 58: 911–60.

Diamond, M., Scheibel, A. B., Murphy, J. G. M. and Harvey, T. 1985. On the brain of a scientist: Albert Einstein. *Experimental Neurology* 88: 198–204.

Dietrich, R., Klein, W. and Noyau, C. (eds.). 1995. *The acquisition of temporality in a second language*. Amsterdam: John Benjamins.

Dijkstra, T. 2005. Bilingual visual word recognition and access. In J. F. Kroll and D. de Groot (eds.), *Handbook of bilingualism: psycholinguistic perspectives*, 179–201. Oxford University Press.

Dijkstra, T. and Haverkort, M. 2004. Costs and benefits of a hybrid model. *Bilingualism: Language and Cognition* 7: 26–28.

Dijkstra, T. and van Heuven, W. J. B. 2002. The architecture of the bilingual word recognition system: from identification to decision. *Bilingualism: Language and Cognition* **5**: 175–97.

Dimroth, C. 2002. Topics, assertions, and additive words: how L2 learners get from information structure to target-language syntax. *Linguistics* **40**: 891–923.

DiNitto, R. 2000. Can collaboration be unsuccessful? A sociocultural analysis of classroom setting and Japanese L2 performance in group tasks. *Journal of the Association of Teachers of Japanese* **34**: 179–210.

Doerr, N. M. (ed.). 2009. *The native speaker concept: ethnographic investigations of native speaker effects*. New York: Mouton de Gruyter.

Dogil, G. and Reiterer, S. M. (eds.). 2009. *Language talent and brain activity*. Berlin: Mouton De Gruyter.

Donato, R. 1994. Collective scaffolding in second language learning. In L. P. Lantolf and G. Appel (eds.), *Vygotskian approaches to second language research*, 33–56. Norwood, NJ: Ablex.

Donzelli, G. 2010. Young learners and foreign language learning: the words they hear and the words they learn. Unpublished PhD dissertation, Swansea University.

Donzelli, G., Milton, J. and Daller, M. H. In press. Journey into the language classroom: how do children learn vocabulary in a foreign language? In A. McLachlan, J. Jones and G. Macrory (eds.), *Primary language: issues in research and practice*. Open University Press.

Dörnyei, Z. 1994. Motivation and motivating in the foreign language classroom. *Modern Language Journal* **78**: 273–84.

2005. *The psychology of the language learner: individual differences in second language acquisition*. Mahwah, NJ: Lawrence Erlbaum.

2006. Individual differences in second language acquisition. *AILA Review* **19**: 42–68.

2009a. *The psychology of second language acquisition*. Oxford University Press.

2009b. Individual differences: interplay of learner characteristics and learning environment. *Language Learning* **59**: Suppl. 1, 230–48.

2009c. The L2 motivational self system. In Z. Dörnyei and E. Ushioda (eds.), *Motivation, language identity and the L2 self*, 9–42. Clevedon: Multilingual Matters.

Dörnyei, Z. 2010. Researching motivation: from integrativeness to the ideal L2 self. In S. Hunston and D. Oakey (eds.), *Introducing applied linguistics: concepts and skills*, 74–83. London: Routledge.

Dörnyei, Z. and Skehan, P. 2003. Individual differences in second language learning. In C. Doughty and M. Long (eds.), *The handbook of second language acquisition*, 589–630. Oxford: Blackwell.

Dörnyei, Z. and Ushioda, E. (eds.). 2009. *Motivation, language identity and the L2 self*. Clevedon: Multilingual Matters.

Doughty, C. and Long, M. (eds.). 2003. *The handbook of second language acquisition*. Oxford: Blackwell.

Doughty, C. and Williams, J. (eds.). 1998. *Focus on form in classroom second language acquisition*. Cambridge University Press.

Duff, P. A. 2007a. Second language socialization as sociocultural theory: insights and issues. *Language Teaching* **40**: 309–19.

  2010. Introduction to volume 8: language socialization. In P. A. Duff and N. C. Hornberger (eds.), *Encyclopaedia of language and education*, vol. VIII: *Language socialization*, xiii-xix. New York: Springer.

Duff, P. A. and Hornberger, N. C. (eds.). 2010. *Encyclopaedia of language and education*, vol. VIII: *Language socialization*. New York: Springer.

Duffield, N. 2009. The kids are alright . . . aren't they? *Second Language Research* **25**: 269–78.

DuFon, M. and Churchill, E. (eds.). 2006. *Language learners in study abroad contexts*. Clevedon: Multilingual Matters.

Dulay, H. C. and Burt, M. K. 1973. Should we teach children syntax? *Language Learning* **23**: 245–58.

  1974a. Errors and strategies in child second language acquisition. *TESOL Quarterly* **8**: 129–36.

  1974b. Natural sequences in child second language acquisition. *Language Learning* **24**: 37–53.

  1975. Creative construction in second language learning and teaching, In M. Burt and N. Dulay (eds.), *New directions in second language learning, teaching and bilingual education*, 22–32. Washington, DC: TESOL.

Dulay, H. C., Burt, M. K. and Krashen, S. 1982. *Language two*. Oxford University Press.

DuPlessis, J., Solin, D., Travis, L. and White, L. 1987. UG or not UG, that is the question: a reply to Clahsen and Muysken. *Second Language Research* **3**: 56–75.

Dupoux, E., Pallier, C., Kakehi, K. and Mehler, J. 1999. Epenthetic vowels in Japanese: a perceptual illusion? *Journal of Experimental Psychology: Human Perception and Performance* **25**: 1568–78.

Dupoux, E., Sebastián-Gallés, N., Navarete, E. and Peperkamp, S. 2008. Persistent stress 'deafness': the case of French learners of Spanish. *Cognition* **106**: 682–706.

Dušková, L. 1969. On sources of errors in foreign language learning. *International Review of Applied Linguistics in Language Teaching* **7**: 11–36.

Dussias, P. 2010. Uses of eyetracking data in second language sentence processing research. *Annual Review of Applied Linguistics* **30**: 149–66.

Dussias, P. and Sagarra, N. 2007. The effect of exposure on syntactic parsing in Spanish–English bilinguals. *Bilingualism: Language and Cognition* **10**: 101–16.

Duyck, W. 2005. Translation and associative priming with cross-lingual pseudohomophones: evidence for nonselective phonological activation in bilinguals. *Journal of Experimental Psychology: Learning Memory and Cognition* **31**: 1340–59.

Eckman, F. R. 1977. Markedness and the Contrastive Analysis Hypothesis. *Language Learning* **27**: 315–30.

Edelman, G. 1987. *Neural Darwinism: the theory of neuronal group selection.* New York: Basic Books.

Edelman, G. and Gally, J. 2001. Degeneracy and complexity in biological systems. *Proceedings of the National Academy of Sciences of the United States of America* **98**: 13763–68.

Edwards, J. G. H. and Zampini, M. L. (eds.). 2008. *Phonology and second language acquisition.* Amsterdam: John Benjamins.

Ehrman, M. 2008. Personality and the good language learner. In C. Griffiths (ed.), *Lessons form the good language learner,* 61–72. Cambridge University Press.

Ehrman, M. and Leaver, B. L. 2003. Cognitive styles in the service of language learning. *System* **31**: 393–415.

Ellis, N. C. 1997. Vocabulary acquisition: word structure, collocation, word-class, and meaning. In N. Schmitt and M. McCarthy (eds.), *Vocabulary: description, acquisition and pedagogy,* 122–39. Cambridge University Press.

2001. Memory for language. In P. Robinson (ed.), *Cognition and second language instruction,* 33–69. Cambridge University Press.

2002a. Frequency effects in language processing: a review with implications for theories of implicit and explicit language acquisition. *Studies in Second Language Acquisition* **24**: 143–89.

2005. At the interface: dynamic interactions of explicit and implicit language knowledge. *Studies in Second Language Acquisition* **27**: 305–53.

2008b. Usage-based and form-focused language acquisition. In P. Robinson and N. C. Ellis (eds.), *Handbook of cognitive linguistics and second language acquisition,* 372–405. New York: Routledge.

Ellis, N. C. and Larsen-Freeman, D. 2006. Language emergence: implications for applied linguistics – introduction to the special issue. *Applied Linguistics* **27**: 558–89.

Ellis, R. 1985. *Understanding second language acquisition.* Oxford University Press.

1989. Are classroom and naturalistic acquisition the same? A study of the classroom acquisition of German word order rules. *Studies in Second Language Acquisition* **11**: 305–28.

1990. *Instructed second language acquisition.* Oxford: Blackwell.

1994a. *The study of second language acquisition.* Oxford University Press.

1994b. Factors in the incidental acquisition of vocabulary from oral input: a review essay. *Applied Language Learning* **5**: 1–32.

1997b. *Second language acquisition.* Oxford University Press.

2002. Does form-focussed instruction affect the acquisition of implicit knowledge? A review of the research. *Studies in Second Language Acquisition* **24**: 223–37.

2007. The differential effects of corrective feedback on two grammatical structures. In A. Mackey (ed.), *Conversational interaction in second language acquisition*, 339–60. Oxford University Press.

2008. *The study of second language acquisition*. Oxford University Press.

Ely, C. M. 1986. An analysis of discomfort, risktaking, sociability, and motivation in the L2 classroom. *Language Learning* **36**: 1–25.

1988. Personality: its impact on attitudes toward classroom activities. *Foreign Language Annals* **21**: 25–32.

Emonds, J. 1970. Root and structure preserving transformations. Unpublished PhD dissertation, Massachusetts Institute of Technology.

Engeström, Y. 2001. Expansive learning at work: toward an activity theoretical reconceptualization. *Journal of Education and Work* **14**: 133–56.

Ensslin, A. 2001. Fremdsprachendidaktische Analyse der Online-Englischkurse *GlobalEnglish* und *Englishtown*. Unpublished MA thesis, Universität Tübingen.

2006. Literary hypertext in the foreign language classroom: a case study report. *Language Learning Journal* **33**: 13–21.

2010. Metalanguage and the ideology of creationist capitalism in Second Life. Paper presented at the Language Development and Cognition Colloquium, Bangor University.

Ensslin, A. and Muse, E. (eds.). 2011. *Creating Second Lives: community, identity and spatiality as constructions of the virtual*. New York: Routledge.

Epstein, S., Flynn, S. and Martohardjono, G. 1996. Second language acquisition: theoretical and experimental issues in contemporary research. *Brain and Behavioral Sciences* **19**: 677–758.

1998. The strong continuity hypothesis: some evidence concerning functional categories in adult L2 acquisition. In S. Flynn, G. Martohardjono and W. O'Neil (eds.), *The generative study of second language acquisition*, 61–77. Mahwah, NJ: Lawrence Erlbaum.

Escudero, P. 2009. The linguistic perception of SIMILAR L2 sounds. In P. Boersma and S. Hamann (eds.), *Phonology in perception*, 151–90. Berlin and New York: Mouton de Gruyter.

Escudero, P. and Boersma, P. 2004. Bridging the gap between L2 speech perception research and phonological theory. *Studies in Second Language Acquisition* **26**: 551–85.

Escudero, P., Benders, T. and Lipski, S. C. 2009. Native, non-native and L2 perceptual cue weighting for Dutch vowels: the case of Dutch, German, and Spanish listeners. *Journal of Phonetics* **37**: 452–65.

Eubank, L. (ed.). 1991. *Point-counterpoint: Universal Grammar in the second language acquisition*. Amsterdam: John Benjamins.

1993/94. On the transfer of parametric values in L2 development. *Language Acquisition* **3**: 183–208.

Evans, N. and Levinson, S. 2009. The myth of language universals: language diversity and its importance for cognitive science. *Brain and Behavioral Sciences* **32**: 429–92.

Faculté de philosophie, arts et lettres. 2010. ICLEv2. *Université catholique de Louvain*. www.uclouvain.be/en-277586.html

Falk, Y. and Bardel, C. 2011. Object pronouns in German L3 syntax: evidence for the L2 status factor. *Second Language Research* **27**: 59–82.

Farley, A. 2004. Processing Instruction and the Spanish subjunctive: is explicit information needed? In B. VanPatten (ed.), *Processing instruction: theory, research, and commentary*, 227–39. Mahwah, NJ: Lawrence Erlbaum.

Faux, N. (ed.). 2007. *Low-educated Second Language and Literacy Acquisition: proceedings of the 2nd Annual Forum*. Richmond, VA: The Literacy Institute at Virginia Commonwealth University.

Fernández, C. 2008. Re-examining the role of explicit information in processing instruction. *Studies in Second Language Acquisition* **30**: 277–305.

Fernández, E. M. 2006. How do second language learners build syntactic structure? *Applied Psycholinguistics* **27**: 59–64.

Firth, A. and Wagner, J. 1997. On discourse, communication, and (some) fundamental concepts in SLA research. *Modern Language Journal* **81**: 285–300.

 2007. Second/foreign language learning as social accomplishment: elaborations on a reconceptualized SLA. *Modern Language Journal* **91**: 800–19.

Flavell, J. H. 1972. An analysis of cognitive-developmental sequences. *Genetic Psychology Monographs* **86**: 279–350.

Flege, J. E. 1987a. A critical period for learning to pronounce foreign languages? *Applied Linguistics* **8**: 162–77.

 1987b. The production of "new" and "similar" phones in a foreign language: evidence for the effect of equivalence classification. *Journal of Phonetics* **15**: 47–65.

 1995. Second language speech learning: theory, findings, and problems. In W. Strange (ed.), *Speech perception and linguistic experience: issues in cross-language research*, 233–77. Baltimore: York Press.

Flege, J. E. and MacKay, I. 2004. Perceiving vowels in a second language. *Studies in Second Language Acquisition* **26**: 1–34.

Flege, J. E., Schirru, C. and MacKay, I. 2003. Interaction between native and second language phonetic subsystems. *Speech Communication* **40**: 467–91.

Flege, J. E., Takagi, N. and Mann, V. 1995. Japanese adults can learn to produce English /r/ and /l/ accurately. *Language and Speech* **38**: 25–55.

Fleming, A., O'Day, D. H. and Kraemer, G. W. 1999. Neurobiology of mother-infant interactions: experience and central nervous system plasticity across development and generations. *Neuroscience and Biobehavioral Reviews* **23**: 673–85.

Flynn, S. 1987. *A parameter-setting model of L2 acquisition*. Dordrecht: Reidel.

 1996. A parameter-setting approach to second language acquisition. In W. C. Ritchie and T. K. Bhatia (eds.), *Handbook of second language acquisition*, 121–58. New York: Academic Press.

Flynn, S., Foley, C. and Vinnitskaya, I. 2004. The cumulative-enhancement model for language acquisition: comparing adults' and children's patterns of development in first, second and third language acquisition. *International Journal of Multilingualism* **1**: 3-17.

Flynn, S., Martohardjono, G. and O'Neil, W. (eds.). 1998. *The generative study of second language acquisition*. Mahwah, NJ: Lawrence Erlbaum.

Fodor, J. D. 1998. Unambiguous triggers. *Linguistic Inquiry* **29**: 1-36.

Fodor, J. D. and Crowther, C. 2002. Understanding stimulus poverty arguments. *The Linguistic Review* **19**: 105-45.

Foote, R. 2009. Transfer and L3 acquisition: the role of typology. In Y.-k. I. Leung (ed.), *Third language acquisition and Universal Grammar*, 89-114. Clevedon: Multilingual Matters.

Foster, P. and Ohta, A. S. 2005. Negotiation for meaning and peer assistance in second language classrooms. *Applied Linguistics* **26**: 402-30.

Foster-Cohen, S., Sharwood Smith, M., Sorace, A. and Ota, M. (eds.). 2004. *EUROSLA Yearbook* 4. Amsterdam: John Benjamins.

Foucart, A. 2008. Grammatical gender processing in French as a first and second language. Unpublished PhD dissertation, University of Edinburgh and Université de Provence.

Foucart, A. and Frenck-Mestre, C. 2011. Grammatical gender processing in L2: electrophysiological evidence of the effect of L1-L2 syntactic similarity. *Bilingualism: Language and Cognition* **14**: 379-99.

Franceschina, F. 2005. *Fossilized second language grammars: the acquisition of grammatical gender*. Amsterdam: John Benjamins.

Francis, W. S. 2005. Bilingual semantic and conceptual representation. In J. Kroll and A. de Groot (eds.), *Handbook of bilingualism: psycholinguistic perspectives*, 251-67. Oxford University Press.

Freidin, R. 1991. Linguistic theory and language acquisition: a note on structure-dependence. *Behavioral and Brain Sciences* **14**: 618-19.

Frenck-Mestre, C. 2005a. Ambiguities and anomalies: what can eye-movements and event-related potentials reveal about second language sentence processing? In J. Kroll and A. de Groot (eds.), *Handbook of bilingualism: psycholinguistic perspectives*, 268-84. Oxford University Press.

2006. Shallow processing? Commentary on Clahsen and Felser. *Applied Psycholinguistics* **27**: 64-65.

Frenck-Mestre, C., McLaughlin, J., Osterhout, L. and Foucart, A. 2008. The effect of phonological realization of inflectional morphology on verbal agreement in French: evidence from ERPs. *Acta Psychologica* **128**: 528-36.

Friederici, A. 2002. Towards a neural basis of auditory sentence processing. *Trends in Cognitive Sciences* **6**: 78-84.

Fries, C. C. 1945. *Teaching and learning English as a foreign language*. Ann Arbor: University of Michigan Press.

Furnham, A. 1990. Language and personality. In H. Giles and W. P. Robinson (eds.), *Handbook of language and social psychology*, 73-95. Chichester: John Wiley.

Gabriele, A. 2005. The acquisition of aspect in a second language: a bidirectional study of learners of English and Japanese. Unpublished PhD dissertation, City University of New York.

2009. Transfer and transition in the SLA of aspect: a bidirectional study of learners of English and Japanese. *Studies in Second Language Acquisition* **31**: 371–402.

2010. Deriving meaning through context: interpreting bare nominals in second language Japanese. *Second Language Research* **26**: 379–405.

Gairns, R. and Redman, S. 1986. *Working with words: a guide to teaching and learning vocabulary.* Cambridge University Press.

Gallagher, S. 2005. *How the body shapes the mind.* Oxford: Clarendon Press.

Gallistel, C. R. and King, A. P. 2009. *Memory and the computational brain: why cognitive science will transform neuroscience.* Malden, MA: Wiley-Blackwell.

García, O. 2009. *Bilingual education in the 21st century: a global perspective.* Malden, MA, and Oxford: Blackwell.

García Mayo, M. P. 2001. Repair and completion strategies in the interlanguage of advanced EFL learners. *ITL: Review of Applied Linguistics* **131**: 139–68.

2002. Interaction in advanced EFL pedagogy: a comparison of form-focused activities. *International Journal of Educational Research* **37**: 323–41.

2005. Interactional strategies for interlanguage communication: Do they provide evidence for attention to form? In A. Housen and M. Pierrand (eds.), *Investigations in instructed second language acquisition* (Studies on Language Acquisition series), 357–79. Berlin and New York: Mouton de Gruyter.

(ed.). 2007. *Investigating tasks in formal language learning.* Clevedon: Multilingual Matters.

García Mayo, P. and Hawkins, R. (eds.). 2009. *Second language acquisition of articles: empirical findings and theoretical implications.* Amsterdam: John Benjamins.

García Mayo, M. P. and Pica, T. 2000. L2 learner interaction in a foreign language setting: are learning needs addressed? *International Review of Applied Linguistics in Language Teaching* **38**: 35–58.

García Mayo, M. P. and Rothman, J. In press. L3 morphosyntax in the generative tradition: from the initial state and beyond. In J. Cabrelli Amaro, S. Flynn and J. Rothman (eds.), *Third language (L3) acquisition in adulthood.* Amsterdam: John Benjamins.

García Mayo, M. P. and Villarreal Olaizola, I. 2011. The development of suppletive and affixal tense and agreement morphemes in the L3 English of Basque–Spanish bilinguals. *Second Language Research* **27**: 129–49.

García Mayo, M. P., Lázaro Ibarrola, A. and Liceras, J. M. 2005. Placeholders in the English interlanguage of bilingual (Basque/Spanish) children. *Language Learning* **55**: 445–89.

2006. Agreement in the English interlanguage of Basque/Spanish bilinguals: a minimalist farewell to pro. *ITL: International Journal of Applied Linguistics* **151**: 83–98.

Gardner, R. C. 1985. *Social psychology and second language learning: the role of attitudes and motivation*. London: Edward Arnold.

2006. The socio-educational model of second language acquisition: a research paradigm. *EUROSLA Yearbook* **6**: 237–60.

2010. *Motivation and second language acquisition: the socio-educational model*. New York: Peter Lang.

Gardner, R. C. and MacIntyre, P. 1993. A student's contributions to second language acquisition. Part II. Affective variables. *Language Teaching* **26**: 1–11.

Gardner, R. C., Smythe, P. C., Clement, R. and Glicksman, L. 1976. Second language learning: a social-psychological perspective. *Canadian Modern Language Review* **32**: 198–213.

Gass, S. 1988. Integrating research areas: a framework for second language studies. *Applied Linguistics* **9**: 198–217.

1989. How do learners resolve linguistic conflicts? In S. Gass and J. Schachter (eds.), *Linguistic perspectives on second language acquisition*, 183–99. New York: Cambridge University Press.

1996. Second language acquisition and linguistic theory: the role of language transfer. In W. C. Ritchie and T. K. Bhatia (eds.), *Handbook of second language acquisition*, 317–45. New York: Academic Press.

1997. *Input, interaction and the second language learner*. Mahwah, NJ: Lawrence Erlbaum.

2003. Input and interaction. In C. Doughty and M. Long (eds.), *The handbook of second language acquisition*, 224–55. Oxford: Blackwell.

Gass, S. and Mackey, A. 2006. Input, interaction and output: a review. *AILA Review* **19**: 3–17.

2007. Input, interaction and output in second language acquisition. In B. VanPatten and J. Williams (eds.), *Theories in second language acquisition: an introduction*, 175–200. Mahwah, NJ: Lawrence Erlbaum.

Gass, S. and Madden, C. (eds.). 1985. *Input in second language acquisition*. Rowley, MA: Newbury House.

Gass, S. and Schachter, J. (eds.). 1989. *Linguistic perspectives on second language acquisition*. New York: Cambridge University Press.

Gass, S. and Selinker, L. 2008. *Second language acquisition: an introductory course*, 3rd edn. London: Routledge.

Gass, S., Fleck, C., Leder, N. and Svetics, I. 1998. A historicity revisited: does SLA have a history? *Studies in Second Language Acquisition* **20**: 407–21.

Gathercole, S. E. and Baddeley, A. D. 1993. *Working memory and language*. Hove: Lawrence Erlbaum.

Gavruseva, E. 2008a. The development of copula and auxiliary *be* and overgeneration of *be* in child L2 English. In B. Haznedar and E. Gavruseva (eds.), *Current trends in child second language acquisition: a generative perspective*, 145–76. Amsterdam: John Benjamins.

Geçkin, V. and Haznedar, B. 2008. The morphology/syntax interface in child L2 acquisition: evidence from verbal morphology. In B. Haznedar and E. Gavruseva (eds.), *Current trends in child second language acquisition: a generative perspective*, 237–67. Amsterdam: John Benjamins.

Genesee, F., Paradis, J. and Crago, M. B. 2004. *Dual language development and disorders: a handbook on bilingualism and second language learning*. Baltimore: Paul H. Brookes (2nd edn 2010).

Gibson, E. and Wexler, K. 1994. Triggers. *Linguistic Inquiry* **25**: 405–54.

Gick, B., Bernhardt, B., Bacsfalvi, P. and Wilson, I. 2008. Ultrasound imaging applications in second language acquisition. In G. J. H. Edwards and M. L. Zampini (eds.), *Phonology and second language acquisition*, 309–22. Amsterdam: John Benjamins.

Giddens, A. 1991. *Modernity and self-identity: self and society in the late modern age*. Cambridge: Polity.

Gillon-Dowens, M. and Carreiras, M. 2006. The shallow structure hypothesis of second language sentence processing: what is restricted and why? *Applied Psycholinguistics* **27**: 49–52.

Gillon-Dowens, M., Vergara, M., Barber, H. A. and Carreiras, M. 2010. Morphosyntactic processing in late L2 learners. *Journal of Cognitive Neuroscience* **22**: 1870–87.

Goad, H. and White, L. 2006. Ultimate attainment in interlanguage grammars: a prosodic approach. *Second Language Research* **22**: 243–68.

 2008. Prosodic structure and the representation of L2 functional morphology: a nativist approach. *Lingua* **118**: 577–94.

 2009a. Prosodic transfer and the representation of determiners in Turkish–English interlanguage. In N. Snape, Y.-k. I. Leung and M. Sharwood Smith (eds.), *Representational deficits in SLA: studies in honor of Roger Hawkins*, 1–26. Amsterdam: John Benjamins.

Goad, H., White, L. and Steele, J. 2003. Missing inflection in L2 acquisition: defective syntax or L1 constrained prosodic representations? *Canadian Journal of Linguistics* **48**: 243–63.

Godson, L. 2004. Vowel production in the speech of Western Armenian heritage speakers. *The Heritage Language Journal* **2**: 1–26.

Goldberg, A. E. 1995. *Constructions: a construction grammar approach to argument structure*. University of Chicago Press.

Goldberg, A. E. and Casenhiser, D. 2008. Construction Learning and Second Language Acquisition. In P. Robinson and N. Ellis (eds.), *Handbook of cognitive linguistics and second language acquisition*, 197–215. New York: Routledge.

Goldschneider, J. and DeKeyser, R. 2001. Explaining the "natural order of L2 morpheme acquisition" in English: a meta-analysis of multiple determinants. *Language Learning* **51**: 1–50.

Golestani, N., Alario, F. X., Meriaux, S., Le Bihan, D., Dehaene, S. and Pallier, C. 2006. Syntax production in bilinguals. *Neuropsychologia* **44**: 1029–40.

Gombert, J. E. 1994. How do illiterate adults react to metalinguistic training? *Annals of Dyslexia* **44**: 250–69.

Gould, S. J. and Lewontin, R. 1979. The spandrels of San Marco and the panglossian paradigm: a critique of the adaptationist programme. *Proceedings of the Royal Society of London.* B **205** (1161): 581–98.

Gould, S. J. and Vrba, E. 1982. Exaptation: a missing term in the science of form. *Paleobiology* **8**: 4–15.

Goulden, R., Nation, I. S. P. and Read, J. 1990. How large can a receptive vocabulary be? *Applied Linguistics* **11**: 341–63.

Green, D. 1998. Mental control of the bilingual lexicosemantic system. *Bilingualism: Language and Cognition* **1**: 67–82.

Greenhill, A., Littlefield, H. and Tano, C. (eds.). 1999. *Proceedings of the 23rd Annual Boston University Conference on Language Development (BUCLD)*. Somerville, MA: Cascadilla Press.

Gregersen, T. and Horwitz, E. K. 2002. Language learning and perfectionism: anxious and non-anxious language learners' reactions to their own oral performance. *Modern Language Journal* **86**: 562–70.

Gregg, K. 1984. Krashen's monitor and Occam's razor. *Applied Linguistics* **5**: 79–100.

  1996. The logical and developmental problems of second language acquisition. In W. C. Ritchie and T. K. Bhatia (eds.), *Handbook of second language acquisition*, 49–81. New York: Academic Press.

  2003a. The state of emergentism in second language acquisition. *Second Language Research* **19**: 95–128.

  2003b. SLA theory: construction and assessment. In C. Doughty and M. Long (eds.), *The handbook of second language acquisition*, 831–65. Oxford: Blackwell.

Grice, P. 1989. *Studies in the way of words*. Cambridge, MA: Harvard University Press.

Griffiths, C. (ed.). 2008. *Lessons form the good language learner*. Cambridge University Press.

Grimshaw, J. 1993. Minimal projection and clause structure. In B. Lust, M. Suñer and J. Whitman (eds.), *Heads, projections and learnability*, 75–83. Hillsdale, NJ: Erlbaum.

Grondin, N. and White, L. 1996. Functional categories in child L2 acquisition of French. *Language Acquisition* **1**: 1–34.

Grosjean, F. 1982. *Life with two languages: an introduction to bilingualism*. Cambridge, MA: Harvard University Press.

  2001. The bilingual's language modes. In J. Nicol (ed.), *One mind, two languages: bilingual language processing*, 1–22. Oxford: Blackwell.

  2004. Studying bilinguals: methodological and conceptual issues. In T. K. Bhatia and W. C. Ritchie (eds.), *The handbook of bilingualism*, 32–63. Malden, MA, and Oxford: Blackwell.

Grüter, T. 2006. Object (clitic) omission in L2 French: mis-setting or missing surface inflection? In M. G. O'Brien, C. Shea and J. Archibald (eds.), *Proceedings of the 8th Generative Approaches to Second Language Acquisition Conference (GASLA 2006)*, 63–71. Somerville, MA: Cascadilla Proceedings Project.

Guasti, M. T., Chierchia, G., Crain, S., Foppolo, F., Gualmini, A. and Meroni, L. 2005. Why children and adults sometimes (but not always) compute implicatures. *Language and Cognitive Processes* **20**: 667–96.

Guerrero, M. C. M. 2005. *Inner speech – L2: thinking words in a second language*. New York: Springer.

Guerrero, M. C. M. and Villamil, O. S. 2000. Activating the ZPD: mutual scaffolding in L2 peer revision. *Modern Language Journal* **84**: 51–68.

Guion, S. 2005. Knowledge of English word stress patterns in early and late Korean–English bilinguals. *Studies in Second Language Acquisition* **27**: 503–33.

Guk, I. and Kellogg, D. 2007. The ZPD and whole class teaching: teacher-led and student-led interactional mediation of tasks. *Language Teaching Research* **11**: 281–99.

Gut, U. 2010. Cross-linguistic influence in L3 phonological acquisition. *International Journal of Multilingualism* **7**: 19–38.

Gyllstad, H. 2007. *Testing English collocations – developing receptive tests for use with advanced Swedish learners*. Lund University: Media-Tryck.

Häcker, M. 2008. Eleven pets and twenty ways to express one's opinion: the vocabulary learners of German acquire at English secondary schools. *Language Learning Journal* **36**: 215–26.

Hagoort, P. and Brown, C. M. 1999. Gender electrified: ERP evidence on the syntactic nature of gender processing. *Journal of Psycholinguistic Research* **28**: 715–28.

Hahne, A. and Friederici, A. D. 2001. Processing a second language: late learners' comprehension mechanisms as revealed by event-related brain potentials. *Bilingualism: Language and Cognition* **4**: 123–41.

Håkansson, G. 1995. Syntax and morphology in language attrition: a study of five bilingual expatriate Swedes. *International Journal of Applied Linguistics* **5**: 153–71.

Hale, K. and Keyser, S. J. (eds.). 1993. *The view from Building 20: essays in linguistics in honor of Sylvain Bromberger*. Cambridge, MA: MIT Press.

Halle, M. and Marantz, A. 1993. Distributed Morphology and the pieces of inflection. In K. Hale and S. J. Keyser (eds.), *The view from Building 20: essays in linguistics in honor of Sylvain Bromberger*, 111–76. Cambridge, MA: MIT Press.

Halliday, M. and Matthiessen, C. 2000. *Construing experience through meaning: a language-based approach to cognition*. London: Continuum.

Hammarberg, B. 2010. The languages of the multilingual: some conceptual and terminological issues. *International Review of Applied Linguistics in Language Teaching* **48**: 91–104.

Han, Z.-H. and Odlin, T. (eds.). 2006. *Studies of fossilization in second language acquisition*. Clevedon: Multilingual Matters.

Han, Z.-H., Park, E. S. and Combs, C. 2008. Textual enhancement of input: issues and possibilities. *Applied Linguistics* **29**: 597–618.

Hankins, T. 1985. *Science and the Enlightenment*. Cambridge University Press.

Hannahs, S. J. and Young-Scholten, M. (eds.). 1997. *Focus on phonological acquisition*. Amsterdam: John Benjamins.

Hansen, J. 2006. *Acquiring a non-native phonology: linguistic constraints and social barriers*. London: Continuum.

Hansen, K. 2005. Impact of literacy level and task type on oral L2 recall accuracy. Unpublished MA thesis, University of Minnesota.

Hanson-Smith, E. 2001. Computer-assisted language learning. In R. Carter and D. Nunan (eds.), *The Cambridge guide to teaching English to speakers of other languages*, 107–13. Cambridge University Press.

Harklau, L. 2000. From the "good kids" to the "worst": representations of English language learners across educational settings. *TESOL Quarterly* **34**: 35–67.

Harris, J. 2008. The declining role of primary schools in the revitalization of Irish. *AILA Review* **21**: 49–68.

Harris, T. and Moreno Jaén, M. (eds.). 2010. *Corpus linguistics in language teaching*. Bern: Peter Lang.

Harris, V. and Snow, D. 2004. *Classic Pathfinder: doing it for themselves: focus on learning strategies and vocabulary building*. London: CILT.

Hassall, T. 2006. Learning to take leave in social conversations: a diary study. In M. DuFon and E. Churchill (eds.), *Language learners in study abroad contexts*, 31–58. Clevedon: Multilingual Matters.

Hatch, E. 1978a. Acquisition of syntax in a second language. In J. Richards (ed.), *Understanding second and foreign language learning*, 34–70. Rowley, MA: Newbury House.

1978b. Discourse analysis and second language acquisition. In E. Hatch (ed.), *Second language acquisition: a book of readings*, 401–35. Rowley, MA: Newbury House.

(ed.). 1978c. *Second language acquisition: a book of readings*. Rowley, MA: Newbury House.

1983. Simplified input and second language acquisition. In R. Andersen (ed.), *Pidginization and creolization as language acquisition*, 64–86. Rowley, MA: Newbury House.

Haught, J. R. and McCafferty, S. G. 2008. Embodied language performance: drama and second language teaching. In J. P. Lantolf and M. Poehner (eds.), *Sociocultural theory and the teaching of second languages*, 139–62. London: Equinox.

Hauser, M., Chomsky, N. and Fitch, T. 2002. The faculty of language: what is it, who has it, and how did it evolve? *Science* **298**: 1569–79.

Hawkins, J. A. 2004. *Efficiency and complexity in grammars*. Oxford University Press.

Hawkins, R. 2001a. *Second language syntax: a generative introduction*. Oxford: Blackwell.
  2001b. The theoretical significance of Universal Grammar in second language acquisition. *Second Language Research* **17**: 345–67.
  2009. Second language acquisition of morphosyntax. In W. C. Ritchie and T. K. Bhatia (eds.), *The new handbook of second language acquisition*, 211–36. Bingley: Emerald.
Hawkins, R. and Franceschina, F. 2004. Explaining the acquisition and non-acquisition of determiner-noun gender concord in French and Spanish. In P. Prévost and J. Paradis (eds.), *The acquisition of French in different contexts: focus on functional categories*, 175–205. Amsterdam: John Benjamins.
Hawkins, R. and Hattori, H. 2006. Interpretation of multiple *wh*-questions by Japanese speakers: a missing uninterpretable feature account. *Second Language Research* **22**: 269–301.
Hawkins, R. and Liszka, S. 2003. Locating the source of defective past tense marking in advanced L2 English speakers. In R. van Hout, A. Hulk, F. Kuiken and R. Towell (eds.), *The lexicon–syntax interface in second language acquisition*, 21–44. Amsterdam: John Benjamins.
Hayes-Harb, R. and Masuda, K. 2008. Development of the ability to lexically encode novel second language phonemic contrasts. *Second Language Research* **24**: 5–33.
Hazan, V., Sennema, A., Iba, M. and Faulkner, A. 2005. Effect of audiovisual perceptual training on the perception and production of consonants by Japanese learners of English. *Speech Communication* **47**: 360–78.
Haznedar, B. 1997. L2 acquisition by a Turkish-speaking child: evidence for L1 influence. In E. Hughes, M. Hughes and A. Greenhill (eds.), *Proceedings of the 21st Boston University conference on language development (BUCLD)*, 245–56. Somerville, MA: Cascadilla Press.
  2001. The acquisition of the IP system in child L2 English. *Studies in Second Language Acquisition* **23**: 1–39.
  2003. The status of functional categories in child second language acquisition: evidence from the acquisition of CP. *Second Language Research* **19**: 1–41.
Haznedar, B. and Gavruseva, E. (eds.). 2008. *Current trends in child second language acquisition: a generative perspective*. Amsterdam: John Benjamins.
Haznedar, B. and Schwartz, B. D. 1997. Are there optional infinitives in child L2 acquisition? In E. Hughes, M. Hughes and A. Greenhill (eds.), *Proceedings of the 21st Boston University Conference on Language Development (BUCLD)*, 257–68. Somerville, MA: Cascadilla Press.
Hebdige, D. 1984. *Subculture: the meaning of style*. New York: Methuen.
Hélot, C. and de Mejía, A.-M. (eds.). 2008. *Forging multilingual spaces*. Clevedon: Multilingual Matters.
Herder, J. G. von. 2002 [1772]. Treatise on the origin of language. In M. N. Forster (ed. and trans.), *Johann Gottfried von Herder: Philosophical writings*, 65–164. Cambridge University Press.

Herdina, P. and Jessner, U. 2002. *A dynamic model of multilingualism: perspectives of change in psycholinguistics*. Clevedon: Multilingual Matters.

Herschensohn, J. 2000. *The second time around: Minimalism and L2 acquisition*. Amsterdam: John Benjamins.

Herschensohn, J. 2001. Missing inflection in second language French: accidental infinitives and other verbal deficits. *Second Language Research* **17**: 273–305.

 2007. *Language development and age*. Cambridge University Press.

 2009. Fundamental and gradient differences in language development. *Studies in Second Language Acquisition* **31**: 259–89.

Hertel, T. J. 2003. Lexical and discourse factors in the second language acquisition of Spanish word order. *Second Language Research* **19**: 273–304.

Hilles, S. 1991. Access to Universal Grammar in second language acquisition. In L. Eubank (ed.), *Point-counterpoint: Universal Grammar in the second language acquisition*, 305–38. Amsterdam: John Benjamins.

Hinkel, E. (ed.). 2005. *Handbook of research in second language teaching and learning*. Mahwah, NJ: Lawrence Erlbaum.

Hirsch, C., Orfitelli, R. M. and Wexler, K. 2007. When *seem* means *think*: the role of the experiencer-phrase in children's comprehension of raising. In A. Belikova, L. Meroni and M. Umeda (eds.), *Proceedings of the 2nd Conference on Generative Approaches to Language Acquisition North America (GALANA)*, 135–46. Somerville, MA: Cascadilla Press.

Hoberg, U. 1981. *Die Wortstellung in der geschriebenen deutschen Gegenwartssprache [Word order in contemporary written German]*. Munich: Hueber.

Hoekstra, T. and Schwartz, B. D. (eds.). 1994. *Language acquisition studies in generative grammar: papers in honor of Kenneth Wexler from the 1991 GLOW Workshops*. Amsterdam: John Benjamins.

Hoffman, M. F. and Walker, J. A. 2010. Ethnolects and the city: ethnic orientation and linguistic variation in Toronto English. *Language Variation and Change* **22**: 37–67.

Holcomb, P. J., Grainger, J. and O'Rourke, T. 2002. An electrophysiological study of the effects of orthographic neighborhood size on printed word perception. *Journal of Cognitive Neuroscience* **14**: 938–50.

Holich, G., Hirsh-Pasek, K. and Golinkoff, R. M. 2000. *Breaking the language barrier: an emergentist coalition model for the origins of word learning* (Monographs of the Society for Research in Child Development). Oxford: Blackwell.

Holland, J. H., Holyoak, K. J., Nisbett R. E. and Thagard, P. R. 1986. *Induction: processes of inference, learning and discovery*. Cambridge, MA: MIT Press.

Holmberg, A. 2009. Parameters in Minimalist Theory: the case of Scandinavian. *Theoretical Linguistics* **36**: 1–48.

Holme, R. 2009. *Cognitive linguistics and language teaching*. Basingstoke: Palgrave Macmillan.

Holmes, J. and Meyerhof, M. 2003. *The handbook of language and gender*. Oxford: Blackwell.

Holtgraves, T. 2007. Second language learners and speech act comprehension. *Language Learning* **57**: 595–610.

Hopp, H. 2002. Constraints on word order variation: learnability and UG in advanced English–German and Japanese–German interlanguage. Unpublished MA thesis, University of Durham.

2005. Constraining second language word order optionality: scrambling in advanced English–German and Japanese–German interlanguage. *Second Language Research* **21**: 34–71.

2006. Syntactic features and reanalysis in near-native processing. *Second Language Research* **23**: 369–97.

2007. *Ultimate attainment at the interfaces in second language acquisition: grammar and processing*. Groningen: Grodil Press.

2009. The syntax-discourse interface in near-native L2 acquisition: off-line and on-line performance. *Bilingualism: Language and Cognition* **12**: 463–83.

2010. Ultimate attainment in L2 inflection: performance similarities between non-native and native speakers. *Lingua* **120**: 901–31.

Horn, L. 1972. On the semantic properties of the logical operators in English. Unpublished PhD dissertation, UCLA.

Horn, L. and Ward, G. (eds.). 2004. *The handbook of pragmatics*. Malden, MA: Blackwell.

Hornstein, N., Nunes, J. and Grohmann, K. 2005. *Understanding minimalism*. Cambridge University Press.

Horst, M. and Meara, P. 1999. Test of a model for predicting second language lexical growth through reading. *The Canadian Modern Language Review / La Revue canadiennne des langues vivantes* **56**: 308–28.

Horwitz, E. K. 2001. Language anxiety and achievement. *Annual Review of Applied Linguistics* **21**: 112–26.

Horwitz, E. K., Horwitz, M. B. and Cope, J. 1986. Foreign language classroom anxiety. *Modern Language Journal* **70**: 125–32.

House, J. and Rehbein, J. (eds.). 2004. *Multilingual communication*. Amsterdam: John Benjamins.

Hovdhaugen, E. 1982. *Foundations of western linguistics: from the beginning to the end of the first millenium A.D*. Oslo: Universitetsforlaget.

Howard, M. (ed.). In press. *The effects of input on foreign language learning*. Berlin: Mouton De Gruyter.

Hu, X. and Reiterer, S. M. 2009. Personality and pronunciation talent. In G. Dogil and S. M. Reiterer (eds.), *Language talent and brain activity*, 97–130. Berlin: Mouton de Gruyter.

Huang, Y. 2000. *Anaphora: a cross-linguistic study*. Oxford University Press.

Huckin, T. and Coady, J. 1999. Incidental vocabulary acquisition in a second language. *Studies in Second Language Acquisition: a review* **21**: 181–93.

Hufeisen, B. and Fouser, R. J. (eds.). 2005. *Introductory Readings in L3*. Tübingen: Stauffenburg Verlag.

Hughes, E., Hughes, M. and Greenhill, A. (eds.). 1997. *Proceedings of the 21st Annual Boston University Conference on Language Development (BUCLD)*. Somerville, MA: Cascadilla Press.

Hulstijn, J. 2007. Fundamental issues in the study of second language acquisition. In L. Roberts, A. Guerel, S. Tatar and L. Marti (eds.), *EUROSLA Yearbook* 7, 191–203. Amsterdam: John Benjamins.

Hulstijn, J. and Laufer, B. 2001. Some empirical evidence for the involvement load hypothesis in vocabulary acquisition. *Language Learning* 51: 539–58.

Humboldt, W. von. 1988 [1836]. *On language: the diversity of human language-structure and its influence on the mental development of mankind*, trans. P. Heath. Cambridge University Press.

Hyltenstam, K. and Abrahamsson, N. 2001. Age and L2 learning: the hazards of matching practical "implications" with theoretical "facts". *TESOL Quarterly* 35: 151–70.

2003. Maturational constraints in SLA. In C. Doughty and M. Long (eds.), *The handbook of second language acquisition*, 539–88. Oxford: Blackwell.

Hyltenstam, K., Bylund, E., Abrahamsson, N. and Park, H.-S. 2009. Dominant language replacement: the case of international adoptees. *Bilingualism: Language and Cognition* 12: 121–40.

Hyman, L. M. 2006. Word-prosodic typology. *Phonology* 23: 225–57.

Hymes, D. 1971. *On communicative competence*. Philadelphia: University of Pennsylvania Press.

1972. On communicative competence. In J. B. Pride and J. Holmes (eds.), *Sociolinguistics*, 269–93. Harmondsworth: Penguin.

Ibrahim, A. E. K. M. 1999. Becoming black: rap and hip-hop, race, gender, identity, and the politics of ESL learning. *TESOL Quarterly* 33: 349–69.

Ilieva, R. 2010. Non-native English-speaking teachers' negotiations of program discourses in their construction of professional identities within a TESOL program. *Canadian Modern Language Review / La Revue canadienne des langues vivantes* 66: 343–69.

Indefrey, P. 2006a. A meta-analysis of hemodynamic studies on first and second language processing: which suggested differences can we trust and what do they mean? *Language Learning* 56: 279–304.

2006b. It is time to work toward explicit processing models for native and second language speakers. *Applied Psycholinguistics* 27: 66–69.

Ingham, R. 1998. Tense without agreement in early clause structure. *Language Acquisition* 7: 51–81.

Ionin, T. 2008. Progressive aspect in child L2-English. In B. Haznedar and E. Gavruseva (eds.), *Current trends in child second language acquisition: a generative perspective*, 17–53. Amsterdam: John Benjamins.

Ionin, T. and Wexler, K. 2002. Why is "is" easier than "-s"?: acquisition of tense/agreement morphology by child L2-English learners. *Second Language Research* 18: 95–136.

Ionin, T., Ko, H. and Wexler, K. 2004. Article semantics in L2 acquisition: the role of specificity. *Language Acquisition* 12: 3–69.

Ioup, G. and Weinberger, S. (eds.). 1987. *Interlanguage phonology: the acquisition of a second language sound system*. Cambridge, MA: Newbury House.

Ivanov, I. 2009. Topicality and clitic doubling in L2 Bulgarian: a test case for the interface hypothesis. In M. Bowles, T. Ionin, S. Montrul and A. Tremblay (eds.), *Proceedings of the 10th Generative Approaches to Second Language Acquisition Conference (GASLA 2009)*, 17–24. Somerville, MA: Cascadilla Proceedings Project.

Iverson, M. 2010. Informing the age of acquisition debate: L3 as a litmus test. *International Review of Applied Linguistics in Language Teaching* **48**: 219–41.

Iverson, P., Hazan, V. and Bannister, K. 2005. Phonetic training with acoustic cue manipulations: a comparison of methods for teaching English /r/-/l/ to Japanese adults. *Journal of the Acoustical Society of America* **118**: 3267–78.

Iverson, P., Kuhl, P. K., Akahane-Yamada, R., Diesch, E., Tohkura, Y., Kettermann, A. and Siebert, C. 2003. A perceptual interference account of acquisition difficulties for non-native phonemes. *Cognition* **87**: B47–57.

Izumi, S. 2002. Output, input enhancement and the noticing hypothesis. *Studies in Second Language Acquisition* **24**: 541–77.

2003. Comprehension and production processes in second language learning: in search of the psycholinguistic rational of the Output Hypothesis. *Applied Linguistics* **24**: 168–96.

Jackendoff, R. 1987. *Consciousness and the computational mind*. Cambridge, MA: MIT Press.

1996. The proper treatment of measuring out, telicity, and possibly even quantification in English. *Natural Language and Linguistic Theory* **14**: 305–54.

1997. *The architecture of the language faculty*. Cambridge, MA: MIT Press.

2002. *Foundations of language: brain, meaning, grammar, evolution*. New York: Oxford University Press.

Jaensch, C. 2008. Defective adjectival inflection in non-native German: prosodic transfer or missing surface inflection. In L. Roberts, F. Myles and A. David (eds.), *EUROSLA Yearbook* 8: 259–86. Amsterdam: John Benjamins.

2009. L3 enhanced feature sensitivity as a result of higher proficiency in the L2. In Y.-k. I. Leung (ed.), *Third language acquisition and Universal Grammar*, 115–43. Clevedon: Multilingual Matters.

James, A. and Leather, J. (eds.). 1997. *Second language speech: structure and process*. Berlin and New York: Mouton de Gruyter.

Jansen, B., Lalleman, J. and Muysken, P. 1981. The alternation hypothesis: acquisition of Dutch word order by Turkish and Moroccan foreign workers. *Language Learning* **31**: 315–36.

Jenkins, L. 2000. *Biolinguistics*. Cambridge, MA: MIT Press.

Jessner, U. 2008. Teaching third languages: findings, trends and challenges. *Language Teaching* **41**: 15–56.

Jia, G. and Aaronson, D. 2003. A longitudinal study of Chinese children and adolescents learning English in the United States. *Applied Psycholinguistics* **24**: 131–61.

Jiang, N. 2002. Form-meaning mapping in vocabulary acquisition in a second language. *Studies in Second Language Acquisition* **24**: 617–37.

2004. Semantic transfer and its implications for vocabulary teaching in a second language. *Modern Language Journal* **88**: 416–32.

Jilka, M. 2009. Talent and proficiency in language. In G. Dogil and S. M. Reiterer (eds.), *Language talent and brain activity*, 1–16. Berlin: Mouton de Gruyter.

Johns, T. 2002. Data-driven learning: the perpetual challenge. In B. Kettemann and G. Marko (eds.), *Teaching and learning by doing corpus analysis*, 107–17. Amsterdam: Rodopi.

Johnson, J. and Newport, E. 1989. Critical period effects in second language learning: the influence of maturational state on the acquisition of English as a second language. *Cognitive Psychology* **21**: 60–99.

Johnson, K. 1996. *Language teaching and skill learning*. Oxford: Blackwell.

Johnson, M. 1987. *The body in the mind: the bodily basis of meaning, imagination, and reasoning*. University of Chicago Press.

2004. *A philosophy of second language acquisition*. New Haven, CT: Yale University Press.

Jordan, G. 2004. *Theory construction in second language acquisition*. Amsterdam and Philadelphia: John Benjamins.

Jordens, P. 2008. The development of finiteness from a lexical to a functional category. In L. Roberts, F. Myles and A. David (eds.), *EUROSLA Yearbook* 8: 191–214. Amsterdam: John Benjamins.

2009. The acquisition of functional categories in child L1 and adult L2 Dutch. In C. Dimroth and P. Jordens (eds.), *Functional categories in learner language*, 45–96. Berlin: Mouton.

Joseph, J. E. 2010. Chomsky's atavistic revolution (with a little help from his enemies). In D. A. Kibbee (ed.), *Chomskyan (r)evolutions*, 1–18. Amsterdam: John Benjamins.

Jourdenais, R., Ota, M., Stauffer, S., Boyson, B. and Doughty, C. 1995. Does textual enhancement promote noticing? A think-aloud protocol analysis. In R. Schmidt (ed.), *Attention and awareness in foreign language learning. Technical report #9*, 183–216. Honolulu: University of Hawai'i.

Juffs, A. 2004. Representation, processing and working memory in a second language. *Transactions of the Philological Society* **102**: 199–225.

2009. Second language acquisition of the lexicon. In W. C. Ritchie and T. K. Bhatia (eds.), *The new handbook of second language acquisition*, 181–209. Bingley: Emerald.

Jun, S.-A. and Fougeron, C. 2002. Realizations of accentual phrase in French intonation. *Probus* **14**: 147–72.

Jusczyk, P. 1997. *The discovery of spoken language*. Cambridge, MA: MIT Press.

Kabak, B. and Idsardi, W. 2007. Perceptual distortions in the adaptation of English consonant clusters: syllable structure or consonantal contact constraints? *Language and Speech* **50**: 23–52.

Kang, K.-H. and Guion, S. G. 2006. Phonological systems in bilinguals: age of learning effects on the stop consonant systems of Korean-English bilinguals. *Journal of the Acoustical Society of America* **119**: 1672-83.

Kang, Y. 2008. Interlanguage segmental mapping as evidence for the nature of lexical representation. *Language and Linguistics Compass* **2**: 103-18.

Kanno, Y. 2003. *Negotiating bilingual and bicultural identities: Japanese returnees betwixt two worlds*. Mahwah, NJ: Lawrence Erlbaum.

Kaplan, R. (ed.). 2002. *The Oxford handbook of applied linguistics*. Oxford University Press.

Karmiloff-Smith, A., Grant, J., Sims, K., Jones, M. and Cuckle, P. 1996. Rethinking metalinguistic awareness: representing and accessing knowledge about what counts as a word. *Cognition* **58**: 197-219.

Kasper, G., and Rose, K. 2002. *Pragmatic development in a second language*. Oxford: Blackwell.

Kathol, A. 2000. *Linear syntax*. Oxford University Press.

Katz, J. and Postal, P. 1964. *An integrated theory of linguistic descriptions*. Cambridge, MA: MIT Press.

Katz, L. and DaSilva Iddings, A. C. 2009. Classroom positionings and children's construction of linguistic and racial identities in English-dominant classrooms. In R. Kubota and A. Lin (eds.), *Race, culture, and identity in second language education: exploring critically engaged practice*, 138-57. New York: Routledge.

Kauffman, S. 2007. Beyond reductionism: reinventing the sacred. *Zygon* **42**: 903-14.

Kayne, R. 1984. *Connectedness and binary branching*. Dordrecht: Foris.
   2005. *Movement and silence*. Oxford University Press.

Keating, G., VanPatten, B. and Jegersky, J. 2011. Who was walking on the beach? *Studies in Second Language Acquisition* **33**: 193-221.

Keck, C., Iberri-Shea, G., Tracy-Ventura, N. and Wa-Mbaleka, S. 2006. Investigating the empirical link between task-based interaction and acquisition: a meta-analysis. In J. Norris and L. Ortega (eds.), *Synthesizing research on language learning and teaching*, 91-129. Amsterdam: John Benjamins.

Kellerman, E. 1979. Transfer and non-transfer: where we are now. *Studies in Second Language Acquisition* **2**: 37-57.

Kellerman, E. and Van Hoof, A.-M. 2003. Manual accents. *International Review of Applied Linguistics in Language Teaching* **40**: 3.

Kenneally, C. 2010. Talking heads. *New Scientist*, 29 May 2010, 33-35.

Kenstowicz, M. (ed.). 2001. *Ken Hale: a life in language*. Cambridge, MA: MIT Press.

Kern, R. and Liddicoat, A. J. 2010. Introduction: from the learner to the speaker/actor. In G. Zarate, C. Kramsch and D. Levy (eds.), *Handbook of multilingualism and multiculturalism*, 23-29. Paris: Editions des Archives contemporaines.

Kerswill, P. 2006. Migration and Language. In K. U. A. Mattheier and P. Trudgill (eds.), *Sociolinguistics/Soziolinguistik, an international handbook of the science of language and society*, 2nd edn, vol. III, 2271–85. Berlin: De Gruyter.

Kettemann, B. and Marko, G. (eds.). 2002. *Teaching and learning by doing corpus analysis*. Amsterdam: Rodopi.

Kijak, A. 2009. *How stressful is L2 stress? A cross-linguistic study of L2 perception and production of metrical systems*. Utrecht: Landelijke Onderzoekschool Taalwetenschap.

Kim, J.-H., Montrul, S. and Yoon, J. 2009. Binding interpretation of anaphors in Korean heritage speakers. *Language Acquisition* **16**: 3–35.

Kindred, K. 2010. Yes/No vocabulary size tests constructed using the BNC. Unpublished MA thesis, Swansea University.

Kinginger, C. 2002. Defining the zone of proximal development in US foreign language education. *Applied Linguistics* **23**: 240–61.

  2008. Language learning in study abroad: case studies of Americans in France. *Modern Language Journal* (issue supplement) **92**: 1–124.

  2009. *Language learning in study abroad: a critical reading of research*. Basingstoke: Palgrave Macmillan.

Kitade, K. 2008. The role of offline metalanguage talk in asynchronous computer-mediated communication. *Language Learning and Technology* **12**: 64–84.

Klassen, C. and Burnaby, B. 1993. "Those who know": views on literacy among adult immigrants in Canada. *TESOL Quarterly* **27**: 377–97.

Klein, C. 1995. Second versus third language acquisition: is there a difference? *Language Learning* **45**: 419–65.

Klein, W. and Perdue, C. 1992. *Utterance structure: developing grammars again*. Amsterdam: John Benjamins.

  1997. The basic variety (or: couldn't natural languages be much simpler?). *Second Language Research* **13**: 301–47.

Kleinmann, H. 1977. Avoidance behavior in adult second language acquisition. *Language Learning* **27**: 93–107.

Klima, E. 1964. Negation in English. In J. D. Fodor and J. Katz (eds.), *The structure of language: readings in the philosophy of language*, 246–323. Englewood Cliffs, NJ: Prentice Hall.

Klima, E. and Bellugi, U. K. 1966. Syntactic regularities in the speech of children. In J. Lyons and R. Wales (eds.), *Psycholinguistic papers*, 183–208. Edinburgh University Press.

Knouzi, I., Swain, M., Lapkin, S. and Brooks, L. 2010. Self-scaffolding mediated by languaging: microgenetic analysis of high and low performers. *International Journal of Applied Linguistics* **20**: 23–49.

Knudsen, E. I. 2004. Sensitive periods in the development of the brain and behavior. *Journal of Cognitive Neuroscience* **16**: 1412–25.

Kohnert, K. and Bates, E. 2002. Balancing bilinguals II. Lexical comprehension and cognitive processing in children learning Spanish and English. *Journal of Speech, Language, and Hearing Research* **45**: 347–59.

Koike, D. A. and Pearson, L. 2005. The effect of instruction and feedback in the development of pragmatic competence. *System* **33**: 481–501.

Kolinsky, R., Cary, L. and Morais, J. 1987. Awareness of words as phonological entities: the role of literacy. *Applied Psycholinguistics* **8**: 223–32.

Kondo-Brown, K. (ed.). 2006. *Heritage language development: focus on East Asian immigrants*. Amsterdam: John Benjamins.

Köpke, B., Schmid, M. S., Keijzer, M. and Dostert, S. (eds.). 2007. *Language attrition: theoretical perspectives*. Amsterdam: John Benjamins.

Kormos, J. 2006. *Speech production and second language acquisition*. Mahwah, NJ: Lawrence Erlbaum.

Kormos, J. and Csizér, K. 2008. Age-related differences in the motivation of learning English as a foreign language: attitudes, selves and motivated learning behavior. *Language Learning* **58**: 327–55.

Koster, J. 1978. *Locality principles in syntax*. Dordrecht: Foris.
  1987. *Domains and dynasties: the radical autonomy of syntax*. Dordrecht: Foris.
  2007. Structure-Preservingness, internal Merge, and the strict locality of triads. In S. Karimi, V. Samiian and W. Wilkins (eds.), *Phrasal and clausal architecture: syntactic derivation and interpretation: papers in honour of Joseph Emonds*, 188–205. Amsterdam: John Benjamins.
  2009a. Word meaning and the preformationist fallacy. MS, University of Groningen. www.let.rug.nl/koster/papers/Word%20meaning%20and%20the%20preformationist%20fallacy%201.pdf

Kotz, S. A. 2009. A critical review of ERP and fMRI evidence on L2 syntactic processing. *Brain and Language* **109**: 68–74.

Kotz, S. A. and Elston-Güttler, K. E. 2007. Bilingual semantic memory revisited: ERP and fMRI evidence. In J. Hart and M. Kraut (eds.), *The neural basis of semantic memory*, 105–32. Cambridge University Press.

Kouritzin, S. 2000. Immigrant mothers redefine access to ESL classes: contradiction and ambivalence. *Journal of Multilingual and Multicultural Development* **21**: 14–32.

Kramsch, C. 2009a. *The multilingual subject: what foreign language learners say about their experience and why it matters*. Oxford University Press.

Kramsch, C. and Vork Steffensen, J. 2010. Ecological perspectives on second language acquisition. In P. A. Duff and N. C. Hornberger (eds.), *Encyclopaedia of language and education*, vol. VIII: *Language socialization*, 17–28. New York: Springer.

Kramsch, C. and Whiteside, A. 2007. Three fundamental concepts in second language acquisition and their relevance in multilingual contexts. *Modern Language Journal* **91**: 907–22.
  2008. Language ecology in multilingual settings: towards a theory of symbolic competence. *Applied Linguistics* **29**: 645–71.

Krashen, S. D. 1977. The monitor model for adult second language performance. In M. Burt, H. Dulay and M. Finocchiaro (eds.), *Viewpoints on English as a second language*, 152–61. New York: Regents.
  1981. *Second language acquisition and second language learning*. Oxford: Pergamon.

1982. *Principles and practice in second language acquisition*. Oxford: Pergamon.

1985. *The input hypothesis: issues and implications*. London: Longman.

Kroll, J. F. and de Groot, A. (eds.). 2005. *Handbook of bilingualism: psycholinguistic perspectives*. Oxford University Press.

Kroll, J. F. and Dussias, P. E. 2004. The comprehension of words and sentences in two languages. In T. K. Bhatia and W. C. Ritchie (eds.), *The handbook of bilingualism*, 169–200. Malden, MA, and Oxford: Blackwell.

Kubota, R. and Lin, A. (eds.). 2006. Race and TESOL (special topic issue). *TESOL Quarterly* **40** (3).

Kubota, R. and Lin, A. (eds.). 2009a. *Race, culture, and identity in second language education: exploring critically engaged practice*. New York: Routledge.

2009b. Race, culture, and identities in second language education: introduction to research and practice. In R. Kubota and A. Lin (eds.), *Race, culture, and identity in second language education: exploring critically engaged practice*, 1–22. New York: Routledge.

Kubota, M., Inouchi, M., Ferrari, P. and Roberts, T. P. L. 2005. Human magnetoencephalographic evidence of early syntactic responses to c-selection violations of English infinitives and gerunds by L1 and L2 speakers. *Neuroscience Letters* **384**: 300–4.

Kuhl, P. 2004. Early language acquisition: cracking the speech code. *Nature Reviews Neuroscience* **5**: 831–43.

Kuhl, P. K. and Iverson, P. 1995. Linguistic experience and the "perceptual magnet effect." In W. Strange (ed.), *Speech perception and linguistic experience: issues in cross-language research*, 121–54. Baltimore: York Press.

Kurvers, J. and Craats, I. van de. 2007. What makes the illiterate language genius? In N. Faux (ed.), *Low-educated Second Language and Literacy Acquisition: proceedings of the 2nd Annual Forum*, 49–57. Richmond, VA: The Literacy Institute at Virginia Commonwealth University.

Kurvers, J., van Hout, R. and Vallen, T. 2006. Discovering language: metalinguistic awareness of adult illiterates. In I. van de Craats, J. Kurvers and M. Young-Scholten (eds.), *Low-educated Second Language and Literacy Acquisition: Proceedings of the 1st Annual Forum* (LOT Occasional Series 15), 69–88. http://lotos.library.uu.nl/index.html. Utrecht: Landelijke Onderzoekschool Taalwetenschap.

2009. Print awareness of adult illiterates: a comparison with young pre-readers and low-educated adult readers. *Reading and Writing* **22**: 863–87.

Kwon, E.-Y. 2005. The "natural order" of morpheme acquisition: a historical survey and discussion of three putative determinants. *Working Papers in TESOL and Applied Linguistics* **5**: 1–21.

Labov, W. 1966. *The social stratification of English in New York City*. Washington, DC: Center for Applied Linguistics.

1972. *Language in the inner city: studies in the Black English Vernacular*. Philadelphia: University of Pennsylvania Press.

1984. Field Methods of the project on linguistic change and variation. In J. Baugh and J. Sherzer (eds.), *Language in use: readings in sociolinguistics*, 28–54. Englewood Cliffs, NJ: Prentice-Hall.

Lado, R. 1957. *Linguistics across cultures*. Ann Arbor: University of Michigan Press.
　1964. *Language teaching: a scientific approach*. New York: McGraw-Hill.
Lakoff, G. 1987. *Women, fire and dangerous things: what categories reveal about the mind*. University of Chicago Press.
Lakshmanan, U. 1994. *Universal grammar in child second language acquisition: null subjects and morphological uniformity*. Amsterdam: John Benjamins.
　1995. Child second language acquisition of syntax. *Studies in Second Language Acquisition* 17: 301–29.
　2009. Child second language acquisition. In W. C. Ritchie and T. K. Bhatia (eds.), *The new handbook of second language acquisition*, 377–99. Bingley: Emerald.
Lamy, M.-N. and Hampel, R. 2007. *Online communication in language learning and teaching*. Basingstoke: Palgrave Macmillan.
Langacker, R. 2008a. *Cognitive Grammar: a basic introduction*. Oxford University Press.
Lantolf, J. P. 1996. SLA theory building: "Letting all the flowers bloom!" *Language Learning* 46: 713–49.
　2006. Sociocultural theory and second language learning: state of the art. *Studies in Second Language Acquisition* 28: 67–109.
Lantolf, J. P. and Appel, G. (eds.). 1994. *Vygotskian approaches to second language research*. Norwood, NJ: Ablex.
Lantolf, J. P. and Pavlenko, A. 2001. (S)econd (L)anguage (A)ctivity theory: understanding second language learners as people. In M. P. Breen (ed.), *Learner contributions to language learning: new directions in research*, 141–58. Harlow: Pearson.
Lantolf, J. P. and Thorne, S. L. 2006. *Sociocultural theory and the genesis of second language development*. New York: Oxford University Press.
Lardiere, D. 1998a. Case and tense in the "fossilized" steady state. *Second Language Research* 14: 1–26.
　1998b. Dissociating syntax from morphology in a divergent L2 end-state grammar. *Second Language Research* 14: 359–75.
　1999. Suppletive agreement in second language acquisition. In A. Greenhill, H. Littlefield and C. Tano (eds.), *Proceedings of the 23rd Annual Boston University Conference on Language Development (BUCLD)*, 386–96. Somerville, MA: Cascadilla Press.
　2000. Mapping features to forms in second language acquisition. In J. Archibald (ed.), *Second language acquisition and linguistic theory*, 102–29. Malden, MA: Blackwell.
　2003. Second language knowledge of [+/−past] vs. [+/−finite]. In J. Liceras, H. Goodluck and H. Zobl (eds.), *Proceedings of the 6th Generative Approaches to Second Language Acquisition Conference (GASLA 2002)*, 176–89. Somerville, MA: Cascadilla Proceedings Project.
　2006. Establishing ultimate attainment in a particular second language grammar. In Z.-H. Han and T. Odlin (eds.), *Studies of fossilization in second language acquisition*, 35–55. Clevedon: Multilingual Matters.

2007. *Ultimate attainment in second language acquisition: a case study*. Mahwah, NJ: Lawrence Erlbaum Associates.

2008. Feature assembly in second language acquisition. In J. Liceras, H. Zobl and H. Goodluck (eds.), *The role of formal features in second language acquisition*, 106–40. New York: Lawrence Erlbaum.

2009a. Some thoughts on the contrastive analysis of feature in second language acquisition. *Second Language Research* **25**: 171–225.

2009b. Further thoughts on parameters and features in second language acquisition: a reply to peer comments on Lardiere's "Some thoughts on the contrastive analysis of features in second language acquisition." *Second Language Research* **25**: 409–22.

Larsen-Freeman, D. 1975. The acquisition of grammatical morphemes by adult ESL students. *TESOL Quarterly* **9**: 409–30.

1997. Chaos/complexity science and second language acquisition. *Applied Linguistics* **18**: 141–65.

2007. Reflecting on the cognitive-social debate. *Modern Language Journal* **91**: 773–87.

Larsen-Freeman, D. and Cameron, L. 2008. *Complex systems and applied linguistics*. Oxford University Press.

Laufer, B. 2005. Focus on form in second language vocabulary learning. In S. Foster-Cohen, M. del P. García Mayo and J. Cenoz (eds.), *EUROSLA Yearbook* 5: 223–50. Amsterdam: John Benjamins.

2010. Form-focussed instruction in second language vocabulary learning. In R. Chacón-Beltrán, C. Abello-Contesse and M. Torreblanca-López (eds.), *Further insights into non-native vocabulary teaching and learning*, 15–27. Clevedon: Multilingual Matters.

Laufer, B. and Eliasson, S. 1983. What causes avoidance in L2 learning: L1-L2 difference, L1-L2 similarity, or L2 complexity? *Studies in Second Language Acquisition* **15**: 33–48.

Laufer, B. and Hulstijn, J. 2001. Incidental vocabulary acquisition in a second language: the construct of task induced involvement. *Applied Linguistics* **22**: 1–26.

Laufer, B. and Sim, D. D. 1985. Reading and explaining the reading threshold needed for English for academic purposes texts. *Foreign Language Annals* **18**: 405–11.

Lave, J. and Wenger, E. 1991. *Situated learning: legitimate peripheral participation*. Cambridge University Press.

Lee, J. F. and Benati, A. 2010. *Processing instruction and discourse level input*. London: Continuum Press.

Lee, J. S. 2005. Through the learners' eyes: reconceptualizing the heritage and non-heritage learner of the less commonly taught languages. *Foreign Language Annals* **38**: 554–63.

Lee, S. 2007. Effects of textual enhancement and topic familiarity on Korean EFL student's reading comprehension and learning of passive form. *Language Learning* **57**: 87–118.

Lee, S. and Huang, H. 2008. Visual enhancement and grammar learning: a meta-analytic review. *Studies in Second Language Acquisition* **30**: 307–31.

Lee, Y.-S., Vakoch, D. A. and Wurm, L. H. 1996. Tone perception in Cantonese and Mandarin: a cross-linguistic comparison. *Journal of Psycholinguistic Research* **25**: 527–42.

Legendre, G., Hagstrom, P., Vainikka, A. and Todorova, M. 2002. Partial constraint ordering in child French syntax. *Language Acquisition* **10**: 189–227.

Leikin, M., Raphiq, I., Zohar, E. and Shimon, S. 2009. Listening with an accent: speech perception in a second language by late bilinguals. *Journal of Psycholinguistic Research* **38**: 447–57.

Lenneberg, E. 1966. The natural history of language. In F. Smith and E. Miller (eds.), *The genesis of language*, 219–52. Cambridge, MA: MIT Press.

  1967. *Biological foundations of language*. New York: John Wiley.

Leopold, W. 1949. *Speech development of a bilingual child: a linguist's record*, vol. IV: *Diary from age two*. Evanston, IL: Northwestern University Press.

Leow, R. 1997. The effects of input enhancement and text length on adult L2 readers' comprehension and intake in second language acquisition. *Applied Language Learning* **8**: 151–82.

  2001. Do learners notice enhanced forms while interacting with the L2? An online and offline study of the role of written input enhancement in L2 reading. *Hispania* **84**: 496–509.

Leow, R., Egi, T., Nuevo, A. M. and Tsai, Y. C. 2003. The roles of textual enhancement and type of linguistic item in adult L2 learners' comprehension and intake. *Applied Language Learning* **13**: 93–108.

Leung, Y.-k. I. 2005. L2 vs. L3 initial state: a comparative study of the acquisition of French DPs by Vietnamese monolinguals and Cantonese–English bilinguals. *Bilingualism: Language and Cognition* **8**: 39–61.

  (ed.). 2009. *Third language acquisition and Universal Grammar*. Clevedon: Multilingual Matters.

Levelt, W. 1989. *Speaking: from intention to articulation*. Cambridge, MA: MIT Press.

  1999. Producing spoken language: a blueprint of the speaker. In C. Brown and P. Hagoort (eds.), *The neurocognition of language*, 83–122. Oxford University Press.

Levinson, S. C. 1983. *Pragmatics*. Cambridge University Press.

  2000. *Presumptive meanings: the theory of generalized conversational implicature*. Cambridge, MA: MIT Press.

Li, S. 2010. The effectiveness of corrective feedback in SLA: a meta-analysis. *Language Learning* **60**: 309–65.

Liceras, J. 1986. *Linguistic theory and second language acquisition*. Tübingen: Gunter Narr.

  2009. On parameters, functional categories and features... and why the trees shouldn't prevent us from seeing the forest... *Second Language Research* **25**: 279–89.

Liceras, J., Goodluck, H. and Zobl, H. (eds.). 2003. *Proceedings of the 6th Generative Approaches to Second Language Acquisition Conference (GASLA 2002)*. Somerville, MA: Cascadilla Proceedings Project.

Liceras, J., Zobl, H. and Goodluck, H. (eds.). 2008. *The role of formal features in second language acquisition*. New York: Lawrence Erlbaum Associates.

Liddicoat, A. 2006. Learning the culture of interpersonal relationships: students' understandings of personal address forms in French. *Intercultural Pragmatics* 3: 55–80.

2009. Sexual identity as linguistic failure: trajectories of interaction in the heteronormative language classroom. *Journal of Language, Identity, and Education* 8: 191–202.

Lightbown, P. and White, L. 1987. The influence of linguistic theories on language acquisition research: description and explanation. *Language Learning* 37: 483–510.

Linden Research. 2003-10. *Second Life*. secondlife.com (22 June 2010).

Lively, S. E., Pisoni, D. B., Yamada, R. A., Tohkura, Y. and Yamada, T. 1994. Training Japanese listeners to identify English/r/ and /l/. III: long-term retention of new phonetic categories. *Journal of the Acoustical Society of America* 96: 2076–87.

Llama, R., Cardoso, W. and Collins. L. 2010. The influence of language distance and language status on the acquisition of L3 phonology. *International Journal of Multilingualism* 7: 39–57.

Locke, J. 1975 [1690]. *An essay concerning human understanding*, ed. P. H. Nidditch. Cambridge University Press.

Long, M. H. 1981. Input, interaction, and second-language acquisition. In H. Winitz (ed.), *Native language and foreign language acquisition. Annals of the New York Academy of Science* 379: 259–78.

1990. Maturational constraints on language development. *Studies in Second Language Acquisition* 12: 251–85.

1996. The role of the linguistic environment in second language acquisition. In W. C. Ritchie and T. K. Bhatia (eds.), *Handbook of second language acquisition*, 413–68. New York: Academic Press.

1997. Construct validity in SLA research: a response to Firth and Wagner. *Modern Language Journal* 81: 318–23.

2003. Stabilization and fossilization in interlanguage development. In C. Doughty and M. Long (eds.), *The handbook of second language acquisition*, 487–535. Oxford: Blackwell.

2007. *Problems in SLA*. Mahwah, NJ: Lawrence Erlbaum.

Long, M. H. and Doughty, C. (eds.). 2009. *The handbook of language teaching*. Malden, MA: Wiley-Blackwell.

Long, M. H. and Richards, J. C. 2007. Series editors' preface. In H. Daller, J. Milton and J. Treffers-Daller (eds.), *Modelling and assessing vocabulary knowledge*, xii-xiii. Cambridge University Press.

Long, M. H. and Robinson, P. 1998. Focus on form: theory, research and practice. In C. Doughty and J. Williams (eds.), *Focus on form in classroom second language acquisition*, 15–41. Cambridge University Press.

Loureiro, C., Willadino-Braga, L. W., Souza, L., Filho, G. N., Queiroz, E. and Dellatolas, G. 2004. Degree of illiteracy and phonological and metaphonological skills in unschooled adults. *Brain and Language* **89**: 499–502.

Louriz, N. 2007. Alignment in L3 Phonology. *Langues et Linguistique* **18/19**: 129–60.

Lovett, M. C., Reder, L. M. and Lebiere, C. 1999. Modeling working memory in a unified architecture: an ACT-R perspective. In A. Miyake and P. Shah (eds.), *Models of working memory: mechanisms of active maintenance and executive control*, 135–83. Cambridge University Press.

Lozano, C. 2002. The interpretation of overt and null pronouns in non-native Spanish. In H. Marsden, S. Pourcel and M. Whong-Barr (eds.), *Durham Working Papers in Linguistics* 8: 53–66. Newcastle upon Tyne: Newcastle University Press.

2006. Focus and split-intransitivity: the acquisition of word order alternations in non-native Spanish. *Second Language Research* **22**: 145–87.

Lüdeling, A. and Ensslin, A. 2009–10. WHiG? What's hard in German? Bangor University. www.bangor.ac.uk/creative_industries/whig.php.en

Lüdeling, A. and Kytö, M. (eds.). 2008. *Corpus linguistics: an international handbook*, vol. I. Berlin: de Gruyter.

Ludlow, P. 1999. *Semantics, tense and time: an essay in the metaphysics of natural language*. Cambridge, MA: MIT Press.

Lyster, R. and Ranta, L. 1997. Corrective feedback and learner uptake: Negotiation of form in communicative classrooms. *Studies in Second Language Acquisition* **19**: 37–66.

MacIntyre, P. D. and Charos, C. 1996. Personality, attitudes, and affect as predictors of second language communication. *Journal of Language and Social Psychology* **15**: 3–26.

MacIntyre, P. and Gardner, R. C. 1991. Language anxiety: its relationship to other anxieties and to processing in native and second languages. *Language Learning* **41**: 85–117.

MacIntyre, P. D., Clément, R. and Noels, K. A. 2007. Affective variables, attitude and personality in context. In D. Ayoun (ed.), *French applied linguistics*, 270–98. Amsterdam: John Benjamins.

MacIntyre, P. D., Baker, S., Clément, R. and Conrod, S. 2001. Willingness to communicate, social support and language learning orientations of immersion students. *Studies in Second Language Acquisition* **23**: 369–88.

MacIntyre, P. D., Clément, R., Dörnyei, Z. and Noels, K. A. 1998. Conceptualizing willingness to communicate in a L2: a situational model of L2 confidence and affiliation. *Modern Language Journal* **82**: 545–62.

MacKain, K. S., Best, C. T. and Strange, W. 1981. Categorical perception of English /r/ and /l/ by Japanese bilinguals. *Applied Psycholinguistics* **2**: 369–90.

Mackey, A. 1999. Input, interaction and second language development: an empirical study of question formation in ESL. *Studies in Second Language Acquisition* **21**: 557–87.

2006. Feedback, noticing and second language development: an empirical study of L2 classroom interaction. *Applied Linguistics* **27**: 405-30.

(ed.). 2007. *Conversational interaction in second language acquisition.* Oxford University Press.

Mackey, A. and Goo, J. 2007. Interaction research in SLA: a meta-analysis and research synthesis. In A. Mackey (ed.), *Conversational interaction in second language acquisition*, 407-72. Oxford University Press.

Mackey, A. and C. Polio (eds.). 2009. *Multiple perspectives on interaction.* New York: Routledge.

Mackey, A., Adams, R., Stafford, C. and Winke, P. 2010. Exploring the relationship between modified output and working memory capacity. *Language Learning* **60**: 501-33.

Maclachlan, K., Tett, L. and Hall, S. 2009. "The more you learn the better you feel": research into literacies, learning and identity in Scotland. In S. Reder and J. Bynner (eds.), *Tracking adult literacy and numeracy skills: findings from longitudinal research*, 329-48. New York and London: Routledge.

MacWhinney, B. (ed.). 1987a. *Mechanisms of language acquisition.* Mahwah, NJ: Erlbaum.

1987b. The competition model. In B. MacWhinney (ed.), *Mechanisms of language acquisition*, 249-308. Majwah, NJ: Erblaum.

1995. *The CHILDES project: tools for analyzing talk*, 2nd edn. Hillsdale, NJ: Lawrence Erlbaum.

(ed.). 1999. *The emergence of language.* Mahwah, NJ: Lawrence Erlbaum.

2005. A unified model of language acquisition. In J. Kroll and A. de Groot (eds.), *Handbook of bilingualism: psycholinguistic perspectives*, 49-67. Oxford University Press.

2010. A tale of two paradigms. In M. Kail and M. Hickmann (eds.), *Language acquisition across linguistic and cognitive systems*, 17-32. Amsterdam: John Benjamins.

Major, R. C. 2004. Gender and stylistic variation in second language phonology. *Language Variation and Change* **16**: 169-88.

2008. Transfer in second language phonology: a review. In J. G. H. Edwards and M. L. Zampini (eds.), *Phonology and second language acquisition*, 63-94. Amsterdam: John Benjamins.

Major, R. C. and Kim, E. 1996. The Similarity Differential Rate Hypothesis. *Language Learning* **46**: 465-96.

Makino, T. 1980. Acquisition order of English morphemes by Japanese secondary school students. *Journal of Hokkaido University of Education* **30**: 101-48.

Marcus, G. 2004. *The birth of the mind.* New York: Basic Books.

Marian, V., Spivey, M. and Hirsch, J. 2003. Shared and separate systems in bilingual language processing: converging evidence from eyetracking and brain imaging. *Brain and Language* **86**: 70-82.

Marinis, T. 2003. Psycholinguistic techniques in second language acquisition research. *Second Language Research* **19**: 144-61.

Marinis, T. and Chondrogianni, V. 2010. Production of tense marking in successive bilingual children: when do they converge with their monolingual peers? *International Journal of Speech-Language Pathology* **12**: 19–28.

Marsden, H. 2004. Quantifier scope in non-native Japanese: a comparative interlanguage study of Chinese, English, and Korean-speaking learners. Unpublished PhD dissertation, University of Durham.

   2008. Pair-list readings in Korean–Japanese, Chinese–Japanese and English–Japanese interlanguage. *Second Language Research* **24**: 89–226.

   2009. Distributive quantifier scope in English–Japanese and Korean–Japanese Interlanguage. *Language Acquisition* **16**: 135–77.

Martin, C. D., Dering, B., Thomas, E. M. and Thierry, G. 2009. Brain potentials reveal semantic priming in both the "active" and the "non-attended" language in early bilinguals. *NeuroImage* **47**: 326–33.

May, R. 1985. *Logical form: its structure and derivation*. Cambridge, MA: MIT Press.

Mayberry, R. I., Lock, E. and Kazmi, H. 2002. Linguistic ability and early language exposure. *Nature* **417**: 38.

McCafferty, S. In press. Zone of proximal development in second language acquisition. In A. S. Ohta (ed.), *Enyclopedia of applied linguistics*, ed. C. Chapelle, vol. XXI: *Social, dynamic, and complexity theory approaches to second language development*. Malden, MA, and Oxford: Wiley-Blackwell.

McCandliss, B. D., Fiez, J. A., Protopapas, A., Conway, M. and McClelland, J. L. 2002. Success and failure in teaching the [r]–[l] contrast to Japanese adults: tests of a Hebbian model of plasticity and stabilization in spoken language perception. *Cognitive, Affective, & Behavioral Neuroscience* **2**: 89–108.

McCarthy, C. 2008. Morphological variability in the comprehension of agreement: an argument for representation over computation. *Second Language Research* **24**: 459–86.

McCarthy, M., McCarten, J. and Sandiford, H. 2005. *Touchstone: student's book 1*. Cambridge University Press.

McDonald, B. A. and Scollay, P. A. 2009. Outcomes of literacy improvement: a longitudinal view. In S. Reder and J. Bynner (eds.), *Tracking adult literacy and numeracy skills: findings from longitudinal research*, 312–28. New York and London: Routledge.

McDonald, J. L. 2006. Beyond the critical period: processing-based explanations for poor grammaticality judgment performance by late second language learners. *Journal of Memory and Language* **55**: 381–401.

McKay, S. L. and Wong, S. C. 1996. Multiple discourses, multiple identities: investment and agency in second-language learning among Chinese adolescent immigrant students. *Harvard Educational Review* **66**: 577–608.

McLaughlin, J., Tanner, D., Pitkanen, I., Frenck-Mestre, C., Inoue, K., Valentine, G. and Osterhout, L. 2010. Brain potentials reveal discrete stages of L2 grammatical learning. *Language Learning* **60**: 123–50.

Meara, P. 1992. *EFL vocabulary tests*. University College Swansea: Centre for Applied Language Studies.

Meara, P. and Jones, G. 1990. *Eurocentre's vocabulary size test: user's guide*. Zurich: Eurocentres.

Meara, P. and Wolter, B. 2004. V_Links, beyond vocabulary depth. *Angles on the English Speaking World* **4**: 85–96.

Meisel, J. 1997. The acquisition of the syntax of negation in French and German: contrasting first and second language development. *Second Language Research* **13**: 227–63.

  2008. Child second language acquisition or successive first language acquisition? In B. Haznedar and E. Gavruseva (eds.), *Current trends in child second language acquisition: a generative perspective*, 55–80. Amsterdam: John Benjamins.

Meltzoff, A. 2002. Elements of a developmental theory of imitation. In A. Meltzoff and W. Prinz (eds.), *The imitative mind: development, evolution, and brain bases*, 19–41. Cambridge University Press.

Meltzoff, A. and Prinz, W. (eds.). 2002. *The imitative mind: development, evolution, and brain bases*. Cambridge University Press.

Menard-Warwick, J. 2008b. The cultural and intercultural identities of transnational English teachers: two case studies from the Americas. *TESOL Quarterly* **42**: 617–40.

Mendoza Denton, N. 2008. *Homegirls: symbolic practices in the making of Latina youth styles*. Oxford: Blackwell.

Mennen, I., Scobbie, J. M., de Leeuw, E., Schaeffler, S. and Schaeffler, F. 2010. Measuring language-specific phonetic settings. *Second Language Research* **26**: 13–41.

Merino, B. 1983. Language loss in bilingual Chicano children. *Journal of Applied Developmental Psychology* **4**: 277–94.

Meskill, C. and Anthony, N. 2010. *Teaching languages online*. Bristol: Multilingual Matters.

Meuter, R. and Allport, A. 1999. Bilingual language switching in naming: asymmetrical costs of language selection. *Journal of Memory and Language* **40**: 25–40.

Meyerhof, M., Schleef, E. and Clark, L. 2009. Sociolinguistics and immigration: variation among Polish adolescents living in the UK. Paper presented at the NWAV 38.

Miller, J. 2003. *Audible difference*. Clevedon: Multilingual Matters.

Miller, W. and Ervin, S. 1964. The development of grammar in child language. In U. Bellugi and R. Brown (eds.), *The Acquisition of Language. Monographs of the Society of Research in Child Development* **29**: 9–34.

Milton, J. 2007. Lexical profiles, learning styles and construct validity of lexical size tests. In H. Daller, J. Milton and J. Treffers-Daller (eds.), *Modelling and assessing vocabulary knowledge*, 45–58. Cambridge University Press.

  2008. Vocabulary uptake from informal learning tasks. *Language Learning Journal* **36**: 227–38.

  2009. *Measuring second language vocabulary acquisition*. Clevedon: Multilingual Matters.

Milton, J. and Meara, P. 1998. Are the British really bad at learning foreign languages? *Language Learning Journal* **18**: 68–76.

Milton, J., Wade, J. and Hopkins, N. 2010. Aural word recognition and oral competence in a foreign language. In R. Chacón-Beltrán, C. Abello-Contesse and M. Torreblanca-López (eds.), *Further insights into non-native vocabulary teaching and learning*, 83–98. Clevedon: Multilingual Matters.

Mitchell, R. and F. Myles. 2004. *Second language learning theories*. London: Edward Arnold.

Miyake, A. and Shah, P. (eds.). 1999. *Models of working memory: mechanisms of active maintenance and executive control*. Cambridge University Press.

Miyawaki, K., Strange, W., Verbrugge, R., Liberman, A. M., Jenkins, J. J. and Fujimura, O. 1975. An effect of linguistic experience: the discrimination of [r] and [l] by native speakers of Japanese and English. *Perception & Psychophysics* **18**: 331–40.

Mobaraki, M., Vainikka, A. and M. Young-Scholten. 2008. The status of subjects in early child L2 English. In B. Haznedar and E. Gavruseva (eds.), *Current trends in child second language acquisition: a generative perspective*, 209–36. Amsterdam: John Benjamins.

Moll, L. 1990. *Vygotsky and education: instructional implications and applications of sociohistorical psychology*. New York: Cambridge University Press.

Möllering, M. 2004. *The acquisition of German modal particles: a corpus-based approach*. Bern: Peter Lang.

Mondria, J.-A. and Wit-de Boer, M. 1991. The effects of contextual richness on the guessability and the retention of words in a foreign language. *Applied Linguistics* **12**: 249–67.

Montaigne, M. de. 1899 [1580]. *The education of children*, trans. L. E. Rector. New York: D. Appleton.

Montrul, S. 2000. Transitivity alternations in L2 acquisition. *Studies in Second Language Acquisition* **22**: 229–73.

2002. Incomplete acquisition and attrition of Spanish tense/aspect distinctions in adult bilinguals. *Bilingualism: Language and Cognition* **5**: 39–68.

2004a. *The acquisition of Spanish*. Amsterdam: John Benjamins.

2004b. Subject and object expression in Spanish heritage speakers: a case of morpho-syntactic convergence. *Bilingualism: Language and Cognition* **7**: 1–18.

Montrul, S. 2007. Interpreting mood distinctions in Spanish as a heritage language. In K. Potowski and R. Cameron (eds.), *Spanish in contact. policy, social and linguistic inquiries*, 23–40. Amsterdam: John Benjamins.

2008. *Incomplete acquisition in bilingualism: re-examining the age factor*. Amsterdam: John Benjamins.

2010. How similar are L2 learners and heritage speakers? Spanish clitics and word order. *Applied Psycholinguistics* **31**: 167–207.

2011a. Morphological errors in Spanish second language learners and heritage speakers. *Studies in Second Language Acquisition* **33**: 155–61.

2011b. First language retention and attrition in an adult Guatemalan adoptee. *Language, Interaction and Acquisition* **2**: 276–311.

Montrul, S. and Bowles, M. 2009. Back to basics: Differential Object Marking under incomplete acquisition in Spanish heritage speakers. *Bilingualism: Language and Cognition* **12**: 363-83.

Montrul, S. and Ionin, T. 2010. Transfer effects in the interpretation of definite articles by Spanish heritage speakers. *Bilingualism: Language and Cognition* **13**: 449-73.

Montrul, S. and Perpiñán, S. 2011. Assessing differences and similarities between instructed L2 learners and heritage language learners in their knowledge of Spanish Tense-Aspect and Mood (TAM) Morphology. *The Heritage Language Journal* **8**: 90-133.

Montrul, S. and Slabakova, R. 2002. Acquiring morphosyntactic and semantic properties of preterite and imperfect tenses in L2 Spanish. In A.-T. Pérez-Leroux and J. Liceras (eds.), *The acquisition of Spanish morphosyntax: the L1/L2 connection*, 113-49. Dordrecht: Kluwer.

  2003. Competence similarities between natives and near-native speakers: an investigation of the preterit/imperfect contrast in Spanish. *Studies in Second Language Acquisition* **25**: 351-98.

Montrul, S. and Yoon, J. 2009. Putting parameters in their proper place. *Second Language Research* **25**: 291-311.

Montrul, S., Foote, R. and Perpiñan, S. 2008. Gender agreement in adult second language learners and Spanish heritage speakers: the effects of age and context of acquisition. *Language Learning* **58**: 502-53.

Morais, J., Bertelson, P., Cary, L. and Alegría, J. 1986. Literacy training and speech segmentation. *Cognition* **24**: 45-64.

Morais, J., Cary, L., Alegría, J. and Bertelson, P. 1979. Does awareness of speech as a sequence of phones arise spontaneously? *Cognition* **7**: 323-31.

Morgan-Short, K., Sanz, C., Steinhauer, K. and Ullman, M. T. 2010. Second language acquisition of gender agreement in explicit and implicit training conditions: an event related potential study. *Language Learning* **60**: 154-93.

Mori, J. and Ohta, A. S. (eds.). 2008. *Japanese applied linguistics: discourse and social perspectives*. London: Continuum.

Morita, N. 2004. Negotiating participation and identity in second language academic communities. *TESOL Quarterly* **39**: 573-603.

Mougeon, R., Nadasdi, T. and Rehner, K. 2002. Etat de la recherche sur l'appropriation de la variation par les apprenants avances du FL2 or FLE. *AILE: acquisition et interaction en langue étrangère* **17**: 7-50.

Moyer, A. 2004. *Age, accent and experience in second language acquisition*. Clevedon: Multilingual Matters.

Mueller, J. L., Hahne, A., Fujii, Y. and Friederici, A. D. 2005. Native and non-native speakers' processing of a miniature version of Japanese as revealed by ERPs. *Journal of Cognitive Neuroscience* **17**: 1229-44.

Müller, G. 1996. A constraint on remnant movement. *Natural Language and Linguistic Theory* **14**: 355-407.

  1998. *Incomplete category fronting*. Dordrecht: Kluwer.

Muñoz, C. (ed.). 2006a. *Age and the rate of foreign language learning*. Clevedon: Multilingual Matters.

Muñoz, C. and Singleton, D. 2011. A critical review of age-related research on L2 ultimate attainment. *Language Teaching* **44**: 1–35.

Muranoi, H. 2007. Output practice in the L2 classroom. In R. DeKeyser (ed.), *Practice in a second language*, 51–84. Cambridge University Press.

Murray, W. S. and Forster, K. I. 2004. Serial mechanisms in lexical access: the rank hypothesis. *Psychological Review* **111**: 721–56.

Muysken, P. 1982. Parametrizing the notion "head." *Journal of Linguistic Research* **2**: 57–75.

Myles, F. 2004. From data to theory: the over-representation of linguistic knowledge in SLA. *Transactions of the Philological Society* **102**: 139–68.

2005. The emergence of morpho-syntactic structure in French L2. In J.-M. Dewaele (ed.), *Focus on French as a foreign language*, 88–113. Clevedon: Multilingual Matters.

Nagy, E. and Molnar, P. 2004. Homo imitans or homo provocans? Human imprinting model of neonatal imitation. *Infant Behavior and Development* **27**: 54–63.

Nagy, N., Blondeau, H. and Auger, J. 2003. Second language acquisition and "real" French: an investigation of subject doubling in the French of Montreal anglophones. *Language Variation and Change* **15**: 73–103.

Naiman, N., Fröhlich, M., Stern, H. H. and Todesco, A. 1978. *The good language learner*. Toronto: Ontario Institute for Studies in Education.

Nassaji, H. and Simard, D. 2010. Introduction: current developments in form-focused interaction and L2 acquisition. *Canadian Modern Language Review / La Revue canadienne des langues vivantes* **66**: 773–78.

Nassaji, H. and Swain, M. 2000. A Vygotskian perspective on corrective feedback in L2: the effect of random versus negotiated help on the learning of English articles. *Language Awareness* **9**: 34–51.

Nation, I. S. P. 2001. *Learning vocabulary in another language*. Cambridge University Press.

2006. How large a vocabulary is needed for reading and listening? *The Canadian Modern Language Review* **63**: 59–82.

Negueruela, E. 2008. Revolutionary pedagogies: learning that leads (to) second language development. In J. P. Lantolf and M. Poehner (eds.), *Sociocultural theory and the teaching of second languages*, 189–227. London: Equinox.

Nelson, C. D. 2009. *Sexual identities in English language education*. New York: Routledge.

Nestor, N. and Regan, V. 2010. New kids on the block: young Poles, language, and identity. In N. Bushin-Tyrrell, M. Darmody and S. Song (eds.), *Ethnic minority children and youth in Ireland*. Rotterdam and Boston: Sense Publishers.

Newman, F. and Holzman, L. 1993. *Lev Vygotsky: revolutionary scientist*. London: Routledge.

Newmeyer, F. J. 1998. *Language form and language function*. Cambridge, MA: MIT Press.

Nice, M. 1925. The speech development of a child from eighteen months to six years. *Pedagogical Seminary* **24**: 204–43.

Nicholas, H. and Lightbown, P. 2008. Defining child second language acquisition, defining roles for L2 instruction. In J. Philp, R. Oliver and A. Mackey (eds.), *Second language acquisition and the younger learner: child's play?*, 27–51. Amsterdam: John Benjamins.

Nicol, J. (ed.). 2001. *One mind, two languages: bilingual language processing*. Oxford: Blackwell.

Niimura, T. and Hayashi, B. 1996. Contrastive Analysis of English and Japanese demonstratives from the perspective of L1 and L2 Acquisition. *Language Sciences* **18**: 811–34.

Norris, J. and Ortega, L. (eds.). 2006. *Synthesizing research on language learning and teaching*. Amsterdam: John Benjamins.

Norton Peirce, B. N. 1995. Social identity, investment, and language learning. *TESOL Quarterly* **29**: 9–31.

Norton, B. 2000. *Identity and language learning*. Harlow: Pearson Education.

Norton, B. 2010. Language and identity. In N. Hornberger and S. McKay (eds.), *Sociolinguistics and language education*, 349–69. Bristol: Multilingual Matters.

Norton, B. and Toohey, K. 2002. Identity and language learning. In R. Kaplan (ed.), *The Oxford handbook of applied linguistics*, 115–23. Oxford University Press.

O'Brien, M. G., Shea, C. and Archibald, J. (eds.). 2006. *Proceedings of the 8th Generative Approaches to Second Language Acquisition Conference (GASLA 2006)*. Somerville, MA: Cascadilla Proceedings Project.

Ochs, E. and Schiefflin, B. 2010. Language socialization: a historical overview. In P. A. Duff and N. C. Hornberger (eds.), *Encyclopaedia of language and education*, vol. VIII: *Language socialization*, 3–15. New York: Springer.

Odlin, T. 2008. Conceptual transfer and meaning extensions. In P. Robinson and N. Ellis (eds.), *Handbook of cognitive linguistics and second language acquisition*, 306–40. New York: Routledge.

O'Dowd, R. 2000. Intercultural learning via videoconferencing: a pilot exchange project. *ReCALL* **12**: 49–63.

O'Grady, W. 2003. The radical middle: nativism without universal grammar. In C. Doughty and M. Long (eds.), *The handbook of second language acquisition*, 43–62. Oxford: Blackwell.

   2005. *Syntactic carpentry: an Emergentist aapproach to syntax*. Mahwah, NJ: Lawrence Erlbaum.

   2008a. The emergentist program. *Lingua* **118**: 447–64.

   2008b. Innateness, universal grammar, and emergentism. *Lingua* **118**: 620–31.

   2010a. Fundamental universals of language. *Lingua* **120**: 2707–12.

2010b. Language acquisition without an acquisition device. www.ling.hawaii.edu/faculty/ogrady/LT.pdf

O'Grady, W., Lee, M. and Choo, M. 2001. The acquisition of relative clauses by heritage and non-heritage learners of Korean as a second language: a comparative study. *Journal of Korean Language Education* **12**: 283–94.

O'Grady, W., Kwak, H.-Y., Lee, O.-S. and Lee, M. 2011. An emergentist perspective on heritage language acquisition. *Studies in Second Language Acquisition* **33**: 223–45.

Oh, J., Jun, S., Knightly, L. and Au, T. 2003. Holding on to childhood language memory. *Cognition* **86**: B53–B64.

Ohta, A. S. 1995. Applying sociocultural theory to an analysis of learner discourse: learner-learner collaborative interaction in the zone of proximal development. *Issues in Applied Linguistics* **6**: 93–121.

1997. The development of pragmatic competence in learner-learner interaction. In L. Bouton (ed.), *Pragmatics and Language Learning* (Monograph Series) 8: 223–42. Urbana-Champaign: University of Illinois.

1999. Interactional routines and the socialization of interactional style in adult learners of Japanese. *Journal of Pragmatics* **31**: 1493–512.

2000a. Re-thinking interaction in SLA: developmentally appropriate assistance in the zone of proximal development and the acquisition of L2 grammar. In J. P. Lantolf (ed.), *Sociocultural theory and second language learning*, 51–78. Oxford University Press.

2000b. Re-thinking recasts: a learner-centered examination of corrective feedback in the Japanese language classroom. In J. K. Hall and L. Verplaeste (eds.), *The construction of second and foreign language learning through classroom interaction*, 47–72. Mahwah, NJ: Lawrence Erlbaum.

2001b. From acknowledgment to alignment: a longitudinal study of the development of expression of alignment by classroom learners of Japanese. In K. R. Rose and G. Kasper (eds.), *Pragmatics in language teaching*, 103–20. Cambridge University Press.

2001c. *Second language acquisition processes in the classroom: learning Japanese.* Mahwah, NJ: Lawrence Erlbaum.

2006. The zone of proximal development and second language acquisition: beyond social interaction. In A. Yoshitomi, T. Umino and M. Negishi (eds.), *Readings in second language acquisition and second language pedagogy in a Japanese context*, 155–78. Amsterdam: John Benjamins.

2008. Laughter and second language acquisition: a study of Japanese foreign language classes. In J. Mori and A. S. Ohta (eds.), *Japanese applied linguistics: discourse and social perspectives*, 213–42. London: Continuum.

2010. Limitations of social interaction in second language acquisition: learners's inaudible voices and mediation in the zone of proximal development. In P. Seedhouse, S. Walsh and C. Jenks (eds.), *Conceptualising "learning" in applied linguistics*, 163–81. Basingstoke: Palgrave Macmillan.

(ed.). In press. *Encyclopedia of applied linguistics*, ed. C. Chapelle, vol. XXI: *Social, dynamic, and complexity theory approaches to second language development.* Malden, MA: Wiley-Blackwell.

O'Keefe, A., McCarthy, M. and Carter, R. 2007. *From corpus to classroom: language use and language teaching*. Cambridge University Press.

Oliveira, A. L. and Ança, M. H. 2009. "I speak five languages": fostering plurilingual competence through language awareness. *Language Awareness* 18: 403–21.

Oliver, R. 2002. The patterns of negotiation for meaning in child interactions. *Modern Language Journal* 86: 97–111.

Oliver, R. and Mackey, A. 2003. Interactional context and feedback in classroom and pairwork. *Modern Language Journal* 87: 519–33.

Oller, K. and Jarmulowicz, L. 2009. Language and literacy in bilingual children in the early school years. In E. Hoff and M. Shatz (eds.), *Blackwell handbook of language development*, 368–88. Malden, MA: Wiley-Blackwell.

Olson, D. 2002. What writing does to the mind. In E. Amsel and J. P. Byrnes (eds.), *Language, literacy, and cognitive development: the development and consequences of symbolic communication*, 153–66. Mahwah, NJ: Lawrence Erlbaum.

Olson, D. and Torrance, N. (eds.). 2009. *The Cambridge handbook of literacy*. Cambridge University Press.

O'Malley, J. M. and Chamot, A. 1990. *Learning strategies in second language acquisition*. Cambridge University Press.

Onderdelinden, L., Craats, I. van de, and Kurvers, J. 2009. Word concept of illiterates and low-literates: worlds apart? In I. van de Craats and J. Kurvers (eds.), *Low-educated Second Language and Literacy Acquisition: proceedings of the 4th Annual Forum*, 35–48. Utrecht: Landelijke Onderzoekschool Taalwetenschap.

Ong, W. J. 2002. *Orality and literacy: the technologizing of the word*, 2nd edn. New York: Routledge.

Opitz, B. and Friederici, A. D. 2004. Brain correlates of language learning: the neuronal dissociation of rule-based versus similarity-based learning. *Journal of Neuroscience* 24: 8436–40.

Oriyama, K. 2010. Heritage language maintenance and Japanese identity formation: what role can schooling and ethnic community contact play? *Heritage Language Journal* 7: 76–96.

Osterhout, L., McLaughlin, J., Kim, A., Greenwald, R. and Inoue, K. 2004. Sentences in the brain: event-related potenials as real-time reflections of sentence comprehension and language learning. In C. Carreiras and M. Clifton (eds.), *The on-line study of sentence comprehension: eyetracking, ERP, and beyond*, 271–308. New York: Psychology Press.

Osterhout, L., McLaughlin, J., Pitkänen, I., Frenck-Mestre, C. and Molinaro, N. 2006. Novice learners, longitudinal designs and event-related potentials: a paradigm for exploring the neurocognition of second-language processing. *Language Learning* 56: 199–230.

Osterhout, L., Poliakov, A., Inoue, K., McLaughlin, J., Valentine, G., Pitkanen, I. *et al.* 2008. Second-language learning and changes in the brain. *Journal of Neurolinguistics* 21: 509–21.

Ostrosky-Solís, F., García, M. A. and Pérez, M. 2004. Can learning to read and write change the brain organization? An electrophysiological study. *International Journal of Psychology* **39**: 27–35.

Oxford, R. L. and Shearin, J. 1994. Language learning motivation: expanding the theoretical framework. *Modern Language Journal* **78**: 12–28.

Oya, T., Manalo, E. and Greenwood, J. 2004. The influence of personality and anxiety on the oral performance of Japanese speakers of English. *Applied Cognitive Psychology* **18**: 841–55.

Pallier, C. 2007. Critical periods in language acquisition and language attrition. In B. Köpke, M. S. Schmid, M. Keijzer and S. Dostert (eds.), *Language attrition: theoretical perspectives*, 155–68. Amsterdam: John Benjamins.

Pallier, C., Dehaene, S., Poline, J.-B., LeBihan, D., Argenti, A. M., Dupoux, E. and Mehler, J. 2003. Brain imaging of language plasticity in adopted adults: can a second language replace the first? *Cerebral Cortex* **13**: 155–61.

Papafragou, A. and Musolino, J. 2003. Scalar implicatures: experiments at the syntax semantics interface. *Cognition* **86**: 253–82.

Paradis, J. 2005. Grammatical morphology in children learning English as a second language: implications of similarities with specific language impairment. *Language, Speech and Hearing Services in the Schools* **36**: 172–87.

  2008. Tense as a clinical marker in English L2 acquisition with language delay/impairment. In B. Haznedar and E. Gavruseva (eds.), *Current trends in child second language acquisition: a generative perspective*, 337–56. Amsterdam: John Benjamins.

  2010. The interface between bilingual development and specific language impairment. *Applied Psycholinguistics* **31**: 227–52.

Paradis, M. 2004. *A neurolinguistic theory of bilingualism*. Amsterdam: John Benjamins.

  2009. *Declarative and procedural determinants of second languages*. Amsterdam: John Benjamins.

Park, G. 2009. "I listened to Korean society. I always heard that women should be this way...": the negotiation and construction of gendered identities in claiming a dominant language and race in the United States. *Journal of Language, Identity, and Education* **8**: 174–90.

Pavlenko, A. 2007. Autobiographic narratives as data in applied linguistics. *Applied Linguistics* **28**: 163–88.

Pavlenko, A. and Blackledge, A. (eds.). 2004. *Negotiation of identities in multilingual contexts*. Clevedon: Multilingual Matters.

Pavlenko, A. and Lantolf, J. P. 2000. Second language learning as participation and the (re)construction of selves. In J. P. Lantolf (ed.), *Sociocultural theory and second language learning*, 155–77. Oxford University Press.

Pavlenko, A., Blackledge, A., Piller, I. and Teutsch-Dwyer, M. (eds.). 2001. *Multilingualism, second language learning, and gender*. Berlin: Mouton de Gruyter.

Pawlikowska-Smith, G. 2000. *Canadian language benchmarks: English as-a-second-language-for-adults*. Ottawa: Citizenship and Immigration Canada.

Pellettieri, J. 2000. Negotiation in cyberspace: the role of chatting in the development of grammatical competence. In M. Warschauer and R. Kern (eds.), *Network-based language teaching: concepts and practice*, 59–86. Cambridge Iniversity Press.

Peng, L. and Ann, J. 2001. Stress and duration in three varieties of English. *World Englishes* **20**: 1–27.

Peperkamp, S., Vendelin, I. and Dupoux, E. 2010. Perception of predictable stress: a cross-linguistic investigation. *Journal of Phonetics* **38**: 422–30.

Perales, S., García Mayo, M. P. and Liceras, J. M. 2009. The acquisition of L3 English negation by bilingual (Spanish/Basque) learners in an institutional setting. *International Journal of Bilingualism* **13**: 3–33.

Perani, D. and Abutalebi, J. 2005. The neural basis of first and second language processing. *Current Opinion in Neurobiology* **15**: 202–6.

Perani, E., Paulesu, N., Galles, S., Dupoux, E., Dehaene, S., Bettinardi, V. et al. 1998. The bilingual brain: proficiency and age of acquisition of the second language. *Brain* **121**: 1841–52.

Perdue, C. 1993. *Adult language acquisition: cross-linguistic perspectives*. Cambridge University Press.

Pérez-Leroux, A.-T. and Liceras, J. (eds.). 2003. *The acquisition of Spanish morphosyntax: the L1/L2 connection*. Dordrecht: Kluwer.

Peterson, M. 2006. Learner interaction management in an avatar and chat-based virtual world. *Computer Assisted Language Learning* **19**: 79–103.

Petersson, K. M., Ingvar, M. and Reis, A. 2009. Language and literacy from a cognitive neuroscience perspective. In D. Olson and N. Torrance (eds.), *The Cambridge handbook of literacy*, 152–82. Cambridge University Press.

Petersson, K. M., Reis, A., Askelöf, S., Castro-Caldas, A. and Ingvar, M. 2000. Language processing modulated by literacy: a network analysis of verbal repetition in literate and illiterate subjects. *Journal of Cognitive Neuroscience* **12**: 364–82.

Petersson, K. M., Silva, C., Castro-Caldas, A., Ingvar, M. and Reis, A. 2007. Literacy: a cultural influence on functional left–right differences in the inferior parietal cortex. *European Journal of Neuroscience* **26**: 791–99.

Peyton, J., Ranard, D. and McGinnis, S. (eds.). 2001. *Heritage languages in America: preserving a national resource*. Washington, DC: Center for Applied Linguistics.

Philp, J. 2003. Constraints on "noticing the gap" nonnative speakers' noticing of recasts in NS–NNS interaction. *Studies in Second Language Acquisition* **25**: 99–126.

Philp, J. and Tognini, R. 2009. Language acquisition in foreign language contexts and the differential benefits of interaction. *International Review of Applied Linguistics* **47**: 245–66.

Philp, J., Oliver, R. and Mackey, A. (eds.). 2008. *Second language acquisition and the younger learner: child's play?* Amsterdam: John Benjamins.

Piaget, J. and Inhelder, B. 1969. *The psychology of the child*. New York: Basic Books.

Piattelli-Palmarini, M. (ed.). 1980. *Language and learning: the debate between Jean Piaget and Noam Chomsky*. Cambridge, MA: Harvard University Press.

Pica, T. 1994. Review article: research on negotiation: what does it reveal about second-language learning conditions, processes and outcomes? *Language Learning* **44**: 493–527.

2009. Second language acquisition in the instructional environment. In W. C. Ritchie and T. K. Bhatia (eds.), *The new handbook of second language acquisition*, 473–501. Bingley: Emerald.

Pica, T., Kanga, H. and S. Sauro. 2006. Information gap tasks: their multiple roles and contributions to interaction research methodology. *Studies in Second Language Acquisition* **28**: 301–38.

Pica, T., Holliday, L., Lewis, N. E. and Morgenthaler, L. 1989. Comprehensible output as an outcome of linguistic demands on the learner. *Studies in Second Language Acqusiition* **11**: 63–90.

Pienemann, M. 1984. Psychological constraints on the teachability of languages. *Studies in Second Language Acquisition* **6**: 186–214.

1989. Is language teachable? Psycholinguistic experiments and hypotheses. *Applied Linguistics* **10**: 52–79.

1998. *Language processing and second language acquisition: Processability Theory*. Amsterdam: John Benjamins.

2003. Language processing capacity. In C. Doughty and M. Long (eds.), *The handbook of second language acquisition*, 679–714. Oxford: Blackwell.

2004. Processing perspectives in SLA research and their compatibility. *Bilingualism: Language and Cognition* **7**: 37–39.

(ed.). 2005a. *Cross-linguistic aspects of Processability Theory*. Amsterdam: John Benjamins.

2007. Processability Theory. In B. VanPatten and J. Williams (eds.), *Theories in second language acquisition: an introduction*, 137–54. Mahwah, NJ: Lawrence Erlbaum.

Pienemann, M. and Johnston, M. 1987. Factors influencing the development of language proficiency. In D. Nunan (ed.), *Applying second language acquisition research*, 45–141. Adelaide: National Curriculum Resource Center.

Pienemann, M., Johnston, M. and Brindley, G. 1988. Constructing an acquisition-based procedure for second language assessment. *Studies in Second Language Acquisition* **10**: 217–43.

Pinker, S. and Jackendoff, R. 2005. The faculty of language: what's special about it? *Cognition* **95**: 201–36.

Pires, A. and Rothman, J. 2009a. Disentangling sources of incomplete acquisition: an exploration for competence divergence across heritage grammars. *International Journal of Bilingualism* **13**: 210–338.

(eds.). 2009b. *Minimalist inquiries into child and adult language acquisition: case studies across Portuguese*. Berlin and New York: Mouton de Gruyter.

Piske, T. and Young-Scholten, M. (eds.). 2009. *Input matters in SLA*. Clevedon: Multilingual Matters.

Pladevall-Ballester, E. 2010. Child L2 development of syntactic and discourse properties of Spanish subjects. *Bilingualism: Language and Cognition* **13**: 185–216.

Poehner, M. E. 2007. Beyond the test: L2 dynamic assessment and the transcendence of mediated learning. *Modern Language Journal* **91**: 323–40.

2009. Group dynamic assessment: mediation for the L2 classroom. *TESOL Quarterly* **43**: 471–91.

Poehner, M. E. and Lantolf, J. P. 2005. Dynamic assessment in the language classroom. *Language Teaching Research* **9**: 1–33.

Polinsky, M. 1997. American Russian: language loss meets language acquisition. *Proceedings of the Annual Workshop on Formal Approaches to Slavic Linguistics (The Cornell Meeting 1995)*, 370–406. Ann Arbor: Michigan Slavic Publications.

2005. Word class distinctions in an incomplete grammar. In D. Ravid and H. Bat-Zeev Shyldkrot (eds.), *Perspectives on language and language development*, 419–36. Dordrecht: Kluwer.

2006. Incomplete acquisition: American Russian. *Journal of Slavic Linguistics* **14**: 191–262.

2008a. Gender under incomplete acquisition: heritage speakers' knowledge of noun categorization. *The Heritage Language Journal* **6**(1). www.heritagelanguages.org.

2008b. Heritage language narratives. In D. Brinton, O. Kagan and S. Bauckus (eds.), *Heritage language education: a new field emerging*, 149–64. New York: Routledge.

2008c. Relative clauses in Heritage Russian: fossilization or divergent grammar? In A. Angtonenko, J. Bailyn and C. Bethin (eds.). *Annual Workshop on Formal Approaches to Slavic Linguistics* (the Stony Brook Meeting 2007), 333–58. Ann Arbor: Michigan Slavic Publications.

2011. Reanalysis in heritage language grammars: new evidence for attrition. *Studies in second Language Acquisition* **33**: 305–28.

Polinsky, M. and Kagan, O. 2007. Heritage languages in the "wild" and in the classroom. *Language and Linguistic Compass* **1**: 368–95.

Pollard, C. and Sag, I. A. 1994. *Head-driven phrase structure grammar*. University of Chicago Press.

Pollock, J.-Y. 1989. Verb movement, Universal Grammar, and the structure of IP. *Linguistic Inquiry* **20**: 365–424.

Porges, S. 2011. *The Polyvagal Theory: neurophysiological foundations of emotions, attachment, communcation, and self-regulation*. New York: W. W. Norton.

Porquier, R. and Py, B. 2004. *Apprentissage d'une langue étrangère: contextes et discours*. Paris: Didier.

Poulisse, N. and Bongaerts, T. 1994. 1st language use in 2nd-language production. *Applied Linguistics* **15**: 36–57.

Prévost, P. 2003. Truncation and missing surface inflection in initial L2 German. *Studies in second language acquisition* **25**: 65–97.

Prévost, P. and White, L. 2000. Missing surface inflection or impairment in second language? Evidence from tense and agreement. *Second Language Research* **16**: 103–34.

Prince, A. and Smolensky, P. 2004. *Optimality Theory: constraint interaction in Generative Grammar*. Malden, MA, and Oxford: Blackwell.

Pullum, G. K. and Scholz, B. C. 2002. Empirical assessment of stimulus poverty arguments. *The Linguistic Review* **19**: 9–50.

Quintilianus, M. F. 1920 [c. 96]. *Institutio oratoria*, vols. I–IV, trans. H. E. Butler. London: Heinemann.

Radford, A. 1990. *Syntactic theory and the acquisition of English syntax*. Oxford: Blackwell.

Rampton, B. 1995. *Crossing: language and ethnicity among adolescents*. London: Longman.

  1999. Sociolinguistics and cultural studies: new ethnicities, liminality and interaction. *Social Semiotics* **9**: 335–73.

Rast, R. 2008. *Foreign language input: initial processing*. Clevedon: Multilingual Matters.

Read, C., Zhang, Y., Nie, H. and Ding, B. 1986. The ability to manipulate speech sounds depends on knowing alphabetic spelling. *Cognition* **24**: 31–44.

Reder, S. and Bynner, J. (eds.). 2009. *Tracking adult literacy and numeracy skills. Findings from longitudinal research*. New York and London: Routledge.

Regan, V. 1996. Variation in French interlanguage: a longitudinal study of sociolinguistic competence. In R. Bayley and D. R. Preston (eds.), *Second language acquisition and linguistic variation*, 177–203. Amsterdam: John Benjamins.

  2004. The relationship between the group and the individual and the acquisition of native speaker variation patterns: a preliminary study. *International Review of Applied Linguistics in Language Teaching* **42**: 335–48.

  2010. Sociolinguistic competence and identity in second language acquisition: a research programme. *EUROSLA Yearbook* **10**: 21–37. Amsterdam: John Benjamins.

Regan, V., Howard, M. and Lemée, I. 2009. *The acquisition of sociolinguistic competence in a study abroad context*. Bristol: Multilingual Matters.

Rehner, K., Mougeon, R. and Nadasdi, T. 2003. The learning of sociolinguistic variation by advanced FSL learners: the case of *nous* versus *on* in immersion French. *Studies in Second Language Acquisition* **25**: 127–56.

Reis, A. and Castro-Caldas, A. 1997. Illiteracy: a cause for biased cognitive development. *Journal of the International Neuropsychological Society* **3**: 444–50.

Reis, A., Faísca, L., Mendonça, S., Ingvar, M. and Petersson, K. M. 2007. Semantic interference on a phonological task in illiterate subjects. *Scandinavian Journal of Psychology* **48**: 69–74.

Reis, A., Guerreiro, M. and Petersson, K. M. 2003. A sociodemographic and neuropsychological characterization of an illiterate population. *Applied Neuropsychology* **10**: 191–204.

Rice, M. L. 2004. Growth models of developmental language disorders. In M. L. Rice and S. Warren (eds.), *Developmental language disorders: from phenotypes to etiologies*, 207–40. Mahwah, NJ: Lawrence Erlbaum.

Ricento, T. 2005. Considerations of identity in L2 learning. In E. Hinkel (ed.), *Handbook of research in second language teaching and learning*, 895–910. Mahwah, NJ: Lawrence Erlbaum.

Richards, B. J. and Malvern, D. D. 2007. Validity and threats to the validity of vocabulary measurement. In H. Daller, J. Milton and J. Treffers-Daller (eds.), *Modelling and assessing vocabulary knowledge*, 79–92. Cambridge University Press.

Rieder, A. 2003. Implicit and explicit learning in incidental vocabulary acquisition. *VIEWS* **12**: 24–39.

Riemsdijk, H. van. 1978. *A case study in syntactic markedness: the binding nature of prepositional phrases*. Dordrecht: Foris.

Riley, K. C. 2010. Language socialization. In B. Spolsky and F. M. Hult (eds.), *Handbook of educational linguistics*, 398–410. Oxford: Blackwell.

Ringbom, H. 2002. Levels of transfer from L1 and L2 in L3-acquisition. In J. Ytsma and M. Hooghiemstra (eds.), *Proceedings of the Second International Conference on Trilingualism*. Leeuwaarden: Fryske Adademie (CD Rom).

Ritchie, W. C. and Bhatia, T. K. (eds.). 1996. *Handbook of second language acquisition*. New York: Academic Press.

(eds.). 2009. *The new handbook of second language acquisition*. Bingley: Emerald.

Rizzi, L. 1990. *Relativized minimality*. Cambridge, MA: MIT Press.

1993/1994. Some notes on linguistic theory and language development: the case of root infinitives. *Language Acquisition* **3**: 371–93.

(ed.). 2004. *The structure of CP and IP: the cartography of syntactic structures*, vol. II. Oxford University Press.

Roberts, L., Gullberg, M. and Indefrey, P. 2008. Online pronoun resolution in L2 discourse: L1 influence and general learner effects. *Studies in Second Language Acquisition* **30**: 333–57.

Roberts, L., Gürel, A., Tatar, S. and Marti, L. (eds.). 2007. *EUROSLA Yearbook 7*. Amsterdam: John Benjamins.

Robinson, P. (ed.). 2001a. *Cognition and second language instruction*. Cambridge University Press.

(ed.). 2002a. *Individual differences and instructed language learning*. Philadelphia: John Benjamins.

2002c. Learning conditions, aptitude complexes, and SLA: a framework for research and pedagogy. In P. Robinson (ed.), *Individual differences and instructed language learning*, 113–36. Philadelphia: John Benjamins.

2005a. Aptitude and second language acquisition. *Annual Review of Applied Linguistics* **25**: 46–73.

2006. Attention, memory, and the "noticing" hypothesis. *Language Learning* **45**: 283–331.

2007a. Criteria for classifying and sequencing pedagogic tasks. In M. P. García Mayo (ed.), *Investigating tasks in formal language learning*, 7–26. Clevedon: Multilingual Matters.

2009. Individual differences, aptitude complexes, SLA processes and aptitude test development. In M. Pawlak (ed.), *Studies in pedagogy and fine arts: new perspectives on individual differences in language learning and teaching*. Poznań-Kalisz: Adam Mickiewicz University, Poznań.

Robinson, P. and Ellis, N. (eds.). 2008. *Handbook of cognitive linguistics and second language acquisition*. New York: Routledge.

Rocca, S. 2007. *Child second language acquisition: a bi-directional study of English and Italian tense–aspect morphology*. Amsterdam: John Benjamins.

Roediger, H. L. III. 2003. Reconsidering implicit memory. In J. S. Bowers and C. J. Marsolek (eds.), *Rethinking implicit memory*, 3–18. Oxford University Press.

Roediger, R. 2009. The critical role of retrieval in enhancing long-term memory: from the laboratory to the classroom. Keynote address at the Annual Meeting of the Pyschonomics Society, 19 November 2009. (Video available online).

Roelofs, A. 1998. Lemma selection without inhibition of languages in bilingual speakers. *Bilingualism: Language and Cognition* **1**: 94–5.

Roeper, T. and Williams, E. (eds.). 1987. *Parameter setting*. Dordrecht: Reidel.

Rogoff, B. 2003. *The cultural nature of human development*. Oxford University Press.

Rohde, A. 1996. The aspect hypothesis and the emergence of tense distinctions in naturalistic L2 acquisition. *Linguistics* **34**: 1115–37.

Rose, K. R. 2005. On the effects of instruction in second language pragmatics. *System* **33**: 385–99.

Rose, K. R. and Kasper, G. (eds.). 2001. *Pragmatics in language teaching*. Cambridge University Press.

Rosenbaum, P. 1967. *The grammar of English predicate compliment constructions*. Cambridge, MA: MIT Press.

Rosenthal, J. W. (ed.). 2000. *Handbook of undergraduate second language education*. Mahwah, NJ: Lawrence Erlbaum.

Rossi, S., Gugler, M. F., Hahne, A. and Friederici, A. D. 2006. The impact of proficiency on syntactic second-language processing of German and Italian: evidence from event-related potentials. *Journal of Cognitive Neuroscience* **18**: 2030–48.

Rothman, J. 2009. Pragmatic deficits with syntactic consequences? L2 pronominal subjects and the syntax–pragmatics interface. *Journal of Pragmatics* **41**: 951–73.

2010. On the typological economy of syntactic transfer: word order and relative clause high/low attachment preference in L3 Brazilian Portuguese. *International Review of Applied Linguistics in Language Teaching* **48**: 245–73.

2011. L3 syntactic transfer selectivity and typological determinacy: the Typological Primacy Model. *Second Language Research* **27**: 107–27.

Rothman, J. and Cabrelli Amaro, J. 2010. What variables condition syntactic transfer? A look at the L3 initial state. *Second Language Research* **26**: 189–218.

Rothman, J. and Iverson, M. 2008. Poverty-of-the-stimulus and SLA epistemology: considering L2 knowledge of aspectual phrasal semantics. *Language Acquisition* **15**: 270–314.

  2010. Independent normative assessments for bi/multilingualism, where art thou? In M. Cruz-Ferreira (ed.), *Multilingual norms*, 33–51. Frankfurt: Peter Lang.

Rothman, J. and Slabakova, R. 2011. Acquisition at the linguistic interfaces. *Lingua* (special issue) **121**(4): 568–76.

Rothman, J., Iverson, M. and Judy, T. 2011. Some notes on the generative study of L3 acquisition. *Second Language Research* **27**: 5–19.

Rothman, J., Judy, T., Guijarro-Fuentes, P. and Pires, A. 2010. On the (un)-ambiguity of adjectival interpretation in L2 Spanish: informing debates on the mental representation of L2 syntax. *Studies in Second Language Acquisition* **32**: 47–77.

Röver, C. 2005. *Testing EFL pragmatics*. Tübingen: Gunter Narr.

Rubin, J. 2008. Reflections. In C. Griffiths (ed.), *Lessons from the good language learner*, 10–15. Cambridge University Press.

Ruiz de Zarobe, Y., Sierra, J. M. and Gallardo del Puerto, F. (eds.). 2011. *Content and foreign language integrated learning: contributions to multilingualism in European contexts*. Bern: Peter Lang.

Russell, E. 1916. *Form and function: a contribution to the history of animal morphology*. London: Murray.

Russell, J. and Spada, N. 2006. The effectiveness of corrective feedback for the acquisition of L2 grammar. In N. Norris and L. Ortega (eds.), *Synthesizing research on language learning and teaching*, 133–64. Amsterdam: John Benjamins.

Rutherford, W. and Sharwood Smith, M. 1985. Consciousness-raising and Universal Grammar. *Applied Linguistics* **6**: 274–82.

Sabourin, L. 2006. Does the shallow structures proposal account for qualitative differences in first and second language processing? *Applied Psycholinguistics* **27**: 81–84.

  2009. Neuroimaging and research into second language acquisition. *Second Language Research* **25**: 5–11.

Sabourin, L. and Stowe, L. A. 2008. Second language processing: when are first and second languages processed similarly? *Second Language Research* **24**: 397–430.

Sabourin, L., Stowe, A. L. A. and de Haan, G. J. 2006. Transfer effects in learning a second language grammatical gender system. *Second Language Research* **22**: 1–29.

Sagarra, N. and Herschensohn, J. 2010. The role of proficiency and working memory in gender and number agreement processing in L1 and L2 Spanish. *Lingua* **120**: 2022–39.

Salaberry, R. and Shirai, Y. (eds.). 2002. *The L2 acquisition of tense–aspect morphology*. Amsterdam: John Benjamins.

Sankoff, G. 2002. Linguistic outcomes of language contact. In J. K. Chambers, P. Trudgill and N. Schilling-Estes (eds.), *The handbook of language variation and change*, 638–68. Oxford: Blackwell.

Sankoff, G., Thibault, P., Nagy, N., Blondeau, H., Fonollosa, M.-O. and Gagnon, L. 1997. Variation in the use of discourse markers in a language contact situation. *Language Variation and Change* 9: 191–217.

Sanz, C. (ed.). 2005. *Mind and context in adult second language acquisition: methods, theory and practice*. Washington, DC: Georgetown University Press.

Saussure, F. de. 1916. *Cours de linguistique générale*, ed. C. Bally and A. Sechehaye (eds.). Lausanne and Paris: Payot.

Sax, K. 2003. Acquisition of stylistic variation in American learners of French. Unpublished PhD, Indiana University.

Scarcella, R. and Krashen, S. (eds.). 1980. *Research in second language acquisition: selected papers of the Los Angeles second language research forum*. Rowley, MA: Newbury House.

Schachter, J. 1974. An error in error analysis. *Language Learning* 24: 205–14.
  1989a. A new look at an old classic. *Second Language Research* 5: 30–42.

Scherer, K. 1984. Emotion as a multi-component process: a model and some cross-cultural data. In P. Shaver (ed.), *Review of personality and social psychology: emotions, relationships and health*, 37–63. Beverly Hills: Sage.

Schlesewsky, M., Fanselow, G., Kliegl, R. and Krems, J. 2000. The subject preference in the processing of locally ambiguous *wh*-questions in German. In B. Hemforth and L. Konieczny (eds.), *German sentence processing*, 65–94. Dordrecht: Kluwer.

Schmid, M. S. and Dusseldorp, E. 2010. Innovative and quantitative methods for bilingualism research. *Second Language Research* 26: 5–11.

Schmidt, R. (ed.). 1995. *Attention and awareness in foreign language learning. Technical report #9*. Honolulu: University of Hawai'i.
  2001. Attention. In P. Robinson (ed.), *Cognition and second language instruction*, 3–32. Cambridge University Press.

Schmitt, N. 2008. Review article: instructed second language vocabulary learning. *Language Teaching Research* 12: 329–63.

Scholz, B. C. and Pullum, G. K. 2002. Searching for arguments to support linguistic nativism. *The Linguistic Review* 19: 185–223.

Schönenberger, M. 1996. Why do Swiss-German children like verb movement so much? In A. Stringfellow, D. Cahana-Amitay, E. Hughes and A. Zukowski (eds.), *Proceedings of the 20th Annual Boston University Conference on Language Development (BUCLD)*, 2: 658–69. Somerville, MA: Cascadilla Press.

Schoonbaert, S., Hartsuiker, R. J. and Pickering, M. J. 2007. The representation of lexical and syntactic information in bilinguals: evidence from syntactic priming. *Journal of Memory and Language* 56: 153–71.

Schreiber, T. and Sprouse, R. A. 1998. Knowledge of topicalization and scrambling in English–German interlanguage. *McGill Working Papers in Linguistics* 13: 162–72.

Schumann, J. 1978a. *The pidginization process: a model for second language acquisition*. Rowley, MA: Newbury House.

1997. *The neurobiology of affect in language*. Los Angeles: Blackwell.

Schumann, J., Crowell, S. E., Jones, N. E., Lee, N., Schuchert, S. A. and Wood, L. A. 2004. *The neurobiology of learning: perspectives from second language acquisition*. Mahwah, NJ: Lawrence Erlbaum.

Schütze, C. 2005. Thinking about what we are asking speakers to do. In S. Kepser and M. Reis (eds.), *Linguistic evidence: empirical, theoretical, and computational perspectives*, 457–85. Berlin: Mouton de Gruyter.

Schütze, C. T. and Wexler, K. 1996. Subject case licensing and English root infinitives. In A. Stringfellow, D. Cahana-Amitay, E. Hughes and A. Zukowski (eds.), *Proceedings of the 20th Annual Boston University Conference on Language Development (BUCLD)*, **2**: 670–81. Somerville, MA: Cascadilla Press.

Schwartz, A. I. and Kroll, J. F. 2006. Bilingual lexical activation in sentence context. *Journal of Memory and Language* **55**: 197–212.

Schwartz, B. D. 1987. The modular basis of second language acquisition. Unpublished PhD dissertation, University of Southern California.

1998a. The second language instinct. *Lingua* **106**: 133–60.

1999. The second language instinct. In A. Sorace, C. Heycock and R. Shillcock (eds.), *Language acquisition: knowledge, representation and processing*, 133–60. Dordrecht: Elsevier.

2003. Child L2 acquisition: paving the way. In B. Beachley, A. Brown and C. Conlin (eds.), *Proceedings of the 27th Annual Boston University Conference on Language Development (BUCLD)*, 26–50. Somerville, MA: Cascadilla Press.

2004. Why child L2 acquisition? In J. Van Kampen and S. Baauw (eds.), *Proceedings of Landelijke Onderzoekschool Taalwetenschap Generative Approaches to Language Acquisition (GALA 2003)*, 47–66. Utrecht: Landelijke Onderzoekschool Taalwetenschap.

Schwartz, B. D. and Sprouse, R. A. 1994. Word order and nominative case in non-native language acquisition: a longitudinal study of (L1 Turkish) German interlanguage. In T. Hoekstra and B. D. Schwartz (eds.), *Language acquisition studies in generative grammar: papers in honor of Kenneth Wexler from the 1991 GLOW Workshops*, 317–68. Amsterdam: John Benjamins.

1996. L2 cognitive states and the Full Transfer / Full Access model. *Second Language Research* **12**: 40–72.

2000. When syntactic theories evolve: consequences for L2 acquisition research. In J. Archibald (ed.), *Second language acquisition and linguistic theory*, 156–86. Malden, MA: Blackwell.

Schwartz, B. D. and Tomaselli, A. 1990. Some implications from an analysis of German word order. In A. Werner, W. Kosmeijer and E. Reuland (eds.), *Issues in Germanic syntax*, 251–74. Berlin: de Gruyter.

Scovel, T. 1978. The effect of affect on foreign language learning: a review of the anxiety research. *Language Learning* **28**: 129–42.

1988. *A time to speak: a psycholinguistic inquiry into the critical period for human speech*. Cambridge, MA: Newbury House.

Searle, J. R. 1969. *Speech acts: an essay in the philosophy of language*. Cambridge University Press.

1995. *The construction of social reality*. London: Penguin.

Seedhouse, P. 2005b. Conversation analysis as research methodology. In K. Richards and P. Seedhouse (eds.), *Applying conversation analysis*, 251–66. Basingstoke: Palgrave Macmillan.

Segalowitz, N. 2010. *Cognitive bases of second language fluency*. London: Routledge.

Sekerina, I. A. and Brooks, P. J. 2006. Pervasiveness of shallow processing. *Applied Psycholinguistics* **27**: 84–8.

Selinker, L. 1972. Interlanguage. *International Review of Applied Linguistics in Language Teaching* **10**: 209–31.

Sharwood Smith, M. 1991. Speaking to many minds: on the relevance of different types of language information for the L2 learner. *Second Language Research* **7**: 118–32.

Sharwood Smith, M. and Truscott, J. 2005. Stages or continua in second language acquisition: a MOGUL solution. *Applied Linguistics* **22**: 219–40.

2009. Short introduction to the MOGUL framework. www.msharwood.pwp.blueyonder.co.uk/mogul/

Shaver, P. (ed.). 1984. *Review of personality and social psychology: emotions, relationships and health*. Beverly Hills: Sage.

Sheldon, A. and Strange, W. 1982. The acquisition of /r/ and /l/ by Japanese learners of English: evidence that speech production can precede speech perception. *Applied Psycholinguistics* **3**: 243–61.

Shook, J. D. 1994. FL/L2 reading, grammatical information, and the input to intake phenomenon. *Applied Language Learning* **5**: 57–93.

Siegal, M. 1996. The role of learner subjectivity in second language sociolinguistic competency: western women learning Japanese. *Applied Linguistics* **17**: 356–82.

Siegal, M., Iozzi, L. and Surian, L. 2009. Bilingualism and conversational understanding in young children. *Cognition* **110**: 115–22.

Siegel, J. 2003. Social context. In C. Doughty and M. Long (eds.), *The handbook of second language acquisition*, 178–223. Oxford: Blackwell.

Silva-Corvalán, C. 1994. *Language contact and change: Spanish in Los Angeles*. Oxford University Press.

2003. Linguistic consequences of reduced input in bilingual first language acquisition. In S. Montrul and F. Ordóñez (eds.), *Linguistic theory and language development in Hispanic languages*, 375–97. Somerville, MA: Cascadilla Press.

Singleton, D. and Ryan, L. 2004. *Language acquisition: the age factor*, 2nd edn. Clevedon: Multilingual Matters.

Skapoulli, E. 2004. Gender codes at odds and the linguistic construction of a hybrid identity. *Journal of Language, Identity, and Education* **3**: 245–60.

Skehan, P. 1989. *Individual differences in foreign language learning.* London: Edward Arnold.

Skilton-Sylvester, E. 2002. Should I stay or should I go? Investigating Cambodian women's participation and investment in adult ESL programs. *Adult Education Quarterly* **53**: 251–86.

Skinner, B. F. 1957. *Verbal behavior.* Englewood Cliffs, NJ: Prentice-Hall.

Slabakova, R. 2001. *Telicity in the second language.* Amsterdam: John Benjamins.

　2005. What is so difficult about telicity marking in L2 Russian? *Bilingualism: Language and Cognition* **8**: 63–77.

　2006a. Learnability in the L2 acquisition of semantics: a bidirectional study of a semantic parameter. *Second Language Research* **22**: 498–523.

　2006b. Is there a critical period for semantics? *Second Language Research* **22**: 302–38.

　2008. *Meaning in the second language.* Berlin: Mouton de Gruyter.

　2009b. Features or parameters: which one makes second language acquisition easier, and more interesting to study? *Second Language Research* **25**: 313–24.

　2010. Scalar implicatures in second language acquisition. *Lingua* **120**: 2444–62.

Slabakova, R. and Ivanov, I. 2011. A more careful look at the syntax-discourse interface. *Lingua* **121**: 637–51.

Slabakova, R. and Montrul, S. 2002. On viewpoint aspect and its L2 acquisition: a UG perspective. In R. Salaberry and Y. Shirai (eds.), *The L2 acquisition of tense–aspect morphology,* 363–98. Amsterdam: John Benjamins.

　2003. Genericity and aspect in L2 acquisition. *Language Acquisition* **11**: 165–96.

　2008. Aspectual shifts: grammatical and pragmatic knowledge in L2 acquisition. In J. Liceras, H. Zobl and H. Goodluck (eds.), *The role of formal features in second language acquisition,* 455–83. New York: Lawrence Erlbaum.

Slobin, D. I. 1985; 1992. *The cross-linguistic study of language acquisition,* vols. I and III. London: Lawrence Erlbaum.

　1996. From "thought and language" to "thinking for speaking." In J. Gumperz and S. Levinson (eds.), *Rethinking linguistic relativity* (Studies in the Social and Cultural Foundations of Language 17), 70–96. Cambridge University Press.

Smith, B. L., Hayes-Harb, R., Bruss, M. and Harker, A. 2009. Production and perception of voicing and devoicing in similar German and English word pairs by native speakers of German. *Journal of Phonetics* **37**: 257–75.

Snape, N. and Kupisch, T. 2010. Ultimate attainment of second language articles: a case study of an endstate second language Turkish-English speaker. *Second Language Research* **26**: 527–48.

Snape, N., Leung, Y.-k. I. and Sharwood Smith, M. (eds.). 2009. *Representational deficits in SLA: studies in honor of Roger Hawkins.* Amsterdam: John Benjamins.

So, C. and Best, C. 2010. Cross-language perception of non-native tonal contrasts: effects of native phonological and phonetic influence. *Language and Speech* **53**: 273–93.

Sommers, M. and Barcroft, J. 2007. An integrated account of the effects of acoustic variability in first language and second language: evidence from amplitude, fundamental frequency, and speaking rate variability. *Applied Psycholinguistics* **28**: 231–49.

Song, H. and Schwartz, B. D. 2009. Testing the fundamental difference hypothesis: L2 adult, L2 child, and L1 child comparisons in the acquisition of Korean *wh*-constructions with negative polarity items. *Studies in Second Language Acquisition* **31**: 323–61.

Song, M. J., O'Grady, W., Cho, S. and Lee, M. 1997. The learning and teaching of Korean in community schools. In Y.-H. Kim (ed.), *Korean language in America*, vol. II: 111–127. Los Angeles: American Association of Teachers of Korean.

Sorace, A. 2003. Near-nativeness. In C. Doughty and M. Long (eds.), *The handbook of second language acquisition*, 130–51. Oxford: Blackwell.

　2011. Pinning down the concept of "interface" in bilingualism. *Linguistic Approaches to Bilingualism* **1**: 1–33.

Sorace, A. and Filiaci, F. 2006. Anaphora resolution in near-native speakers of Italian. *Second Language Research* **22**: 339–68.

Sowell, E., Peterson, B., Thompson, P., Welcome, S., Henkenius, A. and Toga, A. 2003. Mapping cortical change across human life span. *Nature Neuroscience* **6**: 309–15.

Spada, N. and Lightbown, P. 2009. Interaction research in second/foreign language classrooms. In A. Mackey and C. Polio (eds.), *Multiple perspectives on interaction*, 157–75. New York: Routledge.

Sperber, D. and Wilson, D. 1986/1995. *Relevance: communication and cognition*, 2nd edn. Oxford: Blackwell.

Spolsky, B. and Hult, F. M. (eds.). 2010. *Handbook of educational linguistics*. Oxford: Blackwell.

Sprouse, R. A. 2006a. The bankruptcy of the stimulus. In K. U. Deen, J. Nomura, B. Schulz and B. D. Schwartz (eds.), *Proceedings of the Inaugural Conference on Generative Approaches to Language Acquisition – North America, Honolulu, University of Connecticut Occasional Papers in Linguistics* 4: 51–63.

　2006b. Full transfer and relexification: second language acquisition and creole genesis. In C. Lefebvre, L. White and C. Jourdan (eds.), *L2 acquisition and creole genesis: dialogues*, 169–81. Amsterdam: John Benjamins.

Stæhr, L. S. 2008. Vocabulary size and the skills of listening, reading and writing. *Language Learning Journal* **36**: 139–52.

Stam, G. In press. Gesture and second language acquisition. In A. S. Ohta (ed.), *Encyclopedia of applied linguistics*, ed. C. Chapelle, vol. XXI: *Social, dynamic, and complexity theory approaches to second language development*. Malden, MA: Wiley-Blackwell.

Stauble, A. M. 1984. A comparison of a Spanish-English and a Japanese-English second language continuum: negation and verb morphology.

In R. Andersen (ed.), *Second languages: a cross-linguistic perspective*, 323–53. Rowley, MA: Newbury House.

Stavans, A. and Swisher, V. 2006. Language switching as a window on trilingual acquisition. *International Journal of Multilingualism* **3**: 193–220.

Steinberg, F. and Horwitz, E. 1986. The effect of induced anxiety on the denotative and interpretive content of second language speech. *TESOL Quarterly* **20**: 131–36.

Steinhauer, K., White, E. J. and Drury, J. E. 2009. Temporal dynamics of late second language acquisition: evidence from event-related brain potentials. *Second Language Research* **25**: 13–41.

Stevens, K. N., Libermann, A. M., Studdert-Kennedy, M. and Öhman, S. E. G. 1969. Crosslanguage study of vowel perception. *Language and Speech* **12**: 1–23.

Stevens, V. 2006. Second Life in education and language learning. *TESL-EJ* **10**, www.tesl-ej.org/ej39/int.html

Storch, N. 2002. Relationships formed in dyadic interaction and opportunity for learning. *International Journal of Educational Research* **37**: 305–22.

Storch, N. and Wigglesworth, G. 2007. Writing tasks: comparing individual and collaborative writing. In M. P. García Mayo (ed.), *Investigating tasks in formal language learning*, 157–77. Clevedon: Multilingual Matters.

Strange, W. (ed.). 1995. *Speech perception and linguistic experience: issues in cross-language research*. Baltimore: York Press.

Strange, W. and Shafer, V. L. 2008. Speech perception in second language learners: the re-education of selective perception. In J. G. H. Edwards and M. L. Zampini (eds.), *Phonology and second language acquisition*, 153–91. Amsterdam: John Benjamins.

Stringer, D. 2007. Motion events in L2 acquisition: a lexicalist account. In H. Caunt-Nulton, S. Kulatilake and I. H. Woo (eds.), *Proceedings of the 31st annual Boston University Conference on Language Development (BUCLD)*, vol. II: 585–96. Somerville, MA: Cascadilla Press.

2010. The gloss trap. In Z.-H. Han and T. Cadierno (eds.), *Linguistic relativity in SLA: thinking for speaking*, 102–24. Bristol: Multilingual Matters.

Stringer, D., Burghardt, B., Seo, H.-K. and Wang, Y.-T. 2011. Straight on through to Universal Grammar: spatial modifiers in second language acquisition. *Second Language Research* **27**: 289–311.

Stringfellow, A., Cahana-Amitay, D., Hughes, E. and Zukowski, A. (eds.). 1996. *Proceedings of the 20th Annual Boston University Conference on Language Development (BUCLD)*. Somerville, MA: Cascadilla Press.

Swain, M. 1985. Communicative competence: some roles of comprehensive input and comprehensible output in its development. In S. Gass and C. Madden (eds.), *Input in second language acquisition*, 235–53. Rowley, MA: Newbury House.

1995. Three functions of output in second language learning. In G. Gook and B. Seidlhofer (eds.), *Principle and practice in applied linguistics*, 125–44. Oxford University Press.

2005. The output hypothesis: theory and research. In E. Hinkel (ed.), *Handbook of research in second language teaching and learning*, 471–84. Mahwah, NJ: Lawrence Erlbaum.

Swain, M. and Deters, P. 2008. "New" mainstream SLA theory: expanded and enriched. *Modern Language Journal* 91: 820–36.

Swain, M. and Lapkin, S. 1995. Problems in output and the cognitive processes they generate: a step towards second language learning. *Applied Linguistics* 16: 370–91.

2002. Talking it through: two French immersion learner's response to reformulation. *International Journal of Educational Research* 37: 285–304.

Sweet, H. 1964 [1899]. *The practical study of languages.* Oxford University Press.

Tagliamonte, S. 2006. *Analysing sociolinguistic variation.* Cambridge University Press.

Taguchi, N. 2008. The role of learning environment in the development of pragmatic comprehension: a comparison of gains between EFL and ESL learners. *Studies in Second Language Acquisition* 30: 423–52.

Takagi, N. 2002. The limits of training Japanese listeners to identify English /r/ and /l/: eight case studies. *Journal of the Acoustical Society of America* 111: 2887–96.

Tanner, D. 2011. Agreement mechanisms in native and nonnative language processing: electrophysiological correlates of complexity and interference. Unpublished PhD dissertation, University of Washington.

Tarone, E. 1988. *Variation in interlanguage.* London: Edward Arnold.

2007. Sociolinguistic approaches to second language acquisition research 1997–2007. *Modern Language Journal* 91: 837–48.

Tarone, E. and Bigelow, M. 2007. Alphabetic print literacy and oral language processing in SLA. In A. Mackey (ed.), *Conversational interaction in second language acquisition*, 101–21. Oxford University Press.

Tarone, E., Bigelow, M. and Hansen, K. 2007. The impact of alphabetic print literacy level on oral second language acquisition. In N. Faux (ed.), *Low-educated Second Language and Literacy Acquisition: proceedings of the 2nd Annual Forum*, 99–122. Richmond, VA: The Literacy Institute at Virginia Commonwealth University.

2009. *Literacy and second language oracy.* Oxford University Press.

Tarone, E., Swierzbin, B. and Bigelow, M. 2006. The impact of literacy level on features of interlanguage in oral narratives. *Rivista de Psicolinguistica Applicata* (special issue on "Interlanguage," ed. T. Baldwin and L. Selinker) 6: 65–77.

Tesnière, L. 1959. *Éléments de syntaxe structurale.* Paris: Editions Klincksieck.

Teutsch-Dwyer, M. 2001. (Re)constructing masculinity in a new linguistic reality. In A. Pavlenko, A. Blackledge, I. Piller and M. Teutsch-Dwyer (eds.), *Multilingualism, second language learning, and gender*, 175–98. Berlin: Mouton de Gruyter.

Thierry, G. and Wu, Y. J. 2007. Brain potentials reveal unconscious translation during foreign-language comprehension. *Proceedings of the National Academy of Sciences of the United States of America* **104**: 12530–35.

Thije, J. and Zeevaert, L. (eds.). 2007. *Receptive multilingualism: linguistic analyses, language policies and didactic concepts*. Amsterdam: John Benjamins.

Thomas, M. 1989a. The interpretation of English reflexive pronouns by non-native speakers. *Studies in Second Language Acquisition* **11**: 281–301.

  1998a. Programmatic ahistoricity in second language acquisition theory. *Studies in Second Language Acquisition* **20**: 387–405.

  1998b. Corder's insight in the context of medieval and early Renaissance language science. *McGill Working Papers in Linguistics* **13**: 183–96.

  2002. Development of the concept of "the poverty of the stimulus." *The Linguistic Review* **19**: 51–71.

  2004. *Universal Grammar in second language acquisition: a history*. London: Routledge.

Thorne, S. L. 2003. Artifacts and cultures-of-use in intercultural communication. *Language Learning and Technology* **7**: 38–67.

Thornton, R. 1990. Adventures in long-distance moving: the acquisition of complex wh-questions. Unpublished PhD dissertation, University of Connecticut, Storrs.

Tohkura, Y., Sagisaka, Y. and Vatikiotis-Bateson, E. (eds.). 1992. *Speech perception, production and linguistic structure*. Tokyo: OHM.

Tokowicz, N. and MacWhinney, B. 2005. Implicit and explicit measures of sensitivity to violations in second language grammar. *Studies in Second Language Acquisition* **27**: 173–204.

Tomasello, M. 2003. *Constructing a language: a usage-based theory of language acquisition*. Cambridge, MA: Harvard University Press.

  2008. *Origins of human communication*. Cambridge, MA: MIT Press.

Toohey, K. 2000. *Learning English at school: identity, social relations and classroom practice*. Clevedon: Multilingual Matters.

Towell, R. 2002. Relative degrees of fluency: a comparative case study of advanced learners of French. *International Review of Applied Linguistics in Language Teaching* **40**: 117–50.

Towell, R. and Dewaele, J.-M. 2005. The role of psycholinguistic factors in the development of fluency amongst advanced learners of French. In J.-M. Dewaele (ed.), *Focus on French as a foreign language*, 210–39. Clevedon: Multilingual Matters.

Towell, R. and Hawkins, R. 1994. *Approaches to second language acquisition*. Clevedon: Multilingual Matters.

  (eds.). 2004. *Empirical evidence and theories of representation in current research in second language acquisition. Transactions of the Philological Society*, vol. CII. Oxford: Blackwell.

Towell, R., Hawkins, R. and Bazergui, N. 1996. The development of fluency in advanced learners of French. *Applied Linguistics* **15**: 225–43.

Trahey, M. and White, L. 1993. Positive evidence and preemption in the second language classroom. *Studies in Second Language Acquisition* **15**: 181–204.

Trenkic, D. 2007. Variability in L2 article production: beyond the representational deficits vs. processing constraints debate. *Second Language Research* **23**: 289–327.

2008. The representation of English articles in second language grammars: determiners or adjectives? *Bilingualism: Language and Cognition* **11**: 1–18.

Trevarthen, C. 1979. Communication and cooperation in early infancy: a description of primary intersubjectivity. In M. Bulowa (ed.), *Before speech: the beginning of interpersonal communication*, 321–48. Cambridge University Press.

Trofimovich, P. and Baker, W. 2006. Learning second language suprasegmentals: effect of L2 experience on prosody and fluency characteristics of L2 speech. *Studies in Second Language Acquisition* **28**: 1–30.

Trofimovich, P., Gatbonton, E. and Segalowitz, N. 2007. A dynamic look at L2 phonological learning: seeking processing explanations for implicational phenomena. *Studies in Second Language Acquisition* **29**: 407–48.

Truscott, J. 2006. Optionality in second language acquisition: a generative processing-oriented account. *International Review of Applied Linguistics in Language Teaching* **44**: 311–30.

Truscott, J. and Sharwood Smith, M. 2004a. Acquisition by processing: a modular perspective on language development. *Bilingualism: Language and Cognition* **7**: 1–20.

Truscott, J. and Sharwood Smith, M. 2004b. How APT is your theory: present status and future prospects. *Bilingualism: Language and Cognition* **7**: 43–47.

Tryzna, M. 2009. Questioning the validity of the Article Choice Parameter and the Fluctuation Hypothesis: evidence from L2 English article use by L1 Polish and L1 Mandarin Chinese speakers. In M. P. García Mayo and R. Hawkins (eds.), *Second language acquisition of articles: empirical findings and theoretical implications*, 67–86. Amsterdam: John Benjamins.

Tsimpli, I.-M. and Dimitrakopoulou, M. 2007. The Interpretability Hypothesis: evidence from wh-interrogatives in second language acquisition. *Second Language Research* **23**: 215–42.

Tsimpli, I.-M. and Mastropavlou, M. 2008. Feature interpretability in L2 acquisition and SLI: Greek clitics and determiners. In J. Liceras, H. Goodluck and H. Zobl (eds.), *Proceedings of the 6th Generative Approaches to Second Language Acquisition Conference (GASLA 2002)*, 142–83. Somerville, MA: Cascadilla Proceedings Project.

Tsimpli, T., Sorace, A., Heycock, C. and Filiaci, F. 2004. First language attrition and syntactic subjects: a study of Greek and Italian near-native speakers of English. *International Journal of Bilingualism* **8**: 257–77.

Tsubaki, M. 2006. The involvement load hypothesis: an inquiry into vocabulary learning. http://cicero.u-bunkyo.ac.jp/lib/kiyo/fsell2006/EIBUN175_184.pdf

Ullman, M. 2001b. The neural basis of lexicon and grammar in first and second language: the declarative/procedural model. *Bilingualism: Language and Cognition* **4**: 105–22.
  2005. A cognitive neuroscience perspective on second language acquisition: the declarative/procedural model. In C. Sanz (ed.), *Mind and context in adult second language acquisition: methods, theory and practice*, 141–78. Washington, DC: Georgetown University Press.
Uludag, O. and VanPatten, B. In press. The comparative effects of processing instruction and dictogloss on the acquisition of the English passive by speakers of Turkish. *International Review of Applied Linguistics in Language Teaching*.
Unsworth, S. 2003. Child L1, child L2, and adult L2 acquisition: differences and similarities. In A. Brugos, L. Micciulla and C. E. Smith (eds.), *Proceedings of the 28th Annual Boston University Conference on Language Development (BUCLD)*, 633–44. Somerville, MA: Cascadilla Press.
  2004. On the syntax–semantics interface in Dutch: adult and child L2 acquisition compared. *International Review of Applied Linguistics in Language Teaching* **42**: 173–87.
  2005. *Child L2, adult L2, child L1: differences and similarities*. Utrecht: Landelijke Onderzoekschool Taalwetenschap.
  2008b. Comparing child L2 development with adult L2 development: how to measure L2 proficiency. In B. Haznedar and E. Gavruseva (eds.), *Current trends in child second language acquisition: a generative perspective*, 301–33. Amsterdam: John Benjamins.
Unsworth, S., Parodi, T., Sorace, A. and Young-Scholten, M. (eds.). 2006. *Paths of development in L1 and L2 acquisition: in honor of Bonnie D. Schwartz*. Philadelphia: John Benjamins.
Ushioda, E. 2008. Motivation and good language learners. In C. Griffiths (ed.), *Lessons from the good language learner*, 19–34. Cambridge University Press.
Ushioda, E. and Dörnyei, Z. 2009. Motivation, language identities and the L2 Self: a theoretical overview. In Z. Dörnyei and E. Ushioda (eds.), *Motivation, language identity and the L2 self*, 1–8. Clevedon: Multilingual Matters.
Vainikka, A. and Young-Scholten, M. 1994. Direct access to X-bar theory: evidence from Korean and Turkish adults learning German. In T. Hoekstra and B. D. Schwartz (eds.), *Language acquisition studies in generative grammar: papers in honor of Kenneth Wexler from the 1991 GLOW Workshops*, 265–316. Amsterdam: John Benjamins.
  1996a. Gradual development of L2 phrase structure. *Second Language Research* **12**: 7–39.
  1996b. The early stages in adult L2 syntax: additional evidence from Romance speakers. *Second Language Research* **12**: 140–76.
  1998. Morphosyntactic triggers in adult SLA. In M. L. Beck (ed.), *Morphology and its interface in L2 knowledge*, 89–113. Amsterdam: John Benjamins.
  2007b. The role of literacy in the development of L2 morpho-syntax from an organic grammar perspective. In N. Faux (ed.), *Low-educated Second*

Language and Literacy Acquisition: Proceedings of the 2nd Annual Forum, 123–48. Richmond, VA: The Literacy Institute at Virginia Commonwealth University.
  2011. *The acquisition of German under an Organic Grammar approach*. Berlin: de Gruyter.
Valdés, G. 2001. Heritage language students: profiles and possibilities. In J. Peyton, D. Ranard and S. McGinnis (eds.), *Heritage languages in America: preserving a national resource*, 37–77. Washington, DC: Center for Applied Linguistics.
Valdés, G., Fishman, J., Chávez, R. and Pérez, W. 2006. *Developing minority language resources: the case of Spanish in California*. Clevedon: Multilingual Matters.
Valenzuela, E. 2006. L2 endstate grammars and incomplete acquisition of the Spanish CLLD constructions. In R. Slabakova, S. Montrul and P. Prévost (eds.), *Inquiries in linguistic development: in honor of Lydia White*, 283–304. Amsterdam: John Benjamins.
Valsiner, J. 2001. Process structure of semiotic mediation in human development. *Human Development* **44**: 84–97.
Van der Veer, R. and Valsiner, J. (eds.). 1991. *Understanding Vygotsky: a quest for synthesis*. Oxford: Blackwell.
  1994. *The Vygotsky reader*. Oxford: Blackwell.
Van Heuven, W. J. B. and Dijkstra, T. 2010. Language comprehension in the bilingual brain: fMRI and ERP support for psycholinguistic models. *Brain Research Reviews* **64**: 104–22.
Van Hout, R. and Strömqvist, S. 1993. The influence of socio-biographical factors, in Perdue (ed.), 164–72.
Van Hout, R., Hulk, A., Kuiken, F. and Towell, R. (eds.). 2003. *The lexicon-syntax interface in second language acquisition*. Amsterdam and Philadelphia: John Benjamins.
Van Lier, L. 2010. Ecological-semiotic perspectives on educational linguistics. In B. Spolsky and F. M. Hult (eds.), *Handbook of educational linguistics*, 596–606. Oxford: Blackwell.
Van Naerssen, M. 1980. How similar are Spanish as a first and foreign language? In R. Scarcella and S. Krashen (eds.), *Research in second language acquisition*, 146–54. Rowley, MA: Newbury House.
VanPatten, B. 1996. *Input processing and grammar instruction: theory and research*. Norwood, NJ: Ablex.
  (ed.). 2004. *Processing instruction: theory, research, and commentary*. Mahwah, NJ: Lawrence Erlbaum.
  2007. Input processing in adult second language acquisition. In B. VanPatten and J. Williams (eds.), *Theories in second language acquisition: an introduction*, 115–36. Mahwah, NJ: Lawrence Erlbaum.
VanPatten, B. and Cadierno, T. 1993. Explicit instruction and input processing. *Studies in Second Language Acquisition* **15**: 225–43.

VanPatten, B. and Oikkenon, S. 1996. Explanation vs. structured input in processing instruction. *Studies in Second Language Acquisition* **18**: 495–510.

VanPatten, B. and Williams, J. (eds.). 2007. *Theories in second language acquisition: an introduction*. Mahwah, NJ: Lawrence Erlbaum.

VanPatten, B. and Wong, W. 2004. Processing instruction and the French causative: a replication. In B. VanPatten (ed.), *Processing instruction: theory, research, and commentary*, 33–63. Mahwah, NJ: Lawrence Erlbaum.

VanPatten, B., Inclezan, D., Salazar, H. and Farley, A. P. 2009. Processing instruction and dictogloss: a study on object pronouns and word order in Spanish. *Foreign Language Annals* **42**: 557–75.

Varchi, B. 1804 [1570]. *L'Ercolano*, vol. I. Milan: Società Tipografica de' Classici Italiani.

Varghese, M., Morgan, B., Johnston, B. and Johnson, K. A. 2005. Theorizing language teacher identity: three perspectives and beyond. *Journal of Language, Identity and Education* **4**: 21–44.

Vassiliu, P. 2001. Lexical input in the low level EFL classroom. Unpublished PhD dissertation, University of Wales Swansea.

Verhoeven, L. and Vermeer, A. 2002. Communicative competence and personality dimensions in first and second language learners. *Applied Psycholinguistics* **23**: 361–74.

Vermeer, A. 2001. Breadth and depth of vocabulary in relation to L1/L2 acquisition and frequency of input. *Applied Psycholinguistics* **22**: 217–34.

Verspoor, M., de Bot, K. and Lowie, W. (eds.). 2011. *A dynamic approach to second language development: methods and techniques*. Amsterdam: John Benjamins.

Vigliocco, G., Hartsuiker, R. J., Jarema, G. and Kolk, H. H. J. 1996. How many labels on the bottles? Notional concord in Dutch and French. *Language and Cognitive Processes* **11**: 407–21.

Vitanova, G. 2005. Authoring the self in a non-native language: a dialogic approach to agency and subjectivity. In J. K. Hall, G. Vitanova and L. Marchenkova (eds.), *Dialogue with Bakhtin on second language learning: new perspectives*, 149–69. Mahwah, NJ: Lawrence Erlbaum.

Vygotsky, L. S. 1978. *Mind in society: the development of higher psychological processes*. Cambridge, MA: Harvard University Press.

1986 [1934]. *Thought and language*. Cambridge, MA: MIT Press.

1987a [1934]. *The collected works of L. S. Vygotsky*, vol. I: *Problems in general psychology*, ed. R. W. Rieber and A. S. Carton. New York: Plenum.

1987b [1934]. Thinking and speech. In *The collected works of L. S. Vygotsky*, vol. I: *Problems in general psychology*, ed. R. W. Rieber and A. S. Carton, 39–288. New York: Plenum.

Wagner-Gough, J. 1978. Comparative studies in second language learning. In E. Hatch (ed.), *Second language acquisition: a book of readings*, 155–71. Rowley, MA: Newbury House.

Walker, J. A. 2010. *Variation in linguistic systems*. New York; London: Routledge.

Wall, T. and Leong, M. (eds.). 2010. *Low-educated Second Language and Literacy Acquisition: Proceedings of the 5th Annual Forum*. Calgary: Bow Valley College.

Wang, Y., Jongman, A. and Sereno, J. 2006. Second language acquisition and processing of Mandarin tone. In E. Bates, L. Tan and O. Tzeng (eds.), *Handbook of East Asian psycholinguistics*, vol. I: *Chinese*, 250–57. Cambridge University Press.

Warschauer, M. and Healey, D. 1998. Computers and language learning: an overview. *Language Teaching Research* 31: 57–71.

Warschauer, M. and Kern, R. (eds.). 2000. *Network-based language teaching: concepts and practice*. Cambridge University Press.

Wartenburger, I., Heekeren, H. R., Abutalebi, J., Cappa, S. F., Villringer, A. and Perani, D. 2003. Early setting of grammatical processing in the bilingual brain. *Neuron* 37: 159–70.

Watson-Gegeo, K. A. and Nielsen, S. 2003. Language socialization in SLA. In C. Doughty and M. Long (eds.), *The handbook of second language acquisition*, 155–77. Oxford: Blackwell.

Wayland, R., Guion, S., Landfair, D. and Li, B. 2006. Native Thai speakers' acquisition of English word stress patterns. *Psycholinguistic Research* 35: 285–304.

Weasenforth, D., Biesenbach-Lucas, S. and Meloni, C. 2002. Realizing constructivist objectives through collaborative technologies: threaded discussions. *Language Learning and Technology* 6: 58–86.

Weber, A. and Cutler, A. 2004. Lexical competition in non-native spoken-word recognition. *Journal of Memory and Language* 50: 1–25.

Weber-Fox, C. M. and Neville, H. J. 1996. Maturational constraints on functional specializations for language processing: ERP and behavioral evidence in bilingual speakers. *Journal of Cognitive Neuroscience* 8: 231–56.

Weedon, C. 1987. *Feminist practice and poststructuralist theory*. Oxford: Blackwell.

Wei, L. 2006. The multilingual mental lexicon and lemma transfer in third language learning. *International Journal of Multilingualism* 3: 88–105.

Wei, L. and Wu, C.-J. 2009. Polite Chinese children revisited: creativity and the use of codeswitching in the Chinese complementary school classroom. *International journal of Bilingual Education and Bilingualism* 12: 193–211.

Weinberger, S. H. 1996. Minimal segments in second language phonology. In A. James and J. Leather (eds.), *Second language speech: structure and process*, 263–312. Berlin and New York: Mouton de Gruyter.

Weise, H. 2009. Grammatical innovation in multiethnic urban Europe: new linguistic practices among adolescents. *Lingua* 119: 782–806.

Wertsch, J. 1985. *Vygotsky and the social formation of mind*. Cambridge, MA: Harvard University Press.

Westfall, R. 1977. *The construction of modern science: mechanisms and mechanics*. Cambridge University Press.

Wexler, K. 1994. Optional Infinitives, head movement and the economy of derivations. In D. Lightfoot and N. Hornstein (eds.), *Verb movement*, 305–50. Cambridge University Press.

Wexler, K. and Culicover P. 1980. *Formal principles of language acquisition*. Cambridge, MA: MIT Press.

White, L. 1985. The "pro-drop parameter" in adult second language acquisition. *Language Learning* **35**: 47–61.

  1989. *Universal Grammar and second language acquisition*. Amsterdam and Philadelphia: John Benjamins.

  1996b. Universal grammar and second language acquisition: current trends and new directions. In W. C. Ritchie and T. K. Bhatia (eds.), *Handbook of second language acquisition*, 85–120. New York: Academic Press.

  2003a. *Second language acquisition and Universal Grammar*. Cambridge University Press.

  2003b. Fossilization in steady-state L2 grammars: persistent problems with inflectional morphology. *Bilingualism: Language and Cognition* **6**: 129–41.

  2009. Grammatical theory: interfaces and L2 knowledge. In W. C. Ritchie and T. K. Bhatia (eds.), *The new handbook of second language acquisition*, 49–68. Bingley: Emerald.

  2011. Second language acquisition at the interfaces. *Lingua* **121**: 577–90.

White, L., Valenzuela, E., Kozlowska-Macgregor, M. and Leung, Y.-k. I. 2004. Gender agreement in nonnative Spanish: evidence against failed features. *Applied Psycholinguistics* **25**: 105–33.

White, T., Andreasen, N. and Nopoulos, P. 2002. Brain volumes and surface morphology in monozygotic twins. *Cerebral Cortex* **12**: 486–93.

Whong-Barr, M. 2006. What transfers? In S. Unsworth, T. Parodi, A. Sorace and M. Young-Scholten (eds.), *Paths of development in L1 and L2 acquisition: in honor of Bonnie D. Schwartz*, 187–99. Amsterdam and Philadelphia: John Benjamins.

Wigglesworth, G. and Storch, N. 2009. Pair versus individual writing: effects on fluency, complexity and accuracy. *Language Testing* **26**: 445–66.

Wilkins, D. A. 1972. *Linguistics in language teaching*. London: Edward Arnold.

Williams, G. 2010. Language Socialization: a systemic functional perspective. In P. A. Duff and N. C. Hornberger (eds.), *Encyclopaedia of language and education*, vol. VIII: *Language socialization*, 57–70. New York: Springer.

Williams, L. 1977. The perception of stop consonant voicing by Spanish–English bilinguals. *Perception and Psychophysics* **21**: 289–97.

Wilson, C. and Davidson, L. In press. Bayesian analysis of non-native cluster production. *Proceedings of NELS* 40. Cambridge, MA: MIT.

Winitz, H. (ed.). 1981. *Native language and foreign language acquisition. Annals of the New York Academy of Science* 379.

Witelson, S., Kigar, D.L. and Harvey, T. 1999. The exceptional brain of Albert Einstein. *The Lancet* **353**: 2149–53.

Wode, H. 1981. *Learning a second language*, vol. I: *An integrated view of language acquisition*. Tübingen: Narr.

  1996. The reacquisition of languages: some issues. MS, English Department and Center for Bilingualism and Language Contact, University of Kiel.

Wolfram, W. 1985. Variability in tense marking: a case for the obvious. *Language Learning* **35**: 229–53.

Wong, W. 2003. Textual enhancement and simplified input: effects on L2 comprehension and acquisition of non-meaningful grammatical form. *Applied Language Learning* **13**: 109–32.
　2005. *Input enhancement: from theory and research to the classroom.* Boston: McGraw-Hill.
Woodall, B. R. 2002. Language switching: using the first language while writing in a second language. *Journal of Second Language Writing* **11**: 7–38.
Wright, S., Taylor, D. and Macarthur, J. 2000. Subtractive bilingualism and the survival of the Inuit language: heritage-versus second-language education. *Journal of Educational Psychology* **92**: 63–84.
Yashima, T. 2002. Willingness to communicate in a second language: the Japanese EFL context. *Modern Language Journal* **86**: 55–66.
Yavaş, M. (ed.). 1994a. *First and second language phonology.* San Diego: Singular.
Yeni-Komshian, G. H., Flege, J. E. and Liu, S. 2000. Pronunciation proficiency in the first and second languages of Korean–English bilinguals. *Bilingualism: Language and Cognition* **3**: 131–49.
Ylinen, S., Uther, M., Latvala, A., Vepsäläinen, S., Iverson, P., Akahane-Yamada, R. and Näätänen, R. 2009. Training the brain to weight speech cues differently: a study of Finnish second-language users of English. *Journal of Cognitive Neuroscience* **22**: 1319–32.
Yoshida, R. 2009. *Learners in Japanese language classrooms.* London: Continuum.
　2010. How do teachers and learners perceive corrective feedback in the classroom? *Modern Language Journal* **94**: 293–314.
Young, R. and Bayley, R. 1996. VARBRUL analysis for second language acquisition research. In R. Bayley and D. R. Preston (eds.), *Second language acquisition and linguistic variation*, 253–306. Amsterdam: John Benjamins.
Young-Scholten, M. 1993. *The acquisition of prosodic structure in a second language.* Tübingen: Max Niemeyer Verlag.
　(ed.). 2008. *Low-educated Second Language and Literacy Acquisition: proceedings of the 3rd Annual Forum.* Newcastle upon Tyne: Newcastle University.
Young-Scholten, M. and Ijuin, C. 2006. How can we best measure adult ESL student progress? *TESOL Adult Education Interest Section Newsletter*, September, **4**(2).
Young-Scholten, M. and Naeb, R. 2010. Non-literate L2 adults' small steps in mastering the constellation of skills required for reading. In T. Wall and C. Leong (eds.), *Low-educated Second Language and Literacy Acquisition: proceedings of the 5th Annual Forum*, 63–74. Calgary: Bow Valley College.
Young-Scholten, M. and Strom, N. 2006. First-time L2 readers: is there a critical period? In I. van de Craats, J. Kurvers and M. Young-Scholten (eds.), *Low-educated Second Language and Literacy Acquisition: proceedings of the 1st Annual Forum* (LOT Occasional Series 15), 45–68. http://lotos.library.uu.nl/index.html. Utrecht: Landelijke Onderzoekschool Taalwetenschap.
Yuan, B. 2010. Domain-wide or variable-dependent vulnerability of the semantics–syntax interface in L2 acquisition? Evidence from wh-words

used as existential polarity words in L2 Chinese grammars. *Second Language Research* **26**: 219–60.

Zähner, C., Fauverge, A. and Wong, J. 2000. Task-based language learning via audiovisual networks? In M. Warschauer and R. Kern (eds.), *Network-based language teaching: concepts and practice*, 186–203. Cambridge University Press.

Zdorenko, T. and Paradis, J. 2008. The acquisition of articles in child second language English: fluctuation, transfer or both? *Second Language Research* **24**: 227–50.

Zeldes, A., Lüdeling, A. and Hirschmann, H. 2008. What's hard? Quantitative evidence for difficult constructions in German learner data. *Proceedings of QITL* **3**. www.ling.helsinki.fi/sky/tapahtumat/qitl/Abstracts/Zeldes_et_al.pdf

Zhang, Y. and Francis, A. 2010. The weighting of vowel quality in native and non-native listeners' perception of English lexical stress. *Journal of Phonetics* **38**: 260–71.

Zimmerman, K. J. 2004. The role of vocabulary size in assessing second language proficiency. Unpublished MA thesis, Brigham Young University.

Zobl, H. 1980a. Developmental and transfer errors: their common bases and (possibly) differential effects. *TESOL Quarterly* **14**: 469–79.

1980b. The formal and developmental selectivity of L1 influence on L2 acquisition. *Language Learning* **30**: 43–57.

1982. A direction for Contrastive Analysis: the comparative study of developmental sequences. *TESOL Quarterly* **16**: 169–83.

Zobl, H. and Liceras, J. 1994. Functional categories and acquisition orders. *Language Learning* **44**: 159–80.

Zuengler, J. and Miller, E. 2006. Cognitive and sociocultural perspectives: two parallel SLA worlds? *TESOL Quarterly* **40**: 35–58.

Index

access to UG, *see* Universal Grammar
access, lexical, 316, 326, 328, 394, 397–98, 403, 411–13, 415, 573, 575, 678
accommodation theory, 285
Acculturation Model, 255, 261, 702
acoustically varied input, 635
Acquisition by Processing theory (APT), 571–74, 576, 578
activity theory, 70, 256, 258, 649, 650, 651
affect (emotional engagement), 177, 230, 417, 421, 424, 428
affiliation, 426
affixation, 443, 703
affordance(s), 252, 253, 292, 293, 298, 299, 304
African American, 237, 245
agency, learner, 249, 657, 664
agreement, 141, 328–29, 333–34, 350, 362, 415, 505, 508, 509, 512, 514–17, 519, 639, 684, 686, 691, 703
  case, 361, 362, 371, 517, 686, 687, 690, 730
  nominal, 360, 407, 703
  subject–verb, 362, 399, 564, 584, 585, 601, 687, 690
aizuchi ("listener responses"), 656
allophone, 31, 109, 533, 538
alphabetic script, *see* script
alter ("other"), 257
ambiguity, syntactic, 400
American Sign Language (ASL), 319, 336, 678, 700, 701
amygdala, 316, 424, 426–27, 432–33, 435
anaphora, 32, 150, 266, 267, 440, 491, 493, 689, 703
anomia, 703
anxiety, *see* foreign language anxiety
AoA (age of acquisition onset / age of arrival), 75, 112, 288, 315–37, 342, 394, 404–13, 416, 417, 550, 703
aphasia, 408, 703, 704
appetitive reward, 425, 426
aptitude, 39, 50, 60, 63, 96, 160, 165–69, 172, 323, 324, 335, 337, 417, 433, 611, 678
Arabic, 26, 99, 100, 108, 197, 243, 293, 349, 357, 368, 519, 522, 543, 544, 622
Archibald, John, 54, 56, 530, 531, 533, 544, 545

argument structure, 107, 108
Armenian, 360
articulatory settings, 389
aspect
  grammatical, 355, 704, 717, 725
  imperfective, 362, 469, 470–71, 527, 704, 717
  perfective, 280, 343, 362, 469, 470, 471, 526, 527, 704, 725
  verbal, 440, 666
attrition, 316, 335, 353, 355, 356, 358, 360–63, 365, 366, 370, 380, 581, 670
Augustine, 40, 41, 42
automatization, vii, 50, 95, 114, 123–25, 704
Autonomous Induction theory (AIT), 116, 567, 569
auxiliary verbs, 150, 350, 452, 591, 610, 704
AX discrimination task, 110, 704

baby talk, *see* child-directed speech
bankruptcy of the stimulus, 145–47, 158
Barcelona Age Factor (BAF), 323–26, 335
Bardovi-Harlig, Kathleen, 56, 380, 470, 482–86, 488, 498, 499
Basic Variety, 106, 265, 266, 267, 498, 499, 582, 593, 594, 705
Basque, 228, 354, 375, 376, 378, 387
behavioral studies, 316, 705
behaviorism, 13, 19, 22, 32, 705
Bengali, 238, 357
Bialystok, Ellen, 75, 78, 89, 191, 319, 320, 324, 333, 490, 713
Bickerton, Derek, 493, 594
Bigelow, Martha, 221, 222
Bilingual Syntax Measure (BSM), 74, 99, 705
binding, *see* anaphora
Birdsong, David, 50, 78, 112, 317, 318, 320, 324, 333, 527, 670, 671, 675–76, 678, 679, 684, 690
Bley-Vroman, Robert, 38, 57, 60, 137, 315, 318, 321, 340, 341, 385, 480, 582, 591, 674–76, 707
blog, 88, 208, 292, 293, 295, 299, 301, 305
bootstrapping, 386, 565, 612, 615
Brazilian Portuguese, 366, 386, 387, 391, 542
British English, 287
Brocanto, 406
Broselow, Ellen, 54

Brown, Roger, 74, 83, 99, 110, 112, 147, 230, 237, 339, 358, 448, 494, 499, 531, 538, 540, 561, 563, 574, 576, 578, 585–88, 698, 732
Bulgarian, 308, 475, 502, 503
Burt, Marina, 31–33, 37, 42, 74, 99, 102, 103, 339, 341, 508, 588, 589

Cabrelli Amaro, Jennifer, 11
Cambodian, 242, 277, 282
Canada, 171, 173, 191, 217, 245, 279, 287, 545, 603
Cantonese, 77, 550, 551, 614
Carroll, Susanne, 56, 79, 95, 114–20, 133, 214, 453, 561, 565, 567, 569–70, 571, 579, 580, 630, 636, 670, 690
Case, grammatical, 515–17, 687
　filter, 339
　licensing, 463
　structural/inherent, 342, 359, 687, 731
Catalan, 323, 348, 354, 375, 379, 396, 409, 536, 540
causative/inchoative alternation, 107, 108, 112, 706
c-command, 491, 705, 709
chaos theory, 623
character-based script, *see* script
chat, 208, 292, 293, 297, 299, 301, 303, 306, 309, 791
child-directed speech (baby talk, motherese, parentese), 141
child L2 acquisition, 2, 315, 318, 321, 339–46, 349, 352
Child Language Data Exchange System (CHILDES), 80, 90, 143, 308, 706
Chinese, 28, 32, 74, 77, 99, 100, 102, 111, 112, 174, 182, 188, 191, 203, 241, 277, 280, 281, 283, 287, 288, 293, 308, 324, 333, 344, 357, 364, 384, 401, 404, 409, 410, 424, 479, 491–92, 495, 499, 507, 509, 515, 516, 523–24, 525–26, 531, 542, 588, 618, 676, 680, 681, 684, 686, 718
Chomsky, Noam, 9, 11, 12–14, 16–22, 25, 32, 33, 36, 37, 38, 40, 44, 53, 66, 73, 79, 80, 98, 104, 141, 142, 149, 158, 251, 341, 381, 482, 491, 500, 505–7, 512, 516, 526, 567, 568, 584, 585, 587, 591, 594, 597, 670, 671, 672, 679, 700, 706, 707, 709, 711, 716, 719, 721, 723, 732, 734
Chomskyan revolution, 7
Clahsen, Harald, 34, 76, 77, 83, 106, 137, 187–88, 194, 195, 320, 326, 328–30, 340, 342, 344, 401, 405, 413–14, 480, 583, 592–97, 598, 602, 621, 689–91, 748
clarification request, 213, 218
clitics, 58, 108, 340, 343, 344, 369, 501, 502–3, 505, 507, 511, 516, 519–21, 687, 706, 711
coarticulation, 537
code switching (code mixing), 208, 316, 378, 381, 706
cognates, 295, 395, 398
cognitive processes (mental processes), 71, 83, 202, 214, 224, 229, 252, 268, 270, 394, 612, 649, 650, 661
cognitivism, 61
collaborative tasks, 225, 228, 653
Common European Framework of Reference for Languages (CEFR), 308, 374, 446–47, 448, 603, 604, 707

Communicative Orientation of Language Teaching (COLT), 84
community of practice, 233, 234, 260, 285, 291
comparative fallacy, 321, 391, 392, 582, 591, 675
competence
　communicative, 256, 297, 376, 377, 379, 429, 482, 483, 504, 603, 731
　linguistic, 34, 55, 77, 80, 125, 126, 132, 244, 246, 278, 293, 316, 321, 376, 381, 411, 440, 482, 483, 603, 734
　pragmatic, 174, 440, 482, 483, 485, 490, 603
competence/performance, 55, 61, 66, 80, 482, 674, 691
competencies, 122
Competition Model, 132, 708
comprehensible input, 207, 211–12, 214, 296, 312, 428, 629, 708, 722
comprehension/production, 80, 95, 124–26, 128, 329, 367, 406, 482, 577, 645, 707, 727
comprehension check, 212, 213, 215, 633
Computer-Mediated Communication (CMC), 229, 293–98, 300, 665, 700
Computer-assisted Language Learning (CALL), 294–95, 296, 311, 765
Computer-Mediated Communication for Language Learning (CMCL), 208, 294, 295, 297–99, 301–7, 311, 312
concordance, 309–10, 708
condition–action pair, 116, 121
confirmation check, 212, 226
connectionism, viii, 7, 61, 605
constituent (continuous/discontinuous), 116, 150, 153, 154, 462, 476–78, 549, 615, 703, 705, 714, 719, 722, 729
Constraint Hierarchy, 18, 54, 56, 73, 75, 76, 79, 84, 87, 106, 109, 116, 243, 252, 261, 275, 280, 292, 297, 302, 325, 332, 370, 384, 406, 408, 411, 440, 445, 463, 467, 472, 476, 483, 491, 493, 527, 528, 530, 531, 541, 543, 551, 552, 564, 571, 594, 597, 602, 611, 615, 620, 627, 639, 672, 673, 678–86, 691, 701, 703, 705, 706, 716, 720, 734, 735
construal, 15–16, 606, 607, 608, 708
construct validity, 171
construction grammar, 708
constructivism, 61, 708
consummatory reward, 425, 426, 435
Context and Language Integrated Learning (CLIL), 228, 229, 375, 376
Contextual Constraint Principle, 639
Contrastive Analysis (Hypothesis), 75, 95, 97–98, 529, 530, 708, 756
control theory, 105
conversation
　analysis, 84, 88, 90, 208, 254, 256, 258, 264, 270, 285, 295, 299, 483, 728, 800
　conversational: turn, 306, 484; implicature, 483, 486, 487, 488, 490, 709
　conversation: synchronous/asynchronous, 292–94, 297, 301, 302, 664, 665, 732
Cook, Vivian, 49, 178, 247, 373, 379, 392, 590
Corder, Stephen Pit, 37, 98, 276, 278, 450, 628
corpus (corpora), 37, 80, 99, 141, 151, 208, 263, 292, 294, 308–12, 326, 387, 445, 447, 455, 456, 498, 542, 546, 611, 614, 655, 699, 708
corrective feedback, 86, 181, 188–92, 200, 201, 224, 227, 658, 660
cortical arousal, 170

Creative Construction, 32, 42, 611
critical discourse, 258, 709
Critical Period, 54, 74, 315, 317-20, 322, 325, 330, 332, 334, 337, 352, 367, 390, 404, 408, 413, 450, 478, 507, 578, 674, 678, 679
Critical Period Hypothesis, 282, 675
Crosslinguistic Influence (CLI), 281, 376, 380, 382, 383, 388-90, 399, 411
cross over effects, 709, 735
cross-sectional studies, 710
crosstabs, 710
cultural capital, 29, 163, 245, 298
cultural historical psychology, 648
Cumulative Enhancement Model, 386-87
Czech, 31, 308, 544, 547

Dante Alighieri, 29
data-driven learning, 151, 309, 311
de Bot, Kees, 166, 220, 372, 380-81, 385, 396, 398, 581, 623
de Villiers, Jill, 587, 588
declarative/procedural knowledge, 41, 95, 117-21, 124, 125-27, 128, 133, 134-36, 200, 220, 331, 332, 414-15, 434, 448, 458, 698, 710, 727
declarative sentence, 142, 462
decoding, 114, 116, 168, 196, 304, 335, 382, 504
deficits, grammatical, 315, 319, 324
definiteness/indefiniteness, 102, 440, 481, 482, 483, 493-94, 495, 496, 526, 686, 704, 710, 718, 730
deixis, 440, 482-500
DeKeyser, Robert, xv, 61, 74, 100, 123-24, 133, 135, 220, 318, 320, 324, 326, 331, 335, 589, 613, 614, 674, 678, 685, 687, 717, 751, 752, 762, 786
Dekydtspotter, Laurent, 38, 52, 54, 137, 414, 439
deletion, 183, 188, 189, 273, 277, 279, 281, 525, 714, 733
demasking, 395
dependence, 331, 465, 472, 731
desire, 161-64
developmental problem, 581
developmental selection, 418, 421
Dewaele, Jean-Marc, 50, 62, 65, 66, 67, 69, 96, 123, 130, 276, 279, 283, 378, 379, 500
dialogically, 666
dictogloss, 226, 228
Differential Object Marking (DOM), 362, 365, 710
discourse, i, 48, 56, 57, 59, 80, 81, 88, 98, 122, 153, 156, 157, 176, 207, 208, 211, 231-32, 233, 236, 240, 244, 245, 247, 259, 265, 272, 274, 275, 285, 288, 289, 295, 299, 302, 303, 307, 310, 312, 316, 325, 345, 349, 361, 362, 363, 364, 376, 384, 399, 429, 434, 440, 464, 465, 474, 481-83, 491, 493, 494, 496, 498, 500-3, 594, 611, 628, 632, 633, 645, 646, 648, 653, 654, 658, 688, 689, 691, 698, 703, 709, 710-11, 715, 717, 718, 724, 726, 728
Distributed Morphology, 440, 508, 521, 523, 711
distributional contingency, 711
domain specificity, 324, 350, 467, 472, 478, 479, 481, 482
dominant language, 711
Donzelli, Giovanna, 439, 441, 449, 455
dopamine, 170, 425, 426, 427

Dörnyei, Zoltán, 50, 59, 60, 63, 89, 159, 160-63, 165, 167, 226, 227, 294, 309, 320, 332, 422-24, 429, 434, 488
Dulay, Heidi, 32, 37, 42, 74, 99, 102, 103, 339, 341, 508, 587-89
Dutch, 101, 111, 112, 168, 172, 188, 197, 198-99, 279, 283, 308, 321, 324, 330, 333, 340, 348, 349, 375, 382, 385, 395, 396, 397, 399-400, 412, 498, 503, 522, 534, 535, 536, 541, 542, 551, 593, 594, 598, 683, 686, 690, 700, 712
Dynamic Assessment (DA), 295, 299, 651, 658, 659
Dynamic Systems, 207, 381

ecology, 711
efficiency-driven parser, 565, 566
Egyptian, 243
E-language/I-language, 20, 711
electronic interaction, 292, 293, 294
elicited imitation task, 193
Ellis, Nick, 60, 61, 133
Ellis, Rod, 32, 37, 50, 51, 87, 90, 134, 200, 218, 224, 225, 451, 454, 590, 603, 658, 756
email, 208, 292, 293, 298, 301, 304, 306, 523, 664, 665, 704, 724
emergentism, 39, 61, 566
emic/etic, 164, 236, 252, 254, 255, 258, 712
Emonds, Joseph, 16, 158
empiricism, 9, 39, 712
English as a foreign language (EFL), 172, 216-26, 228, 308, 311, 376, 448, 449, 488, 642, 654
English as a lingua franca (ELF), 173, 297, 378
English as a second language (ESL), 196, 197, 216, 217, 221, 222, 226, 228, 242, 245, 246, 263, 268, 302, 431, 448, 488, 493, 603, 640, 657, 737
Ensslin, Astrid, 664
epistemology, 36, 138, 391, 708
equivalence classification, 530, 545, 551
errors, 98, 99
essentialism, 241, 284, 285, 291, 712, 717, 726, 733
ethnography, 72, 84, 87-89, 234, 236, 239-43, 245, 251, 254, 256, 264, 270, 275, 276, 284, 285, 290, 291, 307, 707, 712, 713, 728
Eurocentres Vocabulary Size Test, 447, 713
European Science Foundation (ESF), 77, 80, 187, 498, 519, 593-95, 712
Event Probabilities Principle, 639
event-related potentials (ERP), 82, 83, 127, 328, 329, 333, 403, 405, 407, 408, 412-14, 540, 552, 713, 719
executive control, 167, 713
experiential selection, 418, 419, 421
explanandum, 254, 271
explicit knowledge, 40, 83, 125, 128, 133, 134, 135, 136, 334, 577, 721
Extended Projection Principle (EPP), 506, 507, 713, 714
extensive reading, 455, 460, 713
eye-tracking (recording of eye movement), 82, 398, 402, 403, 411, 414, 415, 533, 552, 646, 713

failure-driven learning (parsing breakdown), 569
Farsi, 281, 342, 368
feature selection, 527
Feature Reassembly Hypothesis, 507, 525-27, 679
features

±Q, 684
±Topic Shift, 689
  formal, 109, 113, 506-8, 515, 527-28, 641, 688
  functional, 514, 515, 517, 679, 691
  interpretable, 506, 515, 527, 688, 714
  selection, 507, 679
  uninterpretable, 506, 507, 515, 527, 528, 682, 714
feedback, 210, 214, 221, 222-24, 227
filler-gap dependencies, 329
finiteness, 347, 348, 349, 350, 510, 516, 518-21, 594, 686, 714, 732, 735
  finite verb, 148, 153, 348, 350, 510, 512, 513, 514, 516, 520-21, 711, 715, 724, 732, 735
  non-finite verb (infinitive), 509, 511, 513, 520, 521, 593, 711, 715, 724, 735
Finnish, 308, 536, 537, 547
first language, 28, 30, 38, 41, 50, 51, 53, 54, 60, 73, 74, 78, 97, 100, 104, 116, 132, 133, 137, 160, 225, 305, 315, 317, 319, 336, 346, 347, 353, 355, 363, 377, 379, 383, 391, 444, 578, 579, 582, 598, 605, 611-17, 622, 623, 706
First Noun Principle, 639, 644
Firth, Alan, 35, 42, 43, 44, 51, 57, 64, 69, 72, 90, 207, 208, 235, 236, 252, 253, 255, 697, 715
Firthian linguistics, 259
fixed sequences, developmental, 49, 69, 346
Flege, James, 109, 112, 282, 318, 320, 322, 360, 530, 533-36, 538, 542, 545, 576, 578, 712
Fluctuation Hypothesis, 340, 344, 494, 495, 496
fluency tasks (semantic fluency, verbal fluency), 166, 184, 185
Flynn, Suzanne, 340, 341, 386, 614
focus, 483, 498, 500, 501-3
foreign language anxiety, 96, 170, 178
foreigner talk, 211, 715
form-meaning connections, 451, 628, 635, 644, 645, 654
fossilization, 76, 121, 321, 338, 345, 673, 675, 676, 685-87, 691
Foucart, Alice, 316, 328, 329, 331
French, 33, 35, 36, 38, 43, 52, 58, 63, 66, 77, 80, 82, 101, 105, 164, 168, 171-75, 189, 208, 211, 217, 223, 225, 259, 273, 277, 279, 281, 283, 287, 288, 290, 293, 308, 317, 324, 327-29, 332, 333, 340, 343, 344, 345, 348, 350, 354, 367, 375, 379, 382, 386, 387, 389, 390, 395, 396, 398, 399, 400, 402, 404, 407, 412, 422, 424, 430, 439, 440, 448, 449, 450, 461, 462, 463, 467, 468, 469, 470, 498, 499, 509, 510, 511-13, 514, 518-22, 532-38, 540, 544-48, 565, 569, 570, 587, 593, 598, 617, 639, 641, 642, 644, 654, 666, 676, 683, 703, 706, 712, 715, 718
Frenck-Mestre, Cheryl, 327, 328, 690
frequency, 38, 61, 63, 74, 80, 84, 100, 101, 132, 136, 156, 178, 223, 301, 322, 327, 334, 357, 378, 402, 412, 449, 451, 452, 454, 460, 533, 546, 583, 589, 606, 613-14, 618, 620-22, 633, 638, 639, 642, 646, 676, 710, 715, 720, 729, 737
Frisian, 376
Full Access Model, 105, 506
Full Transfer / Full Access (FT/FA), 34, 42, 105, 341, 475, 506, 596, 601, 702
functional categories, 315, 346, 506, 521, 563, 585, 595

morphemes, 13, 31, 54, 74, 99, 102, 108, 140, 188, 194, 195, 201, 283, 339, 350-51, 415, 471, 475, 480, 481, 509, 510, 518, 519, 521, 523-25, 528, 542, 564, 584, 586-87, 588, 589, 591, 599, 601, 613, 679, 687, 688, 706, 708, 715, 721, 722, 724, 732
  order of acquisition, 37, 99, 100, 102, 387, 587, 589, 598
  projections, 20, 341, 342, 345-47, 584-91, 596-99, 601, 735
Functional Grammar, 608
functional Magnetic Resonance Imaging (fMRI), 82, 403, 408, 409-11, 413, 715
functionalism, 258, 715

García Mayo, María del Pilar, 385, 387, 495, 508
Gass, Susan, 27, 32, 50, 67, 98, 100, 111, 201, 210, 211, 212, 214, 215, 219, 222, 224, 226, 227, 281, 297, 303, 428, 629, 630, 641, 642
gate-keeping, 258, 261, 262, 263, 264, 716
GB, see Principles and Parameters
gender, grammatical, 58, 334, 636
general genetic law of cultural development, 650, 651
generative grammar, 10, 12, 31, 34, 35, 37, 42, 137, 138, 149, 596, 672, 675, 679, 719
generic interpretation, 465, 471
Genesee, Fred, 81, 98, 319, 340, 348, 354, 375, 680
genetic method, 649
genetics, 417, 419
Georgian, 139, 140, 141
German, 9, 35, 52, 76, 103, 109, 152-57, 168, 171, 172, 208, 264, 283, 308-10, 322, 324, 329, 330, 333, 340, 343, 345, 356, 382, 385, 387-91, 401, 405-7, 410, 443, 498, 499, 503, 509, 510, 513, 514, 519, 520, 522, 536, 541, 543, 545, 582-85, 588, 589-601, 602, 603, 611, 621, 683, 687, 691, 715
global impairment, 732
globalization, 239, 284, 374
Government and Binding, see Principles and Parameters
grammatical architecture, 463-65, 469, 478, 691
grammaticality judgment task (GJT), 77, 78, 369, 403, 503
grammaticalization, 265, 328
grapheme-phoneme correspondence, 191, 197, 199, 200, 390, 716
Greek, 29, 30, 40, 41, 103, 164, 243, 340, 344, 368, 401, 457, 503, 515, 534, 551, 609, 687
Gregg, Kevin, 47, 59, 132, 214, 254, 563, 580, 581, 582, 584, 588, 591, 625, 670
grey matter / white matter, 166, 186
Grosjean, François, 320, 327, 328, 377, 398

Halliday, M. A. K., 35, 55, 259, 716, 764
Hawkins, Roger, 49, 50, 52, 55, 57, 58, 60, 77, 123, 137, 320, 340, 388, 480, 508, 514, 515, 523, 524, 560, 584, 589-90, 597, 602, 673-74, 679, 680, 681-82
Haznedar, Belma, 77, 509-18
Hebrew, 101, 164, 191, 375
heritage language speakers, 359, 362, 364, 369, 670
hermeneutic, 254, 255, 269, 716
Herschensohn, Julia, 50, 58, 137, 402, 407, 413, 415, 521, 674, 683, 767, 789, 797
heterosyllabic, 540

Hindi, 354, 357, 368, 532
Hmong, 268, 359
Hokkien, 523, 676
Holme, Randal, 38
Homo sapiens sapiens, 139, 716
Hopp, Holger, 55, 56, 112, 154-57, 327, 329-32, 334, 413, 414, 415, 503, 677, 683, 686, 687, 690, 691
Hungarian, 281, 335, 390, 543, 544, 545, 547
hybrid/hybridity, 66, 207, 208, 230, 232, 238, 241, 243, 248, 250, 585, 710, 717
hypothesis formulation, 219

identity, 230-38, 241, 242-50, 252, 255, 260, 263, 265, 269, 271, 278, 285-90
  gendered, 231, 233, 241-44
  heritage language, 231, 236-39, 249
  multilingual, 239, 241
  non-native teacher, 208, 246, 247
  racialized, 195, 231, 233, 244, 245, 606, 607, 615-17
i-learning, 570, 571
image schema, 616, 620
immigrants, 180, 187, 189, 190, 198, 240, 243, 262, 263, 268, 287, 288, 317, 322, 324, 356-59, 363, 594, 599, 634, 705, 716
implicit knowledge, 95, 114, 125, 132, 134-36, 171, 319, 332, 334, 716, 721
incidental recast, 658
incomplete acquisition, 355, 784, 793
induction, 36, 116, 119, 462, 561, 565, 570, 746
inflectional morphology, 75, 99, 348, 349, 351, 361, 369, 405, 509, 517, 519, 525, 528, 583, 602, 673, 685, 686, 687
Information Structure, 11, 13, 14, 16, 365, 440, 500, 543, 593, 594, 688, 698
initial state, *see* Full Transfer / Full Access
inner speech, 68, 650, 661, 717
innervation, 170
input, 13, 15, 28, 38, 46, 49, 50-52, 56, 61, 63, 65, 66, 67, 69, 74, 76, 77, 81, 84, 96, 102, 114, 115, 138-44, 145-49, 156, 158, 179, 186, 195, 196, 198, 200-2, 207-18, 220, 221, 224, 226, 227, 229, 236, 252, 264, 279, 280, 284, 287, 288, 292, 294, 296, 297, 301, 310, 311, 316, 319, 320, 321, 323, 325, 326, 330, 334, 336, 346, 357, 360, 364, 366, 367, 368, 369, 370, 407, 426, 428, 439, 440, 442, 449-51, 454, 455-57, 460-62, 465, 469, 472, 473, 479-81, 488, 493, 494, 503, 531, 533, 537, 541, 542, 545-47, 552, 553, 563, 565-66, 568-71, 573-78, 582, 584, 587, 589, 593, 595, 602, 605, 613, 614, 618, 620, 621, 623, 625, 627-47, 673, 675, 677, 680, 698, 708, 710, 712, 714, 717, 718, 720, 722, 723, 734
  enhanced, 201, 214
  modified, 214-17
  structured, 214, 635, 636, 643-47, 692
input enhancement
  acoustically varied, 634, 635
  flood, 642, 644
  interactional/non-interactional, 634
Input Hypothesis (Krashen's i + 1), 211, 214, 296, 297, 628, 708
Input Processing, 451, 627-31, 636-47, 808
intake, 200, 215, 218, 252, 296, 451, 628, 630, 641, 644, 645, 723, 724
integration, 284

interaction, conversational, 209, 210, 211, 214, 220, 222-29, 723
interactional modifications, 207, 212, 215, 221, 223, 707
Interface Hypothesis, 483, 500, 677, 688, 689
interface vulnerability, 345, 718
International English Language Teaching System (IELTS), 76, 172, 448
Interpretability Hypothesis, 320, 514, 679, 806
interpretation task, 363, 718
interrogatives, 142, 143, 144, 150, 462, 476, 478, 479
intonation, 157, 195, 298, 389, 440, 534, 542, 543, 550-52, 590, 596, 659, 718, 733
Inuktitut, 354, 367
investment, 161, 163-65, 235, 245, 289, 377, 782, 787, 801
Ionin, Tania, 338, 340, 343, 344, 348, 349, 350, 365, 369, 476, 481, 493-96
Irish, 277, 279, 281, 283, 287-89, 354, 358, 359, 368, 699
islands, *see wh*-movement, subjacency
Italian, 103, 224, 282, 287, 289, 308, 333, 340, 343, 345, 348, 362, 363, 386, 390, 399, 406, 409, 439, 442, 443, 463-67, 490, 501-22, 544, 592, 597, 639, 689, 703, 717

Jackendoff, Ray, 15, 18, 54, 115, 470, 500, 567-69, 570, 571, 580
Japanese, 41, 66, 78, 99, 100, 102, 104, 110, 157, 158, 162, 167, 173, 174, 216, 219, 220, 223, 225, 226, 237, 243, 282, 293, 308, 323, 333, 335, 342, 344, 389, 401, 405, 407, 409-11, 439, 471-75, 478, 479, 488, 489, 498, 499, 515, 524, 531, 533, 534, 537, 538, 539, 540, 543-45, 550, 551, 561, 562-63, 574, 576, 578-80, 590, 614, 625, 655, 656, 658, 661, 662, 664, 680-84, 699, 701, 725
jigsaw task, 225

Kasper, Gabriele, 65, 67, 229, 482-85
Klein, Wolfgang, 55, 56, 77, 106, 256, 265, 386, 387, 484, 496-98, 500, 593, 594, 705, 753, 773
Korean, 76, 77, 78, 99, 112, 242, 293, 324, 332, 333, 342, 344, 357, 360-64, 390, 410, 439, 476-79, 489, 491, 493, 495, 499, 526, 532, 536, 538, 539, 541, 545, 548, 549, 597, 631, 680, 683-84
Koster, Jan, 697
Krashen, Stephen, 32, 99, 102, 126, 132, 165, 202, 211, 214, 217, 294, 296, 297, 428, 508, 588, 592, 593, 628, 629, 708, 722, 723
Krummes, Cedric, 664
Kubota, Ryuko, 409, 649

L1, *see* first language
L1 acquisition, 41, 60, 83, 88, 90, 102, 105, 106, 147, 150, 339, 340, 341, 342, 345, 348, 349, 351, 353, 355, 357, 366, 371, 385, 414, 535, 581, 582, 601, 671, 672, 678, 689, 699, 717
L1 influence, *see* transfer
L2 Motivational Self, 423
Ladin, 376
Lado, Robert, 1, 30-32, 34, 42, 75, 98, 332, 338, 378, 529, 581
language acquisition device (LAD), 15, 25, 565, 569-71, 719
language faculty, *see* Universal Grammar

language shift, 358
language-related episodes (LRE), 221, 654
languaging, 666, 719, 773
Lao, 243
Lardiere, Donna, 109, 340, 342, 346–49, 440, 476, 480, 481, 507, 508–9, 515–18, 521–24, 526, 527, 528, 596
Larsen-Freeman, Diane, 32, 60, 207, 253, 380, 381, 434, 508, 613, 623
latency, 403–5, 408, 713, 719, 720
Latin, 26, 29, 30, 36, 40, 41, 164, 317, 354, 365, 499
Latino, 263
learnability, 61, 147, 157, 464, 465, 467, 468, 527, 682, 700
Left Anterior Negativity (LAN), 127, 404–6, 413
left dislocation, 369, 719
lemma, 111, 119, 384, 443–45, 447–49, 810
length of residence (LoR), 91, 322, 325, 382, 682, 719
Levelt, Willem, 95, 111, 114, 117–20, 443, 595
lexeme, 384, 719
Lexical Functional Grammar, 18, 60, 567, 595
Lexical Semantics Principle, 639
lexis, 31, 38, 48, 50, 81, 117, 298, 301, 448, 451, 456, 459, 608–12, 615, 624, 628, 640, 708
light verb, 563, 719, 720
Linguistics and Language Behavior Abstracts (LLBA), 496
literacy
   illiterate, 181, 198
   low-literate, 195, 196, 198, 223, 263, 603
   non-literate, 96, 181–89, 197, 198, 199, 201, 202, 291
local impairment, 514, 732
locality, 491, 492
logical problem of language acquisition, *see* poverty of the stimulus
long-distance dependencies, 413
Long, Michael, 83
longitudinal studies, 77, 181, 187, 275, 277, 341, 356, 371, 407, 414, 589, 646, 653
Low-Educated Second Language and Literacy – for Adults (LESLLA), 196, 198, 199, 268, 719
Luxembourg, 300, 373

Mackey, Alison, 50, 65, 67, 69, 131, 133, 201, 209–11, 214, 216, 222–24, 227
magneto-encephalography (MEG), 403, 408, 409, 411, 720
majority languages, 354, 374
Malagasy, 364
Malay, 241
Mandarin, 110, 221, 241, 357, 364, 499, 523, 524, 525, 531, 536, 542, 544–45, 548, 549–51, 676, 683, 684, 778, 806, 810
markedness, 529, 530, 533, 538–40, 542
maturation, 315, 316, 317–33, 345, 346, 488, 597, 698, 709
mean length of run, 123, 720, 732
mean length of utterance (MLU), 351, 586, 721
Meisel, Jürgen, 137, 187–88, 276, 283, 317, 319, 338, 344, 346, 348, 480, 498, 520, 583, 590, 592, 595
memory, 8, 24, 36, 61, 114, 115, 117, 120, 124, 126, 127, 129, 131, 167, 170, 179, 331, 335, 410, 459, 541, 567, 569, 571, 603, 622, 647, 702, 726
   long-term, 62, 114, 128, 129, 130, 571–73

short-term, 160, 166, 185, 194, 500
working, 39, 59, 62, 95, 114, 115, 120, 128–31, 135, 136, 160, 167, 168, 170, 172, 181, 185, 571, 573, 661, 691, 704, 707, 713, 735
Merge, 17, 19, 20–22, 721
meta-analysis, 85–86, 100, 133, 210, 224, 485, 643
metalinguistic awareness, 46, 53, 126, 134, 181, 189, 190, 193, 197–201, 219, 223, 227, 297, 307, 334, 373, 392, 490, 576–79, 653, 654, 664, 666, 721, 772, 775
Mexican, 241, 245, 367
microgenesis, 65, 68, 653
migrants, *see* immigrants
miking, 662
Miller, Elizabeth, 208, 649
Minimal Trees Hypothesis, 35, 106
Minimalist Program, 16–21, 104, 150, 506, 526, 567, 585, 597, 672, 713, 714, 721
minority languages, 240, 316, 353, 354, 358, 359, 367, 368, 374, 377, 378
Missing Surface Inflection Hypothesis (MSIH), 388, 515, 711
Modern Language Aptitude Test (MLAT), 167
Modular On-line Growth and Use of Language (MOGUL) framework, 707
modularity, 97, 113, 115, 569, 721
modulated structure building, 597, 698
Monitor Model, 628, 722
Montrul, Silvina, 106–9, 112, 208, 316, 318, 319, 334, 336, 387, 388, 470, 471, 516, 526–28, 689
Moroccan, 197, 266, 349, 382, 390, 519, 522
morpheme order studies, 74, 508, 582, 588, 598
morphological variability, 315, 340, 341, 347, 349
morphology, 31, 38, 48, 54, 56, 75, 98, 102, 106–9, 111, 194, 197, 217, 225, 298, 316, 325, 334, 345, 347–51, 356, 364, 370, 440, 443, 448, 464, 469, 470–72, 479, 480, 499, 507–9, 514–19, 520, 521, 523, 525, 528, 594–98, 602, 603, 622, 628, 631, 670, 683–88, 691, 703, 704, 712, 715, 716, 724
morphosyntax, 32, 37, 49, 52, 54, 57, 73, 95, 96, 105, 107, 109, 217, 315, 319, 320–22, 325, 326, 337, 349, 350, 359–61, 440, 462, 465, 467, 472, 478, 480, 505, 507–9, 514, 515, 523, 525, 528, 581, 593, 602, 603, 628, 631, 636
motivation, 39, 50, 59, 60, 63, 87–91, 96, 149, 160–65, 176, 179, 226, 230, 235, 237, 294, 295, 298, 302, 316, 318, 321, 322, 323, 336, 377, 379, 417, 421–25, 429, 433–35, 458, 459, 676, 677, 678, 718, 722
movement rules, 16, 461, 722, 731
Multidimensional Model, 595
multilingualism, 51, 57, 89, 231, 239–41, 259, 269, 273, 286, 293, 316, 373–87, 391, 392, 722, 739, 741, 747, 751, 753, 759, 764, 766, 774, 779, 790, 803, 810
Myles, Florence, 28, 256, 272, 276, 338, 451, 590, 593, 611

N400, 127, 327, 328, 404, 405, 407, 408, 412, 415
native language influence, *see* transfer
Native Language Literacy Screening Device, 191, 722
nativelikeness, 90, 325, 672, 674–76, 678, 690, 691
nativism, 150, 723
natural analogical extension, 144, 155, 723
natural language, 12, 21, 24, 33, 124, 129, 137, 143, 146, 149, 406, 461, 592, 723, 734

naturalistic learning, 8, 51, 55, 80, 89, 90, 140, 208, 251, 252, 261–63, 265, 270, 278–80, 283, 291, 323, 325, 326, 331, 338, 340, 344, 351, 359, 367, 369, 377, 392, 451, 498, 509, 581, 585, 592, 595, 597, 598, 634, 635, 712
nature/nurture, 9, 165, 712
ne deletion (French), 273, 277, 279, 281
negation, 52, 80, 103, 201, 265, 277, 333, 339, 385, 489, 507, 510–12, 516, 518, 520–22, 561–64, 582, 585, 588, 589–91, 597, 598, 601, 715, 723, 730, 735
negative/positive evidence, 132, 138, 143, 145, 147, 150, 151, 217, 472, 682, 685, 723, 725
negotiation, 50, 85, 207, 209–15, 228, 253, 286, 298, 634
netiquette, 293, 723
neural networks, 63, 327, 330, 331, 337, 419, 620
neurobiology, 9, 23, 64, 417–35
neuroimaging methodology, 403, 408, 409, 646
neurophysiology, 115, 126, 127, 375, 416
Next-Turn-Repair Initiation (NTRI), 659
Nigerian, 546
norms, 485
Norton, Bonnie, 51, 64, 67, 163, 230–31, 233–35, 241, 243, 249, 255, 260, 261, 263, 267, 282, 288
Norwegian, 308, 348, 590
Noticing Hypothesis, 200, 201, 202, 218, 457, 485, 723, 724
null subjects, 33, 76, 103–5, 342, 347, 363, 364, 386, 501, 505, 584, 592, 597, 689, 716, 724

object-regulation, 724, 729, 730
offset, 319, 320, 337, 481, 709
O'Grady, William, 61, 63, 364, 381, 561, 565–67, 580, 630–31, 723
Ohta, Amy, 41–43, 65, 67, 69, 208, 223, 225
ontology, 724
opiates, 425, 426, 427
Optimality theory (OT), 109, 390, 530, 531, 542, 550, 553
optional infinitives, 342, 343, 348, 766
oral production data, 74, 80, 590, 593
order of acquisition of functional morphemes, *see* morpheme order studies
Organic Grammar, 3, 106, 196
Osterhout, Lee, 326–28, 331, 332, 406–8, 413, 414, 415
other, *see* alter
other-regulation, 650, 724, 729
output, 8, 37, 49, 50, 55, 65, 67, 69, 84, 115, 131, 142, 207, 209, 210, 213, 214, 216–27, 294, 296–97, 309, 396, 420, 451, 620, 623, 629, 630, 636, 645, 647, 675, 723, 724, 734

P600, 127, 128, 327, 328, 333, 403–7, 413, 415, 719
Paradis, Johanne, 98, 340, 344, 348–51, 354, 495, 542
Paradis, Michel, 95, 125, 131, 331, 408
parameters, 439, 673, 676
parsing, 81, 82, 117, 329, 400, 401, 565, 569–71, 580, 630, 674, 689, 690
perceived fluency, 325
perceptual assimilation, 530, 724
Perdue, Clive, 55, 56, 106, 187, 256, 264, 265, 498, 519, 593, 594, 705
perfectionism, 160, 170, 178

performativity, 208, 233, 245, 285, 286, 725, 726
personality traits, 96, 160, 161, 169, 174, 429
phonation/time ratio, 123, 725, 732
phoneme, 31, 54, 110, 140, 180–86, 191, 196–201, 336, 390, 396, 440, 530–35, 538, 542, 547, 551, 561, 578, 613, 703, 716, 725
phoneme deletion, 183
phoneme reversal, 183
phonological awareness, 168, 181, 182, 195, 196, 197, 198, 725
phonological development, 572
phonology, 17, 31, 38, 48, 54, 56, 57, 73, 95, 98, 107, 109–12, 118, 133, 166, 184, 197, 315, 316, 318, 320, 321–26, 330, 333, 336–37, 360, 381, 388–90, 391, 440, 500, 523, 531–53, 562, 567, 569, 570, 571, 581, 603, 628, 646, 670, 673, 688, 691, 716, 727
phonotactics, 440, 534, 539, 540, 542, 725
Piaget, Jean, 25, 583, 584, 708
Pienemann, Manfred, 50, 59–63, 124, 187–88, 190, 216, 443, 565, 579, 583, 592–96, 602, 606, 615, 624, 727
pitch accent, 534, 542, 545, 546, 549, 550, 725
polarity, 141–43, 403, 478, 684, 691, 704, 713, 725
Polish, 167, 242, 287–90, 308, 322, 384, 389, 390, 495, 534, 543, 544, 545, 547–49, 622
Portuguese, 100, 164, 165, 181–86, 240, 293, 366, 367, 387, 471, 519, 534, 536, 542, 551, 592
positivism, 254, 725, 726
positron emission tomography (PET), 186, 408, 409, 411, 725
postmodernism, 163, 164, 230–33, 240, 248, 249, 259, 709, 726, 733
poverty of the stimulus (POS), 79, 96, 137–58, 211, 439, 462, 481, 671, 682, 683, 699, 716
power, 230–34, 236, 241, 244, 245, 249, 251, 254, 259, 260, 262–64, 270, 271
pro-drop, *see* null subjects
Praat (software program), 125
praxis, 653, 726
prefix, 140–41, 443, 475, 703, 726
presupposition, 11, 30, 482, 494, 726
priming effects, 64, 82, 222, 399, 400, 404, 573, 726
primitive, 568, 571, 579, 726
Principles and Parameters, 14, 18, 79, 150, 505, 527, 591, 716
private speech, 41, 67, 225, 650, 658, 662, 717, 727
proceduralization, 95, 119, 121, 123, 124, 126, 332, 704, 727
Processability theory, 60, 61, 62, 188, 443, 565, 595, 602, 615, 624, 727
processing, 28, 39, 43, 46, 48–52, 54–64, 69, 79–83, 88, 96, 108, 112, 114, 116, 118, 119, 125, 126, 127, 131, 132, 133, 135, 136, 167, 172, 179, 180, 181, 183–88, 191, 192–97, 199, 200, 202, 217, 220, 227, 228, 252, 253, 264, 277, 295, 307, 315, 316, 318–21, 326, 328–32, 335, 337, 363, 372, 373, 381–82, 384, 394, 396–415, 417, 424, 426, 439, 443, 457, 458, 459, 463, 469, 474, 480–81, 488–90, 502, 503, 521, 525, 533, 535, 540, 547, 552, 561, 563–69, 571–80, 595, 602, 606, 613, 614, 618, 619, 620, 628–32, 636–40, 643–47, 649, 650, 668, 674, 678, 685, 687, 689–91, 693, 696, 700, 702, 705, 707, 708, 713, 714, 718, 720, 721–23, 724, 726, 727
bottom-up, 705

semantic, 185, 188, 192, 194, 195, 328, 403, 404, 408–10, 412, 413, 415, 640, 641, 721
top-down, 733
pro-drop, *see* null subjects
prompt, 193, 297, 307, 590, 602, 629, 659, 663, 712, 727, 728, 734
property theory/transition theory, 47, 54, 79, 563, 580, 584, 602
propositional content, 461
Prosodic Transfer Hypothesis, 110, 388, 493, 523, 524, 688, 691
prosody, 75, 110, 330, 336, 507, 534, 542, 546, 552, 657, 691, 727
Prototype Hypothesis, 280
pseudo-word, 182, 184, 186, 188, 728
Punjabi, 239

qualitative study, 163, 263, 728
quantification, 462–65, 474, 563, 728, 730
quantitative study, 67, 273, 485, 728
Quebec, 358, 367, 384, 532
queer theory, 244
questions, *see* interrogatives
quotative *like*, 289

rationalism, 19, 25, 712, 728
reaction time (RT), 64, 81–82, 124, 316, 321, 325–29, 337, 547, 636, 705, 728
real time, 80, 89, 125, 127, 303, 316, 568, 674, 727, 789
recasts, 67, 133, 192, 200, 223, 227, 728
recycling, 24, 25
reductionism, 22, 649, 728, 772
Regan, Vera, 65, 67, 69, 208, 252, 261
register, 210, 229
Regressive Transfer, 390
regulation, 41, 128, 419, 432, 650–52, 668, 724, 729, 730
  object, 650, 724, 729, 730
  other, 650, 724, 729
relativism, 254, 259, 729
remnant movement, 154–57, 729, 785
Representational Deficit Hypothesis, *see* syntactic deficit
resting levels of activation, 702, 729
restructuration, 608
Rizzi, Luigi, 18, 340, 348, 505, 516, 522, 585, 590, 597
role of L1, *see* transfer
Romanian, 365
root infinitives, 348, 522, 724, 795, 799
Rothman, Jason, 56, 112, 316, 359, 364, 366, 367, 469, 471, 501, 502, 503
Russian, 28, 41, 235, 240, 293, 308, 330, 333, 342–43, 346, 347, 357, 360–64, 365, 368, 371, 390, 401, 405, 410, 475, 495, 503, 509, 516, 518, 536, 537, 541, 544, 593, 648, 657, 686, 690, 731

Saussure, Ferdinand de, 10, 21, 30, 66, 729
scaffolding, 65, 67, 68, 70, 133, 201, 257, 298, 301, 303, 660, 666, 668, 729
scalar implicature, 487–91
Schumann, John, 99, 230, 252, 255, 261, 278, 283, 298, 316, 331, 339, 346, 418, 421–27, 434, 677, 702
Schwartz, Bonnie D., 34, 38, 47, 56, 59, 61, 63, 98, 103, 105, 106, 117–21, 126, 321, 338, 340–44,

348, 349, 395, 398, 414, 415, 468, 475–78, 506, 515, 516, 569, 592, 593, 596, 601, 672, 678, 690
scope (wide, narrow), 157, 158, 729, 730
scrambling (German, Japanese), 153, 154–57, 329, 330, 340, 349, 681, 683, 687, 691
script, 191, 203, 720
  alphabetic, 180, 182–86, 189, 191, 203, 703, 716
  character, 191
Second Life, 250, 293, 296, 298, 301, 307
self-efficacy, 163, 177, 179
self-report, 88, 89
Selinker, Larry, 32, 37, 52, 98, 99, 100, 111, 252, 276, 339–40, 379, 581, 715
semantics, 3, 38, 48, 54–56, 184, 185, 320, 344, 345, 360, 367, 439, 461–81, 500, 527, 603, 639, 673, 679, 683, 715, 718, 730
semiotics, 794
sentence structure, 11, 167, 195, 430, 584, 590, 644, 734
Serbo-Croatian, 103
shadowing, 168
Shallow Structure Hypothesis, 316, 413, 690
Sharwood Smith, Michael, 9, 56, 214, 560, 561, 565, 567, 569, 571, 576, 580, 641, 642, 643
Singlish, 241
Skinner, B. F., 13, 22, 25, 32, 235, 697
Skype, 292, 303
Slabakova, Roumyana, 56, 76, 79, 137, 345, 388, 440, 464–67, 470–71, 475, 478, 480, 481, 482, 527, 682–86, 689, 691
slave system, 129
social engagement system, 417, 427, 432
socialization, 178, 208, 229, 235, 251–71, 379, 420
sociocultural theory, 44, 201, 208, 225, 235, 258, 296, 483, 648–53, 711, 719, 721, 729
sociodiscursive theory, 483
sociolinguistic variation, 67
Somali, 189, 190, 192, 195–98, 268, 599
sonority, 539, 546, 730
Sorace, Antonella, 54, 55, 56, 345, 362, 363, 483, 500, 501, 670, 677, 688, 689, 690
Spanish, 32–34, 56, 74, 76, 80, 99–105, 107–8, 112, 131, 168, 172, 191, 216, 225, 228, 240, 244, 263, 281, 282, 293, 300, 303, 308, 321–23, 324, 327–29, 332–34, 335, 339, 340, 345, 346, 348, 354–65, 367–69, 375, 379, 386–91, 396, 399, 401, 402, 405, 406, 409, 431, 439, 469–71, 485, 492, 495, 499, 502, 506–7, 515, 519, 522, 527, 534, 535, 536, 537, 543–50, 562, 588, 590, 592, 597, 617, 631, 636, 640, 644, 659, 691, 692, 693, 696, 716, 724
Specific Language Impairment (SLI), 347, 349, 730
specificity, 495
speech acts, 215, 259, 440, 482–86, 504
speech community, 13, 138, 148, 239, 274, 354, 611, 700, 723
speech production, 495
Sprouse, Rex, 34, 38, 52, 105, 106, 340, 341, 414, 415, 461, 463, 467–68, 474, 475, 506, 516, 596, 601, 672, 683, 690
stabilization, *see* fossilization
stage seepage, 584
Stimulus Appraisal, 316, 421–28, 431–33, 435
strategic competence, 122, 707, 731
stress (phonological), 158, 195, 390, 440, 525, 534, 537, 542–52, 564, 633, 731

Strong Continuity, 345, 347, 587, 596, 601
Stroop test, 382, 705, 731
structuralism, 10, 14, 15, 31, 34, 729, 731
structure building, 106, 586, 589, 597, 601, 602
structure dependent rule, 142
subdoxastic knowledge, 140, 149, 732
subjacency, *see wh*-movement
suffix, 140–41, 442, 443, 509, 520, 526, 703, 714, 717, 732
Suppliance in Obligatory Contexts (SOC), 517, 587, 686, 732
Surinam, 382
Swain, Merrill, 201, 210, 217–21, 223, 225, 227, 297, 429, 648, 652, 653–55, 658, 664, 665, 666, 707, 723, 724, 731
Swedish, 101, 308, 322, 324, 325, 335, 336, 382, 385, 390, 498, 537, 590, 593, 594, 712
Swiss German (Lucernese), 147–49
syllable, 129, 180, 182–84, 193, 196–98, 325, 330, 524, 525, 530, 538–52, 725, 731, 732
syllable coda, 540, 541
synchronous discourse, 292, 294, 297, 298, 300–3, 704
syntactic impairment, 440, 522, 528
  global, 732
  local, 514, 732
  representational deficit, 415, 674, 679, 681, 682, 688
syntax-semantics interface, 812

Tagalog, 357
Tarone, Elaine, 65, 67, 96, 208, 272, 276, 285, 297
temporal variable methodology, 124, 732
temporality, 499, 732, 753
tense, verbal, 18, 57, 174, 201, 279–81, 320, 333, 334, 340, 342, 345–51, 356, 357, 360, 362, 370, 371, 406, 443, 498, 499, 505–11, 512, 515–17, 519, 521, 523–27, 584–86, 595, 596–98, 638, 639, 640, 670, 683, 686, 688, 691, 711, 712, 714, 715, 732, 735
  agreement, 509, 517, 525, 686
  and aspect, 279, 371, 527, 596
  features, 57, 342
  morphology, 350–51, 499
  past, 86, 147, 194, 226, 277, 280, 283, 303, 347, 350, 351, 469–70, 499, 506, 507–10, 517, 526, 601, 618, 621, 638, 714, 715, 724, 725
  present, 139, 140, 510, 715
Test of English as a Foreign Language (TOEFL), 76, 111, 172, 448
Test of Spoken English, 191
text coverage, 447, 453, 733
Thai, 221, 499, 535, 540, 549, 550, 564, 750, 810
thematic verbs, 342, 343, 387, 510–13, 518, 733, 735
thetic construct, 267, 733
third language (L3) acquisition, 316, 372
third space, 232, 733
Thomas, Margaret, 138, 149, 492, 493
Tomasello, Michael, 17, 60, 61, 132, 415, 607, 611, 612
tone, phonemic, 534, 542–46, 548–51, 651, 656
topicalization, 153–56, 502, 594, 733
Towell, Richard, 50, 55, 60, 95, 168
transfer, 2, 33, 34, 52, 54, 58, 63, 73, 75, 82, 95, 98–113, 121, 160, 168, 191, 279–81, 302, 316, 334, 338, 341–45, 352, 356, 360, 364–66, 369, 372, 377, 380, 385–91, 392, 400, 401, 406–8, 410, 413, 416, 440, 473, 474, 483, 484, 487, 492, 493, 495, 503, 506, 508, 515, 517, 525, 526, 528, 529, 530, 535, 536, 539, 541, 544–47, 549, 552, 553, 581, 588, 598, 606, 616, 622, 640, 690, 698, 734
  lexicon, 101
  morphosyntax, 52, 58, 75, 101, 108, 334, 342, 344, 365, 515, 526, 598
  phonology, 389, 523
transition problem, 561, 572
transition theory, *see* property theory / transition theory
triggers, 54, 57, 108, 164, 213, 560, 584, 602
Truncation Hypothesis, 340
Truscott, John, 56, 108, 221
truth-value judgment (TVJ), 78, 466, 681
Tsimpli, Ianthi-Maria, 137, 320, 345, 493, 514, 515, 679, 687, 689
Tswana, 308
Turkish, 103, 106–8, 197, 264, 308, 341–44, 347, 349, 351, 368, 382, 492, 503, 509, 516, 517, 522, 523, 525, 532, 586, 593, 596, 597, 686, 688
typical development, 350
Typological Primacy Model, 796

Ullman, Michael, 83, 95, 126–28, 331, 413–15
ultimate attainment, 76, 91, 179, 315, 318, 321, 324, 326, 338, 352, 380, 386–88, 392, 433, 439, 500, 503, 530, 670–91, 700, 715, 734
unanalyzed chunks, 586, 734
underspecification, 508, 522
Universal Grammar (UG), 7–9, 15, 17, 18, 25, 33, 53–61, 76, 77, 79, 95, 96, 98, 103–06, 116, 117, 137–39, 142–45, 147, 155–58, 272, 338, 339, 341, 345, 346, 348, 366, 373, 380, 381, 440, 462, 463, 464, 467, 480, 491, 494, 506, 516, 527, 565, 567, 568, 570, 571, 579, 581, 583, 587, 591, 592, 593, 595, 596, 598, 601–2, 614, 627, 672–74, 679, 682, 698, 699, 702, 706, 717, 719, 723, 724, 734, 735
  access to, 506
  Principles and Parameters, 14, 18, 79, 150, 505, 527, 591, 673, 716
  sequences, 339
universals of language, 149, 280, 388, 483
Unsworth, Sharon, 321, 334, 338, 340, 349, 352, 683
U-shaped learning, 618

Vainikka, Anne, 35, 57, 106, 137, 196, 340, 341, 342, 346
Valley Girl speech, 288
VanPatten, Bill, 50, 60, 364, 565, 628, 629, 630, 636–47
Varbrul, 274, 277, 279, 280, 282, 283, 734, 812
variable, 40, 48, 50, 53, 56, 57, 61, 62, 64, 72, 75, 83–87, 91, 111, 123, 135, 160, 165, 166, 171–73, 176, 178–79, 192, 222, 223, 261, 268, 279, 281, 287, 291, 328, 334, 352, 372, 375, 377, 378, 386, 389, 392, 423, 429, 433, 434, 623–25, 643, 683, 684, 710, 731
  dependent, 160, 166, 171, 279
  independent, 159, 166, 171, 178, 735
variationism, 202, 208, 252, 256, 272–90, 735
variationist, 741
verb final, 735

verb raising (verb movement), 345, 346, 352, 511, 593, 595, 732, 733, 735
verb second (V2), 147–49, 152, 346, 385, 513, 514, 735
verbal inflection, 508
Véronique, Georges Daniel, 208, 251, 283
vicarious response, 658, 659, 660
video conferencing, 294, 301, 303
Vietnamese, 99, 196, 240, 268, 277, 282, 333, 335, 499, 549, 599
virtual environments, 293, 294, 298, 301, 303, 306, 307
voice onset time (VOT), 323, 360, 389, 534–35, 678, 735
Vygotsky, Lev, 41–44, 50, 225, 235, 256–59, 296, 624, 648–68, 708

Wagner, Johannes, 42, 43, 44, 51, 57, 64, 69, 72, 90, 207, 208, 235, 236, 252, 253, 255, 697
Weak Continuity, 345, 346, 586, 596
Web 2.0, 292, 294, 301, 305
Welsh, 354, 368

White, Lydia, 32–35, 42, 49, 54, 56, 58, 76, 79, 81, 98, 104, 110, 127, 132, 137, 212, 215, 297, 340, 345, 348, 380, 387, 388, 418, 493, 501, 506, 509, 510, 512–31, 582, 596, 597, 602, 642, 672, 674, 675, 680, 682, 686–89
wh-movement, 16, 81, 505, 508, 670, 680–83, 686, 701, 735
wiki, 293, 301, 303, 305, 306
willingness to communicate, 173

X-bar theory, 16–18, 20, 21, 346

Young-Scholten, Martha, 35, 57, 106, 109, 137, 196, 199, 267–69, 336, 340, 341–43, 346, 531, 545, 553

Zobl, Helmut, 101–4, 109, 113, 415, 508, 509
zone of proximal development (ZPD), 70, 201, 257, 648–69
Zweitspracherwerb italienischer (portugiesischer) und spanischer Arbeiter (ZISA), 77, 187–88, 252, 592–95, 598, 602, 736